# Brooks/Cole Empowerment Series and the Council on Social Work Education's Educational Policy and Accreditation Standards

 The Council on Social Work Education's Educational Policy and Accreditation Standards requires all social work students to develop ten competencies and recommends teaching and assessing 41 related practice behaviors, listed as Educational Policy (EP) 2.1.1 – 2.1.10m below. "Helping Hands" icons throughout this text, "Competency Notes" sections at the end of each chapter, and the supplemental *Practice Behaviors Workbook* connect class work to these important standards.

## Competencies and Practice Behaviors

**EP 2.1.1 Identify as a professional social worker and conduct oneself accordingly:**
  a. Advocate for client access to the services of social work
  b. Practice personal reflection and self-correction to assure continual professional development
  c. Attend to professional roles and boundaries
  d. Demonstrate professional demeanor in behavior, appearance, and communication
  e. Engage in career-long learning
  f. Use supervision and consultation

**EP 2.1.2 Apply social work ethical principles to guide professional practice:**
  a. Recognize and manage personal values in a way that allows professional values to guide practice
  b. Make ethical decisions by applying standards of the National Association of Social Workers Code of Ethics and, as applicable, of the International Federation of Social Workers/International Association of Schools of Social Work Ethics in Social Work, Statement of Principles
  c. Tolerate ambiguity in resolving ethical conflicts
  d. Apply strategies of ethical reasoning to arrive at principled decisions

**EP 2.1.3 Apply critical thinking to inform and communicate professional judgments:**
  a. Distinguish, appraise, and integrate multiple sources of knowledge, including research-based knowledge and practice wisdom
  b. Analyze models of assessment, prevention, intervention, and evaluation
  c. Demonstrate effective oral and written communication in working with individuals, families, groups, organizations, communities, and colleagues

**EP 2.1.4 Engage diversity and difference in practice:**
  a. Recognize the extent to which a culture's structures and values may oppress, marginalize, alienate, or create or enhance privilege and power
  b. Gain sufficient self-awareness to eliminate the influence of personal biases and values in working with diverse groups
  c. Recognize and communicate their understanding of the importance of difference in shaping life experiences
  d. View themselves as learners and engage those with whom they work as informants

**EP 2.1.5 Advance human rights and social and economic justice:**
   a. Understand the forms and mechanisms of oppression and discrimination
   b. Advocate for human rights and social and economic justice
   c. Engage in practices that advance social and economic justice

**EP 2.1.6 Engage in research-informed practice and practice-informed research:**
   a. Use practice experience to inform scientific inquiry
   b. Use research evidence to inform practice

**EP 2.1.7 Apply knowledge of human behavior and the social environment:**
   a. Utilize conceptual frameworks to guide the processes of assessment, intervention, and evaluation
   b. Critique and apply knowledge to understand person and environment

**EP 2.1.8 Engage in policy practice to advance social and economic well-being and to deliver effective social work services:**
   a. Analyze, formulate, and advocate for policies that advance social well-being
   b. Collaborate with colleagues and clients for effective policy action

**EP 2.1.9 Respond to contexts that shape practice:**
   a. Continuously discover, appraise, and attend to changing locales, populations, scientific and technological developments, and emerging societal trends to provide relevant services
   b. Provide leadership in promoting sustainable changes in service delivery and practice to improve the quality of social services

**EP 2.1.10 Engage, assess, intervene, and evaluate with individuals, families, groups, organizations and communities:**
   a. Substantively and affectively prepare for action with individuals, families, groups, organizations, and communities
   b. Use empathy and other interpersonal skills
   c. Develop a mutually agreed-on focus of work and desired outcomes
   d. Collect, organize, and interpret client data
   e. Assess client strengths and limitations
   f. Develop mutually agreed-on intervention goals and objectives
   g. Select appropriate intervention strategies
   h. Initiate actions to achieve organizational goals
   i. Implement prevention interventions that enhance client capacities
   j. Help clients resolve problems
   k. Negotiate, mediate, and advocate for clients
   l. Facilitate transitions and endings
   m. Critically analyze, monitor, and evaluate interventions

**For more information about the standards themselves, and for a complete policy statement, visit the Council on Social Work Education website at www.cswe.org.**

Adapted with permission from the Council on Social Work Education

# The Skills of Helping Individuals, Families, Groups, and Communities

BROOKS/COLE EMPOWERMENT SERIES

**LAWRENCE SHULMAN**

*University at Buffalo*
*The State University of New York*

BROOKS/COLE
CENGAGE Learning™

Australia • Brazil • Japan • Korea • Mexico • Singapore
• Spain • United Kingdom • United States

BROOKS/COLE
CENGAGE Learning

**Brooks/Cole Empowerment Series:**
*The Skills of Helping Individuals, Families,*
*Groups and Communities,* **Seventh Edition**
**Lawrence Shulman**

Executive Editor: Linda Schreiber-Ganster

Acquisitions Editor: Seth Dobrin

Assistant Editor: Alicia McLaughlin

Editorial Assistant: Suzanna Kincaid

Media Editor: Elizabeth Momb

Marketing Manager: Christine Sosa

Marketing Assistant: Gurpreet Saran

Marketing Communications Manager:
Tami Strang

Content Project Manager: Michelle Clark

Design Director: Rob Hugel

Art Director: Caryl Gorska

Print Buyer: Karen Hunt

Rights Acquisitions Specialist:
Tom McDonough

Production Service: Suwathiga Velayutham

Copy Editor: Linda Ireland

Cover Designer: Natalie Hill

Cover Image: Lawrence Lawry/SPL/Science
Photo Library/Getty Images

Compositor: Integra

Library of Congress Control Number: 2011923503

International Edition:
ISBN-13: 978-1-111-52126-4
ISBN-10: 1-111-52126-3

Cengage Learning International Offices

**Asia**
www.cengageasia.com
tel: (65) 6410 1200

**Australia/New Zealand**
www.cengage.com.au
tel: (61) 3 9685 4111

**Brazil**
www.cengage.com.br
tel: (55) 11 3665 9900

**India**
www.cengage.co.in
tel: (91) 11 4364 1111

**Latin America**
www.cengage.com.mx
tel: (52) 55 1500 6000

**UK/Europe/Middle East/Africa**
www.cengage.co.uk
tel: (44) 0 1264 332 424

**Represented in Canada by Nelson Education, Ltd.**
tel: (416) 752 9100 / (800) 668 0671
www.nelson.com

Cengage Learning is a leading provider of customized learning solutions with office locations around the globe, including Singapore, the United Kingdom, Australia, Mexico, Brazil, and Japan. Locate your local office at **www.cengage.com/global**

For product information: **www.cengage.com/international**
Visit your local office: **www.cengage.com/global**
Visit our corporate website: **www.cengage.com**

AVAILABILITY OF RESOURCES MAY DIFFER BY REGION. Check with your local cengage learning representative for details.

Printed in the United States of America
1 2 3 4 5 6 7 15 14 13 12 11

-----------------------------------------------------

*To my wife Sheila, with love*

# Brief Contents

# Contents

# Beginnings and the Contracting Skills 97

CHAPTER 5

# Skills in the Work Phase 146

CHAPTER 8

# The Middle and Ending Phases in Family Practice 294

CHAPTER 9

# Variations in Family Practice 313

PART IV   Social Work with Groups 341

CHAPTER 10

# The Preliminary Phase in Group Practice: The Group as a Mutual-Aid System 342

**CHAPTER 14**
# Endings and Transitions with Groups  574

PART V  Macro Social Work Practice: Impacting the Agency/Setting, the Community, and Effecting Social Change  601

# Council on Social Work Education Educational Policy and Accreditation Standards by Chapter

In social work, the words "competence and practice behavior" have a unique meaning beyond the typical dictionary definitions. *Competence* in the usual sense means that a person possesses suitable skills and abilities to do a specific task. Competent social workers should be able to do a number of job-related duties, think critically, and understand the context of their work.

*The Skills of Helping Individuals, Families, Groups, and Communities*, Seventh Edition now includes explicit references to the Educational Policy and Accreditation Standards' (EPAS) 10 core competencies and 41 recommended practice behaviors. The column on the right informs the reader in which chapters the icons appear.

| The 10 Competencies and 41 Recommended Practice Behaviors (EPAS 2008) | Chapter(s) Where Referenced |
| --- | --- |
| **2.1.1 Identify as a professional social worker and conduct oneself accordingly** | |
| a. Advocate for client access to the services of social work | 1, 4, 5, 6, 9, 13, and 15 |
| b. Practice personal reflection and self-correction to assure continual professional development | 1, 4, 5, 6, 7, 8, 10, 11, 12, and 13 |
| c. Attend to professional roles and boundaries | 1, 5, 10, and 16 |
| d. Demonstrate professional demeanor in behavior, appearance, and communication | 4, 5 |
| e. Engage in career-long learning | 5 and 12 |
| f. Use supervision and consultation | 3, 5, 6, 9, 12 and 17 |
| **2.1.2 Apply social work ethical principles to guide professional practice** | |
| a. Recognize and manage personal values in a way that allows professional values to guide practice | 1, 4, 5, and 10 |

b. Make ethical decisions by applying standards of the National Association of Social Workers Code of Ethics and, as applicable, of the International Federation of Social Workers/International Association of Schools of Social Work Ethics in Social Work, Statement of Principles

1, 4, 10, 11, 12, and 17

c. Tolerate ambiguity in resolving ethical conflicts

1, 4, and 5

d. Apply strategies of ethical reasoning to arrive at principled decisions

1, 4, and 10

### 2.1.3 Apply critical thinking to inform and communicate professional judgments

a. Distinguish, appraise, and integrate multiple sources of knowledge, including research-based knowledge and practice wisdom

2, 7, 13, 14, 16, and 17

b. Analyze models of assessment, prevention, intervention, and evaluation

2, 3, 5, 7, 13, 15, and 16

c. Demonstrate effective oral and written communication in working with individuals, families, groups, organizations, communities, and colleagues

3, 5, and 15

### 2.1.4 Engage diversity and difference in practice

a. Recognize the extent to which a culture's structures and values may oppress, marginalize, alienate, or create or enhance privilege and power

1, 2, 3, 4, 7, 9, 10, 11, 13, 15, 16, and 17

b. Gain sufficient self-awareness to eliminate the influence of personal biases and values in working with diverse groups

1, 2, 3, 4, 7, 15, and 17

c. Recognize and communicate their understanding of the importance of difference in shaping life experiences

1, 2, 3, 4, 7, 8, 10, 13, 14, and 15

d. View themselves as learners and engage those with whom they work as informants

1, 4, 6, 7, 8, 10, 11, and 13

### 2.1.5 Advance human rights and social and economic justice

a. Understand forms and mechanisms of oppression and discrimination

2, 7, 8, 10, 13, 14, 15, 16, and 17

b. Advocate for human rights and social and economic justice

1, 2, 14, and 16

c. Engage in practices that advance social and economic justice

1, 14, and 15

### 2.1.6 Engage in research-informed practice and practice-informed research

a. Use practice experience to inform scientific inquiry

1, 2, 4, 10, and 17

b. Use research evidence to inform practice

1, 2, 3, 4, 9, 11, 12, 13, 16, and 17

**2.1.7 Apply knowledge of human behavior and the social environment**

  a. Utilize conceptual frameworks to guide the process of assessment, intervention, and evaluation

1, 2, 3, 4, 5, 6, 7, 8, 9, 10, 11, 12, 13, and 17

  b. Critique and apply knowledge to understand person and environment

1, 2, 3, 5, 7, 9, 10, 13, and 15

**2.1.8 Engage in policy practice to advance social and economic well-being and to deliver effective social work services**

  a. Analyze, formulate, and advocate for policies that advance social well-being

15

  b. Collaborate with colleagues and clients for effective policy action

9, 10, 11, and 15

**2.1.9 Respond to contexts that shape practice**

  a. Continuously discover, appraise, and attend to changing locales, populations, scientific and technological developments, and emerging societal trends to provide relevant services

1, 15, and 17

  b. Provide leadership in promoting sustainable changes in service delivery and practice to improve the quality of social services

9, 10, and 15

**2.1.10 Engage, assess, intervene, and evaluate with individuals, families, groups, organizations, and communities**

  a. Substantively and affectively prepare for action with individuals, families, groups, organizations, and communities

1, 3, 4, 5, 7, 8, 10, 11, 12, and 14

  b. Use empathy and other interpersonal skills

1, 3, 4, 5, 6, 7, 8, 9, 10, 11, 12, 13, and 14

  c. Develop a mutually agreed-on focus of work and desired outcomes

4, 5, 7, 8, 9, 10, 11, 15, and 17

  d. Collect, organize, and interpret client data

3, 4, 5, 7, 8, 11, and 12

  e. Assess client strengths and limitations

3, 5, 7, 9, 10, 12, 14, 16, and 17

  f. Develop mutually agreed-on intervention goals and objectives

4, 5, 6, 7, 9, 11, and 12

  g. Select appropriate intervention strategies

3, 7, 10, 11, and 13

  h. Initiate actions to achieve organizational goals

15

  i. Implement prevention interventions that enhance client capacities

3, 5, and 16

  j. Help clients resolve problems

7

  k. Negotiate, mediate, and advocate for clients

6, 7, 15, and 16

  l. Facilitate transitions and endings

5, 12, and 14

  m. Critically analyze, monitor, and evaluate interventions

5, 11, 13, and 14

# Preface

## Introduction and Underlying Assumptions

The focus of this book is method—what social workers do as their part in the helping process. I believe that the dynamics of giving and taking help are not mysterious processes incapable of being explained. Helping skills can be defined, illustrated, and taught. The helping process is complex; it must be presented clearly and broken down into manageable segments. Theories and simple models need to be developed to provide tools for understanding and guiding interventions.

This book represents an effort to conceptualize and illustrate a generalist practice model without losing the detail of the specific ways that social workers practice. The term *generalist* has been used in different ways over the years, sometimes to refer to practice models so abstract and on such a high theoretical level that one has difficulty finding the social worker or client in the description. The focus here is not just on what is common about what we know, value, and aspire to, nor on our common models for describing clients (e.g., systems, strengths perspective, cognitive-behavioral, ecological, or psychodynamic theory), but on the common elements and skills of the helping person in action.

Underlying this approach is the belief that social workers need to be prepared to offer clients service in the modality (individual, group, family, community) that is most suitable to the client, rather than the one that is most comfortable for the worker. One goal of this book is to help the reader appreciate that once a level of skill is developed in working with individuals, it is possible to expand on that understanding and elaborate that skill when working with more than one person at a time (e.g., family, group, or community organization). A number of additional assumptions follow.

### The Assumption of a Core (Constant) Element to the Helping Process

This book is based on the assumption that we can identify an underlying process in all helping relationships. This process and its associated set of core skills can be observed whenever one person attempts to help another. These dynamics and skills are referred to as the constant elements of the helping process. The reader will note how central concepts and skills appear first in the chapters on working with individuals and then reappear as the focus shifts to families, groups, communities, organizations, agencies, and even social action activity in pursuit of social policy change.

For example, the importance of developing a positive working relationship, sometimes referred to as the "therapeutic alliance" in clinical practice, and the interactional skills required to develop this relationship cut across modalities of intervention (e.g., individual, family, or group work) as well as theoretical orientation (e.g., solution-focused therapy, cognitive-behavioral therapy, or motivational interviewing).

The impact of time on the helping relationship as well as on each individual contact also introduces constant elements. Understanding the helping interaction to have preparatory, beginning, middle, and ending phases helps to explain certain dynamics, such as the indirect ways clients may raise difficult issues at the start of a session as well as the phenomenon known as "doorknob therapy"—when clients reveal a powerful issue at the end of the session, sometimes literally as they leave the office.

## Variant Elements to the Helping Process

As you read this book, these common elements and skills will become clearer and will be observable in any situation in which you see a social worker in action. Although there is a constant core to helping, there are also variant elements introduced by a number of factors.

For example, the reader will note the importance of the concept and skill of contracting in first sessions that is central to all helping relationships. The skills of clarifying purpose and the social worker's role, reaching for client feedback, finding the common ground between the two, and addressing issues of authority are of crucial importance to develop an initial structure that frees the client to begin the work. However, the manner in which the contracting takes place and the issues—or what I will call "themes of concern" to the client—will vary according to the impact of these variant elements. These factors can include the following:

- The setting for the engagement (e.g., school, hospital, family counseling agency, child welfare agency, or community-action–focused organization)
- The modality of practice (e.g., individual or family counseling, group practice, community organizing or policy advocacy)
- The age and stage of the client's life cycle (e.g., child, teenager, young adult, or elderly and retired)
- The particular life problems the client brings to the encounter (e.g., emotional and/or physical health issues, addiction, unemployment, physical or sexual abuse, poverty, or parenting)
- Whether the client is participating voluntarily or involuntarily (e.g., the difference between a voluntary group for parents of teenagers seeking help in dealing with their kids and a group of clients mandated to attend by the court because of a driving-while-intoxicated conviction)

- Demographic elements that may interact with the social and/or emotional problems (e.g., race, ethnicity, sexual orientation, physical ability, or economic class)
- Whether the client is being seen in an agency or host setting (e.g., school or hospital) or in a private practice setting

The discussion of specific and detailed examples of practice in action, not just general case presentations, will help the reader to see both the constant and variant elements in all of these examples as well as many others that are common to our practice.

The social worker also brings personal elements to the process related to such factors as education and experience, life events, and the effectiveness of the support and supervision available to the worker. For example, there is some benefit to having been a parent when one is leading a parenting group. However, a skilled worker who understands that the process of mutual aid involves group members helping one another, and that the group leader learns at least as much from the group members as he or she teaches, can still effectively lead such a group. A social worker does not have to have "walked the walk" and "talked the talk" (i.e., been in recovery and participated in recovery groups such as Alcoholics Anonymous [AA]) in order to be helpful to a client struggling to begin or maintain the recovery process as long as the social worker is open to new learning from a range of sources (e.g., literature, supervision, workshops) as well as learning from the client.

Despite the varying aspects of practice, when we examine interactions closely, the similar aspects become apparent. This book addresses a range of helping situations in the belief that each social worker can incorporate the model into his or her own work context. In addition, findings drawn from my studies of social work practice, supervision, management, and medical practice—as well as the research of others—-provide empirical support for the importance of the core skills that make up the constant elements of practice. The book reviews "evidence-based" practice models, when available, but also draws on practice wisdom—what I refer to as emerging models—that still awaits research support that would qualify these approaches to be formally described as evidence-based.

## The Skills of Professional Impact

An additional assumption in this text is the existence of common elements that help make us more effective when we work with other professionals. This area of skill development is termed *professional impact*. The argument will be made, and illustrated using numerous examples, that the skills of direct practice (e.g., contracting, listening, the ability to empathize, and being honest with one's own feelings) are just as important in work with other professionals (e.g., teachers, doctors, judges, other social workers) and systems (e.g., schools, hospitals, courts, agencies) as they are in work with our clients.

These skills and others are important when one is mediating a client-system engagement (e.g., the high school student in conflict with a teacher) or is actively advocating for a client to receive services (e.g., those withheld by a health insurance company). In fact, these skills take on an increased importance when working with other professionals. A social worker who wants another professional, perhaps from another discipline, to understand and emphasize with a client can be more effective if the worker can understand and empathize with the other professional. The argument will be made in this book that one must at times "speak loudly," that is, confront other systems, while also being prepared to "speak softly," that is, work effectively with other professionals. A range of encounters illustrates the professional impact skill model developed in this book.

Although the subject of professional impact is addressed and illustrated in detail in Chapter 15 dealing with macro practice (working with larger systems), it is not possible to address practice with individuals, families, and groups without introducing the importance of the social worker's role in dealing with the system. Therefore, the idea of the system (e.g., agency, school, hospital) as the "second client" is a theme in all of the chapters leading up to the more detailed discussion in Chapter 15.

## Organization of the Book

To simplify the complex task of describing the core methodology, a single frame of reference described as the Interactional Model (IM) is presented. Included is a description of a theory of the helping process, several models (middle-range descriptions) that connect theory and practice, the identification of skills needed to put the framework into action, and empirical data that support the major elements of the framework. A summary of other models, both evidence-based and emerging models, is provided in Chapter 17 to help place the interactional model into context. Elements of other practice models in Chapter 17 are also referenced throughout the text as examples of how concepts can be integrated into a single framework to both elaborate and strengthen the approach to practice.

In considering how to organize this book, suggestions by some reviewers of the sixth edition that Chapter 17 should appear in Part I had validity. On the other hand, some reviewers argued for less theory in Part I while moving as quickly as possible to the practice skills and illustrations. This view also made sense. Based upon my own experiences as a practice teacher, I decided to maintain the current organization but add greater emphasis in the early chapters on brief descriptions of the other models as I drew upon them for their useful concepts and interventions. The reader will have to wait until Chapter 17 for a fuller discussion of the evidence-based and emerging models now available to social workers; however, it is quite possible for someone to read Chapter 17 earlier.

### Organization of the Six Parts of the Book

Part I of the book consists of two chapters that introduce the major theoretical constructs of the interactional model and set the stage for the text. An introduction to the impact of values, ethics, law, and so forth on practice is also provided, as is a discussion of the types of ethical dilemmas social worker may face and methods for resolving them if possible. The four chapters in Part II focus on work with individuals, examining this process against the backdrop of the phases of work: preliminary, beginning, work, and ending/transition phases. Illustrations drawn from a range of settings point out the common as well as variant elements of the work.

In Parts III and IV, we examine the complex issues of working with more than one client at a time. These parts focus on social work with families and groups, respectively. The common elements of the model established in Part I are reintroduced in the context of work with families and groups. These sections are also organized using the phases of work; once again, we examine the unique issues involved in the contexts of preparing, beginning, working, and ending with families and groups.

Part V moves from the micro or clinical level to include two chapters that focus on the macro level, exploring the skills involved in work with communities and with people in the larger systems and organizations that are important to clients. Chapter 15 illustrates the dynamics and skills involved in influencing one's own agency or setting as well as other organizations. Many of these ideas and strategies are introduced and illustrated in earlier chapters as integral elements of any social worker's role. Chapter 16 introduces the core concepts of community and principles of community practice. The chapter provides examples that illustrate how social workers help members of a community (e.g., a neighborhood, a housing project, or a ward group in a psychiatric hospital) to empower themselves by focusing on community issues that relate to their personal concerns. Conversations with teachers, doctors, and politicians help illustrate effective impact on other professionals. The social worker's responsibility to engage in social action within the community and in political action is also highlighted in Chapter 16. Once again, the core skills and the impact of time and the phases of work are used as organizing principles.

Part VI of the book contains a final chapter that provides an overview of a number of different models of practice. This allows the reader to put the interactional model into context. Concepts from evidence-based models such as cognitive-behavioral therapy, solution-focused therapy, and motivational interviewing are presented and illustrated with individual and group examples. An introduction to the concept of evidence-based practice as well as the criteria for evaluating models puts the three presented models in context.

Additional models that have emerged from research and practice wisdom, but do not yet qualify as evidence-based, are presented in the second part of Chapter 17. These include: self-in-relation, feminist, psychodynamic, brief treatment, religion and spirituality, trauma and extreme events, and social work with lesbians, gays, bisexuals, and transgender clients. Also addressed are models for dealing with secondary trauma experienced by helping professionals. Many concepts from these models are introduced and incorporated throughout the earlier chapters wherever they can help the reader understand and practice more effectively. In Chapter 17, the models themselves come to the foreground for a more in-depth discussion.

# What's New in This Edition?

In approaching this major edition revision, I was fortunate once again to have input from a number of social work faculty, solicited by my publisher, some of whom use the book for their classes and others who currently do not. Some suggestions were minor, but others called for rebalancing of the method content and reorganization of some sections. I have been able to incorporate a significant number of suggestions, and I am grateful to the reviewers who took the time to respond. Of course, I could not integrate all of the suggestions, especially when some were inconsistent with my assumptions and practice model or conflicted with other reviewer suggestions. A brief list of some critical changes as well as a discussion of the changes follows.

- The method sections have been rebalanced, with a decrease in the chapters dealing with group work and a decrease in the number of illustrations provided in all of the chapters.

- Each modality (individual, family, group, and community) section includes at least one case that demonstrates the intervention over time.

- There is increased emphasis on the latest findings related to evidence-based practice and how they can be integrated into a generalist framework.

- The discussion of practice models has been expanded to include additional content on evidence-based practices (solution-focused, cognitive-behavioral, and motivational interviewing), feminist practice, religion and spirituality, working with LGBT clients, and practice in response to trauma and extreme events.

- There is an expanded discussion of the role and skills of the social worker when advocating policy changes.

- The content of the last chapter in the sixth edition on values, ethics, ethical dilemmas, legislation, and so forth has been integrated in segments into earlier chapters. For example, the introduction to values, ethics, codes of ethics, and similar topics can now be found in Chapter 1. Specific ethical and legal issues can now be found in related chapters. Thus, a discussion of informed consent and confidentiality concludes Chapter 4 that deals with beginnings and contracting. Issues related to the duty to warn if a client is considered dangerous are now included in Chapter 5 dealing with the middle phase of practice. Unique ethical issues related to group work are presented in the group work chapters. All of the previous content has been retained, only updated and presented in segments and in context earlier in the book.

## Evolving Practice Knowledge in Response to Disasters

The sixth edition was published in 2009. Since that time, social workers have continued to deepen their understanding and skill in many emerging practice areas. The changes in the nature of practice in response to the AIDS epidemic, homelessness, the elderly, problems of addiction to crack cocaine and other substances, the powerful impact of economic changes including loss of jobs and loss of homes, and sexual violence remain at the forefront of practice. The impact of posttraumatic stress and other emotional and physical problems experienced by soldiers returning from both wars has finally received a well-deserved increase in attention and treatment. Our understanding of the effects of community traumas—such as 9/11, the Katrina hurricane, and, most recently, the deep oil drilling disaster in the Gulf of Mexico—and the accompanying devastation is growing, as are our strategies for responding. As this edition is being written, the ecological and human tragedies associated with the oil spill in the Gulf will be occupying our efforts to respond as many in these communities attempt to cope with life-shaking experiences. Work in each of these areas has also changed at a rapid pace, as new understanding of the issues has led to new strategies for intervention

## Current Issues Affecting Practice

In addition, clients and social workers have been impacted by the implementation of significant social policies, such as managed care and welfare reform, and now the implications of the recently passed health care legislation. These continue to profoundly affect the lives of clients and the nature of our practice. Many of these major social changes have also challenged our profession to consider professional ethical issues that have arisen, such as our responsibility to provide end-of-life care or how we can ethically work within restrictions raised by legislation in respect to abortion and other issues. Illustrations drawn from these areas bring practice theory closer to the realities of today's students and practitioners. Finally, an expanded body of knowledge with respect to work with lesbian, gay, bisexual, and transgender (LGBT) clients is also included.

As in each of the earlier editions, this book shares theories and constructs about human behavior—some supported by research, others drawn from experience in practice—when relevant to specific practice issues. In this way, what is known about the dynamics of helping, oppression and vulnerability, resilience, group process, substance abuse, family interaction, the impact of critical social and personal events (e.g., 9/11), and so on is directly linked to the worker's interactions with the client and with relevant systems.

## Integration of Interactional Research

My research and theory-building work (Shulman, 1991), designed to develop a holistic theory of practice, is more thoroughly integrated into this edition. This theory recognizes the complexity of social work practice. Focusing solely on the social worker-client interaction ignores many factors such as supervision, availability of resources, client motivation and capacity, the impact of cost-containment efforts, and the effects of trauma on the client and secondary trauma impact on the worker (e.g., death of a client). Chapter 1 contains a description of these studies and their central findings.

This book systematically addresses these findings along with other elements of practice. It also updates our current knowledge base of research findings from the work of other researchers both within social work and in related professions. All too often professions operate as if in an information silo, only reading their own professional literature, for example, without integrating knowledge developed by related professions. My experiences as cofounder and cochair of a five-year international and interdisciplinary conference on clinical supervision, funded by the National Institute of Drug Abuse, and as coeditor of a clinical supervision journal have brought me into close professional contact with a number of outstanding colleagues from related professions (e.g., psychology, counseling, nursing, and marriage and family counseling). This joint work has strengthened my belief in the need to incorporate related models and research where appropriate.

## Strengths and Resiliency Perspectives

The book also continues to build on a strengths and resiliency perspective when considering practice with oppressed and vulnerable populations. Social workers not only need to understand the socio-economic factors that contribute to individual, family, and community problems, but also must recognize, understand, and respect the existing strengths and resiliencies that have helped people cope. The major ideas of this socially oriented framework for understanding individual, family, group, and community behavior are presented in the first chapter of the book and then illustrated with appropriate examples throughout the text. The material on this topic has been updated to reflect our current knowledge in these areas.

## Evidence-Based and Emerging Models

This concept of working with clients' strengths is continued and expanded in this edition and incorporates promising new emerging models (e.g., the importance of religion and spirituality) and evidence-based practices that have been identified as consistently helpful to different populations (e.g., motivational interviewing, cognitive-behavioral therapy, and solution-focused therapy). In addition to discussing and illustrating these models and intervention strategies in work with individuals and families, the discussion of evidence-based intervention in groups has been significantly expanded.

I also take the position that the adoption of any one model to fit all situations and clients is not advocated. It can be seductive, especially for students or beginning practitioners, to try to achieve some level of certainty in their work. It is part of human nature to try to come to closure and to avoid or ignore ambiguity in a quest for certainty. However, this effort can lead to trying to fit the client to the model rather than responding with an intervention that fits the client.

An alternative suggested in this book is to use concepts, theories, and intervention strategies from a range of evidence-based practices in designing and implementing a framework that fits the client, the setting, the modality of practice, the problem, and so forth, making effective use of some of the excellent concepts and interventions that are proving to be helpful.

### Textbook Features

A major change for this edition is the inclusion of Practice Points and Practice Summaries within the text. I have used the term "**practice points**" in bold at the start of a paragraph that contains a discussion of the important ideas that are illustrated in the example that follows. I have used the words "**practice summary**" at the start of a paragraph that follows a practice example. These two additions should make the connections between the practice model and the illustration that follows or precedes it stand out more clearly to the reader. Thus, even in the longer examples, the reader will have a concurrent discussion and analysis of the practice excerpts.

A reference list and glossary are provided at the end of the book. In addition, subject, author, and case example indexes are provided. This will allow for quick access to specific material. For example, the subject index will direct readers interested in adolescents to all of the places in the book that address that age group. Readers could also go to the case example index and find references to the case material that involves adolescents, whether in individual, family, group, or community work.

The book is intended to address the practice needs of the foundation-year social work student in either a bachelor or master of social work program. It is substantive enough to serve as a text for a full-year practice course. It is designed so that it can be used over a number of courses, starting with a one-semester practice course and then continuing in method-specific courses. For example, the depth of discussion and the large number of examples in the book and online make it useful for advanced courses, such as one on group work. (Note: The group practice described in this model is presented in detail in a new book entitled *Dynamics and Skills of Group Counseling*, Cengage Publishers, 2011.)

The more experienced practitioner will also find this book helpful for continued learning. It provides models that help articulate concepts that the practitioner may have already developed through experience in practice. Using these models, any practitioner can become more systematic and effective. A clearly developed framework will increase consistency and help explain why some sessions go well and others do not.

## Additional Resources for the Seventh Edition

Additional resources have been provided for this edition for both the student reader and the instructor.

### Student Ancillaries

There are two significant video student supplements to this edition, which were first introduced in the fifth edition. These two programs are contained on a DVD designed to provide the reader with illustrations of the identified skills as well as excerpts from a workshop I have conducted. (If the book was purchased without this supplementary DVD, students can purchase the DVD at www.cengagebrain.com. These videos are also included on Cengage Learning's Social Work CourseMate, also available for purchase.)

The first program, entitled *The Interactive Skills of Helping* (ISH), was produced by two of my colleagues, Mark Cameron and Denise Krause, with the production assistance of Steven Sturman. The program contains role-play excerpts that illustrate the core skills, such as tuning in and contracting. For each skill, there are three segments. The first demonstrates the skill in a role-play graciously acted out by University at Buffalo colleagues and students. A variety of worker-client situations provide the substance of the practice. By way of contrast, the second excerpt, called "the blooper," demonstrates lack of the skill. The third element is a brief discussion and debriefing between the "worker" and me, exploring her or his thinking and feelings during the previous two segments. This can also serve as an illustration of a clinical supervision process. (For a discussion of this model in the supervision process, see Shulman, *Interactional Supervision,* 3rd edition, NASW Press, 2010.)

A second program on the DVD, entitled *Engaging and Working with the Hard-to-Reach Client* (EWHRC), consists of video excerpts from an interactive workshop I conducted with a volunteer group of child welfare workers. Although the examples come from child welfare, the principles discussed can easily be applied to other populations. The workshop is organized using the phases-of-work framework that provides structure for this text. The workshop segments combine a presentation by me, discussion, detailed case examples, and an illustration of the mutual-aid process as participants support one another. In many ways, the workshop is an example of an educational mutual-aid support group, with the workshop leader attempting to demonstrate many of the dynamics and skills of the interactional model in his role as teacher.

To become familiar with the contents, the reader should first view the welcome section of the first program and the introduction section of the EWHRC program, as well as the table of contents of both. The reader will note an icon ▣ that connects the content in the book to the particular segments of the DVD.

A student tutorial quiz, organized by chapter, is also available on Cengage Learning's Social Work CourseMate. And finally, a text-related Course Book is available organized by chapter and the Council on Social Work Education (CSWE) Competencies and Practice Behaviors (see below).

## Instructor's Ancillaries

An online Instructor's Manual, electronic Test Bank, and Microsoft PowerPoint® presentations slide show developed by the author are available on the instructor's companion website and on the PowerLecture DVD that can be requested from a Cengage Learning representative. The PowerLecture DVD also contains a link (http://www.socialwork.buffalo.edu/facstaff/skills_dynamics.asp) to seven 1-hour workshops I conducted with PhD students, adjuncts, and full-time faculty at the University at Buffalo School of Social Work who teach in all areas of the curriculum. The workshops deal with many of the difficult issues faced by new and experienced bachelor and master of social work teachers as they work to strengthen their teaching skills.

Finally, the PowerLecture DVD now includes the original video of two sessions of the married couples' group led by myself (Session 1—two parts and Session 19). Session 1 includes my conversation with a group of social work students prefacing the excerpts from the first session. This is the same session as the one presented in Chapter 11 on the beginning phase in group practice. (Note: The names of the group members have been changed in the text.) Session 19 illustrates the dramatic changes in group participation and provides an illustration of a middle phase group session with segments narrated by myself.

## Finally, Some Advice to Social Work Students

While serving as Dean at the University at Buffalo School of Social Work for 6 years, I gave the same advice to each of our master of social work graduating classes. I told them that I thought we would have done our job as faculty well if we accomplished the following:

- Equipped them with a beginning professional understanding and skill level for practice

- Helped them to understand that they needed to tolerate ambiguity and stay open to new ideas so as not to come to premature closures

- Taught them how to continue their learning using client feedback, research findings, their supervisors, and their colleagues, both from within the profession and from other disciplines

- Helped them to understand that, as social workers, they always had two clients: the one(s) they worked with directly as well as their second "client"— the agency, the host setting (e.g., school or hospital), the community, the political systems, and the social policies that powerfully impacted their clients

- And finally, challenged them to see their professional development as a lifelong task, during which they would not be afraid to risk, to learn from mistakes, to shorten the distance between when they made a mistake and when they returned to the client to correct the mistake, and to continue to grow by making ever more sophisticated mistakes

I share these same suggestions with the readers of this text, who may just be embarking on their exciting and satisfying careers as professional social workers.

# Acknowledgments

I would like to acknowledge the many people who contributed to this book. William Schwartz first described the interactionist perspective on which much of my work has been based. Bill's substantial body of work initiated a paradigm shift for our profession and was the first to introduce to social work the ideas of mutual aid, contracting, the demand for work, and other concepts. He died in 1982 and is still missed; however, he remains very much alive in this text.

I would also like to thank my wife, Sheila, who has always been supportive of my work in more ways than I can say.

Early research of mine reported in this book was supported by the Edna McConnell Clark Foundation; the Welfare Grants Directorate of Health and Welfare, Canada; and the P. A. Woodward Foundation of Vancouver, British Columbia. More recent research, into child welfare and school violence, particularly during my tenure as Dean of the School of Social Work at the University at Buffalo, was supported by the New York State Department of Education and a number of local foundations including: The Community Foundation for Greater Buffalo; The John R. Oishei Foundation; The Margaret L. Wendt Foundation; and the Goodyear Foundation.

Various colleagues have helped along the way. Several faculty members at the School of Social Work of the University of British Columbia and at Boston University have offered valuable advice. More recently, collaboration with colleagues at the University at Buffalo School of Social Work (UBSSW) has also been helpful; thanks in particular to Denise Krause, Mark Cameron, and Steve Sturman, who developed the *Interactive Skills of Helping*, one of the video-teaching programs on the related DVD that enhance this book. Denise also worked on preparing the ExamView questions and the Workbook that accompanies this text. Steve also worked with me to develop a companion DVD on teaching entitled *The Skills and Dynamics of Teaching: Addressing the Hidden Group in the Classroom*. This DVD can be accessed directly on the School of Social Work Web page at http://stream.buffalo.edu/shared/sw/teachingseminar/.

Alex Gitterman of Columbia University is a colleague who has been a sounding board for my ideas about practice. Our joint editorial work and coleadership of workshops have also enriched my understanding.

I am especially grateful to several social work faculty members who responded to a request for suggestions for revisions. Many of their suggestions have been carried forward in this edition. An additional group of faculty reviewers made many excellent suggestions after reading the seventh edition draft outline. These included: Parris J. Baker, Gannon University; Mark Cameron, Southern Connecticut State University; Marcia Cohen, University of New England; Brian Flynn, State University of New York, Binghamton; Jennifer Holland, Clemson University; Catherine Kalob, New England University; Marlys Peck, University of Central Missouri; Jean Nuernberger, University of Central Missouri; and Desiree Stepteau-Watson, University of Mississippi.

I would also like to thank the editorial team at Cengage, headed by social work and counseling editor Seth Dobrin. The team included: Suzanna Kincaid, Editorial Assistant; Alicia Mclaughlin, Assistant Editor; and Elizabeth Momb, Media Editor. I also need to express my special appreciation for the work of Linda Ireland who served as copyeditor of this edition, and whose understanding and appreciation of the content significantly improved the manuscript. Moving the book from manuscript through production was overseen by Michelle Clark and Integra's Suwathiaga Velayutham who served as project manager.

Finally, I want to thank the staff and clients who participated in the cited studies, the workers and students who shared examples of their practice, and my own clients who allowed me to share their experiences in the interest of helping others. These illustrations of the joint efforts of workers and clients give life to the theory and stand as a tribute to their professional commitment and courage.

# A Model of the Helping Process

P art I consists of two chapters that introduce and illustrate the major themes of the interactional approach to social work practice. Chapter 1 sets the stage for the rest of the book with a discussion of the underlying assumptions of the model, a brief history of the profession, and the importance of integrating the personal and professional selves. Chapter 2 explores two central theories of human behavior and the social environment: an oppression model and one that focuses on the client resilience that informs our practice. Other theoretical frameworks are integrated in the chapters that follow.

# An Interactional Approach to Helping

## Problematic Social Work Encounters in Early Sessions

In the hundreds of workshops on practice I have conducted over the past years, a number of common problems are usually raised by participants. These are the moments when experienced, novice, and student social workers feel at a loss on how to respond. Some examples follow:

- A young, unmarried social worker is having her first interview with a middle-aged mother of six children who is having parenting problems when the client suddenly turns to her and asks: "And how many children do you have?" Having none, and feeling defensive, the worker responds by saying, "We are here to talk about you, not me." The social worker can then sense the mother shutting down.

- A social worker with some experience but new to working in a substance abuse recovery agency starts a group first session for men who have been mandated to attend by the court, or go to jail, and finds all of the men staring ahead with arms folded sending a nonverbal signal about not wanting to be there. He wants to get some conversation going but, after introducing himself and explaining the purpose of the group, is greeted by silence. He wonders if he should have brought a film!

- A social work first-year student is assigned to lead an "anger management" group in a middle school for students who have been referred by their teachers for behavioral problems but can't get past the first few minutes because the students respond to his opening statement with loud, boisterous, angry, acting out behavior demonstrating exactly why they were referred to the group. The Assistant Principal looks into the room and asks: "Do you need some help controlling these kids?"

- A new social worker in a hospital stops in to see a 90-year-old female patient to ask if she needs any help from social services. After a nice conversation, as the worker is about to leave, she asks if the patient would like to speak with her again the next day. The woman says she would like that very much, "God willing!" As the social worker walks to the elevator she says to herself: "Oh, my G-d, she doesn't know if she will be alive tomorrow."

- An African American, male, child welfare worker in the protection unit is assigned to visit a Caucasian family in a mostly white, working-class neighborhood as a result of an anonymous telephone call suggesting parental neglect. The wife responds to his questions referring to him as "Sir." After a few minutes, the silent husband says to the wife, with a sarcastic tone: "You don't have to call him sir." The social worker feels angry at what he perceives as a racist comment but keeps going as if he did not hear it.

- A Latina worker meets with a Latina client for a first session in an agency in which she is the newest and only Hispanic staff member. After introductions, the client says: "I am glad you are my worker because you know these other workers I have met here don't understand our people." The worker senses the effort to make an alliance but is not sure how to respond. Her feelings are compounded by her reactions to her first few agency staff meetings when she also felt the staff did not understand Hispanic clients.

- At a first family counseling session the father reports, with anger, examples of his teenage daughter's misbehaviors. The mother sits silently staring at the ground. The daughter looks close to tears. The father demands of the worker how long it will take for the worker to "fix" his kid. The worker is thinking, "With a father like this I'd be acting out as well."

- The community organization (macro) social work student is assigned to help develop a tenants' association in a public housing projects. After door-to-door recruitment a large group of tenants arrive for the first meeting and share angry stories of mismanagement and bad treatment by the staff and the housing manager. After listening and acknowledging the strong feelings the social worker asks for volunteers to form a tenants' committee to address the problems. The request is greeted with silence. The social worker responds: "Well, to get started, maybe I should speak to the manager."

- Family support workers from a family counseling agency attend an interdisciplinary meeting with professionals from the referring child welfare agency, the clinic psychologists working with the child, and the visiting nurse meeting with the mom once a week. From the start of the meeting it is clear that each discipline has its own ideas of how to assess the issues and develop an appropriate treatment plan. The social worker is frustrated at what she experiences as a subtle battle over "Who owns the client?" The actual conversation is an "illusion of work" with nothing real happening. The social worker leaves frustrated by the meeting and no further ahead in figuring out how they can all best help this client.

- The social worker has a new client—a teenage boy referred by the school—who responds to every question in the first session with either a "yes" or a "no" without elaboration. It feels to the worker like pulling teeth.

- A hospital-based group for parents dealing with children who have a serious illness meets every week, but as soon as the discussion gets close to painful feelings one parent takes the conversation off to what seems like an unrelated topic and monopolizes the meeting. The other parents are obviously frustrated, as is the group leader as well.

These and many other specific examples are addressed in this book in an effort to understand the process (the interaction) in new ways and to develop strategies for the social worker to respond more effectively. In each case there is a "next step" that can be taken by the social worker that has the potential to move the work ahead assuming the worker can reach the part of the client, even the mandated clients, ready to change. These interventions are guided by an interactional practice theory that can provide a structure for analyzing issues and responding effectively.

This chapter introduces the central ideas of this interactional social work practice theory. First, a brief discussion of the process of theory building in social work will place this effort in context. Clients will be viewed in a dynamic interaction with many important social systems, such as the family, peers, school, and hospital. This chapter also presents the underlying assumptions about the nature of the relationship between people and their social surroundings.

Our discussion of the assessment process will center on a strengths perspective rather than on client pathology (the medical model). The role of the social work profession in mediating the individual-social engagement will be traced to the roots of the profession, which has historically been concerned with both private troubles and public issues.

Social work practice skill will then be described as the method by which the social worker strives to develop a positive working relationship with the client, a relationship that allows the social worker to be helpful. The impact of the social worker's personal self—that is, the effect of his or her feelings, ethics, or values—on his or her professional practice will also be examined.

## The Interactional Social Work Practice Theory

**EP 2.1.7a**

This book builds on the interactional model of social work practice, which draws on a number of diverse theories that guide the helping professions. By the late 1980s, the helping professions were in what Kuhn described as a "pre-scientific stage" (1962). The social work profession had just begun to use theories to translate empirical research into practice. In a scientific stage, by contrast, the results of research are used to modify theories, which are then used to guide new research.

In the 1990s, the profession was moving toward a scientific stage and beginning to develop an empirically based practice theory. Today, I believe that the helping professions have made the transition and are now, in Kuhn's term, in the early phase of a scientific stage of development. As such, this book integrates recent research results from both quantitative and qualitative methods.

Because the social work profession is still in the early stages of this crucial theory-building process, a wide range of views is possible. In recent years, social work has seen a significant expansion of efforts to strengthen theory building by employing empirical approaches. I have completed my own effort to develop a holistic, empirically based theory of social work practice, which has at its center the interactional approach to helping (Shulman, 1991). Ideas from that model have been included in this book, as have findings from my studies associated with that effort.

In particular, I emphasize the impact of oppression on clients experienced because of their race, gender, sexual orientation, physical and mental ability, and so forth; this is countered by a discussion of resilience theory and the strengths perspective as models for understanding human behavior and how clients can overcome powerful obstacles in their lives.

All practitioners eventually develop their own practice frameworks, some more and some less explicit, and judge them by how well they explain their practice. The framework for social work described in this book has been most helpful to me in my practice, theory building, and research. It is not engraved in stone, however. Having evolved for over 50 years, it will continue to be used as a framework only as long as it appears to do the job. You should test its ideas, as with all models, against your own sense of reality and use those portions that seem helpful. I encourage my students to "write your own book." I do not mean that literally—although I hope and expect that some will—but rather to suggest that they need to create their own models of the helping process.

Many of the skills and intermediate models in this book are not bound by one approach and can easily fit into other theoretical frameworks. Ideas from other models, some of which are identified and summarized in Chapter 17, are integrated whenever they help to enrich the core framework. For example, strategies and interventions from solution-focused practice (SFP) models join the list of available practitioner tools in the beginning phase of practice. Concepts that underlie the motivational interviewing (MI) approach also fit nicely within this framework when considering how to engage clients—particularly those who are mandated and resistant. Assessment and intervention concepts described in cognitive-behavioral therapy (CBT) are also useful in helping clients in the early stages of practice become unstuck in self-defeating internalizations.

## Elements of a Practice Theory

Because I refer to practice theory, models, and skills throughout the text, a brief explanation of how I use these terms may be helpful. A *practice theory* first describes what we know about human behavior and social organizations. The social worker then establishes a set of specific goals or outcomes based on these underlying assumptions. Finally, a description of the worker's interventions to achieve these specific goals completes the practice theory. Simply put, what we know about people (knowledge) informs our thinking about what we wish to achieve in our practice (valued outcomes) and this in turn guides our interventions (skills).

This approach to theorizing about practice is used throughout the text. For example, when we examine the beginning phase of work, assumptions about how people behave in new situations are related to outcomes the worker wishes to achieve during the first sessions. These outcomes, in turn, are linked to specific activities of the worker, described in more detail later as *contracting*.

As an example, clients have some degree of uncertainty about if and how a counseling relationship can be helpful to them and whether the social worker will understand their concerns. This understanding of how clients generally approach a new counseling relationship leads the social worker to set a goal in the first sessions of aiding the client to understand the kind of help that can be offered, the social worker's role, and the potential overlap—or common ground—between the client's presented need and the agency service. Based upon this understanding and these immediate goals, the social worker will use the skills of clarifying purpose, clarifying his or her role, and seeking client feedback. (These specific skills are described in more detail in Chapter 4.) For our purpose here, they demonstrate how what we know about clients in new situations (knowledge) relates to our immediate goals (valued outcomes), which in turn inform the social worker of the skills and interventions (contracting) needed in the beginning phase of work. These are the elements of a practice theory as described in this book.

## Models, Skills, and Empirical Support

The term *model* is used to describe a representation of reality. One would construct a model to help simplify the explanation or description of a complex process or object. Anyone who has visited a planetarium knows (at least after a certain age) that the balls circling the sun on the ceiling are not real planets. This is a model of the solar system and as such is a representation of reality.

In this text, models are used to describe helping processes (e.g., the dynamics and skills required in a beginning, middle, or ending phase session), individual and social psychologies (e.g., resiliency and oppression theory), and the entities with which professionals work (e.g., families, groups, communities, or organizations).

The term *skill* refers to a specific behavior that the worker uses in the helping process. Many of the skills described in this text are core relationship skills, which are useful in the performance of professional as well as personal tasks. For example, empathic skills are needed by parents, spouses, and friends. I have come to believe that, for many helping professionals, the development of self-knowledge and the enhancement of personal skills are an important part of what originally inspired us to consider the helping professions. Helping others—as every candidate's application for admission to a school of social work identifies as a core motivation—is also important. The focus here will be on the use of these skills as they relate to the social work professional function, but it would not be surprising if readers associate them, at times, to other important interpersonal relationships in their lives.

Finally, although I have been conducting empirical testing of the hypotheses contained in this practice theory, this work should be seen as an ongoing process. The grounded theory approach to theory building, first described by Glaser and Strauss (1967) in the field of sociology, guides my work. Formal and informal observations from practice are used to develop constructs of the theory. Formal research is conducted both to test propositions and to generate new ones. Some of the most interesting findings of my earlier studies did not support my initial hypotheses. These helped me to expand the theoretical constructs and led to the development of the more general and holistic theory presented in the text that complements this book (Shulman, 1991).

Many of the core findings about skill from my earlier research have been supported by research in social work and related fields. Some propositions have begun to reach the replication level at which they may be described, in Rosenberg's term (1978), as theoretical generalizations. These propositions have received repeated support from many research efforts. As these ideas are presented, I shall provide citations to the supportive literature. However, even these propositions must be open to modification as further empirical efforts direct. It is in this spirit of continuous evolution that the ideas in this book are shared.

## The Client-System Interaction

**EP 2.1.7a**

A critical factor in the helping process is the way one views the client. In early attempts to conceptualize this process, the helping professions borrowed the medical model developed by physicians. The term *medical model* has also been used in recent years to characterize a view of the client that focuses on illness and pathology; however, I use it in another sense. The medical model is defined here as the four-step process of thinking about practice commonly described as study, diagnosis, treatment, and evaluation. In this framework, the knowing professional studies the client, attempts to make an accurate assessment or diagnosis, develops a treatment plan, and evaluates the outcome. The result of the evaluation, if not positive, may lead to a rethinking of the assessment or the specific treatment plan.

### The Medical Model

**EP 2.1.7b**

To be clear, it is not the elements of the model (study, diagnosis, treatment, and evaluation) that I question here but rather the linear way in which the process is described. I believe that the helping process does not proceed in such an orderly manner and that an "interactional model," in which both client and practitioner are affecting and being affected by each other almost moment by moment, provides a more accurate description of the helping process. The helping professional who works with an individual, a couple, a family, a group, a community, or other professionals will do a great deal of thinking before and after the encounter, but his or her responses to the moment will be guided by a clear sense of purpose and role, instinct, affect, and the immediate behavior of the client. This way of thinking and responding, acting and reacting—affecting and being affected by the client, will be illustrated throughout this text.

One of several problems with the medical model has been the heavy emphasis on the study phase, in which the social worker attempts to obtain a great deal of information about the client (e.g., family history, work history, and medical history) to develop the psychosocial study on which the diagnosis and resulting treatment plan are based. Obtaining such information in the early stage is important and, in some settings, essential for reimbursement of the service, yet the question-and-answer format could lead workers to ignore the equally important processes required to engage the client and to begin to develop the working relationship. We will return to issues of assessment and diagnosis, an essential part of current social work practice, in a later chapter. For now, the argument is that the social worker needs to at one and the same time be obtaining information needed for a proper assessment and eventual treatment plan while engaging the client through a skillful contracting process as illustrated in the following example.

### First Interview with a Depressed Client

**Practice Points:** (Note that the term **Practice Points**, used throughout this book, at the start of a paragraph indicates the text is an explanation of the detailed example that follows.) The following example illustrates how a social work student begins to connect with her new client during their first session, loses the client as she switches to taking the family history, and then catches herself as she reconnects with her client on an emotional level. Also note that rather than responding defensively to the question about experience the student/social worker answers the question directly and then inquires as to the reason for the visit.

WORKER: Come on in and sit down. If you get too cold, just tell me and I'll close the window.

CLIENT: No, that's fine, it's very nice outside. So, what is your experience, your specialization? They tell me this is an important question to ask.

WORKER: Well, I'm a second-year graduate student at the School of Social Work. This is my second internship. My first one was at a child welfare office. I could tell you all of the theories I have learned and books I have read, but I think it is more important for you to see how comfortable you are with me.

CLIENT: I never had therapy before, so I guess we'll make a good team.

WORKER: What brought you here today?

CLIENT: I felt like driving my car into the canal. I left my husband in Florida, and I came home. I feel like this is where I belong. Basically, I feel like I'm drowning. (Tears fill her eyes.)

**Practice Points:** It is important that the social worker respond to the expressed emotion using a skill of articulating the client's feelings (to be discussed in detail in a later chapter). The client has not said the word *painful*; however the social worker senses the pain from her words and her facial expressions. By saying "painful," rather than simply asking how the client is feeling, the social worker is already demonstrating her capacity for empathy and understanding. She is also giving the client permission to express her feelings.

WORKER: Sounds like this is a very painful time for you. (Client is silent, head down.) When did you leave Florida?

CLIENT: Two and a half weeks ago. I went to Florida a year ago to save my marriage. I gave up everything for him—my friends, family, job—and I realize the sacrifice is not worth it. I'm going through the empty-nest syndrome without the children. I had to adjust to his family, his way of living. There was no communication between us. I got scared! I felt more like his roommate. I always have to take care of everyone!

WORKER: You sound angry.

CLIENT: Yes, and I'm tired of it!

**Practice Points:** Note that the social worker picked up the angry tone in the client's statement and even named it when she says: "You sound angry." However, at this moment, the social worker changes the tone, mood, and content of the conversation by switching to a "study" process and asking questions. In part, this is necessary to obtain the information needed by the agency, for example, for documentation in the file and/or for billing purposes. However, it is my sense that this student worker, who felt comfortable with expressions of pain, did not feel quite so comfortable with expressions of anger. Note that the client gets back to her emotions in response to the questions and for a time the worker drops the information gathering and responds once again to the feelings.

**WORKER:** Because this is an intake, I need to ask you some questions in order to complete the paperwork portion of our meeting.
**CLIENT:** Oh, I'm sorry. Go ahead.
**WORKER:** Don't be sorry. I just wanted you to know we needed to shift gears for a while.
**CLIENT:** Go ahead; that's fine.
**WORKER:** Tell me about your family.
**CLIENT:** I have five grown children: Pam, Jane, John, Cathy, and Tina. She's my baby. She recently had a baby and. . . . (Tears fill her eyes.) That's another subject.
**WORKER:** Seems like babies are a tough subject for you to talk about.
**CLIENT:** (Beginning to cry) It's OK. Go ahead, ask your questions.
**WORKER:** They are not as important as your feelings are right now. We'll have plenty of time later to complete the forms.

**Practice Summary.** (The term **Practice Summary** will be used throughout this text to introduce summary comments about the prior described practice example.) When this example was discussed in class, the student worker recognized that she had switched to the questioning format just when the client expressed strong feelings of anger. Other students in the class acknowledged that having a structured first interview in which they could focus on asking a series of questions made them feel more comfortable, whereas it possibly made the client feel less comfortable. They could also see how important it was to stay close to the feelings of the client. Many of the questions would be answered in the course of the interview, and the social worker could always leave some time at the end to obtain the missing data.

## Integrating Assessment and Engagement: Behavior as Communication

Because assessment and diagnosis is usually, and appropriately, integrated into the practices of social agencies, I try to help my students develop a workable approach even while recognizing the limitations of the medical model. We develop creative approaches for obtaining the required information and skillfully engaging the client during the first interview. Involving the client actively in the process, discussing the reasons for the information gathering, and making sure that the study phase does not substitute for contracting work are essential elements.

Students are also encouraged to find ways of relating to the team when discussing specific clients, such as in a case conference, which may effect a shift in attitude toward clients from pathology to strengths. In later chapters, we examine assessment models and work with other professionals and systems in more detail. To preview this discussion, I will be suggesting that the social worker always has two clients—the client in the interview and the agency or host setting (e.g., school, hospital). In fact, I will argue that one of the unique aspects of the social work professional role is attending to and attempting to skillfully impact this "second" client.

Another problem with the medical model is that it tends to present clients in static terms. The model emphasizes attributing descriptive characteristics to the client (e.g., resistant, hard to reach). In extreme cases, workers refer to clients as diagnoses, as in "I'm working with a borderline" rather than "a client with a borderline diagnosis." Even the term *therapy*, often used by social workers to describe work with individuals, families, and groups (e.g., group or family therapy), implies that something is wrong with the client that requires fixing.

## Dynamic Systems Theory: The VISA Center Example

For many years now, dynamic systems theory has profoundly influenced the way that helping professionals view their clients. One central idea has been the emphasis on viewing a client in interaction with others. Instead of seeing a client as the object of analysis, workers began to focus on the way in which the client and the client's important systems were interacting. In fact, according to this viewpoint, one can never understand the movements of the client except as affected by the movements of others. Clients are viewed in interaction with their immediate and larger social surrounding, each affecting and being affected by the other in a reciprocal manner. A client may be considered resistant, for example, until one looks closely at the way the social worker is attempting to engage the client. The resistance may be a direct result of the efforts of the worker, or past experiences with other workers, and not inherent to the client.

For example, consider the work I directed during a project to address the problem of school violence in a midsize, inner-city school district, in which a significant percentage of students suspended from school for violent acts against teachers or other students, drug possession, or weapon possession were students of color who were also economically disadvantaged and at least one year behind in school. The center we established on the university campus, Vision-Integrity—Structure-Accountability, or VISA, provided a short-term, two-week academic and behavioral intervention program as well as services for the students' families.[1]

From the perspective of the school system, the problem was with the student, and the diagnosis was often "learning disability," "oppositional behavior disorder," "borderline personality," or "emotionally disturbed." The usual treatment was to formally suspend the student and send him or her home for two weeks, to receive home instruction from a teacher for one hour a day, or to enroll the student in anger management programs at the school or through local agencies. The school district recidivism rate was high, and many of the students were resuspended soon after they returned to school.

From our perspective, the students' behavior was instead a call for help to deal with some life situation that these students faced. We started with the assumption that the behavior was not the problem but the symptom of a maladaptive way of coping with interactional struggles that existed for them with their families, their schools, the community, and—on a larger social level—society.

The VISA Center was a voluntary alternative offered to the students and their parents at the time of the formal suspension hearing. In addition to academic instruction, the behavioral modules were all designed to focus on the issues and concerns that faced students from their perspective. For example, modules on substance abuse were not used as lectures on the damage done by drugs but instead focused on the damage done to the students' lives. These included, for example, substance abuse issues in their families, the difficulty they faced from peer pressure to use drugs, and friends who were heavy users and whom they worried about but did not know how to help.

Mutual-aid support groups focused on issues in their lives that ranged from physical or sexual abuse to involvement in fights for fear of "losing face," pressure to join

---

1. For more information, see the VISA Center Report at http://www.socialwork.buffalo.edu/research/visa.asp.

gang activity in the neighborhood (if only for protection), posttraumatic stress as a result of witnessing family violence or drive-by shootings, depression because of the loss of family members to violence and prison, anger about perceived racism within the schools they attended and the larger community, and a sense of hopelessness about their futures. The latter issue was poignantly characterized by one 16-year-old who said, "Why do I need to finish school? I'm not going to live past 20 anyway!"

This interactional perspective led to interventions that were designed to work "with" the students rather than "on" the students. More detail on this program will be shared later in the book; for now the point is that, by avoiding seeing the student as the problem and instead focusing on the reciprocal interaction between the student and the immediate and larger environment, we were able to shift the conversation. By understanding that the student's behavior in the VISA Center was constantly affecting and being affected by the interaction with staff and other students (e.g., group dynamics), we were able to see the student in a more dynamic and individualized way.

***An "Anger Management" Group for Angry 15- and 16-Year-Old Girls*** Another illustration of understanding behavior as communication would be work done with a group of 15- and 16-year-old African American girls on probation for criminal activity referred to an "anger management group" by a judge as an alternative to going to jail. Brief excerpts from a number of sessions illustrate the importance of dealing with the issues and feelings leading to the maladaptive behavior.

In the early sessions, the two young, Caucasian, female middle-class group leaders need to clarify the purpose of the group, clarify the members' reactions to being mandated to attend, explain their roles as group leaders, and address the intercultural issues of having Caucasian workers with African American clients. After opening up the issue of their involuntary attendance, one member, Monica, responds:

> What is it gonna matter if we decide we want to stay or not? We have to be here. I really just think it's stupid that I have to sit here with people I don't know and learn from two old women how I'm supposed to act.

**Practice Points:** The group leaders, both in their early twenties, particularly reacted to the "old women" part of the comment. Their immediate responses are defensive and they quickly change the subject and introduce an exercise. In a later session, the leaders address the issues of race, age, and class directly:

> I opened the session by asking the girls to go around the room and say one thing about their week. The girls did this with no problems until it came to Monica, who stated, "Why do you care about my week? None of you would understand what I'm going through anyway." I responded by asking Monica if she was concerned that Kim and I wouldn't understand because we are white and much older than her. Monica said that was part of it and that we both come from places that are different than where she lives. At this point, we were right in the thick of the authority theme (once again). I said, "Monica, I realize that Kim and I may look different than you, and we are. And, to be completely honest with you, we probably won't understand all of the time what you or any of the other members are experiencing. The only thing that I can tell you is that we want to try and understand, but that we can only do that if you'll give us the chance."

**Practice Points:** This courageous and direct response to an otherwise taboo issue helps to build a more positive relationship between the leaders and the group members. It becomes clear through discussion that these girls had experienced early sexual and physical abuse. They also described incidents in detention centers (and one in an adult jail) where they witnessed or heard about other inmates forced to provide "sexual favors" to guards. The group leaders decide to introduce the idea of "forgiveness" as a way of getting past their continued underlying anger. Monica, who has emerged as an internal leader in the group, once again responds:

> Monica started talking right away. She said, "I hope you don't think I'm ever going to forgive my f---in' father—when he's dead, I'll forgive him." I asked Monica if she was saying that because she was still angry with him for some of the things that he had done to her. Monica agreed. I then asked her if she would mind sharing a little bit about what happened. She began explaining a situation with her father. When she was very little, he had broken her arm in five different places because he was trying to keep his beer from rolling down the hill, and he slammed her arm in the car door. She went on to explain that, when she was 10 years old, her stepbrother had molested her; her father knew about it and didn't do anything.

**Practice Summary:** One can easily understand the anger carried around by these girls. Expressions of rage and escalation of negative behavior are often a call for help. They will continue until someone hears the hurt and begins to respond to the meaning of the behavior. These two group leaders are quickly learning that persistent and ongoing oppression and trauma can lead to expressions of anger that are then responded to by the systems (e.g., school, juvenile justice) as the problem, which misses the underlying message. It serves as a striking example of the need to understand behavior as communication.

***Work with a Depressed, Middle-Aged Woman in a Psychiatric Ward*** In another, very different example, this shift in thinking is illustrated by the case of a depressed, middle-aged woman who was admitted to the psychiatric ward of a hospital. Initially, one could choose to focus only on her depression and other symptoms. In fact, current knowledge about the biological sources of some forms of depression requires that professionals be aware of treatment possibilities that can include the use of psychotropic drugs.

An alternative framework would seek to identify those important systems in her life with which she must deal: her husband, her children, her job, her peer group, her parents or siblings, her society and its many sexist attitudes, and so on. In addition, one could include the hospital, her doctor, the ward staff, and other patients. Figure 1.1 presents a diagrammatic view of this framework.

FIGURE 1.1

------------------------------------------------------------

### *Relationship of Client and Systems*

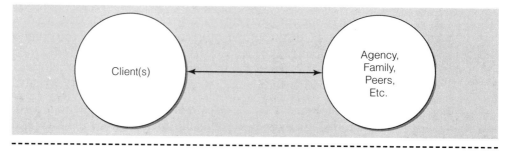

This important change in perspective alters the kind of questions that the worker mentally asks. Instead of simply focusing on the state of the patient's mental health, the degree of the depression, and its possible cause (e.g., early childhood trauma or substance abuse), the worker is equally curious about the state of the interactions between the patient and each of the relevant systems.

What is the nature of the relationship between the woman and her husband? Can they talk to and listen to each other? Is the relationship emotionally or physically abusive? The worker would also be interested in the relationship between the patient and the hospital. How well has the patient integrated into the ward? Is she reaching out to other patients and creating an informal support group, or is she cut off and isolated?

These are not questions the worker will be asking the client in the early interviews (the structure of first sessions will be discussed later). Rather, they are examples of the potential areas of work on which the helping process may focus. Furthermore, the worker will not focus only on the client's part in the interaction. As stated earlier, the client's movements can only be understood in relation to the movements of those around her. How well do family, friends, and other clients reach out to her? Part of the outcome of these interactions will be determined by the client's input, but other parts will be a result of the system's responses. In fact, as mentioned earlier, the relationship will be reciprocal, with the movements of each constantly affecting the movements of the others.

In addition to understanding the client in interaction with her environment it is important to consider societal context related to her gender and its impact on her life. Feminist practice consists of a number of models and frameworks that attempt to address the unique issues facing women in our society. These include issues of social and political oppression and the impact of having been generally placed in a subordinate position in respect to their gender. Efforts have also been made to develop a unique psychology of women in terms of how they relate and connect to others. This model will be explored in more detail in later chapters.

One example of how to integrate various theories into a single framework taking gender into account is the self-in-relation theory that emerged from efforts to rethink women's psychology initiated by Miller (1987, 1988; Miller & Stiver, 1991, 1993) and Gilligan, Lyons, and Hammer (1990) as part of the Harvard Project on Women's Psychology and Girls' Development, as well as by others at the Stone Center in Wellesley, Massachusetts (e.g., Fedele, 1994; Jordan, 1991, 1993).

It's important to note that following the early publications addressing the relational model, Stone Center researchers focused on an inherent and acknowledged bias in their original work. Jordan (1997), referring to the early work, said that

> it represented largely white, middle-class, well-educated heterosexual experience. While we struggled not to reproduce the errors that occur when one subgroup speaks as if its reality is the reality, we inevitably were bound by our own blindspots and biases. We became more and more aware of the dangers of speaking about or for "all women." We were indeed speaking about "some women" or about partial aspects of many women's experience. Our appreciation of diversity needed to be broadened and deepened. (p. 1)

Jordan points out that the work in these later publications continued to elaborate and explore the relational theory with an emphasis on topics such as sexuality, shame, anger, and depression, as well as the complexity related to women's diverse life experiences.

While all women suffer in a patriarchal society where our experience is not presented in the dominant discourse, women in various cultural/ethnic groups suffer additional marginalization based on race, sexual orientation, socioeconomic standing, able-bodiedness, and age. Women who are marginalized also develop strengths that may differ from those of white, privileged heterosexual women. (p. 1)

Keeping in mind Jordan's concerns about generalizing, if we were to apply some of this theory, we might rethink this client's situation in terms of paradoxes. For example, in an article on the use of relational theory in group work practice, Fedele (1994) describes a central paradox first identified by Miller as follows:

This paradox states that during the course of our lifetime, in the desire to make connections and be emotionally accessible, we all experience harm or violation that leads to a need to develop strategies to keep large parts of ourselves out of connection. In the face of intense yearning for connection and in order to remain in the only relationships available, we develop strategies that keep more and more of ourselves out of connection. Simply put, the paradox is that in order to stay in connection, we keep parts of ourselves out of connection. (Miller, 1988, p. 10)

The paradox of maintaining connection through disconnection offers additional insights into the potential causes of a client's depression, rooted in her current and possibly past experiences. It also suggests how to help clients find ways to make new connections (with family members, the hospital, other women in a mutual-aid support group, etc.) without the need to maintain the disconnection defenses. (The relational model will be discussed in more detail in Chapter 13.)

In addition, to truly understand clients, workers need to understand clients' interactions in the context within which they take place. We are much clearer now about how our society's stereotypes of women and men affect relationships. In many examples, when one looks beneath the depression of some middle-aged women, one finds an understandable anger, even rage, related to sex-role stereotyping and oppression by a male-dominated and privileged society. Does the woman experience herself as able to influence her social environment, or does she feel powerless (Weick & Vandiver, 1982)? Has she experienced significant victimization in her life (Berlin & Kravetz, 1981)? Is this a situation in which it is important to empower the client (Smith & Siegal, 1985)? Does the view of her situation change if workers apply one of the many feminist models more recently summarized by Saulnier (1996, 2000), such as liberal feminism, radical feminism, or postmodern feminism?

If the client is also a person of color and economically disadvantaged, then we have the classic triple oppressions related to gender, race, and class. A severe depression may well represent an understandable, but maladaptive defensive reaction in response to the oppressive conditions imposed by the increasing feminization of poverty or the impact of welfare reform efforts that require recipients to find work when jobs are unavailable and resources are limited.

### Intersectionality, Interlocking Oppressions, and Social Location

EP 2.1.4a
EP 2.1.4b
EP 2.1.4c
EP 2.1.4d

More recently, feminist scholarship has turned to developing concepts such as *intersectionality, interlocking oppressions,* and *social location* (Butterfield, 2003; Hancock, 2007; Hulko, 2009). Intersectionality refers to the way in which different identities intersect, for example, being a woman, a person of color, and a Lesbian has a different level of impact than just being a woman. Interlocking oppressions refers to the oppression and privilege (or lack of privilege) that may be associated with intersectionality. Hulko refers to social location as follows:

> Social location is a dynamic concept; it is context contingent, and its attribution reflects processes of subordination and domination—both contemporary and historical. The ways in which identities intersect and oppressions interlock are fluid and varied because the meanings that are ascribed to identify categories and the power afforded or denied to specific social groups are based on the sociocultural context in which these social processes occur. (p. 52)

Hulko and others stress the importance of social workers and social work students learning to acknowledge holding "unearned privileges," for example, those associated with their Whiteness or straightness. She suggests the importance of helping individuals "to move beyond guilty feelings towards responsible actions" (p. 53).

## Fanon: The Oppressor Within and the Oppressor Without

Oppression psychology, as described by Fanon and elaborated by Bulhan (1985), is discussed in more detail in the next chapter. Fanon suggested that prolonged exposure to oppression could lead clients to internalize the "oppressor without" and adopt negative self-attitudes and self-images. Internalized rage, often masked by depression, can lead clients to behavior that is maladaptive and destructive to themselves and others. "The oppressor without becomes an introppressor—an oppressor within" (p. 126). Such a person, according to Fanon, becomes an "autopressor" by participating in her or his own oppression.

Ironically, and conveniently, the maladaptive behavior that results from prolonged experience of oppression is then used by the majority and the more privileged group to justify continued stereotyping and oppression, maintaining a vicious cycle. We certainly observed this maladaptive pattern and the social response in respect to the students we worked with at the VISA Center who were suspended for violence. Many of their behaviors were self-destructive, and even their use of language and self-deprecating names and expressions often revealed a form of internalized negative image.

If the client is also a vulnerable client—for example, he or she lacks a strong social support system of family or friends—then his or her essentially maladaptive responses become all the more understandable. In addition, given the client's situation, one has to be impressed by the strength the client has shown by simply surviving and continuing to struggle. By viewing the client from a strengths perspective and a resiliency model as well as incorporating solution-focused strategies, discussed later in this book, the social worker can focus on the part of the client that has demonstrated a capacity to deal effectively with life. Certainly, as we worked with more than 350 suspended students during the duration of the VISA project, we were impressed with their survival skills and wondered whether we would have been able to cope, even maladaptively, if faced with their often overwhelming life situations.[2]

A worker starting from this perspective will be more interested in identifying what is right than what is wrong with clients. For example, the worker will want to help them identify times in their lives when they effectively coped and the resources

---

2. The VISA Center was funded by a New York State legislative initiative and operated over 2 school years. The center closed after the 9/11 attacks, when state funding shifted to focus on recovery efforts in lower Manhattan.

they needed rather than concentrating on when they were in trouble. Instead of focusing only on the causes of relapses in substance abuse recovery, the worker will want to help clients consider how they maintained their recovery between relapses. For our suspended students, their ability to survive longer periods of time in school before they were resuspended was viewed as a positive outcome. If they were first suspended for a violent act and then resuspended for nonviolent behavior, this was also viewed as progress. These often-subtle signs of life and strength are what the worker will reach for in trying to help clients overcome the effects of oppression.

To return to our earlier example of the depressed female client, as the client-system interactions are identified, the woman's depression may take on new meaning. The sadness and passivity are not the problems; rather, they are the symptoms of the breakdown in these important interactions and the result of the experienced oppression. The depression is not the illness to be cured but a signal that important areas of interaction in the woman's life have broken down. The worker will not try to "cure" the client but instead affect the client's capacity for coping and change, the way she thinks about her feelings and problems and herself, and how she and these important systems interact.

The cure for the problem will emerge not from the professional's treatment plan but from the client's increasing understanding of her situation and her own efforts, with the support of the worker, to find new ways to interact with the systems that matter to her—either by reaching out to them or cutting herself off from them and finding new sources of support. Similarly, the systems (e.g., the family) may have to find new ways to reach out to this client to reengage her. Both the client and the systems may find implementation of this process difficult. Here, the job of the social worker plays a crucial role. Psychotropic drugs may be needed in some cases to deal with the biological/physical causes of the depression but that will not remove the need to help the client through counseling as well.

At this point, you may have many questions and possibly some objections. What if the client is too weak to deal with the system, doesn't want help, or refuses to work on the interaction? Perhaps the problem is with the system—for example, the school. As mentioned earlier, what happens if the depression is related to biological factors for which pharmaceutical treatment is needed, perhaps in conjunction with counseling? These and other objections are pursued in some detail in the discussions that follow. For the moment, try to set them aside. At this point, the most important concept to grasp is that the client to be helped, the suspended middle or high school student, the recovering addict or the depressed wife, is viewed as an interactive entity, often ambivalent, acting and reacting to the various demands of the systems he or she must negotiate. The systems will be viewed in this way as well and will be referred to as the "second client" throughout the book.

Each client is a special case within this general model. The unwed pregnant teen in a child welfare agency might be dealing with the systems of the agency, the child's biological father, family, friends, societal attitudes as reflected in welfare legislation, prejudices toward women and sexuality in general, antiabortion pressures, and so on. Of equal concern to her may be issues of income (welfare or work), housing, child care, and the medical system. If she lives in a group care home, the house parents and other residents become part of the active systems in her life. Her feelings about herself as a woman, her reactions to society's norms, and her own, often harsh, judgments of herself (the oppressor within) may all be part of her agenda, but always in relation to the way in which she deals with those systems that matter to her.

Whatever the category of client discussed in this book—the child in the residential center, the husband in marital counseling, the student who is failing, the client with a terminal illness, the client learning to live with AIDS, the client in the early stages of recovery from substance abuse, the soldier returning from a war and experiencing posttraumatic stress symptoms, or the member of a citizens' community action group—all will be viewed in the context of the interaction with their social surroundings and an understanding of their potential strengths.

## Underlying Assumptions in the Interactional Model

**EP 2.1.7a**

All models of social work practice are based on underlying assumptions about people and their social surroundings. These are the starting points for theory building, and they need to be made explicit. Although many assumptions about people and the helping process will be examined throughout this book, three core ideas that underlie the interactional model are presented here. The first is the symbiotic assumption: a belief in the essential symbiotic relationship between people and their social surroundings. The second is the assumption that this mutual need is systematically blocked by obstacles, some raised by the client and others by the systems the client must negotiate. The third basic assumption is that the social worker must always assume and reach for the client's (and system's) strengths for change. These assumptions are explored in the sections that follow.

### Assumption of Symbiosis

Now that we have placed clients in interaction with the various systems that affect them, we need to examine the nature of this relationship. If we return to the example in the previous section of a depressed, middle-aged woman, our view of how to help this client will depend on our assumptions about the individual-social engagement. If we examine her interactions with her environment, we can perceive a certain amount of ambivalence. Some part of her will seem to be reaching out, however faintly, toward life and the people around her. On the other hand, her withdrawal, depression, and general communications appear to signal a retreat from life. She may have experienced life as too difficult, her feelings too painful to face, and the demands seemingly impossible to meet.

A part of her seems to be giving up and saying that the very struggle seems useless. She can be observed placing barriers between herself and these systems, including that part of the system (the worker) that is reaching out to help her. She is simultaneously reaching out for life, growth, and the important systems around her, and moving away from each.

The assumption that a part of us is always striving toward health lies at the core of the practice theory formulated by Schwartz (1961). Borrowing a "symbiotic" model of human relationships, he views the individual-social interaction as

> a relationship between the individual and his nurturing group which we would describe as "symbiotic"—each needing the other for its own life and growth, and each reaching out to the other with all the strength it can command at a given moment. (Schwartz, 1961, p. 15)

The term *symbiotic* is used to describe the mutual needs of individuals and the systems that matter to them. This woman's needs can best be met through interaction with the world around her and not through complete withdrawal from it. Similarly, society has a stake in maintaining this client as an active, involved, unique, integrated individual. The idea of symbiotic striving fits comfortably with the constructs of the relational model described earlier.

Unfortunately, the term *symbiotic* has taken on a professional connotation of unhealthy mutual overdependency, as between a mother and child. In the world of biology, symbiosis actually describes two organisms living in a mutually beneficial relationship. The exploitation of one organism by another would be described as a parasitic relationship.

Schwartz uses the term to underline our mutual dependency and our essential interest in each other. It is a statement of the interdependence that is fundamental to a belief in social responsibility for the welfare of each individual. It also recognizes that each individual finds life's needs best satisfied through positive relationships with others. Although not always explicitly stated, this assumption underlies much of our profession's advocacy efforts on behalf of the poor and other left-out populations. Providing adequate health care and an adequate education for all, as examples, are not only in the client's interest; it is also in the interest of the larger society that needs a healthy and educated population to contribute to the nation's growth.

You may be wondering at this point how this assumption of a symbiotic model relates to experiences in which the individual-social interaction appears to be far from symbiotic and, in fact, has often been defined as oppressive. Schwartz (1961, p. 15) points out that, in a complex and often distorted society, the individual-social symbiosis grows diffuse and obscure in varying degrees, ranging from the normal developmental problems of children growing into their culture to the severe pathology involved in situations where the symbiotic attachment appears to be all but severed.

The very fact that the mutual self-interest of people and their surrounding systems is often obscured creates the working ground for the helping professional. The observation that people and their systems often appear to be acting against each other's self-interest is not an argument against the symbiotic model; rather, it is an argument to help both system and client regain their sense of mutuality.

Following this model, the worker will search not only for the part of the client that is reaching out toward systems but also for the part of the family, friends, peer group, and hospital system that is reaching out toward the patient. For instance, if the husband appears to turn away from his wife during the family session, closing off his feelings, the worker might reach for the underlying sense of loss and hurt that he attempts to hide even from himself. When the hospital rules, procedures, and services seem to work against the best interests of a patient, the helping person will attempt to influence the part of the system that cares about the people it serves; in doing so, the worker will employ several strategies such as mediation, brokering, or advocacy.

In example after example throughout this book, you will observe that the helping person's movements with the client, the moment-by-moment interventions, are affected by the worker's view of the individual-social relationship. At critical moments in the interactions, connections will be discovered between husbands and wives, parents and children, students and teachers, community groups and politicians, individual group members and the group, and so forth, because the helping person was searching for them. This idea is termed the *two-client construct*, in which the social worker will always be seen as having two clients. The second client will change in each situation. In the current example, it may be the woman's family, hospital system, friends, and so on.

The practical implications of this philosophical assumption are important. For example, in the case of our female client, the worker's belief in the importance of helping her find connections to people around her and the belief in this woman's partial striving for this connection will cause the worker to search for faint clues that the client is still emotionally alive and trying. The worker will not be fooled by the defenses thrown up by the client but will concentrate instead on the spark of life that still exists, often associated with the anger—even rage—that is buried under the depression and apathy. The work of the helping person is not to remotivate the client but to discover and support the motivation that is already there. Helping the client understand the nature of her internalized oppressor is an important step in helping her take control over her life and begin dealing with the oppressor without.

Belief in this symbiotic model does not necessarily exclude the existence of important tensions and real conflicts of interest between the individual and the systems. Interactions in life involve conflict and confrontation. Not all interests are mutual. Oppression happens for a reason. The effective helping person brings these underlying differences into the open so that the engagement is a real human process invested with a range of feelings. Examples abound in which the skilled helper challenges the illusion of agreement between the parties in conflict by reaching for and demanding real work. The model provides the worker with a sense of the potential common ground on which both the client and the important life systems can build.

For workers to be effective in this role, they need to recognize that oppression clearly has some psychological and concrete payoffs for the majority group in any situation. Our more recent literature has focused on the issue of privilege, in which certain groups gain an advantage and have an ongoing stake in protecting it. For example, when a man uses battering and intimidation to attempt to control a woman in his life, he receives psychological and concrete benefits from the interaction. If we consider the "master-slave" paradigm developed by Hegel in 1807 (1966), elements of which underlie oppression theory, the insecure "master" seeks to "recognize" or define himself through the unreciprocated recognition by the "slave" (Bulhan, 1985). In effect, the male batterer uses the subjugation of his female partner to bolster his sense of self by his partner "recognizing" him without his having to "recognize" her.

In considering such relationships, social workers' first concern should be to protect oppressed clients and hold the oppressors accountable for their actions. Battering is a criminal offense and must be treated as such. Work with a battered woman often involves helping her find her own strength and the social resources needed to leave the abusive relationship safely.

However, when also working with the male batterer, workers need to recognize that this use of violence for control can have significant negative effects on him, including legal consequences, emotional damage to the self, and preclusion of an intimate relationship based on mutuality and equality—a relationship of mutual recognition. Work with men who batter often reveals that these men were childhood victims of abuse (emotional, sexual, and physical), which helps to explain but not excuse their behavior. We have learned that if we wish to help them break the pattern of use of abuse and the need for control when dealing with others, we need to address them as clients in their own right. This often also means addressing their substance abuse, which is often a form of flight from their own early oppression.

We can extend this individual psychology to a social psychology when we recognize that the wider sexist attitudes that support this brutal form of oppression can be explained by the same psychological dynamics. The payoffs for sexism are not only psychological but concrete and financial as well. When women are consistently paid less than men for the same jobs, profits are higher, even in nonprofit organizations. When a "glass ceiling" stops women (and other minority groups) from advancing in business or government agencies, more senior positions are available for men and members of the majority and privileged groups. Even these gains, however, are offset by the long-term social, moral, and economic prices paid as a result of such short-sighted practices.

On a broader scale, oppression by all majority groups against all minority groups—such as people of color, women, immigrants, Jews, gays and lesbians, and people with mental illness, mental retardation, or significant physical challenges—results in specific economic and psychological benefits for the majority group. However, the significant personal, social, and even economic costs are often ignored.

For example, when the AIDS epidemic was viewed as a problem that affected only gays, Haitians, and intravenous drug users, many of whom live in inner-city ghettos, the U.S. government—including then-president Ronald Reagan—largely ignored it. Some extreme religious groups actually pointed to the disease as retribution for "immoral" behavior and saw the growing numbers of deaths as a cleansing of society. Although these views were extreme, they may have represented a more general undercurrent of racism and homophobia that fostered lethargy and inaction among the larger community. One has only to imagine the difference in the response if such an epidemic had initially struck middle-class, heterosexual Whites instead of these minority populations.

The differential provision of medical research and support to minority populations represents a deadly form of oppression. Only more recently has the majority group come to grips with the incredible social and health-related costs associated with the increase in this epidemic and its spread to the majority population. The same is true if one considers the true costs of the inadequate health care services provided in the United States to the poor and the oppressed. Lack of a universal health care system in this country stands in stark contrast to programs developed in Canada, Europe, and some Latin American countries.

These examples can be added to the list of the many documented incidents of racism in medicine, including the "shocking and scandalous relatively recently halted Tuskegee experiment on syphilis among blacks in Macon County, Alabama" (Bulhan, 1985, p. 87), in which the effects of the untreated disease on 400 Black men and their families were observed for more than 40 years without the knowledge of the study participants or the provision of available treatments. It was only in 1997 that then-president Bill Clinton publicly acknowledged and apologized for these actions on behalf of the American people.

The existence of the many powerful examples of oppression and exploitation of vulnerable populations in U.S. history does not change the essential, symbiotic nature of the relationship between people and their social surroundings. These instances instead reveal how much we have lost sight of these connections. They also provide a rationale for the unique functional role of the social work profession described later in this chapter.

## Assumption of Obstacles in the Engagement

Thus far we have focused on the client's interactions with important environmental systems. Both the individual and the systems are vitally linked through mutual need. Each is seen as reaching out to the other with all the strength available at the moment and with the capacity to reach out more effectively. The next logical question is: What goes wrong? The mutual dependence can be blocked or obscured by any number of obstacles. We now briefly examine three potential obstacles to interaction between the individual and the social system: changing social systems, conflicts between self-interest and mutual interest, and the dynamics of interpersonal communication.

***The Increasing Complexity of Human Social Systems*** One problem is the increasing complexity of human social systems, such as the family. The relationships between parents and children and husbands and wives (or same-sex partners) have become increasingly difficult. Important sources of social support across generations have diminished as modern nuclear families tend to live apart from grandparents and other relatives. As society's norms and values change more rapidly than they did in past generations, parents are forced to reconcile their own beliefs with the newer values of their children. Furthermore, the world of work absorbs more time and energy, often allowing parents less opportunity to foster family stability. The significant increase in single-parent families puts an additional burden on a parent to be the provider and fill all other roles as well. It can be done—and is done—but usually at some cost to the parent and the child.

EP 2.1.9a

Middle-aged parents find themselves attempting to provide support for their adolescent (and often young adult) children while simultaneously feeling responsible for the well-being of their aged parents. Called by some the "sandwich generation," they often ask, "When will I have time for me?" This was a common expression of the so-called "baby boomer" generation, those born during the post–World War II baby boom. Now, as a record number of the members of this generation are reaching retirement and their own old age, the question has become, "Who will have time for me?" The growth in interest in geriatric social work and the significant input of geriatric information to our curriculum is one sign of this major population change. Given all of these changes, is it any wonder that family members at times find dealing with one other quite complicated?

Our definition of family has changed dramatically. The typical two-parent family of a few generations ago has been replaced by an ever-higher percentage of single-parent families. These families, as well as low-income two-parent families, face increasing stress because of the breakdown of the formal support network—the government "safety net"—as a result of budget cuts. The full impact of the 1996 Welfare Reform Act has now been felt, and studies suggest that at least some of the families cut off from welfare have not been able to make the predicted transition to work and independence and are now far worse off than they were before. We are starting to recognize that early positive findings may have been related more to a booming economy than to programmatic changes.

The availability of day care, low-cost housing, financial subsidies, and adequate health care has decreased almost in proportion to the increase in need. Some political and economic leadership has stressed a "me-first" ethic that has encouraged the majority to ignore the needs of disenfranchised populations. We were at first shocked by the appearance of the homeless on our urban streets, and then encouraged to be angry at them by political leaders who suggested that shelter was available for anyone who really wanted it.

Periodically, and currently, we have experienced severe problems in the economy that have undermined employment stability. Employment patterns that rely on temporary workers, corporate restructuring, and the layoff of middle level managers are more common now than before. The increased globalization of the economy and the ability of corporations to outsource—or move jobs to other countries to increase profits—have led to fears that unemployment in the United States may be an ongoing problem even when the economy appears to be robust.

When higher-paying jobs are lost and replaced by lower-paying ones, often without benefits, a larger portion of our population moves into poverty and vulnerability rather than into economic and social security. The high levels of unemployment and uncertainty have led to increased family tension. In one of my early research projects (Shulman, 1991), Canadian workers in British Columbia reported significant increases in the number and severity of child abuse cases, which appear to be linked to economic stress (e.g., loss of a job or fear of such a loss). Normal family tensions, such as parent-teen conflicts, become exacerbated when parents face economic stress or must cope, in the words of one study participant, with the "earthquake" of unemployment.

The recent crash of the housing market and the revelations of mortgage irregularities that may have led to many finding themselves "underwater"—meaning their houses were worth less than the principal of their mortgages—have led to foreclosures and the obvious family stresses associated with a loss of housing. Many who had counted on their home equity to provide substantial support as they approached or were in the retirement stage of life have been disappointed.

Even during stable economic conditions, a politically divided federal government, debates over a balanced budget, pressures to provide tax breaks (which mostly benefit the wealthy), the rising costs of health care in general and prescription drugs in particular, demands for "smaller government," and the abandonment of federal responsibility—to be replaced by state control over health and social welfare programs—have led to an increasing gap between the rich and the poor, the healthy and the sick, the fully participating members of our communities and those who are left out.

More generally, as the poor collect in cities, and as the institutions (welfare, medical, educational) designed to serve them grow more complex, the basic relationship between people and these important systems is bound to become obstructed. One need only think of one's reactions to the first day at a new school or to entering a busy hospital to remember how strange, overwhelming, and impersonal the system can seem. The obstacles related to complexity are inherent, and they often emerge inadvertently from the realities of the system.

Immigration, both legal and illegal, has emerged as a powerful social and political issue. It is interesting to note that an emotional backlash against the growing number of immigrants, particularly from Mexico and other countries in Central and South America, is often based on myths advanced by those who seek political gain or talk show hosts who cater to the prejudices of their audiences. For example, the myth that large-scale immigration leads to lower wages has been challenged by research that suggests that larger immigration actually leads to higher wages for the general population. It is also interesting to note that major industries that depend on immigrants to do jobs that others will not have joined together to propose revisions of the immigration laws and paths to citizenship that they see as essential to their industry's survival. This is one example of how, even at points of social conflict, it is possible to identify the essential symbiotic nature between our larger society and oppressed and vulnerable populations.

***Divergence in Self-Interest and Social Interest*** A second set of obstacles is associated with the divergent interests of people and the systems that matter to them. Life does not consist only of mutual interest and interdependence. There are times when self-interest directly conflicts with the interests of others. In fact, each individual, as part of the growth process, must learn to set aside his or her own immediate needs to integrate into the social order.

For example, in marriage or partnerships, the man may believe that he has some stake in maintaining a traditional and privileged gender role. The rules of behavior, norms, and the traditional structures in such relationships provide some payoffs for the privileged male partner. A confident woman who is able to develop a sense of her self differentiated from her husband and her family may be a more interesting person, but she may also intimidate a partner who is struggling with his own sense of worth. Obstacles to the symbiotic relationship can be generated by the ambivalence that family members feel toward change. Rapid changes produce anxiety for all in our society, so we often attempt to maintain the status quo and preserve continuity.

Complex systems are also ambivalent toward the people they serve. For example, politicians may view community action pressure groups as thorns in their sides. As these groups expose important unmet needs, they also reveal problems that are difficult to handle. Government bodies face demands from many sources for a share of the economic pie, and to have this pressure heightened by citizen groups creates new difficulties. School boards may encourage the development of parent groups but are not quite so positive when the groups openly challenge the quality of the education rather than sticking to bake sales and school trips.

Although society has a fundamental stake in strengthening and incorporating its most vulnerable populations, it also has an element of economic self-interest in maintaining the poor and fostering a stereotype that blames them for their own problems. It is easy to see how the need for strong, active, community pressure groups as sources of feedback for our society can be obscured by the immediate need for peace and quiet. Similarly, large institutions such as schools find it easier to deal with students and parents who conform, make no trouble, and go along with the present order. These same schools often fail to realize the price they pay in terms of parent involvement in their children's learning.

***Problems of Interpersonal Communication*** A third major set of obstacles involves problems associated with interpersonal communication. Sharing and understanding painful or taboo thoughts and feelings is hard. People find it difficult to speak of feelings about sex, authority, race, intimacy, dependency, loss, sexual orientation, and so on. The powerful norms of our society are brought to bear in each interpersonal relationship, often making achievement of mutual understanding difficult. Most important conversations between people take place through the use of indirect communications that can be extremely hard to decipher.

For example, the husband who feels hurt and rejected by his wife's apparent lack of interest in sexual relations may express this through hostile or sarcastic comments in a totally unrelated area. The wife, in turn, may be expressing her own reactions to the husband's continual criticism through lack of interest in sexual contact. Each may be feeling a powerful and important need for the other that is obscured by the built-up resentment developed by their immature means of communication.

Students who feel that a teacher is always on their back, or is racist, or does not like them, or makes them feel academically incompetent, or has lower expectations for them, may respond with failure, lack of preparation, aggressive behavior, and cutting classes.

In one example of a student in our VISA program, a young girl who was suspended from school after a verbal and almost physical altercation with a teacher in a hallway, the lack of clear communications was poignant and striking. As the student described it in one of our mutual-aid support groups—and only after a great deal of effort to make her feel safe to share the incident—she was walking with her friends toward one part of the school when the teacher told her she should be heading in the other direction. What was not said was that she had been recently referred to a special education class, which her friends did not know about. She was walking in the wrong direction because she was hiding the fact that she needed to attend a class, as she put it, for "dummies." Her resistance to turning around was an indirect communication that her teacher missed. Instead of an opportunity to talk with the student about the incident, it became a battle of wills in which everyone lost. The support group became a way to help the student rethink her self-image and develop better strategies for communication to avoid self-destructive behavior.

Teachers, out of frustration at not being able to reach children, often respond with increased exhortation or punishment or in some cases by developing stereotypes based on race, class, ethnicity, or gender. To the children, the message is that the teacher does not care. To the teacher, the message is that the children (or their parents) do not care.

In most cases, they are both wrong. The children's stake in the successful completion of their education and the teacher's stake in helping students through a difficult learning process may be overwhelmed by their mutual misconceptions. Instead of strengthening the relationship, the student and the teacher turn away from each other. The difficulty of overcoming these obstacles is heightened when reduced financial support for education results in larger classes, diminished support services, and reduced resources for children with special needs.

The teacher might not recognize the community and family issues that profoundly affect the student. Substance abuse, physical and sexual abuse, vicarious trauma from witnessing community violence, the incarceration of relatives for drug and other offenses, and other problems can severely impact even the healthiest people. Often, behavior problems in school are a cry for help.

In another inner-city middle school violence-prevention project under my direction, trained workers used a "restorative justice" model to meet with students and their teacher three times a week to identify issues of conflict and ask the whole group to work on ways of resolving them. Issues of bullying, negative bystander behavior, and so forth were discussed and led to significant reductions in stress and conflict for students and their teachers.

Consider another example: The gay man who was previously rejected by his family for being gay, and who has since been diagnosed as HIV positive, may feel a strong need to repair a fractured family-of-origin relationship. Having been hurt deeply by his family, he may be reluctant to contact his parents and inform them of his illness. For the family, the crisis of their son's illness may be the very catalyst needed to break the cycle of rejection and allow for some form of family reunification and healing. An understandable fear of another painful rejection may cut a client off from his ability to communicate his need for renewed family relationships.

In relationships between parent and child, hospital ward and patient, student and school, the person with AIDS and his family, individual and group—that is, in each special case of the individual-social engagement—the essential mutual need is fragile and easily obscured by the complexity of the situation, by divergent needs, or by the difficulty involved in communication.

From this ever-present possibility of symbiotic diffusion and the loss of a clear sense of the symbiotic striving, the need for the social work profession emerged (Schwartz, 1961). The profession's tasks relate directly to the fact that obstacles can easily obscure the mutual dependence between the individual and important systems. When both sides have lost sight of this important connection, a third force is needed to help them regain this understanding. According to Schwartz (1961), the social work profession, with its historical roots firmly planted in two streams—concern for individual well-being and social justice—is uniquely suited to this role. This idea of the third force leads to the mediating function of the social work professional described later in the chapter.

## Assumption of Strength for Change

Belief in the existence of symbiotic striving is closely linked to another assumption about the individual-social engagement: that both the individual and the system contain within them the strength to implement this mutuality. This assumption depends on a view of people (and complex systems) as able to act in their own interest without being bound by their past experiences. An alternative approach considers that people fundamentally act according to the sum of the strengths and skills accumulated by past experiences. Causal links can be drawn between a person's present apparent immobility and earlier traumatic events.

Although it seems logical that past experiences affect the ways in which an individual attempts to negotiate new surroundings, the danger exists within this view of prejudging and underestimating a client's (or the system's) resiliency, strength, and capacity for change. Within the framework presented here, the individual is best described by actions and is as strong or as weak as he or she acts in the present moment. The practice implication of this attitude is that the worker must believe that the individual or the system has the capacity to move in its own self-interest, even if only by small steps, and that this movement will lead to increased strength and more change. These strengths and resiliency perspectives will be discussed more fully in the next chapter.

With this basic assumption in mind, the interactional perspective calls for the helping person always to place a "demand for work" before the client. The demand for work occurs when the worker exhorts the client to work effectively on her or his tasks and to invest that work with energy and affect. The work itself—the goals of the process (even with mandated clients)—must be shared by the client, not merely imposed by the worker. In this way, the demand is to work on the very tasks that the client has agreed need to be addressed. This demand also must be integrated with support in what could be called an *empathic* demand for work. When we press the client to take a difficult next step, to face painful feelings, to reach out to people who are important to him or her, or to take a risk, is exactly when the client most needs our support and empathy. A similar demand for work will be placed on the system (e.g., doctors and teachers), and I argue that our capacity for empathy with other professionals is just as important.

A familiar expression in this connection is "reach for the client's strength," which suggests that the very act of reaching for strength—an expression of belief in the potential of the work and refusing to accept even the client's own self-description of weakness—is a central part of what helps a client to act. Possibly the client has reached the present impasse precisely because all the signals received from important others have reinforced belief in the client's own impotence. The social worker, by contrast, operates on a basic principle: No matter how hopeless it seems, *there is always a next step.*

In an example from my own group work practice, I confront a group of people with AIDS in early recovery who have apparently given up on their ability to have nonexploitive and drug- and alcohol-free intimate relationships with others; I tell them that they must set aside their own concerns and issues and become a mutual support group for one another. I suggest that they have the capacity to help one another and that, by giving help to others, they will be getting help themselves. This is a key concept in mutual-aid support groups. My demand for work is rooted in the belief that even these clients, who have experienced years of polysubstance abuse, prison sentences, prostitution, and traumatic childhood experiences, still have the strength to reach out to one another within the group, which serves as a microcosm of larger society. The group members' response and their ability to care for one another is a tribute to themselves and an affirmation of the strengths perspective.

The assumptions just demonstrated will interact in important ways in the models and examples shared in this book. Workers will always search for subtle connections and demand that clients and systems act on their potential for change. This view of practice is built on a deep investment in the concept of interdependence; a view of the client as the source of energy for change, healing, and growth; a belief in client strength; and a preoccupation with health rather than sickness.

This stance does not negate the fact that some clients and some systems, for many complex reasons, will not be able to use the worker's help at a given moment. The helping process is interactional, with workers carrying out their parts as best they can. As such, clients have a part to play, and their strength helps to determine the outcome. For example, no matter how skillful the worker, he or she may not be able to reach a substance-abusing client until the client enters a detoxification center and stops using cocaine.

Using findings from my own research and that of others, we shall throughout this book explore the ways in which stress, acceptance of a problem, and motivation affect the client's ability to receive and use help at any given moment. Another core concept, however, will be that a client's inability to use help at a certain point in life does not mean that he or she cannot use it at a later time. In a project I recently directed, working with older foster children who were about to make the transition to independence (aging out of the foster care system), we found client readiness to address problems at ages 17 and 18 that clearly was not there at ages 15 and 16. I believe that skillful work done by social workers during the early years may have laid the groundwork for our progress once the clients were ready.

Socioeconomic factors, such as income, housing, and employment trends, also profoundly affect social work outcomes. Social workers must therefore be concerned with social policies that affect the human situation. Becoming aware of and working for changes in social policies is part of the task of helping. Recognizing that a particular client may be unable to use help at that time, the worker will nevertheless always attempt to reach for the client's strength because this is the way in which help is given.

## The Social Work Profession: A Brief Historical Perspective

Thus far, we have tried to view each client as presenting a special case of the more general individual-social interaction in our society. The issue we now explore is the role that the social work profession plays in this process. Although a detailed discussion of the complex history of the profession's development lies beyond the scope of this book, a general understanding of its unique historical roots will place the helping role in perspective.

**EP 2.1.1a**
**EP 2.1.1b**
**EP 2.1.1c**

Why is this important? I believe that every profession has developed over the years to meet specific needs in our society. For example, education is designed essentially to transmit the knowledge of our society to each generation to meet our social and individual needs for an informed, knowledgeable, and skilled population. Medicine and nursing are examples of professions that possess the essential role of addressing our health needs through both prevention and treatment. The legal profession, on the other hand, has a general mandate to deal with the rules that are developed to guide our ability to work and live together in an organized manner. Of course, each profession has a broader mandate as well (e.g., research for medicine), but there is a core purpose behind the invention of each. So why was our profession, social work, invented?

## The Roots of the Profession

The social work profession, as we know it now, was created through the merger of two basic streams of thought about the helping process. One was rooted in the work of those interested in issues of social change. One example is the early settlement house movement, most often associated with the work of Jane Addams at Hull House, founded in 1889 (Addams, 1961). This movement, which began in England, was one of many established at the turn of the century to cope with the stresses created by urbanization, industrialization, and the large-scale influx of immigrants to North America. The mission of these early, community-oriented social agencies included an attempt to help immigrant and other poor families integrate into U.S. society more effectively. At the same time, the leadership of these movements, mostly middle- and upper-class liberals of the day, waged a fight against the social conditions that faced these populations. Poor housing and health services, child labor, sweatshop conditions in urban factories—all became targets for social change.

Although Jane Addams was known for her relatively radical approach to actively involving the oppressed people for whom she worked, many in the settlement house movement instead incorporated a "doing for" approach to their targeted populations. Little effort was directed at actually organizing the poor, through an empowerment process, to fight effectively against the forces of oppression related to class, gender, race, ethnicity, and so forth. An empowerment process involves engaging the client (individual, family, group, or community) in developing strengths to personally and politically cope more effectively with those systems that are important to them. It is likely that, should the leaders of these early social movements have attempted to mobilize client groups in this way, they would have been viewed as too radical and faced political repression, as did the early labor unions.

In addition, this early social justice movement also saw as one of its major roles the acculturation of the poor to the values and beliefs of their own upper-middle-class society. Developing an appreciation of the arts, such as classical music and literature, and participating in other "refined" activities were seen as paths for self-improvement and building character. Workers often lived with clients in the settlement houses; helping was seen as practical in nature. For example, if cities were overcrowded and unhealthy, then children needed to be removed to camps in the country during the summer. Not until the 1930s did this social-change orientation join the mainstream of the emerging social work profession. This early driving concern for social justice for vulnerable populations gave the social work profession an important element of its current identity. The early roots of the group work and community organization methods can be traced to these professional pioneers.

The other major stream of professional development was rooted in a focus on fulfilling individual needs. The founder of this stream is often identified as Mary Richmond (1918), whose work at the Charities Organization Society made a major contribution toward the professionalizing of social work. Her efforts were directed at moving social work beyond the notion of "friendly visitors" who were charitable to the poor toward a systematic, professional approach to helping. Richmond was interested in the helping process and wanted it to be recorded, analyzed, and then taught.

By the 1930s, two new specializations in social work had developed: group work and community organization. Group work was closely associated with the informal education and socialization movements. Early leaders included Grace Coyle (1948) and Gertrude Wilson and Gladys Ryland (1949). Their work focused on using the peer group to help people cope with the normative tasks of life. A typical group might consist of teenagers who formed a social club in a community center; a group worker would be assigned to help them learn to work effectively together. Activities such as games, singing, crafts, or bowling provided ways through which group members could enjoy recreation and work on appropriate individual and group developmental tasks.

I was a group work major at the Columbia University School of Social Work from 1959 to 1961. Of our group of 30 students, 29 had field placements in community centers, settlement houses, and Young Men's Christian Associations (YMCAs). In addition to our core social work courses—also attended by the casework and community organization students—the group work students participated in activity courses that included games, singing, dancing, and other program activities. I remember distinctly the envious looks of our casework colleagues as they walked by our open classroom doors.

Early community organization activity was designed to coordinate social services through, for example, councils of social agencies. A second function was to raise funds for private social welfare activities through organizations such as community chests, the forerunners of today's United Way campaigns. Not until the late 1950s and early 1960s, in a reflection of the social activist themes of that time and the civil rights movement—and borrowing from community action and organizer models developed by activists such as Saul Alinsky (Reitzes & Reitzes, 1986)—did community organization practice shift to an approach that emphasized organizing and empowering clients and other members of the community to achieve social changes.

Specht[3] and Courtney (1993) describe the convergence of the three streams of casework, group work, and community organization in the mid-1930s as creating the social work trinity:

Social work practice had evolved into specializations: social casework, social group work, and community organization. Each drew on different theories.

---

3. Harry Specht was a central figure in the development of a community action program of the early 1960s. The project, funded by the Kennedy administration, devoted $13 million to combat juvenile delinquency through a comprehensive effort to impact welfare, education, and social services on the lower east side of New York City. The program, called "Mobilization for Youth," was designed and led by social workers. It was the basis for many social work community organization models and was the prototype for the development of the national Volunteers in Service to America (VISTA) volunteer program. Dr. Specht went on to become dean of the Berkeley University School of Social Work. Dr. Specht was also my first-year field instructor at the Mt. Vernon Young Men's and Young Women's Hebrew Association (YM & YWHA) and helped shape my views on the role of social work in the arena of social justice.

Community organization was related clearly enough to the organizational frameworks within which social casework was practiced to make the relationship practical even though it was not compatible philosophically and theoretically. Social group work began with a philosophical concern for social improvement and moral uplift of disadvantaged people. However, social casework focused on individual causes of problems, while social group work concentrated on citizen education for social action and social development. (p. 36)

Thus, these three major modalities of practice, each defined by its targeted client (individual, family, group, and community), merged to become the modern-day social work profession.

The creation of a unified profession was consummated in 1955, when seven separate social work organizations—the American Association of Group Workers, the American Association of Medical Social Workers, the American Association of Psychiatric Social Workers, the American Association of Social Workers, the National Association of School Social Workers, the Social Work Research Group, and the Association for the Study of Community Organizations—united to form a common professional organization, the National Association of Social Workers (NASW). Social workers shared a code of ethics, a value system, knowledge, and skills; however, social workers still differentiated themselves into groups by methodology, describing themselves either as caseworkers, group workers, or community organizers.

For the caseworkers, the "friendship" of the original friendly visitors became the "relationship" of the clinician with the client. The strong influence of psychoanalytic theory was evident in schools of social work, and, with few exceptions, the diagnostic model of medicine—the three-phase process of study, diagnosis, and treatment—was seen as a model of professionalism worthy of emulation.

In its next evolution, the three modalities of practice were subsumed under two more general categories. Casework, family work, and group work were combined into "micro" or "clinical" practice. Community organization practice became more closely linked to policy and management-oriented social work in a "macro" subgrouping. A trend toward the deemphasis of specialization has led to the wider use of the term *generalist practice*, which describes a social work practitioner whose knowledge and skills encompass a broad spectrum and who assesses problems and their solutions comprehensively. The term *generic social work* is often used interchangeably with generalist practice, although the former refers more specifically to the social work orientation that emphasizes a common core of knowledge and skills associated with social service provision.

This historical review presents an oversimplified description of the development of the social work profession. For our purposes, the main point is that the profession is the product of a unique merger of interests in individual healing and social change for social justice. This is the historical basis for what will be presented as the "two-client" idea, which is central to the interactional model of social work. With regard to the complex interaction between the individual client and her or his social surroundings (the "second client"; e.g., society, community, family, small group), the social work professional will always be identifiable by her or his attention to both clients. Although common values, knowledge, beliefs, skills, professional associations, codes of ethics, and so on help unify the profession, it is the shared sense of social workers' function in society that makes their profession unique.

# The Function of the Social Work Profession

**EP 2.1.5b**
**EP 2.1.5c**

In developing his view of the social work profession's function in society, Schwartz (1961) did not accept the broadly held idea that the profession was defined solely by a base of shared knowledge, values, and skills. He also rejected the notion that one could describe the profession's function solely in terms of aspirations for positive general outcomes, such as "enhancing social functioning" or "facilitating individual growth and development." He understood that the profession required a general and unique functional statement that would direct the actions of all social workers regardless of the setting in which they practiced. Although many elements of practice would be introduced by the particular problems the client faced—the mission of the agency or host setting, the modality of service (e.g., individual, group, or family counseling), the age and stage of life of the client, and so forth, Schwartz viewed professional function as a core and constant element of any social work practice theory.

*Function* is defined here as the specific part that each social work professional plays in the helping process. To understand the term better, consider how an automobile engine might work if all the parts were like people. If we defined the function of the carburetor as "helping to make the car move," we would be defining function in terms of outcome. This would not provide specific direction to the carburetor, which would be left on its own to figure out how to play its part in the process. On the other hand, if we specifically defined the carburetor's function as mixing air and gasoline to create a vapor that could then be ignited by a spark plug, our anthropomorphic carburetor would have a clear idea of how to do its part. If all parts of the engine understood clearly their functional roles and implemented those roles effectively, the car would start to move.

This kind of functional preciseness is what Schwartz felt every social worker needed to understand his or her role in the many complex situations faced in everyday practice. This professional role would travel with the social worker to any agency or host setting and would, in part, define the social worker's interventions at any given moment. We would be able to recognize social workers in action and distinguish them from other professionals with similar knowledge, values, and skills because we would see the functional role underlying their interventions.

Schwartz's definition of the function of the social work profession was based on the previously described underlying assumptions about the essentially symbiotic nature of the individual-social relationship. He examined the history of the profession and tried to identify the essential functional assignment that might define a unique role for social work. His definition of the professional function is "to mediate the process through which the individual and his society reach out for each other through a mutual need for self-fulfillment" (Schwartz, 1961, p. 9). As a result, a third force is introduced to the diagram of a hypothetical client attempting to deal with several important systems (see Figure 1.2).

With the addition of the worker, the basic triangular model is complete. On the left side is the client reaching out with all available strength, attempting to negotiate important systems while often simultaneously throwing up defenses that cut him or her off from the needed systems. On the right side are the systems reaching out to incorporate the client—but often reaching ambivalently. At the bottom is the social worker, whose sense of function and skills is mobilized in an effort to help both client and system overcome the obstacles that block their engagement.

FIGURE 1.2

## Relationship of Client, Systems, and Worker

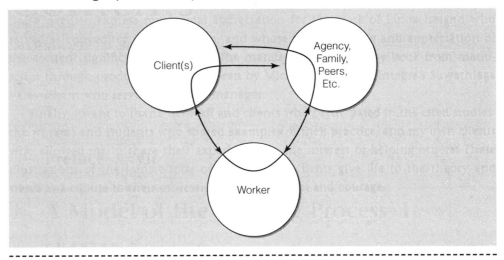

Consider the application of this functional role in working with the students we described earlier who were suspended from school for violent or other negative behavior. Whereas other professions (e.g., guidance and attendance counselors, psychologists, school nurses) might limit their role to working directly with the student, and in fact be somewhat effective, a social worker who was clear about his or her role would have to view the school, its administration and staff, the family, and even the community as the second client. The functional role would require skillful work to influence the system so that it could both understand and respond to the student behavior more effectively.

Inherent in this role would be concern with social and educational policies, funding decisions, and anything else that impacted the school and the students. This unique responsibility and functional role may also be seen in social workers who attempt to impact a hospital, a home for the aged, a residential institution, and so on. Chapter 15 will focus on this unique social work role and the dynamics and skills required for the worker to implement the role in a range of settings.

One could argue, and I would agree, that all helping professions have some responsibility for social change within their specific settings and, more broadly, in society. However, social work is the only one of the professions that has inherited this role that, in fact, helps to define our work in a unique way. As we move through this text and look at work with individuals, families, groups, and communities, the reader will repeatedly see how clarification of this role gives direction and power to social work intervention. At key moments, when the social worker seems uncertain about what should be his or her next step, the reader will also see how functional confusion can be immobilizing and lead to less-than-effective interventions.

Some may consider this functional statement too limited. I have already indicated that the term *mediation* is used in a broad sense and can include other activities such as confrontation and advocacy. There are times when the crucial work in the area between the helping person and the system requires conflict and social pressure. In one example cited in the book, a social worker helps a tenant group confront the housing authority and the political system because of the unresponsiveness of the housing project administrator (see Chapter 16).

Even using a broad interpretation of *mediation,* one might still argue that this functional statement is too limited. However, if the helping person is clear about the helping function and that function is specifically defined, the chance of consistently performing it improves. Jessie Taft (1942), one of the early leaders of the functional school of social work practice developed at the University of Pennsylvania School of Social Work, stressed this view. In addition, the client who understands what the helping person does—the way in which help is given—will be better able to use the worker's services.

Couples' counseling provides a good illustration. The division between the couple often causes most people they know (family, friends, coworkers) to take sides with one person or the other. An early, often unstated question on the minds of both partners as they enter the counseling process is "Whose side will the social worker be on?" Only through explanation and demonstration can the skillful worker help the couple understand that the worker must be on both sides at the same time to help them. Practice experience has taught most workers that the moment they identify with one side versus the other, an example of functional confusion, they lose their usefulness to the client who feels cut off.

Clarity about one's professional function and role in the helping process is essential for effective practice. When a social worker is clear about his or her part in the interaction, the worker will be less likely to take over the client's part—in other words, doing things *for* the client instead of *with* the client. Once a social worker has integrated a sense of professional function and role, the communications, relationship, and problem-solving skills become the tools through which the social worker puts her or his function into action.

I have long believed and observed that most students and new practitioners already have many of the basic human relations skills needed to be helpful. Once they have integrated a clear sense of their general function as social workers, and the specific way it emerges in a particular setting with a particular client, in a particular modality of practice (e.g., family work or groups), the development of more sophisticated skills will follow. Clearly knowing one's role, then, matters a great deal; beginning workers can do well from the start with a clear understanding of their role and purpose.

Again, a profession is differentiated from other professions by its functional role, not by its knowledge, values, and skills. For example, in a hospital, empathy skills are important for the social worker, the doctor, and the nurse. Each professional must harness these skills in pursuit of his or her separate functions.

In the scores of examples included in this book, you will see that social workers often get in trouble in their practice when they lose their sense of functional clarity. For example, you will read about incidents in family work in which the social worker identifies with the children and loses the connection with the parents. Such a worker can no longer help the family work on its issues. In another example, a new worker who claims that he has "solved" the client's problem by taking him to church on Sunday may once again be unclear about the boundaries that delimit the social worker's role.

One might see ongoing professional development as a continual deepening of the social worker's understanding of the helping function and of those situations that may lead to functional confusion and diffusion. Functional diffusion occurs when the social worker tries to be everything to everyone and, in so doing, loses sight of the core job. Functional diffusion is not a terminal illness, however, and is usually cured by a dose of functional clarity.

At this point, you may be wondering how generally applicable this mediation assignment can be. We shall work toward the answer in the rest of the book, drawing illustrations from a range of settings with varying types of individuals, families, groups, and communities. In each example, you should mentally step into the shoes of the worker. The argument is that the worker's sense of the next step at specific moments of interaction will be vitally affected by an internalized sense of function.

These introductory comments have laid out the general model applied in each step of analysis throughout the book. A further elaboration of this function and the worker tasks will be shared in the context of practice illustrations.

## Social Work Skill and the Working Relationship

**EP 2.1.10a**
**EP 2.1.10b**

At the core of the interactional theory of social work practice is a model of the helping process in which the skill of the worker helps to create a positive working relationship, referred to elsewhere as the "therapeutic alliance." In turn, this relationship is the medium through which the worker influences the outcomes of practice. This simple model can be visualized as shown in Figure 1.3.

Although the model suggests that the applied skill leads to relationship, which then influences outcomes, the double-pointed arrows imply that the model is dynamic. For example, a change in the working relationship will affect the worker's use of skill. A worker may be influenced in her or his interaction with a client by the changing nature of the relationship (e.g., a positive relationship leads to more empathy on the worker's part). Similarly, positive or negative outcomes for the client may influence his or her sense of the relationship.

Another model incorporated into this theory involves the relationship between clients' ability to manage their feelings and their ability to manage their problems. These ideas were developed as part of the theory-building effort I have described in other publications (Shulman, 1978, 1981, 1991). The construct is based on the assumption that how we feel powerfully affects how we act. The relationship between feelings and action is reciprocal: How we act also influences how we feel.

To this feeling-behavioral connection we can add a third element: cognition. *Cognition* refers to the way that clients think about themselves and their environment. The contributions of cognitive-behavioral theory (Berlin, 1983) have helped us to broaden our understanding of how a client's perception of reality can have a powerful impact on self-image, identification of the nature of a problem, and self-assessment of the ability to cope. I argue throughout this book that how clients think affects how they feel, which affects how they act, in a circular and reciprocal

**F I G U R E   1 . 3**

*Worker Skill and the Working Relationship*

manner. The model presented could be termed a cognitive-affective-behavioral framework without confusing it with other models that incorporate cognitive-behavioral approaches.

For example, some female survivors of childhood sexual abuse describe themselves as "damaged goods" as they enter their teenage years. These clients may respond to the oppression they have experienced by internalizing a negative self-image and assuming some form of responsibility for what was done to them. They could express feelings of guilt and concern that they may have been seductive toward the offending adult, thus shifting responsibility for the problem to themselves—a form of self-blame. This is an example of the internalized oppressor at work (an oppression model is discussed in more detail in Chapter 2). Symptoms of depression and personal apathy often cover an underlying rage that the child learned to suppress in order to survive. The use of alcohol and drugs also provides an escape, a flight from the pain associated with the abuse, and is an example of the self-destructive behavior described earlier, in which oppressed clients become autopressors.

The association between these perceptions of low self-image and the feelings (e.g., shame) that they can generate may lead these teenage survivors to enter into relationships and life patterns that perpetuate their exploitation. For example, a woman's low sense of self-esteem may lead her to relationships with exploitive men who use physical, emotional, and sexual violence to maintain control over the lives of women. The use of drugs and involvement in the street culture may lead to prostitution. These actions on the client's part, related to the client's feelings, may in turn deepen the sense of being "damaged." Thus, negative reciprocal relationships among how the client feels, thinks, and acts result in a deepening of the problems in living. Of course, for many survivors, protective factors (described in the next chapter) mitigate the impact of the abuse on their lives.

An intervention is needed to disrupt this vicious cycle. As the worker helps the client to examine the underlying pain and rage and to face the oppressor within, the client can begin to take control of his or her emotions and more effectively manage them rather than being managed by them. Effective practice can help the client cognitively reframe the source of the problem and begin to perceive himself or herself as a survivor rather than a victim. Techniques associated with solution-focused practice, also described later in this book, can help the client see his or her strengths and begin the healing process. In the words of a poem written by a member of a support group for survivors, described in Chapter 14, clients can work through their pain and see themselves as "surviving and thriving."

The principle of dealing with feelings in pursuit of purpose will lead the worker to help the client connect her or his feelings and perceptions with her or his actions. Being aware of the connections among how we think, feel, and act is an early step in taking control over these thoughts and feelings and our resultant behaviors. As the client better manages these feelings and develops a more accurate assessment of self and the situation, she or he can begin to manage her or his life problems more effectively. Success with life's problems, in turn, will influence her or his thoughts and feelings.

For example, a teenage survivor may begin to change her self-destructive behavior by taking a first step on her own behalf. Obtaining help with her addiction, leaving the streets for a shelter, or attempting to break off an abusive and exploitive relationship may be the first step toward breaking out of her trap. Each step that she takes in her own self-interest, however small, can contribute to a more positive feeling about herself and strengthen her to take the next step. Thus, managing her feelings helps her to manage her problems, and managing her problems helps her to manage her feelings.

As this model is explored, we shall see that if the worker is to help clients manage their feelings, the worker must be able to manage his or her own emotions. For example, as a result of feeling a client's pain, a worker who is helping a survivor of sexual abuse may prematurely attempt to reassure the client that she is not damaged. Or the worker may take on the woman's anger against the men who have exploited her, which may preempt the client's essential work in facing her own anger. Both of these understandable emotional reactions by the worker may block the client's ability to manage her own feelings. The worker instead needs to share his or her sense of the client's pain without trying to relieve it. For example,

> As I listen to you I'm feeling how much pain you are in, how damaged you must feel. A big part of me wants to say, "Don't feel that way! You are a person of value." But I know that no matter what I say, the pain is there, and I can't make it go away.

The anger against the exploitive men—for example, a sexually abusive father—can also be shared, but in a manner that helps the client face her own anger rather than doing the work for her. For example,

> It makes me angry when I think of what was done to you by people you expected to take care of you and to protect you. But from what you are saying to me, it seems that your feelings are mixed right now. It sounds like a big part of you wishes your family could be different, could change, and that you could still be like a real family.

The worker's sharing of her or his feelings, in what I refer to as the integration of personal and professional selves, is a crucial and somewhat controversial element in this model. Once again, borrowing from the medical profession, a general injunction has been suggested by many in the field, as well as in the social work literature, whereby the social worker does not share his or her feelings at any time. I will argue and illustrate throughout the book that this is a false dichotomy, and, in fact, based on some of my own research into the doctor-patient relationship (Shulman & Buchan, 1982), it does not even work for the medical profession from which it was borrowed. The issue is, instead, how do we "use ourselves" appropriately and professionally, within appropriate boundaries, rather than "losing ourselves" through the presentation of a supposed blank slate of emotions. Much more will be said about this question throughout the book.

The eight skills examined in my study (Shulman, 1991) were drawn from those that proved to be most important in my prior research (1978, 1979b). (The last section of this chapter provides an overview of the research and the findings.) Twenty-two specific skills were examined in the earlier research, with 10 of the 22 associating at a significant level with developing a positive relationship and worker helpfulness. Although all of these skills (and others) are discussed in the chapters that follow, a particular emphasis is placed on the eight skills examined in the more recent work. These eight skills have been organized into two groupings, as follows:

### Workers' Skills for Helping Clients Manage their Feelings

- Reaching inside of silences
- Putting the client's feelings into words

- Displaying understanding of the client's feelings
- Sharing the worker's feelings

***Workers' Skills for Helping Clients Manage their Problems***
- Clarifying the worker's purpose and role
- Reaching for client feedback
- Partializing concerns
- Supporting clients in taboo areas

All of these skills are important in all phases of practice. However, each skill may have various meanings or impacts at different stages of the relationship. Because the helping process is so complex, it is useful to analyze it against the backdrop of the different phases of work. The four phases of work described in this book are as follows:

Preliminary (or Preparatory) Phase

Beginning (or Contracting) Phase

Middle (or Work) Phase

Ending and Transition Phase

Each phase of work—preliminary, beginning, middle, and ending and transition—has unique dynamics and requires specific skills. Jessie Taft (1949), referring to the beginning, middle, and ending phases, was one of the first to draw attention to the impact of time on social work practice. Schwartz (1971) incorporated this dimension into his work, adding the preliminary phase and modifying the ending phase to the "ending and transition" phase.

The preliminary (or preparatory) phase is the period prior to the first encounter with the client. The beginning (or contracting) phase refers to the first sessions in which the worker develops a working contract with the client and begins developing the working relationship. The middle (or work) phase is the period in which the work is done. Finally, in the ending and transition phase, the worker prepares the client to bring the relationship to an end and to make transitions to new experiences.

Another way of thinking about these phases is as a series of decisions. The client (individual, family, group, or community) must first make a decision in the beginning phase about whether or not to face her or his problems and engage with the worker. Even mandatory clients (e.g., child welfare, court-ordered, or probation) must make that decision for the work to be effective. The second decision comes as the client makes the transition to the middle phase and decides to deal with more difficult and often painful issues. The third decision is made by the client as she or he prepares for the termination of the relationship and, in a manner often described as "doorknob therapy," raises the most powerful and difficult issues of the work. These processes are identified in the balance of this book using examples of micro-(clinical) and macro-practice.

We begin the exploration of these constructs in Chapter 3, which focuses on the preliminary phase of practice in work with individuals. The phases of work serve as an organizing principle for each modality—family, group, and community—throughout the rest of the book as well.

# The Integration of Personal and Professional Selves

As suggested earlier, another carryover from the medical model was the importance placed on maintaining one's professional self. Most helping professions stressed the professional role and the need to suppress personal feelings and reactions. For example, when working with stressful patients, one might have to keep one's real reactions in check to avoid appearing judgmental. A professional worker was previously described as one who maintained control of emotions and would not become angry or too emotionally involved, would not cry in the presence of a client, and so forth. The injunction to the worker appeared to be "Take your professional self to work and leave your personal self at home." This image of professionalism was (and still is) widely held; many of my social work students started their careers wondering if they would have problems as a social worker because they "felt too much."

The practice model presented in this text will suggest that we are faced with a false dichotomy when we believe we must choose between our personal self and our professional self. In fact, I argue that we are at our best in our work when we are able to synthesize the two by integrating our personal self into our professional role.

The conflict of views about what defines the professional self was brought home dramatically in a workshop I led on direct practice. One pediatric oncology social worker described an incident in which a mother appeared at her door after being referred by the attending physician. The mother had just been told that her 7-year-old daughter had a terminal illness. After explaining this to the social worker, the mother broke down and cried.

When I asked the worker what she did, she described how overwhelmed she felt by the mother's grief. All that the worker could do was sit and hold the mother's hand, softly crying with her. I maintain that, although much work would need to be done in this case (such as helping the mother deal with her dying daughter and her family over the next few months), at this point what the mother needed most was not advice but someone to be with her. In fact, as the worker partially experienced the mother's pain and shared it with her through her own tears, she gave that client the important gift of her own feelings. The worker was being professional in the best sense of the word. Other workers, who might not cry with a client, may make the same gift in different ways— through facial expressions, a respectful silence, or a hand on the shoulder—each worker responding in a way that is consistent with his or her own personality. The crucial factor is the worker's willingness to be honest and to share his or her own feelings.

In this example, the worker continued her story by telling us that her supervisor passed the open door, called the worker outside, and berated her for unprofessional behavior. The supervisor said, "How could you let yourself break down that way? You can't help your clients if you become overwhelmed yourself." When I asked the worker what she took from the experience, she replied, "I learned to keep my door closed." Although many who hear this story are upset with the supervisor, I am not. I realize that she may have been trained as I was, during a time when personal expressions of emotion were considered unprofessional.

I encouraged this social worker to talk to her supervisor, because I felt that it was crucial for her to obtain support from her supervisor and colleagues if she were to continue to provide this kind of help to clients. My research (Shulman, 1979b) has emphasized the importance of formal and informal sources of social support for social workers. This worker was making a gift to the client of her willingness to "be with" her at a terrible moment in her life. The worker's capacity to continue to be there for the client depends somewhat on her having someone—supervisor, colleague, or both—be there for her. This issue of needing support to provide support to clients is now discussed in the literature dealing with "secondary trauma." Chapter 17 includes some of the more recent thinking and research in this area.

This often artificial split between personal and professional selves was created from the profession's understandable concerns with the inappropriate use of self by helping professionals. For example, concern arose about *countertransference*, a process in which workers may project onto clients their own unfinished family business (e.g., relating to a father in a client's family as if he were one's own parent). The profession was troubled by workers who used the argument of spontaneity to justify acting out with clients, such as getting inappropriately angry or judgmental or sharing personal problems ("If you think you have troubles with your kids, let me tell you about my family").

Unethical behavior with clients, such as abusing the powerful forces of the helping bond to sexually exploit a vulnerable client, provides another example. Each of these examples illustrates a lack of integration of personal and professional selves. The concerns about the use of the personal self were—and continue to be—well founded. Unfortunately, the solution of separating the personal from the professional led to more problems than it resolved.

The argument advanced throughout this text will be that each of us brings our own personal style, artistry, background, feelings, values, and beliefs to our professional practice. Rather than denying or suppressing these, we need to learn more about ourselves in the context of our practice, and find ways to use ourselves in pursuit of our professional functions. We will make many mistakes along the way—saying things we will later regret, apologizing to clients, learning from these mistakes, correcting them, and then making what I call "more sophisticated" mistakes.

In other words, we will be real people carrying out difficult jobs as best we can, rather than paragons of virtue who present an image of perfection. As we demonstrate to our clients our humanness, vulnerability, willingness to risk, spontaneity, honesty, and lack of defensiveness (or defensiveness for which we later apologize), we model the very behaviors we hope to see in our clients. Thus, when workers or students ask me, "Should I be professional or should I be myself?" I reply that the dualism implied in the question does not exist. They must be themselves if they are going to be professional. Fortunately, we have the whole of our professional lives to learn how to effect and refine this synthesis.

## Research Findings

**EP 2.1.6a**
**EP 2.1.6b**

Many of my research studies have contributed to the insights shared in this book. Over a number of years I developed instruments to measure social work practice skills and to relate the use of those skills to the development of positive working relationships with clients (also referred to as a therapeutic alliance) and the impact of the skills and the relationships on effective helping. The findings were then used to analyze the practice approach critically—to confirm some hypotheses while generating new assumptions for future research. Each successive study built on the preceding one, as well as on the knowledge base developed in social work and related professions and disciplines.

I would note that my interest has always been in what I would call "process research." Perhaps, stemming from my own identity as a practitioner, researcher, and educator for all of my professional life, I was as much interested in the mechanics of the helping process as in the outcomes of the interventions. Put another way, whereas many studies asked: "Is social work practice (or a particular model) effective?" I was equally interested in the question: "What does social work practice look like when we examine it?" I was curious about and focused on operationalizing the independent variable (practice skill) and then understanding its impact on the mediating variables (working relationship) as well as on the dependent or outcome variables. In keeping with the interactional model, my studies always tried to understand and measure the interaction between social workers and clients using a range of instruments that included questionnaires and observation systems developed and tested for the purpose.

To further explore this research paradigm, the reader is also referred to my other publications (1970, 1978, 1979a, 1979b, 1981, 1991) for more detailed descriptions of the methodology of each study and their findings. Although all findings reported in this text are tentative and should be considered in light of the limitations of each study, some findings have been repeated in my studies and the studies of other researchers. Confidence in these findings increases with each replication.

Although the reader is urged to read the more complete discussion of methodology in the publications just cited, a brief summary of the author's major study most often quoted in this text follows.

## Study Design

The major study of this framework was conducted in a government child welfare agency in British Columbia, Canada. Project staff reviewed family files that had been recently opened in 68 district offices. Of the 1,056 families identified as potential subjects, 348 (33 percent) agreed to participate. The final sample consisted of 305 families with 449 children served by 171 social workers in 68 district offices.

Most of the data were gathered during the first 3 months of the project. Home interviews were conducted with the parent(s). A mail survey of staff at all levels (workers, supervisors, managers, and so forth) was carried out at the same time. Project staff also read the participating clients' files. Much of the analysis is based on the data obtained during this time. Follow-up data were obtained through surveys mailed to clients and staff at intervals during the subsequent 15-month period. Project staff also reviewed the family files every 3 months. Twenty-three questionnaires and interview guides were developed and tested for this study.

## Description of Study Participants

The five executive directors had master of social work (MSW) degrees; however, only 60 percent of the regional managers, 44 percent of the district supervisors, and 20 percent of the social workers held that degree. When MSWs, bachelor of social work (BSW) degrees, and other professional degrees were included, 90 percent of the managers, 60 percent of the supervisors, and 68 percent of the social workers held professional degrees.

Two-thirds of the families were headed by a single parent. One-third of the families also reported "some" or "severe" disability with respect to physical and emotional health, learning problems, or drug and alcohol problems. Fourteen percent reported some or severe alcohol or drug problems for themselves. Eight percent reported that their spouses had similar problems. Unemployment was present for one-third of the families. Forty-seven percent of the families were living on welfare or unemployment insurance benefits. Finally, in 10 percent of the families, at least one family member was of Canadian Native origin.

Family problems included periodic and severe neglect of children, inability of parents to care for children (because of illness, addictions, and so forth), and physical and sexual abuse. By the end of the study, 28 percent of the families had been listed on the child abuse registry. Forty-nine percent of the families had at least one child in care during the study period.

### Study Limitations

The study is limited by the self-selection of the families involved. We compared the participating and nonparticipating groups on several variables and found no significant differences between the groups. An additional limitation was added when the Province of British Columbia cut back funding and services to the province-wide child welfare program. In particular, these cutbacks led to the nonrenewal of more than 600 family support workers. Because the cutbacks were implemented differentially in regions, we could gather data on the impact over time. Thus, we could incorporate the impact of these cutbacks into the study design.

The findings of this aspect of the study take on added meaning today, as social workers face an increasingly conservative climate that encourages politicians to compete in their efforts to demonstrate their ability to shred the safety net developed over the years to protect our most vulnerable populations. The current economic problems are impacting budgets on every level of government—with social services, both public and private, some of the first to be sacrificed to balancing the budget. Given the impact on individuals and families of wide-scale and sustained unemployment, as well as the loss of homes through foreclosures, these are exactly the times we should be expanding, not contracting, services to at-risk clients.

These findings are reviewed in the current sociopolitical context, and the call for social workers to become more actively involved in policy and political efforts is clearly articulated. My own experiences as a politically active social worker are used as illustrations.

## Values and Ethics in Social Work Practice

**EP 2.1.2a**
**EP 2.1.2b**
**EP 2.1.2c**
**EP 2.1.2d**

In addition to knowledge and a sense of professional function, specific values and ethics also guide the social worker's practice. In preparing to meet clients, a social worker needs to consider these areas, which will affect the process and content of practice in significant ways. Although preparing for every eventuality is impossible, familiarity with basic expectations of professional practice will alert a worker to potentially serious situations and possible missteps, thus encouraging consultation with colleagues or a supervisor.

In this chapter, I focus first on a general introduction to values and ethics and their impact on social work practice. In later chapters I will focus on those issues more specifically related to the chapter content such as the importance of informed consent in the beginning phase of practice and contracting. This introduction will set the stage for later discussions of more specific ethical issues related, for example, to working with families, first client group sessions, and so on. But first, some definitions are needed.

## Definitions of Values and Ethics

Values are defined in the *Social Work Dictionary* as "the customs, beliefs, standards of conduct, and principles considered desirable by a culture, a group of people, or an individual" (Barker, 2003, p. 453). The same dictionary defines ethics as "a system of moral principles and perceptions about right versus wrong and the resulting philosophy of conduct that is practiced by an individual, group, profession, or culture" (p. 147).

Loewenberg and Dolgoff (1996) define professional ethics as

> a codification of the special obligations that arises out of a person's voluntary choice to become a professional, such as a social worker. Professional ethics clarify the ethical aspects of professional practice. Professional social work ethics are intended to help social work practitioners recognize the morally correct way of practice and to learn how to decide and act correctly with regard to the ethical aspects of any given professional situation. (p. 6)

Dolgoff et al. (2005) highlight the difference between ethics and values as follows:

> Social workers, like so many others, often fail to distinguish between such terms as *values, ethics* and *morality* (or *virtues*). They use them rather loosely as if they all have the same meaning. Values, however, are not the same as virtues, though the two terms are often used interchangeably. Neither are values the same as ethics. (p. 16)

The authors argue that values imply a priority or preference, and that social work values are generally drawn from the values of the larger society. They suggest that

> There is a general consensus about social work values. For example, most professional social workers agree that client participation, self-determination, and confidentiality, are among basic social work values. However, disagreements are likely to occur when it comes to implementing these generalized professional values. Social workers may disagree about priorities, specific objectives, and the means necessary to put these generalized values into practice. . . . Thus, the value "enhancing the dignity of life" may be used by one social worker to support a client's request for an abortion or assisted suicide, while her social work colleague may call on the same generalized value to support her professional decision to try to persuade the client to go through a full-term pregnancy. In fact, these examples illustrate how "nonprofessional" or "higher" values can affect practice decisions. (Dolgoff et al., 2005, p. 18)

## National Association of Social Workers Code of Ethics

The National Association of Social Workers (NASW) has developed a code of ethics that is defined as the explication of the values, rules, and principles of ethical conduct that apply to all social workers who are members of the NASW. The original code of ethics for social workers was implicit in the 1951 Standards for Professional Practice of the American Association of Social Workers (ASSW). NASW developed a formal code in 1960 and has since made subsequent revisions, the latest in 2002 (Barker, 2003, p. 286).

For a link to the NASW Code of Ethics and the Code of Ethics of the Canadian Association of Social Workers (CASW), consult the CourseMate website at www.cengagbrain.com and enter your personal access code.

The drafters of the NASW code recognized the difficulties involved when professionals attempt to make specific decisions based on general principles. They also introduced the notion of peer review and peer standards for judging ethical behavior.

By itself, this code does not represent a set of rules that will prescribe all the behaviors of social workers in all of the complexities of professional life. Rather, it offers general principles to guide conduct, as well as the judicious appraisal of conduct, in situations that have ethical implications. It provides the basis for making judgments about ethical actions before and after they occur. Frequently, the particular situation determines the ethical principles that apply and the manner of their application. In such cases, not only the particular ethical principles but also the entire code and its spirit are taken into consideration. One must judge specific applications of ethical principles in context. Ethical behavior in a given situation must satisfy not only the judgment of the individual social worker but also the judgment of an unbiased jury of professional peers.

## Ethical Problems and Dilemmas

Of course, if all situations were clear and unambiguous, and if ethical codes were explicit enough to provide specific guidelines for all occasions (and all professionals could agree on these), ethical practice would simply involve a learning process and the strict implementation of agreed-on standards of practice. In reality, however, it does not work that way. For example, Loewenberg and Dolgoff (1996) describe an important distinction between "ethical problems" and "ethical dilemmas":

> Ethical problems raise the question: What is the right thing to do in a given practice situation? How can a social worker avoid unethical behaviors in that situation? Ethical dilemmas occur in situations where the social worker must choose between two or more relevant, but contradictory, ethical directives, or when every alternative results in an undesirable outcome for one or more persons. (p. 8)

The interplay among values, ethics, and practice is rarely simple and clear-cut. Workers often face an ethical dilemma in which several possible solutions are equally desirable or undesirable.

***An Elderly Client and his Adult Child: A Conflict of Values and Ethics*** Consider, for example, the situation of a geriatric social worker working in an outreach program—a program that attempts to bring services (e.g., homemaking services) directly to clients, usually in their own homes or neighborhoods. The social worker in this case is assisting an elderly man and his adult child. A not-uncommon example of value conflicts may emerge when during the first sessions the client indicates he wants to remain in his home but his adult children want him to move to a nursing home for his own safety. The value systems of many parties and organizations may ultimately impinge on the worker's decision: the values of the elderly client, his family (the second client), the agency, the community, society in general, the social work profession, and the individual social worker. If any of these are in conflict, which ethical rules will guide the worker?

For example, a generally accepted social work ethical principle is self-determination—the client's right to make her or his own choices—which seems to provide a clear direction. The worker must support the client's decision. What happens, however, if the client is so frail that his living independently may pose some danger to himself and to his neighbors? Although the client adamantly insists that he can care for himself, his apartment desperately needs cleaning. The client mentions that he is not feeling too well today because he sometimes forgets to take his medicine. He excuses himself to get his pills but opens the closet door instead of the door to the kitchen, appearing momentarily confused. His still-lit cigarette sits on the edge of the ashtray, close to falling off, the long ash suggesting it may have been forgotten. Old newspapers are strewn around the floor and under the coffee table.

Add to the mix a social worker whose elderly grandfather, living alone and unable to safely care for himself, accidentally set his house on fire by leaving a pot on a hot stove. The resulting fire almost killed the grandfather and posed a serious threat to the neighbors.

The client in this example values his independence, and the value system of the social work profession supports his right to make the decision. The agency also values outcomes that help elderly people remain at home. The funding for the agency may even depend on how many elderly people it can keep out of nursing homes. A recent memo from the agency director has encouraged staff to "keep the numbers up" as the agency prepares to renegotiate, with the health insurance provider, the contract on which its very existence depends.

The family members value the client's safety and their own peace of mind. The social worker's professional and personal value system, in part based on his own life experience, causes him to identify with the family. The community's value system, which may even be embodied in state legislation, may make the social worker a mandated reporter, required to report to the proper authorities if this elderly client is a potential threat to himself or others. The degree of seriousness of the danger is ambiguous in this case, and the regulations of the legislative act are somewhat unclear in providing specific guidelines. What ethical principles can guide this social worker's actions? What does the worker do when some of the ethical principles appear to conflict with others?

## Factors that may Affect Ethical Decision Making

Some ethical issues are reasonably clear-cut and provide unambiguous guidelines that are universally agreed on. Take, for example, the injunction against a social worker engaging in sexual activity with a client. Given the power differential between the helper and the client, as well as the serious potential for long-range damage to the client, such activity is universally condemned. The NASW Code of Ethics is very clear on this point:

> Social workers should under no circumstances engage in sexual activities or sexual contact with current clients, whether such contact is consensual or forced. (National Association of Social Workers, 1999, Section 1.09)

In some places, legislation has defined such unprofessional acts a crime, with violators subject to criminal penalties. Many ethical dilemmas, however, are less clear-cut and require careful thought and even consultation before action.

Loewenberg and Dolgoff (1996) identify several factors that can contribute to such moments of serious uncertainty. For example, in the illustration of the elderly client, we saw competing values (self-determination and the need to protect a client), multiple-client systems (the elderly client and the family), worker difficulty in maintaining objectivity (the impact of the worker's life experience), and ambiguity in the case (lack of clarity on the degree of danger to the client). By simply recognizing the factors contributing to the dilemma, the worker begins the processes of managing the problem rather than having the problem manage the worker.

***Agency Ethics Committees for Value Conflicts Consultation*** Rather than naively operating under the assumption that social work practice is "value free," social workers must recognize that the very act of intervening in a situation is based on value assumptions. In an increasingly complex and changing society, with value systems constantly in flux, every social worker must be knowledgeable about current ethical dilemmas and must develop a methodology to analyze value and ethics conflicts when they emerge. Many agencies and health settings have ethics committees in place to assist in this process.

For example, in the illustration of the elderly client, the social worker should have a forum either in supervision or in staff groups to raise this case for consultation. An atmosphere should exist in which a social worker can feel free to share honestly his or her own personal value conflicts in such a situation and thereby sort through the conflicting pressures.

Perhaps the agency should set up a committee to examine the specific criteria used to make decisions about the degree of danger required before a worker must implement the mandated reporter role. Would a checklist based on these criteria help to reduce the amount of ambiguity in such cases? Can the worker be helped to see a role in mediating the conflict between the client and his family so that their mutual concerns can be made clear to each other? Can the client and the family members be involved in a process of decision making in which they all feel that their concerns are respected? The agency would not provide a simple answer to a complex problem but would implement a process for recognizing and dealing with the complexity itself. In addition, the agency would take responsibility for actively assisting workers to deal with these issues.

***Ethics Audit and Risk Management Strategy*** Given the complexity involved in trying to respond appropriately when ethical dilemmas emerge, Reamer (2000) proposes a social work ethics audit and a risk management strategy (p. 355). Pointing out that agencies routinely conduct financial audits, he suggests that an ethical audit might determine:

1. The extent of social workers' familiarity with known ethics-related risks in practice settings, based on empirical trend data summarizing actual ethics complaints and lawsuits filed against social workers and summarizing ethics committee and court findings and dispositions; and

2. Current agency procedures and protocols for handling ethical issues, dilemmas, and decisions. (p. 356)

Reamer (2000) further suggests that each topic, such as confidentiality procedures, can be assessed and assigned one of four risk categories:

1. No risk—current practices are acceptable and do not require modification;

2. Minimal risk—current practices are reasonably adequate; minor modifications would be useful;

3. Moderate risk—current practices are problematic; modifications are necessary to minimize risks; and

4. High risk—current practices are seriously flawed; significant modifications are necessary to minimize risks. (p. 356)

He identifies the areas to be addressed in an audit to include client rights, confidentiality and privacy, informed consent, service delivery, boundary issues and conflicts of interest, documentation, defamation of character, supervision, training, consultation, referral, fraud, termination of services, and practitioner impairment (pp. 357–359).

Several texts have addressed in detail the issues introduced in this section and provide useful models for workers faced with an ethical dilemma. See, for example, Gambrill and Pruger (1997); Dolgoff, Loewenberg, and Harrington (2005); and Reamer (1990, 1998, 2000).

## Chapter Summary

The interactional theory of social work practice views the client as being in a symbiotic relationship with his or her social surroundings. The mutual need between the individual and his or her social surroundings is blocked by obstacles that often obscure it from view.

A historical perspective of social work shows the profession rooted in the twin streams of concern for individual well-being and for social change. As such, the functional assignment for the social work profession is that of mediating the engagement between the client and the systems important to that client. Practice methods and communication and relationship skills are the tools that enable the social worker to put his or her function into action. Practice skills are the instruments needed to develop a positive working relationship that serves as the medium through which the social worker influences the client.

Central to the effectiveness of the worker is her or his ability to integrate the personal self with the professional self. The social worker's practice is guided as well by a set of professional and personal values and by a well-defined professional code of ethics. Value and ethical issues, as well as codes of ethics and legislation, may influence practice and must be taken into account. When ethical dilemmas exist social workers need an opportunity to use agency ethics committees for consultation. Agencies have an obligation to perform ethical audits and to develop risk management models in order to monitor agency practices.

## Related Online Content and Activities

Visit *The Skills of Helping Individuals, Families, Groups, and Communities*, Seventh Edition, CourseMate website at **www.cengagebrain.com** for learning tools such as glossary terms, links to related websites, and chapter practice quizzes. The website for this chapter also features additional notes from the author.

## Competency Notes

The following is a list of Council on Social Work Education (CSWE) recommended competencies and practice behaviors for social work students defined in Educational Policy and Accreditation Standard (EPAS).

**EP 2.1.1a** Identify as a professional social worker and conduct oneself accordingly (p. 27)

**EP 2.1.1b** Attend to professional roles and boundaries (p. 27)

**EP 2.1.4a** Recognize the extent to which a culture's structures and values may oppress, marginalize, alienate, or create or enhance privilege and power (p. 14)

**EP 2.1.4b** Gain sufficient self-awareness to eliminate the influence of personal biases and values in working with diverse groups (p. 14)

**EP 2.1.4c** Recognize and communicate their understanding of the importance of difference in shaping life experiences (p. 14)

**EP 2.1.4d** View themselves as learners and engage those with whom they work as informants (p. 14)

**EP 2.1.6a** Use practice experience to inform scientific inquiry (p. 38)

**EP 2.1.6b** Use research evidence to inform practice (p. 38)

**EP 2.1.7a** Utilize conceptual frameworks to guide the process of assessment, intervention, and evaluation (pp. 4, 7, 17)

**EP 2.1.10a** Substantively and affectively prepare for action with individuals, families, groups, organizations, and communities (p. 33)

**EP 2.1.10b** Use empathy and other interpersonal skills (p. 33)

# Oppression Psychology, Resilience, and Social Work Practice

In the discussion of theory building in Chapter 1, I indicated that what we know about people in general and clients in particular makes up the underlying foundation of knowledge about human behavior and the social environment that guides our work. This knowledge helps us to develop our valued outcomes at particular points in our work (e.g., what we want to achieve in the beginning or contracting phase of work). This, in turn, guides our strategies and specific interventions.

Although it is beyond the scope of this book to explore the wide range of theories, models, and research findings that our profession has drawn upon, two models—oppression psychology and resilience theory—have been particularly central to the development of the interactional perspective and will be briefly presented.

This chapter sets out some of the basic principles and research findings of these models of human behavior and the social environment. The chapter also connects this underlying approach to understanding clients with our practice framework by providing illustrations. Other frameworks that relate to human psychology, to the process of change, to family, group, community, and organizational dynamics, and so forth are explored in more detail in later chapters. The centrality of these perspectives requires that they be introduced in a chapter of their own.

# Oppression Psychology

**EP 2.1.4a**
**EP 2.1.5a**
**EP 2.1.7a**

Social workers need to draw on the social sciences and the large theory and knowledge base about human development, behavior, and the impact of the social environment. This theory base can help the practitioner understand the client in new ways and hear underlying client communication that might otherwise be missed. It also provides suggestions for increasing the effectiveness of our interventions.

## The Oppression Psychology of Frantz Fanon

As one example of a theory that can guide social work practice, I have selected the classic oppression psychology of Frantz Fanon. A brief introduction to the life, views, and psychology of Fanon will help to set the stage for the use of his central ideas and those of others who have built on his work. Fanon, an early exponent of the psychology of oppression, was a Black, West Indian revolutionary psychiatrist who was born on the French-colonized island of Martinique in 1925 and died at age 36.

His short life was chronicled by Bulhan (1985). At age 17, Fanon enlisted in the French army to fight against the Nazis in World War II. He later became interested in and studied psychiatry. While working as a chief of service at a psychiatric hospital in Algeria, he secretly provided support and medical services to the National Liberation Front (FLN) fighting against the French colonial government. When he resigned his position, he became a spokesperson for the FLN and was based in Tunisia. These experiences and others shaped his views of psychology, which challenged many of the constructs of the widely held, European American, White, male-dominated psychology of the day. Bulhan states,

> In the first chapter of his classic book *The Wretched of the Earth* (Fanon, 1968) Fanon elaborated the dynamics of violence and the human drama that unfolds in situations of oppression. He boldly analyzed violence in its structural, institutional, and personal dimensions. Fanon analyzed the psycho-existential aspects of life in a racist society. He emphasized the experiential features and hidden psycho-affective injuries of blacks and the various defensive maneuvers they adopted. Another unstated objective was quite personal: He himself had experienced these injuries, and writing about them was a way of coming to terms with himself. (1985, p. 138)

Although Fanon's psychology emerged from his analysis of race oppression—particularly associated with White, European colonial repression of people of color—many of his key concepts apply to any oppressed population. Using such an application, workers need to recognize the significant differences in degrees and types of oppression experienced by clients. The results of the oppression of African Americans, for example, rooted in the unique experience of slavery, must be seen as one of the most critical, major social problems that still faces urban areas in the United States.

In addition, we must be cautious in how we think about the impact of oppression, because we might inadvertently ignore the significant strengths and resiliency demonstrated by oppressed clients and communities. Such a one-sided view can lead to a practice that does not recognize or work with existing sources of support (e.g., the extended family, the church, community leadership). The next sections of this chapter complement this oppression model with a summary of a resiliency model and strengths perspective that helps uncover clients' strengths for coping.

If social workers think broadly about issues of oppression, vulnerability, and resiliency, they can use such a model, in part, to understand many of their clients. People with mental illness, survivors of sexual abuse, people with AIDS, people with significant physical or mental disabilities, long-term unemployed people, people of color, the homeless, aged nursing home residents, neglected and abused children, clients addicted to substances or in recovery—all of these clients and others can be viewed from a framework that takes oppression, vulnerability, and resiliency into account.

These concepts will be illustrated in the examples of practice explored in this book. Strategies for social worker intervention, based on understanding that emerges from this psychology, will be directed toward helping clients deal with both the oppressor within—internalized negative self-images—and the oppressor without. In fact, it will be argued that unless they broaden their understanding of many of their clients' problems by seeing them as dynamic and systematic in nature and related to oppression, the social agencies, social work departments, and helping professionals who are trying to help these clients can inadvertently become part of the system of oppression.

## Internalized Negative Self-Images

Repeated exposure to oppression, subtle or direct, may lead vulnerable members of the oppressed group to internalize the negative self-images projected by the external oppressor, or the "oppressor without." The external oppressor may be an individual (e.g., the sexual abuser of a child) or an aspect of society (e.g., the racial stereotypes perpetuated against people of color). Internalization of the negative self-images and repression of the rage associated with oppression may lead to destructive behaviors toward oneself and others as oppressed people become autopressors who participate in their own oppression. Thus, the oppressor without becomes the oppressor within.

Evidence of this process can be found in the maladaptive use of addictive substances and the internal violence in communities of oppressed people (e.g., urban or rural areas populated by people of color who may also be poor and/or unemployed). Bulhan (1985) noted that:

> Oppressed people may develop a victim complex, viewing all actions and communications as further assaults or simply other indications of their victim status. This is an example of "adaptive paranoia" seen among the oppressed. (p. 126)

The paranoia is adaptive because oppression is so omnipresent that it would be maladaptive for a person not to be constantly alert to its presence. During a supervision workshop I led, one African American participant, a child welfare supervisor, put it this way: "I have experienced direct and indirect racism so often in my life that I have to have my antennae up all of the time. What I sometimes worry about is that if my antennae are up too high I may see it when it is not really there."

## Oppression Models and Inter- and Intracultural Practice

For the White worker with a client of color, the male worker with a female client, the straight worker with a gay or lesbian client, and so forth—what I refer to as "intercultural" practice—this notion raises important implications for the establishment of an effective and trusting working relationship. Important issues related to oppression also arise when we work with people who are like us—what I call "intracultural" practice. For example, a middle-class Native American social worker and a Native American client who is on welfare may face a similar adaptive paranoia; the client could, directly or indirectly, view the worker as a "sellout" or an "apple": red on the outside and white on the inside. It has been my observation that social work education focuses on intercultural practice and often ignores the even more difficult and often painful issues associated with intracultural practice.

It is not uncommon to think that, because social work educational programs teach about racism and oppression or cultural diversity, the trained worker will know what to do when he or she is face-to-face with a client. I call this the "inductive" fallacy; if we have enough information about the client, we will be able to induce how to act. As outlined earlier, this information is important but we need to use it to deduce our hoped-for outcomes and required interventions.

For example, my understanding of the importance of extended family for most Hispanics, and my desire to engage all of the potential sources of help, might lead me—with the permission of the client—to include or even invite all family members into the process. I include the word "most" before "Hispanics" here because another common mistake is not to recognize diversity within diversity. When we refer to Spanish-speaking clients are we thinking of Chicanos, Puerto Ricans, or Central Americans? While speaking a similar language, elements of culture may be significantly different. The same would be true of Native Americans who come from different tribes with different histories and different cultures. All members of a particular group are not the same, and we need to respect differences as well as similarities. These implications are explored in later chapters that deal with the dynamics and skills involved in developing a positive working relationship between worker and client.

## Indicators of Oppression

**EP 2.1.4a**
**EP 2.1.5a**

Bulhan (1985) identifies several key indicators for objectively assessing oppression. He suggests that "all situations of oppression violate one's space, time, energy, mobility, bonding, and identity" (p. 124). He illustrates these indicators using the example of the slave:

> The male slave was allowed no physical space which he could call his own. The female slave had even less claim to space than the male slave. Even her body was someone else's property. Commonly ignored is how this expropriation of one's body entailed even more dire consequences for female slaves. The waking hours of the slave were also expropriated for life without his or her consent. The slave labored in the field and in the kitchen for the gain and comfort of the master. The slave's mobility was curbed and he or she was never permitted to venture beyond a designated perimeter without a "pass."
>
> The slave's bonding with others, even the natural relation between mother and child, was violated and eroded. The same violation of space, time, energy, mobility, bonding and identity prevailed under apartheid, which in effect, is modern-day slavery. (p. 124)

The slave model is an extreme example of the violation of space, time, energy, mobility, bonding, and identity as indicators of oppression. One can also find current examples of these restrictions. Institutionalized racism in North America toward people of color (e.g., African Americans, Native Americans, Hispanic immigrants) currently provides examples of restrictions on all six indicators. Recent efforts in some communities to provide law enforcement with the power to stop Hispanics and to check for their papers to prove that they are legal, with undefined criteria to justify a suspicion that they are illegal, can be viewed as an example of violation of space, time, and mobility. This expansion of police power is currently under challenge as a violation of civil rights. It was not that long ago, as Bulhan's comments attest, that an oppressive, White government dominated South Africa through apartheid.

Although the slavery experience of African Americans in North America must be considered a unique example of oppression, the indicators may be used to assess degrees of oppression for other populations as well. In this way, a universal psychological model can help us to understand the common elements that exist in any oppressive relationship. Consider the six indicators cited by Bulhan (1985), *violations of space, time, energy, mobility, bonding, and identity* as you read the following excerpt of a discussion among battered women in a shelter as they describe their lives.

### Battered Women and Indicators of Oppression

**Practice Points:**   Note that the first worker intervention is to challenge what she perceived as a justification for abuse:

> Candy said one thing that she didn't like was that her husband had to be number one all the time. He felt he should come first even before the children. She said, "The man's got to be number one. Just like the president. He's a man and he's number one. You don't see no female presidents, do you?" I said, "Are you saying that a man has the right to abuse his partner?" She said no and then turned to the women to say, "But, who's the one who always gives in? The woman does." All the women nodded to this remark. Linda said, "To keep peace in the family."
>
> Candy said, "In the long run, we're the ones who are wrong for not leaving the abusive situations." She said she finally came to the realization that her man was never going to be of any help to her. In the long run, she felt that her children would help her out if she gave them a good life now. She feels very strongly about her responsibilities to her children.

**Practice Points:**   Note how the worker in the next excerpt contains herself—stays silent—as the members describe their experiences. At one point the group leader uses her empathy to articulate the feelings of humiliation experienced by the women.

> Another woman, Tina, said that when she called the police for help, they thought it was a big joke. She said when she had to fill out a report at the police station, the officer laughed about the incident. The women in the group talked about their own experiences with the police which were not very good. One woman had to wait 35 minutes for the police to respond to her call after her husband had thrown a brick through her bedroom window. I said, "Dealing with the police must have been a humiliating situation for all of you. Here you are in need of help and they laugh at you. It's just not right."
>
> Joyce said that she wanted to kill her husband. This desire had been expressed by an abused woman in a previous group session. Other women in

the group said it wouldn't be worth it for her. "All he does is yell at me all the time. He makes me go down to where he works every day at lunch time. The kids and I have to sit and watch him eat. He never buys us anything to eat. Plus, he wants to know where I am every minute of the day. He implies that I sit around the house all day long doing nothing."

Marie said her ex-husband used to say that to her all the time. She said, "But now I'm collecting back pay from my divorce settlement for all the work I never did around the house."

**Practice Points**:   As the trust in the group grows, one woman uses the moment to share her painful experience of being molested at an early age. When she starts to cry the social worker provides support and recognizes the difficulty in raising this in the group. It was not necessary to acknowledge the pain of the experience, expressed through the client's tears, but it was important to credit the client's strength in raising the experience.

Then Joyce said she was going to tell us something that she had only told two other people in her life. Joyce said that she had been molested from the ages of 5 to 7 by her next-door neighbor, Pat. She said that Pat was friendly with her parents. Her mother would say, "Bring a glass of lemonade over to Pat." The first time she did this, he molested her. After that incident, when her mother told her to bring something over to Pat, Joyce would try to get out of it, but her mother insisted that she go over. Pat had told Joyce not to tell anyone what went on.

At this point in the session, Joyce began to cry. I said that I understood this was a difficult situation for her to talk about. Candy said, "Joyce, it wasn't your fault." Joyce said she had kept this incident to herself for approximately 25 years. Finally, when she told her husband, he said, "You probably deserved it." Joyce said she felt like killing him for saying that.

**Practice Points**:   The conversation turns to the issue of leaving the abuser. Once again, the social worker contains herself even though she may feel like saying: "Why don't you leave him?!" The issue of staying or leaving an abusive relationship is a complex one and if the worker intervenes with what may be experienced as a judgmental comment she may close off the ability of the women to admit to ambivalent feelings. As is often the case, a member of the group picks up the conversation and expresses both the struggle and the importance of asserting oneself, if not for themselves then at least for their children.

Candy said she watched while her father beat her mother. She said she used to ask her mother why she put up with it. She said now she sees that it's easier to say you want to get out of a relationship than it is to actually do it. Candy said that leaving was better in the long run. By staying, the children will see their father abusing their mother. "What kind of example is that going to set for the children?" She felt her children would be happier by their leaving.

Joyce said her children were happy to leave their father. She said, "They're tired of listening to him yell all the time." She said her son was more upset about leaving the dog behind than he was about leaving his father. Linda said another good reason for leaving is self-love. She said, "It comes to a point where you know he's going to kill you if you stay around."

**Practice Summary**:   Careful reading of the preceding excerpts provides examples of the violation of these women's space, time, energy, mobility, bonding, and identity—the six identified indicators of oppression. Other examples of differing numbers of indicators violated, and different degrees of violation, could include an inpatient in a rigidly structured psychiatric setting; a wheelchair-bound person who faces buildings that are not accessible; an African American woman who is the only person of her race in an organization and who is held back from advancement by the "glass ceiling" and excluded from the "old boys' network"; an unemployed, 55-year-old man who cannot get a job interview because of his age; an elderly person in a home for the aged who is tied to a chair or tranquilized all day because of staff shortages; and a large, poor family forced to live in inadequate housing, a homeless shelter, or on the street. To one degree or another, space, time, energy, mobility, bonding, and identity may be violated for each of these clients.

***Survivors of Sexual Abuse: The "Damaged Goods" Syndrome***  Examples in the chapters that follow illustrate how oppression can lead to symptoms that are then viewed as pathological. In one illustration, discussed in detail in Chapter 13, a group of survivors of childhood sexual abuse describes the pattern of capitulation that led to their loss of self-identity and their identity as women. The resultant internalization of the belief that they are "damaged goods," as well as their willingness to feel guilty about what was done to them, profoundly affects their current lives and relationships.

**Practice Points:**   A revitalization of their selves and their sense of identity as women can be seen to develop, enhanced by the social support of the group. As the group moves into the ending stage of their work together, a form of radicalization is noted, one of the responses to oppression noted in Fanon's psychology, when the group decides to join a "Take Back the Night" march in the community and protest actively against violence toward women. This leads to their making a commitment to work for changing community understanding and attitudes toward children who have been sexually abused.

### September 18

Then group members asked me to review information about the local "Take Back the Night" march with them. We had told them about the march against sexual violence against women a few weeks before and, after some exploration of their fears about participating in a public demonstration, they decided to march as a group. I supported the group's readiness to act independently and support one another in new experiences. I shared with them how good I felt that they wanted to march together, and I gave them the information they needed.

### September 25

We supported the group's growing independence and shared our feelings with them: As the group processed how the march had felt for them, Jane and I shared how powerful it had felt for us to see them there, marching, chanting, and singing. We also shared that it was hard for us to see them and know that the group was ending. The group was special for us, and it would be hard to let it go.

**Practice Points:**   As the group comes closer to the impending ending we see how this internalized negative self-image, the idea that they are "damaged goods," begins to change as they realize they were not responsible for what was done to them. This change is embodied in a poem written by one member and shared in the group. The poem is an example of the resilience and strength that can be mobilized in clients and will be discussed in the next section.

Linda and various group members talked for some time about how hopeless she felt. I reached for her ability to cope with her pain. "I'm just hearing that you have so much pain and sadness right now, Linda, and I wonder, what are you doing with all this hurt?" She said that she was crying a lot, just letting herself feel the sadness, and that she was also writing in her journal and writing poems. She mentioned that she had just written a poem today about her pain and where it was taking her. Several people asked her if she would read it, and she did. It was called "Children of the Rainbow," and it described how beams of light are shattered and broken as they pass through a drop of water and how they emerge to form the vibrant colors of the rainbow. The poem said that she and all survivors in recovery are like beams of light; if they can make it through their pain, they will become vibrant, beautiful, and whole. Several of us had tears in our eyes (me included), and there was a powerful silence when she finished.

This brief summary of some central ideas in oppression psychology theory sets the stage for the use of these constructs in later chapters. Although there are many other models that can help workers understand their clients and develop effective intervention strategies, this is a very useful model for thinking about work with oppressed and vulnerable populations, which make up a large part of the social worker's practice. As we consider the impact of oppression, we must also understand the elements of resilience that help individuals, families, communities, and entire population groups survive—and often thrive—in the face of adversity.

## Resilience Theory and Research

**EP 2.1.3a**
**EP 2.1.3b**
**EP 2.1.6b**

During the 1970s and 1980s, developmental research focused on risk factors that appeared to be associated with negative outcomes for clients. A child growing up in an inner-city neighborhood besieged by drugs and violence faced a degree of risk in attempting to negotiate the passage to young adulthood and beyond. If the same child also experienced childhood trauma (physical or sexual abuse, abandonment, and so on) and had parents and family members who were active abusers of drugs and alcohol, research indicated that the degree of risk for the child's negative developmental outcome increased exponentially. However, a recurring anomaly in social work practice experience and literature indicated that not all children exposed to high degrees of risk and trauma had negative developmental outcomes. Examining the "anatomy of resilience," Butler (1997) pointed out that

> a growing number of clinicians and researchers were arguing that the risk factor model burdens at-risk children with the expectation that they will fail, and ignores those who beat the odds. Broad epidemiological studies, they say, don't explain why one girl, sexually abused by a relative, becomes an unwed mother or a prostitute while another becomes an Oprah Winfrey or a Maya Angelou. Retrospective studies can't explain why one man, raised in a harsh, crowded household in impoverished Richmond, California, becomes addicted to crack cocaine and dies of AIDS, while his younger brother—Christopher Darden—graduates from law school, and goes on to prosecute O. J. Simpson. It's time, they say, to see what the Dardens and Winfreys of the world have to teach. (p. 25)

Given the widespread nature of substance abuse; the evidence of substantial emotional, physical, and sexual abuse; the increase in the nature and degree of violence in many communities; and the growing numbers of children living in poverty, it is little wonder that research shifted toward understanding why some children, families, and communities still thrive under these conditions. This focus lends itself to the development of both preventive and curative approaches to clients at risk.

Rak and Patterson (1996, p. 369) identified four major groupings of protective factors associated with the "buffering hypothesis"—that is, variables that may provide a buffer of protection against life events that affect at-risk children:

1. The personal characteristics of the children (e.g., an ability from infancy on to gain others' positive attention)
2. Family conditions (e.g., focused nurturing during the first year of life and little prolonged separation from the preliminary caretaker)
3. Supports in the environment (e.g., role models, such as teachers, school counselors, mental health workers, neighbors, and clergy)
4. Self-concept factors (e.g., the capacity to understand self and self-boundaries in relation to long-term family stressors such as psychological illness)

Masten (2001) reviewed the existing resilience models and research and identified two major streams of thought. One is the variable-focused study, which suggests that parenting qualities, intellectual functioning, socioeconomic class, and so forth correlate with positive adaptive behavior. The second line of inquiry is the person-focused study, which tries to understand the whole individual rather than specific variables. Researchers who use the latter approach seek to identify groups of individuals with patterns of good-versus-poor adaptive functioning in life contexts of high-versus-low risks and then compare outcomes. After reviewing studies that use both approaches, Masten (2001) drew the following conclusions:

> The accumulated data on resilience in development suggest that this class of phenomena is more ordinary than one was led to expect by extraordinary case histories that often inspired the study. Resilience appears to be a common phenomenon arising from ordinary human adaptive processes. The great threats to human development are those that jeopardize the systems underlying these adaptive processes, including brain development and cognition, caregiver-child relationships, regulation of emotion and behavior, and the motivation for learning and engaging the environment. (p. 238)

## Developmental Psychology Theory and Research

A landmark study in developmental psychology involved 698 infants on the Hawaiian island of Kauai who, in 1955, became participants in a 30-year longitudinal study of "how some individuals triumph over physical disadvantages and deprived childhoods" (Werner, 1989, p. 106). Werner described the goals that she and her collaborators shared "to assess the long-term consequences of prenatal and perinatal stress and to document the effects of adverse early rearing conditions on children's physical, cognitive, and psychosocial development" (p. 106). She described their growing interest in resilience as follows:

> But as our study progressed we began to take a special interest in certain "high risk" children who, in spite of exposure to reproductive stress, discordant and impoverished home lives and uneducated, alcoholic, or mentally disturbed parents, went on to develop healthy personalities, stable careers, and strong

interpersonal relations. We decided to try to identify the protective factors that contributed to the resilience of these children. (p. 106)

The researchers identified 201 "vulnerable" children (30 percent of the surviving children) as high risk if they encountered four or more risk factors by the age of 2 (severe perinatal stress, chronic poverty, uneducated parents, or troubled family environments marked by discord, divorce, parental alcoholism, or mental illness). Two-thirds of this group (129) developed serious learning or behavior problems by the age of 10 or had delinquency records, mental health problems, or pregnancies by the time they were 18.

It was the other third (72) of these high-risk children—those who "grew into competent young adults who loved well, worked well and played well"—that attracted the researchers' attention (Werner, 1989, p. 108). They identified several constitutional factors as sources of resilience (e.g., high activity level, low degree of excitability and distress, high degrees of sociability, ability to concentrate at school, problem-solving and reading skills, and effective use of their talents). They also identified the following environmental factors:

- Coming from families with four or fewer children
- Spaces of two or more years between themselves and their next siblings
- The opportunity to establish a close bond with at least one caretaker who provided positive attention during the first years of life

These resilient children were found to be "particularly adept at recruiting such surrogate parents when a biological parent was unavailable or incapacitated" (Werner, 1989, p. 108). These children were also able to use their network of neighbors, school friends and teachers, church groups, and so forth to provide emotional support in order to succeed "against the odds" (p. 110).

The researchers concluded on a hopeful note:

As long as the balance between stressful life events and protective factors is favorable, successful adaptation is possible. When stressful events outweigh the protective factors, however, even the most resilient child can have problems. It may be possible to shift the balance from vulnerability to resilience through intervention, either by decreasing exposure to risk factors or stressful events or by increasing the number of protective factors and sources of support that are available. (Werner, 1989, p. 111)

Researchers and theorists have built on this basic set of ideas: Life stressors can lead to negative outcomes for people at high risk; however, personal and environmental factors can buffer the individual, thereby providing the resilience to overcome adversity. For example, Fonagy, Steele, Steele, and Higgitt (1994) examined attachment theory, which focuses on the impact of early infant-caregiver attachments on a child's development and the security of such attachments. They examined the intergenerational transmission of insecure attachments, focusing on factors that might disrupt a negative cycle—in other words, ways to help mothers who had themselves experienced insecure attachments avoid transmitting these to their own children.

Other researchers have applied the basic model to specific populations (as defined by race, ethnicity, and so forth), economic status (poverty), or community variables (inner-city, level of violence). For example, Daly, Jennings, Beckett, and Leashore (1995) make use of an "Africentric paradigm" to describe an emphasis on collectivity that is expressed as shared concern and responsibility for others: "Scholarship using this perspective identifies positive aspects of African American life richly embedded in spirituality and a world-view that incorporates African traits and commitment to common causes" (p. 241).

As an example on the individual level, specifically referring to the resilience of successful African American men, the authors cite research findings (Gary & Leashore, 1982; Hacker, 1992) that suggest the following:

> Much of their success can be attributed to individual and family resilience, the ability to "bounce back" after defeat or near defeat, and the mobilization of limited resources while simultaneously protecting the ego against a constant array of social and economic assaults. To varying degrees, success results from a strong value system that includes belief in self, industrious efforts, desire and motivation to achieve, religious beliefs, self-respect and respect for others, and responsibility toward one's family and community, and cooperation. (Daly et al., 1995, p. 242)

In another example, researchers examined age, race, and setting by focusing on risk and resilience for African American youths in school settings (Connell, Spencer, & Aber, 1994). They developed a theoretical model that they tested using data from two large samples in two cities: New York and Atlanta. Their findings confirm that family involvement is an important target for these interventions. This study's results also support efforts to develop intervention strategies that increase poor African American youths' beliefs in their own abilities to affect their academic outcomes and for improving their relationships with peers in the school context.

Perhaps the most intriguing and disturbing implication of this study for our understanding of risk and resilience is that disaffected behavior in low-income African American youth can lessen parental involvement, which in turn contributes to negative appraisals of self that exacerbate disaffected patterns of action and contribute to negative educational outcomes.

Christian and Barbarin (2001) also examined the importance of parental involvement on the adjustment of low-income African American children. They found that children of parents who attended church at least weekly had fewer behavior problems than did those who attended church less frequently. This supported the importance of religiosity as a sociocultural resource for African American families with children who are potentially at risk for behavioral and emotional maladjustments related to growing up in poor families and communities. In a second and related line of inquiry, the researchers hypothesized that parents who reported a positive racial identity, as well as those who tended to externalize by attributing the causes of negative African American life outcomes to outside forces, would have children with fewer behavioral problems. Although these two variables might relate to parental self-esteem, they did not directly affect the children's incidence of behavioral problems. In fact, parents who tended to internalize explanations of poor outcomes (e.g., not working hard enough, lack of persistence) had children with fewer behavioral problems. The authors concede that the limitations of the study do not allow wider generalizations; nonetheless, their findings were both unexpected and intriguing.

Richters and Martinez (1993) offer an example of resilience research that examines the impact of community violence on childhood development. They examined factors that contributed to resilience on the part of 72 children attending their first year of elementary school in a violent neighborhood of Washington, D.C. Their findings indicate the following:

> Despite the fact that these children were being raised in violent neighborhoods, had been exposed to relatively high levels of violence in the community, and were

experiencing associated distress symptoms, community violence exposure levels were not predictive of adaptational failure or success. Instead, adaptational status was systematically related to characteristics of the children's homes. (p. 609)

The authors point out that only when the environmental adversities contaminated the safety and stability of the children's homes did their odds of adaptational failure increase.

In a study of the risk and protective factors associated with gang involvement among urban African American adolescents, researchers found that youths with current or past gang membership documented higher levels of risk involvement, lower levels of resilience, higher exposure to violence, and higher distress symptoms than did youths with no gang affiliations (Li et al., 2002). The findings persisted when controlled for age, gender, and risk involvement. The authors suggest that gang membership itself is associated with increased risk and ill effects on psychological well-being. They also found that strong family involvement and resiliency protects against gang involvement.

Garmezy (1991) focused on the resilience and vulnerability of children in relation to the impact of poverty. He states:

> The evidence is sturdy that many children and adults do overcome life's difficulties. Since good outcomes are frequently present in a large number of life histories, it is critical to identify those "protective" factors that seemingly enable individuals to circumvent life stressors. (p. 421)

The author points to a core of variables that serve as resilience factors. These include "warmth, cohesion, and the presence of some caring adults (such as a grandparent) in the absence of responsive parents or in the presence of marked marital discord" (p. 421). Similar findings in studies that examine the resiliency of children who are exposed to poverty and other traumas have identified emotional responsivity in the parent-child relationship as a buffering factor (Egeland, Carlson, & Sroufe, 1993).

In one example of a study that focused on children from maltreating homes, Herrenkohl, Herrenkohl, and Egolf (1994) report on a longitudinal study of the effects of abuse and neglect on 457 children. The study began in 1976 and continued with follow-up studies of 345 of the children in 1980–1982 (when the children were of elementary school age) and again in 1990–1992 (during late adolescence). The 1980 phase included children who received services from the local child welfare agencies for abuse ($N = 105$) or neglect ($N = 86$), as well as a control group of children in day care ($N = 52$), Head Start programs ($N = 52$), and private nursery schools ($N = 50$). All of the children were rated on several variables and then grouped into high-functioning, low-functioning, and middle-functioning categories. School success (as in attendance, graduation) was one of the key outcome measures for determining success.

Their data suggested that "the presence of at least one caretaker throughout childhood appeared to be a necessary, although not sufficient, condition for school achievement" (p. 304). Finally, positive parental expectations for self-sufficiency on the part of parents with children who experienced severe physical health problems appeared to "stimulate the child's goal-setting and determination, with good effect on their academic work" (p. 304).

In a review of the literature on resilience and poverty, Garmezy (1993) suggests that these findings provide new questions and avenues for research. What factors are involved in the seeming diminution over time of resilience in some hitherto adaptive children and adults? Prolonged and cumulated stress would appear to be a prime candidate for examination. Another factor worthy of consideration would be the absence of a support structure and its availability over time. Other candidates for effecting change may include critical modifications in the child's environment, such as the physical dissolution of the family (p. 130).

Other examples of population-specific resilience studies include research on youths with high incidence of disabilities (Murray, 2003), homeless students (Reed-Victor & Stronge, 2002), and adolescents who experience marital transitions (Rodgers & Rose, 2002).

## Resilience and Life-Span Theory

Resilience theory does not apply only to children and families. Staudinger, Marsiske, and Baltes (1993), working in the area of aging, have attempted to integrate the notion of resilience with work concerning developmental reserve capacity emerging from the field of life-span psychology. Life-span theory suggests that development throughout life is characterized by the joint occurrence of increases (gains), decreases (losses), and maintenance (stability) in adaptive capacity (p. 542).

Staudinger et al. (1993) suggest that this theory challenges a one-dimensional model in which aging, for example, might be seen as simply the loss of capacity. Plasticity, which can be positive or negative, is another central notion of life-span theory. Plasticity can be defined as the individual's ability to be flexible in response to stress. This idea suggests that variable components of change can be attributed to individuals or populations and may be associated with cross-cultural or historical differences. The degree of an individual's plasticity may depend on the individual's reserve capacity, which is constituted by the internal and external resources available to the individual at a given point in time. Cognitive capacity and physical health are examples of internal resources; one's social network and financial status are external ones. Note that an individual's resources need not be fixed but may change over time (p. 542).

The authors describe two types of reserve capacity. Baseline reserve capacity is the individual's current "maximum performance potential" with existing internal and external resources. Developmental reserve capacity refers to resources that can be activated or increased. The life-span theory argues that, as reserve capacity increases, so does the potential for positive plasticity.

Social work intervention activities (e.g., case management) may be seen as focusing on helping elderly clients, for example, to use their baseline reserves while intervening to activate the clients' developmental reserves. For example, increasing the client's social network (external reserves) through involvement in a senior citizens' program could directly improve the internal reserve capacity (health, emotional state, cognitive capacity), which in turn strengthens the client's capacity for developing stronger social networks. This client would have demonstrated positive plasticity in the area of social relationships.

## Cognitive Hardiness

Researchers have also examined the concept of "cognitive hardiness" and coping style as buffering or moderating variables between life stress events and trauma and psychological and somatic distress (Beasley, Thompson, & Davidson, 2003). The study involved analysis of questionnaires completed by 187 students who had returned to the university as mature adults. In general, findings supported a direct effect on outcomes of life stress and psychological health. Cognitive hardiness, coping style, and negative life events also impacted outcomes. Several cases supported the concept that cognitive hardiness moderated the impact of emotional coping styles and adverse life events on psychological distress. The researchers used Kobasa and Pucetti's (1983) definition of cognitive hardiness as a personality variable; specifically, the quality of hardy individuals who

> believe that they can control or influence events, have a commitment to activities and their interpersonal relationships and to self, in that they recognize their own distinct values, goals and priorities in life, and view change as a challenge rather than a threat. In the latter regard, they are predisposed to be cognitively flexible. (p. 841)

## Implications for Social Work Practice

The growing interest in resilience theory and research, along with the concept of life-span theory, fits nicely with evolving theory and practice in social work and also with the interactional model. For social workers who have long held a psychosocial approach to understanding and working with clients and who have more recently embraced ecological models and a strengths perspective, these theoretical models and research findings tend to confirm what their practice wisdom and research has told them. These models also reinforce the first practice principle I was taught in graduate school: "Always reach for the client's strength!"

The strong emergence of a resilience model, with its concepts of reserve capacities and plasticity, together with the life-span idea of cognitive hardiness, can influence social work practice on many levels. For example, we have just seen in this chapter, through our own exploration of theory development, how theories provide underlying propositions about people and their behavior that can guide our interventions.

Gilgun (1996) provides one example of an effort to integrate resilience theory with social work practice theory—what has been commonly described as the systems or ecological approach or framework. She suggests that this framework leads to social work interventions that are "wide-ranging, covering research, program development, direct practice, and policy formulation, implementation, and evaluation" (p. 399). She points out that developmental psychopathology introduces social work to a language full of generative concepts and theory, whereas social work provides the ecological framework, strengths-based focus, and phenomenological perspectives. In combination, social work and developmental psychopathology can greatly advance knowledge to inform research, program development, practice, and policy.

In the earlier discussion of resilience and life-span theory, the concept of developmental reserve capacity was introduced. Life-span theory suggests that development throughout life is characterized by the joint occurrence of increases (gains), decreases (losses), and maintenance (stability) in adaptive capacity. The concept of "cognitive hardiness" and coping style as buffering or moderating variables between life stress events and trauma and psychological and somatic distress was also discussed.

### Older People's Strategies and Ways of Coping

Tanner (2007) focused on the strategies and mechanisms for coping employed by older people to manage changes and difficulties that accompany aging. They suggested that a good starting point for social workers is to focus on the clients' present lives. Using a small-sample qualitative analysis study they identified three major themes for sustaining one's self. These were "keeping going" and "staying me" and the "slippery slope."

The theme of keeping going refers to practical or "doing" strategies employed by participants, while the theme of staying me refers to their cognitive ways of coping. The third theme, the slippery slope, refers to factors that support or undermine strategies and ways of coping. (p. 11)

The study sample included 12 older people who were referred or self-referred for services but were refused service from a local social services department. The sample resulted from 53 invitations to participate to people who met the study criteria. The difficulties for which they had originally sought help concerned domestic tasks (e.g., cleaning and shopping, getting in and out of the bath). The design of the study was to carry out five in-depth semistructured interviews with each participant over the course of three years to determine how they had managed their difficulties. Four participants did not complete the study because of death or moving way. The qualitative analysis of interviews identified the following three subcategories for keeping going:

- *Activity*. "Participants took a proactive role in managing their situation, keeping themselves busy, making efforts to deal with difficulties, endeavoring to take charge of their situation and adapting their usual ways of doing things to accommodate loss and change" (p. 12).

- *Stability*. Participants made "efforts to keep some stability in life, often in the face of threats brought about by illness, disability and other forms of loss. Two sub-categories identified here were maintaining routines and maintaining standards" (p. 13).

- *Balanced Relationships*. "Participants endeavored to maintain an acceptable balance between giving and receiving within relationships, seeking to preserve accepted relationship boundaries and maintain reciprocity" (p. 15).

The theme of staying me was "comprised of two categories: continuity, referring to ways in which a sense of connection between the past, present and future is preserved, and self-affirmation, referring to cognitive processes by which a positive view is supported" (p. 16).

The third and final theme, the slippery slope, "acknowledges that experiences of illness, disability and ageing, and ways of managing them, have to be understood in the social context. Threats and resources that impinge on how difficulties are experienced and managed were identified at person, social and community levels" (p. 20).

The use of support groups for the geriatric population illustrates how a social work program can maintain or increase adaptive capacity, and strengthen cognitive hardness in the face of losses of family, friends, health, work role, physical functioning, neighbors, and so on, to help the elderly with difficulties often associated with this stage of life. These groups can also provide the medium for maintaining activity and reciprocal social relations as well as helping the elderly with the cognitive issues involved in "staying me." The example that follows illustrates how all of these support strategies for coping can be employed.

***Geriatric Reminiscence Group: Strengthening Social Connections*** In the example that follows, a geriatric reminiscence group is organized at a day center to help older members, 68 to 101, to make social connections and to strengthen external and internal reserves. This programmatic social work response provides a place where otherwise lonely clients can come each day to share food, play cards, and find support from social connections.

**Practice Points:** We can see the impact of age and stage of the life cycle as members of this group, who have experienced many losses in their lives, start to face some of the painful as well as positive feelings associated with their reminiscences. In addition to losses of friends, relatives, and their work as homemakers or in other capacities, they also have experienced the loss of being able to prepare foods that had important meaning to them. The leaders note a pattern of joking in the early sessions, which may be a form of "flight," as they signal to the leaders that these are difficult areas for discussion. After a number of chaotic and often frustrating (for the leaders) meetings, the members finally begin to work on the purpose of the group.

### February 18

Before the group meeting, my coleader and I realized that, although the conversations were funny and people were socializing, we were not accomplishing the group's purpose, which was to reminisce about the past. After getting seated, I stated, "Is everyone ready to work today?" Florence replied by saying, "What's the job?" The group started laughing. I stated again that the purpose of the group was to reminisce. Grace began by talking about birth order. The group talked about family, siblings, and children. The topic then turned to the discussion of medical care and how much things have changed with technology. I was actually amazed. The group was communicating, listening to one another and sharing opinions. I encouraged the communication to continue. Everyone was listening and respecting one another. When the group was over and I was getting my coat on, Lena grabbed my arm and stated, "Oh yeah, Joan, what does reminiscing mean?"

**Practice Points:** Unfinished business from the first (contracting) session reemerged because the group leader had used the term *reminiscing* without illustrations or further explanation. Lena gives her an opportunity to recontract. Once again the group members, through Rose, use a member (Paul) to both avoid a discussion and at the same time raise an issue: lost love relationships.

### February 25

I started the group by asking if anyone knew what *reminiscing* means. My purpose for doing this was because that is where the group left off last week. A group member volunteered with an answer by saying, "Thinking and talking about stuff from long ago." Other members chimed in to give their definition. I asked the group if they knew why we reflect on memories from the past. Rose stated, "More importantly, do you all know that Paul has a girlfriend?" Everyone started laughing. I asked Rose how that was relevant to the conversation. Rose stated that the present was better than the past. I asked if the past was too painful to talk about. Rose told me that the past was dead. Another member asked Paul if he was in love. I ignored the comment and asked the group if they thought that Paul wanted his love life told to everyone. I now realize that I was adding to the "flight" behavior. Fran looked at me and then said something to Rose in Italian.

**Practice Points:** When the group starts to talk about Paul's "love" they are actually working on an important issue—their own lost loves. The social worker's first response is to experience only the flight; however, she quickly catches this mistake and finds the connection between the joking and the theme for the day. Her acknowledgment of an intercultural issue, her being Jewish and most of the members Catholic, helps the group members to discuss the sensitive area of intercultural romantic relationships. Note how Fran actually introduces a response about first loves by asking the group leader if she is Jewish.

> I tried to turn an awkward moment into work and asked the group if anyone would like to talk about their first love. Fran turned to me and stated, "You're Jewish, aren't you?" After I answered yes, Fran turned to Rose and continued having a conversation in Italian. I avoided questioning Fran's comment because I knew they were angry and looked at my coleader for help. My coleader asked the group to share one trait that makes them different. Everyone started saying what makes them different from others. After the conversation ended, I took a chance and stated, "Everyone has different abilities and traits. One thing that makes me different is that I am Jewish while most of you are Catholic, but we are all the same inside." Fran seemed to get a kick out of my statement. She came over to me, gave me a hug, and then stated, "My first love was Jewish, but I was not allowed to date him." From there, the work began.

**Practice Points:**   By now the leader has learned to understand the group's pattern of raising issues indirectly and using humor to do so. Each group develops their own culture and the method of discussing difficult topics. The group leader needs to learn the "language" of the group which helps her to "hear" the underlying issues. Real intimacy between members means real sharing of memories both positive and negative.

> My coleader asked the group what they wanted to talk about. Frank stated, "We talk about the same things over and over. Let's play cards." I asked if the past was too painful to talk about. Mary commented, "Why talk about the past? Who cares about the past? I agree with Frank. Let's play cards." Before I could respond, Rose states, "I live in the future, not the past." I tried to get Rose to elaborate. I asked her to describe her future, but she could not. I tried to keep a focus on the group and stated that, if we played cards today, then tomorrow that too would be in the past. I asked if that would be difficult to talk about. The group said no.

**Practice Points:**   The underlying issue of the pain that can be associated with reminiscing for this population has finally emerged directly. Ethel, who questions the value of talking about the past, is actually the leader's ally by raising an issue felt by others in the group. The group leader credits her since it has been raised so indirectly in the past and needs to be discussed.

> Ethel said in a strong voice that so many people have so little time left that it is better to plan tomorrow than think about yesterday. I thanked the group member who stated this comment and acknowledged the fact that it took a lot of courage to make that statement. I then commented that it must be tough having so many losses. Lena said, "Enjoy it while you're young because it goes by too fast." With that comment, I truly empathized with what the members were feeling. I realized that they did not want to discuss the pain because they could almost count the time they had left. They would rather enjoy the time that they had left. I voiced my thoughts to the group. The response I received was, "Exactly. Now let's play cards."

**Practice Points:** As noted earlier in the example of survivors of sexual abuse, the leaders introduce the impending ending of the group a few sessions in advance. They share their own feelings of loss and this evokes an expression of feelings by the members. In an example of the integration of process and content, discussion of the ending of the group brings forth the issue of loss in the lives of the members.

### March 18

My coleader and I mentioned that there would only be four more group meetings and that then the group would end. My coleader explained that school would be over and so would our internships, which would be another loss in their lives. Mary said, "Four weeks is far away. Why are you bringing this up now?" I explained that termination is a process and that, although I would be leaving, I would miss all the members and wanted to start preparing myself to leave. I explained that it would be a loss for me as well. The group expressed sadness. Joe said, "Oh well, just another person leaving my life." I validated that loss is difficult and facilitated a conversation on loss and sadness. Group members openly shared their sadness and grief with the group.

Mary shared with the group, "I may give these girls a hard time, but it is only because I know I can, because I know they care." The group turned its focus to friends that have left through the years. Frank seemed to get uncomfortable and started singing. I confronted Frank about his feelings and universalized to the group. As my coleader and I left the group for the day, the group continued to share feelings with one another.

**Practice Summary.** These group leaders have learned to understand the language of the group and to realize the meaning of the active resistance ("Let's play cards") as a signal to them of the importance of addressing the difficulty and pain involved in reminiscence. They believe in the healing power of mutual aid, described in more detail in the group work chapters of this book, and encourage the members to embrace both the sad and happy moments of their past. It can strengthen clients to find out they are not alone and that others in their stage of life are "all in the same boat," another concept explored in detail in Part IV of this book.

***Resilience Theory and Research and Child Welfare Practice*** We find another example of the use of resilience theory and research in its implications for child welfare practice among African American families. Scannapieco and Jackson (1996) review the historical response of African American families to separation and loss, starting with slavery and continuing through the reconstruction period, World War II, the civil rights years, the 1970s and 1980s, and on to the 1990s.

In each stage, they describe the resilience of the African American family and the ways in which it has coped with life stresses brought about by racism in U.S. society. Current stresses associated with poverty, AIDS, child abuse and neglect, and reductions in services have elevated childhood risks to crisis proportions. These authors point to "kinship care" placements, in which the resources of extended African American families are used to provide some of the resilience factors described in the previous discussion of the research. The authors suggest that all members of the extended family should be involved in case planning, because any of them may need to take over as full- or part-time caregivers:

Social work practice within kinship care programs must recognize the resilient nature of the African-American family and work with the "kinship triad," made up of the children, the biological parents, and the caregiver relatives. A system of services should be directed at this union of three to ensure a permanent living arrangement for the children. (p. 194)

This same example could be conceptualized in life-span theory terminology as focusing on resources (internal and external, baseline and developmental) that have increased the positive plasticity of the African American family, thus allowing not only for recovery from trauma but also for the optimizing of individual, family, and community growth and development.

## Section Summary

For the purposes of this chapter, I suggest that resilience and life-span theory and their related research provide an important framework for understanding and engaging any client. If we understand that clients—even those who appear to be totally overwhelmed—have the potential to overcome adversity, we will always look for what is right with them rather than what is wrong. By doing so—and by representing to the client a professional who believes in the client's capacities for growth, change, and adaptation—the social worker becomes a source of resilience for the client. This strengths perspective also provides a rationale for the integration of solution-focused interventions, which are discussed later in this book.

## Chapter Summary

This chapter presented an oppression model designed to help the reader understand some underlying causes of maladaptive behavior observed in many of our clients. Using the oppression psychology of Frantz Fanon, we explored the negative impact of long-term oppression and some of the adaptive and maladaptive defenses that were developed to cope with its impact.

The oppression model was offset by theory and research related to resilience, emphasizing the many ways in which the impact of oppression of all kinds can be overcome by clients. This strengths perspective provides a model for viewing every client as able, at certain times in his or her life, to overcome the many obstacles he or she faces. The argument is made for reaching for a client's strengths instead of being preoccupied with signs of pathology.

Concepts such as "cognitive hardiness" and strategies for staying active and maintaining positive cognitions were described as ways in which the elderly cope with problems as they face the "slippery slope" of aging. These were illustrated by excerpts from a geriatric remembrance group at a senior center.

## *Related Online Content and Activities*

Visit *The Skills of Helping Individuals, Families, Groups, and Communities*, Seventh Edition, CourseMate website at **www.cengagebrain.com** for learning tools such as glossary terms, links to related websites, and chapter practice quizzes. The website for this chapter also features additional notes from the author.

# Competency Notes

The following is a list of Council on Social Work Education (CSWE) recommended competencies and practice behaviors for social work students defined in Educational Policy and Accreditation Standard (EPAS).

**EP 2.1.3a** Distinguish, appraise, and integrate multiple sources of knowledge, including EP research-based knowledge and practice wisdom (p. 54)

**EP 2.1.3b** Analyze models of assessment, prevention, intervention, and evaluation (p. 54)

**EP 2.1.4a** Recognize the extent to which a culture's structures and values may oppress, marginalize, alienate, or create or enhance privilege and power (p. 48)

**EP 2.1.4b** Gain sufficient self-awareness to eliminate the influence of personal biases and values in working with diverse groups (p. 13)

**EP 2.1.4c** Recognize and communicate their understanding of the importance of difference in shaping life experiences (p. 13)

**EP 2.1.5a** Understand forms and mechanisms of oppression and discrimination (p. 48)

**EP 2.1.5b** Advocate for human rights and social and economic justice (p. 29)

**EP 2.1.6a** Use practice experience to inform scientific inquiry (p. 37)

**EP 2.1.6b** Use research evidence to inform practice (p. 54)

**EP 2.1.7a** Utilize conceptual frameworks to guide the process of assessment, intervention, and evaluation (p. 48)

**EP 2.1.7b** Critique and apply knowledge to understand person and environment (p. 6)

# Social Work with Individuals

P art II of this book consists of four chapters that elaborate and illustrate the interactional approach to social work in the context of work with individuals. Chapters 3 through 6 use the model of the four phases of work—preliminary, beginning, middle, and ending/transition—as their organizing framework. In Chapter 3, which covers the preliminary phase, we examine the skills required to prepare for a new contact with a client. In Chapter 4, which covers the beginning phase, we focus on the contracting skills needed to create a clear structure for work. In Chapter 5, we examine the middle (work) phase of practice and provide a model of the stages of an individual session. Finally, in Chapter 6, we explore the ending and transition phase of practice, in which the worker and client bring their relationship to an end and prepare the client to move on to new experiences.

Each chapter describes the specific dynamics and skills associated with the particular phase as well as briefly discussing relevant ethical and legal issues (e.g., informed consent and confidentiality). Research findings are cited to provide an empirical basis for the work. Detailed illustrations of social workers interacting with clients help connect the theory to day-to-day realities that are familiar to the reader. These examples illustrate the constant or core elements of practice while demonstrating the many variations introduced by the nature of the client population, each client's particular problems, and the impact of the practice setting.

# The Preliminary Phase of Work

I n Chapter 1, we outlined four phases of work: the preliminary, beginning, middle, and ending/transition phases. In this chapter, we begin to explore the constructs introduced in Chapter 2, starting with the preliminary phase of practice. The indirect nature of the communication process is examined, with suggestions provided for ways in which the worker can respond directly to indirect cues. We then look at an approach for developing preliminary empathy—prior to the first interview—with potential client feelings and concerns related to the worker, the agency or setting, and the client's problems. The importance of a social worker "tuning in" to his or her own feelings is also stressed.

The rationale for the preliminary phase of practice is based on the idea that preparing for social work interactions can increase the likelihood of establishing a positive worker–client relationship and of hearing and understanding what the client has to say. We start this chapter by looking at the complexity of the human communication process in general, and then we move on to explore issues specific to social work practice.

EP 2.1.3b
EP 2.1.3c
EP 2.1.7a
EP 2.1.7b
EP 2.1.10a
EP 2.1.10b

# Communications in Practice

Human communications can be complex under any circumstances. Let us examine the nature of a single communication. We start with a sender, or an individual who has an idea to transmit. This idea must first be encoded—that is, translated from ideas into symbols. Then it is transmitted to the intended receiver through spoken or written words, touch, or nonverbal means (e.g., facial expression or posture). The message must next be received. This involves hearing, reading, seeing, or feeling by the recipient. Next, the message must be decoded—that is, translated by the recipient from symbols to the ideas that they represent. The recipient must then acknowledge the message through some form of feedback to the sender, thus completing the cyclical process.

## Obstacles to Direct Communication

Considering how complicated even the simplest communications can be and how many points in the process there are at which meanings can be distorted, we might wonder how any communication is ever completed. In the helping relationship, additional factors can complicate the process. These obstacles to open communication often cause a client to employ indirect methods of expressing thoughts and feelings.

*Client Ambivalence* One obstacle may be the feeling of ambivalence associated with accepting help. Our society responds negatively to almost all forms of dependency, stressing instead the norm of independence—being able to handle things on one's own. For the client, however, the urgency of the task at hand counters society's pressure. The result of conflicting forces is often an ambiguous call for help. Particularly in early sessions, before a working relationship has been established, clients may present concerns in an indirect manner; they also may present "near problems," that is, real issues that are not the ones they really need to talk about.

*Societal Taboos* A second potential obstacle to direct communication, societal taboos, reflects a general consensus to block or prohibit discussion in areas of sensitivity and deep concern. The client enters the helping relationship with a conscious or unconscious internalization of these taboos, which hinders free speaking. Major taboos in our society discourage "real" talk about topics such as sex, dependency, substance abuse, authority, and money. The discomfort that clients experience when talking about issues and feelings in certain areas may cause them to use indirect methods of communication.

*Impact of Painful and Frightening Affect* A third obstacle is associated with the feelings that accompany concerns. Clients may find certain feelings painful and frightening. The raising of a concern may be blocked by conscious or unconscious defenses that clients use to avoid moving into areas that produce these feelings. This can lead to clients sharing the facts of an issue but ignoring their own feelings. Because all issues of concern are invested with both facts and feelings, the sharing of the facts represents only a partial communication.

In one example, a client with a chronically ill child was able to share her anger but was less in touch with the pain that contributed to her rage. She was using a form of flight-fight response that served as a defense against her own distress. Fight and flight, in this case, are the emotional versions of what we observe in humans and animals when faced with a threatening situation. Bion (1961) suggested that individuals and groups that are unable to deal directly with painful emotions use fight (e.g., an argument) or flight (e.g., humor) to avoid the pain. Because it cut this client off from the support she desperately needed, it was a maladaptive defense.

***Context of the Engagement*** Finally, the context of the contract with the helping person may contribute factors that block real talk. For example, in a child welfare agency, workers carry dual functions and—in some cases—may have to act for the state in apprehending (removing) a child. Parents are quite aware of the worker's authority and power and thus will be wary of sharing information or feelings that can be used against them. An officer who can revoke parole, a nurse who can make a hospital stay unpleasant, a psychiatrist who can decide when a patient can go home, an adoption worker who can decide if a person gets a child, a worker in a mandatory group for male batterers—all of these helping people have power over the lives of their clients, and this power may become an obstacle to real talk.

## Examples of Indirect Communication in Practice

Because of the obstacles that block the direct expression of feelings, clients may use indirect means to present them, as in the classic case of the teenage client who has "a friend with a problem." Hinting is an important indirect cue; the client makes a comment or asks a question that contains a portion of the message. The mother who asks the worker if she has children, for example, may be using a question to raise, very tentatively, a more complex and threatening issue: "Will this worker understand what it is like for me?" Clients may also raise their concerns through their behavior. For example, a child in a residential setting who has not been asked to return home for a family visit over a holiday may let his child-care worker know how upset he is by acting out. Adults in counseling sessions who come across negatively may be doing the same thing.

EP 2.1.10b
EP 2.1.10d
EP 2.1.10e
EP 2.1.10g
EP 2.1.10i

***Indirect Communications: A Young, Single-Parent Mother*** Another illustration can be drawn from the child welfare setting. A social worker was visiting a young, single-parent mother who had three children under the age of 4. The worker had been brought in to investigate a neglect complaint that was called in by a neighbor. As the worker spoke to the harried mother, the youngest child pulled at her mother's leg until the mother said, "Leave me alone, I'm talking now." The child continued to try to engage the mother, who finally grabbed the little girl by the shoulders and shouted, "Leave me alone!"

The worker was stunned and, responding to that part of her job function that called for the protection of children, began to counsel the mother: "Mrs. Jones, don't you think there might be other ways in which you can tell your child you wish to be left alone?" The mother understood the implied criticism and immediately began to feel more tense and defensive with this worker.

If the worker were in touch with her own feelings and those of the mother, and if it had been clear to the worker that the mother was a client in her own right and not just an instrument for providing service to the child, she might have recognized the indirect cues of the mother's negative behavior and responded as follows: "Is this what it's like for you all the time—no chance to be alone, to talk to other people without the kids pestering you?" If said with genuine understanding of the plight of a single mother who is young, trying to raise kids on her own, probably struggling with an inadequate income, and so on, this type of direct response to indirect cues would likely strengthen the working relationship. In one of my studies, for example, the use of this skill contributed directly to the client's perception that the worker was there both to protect the child and to help the mother (Shulman, 1991).

The worker also might acknowledge how hard it must be on the mother to have a social worker talk to her about these things. It might still be necessary for the worker to intervene by offering respite care to give the mother a break. Because protecting the child matters most, the worker may have to remove the child, with or without the mother's agreement. Nonetheless, the impact of exercising this authority would be somewhat moderated by the worker's caring for the mother as a client in her own right.

***Metaphor and Allegory: A Depressed Adolescent Foster Child*** Clients sometimes use metaphor and allegory as means of indirect communication. As in literature, the intent is to send a message without necessarily expressing its content directly. This is illustrated by an interview with a depressed adolescent foster child who has recently lost his parents. The youngster is getting ready to leave the care of the agency because he is 18, and he is worried about where he will live. He has had eight changes of residence during the past year.

**Practice Points:**   Note both the indirect communications and the means by which the worker uses her preparatory empathy (tuning in) to reach for the underlying message:

> Frank asked me if I ever thought of the fact that space never ended. I said I hadn't really. I wondered if he had, and if it worried him somehow. He said it did, because sometimes he felt like a little ball, floating in space, all alone. A little bit higher and more to the right, and bye, bye world—just like a wee birdie. I said he really has been floating in space, moving from place to place, and that he must be feeling all alone. Frank's eyes filled with tears and he said, emphatically, "I am all alone!"

**Practice Summary.**   Although the worker skillfully responded to one part of the indirect communication, she did not pick up on the second, more difficult and disturbing, part, in which he says "bye, bye world." The client might have suicidal fears, and the worker should explore what he meant by this part of his statement.

Nonverbal forms of communication can also be used to send important indirect messages. The client who always arrives late or early or who misses sessions after promising to attend may be commenting on his reactions to the process of helping. The children in the family session who arrive looking tense and angry and refuse to take off their coats may be conveying their feelings about being there. The client who sits back looking angry, with arms firmly folded across his chest, may be saying, "Go ahead, try and change me." These are all important messages; however, the common element is that the clients are not using words.

The crucial point here is that indirect communications often make it hard to understand what clients are trying to say. In particular, negative behavior is difficult to understand, particularly for new workers, because it throws them off balance. The capacity to reach beyond negative behavior for the client's real message comes with the growth of the worker's sense of professional competency.

With such complex communications, how can the worker ever hear what the client is trying to say? This is where developing preliminary empathy prior to a session through the use of the "tuning in" skill can be helpful. It can substantially increase the odds in favor of understanding, particularly in the beginning stage of work, when the conversation tends to be indirect. In the next section, we examine tuning in more closely.

# Preliminary Phase: Tuning In to the Self and to the Client

**EP 2.1.10a**
**EP 2.1.10b**

A major skill in the preliminary phase of work is the development of the worker's sense of empathy. This technique can be employed before contact with the client has taken place. Schwartz (1961) termed this process *tuning in*; it involves the worker's effort to get in touch with potential feelings and concerns that the client may bring to the helping encounter. The purpose of the exercise is to help the worker become a more sensitive receiver of the client's indirect communications during the first sessions. For reasons discussed earlier, some of the most important client communications are not spoken directly. By tuning in, the worker may be able to hear the client's indirect cues and respond directly. A direct response to an indirect communication is one of the skills a worker can use to help clients manage their feelings. It is called "putting the client's feelings into words."

In the sections that follow, we explore the importance of tuning in to issues related to the worker's authority, the differences between affective and intellectual tuning in, tuning in to the worker's own feelings, and different levels of tuning in.

## Tuning In to the Authority Theme

All levels of tuning in will be illustrated in this book. I believe, however, that the first question on the client's mind is "Who is this worker, and what kind of a person will she or he be?" For that reason, I will begin with what I call the *authority theme*, focusing on issues related to the relationship between the client and the social worker. An example from practice will illustrate the general issues involved. This particular experience has been shared by workers in consultation sessions so often, with only slight variations, that it probably represents an archetype.

***The Authority Theme: Young Worker Meets Middle-Aged Mother*** The presenter was a social worker in a child welfare agency. She was 22, unmarried, and new to the job. Her first interview was with a 38-year-old mother of seven children who had come to the agency's attention because of a neighbor's complaint about her care of her children. Another worker had met with her for 4 months but was leaving the agency. The new worker was the replacement, and she was making her first visit.

**Practice Points:**   Note the indirect communication and how the worker, unprepared for the question, responds defensively.

> After introductions, the worker and client had been sitting in the living room chatting for a few minutes when the client suddenly turned to the worker and said, "By the way, do you have any children?" There was a brief silence after this embarrassing question. Recovering quickly, and hiding her feelings, the worker said to the client, "No, I don't have any children. However, I have taken a number of courses in child psychology." Another common technique used to avoid having to respond to the client is to say, "We are here to talk about you, not me." Discussing this incident later, in a consultation session, the worker reported her internal feelings and thoughts: "I panicked! I thought, 'Oh my God, she knows I don't have any children—how am I supposed to help her?'"

This is just one example of this situation, but many variations exist on the same theme: the recovering alcoholic who wonders if the worker has "walked the walk" (been an alcoholic) or "talked the talk" (been a member of Alcoholics Anonymous), the gay man with AIDS who inquires whether the worker is straight, or the person of color who describes prior White workers who "didn't understand our people." These variations and others will be explored throughout the book. For now, however, let us return to our first example.

The conversation with the mother shifted back to the worker's agenda of agency business and never returned to this area. An important issue had been raised indirectly, however, and an unprepared worker had responded defensively. If we were to analyze the more subtle, indirect communications involved in this incident, we could interpret the client's question in the following manner:

**Client:** By the way, do you have any children? (The client is thinking, *I wonder if this one will be like the other worker. They have all kinds of ideas about how I should raise children and have never changed a dirty diaper themselves. How can they understand what it's like for me?*)

**Practice Points:** Other interpretations are possible; however, I believe that this question is significant for all clients in first sessions. The crucial part of the message—left unsaid—was the client's concern that she would not be understood. The worker's response, a product of her own concern about her capacity to help, only confirmed the client's apprehension. It is quite normal for clients to wonder if a new worker will be like other helping professionals whom they have met—in this case, the stereotypical cold, unfeeling "expert" who thinks she has all the answers. This thought was too dangerous to express openly, so it was only hinted at. The worker's reaction was also quite normal, especially for a new worker who did not anticipate the question.

If the worker had been tuned in to the client's potential concern, not intellectually but by actually trying to get in touch with the way this (or any) client might feel, she may have been able to hear the real question behind the question. If she had been helped to understand her own feelings, either by a supervisor or by colleagues, she might have been able to consider in advance how to respond directly to an indirect cue in this important area. Each worker develops his or her own unique responses, but one way to deal with this situation might be to say:

**Worker:** No, I don't have any children. Why do you ask? Are you wondering if I'm going to be able to understand what it's like for you having to raise so many? I'm concerned about that as well. If I'm to help you, I'm going to have to understand, and you are going to have to help me to understand.

Such a response might have opened up a discussion of the woman's past experiences with other workers, some helpful and some not. The response also allows the worker to share her own feelings of concern without overdoing them. She says, "I'm concerned about that as well." If the worker withholds his or her own affect, then the energy invested in suppressing the worker's feelings will not be available to invest in the affect of the client. Of course, integrating personal and professional selves requires some restraint on the worker's part.

It would not have been appropriate for the worker to have said, however truthfully, "You're absolutely right! What are they doing sending me out to work with you when I've never changed a diaper or heated a bottle?" The client does not want to hear that level of concern. These feelings need to be shared with supervisors and colleagues before the interview.

As the client begins the worker's education, the work gets under way. Instead of the working relationship being closed, the potential exists for this one to begin to grow. If nothing else, the client might end the interview thinking, as one client in an earlier study of mine said, "This worker is different. Perhaps I can train her."

**EP 2.1.10b**

***The Importance of Being Genuine*** Although the empathic skills will be discussed in more detail in Chapter 4, we should focus for a moment here on the issue of genuineness. One of the key reasons to tune in is to combat the ease with which helping professionals can learn to say the words related to affect without really experiencing the feelings. For example, a popular technique advocated in some texts on practice involves the use of reflection. That is, the worker reflects back to the client the affective words. If a client says, "I'm really angry at my kids," the worker might repeat, "You're really angry at your kids." If I were the client in that situation, I probably would feel like saying, "I just *told* you I was angry at my kids."

The problem with a reflective response is that it is often mechanical and artificial. The worker is not really feeling the client's anger. When I press practitioners on this question, they usually admit that they reflected because they did not know what else to say. Unfortunately, the client perceives the response as uncaring. The workers would have been better off being honest and admitting that they did not know what to say.

An even better response might be to remain silent for a few moments—this is the skill of containment—to try to feel how angry parents can get with their children, and then to respond with reactions that might deepen the conversation. For example, instead of being slightly behind the client, as illustrated in the reflective response, one approach might be to try to be one half-step ahead of the client by putting the client's unstated feelings into words: "That's the thing, isn't it—how can you be so angry at the kids but at the same time love them so much?"

The exact words one uses are not crucial, because each of us develops our own personal style and way of expressing our feelings and those of clients. What is crucial is that the worker should be feeling *something*. My students have pointed out that this is easy for me to say and hard for them to do. The fact is, most of us have not learned how to deal well with our feelings, let alone those of others, in most areas of our lives. As one mature student put it, "I have trouble dealing with my kids' feelings; how am I going to help this client deal with hers?"

Fortunately, helping professionals have their whole practice lives in which to develop their ability to be genuinely empathic. As they listen to clients and try to tune in, they will discover feelings within themselves that may have been earlier ignored. In the beginning, they will borrow the words of others. It is not uncommon for my students to bring to an early class the audiotape of an interview in which the students use my words as they try to empathize. In some of the tapes, you can even pick up traces of my New York City accent. When this was pointed out once by a fellow student, the presenting student replied, with some feeling: "I know, and I don't want to be a little Shulman." I try to reassure my students and suggest that they can borrow whatever words they need in the beginning. With continued work at developing their skills, they soon become more comfortable and find their own voice. This point is elaborated in Chapter 5.

***The Working Relationship or the Therapeutic Alliance*** In describing the situation with the young mother and the new worker, I mentioned the term *working relationship*. This is similar to the concept of *therapeutic alliance*. A generally accepted concept contained in most practice theories suggests that the activities of the helping person can help him or her develop a positive working relationship with the client. Something about the way the worker and client talk to and listen to each other—the flow of both positive and negative feelings between them—can affect the outcome. I believe that the development of a working relationship is a precondition for helping.

Note the use of the word *working* to differentiate this relationship from those that may be personal in nature, such as a parent–child relationship or a friendship. This is a simple yet crucial idea. The relationship is based on the work to be done together. The purpose of the encounter will affect the relationship directly, and the relationship will be the vehicle through which this purpose is achieved. A common misconception about practice is that the worker must establish a relationship first and then begin to work. This leads to a practice of "chatting" with a client during the first contact, discussing the weather or other superficial matters, supposedly to set the client at ease. Actually, the reverse is often true, with the worker feeling more at ease and the client more uncomfortable. I suggest in Chapter 4 that the relationship grows out of the work itself and that a worker needs to get down to business quickly. The relationship is not separate from the work; rather, it is part of the work. The very act of defining the nature of the work together (contracting) helps to develop the working relationship.

## The Impact of Diversity and Culturally Competent Practice

Of course, the worker must also be aware of cultural diversity issues that may moderate the just-stated rule of getting to work quickly. In some cultures, directness might be perceived as offensive; this is true, for example, in some Asian and Native American cultures. Cultural awareness can help a worker distinguish those situations in which small talk about families or appropriate discussions of life experiences might be exactly what is needed to set the stage for the development of a working relationship. While always recognizing the existence of diversity within diversity (e.g., generational differences and acculturation variables), workers need to attend to the client's view of what makes an effective counselor and what kind of help is needed.

In one study of client adherence to Asian cultural values, Kim, Ng, and Ahn (2009, p. 131) gathered data from 61 Asian American clients at a university counseling center building on earlier research that suggested "that Asian Americans favor a logical, rational, directive and culturally attentive counseling style over a reflective, affective, nondirective, and less culturally attentive one" (Atkinson, Maruyama, & Matsui, 1978; Gim, Atkinson, & Kim, 1991). The earlier research had mostly relied on Asian American participants, not counseling clients, rating transcripts, audio recordings, or audiovisual recordings of mock counseling sessions. The Kim et al. study used data from actual counseling clients and its purpose was described as to examine the following:

> (a) Asian American client's adherence to Asian cultural values, (b) expectation for counseling success, (c) perception of client-counselor match on belief about problem etiology, and (d) the relationship of these variables to client evaluation of the counselor and the counseling session (p. 133).

Dependent variables included counselor credibility, empathic understanding, cross-cultural counseling competence, client-counselor working alliance, session depth, the likelihood of recommending the counselor to another person in need of counseling, and the likelihood of returning for the next counseling session.

While recognizing the limitations of the study design, the authors suggested:

The results of the current study showing the pervasive and positive effects of client-counselor worldview match suggest that this is an important variable that needs to be focused on in the field. For instance, to enhance the session outcome, it would be beneficial for counselors to focus on establishing an agreement with clients on the belief about problem etiology, at least during the initial stage of counseling. One way to achieve this goal is for counselors to explore in great detail the ideas their clients have about the source of the problem before coming to their own conclusions about this cause. (p. 140)

The authors point out that etiology of the problem agreement is one form of worldview match and that others, such as the method of treatment, length of treatment and indicators of success, are others that can be explored to increase this match. Of course, one could argue that this would be important with any client of any culture. The issue may be the degree of importance for some clients as opposed to others.

***Intercultural Practice: A Native American Example*** Lum (1996) addresses the issue of intercultural practice directly. He identifies the many barriers that may exist during the beginning stage in cross-cultural, or what I term *intercultural,* practice. The author provides an example:

A common question asked by Native Americans in formal helping situations is: "How can I tell you about my personal life, which I share with my lifelong friends, when I have just met you only a half hour ago?" Mistrust and reservation are typical responses of ethnic clients until the social worker moves out of the category of stranger. Taking the first step of professional self-disclosure sets the stage for openness and relationship-building. (p. 145)

Lum (1999) also provides the following "practical suggestions for professional self-disclosure":

### Introduce Yourself

Share pertinent background about your work, family, and helping philosophy. Find a common point of interest with the client. (p. 145)

Lum (1999) has addressed the larger issue of developing a culturally competent practice. He sets forth a framework for describing and measuring culturally competent practice at both the generalist and the advanced levels. The framework includes the following elements:

- *Cultural Awareness:* "to develop an awareness of ethnicity and racism and its impact on professional attitude, perception and behavior" (p. 31).
- *Knowledge Acquisition:* "the acquisition of a body of information that organizes material about a topic into sets of facts that plausibly explain phenomenon" (p. 34).
- *Skill Development:* "when the worker applies what he or she knows to the helping situation, is based on cultural awareness and knowledge acquisition. Skills are developed in the course of working with a client from a set of practice principles" (p. 37).
- *Inductive Learning:* "is concerned with teaching social work students and social workers creative ways to continue developing new skills and insights relating to multicultural social work so that new contributions are made to this field" (p. 41).

***General Issues and Client Concerns*** Proctor and Davis (1994) identify three concerns that clients experience when working with practitioners of different races: (1) whether the practitioner is a person of goodwill, (2) whether she or he is trained and skilled, and (3) whether the help offered is valid and meaningful to the client. Although these questions are common for all helping relationships, they take on a special meaning when interethnic factors are involved. In this book, the term *intercultural* will be used broadly to include a range of differences not limited to ethnicity—for example, a male worker with a female client or straight worker with a gay client.

A study of the differences between the culturally sensitive practices of White and Latino clinicians with Latino immigrant clients found that Latinos responded with more culturally relevant interpretations, whereas non-Latinos were more directive and instrumental (Lu et al., 2001). Reinforcing the notion that there is diversity within diversity, Castex (1994) suggests that factors that need to be taken into account when working with the U.S. Hispanic/Latino population include national origin, language, names, religion, racial ascription, and immigration or citizenship issues. Mendez-Negrete (2000) suggests that practitioners need to begin with a broad understanding of what constitutes the idea of "family" and to recognize the "myriad" of forms that families can take. Congress (1994) proposes the use of culturegrams (charts drawn to illustrate the impact of various aspects of culture on the family) to assess and empower ethnic families. Chung and Bemak (2002) focus on the relationship between culture and empathy when working with diverse populations and suggest guidelines for establishing "cultural empathy."

The increased attention of the helping professions to diversity issues can be seen in the growth of publications that address specific populations and issues. For example, De Anda (2002) focused on issues related to practice with multicultural youth; chapters are devoted to populations including African American, Latino/a, and Asian American youth.

These findings reinforce the importance of cultural education. However, in a study of undergraduate social work students, researchers found that most students indicated only partial support for multicultural goals (Swank, Asada, & Lott, 2002). Although they agreed that multicultural information should be used and that more minority faculty and staff should be hired, their acceptance was conditional in that they were reluctant to make classes on this content conditional for graduation. In addition, only one-fourth of the respondents felt personally compelled to learn more about cultural diversity. The study also found that these attitudes changed as students initiated interracial exchanges and completed social diversity classes. Boyle and Springer (2001) point out that, although cultural competence is crucial to social work practice, there are gaps in the ability to measure the achievement of competency as well as the gap between social work education and implementation in practice.

Appleby et al. (2001) focus their attention on the impact of diversity and oppression on social functioning using a person-in-environment assessment and intervention model. They provide a comprehensive exploration of the many types of diversity we can find in our client populations. Building on an ecological and strengths perspective framework, they examine how culture, class, race, gender, physical disability, sexual orientation, and mental and emotional challenges interact with the dynamics of oppression and discrimination to affect social functioning.

***Intracultural Practice*** Sensitivity to issues of race, gender, ethnicity, sexual orientation, physical and mental ability, and so forth can be just as important in intracultural practice—that is, when you work with someone with whom you share an important characteristic. For instance, an African American male student presented an example during a videotaped discussion of diversity issues and practice (Shulman & Clay, 1994). He was working interculturally with an African American female client. The student recognized, however, that gender and class (he was from an upper-middle-class, suburban background, and she was poor and lived in the inner city) meant that he was also working interculturally and would have to deal with these potential barriers. Tuning in to his own feelings about working with people of color as a part of the "system" would also be essential to his development as a social worker and his ability to deal with the authority theme.

In another publication that addressed intracultural practice, Drescher et al. (2003) focuses on contemporary dynamic approaches to working with gay men and lesbians. In particular, they address issues that are raised when a gay therapist works with a gay patient, erotic transference and countertransference processes, gender identity issues, and the impact of AIDS.

In the chapters that follow, special attention will be paid to both intercultural and intracultural issues that affect our practice with individual clients, with couples and families, and in groups and communities. We will draw on the previously mentioned publications, as well as others, to deepen both our understanding of diversity and our understanding of appropriate interventions. Even as we consider these issues, we will have to remember that there is diversity within diversity (not all Native Americans, Latinos, etc. come from the same tribes or countries) as well as exceptions to all rules. Consideration of diversity issues should enhance our ability to tune in to and to understand our clients rather than provide us with restrictive perceptions and unhelpful stereotypes.

## Elements of the Working Relationship: The Therapeutic Alliance

Many elements make up the working relationship, also termed the *therapeutic alliance*. Three included in one of my studies (Shulman, 1991) are *rapport, trust,* and *caring*. *Rapport* refers to the client's general sense of getting along well with the worker; *trust* refers the client's willingness to risk sharing thoughts, feelings, mistakes, and failures with the worker; and *caring* means that clients sense that the worker is concerned about them as clients in their own right, and that the worker wishes to help them with concerns that they feel are important. For example, a middle-aged son of an aging parent would sense that an elder-care worker is concerned both about him, as a stressed caretaker, and about the well-being of his aged parent.

Using another example, a parent who has been reported as neglectful of her child would sense that the child welfare worker is simultaneously attempting to help her cope with stresses that may cause the neglect and attempting to investigate the child's situation for protective purposes. In later chapters, I show how these elements of rapport, trust, and caring are affected by issues of confidentiality, the fact that the worker may be a mandated reporter who is required by law to report certain abuses, and so on. For now, I simply wish to put into operation the construct of the working relationship.

I believe that many elements of a working relationship, such as trust and a sense of caring, also matter greatly in other areas of our lives. This is sometimes a source of confusion about the differences between relationships in general and the working relationship. As numerous examples in later chapters will show, these elements take on special meaning in the context of social work.

I have defined the working relationship at this point in the discussion because my research suggests that the ability of the worker to be tuned in to and articulating the client's unspoken feelings and concerns in the preliminary phase of work contributes to the establishment of a positive working relationship (Shulman, 1991, 1978). In fact, all of the skills for helping clients manage their feelings, when used in the beginning phase of practice, have been found to affect the working relationship (Shulman, 1991). This underscores the importance of preparatory empathy and the worker's ability to respond directly to indirect cues.

While the focus in my studies, and in this book, is on intervention strategies and behaviors such as the ability to respond to the client empathically, other studies have indicated that even seemingly small (micro) behaviors can have an important impact. In a recent study of client perception of counselor behaviors that predict the development of the therapeutic alliance with ($N = 79$) adult clients, Duff (2010) found that 11 of the 15 behaviors studied moderately to strongly correlated with the strength of the alliance, and

> hierarchical regression analyses found that three particular counselor behaviours (making encouraging statements, making positive comments about the client, and greeting the client with a smile) accounted for 62% of the variance in *alliance* scores. The findings suggest that seemingly small, strengths-fostering counselor micro-behaviours can play a key role in strengthening *therapeutic alliances*. Given the role that *alliance* plays in positive counseling outcomes, it is suggested that these behaviours be tactfully implemented early on in the counseling process. (p. 91)

Other behaviors that also positively correlated with the therapeutic alliance, more closely associated with those examined in my reported studies, included: asked me questions, identified and reflected back my feelings, was honest, told me about similar experiences that he/she had, and let me decide what to talk about.

In a study of the impact of the therapeutic alliance on client outcomes during routine outpatient treatment, the researchers found that the ($N = 76$) patients' reports on the alliance at the beginning of treatment did not impact on outcome measures (Håkan, 2010). However, the results on the same questionnaire at the end of treatment did significantly explain 15 percent of the variance in outcome and improvement in the alliance significantly correlated with most of the outcome measures. The author suggested that

> The results showed that the therapeutic alliance is an important variable for treatment outcome in routine psychiatric treatment, and improving the *therapeutic alliance* may be one of the most important factors for increasing the total effectiveness of a treatment unit. (p. 193)

When I present these ideas in classes or workshops, the eyes of the participants often indicate that they have begun to free-associate to their own caseloads. This may be happening right now to you as well. When I ask them what is happening, they share that they are feeling guilty for passing over the indirect cues of their clients, particularly in taboo and sensitive areas. I try to reassure them with the following advice.

If they still have a particular client active on their caseload, they can always go back and reopen what they may feel is unfinished business. For example, the worker in the earlier example who responded defensively could return and say, "I was thinking about your question last week about whether or not I had children. I think you were really wondering if I could understand what it is like for you." Three months later, it might sound like this: "I think I ducked your question when we first met, about whether or not I had children. It made me feel uncomfortable. I suspect you were really wondering whether or not I would understand what it is like for you raising seven children. I am wondering if, during our 3 months together, I have come across as not understanding." I believe that clients appreciate it when a worker shares a mistake and therefore can be perceived, as one client in my study reported, as "more like a real human being."

## Making and Catching Mistakes: First Session of a Parents' Group

At this point I believe it is worth repeating my earlier comments about making mistakes. Skillful practice involves learning how to shorten the distance between the point at which a worker makes a mistake and when he or she catches it. Very skillful workers catch their mistakes during the same session in which they make them. Furthermore, becoming an effective practitioner involves learning from active mistakes (as opposed to inactivity resulting from fear of making a mistake), developing better intervention skills, and then making more sophisticated mistakes.

For example, a second-year student was preparing to take over as a new group leader for an ongoing group of mothers with children who had a chronic disease. The group met in a hospital. This student had read my book and had done his tuning in. His field instructor had helped him explore his feelings about being a young, unmarried man working with a group of mothers. He had role-played how he would respond to the questions "Are you married?" and "Do you have any children?" He had prepared for everything except what actually happened.

Before he could make his prepared opening statement, one group member said, "Before you start, I want to let you know what we think of this damned hospital!" The force of the anger in her voice stunned him. She continued, "We have doctors who patronize us, nurses who push us around, and we keep getting young social workers like you who don't even have kids!" You can probably imagine what happened to all of his tuning in. As he put it later, "It went right out the window." When I asked him what he had felt like saying, he replied, "I may be in the wrong room!"

Fortunately, he was so thrown by the comment that he did not switch to what I call a "counseling voice"—that is, he did not suppress the feelings that were churning away inside of him and respond mechanically by saying, "I'm glad you could share that with me," or "Go with that feeling, Mrs. Smith." He was so thrown that he responded spontaneously, saying, "I may not have any children, but I have a mother just like you!"

**Practice Points:** He was surprised, and the group members were surprised. The angry Mrs. Smith looked again at this new worker and probably saw him for the first time. Up to that moment, she had seen him as a stereotype—he was most likely concerned about what he was going to put in his process recording for his field instructor. The group was an ongoing one, so other members moved in and shifted the conversation to a more general discussion. The remainder of the meeting could be characterized as an *illusion of work*, an idea to be more fully defined later in this text. In this case, it meant conversation without real focus, meaning, or feelings. He returned the following week, after further discussion and tuning in with his supervisor, and began as follows:

> Mrs. Smith, I would like to discuss last week for a moment. I was unready for so much anger from you, and, as a result, I think I missed the pain that must be under that anger for you and for all of the group members. You must have run into a lot of professionals who simply did not understand how much it hurts to have a child who is always ill and who never gets better. You saw me, a young worker, and thought "Here comes another one."

**Practice Points:**   His comment was greeted with silence. Silences will be discussed in detail later in the text; for now, I suggest that they are full of meaning, but they are sometimes hard to interpret. Most people guess that, inside the silence, some of the members are getting in touch with their pain or experiencing a positive response to the human quality of this young worker.

> Mrs. Smith, who had been so angry, started to cry and said to the other women in the group, "You are all married. You have someone to help you. I'm a single parent. Who helps me cope? I never have time for myself!" Another woman responded to her, "I'm married, but big deal!" She went on to describe her husband working 12 hours a day, 6 days a week, since the birth of the ill child (his form of flight from pain). The group opened up as the worker listened and began his education.

**Practice Summary.**   I do not believe that this worker was able to reach for the underlying pain the first week. I am not sure he could have done it the second week had he not risked his spontaneous response the first week. He would still have been struggling with the suppression of his own feelings. Some might argue that it is possible to get to empathy in the second week without having to risk the spontaneous expression of feelings in the first week. That has not been my experience—you will need to explore the question in your own practice. In any case, this young worker is probably better able to share some of his feelings when faced with anger in a first session and then more quickly move to reach for the client's underlying pain. He now makes more sophisticated mistakes.

A second line of reassurance I give to workers is that they are usually more effective than they think. More than two-thirds of the clients in one of my studies found their workers to be helpful (Shulman, 1991). This is similar to the findings in my earlier work (Shulman, 1979b). Workers tend to underestimate their positive impact on clients. They eventually communicate their caring and concern for the client. In some cases it just may take longer and include a period of testing that might not have been necessary had the worker tuned in and responded directly.

Finally, with regard to those clients they did not reach and who are no longer on their caseload, I suggest that they realize that they did the best they could, given the training and level of support they had at the time. Somewhat like an artist who must hang up an early painting that reflects limited skill and knowledge, learn from it, and begin a new painting, the worker must start anew with the next client. I suggest that a little guilt is helpful, because it keeps the worker in a self-discovery and learning mode of practice. A lot of guilt would be overwhelming and counterproductive. Workers who are overly judgmental of their own work will find it hard to help clients manage their feelings of guilt.

The practice described in the preceding examples raises the following three areas for further discussion: affective versus intellectual tuning in, tuning in to the worker's feelings, and the different levels of tuning in. Each of these is explored now in more detail.

## Affective Versus Intellectual Tuning In

**EP 2.1.10b**

To tune in effectively, a worker must try to experience the client's feelings. One way to do this is to recall personal experiences that are similar to the client's. For example, in coming to see you, the client is having his or her first contact with a person in authority. This is true even if the client is there voluntarily and the helping person has no specific control functions (e.g., protection of children or maintenance of parole). The first encounter is also a new situation, filled with unknown elements. What new experiences or first encounters with people in authority has the worker had in the past? Can the worker remember how it felt, and what his or her concerns were? A new school, a new teacher, or the first experience of hospitalization—any of these might serve to remind workers and put them in touch with feelings that relate to those of the client. The important point is that workers need to experience these feelings.

## Use of Supervision in Learning to Tune In

**EP 2.1.1f**

Supervision in practice, or field instruction in social work education, can provide important assistance to the worker or student in developing genuine empathy as part of the tuning-in process (Shulman, 1993a, 1993b, 2010). For instance, in a preparatory consultation session with a social worker who is working with AIDS patients, their family members, friends, and lovers, the supervisor attempts to help the worker get in touch with issues facing all of the parties concerned.

***Working with the Partner of a Gay Male Diagnosed with ARC*** In this excerpt, the tuning in is to a gay male client whose lover has recently been diagnosed with AIDS-related complex (ARC), which is a precursor to an AIDS diagnosis.

**Practice Points:** Note how the supervisor does not let the worker get away with an intellectual tuning in but instead asks the worker to remember some traumatic moment in his own life. The supervisor also makes clear the boundary in that he is not opening up a discussion of the worker's experiences, but just asking the worker to use the experience to actually try to feel, as closely as possible, what the client may be experiencing. The focus remains on the client. The supervisor also gives an example from his own life.

SUPERVISOR: What do you think John must be feeling right now?
WORKER: Devastated! It must be as if an earthquake has hit him and his lover.
SUPERVISOR: Are you really feeling devastated right now?
WORKER: Really feeling it? Well no, but I can imagine how it must feel.
SUPERVISOR: Try to take it further. Can you remember a time in your life when you
    felt devastated by a family earthquake? I'm not asking for the details of your
    personal life. I'm just trying to help you get in touch. For me, it was a breast
    cancer diagnosis for my sister. I can still remember the feelings well.
WORKER: The closest I can remember was when my grandfather had a heart attack.
    We were close to each other. He was old, but I still couldn't believe it, and it
    took a long time until I really faced it.
SUPERVISOR: Now you're closer. So tell me, what would you be feeling right now if
    you were John?
WORKER: Oh my God, this can't be happening. It must be a mistake. Maybe the
    diagnosis was wrong. I can't believe I'm going to lose him. What am I going to do?
SUPERVISOR: What do you mean—"going to do"?

**Practice Points:** The supervisor is trying to help the worker tune in to possible areas or themes of concern that may be important to this client. The emphasis should be on "possible" and "may" since this tuning in must be tentative. The worker has to be ready to hear what the client has to say. In a sense, the worker has to clear his tuning in from his mind at the actual session and listen to the productions of the client.

WORKER: We have been sleeping together for over a year. What if I have it? Am I going to stay with him? I must stay with him; he needs me now more than ever. What about my life? I've seen so many friends in these relationships. I want to help him—I must help him—but what about my own life?

SUPERVISOR: As John, how are you really feeling right now?

WORKER: I'm overwhelmed, depressed, and I think I'm even angry at him for having AIDS. But how can I be angry at him when I love him?

SUPERVISOR: I think you are getting closer to possible themes. We have to remember to be prepared for a totally different response from John. Each person may be quite different. What are your feelings right now about working with John and with his lover, Rod?

**Practice Points:** In the next excerpt we see what I have called the *parallel process* at work as the supervisor models the empathic skill by reaching for what the worker might be feeling. It is an example of how a good supervisor must be with the worker and the client at the same time. It would be ironic if the supervisor asked the worker to tune in to the client while at the same time not tuning in to the worker.

WORKER: I'm not sure how I feel about anything right now. I know I'm a little scared. A part of me is not sure I want to get close to this pain. I'm not sure what it will do to me. If I get close to Rod, I'm going to lose him as well.

SUPERVISOR: I'll try to help you through this. It is going to be tough, in part, because it's the first time around for you. My problem is that I have gone through it so often, with so many clients, that I sometimes forget what it was like the first time. (Silence.) No, to be honest, I don't forget—I just feel like closing it off myself. We should both monitor this process and help each other if our defenses get in the way. Also, raise this at the next staff meeting. I think others can offer some support.

**Practice Summary.** I believe workers watch their supervisors closely and that more is "caught" than "taught." The crucial skill modeled by the supervisor is his capacity to be tuned in to the worker and the client at precisely the same time. This theme is central to my supervision model and field instruction models (Shulman, 1984, 2011). In tuning in to the worker's feelings, the supervisor explores the worker's sense of failing with the client and how that affects his practice.

Perhaps the most important contribution made by the supervisor to the worker's growth was his willingness to admit that the struggle to deal with one's own feelings persists throughout one's professional life. The supervisor provided a model for the worker to emulate. The suggestion that the worker reach out for additional support from colleagues was also helpful. In one of my studies, workers who reported access to support from supervisors and colleagues were more effective at providing that same support to their clients than were those who did not have such support (Shulman, 1991, 1993a). The study also indicated that the supervisor needed access to support as well.

## Tuning In to One's Own Feelings

The AIDS example emphasizes how important it is for workers to get in touch with their own feelings. How we feel can have a great deal to do with how we think (cognition) and act. Because of their preoccupation with their own feelings of inadequacy, the young, unmarried workers in the earlier examples could not immediately respond to the clients' concerns. The worker in the AIDS example, as he explores his own reactions to working with the terminally ill, will discover many of the same feelings of helplessness and impotency often felt by friends, lovers, and family members of a person with AIDS. Health professionals often feel quite deeply their inability to save a dying patient.

Precisely because the helping person's feelings are similar to the client's, it may be difficult to listen and respond. In a recent experience coleading a group for people with AIDS in early substance abuse recovery, I commented to my coleader—a full-time, experienced staff person at the AIDS agency—that I would need his help in dealing with the serious decline in health of one of our clients. He responded, "And what makes you think it ever gets any easier for me?" By tuning in to one's own feelings and experiencing them before the engagement, their power to block the worker can be lessened. In many ways, the helping process is one in which workers learn a great deal about their own feelings as they relate to their professional function. One's capacity to understand others and oneself can grow while one engages in this continual process. In fact, I believe this is one of the reasons many workers have entered the social work profession.

This stress on the importance of the worker's own feelings runs counter to many conceptions of professionalism. As pointed out in Chapter 1, a central construct of the medical model stresses the hiding of real feelings, which are seen as interfering with one's professional role. In a study of the effects of family physicians' communications and relationship skills, the strongest predictor of positive outcomes—such as patient satisfaction and comprehension—was whether the doctor felt positively or negatively toward the patient (Shulman & Buchan, 1982). In addition, patients were very good perceivers of their doctors' attitudes toward them. The crucial point is that we need to learn to understand and use our feelings, instead of pretending to deny their existence. This core issue will be explored in many different ways throughout the rest of the book.

## Different Levels of Tuning In

Tuning in can be done at many different levels. Take, for example, the task of a social worker at a residential center for delinquent adolescent boys. A first level of tuning in would be to the general category of adolescents. The literature on stages of development and the worker's own recollections can help in this process. The adolescent is going through a time of normative crisis in which he must begin to define himself in a new role. Several central questions dominate his thinking. He is trying to sort out conflicting messages in our society about the qualities that make a "real man."

Sensitivity to underlying currents of feelings—to the ways in which clients struggle to deal with the normative crises of life—can also be enriched through reading works of fiction. The adolescent's efforts to develop his sense of differentiation from his family, to further his independence while at the same time trying to maintain some sort of relationship, has been explored with great perceptiveness by various authors.

Workers must tap into their own adolescent experiences in an effort to remember the feelings associated with this stage of life. Following are some examples from a training session in which workers, using the first-person voice, attempted to express some of the problems of adolescence.

### First Level of Tuning in

*There are so many things I need to know about sex and girls. When I talk to adults about these things, they make me feel dirty or try to scare me with AIDS. It's important to me that I get accepted by the guys—be one of the gang. It feels great when we hang out together, kid around, talk about girls, gripe about parents and other adults. I'd be willing to do almost anything, even things I don't feel comfortable about, to be in and not left out.*

*I'm feeling a bit trapped by the drugs at school. I'm under a lot of pressure to use—and I've tried to resist—but it's hard not to go along. I'm worried about my friend. He's gone over the edge and could get himself in trouble. Who can I talk to? I don't want to be a rat. If I talk to a teacher, all I will get is a lecture, and my friend could get thrown out of school. I can't talk to my parents. My mother would have a fit, and Dad is so drunk himself most evenings I can't talk to him.*

**Second Level of Tuning in**  The second level of tuning in is the specific client: in this case, youngsters who are in trouble with the law. Information on the background of the boys, the nature of the delinquent acts, their relationships with their families, and so forth can prove useful in attempting to orient oneself to the thoughts and feelings of a specific group of adolescents.

They probably feel that society is starting to define them as outcasts who can't fit in. Their feelings must be mixed. They must think:

*To hell with them! Who wants to be part of all of that crap anyway? Parents, teachers, and social workers—they are always pushing you around, telling you what to do. I don't give a damn. What the hell is happening to me? I'm getting deeper and deeper in trouble. People are taking control over my life. Maybe I am a loser—how the hell am I going to end up?*

**Third Level of Tuning in**  The third level of tuning in relates to the specific phase of work. For instance, consider an adolescent who has been judged delinquent and is about to enter a new residential setting. What are the feelings, questions, and concerns on his mind about this new experience, and what are some of the indirect ways they may be communicated?

*I'm scared stiff but I'm going to act cool—I won't show it. I wonder about the workers; what kind of people are they? How do they treat kids like me? And the other kids, what will they be like? Is it going to be hard to break in? I've got to watch my ass.*

Many of the general fears that people bring to new situations will be present. For example, the client may be apprehensive about the new demands placed on him and concerned about whether he will be able to meet them. At the same time, his feelings may include a sense of hope.

*Maybe this place will be OK. Maybe these workers and the kids will accept me, make me feel at home. Maybe I can get some help here. Anything is better than going back home.*

The key element to all tuning in is the recognition of ambivalence. Part of the client is moving toward the service, hopeful but guarded. Another part is using past experiences or hearsay about the service, workers, and so on, and is defensively holding back.

*Adding Race and Class to the Tuning in* Finally, what happens if we add race and class to the example? Consider an African American teenager from a poor, inner-city neighborhood who has been mandated by a judge to a residential program for delinquent boys in a rural, middle-class, White community. The core focus of the program is on anger management skills. Not only is he in a new and potentially frightening situation, but he is also entering a community in which he will be an outsider. For teens of color, finding themselves in a White neighborhood is threatening. If the staff of the center are also White, he will probably begin (and possibly end) the experience wondering what any of it has to do with what he faces when he returns to the city streets.

At another level, researchers in the counseling field area have explored the Black student's experience at predominantly White colleges. Guiffrida and Douthit (2010) surveyed the literature in this area and identified major themes as well as their implications for college counselors. They identified three major sources of potential stress and how they can be addressed. These included the following:

- *Experiences with Faculty.* "Research indicates that strong relationships with faculty are crucial to student success at college" (p. 312). The authors pointed out that Black students are often unable to form these relationships with White faculty with one reason being their perception of cultural insensitivity on the part of White faculty.

- *Family and Friends from Home.* The authors reported mixed views on the importance of "breaking away" from family and friends in order to more fully integrate into a college community. The argument that students should break away applies to all students with some studies suggesting this may be even more important for minority students from poor neighborhoods. Other researchers have challenged this argument with findings that high-achieving Black students reported financial, emotional, and academic support received from families as crucial to their success and low-achieving students cited lack of family support as contributing to their attrition (p. 313).

- *Black Student Organizations.* The authors summarized a number of studies that support the importance of involvement in formal Black organizations on campus as a source of support. They suggested that unlike White students at these institutions, "Black and other underrepresented racial/ethnic minority students at PWIs socially integrate mostly through more formal associations, such as those inherent among members of racial/ethnic minority student organizations" (p. 314). These organizations may provide Black students with opportunities to connect with Black professionals who can provide support and mentoring; to "give back" to other Blacks through community service projects; to advocate for changes on the campus; and finally, to find "respite" from the White world, "a place where they felt comfortable letting their guards down to dress, talk and socialize in ways that were comfortable and familiar without fear of perpetuating negative Black stereotypes" (p. 315).

Keeping the caveat in mind that tuning in to potential themes of concern does not assume that all clients have the same thoughts, feelings, experiences, and attitudes, and that there is significant diversity within diversity, the two examples above suggest some potential significant themes that may be present for these populations. With the often-taboo subject of race present in intercultural practice (e.g., White counselor with client of color), preparing for these potential concerns by tuning in can help to bridge the race and class gap. Consider this next example, in which a White, high school social worker talks to Dean, an African American teen, about Dean's expressed desire to return the following year to a public school in his inner-city community.

***White High School Worker with an African American Teenager*** Dean had been part of a special program that bused volunteer teens of color from the inner city to White, suburban private schools for enriched educational programs.

**Practice Points:** Because the worker had already acknowledged and explored their racial difference early in their work together, the stage was set for the worker to reach for the reasons behind the desire to change. After tuning in to the possible reasons, the worker reached for underlying issues, although he was still reluctant to name race as one of them.

WORKER: I remember, a couple of weeks ago, you mentioned you wanted to go to the public school next year. I'm curious why you would want to do that if you like getting away from the city to come to school.
DEAN: I do like it here, but my brother and cousin go to public schools in the city.
WORKER: Is that why you want to go to the public school?
DEAN: Sort of. I don't think they get as good of an education as I do, though.
WORKER: I see. I guess I'm still a little confused why you would want to go the public school. Maybe you're not sure yourself? I'm thinking that it may be difficult to come to school out here where you have a totally different atmosphere from what your brother and cousin experience in the public schools. Then you have to go back home and fit into the routine there, which is very different from what your friends at this school experience.
DEAN: It really is different.
WORKER: Tell me how it is different.
DEAN: Well, it's like I have to act different when I am at school than when I am home.
WORKER: Like you're struggling with two different identities? You are expected to act a certain way at this school, and that way doesn't fit in with how you are supposed to act at home?

**Practice Points:** After the worker opens the door to the subject of race the student accepts the invitation. It's important to remember that some prior work had been done on the intercultural issues of a White worker and a Black student.

DEAN: Right! Here, I'm supposed to act "White," and at home I have to act "Black" or people will accuse me of being too "White." I have to be mean at home, but I can be nice here.

**Practice Summary.** This conversation, aided by the worker's tuning in, created the opportunity for the young man to explore with the social worker his ambivalent feelings about making the change. Of course, because social workers have experienced the same set of taboos and have observed the same set of norms of behavior as their clients, it will take training and support from supervisors and/ or peers for the workers to feel comfortable enough to give clients permission to explore these areas of work.

I would argue that, for most clients, their difficulty in articulating their own feelings at the beginning of a new relationship—perhaps even being conscious of what they feel—requires workers to take the risks represented by tuning in and responding directly to indirect cues. I believe the client is often ready early in the contacts to discuss tough issues, explore taboo subjects, and even deal with the worker–client relationship, if only the worker will extend the invitation.

Workers have said, in consultation sessions, that they often hesitate because they are not sure whether the clients are ready. After some reflection, they usually acknowledge that they are not sure they are ready. Thus, the worker's own ambivalence about exploring an area of work can produce the block. In the guise of protecting the client, workers are actually protecting themselves. As one worker put it, "I don't reach directly for those cues early in the work, because I'm afraid the client may take up my invitation. What will I do with all that feeling if I get it?" This excellent question is explored in more detail in later chapters.

***Tuning in to Ambivalence*** With regard to the tuning-in exercises of workers who are preparing to meet new clients, I have observed that the first efforts usually pick up the client's resistance—the defensive side of the ambivalence. This often reflects the worker's frustrating past experiences. It also embodies the worker's concerns that the client will not want help. This can be a self-fulfilling prophecy unless the worker has a sense of the client's potential for resilience and change, as well as a belief that part of the client is reaching out to the worker. Otherwise, the worker's pessimistic stereotype of the client will meet head-on with the client's pessimistic stereotype of the worker. The tuning-in process is a first step in trying to break this self-defeating cycle.

An important objection often raised to the tuning-in skill is that the worker may develop a view of the client that is far removed from what the client actually feels and thinks. The worker may then make sure the client fits the preconceived picture. This is a real danger if the tuning in is not tentative. In a sense, the key to the successful use of tuning in rests in the worker putting all hunches aside when he or she begins the engagement. What the worker responds to in the first contacts are the actual "productions" of the client—that is, the direct and indirect cues that emerge in conversation.

For example, if the worker in the residential setting has tuned in to the front a tough kid might put up on the first day as well as the concerns that could underlie the client's attitude, the worker will have to see evidence of this behavior before acting. The worker reaches only tentatively for indirect messages and remains prepared to have the client share totally unexpected responses. Each client is different. Tuning in is an exercise designed to sensitize the worker to potential concerns and feelings. It does not dictate what the client's feelings must be. The assumption is that, after tuning in to both the client's and the worker's feelings, there is a better chance that the worker's spontaneous reactions to the client's productions will be more helpful.

If, however, the tuning in simply produces a new stereotype of the client, it is self-defeating. I remember one example in which a worker tuned in to what he believed would be the client's anger at having to come to counseling. Appropriately, the worker reached for these feelings. The client indicated that he was not angry, and the worker provided a second chance by suggesting that other clients had felt angry under the same circumstances. The client, with some exasperation in his voice, answered a second time, indicating that he was not angry. When the worker, on automatic pilot, then said: "Well, I can't understand why you are not angry!" the red-faced client responded, "Well, damn it, now I am angry!" The lack of tentativeness on the part of the worker led to a self-fulfilling prophecy.

This section of the chapter has highlighted the importance of preparatory empathy in the beginning phase of practice. In later chapters, we shall return to tuning in as we explore different phases of work, different modalities of practice (e.g., family and group), and even the importance of tuning in when working with other professionals.

# Responding Directly to Indirect Cues

The importance of tuning in during the preliminary phase lies in preparing the worker to hear indirect cues in the first contacts and to respond directly to these cues. In the first example given in this chapter, the new worker would have demonstrated this skill if, in response to the client's question "Do you have any children?" she had said something like, "No. Why do you ask? Are you wondering if I'm going to be able to understand what it is like to raise kids?"

A direct response to the indirect cue would have been just as important if the worker did have children. In one example, a worker in an agency dealing with physically challenged children was asked by a new client if she had children. When the worker responded positively, the client asked, "Teenage children?" The worker shared that her children were teenagers. After a brief silence, the mother inquired, "A handicapped teenaged child?" The worker in this case was able to respond, "As a matter of fact, the reason I was attracted to work in this agency was that my own teenager does have a physical handicap." After a long pause, the client responded, "But not like mine!"

The client was not satisfied with the responses, because the real question was not related to the worker's family situation. I believe this worker would have been better off answering, "I do have a handicapped teenaged child; however, the experience is different for each of us. You'll have to let me know what it has been like for you." The advantage of a direct response in this example is that it opens up an important area of conversation that can then deepen the working relationship. A common objection is that the worker may lead the client by putting words into his or her mouth that are not really there. In addition, the argument goes, even if the worker guesses correctly, the client may not be ready to deal with that particular feeling or concern and may react defensively, become overwhelmed, and not come back. Because of this fear, the worker may be cautioned to withhold hunches and to wait for clients to raise a concern or feeling when they are ready to do so.

Nonetheless, I argue in favor of risking direct responses early in the first contacts. As the working relationship develops, the client is watching the worker and trying to sense what kind of a helping person she or he is. If the relationship includes diversity (e.g., a Latino family and a non-Latino worker), the question carries even more potency. Indirect communications are employed because the client is reluctant to risk communicating directly some of the more difficult and taboo feelings. Let us consider what happens when the worker responds directly to the indirect cues by articulating the client's feelings. If the worker's guess misses the mark, the client will usually let it be known. Even if the client goes along reluctantly, hesitation in the voice and lack of affective response will tip the worker off to the artificial agreement. The worker can then respond directly to that cue. This is one example of how the worker can learn and grow from an active mistake.

***A New Client's Complaints or Praises for the Former Worker*** In a common example of indirect communication, the client—early in the interview with a new worker—says,

"I'm glad to see you. My last worker was really terrible!" Few comments strike more fear into the heart of a new worker; the usual response is to change the subject immediately. Workers claim to be uncomfortable discussing another professional. In my experience, they are particularly quick to change the subject if they secretly agree that the other worker is terrible.

The mistake these workers make is to think the client is really talking about the previous worker. During early contacts, if clients refer to other people (e.g., social workers and doctors who have not helped), it is usually the new worker they are talking about, albeit indirectly. A direct response to this indirect cue might be: "It sounds like you experienced a hard time with John. Can you tell me what went wrong so that I can understand what you are expecting from me? I'd like to try to make our relationship a positive one." The discussion of the past relationship is cast in the context of the beginning of the new relationship. The worker is not making a judgment about the previous worker—rather, the intent is simply to acknowledge what the client has experienced.

Another early client statement, which is even harder for the new worker to hear, often sounds like this: "My last worker was really terrific! My kids used to look forward to his visits." Once again, if the new worker can handle his or her own feelings, a direct response to the indirect cue might be the following: "It sounds like you and your children really got close to John. You must really miss him. Can you tell me why you felt he was terrific? I may not be able to be just like him, because I'm a different person, but it would help to know what you are looking for in a worker." Once again, the ensuing discussion moves the worker and the client quickly into the authority theme—the relationship between the giver and taker of help. The worker both acknowledges the feelings of loss and reaches for the client's concern about how well the new worker will replace the previous worker. In effect, the new worker starts to answer the client's implied question.

Students and workers have said to me, "That sounds great, but how do you say that when you are scared spitless?" I point out that workers usually do not say it the first time, but with practice they catch themselves before the end of the interview or during the next contact. For example, one might say, "I was thinking about our last conversation, and I wondered if, when you were talking about your problems with John, you might also have been thinking about what kind of a worker I'm going to be?"

A second objection raised by workers, particularly those with elements of mandated authority (e.g., financial aid workers or probation officers), is that they fear the client who is positive about the last worker might say something like "Well, John, he didn't hassle me. When I needed something extra, he came up with the money." Or they might say, "John wasn't all uptight about every beer I had."

If the comment about the last worker is an indirect communication that relates to how the new worker is going to enforce his or her authority, a direct response opens up the discussion for the worker to be clear about how he or she will operate—what the client can expect from the worker, and what the worker will expect from the client.

If a child welfare client is angry at the last worker for "always trying to prove I was a bad mother and trying to take away my kids," a direct response about this worker's perspective on the use of authority would be helpful. For example, the worker might say, "Mrs. Smith, my agency is not trying to take away children. There are too many in care already. I would like to try to help you keep your family together. I would only recommend removing your children if I felt they were in danger through abuse or neglect. And even if that ever happened, I would still want to try to help you get them back. I hope I can convince you that I really mean this."

This is an important part of the contracting process, and getting the issue on the table early can speed up the work. The issue of authority and contracting is discussed in more detail in Chapter 4. In early sessions, clients not only respond to workers as symbols of authority and stereotypes based on prior experiences, but they sometimes operate on the basis of specific information about the particular worker (or agency) that has been provided through the grapevine. For example, one parole officer reported a first session with a recently released ex-convict in which they got into a battle of wills over whether or not the client's last parole officer had been too tough.

The new parole officer tuned in, between sessions, and inquired during the next session, "Were you really asking what kind of a parole officer I'm going to be?" After a long pause, the ex-con said, "The word back at the pen is that you're a real dink." The parole officer asked what that meant, and the ex-con revealed that he had left the penitentiary with a dossier on the parole officer at least as long as the one the officer had on him. The parolee came in with a stereotype of the worker that needed to be dealt with early in the work. Even if the parolee had not possessed any information on this particular parole officer, there would have been a general stereotype of parole officers to contend with. In reverse, the parole officer has to be careful not to worry so much about being "conned" that he or she relates to the client as a stereotype rather than a person.

If the client is not ready to pick up on the worker's direct response to an indirect cue because of lack of trust or lack of readiness to share the concern or feelings, particularly in taboo areas, the client can choose not to respond. The worker must give the client that room. The most important outcome of the worker's direct responses is not that the client will always immediately deal with the concern. The crucial message to the client is that the worker is prepared to discuss taboo, tough issues (e.g., authority), or painful concerns when the client is ready. In effect, these interventions give the client permission to deal with these issues while simultaneously showing the worker to be a feeling, caring, direct person who can see the world through the client's eyes and not judge harshly.

## My Research Findings

**EP 2.1.6b**

My research findings have repeatedly supported the importance of using the tuning-in and direct-response skills. Specifically, my study in a Canadian provincial child welfare program (Shulman, 1991) replicated earlier findings (Shulman, 1978) that supported this view. Although findings in any study are always tentative, even when replicated, these shed some interesting light on this issue. I was able to examine whether a specific skill, or group of skills, contributed to strengthening the worker–client relationship. The working relationship construct consisted of the two elements described earlier as trust and caring. This working relationship, in turn, provided the medium for effective helping and positive outcomes.

Clients in the study were asked to rate their workers' use of eight specific skills. The scores for the four skills that relate most to this discussion were averaged to create a scale called "Skills for Helping Clients to Manage Their Feelings." These skills were:

- *Reaching Inside of Silences:* Exploring the meaning of a silence by putting the client's possible feelings into words (e.g., "Are you angry right now?").

- *Putting the Client's Feelings into Words:* Articulating the client's feelings, in response to tuning in or perceiving the client's indirect communications, prior to the client's direct expression of affect.

- *Displaying Understanding of the Client's Feelings:* Acknowledging to the client, through words or nonverbal means, that the worker has understood how the client feels after the affect has been expressed by the client (e.g., a response to crying).
- *Sharing the Worker's Feelings:* Appropriately sharing with the client the worker's own affect. These feelings should be shared in pursuit of professional purposes as the worker implements the professional function.

In one explanation, in which a technique called *causal path analysis* was employed, I determined the path and strength of influence of these skills on the development of the working relationship and a number of outcome measures.[1] Findings indicated that the use of this group of skills positively affected the client's perception of the worker's caring; in turn, the caring dimension of the working relationship had a moderately positive impact on the client's perception that the worker was helpful. In addition, caring had a small but statistically significant impact on two other outcome measures: the final court status of the child (e.g., permanent custody) and the number of days the children spent in care. These findings provide further support for the central construct of this practice model—that worker skills affect outcomes through their influence on the working relationship.

The average scores achieved for each skill by workers also revealed an interesting pattern. Although clients reported that their workers acknowledged their feelings "fairly often," their rating of the workers' articulating their feelings for them was between "seldom" and "fairly often." Exploring silences was rated closer to "seldom," and sharing of the worker's feelings was rated "seldom" by study clients. This pattern, repeated in several of my studies, provides some sense of the degree of difficulty in developing these skills as well as support for my argument of the dominance of the medical paradigm in the social work profession (see Chapters 1 and 2).

Because 81 families out of the 305 in the study provided us with ratings of their workers' use of skills at the time my team and I interviewed them, as well as a retrospective rating of skill use when they first met their workers, I was able to do some tentative analysis of the impact of time on the model. Employing a statistical method called *regression analysis*, I found that the use of these skills to help clients manage their feelings in the beginning phase of practice had a moderately strong predictive ability for both the caring and trust elements of the working relationship. When the use of these skills in the middle phase of practice was examined, they still had a moderate impact on the relationship, although less than in the beginning phase. Both of these findings are consistent with the constructs of the practice theory.

Finally, I examined each specific skill in the study, when used in both the beginning and middle phases, and analyzed their simple correlations with the elements of trust and caring as well as the client's perception of the worker's helpfulness. All four skills for helping clients manage their feelings were found to have moderate positive correlations with relationship and outcome measures, which increased to moderately strong correlations in the middle phase of practice. In general, the positive impact of the use of these skills appears to be supported by research findings.

---

1. Essentially, the statistical technique allows a researcher to construct a model of the process under examination and to estimate the influence of variables along a defined causal path. For example, the model of worker skill (the independent or predictor variable) that influences the development of a working relationship (an intervening or mediating variable), which in turn influences the outcome of the client's perception of the worker's helpfulness (the outcome or dependent variable), was examined in the cited study.

# The Impact of Agency Culture: The "Agency Client"

One worker reported a first session with a client who had a long history of contact with the agency. Before the worker could begin, the client, in a good-humored manner, said, "I bet you've read all about me." Many helping contacts involve clients who have had prior contact with the particular setting or with other professionals. The agency file system may contain detailed records on past experiences or a report from an intake worker, whose job is to make the first contact with a client and conduct some form of assessment of suitability for services. Referrals from other professionals often include descriptions of the client, family, problems, and past history. Depending on how it is used, this prior information can be helpful or it can become an obstacle to the work.

On the positive side, information about the client may help the worker develop the preliminary empathy needed to prepare for the first session. A review of past experiences with workers or a report of the intake conversation may reveal potential themes of concern to which the worker can be alerted. Understanding the recent strains that have brought the client to the attention of the worker may help the worker develop a feel for the emotional state to be expected in early sessions. A summary of past experiences may also yield insight into the client's attitude toward helping professionals. If the records reveal that the going has been rough in the past, the worker may want to plan how to change the client's stereotype of workers.

On the other hand, if the worker uses the information to develop a stereotype of the client, the preparatory work can block the development of a working relationship. For example, say a worker begins a contact with a parent in a child welfare setting. If the worker believes that the client is defensive, resistant, hostile, and not open to help, this mind-set may be the start of a self-fulfilling prophecy. Furthermore, when one stereotype (e.g., the worker's) tries to deal with another stereotype (e.g., the client's), no real communication takes place. As one of my clients once described this problem, "It's like two ships passing in the night." In particular, the worker will miss seeing the potential resilience already demonstrated by the client's ability to survive in the face of adversity.

## Avoiding Stereotyping: The "Agency Client"

The agency culture often sets the stage for the new worker or student to develop a stereotypical view of a particular client or clients. A common example is what I call "the agency client." This is a family or client who has been with the agency for a long time, sometimes two or three generations, and who has developed a reputation for being "unworkable." These are the cases that staff may assign to students or new workers. A common experience is for the new worker or student to mention this client to a colleague, who exclaims, in amazement, "Oh no! They gave you the Smith family?" Even before the first contact, the worker has been set up for a negative experience.

## Stereotyping a Group of Clients

**EP 2.1.4a**
**EP 2.1.4b**

Sadly, agency cultures can foster stereotypes of a whole class of clients—a process that at its worst can be racist, sexist, ageist, homophobic, and so forth. In one of my studies, negative outcomes were associated with a worker's perception that Native families were more difficult to help than non-Native families. For example, there was a negative association with the Native family's perceptions of their workers' availability, their trust in their workers, and outcomes such as workers' helpfulness and Native children going into care (Shulman, 1991). These workers' perceptions may have been rooted in the oppressive attitudes toward others that we all must acknowledge within ourselves. When we experience difficulty working with others who are different, our inherent racism, sexism, or homophobia may emerge as part of our efforts to explain our feelings of being ineffective.

Study findings also revealed positive practice outcomes related to workers' sensitivity to the impact of differences between the workers and their clients. A worker's cultural awareness and sensitivity was associated with positive outcomes, as was the general attitude of the office involved. For example, the existence of cooperative rather than conflicted relationships between an office or region and the minority group's formal support system (e.g., Native court workers or homemakers, Native social workers, Native friendship centers) was associated with positive outcomes (e.g., fewer Native children going into care). This finding was significant in the context at that time when approximately 40 percent of the children in care in the Province were Canadian Native even though they made up less than 10 percent of the child population.

If most or all of the staff are members of the majority group (e.g., White), the chance of negative attitudes and stereotypes being maintained or heightened in an office increases. Agencies have begun to understand the importance of diversity in the management and frontline staff. Increasingly, affirmative action programs have been developed to address this issue.

In general, to avoid responding to clients as if they were stereotypes, workers need to remember that a client described in a report is constantly acting and reacting to systems, including the worker who wrote the report. One simply cannot know clients without understanding them in terms of this process. Their actions need to be viewed in relation to the actions of others.

I have found it interesting to sit in on case conferences in which a client is being discussed. The helping professional will report on a home visit or a contact, describe the client in some detail, review the client's history, and then offer a diagnosis of the problem, a prognosis, and a proposal for treatment. If the worker reports that the client was defensive or hostile, this is discussed. This type of conference follows the medical paradigm described in Chapter 1; the discussion centers on assessing the client.

If I suggest that we shift from talking about the client as an entity to discussing the details of the interview between the worker and the client, the conversation changes dramatically. This represents a shift to what I described in Chapter 1 as the interactional model. I ask the worker to describe how the interview began, what was said to the client, and how the client responded. As the detailed description continues, the staff members begin to get a feeling for the reciprocal interaction between client and worker. The worker's and client's feelings are explored in the process; not surprisingly, the actions of the client often become quite explainable in relation to the worker's efforts. For example, the worker sensed the underlying resistance but did not respond by directly exploring it. Perhaps the worker read a previous report on the client and began the interview expecting trouble, thereby bringing it about. The worker's own feelings may have made empathy with the client's struggle difficult, thus closing off openings for work.

The result of such discussion, even when the worker was skillful in the first interview, is the emergence of a client who is more multidimensional than he or she at first seemed. Workers can see ambivalence rather than just defensiveness. In addition to the anger, they can sense the client's underlying hurt, distrust, and bitterness that may have resulted from poor past experiences with professionals. What might have seemed like a hopeless case changes through this discussion to a difficult case with some important openings for work.

If workers using prior record material or referral material can keep in mind not only the tentativeness of the information but also the need to see the client in interaction rather than as a static entity, this material can help them prepare for the first interview. As this interview begins, workers need to clear their minds of all of these facts, opinions, and even the workers' own tentative tuning-in guesses. The preparatory work has helped pave the way; now the workers will demonstrate skill in responding not to what was expected but to the actual productions of the client.

## Chapter Summary

The complexity of human communications often makes it difficult, particularly in relation to taboo subjects (e.g., authority and dependency), for the worker to hear and understand what a client is thinking and feeling. A worker can increase his or her sensitivity to indirect communications by employing a skill called *tuning in*, or putting oneself in the emotional shoes of the client, prior to the first contact. The worker must also tune in to his or her own feelings first, particularly those related to anxiety about the first meetings. A set of four skills can particularly assist workers to help their clients manage their feelings: (1) reaching inside of silences, (2) putting the client's feelings into words, (3) displaying understanding of the client's feelings, and (4) sharing worker's feelings. Many research results suggest the importance of using these skills in the beginning phase of practice to develop a positive working relationship and to be helpful to the client.

## *Related Online Content and Activities*

Visit *The Skills of Helping Individuals, Families, Groups, and Communities*, Seventh Edition, CourseMate website at **www.cengagebrain.com** for learning tools such as glossary terms, links to related websites, and chapter practice quizzes. The website for this chapter also features additional notes from the author.

## *Competency Notes*

The following is a list of Council on Social Work Education (CSWE) recommended competencies and practice behaviors for social work students defined in Educational Policy and Accreditation Standard (EPAS).

**EP 2.1.1f** Use supervision and consultation (p. 82)

**EP 2.1.3b** Analyze models of assessment, prevention, intervention, and evaluation (p. 69)

**EP 2.1.3c** Demonstrate effective oral and written communication in working with individuals, families, groups, organizations, communities, and colleagues (p. 69)

**EP 2.1.4a** Recognize the extent to which a culture's structures and values may oppress, marginalize, alienate, or create or enhance privilege and power (p. 93)

**EP 2.1.4b** Gain sufficient self-awareness to eliminate the influence of personal biases and values in working with diverse groups (p. 93)

**EP 2.1.6b** Use research evidence to inform practice (p. 91)

**EP 2.1.7a** Utilize conceptual frameworks to guide the process of assessment, intervention, and evaluation (p. 69)

**EP 2.1.7b** Critique and apply knowledge to understand person and environment (p. 69)

**EP 2.1.10a** Substantively and affectively prepare for action with individuals, families, groups, organizations and communities (p. 69)

**EP 2.1.10b** Use empathy and other interpersonal skills (pp. 69, 72, 74, 82)

**EP 2.1.10d** Collect, organize, and interpret client data (p. 70)

**EP 2.1.10e** Assess client strengths and limitations (p. 70)

**EP 2.1.10g** Select appropriate intervention strategies (p. 70)

**EP 2.1.10i** Implement prevention interventions that enhance client capacities (p. 70)

# Beginnings and the Contracting Skills

In this chapter, we explore the dynamics of new relationships in general and new helping relationships in particular. A model for contracting with the client in the first sessions is presented and illustrated. I will be using the term *contracting* to describe the way in which the social worker makes clear the service to be offered, identifies the client's felt needs, identifies the potential common ground between service and needs, describes the worker's role, and addresses issues related to the worker's formal or informal authority.

I then describe specific skills to help clients manage their problems, including clarifying the worker's purpose and role, reaching for client feedback, and dealing with issues of authority. The contracting process is presented as flexible, and the agreed-upon areas of work may change over time. We also discuss the special concerns involved in contracting with resistant clients.

Next, we explore several models for assessment that can be useful in helping the social worker obtain a clearer picture of the client in relation to the environment. Issues of diversity and culturally competent assessment and practice are addressed, and research on the intervention process is shared.

Finally, I will provide a general introduction to the concept of ethics and how they affect our practice with a focus on those ethical or legal issues that present themselves in the first session or sessions. I will do the same, where appropriate in each of the chapters that follow. For example, unique ethical issues in first group sessions will be discussed in that chapter.

## "The First Meeting Is Really Important, You Know!"

**EP 2.1.7a**
**EP 2.1.10a**
**EP 2.1.10b**
**EP 2.1.10c**
**EP 2.1.10d**

During a first interview, a 25-year-old client put his social worker through an indirect test to see if she would be honest with him. The worker, responding directly to the indirect cues, asked, "Did I pass?" After acknowledging that the worker had passed, the client said, "I had to see where we stand. The first meeting is really important, you know."

First meetings in all helping relationships are important. If handled well, they can lay a foundation for productive work and begin the process of strengthening the working relationship between client and worker. If handled badly, they can turn the client away from the service offered. In this chapter, we explore the special dynamics associated with new relationships.

In Chapter 2, we focused on skills designed to help clients manage their feelings. This chapter explores an associated set of skills—called *worker's skills*—that can help *clients* manage their problems. These skills are described in detail later in this chapter. They include:

- *Clarifying the worker's purpose and role:* A simple, "nonjargonized" statement made by the social worker (usually incorporated into the opening statement to a client) that describes the general purpose of the encounter (and/or services of the agency) and provides some idea of how the social worker can help.

- *Reaching for the client's feedback:* An effort made by the worker to determine the client's perception of his or her needs. The working contract includes the common ground between the services of the setting and the felt needs of the client.

- *Partializing the client's concerns:* Helping a client break large and often overwhelming problems into manageable parts.

- *Supporting clients in taboo areas:* Helping clients talk about issues and concerns that are normally treated as taboo (e.g., sex, death, authority, dependency).

- *Dealing with issues of authority:* The worker's efforts to clarify mutual expectations, confidentiality issues, and the authority theme.

The following sections discuss each of these skills and others. Because not all clients are pleased to have the social worker and the agency involved in their lives, this chapter also explores the special dynamics of working with involuntary (mandated) or semi-voluntary clients. Although I cautioned in Chapter 1 against using the study process in a manner that interferes with the engagement process, social workers nonetheless need to obtain an accurate picture of the relationship between the client and his or her environment. We shall look at several models for developing this framework.

Issues in the beginning phase that relate to culturally sensitive practice and assessment will also be explored. In this book, *culturally sensitive practice* refers to the ways we shape our assessment and interventions in order to be respectful of the particular culture of the population with which we work. For example, the importance of respect for elders may shape our intervention with a Native American family, determining in part who needs to be present in family counseling and even to whom we address our interventions.

Now let us begin our exploration of the beginning phase of work by examining what we know about the dynamics of new relationships.

## The Dynamics of New Relationships

All new relationships, particularly those with people in authority, begin tentatively. Clients perceive workers as symbols of authority with power to influence their lives. Clients often bring with them a fund of past experiences with professionals or stereotypes of them passed on by friends or family. As a result, the first sessions are partly an effort to explore the realities of the situation. Encounters with people in authority usually involve risks, and clients will be careful to test the new situation before they expose themselves.

Ambivalent feelings will occur in any new situation. The client's doubts about adequacy and competency increase, as do fears concerning the worker's expectations. The other side of ambivalence is hope of receiving help. Depending on the individual and the helping context, one side of the ambivalence may be stronger than the other.

The two main questions on the client's mind in individual work, though they are rarely spoken, are *What is this going to be all about?* and *What kind of worker is this going to be?* The urgency of these questions stems from the client's fear of the demands to be made. People in authority often have hidden agendas, and the client may fear that the worker will try to change him or her. This suspicion will affect the client's actions until the two questions are answered. Fear of feelings of dependency will be present until the client can see the helping person not in the imagined role as the all-powerful authority doing things *to* the client, but as someone with skills who will do things *with* the client. Even when social workers deal with mandated clients, acknowledging that the client will be the one who is really in control is crucial. The worker must be viewed, in the final analysis, as helping the client to work on the client's own concerns.

Another way to consider this early process is to realize that the client is making what I call the *first decision*. The first decision is essentially whether or not the client will engage with the worker in a meaningful way and begin to develop what has been called the *therapeutic alliance*. Without a client's real commitment to the work and the worker, the relationship is doomed to failure. Clients can drop out by not returning, or they can continue to come and engage in the "illusion of work," in which they go through the motions but no real work or change is occurring. With regard to a mandated client, this illusion can be a form of conning the worker, whereby the client says what she or he thinks the worker wants to hear and not what the client really feels.

The *second decision* is made as the worker and the client make the transition to the middle, or work, phase. In the beginning phase, clients may not be aware of the hard work they face, the painful issues they must confront, and their own responsibilities to address their problems. As they become more aware of these things, they have to decide, once again, whether to continue the engagement.

The *third decision* comes as the client approaches the ending and transition phase and realizes there is little time left in the working relationship. At this point—in a process that has been termed *doorknob therapy*—the client must decide whether or not to face the most difficult (and important) issues in the work.

### Hospital Social Worker: Poor First Interview with a Patient

**Practice Points.**   In the illustrative interview that follows, some of the concerns of the beginning phase arise in the client's indirect communication. The worker heightens the client's feeling of concern by not addressing her questions about the purpose of the session and the role of the worker. The setting is a hospital, and the patient a 43-year-old woman with three young children. Although laboratory tests have been negative, persistent symptoms have necessitated exploratory surgery and raised the specter of cervical disk disease. Referral to the social worker was made because a long convalescence would be required, during which household duties and child care would be impossible. In his written introduction to the recording of the interview, the worker describes his purpose as exploring aftercare possibilities and determining whether homemaker or alternative services might be necessary.

WORKER: Good day, Mrs. Tunney. I'm Mr. Franks from the social service department. Your doctor asked me to visit you and to see in what way we could be of help.

PATIENT: Is this a habit? Do you visit all the patients or only me? (She was smiling but seemed anxious.)

WORKER: We interview patients whenever it seems to be indicated, when there is such a medical request.

**Practice Points:**   The patient is asking "What's this all about?" and expressing a natural anxiety. She might be wondering but not saying, "Oh my God! It must be more serious than they told me." The worker's response does not answer this question and does little to address the patient's concern. Instead of clarifying the reasons for the referral, such as concern over a possible need for homemaking services, the patient is left in the dark. She responds with an unusually direct demand.

PATIENT: All right, in what way do you think you can help me? I am in the hospital for the second day. My children are being looked after by their father. Most probably I will be operated on in the near future. You know this started because I felt I had arthritis. I had difficulty in moving my hands and fingers, so I decided to come here and see what I really have. (Occasionally she works on her crocheting while she speaks.)

WORKER: I would like to ask a few questions, Mrs. Tunney. But first, tell me, do you feel more comfortable talking while you are working?

PATIENT: Perhaps. I always do something with my hands. I have to.

**Practice Points:**   Once again, the worker has not responded to a direct question. The worker is proceeding according to his agenda, conducting a fact-gathering interview. The client is left out of the process. As long as the patient is unclear why this worker is talking to her and what his purpose and role as a social worker are, she will be unable to use him effectively. The client will experience the interview as being "acted on" by the worker. Her sense of dependency and her fears of intrusion into her personal life will increase. She will remain uncertain of what to say because she has no framework within which to weigh her responses. The interview continues:

WORKER: You said, Mrs. Tunney, that your husband is taking care of the children. If I am correct, you have three children. Is that right?

PATIENT: Yes, but the 8-year-old is a very hard one. He cannot be left alone. Fortunately, my husband's superiors are understanding people, and he can take off time whenever he needs to, and now he needs it. Usually, he is away on trips, and sometimes he is gone for weeks.

WORKER: I understand your husband is in the army. In what capacity does he serve?

**Practice Points:**  The client might understandably be thinking at this point, "Why do you want to know about my husband?" The worker's questions are designed to elicit family information for the worker's study, but the client must wonder how disclosing this information is meant to help her.

Clients do not usually ask why the worker wants to know something, because that is not considered polite in our society. They may even cooperate, providing answers to all of the social worker's questions. As long as the doubt persists, however, suspicion and tension will remain.

The interview continues with the worker asking questions about how the pain began, how the husband helps out at home, where the patient was born, and if she has family in this country. The patient's responses become shorter and consist only of direct answers to the worker's questions. When the worker suggests meeting with the husband and children "to get a clearer picture of how we can be helpful," the client agrees and says, "Jeez! Do you do this for all of the patients?"

**Practice Summary.**  In his summary of the first interview, the worker reports that the client showed "inappropriate, almost childish smiling and expressions of distress. Distress is covered by rigid attitudes and a compulsive personality. There are rules and consequently a role distribution which for some reason she would not negotiate."

Alternatively, one might interpret the "childish smiling and expressions of distress" as signals of the client's feelings about the interview.

These feelings can be expressed in many indirect forms. The new boy at the residential institution who acts out his anxiety by immediately breaking rules and picking fights is one example. The adolescent whose total vocabulary during a first interview consists of the words "yes" and "no" and the parent who responds to the child welfare worker with open hostility are others. When the worker interprets the behaviors as a reflection of the client's personality or resistance, the worker is viewing the client as an object rather than as someone in dynamic interaction with the worker—that is, an interaction in which both parties affect each other reciprocally, moment to moment. As a result, the initial client behavior often becomes part of a stereotyped view of the client and initiates an endless cycle. The interactional framework alternative, incorporating the notion of reciprocity in relationships, would require that the social worker understand the client's behavior as, in part, responsive to the worker's interventions. The worker's interventions are also dynamically affected by the client's responses.

## Factors Affecting First Interviews

Many factors can lead workers into first contacts such as the one just described. First, the medical paradigm itself, borrowed from physicians, suggests a four-stage approach to conceptualizing practice. Recall that, in this model, one studies the client, develops a diagnosis, plans treatment, and then evaluates the results. The evaluation may then feed back to the diagnosis and influence a change in treatment plan. The emphasis on a first stage of study encourages some workers to see the initial interview as a fact-gathering exercise in which the client's function is to provide information. This can lead to an interview somewhat like our earlier extreme example.

***Need to Obtain a Psychosocial History*** The discussion of the medical model always leads to some anxiety from students and workers who may be in agencies that require this format for a first interview. In some situations, workers must complete a detailed intake form that requires them to obtain a psychosocial history—the client's psychological and social life story—elements of which may have some bearing on the current problems. The worker must then provide an initial diagnosis or assessment. In some settings, a checklist is provided to guide the worker's responses. Students and workers often ask me, "How can I conduct a first interview in the way you describe if I'm expected to complete this form?"

Examination of these forms and detailed analyses of such first sessions often reveal the following. First, although he or she may protest the rigidity of the structure, the worker often feels much more comfortable using the form to guide the first interview. Use of the form allows the worker to maintain control, makes the first session more predictable, and gives the worker time to become comfortable. Of course, the opposite may be true for the client, who may feel more and more uncomfortable as the interview goes on.

Second, one can design the first interview so that the worker can, without undue effort, simultaneously contract with the client, try to help the client feel more at ease, and still obtain the required information. For example, a worker could say, "There are several questions I need to ask you for us to be able to obtain insurance reimbursement, but before I do so, I thought I would explain how I might help, and find out what's on your mind."

In example after example, students discovered that this preliminary discussion often yielded much of the information they needed to obtain for the form, but it followed an order that fit the client's sense of urgency instead of the worker's. Time could be set aside in the second half of the interview for covering missing information by going through the form. The client was often ready to provide the data at that point, especially if the worker explained why it was required (e.g., for medical insurance, obtaining a more complete understanding of the family's health experiences, and so forth).

An explanation of how the information would be used is important not just to help build trust, but also to maintain the worker's ethical responsibility with regard to the client's informed consent. (Informed consent will be discussed in more detail later in this chapter.) The client has a right to know how his or her personal information will be used by the worker and the agency. The client also has a right not to share such information as a condition of service, unless the worker shows that the information is essential for the client to receive service. The National Association of Social Workers' Code of Ethics provides direction for a social worker on this question. (See the book's companion website, www.cengagebrain.com.)

***Developing a Dynamic Assessment and Diagnosis*** Although students can structure the interview to work within the framework provided by their setting, they still have to deal with the requirement of creating an assessment and diagnosis. Even this can be dealt with if one thinks of diagnosis as a description of the state of the relationship between the client and the various systems to be negotiated, as well as an assessment of the client's sense of strength and readiness to cope with the problem. The discussion of the resilience research in Chapter 2 provided more than enough evidence of factors that could be included in the assessment, thus focusing on what is right with clients rather than what is wrong.

Diagnosis could be seen dynamically as something that changes and shifts, often moment to moment, as opposed to a fixed description of a client's problems. Thus, in most settings, students and new workers can adopt more flexible structures for first interviews while still working within the framework of the setting. Even in situations in which a worker must make a specific assessment, such as a medical insurance requirement to provide a specific diagnosis, the worker needs to incorporate elements of contracting in the first session. Simply recognizing the difficulty of actually listening to a client and empathizing with him or her, while trying simultaneously to "categorize" the client, will often free the worker to respond more and with greater affect. In turn, the client will sense the worker's interest in and concern for what the client has to say, not just the information required by the intake form.

***Developing the Working Relationship*** After the medical paradigm, a second factor that can contribute to the worker's reluctance to be direct about purpose is the notion that one must build a relationship before the work begins. In the model described thus far, the term *working relationship* has been used. The hypothesis advanced now is that the working relationship will develop only after the purpose of the encounter has been clarified and the worker's role explicitly described. In effect, the relationship emerges *from* the work, rather than preceding it.

Of course, the nature of the relationship can change over time. A client may be less likely to share a particularly difficult or embarrassing problem in the beginning, before a positive working relationship has been developed. This is one of the reasons for the common phenomenon of clients raising *near problems*—the real issues in their lives that are close to the most difficult concerns—at the start of the work. The contracting skills described here are designed to build up a fund from which both the worker and the client can draw. As the working relationship strengthens, clients may move on to more powerful themes of concern. I referred to this process earlier as making the "second decision," which allows for the transition to the middle phase and the discussion of more difficult and often painful material. The skills of clarifying purpose and role, used in the beginning phase of practice, provide the groundwork for this transition by helping to develop a positive relationship, in particular the element of trust, between worker and client (Shulman, 1982, 1991). Again, the worker's initial directness enables the relationship building, not the other way around.

***Discomfort Addressing Problems: Worker and Client Embarrassment*** A third factor that prevents directness is the worker's tendency to be embarrassed about either the client's problem or the worker's intentions. In our society, having a problem has become identified with weakness and dependency. Workers therefore sometimes feel uncomfortable talking about a client's problems. Some of the client's difficulties, such as a physical or mental ability that some people judge negatively and to which our society attaches a stigma, are considered so challenging to discuss directly that workers have invented euphemisms to describe them.

One group for teenage unwed mothers met for four sessions, during which no mention was made of their pregnancies, although their midsections grew with each passing week. Children who have difficulty in school have been brought together by school social workers to participate in after-school activity groups with no mention of why they were selected. They are not usually fooled, because they all know they are considered to be the "dummies" or the "problem kids." The worker is embarrassed about mentioning the problem, so the client gets a message that reinforces reluctance to discuss painful areas.

When workers begin their sessions with hidden agendas, they are equally ill at ease about making a direct statement of purpose. If a worker believes the client's problem is all figured out and the task is to change the client's behavior, then reluctance to be direct is understandable.

***The Use of Professional Jargon*** A final factor that leads to difficulty in being direct is the use of professional jargon. When I graduated with an MSW, my professional degree in social work, my mother asked me at a dinner in my honor, "Now that you're a social worker, tell me, what do you do?" I replied, "I work with people to enhance their social functioning, to facilitate their growth, and to strengthen their egos." She smiled at me and said, "But what do you do?"

In fact, I was unclear about how to articulate my professional role. What made it worse was that the other social work graduates appeared to be clear about theirs. I thought, desperately, that perhaps I had missed a key lecture or had not completed an important reading. In reality, all of the helping professions, not just social work, have had trouble with direct statements of purpose and role and have tended to obscure this confusion using jargon. Keywords such as "enhance," "facilitate," and "enable," followed by a statement of hopes and aspirations (such as "enable clients to be empowered"), avoid the functional question. If, in training sessions with professionals, I restrict their use of jargon and insist that they describe what they have to offer me as a client in simple, clear sentences, they usually find it difficult to do so. The more ingenious try to avoid the difficulty by asking me, the client, "What is it that you want?" I point out at such moments that they are answering a question with a question.

Although it is a good question, in that it reaches for client feedback, I do not think I, as the client, can really answer it without some structure from the worker. In effect, the structure provided by the worker through a clear opening statement will potentially free the client to respond. This is another example of a false dichotomy: structure versus freedom. In effect, freedom emerges from structure, but it has to be a structure that encourages freedom.

Sometimes the client has come to the worker for service—for example, a voluntary client who visits a family counseling service. In such a case, the worker may well begin by explaining the purpose of the first visit as one in which the client can tell the worker what brought him or her to the agency so that the worker can see whether she or he can be of any help. The worker listens for the client's sense of urgency; when that is clear, the worker can explain how she or he can help.

In the section that follows, I present a model that depicts how to use a first session to clarify the worker's purpose and professional role directly and simply, without jargon or embarrassment.

# Contracting in First Sessions

The first sessions described in this book take place in the context of an agency or a host setting, such as a hospital, school, or residential institution. Many of these helping concepts apply equally to social work that occurs in individual private practice, group practice, or fee-for-service managed care clinics in which workers are reimbursed for the number of counseling hours they provide. However, the issues involved in private practice—and the profound implications for private practice as a result of changes in managed care in our country—mostly go beyond the scope of this text, which focuses on social work that takes place in more traditional and formal settings.

## The Impact of Context on Practice

Because the effect of the context of practice is particularly important in the contracting phase, we explore it here. Social workers usually work for an agency or institution (the host setting). The setting is more than a convenient place for sessions to take place. It has a function in society, which means it has a stake in the proceedings.

In the societal distribution of tasks, each setting deals with a particular area of concern. The hospital is concerned with the emotional and physical health of patients, the school with the education of students, the family agency with strengthening family functioning, the parole agency with monitoring released prisoners and helping them function in the outside world, and so on. The mission of the setting significantly affects the helping person's actions. I have argued that there is a common core or constant element to social work practice, but that there are also variant elements. Context introduces important variant elements to our work with clients.

In the first chapter, I identified some of the pressing life tasks that face clients: dealing with school, family, work, the welfare or medical systems, and so on. The client sees successfully accomplishing these tasks as the immediate need. In each illustrative example, I described some life tasks that might be important to the client.

The tasks of the agency and the client, as well as their possible convergence, are what Schwartz (1971) considered in developing the contracting concept. Writing in the context of group work practice, he said:

> The convergence of these two sets of tasks—those of the clients and those of the agency—creates the terms of the contract that is made between the client group and the agency. This contract, openly reflecting both stakes, provides the frame of reference for the work that follows and for understanding when the work is in process, when it is being evaded, and when it is finished. (p. 8)

In the beginning phase of work, the worker can be viewed as mediating the initial engagement between the client and the service, searching for the connection between these two sets of tasks. Although many obstacles (e.g., the authority of the worker, an involuntary client, an insensitive doctor in the hospital) might block the mutual interests of the setting and the client, the worker searches for the often elusive common ground, the overlap between the specific services of the setting and the felt needs of the client.

Schwartz (1971) describes three critical skills in this phase of work: clarifying purpose, clarifying role, and reaching for client feedback (the client's perception of his or her stake in the process). Although these skills are central to all beginning engagements, many variations in their implementation exist. For example, the setting introduces a variety of elements. The issue of authority—whether the client is voluntary or the worker makes the first contact—can also introduce variations. The rest of this section details these three skills, illustrates them in different contexts, and describes the results of research on their effects.

***Hospital Contracting Example: An Alternative Approach*** Given the dynamics of new relationships described earlier in this chapter, the worker must attempt to clarify the purpose of the meeting with a simple and direct opening statement that is free of jargon. This statement should openly reflect both the stake of the setting and the possible stake of the client. For example, in the hospital interview described earlier, the worker could have begun in the following way:

> My name is Mr. Franks, and I am a social worker from the social services department. Your doctor asked me to see you to determine whether there was any way I could help with some of the difficulties you might be facing in taking care of your children or your home while you're recovering from the operation. I know that can be a difficult time, and I would like to help, if you wish. I would like to discuss this with you to see if you want some help with these problems or with any other worries you might have about the operation or your hospital stay.

Such a simple statement of purpose sets the stage for the discussion that is to follow. The purpose of the visit is to discuss the service and to see how that service fits with what the client feels she needs. With this simple framework in place, the client's energy can be involved in examining areas of possible work. With a clear boundary in place, the client does not have to worry about why the worker is there. Conversation and the worker's subsequent questions should be related to this task, a mutual exploration of potential service areas.

The worker also needs to be prepared for the client's inevitable question about how the worker can help. In this example, clarifying the worker's role might consist of spelling out several possible forms of assistance. For example, "I can help you examine what you may be facing when you return home, and, if you think you need some help, I can connect you with some homemaking resources in the community." Another form of assistance could be presented in relation to the family: "If you're worried about your husband's ability to help at this time, I can meet with the two of you and try to sort this out." Still another could relate to the hospital and the illness:

> When you're a patient in a big, busy hospital like this, you sometimes have questions and concerns about your illness, medication, and the operation that are not always answered; if you do, you can share these with me and I can see if I can get the staff's attention so that they can help out, or perhaps I can do so myself.

Each of these simple statements defines a potential service the client may wish to use immediately or at some future date. They may seem overly simple, but—for a worried patient on the ward—these statements provide an orientation to services that she simply may not know about. They can be described as "handles" that provide a way for the client to "grab onto" the offer.

The specific examples shared by a worker reflect his or her tuning in to the particular situation faced by the client (see Chapter 3). Previous clients may have taught the worker about the themes of concern that are most common in a particular situation. Thus, the worker not only speaks directly to the heart and mind of the specific client but also normalizes the problems because they have been shared by so many clients in similar situations.

Contracting is a negotiating period that involves both the client and the worker. The skill of reaching for client feedback is essential. In the hospital example, this skill might sound like this: "Are any of these issues of concern to you, and would you like to discuss how I might help?" It is quite possible that, during the feedback stage, the client may raise issues that were not part of the worker's tuning-in process. The agenda for work can expand. The only limitations are the tasks of the setting: The worker cannot offer services that are not relevant to those tasks. For example, the acute care hospital social worker in this example would not get involved in long-term marital counseling with this woman and her husband, even if early contacts indicated that this was needed. Instead, he would focus on the marital issues associated with the illness and hospitalization. He might also make a referral to an appropriate family counseling agency or hospital service.

The boundaries to the work created by the agency service and the needs of the client help the worker focus; they also relieve the client's anxiety that private areas may be intruded on. Contracts are negotiated continuously through recontracting and can be openly changed as the work proceeds. Often a client, not fully trusting the worker, will discuss only the near problems during early interviews. When the working relationship strengthens, areas of concern that were not part of the initial agreement may enter the working contract.

Here I want to distinguish between my use of the term *contracting* and some other uses in the field. Sometimes the term refers to a specific written document, or *service plan*, that the client literally signs and agrees to fulfill. In the case of an involuntary client, or perhaps a teenager in a residential setting, the contract specifies the agreed-on goals and the way they will be achieved; for example, a substance-abusing child welfare client might agree to attend meetings of Alcoholics Anonymous or some other self-help group. In many cases, such documents represent the agency's or the worker's perception of what needs to be done, which the client will go along with to obtain the service or to create the illusion of cooperation. Although a genuine, mutually agreed-on contract may be put into writing in appropriate settings, this is not required in my broader use of the term.

---

### Engaging and Working with the Hard-to-Reach Client

Use the accompanying DVD or visit *The Skills of Helping Individuals, Families, Groups, and Communities*, Seventh Edition, CourseMate website at www.cengagebrain.com and enter your personal access code to watch this video:

**BEGINNING PHASE: CONTRACTING** The author presents the elements of contracting.

## Some Additional Variant Elements in Contracting

The contracting procedure is not mechanistic; variations in the first sessions are often required. As pointed out earlier in this chapter, the helping person who is contacted by a client for assistance may begin the first interview by indicating a wish to understand what brought the client to the agency—in other words, to know what is on the client's mind. As the client shares concerns, the worker tries to connect these to potential service areas and to explain available help. The important point is not the order of skills used, but rather that the contracting is started, that it is an open process, and that both parties are involved. Some illustrations of statements of purpose and role in various settings are as follows:

MARRIAGE COUNSELOR: Living together over a long period can be tough, with many ups and downs. You have been describing a crisis in your marriage, which I am sure is a frightening time. It's also an opportunity for change, perhaps to make a new marriage out of the one you already have. One of the ways I may be able to help is by helping both of you talk and listen to each other about the problems you are having. I can help you tell each other how you are feeling, try to help you figure out how you get into trouble, and help you do some thinking about what each of you can do to strengthen the relationship. As we work, I'll throw in some of my own ideas about living together, and some of these may be helpful.

SCHOOL SOCIAL WORKER: Your teacher told me that you were having trouble in her class and that she thought school was not much fun for you. My job at the school is to meet with kids like you to see if we can figure out, together, what's going wrong for you at school and to see if there are things we can do to make it better. How about it—how is school for you right now? (After some discussion of the problems, the worker tries to define her role.) If you really feel that Mrs. T. (the teacher) is down on you, maybe I could talk to her a bit about how you feel and help her understand that it makes it harder for you to work. With so many kids, she may just not understand that you feel that way.

RESIDENTIAL TREATMENT SOCIAL WORKER: (First contact with new resident) I thought I should tell you what I do around here so if there is any way I can help, you can let me know. My job includes being interested in how you guys are making out. For example, right now, you're new to the house and that can be a scary time; if there is some way I can help you get connected with the other staff or the kids, or if you want me to answer any of your questions about the place, I'd be happy to. (In the course of the conversation, other functions can be clarified.) Sometimes you may have troubles on your mind and need someone to talk to about them. For example, if it's not going well at school, or you're having problems with the guys in the house or your family when you visit, or you're mad at the staff or the rules, I'll be around to listen to your troubles, if you want me to, and to try to help you figure out how you might handle them.

CHILD WELFARE WORKER: (With a young, unmarried mother who is rejected by her family) I know it's tough when you're young, pregnant, and feeling very alone. We could meet each week and talk about some of the things on your mind right now. Perhaps I can help you think them through and figure out some answers to some of your concerns, such as trouble with your parents or your boyfriend, or uncertainty about whether you can make it if you keep the baby, or if you need to give the baby up. How about it, are some of these things on your mind right now?

Workers may need to tailor the opening statement to the specific capabilities of the client population. Young children need to be addressed at a level of language that they can understand. In a sexual abuse investigation, for example, purpose might be explained in terms of adults touching children in places that make them feel uncomfortable. Realistic dolls are often used to help the child understand the areas of the body involved.

In a back ward of a psychiatric hospital, an opening statement that details a discussion group to provide mutual support would have little meaning to a group of patients described as catatonic (i.e., appearing to be completely out of contact with their environment). A worker who says, in a loud voice, "I'm going to try to get all of you to talk to one another" might be more appropriate. In just such a discussion group, one worker met with the patients every day for months and showed them magazine pictures. Initially, there was little response. Just before Christmas, while looking at a picture of a family around a Christmas tree, one patient began to cry. A patient next to him began to cry as well. The purpose of this group—to establish contact of any kind between patients—was appropriate to the population. The crying served as a successful form of contact.

 **Interactive Skills of Helping**

Use the accompanying DVD or visit *The Skills of Helping Individuals, Families, Groups, and Communities*, Seventh Edition, CourseMate website at www.cengagebrain.com and enter your personal access code to watch this video:
**CONTRACTING IN FIRST SESSIONS** This example demonstrates the single-session work of a hospital social worker interviewing a mother and her teenage daughter who are facing medical expenses without having health coverage. Issues of privacy are raised when the worker receives a telephone call about another client.

These illustrations show how one can fashion the contracting to reflect the particular service of the setting and the possible needs of specific clients. This is where the tuning-in process can help. Later in this chapter, an example of contracting with a voluntary yet resistant client, as well as another with a mandated client, will provide an opportunity to discuss the importance of clarifying issues of authority (e.g., confidentiality and the worker's potential use of authority), which are also essential elements in the contracting process.

# Author's Research Findings on Contracting

**EP 2.1.6a**
**EP 2.1.6b**

**EP 2.1.10c**
**EP 2.1.10d**
**EP 2.1.10f**

In my research studies (Shulman, 1978, 1991), the skill of reaching for client feedback about purpose was significantly associated with a worker's ability to be helpful. This supports the concept that the areas in which the worker can be most effective are those in which the client perceives some stake. Garvin (1969) found the same principle to be true for group work practice.

The four skills for helping clients to manage their problems are (1) clarifying the worker's purpose and role, (2) reaching for client feedback, (3) partializing the client's concerns, and (4) supporting clients in taboo areas (Shulman, 1979b, 1991). The scale that included these skills was predictive of the development of trust in the working relationship. Trust, in turn, was the medium through which the worker influenced outcomes of service. These findings supported the idea that contracting creates a structure that is freeing to the client.

The skill of exploring taboo areas is included in this grouping, because some of the most important client issues are taboo in nature. This skill helps a client to move from the near problems to the real problems. Partializing is included in this grouping because it also serves a contracting purpose. By listing specific issues, the worker provides potential handles for the client. The worker also breaks down big problems into more manageable components and suggests that some next steps are possible. Even if a client faces a terminal illness, there is still some work that can be done during the remaining time in relation to friends, family, lovers, and general quality of life.

# Contracting over Time

Our discussion thus far has focused on the initial contact with the client and the beginning of the contracting process. In practice, the contracting process takes place over time, with both the worker and the client deepening their understanding of the content to be covered and of the expectations each can have of the other. For example, as pointed out earlier, clients often share near problems in the early sessions as a way of testing a worker. If the worker deals with these in a manner that helps the client lower his or her defenses, more serious (and often frightening) themes may emerge as a result. With regard to the worker's part, even a clearly stated description of purpose and role might not be heard or remembered by a client who is overwhelmed with anxiety during a first session. Thus, contracting should be understood as a process that, in some ways, may continue throughout the life of the relationship.

### First Session with a Depressed and Angry Client

**Practice Points:**   The worker can also feel overwhelmed in a first session and, as a result, miss or skip over clues to crucial issues that relate to contracting. In the following example, a client uses the device described in Chapter 3—of referring to a former helping professional who was not helpful—as an indirect cue to her concerns about this new worker. The strength of her feelings frightens the worker, a student with some social work experience, who ducks the issue. The client also raises her past suicide attempts, further upsetting the student. The student starts to catch her mistakes at the end of the first session and continues to clarify the contracting at the start of the second session.

> Right at the beginning of our first session, Mary indicated that she had been to see a psychiatrist over a year ago, shortly after her husband had left her. When I asked if that experience had been helpful, she described at length how terrible it had been. She stated laughingly that if she was violent she would like to go and punch him out right now. I failed to respond to this message—failed to relate it to me—and instead asked her to elaborate.

MARY: He told me more or less that I was just feeling sorry for myself and that the relationship had ended, and that I had to accept it and get on with my life. I knew I was feeling sorry for myself, but I couldn't help it. I didn't need him to tell me what I already knew. I just wanted an assist—not for him to solve my problems. He wanted to give me pills but I wouldn't take them. I was afraid enough of myself that I would do something stupid—like I have.

**Practice Points:**   Note that the worker appropriately responds to the hinted concern over possible suicidal behavior. This is a first priority and must be attended to in order to protect the client.

WORKER: Like you have?

MARY: Yeah, I've tried to commit suicide a few times—a number of times—lots of times (pause; a strange laugh)—and one of these days I'm going to succeed.

WORKER: Have you been thinking of suicide lately?

MARY: (Silence) Yeah, that's a good question. I think I hit the age of 12 and I really felt like I was 95 in my mind.

**Practice Points.** The client continued to talk about suicide and described how she was not afraid to die, how nobody would miss her, and so on. The worker, feeling anxious about the topic of suicide, changed the subject by picking up on the problems the client faced. Note also the "doorknob" therapy response as the client leaves referring to previous workers who did not believe her. The worker described her feelings as follows:

> I felt that Mary was trying to manipulate me into feeling sorry for her, and I was angry at her for doing this. I also felt a little bit nervous at what I'd gotten myself into—this was my first client at field placement number three (my first two did not work out). All I needed was someone to commit suicide on me. I wasn't able to empathize with Mary because I was caught up with my own feelings.
>
> I had heard her message loud and clear that she was desperate for help; however, I didn't let her know that I'd heard or that I was prepared to help. I didn't realize at the time that this was her way of saying: "Hey, are you sure you can handle me?" Although I didn't reassure her at the beginning that I was prepared to take her on, because I was feeling ambivalent myself, I had my opportunity at the end of the interview. As we were leaving at the end of the session, Mary suddenly stated, "You know, I once called a crisis center and told the person I felt like killing myself. They told me I might as well go ahead and do it."

WORKER: I'm wondering if you are worried that I might tell you something like that. I guess you're worried about whether I'm going to be able to help you. You know, I can't decide for you if you want to live or die—that's something only you can decide. But if you want to live, I can help you to begin sorting through some of your problems, one step at a time. I don't have any magic cures to help you feel better—I wish I did, because I know you're feeling pretty low right now. It'll take lots of hard work for both of us. I'll try my hardest if you want to continue. (Long silence)

MARY: Yeah, I guess that's fair. At least I can talk to you.

> I had some anxieties about whether or not Mary would show up the following week. She was 10 minutes late, and I was on pins and needles thinking the worst had happened. I couldn't believe how relieved I felt when she finally arrived. I tried to own up to my mistake, declare myself human, and return to some of Mary's concerns I had missed the week before.

**Practice Points:** The second week's response is a good demonstration of quickly catching one's mistake and owning up to having missed the previous week's communications. If, however, the worker felt these concerns during the week, a follow-up telephone call would not have been inappropriate. A discussion of a plan of action if the client has these feelings during the week would also be important in the first session.

WORKER: Mary, you know, I was going over the tape of last week's session and I think a lot of what you were trying to tell me went right over my head. It seems like you were quite worried that you wouldn't be able to get the kind of help you needed.

Who wouldn't be after the experience you had with the psychiatrist? I guess I first want to let you know that I am going to make mistakes too and I'm probably going to say things that you don't agree with, so you're going to have to let me know if you feel I've screwed up. It'll be hard, but please don't keep it in.

**MARY:** Well, at least you seem real—and I'm glad you're not a guy. I didn't trust him. It was all a big game of verbal semantics, with him trying to guess what I was thinking and feeling and me going along with him because I wanted to give the right answers. I wanted him to like me. I didn't realize it at the time.

**WORKER:** Do you find it hard to say things sometimes because you're afraid the person won't like you?

**MARY:** Yeah, I think I do that, especially with men.

When I asked her to elaborate, she described her relationships with men, her fear of making demands, how she gets angry and "starts acting like a bitch." When I asked if that was what was happening with her current boyfriend, she elaborated in some detail, and we spent the remainder of the session on this theme.

**Practice Summary:** The contracting process in this example is not yet complete; both worker and client will have to come back to discussions of their way of working, as well as expansions on the content (themes of concern) of their work. The worker has laid the groundwork for the discussion of their process by letting the client know that she will make mistakes and that it is the client's job to help keep her honest. The worker's job will be to create the conditions that will help the client do just that. This is one example of the skill referred to earlier as *helping the client deal with authority* in the relationship with the worker. The goal is to help the client deal with the worker as a real person, not just as a symbol of authority.

The discussion thus far has described contracting work with clients who appear open to help or who have sought it out. What about work with clients who are resistant? How can you find common ground when the client appears defensive and not open to your intervention? How can you contract with a client when your function includes authority over the client's life (e.g., parole supervision or child welfare protection)?

In the next section, we explore this variation on the contract theme and stress the importance of dealing directly with the issue of authority. The analysis of first sessions expands to include discussion of the skills required to begin to strengthen the working relationship.

## Contracting with Resistant Clients

All clients bring to the first interview some ambivalence toward the idea of accepting help. Resistance to the worker may be strong for some clients because of their past experiences with professionals, their particular concerns, or the problems created by the authority of the helping person. It may be expressed passively (e.g., an apathetic response during the interview) or actively (e.g., open hostility). Although students and inexperienced workers often indicate that they prefer apathy over anger, they soon come to realize that an angry client who is openly resistant can be much easier to work with than one who sits quietly, nodding and agreeing with the worker, while inside he or she feels exactly the same as the openly resistant client.

A key to working with a resistant client is to recognize that resistant behavior has meaning and the social worker's efforts should be to explore resistance and not try to overwhelm or control it. This is the meaning of the expression "resistance is part of the work." It is also a crucial instance where process (the resistance) if explored can lead directly into the content of the work. Let's explore a few of the potential reasons for the emergence of resistance.

First and foremost is the lack of a real, mutually agreed-upon contract with the client. If the social worker is working on his or her perception of the problem and does not find a way to connect to the client's perception in the beginning phase, whether it is accurate or not, resistance is then being generated by the interaction with the worker. Some examples of more effective contracting follow in this section.

Second is that the client is sending a signal to the worker that the discussion is entering a difficult and well-defended area. This is why the skill of exploring resistance, noting the direct or indirect resistance to discussing a particular area, and inquiring what it is about that area that is hard to talk about is an important strategy for helping a client move through the resistance. The worker's genuine empathy with the difficulty and expressed caring may be what is needed at moments like this.

Shallcross (2010), in an article summarizing current thinking about resistance among counseling experts, points out some additional interpretations of resistance:

- The client is being pressed by the counselor to explore difficult themes too early in the work.
- The counselor-client relationship has not been sufficiently established.
- The counselor does not have a sufficient understanding of the client's world.
- The counselor and client have not reached a mutually agreed-upon goal.
- The client is reacting to the counselor's inappropriately assuming the role of "expert."

As seen in the examples that follow, being tuned in and aware of the potential issues allows the social worker to help the client take some control over the process and move past the issues in the beginning phase of work.

*A Young Mother on Probation for Substance Abuse Offenses* Consider the following example of a mandated client, a young mother who was on probation for substance abuse offenses. She was required to meet regularly with her probation officer, attend a group program, see a social worker at a court clinic, and stay free of drugs and alcohol.

**Practice Points:** The social worker, a first-year student, tried to be understanding and to engage with the client but never made clear her expectations. After repeated appointment cancellations, the worker finally decided to confront the client and set limits.

(Session 4) In keeping with the client's pattern of canceling and rescheduling her appointments, it was no surprise that she called the court clinic at 12:05 today. I answered the phone and spoke to her briefly. She asked if she could change her 12:30 appointment to 1:30 because her "kid was sick" and she was at home taking care of him. I asked her if it would be possible for her mother to watch over him while she came to the clinic, but she told me that her mom "wasn't up yet because she takes medication."

I told Deedee that this recurring problem with her appointments cannot continue. She admitted that she realized that this was a problem and offered a variety of excuses. Yesterday, the problem was that she went into work early; today, it is her son. I told Deedee that, if she would like, she could "come in at 2:30 today." "Two-thirty is no good," she replied, because of her work. I explained to Deedee that I was busy until then, as other clients were scheduled to come to the clinic. I was not prepared to change their appointments or to keep others waiting because of this problem. Consequently, Deedee became very abrupt and angry. She raised her voice and said, "Fuck it all. I'll try to get in. What time is it now?"

**Practice Points:** Once again, while the worker may be somewhat upset at the expression of anger, she is actually in a better place with the client with this reaction out in the open. Active resistance is always easier to deal with than continued passive resistance representing the "illusion of work."

This confirmed for me that she had no idea of the exact time. She was just trying to get out of today's meeting. "My kid's sick" was the last I heard before she hung up. Deedee had tried to get me to let her off the hook for her appointment by employing her manipulative techniques, including guilt. (She told me that she didn't want to have to take Stevie out in the heat with a fever.) She asked if she could just see her probation officer next week, as she was already scheduled to see him on Tuesday. I explained to Deedee that, regardless, she had to see me on a weekly basis.

**Practice Points:** This is another good example where process, the way in which the social worker deals with the client, is actually integrated with the content. The client is acting immaturely and not taking responsibility. This is why she was getting in trouble with drugs in the first place. By confronting the client and setting limits, the worker is actually helpful to the client.

At 12:45, and with still no sign of Deedee, the telephone rang. Obviously, after some rethinking, Deedee had called the court clinic to apologize for her behavior. She began by apologizing immediately. "I'm sorry, Lois. I'm so sorry. I'm disgusted with myself. I have split personalities, you know. That wasn't me. I had to cool down." I excused Deedee and asked her when she would be coming in. She told me that she would be able to make it in at 2:30 today, as I requested. She arranged with her coworker to fill in for her, as she would be a few minutes late (according to Deedee, "work" now starts at 3:00). I told Deedee that her schedule was something that we were going to have to review again, as this seems to be a recurring problem. She explained that "I wouldn't want someone to do it to me" (i.e., hang up), and that she wasn't brought up that way. She told me that she hangs up on her mother, too. I told Deedee that I appreciated her apology. She thanked me once again.

**Practice Points:** The worker's beginning efforts to confront the client and to set limits open up a discussion of the authority theme and the client's difficulty in responding to demands placed on her by people in authority. It is not uncommon for clients who begin serious substance abuse programs to appear developmentally stuck at the stage of the life cycle associated with the start of the addiction. If the client sounds like a teenager in the interviews, it may well be because she is stuck in that stage of her growth. In part, the helping process involves beginning to work through these developmental issues.

Deedee arrived promptly at 2:30. As soon as I greeted her, she apologized. We were unable to sit in our usual meeting place because hearings were being held, so we sat at a table in the hall. I began by explaining to Deedee that I was concerned about her difficulties arriving at the clinic each week. I asked her what the problem was. She explained that it was nothing personal; however, she hated feeling "trapped by the court." I asked Deedee if she felt that the terms of her probation were unfair.

**Practice Points:**   The authority theme emerges in full force with the client now openly discussing her negative reactions to being mandated to service. This is the start of helping her to stop acting out her resistance through actions like missing her appointments. The worker begins to help her through the skill of partializing the issues that the client experiences as overwhelming.

Deedee recognized that she was the cause of these terms and admitted that they existed because of her actions. (Too bad that, next week, she'll forget she admitted this.) Deedee explained that she wished "all of this didn't happen." She hated to see her friends "lead a normal life"—they didn't have to comply with the terms of the court, could "go shopping when they want," and "don't have to worry about their appointments." Deedee expressed a sense of feeling overwhelmed by having to "go to a special group program, the court clinic, see the probation officer, and go to work" while managing her own responsibilities. I tried to help Deedee with this feeling by partializing her responsibilities. I focused on our task of meeting weekly. I explained to Deedee that I think picking a firm meeting time that we would adhere to strictly would best serve us. We agreed on Fridays at 12:30. I suggested that, by having a permanent appointment, it would make it easier for her to organize her other meetings and priorities. This way, she would not have to think about or try to remember when we were scheduled to meet, thereby increasing her anxiety and frustration, and resulting in her changing or canceling our appointment.

Furthermore, I told Deedee that she should use these meetings for her benefit, as that was their purpose. It was her chance to outline her goals and discuss any pressing issues. Deedee told me that she loves to talk and "could do so." She explained that, once her job is finished in two weeks, she will have more time. However, she likes working, because it gives her money, which she plans to use for Christmas gifts. She told me that she loves to buy gifts for everyone, especially her son. I asked her how he was doing (aside from feeling sick today). She said he is "doing great" and that he knew that she was supposed to be seeing me weekly. It was Stevie, Deedee explained, who told her to call me back and to come in today.

**Practice Points:**   The worker recognizes that the pattern of irresponsibility and anger at authority is a core one for this client and deftly shifts to that discussion. One way to look at the prior pattern of passive resistance would be to see the client's behavior as actually sending a signal to the worker: "Do you want to see my biggest problems that I need help with? Watch!"

I asked Deedee if she hangs up on everyone, not just her mother. She said she does it all the time, to everyone, when she gets mad. I asked her how she feels once she's hung up, whether or not she's still mad. Deedee told me that she felt "like running away, escaping to a far-off place." These are the same feelings she was having prior to her encounter at Burger King that led to her arrest.

Clearly, Deedee was feeling overwhelmed and tried to escape today rather than confronting her anger. I told her that her hanging up is "not acceptable," while, at the same time, I appreciated her apology. I told her that, next time, she should tell me what the matter is instead, if possible. (I realize that Deedee has certain limitations that I and others do not.)

I reminded Deedee that she had told me over the phone that she "didn't care" if I was going to give her a bad report when she hung up, and wanted to "fuck it all." She said that she was ashamed of her previous behavior and that coming to the court is a "bad reminder" for her. However, she recalled what I had just said to her, that she "must take everything one step at a time." She mustn't look at everything that she has to do as one task, but as many smaller ones. Stevie had helped her today by making her realize that she had to go to the clinic. Deedee asked me if I'd ever met him, and recalled that he used to come in for a group last year. I told her that we would arrange a time for him to come in. She told me that she was excited by that idea.

I reviewed briefly with her how the rest of her week had been otherwise. No drug or alcohol problems. She asked what Dr. Simms had said about her taking the Valium last week. I explained that, because it was not condoned, she must focus on not taking any more and remain drug-free. I asked her what her plans were for the long weekend. She was planning to pick up groceries, as she had just received her check the day before.

We then chatted briefly about what else she had to do, and Deedee asked if she could go. I reminded her that I would see her next week, and to have a good weekend and week. She said one last time that "it wasn't me before." I explained to her that over the phone it was her voice, and that's "all I have to go on." She said she understood and that I must have thought she was "crazy." I told her that today's conversation was forgotten and that, from now on, this shouldn't be a problem because we have contracted an agreement and are beginning to formulate goals (who am I kidding?).

The question of how long these meetings would continue resurfaced again. At the beginning of the meeting I had told her that, unless I heard otherwise from her probation officer, she would go to the group program for two months and remain at the clinic for the duration of her probation. I feel, though, that this issue was dealt with by telling her the meetings are permanent.

Although I realize that today Deedee agreed with these terms, chances are that our next meeting will reflect a lack of compliance. Finally, when Deedee left she seemed to be in brighter spirits. As she said good-bye, she said, "Have a good weekend, hon. See you Friday."

**Practice Summary.**   When the client has not made the first decision (to engage the worker)—whatever the specific reasons or the form of expression—an obstacle sits squarely on the line between worker and client (see Figure 4.1). Therefore, the worker's efforts to turn the client toward the service must be integrated with efforts to deal with this obstacle.

***The Social Worker's Ambivalence about Working with Mandated Clients*** The first step in the process of engaging a resistant client begins with the worker honestly facing his or her own feelings about the engagement. Workers are human, and a new client who appears not to want help or who seems volatile or hostile can cause the worker to hold back on efforts to reach for the client. Workers experience difficulty with offering help in the face of possible rejection.

**EP 2.1.2a**

FIGURE 4.1

## *Obstacles in the Worker-Client Relationship*

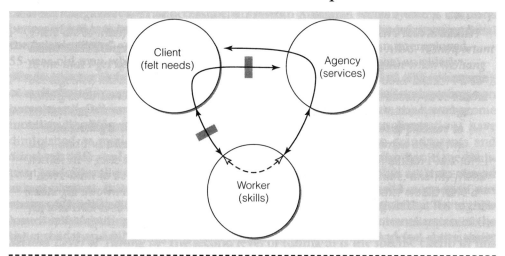

**Engaging and Working with the Hard-to-Reach Client**

Use the accompanying DVD or visit *The Skills of Helping Individuals, Families, Groups, and Communities,* Seventh Edition, CourseMate website at www.cengagebrain.com and enter your personal access code to watch this video:

**CONTRACTING WITH A DRUG-ABUSING FEMALE CLIENT** The social worker has difficulty just getting a time for an interview with a client who is court-ordered to meet with the worker. The client is denying that she has a problem with drugs.

In the example just described, the student shared that Deedee was her only client at the time (the start of the year at her school of social work) and she was afraid of losing her. This fear caused the student to wait three sessions to confront the client. I had pointed out to her that she really couldn't "lose" the client because, at this point, she didn't "have" the client.

If a worker feels relief when the client misses appointments, the worker's offer of service may contain the same elements of ambivalence the client is feeling. This can easily lead to a self-fulfilling prophecy of the first engagement breaking down. Social work professionals have debated whether one can work effectively with mandated clients; some believe that the use of authority to require engagement so profoundly distorts the helping relationship that it can only be an illusion of work.

In some cases it is clearly true that, no matter what the worker says or does, the client refuses to accept the service. In some situations, the client may not yet be ready; in others, the client may never be. This is one of the reasons children must be removed permanently from some abusive homes, some men need to go to prison for battering their partners, and some heroin addicts end their lives overdosing on the street. The worker can only do her or his best to maximize the possibility that the client will use the help, leaving the final decision to the client. This is a core concept of the interactional approach. In the final analysis, real change always rests in the hands of the client. The social worker only has a small, although important, part to play in the process.

***A Group for Mandated Clients: Men Who Batter*** For some categories of clients, however, the requirement that forces them to seek help serves as the beginning of a process of change. Writing about his development as a professional working with men who batter, Trimble (1994) describes his own understanding of this process:

> I was idealistic when I started this work. I wanted men to come to the service because they realized they had a problem which had hurt another person physically and psychologically and had hurt themselves. I hoped they would come to realize that they needed to change themselves even if their wives would never return. In reality, few of us face our problems unless we have to. It has been my experience that most violent men who come to our group and stay long enough to make a change are there because they have to be. That "have to" is either a court order or their wives saying they won't return unless the men get some help. This does not mean that most men want to be violent but rather that most of them cannot tolerate for very long the pain and fear I mentioned earlier. Their inability to tolerate pain, fear, and loneliness forms a part of the foundation for both their violence and for the impulsivity which carries them out of the group. Because of this impulsivity an outside pressure is needed to keep them in the group past their usual tolerance level for self-confrontation. (p. 261)

The skills needed to begin discussion with a resistant client are the same as those described earlier: clarifying purpose, clarifying role, and reaching for feedback. A negotiating process is taking place, but this time the potential obstacles to a working relationship must be part of the discussion. In effect, the worker is asking the client if they can work together in spite of the barriers that may block their efforts. Often, when an obstacle has been identified and explored, it loses its power, and the client and the worker are free to move past it to a deepening relationship.

***First Session with a Voluntary, Resistant Father: The "Agency Client"*** To see how this might work, consider an example of a first session with a voluntary but resistant client in a child welfare agency. The client, Mr. Gregory, is 25 years old. He has recently separated from his wife. She has applied to place their three children in temporary care of the agency. Mr. Gregory has a long record with the agency, in which different workers have consistently characterized him as hostile and defensive. In fact, when this worker told her colleagues she was going to see him, their comment to her was "Good luck!" I sometimes refer to clients such as this as "agency clients," since they and even their families may have had a long history of confrontational contacts with more than one worker. These are the clients who are often assigned to new workers and students because no one else in the agency wants to work with them. In this case, the social worker was a former student of mine working half-time in the agency as my research assistant and carrying a partial caseload.

**Practice Points:** The worker described the purpose of her first interview as informing the client of his legal rights, describing the meaning of the agency's intervention, having him sign consent forms, and seeing if some help could be offered to him for his own concerns. The interview began with the worker's efforts to clarify purpose.

**Worker:** You know that your wife has signed forms to place your children under the care of this agency. I wanted to meet with you to have you sign agreements but, before that, to discuss what this means for you and your children. I know it can be an upsetting time, and I thought you might also have things on your mind you want to discuss.

**Mr. Gregory:** For how long are my kids going to be in care?

**Practice Points:** The worker's opening statement clarified the purpose of the interview and placed strong emphasis on the offer of service to the client. The client is not just someone called in to sign forms—he is someone with feelings and concerns as a client in his own right. In a sense, her direct reaching for him represents a skill called *making a demand for work* (see Chapter 5). In the present context, it means the worker is gently attempting to involve the client actively in the engagement. The demand is synthesized with the worker's ability to express some genuine empathy with the client's situation. This is demonstrated in the sentence, "I know it can be an upsetting time."

In the client's response, "For how long are my kids going to be in care?" we see a shift back to the children—a polite way for him to refuse her offer. The interview continued with the worker responding to the direct question but also refusing to be put off by the client's first refusal. Note how she comes back to his feelings.

**Worker:** Your wife has signed forms for 6 months. That means that we are responsible to look after your children for that time, but with 24 hours' notice, you or your wife can have your children home at any time. If you wish, after 6 months, the time can be extended.

**Mr. Gregory:** It's a long time for the kids.

**Worker:** Yes, it is, and for you also.

**Mr. Gregory:** Yeah, I haven't seen them yet, but I hear they're doing fine.

**Worker:** Would you like to see them?

**Mr. Gregory:** I thought I wasn't allowed to.

**Worker:** Sure you are. You have the right to see your children whenever you wish.

**Mr. Gregory:** I was told that it would upset the kids, especially Alan, to see me, so it would be better not to.

**Worker:** Sure it will upset him. It will upset you, too. It's hard to see someone you love and can't be with.

**Practice Points:** The worker's continued "empathic demand" is contained in the phrase "and for you also." In response, the client began to explore the visiting issue. The issue of visiting is important to the client and provides an example of feedback on the contracting. The worker continued her emphasis on his feelings with the comment, "It will upset you, too. It's hard to see someone you love and can't be with." This persistence resulted in the client's beginning to explore the difficult feelings surrounding visits. In the next segment, the worker opened up this area by using the skill of putting the client's feelings into words. She used her tuning-in preparation to articulate the underlying difficulty clients face in visiting children who have been placed in care.

**Mr. Gregory:** Yeah, Alan has been in care before, and he's confused and sad.

**Worker:** Yes, that must make it hard on you to see him.

**Mr. Gregory:** Yeah. Like what do I say to him?

**Worker:** Like when he asks, "When do I come home?"

**Mr. Gregory:** Well, yeah.

WORKER: What do you say?

MR. GREGORY: Oh, I change the subject and cheer him up.

WORKER: Does it work?

MR. GREGORY: Not really.

WORKER: What do you want to say?

MR. GREGORY: Well, I don't know when he's coming home.

WORKER: I guess that hurts you.

MR. GREGORY: Well, kids don't understand.

WORKER: Have you tried telling him?

MR. GREGORY: No, not really.

WORKER: I think it's hard to tell your child you don't know when he's coming home, but clearing that up might make it easier for you both once it's discussed.

MR. GREGORY: Yeah, I won't feel like I'm holding out. But I won't be seeing him until he comes to my wife on the weekend. Can I do that?

**Practice Points:**   The worker's persistent and genuine concern with his feelings caused the client to begin to open up and deal with a real concern. When she responded to his comment, "Like what do I say to him?" by saying, "Like when he asks, 'When do I come home?'" she effectively opened the door for him to explore one of the roughest issues that faces parents who place children in care—the guilt they feel, which often results in difficulty visiting. Even in these first few minutes, the relationship has opened up, with the worker not acting the way previous workers have acted. Before he can allow himself to go further, he has to clarify how things stand between them. The next excerpt demonstrates how a discussion of the authority theme emerged as the client asks the "which side are you on" question.

WORKER: Whatever visiting arrangements you want to make will be done. I have to know in advance to help plan and to know where he is, since he's our responsibility. Seeing him at your wife's place is fine if your wife wants that.

MR. GREGORY: (In a louder voice) I want to know something. Are you going to be my social worker? I know you see my wife and you help her. So how does it work? Are you on her side or mine, or do I get another social worker?

**Practice Points:**   The directness of the client, which workers in the past may have confused with aggressiveness, is apparent. Consider the effect of this question on the worker. When asked about her reactions to the client's question, the worker admitted to being taken aback and feeling put on the spot by his assertiveness. Clients often ask questions or make statements that throw a worker off balance. This worker responded to her own feelings of defensiveness by delivering a substantial lecture that contrasted with her earlier terse reactions.

This type of response is not uncommon when workers feel put on the spot. Rather than responding with their gut reaction—their honest feeling at the moment—they try to control the situation through the use of words. Compare the following speech, which was delivered quickly, with the worker's previously terse, focused, and on-target responses. I have come to call this "bebbering," a New York City term meaning running off at the mouth. The Native Canadian clients I have worked with have a different term. They call it "nattering." As one said to me, when you stay quiet long enough with white workers, they will get so anxious they go "natter, natter, and natter."

WORKER: I'm on no one's side. I try to help your wife with what's on her mind. I'm here to help you with whatever you want. I do this so you can both come to the point of finally making a decision about your children—do you want them home? If yes, when, and how many of them? Whatever we discuss is confidential, and the same goes for your wife and me. When the two of you make decisions that will affect each other, we'll do it together. Then I won't take sides but try to help the two of you talk to each other and work together on arriving at a decision. (Quiet)

**Practice Points:**   The silence that followed this speech was important, because it contained a message for the worker. Several possibilities existed. It could simply have been that the client was confused by the words ("What did she say?"). He also may have felt that he was not getting a direct answer to his question ("She must be on my wife's side").

In an earlier research project of mine, we viewed more than 120 hours of video-taped social work practice and rated sessions according to an observation system we developed (Shulman, 1979a, 1981). Often, silences occurred just after the worker appeared to misunderstand the client's concern. Silence was many times, but not always, a message that the client felt cut off. Other times, silence was not a signal that the worker was off base, but rather that the worker had hit home. In this study, workers responded to silences most often by changing the topic of discussion. Workers often experience silences as uncomfortable because they sense negative feedback. Silences can, of course, mean other things as well. For example, the client may be reflecting on the worker's comments, or he or she may be experiencing strong emotions. (The different meanings of silence will be discussed further in the next chapter.)

In the next segment, the worker demonstrates the important skill called *reaching inside of silences* (see Chapter 3). Recall that this is the worker's effort to explore the meaning of the silence to better understand what the client is thinking or feeling. As illustrated in this segment, by reaching inside the silence, the worker demonstrated skill in catching her error at the same time she was making it. Workers often have the mistaken notion that, in good practice, one never makes errors. In reality, good practice involves spontaneity on the worker's part—mistakes will be a natural part of the work. If workers always wait for exactly the right thing to say, they will always be thinking and analyzing while the client is working well ahead of them. This was a key moment in the interview, and this skilled and experienced worker proved that she was up to the challenge.

(Silence)
WORKER: Why did you ask? It sounds like you may have had trouble with social workers before.
MR. GREGORY: I did. All the other social workers seemed to be with my wife and against me. I was always the bad one.
WORKER: And you're worried that I might do the same thing?
MR. GREGORY: Well, yeah, you might.
WORKER: I try to help the two of you decide to do what's best for you and the children. If you feel I'm siding or if you don't like how things are going with me, I want you to tell me because I want to help you both.
MR. GREGORY: Don't worry, you'll know. Are you new at this job?

**Practice Points:**   As a result of tuning in, the worker correctly guessed the meaning of his earlier question, "Are you on her side or mine?" She knew that his past experiences might well have led to the development of a stereotype about social workers and that, at some point, she would have to deal with this.

By reaching directly for this in her comment "It sounds like you may have had trouble with social workers before," she gave him permission to talk directly about what some clients would consider a taboo subject.

Workers sometimes express concern about exploring such a question. They feel it would be unprofessional to discuss other workers or other professionals. They say that they might be perceived as not identifying with the agency or as simply trying to get on the client's good side. If one views discussion of other helping professionals as the client's way of indirectly exploring the present working relationship, then the problem does not exist. This worker picked up the indirect cue and reached for the client's present concerns with her comment "And you're worried I might do the same thing?"

The client responded directly and acknowledged that this was what he meant. Many clients who lack the strength and ability to be direct hold back at this point. Because the obstacles are powerful, they need to be explored openly in first sessions. The worker needs to push, gently, a bit harder for such concerns. For example, in response to a client who says, "Oh no, I wasn't worried about you," the worker might continue, "It would be easy to understand how you might be concerned about me. After all, I'm a social worker, too, and you have had some tough experiences. How about it—perhaps you are just slightly concerned?"

The client will often sense in this second invitation that the worker really means that it is all right to talk about their relationship. If not, the worker can let things be and try to return to this topic at another time, when the client's trust has grown. Meanwhile, the client knows that this issue can be discussed when he or she feels ready. (Other examples in this book demonstrate the process of a client accepting a second invitation.)

**Practice Points:** Returning to the interview, we have the interesting question posed by the client, "Are you new at this job?" When students discussed the possible meaning of the client's question, they considered several alternatives: "Maybe he was trying to figure out what kind of worker she is, because she doesn't talk like a social worker." "Maybe he was thinking that, after she had been around for a while, she would change." This time, in contrast to her reaction to the earlier direct question, the worker tried to explore its meaning. This involved the skill of elaboration, inviting the client to expand on what he meant.

WORKER: No, I've been here for a while. Why do you ask?
MR. GREGORY: Well, the last worker I had was really green. She knew nothing. She took me to court—didn't get anywhere, but what a mess.
WORKER: Are you wondering if I'll take you to court?
MR. GREGORY: Oh, no. And if you did, I'd go and fight.

**Practice Points:** Once again, the worker reached into the client's description of past experiences to find the implications for their current relationship. In the next excerpt, the worker tries to clarify some of the terms of their working relationship in the context of the agency and her dual responsibility of trying to offer him a service while carrying statutory responsibility for the protection of his children. This is part of the contracting process; the terms of the relationship must be defined openly. The client may be able to overcome the obstacle posed by the worker's dual function if there is an honest discussion of it and a clear definition of the worker's responsibilities.

This is just as true with the elder care worker who, during a first visit, must deal with the elderly client's fears of being "put in a home," or with the adoption social worker who must make a report on the suitability of prospective parents. When these realities are openly discussed during the first sessions—when the responsibilities and mutual expectations are clearly defined for both the client and the worker—the client often can overcome the obstacles the realities pose. The worker in this illustration attempted to define this part of the contract. Note that this savvy client tries to test her right away.

WORKER: I think it's important for me to let you know under what conditions I'd go to court. Children can be in care of the agency either by court custody or voluntary agreement. In your case, it's voluntary, so there is no court involvement. But if I see the kids harmed when they're with your wife or you while visiting—by "harmed," I mean beaten, black and blue, bones broken, or not fed or supervised for the whole weekend home—then I go to court. But only under those circumstances—beaten or neglected.

MR. GREGORY: What if I want to take my kids home? Can you stop me, go to court and stop me?

WORKER: No. You can take your children whenever you want.

MR. GREGORY: That can't be. What if I'm not working, can't care for them—you won't let them come home.

WORKER: I can't stop them. If, however, once they're home and they don't get fed, clothed, or taken care of, then I can go to court and bring them back.

MR. GREGORY: (Smiling) I really knew the answers to this, but I was misinformed by other people in the past. I used to sort of test my last worker to see if she would tell the truth.

WORKER: Did I pass?

MR. GREGORY: Not you, her. (Quiet) Yeah, you passed. (Smiling) I had to do it to see where we stand. The first meeting is really important, you know.

WORKER: Yes, it is. And it is also scary, since you don't know what to expect.

MR. GREGORY: Yeah, but it looks OK.

**Practice Summary.** They talked some more about procedures, rules, and regulations, and then summed up. The worker asked whether Mr. Gregory would like to meet again to discuss his children and their care. Mr. Gregory declined this invitation, indicating that he was too overwhelmed with trying to find a new job.

I contacted the worker several months after I obtained the process of this interview. Because so many people had asked me about Mr. Gregory, I asked if she had seen him again. The worker told me that, a few months after this interview, Mr. Gregory had called the agency and asked for her by name. When they met, he told her he now had a job and an apartment of his own, and he felt he could take his children home. He indicated that he could not handle this by himself, and that he would need her help. She agreed, and they discussed possible support services. Soon afterward, the children returned to their father.

He may not have been ready to use her help after the first interview; however, she had laid the groundwork in the first session so that, when he was ready, he saw her as a source of real help. Imagine the difference in this interview if the worker had accepted the negative stereotype of this person as an "agency client" instead of reaching for his strength and his potential for growth under all of his anger. The interview might have turned out quite differently. This is also a good example of the other false dichotomy: "Am I with the father or am I with the child?" What is clear is that by being with the father, the worker was, at exactly the same time, with the child.

**Engaging and Working with the Hard-to-Reach Client**

Use the accompanying DVD or visit *The Skills of Helping Individuals, Families, Groups, and Communities,* Seventh Edition, CourseMate website at www.cengagebrain.com and enter your personal access code to watch this video:

**CONTRACTING WITH A RESISTANT MALE CLIENT** The author and workshop participants discuss the previous interview in depth.

After reviewing this interview, many students and workers comment on the client's directness. They even ask, with a touch of hopefulness in their voices, whether clients like this come into agencies often. The key point is that he seems like such a good client only because the worker responded to him with skill. Another worker— even this worker, in her early student days (she was a student of mine, so I know)— would have been put off by an assertive client such as this. The interview might have had a much different ring to it if the worker had not tuned in and prepared herself to reach for the part of this client that, in spite of his ambivalence, was still reaching out to the agency, the worker, and his children. The directness and anger were actually a sign of his caring.

We could conduct a similar analysis of a social worker in a residential setting who is dealing with a new resident and trying to reach past the false bravado put up by the "tough" teenager. Even if the teenager does not immediately accept the worker's offer to help, it is important that the worker acknowledge the teenager's feelings, especially with regard to the fear and stress associated with suddenly finding oneself in a strange setting among potentially threatening peers.

Another example might be an alcohol addiction counselor who faces a client whose arms are tightly folded across his chest, thus expressing physically his feelings about being referred to the program by his boss indicating he had to go to keep his job. The worker needs to make clear her or his recognition that the client is present on an involuntary basis, and that the worker is powerless to help the client without his active involvement.

**Practice Points:** Trimble (1994) learned to understand the value of mandated attendance to his group. In a first session with a group for men referred for battering their wives, Trimble also told the men he recognized that they could continue to attend and meet the requirements of the group without ever changing, thus acknowledging that control—a crucial issue for male batterers—remained in their hands. Trimble incorporated this reality into his opening statement:

> I'm sure it is possible to follow all these rules and not change, not open up to facing yourself or to the other men here. You can probably get through this group and really not change. That's up to you. The judge may order you to be here or your wife may be saying that she won't come back unless you get help. And as I have just said, we require your anger diary and regular attendance in order for you to stay here, but no one can reach into your mind and heart and order a change. That's where you have complete control. (p. 262)

In each case, the worker must tune in to prepare for indirect cues and to get in touch with his or her own feelings about the engagement. A clear statement of purpose and role that incorporates the client's potential sense of urgency is needed.

An opportunity must be provided for client feedback about purpose in addition to the exploration of the potential obstacles to developing a working relationship.

As with any client, the worker begins in the first session to use skills to start developing a positive working relationship while the contracting process is taking place. These skills include elaboration, reaching inside of silence, empathizing with expressed feelings, and articulating unexpressed feelings slightly ahead of the client.

The worker attempts to carry out the helper role as well as her or his abilities permit, making mistakes along the way but correcting them as soon as possible. The client also has a part in the proceedings: the decision to use this worker, to trust, to take some responsibility for part of the problems. If worker and client are both up to their interdependent tasks, in the first sessions they can lay a foundation for movement into the work phase. This phase is examined in the next chapter, which includes a more complete discussion of many of the skills mentioned in this one.

## Models for Assessment in the Beginning Phase

As mentioned earlier, the medical paradigm (study, diagnosis, treatment, and evaluation) is one model that has guided our profession's practice, theory development, and research. The individual elements contained in this model can be useful tools for the practitioner. Thus—within the interactional paradigm described in this book—obtaining relevant information (study), using models to guide our understanding of our client's circumstances (diagnosis), developing intervention strategies (treatment), and assessing our impact on the process and outcome (evaluation) all play important roles. However, several specific characteristics of this model have led me to reject it as a useful paradigm for my teaching, research, and practice:

1. The fact that it is a four-stage linear model, in which each stage appears to follow the other. The reality of practice is that it is much more fluid and interactive. For example, the way in which the "study" phase is handled is already starting the treatment process.

2. The associated trappings borrowed from medicine including the problems associated with the "expert" model discussed earlier.

3. The focus on pathology rather than a strengths perspective.

4. The often-observed underlying assumption that changes come from the worker rather than the client.

### Social Work's Approach to Assessment and Diagnosis

Keeping these reservations in mind, we should explore some of the questions associated with assessment and examine some innovative models for determining "where the client is." Kirk, Siporin, and Kutchins (1989) reviewed the history of social work and diagnosis in an article that focused on the profession's apparent ambivalence toward a formal classification system and the impact of the *Diagnostic and Statistical Manual of Mental Disorders* (DSM). The DSMs are a series of psychiatric manuals used to describe and classify mental disorders for the purpose of developing responsive treatment plans. (These researchers cited the DSM-IIIR, but the most recent version is the DSM-V.) Referring back to the publication of *Social Diagnosis* by Mary Richmond (1918) as the beginning of social work's "distinctive model of assessment, on which a distinctive approach to treatment was based," Kirk et al. (1989, p. 296) point out the following:

> The conception of "social diagnosis," as Richmond named this process, was a complex one. It consisted of analysis of three interacting elements: the social situation, the personality of the client or client group, and the problem. This process of diagnosis did not result in the affixing of a label, but rather in an accurate assessment of the dynamics of the problem in its life context. Richmond further contributed to this change by leading a movement within the social work profession to adopt a medical model for assessment and intervention and to view charity/social workers as "social physicians" who provide "social therapeutics."

The authors trace the evolution of social work's unique approach to assessment through several models leading up to the "person-in-situation" perspective, more recently reframed as the ecological approach, which has been widely adopted in the field. Although their analysis raises many important questions about the suitability of the DSM system for social work assessment, and they call for work in developing a unique social work system rather than borrowing from psychiatry, they do not challenge the core of the medical paradigm in terms of the stages of the process.

Mailick (1991) calls for "reassessing" assessment in clinical social work practice, according to changes in client populations, agency services, and treatment technologies (p. 3). For example, she highlights emerging controversies that influence assessment; this approach is associated with the "social constructivism" of postmodern theory:

> Customary ways of thinking about how information is obtained and how it can be confirmed are being re-examined. Social workers are debating whether it is the context in which information is sought, the purpose for seeking it, and the theoretical framework that shapes the investigator's search that critically influences the meaning of what is obtained. Social constructivism suggests just such an argument. For social work clinicians, it both raises the question of whether facts exist and can be discovered and challenges the usefulness of a monolithic model of assessment. (p. 4)

Her proposal for a new approach to differential assessment calls for acknowledging three major determinants that contribute to assessment: the nature and scope of agency service (e.g., goals of the service, identified population, time frame of service); the theoretical and value orientation of the practice (psychodynamic, behavioral); and the unit of attention (individual, family, small group). Thus, an assessment of an individual client might read (or be constructed) quite differently depending on the setting, the practice orientation, whether the service was individual or family oriented, and the time limits placed on the service.

## Alternative Assessment Approaches

Several authors have developed assessment frameworks or instruments that ask the social worker to pay attention to variables that might otherwise be overlooked. For example, Gutheil (1992) points out the importance of understanding the physical environment and its impact on behavior in the home, the family, the agency, and the interview. For example, the placement of the worker's chair behind a desk or the type and arrangement of furniture in a waiting room can convey a message to clients about the formality or informality of the practice. In the client's home, issues associated with personal space, crowding, privacy, and territory can influence family functioning and individual behavior. The author argues for training to help social workers be more observant and skillful in assessing physical space and its impact on clients.

Tracy and Whittaker (1990) propose using a "social network map" as a means of assessing a client's sources of social support. This instrument, which has been developed and tested by the authors, allows both clinicians and clients to evaluate several aspects of informal support, including: (1) existing informal resources, (2) potential informal resources not currently used by the client, (3) barriers to involving social network resources, and (4) factors to be considered in the decision to incorporate informal resources in the formal service plan (p. 462).

The social network map provides a tool a client can use to identify both the number of significant people in different domains (e.g., household, friends, and neighbors) and the nature of the interaction (e.g., concrete support, emotional support, information, advice). Given the contributions of social support networks to resilience (see Chapter 2), the identification of these actual and potential resources can play an important role in helping the client develop strategies to buffer stress.

The emergence of computer social networking, using online programs such as Facebook, introduces a new and potentially important avenue for connections between clients and others. A social worker might want to explore this avenue of support with a client already connecting to others online, or suggest it for those who are not.

Finally, the use of a culturagram to assess and empower culturally diverse families is described by Congress (1994) as a means to strengthen ethnic-sensitive practice, particularly in relation to immigrant families. The author created an assessment model that allowed social workers to move past generalizations about ethnic groups and to recognize significant levels of diversity within diversity, as well as unique cultural factors that may be client- or family-specific. As the author points out,

> A Puerto Rican family that has lived in the United States for 30 years may be very different from a Mexican family that came to the United States without legal documentation in the past year. An African American family that relocated from a small southern town to a northern city will be unlike a Haitian family. (p. 533)

Use of the culturagram helps the social worker clarify differences among individuals and families from similar racial and ethnic backgrounds (p. 533). Topics included in the culturagram include reasons for immigration, length of time in the community, legal or undocumented status, age at time of immigration, language spoken at home and in the community, contact with cultural institutions, health benefits, holidays and special events, and values about family, education, and work. The author provides examples of information that workers gained through the assessment that helped them understand values, attitudes, and behaviors that would have been differently (and incorrectly) assessed in the absence of cultural sensitivity. Examples include a 2-year-old Mexican child who was brought to a hospital by a mother who had not previously sought medical care—not because of neglect but because of fear of deportation as an undocumented alien, and a 7-year-old Haitian schoolchild whose increasing depression was connected to his family's emigration from Haiti for political reasons and the family's increasing sense of hopelessness about returning to their homeland.

## The Impact of the Use of Structured Assessment Instruments

A more recent Swedish study examined the question of how clients experience the assessment (or investigation) process when a particular instrument is used by the social worker (Engstrom, 2009). This is an interesting line of research in that rather than validating the assessment instrument itself, the focus is on how the client and the worker experience the process. In other words, does the use of the instrument affect the client's or worker's perception of the interview? The method was described by the researchers as follows:

> Two groups of social workers (n = 19, n = 13) carried out two different forms of assessment session, one involving an ASI (Addiction Severity Index) interview (n = 40) and one without (n = 43). After the sessions the social workers were requested to assess both the clients' experience and their own experience of the session. The clients also reported their own experience of the sessions. (p. 309)

A factor analysis created three scales: client's sense of alliance with the worker, the client's sense of own competence, and the client's sense of negative experience. The comparison between the two groups (ASI and non-ASI) provided three perspectives: the client's perspective, the social worker's perspective, and the social worker's perception of the client's perspective.

The results indicated that there were no significant differences between alliance measures for the interview group using the ASI compared to the group that did not. There was a significant difference in the client's sense of own competence, with the clients experiencing the interview without the ASI instrument rating this variable higher. There was no significant difference between the two groups on the client's rating of negative experience.

The researchers did find that "the social workers underrate the clients' experience of alliance and sense of own competence but make a correct assessment of the clients' negative experience of the session" (p. 317). This is a very preliminary and limited finding, but it does suggest that the use of a formal instrument, which structures the assessment interview, may affect the worker's perception of the process. The authors speculate that the difference may be the difficulty in assessing these variables while participating in the session; the nature of the structured session may make it more difficult for the worker to perceive how the client experiences the session, since the primary focus is on obtaining information and not to establish a close relationship. The authors also mention the difficulty of making such an assessment with clients with alcohol and drug problems.

From my perspective this preliminary finding may illustrate the difficulty of integrating in one session the assessment process, at least a formal and structured procedure in which a series of questions are presented to the client, with the also important relationship development process.

## A Model for Assessing Assessment Models

Other assessment instruments that deal with family and group practice, child welfare, and substance abuse will be described in later chapters. I want to end this section with some suggestions for how a worker can judge the assessment process before deciding whether to use a particular instrument in the beginning phase of practice or how to use it if prescribed by agency or funding policy. If an instrument is appropriate, a worker should be able to answer "yes" to each of the following questions:

- Will the information gained through this process provide specific understanding that will directly help me and the client in our work together?
- Is the client fully aware of the reason for using the assessment tool?
- Has the client provided informed consent for the use of the tool, and is the client in control of the process?
- Can the assessment process be used in a manner that does not interfere with the crucial contracting and engaging process of the beginning phase?
- Is the use of the assessment tool critical to the work, as opposed to providing a structure that makes the social worker feel more comfortable?

If the answer to each of these questions is "yes," then I believe use of the instrument early in the development of the working relationship can enhance the process.

## Culturally Diverse Practice in the Beginning Phase

**EP 2.1.4a**
**EP 2.1.4b**
**EP 2.1.4c**
**EP 2.1.4d**

Lum (1996) defines culturally diverse practice as follows:

> Culturally diverse social work practice recognizes and respects the importance of difference and variety in people and the crucial role of culture in the helping relationship. Its primary group focus is on people of color—particularly African Americans, Latino Americans, Asian Americans and Native Americans—who have suffered historical oppression and continue to endure subtle forms of racism, prejudice, and discrimination. In working with an individual, family, group, and/or community, the practitioner draws upon the positive strengths of diverse cultural beliefs and practices and is concerned about discriminatory experiences that require approaches sensitive to ethnic and cultural environments. (p. 12)

Rapid changes in demographics in the United States and Canada have been brought about by a surge of immigration during the past two decades. Social workers often find themselves working with clients of different races and ethnicities whose cultures are foreign to them. Differences may also relate to gender, sexual orientation, class, physical and mental ability, and so on, with distinct cultures associated with each population group.

Significant differences also exist within general population groups. For example, when one refers to a Native American client, one also needs to know to which tribe or nation the client belongs. An Asian American client can be Chinese American, Japanese American, or a recent immigrant from Southeast Asia. Although many experiences and cultures are shared, an African American client from the rural South may seem very different from one raised in Chicago. A Black immigrant from the West Indies will bring a perspective that is quite different from that of an immigrant from Haiti. Among Latin American clients, one would expect to find differences between Puerto Rican Americans in New York City, Mexican Americans in southern California, and Hispanics from Central America living in Boston. Cultural sensitivity that leads to the stereotyping of clients according to general population groups—and does not allow for diversity within diversity—is actually a form of cultural insensitivity.

I remember working with White child welfare workers in British Columbia, Canada, who described their Native Canadian clients as very "passive" and often "silent."

They interpreted this behavior as a cultural trait when they worked with Native Canadian clients on the reservations or in the cities. There is some truth to this notion, in that thoughtful pauses before responding often characterize such conversations. When I conducted workshops for Native counselors, however, they had another interpretation. One counselor told me that a Native client had noted, as mentioned earlier in this chapter, "When you stay very quiet long enough, the White workers get so nervous, they go 'natter, natter, and natter.'" The White social workers in this example explained the silence as a cultural trait instead of understanding it as a form of indirect communication between a particular Native Canadian client, in a particular interview, and a particular White child welfare worker.

A lack of understanding of cultural differences can create barriers between the social worker and the client, particularly during the beginning phase of practice. As described earlier in this chapter, a social worker risks misinterpreting client behaviors, values, and attitudes if he or she cannot see through the cultural eyes of the client. As Weaver and Wodarski (1995) point out:

> Clearly, professionals cannot be expected to know everything about every cultural group; however, rather than judging a client by dominant society standards, it is the practitioner's responsibility to seek out relevant information, just as a social worker must seek out information when a client is referred to them with an unfamiliar case situation; for example, a particular disability, a need for advocacy, a question of eligibility for an entitlement program. Often one of the best sources of information about clients' culture are the clients themselves. (pp. 219–220)

In those settings and geographic locations in which a particular population group is regularly a part of the caseload, the additional responsibility to learn about the group and appropriate culturally sensitive practices rests with the individual social workers and the social work department or agency. In workshops I have presented and in my social work classes, I have included an exercise that tries to explore what makes it hard to talk about sensitive and taboo areas such as race, gender, sexual orientation, and so forth, as well as what would make it easier.

It is not unusual for a student or participant of color, sometimes the only one in the class, to describe a moment in other classes or workshops when they are asked the equivalent of "And what do your people think about this?" Their usual reaction—at times with some irritation—is to explain that they cannot speak for "their people." When I ask them when they do feel all right sharing their personal experiences—not as spokespersons but as people who have had personal experience with, for example, racism—they indicate that they would feel okay "if the person really wanted to hear." Many have also indicated that they would feel all right sharing if the person had done his or her own homework on the issues and not just tried to learn from them.

It is beyond the scope of this book to explore fully the wide range of diversity issues and populations and how they affect practice. Note that several excellent social work texts have addressed these areas, including a number of those cited in Chapter 3. In this section, I instead set the stage for how one might address diversity issues, and I provide some illustrative examples of research and practice with different populations. Discussions in later chapters—for example, on work with couples and families, treatment of substance abuse, group work, and community practice—will expand on this initial discussion by addressing other important populations (e.g., Asian Americans, immigrants) and by identifying other diversity issues (e.g., sexual orientation) as they emerge from the work.

## Working with Mexican Americans

In one study, Lum (1996) discusses how Mexican Americans value the family as a "source of identity and support in times of crisis" (p. 51). The author further points out that

> Mexican American "familism," or concept of family identity, extends beyond the immediate family unit (*la casa*) to include two other similar but distinguishable systems—*la familia* (extended family) and *los compadres* (godparents). In times of crisis, Mexican Americans are inclined to seek the family first for support. . . . Mexican Americans frequently extend the definition of family membership beyond *la casa* to include individuals labeled *compadre* and *familia*. *Los compadres* are important individuals who are often, but not always, related in some manner. *Familia* is variably defined in the literature. Generally, it connotes a social network resembling a modified nuclear structure. Elder males in the community may hold positions of respect and authority, and other members may or may not be related, but have some sort of significant interaction with the family. (pp. 51–52)

Lum (1996) continues that each of the three systems has a sense of responsibility that leads to "volunteerism," where *la casa* serves as "the center of Chicano identity and commitment" (p. 52). Lum uses this understanding to develop guidelines for practice with Mexican American families; these guidelines take into account and work through this "triad of systems" that can provide support for the family members involved. Once again, this example emphasizes the importance of the worker respecting and involving the social support system, which has proven to be an important element of resilience in the face of adversity.

***Cultural Values in the Hispanic Population*** More recently, Garza and Watts (2010) echo Lum's views while arguing for a good fit between Hispanic values, in general, and filial therapy approaches to practice. They point out that the Hispanic population is the fastest-growing minority group in America, with predictions of Hispanics becoming the majority of the population in some states. While acknowledging that society is starting to prepare for this rapid change in demographics, they point out that

> there remains a dearth of information in the area of treatment of culturally diverse populations, particularly related to children. This dilemma is further complicated by a critical lack of appropriate mental health services for children. (p. 108)

The authors also suggest reluctance on the part of Hispanic families to use community mental health services because of the associated stigma, lack of knowledge of services, and low financial resources. In addition, the growing negative reaction to the presence of illegal immigrants, a desire to remain inconspicuous if a family is illegal, and the limits on access to public services aggravates the problem. The authors argue for the use of filial therapy for services to young children which are actually delivered by the parents or other family members after training in the program.

The linking of culture and help-seeking behaviors has been questioned by a recent study (Ramos-Sanchez & Atkinson, 2009):

> This study examined the relationship between Mexican acculturation, cultural values, gender, and help-seeking intensions among Mexican American community college students. Findings suggest that as Mexican Americans lose

their culture of origin and increase their generational status, their attitudes toward help seeking become less favorable. This contradicts cultural barrier theory as an explanation for the underuse of mental health services by Mexican Americans. Furthermore, adherence to traditional Mexican culture and cultural values may actually encourage help seeking. (p. 62)

These findings, which are contradictory to the Garza and Watts (2010) position, may be related to the nature of the sample, which consisted of 262 (80 men, 182 women) Mexican American community college students. One hundred and twenty-nine students were from English as a second language (ESL) courses, and 133 students were from social science courses. Other explanations are also possible. However, whatever the cause of the reluctance to seek help, whether related to culture or not, social workers must understand the unique nature of the culture in order to treat Hispanic clients when they are engaged.

Garza and Watts (2010) suggest the existence of common ground between Hispanic values and the filial therapy approach. They point to *familismo* in which families include both nuclear and extended family members as sources of support in regard to health care decisions. *Familismo* represents a cultural value in which family members are seen as extensions of the self. The authors point to another important cultural value, *respecto:*

Hispanic communities follow a hierarchical, systemic understanding with differential behaviors toward others based on age, gender, social position, economic status, and authority. In health care, providers are, by virtue of the education, afforded a high level of *respecto* as authority figures. Nevertheless, if providers do not work from an understanding of the hierarchical system, this behavior may be viewed as disrespectful and result in clients terminating therapy early. (p. 110)

Another Hispanic cultural value posited by the authors is *personalismo,* referring to behaviors and actions that demonstrate a direct interest in and concern for others. The Hispanic community tends to deemphasize the health care institution while stressing the importance of personal relationships within the institution. Social workers can recognize this value by referring to adults in a respectful manner, attentiveness, as well as including content in conversations that are not directly related to the counseling situation.

Finally, Garza and Watts (2010) suggest that *confianza* "can be understood as the sum total experiences of the counselor's understanding and expression of the core Hispanic values of *familsmo, respecto* and *personalismo,* and the concomitant perception of these values by Hispanic clients in the filial therapy process (p. 111).

## Working with African Americans

Lum (1996) suggests that from a historical perspective:

The African American family has long existed within a well-defined, close-knit system of relationships. Authority and responsibility have been clearly assigned, and complex rules of behavior have embedded them in village and regional linkages. Family life in the United States was impaired by slavery, but the African American community has survived as an active unit to meet the needs of its members. The church is still a central community institution. (p. 95)

Lum identifies underlying themes of the African American community to include "strong bonds of household kinship, an orientation to work for the support of family, flexible family roles, occupational and educational achievement, commitment to religious values, and church participation" (p. 95).

This description of the essential values of the African American community often clashes with perceptions held by social workers who deal with clients who do not appear to fit this general model. For example, the frequency of—and problems associated with—adolescent pregnancy in inner-city communities suggests a breakdown of this value system.

Stevens (1994) studied adolescent development and pregnancy among African American women. She suggests that current paradigms of adolescent pregnancy "tend to view the female adolescent's behavior as disordered, diseased or as an intergenerational transmission of psychological dysfunction" (p. 435). She argues that nonpathologic analysis of problematic behaviors is required to better understand and respond to this pattern. Her findings support the following theoretical perspectives: (1) Pregnancy can serve as a primary way of confirming existence and providing a sense of identity rather than the result of sexual acting-out behavior; (2) parenthood is perceived as a viable route to an adult social identity when opportunities for alternate routes of negotiating an adulthood status are blocked; (3) the adolescent does not have to disconnect or individuate from familiar relationships for the development of self (p. 434).

In comparing a group of 20 pregnant teens with 16 nonpregnant teens, she found that the nonpregnant females manifested a sense of care and responsibility to others in varied relationships and articulated more frequent self-expectancies for social mobility. They were actively engaged in church, work, and school environments. They demonstrated civic competency by being registered voters. Nonpregnant females were less restrictive in their dating and mating behaviors and experienced multiple dating partners (Stevens, 1994, p. 449).

Stevens (1994) suggests that the findings supported the view that both pregnant and nonpregnant participants saw pregnancy as a way of "managing concerns for personal and social maturation" and providing a maturational experience and an indicator of adult status, and that they felt that their age group was mature enough to deal with parenting (p. 449). In summary, Stevens suggests that adolescent pregnancy, rather than being viewed as a sign of pathology, may be better explained as an alternate lifestyle choice. With this understanding, the social worker might well be advised to engage such a client with a nonpathologic orientation, focusing instead on both the adaptive and maladaptive aspects of this behavior. Stevens advocates for early intervention with troubled populations, before sexual decisions are made (e.g., primary and middle school prevention programs). She also suggests that social workers emphasize mother-daughter dyads, the adolescent peer group, mentor-apprenticeship programs, and collaborative programs with inner-city institutions.

Nonpathologic approaches to troubled clients are crucial to develop the working alliance in the early stages of engagement; however, the impact of long-term and persistent racism and discrimination have influenced many members of the African American community in their perception of social workers and others from the dominant society. Davis and Proctor (1989) suggest that "persons of African descent are especially reluctant to disclose themselves to whites, due to the hardships they and their forebears experienced in the United States" (p. 23). They suggest that this represents a special case of unwillingness to disclose themselves to any representatives of the White world, and that

Practice with black families may also be facilitated by the employment of certain practitioner styles. Practitioners should keep in mind that blacks in the United

States have historically received less respect from this society than perhaps any other ethnic group. Hence, a style that indicates respect for them by the therapist will be positively received. As an example of demonstrating respect, the adult members of these families should be referred to, upon introduction, by their last names. The practitioner should not supplant the family's desire to be respected with his or her desire to be informal or even to establish a positive therapeutic rapport. Specifically, in the interest of establishing rapport, informality does not automatically facilitate the establishment of a sincere relationship. (Davis & Proctor, 1989, p. 82)

The importance of showing respect through the use of the last name was brought home by a participant in one of my workshops. Referring to her work with African Americans in the South, she emphasized the relatively recent history of slavery during which slaves had their last names ignored and were referred to by first names in a manner that was demeaning. Thus, efforts by young White workers to establish informality with elderly clients by using their first names were actually perceived as insulting.

***Racial Microaggressions in White-Black Counseling Relationships*** Constantine (2007) raises a concern about what are subtler and oftentimes unrecognizable behaviors in the counseling process that are likely to occur outside the awareness of well-intentioned therapists referred to as racial *microaggressions*. These are "subtle and common place exchanges that somehow convey insulting or demeaning messages to people of color" (p. 1). The example cited above of the young White worker's efforts to be informal with elderly Black clients by using their first names would fall into that category.

Constantine points out that many White therapists, even those with multicultural training in their background, may well have internalized attitudes and stereotypes and are unaware of the subtle ways they may influence their practice. She challenges the argument that practice is color-blind, citing a study by Burkard and Knox (2004) that identified a relationship between greater color-blind racial attitudes expressed by therapists and lower levels of therapeutic empathy and a greater tendency for the psychologist to assign responsibility to African American clients for overcoming their problems.

The general purpose of the Constantine (2007) study was to test a path model exploring the associations among (a) African American clients' perceptions of racial microaggressions in counseling by White therapists, (b) their therapeutic working alliance, (c) their counselors' general and multicultural counseling competence, and (d) their satisfaction with counseling. Initial focus groups with African American students involved in counseling led to the development of the following 12 racial microaggression categories as perceived by the students/clients: (1) color-blindness, (2) overidentification, (3) denial of personal or individual racism, (4) minimization of racial-cultural issues, (5) assignment of unique or special status on the basis of race or ethnicity, (6) stereotypic assumptions about members of a racial or ethnic group, (7) accused hypersensitivity regarding racial or cultural issues, (8) the meritocracy myth, (9) culturally insensitive treatment considerations or recommendations, (10) acceptance of less-than-optimal behaviors on the basis of racial-cultural group membership, (11) idealization, and (12) dysfunctional helping or patronization.

In the second phase of the study, 40 African American clients seen by 19 White counselors participated by completing a questionnaire at the termination of their treatment. The participating counselors provided demographic information. A Racial

Microaggressions in Counseling Scale (RMCS) was developed for the study consisting of 10 items for which the client could rate frequency of occurrence during counseling and whether or not the client was bothered by it. The scores on the RMCS ranged from 0 to 20 with the higher score associated with a greater perceived number and a stronger emotional impact of microaggressions in the counseling experience. Data were also obtained through other measures on the working alliance, counselor effectiveness, cross-cultural competency, and client satisfaction.

The findings of the study indicated that perceived microaggressions were negatively associated with client perception of the therapeutic working alliance as well as client perception of the White therapists' general and multicultural counseling competence. In another analysis, testing whether a positive working alliance and the counselors' general multicultural counseling competence would mediate the impact of the microaggressions on client satisfaction, the finding was that they did not.

Constantine argues that some African American clients may find it difficult to respond to racial microaggressions in counseling situations and, instead, question their own perceptions and thus be less likely to confront their counselor. Since the counselor is in a position of authority in the relationship, the responsibility to monitor this process and to create conditions designed to allow the often-taboo subject of racial-cultural issues to be part of the conversation rests with the counselor.

***Color-Blind or Blind about Color: A Personal Experience*** I think we all would like to believe that we can judge people by who they are and what they do rather than by the color of their skin. It appears, however, that believing we are color-blind really means we are blind about color. I would like to share a personal experience at this point that brought home to me, once again, how deeply ingrained are our internalized stereotypes and biases. I reported this incident in an article on group work practice (Shulman, 2002).

I was leading a two-day, continuing education workshop on leading mutual aid support groups with a special focus on dealing with inter- and intracultural issues between leaders and members and between members as well. There were more than 100 participants in the workshop. It was held on a Friday and Saturday, and on the first day the heat in the room was much too high. I had complained to the building and grounds department, but since the thermostat was locked I could not adjust it myself.

On the second day, a Saturday, most participants dressed informally, and I did as well. Approximately 20 minutes after we started a young, African American male wearing a baseball cap stopped at the entrance door and appeared to be looking around the room. When I saw him I said I was glad to see him and that the thermostat was on the wall to the left. After a brief pause he explained that he was not the maintenance man but was a participant from the previous day looking for an empty seat in the crowded room. I apologized and went back to the presentation.

As I spoke I had this strong, sinking feeling in my gut and I believe I began to sweat. Here I was teaching a workshop for group work with intercultural issues front-and-center, had just made this mistake, and was trying to continue as if nothing had happened. After 5 minutes (that seemed like 25) I stopped and pointed out what had just happened and how I was trying to avoid dealing with my feelings and their feelings as well. I was not practicing what I was preaching, and since more is "caught" than "taught," I was modeling the opposite of what I believed should be done in situations such as this.

Three African American women sitting in the first row smiled and told me they were wondering how long it would take me to catch and raise the issue. After apologizing to the young man again, this time for my apparent racially based assumption that he was the maintenance man (I was not familiar with the term *microaggression* at the time), a wonderful discussion started as the workshop participants moved past the more superficial conversation that just hinted at issues related to race to a deeper and more profound examination of our stereotypes and feelings, both on the part of Whites and Blacks, that affect our practice.

The discussion broadened from race to ethnicity, gender, physical ability, and sexual orientation. For example, workshop participants who were gay but still in the closet spoke about the pain they experienced when clients and colleagues made homophobic comments and jokes. The admission of my own mistake, rooted perhaps in deeply held biases and stereotypes, became an example of how crucial self-reflection is and how honesty can help to open up taboo areas, and to move across boundaries to deeper and more meaningful connections. The young man who I had mistakenly thought was a maintenance man said it meant a lot to him for me to come back to the comment in the way I had. Other African American participants echoed his feelings. Some White participants commented on how hard it would be for them to do what I did and even to recognize a comment was hurtful to another. I had finally relaxed because I was now modeling what I believed to be the right way of working. Even more important, the incident illustrated the lesson that we can make mistakes but still catch them and try to correct them, and that learning about who we are is a lifelong professional endeavor.

## Working with American Indians

Williams and Ellison (1996) address issues of culturally informed health and mental health practice with American Indian clients and provide guidelines for non-Indian social workers. For example, American Indian clients will involve themselves in interventions they perceive to be appropriate. Enlisting the aid of a traditional healer may increase the desirability of an intervention. Social workers should use ceremony and ritual—two important aspects of healing—in an intervention. Giving gifts, serving food, and involving family and friends emphasize the importance of an intervention. The inclusion of family members underscores that the family is a supportive and protective unit whose help is valued (p. 148).

Weaver and White (1997) raise the issue of the impact of historical trauma on Native families:

> In order to work effectively with Native families, social workers must first acquire an understanding of the historical influences on contemporary issues and problems. The root of many current social and health problems among Native people lies in the past. Specific and deliberate attempts were made to destroy Native people both physically and culturally. The impact of these actions cannot be minimized. Although Native people have survived, tremendous damage was done to individuals, families, and communities. The trauma experienced by Native families has never healed. Social workers must be prepared to acknowledge and confront the historical trauma and grief experienced by Native people if they are to successfully assist contemporary Native families. (p. 67)

Weaver and White's injunction was brought home to me personally when I met with a group of Native leaders, homemakers, counselors, friendship center workers, and clients to conduct a group key informant interview in preparation for my child welfare research project in British Columbia, Canada, reported in this book. In the early part of the meeting, I listened to stories of recent abuses experienced by Native families and communities as, one by one, participants shared with great anger and frustration their experiences with child welfare services. As I attempted to listen and understand, without defensiveness, their stories moderated and began to reflect the anguish that seemed to lie just beneath the surface of their anger. Although I was in the role of researcher attempting to enlist their aid in designing and implementing my study, many of the practice principles for effective cross-cultural social work proved important.

Weaver and White (1997) point out that a "deep respect for people is a basic value for even many non-traditional Native people and Native children. In particular, a strong respect for elders is common among Native people" (p. 69). They explain that sharing and giving are highly valued, and that even families in poverty will express generosity through "giveaways" that earn respect. This culturally appropriate behavior can create problems if the social worker does not understand its meaning and importance. Resources expected to last for a period of weeks may be gone within a day or two because they have been shared with other relatives. From the point of view of many Native people, it is inconceivable not to share resources with needy family members. However, from the point of view of the social worker, limited resources designated for a nuclear family in need might be squandered on people who may not deserve them and, in any event, were not part of the case plan (p. 70).

Weaver and White (1997) point to the importance of humor, which Native people often use to teach norms and values, as well as the Native sense of connection to land and the environment. Time is measured "in terms of natural phenomena, not the movements of a clock" (p. 70). Additional strong Native values include privacy, the primacy of the group over the individual, decision by consensus, cooperation, and decentralization of power.

These researchers also illustrate differences between Native family structure and the dominant culture's extended and nuclear family models. They point out that the Lakota Indian word for family, *tiospaye*, includes a variety of people. In the dominant culture, this grouping of people would be called an "extended" family, whereas in most Indian cultures the word simply refers to "family." In the dominant society, a common question when meeting someone for the first time might be "What do you do?" while among Native people it might be "Who are your relations?" (Weaver & White, 1997, p. 72). The Native community also emphasizes the importance and influence of tribal elders and grandparents.

Weaver and White (1997) offer specific suggestions for practice interventions to provide culturally competent services to Native people:

- Seek the sanction and support of people in gatekeeping roles.
- Include Native people in a variety of supportive roles.
- Maintain a positive, objective approach to each Native American family assessment.
- Advocacy around the issues of tribal sovereignty and treaty rights by the client should not be considered a threat to the service plan for the family.
- Members of tribes/nations may be able to get services or funding for services through their nations. (pp. 77–78)

## Working with Canadian Indians

Much of the discussion of the American Indian culture can also be applied to Canadian Indians. In fact, some of the tribes and nations extend across the border, with the Indian identity viewed as primary. In the Canadian Indian community of western Canada, I found similar extensions of support that started with the family and included extended family members, neighbors, and the leadership of the band. My own child welfare research (Shulman, 1991) indicates that workers whom Native clients perceived as understanding and respectful of the Native Canadian culture were more effective in establishing strong working relationships and influencing positive outcomes for the children involved. On a macro level, those regional offices of the province-wide child welfare agency that involved and worked cooperatively with the band leadership, Native Canadian friendship workers, homemakers, or court workers, and who involved this Native Canadian social support system in deliberations on how to help the family, had a better record than others of maintaining children in their own homes, finding kinship placements in the Native Canadian community, or being able to return children to their own families.

## Issues in Cross-Racial Practice

Proctor and Davis (1994) address their perception of the reasons for "the sustainment of race as a salient issue for practice" (p. 314) and the roots of the lack of understanding in cross-racial practice. They suggest that the higher growth rates of populations of color (compared with White populations), the fact that non-Whites continue to be segregated from Whites and the mainstream of America, and the negative connotation associated with race issues "leave both groups uncomfortable discussing race" (p. 315). They continue:

> The combination of these social forces may be quite ominous for personal and professional cross-racial interactions. Although economic problems are likely to increase the numbers of minority group members who need social work services, the white professionals who will be asked to help them may have little prior contact with these groups and hence little substantive knowledge of them. At the same time, minorities are apt to be increasingly distrustful of representatives from "the system." As a worst-case scenario, society may confront increasing numbers of minority clients who must be helped by white practitioners who understand too little about them and for whom their clients have too little trust. (p. 315)

The authors state that one of the questions on the mind of a minority client when dealing with a majority worker (actually, on the minds of all clients) is whether the helper is a person of goodwill. This is the equivalent of the "Who is this worker, and what kind of person will she or he be?" questions I posed in previous chapters. Proctor and Davis (1994) explain that "respect and professional courtesy are particularly important with minority clients, to whom society frequently gives less" (p. 317). They suggest how to show that respect, as follows:

> Signals of respect and goodwill may be conveyed in several ways. Social workers are advised to extend a warm greeting to the clients, to move physical barriers that inhibit communication out of the client's way, and to address the client by his or her last name. The client should be given an opportunity to get settled before the worker begins to talk. Privacy should be maximized, and the worker

should appear unhurried with the client and refer to the shortage of time only in the final minutes of the session. (p. 317)

If you are thinking that these are good principles to apply to practice with all clients, you are right. However, social workers must also understand the differential perceptions based on race, culture, ethnicity, and so forth that the client may bring to an experience. The ease with which majority workers can miss these crucial differences was clarified in a workshop I led for county child welfare investigators in Florida. An African American worker described his experience of making an investigation call to an upper-middle-class, White family who lived in a gated, almost all-White community. He further described his feelings as the guard at the community entrance gate scrutinized his identification card and seemed reluctant to admit him to the property. His White, female colleague, who was sitting next to him at the workshop, said, "But they wanted to see my ID as well." I pointed out that I suspected the first worker experienced the examination differently because he was Black. He agreed, adding, "I always wear a suit, even on dress-down day, because I know I will need to be wearing one to be treated seriously if I get a call from that community."

Davis and Proctor (1989) offer specific suggestions to manage early treatment interaction in which race is a salient factor:

First, racial difference and its potential salience should be acknowledged. Acknowledgment, by the worker, of worker-client dissimilarity will convey to the client the worker's sensitivity and awareness of the potential significance of race to the helping relationship. It will also convey to the client that the worker probably has the ability to handle the client's feelings regarding race. It is probably best to introduce this topic by asking if the client has racial concerns and issues, rather than problems. Obviously the most likely answer to the question, "Do you have problems with my race?" is "No"! Thus we suggest a question such as, "How do you think my being white and your being nonwhite might affect our working together?" Or the practitioner might ask, "If during the course of our meetings you have concerns or issues pertaining to race, please feel free to discuss them." If the client hastens to assure the worker that race is not an issue, the worker can reply, "I don't think it will be a barrier either. But if at any time you feel that I don't understand something you say or mean because our backgrounds are different, I hope you will feel free to tell me. I want to help and I will work hard at understanding you and your situation." (pp. 120–121)

These types of comments, when used in appropriate situations, convey openness to the client and sensitivity to the impact of the difference. Variations on this theme can apply to early sessions in which the differences involve gender, sexual orientation, age, religion, physical or mental ability, or any other factor that could create a barrier if not addressed.

## Education and Training for Culturally Sensitive Practice

Today, the social work education field and agency training programs grant increased attention to cultural sensitivity. There are many obstacles to culturally sensitive training, such as the structure and organization of the school (e.g., the absence or underrepresentation of Black faculty and students; Hardy & Laszloffy, 1992), but strategies for teaching clinical practice with specialized populations are emerging (e.g., working with Asian and Pacific Island elders; Richards, Browne, & Broderick, 1994). Proposals have been advanced for using ethnographic research methods that encourage practitioners to become sensitive observers of cultures and to learn how to form assessments within culturally relevant frameworks (Thornton & Garrett, 1995).

For many students and practitioners, peers can enrich the common learning process by sharing their experiences in life and practice. Unfortunately, in our society it is difficult to hold conversations that allow for honest self-reflection on attitudes, values, and stereotypes in areas such as race, gender, sexual orientation, and ethnicity. Supervisors or teachers must create an atmosphere in the class or work group that allows for such discourse while maintaining mutual respect and openness.

I once worked with an African American colleague to create videotapes that would demonstrate this process for faculty and students (Clay & Shulman, 1993). The key element in setting the stage for a frank and constructive conversation was a preliminary exercise that asked participants to identify factors that made this kind of conversation hard. Participants were also asked about conditions that might make the effort easier. As the discussion on the process of talking about taboo subjects began, the social work students found themselves actually talking about taboo subjects. It was also important for the two faculty members to disclose their own struggles with these issues through the presentation of brief examples.

Issues of inter- and intracultural practice and culturally sensitive practice will emerge throughout the remainder of the book as they relate to other phases in the social work process as well as working with clients other than individuals. Clearly, these issues and others speak of the many challenges that workers must face in first sessions with a client.

# Ethical and Legal Considerations in the Beginning Phase

**EP 2.1.1d**

Chapter 1 introduced the general topic of the impact of values, ethics, legislation, and the social work Code of Ethics on practice. Ethical problems and ethical dilemmas were also discussed, as were methods by which agencies could provide support for social workers in considering ethical choices and managing risks. In this chapter we return to this content, this time focusing on the issues related to the beginning phase of practice, informed consent and confidentiality.

## Informed Consent

The requirement that the client provide informed consent to services offers an example of how legislation and the resulting codes of ethical practice influence a social worker's obligations particularly in the beginning or contracting phase of practice. (Other examples such as the duty to warn are addressed in later chapters.) Informed consent is the client's granting of permission to the social worker and agency or other professional person to use specific intervention procedures, including diagnosis, treatment, follow-up, and research. This permission must be based on full disclosure of the facts needed to make the decision intelligently. Informed consent must be based on knowledge of the risks and alternatives (Barker, 2003, p. 114). Further guidance is available from the NASW's Code of Ethics:

> Social workers should provide services to clients only in the context of a professional relationship based, when appropriate, on valid informed consent. Social workers should use clear and understandable language to inform clients of the purposes of the services, risks related to the services, limits to services

because of the requirements of a third-party payer, relevant costs, reasonable alternatives, clients' right to refuse or withdraw consent, and the time frame covered by the consent. Social workers should provide clients with the opportunity to ask questions. (NASW, 1997, p. 2, Section 1.03a)

Generally, true informed consent contains the following five elements:

- The worker makes full disclosure of the nature and purposes of the service, including associated potential benefits and risks. The availability of alternatives must be explored.
- The client demonstrates an understanding of the information offered in the disclosure.
- The client must be competent to provide informed consent.
- The client's consent must be voluntary, with no coercion.
- The decision must be explicit and involve either consent to or refusal of services.

Although the guidelines for informed consent seem clear, one study (Lidz, 1984) identified several practical problems observed in an analysis of how informed consent actually works. For example, the study pointed out that the person responsible for obtaining informed consent was not always clearly identified. Informed consent was, in some cases, a "floating" responsibility. In addition, clients reported that family members often pressured them to act in a specific manner. Was consent under these circumstances really voluntary? Workers were not always trained to educate clients. A worker's perception of the client's intelligence and ability appeared to influence the disclosure process. Informed consent was often obtained after the caregiver had made an assessment and decision in favor of a specific intervention. Were other alternatives really considered? The authors also observed that a client's understanding appeared to occur over time rather than immediately. True informed consent might require revisiting the consent issue periodically as the client's understanding grows. The authors argue that it is important to review the informed consent procedures in every setting and to actively promote strategies to ensure that informed consent is real rather than illusionary.

## Confidentiality and Privileged Communications

Another ethical and legal area that needs to be considered and addressed in the beginning phase is confidentiality is the right of a client not to have private information shared with third parties. To see the influence of legislation on practice, let us examine how confidentiality and the client's right to privacy can be protected or limited. Since this area of law is usually determined by state legislatures, I will use the Commonwealth of Massachusetts as an example. (The laws may differ in other states, and federal legislation in this area will be discussed later in this section.)

*State Regulations* The Commonwealth of Massachusetts passed an act regulating social work practice a number of years ago. A state licensing board was established to administer its provisions. Legislation amending that act in 1989 was designed to further protect communications between social workers and clients. These communications are held to be privileged, so that the social worker cannot disclose them without the client's permission, even in the course of legal proceedings. Social worker–client privileged communications are thus in a similar category to the privileges associated with doctor-patient or lawyer-client communications, although the exceptions differ. The client's or patient's right to privileged communications strengthens the confidential nature of the professional relationship. When the client's right to privacy is protected, the client will tend to share private information more freely.

The statutory exceptions to privileged communications in Massachusetts arise in the following circumstances:

- A child custody and/or adoption suit
- When the client introduces her or his mental health as an issue in a court
- When it is necessary to commit a client to a hospital in the event of danger to the client or someone else
- When a social worker is conducting a court-ordered evaluation
- In a malpractice action brought by the client against the social worker
- After the death of the client
- In the case of a child abuse investigation or certain other state investigations

Exceptions are also found in other state regulations. For example, professionals are required to report suspicions of child and elder abuse or neglect. Although there are still gray areas in which professional judgment will come into play, regulations such as these provide helpful guidelines to workers and clients. For example, limits of confidentiality may be spelled out in the first interview with a client.

In any case, social workers must be aware of the rights and obligations that flow from legislation and case law. Consider the example of a social worker who is approached by a police investigator requesting information about the worker's client. The protections of confidentiality, and in some instances, privileged communications, mean the worker cannot be forced to disclose any information unless a clear exception exists or the client expressly consents. A social worker needs to be prepared to respond, for example, by stating, "I am not saying Mr. X is or is not my client; however, if he were my client, my communications with him would be confidential and protected, and I would not be able to share them with you."

*Federal Legislation and Court Decisions* Until the 1996 U.S. Supreme Court decision in *Jaffee v. Redmond* clarified the matter, the federal court system had held different views on whether communications between a social worker and a client were privileged. Although communications with psychotherapists were privileged in all 50 states and the District of Columbia, the inclusion of clinical social workers remained in question. Alexander (1997) points out that, in its 1996 decision, the Supreme Court recognized the "absoluteness of social workers' right to privileged communications; social workers can no longer be compelled to disclose confidential information in civil lawsuits filed in federal court" (p. 388). For example, if a licensed social worker is treating a child protective services worker by providing counseling to assist in overcoming grief related to the death of a child on a caseload, the social worker cannot be compelled to testify in federal court.

Alexander (1997) also points out that the absoluteness of privileged immunity does not carry over to nonfederal cases in state court systems. He describes one difficult situation in which a criminal defendant may request access to a sexual assault victim's records. Based on *Jaffee v. Redmond,* the privilege is absolute in a case that occurs on federal property and is tried in a federal court. In most states, however, if the defense meets certain standards, such as demonstrating the relevance of the information to the defense, the trial judge will review the records and decide whether any information should be disclosed. Alexander emphasizes the importance of keeping these distinctions clear:

> On the whole, *Jaffee v. Redmond* recognizes and elevates the prestige of social work. The U.S. Supreme Court spoke positively of clinical social workers and stated that social workers are entitled to the same consideration in counseling that is given to psychologists and psychiatrists. However, social workers should keep in mind that *Jaffee* involves federal issues, and state laws do not provide absolute confidentiality to psychotherapists and differ in their exceptions for privileged communication. Thus, social work agencies should provide in-service training on the conditions of privileged communications in their states. (p. 390)

As pointed out by Alexander (1997), this absoluteness of privileged communications in federal cases can raise significant moral dilemmas for the social worker (p. 390). As recognized by the Court of Appeals and the Supreme Court in *Jaffee v. Redmond* (1996), the privilege is qualified and may not apply if "in the interest of justice, the evidentiary need for the disclosure of the contents of a patient's counseling sessions outweighs that patient's privacy interest." The Supreme Court itself, in a significant footnote to the *Jaffee* case, stated the following:

> Although it would be premature to speculate about most future developments in the federal psychotherapist privilege, we do not doubt that there are situations in which the privilege must give way, for example, if a serious threat of harm to the patient or to others can be averted only by means of a disclosure by the therapists.

***Health Insurance Patient Protection Act (HIPPA)***  The passage of the federal Health Insurance Patient Protection Act (HIPPA) in 2002 has further clarified and set limits on the ability of a social worker or other health professional to share confidential information and with whom such information can be shared. You have likely experienced these changes when visiting a doctor's office since the passage of this act. Patients now receive a description of their rights under HIPPA and must sign a release form that specifies what information can be released and to whom.

One immediate implication for students in social work programs is that case information presented in class or in papers needs to have all identifying information removed. That is, any information that would allow someone to know the identity of the person needs to be changed or eliminated. This includes obvious things like names and birth dates but may also include other information that is so unique to the person that it will allow for identification (e.g., diagnosis, race/ethnicity, or gender). If diagnosis, race/ethnicity, or gender is directly related to the case presentation, students can include it if they are confident it will not allow for identification.

● - - - - - - - - - - - - - - - - - - - - - - -

## Chapter Summary

All new relationships, particularly those with people in authority, begin somewhat tentatively. Clients perceive workers as symbols of authority with power to influence their lives. Clients often bring with them a fund of past experiences with professionals, or stereotypes of helping professionals passed on by friends or family. Thus, the first sessions are partly efforts to explore the realities of the situation.

A structure is needed to free the client to accept the offer of help. The crucial skills involved in the beginning phase of practice include clarifying the purpose of the interview, clarifying the worker's role, reaching for the client's feedback, and exploring issues of authority. Contracting is never completed in the first session; it is an ongoing process, and the common ground between the client's felt needs and the agency's services will evolve and change over time. With regard to resistant and mandated clients, it is important that the worker bring up the obstacles that may block the client's ability to accept help. Mutual expectations need to be defined and are part of the contracting process.

Social workers must also take into account how the diversity of client populations affects practice. Models of practice need to be adapted to ethnically sensitive variations introduced by knowledgeable and responsive social workers. Awareness of the issues raised in intercultural practice, such as the White worker with the Black client, is essential to developing strong working relationships. Workers also have to be aware of the potential for "microaggressions" in which seemingly small and subtle slights can have a powerful impact on the working relationship.

Finally, informed consent and confidentiality were discussed in terms of ethical and legal requirements in the beginning or contracting phase of practice.

---

## Related Online Content and Activities

 Visit *The Skills of Helping Individuals, Families, Groups, and Communities*, Seventh Edition, CourseMate website at **www.cengagebrain.com** for learning tools such as glossary terms, links to related websites, and chapter practice quizzes. The website for this chapter also features additional notes from the author.

---

## Competency Notes

The following is a list of Council on Social Work Education (CSWE) recommended competencies and practice behaviors for social work students defined in Educational Policy and Accreditation Standard (EPAS) and addressed in this chapter.

**EP 2.1.1a** Identify as a Professional Social Worker and Conduct Oneself Accordingly (p. xx)

**EP 2.1.1b** Attend to professional roles and boundaries (p. 102)

**EP 2.1.1d** Demonstrate professional demeanor in behavior, appearance, and communication (p. 140)

**EP 2.1.2a** Recognize and manage personal values in a way that allows professional values to guide practice (p. 116)

**EP 2.1.2b** Make ethical decisions by applying standards of the National Association of Social Workers Code of Ethics and, as applicable, of the International Federation of Social Workers/International Association of Schools of Social Work Ethics in Social Work, Statement of Principles (p. xx)

**EP 2.1.2c** Tolerate ambiguity in resolving ethical conflicts (p. xx)

**EP 2.1.2d** Apply strategies of ethical reasoning to arrive at principled decisions (p. xx)

**EP 2.1.4a** Recognize the extent to which a culture's structures and values may oppress, marginalize, alienate, or create or enhance privilege and power (p. 129)

**EP 2.1.4b** Gain sufficient self-awareness to eliminate the influence of personal biases and values in working with diverse groups (p. 129)

**EP 2.1.4c** Recognize and communicate their understanding of the importance of difference in shaping life experiences (p. 129)

**EP 2.1.4d** View themselves as learners and engage those with whom they work as informants (p. 129)

**EP 2.1.6a** Use practice experience to inform scientific inquiry (p. 109)

**EP 2.1.6b** Use research evidence to inform practice (p. 109)

**EP 2.1.7a** Utilize conceptual frameworks to guide the process of assessment, intervention, and evaluation (p. 98)

**EP 2.1.10a** Substantively and affectively prepare for action with individuals, families, groups, organizations, and communities (p. 98)

**EP 2.1.10b** Use empathy and other interpersonal skills (p. 98)

**EP 2.1.10c** Develop a mutually agreed-on focus of work and desired outcomes (p. 98, 109)

**EP 2.1.10d** Collect, organize, and interpret client data (p. 98, 109)

**EP 2.1.10f** Develop mutually agreed-on intervention goals and objectives (p. 109)

# Skills in the
# Work Phase

I n the course of a training workshop, one participant expressed her feelings about the work phase in a manner that sums up the experiences of many helping professionals: "I'm good at the beginning phase, and I can even deal with the endings, but I'm at a loss when it comes to what happens in the middle." Following a discussion session with social workers about the problems of contracting clearly with children in a group home, one of the participants echoed this sentiment, saying, "I'm afraid that if I make a direct and clear offer to help the kids with their problems, they might take me up on it, and I would be in the middle phase. What do I do then?"

This chapter explores the answer to the question "What do I do then?" That is, what is done after tentative clarity about the working contract has been achieved in the beginning phase? Remember, the beginning phase and contracting may take place over a number of sessions. We shall examine the processes of a middle phase session by using time and the concepts from the phases of work as a background: tuning in, beginning, work, and ending and transitions.

In order to avoid any confusion, when analyzing a single session, I will refer to *stages* of the session instead of *phases.* Thus any single session can be analyzed as having a preliminary stage, a beginning stage, a middle stage, and an ending and transition stage. Simply put, we prepare for a session, we begin the session with a form of contracting, we do the work of the session in the middle stage, and we bring the session to a close by making necessary transitions to the next session or the next steps for the client.

For example, the preliminary phase and the associated skill of tuning in was referred to in Chapter 3 as a form of preparation before meeting a client (individual, family, group, or community) for the first time. In this chapter, this concept will be applied to each session or contact with a client. I will also use the modifier *sessional* before the stages or skills where appropriate; so, for example, preparation before a specific session will be termed *sessional tuning in,* and the beginning stage of each encounter will be termed *sessional contracting.* Each individual interview, family session, and group or community meeting can be analyzed using the model of the stages of work. The complex process of helping will become clearer when we examine a session against the backdrop of time.

First, however, we look at a simplified, general model of a work phase interview. Then we move on to a detailed analysis of each segment of a typical interview. Specific skills are identified and illustrated using examples from a variety of practice situations. Findings from research projects are discussed where relevant. Later chapters will return to the model in relation to family, group, and community work as well.

## A Model of the Work Phase Interview

In Chapter 1, the idea of the phases of work—preliminary, beginning, middle, and ending/transition—was introduced as a model for understanding the dynamics of practice with clients over time. These four phases are revisited in this chapter, but this time we use them to understand each individual worker-client encounter. Every interview, family, or group session can be understood to have certain unique dynamics associated with its beginning, middle, and ending. Specific practice skills are useful in each phase of a session. Some of these general skills, such as tuning in, have been discussed in previous chapters, but we will now examine them in a more specific context.

The second decision, defined in the previous chapter, is associated with the middle phase of work. Once clients understand that emotional pain might be involved and that they may have to take some responsibility for their own part in their problems, they must decide whether they will continue the work. This decision marks the transition from the beginning to the middle phase of practice.

In earlier chapters, eight of the core skills of helping were combined into two groupings: skills to help clients manage their feelings, and skills to help clients manage their problems. Some of these skills are discussed in more detail in this chapter, and additional skills are also examined. To simplify the description of this phase, the skills of the work phase have been reorganized into general categories called *skill factors.* A skill factor consists of a set of closely related skills. The general intent of the worker who is using the skill is the element that is common to a given set of skills. For example, in this model all behaviors associated with the efforts of the worker to deal with client affect are grouped together under the title "empathic skills."

------------------------------------------------------------------------

### The Work Phase Model

1. **Preliminary (Sessional)**

    Sessional Tuning-In Skills

2. **Beginning (Sessional)**

    Sessional Contracting Skills

    Elaborating Skills

3. **Middle (Sessional)**

    Empathic Skills

    Sharing Worker's Feelings

Exploring Taboo Subjects

Making a Demand for Work

Pointing Out Obstacles

Identifying Content and Process Connections

Sharing Data

Helping the Client See Life in New Ways

4. **Ending and Transition (Sessional)**

    Sessional Ending/Transition Skills

------------------------------------------------------------------------

First, an important caution is needed. Sessions do not usually unfold in such a simple and organized manner. For example, an overwhelmed client may need a worker's empathic response at the start of the session before it is clear exactly what the client is overwhelmed about. The model simplifies the processes of a middle phase session for clarification purposes only while recognizing it doesn't always work this way in reality.

Table 5.1 lists the skill factors included in this middle phase model.

## Work Phase Summary

**EP 2.1.3b**
**EP 2.1.3c**
**EP 2.1.7b**
**EP 2.1.10a**
**EP 2.1.10b**
**EP 2.1.10c**
**EP 2.1.10d**
**EP 2.1.10e**
**EP 2.1.10f**
**EP 2.1.10i**
**EP 2.1.10l**

This first section summarizes the work phase model. The sections that follow elaborate and illustrate each skill factor included in the model.

### Preliminary Phase (Sessional)

In the preliminary stage, the worker attempts to sensitize herself or himself, before each session, to themes that could emerge during the work. A review of the previous session, information passed on by the client or others, or the identification of subtle patterns emerging in the work can alert the worker to the client's potential current concerns. The worker also develops some preliminary strategies for responding directly to indirect cues. This involves the use of the skill described earlier as *putting the client's feelings into words*.

### Beginning Phase (Sessional)

In the beginning stage of each session, the central task of the worker is to find out what the client is concerned about or working on at the moment. Sessional contracting skills are used to clarify the immediate work at hand. In some cases, the worker may bring up issues that need to be addressed, and these will then be included in the contracting discussion. Because clients often use indirect communication to indicate their concerns, workers must take care to determine the client's agenda before moving quickly into the work. Elaborating skills are also important in this phase to help the client tell his or her story. A common mistake is for the worker to answer the client's question before the worker really knows what the question is.

## Middle Phase (Sessional)

When the sessional contract has been tentatively identified, the process shifts into the middle or work stage of the session. A priority in this stage is the worker's use of empathy to help the client share the affective part of the message. The worker must also be ready to share the worker's feelings as spontaneously as possible. Because many concerns touch on taboo areas, the worker must be ready to help clients overcome social norms that often block free discussion and to explore taboo feelings.

As the work progresses, it is not unusual to encounter some resistance from the client, who is often of two minds about proceeding. One part of the person is always reaching out for growth and change, but another part is pulling back and holding on to what is comfortable and known. This ambivalence often emerges just as the work in the session starts to go well. It can be seen in evasive reactions (e.g., jumping from one concern to another), defensiveness, expressions of hopelessness, or other forms.

The worker needs to realize that resistance is a normal part of the work. Workers often assume that client resistance is a sign that the workers have done something wrong. Ironically, just the opposite is often true. Lack of resistance may mean that the worker has not pushed hard enough; resistance is often a sign that the worker is doing something right. If we think of resistant behavior as the client's way of communicating that there is a difficult area to face, hard emotions to experience, a problem with taking responsibility for behavior, and so forth, the worker will welcome resistance rather than fearing it. This is easier to do with some experience and very difficult for the beginning student or worker.

It's almost as if the client is saying: "Look here, social worker. We are getting close to a tough area and I need your help to explore what makes it tough." In the framework presented in this book, a premium is placed on exploring client resistance, or the ability of the worker to identify and discuss this resistance with the client, which includes making a demand for work that can help the client prepare to take the important next steps. Some other practice models suggest "rolling with," "circumventing," or simply "avoiding" areas that create resistance. I disagree. Although I agree that timing is important—for example, respecting resistance in the early phase of work before a solid working relationship is established—I believe it is a mistake to avoid it in the work or middle phase of practice. Such avoidance can lead to the illusion of work, in which the client says what he or she thinks the worker wants to hear. It also means that the issues, concerns, and feelings signaled by the resistance remain unexpressed, unexplored, and unresolved.

As the work phase proceeds, obstacles may emerge that frustrate the client's efforts on his or her own behalf. For example, the flow of feeling between the client and the worker may itself become an obstacle. As the worker makes demands for work, the client may react to the worker, and this reaction in turn will affect the working relationship. Workers and clients must pay attention to such obstacles as they emerge. Because the worker-client relationship resembles the client's other relationships, discussion of such obstacles can contribute to the client's understanding of his or her larger concerns. These obstacles are usually brought to light when the worker notices patterns in the work.

Another skill grouping is called *identifying process and content connections*. The central idea underlying this category of skills is that the process, or way of interacting between the worker and the client, often offers clues about the content of the work. In effect, the client may (consciously or not) use the working relationship as a medium to raise and work on issues that are central to the substantive issues under discussion. For example, a client working on developing independence of thought and action may demonstrate extreme dependence on the worker. It is as if the client were saying, "Do you want to see what my problem around dependence and independence is all about? Watch me!"

***African American High School Student Suspended from School*** In another example, an African American high school student suspended from school for violence was confrontational with a White social worker during a group session at the Vision-Integrity-Structure-Accountability (VISA) Center we established at the University at Buffalo. When the worker skillfully addressed the just-below-the-surface and taboo intercultural issue that had emerged between the Black teenager from the inner city and the White worker from the suburbs, it was a major step in strengthening the working relationship. With an understanding of the connection between process and content, the discussion quickly moved to the conflicts between this student and his White teachers and administrators, who he experienced as racist. Thus, process and content were integrated.

Take a moment to consider this important concept. The often-raised false dichotomy between process (the way of working) and content (what the work is about) is resolved as we realize that the interaction between the client and the social worker actually models the central but taboo issue the client must deal with. By addressing the process the worker actually helps the client get into the content. One more false dichotomy bites the dust! More will fall as we continue the discussion.

Two worker skills are associated with identifying content and process connections: (1) identifying these connections, and (2) pointing them out to the client. Clients who are aware of the way in which they use process to deal with content may be able to learn from that awareness and take control of their interactions with others. For example, recognition of the meaning of the dependency on the worker may free a client to become more independent in the helping relationship by taking more responsibility for the work. In turn, this serves as a training medium for the client to practice new skills of independence—skills that can later be transferred to other significant relationships.

Returning to the example of the African American high school student, the discussion may help the student make a better assessment of when he actually experiences racism or when he, for many good reasons, may see it when it is not always there. It may also help him find more adaptive ways of coping with these highly charged interactions that will create fewer problems for him. He may still have to confront racist professionals, but he may be able to develop more effective strategies and interventions.

Another example was cited in Chapter 3, in which an angry mother in a mutual-aid support group for mothers with chronically ill children in a hospital attacked a new worker during the first meeting. I suggested then that the mother was actually showing the worker how she used anger to avoid dealing with her painful feelings, and how she pushed helpful people away when she most needed them. This demonstrated how addressing the process (the authority theme) directly connected to the work of the group.

Moving on to the skill of sharing data, I take the position that the client must also be allowed access to the worker's own relevant data. Contrary to some views, which require a form of neutrality on the part of the worker, I argue that worker sharing of data such as facts, opinions, and value judgments is an important part of the helping process. However, the worker needs to consider when sharing data is appropriate and how the data are shared. For example, the worker must take care to share only data that would otherwise be unavailable to the client and that are relevant to the client's work. Such data need to be shared openly and in such a way that the client is left free to accept or reject the worker's views.

Another skill grouping is called *helping the client see life in new ways*. It could also be called "reframing," "helping clients see systems people in new ways," or any of several other terms based on the idea that clients' thoughts (cognitions) contribute to their difficulties. Many of the solution-focused practice techniques described later in Chapter 17 could be included in this skill group. These skills involve helping the client to revisit cognitions—about themselves, their problems, other people, and so forth—and then examine them, with the goal of developing a more accurate picture. For example, a client with a mental illness may see himself as a failure in life. Reviewing events of his life in which he has succeeded, including those he had not conceived of as successes, may help him to change his self-image. This process can affect his feelings and behaviors, and help him to cope with current issues in his life. A person in relapse from substance abuse recovery may be able to identify times in his or her life when sobriety was maintained for a longer period, so that the client begins to understand relapse as a part of recovery as long as learning can come from it. Students returning to school after a suspension for violent behavior could be helped to consider how long they had been able to maintain positive behavior since the prior suspension and what was going on in their lives that helped them do that.

## Endings and Transitions (Sessional)

Endings and transitions of sessions present important dynamics and require the worker's attention. In addition, issues that have been raised indirectly throughout the session may emerge with some force when the client is preparing to leave (the classic "doorknob therapy" phenomenon, discussed later)—for example, the teenage female client who talks about a friend with a problem and only in the last minutes of the session reveals that she is pregnant. Finally, transitions need to be made to next sessions and future actions. Sessional ending and transition skills are used by the worker to bring a session to a close and to make the connections between a single session and future work or issues in the life of the client.

Once again, in an effort to describe this complex process in simple terms, I have had to oversimplify the central ideas. The work phase session does not proceed as neatly as I have outlined it here. Furthermore, the skill categories are not mutually exclusive. For example, as the sessional contracting proceeds, the worker will use elaborating, empathic, and demand-for-work skills. The advantage of describing this complex process in an oversimplified form is that it gives us a model with which to orient ourselves as we explore each stage and each skill factor in further detail.

**Engaging and Working with the Hard-to-Reach Client**

Use the accompanying DVD or visit *The Skills of Helping Individuals, Families, Groups, and Communities*, Seventh Edition, CourseMate website at www.cengagebrain.com and enter your personal access code to watch this video

**THE MIDDLE OR WORK PHASE OF PRACTICE** The author presents each of the elements for the framework of analyzing a work phase session, with illustrations drawn from practice.

# Sessional Tuning-In Skills

All the principles of tuning in described in Chapter 3 apply equally to each encounter with the client. This process involves efforts by workers to sensitize themselves to potential concerns and feelings that may emerge during the session. The worker must also tune in to her or his own feelings about the encounter. This is a time when workers can draw on personal memories, the literature on human behavior, or input from clients or colleagues and supervisors to deepen understanding of the client's struggle and, especially, of the symbiotic connection between the client and the people and systems that matter. Each of these types of preparatory work, or sessional tuning-in skills, is now explored.

## Tuning In to the Client's Sense of Urgency

Because of the client's ambivalence or lack of conscious awareness of concerns, client communications are often indirect. For example, a client may begin a conversation by describing "how great the weekend was compared with the week before." The client may continue to describe in positive tones the details of the "great" weekend.

*Opening with the Opposite Feelings* In the midst of all of these words is the phrase "compared with the week before." This comment is a red flag for the worker who is really listening—a signal to the worker of the real work of the session. The client may be ambivalent about raising painful feelings and unsure that the worker really wants to hear them. Thus, the client has opened the session by expressing emotions that are the opposite of what he or she feels underneath. The client waits to see if the worker will notice the first offering—the initial hint of a concern—and respond to it in a direct fashion. The worker significantly increases the chances of catching the crucial issue early in the work by being prepared to "hear" it. For example, in this case, the worker might be aware of events in the client's life that have taken place between sessions and that may affect the client's sense of urgency.

*Client Just Diagnosed as HIV Positive* In another example, a worker was preparing for a conversation with an ongoing client who was being seen because of an HIV-positive diagnosis, a signal of the possible onset of AIDS. The client had called the worker for an appointment and informed the worker that his doctor had indicated that he had developed ARC (AIDS-related complex), a set of mild symptoms that indicates the next step in the progression to full-scale AIDS. The worker in this case attempted to tune in, once again, to the shock, pain, and fear associated with this change in diagnosis. First, however, the worker needed to tune in to his own feelings about another of his clients becoming progressively sicker and, even with the new drug treatments, possibly facing death. This triggered many feelings about other clients and friends who had already died. The worker found it helpful to share some of his own distress with a colleague prior to the session.

*Residential Treatment and the Missed Parent Visit* In another illustration, a social worker in a residential institution might be informed by child-care staff of an incident in the house that had been difficult for a resident, or told that the resident's parent had not shown up for a visit on the weekend. The worker would prepare by tuning in to the sense of rejection and hurt that the client might be feeling. The worker would also anticipate from past experiences in general, or observed patterns with this resident in particular, some of the indirect ways in which the feelings might be raised. For example, a pattern of "flight or fight" when a person faces pain is not unusual. Various residents might demonstrate "flight" from the pain through hyperactivity, passivity, and withdrawal, or the use of drugs or alcohol. Others might respond with "fight" by provoking a confrontation with peers, child-care workers, or even the social worker. It's easier to deal with the anger against the parent by acting it out against the worker.

***Residential Treatment and the Death of a Parent*** In another example from a residential setting, a worker was told that a teenager had just heard about the death of his father and that he had to leave the residence the next day to return home for the funeral. The youngster appeared to take the news badly but handled it by withdrawing. The worker tuned in to the effect this had on the resident. He did this by getting in touch with his own feelings about the death of a close relative. He thought of the mixed feelings that must exist—wanting to be alone and not talk about the hurt but desperately wanting to share the feelings with another person. He thought about the boy's need to cry, despite the societal injunction that crying is supposedly not "manly." He worked hard to be in touch with his own sense of sadness so that he would not run from the sadness of this youngster.

He guessed that the cues would be indirect. In this case, the youngster was hanging around in the lounge, looking sad but not saying anything. As such, the worker prepared to reach for the feelings and make an offer to talk while still respecting the boy's right to be left alone. Even if the boy did not respond immediately, or at all, at least he would know the worker cared. At an appropriate time, the worker made his offer:

> I heard about your father's death, and I wanted you to know how sorry I am. I think I can understand how much it must hurt. If you want to talk with me about it, or just spend some time together this evening, I'd be glad to. If you just feel like being alone for a while, I'd understand that as well.

In this case, the youngster said he wanted to be left alone. He had heard the message, however, and at bedtime—when the worker stopped by to say goodnight—he began to cry. The worker sat for a while, sharing some of the hurt and then listening as the boy spoke of his father. (Residential workers on the night shift often report that bedtime, when children feel most vulnerable, is the time they will raise the painful issues.)

When an incident is traumatic, the worker can strategize to reach for it directly during the sessional contracting stage. If other, less urgent themes arise, the worker can be alert to their potential emergence. However, clients have a life between meetings and new issues may have emerged since the last session. In most situations, not all, when the session starts, the worker will clear all these potential themes from her or his mind and listen to and watch the client. Tuning in is tentative, and the worker must be open to the possible emergence of feelings, issues, and responses that are completely different from those that emerge from the tuning-in process. Sessional tuning in may help the worker hear and correctly interpret the indirect communications. It is not unusual, when closely examined, that you can find hints of the issues raised at the doorknob in the opening stage of the session.

## Tuning In to the Worker's Own Feelings

EP 2.1.1b
EP 2.1.1e
EP 2.1.1f

The worker's feelings can either facilitate or block the work to be done. For example, when thinking about an interview, a worker may believe that she or he has "blown it" by not listening to the client, by attempting to impose an agenda, or by preaching to the client. The worker can easily tune in to the client's frustration and anger, then plan to begin again by apologizing and pointing out how the worker had "missed" the client, and inviting the client to discuss his or her reactions.

It is important in this case for the worker to tune in to his or her own feelings about receiving negative feedback. Reaching for negative feedback is one of the hardest skills for inexperienced workers to develop. Students will often say: "I sensed he was unhappy with me but I didn't reach for it because I was afraid he might tell me he was." How will it feel if the client accepts the invitation and provides negative feedback? If the worker can get in touch with his or her own feelings of doubt, insecurity about the work, and possible panic if the client were to get angry, that worker will have a better chance of avoiding defensiveness. This can then be the start of a new idea about what makes a professional.

Specifically, instead of believing that a professional is always right and never makes mistakes—as is often portrayed in the practice literature—the worker can begin to become more comfortable with the notion of a professional as someone who can own up to mistakes. The worker's honesty and lack of defensiveness provide a model for the client to develop the same ability. For example, working with a defensive father the worker can model how not to be defensive about mistakes (the process) and then help the client see the application to his own defensiveness with his children (the content).

***Recent Immigrant Clients Who Lie to or Try to Bribe the Worker*** Another illustration might be an interview wherein the helping person anticipates having to set limits or carry out the part of the helping function that involves control over the client's access to resources. For example, a social worker in an agency that works with recent immigrants from Eastern European countries may find out that a client has lied about available family resources to obtain certain benefits from the agency. If the worker has developed a good relationship with the client, the worker will likely feel hurt and disappointed by the client's actions. The worker may grow angry and wonder if the client has "conned" him or her all along.

Client behavior often serves as an indirect signal of an important work issue, as a sign of some difficulty in the helping relationship, or as a way of testing limits. In this example, the deceptive behavior was related to the client's perceptions of how to deal with authority—views that had been firmly developed while the client was living under an oppressive, Eastern European government. Social workers were seen as agents of the government who had significant power to control the client's life. The client was also extremely anxious about protecting whatever family resources he had been able to bring with him from his former country. Once the behavior had been confronted, the social worker could both set limits on the client in terms of the benefits and use the incident as a way to help the client develop a new perspective on the role of social agencies and government—an important shift in thinking required for successful adaptation to the client's new country.

I remember a group of workers in an immigrant assistance agency who described, with good humor, their first reactions when they began to work with some Russian immigrants who offered bribes during the first interviews. They were shocked at first, until they began to understand that this was the only way one received services in the country the clients had just left. Rather than responding with anger, the social workers could use such incidents to help the immigrants with their transition.

Helping professionals are just as vulnerable as clients and often refuse to take risks because of their fear of being emotionally taken for a ride. If the social workers in these examples can get in touch with their feelings, they stand a better chance of using the incident as a critical turning point in the relationship rather than feeling that it signals an end to the work.

The line of argument pursued here is that, like the client, the worker is a human being with a special function and skills to put that function into action. The worker's feelings can affect actions as profoundly as the client's feelings can. For example, a child welfare worker who has developed a beginning relationship with a mother will often dread the interview following a neighbor's report of neglect of her child. As one worker put it, "I feel like a rat. I have encouraged this woman to open up to me, to share her feelings, and now I may have to take her kid away." At a time in the work when the most help is needed, this feeling can lead workers to harden themselves, put up a front, and cut themselves off from the very feelings they need in order to be helpful.

---

**Engaging and Working with the Hard-to-Reach Client**

Use the accompanying DVD or visit *The Skills of Helping Individuals, Families, Groups, and Communities,* Seventh Edition, CourseMate website at www.cengagebrain.com and enter your personal access code to watch this video

**MIDDLE PHASE WORK WITH A 15-YEAR-OLD SURVIVOR OF SEXUAL ABUSE** This excerpt demonstrates the difficulty involved in helping a client discuss a taboo area such as sexual abuse.

---

## Tuning In to the Meaning of the Client's Struggle

As patterns emerge in work with a client, the worker must often step back and attempt to understand the client's struggles in a new way. A single incident may have one meaning, while a pattern of client responses to issues, conflicts, stresses, anxiety, and so on may mean something else.

*A Father in Conflict with a 17-Year-Old Son's Efforts to Break Away: Searching Out the Common Ground* For example, consider the worker meeting with a father who is attempting to deal with his 17-year-old son's efforts to break away. The battle is a classic one, but the worker must consider what the special meaning of the struggle might be for this father. Understanding the stage of life development that the father may be going through can be helpful in getting at the unique qualities of this particular father-son engagement. The literature on midlife crisis tells us something of the struggle people face in their late thirties to work on their own sense of differentiation as individuals within their marriage. The father may be seeing signs of rebellion in his son that mirror feelings in himself that he is still trying to deal with.

The worker who sensitizes himself or herself to the father's potential conflict will be better able to hear this theme if it emerges in discussion. Helping the father face his own crisis may be the best way to help him understand and deal with his son's experience. The worker's understanding can be gained through life experience, work experience, professional literature, supervision, from other clients and fiction. In many ways, the work experience is an education about life, and the worker is an eager learner. Each client will teach the worker something new. If the worker is listening and feeling, every encounter with a client will result in some change in the worker. In fact, if the worker has not been moved or educated in some way, something is probably wrong with the worker's approach.

One particularly important aspect of the tuning-in process in the interactional practice approach is the worker's ability to find the threads of common ground when obstacles frustrate both parties. In developing his practice approach, Schwartz (1961) described *method* as the means by which the worker implements the helping function. He then identified five general tasks of the worker that constitute social work method. The first of these is "the task of searching out the common ground between the client's perception of his own need and the aspect of social demand with which he is faced" (p. 17). The worker can carry out this task in many and various ways; in our current example, the connection between the father and the son would need to be explored.

I have already pointed out one possible connection: The son's struggle may not be so different from that of the father. Let us explore others. For example, as a young man pursues independence, some part of him will also want to hold on to the security of home and the people who care about him. The connection between the son's need for security as he moves into adulthood and the father's concern about his son's budding independence may be only partial and thus difficult for the father or the son to perceive, but present nevertheless.

On the other side of the coin are the father's hopes and aspirations for his son's growth into adulthood. What connections exist between these aspirations and the son's effort to find some form of independence? Clearly, these connections are subtle and can easily be lost by both parties as they become overwhelmed by the obstacles related to their ambivalent feelings. This is why the worker must tune in to the common ground to be sensitive to it when it emerges. Beneath any anger and recriminations of the father and son is a fund of feelings for each other that needs to be identified and nurtured. It will not make the son's struggle for independence or the father's struggle to let go easy—both are always difficult. It may, however, allow the parties to hang on to what matters most between them.

## Tuning In and the Worker's Realities of Time and Stress

Workers often say to me, "It sounds great, but who has the time?" Allowing time to prepare for a session is often prevented by large caseloads or the speed with which events happen. In fact, many social workers, particularly those in the public services, face overwhelming caseloads. More recently, workers talk of "compliance pressures," usually in the child welfare field, where they are required to comply with a number of visits to clients per month or a 24-hour response time to an abuse complaint. They describe scrambling to make foster care visits, for example, when the situation does not really warrant this close supervision. Usually it is public pressure, a newspaper article, or political pressure, as a result of a traumatic case or a judicial ruling, that results in the compliance pressure. In developing the Interactional Social Work Practice Theory research design (Shulman, 1991), I included variables that measured the worker's job stress and job manageability over a period of time (every 3 months) as elements of the final model.

***Research on Job Stress and Job Manageability*** The findings of my own associated research, in a large, public, child welfare agency, indicated that—on average—over time 84 percent of the frontline workers felt that their jobs were stressful ("strongly agree" and "agree" combined). Only 25 percent of the workers felt that their jobs were manageable (Shulman, 1991, p. 140). More recently, restrictions imposed by managed care agencies and funding requirements for those in private practice have added to these stresses. Clients in private agencies may be booked back-to-back, with workers under pressure to generate "billable hours," with very little time for either recording or tuning in.

***Tuning In in High-Stress Agencies: The Agency Hyperactivity Syndrome*** Given these realities, workers with heavy caseloads need to tune in whenever possible and to recognize the limits of their ability to provide service for all their clients. Workers will often admit that they have time to connect emotionally with some of their clients while they drive home or as they review the work of the week. In addition, many examples can be identified in which a lack of a few tuning-in moments resulted in the worker missing early cues to a problem (the client's first offering), thereby escalating the problem until it became much more difficult to deal with. For example, when cues of stress in a foster home are ignored, the amount of time required for a worker to transfer a foster child to a new setting can easily become a major contributor to job stress and unmanageability. Thus, workers get caught in a vicious cycle of reacting to crises rather than providing ongoing preventative services.

A pattern often emerges in high-stress agencies, which deal with difficult problems such as sexual abuse or terminal illness. Workers and managers engage in what I call "agency hyperactivity." The heavy demands of their jobs indeed require them to work hard. However, some element of the "busyness" appears to be a maladaptive way in which staff members run from the pain of their work. They are simply too busy to tune in. Workers who continue to connect affectively with their clients but lack their own sources of support often experience burnout, or what is now referred to as "secondary trauma." Closing off feelings is not a solution, because that can also lead to burnout.

In one of my studies, I found that the availability of support for the worker from the supervisor and/or colleagues, as well as the worker's willingness to use this support, were predictive of the worker's ability to tune in to the client (Shulman, 1991).

## Tuning In to the Worker's Own Life Experiences

**EP 2.1.1b**
**EP 2.1.1e**
**EP 2.1.1f**
**EP 2.1.2a**

In my view, a worker's capacity for empathy expands with use. This exciting part of the worker's growth comes from engagement with clients. Within limits, the worker gradually can feel more often, more accurately, and more deeply what the clients are experiencing. Life and work experiences contribute to understanding, and this understanding can be drawn on when needed. Workers may discover their own feelings about many of the issues their clients deal with, some of which may touch on unresolved concerns in their own lives. This is one of the payoffs in the field that motivates many to enter it. Social workers rarely come into the field because they look forward to the great working hours or the high financial compensation. The motivation to help others is there, but so is an understanding that they help themselves when they help others.

This is one sense in which the work is interactive—the feelings of the client affect the feelings of the worker. This idea is easier to understand when one views the professional worker not as someone who has found all of the answers to life's problems and is now prepared to share them with the client but rather as a fellow learner with a special functional role and skills for implementing that function.

Because of the close parallels between the social worker's life experiences and those of the clients, the worker must guard against a process called *countertransference,* defined as the complex of a worker's feelings toward a client. For example, young workers still close to the battle for independence from their own families may discover that their own feelings lead them to identify with the child in the struggle with the parent. The worker may start to relate to a parent in the family as if she or he were his or her own parent.

A supervisor can be very helpful to the worker in the lifelong educational process of discovering oneself through practice. A common danger, however, is that the supervisor may lose her or his sense of function and begin to relate to the social worker as a client rather than as a student or employee. Supervision can turn into an inappropriate form of personal therapy as the conference explores the worker's unresolved issues with his or her own family of origin rather than focusing on the impact of personal experiences on practice with clients.

## Sessional Contracting Skills

In a sub-design of one of my early research projects, I videotaped and analyzed client interviews, with their permission (Shulman, 1991). The clients knew that these tapes would be analyzed at the university by researchers unknown to them; however, during the interview, the client and the worker were alone in the room with the camera.

One videotape illustrated dramatically the issues related to sessional contracting. As the session began, the client touched on a concern she was feeling about her child, hinting at it instead of raising it directly. The worker listened to the concern, but it soon became obvious that she had her own agenda for the session as her questions attempted to lead the client to other issues. After a few minutes, the client hinted again and made a second offering of her concern, this time a little more strongly and clearly. The worker still did not "hear," because she was preoccupied with her own agenda. The client made a third attempt a few minutes later, which the worker once again missed. At this point, with a look of complete frustration, the client turned to face the video camera and said, "Do you understand?"

This interview illustrates the problems that occur when the client and the worker are operating on two different agendas. It also raises the larger issue of control over the interview. This, in turn, stems directly from the paradigm that guides the helping professional in thinking about his or her work. The sessional contracting skill provides us with a good opportunity to elaborate on this general issue.

### Working from the Client's Sense of Urgency

In an interactional approach, clients attempt to work, as best they can, on issues that matter to them. Clients find that their sense of urgency about problems shifts from week to week, depending on the realities of their lives. A major assumption of the interactional practice theory is that clients will only invest in those areas of concern that they feel are important. The worker's task is not to *decide* what the client should be working on. Instead, using sessional contracting skills, the worker attempts to *discover* what the client actually is working on.

I have already discussed some of the difficulties clients experience in communicating their thoughts and feelings directly, especially at the beginning of each session. Clients often raise their concerns ambivalently and express this ambivalence through indirect forms of communication. For example, a client may begin a session describing how great things have been that week, while actually facing a difficult problem. An example from a couples' group illustrates this situation:

### Sessional Contracting in a Couples' Group Session: The Taboo Subject

**Practice Points:**   Note the indirect way the client raises the sexual issue. It is an expression of ambivalence which the worker picks up by responding to the comment about the previous week rather than the comment about how "it has been really great" this week.

WORKER: Does anyone have anything they would like to be discussed?
FRAN: We've had no problems this week; it has been really great. We have been communicating with each other better than ever before. (Silence.) We had a problem last week that I used to get really angry about, but I think I was more helpful to Ted this time (looking over to her husband).
WORKER: Can you tell us a bit about it?
FRAN: It was a problem that had to do with our sexual relations (looking nervously over at Ted now), but I'm not sure Ted wants to discuss it.

**Practice Points:**   Further discussion revealed that the concern was over Ted's premature ejaculations, a major concern for this couple. This client offered her concern this first time by emphasizing something opposite to the true state of affairs.

### Foster Child Transitioning to Independence

**Practice Points:**   In another example (touched on in Chapter 3), an 18-year-old foster child, who is about to leave the care of the child welfare agency, used a metaphor to introduce a discussion of his feelings of lacking roots and terrible loneliness:

CLIENT: Have you ever thought about space, about space never ending?
WORKER: Yes, I have. Have you thought about it, and does it bother you?
CLIENT: Sometimes I imagine that I'm a little bird and that I'm floating up into never-ending space. A little bit higher and a little bit to the right, and it's "bye, bye world."
WORKER: You have been floating in space this year, with all of the changes you've made.

**Practice Summary:**   The client responded by detailing—with great feeling—all of the places he had stayed during the year (eight of them), the deaths of his mother and an uncle, and his feelings of being alone in the world. The discussion continued with a poignant description of what it was like to spend important family holidays, such as Christmas, alone in a movie theater. The worker noted, but did not respond to, the client's hinting of suicidal ideation in the comment "bye, bye world." In her next session, she listened carefully for additional hints of how deep his desperation was and asked him directly if he had considered suicide. He indicated that he had felt "low" enough but that he wanted too much out of life not to keep fighting.

### Other Examples of Indirect Communications   Examples of indirect first offerings of concerns are almost endless. A parent who is dreadfully worried about how her child is doing, and who feels guilty about her own parenting, raises the concern by attacking the worker's competency to help her child. A child in the residential treatment center who found out his parents were not taking him home for a visit over Christmas acts out his feelings by fighting with other residents and staff. Or conversely, a child

who is going home acts out his anxiety about the visit and family conflict. A mother of a young man who has just died from AIDS begins her first session with a worker by talking nonstop about all of the things she did that week to keep busy, thus demonstrating to the worker her use of activity as a form of flight from her pain.

The adult child of an elderly patient in a nursing home who still feels guilty for not taking her mother into her own home questions the quality of care provided by the nursing staff. An attractive, female teenage survivor of sexual abuse wears provocative clothing and "comes on" to her young male social worker in a residential setting, which turns out to be her way of signaling her need to work on issues of relationships with males and her own sense of self-worth as a woman after feeling so long like "damaged goods."

In each case, the clients are working on important issues. Sometimes they are aware of the concern but have difficulty expressing it. Other times the feelings are there, just below the surface, but the clients themselves are unaware of the central theme. Whatever the circumstances, the clients' offerings are present, but they are hard to understand in their early forms. Because of the complexity of communication, a worker often feels that the client is not working and so decides to take over the task of determining the client's agenda. However, as seen in the example that opened this section, the worker can rarely understand the client's agenda without actively attempting to determine what it is.

## Research on Sessional Contracting

One of the findings of a sub-design of another one of my research projects concerned the question of sessional contracting (Shulman, 1981). It centered on the practice of 11 workers, out of 118 included in the major study, who agreed to have their practice videotaped and analyzed. It would be a mistake to generalize the findings beyond this sample. In my experience as a consultant in various settings, however, I have found this pattern to be persistent.

Each videotape was analyzed by a trained rater who assigned a number that represented a category of behavior (e.g., clarifying purpose, encouraging elaboration, dealing with feelings) every 3 seconds. A numerical record of the session was available for computer analysis, and more than 120 hours of individual and group practice were analyzed in this manner.

It was possible to determine whether workers were relating to the client's concerns, as judged by the raters, or working on their own agendas. According to this analysis, workers related to the client's concerns only 60 percent of the time. We further analyzed separately each third of every session. This roughly approximated the beginning, middle, and ending phases of work. Workers began by relating to client concerns 65 percent of the time but dropped to 58 percent in the middle and ending phases. This finding was interpreted as suggesting a high incidence of unsuccessful sessional contracting in the beginning phase.

In a more recent study (Shulman, 1991), the overall score for all of the workers on the skill called *reaching for feedback* (asking for the client's perception of his or her sense of urgency) was between "seldom" and "fairly often." This skill was ranked sixth out of the eight skills studied. When time was introduced as a factor, we found that the correlation (a nondirectional measure of association between two variables) of this skill with the development of the working relationship was stronger when used in the middle phase than in the beginning phase. This finding could be interpreted as supporting the continued and increased importance of sessional contracting.

## Impact of the Medical Paradigm on Sessional Contracting

Earlier, I suggested that the question of sessional contracting was related to the larger concerns of control of the interview and which paradigm of the helping process guides the worker. I believe that some of the workers in the study operated from a paradigm of helping that gave them the central responsibility for determining the agenda. They saw a good worker as one who controlled the interview to reach selected goals for the clients. Case conferences with supervisors and colleagues might even develop an agenda for the session, with specific goals to be accomplished by the worker. Unfortunately, clients, not having been involved in the conference, would remain unaware of the plan. Workers who operated solely from this model would find it impossible to hear the clients' indirect efforts to communicate their own sense of urgency because they would be preoccupied with accomplishing their goals for the session.

Clearly, there are times when the worker must bring an agenda to the session. Agency issues, information to be shared or obtained, and other topics may have to be part of a session. Sessional contracting suggests that the worker can openly and directly raise these issues with the client while simultaneously attempting to determine the client's perception of the sense of urgency. The sessional contract emerges from the convergence of the worker's agenda items and the acuteness of the client's felt needs. Either client or worker may have to set his or her own issues aside for a moment.

It is clear that, even as we discuss specific skills such as sessional contracting, we need to consider the worker's sense of function. If one believes that the worker's tasks include selecting the agenda for the work, then sessional contracting, as discussed here, is impossible. If one believes that this is the task of the client, however, and one has faith in the client's ability to do this with help from the worker, then all beginnings are tentative. The worker begins each session by listening for the client's concern, and the question of control of the interview is settled. The important point is that this is a joint process—no matter what the worker's view, the client will "own" the session.

A common concern raised at this point is that the client may raise other issues as a means of avoiding the work and collaborating if the worker always responds to the client's agenda. This is an important observation. For example, a mandated (by the court) substance-abusing client may actively create an "illusion of work" by talking about issues not related to the addiction. Or, another client may constantly raise "near issues" to avoid dealing with the painful ones. This is not uncommon. However, reflect a moment on these two patterns of behavior. What are these clients actually saying through the pattern? The mandated client may be saying, "I don't want to be here and I don't believe I have an addiction problem," and the client who only raises near and safe issues may be saying, "I'm afraid to talk about the real problem because it is scary and painful." Sessional contracting is still crucial, only the issue to be discussed is the pattern of resistance.

 **Interactive Skills of Helping**

Use the accompanying DVD or visit *The Skills of Helping Individuals, Families, Groups, and Communities,* Seventh Edition, CourseMate website at www.cengagebrain.com and enter your personal access code to watch this video

**CONTRACTING AND SHARING THE WORKER'S FEELINGS** This is an interview with a high school student who is under peer pressure to use drugs.

# Elaborating Skills

EP 2.1.1f
EP 2.1.10b
EP 2.1.10d
EP 2.1.10f
EP 2.1.10i

When a client begins to share a particular concern, the first presentations of the problem are usually fragmentary. These initial offerings provide a tool that the worker can use to deepen the work. The elaborating skills are important in this stage, because they help clients tell their own story. The worker's questions and comments focus on helping the client elaborate and clarify specific concerns. The examples of elaborating skills explored in this section include containment, moving from the general to the specific, focused listening, questioning, and reaching inside of silences.

## Containment

As clients begin to tell their stories, workers too often attempt to "help" before the whole story is told. This is especially true for people who are new to helping; the desire to help is so strong that they will often rush in with unhelpful suggestions that are not directed at the client's actual concerns. The elaborating skill of containment is an interesting one, because it suggests that not acting—that is, a worker's ability to contain himself or herself—is an active skill (see Chapter 3).

### Welfare Client Considering a Career: Lack of Worker Containment

**Practice Points:**   In the following example, we see a new worker in a public welfare setting who fails to contain herself in response to a mother whose children have grown up and who is thinking of pursuing a career.

CLIENT: I've been thinking that, now that the kids are older, perhaps I can find a job. But you know, finding jobs is difficult these days.
WORKER: I think that's a great idea. You know, we have a job-finding service, and I bet if you speak to one of the workers, he could come up with something for you.
CLIENT: (Hesitantly) That sounds like a good idea.
WORKER: Let's set up an appointment. How about next Wednesday at 3:00 P.M.?

**Practice Points:**   Although the client agreed to the appointment, she did not show up. When we explore the worker's feelings in interviews such as this, they often exemplify what I call the "heart-soaring" sensation. The worker is pleased at the client's interest in doing something about the problem and is feeling like a very successful worker indeed. If job referral is one of the ways in which practice is evaluated, we can imagine the worker mentally checking off one more successful referral for the month. Containment in response to the client's interest in a job, and further exploration of the client's feelings and concerns about returning to the workforce, would be much more helpful.

Specifically, picking up the hesitancy in the client's voice as a signal of unexplored issues would be a good place to start. Even when the client enthusiastically says that she will go to the appointment, using the containment skill of *looking for trouble when everything is going the worker's way* is important. This less-often-used skill will come back in this book in a number of contexts. It means that the worker, from tuning in or experience or knowledge of the particular client, realizes that it may not be so easy for the client to take a next step, even when she or he provides verbal agreement. Looking for trouble in this case means naming and exploring the ambivalence or fears that may impede the client's ability to follow through. For example:

**WORKER:** You sound excited about the appointment, and I'm happy for you. However, you have not been in the workforce for quite a while, and you have not had to deal with an employment interview, either. I wonder if, after you leave the office, you might have some second thoughts.

**Practice Points:** By reaching for the concerns, the worker gives the client an opportunity to explore them with the worker, rather than having to face them on her own the night before the interview. However, the worker can always go back and catch a mistake. At the next interview, the disappointed worker asked the client why she missed the appointment. The client said that she forgot, and this time the worker contained herself and did not schedule a new appointment. Instead, she attempted to explore further the client's perception of what was involved in taking a job.

**WORKER:** I was thinking about this business of taking a job, and it struck me that it might not be so easy for you after so many years at home.
**CLIENT:** That's what I'm worried about; I'm not sure I can handle work again—you know, I've been away so long. I'm even nervous about what to say at a job interview.

**Practice Summary:** Feelings of fear and ambivalence are usually associated with most concerns. Workers who attempt to find simple solutions often discover that, if the solutions were indeed that simple, the client could have found them without the help of the worker.

## Moving from the General to the Specific

Clients often raise a general concern that relates to a specific event. The general statement can be viewed as a first offering from the client to the worker. It may be presented in universal terms because the client experiences it that way at the moment. The general nature of its expression may also reflect the ambivalence the client feels about dealing with the concern in depth.

In one example, at the beginning of an interview a mother stated, "It's impossible to raise teenagers these days." Responding to the general theme, the worker might have engaged in a discussion of changing mores, peer group pressure, drug availability, and so on. An example of moving from the general to the specific would be to ask, "Did you have a tough time with Sue this week?" The client's response in this case was to describe a fight she had with her 15-year-old daughter, who had returned home after 2:00 A.M. and refused to say where she had been. This second offering of the concern was a more specific and manageable piece of work; in other words, the general problem of raising teenagers is pressing in our society, but this client and this worker could not do much about it. However, this mother's relationship with her daughter was open to change.

Behind most early general statements is a specific concern and often some pain. If the worker does not encourage elaboration, the concern might emerge at the end of the session as a doorknob communication (offered as the client is leaving the office). The teenager in the living room of the group home who casually comments during a general discussion that "parents just don't understand" may be reacting to a letter or phone call received that morning. The patient on the ward who mentions to the nurse that "doctors must work hard because they always seem so busy" may still be reacting to terse comments overheard during rounds, which the patient was too frightened or overwhelmed to inquire about. In each case, the worker skill would involve reaching for more specific information.

***Reasons Workers Stay General and Do Not Reach for the Specifics*** Helping professionals have suggested to me two major reasons why they might refrain from reaching for the specifics behind general comments. First, they are unaware of how specific work must be; that is, they do not realize that they can only give help in terms of the details of a problem. One cannot help a parent to deal with teenagers through general discussion alone. The learning will take place through the discussion of the specific interactions between parent and child. The worker can help the parent develop general principles about her relationship with her daughter, but these principles must emerge from discussions of the specific events. Without the specific discussions, the worker's attempts to generalize may be perceived by the mother as theoretical advice.

For example, the parent in the earlier encounter might describe a conversation with her daughter in which she did not share her distress and hurt but instead gave way to the surface feelings of anger. After a while, the worker may be able to help the client see how, in incident after incident, she finds it hard to be open with her daughter about certain feelings. The client may be able to understand this point because of the discussion of specific incidents. The discussion should develop an experiential base on which the client can build new understanding, a reframing of her perceptions about the problem, and possible solutions. The client may not be able to do much about changing mores in our society, but she can conduct her next conversation with her daughter in a different way. Lack of understanding of the power of specific discussion may lead the worker to overlook the usefulness of this elaboration skill.

The second reason why workers do not reach for the specifics—even when they sense the concrete problem connected to the client's general offering—is that they are not sure they want to deal with it. Hospital social workers, for example, suggest that they do not reach for a patient's comment about busy doctors because they are not sure what they can do about it. As one put it, "I find the doctors too busy to answer *my* questions, so how can I help the patient?" The source of the worker's ambivalence may vary, but feelings of ambivalence are common. I believe that, when workers feel more confident about offering help, they reach more easily for specifics.

I propose a third, and less obvious, reason for failure to reach for elaboration from the general to the specific that has to do with the parallel process between workers and supervisors described earlier. Often, a worker or student raises a question with a supervisor such as "Do you have any thoughts about techniques for handling angry clients?" Unless the supervisor inquires, "Did you have a tough interview?" the remainder of the conversation may stay at a general level. If the modeling is sound, the supervisor will always move from the general to the specific, thus teaching by modeling the skill. In turn, the supervisor is aided by having an administrator reach for her or his specific concerns behind the general offerings. My research on supervision of supervisors, however, has indicated that this is rarely done (Shulman, 1994, 2010).

## Focused Listening: The Complex Communication Process

Listening is something we do all the time; however, focused listening involves attempting to concentrate on a specific part of the client's message. I discussed earlier how complex even the simplest interchange of communication can be. In complex communications at the beginning of sessions, the worker must focus on whatever the client is working on at that particular moment. By listening to the early communications with this purpose in mind, the worker has a better chance of hearing the message.

A simple analogy is the difficulty of hearing two simultaneous conversations at a crowded social event. If one listens in a general way, all one hears is a loud buzz. If one attempts to focus on one particular conversation, however, it begins to stand out clearly, and the buzzing noise recedes. Similarly, when one is driving at night in a rural area, sometimes two radio stations are heard at once. The driver must tune in one station and tune out the other in order to really hear anything. In the same way, the "noise" of the client's early communications may make it difficult for the worker to understand the single strand that represents the basic concern. Focused listening—directed toward determining the concern—often makes the theme stand out clearly.

A common mistake a worker makes is to take control of the interview when he or she does not immediately understand the meaning of the communication. In effect, a worker may answer a question before he or she actually knows what the question is. Focused listening involves an attempt to hear the communication as the client's effort to work, and to search for the connections when they are not apparent. The worker can ask for the client's help. For example, "Could you help me connect this discussion with the concern you raised about your daughter at the start of the session?" Clients will often be able to do so, either immediately or after some reflection. They do not get the opportunity if the worker has already decided they are simply not working and more worker activity is needed.

Workers often ask me how to handle a situation in which there is no real connection and the client evades work by changing the subject. Focused listening will clarify this as well. The client is actually working by avoiding the work; this may sound contradictory, but the client is signaling resistance to a particular topic—perhaps because it is too painful or embarrassing—and this resistance is what the worker should hear and address. Once again, **the resistance is part of the work** if the social worker hears it for what it is; a call for help in facing difficult issues. There is no dichotomy between process and content. Addressing the process (resistance) takes the conversation into the content.

## Questioning

Questioning in the elaboration process involves requests for more information about the nature of the problem. As a fledgling high school journalist, I was encouraged to answer the "five Ws" early in my articles: the *who, what, when, where* and *why* of the story. These are useful areas for exploring the details of a client's concern.

### The Mother-Daughter Conflict: A Continuation of the Session

**Practice Points:** For example, in the earlier illustration with the mother and daughter, we left the process at the point where the client responded to the worker's effort to move from the general to the specific by describing a fight with her daughter. In the next part of the session, we can see that the worker's questions are designed to elicit more detail about what happened during the encounter.

CLIENT: We had some row last night when Sue came home at 2:00 A.M.
WORKER: What happened?

CLIENT: She had told me she was going to a movie with a friend, but when she didn't get home by 11:00, I was really worried.

WORKER: You were afraid something might have happened to her?

CLIENT: Well, you know we have had some problems in the neighborhood with men.

WORKER: What did you say to Sue when she came home?

CLIENT: I let her have it good. I told her she was irresponsible and that I was going to keep her home for 2 weeks.

WORKER: What did she say back to you?

**Practice Summary:**   As the conversation proceeded, the worker helped the client elaborate on the details of the interaction. A term to describe this process between worker and client is *memory work,* in which the client reaches back into her memory to recall the incident. In other situations, the worker may aim her questions at getting a fuller picture of the client's concern. In the earlier example of the woman considering a return to the workforce, the questions would be designed to elicit the *what* and *why* of the concerns she might have about returning to work. Once again, if frontline workers experience a similar process in supervision—when the supervisor uses all of these elaboration skills—there is a greater chance that workers will integrate the same skills in their practice with clients.

## Reaching Inside of Silences

Recall from Chapter 3 that silence during a helping interview may be an important form of communication. The difficulty with silences is that it is often hard to understand exactly what the client is "saying." In one situation, the client may be thinking and reflecting on the implications of the conversation. In another, a discussion may have released powerful emotions that are struggling to surface in the client. The client may be at the critical point of experiencing suppressed and painful feelings. Silence can indicate a moment of ambivalence as the client pauses to decide whether or not to plunge headlong into a difficult area of work. This is not uncommon when the conversation deals with an area generally experienced as taboo. Silence may also signal that the worker's preceding response was off base in relation to the client's expressed concern. The worker has "missed" the client, and the silence is the client's polite way of saying so. Finally, the client may be angry with the worker. Frequent silence in an interview may reflect a systematic attempt to express this anger passively by withholding involvement.

*Silence as an Expression of Difficult Feelings* Because silences carry a variety of meanings, the worker's response must vary accordingly. An important aid is the worker's own set of feelings during the silence. For example, if the silence represents the emergence of difficult feelings, the worker may have anticipated this reaction based on the content of the conversation or from the nonverbal communications the client sent. Posture, facial expressions, and bodily tension all speak loudly to the observing worker and can trigger empathic responses. As such, the worker may experience the same emergence of feeling as the client. At moments like this, the worker can respond to silence with silence or with nonverbal expressions of support. All of these responses offer some support to the client while still allowing time to experience the feelings.

*Silence Because the Client is Just Thinking* If the worker senses that the client is thinking about an important point of the discussion or considering a related problem, responding with a brief silence allows the client room to think. Silence demonstrates respect for the client's work. However, a problem can arise if the worker maintains the silence for too long. Silence can also be particularly troublesome if the worker does not understand it or if it is used to communicate either a negative reaction or passive resistance. In such cases, the client may experience the silence as a battle of wills. What started as one form of communication may quickly change to a situation in which the client is saying, "I won't speak unless you speak first." In this battle, both worker and client always lose. The skill of reaching inside the silence matters most during these kinds of silences.

This skill involves attempts to explore the meaning of the silence. For example, the worker who responds to a silence by saying, "You've grown quiet in the last few moments. What are you thinking about?" is encouraging the client to share her or his thoughts. In another case, the worker could try to articulate what the silence may mean. For example, the client who hesitates as he describes a particularly difficult experience might be offered this response: "I can see this is hard for you to talk about." Once again, the worker's own feelings guide her or his attempts to explore or acknowledge the silence. The worker must be open to the fact that the guess may be wrong and must encourage the client to feel free to say so.

***The Worker's Difficulty in Tolerating Silences*** Workers often find silences in interviews to be difficult moments. They have been affected by societal norms that create the feeling that a silence in conversation is embarrassing, and they may feel that the most helpful thing to do is fill the gap. When one works with clients from different cultures, one is struck by the differences in these social norms. For example, American Indian clients describe how talking to non-Indian workers is hard because the workers never keep quiet. As one Native worker said to me, "The problem with White workers is that they never stop 'nattering.'" She pointed out that Indian culture respects silence as a time to reflect, but non-Indian workers continue to talk because of their own anxiety, without giving the Native person a chance to think. In some cases, the Indian client might simply be trying to translate the non-Indian worker's English into the Indian language and then back to English.

***Some Research Findings on Worker Responses to Silence*** In my early research project on practice, the skill of reaching inside silences was one of the 5 skills used least often of the 27 skills studied (Shulman, 1978). However, another analysis showed it to be one of the most significant. The 15 workers (of 155 total) who had the most positive overall skill scores were compared with those workers who had the most negative. The former were found to have more positive working relationships and were more helpful than were the latter. The practice skill profiles of the workers were compared according to their scores on 27 specific skills. The skill of reaching inside silences was one of the three most important in which the positive skill group of workers differed from the negative skill group (p. 281).

In my more recent study, reaching inside of silences was one of the four skills included in the skills to help clients manage their feelings (Shulman, 1991). This grouping was related to the client's sense that the worker cared—one element of the working relationship. When the skill was examined by itself, workers were perceived by their clients to use it seldom. In fact, out of the eight skills examined, it was almost the least-used skill, only slightly ahead of the worker sharing his or her own feelings (p. 61).

The particular impact of each of the four skills on the development of the working relationship (caring and trust) as well as the client's perception of the worker's helpfulness was also examined (Shulman, 1993b). The striking results, which replicated the general findings of the 1978 study, indicated that this skill—when used in the beginning phase of practice—showed the highest correlation with the client's perception of the worker's caring (.56) and trust in the worker (.68). It was fifth in importance in terms of helpfulness (.51). The findings of both studies support the notion that the worker needs to actively explore the hidden meaning of silences in interviews.

Another finding from a separate design of the 1978 study yielded additional evidence that this important skill may often be lacking. In this part of the study, the individual interviews and group sessions of 11 volunteer workers were videotaped and then analyzed by trained raters using a system I developed. In an analysis of 32 individual interviews, raters scored the worker's or the client's behavior by entering a number that described the interaction at least every 3 seconds. A total of 40,248 individual observations of sessions were scored and then analyzed by computer. In one analysis, we were able to determine which behaviors of the workers most often followed silences of 3 seconds or longer.

The findings were striking. Of all the entries scored, only 1,742 (4 percent) indicated that a silence of 3 seconds or more had taken place after the client was silent for 3 seconds or more. Raters found that client comments followed silences only 38 percent of the time. A 3-second silence was followed by another 3-second silence 26 percent of the time. Workers' active comments in response to silences occurred 36 percent of the time. When these ratings were examined more closely, they revealed the following results:

- When workers actively intervened after a silence, they attempted to encourage elaboration 31 percent of the time.

- Their efforts to deal with the client's feelings or share their own feelings were noted in only 4 percent of their responses.

- The most common active action in response to silence was to direct the client away from the client's presented theme of concern (as our raters perceived it). This occurred 49 percent of the time.

Remember, however, that this sub-design involved only 11 workers in one child welfare agency, each of whom faced the unusual pressure of being videotaped as part of a research project. My attempt to generalize from these findings to other settings or workers is tentative; even so, my observations as a training consultant and the findings of the more recent study support these conclusions (Shulman, 1991).

I share these tentative findings with you because they reflect statistically my own observations that workers often seem reluctant to explore silences. In addition to the reasons already advanced, workers have suggested that they often perceive silences to represent a problem in the interview. If there is silence, the worker must have done something wrong. The irony in the situation is that silence results more often from a worker doing something right. The worker often sees silence as negative feedback, even in those cases when it may mean other things.

A worker's willingness to reach inside the silence when there is a possible negative response is directly related to feelings of comfort in the work and willingness to deal with negative feedback. (This aspect of the process will be discussed more fully in the skill factor called "pointing out obstacles.") Understandably, a worker may be unsure about what to do with the feelings and concerns that might reside within the silence, and she or he may choose to change the subject rather than reach inside the silence.

When these findings are shared with workers in training sessions, their reactions provide further clues to the apparent low frequency of use of this important skill.

Many indicate that their skill training specifically cautioned them not to put a client's thoughts or feelings into words. They report having been encouraged to ask questions but to avoid "putting words into the client's mouth" or "doing the clients' work for them." One worker reported being told by a supervisor that it was "like tying a client's shoelaces for him." Although these are legitimate concerns, these repeated findings suggest that workers make more errors of omission (failing to articulate the feelings) than errors of commission (articulating the wrong feelings).

### Interactive Skills of Helping

Use the accompanying DVD or visit *The Skills of Helping Individuals, Families, Groups, and Communities,* Seventh Edition, CourseMate website at www.cengagebrain.com and enter your personal access code to watch this video

**ELABORATING** This is an interview conducted in a college counseling center with a graduate student who feels stress from trying to manage her relationship with her partner and the demands of school. This example may hit close to home for many readers in similar situations.

At this point, after (and while) the worker has successfully helped the client elaborate concerns, our discussion needs to move to the question of feelings and how to deal with them.

## Empathic Skills

**EP 2.1.1f**
**EP 2.1.10b**

As clients tell their stories, workers may use a number of skills designed to keep the discussion meaningful by having clients invest it with feelings. Clients often share difficult experiences while seeming to deny the affect associated with them. For some, the experience may be so painful that they have suppressed the emotion to the point that their own feelings are not clear to themselves. For others, the emotions may seem strange or unacceptable, and they are fearful of discussing them with the worker.

Taft (1933) was one of the first social work theorists to discuss the power of feelings:

There is no factor of personality which is so expressive of individuality as emotion. The personality is impoverished as feeling is denied, and the penalty for sitting on the lid of angry feelings or feelings of fear is the inevitable blunting of capacity to feel love and desire. For to feel is to live, but to reject feeling through fear is to reject the life process itself. (p. 10)

***Impact on the Client of Addressing and Experiencing Emotions*** Whatever the reason, the affect is there, and it will exert a powerful force on the client until it can be acknowledged and dealt with. When clients deal directly with affect, it can affect them in at least three different ways: (1) Clients' sharing of feelings with the worker can release an important source of energy that has been suppressed along with the emotions; (2) clients can learn how emotions directly affect their thoughts and actions; and (3) clients can develop skills that allow them to understand the sensations, accept them without harsh self-judgment, and disclose them to those who matter.

As workers allow themselves to get closer to clients—to experience clients realistically and not necessarily as clients present themselves—workers also give their clients permission to be natural. The acceptance and understanding of emotions, and the worker's willingness to share them by experiencing them, frees a client to drop some defenses and to allow the worker and the client more access to the real person. The worker also serves as a model of an adult with empathic ability. The client can learn to develop powers of empathy to be used, in turn, with those who need support. On the other hand, a worker might so identify with a child in a family conflict situation that the worker pushes the parent to understand the child's feelings while expressing little understanding of the parent's feelings. Providing genuine empathy for the parent's dilemma is often the key to helping the parent understand the struggles of the child.

This can be described as the feeling-thinking-doing connection. How we feel affects how we think and act, and how we act affects how we think and feel. This interaction among feeling, thinking, and doing leads to the model described in this book, in which a worker's skills for helping clients to manage their feelings takes on such importance in helping clients to manage their problems.

***Research on the Rogerian Conditions*** Rogers (1961) stressed the importance of the helping person listening for the affective component of the communication:

> Real communication occurs when the evaluative tendency is avoided, when we listen with understanding. It means to see the expressed idea and attitude from the other person's point of view, to sense how it feels to him, to achieve his frame of reference in regard to the thing he is talking about. (pp. 331–332)

Rogers's communication model was the basis for early work on the impact of the therapist's behavior on patient outcomes. Truax et. al. (1966) studied what became known as the "Rogerian conditions." These behaviors included therapists' capacity for empathy, nonpossessive warmth, and genuineness in their work with clients.

> An equal number of "good" or "poor" therapy prospects were randomly assigned to 4 resident psychiatrists (10 patients each) for 4 months of psychotherapy. Results tended to confirm the importance of the 3 therapeutic conditions in combination and of empathy and genuineness separately. Negative findings for separate analysis of therapists' warmth were interpreted in terms of its negative correlation with empathy and genuineness in the present sample. On the overall measure for all patients, therapists providing high therapeutic conditions had 90 percent patient improvement while those providing lower conditions had 50 percent improvement. (p. 1)

More recently, Zuroff et. al. (2010) reexamined the impact of the Rogerian conditions in the treatment of 157 depressed patients treated by 27 therapists using a cognitive-behavioral therapy, interpersonal therapy, or placebo. Their central finding, confirming a number of earlier studies, was as follows:

> [P]atients whose therapists provided high average levels of the perceived Rogerian conditions across the patients in their caseloads experienced more rapid reductions in both overall maladjustment and depressive vulnerability (self-critical perfectionism). Within each therapist's caseload, differences between patients in perceived Rogerian conditions had weaker effects. The results underline the importance of differences between therapists as determinants of outcome in the treatment of depression. (p. 682)

***Worker Difficulty in Relating to a Client's Emotions*** Expressing empathy with the client can prove difficult for the worker in many ways. The capacity to be in touch with the client's feelings is related to the worker's ability to acknowledge his or her own feelings. Before workers can understand the power of emotion in the lives of clients, they must discover its importance in their own experience. Workers often find it hard to express empathy in specific personal areas. Workers are human, and they face of all the stresses and difficulties associated with daily living, including crises. When workers hear their own difficult feelings expressed by clients, the capacity for empathy can be blunted. The worker's authority over the client may serve as another major block to empathy. For example, a child welfare worker who has removed a child from an abuse situation may find her or his empathic responses to the parent-client blocked at the time when they may be most needed.

***A Mother Undergoing Psychiatric Treatment: The Uncaring Worker*** The following example effectively illustrates this difficulty and how it can lead to a relationship that is devoid of feeling, in which the worker seems cold and uncaring.

**Practice Points:** The excerpt is from a recorded interview with a mother who had undergone psychiatric treatment for a time and was separated from her husband. Her 9-year-old adopted and only daughter had come into care of the agency one year before this interview because the mother had found her unmanageable. A short time into the interview, there was a pause followed by this comment:

CLIENT: You know I'm afraid of you.
WORKER: Why?
CLIENT: Because you are sitting in judgment of me. You're only human—you might make a mistake.
WORKER: I'm only judging how we can help you—help you to improve.
CLIENT: No, you are judging whether or not I can be a mother to Fran—whether I can have my child back. (Silence.) I feel at the moment I am not capable of caring for Fran on a full-time basis—I know that. Don't you understand? I'm grieving—I'm grieving for Fran. Wouldn't you be upset and worried and confused?
WORKER: I'm worried about other things as well.

**Practice Points:** The worker was not in tune with the client's feelings. She regarded the child as her only client and did not respond to the mother as a client in her own right. The two-client concept—which is central to this interactional model—would have been helpful at this moment. After further discussion, in which the worker indicated that the client was not working hard enough during her contacts with her psychiatrist, the worker asked how long the client had been seeing the doctor.

CLIENT: I'm not sure—I don't remember—(with tremendous feeling)—it's absolutely terrible not to be able to remember. It makes me feel incompetent, incapable. (Silence.) There are some things in my head I know can't be real. (Silence.) But I feel I can be competent and capable of looking after Fran—or I wouldn't want to—because I know she is a problem to look after. But I love her even with her faults.
WORKER: When you think of Fran, what do you think of most—her faults?
CLIENT: No! Fran wants to laugh—enjoy people—not to analyze them. She's a baby bird, full of life, receptive, loving people. I may seem aloof, but I'm really just shy.
WORKER: You say Fran is sociable, but before, you told me she had no friends.

**Practice Points:** The worker ignored the client's offering of sensitive subjects for discussion, including her self-depreciation and her expression of loss and guilt. She missed the meaning of the comment about enjoying people—"not to analyze them"—which is probably what the client felt the worker was doing. The worker's capacity to help this mother was minimal, because she saw her intellectually, not affectively. Smalley (1967) described this process as follows:

> The self of another cannot be known through intellectual assessment alone. Within a human, compassionate, and caring relationship, selves "open up," dare to become what they may be, so that the self which is known by a worker, a worker at once human, caring, and skillful, is a different self from that diagnosed by one who removes himself in feeling from the relationship in an attempt to be a dispassionate observer and problem solver. As an adolescent girl once said to her new social worker, in referring to a former worker, "She knew all about me, but she didn't know me." (p. 86)

Because of the difficulty of this skills area, workers must develop over time their ability to empathize. The capacity for empathy grows with experience. Workers who are open to this development can learn more about life from each client, which will help them to better understand the next client. Workers also learn more about their own feelings and true reactions to the plight of others. Awareness of the sensitive areas in one's own emotional armor will help one avoid the denial or intellectualization of difficult emotions when they are presented. The worker will more readily allow a client to share more difficult emotions as the worker becomes comfortable with their effects, particularly those of negative feelings—both the worker's and the client's—which form a natural part of any helping relationship.

*Supervision and Worker Development of Emotional Skills* Supervision can play an important part in a worker's emotional development. The concept of the parallel process suggests that the helping relationship between a supervisor and a worker, or a field instructor and a student, parallels the relationship between the worker (student) and the client. Thus, a supervisor must model effective empathic skills in the supervisory relationship. This is the meaning of the phrase "more is caught than taught"—supervisees watch their supervisors closely and learn a great deal from the nature of the interaction.

For illustration, consider the supervision session between the field instructor and the student involved in the interview, just described, with the mother who was fearful of losing her child. If, as they listened to the tape together, the supervisor simply criticized the student for her lack of affective response to the client, the student might remain stuck and show little growth. The supervisor's words might be teaching empathy for the client, but his or her actions would be repeating the student's mistake. In effect, she would be asking the student to "be with" the mother; however, at exactly the same moment, the supervisor would not "be with" the student.

In contrast, if the supervisor asked the student, "What were you feeling when she was describing her relationship with her daughter?" the crucial affective work would begin. If the supervisor could genuinely acknowledge the student's struggle to be emotionally with the parent and the child at the same time, a powerful lesson could be taught. The supervisor would model by demonstrating her ability to be with the student as a social worker and a client at exactly the same time.

In my most recent supervision study, we found that the worker's perception of the effectiveness of supervision was a powerful predictor of the worker's morale

(Shulman, 1993a, 2010). Supervisory skill also contributed to the development of a positive working relationship with staff and to their sense of the supervisor's helpfulness. When I share these findings with supervisors, a short period of silence usually follows. When I reach inside of the silence, one supervisor will often say, "But who listens to me?" The appropriateness of that question was suggested by other findings in the supervision study. The skill of articulating the supervisee's feelings—the skill parallel to articulating the client's feelings—was positively associated with relationship and helpfulness on every level of the study (supervisors–workers, managers–supervisors, executives–managers).

The three empathic skills described in the rest of this section—reaching for feelings, displaying understanding of the client's feelings, and putting the client's feelings into words—will be illustrated using excerpts from practice with a mother whose child is about to be apprehended because of parental abuse. This example provides a contrast to the earlier one and demonstrates how the functions of protecting a child and caring for the parent can be integrated. That is, it will illustrate how a worker can "be with" the parent and the child at the same time.[1]

## Reaching for Feelings

Reaching for feelings is the skill of asking the client to share the affective portion of the message. Before proceeding, however, I should clarify one point. This process is sometimes handled superficially, in a ritualistic manner, thus negating its usefulness. The worker who routinely asks a client, "How do you feel?" while not really being open to experiencing the feeling, may be perceived by the client as not really caring. Experienced clients have been known to say at that moment, "Stop social-working me." Of course, what they are reacting to is the worker's intellectualizing, which is not effective social work. Genuine empathy involves stepping into the client's shoes and summoning an affective response that comes as close as possible to the experience of the other.

With the emergence of technique-centered training programs that focus on developing a patterned response from the worker, the danger of expressing an artificial response increases. One worker described how she had been taught by one program to reflect back the clients' feelings with the phrase, "I hear you saying...." When she used this technique in one interview, her client looked surprised and replied, "You *heard* me saying that!" The reaching for feelings must be genuine. The worker must be feeling something as he or she addresses the client's affect.

***Hospital Social Work: An Abusing Mother After Removal of a Child*** In the illustration that follows, a worker talks with a mother about her reactions to one of her five children being taken into the care of the agency after being admitted to the hospital with bruises. In discussions with the hospital social worker, the mother had admitted to having beaten the child. The child welfare social worker discussed the placement with the mother.

WORKER: We have to be honest with you, Mrs. Green. Did the hospital social worker talk to you about the possibility of your child being placed?
CLIENT: Yes, but not with my mother; anywhere else but there.
WORKER: I guess your mother has enough kids already.
CLIENT: It's not that; it's that we don't get along.

---

1. For a full discussion of the author's supervision model, see *Interactional Supervision*, 3rd edition, 2010, NASW Press.

WORKER: Can you think of anyone else your son can live with?

CLIENT: I have a friend, Sara, who helped me when my husband died and when I had my baby.

**Practice Points:** Note how the worker tries to empathize with the mother by asking directly about her feelings. This is difficult because the worker will have feelings about the abuse of the child. However, in the long run, if the worker can really help the mother as a client in her own right she will actually be helping the abused child as well as the other children.

WORKER: This must be a hard time. How are you feeling about the possibility of your son being placed?

CLIENT: I can't stand the idea. I don't want the other children with me if John is placed. I have often said this to the kids when I was angry at them—I told them I would place them all, and the kids remember that.

This interview continues in the next section.

## Displaying Understanding of the Client's Feelings

The skill of displaying understanding of the client's feelings (introduced in Chapter 3) involves indicating through words, gestures, expression, physical posture, or touch (when appropriate) the worker's comprehension of the expressed affect. The worker attempts to understand how the client experiences the feelings even if the worker believes that the reality of the situation does not warrant the reaction. The worker may believe that the client is being too self-punishing or taking too much responsibility for a particular problem. Even so, the client may not agree at that moment, and the worker must respond to the client's sense of reality. Furthermore, the worker needs to resist the natural urge to rush in with reassurances and attempts to help the client feel better. The reader should think back to moments when he or she had strong feelings of any kind and someone, a friend or relative, said "you shouldn't feel that way." All that did was emphasize that the other person really did not understand the power and the reality of the emotion.

**Practice Points:** Efforts at reassurance are often interpreted by the client as the worker's failure to understand. As one client put it, "If you really understood how bad I felt, you wouldn't be trying to cheer me up." We return to the interview with the mother at the point where she commented, "I told them [the children] I would place them all, and the kids remember that." The worker needs to stay with the client's feelings rather than responding to an understandable urge to try to convince the client that she should not feel this way.

WORKER: We often say things when we are hurt or angry that we regret later.

CLIENT: I told the hospital social worker that if John was placed, all of the kids might have to be placed. I feel very strongly about this. It will hurt me to lose my kids, but I can't bear to think about getting up in the morning and only counting four heads instead of five.

WORKER: You mean that together you are a family, and, if one is missing, you're not? (She nodded when I said this and began to cry softly.)

**Practice Points:** The worker's gentle restatement of the client's feelings has communicated to the client that the worker understands and is compassionate. The client expresses her emotions by crying. This is an important form of communication between worker and client. Part of the healing process includes the client's sharing of feelings with a caring person.

***The Importance of Encouraging the Expression of Strong Emotions*** Workers often express their fear of strong emotions. They are concerned that a client might become too depressed and that the worker's effort to bring the emotions to the fore could result in more problems. Some workers worry that clients' feelings will overwhelm them to the point where they feel equally depressed and hopeless—the workers would then lose their ability to be effective. For many workers, the ultimate fear is triggering such deep feelings in the client that the client feels overwhelmed and commits suicide.

Note that the emotions themselves do not create the problems; rather, clients' inability to face their feelings or to share them with someone important does. The power that feelings can have over clients may be dissipated when these feelings are expressed and dealt with. The greater danger is not in the facing of feelings but in their denial. The only thing worse than living with strong emotions is the feeling that one is alone and that no one can understand.

The worker's fear of being overwhelmed by emotions can be alleviated somewhat if the worker is clear about the worker's role and the purpose of the engagement. The worker's sense of function requires placing a demand for work on the client (as discussed in the next section). No matter how strong the client's feelings of hopelessness, some next step can always be taken. The worker needs to experience the client's feelings of being overwhelmed (the empathy) while still indicating a clear expectation (the demand) that the client will do something about the situation, even in those cases in which doing something means coming to grips with the reality (e.g., the death of someone close) and picking up and beginning again (e.g., searching out new significant relationships). Belief in the strength and resilience of the client enables a worker to make this demand.

With clarity of purpose in mind, the worker can help the client find the connections between the emotions and the purpose of the discussion. Significant work with clients in painful areas can be done only after the expression and acknowledgment of feelings. The flow of affect and understanding between worker and client is a necessary precondition for further work. Workers who attempt to make demands on clients without first having experienced the affect with them will be perceived as "not understanding," and their demands will be experienced as harsh and uncaring. Empathic responses build a fund of positive work that the worker can draw on later. This fund is a buffer that helps the client experience a worker's later confrontation as a caring gesture from someone who does understand.

## Putting the Client's Feelings into Words

Thus far, I have described how a worker might reach for feelings and acknowledge those that have already been stated. There are times, however, when a client comes close to expressing an emotion but stops just short. The client might not fully understand the feeling and thus be unable to articulate it. In other cases, the client might not be sure it is all right to have such a feeling or to share it with the worker. Putting the client's feelings into words is the skill of articulating the client's affect a half step ahead of the client. This occurs when the worker's tuning in and intense efforts to empathize during the session result in emotional associations as the client elaborates a concern.

**Practice Points:** In our previous example, the hospital social worker asked, "You mean that together you are a family, and, if one is missing, you're not?" and the client responded by crying softly. The worker gave the client a tissue and waited a few minutes. The client sat and looked at the floor.

WORKER: You must be feeling like a terrible mother right now. (The client nodded.) It must be really rough with all of the problems with the house, everything breaking down on you, having these hassles every day, and five kids also must make it pretty rough sometimes.

**Practice Points:** The client had not directly said anything about her parenting or about feelings of guilt, but, by articulating this emotion, the worker gave the client permission to discuss her own feelings about herself. If, as in the first negative illustration in this section, the worker is so busy trying to consciously or unconsciously communicate disapproval of the client's actions, she cannot hear the client's own harsh judgment of herself. The assumption here is that how we feel about ourselves has a great deal of influence on how we think about ourselves and how we act.

The way the worker can begin to help this mother is to break a vicious cycle in which her own guilt leads to feelings of helplessness and hopelessness and a negative self-image, which in turn leads to poor parenting, and so on. The ability to articulate and face her feelings—to share them with a caring and yet demanding worker—can be a beginning. The worker's acceptance of the client, including her feelings, can be the starting point for the client's acceptance of herself.

**Interactive Skills of Helping**

Use the accompanying DVD or visit *The Skills of Helping Individuals, Families, Groups, and Communities,* Seventh Edition, CourseMate website at www.cengagebrain.com and enter your personal access code to watch this video

**EMPATHIC SKILLS** A social worker meets with an elderly client who is in a wheelchair and has great difficulty speaking. The empathic skills under difficult circumstances are demonstrated in the practice excerpt. In the "blooper," the worker ignores the feelings of the client and tries to rush the interview because he is having difficulty understanding her words.

## Research on Empathy

Empathic skills have consistently been identified as important in helping relationships. One of the early pioneers in this area—working in the field of psychotherapy—Truax (1966) found a relationship between personality change and therapist empathy, warmth, and genuineness. Rogers (1969) points to several studies that found empathy to be central to the worker's effectiveness. In the field of educational research, Flanders (1970) found empathy to be an important skill for teachers in improving student performance. A growing body of evidence following these early studies suggests that this is one of the core skills for all helping functions.

My own research supports these findings. The skill of acknowledging the client's feelings appears to contribute substantially to the development of a good working relationship between worker and client as well as to the worker's ability to be helpful

(Shulman, 1978). It was the second most powerful skill in my research, ranking only behind the skill of sharing worker's feelings, which is discussed in a later section. This finding was replicated in both the study of supervision skill (Shulman, 1981, 1984, 2010) and the study of the practice of family physicians (Shulman & Buchan, 1982).

Videotape analysis data indicated less concern with affect on the part of workers than the overall study suggested. Workers shared their own feelings or dealt with client feelings in only 2.3 percent of their interventions in the individual sessions and in 5.3 percent of their interventions in the group sessions. When total interactions in the session were analyzed, including times when the client was speaking and the worker listening, the total interventions that dealt with the affect in the group sessions dropped to 1.4 percent. This figure is very close to Flanders's results from analyzing teaching behaviors (Flanders, 1970).

When examining the skill profile of the average worker, I found that clients perceived their workers as acknowledging their feelings "fairly often" and as articulating their feelings without their having to share them between "seldom" and "fairly often" (Shulman, 1993b). When the correlation between this skill and the development of the caring dimension of the working relationship was examined, it was the second strongest associating skill when used in the beginning phase of practice ($r = .54$) and the strongest associating skill when used in the middle phase ($r = .77$). Similar patterns were found in relation to trust and worker helpfulness.

In a more recent qualitative study of empathy as an interpersonal phenomenon, Hakansson and Montgomery (2002, 2003) examined the experiences of 28 empathizers and 28 targets through analysis of their narrative accounts of situations in which they experienced empathy. Their subjects were 20 to 64 years old. The researchers focused on the constituents of both the empathizers' and the targets' experience of empathy. They examined four constituents: (1) The empathizer understands the target's situation and emotions, (2) the target experiences one or more emotions, (3) the empathizer perceives a similarity between what the target is experiencing and something the empathizer has experienced, and (4) the empathizer is concerned for the target's well-being. The data suggested that the actions associated with the fourth constituent concern make empathy an interpersonal phenomenon (2002, p. 267). The researchers' definition of the dimension of concern included such acts as "giving time, paying attention, giving the target advice, doing something for the target, being concerned for the target, being respectful towards the target, and performing coordinated acts demonstrating concern" (2002, p. 279).

This finding offers additional support for my construct that describes how skill—including empathy—develops a working relationship with the client. The expression of concern for the client corresponds to the term *caring* in my own research. All of the behaviors associated with concern could be perceived as contributing to the client's perception of the worker as "caring as much about me as my children" and "here to help me, not just investigate me" (Shulman, 1978, 1991).

Although there is a consensus that the skills of empathy are important in the helping relationship, or "therapeutic alliance," some researchers have suggested that some clients (e.g., unmotivated and volatile ones) would be better served by "therapeutic detachment" (Galloway & Brodsky, 2003). This view suggests the need for research that further defines and differentiates the mechanics of the process through which empathy affects a working relationship and outcomes. These researchers suggest addressing questions such as: "Under what circumstances does empathy help?" "With which clients?" and "For what kind of problems?" Additionally, can the helper determine whether detachment would be more appropriate?

# Sharing the Worker's Feelings

EP 2.1.1b
EP 2.1.3c
EP 2.1.10b

An essential skill relates to the worker's ability to present himself or herself to the client as a "real" human being. Theories of the helping process that follow the medical paradigm have presented the ideal worker as an objective, clinical, detached, and knowledgeable professional. In these models, direct expression of the worker's real feelings is considered unprofessional. This has resulted in a concept of professionalism that asks the worker to choose between the personal and the professional self. I believe this is another of the many false dichotomies that plagues our practice; the real skill lies in integrating the personal and the professional. Rather than losing one's personal self in practice, learning how to use one's personal self is, I believe, a lifelong professional development task.

## Integrating the Personal and the Professional

In an earlier example, one worker illustrated the effect of the personal/professional dichotomy in one of my training workshops. She described her work with a woman who had just discovered that her child was dying of cancer. As the woman spoke, grief overcame her and she began to cry. The worker felt compassion and found herself holding the woman's hand and crying with her. Recall that a supervisor, passing by the open door, criticized the worker for her "unprofessional" behavior.

My view is that the worker was helping at that moment in one of the most important and meaningful ways we know. She was sharing the pain with the client, and, in expressing her own sorrow, she was making a gift of her feelings to the client. This worker was responding in a deeply personal way, yet, at the same time, she was carrying out her helping function. The interactional practice theory suggests that the helping person is effective only when able to synthesize real feelings with professional function. Without such a synthesis of personal and professional, the worker appears as an unspontaneous, guarded professional who is unwilling to allow clients access to the worker's feelings. The irony is apparent: The social worker asks clients to take risks and to be open, honest, and vulnerable in sharing feelings, while—in the name of professionalism—he or she is doing just the opposite. The result will be the "mechanical" worker who always maintains self-control, who has everything worked out, and who is never at a loss for words or flustered—in short, a person who is difficult to relate to in any helpful way.

Clients do not need a perfect, unruffled worker who has worked out all of life's problems. They require someone who cares deeply about the clients' success, expresses the clients' own sense of urgency, and openly acknowledges feelings. When clients experience the worker as a real person rather than mechanical, they can use the worker and the helping function more effectively. If the worker shows no signs of humanity, the client will either constantly test to find the flaws in the facade or idealize the worker as the answer to all problems. The client who does not know at all times where the worker stands will have trouble trusting that worker.

## When the Worker Is Angry with the Client

If the worker is angry with the client, it is much better to get the anger out in the open where it can be dealt with honestly. Workers who fear the expression of angry feelings as signs of their own "aggressiveness" often suppress them, only to have them emerge indirectly in ways to which the client finds it harder to respond. Professional expressions of anger, for example, through an unfeeling interpretation of a client's behavior, can be more hurtful than an honest statement of the feeling.

Direct expression of feelings is as important for the worker as it is for the client. A worker who suppresses feelings must use energy to do so. This energy can be an important source of help to the client if it is freed for empathic responses. The worker cannot withhold feelings and experience those of the client at the same time. The worker may also become cut off from important forms of indirect communication in which the client uses the worker's feelings to express his or her own.

***Residential Social Worker with an Angry Parent*** Consider the following example of this process. A worker in a residential center for children was confronted by an angry parent after an incident on an excursion in which the child was left on a bus during a field trip and lost for a time. This child had been apprehended by the agency because of numerous complaints of neglect and abuse. During a visit to the center, the client began a loud, angry tirade directed at the worker.

CLIENT: What kind of a place do you run here anyway? He's only been here 3 weeks, and already he's sick, had a bump on his head, and you jerks lost him on a bus.
WORKER: (Obviously upset but trying to control himself) Look, Mr. Frank, we do the best we can. You know, with 15 kids on the bus, we just lost track.
CLIENT: Lost track! For God's sake (his voice getting louder), you mothers are paid to keep track, not lose track of my kid. Do you realize what could have happened to him on that bus alone?

**Practice Points:** The client screamed the last question. The worker felt embarrassed, overwhelmed, backed against the wall, conscious of the other workers and the kids watching, and angry at the client. Instead of addressing his angry feelings, he responds with a threat that is an indirect expression of anger.

WORKER: (With great control in his voice) You know, we simply can't tolerate this behavior in the house. You're upsetting all of the children, and if you don't calm down, I'm going to have to stop your visiting.

**Practice Points:** The truth of the matter is that the client was upsetting the worker, who did not know what to do about it. His anger was expressed in a controlled fashion, which turned it into an attempt to exert his authority over the client. He tried to tame the client by using his ability to influence access to the child. The calmer and more controlled the worker seemed, the angrier the client became. With his own feelings racing in all directions, the worker's efforts to put up a calm front actually cut him off from a professional response. He had no way of understanding that parents who have had children apprehended also often feel guilty, embarrassed, overwhelmed, backed against the wall, and quite conscious of the reactions of their children.

The client may have unconsciously used the incident to make the worker feel exactly how he himself had felt for the past 3 weeks. In this sense, the client's feelings were projected onto the worker, and the attack was a form of indirect communication. (In the group work chapters of this book, I will present the work of Bion [1961] who would describe this as "projective identification.")

Unfortunately, the worker expended his energy on defending himself and suppressing anger. He could not work with this client in a meaningful way as long as he blocked expression of his own feelings. The client needed to keep pushing him until he got some reaction. Returning to the interview, we see that the worker's attempt to "read the riot act" to the client resulted in an escalation on the client's part.

CLIENT: You can't stop me from seeing my kid. I'm going to call my lawyer and bring charges against you and the agency for incompetence.

**Practice Points:** When the worker finally responds with some honesty, the energy is released to actually hear and begin to understand the father's feelings under the anger. He then asks the client to start all over. He is also able to place the importance of their repairing their relationship in the context of helping the father's child.

WORKER: (Finally losing his temper) Well, go ahead and call. I'm tired of hearing you complaining all the time. Do you think it's easy to deal with your kid? Frankly, I'm tired of your telling me what a lousy worker I am.

CLIENT: (With equal intensity) How the hell do you think I feel? (Silence)

WORKER: (A deep sigh as the worker seems to be catching his breath) You've been feeling this way ever since they took Jim away from you, haven't you?

CLIENT: (Subdued, but still angry) It's no picnic having your kid taken out of your house and then being told you're an unfit parent.

WORKER: Look, we can start all over. I felt angry, guilty, and very defensive when you put me on the spot, and that's why I threatened you about the visiting business. I guess I just didn't know how else to handle you. You know, we really need to get along better in spite of your being angry at the agency, for your sake, for mine, and especially for Jimmy's. How about it? (Silence)

CLIENT: I guess I was a little rough on you, but you know, I worry about the kid a lot and when he's not with me, I feel . . . (struggling for the right word)

WORKER: Powerless to help him, isn't that it?

**Practice Summary:** The worker's expression of his own feeling freed his energy to respond to the client's question, "How the hell do you think I feel?" The results of this important step were threefold. First, the worker began to strengthen the working relationship between himself and the child's parent. This parent cared, and his anger and assertiveness could make him an excellent client to work with. I know that may be hard to believe, given our own feelings about dealing with anger; however, a passive-aggressive client would really be more difficult in the long run.

Second, it allowed the worker to begin to respond empathically to the client, which is a crucial skill in the helping process. Finally, it demonstrated openness on the part of the worker to admitting feelings and mistakes. The client perceived an adult, a helping professional, who understood the connection between his own feelings and his actions. It is precisely this kind of openness to self-examination that the father will need to develop if the family relationship is to be strengthened.

## A Worker's Investment in the Success of the Client

In the two illustrations presented thus far, we have seen how the worker's feelings of caring and anger, when expressed openly, can help clients. This honest and spontaneous expression of feelings extends to a broad range of worker responses. Another example is the feeling of investment a worker can have in a client's progress. For some reason, the idea of self-determination has been interpreted to mean that the helping person cannot share a stake in the client's progress and growth. At points in the struggle toward change when clients feel most hopeless and ready to quit, workers sometimes suppress their own feelings of disappointment. This is a misguided attempt not to unduly influence the client's choices.

***Social Work with a Paraplegic Young Adult in a Rehabilitation Center*** The following example illustrates the importance of direct expression of a worker's hope and expectations. A professional is working with a paraplegic young adult in a rehabilitation center. A relationship has developed over months as the worker has helped the patient deal with his feelings about this sudden change in his life. The exercise program to help the patient develop some limited functioning in his limbs has gone slowly and painfully, and with no signs of a quick recovery.

**Practice Points:**   Disappointed by the pace of his progress, the patient has become depressed and apathetic, refusing to continue. It is at this point that the following dialogue begins. Keep in mind that this excerpt follows months of developing the working relationship. The professional has a fund of positive feelings to draw on as she makes this facilitative confrontation, a confrontation designed to move the client forward in his work.

PATIENT: It's no use continuing—I quit!

WORKER: Look, I know it's been terribly frustrating and damn painful—and that you don't feel you're getting anywhere—but I think you are improving and you have to keep it up.

PATIENT: (With anger) What the hell do you know about it? It's easy for you to say, but I have to do it. I'm not going to get anywhere, so that's that.

WORKER: (With rising emotion) It's not the same for me. I'm not sitting in that wheelchair, but you know, working with you for the past 3 months has not been a picnic. Half the time you're feeling sorry for yourself and just not willing to work. I've invested a lot of time, energy, and caring in my work with you because I thought you could do it—and I'm not about to see you quit on me. It would hurt me like hell to see you quit because the going gets rough.

**Practice Summary:**   The patient did not respond immediately to the "demand for work" expressed in the worker's affective response. However, the next day, after some time to work through the feelings, he appeared for physiotherapy without a word about the previous conversation. Once again, we see how a worker's statement of feeling can integrate a highly personal and at the same time highly professional response. The worker's feelings are the most important tool in the professional kit, and any efforts to blunt these feelings results in a working relationship that lacks substance.

## A Worker Sharing Feelings Associated with Life Experiences

Another way in which sharing the worker's feelings can be helpful in a relationship is when the affect is directly related to the content of the work, as when the worker has had a life experience similar to that of the client. Self-disclosure of personal experiences and feelings, when handled in pursuit of purpose and integrated with the professional function, can promote client growth.

**EP 2.1.1c**

***Mentally Challenged Young Men Dealing with Grief: The Worker's Parent Dies*** In one dramatic example, a student social worker was describing in my practice class her work in a residential setting with a group of young men who were mildly mentally challenged. All of these clients had recently lost a significant family member.

They had been brought together to discuss their losses because they had been exhibiting ongoing depression and denial. The group was started to help them face their feelings and to accept, or at least learn to live with, their sadness. Two weeks into the group, the student's father died, and she had to return home to take care of her own grieving. The clients were aware of her loss.

When she returned, she picked up with the group but did not mention the reason she had been away, even though she knew the members had been informed. One of the members said to her, "Jane, your father died, didn't he?" The worker later described feeling overwhelmed by his comment and struggling to maintain her "professional composure." She reported that the group members must have sensed her emotions, because another member said, "It's OK to cry, Jane, God loves you too!" In response to his comment, she began to cry and was joined by most of the group members. After a few moments, she commented to the members that she had been encouraging them to share the pain of their losses, but she had been trying to hide her own. The group members began their first serious and emotion-filled discussion of their own losses and why they tried to hide their feelings, even from themselves. As the student described the incident in class, she cried again and was joined by many other students and this instructor as well.

Even as I write about this incident, I can remember the many objections raised by workers when I advance the argument in favor of sharing the worker's feelings. Let us take some time to examine these.

### Boundary Issues in Sharing the Worker's Feelings

The first concern relates to the boundaries within which personal feelings can be shared. I believe that, if a worker is clear about the contract (the purpose of the work with the client) and the particular professional function, these will offer important direction and protection. For example, if a client begins an interview by describing a problem with his mother-in-law, the worker should not respond by saying, "You think you have problems with your mother-in-law? Let me tell you about mine!" The client and worker have not come together to discuss the worker's problems, and an attempt by the worker to introduce personal concerns, even those related to the contract area, is an outright subversion of the contract. If the student in the previous example had started to discuss the death of her father and her own loss, rather than using the moment to return to the clients' issues and to deepen their work on their losses, she would not have been synthesizing the personal and professional—she simply would have been unprofessional.

The client seeks help from the worker, and the worker's feelings about personal relationships can be shared only in ways that relate directly to the client's immediate concerns. For example, take a situation in which a worker feels that the client is misinterpreting someone's response because of the client's feelings. The worker who has experienced that kind of miscommunication might briefly describe his or her experience as a way of providing the client with a new way to understand an important interaction.

A second area of major concern for workers is that, in sharing their feelings spontaneously—that is, without first monitoring all of their reactions to see if they are "correct"—they risk making inappropriate responses. They worry that they will make a mistake, act out their own concerns, and perhaps hurt a client irretrievably. This fear has some basis because workers do, at times, respond to the client based on their own needs. A young worker gets angry at an adolescent client's mother because this mother seems as overprotective as the young worker's own. Another worker experiences great frustration with a client who does not respond immediately to an offer of help but moves slowly through the process of change. Although the client makes progress at a reasonable pace, it still makes the worker feel ineffective. Still another worker misses several indirect cues from a group home resident about a serious problem with his family, whom he is about to visit during the holidays. The worker responds to the resident's acting out of the feelings through negative behavior by imposing angry punishment instead of hearing the hidden message.

Spontaneous expression of feeling leads to all of these mistakes and others. In fact, a helping professional's entire working experience will inevitably consist of making such mistakes, catching them as soon as possible, and then rectifying them. In these cases, a good worker will learn something about his or her personal feelings and reactions to people and situations. As this learning deepens, these early mistakes diminish. The worker then becomes conscious of new, what I like to describe as more sophisticated mistakes.

When teachers, supervisors, theorists, and colleagues convey the idea that the worker should try during interviews to monitor her or his feelings continuously, to think clearly before acting, and to conduct the perfect interview, they are setting up blocks to the worker's growth. Only through continuous analysis of some portion of their own work after the interview has taken place can workers develop the ability to learn from their mistakes. The more skilled workers, who are spontaneous, can catch their mistakes during the interviews—not by withdrawing and thinking, but by using their own feelings and by reaching for the cues in the client's responses. This is what the residential counselor with the angry parent in the earlier example was able to do.

What is often overlooked is that clients can forgive a mistake more easily than they can deal with the image of a perfect worker. They are truly relieved when a worker owns up to having "blown" an interview, not having understood what the client was saying or feeling, or overreacting and being angry with a client. An admission of a mistake both humanizes the worker and indirectly gives the client permission to do the same. Workers who feel clients will lose respect for their expertise if they reveal human flaws simply misunderstand the nature of helping. Workers are not "experts" with the "solutions" for clients' problems, as suggested by the medical paradigm. Instead, workers possess skills that can help clients develop their own solutions to their problems. One of the most important of these skills is the ability to be personally and professionally honest.

## Sexual Transference and Countertransference Feelings

Finally, some worker feelings are seen as too potentially harmful to be expressed. This is true; however, there are few such feelings. For example, many feelings of warmth and caring may flow between a worker and a client. These positive feelings constitute a key dynamic that helps to power the helping process. Under certain circumstances, feelings of intimacy are associated with strong sexual attraction. These mutual attractions are often understandable and normal. However, a client would find it difficult to handle a worker who honestly shared a sexual attraction.

Because of the authority of the worker, as well as the process of transference, sharing feelings of sexual attraction—and, even worse, acting on them—constitutes a form of unethical sexual exploitation. Clients are vulnerable in the helping relationship and need to be protected. It is especially tragic and harmful when clients who are seeking help to heal their wounds from exploitive relationships find themselves in yet another one, this time with an exploitive worker. Again, the problem is not that the worker is sexually attracted to a client. This can be understandable, and the worker should be able to discuss these emotions with a supervisor and/or colleagues. The unethical part is acting on feelings with the client.

*Female Worker Reacts to a Paraplegic Male's "Come-on"* Workers sometimes feel that they are in a bind if clients begin to act seductively toward them and even directly request some response from the worker. For example, a young and attractive female worker described her reactions to the "come-on" of the paraplegic male client in a rehabilitation setting as "stimulating." She felt somewhat ashamed of her feelings, because she thought they revealed a lack of professionalism. Most workers in the consultation group in which this illustration was presented reported that they, too, had experienced these feelings at times. They had not discussed them with colleagues, supervisors, or teachers because they felt a professional taboo against doing so.

When the discussion returned to the interaction in the interview with the paraplegic, I asked the participants to tune in to the meaning of the sexual "come-on" in the context of the contract. They speculated that the young client feared he could not be sexually attractive as a paraplegic. With a new handle for approaching the issue, it was clear to the worker that the client's feelings and fears about his sexual attractiveness might be a central issue for work that the worker would miss if overwhelmed by her own feelings.

This illustrates how the worker can use the process (interaction with the client) as a tool to explore the content (the substantive content of the working contract). In this example, the worker confronted the client directly about his comments to her, clarified her professional and ethical responsibilities and boundaries, and then reached directly for his issues with regard to relationships to the opposite sex. The work proceeded to explore this painful, yet crucial, area of content. (A later section discusses process and content connections in greater detail.)

**Engaging and Working with the Hard-to-Reach Client**

Use the accompanying DVD or visit *The Skills of Helping Individuals, Families, Groups, and Communities,* Seventh Edition, CourseMate website at www.cengagebrain.com and enter your personal access code to watch this video

**MIDDLE PHASE CONTINUES** Integrating False Dichotomies: The author addresses the apparent dualisms or dichotomies that can negatively influence practice. These include the suggested dichotomies between personal and professional, structure and freedom, support and confrontation, and content and process.

## Research on Sharing Feelings

A number of helping professions have produced research on the impact of sharing workers' feelings. The findings indicate that this skill plays as important a part in the helping process as the empathic skills described earlier. The skill has been called "self-disclosure" or "genuineness," among other labels. In my 1978 study, the worker's ability to "share personal thoughts and feelings" ranked first as a powerful correlate to developing working relationships and being helpful. Further analysis of the research data suggested that the use of this skill contributed equally to the work of developing the working relationship and the ability of the worker to be helpful.

The importance of this skill was replicated in the more recent practice study (Shulman, 1991). It was one of the four skills in the grouping called *skills to help clients manage their feelings.* These skills had a strong impact on the development of the caring element of the working relationship and, through caring, a strong impact on the client's perception of the worker's helpfulness as well. In addition, there was a low but significant influence on hard outcome measures (final court status of the children and days spent in care).

Examined by itself, the skill was found to correlate significantly with caring, trust, and helpfulness when used in the beginning and middle phases of practice, but it was usually at the low end of the list of eight skills. The difference in the importance of this skill in this study, compared with the 1978 study, may be related to a change in study design.

What inferences can we take from these findings? It may be that, in sharing personal thoughts and feelings, the worker breaks down the barriers that clients experience when they face the feelings of dependency evoked by taking help. As the worker becomes more multidimensional—more than just a professional helping person—there is more "person" available for a client to relate to. In addition, thoughts and feelings of a personal nature appear to provide substantive data for the client's tasks and therefore increase the worker's helpfulness. Perhaps the personal nature of the data is what makes it appear more relevant to the client, easier to use and to incorporate into a sense of reality. This skill, like many others, may simultaneously serve two functions. By sharing feelings freely, a worker effectively strengthens the working relationship (the process) while contributing important ideas for the client's work (the contract).

When the skill-use profiles of the average worker in the 1978 and 1991 studies were examined, I found that clients perceived their workers as seldom sharing their personal thoughts and feelings. When these findings were later shared with workers in various training groups, they always provoked important discussions in which workers explored the reasons why they found it difficult to reveal themselves to clients. The group's first response was to cite a supervisor, book, or former teacher who had made it clear that sharing feelings was unprofessional. As one worker put it, "I was told I had to be a stone-faced social worker."

After a discussion of these injunctions and their impact on the workers, I would say, "Based on my research, my practice experience, my expertise, I am now telling you that it is no longer 'unprofessional' to be honest with clients and to make your feelings part of your work." I would then inquire how this new freedom would affect their work the next day. After a long silence, a typical response from a worker would be "You have just made things a lot tougher. Now I'm going to have to face the fact that it's my own feelings that make it hard for me to be honest. I'm not really sure how much of myself I want to share." At this point in the workshop discussion following this honest admission the work would deepen.

I will also share the findings of my early doctor-patient interactional research related to the issue of sharing feelings (Shulman & Buchan, 1982). Although physicians believed that they were able to hide their feelings toward patients, especially negative ones, this study showed a high correlation between the doctor's expressed attitude toward the patient (positive, neutral, or negative) and the patient's perception of the doctor's attitude. In fact, the doctor's attitude was an important predictor of the outcomes. Thus, some members of the profession from which we borrowed the medical model may believe in a *myth* of emotional neutrality.

Developing the ability to be honest in sharing feelings is difficult, but workers ask clients to do it all the time. It is an essential skill to provide effective helping. As one client said of her worker, "I like Mrs. Tracy. She's not like a social worker. She's like a real person." This model suggests that Mrs. Tracy was both a real person and a real social worker.

# Making a Demand for Work

In constructing this model of the helping process, thus far we have seen the importance of five components: establishing a clear contract, identifying the client's agenda, helping the client to elaborate concerns, making certain the client invests the work with feeling, and sharing the worker's feelings.

## Client Ambivalence and Resistance

At this point, we should examine the question of ambivalence and resistance. Clients will be of two minds about proceeding with their work. A part of them, which represents their strength, will move toward understanding and growth. Another part of them, which represents their resistance, will pull back from what is perceived as a difficult process.

Work often requires lowering long-established defenses, discussing painful subjects, experiencing difficult feelings, recognizing one's own contribution to the problem, taking responsibility for one's actions, giving up long-held cognitive frameworks about life, and confronting significant people and systems. Whatever the difficulty involved, a client will show some degree of ambivalence.

Perlman (1957) describes client ambivalence as follows:

> To know one's feelings is to know that they are often many-sided and mixed and that they may pull in two directions at once. Everyone has experienced this duality of wanting something strongly yet drawing back from it, making up one's mind but somehow not carrying out the planned action. This is part of what is meant by ambivalence. A person may be subject to two opposing forces within himself at the same moment—one that says, "Yes, I will," and the other that says, "No, I won't"; one that says, "I want," and the other, "Not really"; one affirming and the other negating. (p. 121)

Relating client ambivalence to the relationship with the worker and the process of taking help, Strean (1978) describes resistance as follows:

> Recognizing that every client has some resistance to the idea and process of being helped should alert the social-work interviewer to the fact that not every part of every interview can flow smoothly. Most clients at one time or another will find participation difficult or may even refuse to talk at all; others will habitually come late and some may be quite negative toward the agency, the social-work profession, and the social worker. (p. 193)

***Adolescent Foster Boy: Ambivalence and the Demand for Work*** An example of this ambivalence at work is found in the following excerpt from a videotaped interview with an adolescent foster boy.

**Practice Points:** Early in the interview, the 18-year-old indirectly hinted at his feelings about leaving a group home and particularly about the warm feelings he had established for the head child-care worker. The worker missed the first cues because she was preoccupied with her written agenda that rested on the table between them. Catching her mistake during the session, the worker moved her agenda aside and began to listen systematically to this theme, to encourage the client to elaborate, and to reach for and articulate his feelings. The following excerpt picks up the interview at the point at which the worker responded to the client's second offering of this concern.

**Worker:** Is it going to be hard to say good-bye to Tom (the head child-care worker)?
**Client:** It's not going to be hard to say good-bye to Tom, but I'll miss the little kittens that sleep with me. Last night one dug his claws into me and I screamed and screamed and yelled to Tom—"Come and get this goddamn kitten—do you think I'm going to go around ruptured all my life?" (At this point, the client had told the story with such exuberance that the worker was laughing along with him. The client quickly reached over the table for the worker's written agenda and said, "OK, what's next?")

**Practice Points:** When the worker was distracted by the agenda, the client continually offered indirect cues related to this important theme. As the worker began to deal seriously with the theme, the part of the client that feared the discussion and the accompanying feelings found a way to put the worker off by using the worker's own agenda. The client might also be testing to see if the worker is ready for the discussion. By allowing herself to be put off, the worker sent the message, "I'm not ready, either." When this was explored with the worker in a consultation, her reflections on the process led her to recognize that she was also about to end her work with this client—an ending she was avoiding. In effect, she had a stake in putting off the discussion as well because she had become close to the client and was already feeling the loss as he prepared to make the transition to independence. Once again, the ability of the worker to manage her own feelings influenced her ability to help the client manage his. (The ending phase of practice is discussed in detail in Chapter 6.)

The important thing to remember is that resistance is quite normal. In fact, a lack of resistance may mean that the progress of the work is an illusion and the real issues still unexplored. If this client could have easily dealt with his feelings about terminating his relationship with Tom, he would not have needed the worker's help. Termination feelings form the core of the work for foster children who must struggle to find ways to invest in new, meaningful relationships despite deep feelings of rejection by their biological parents. Many of these children have experienced a number of losses in their life, including the loss of a normal childhood. This client was losing Tom, the residence, and this caring social worker as well. When the worker approached the core area of feeling, it would be surprising if resistance did not appear.

A crucial concept is that resistance is a part of the work. Less experienced workers who do not understand this may back off from an important area. Their own confidence in what they are doing is fragile, so when the client shows signs of defensiveness or unwillingness to deal with a tough problem, they allow themselves to be put off. This is especially true if workers experience their own ambivalence about the area.

Communication of ambivalence in tough areas can be seen as the client's way of saying, "This is tough for me to talk about." It can also be a question to the worker: "Are you really prepared to talk with me about this?" It is one of those life situations in which the other person says he is reluctant to enter the taboo area, hoping you will not really believe him. The surface message is "Leave me alone in this area," while the real one is "Don't let me put you off." These are the moments in interviews when the skills of making a demand for work are crucial.

The notion of a demand for work is one of Schwartz's (1961) most important contributions to our understanding of the helping process. He describes it as follows:

> The worker also represents what might be called the demand for work, in which role he tries to enforce not only the substantive aspects of the contract—what we are here for—but the conditions of work as well. This demand is, in fact, the only one the worker makes—not for certain perceived results, or approved attitudes, or learned behaviors, but for the work itself. That is, he is continually challenging the client to address himself resolutely and with energy to what he came to do. (p. 11)

The demand for work is not limited to a single action or even a single group of skills; rather, it pervades all the work. For example, the process of open and direct contracting in the beginning phase of work represents a form of demand for work. The attempt of the worker to bring the client and feelings into the process is another form of demand for work. The illustration of the earlier described interview with the angry father (the "agency client"), Mr. Gregory, in which the worker kept coming back to his feelings in the situation is a good example. The father said, referring to how long his children would be in care: "It's a long time for the kids." The worker responded, "And for you too." Similarly, in the interview with the foster child, the youngster was discussing, at one point, the feeling that had grown between Tom (the child-care worker) and himself, and he said to the worker, "How does it hit people like him?" The worker's response was "How does it hit you?" This is another illustration of the demand for work, or what might be better described as an empathic demand for work.

## Integrating Support and Confrontation: The Empathic Demand for Work

Note that this demand can be gentle and coupled with support. It is not necessarily confrontational. I underline this point because of a tendency for people to see confrontation as negative and uncaring. Some models of practice, particularly in the substance abuse area, have been designed to use confrontation to break down defenses. It is quite possible for the worker to make an empathic demand for work—and, as emphasized earlier, confrontation is experienced as caring if carried out in the context of a positive working relationship.

Several specific skills can be categorized as demand-for-work skills:

- Partializing client concerns
- Holding to focus
- Checking for underlying ambivalence
- Challenging the illusion of work
- Pointing out obstacles

Each is related to specific dynamics in interview situations that could be interpreted as forms of resistance. Note that the consistent use of demand-for-work skills can only be effective when accompanied by the empathic skills described earlier. As the workers express their genuine caring for the clients through their ability to empathize, they build up a fund of positive affect that is part of the working relationship—almost like a bank account that the worker can draw on when needed. Only when clients perceive that their worker understands, and is not judging them harshly, can they respond to the demands.

An integration of empathy and demand for work is needed. On one hand, workers who have the capacity to empathize with clients can develop a positive working relationship but not necessarily be helpful. On the other hand, clients will experience workers who only make demands on their clients, without the empathy and working relationship, as harsh, judgmental, and unhelpful. The most effective help will be offered by workers who can synthesize caring and demand in their own way.

This is not easy to do, either in the helping relationship or in life. There is a general tendency to dichotomize these two aspects of relationships, and workers might see themselves as going back and forth between the two. For example, caring about someone, expressing it through empathy, but getting nowhere leads to anger and demands, with an associated hardening of empathic response. However, it is precisely at this point, when crucial demands are made on the client, that the capacity for empathy is most important. With this stipulation clearly in mind, in the next section we explore four specific demand-for-work skills.

### Partializing Client Concerns

**EP 2.1.1a**

Clients often experience their concerns as overwhelming. A worker may find that a client's response to an offer of help in the contracting phase consists of the recitation of a flood of problems, each having some impact on the others. The feeling of helplessness experienced by the client is as much related to the difficulty of tackling so many problems as it is to the nature of the problems themselves. The client feels immobilized and does not know how or where to begin. In addition, maintaining problems in this form can represent resistance. If the problems are overwhelming, the client can justify the impossibility of doing anything about them.

***Interview with an Overwhelmed Single Parent: The Power of Partializing*** Partializing is essentially a problem-management skill. The only way to tackle complex problems is to break them down into their parts and address these parts one at a time. The way to move past perceptions of helplessness and feelings of being immobilized is to begin by taking one small step on one part of the problem. This is one way the worker can make a demand for work. When a worker listens to the concerns of the client and attempts to understand and acknowledge the client's feelings of being overwhelmed, the worker simultaneously begins the task of helping the client to reduce the problem to smaller, more manageable proportions.

**Practice Points:** This skill is illustrated in the following excerpt of an interview with a single parent. Note that the worker empathizes with the client's feeling of being overwhelmed but then, having listened carefully, breaks the overwhelming problem into manageable pieces. In this case, the worker also asks the client to identify which issue is most important.

WORKER: You seem really upset by your son's fight yesterday. Can you tell me more about what's upsetting you?

CLIENT: All hell broke loose after that fight. Mrs. Lewis is furious because he gave her son a black eye, and she is threatening to call the police on me. She complained to the landlord, and he's threatening to throw me out if the kids don't straighten up. I tried to talk to Frankie about it, but I got nowhere. He just screamed at me and ran out of the house. I'm really afraid he has done it this time, and I'm feeling sick about the whole thing. Where will I go if they kick me out? I can't afford another place. And you know the cops gave Frankie a warning last time. I'm scared about what will happen if Mrs. Lewis does complain. I just don't know what to do.

WORKER: It really does sound like quite a mess; no wonder you feel up against the wall. Look, maybe it would help if we looked at one problem at a time. Mrs. Lewis is very angry, and you need to deal with her. Your landlord is important, too, and we should think about what you might be able to say to him to get him to back off while you try to deal with Frankie on this. And I guess that's the big question, what can you say to Frankie since this has made things rougher for the two of you? Mrs. Lewis, the landlord, and Frankie—where should we start?

**Practice Points:** The demand implied in the worker's statement is gentle yet firm. The worker can sense the client's feelings of being overwhelmed, but she will not allow the work to stop there. In this example, one can see clearly two sets of tasks: those of the worker and those of the client. The client raises the concerns, and the worker helps her to partialize her problems; the client must begin to work on them according to her sense of urgency. This is the sense in which work is interactional, with the worker's tasks and those of the client interacting with each other. (This interview is continued in a later section of this chapter.)

When a worker partializes an overwhelming problem and asks a client to begin to address the issues, she or he is also acting on a crucial principle of the helping process: **There is always a next step.** The next step is whatever the worker and client can do, together, to begin to cope with the problem. Even when a client is dealing with a terminal illness, the next steps may mean developing a way of coping with the illness, getting one's life in order, taking control of the quality of one's remaining time, and so on. When social supports, such as adequate housing, are not available for a client, the next steps may involve advocacy and confrontation of the system or, if all else fails, attempting to figure out how to minimize the impact of the poor housing. Although the worker may not be able to offer hope of completely solving the problem, the worker needs to help the client find the next step. When a client feels overwhelmed and hopeless, the last thing he or she needs is a worker who feels exactly the same way.

***Research Findings on Partialization Skill*** In my more recent practice study, partializing was one of the four skills for helping clients manage their problems that contributed to the development of the trust element in the working relationship (Shulman, 1991). The other skills in the managing problems grouping included clarifying purpose and role, reaching for client feedback, and supporting clients in taboo areas. The trust element of the relationship, in turn, contributed to the client's perception of the worker as being helpful. This is a logical finding, because workers who help their clients to deal with complex problems are going to be seen as more helpful.

Furthermore, when used in the beginning phase of practice, the partializing skill ranked fifth out of eight skills in the strength of its correlation with the caring element of the working relationship. It moved to second place in relation to the trust element of the relationship, and to first in importance in terms of its impact on helpfulness. This association between partializing and the working relationship replicated a finding in my earlier study, in which the skill appeared to contribute to the outcome of helpfulness through its impact on relationship (Shulman, 1978).

Why, then, does use of the partializing skill positively affect relationship building? One explanation may be that the worker's use of the partializing skill conveys several important ideas to the client. First, the worker believes the tasks facing the client are manageable. Second, the worker conveys the belief that the client can take some next step—that is, that the client has the strength to deal with the problem when it is properly broken down into manageable pieces. Third, because partializing also serves to focus the work clearly, it may be another form of clarifying role and purpose. In any case, the findings on the partializing skill suggest that workers might do well, especially early on, to help clients identify clearly the component parts of the concerns they bring to the worker.

These ideas are consistent with the more recent evolution of the strengths perspective and solution-focused approaches (introduced in Chapter 2 and discussed in more detail in Chapter 17). Essentially, the worker conveys to clients a belief in their ability to manage their problems if they can address them step by step. Asking clients to reflect on times in their lives when they were able to deal with issues more effectively—one of the basic solution-focused techniques—is an effort to help change clients' cognition about their life and their abilities.

## Holding to Focus

As a client begins to deal with a specific concern, associations with other related issues often result in a form of rambling in which the client has great difficulty concentrating on one issue at a time. *Holding to focus*—asking the client to stay on one question—is a second problem-solving skill that incorporates a demand for work. Moving from concern to concern can be an evasion of work; if the client does not stay with one issue, he or she does not have to deal with the associated feelings. Holding to focus sends the message to the client that the worker intends to discuss the tougher feelings and concerns. This skill is illustrated in the earlier interview with the single parent. After the client decided to deal with Mrs. Lewis first (because of her fear of police involvement), the discussion continued:

CLIENT: When Mrs. Lewis came to the door, all she did was scream at me about how my Frankie was a criminal and that she would not let him beat up her son again.

WORKER: You must have been frightened and upset. What did you say to her?

CLIENT: I just screamed back at her and told her that her son was no bargain and that he probably asked for it. I was really upset because I could see the landlord's door opening, and I knew he must be listening. You know he warned me that he wouldn't stand for all of this commotion anymore. What can I do if he really kicks me out on the street?

WORKER: Can we stay with Mrs. Lewis for a minute and then get back to the landlord? I can see how angry and frightened you must have felt. Do you have any ideas about how Mrs. Lewis was feeling?

**Practice Points:** By acknowledging the distress (support) and then returning to the issue of dealing with Mrs. Lewis (demand), the worker helped the client stay focused on this issue instead of allowing the client's anxiety to overwhelm her.

## Checking for Underlying Ambivalence

One of the dangers in a helping situation is that a client may choose to go along with the worker, expressing an artificial consensus or agreement, while really feeling ambivalent about a point of view or a decision to take a next step. I have called these agreements "New Year's Resolutions" meant to be broken. Checking for underlying ambivalence is thus another important task of the worker.

Clients may go along with the worker in this way for several reasons. A client who feels that the worker has an investment in the "solution" may not want to upset the worker by voicing doubts. The client may also be unaware at this moment of his or her current doubts or the ones that might appear later, when implementation of the difficult action is attempted. Finally, the client may withhold concerns as a way to avoid dealing with the core of the issue. In this sense, the client shows another form of resistance that is subtle because it is expressed passively. In these circumstances, when words are being spoken but nothing real is happening, we have the illusion of work, which is the single most dangerous threat to effective practice. Having lived for six years in French Canadian Montreal, Quebec, I call this the "therapeutic pas des deux"—a form of a dance in which workers and clients develop marvelous ways of maintaining the illusion, each for his or her own reasons.

Sometimes workers are aware of clients' underlying doubts, fears, and concerns but simply pass over them. As one worker put it, "I knew we were just spinning our wheels, but I was afraid to confront the client." Workers believe that raising these issues may cause the client to decide not to take the next step. They believe that positive thinking is required, and they do not wish to heighten the client's ambivalence by acknowledging and discussing it. However, the reverse is true. It is exactly at moments such as these that the worker should check for the underlying ambivalence.

When a client has an opportunity to express ambivalence, the worker has access to the client's real feelings and can be of help. When discussed with the worker, negative feelings usually lose much of their power. Perhaps the client is overestimating the difficulties involved, and the worker can help clarify the reality of the situation. In other cases, the next step will indeed be difficult. The worker's help consists of empathic understanding of the difficulty and expression of faith in the client's strength and resilience in the face of these feelings. Whatever the reasons for hesitation, they must be explored so that they do not block the client's work outside the session.

***Looking for Trouble when Everything is going your Way*** Workers need to struggle against a sense of elation when they hear clients agree to take an important next step. Schwartz (1961) describes the need for workers to "look for trouble when everything is going your way." For example, in working with a client with a substance abuse problem, an enthusiastic worker might accept the client's agreement to enter a treatment program and then be disappointed when the client does not show up for the intake appointment. Careful examination of the session reveals that the client sent signals that he was still in the "contemplative" stage and not yet ready to move into the "action" stage of seeking help. Workers often admit to sensing a client's hesitancy but believing that it can be overcome through positive encouragement. This mistake comes back to haunt the worker when the ambivalence and fears emerge after the session.

All is not lost if, in the next session, the worker can admit to having moved too quickly and can encourage the client to explore his mixed feelings, which are normal at this stage of the process. This provides a good opportunity to elaborate on the earlier comment that resistance is part of the work. It would be a mistake simply to think of client resistance as an obstacle to progress; rather, there are important "handles for work" within the resistance itself. In the example of the client with a substance abuse problem, as the worker explores the client's resistance, important work themes may emerge: concerns regarding acceptance of a problem with substances, how employers would view him, feelings of shame, memories of traumatic events that serve as triggers, and so on.

In another example, a young university student who had been admitted to a psychiatric unit after a suicide attempt announced early in the first interview that she would not discuss her boyfriend or her family because that would mean she blamed them. She simultaneously expressed resistance (what she wouldn't discuss), and one of her central concerns related to guilt over her anger and resentment. Exploring why she did not want to discuss them could lead directly to a central theme of concern—perhaps that she really did blame them.

## Challenging the Illusion of Work

As mentioned earlier, perhaps the greatest threat to effective helping is the illusion of work. Although helping can be achieved through nonverbal means such as touch or activity, much of the helping process takes place through an exchange of words. We have all engaged in conversations that are empty of real meaning. It is easy to see how this ability to talk a great deal without saying much can be integrated into the helping interaction. This represents a subtle form of resistance: By creating the illusion of work, the client can avoid the pain of struggle and growth while still *appearing* to work. For the illusion to take place, however, two must engage in the ritual. The worker must be willing to allow the illusion to be created, thus participating actively in its maintenance. Workers have reported helping relationships with clients that have spanned months, even years, in which the worker always knew, deep inside, that it was all illusion.

Schwartz (1971) describes the illusion of work in this passage about group work:

> Not only must the worker be able to help people talk but he must help them talk to each other; the talk must be purposeful, related to the contract that holds them together; it must have feeling in it, for without affect there is no investment; and it must be about real things, not a charade, or a false consensus, or a game designed to produce the illusion of work without raising anything in the process. (p. 11)

### *Marriage Counseling Example: The Illusion of Work*

**Practice Points:** The skill involves detecting the pattern of illusion, perhaps over a period of time, and confronting the client with it. An example from marriage counseling illustrates this process. A couple had requested help for problems in their marriage. As the sessions proceeded, the worker noted that most of the conversation involved problems they were having at work, with their parents, and with their children. Some connection was made to the impact on their marriage; however, they seemed to have created an unspoken alliance not to deal with the details of their relationship. No matter how hard the worker tried to find the connections to how they got along, they always seemed to evade him. Finally, the worker said,

> You know, when we started out, you both felt you wanted help with the problems in your marriage, how you got along with each other. It seems to me, however, that all we ever talk about is how you get along with other people. You seem to be avoiding the tough stuff. How come? Are you worried it might be too tough to handle?

**Practice Summary:**  The worker's challenge to the illusion brought a quick response as the couple explored some of their fears about what could happen if they really began to work. This challenge to the illusion was needed to help the couple begin the difficult, risky process of change. In addition, their resistance itself revealed a great deal about their underlying problems. They were demonstrating to the worker how they avoided talking to each other about their real problems.

 **Interactive Skills of Helping**

Use the accompanying DVD or visit *The Skills of Helping Individuals, Families, Groups, and Communities,* Seventh Edition, CourseMate website at www.cengagebrain.com and enter your personal access code to watch this video

**DEMAND FOR WORK: PART I** This is a private practice interview with a gay man who has come for counseling after being assaulted. The example demonstrates demand-for-work skills and the skills involved in challenging the illusion of work.

# Pointing out Obstacles

When developing his theory of the mediation function for social work, Schwartz (1961) broke down the function into five general sets of tasks. One of these was the task of searching out the common ground between the client and the systems to be negotiated. This task is evident when workers attempt to contract with clients—to find the connections between the felt needs of the client and the services of the agency. It is also apparent when the workers attempt to alert themselves, for example, to the subtle connections between a teenager's need for independence and the parents' desire to see their youngster grow and actually become independent.

Because the common ground between the individual and the system may appear to each to be diffused, unclear, or even totally absent, Schwartz elaborated his mediation function with a second set of important activities, the task of detecting and challenging the obstacles to work as these obstacles arise. Like all of Schwartz's tasks, this one is repeated, moment by moment, in every helping encounter. Two major obstacles that tend to frustrate people as they work on their own self-interest are the blocking effects of social taboos and the effect of the authority theme—the relationship between the person who gives help and the one who takes it.

In one example of the impact of societal taboos, a social worker working with a teenager who is exhibiting behavior problems in her high school picks up hints that there may be a problem at home, including indirect suggestion of sexual abuse. The social worker points out the obstacle by commenting at the end of the session that a number of the girls he sees have experienced some form of abuse at home, and that this is always difficult for them to talk about for a number of reasons. The teenage girl does not respond in the moment; however, at the beginning of the next session, she discloses that she has experienced incest with her father and has been too ashamed to tell anyone.

In another example of the impact of race and the authority theme, an African American high school student in a largely White school has difficulty discussing his experiences being bullied by White students with his White social worker. The social worker points out that it might be hard for the student to talk about what he is going through as a Black in a mostly White school with a White social worker. By pointing out this obstacle, the social worker opened the door for the discussion that followed.

## Supporting Clients in Taboo Areas

When moving into a helping relationship, the client brings along a sense of society's culture, which includes taboos against open discussion about certain sensitive areas. For example, we are taught early in life that direct questions and discussions about sex are frowned on. Other areas in which we are subtly encouraged not to acknowledge our true feelings include dependency, authority, loss, and financial issues. The last two examples in the previous section illustrate the power of discussing sex, incest, race, and authority.

Feeling dependent is often experienced as being weak. The unrealistic image of a "real man" or a "real woman" presents one who is independent, who can stand on his or her own feet, and who deals with life's problems without help. In the real world, however, life is so complex that we are always dependent on others in some way. Most people experience the bind of feeling one way, consciously or not, but thinking they should feel another way. The norms of our culture include clear taboos that make real talk about dependency difficult.

Money is considered a taboo subject as well. Many families deeply resent questions related to their financial affairs. Having enough money is equated with competency in our society, and poverty is embarrassing. Reluctance to discuss fees with professionals is one example of the effect of the taboo in social work practice. Clients sometimes contract for services without asking about the fee, feeling that it would be embarrassing to inquire.

One of the most powerful taboos involves feelings toward authority. Parents, teachers, and other authority figures do not generally encourage feedback from children on the nature of the relationship. We learn early on that commenting on this relationship, especially negatively, is fraught with danger. People in authority have power to hurt us, so we can only, at best, hint at our feelings and reactions. Revealing positive feelings to people in authority is almost as hard, because it is considered demeaning. The authority taboo creates an important problem in the working relationship between the worker and the client, as I shall demonstrate in the next section.

Loss represents another taboo—one that takes many forms and affects various types of clients and areas of work. For example, the loss of a relationship because of death or separation may be considered too difficult to discuss directly. A parent whose child has been born with a physical or mental problem may secretly mourn the loss of the perfect child he or she had wished to have. A survivor of sexual, emotional, or physical abuse may mourn the loss of childhood and innocence. The adult child of an alcoholic may mourn the loss of the family once hoped for, but he or she may not feel free to discuss this because the family taught that the problem must be kept a family secret. Many of the messages of our society indicate that direct discussion of loss is not acceptable.

***Creating the Culture for Work: Taboos and other Obstacles*** To help a client discuss taboo feelings and concerns, the worker has to create a unique "culture" in the helping interview. In this culture, it is acceptable to discuss feelings and concerns that the client may experience as taboo elsewhere. The taboo will not be removed for all situations, however. There are some good reasons for us not to talk freely and intimately on all occasions about our feelings in taboo areas, as the discussion on sharing worker feelings showed (e.g., a worker's sexual attraction to a client).

Discussing taboos during the interview is meant not to change the client's attitudes forever but rather to allow work in the immediate situation. The worker enables such discussion by monitoring the interaction of the work with the client and listening for clues that may reveal a taboo-related block in the process. Past experiences with clients and the tuning-in process may heighten the worker's sensitivity to a taboo that lies just beneath the surface of the interview. On recognizing the taboo, the worker brings it out in the open and begins the negotiation of a new norm of behavior for the interview situation.

***Forty-Eight-Year-Old Male and Sexual Dysfunction*** The following illustration concerning taboos is from an interview between a female helping professional and a 48-year-old male patient:

PATIENT: I've been feeling lousy for a long time. It's been especially bad since my wife and I have been arguing so much.

WORKER: Tell me more about the arguments.

PATIENT: They've been about lots of things—she complains I drink too much, I'm not home often enough, and that I always seem too tired to spend time with her. (At this point, the worker senses the patient's difficulty in talking. His hesitation and an inability to look directly at her are the cues.)

**Practice Points:**   Given the difference in gender and the general difficulty of talking about sexual dysfunction, the worker opens the door to this discussion while still leaving room for the client to decide whether to enter or not. She then openly acknowledges the difficulty and raises the gender difference as well.

WORKER: Often when there is a lot of difficulty like this, it spills over into the sexual area.

PATIENT: (After a long pause) There have been some problems around sex as well.

WORKER: You know I realize that it's tough to talk about something as intimate as sex, particularly for a man to discuss it with a woman. It's really not something one can do easily.

PATIENT: It is a bit embarrassing.

WORKER: Perhaps you can speak about it in spite of your embarrassment. You know, there is not much I haven't heard already, and I won't mind hearing what you have to say. Anyway, we can't do much about the problems if we can't discuss them.

PATIENT: I've been tired lately with a lot of worries. Sometimes I have too much to drink as well. Anyway, I've been having trouble getting it up for the past few months.

WORKER: Is this the first time this had happened?

PATIENT: The first time. I usually have no trouble at all.

WORKER: It must have come as quite a shock to you. I guess this has hit you and your wife hard.

**Practice Summary:**   The discussion continued as the client went into more detail about the nature of the problem. Other symptoms were described, and the worker suggested that a complete physical was in order. She pointed out that it was not at all unusual for these things to happen to men of this age and that often there were physiological reasons.

At the end of the interview, the worker reinforced the development of the new norm in their working relationship by commenting, "I know how hard it was for you to speak to me about this. It was important, however, and I hope this discussion will help you feel free to talk about whatever is on your mind." The patient answered that he felt better now that he had been able to get it off his chest.

Although this conversation would still be difficult for most men in our society, changes in the culture may have made it a bit easier. It's hard to turn on the TV without seeing a commercial for Viagra or other impotency treatments. At first, these commercials featured an elderly former U.S. senator who took the first step toward challenging the taboo. These commercials now include athletes, a former football coach with a reputation for being tough, and younger men. Clearly the pharmaceutical companies are trying to make the discussion and treatment of erectile problems acceptable and to change the norm of what makes a "real man."

It is important to see that identifying the taboo or any other obstacle is done to free the client's energy to work on the mutually agreed-on contract. Sometimes simply naming an obstacle will release the client from its power. In other situations, some exploration of the obstacle may be needed before its impact abates. For example, a client might need to talk briefly about the difficulty he feels in discussing issues related to sex. His family norms might have added to the pressure against such open discussion. Once again, as the client discusses the difficulties in talking about sex, he is actually beginning to talk about sex.

This idea needs to be emphasized. By addressing the process (the difficulty talking to the worker about the taboo subject), the client actually begins a discussion of the content (discomfort in this area). The integration of process and content is very clear when one understands that the client may be having the same problem talking openly—in the case of sexual issues—with his wife. By learning to talk to the worker, he is actually rehearsing the conversation he will need to have with his wife.

The worker needs to guard against a subtle subversion of the contract that can easily occur if the discussion of the obstacle becomes the focus of the work. The purpose of the helping encounter is neither to examine the reasons why the taboo exists nor to free the client from its power in all situations. Clarity of purpose and role can assist the worker to avoid the trap of becoming so engrossed in the analysis of the process that the original task becomes lost. In the preceding example, the discussion should move from a discussion of the taboo and the authority theme to the client's difficulty in having this conversation with his wife.

***My Early Research Findings*** In my early study, the skill of supporting clients in taboo areas was one of four skills that distinguished the most effective workers from the least effective, from their clients' perspective (Shulman, 1978). In the more recent study, this skill was only the sixth most used out of the eight skills examined (Shulman, 1991). Clients reported that their workers used this skill between "seldom" and "fairly often." This is not unexpected, because workers face the same taboos that clients do. Workers need experience and supervision to find the courage to speak directly about many of these issues.

The introduction of time to the analysis of this skill yielded some interesting findings. Supporting clients in taboo areas, when used in the beginning phase of work (first sessions), was the third strongest skill (out of eight) that correlated with the client's perception of the worker's caring ($r = .52$). The correlation for the use of the skill in the middle phase of work was slightly higher ($r = .58$). These findings were expected, because support of any kind, particularly in sensitive and painful areas of work, could contribute to the client's perception that the worker was concerned about him or her.

When the association between the beginning phase use of this skill and trust was examined, however, it was significant but smaller ($r = .37$). The correlation was higher when the skill was used in the middle phase ($r = .57$). A similar pattern was found when the skill use was correlated with client perception of the worker's helpfulness ($r = .39$ in the beginning phase, and $r = .50$ in the middle phase). One inference from these findings might be that the use of this skill in the early phases of work, before a solid working relationship has been established, primarily contributes to the working relationship through the development of a client's sense of the worker's caring. This provides some justification for the argument that it is better for the worker to risk and be too far ahead of the client than to be overly cautious and too far behind.

The use of the skill may have less of an impact on trust and helpfulness early in the work because of the lower levels of trust in the beginning phase of any relationship. In short, the client needs to feel somewhat safe with the worker before the worker's efforts to explore taboo areas have their largest impact on trust.

 **Interactive Skills of Helping**

Use the accompanying DVD or visit *The Skills of Helping Individuals, Families, Groups, and Communities,* Seventh Edition, CourseMate website at www.cengagebrain.com and enter your personal access code to watch this video

**Demand for Work: Part II** This is an interview with a young Latina woman. The client understands English but has difficulty speaking easily, so the interview is conducted through a translator. The issue that appears to be under the surface is domestic violence; however, the client is reluctant to discuss this part of her problem. The discussion looks into the meaning of resistance and how to explore it in a facilitative manner.

## Dealing with the Authority Theme

Schwartz (1971) describes the authority theme as a reference to "the familiar struggle to resolve the relationship with a nurturing and demanding figure who is both a personal symbol and a representative of a powerful institution" (p. 11). The authority theme is not one that just emerges in the beginning phase of practice. As the client uses the worker's help to deal with the task, positive and negative feelings will arise. At times, the client will think fondly of this caring and supportive figure. At other times, the client will feel anger toward a worker who demands that the client take responsibility for the client's own part in the events of her or his life. I often suggest to students and workers that if their clients are never angry at them, they probably are not pushing them hard enough. I also suggest that if their clients are always angry at them, they may not be supportive enough and this is also a problem.

Workers are not perfect individuals who never make mistakes. Even the most skilled worker will sometimes miss a client's communications, lose track of the real function and begin to sermonize, or judge the client harshly without compassion for real struggles. Reactions and feelings on the part of the client will result. As one enters a helping relationship, problems with the authority theme should be anticipated as a normal part of the work. In fact, the energy flow between worker and client, both positive and negative, can provide the drive that powers the work.

***Transference and Countertransference in the Authority Theme*** Two processes central to the authority theme are transference and countertransference. Drawing on Freud's psychoanalytic theory, Strean (1978) describes their effects on the worker-client relationship as follows:

> This relationship has many facets: subtle and overt, conscious and unconscious, progressive and regressive, positive and negative. Both client and worker experience themselves and each other not only in terms of objective reality, but in terms of how each wishes the other to be and fears he might be. The phenomena of "transference" and "countertransference" exist in every relationship between two or more people, professional or nonprofessional, and must be taken into account in every social-worker-client encounter. By "transference" is meant the feelings, wishes, fears, and defenses of the client deriving from reactions to significant persons in the past (parents, siblings, extended family, teachers) that influence his current perceptions of the social worker. "Countertransference" similarly refers to aspects of the social worker's history of feelings, wishes, fears, and so on, all of which influence his perceptions of the client. (p. 193)

Unfortunately, the authority theme is one of the most powerfully taboo areas in our society. Clients have as much difficulty talking about their reactions and feelings toward their workers as they do discussing subjects such as sex. When these feelings and reactions remain undiscussed, the helping relationship suffers. These strong feelings operate just below the surface and emerge in many indirect forms. The client becomes apathetic, is late for appointments, or does not follow up on commitments. The worker searches for answers to the questions raised by the client's behavior. In Strean's view, workers attempt to understand this behavior in terms of the client's "personality." However, the answers to the worker's questions are often much closer to home and more accessible than the intangible notion of personality. The answers often may be found in the interactional process between the worker and the client.

The skill of dealing with the authority theme involves continual monitoring of the relationship. A worker who senses that the work is unreal or blocked can call attention to the obstacle and respond directly to it if she or he thinks it centers on the authority theme. Once again, as with other taboo subjects, the worker is trying to create a culture in this situation in which the client perceives a new norm: "It is all right to treat the worker like a real person and to say what you think about how the worker deals with you." The worker can begin this process in the contracting stages by responding directly to early cues that the client wants some discussion about what kind of worker this will be (see Chapter 4). The new culture will develop slowly as the client tests this strange kind of authority who seems to invite direct feedback, even the negative kind. As the client learns that the worker will not punish her or him, the feedback will arise more often and more quickly than before. Also of importance, the client gets to see a nondefensive worker demonstrate the capacity to examine his or her own behavior and to be open to change—exactly what the worker will be asking the client to do. This is another example of integrating content and process.

***Conflict between a Worker and a 14-Year-Old in a Group Home*** The following illustration demonstrates this skill in action. It describes a brief interaction between a worker and John, a 14-year-old resident in a group home. The resident had been disciplined by the worker earlier in the afternoon for a fight he appeared to have provoked with another resident, Jerry.

**Practice Points:** The worker's one-sided intervention had shifted the fight to a battle of wills between John and himself, which then escalated until he finally imposed strict consequences. John had been quiet and sullen throughout dinner and the early evening. The worker approached him in the lounge.

WORKER: John, you have been looking mad all evening, ever since the fight. Let's talk about it.

CLIENT: F—k off!

WORKER: Look, I know you're mad as hell at me, but it won't help to just sit there and keep it in. It will be miserable for both of us if you do. If you think I wasn't fair to you, I want to hear about it. You know I'm human, and I can make a mistake, too. So how about it, what's bugging you?

CLIENT: You're just like all the rest. The minute I get into trouble, you blame me. It's always my fault, never the other kids'. You took Jerry's side in that fight without ever asking me why I was beating up on him.

WORKER: (Short silence) I guess I did come down hard on you quickly. You know, you're probably right about my figuring it was your fault when you get in trouble—probably because you get into trouble so often. I think I was also a little tired this afternoon and maybe not up to handling a fight on my shift. Look, let's start again. OK? I think I can listen now. What happened?

**Practice Points:** The discussion carried on about the fight and the issues that led up to it. It became clear that there were some ongoing questions between John and Jerry that needed to be dealt with. The worker suggested another meeting with Jerry present, at which time he would try not to take sides and try to help both John and Jerry work this out. John seemed willing but showed a great deal of skepticism. The interview continued, and the worker returned to the authority theme.

WORKER: You know, I really wasn't helpful to you this afternoon, and I'm sorry about that. But you know, I'm only human, and that is going to happen some-times. What I'd like you to do, if it happens again, is not just sit around upset but to call me on it. If you do, I may catch myself sooner. Do you think you can do that?

CLIENT: Don't worry—I'll let you know if you get out of line.

WORKER: I guess this kind of thing happens a lot to you, I mean with the other staff here and maybe even the teachers at school.

CLIENT: You bet it does! Mr. Fredericks is always on my back, the minute I turn around in my seat.

**Practice Summary:** In this illustration the worker caught his mistake, and he had an important discussion with his client about how they worked together. His willingness to own up to his mistake and to take negative feedback contributed to a change in the subtle rules that had governed John's reaction to adults in authority. The worker was very conscious that one of the most important outcomes of the young man's stay in the group home may be his development of greater skill in dealing with people of authority, who are not always skillful in dealing with him. In many ways, the helping relationship itself is a training ground in which the client develops new skills for dealing with authority. For some clients, particularly children in alternative-care facilities, the ability to trust adults and to risk themselves is so limited that learning to relate in a new way to the worker represents a profound change. It becomes a first step in developing their skills to deal with the outside world.

The worker also demonstrated an advanced level of skill when he deftly integrated process and task toward the end of the illustration. Part of his work involved helping John deal with the other systems of his life, such as his school. By generalizing to another situation, the worker found the work element related to their contract that was contained in the process. Dealing with the authority theme is not only a requirement for maintaining a positive working relationship; it may also provide important material to help clients work on the substance of the contract. The process-content integration issue is discussed in more detail in the next section.

## Identifying Process and Content Connections

*Process* refers to the interaction between the worker and the client (the authority theme) and between the client and other clients, such as family or group members (the intimacy theme). Another way to describe process is that it refers more to the way of working than to the substance or content of the work. *Content* is defined here as the substantive issues or themes that have been identified as part of the working contract.

### Process and Content that Address the Authority Theme

At any one time, the work in an interview (or family or group session or community meeting) is related to either process or content. However, because of the indirect nature of client communications, it is often hard to know which is really under discussion. For example, a single parent may have contracted to work on issues related to dealing with her children, employment, and relationships with friends and family. She may begin a session apparently talking about content—how none of her friends or relatives understands her pain. The issue is real to her, but she has also been angry with the worker since the previous session, when the worker missed her signals of distress.

This example emphasizes the importance of tuning in and worker tentativeness in the sessional contracting phase of a session, discussed earlier in this chapter. The worker who is tuned in to the client's pattern of indirect communications around issues of authority may be better prepared to hear that the discussion is really about process (the worker's ability to understand) rather than content (friends and relatives). If the worker prematurely assumes that the discussion is only content related, the session may turn into the illusion of work, with the process issues buried under the surface.

Thus far, the terms *content* and *process* have been described and illustrated; however, the concept of the integration of the two, cited often thus far, requires further elaboration. One major, common mistake made by workers is to fail to see the possible connections between process and content that allow for synthesizing of the two. Workers often describe being torn between process and content. Group leaders describe trying to balance the two, spending some time on process (how the group is working) and some time on content. What they do not realize is that they have fallen into the trap of accepting the false dichotomy of process *versus* content. When workers embrace this false dualism, they cannot avoid getting stuck. Instead, the worker must search out the connections between process and content so that the discussion of process deepens the work on the content, and vice versa.

**Practice Points:** Returning to our earlier angry single-parent example, the worker who looks for this synthesis may recognize (usually between sessions, rarely during a session) that the way in which the client indirectly raised her anger and hurt feelings at the worker's lack of compassion is a good example of the way this client deals with friends and other important people in her life. When her needs are not met, she gets angry because she expects other people to intuitively sense her feelings. This is a source of major communication problems, when we expect others to "divine" our feelings without being direct about them.

She does not take responsibility for being direct about her pain and thereby helping others to understand. In this case, if the worker opens up a discussion of the authority theme, the client can gain a deeper understanding of the skills she must develop to create and maintain a social support system. The client can be held accountable for her own responsibility in the relationship with the worker as well as in relationships with other significant people in her life. Thus, we see in this example that the content of the work can be synthesized with process issues, and the process issues can be integrated into the content. After discussing the authority theme, the worker can move from the specific issue of the client's way of dealing with the worker to the general issue of how the client seeks to have needs met by friends and family.

In another illustration, a social worker used her discussion with a foster teenager about the termination of service to open up a discussion of the difficulty the youth encountered in forming new relationships after so many had ended badly. They were able to explore this pain over the ending with the worker, as well as the many other losses he had experienced in his life. The teenager was able to see how difficult it was for him to invest in new relationships that might also end and therefore cause pain. The worker used a review of their relationship (the authority theme) to help the client understand and take some control over the feelings that affected him and his life. The importance of being willing to risk by getting close to other people was a central theme of the ending discussions, helping in the transition work. Their own ending provided an important opportunity for substantive work on how he could deal with new relationships now that he was transitioning to independence and leaving the care of the agency.

In a final example, one worker explored the difficulty a married client was having in allowing himself to feel dependent on the female worker and the discomfort he felt at expressing his need for help. The difficulty seemed to relate to many of his notions of what a "real man" should feel. The work on the authority theme led directly to discussions of how hard it was for him to let his wife know how much he needed her.

In each of these examples, dealing with the authority theme served two distinct functions: It freed the working relationship from a potential obstacle and led directly to important substantive work on the contract. But this can only happen if the worker rejects the process-content dichotomy and instead searches for the potential connections between the two.

## Impact of the Worker's Emotions

At times, the difficulty the worker has in being able to see and make use of the process-content connection relates to the emotions engendered in the worker by the manner in which the client uses process to communicate.

***Process-Content Connection in a Married Couples' Group*** In one example from the first session of a married couples' group I led and videotaped, all five men indicated on arrival that they were there to do whatever they could to help "straighten out" their wives. All of the wives indicated that they were depressed and seemed to accept the role of "patient," the client in a family system who is identified as having the problem. When clients accept the designation, the family cannot address the problems of the whole family and its dynamics. Two women in the group indicated that they were being seen by psychiatrists (all male, in this example) who prescribed drugs for their depression.

When I show this tape in my classes, many students express anger at one of the men, a 69-year-old who talks at great length about his wife's depression while she sits passively and silently. They become angry with me for not confronting this man at the start of the session, not demanding that he not speak for his wife. Some want me to "tell him to use 'I' statements!" The students are understandably upset about the sexist attitudes and myths that allow the male partner to deny his responsibility in the problem and to project all the difficulty onto his wife. I try to point out that the couples are letting me know in the first few minutes of the session exactly what the core of their problem is. This husband is saying to me:

> Social worker, if you want to see how we mishandle our marital relationship, just watch. I defend myself by taking no responsibility and defining my wife as the problem, while my wife accepts the blame outwardly, covering her rage with apathy and depression. Most helping professionals we have seen have colluded in accepting this maladaptive pattern of behavior as the definition of the problem.

I explain to my students that I can't get angry in a first session at clients who are acting out the very problem that brought them to the group for help. Understanding the connection between process and content reframes the interaction into a positive call for help. The process is the content.

In the detailed discussion of this example in Chapter 11, as I kept coming back to the male partner and reaching for his feelings while he was trying to talk about his wife, a noticeable lowering of his defenses took place. For example, he said, "My wife has been an inpatient in the psychiatric hospital for 6 weeks, and it has been a long time for her." I responded, "And it hasn't been easy for you either." After a short while, in a dramatic moment, he accepted some responsibility for his part in the problem when he revealed an incident of his verbal abuse of his wife, which caused him to cry in the session. As is often the case, during the group meetings that followed this first session, the women who were defined as the problem emerged as strong partners in the relationship and internal group leaders. In effect, the depression was their call for help—a signal of their strength rather than their weakness. During later sessions, for some of the men, a confrontation by the worker was needed as they continued to defend themselves and minimize their own part in the problem.

Once again, workers' ability to manage their own emotions powerfully affects their ability to help clients manage their feelings and problems. As a male group worker in the previous example, I found it fairly easy to tolerate the men's denial in the first session, to reframe the process as a call for help, and to reach for the related content. For a female worker, the struggle might be greater, as she would have experienced the oppression associated with sexism firsthand.

*A Female Worker with an Imprisoned Male Rapist* This important understanding was reinforced for me by an incident that occurred when I was teaching a class on group social work. By chance, the class consisted of all female students and me, the only male and a symbol of authority. I commented on this class composition issue in our first class and pointed out that we all might want to monitor this to see if it affected our work. There was no immediate response.

A turning point came in the sixth class when Jane, a student working in the criminal justice system, presented her work with a client who had been convicted of assaults. She related his story, in which he told how he had assaulted and raped his wife. She had experienced the manner in which he told the story as threatening to herself—it was as if he were trying to intimidate her in the telling of the story. The class discussion proceeded as follows:

> I asked Jane and the class to take a few minutes and explore what it felt like to work with clients who had done things that were very upsetting to them. In this case, it was rape of a woman; in another situation, it might be an adult who had sexually abused a child. We were discussing examples of male oppression of women and children. I wondered what Jane and the other students experienced as they heard this client's story. There was a brief silence, followed by Jane saying, "I was furious at him!" The class members began to tell stories of clients who had engendered similar feelings in them. Some indicated that their feelings were so strong that they didn't think they could ever work with a client like this.
>
> After several minutes, I intervened and said, "I think this is going to be the hard part for you, trying to examine the feelings provoked by clients like this and deciding whether or not you can work with them as clients in their own right." There was a momentary silence, following which one student said to me, with great feeling and anger, "You could never understand what this means to us!"

**Practice Points:**   I was stunned by the force of her comment. The other students stared at me to see how I would respond. I remained silent for a moment (containment) and realized that, as I was giving them my sage advice about examining their own feelings, I had not been feeling a thing.

> I broke the silence by saying, "You are absolutely right! I gave an intellectual response just then. It was easy to do, since I have not experienced the kind of gender oppression you have. What you said just now, about my never being able to understand, hit me very hard. I guess, on this issue, you are going to have to help each other."

After I spoke, I could sense the tension lifting. I remained silent as they began to talk with one another about how they tried to handle these situations. One student with work experience in shelters for battered women said she had felt she could never work with batterers, because she so strongly identified with the women. She went on to describe how she had taken a risk and co-led a group for male batterers with a male colleague. She had been amazed to find that she could retain her anger at the men but still start to overcome the stereotype of them she had developed. She found that she had been able to hold the men accountable for their actions and to take steps needed to protect the women still in their lives. Furthermore, she could see the men as clients in their own right. She said she felt that she now did a better job with women after having worked with the men. Discussion continued along these lines, with some students feeling they would be able to do it and others sure they could not.

As we neared the end of the class, I pointed out that Jane was going to be seeing this client again this week. I wondered if we could help her think through how she might handle the next interview. Last time she had sat on her feelings because she needed to be "professional." What advice did [the students] have for her now? Jane indicated that the discussion had helped already. She realized that she wanted to work with this client in spite of her feelings. If she didn't reach him, he eventually would abuse other women. She felt she should confront him with his behavior toward her the previous week. Others in the class supported this. I asked her what she might say. She tried to role-play how she could get back to the issue. Other students provided suggestions and feedback. I pointed out that she could also view his behavior toward her as demonstrating how he related to women—how he tried to exercise control through intimidation. Perhaps she could use the process in their work together and generalize to his relationship with other women. She agreed that it was worth a try, saying that at least she now felt she had a next step with him.

I credited Jane and the class with their fine work. I thanked the student who had confronted me. I asked them all to keep an eye on this issue and said that, if they ever felt in future classes that I did not really understand their struggle, they should say so as soon as possible.

This example is another illustration of process and task integration. The process in this class in relation to the authority theme (the relationship of the students to me) and issues of gender (a male teacher with female students) provided a medium for an important learning experience for the class. As the instructor, I had to model for the class a way of using process to deepen the work on the content, especially at a time when my own feelings were influencing me in a powerful way. This was exactly what I was attempting to help them do with their clients. As is often the case in teaching and learning, more is "caught" than "taught."

# Sharing Data

In a social work setting, we define worker data as facts, ideas, values, and beliefs that workers have accumulated from their own experiences and education and can make available to clients. Furthermore, as Schwartz (1961) argues,

> The worker's grasp of social reality is one of the important attributes that fit him to his functions. While his life experiences cannot be transferred intact to other human beings, the products of these experiences can be immensely valuable to those who are moving through their own struggles and stages of mastery. (p. 23)

Sharing worker data is important not only because of the potential usefulness to the client, but also because the process of sharing the data helps to build a working relationship. The client looks to the worker as a source of help in difficult areas. If the client senses that the worker is withholding data, for whatever reason, this can be experienced as a form of rejection. As a client might put it, "If you really cared about me, you would share what you know."

During my social work training, a student who was majoring in group work described his work with a group of teenage boys in a residential institution. They were planning their first party and were obviously underestimating the quantities of food and drink required. When I asked if he had pointed this out to them, he replied that he had not interfered, feeling that they would learn something important about planning. I was shocked and felt that if they ever found out he knew their supplies would fall short and had not told them, their significant learning would be about him.

Although the skills of sharing data may sound simple, several misconceptions about how people learn—as well as a lack of clarity about the helping function—have served to make a simple act complex. These problems are also apparent in the actions of workers who indirectly "slip in" their ideas. This is most easily recognizable in interviews wherein the worker leads a client to the answer that the worker already has in mind. The belief is that learning takes place if the client speaks the words the worker wants to hear.

In the balance of this section, I shall identify some of the skills involved in sharing data and discuss some of the issues that often lead workers to be less than direct.

## Providing Relevant Data

The skill of providing relevant data is the direct sharing of the worker's facts, ideas, values, and beliefs that relate to the client's immediate task at hand. The three key requirements for effective communication of data are that the data be related to the working contract, that they be necessary for the client's immediate work, and that the client actually hears, understands, and remembers what has been said. The third requirement is more likely to be met if the first two are respected.

Regarding the first requirement, if the worker is clear about the purpose of the encounter and that purpose has been openly negotiated with the client, then the worker has a guideline as to what data to share. A problem is created when the worker wants to teach something indirectly to the client and uses the interchange to subtly introduce personal ideas. The problem is that the client soon senses that the worker has a hidden agenda, and, instead of using the worker as a resource for the client's own agenda, he or she must begin to weigh the worker's words to see what is "up her sleeve." If data are related to an openly agreed-on purpose, however, the worker is free to share them directly.

The second requirement for directly sharing data is that the data be connected to the client's immediate sense of concern. Clients will not learn something simply because the worker feels it may be of use to them at some future date, even if it relates to the working contract. The attraction people feel toward ideas, values, and so forth is related to their sense of their usefulness at the time. One reason for the importance of sessional contracting is that the worker needs to determine the client's current sense of urgency and must share data that the client perceives as helpful at that moment in time.

The third requirement is that the client invests energy and feeling into the content and that the client is able to actually hear, understand, and remember what is said. A myth exists that words are magic and once spoken they have the desired impact. When teaching in a class or presenting a workshop I often point out that if we have 30 or 100 participants, they will each be hearing a different workshop as filtered through their personal and professional experiences, their preconceived ideas about practice, and their attentiveness that day or their emotional state. Although this is a slight exaggeration, since the core content does get through to most participants, I have had experiences where I am cited the next day for something I never said but the participant heard.

In my doctor-patient research (Shulman & Buchan, 1982), one finding was a high correlation between the patients reporting that they understood what their doctor had said (e.g., the nature of their illness, the treatment plan) and a second variable, the patients reporting that they believed the doctor had understood them. In other words the information shared by the doctor was selectively heard and understood by the patient depending, in part, on how skillful the doctor was in listening to the patient. Other factors also affected this process (e.g., the doctor's empathic skill), making it clear that simply saying the words was not enough.

## Providing Data in a Way that Is Open to Examination and Challenge

Workers are sometimes fearful of sharing their own fears, values, and so forth because of a genuine concern with influencing clients who need to make a difficult decision. The unwed mother, for example, who is trying to decide whether to abort her child, to have it and keep it, or to have it and give it up for adoption faces some agonizing decisions—none of which will be easy. Each option holds important implications for her future. The skillful worker will help such a client explore in detail these implications and her underlying feelings of ambivalence. During this work, the client may turn to the worker at some point and say, "If you were me, what would you do?" Workers often have opinions about questions such as these but hold them back, usually responding to the question with a question of their own. I believe it is better for workers to share their feelings about revealing their opinions and then to allow the client access to their views as representing one source of reality. For example,

> When you ask me that question, you really put me on the spot. I'm not you, and no matter how hard I try, I can't be you, since I won't have to live with the consequences. For what it's worth, I think the way you have spelled it out, it's going to be an awfully tough go for you if you keep the baby. I probably would place the child for adoption. Now, having said that, you know it's still possible that you can pull it off, and only you know what you're ready for right now. So I guess my answer doesn't solve a thing for you, does it?

Workers who withhold their opinion do so because they fear that the client will adopt it as the only source of reality. Rather than holding back, however, a worker can simultaneously allow the client access to his or her opinions while guarding against the client's tendency to use them to avoid difficult work. Schwartz (1961) describes this consideration that guides the worker's movements as follows:

> The first [consideration] is his awareness that his offering represents only a fragment of available social experience. If he comes to be regarded as the fountainhead of social reality, he will then have fallen into the error of presenting himself as the object of learning rather than as an accessory to it. Thus, there is an important distinction to be made between lending his knowledge to those who can use it in the performance of their own tasks and projecting himself as a text to be learned. (p. 11)

## Providing Data as a Personal View

Thus far, I have described how a worker can provide data to a client in a way that is open to examination by making sure that the client uses the data as just one source of reality. An additional consideration is to make sure that what is shared is presented as the worker's own opinion, belief, values, and so forth, rather than as fact. This is one of the most difficult ideas for many workers to comprehend, because it contradicts the normal societal pattern for exchanging ideas. Workers have an investment in their own views and will often attempt to convince the client of their validity. We are accustomed to arguing our viewpoint by using every means possible to substantiate it as fact. New workers in particular feel that they must present their credentials to clients to convince them that they know what they are talking about.

In reality, however, our ideas about life, our values, and even our "facts" are constantly changing and evolving. A cursory reading of childrearing manuals would convince anyone that the hard-and-fast rules of yesterday are often reversed by the theories of today. I have found that inexperienced workers are often most dogmatic in areas where they feel most uncertain.

The skill of sharing data in a way that is open for examination means that the worker must qualify statements to help clients sort out the difference between their reality and the worker's sense of reality. Rather than being a salesperson for an idea, the worker should present it with all of its limitations. A confident and honest use of expressions such as "This is the way I see it" or "This is what I believe, which doesn't mean it's true" or "Many people believe this, but others do not" will convey the tentativeness of the worker's beliefs. The worker must encourage the client to challenge these ideas when they do not ring true to the client.

Any nonverbal signals of disagreement mean that the worker needs to reach for the underlying questions. For example, "You don't look like you agree with what I just said. How do you see it?" The client's different opinions need to be respected and valued. Even if all the experts support the idea, fact, or value at issue, it will only have meaning for the client if and when the client finds it useful. In many ways, the worker is a model of someone who is still involved in a search for reality. Every idea, no matter how strongly held, needs to be open to challenge by the evidence of the senses. The worker is asking the client to do the same in relation to life, and the client should not expect any less of the worker. Schwartz (1961) sums this up:

> As he [the worker] helps them to evaluate the evidence they derive from other sources—their own experiences, the experiences of others, and their collaboration in ideas—so must he submit his own evidence to the process of critical examination. When the worker understands that he is but a single element in the totality of the [group] member's experience, and when he is able to use this truth rather than attempt to conquer it, he has taken the first step toward helping the member to free himself from authority without rejecting it. (p. 25)

## Helping the Client See Life in New Ways

A specific form of data is important enough to be included as a separate skill category. These are the skills with which the worker helps clients reexamine perceptions (cognitions) about themselves, their life situations, or important people or systems in clients' lives (e.g., husband, parent, school). This skill can be central to a form of practice called cognitive-behavioral therapy (for a fuller discussion of this approach and others, see Chapter 17). To summarize briefly, clients have developed their views of life subjectively. Given the difficulties involved in communications, they quite possibly have distorted other people's actions or have internalized perceptions of themselves and their life experiences which has led to negative feelings and self-defeating behaviors. By exploring alternative views in collaboration with the client, the worker attempts to help a client rethink his or her life situation and correct negative and inaccurate "automatic thoughts" and perceptions. This approach is consistent with some of the solution-focused techniques and strategies also discussed in Chapter 17.

One way the worker can do this is by identifying the person or part of the system that may still be reaching out to the client. In a way, the worker plays the role of the missing person, articulating during the interview the thoughts and feelings that might lie beneath the surface.

***A School Social Worker and an Adolescent Having Trouble in Class*** For example, following is an excerpt from an interview between a school social worker and an adolescent who is having trouble in a class.

CLIENT: Mr. Brown is always after me, always putting me down when I'm late with my work. I think he hates me.

WORKER: You know, it could be that Mr. Brown knows that you're having trouble keeping up and is really worried about your failing. He may be keeping after you to try to get you going again.

CLIENT: Well, it doesn't help. All it makes me do is want to miss his class.

WORKER: He might not realize that what he says makes you feel so bad. Maybe it would help if I could let him know that you feel he is really mad at you.

**Practice Summary:** The work continued with a discussion of the student's fears about what might happen if the social worker talked to the teacher and the social worker's reassurance about how he would handle it. Mr. Brown was surprised by the student's feelings. He had been frustrated because he felt the student did not care about school. A joint meeting was held to begin to discuss what each really felt in relation to the child's schoolwork. This started to open doors for collaboration.

After a period of bad experiences, the blocks in the reality of the relationship become the client's (and sometimes the system's) only view of reality itself. The worker needs to help the client explore this maladaptive pattern and to break the cycle that prevents the client from connecting to people and systems that are important for success. At these moments, a worker offers the possibility of hope and a next step by sharing a view of others in the system that allows the client to glimpse some possibility of mutual attraction. This is only possible when workers themselves see these possibilities, described earlier as the *areas of common ground*. For example, when a worker helps a teenager see that his parents' setting of curfew limits may show that they care for him and recognize that he is growing up, the worker has not solved the problem, but at least he has shed a new light on the interaction. The child-care worker who helps a resident see that a parent who misses visits may not be saying that he does not care for the child, but that he really cares too much, also holds out the possibility of reconciliation.

The findings of my earlier research on this particular skill were not strong; however, the skill correlated with helping to develop a working relationship, perhaps indicating that the importance of sharing new ways to perceive other people lies not in its content but in its impact on the relationship with the worker (Shulman, 1978). The client will have to use personal experiences to revise some thinking about people and systems during the time between sessions. It takes many years to build up stereotypes of oneself, parents, systems, and people in authority, and it will take more than the worker's words to change them. In expressing these alternative views, which can help the client see strengths and mutual attraction, the worker makes an important statement about views of life. The willingness to see the positive side of people's behavior and not to judge people's weaknesses may say a great deal to clients about how the worker might view them. This could contribute to strengthening the working relationship.

# Sessional Ending and Transition Skills

As with beginnings and middles, endings contain unique dynamics and special requirements for worker skills. I call this stage the *resolution stage*. It is not unusual to find workers carrying out their sessional contracting and demonstrating sensitive work with clients with regard to their concerns, but then ending a session without a resolution of the work.

By "resolution of the work," I am not suggesting that each session end neatly, with all issues fully discussed, ambivalence gone, and next steps carefully planned. A sign of advanced skill is a worker's tolerance for ambiguity and uncertainty, which may accompany the end of a session that has dealt with difficult work. If uncertainty is present for a client at the end of a session, the resolution stage might consist of identifying the status of the discussion. The five specific skills discussed in the balance of this section include summarizing, generalizing, identifying next steps, rehearsing, and identifying doorknob communications.

### Interactive Skills of Helping

Use the accompanying DVD or visit *The Skills of Helping Individuals, Families, Groups, and Communities,* Seventh Edition, CourseMate website at www.cengagebrain.com and enter your personal access code to watch this video

**SESSIONAL ENDINGS AND TRANSITIONS** In an interview with a young lesbian woman who is anxious about "coming out" to her family, the client shares an important issue as the session comes to a close.

Before we examine these skills, a word on client activity between sessions is in order. Workers sometimes act as if clients have no life between sessions. They review an individual counseling session or a group meeting and then prepare to pick up the next session "where we left off." The worker needs to realize that the client has had life experiences, contacts with other helping systems, new problems that may have emerged during the week, and time to think about problems discussed in the previous session. After giving much consideration to how to help a client with a particular problem, a worker may be surprised to discover that the client has resolved the issue between sessions. It would be a mistake not to recognize and legitimate these between-session activities. That is one reason why the sessional contracting skill, described at the beginning of this chapter, is so important.

## Summarizing

Often, the client is learning about life and trying to develop new skills to manage life in more satisfying ways. It can be important to use the last moments of a session to help the client identify what has been learned. How does the client add up the experiences? What new insights does the client have about understanding relationships to others? What has the client identified as the next, most urgent set of tasks? What areas does the client feel hopeless about and need more discussion on? I believe that the process of summarizing can help a client secure what he or she has learned. Sometimes the client summarizes the work, other times the worker does it, and sometimes they do it together. Note that summarizing is not required in all sessions. This is not an automatic ritual but a skill to be employed at key moments.

*An Interview with a Mentally Challenged 16-Year-Old Boy*  The skill is illustrated in the following excerpt from an interview with a mildly mentally challenged 16-year-old boy. He is discussing his relationship with his mother, who he feels is overprotective. After a painful session in which the worker asked the youngster to examine his own part in maintaining the problem, the resolution stage begins.
(John paused and seemed thoughtful.)

WORKER: This hasn't been easy, John; it's never easy to take a look at your own actions this way. Tell me, what do you think about this now? (Silence)

JOHN: I guess you're right. As long as I act like a baby, my mother is going to treat me like a baby. I know I shouldn't feel like such a dummy, that I can do some things real well—but you know that's hard to do.

WORKER: What makes it hard, John?

JOHN: I have felt like a dummy for so long, it's hard to change now. I think what was important to me was when you said I have to take responsibility for myself now. I think that's right.

WORKER: If you did, John, then maybe your mother might see how much you have grown up.

**Practice Points:**  The worker's request to summarize the work constitutes a demand for work. Her silence allows time for the response, and her support ("This hasn't been easy") helps the client face a painful realization.

## Generalizing

Earlier discussion stressed the importance of the elaborating skill of moving from the general to the specific as a way of facilitating the immediate work of the client. In addition, the worker often must work with the specific example and then move back to the general. In this way clients can develop a broader view of how to deal with similar problems as they emerge.

For example, in a situation presented earlier in the elaboration section of this chapter, one worker responded to a general comment from a mother about the difficulty of raising teenagers by requesting specific information on conflicts that week. As the mother gave details of the specific encounter when her daughter arrived home late, the worker helped her consider her feelings and actions and how she might have been able to handle that specific situation differently. The next step would be to help the client to generalize the learning from the specific incident to the general category of conflict with her daughter and perhaps other experiences as well.

This is a key skill of living, because it equips the client to continue without the worker and to use the newfound skills to deal with novel and unexpected experiences. This skill is demonstrated in the continuation of the interview with the mentally challenged adolescent in the preceding section. The discussion has moved to the importance of talking more honestly with his mother about his feelings. He balks and expresses doubts about being able to do this.

JOHN: I could never tell her how I felt, I just couldn't.

WORKER: Why not? What would make it hard?

JOHN: I don't know why, I just couldn't.

WORKER: Is it anything like what you felt when we discussed talking to your teacher, Mr. Tracy, about how dumb he sometimes makes you feel in class?

JOHN: I guess so; I guess I'm afraid of what she would say.

WORKER: You were afraid then that he would get angry at you or laugh at you, do you remember?

JOHN: Yeah, I remember. He didn't get mad. He told me he hadn't realized I felt that way. He has been nicer to me since then.

WORKER: Maybe it's also like that with other people, even your mother. If you could find a way to tell her how you felt, she could understand better. Do you remember how proud you were of yourself after you did it, even though you were scared?

**Practice Summary:** Generalizing from the experience with the teacher is an important learning tool. Any life skill, such as the importance of being direct with one's feelings, becomes clearer as clients observe its power in different situations and then learn to generalize it to others.

## Identifying the Next Steps

We have all experienced, at one time or another, frustration when we participate in some form of work that goes nowhere because of lack of follow-up. A good example is a committee or staff meeting in which decisions are made but the division of labor for implementing the decisions is overlooked, and no action follows. The worker must make a conscious effort to help the client identify the next steps involved in the work. No matter what the situation is, and no matter how impossible it may seem, some next step is possible, and the worker will ask the client to discuss it. I call this the principle of "there is always a next step." The next step may be a small one and not an easy one, but it will be available when all else fails.

Next steps must be specific; that is, the general goal the client wishes to achieve must be broken down into manageable parts. In the preceding example, next steps included helping the young man plan to spend time thinking of some of the things he can do differently to help his mother see another side of him, identifying what he felt about the relationship, and deciding to confront his mother with his true feelings.

The next steps for an unemployed mother on welfare who needs to find a job might include exploring day-care centers for her child and meeting with an employment counselor. The next step for a couple in marital counseling who feel their relationship is worsening might be to identify specific areas of difficulty for discussion the following week. In essence, the identification of next steps represents another demand for work on the client.

Lack of planning by the client does not always represent poor life-management skills; it may be another form of resistance. Talking about a tough subject may be difficult, but doing something about it may be even harder. By demanding attention to future, specific actions, the worker may bring to the surface another level of fear, ambivalence, and resistance that needs to be dealt with.

Sometimes the expression of understanding, support, and expectation by the worker is all the client needs to mobilize resources. There may be no easy way for the client to undertake the task, no simple solution, and no easy resolution when two genuinely conflicting needs arise. For the client, verbalizing the dilemma to an understanding and yet demanding worker may be the key to movement. At other times, the client may need help figuring out the specifics of how to carry out the act. For example, the client might need some information about community resources.

## Rehearsing

In the example of our adolescent, where the next step involved implementing some difficult interpersonal strategy, the skill of rehearsal was crucial; that is, he practiced what to say. Talking about confronting another person with regard to difficult, interpersonal material is one thing, but actually doing it is quite another. A client who protests "I don't know what to say" may be identifying an important source of blockage. A worker can help by offering the safe confines of the interview situation as a place for the client to rehearse. The worker takes on the role of the other person (boss, teacher, husband, mother, doctor, and so forth) and feeds back to the client possible reactions to the client's efforts. All too often, the worker skips this simple and yet powerful device for aiding a client by saying, "When the time comes, you will know what to say." Words do not come easily for most people, especially in relation to their most difficult feelings.

**Practice Points:**   With the help of a worker, clients may be able to say what must be said and, with some successful rehearsal under their belts, may feel a bit more confident about doing it. We return to the illustration at the point at which the teenager says that he does not know what to say to his mother.

WORKER: Look, John, perhaps it would be easier for you if you practiced what you would say to your mother. I'll be your mother, and you say it to me. I can tell you how it sounds.
JOHN: You will be my mother? That's crazy! (Laughing)
WORKER: (Also laughing) It's not so crazy. I'll pretend I'm your mother. Come on, give it a try.
JOHN: (With a lot of anger) "You have to stop treating me like a baby!" Is that what you mean; is that what I should say?
WORKER: Yes, that's what I mean. Now if I were your mother I could tell you were really angry at me, but I'm not sure I would understand why. I might think to myself, "That's just like John, he always runs around hollering like that." Maybe you could begin a bit calmer and tell me what you want to talk about.
JOHN: I don't understand.
WORKER: Let me try. I'll be you for a minute. "Mom, there is something I want to talk to you about—about the way we get along. It's something that really bothers me, makes me sad and sometimes angry." Now I don't know, perhaps that's not so good either. What do you think?

**Practice Points:**   Reversing roles in the rehearsal process is an excellent way of modeling how to handle a situation—what the words might sound like. The worker has made the suggestion but left open the option that the client may not find these words helpful. Note also that the worker has included "sad" in the sentence. The client has only said he is angry but the worker reaches for the part under the anger and the associated pain. The worker then has to address why it's hard for the client to admit to sadness.

JOHN: I see what you mean. Tell her I want to talk to her about how we get along. That's good, but I don't like the part about being sad.
WORKER: Why not? It's true, isn't it?

JOHN: I don't like to admit that to her.

WORKER: You mean you don't want to let her know how much it hurts. (John nods.) How will she ever understand if you don't tell her? Maybe there are things she would like to tell you, but she feels the same way.

**Practice Summary:** As the conversation continues, the worker and John explore the difficult problem of real communication between a teenager and his mother—in this case, a special variation on the theme because of the mental challenge. John tries to formulate what he would say, using some of the worker's ideas and incorporating some of his own. The worker offers to speak to John's mother or to be there during the discussion, if John wishes. The illustration underscores the value of rehearsal, as well as the way in which role-play can reveal additional blocks to the client's ability to deal with important people in his life. A worker who thinks she has done a marvelous job in helping a client learn to deal effectively with an important person may find that additional work needs to be done when the client formulates the words to be used. In this case, the difficulty in sharing the client's sense of hurt with his mother was important, unfinished business.

## Identifying "Doorknob" Communications

A "doorknob" communication is shared as the client leaves the office, often with his or her hand on the doorknob, or during the last session or sessions. This commonly observed phenomenon, described in the literature of psychotherapy, refers to any comments of significance raised by the client toward the end of a session when there is too little time to deal with them. We have all experienced a session with a client, or a conversation with a friend, when—after a relatively innocuous discussion—he says, "There is just one thing that happened this week." Then we hear that he lost his job or found out that his girlfriend was pregnant or received an eviction notice or noticed a strange lump in his groin. Reflecting on the session, the worker may see that the first clues to the concern were presented indirectly during the beginning phase. On the other hand, there may have been no clues at all.

A doorknob comment signals to the worker the client's ambivalence about discussing an area of work. The concern is raised at a time when it cannot be fully discussed. It may be a taboo area or one experienced as too painful to talk about. Whatever the reason, the desire to deal with the concern finally overwhelms the forces of resistance. The urgency of the concern, coupled with the pressures created by the lack of time left in the interview, finally results in the expression of the issue. This kind of comment is actually a special case of obstacles that block the client's ability to work. As with all forms of resistance, it is a natural part of the process and provides the worker with an opportunity to educate the client about the client's way of working.

*A Young Woman Raising Marital Concerns and a Sexual Problem* The skill involves identifying the process for the client. For example, at the end of a second session with a young woman concerned about her marriage, the client directly revealed a difficult sexual problem between her husband and herself. The worker responded directly:

WORKER: You know, you have just raised a really important issue, which we will not have time to talk about. You raised it at the end of a session. Were you feeling it was too tough to talk about, too uncomfortable?

CLIENT: (Brief silence) It is embarrassing to talk like this to a stranger.

WORKER: I can understand how it would be hard to discuss sex; I mean really talk about it, with anyone. You know, it's quite common for people to be reluctant to discuss this subject directly, and they often raise these kinds of difficult areas right at the end of the session, just like you did. (The client smiles at this.) Would it help if we started next session talking a bit about what makes it so hard for you to talk about sex? That might make it easier for us to discuss this important area. What do you think?

CLIENT: That sounds OK to me. This is a hard one for me, and I would like to discuss it.

WORKER: I think you are making a good start even by raising it at the end.

Practice Summary: The worker did not blame the client for her difficulty but instead offered support for the strength she had shown in raising the issue. By identifying the lateness of the comment, she built into the interview comments on the way in which the two of them work. The client's sophistication about how she works will increase, and, after more incidents like this one, she can begin to understand and control how she introduces material into the interviews. In addition, the discussion of the source of the embarrassment in the interview will open up related feelings about the difficulty of discussing sex in our society, as well as the couple's problems with open communication with each other in this area. The discussion of the process in the interview will lead directly to work on the content—another illustration of the process-content connection.

This discussion of sessional ending skills brings to a close our analysis of the work phase. The purpose of this analysis has been to identify some of the key dynamics in giving and taking help that follow the negotiation of a joint working contract. The next section will review some of the ethical issues that may arise during this phase, or really any phase of work.

The discussion of doorknob comments is an appropriate one to serve as a transition to the next chapter on the skills of the ending and transition phase. In many ways, the last portion of the work with a client may have a doorknob quality in that some of the most important and hard-to-discuss issues may make their appearance at this time. This phase of work provides an opportunity for the most powerful learning of the entire encounter. It does not always happen that way, however, and in the next chapter we discuss why the ending phase can create problems if not handled well, or solve others if the worker is skillful.

## Ethical and Legal Issues in the Middle Phase

EP 2.1.2c

In this section I will continue the discussion begun in earlier chapters of ethical and legal issues that can impact practice. I realize that for a student, and even an experienced practitioner, keeping track of ethical responsibilities and legal obligations, both state and federal, can be daunting. This is why the idea of having an agency committee or at least a supervisor who can be consulted when in doubt is important. Although I have chosen to list the following issues in this chapter on the middle phase, they can also easily emerge at a first session or during the ending phase as well.

### Ethical Issues in Withholding Information

An earlier discussion in this chapter on providing data raised the issue of withholding information. I argued that a client had a right to the worker's views when relevant to the purpose of the engagement. There are times, however, when the worker may face restraints and/or dilemmas. For example, the issues raised in the preceding section on providing data have taken on increased complexity as governments and other funding agencies have introduced economic and political issues into the equation.

***Patient Rights When Faced with Cost-Containment Decisions*** A social worker may face a conflict when agency or setting policy appears to come in conflict with professional ethical responsibilities and/or the National Association of Social Workers' (NASW's) Code of Ethics. As one example, cost-containment efforts in the health care system have led government and private third-party payers to develop a standard of care that dictates how long, on average, a patient should remain hospitalized after a specific procedure. Reimbursement to the hospital is a fixed amount, which means that patients who leave the hospital early earn money for the hospital, whereas those who stay longer lose money for it. Social workers may feel pressured to help "empty the bed" as quickly as possible. In some settings, the social work department has defined this as one of its major roles and may even be viewed by administration as a "revenue-generating center" if it does its work effectively.

The ethical dilemma emerges when a patient, family members, or even the social worker feels that a patient may not be ready for discharge for any of various reasons, perhaps related to psychosocial issues or the availability of suitable community resources. The social worker has a responsibility to help the client to negotiate the system, which includes working to advocate with the hospital for the client's interest (see Chapter 15). The question here is whether the social worker should inform the patient of his or her right to appeal a decision to discharge the patient early, even if the patient does not ask. What if the medical or administrative staff asks frontline staff not to share such information unless it is requested (sometimes referred to as a gag rule)? In some states, legislatures have specifically addressed this issue making the gag rule illegal. The implementation of the recently passed health care legislation may impact national regulations providing protection for patient rights and resolve the dilemma for the social worker.

For the worker in this situation, the NASW Code of Ethics states, "The social worker should be alert to and resist the influences and pressures that interfere with the exercise of professional discretion and impartial judgment required for the performance of professional functions" (NASW, 1997). This is one of those situations where advice and support of colleagues, other professionals, and professional associations and legislation may be needed as well as courage to resist what would amount to unethical practice.

***Withholding Family Planning Information*** Another, even more striking example comes from the political controversy surrounding a decision by the U.S. Supreme Court in May 1991, which supported the right of the government to cut off funding for family planning centers that informed pregnant clients of the option of abortion. Many of these clients were young, poor people of color. Even if clients requested information on this option for dealing with an unwanted pregnancy, or even if the client's health and safety might be in danger, any center that provided such information or referred a client to an alternative source of counseling where such information might be available would lose its funding. More recently, the Bush administration continued this approach on an international and national level, while the current Obama administration has modified it on the international level through an Executive Order. For a number of reasons, addressing and correcting this censorship of important information is one of the "third rails" of politics.

Many health care centers have indicated an unwillingness to accept such restrictions on free speech and a client's right to be fully informed so that she can make a sound, personal decision on the issue. However, what if a center decided that continuing to provide family planning services to poor women was so important that they would accept this restriction rather than close down for lack of money? For many social workers—regardless of their views on the issue of abortion—denying access to this information to women who are dependent on public social services may be sexist, racist, and classist. Should a social worker try to subvert the policy? Should a social worker refuse to work in such a setting?

The NASW Code of Ethics (NASW, 1999) makes clear the social worker's responsibility to the client in both of these examples. The ethical worker would need to make available to the client all information required by the client to make a sound personal decision about her health care or her options in the face of unwanted pregnancy. Acting ethically, however, might require courage and might well involve personal risk. This represents another example of how practice may be affected as much by ideological, financial, and political issues as by theories of human behavior.

A related issue is the legislation of "conscience clauses" passed by Congress shortly after the 1973 *Roe v. Wade* Supreme Court decision guaranteeing a women's right to an abortion. These clauses protected health care providers from having to perform legal medical services that conflicted with their religious or moral values. Although one might be able to make a case for respecting a provider's personal reluctance to provide a service, it has been generally accepted that there is an ethical requirement to refer a client to other resources or at least make them aware of their availability. More recently, however, one state (Idaho) has extended the conscience clause to indicate that health providers do not have to offer a referral service or even information about resources for procedures that they are unwilling to perform. At the time of this writing, other states were considering this as well. While social workers may have legal conscience clause protection in some states, exercising this legal right violates the ethical requirements of the profession.

 **Interactive Skills of Helping**

Use the accompanying DVD or visit *The Skills of Helping Individuals, Families, Groups, and Communities,* Seventh Edition, CourseMate website at www.cengagebrain.com and enter your personal access code to watch this video

**SHARING DATA** This is an interview conducted in a faith-based agency in which a worker counsels a 17-year-old woman who has just found out that she is pregnant. The worker's struggle—feeling caught between the agency policy against discussing abortion and the ethical issues of practice—is illustrated and then discussed in the debriefing.

## The Duty to Warn

Another court decision has had a powerful impact on practice by defining the duties and obligations of a social worker in respect to her or his duty to warn (in some states, the "duty to protect") a third party if information shared by a client indicates that the third party may be in danger. An important California decision, *Tarasoff v. Regents of the University of California* (1976), severely limited privileged communications under certain circumstances involving duty to warn.

In this case, a client of a therapist at the Berkeley University Clinic indicated murderous fantasies about his former girlfriend, Tatiana (Tanya) Tarasoff. The therapist became concerned and notified campus police, requesting that they have the client committed. After a brief confinement, the police, believing the client was rational, released him. No further steps were taken, on the orders of the therapist's superior. Neither Tarasoff nor her immediate family was notified. The family sued after the client followed through on his threats to kill Tarasoff. The court held that the therapist had been negligent in not notifying Tarasoff directly or taking other steps to prevent the attack. The court said the following: When a doctor or a psychotherapist, in the exercise of his professional skill and knowledge, determines, or should determine, that a warning is essential to avert danger arising from the medical or psychological condition of his patient, he incurs a legal obligation to give that warning.

This is an example in which the evolving rules for professional behavior provide structure and clarity for the professional. In this case, if a client communicates a threat toward a specific person and either has the intent and ability to implement a violent act or has a history of such acts, the social worker is required to take appropriate actions. These may include warning the victim, calling the police, asking the client to accept voluntary hospitalization, or attempting to arrange an involuntary hospitalization. Although helpful guidelines have emerged from legislation and court decisions, the worker's judgment is still required.

## Staying Up-to-Date with Evolving Circumstances and the Law

Given the importance of understanding evolving legal requirements as they affect the obligations of the social worker, practitioners need to stay up-to-date with the law and its application to new sets of circumstances. Membership in a professional association, such as the NASW, can provide a means for keeping abreast. Consider, for example, an issue in the Massachusetts NASW chapter's (1996) monthly newspaper, which provides advice on the duty to warn:

> A clear case of duty to warn occurs when a client reports a clear intent to harm another and has the motivation, intention and means to fulfill this threat. It becomes incumbent on the clinician to report the client to both the police and the third party. A situation not involving weapons or arson, but where there is an explicit threat, would be the client who is HIV-positive, is aware of the risks of transmission, knows how to avoid such risks, but has no intention of doing so and wants to infect his partner(s). A more complicated case would be in the instance of an HIV-positive client who is not overtly threatening to harm a spouse or partner but is unwilling to disclose or take precautions against the risk of transmission. Although there may be no explicit oral threat, there may be an explicitly behavioral threat.

Many states now have statutes requiring duty to warn in such instances. To date, however, a number of states do not require partner notification. The other side of the coin, however, is that the clinician, by not disclosing, runs the risk of suit should the partner at a later point become infected and learn that she/he had not been informed by either the infected client or the client's therapists. The therapist has a difficult decision here and should probably seek legal consultation on a case-by-case basis.

After reviewing the previous sections from the perspective of a student or any practicing social worker, it would not be surprising if, rather than feeling more prepared to meet a client, you might be having second thoughts about engaging in practice at all. Ethical issues, rules of professional conduct, and the still-evolving case law highlight the increasing clarity as well as the growing complexity of guidelines that affect practice. Understand that developing competency in practice takes time. The purpose of highlighting these issues is not to discourage you but to sensitize you to be more alert to the signs of ethical dilemmas or legal questions. This awareness should encourage all workers to make use of supervisors, colleagues, agency procedural manuals, and other resources whenever such issues emerge. Thus, in a case-by-case manner, as the social worker raises her or his concerns about client disclosure in an interview or group meeting, the worker will gradually learn when such a disclosure triggers the duty to warn or give an otherwise mandated report. This is an important part of the learning process, which in the long run will significantly strengthen a worker's competency and practice effectiveness.

## Chapter Summary

A session in the middle phase of practice has four stages: preliminary (sessional tuning in), beginning (sessional contracting), middle (sessional work), and sessional ending and transition. The indirect nature of client communications at the start of a session—often related to client ambivalence—means that the worker must tune in to potential themes of concern prior to the session and remain tentative in the beginning phase, listening for cues of underlying issues. As a middle phase session proceeds, the worker uses several groups of skills called *skill factors*. These are designed to help the client tell his or her story and to do so with affect. They are also important for the worker to be able to challenge the illusion of work and to find the connections between the process (way of working) and the content (substantive areas of work) in a session. These skill factors include elaboration, empathy, sharing worker's feelings, making a demand for work, pointing out obstacles to work, identifying process and content connections, sharing worker data, and helping the client see life in a new way. Several skills were also identified for bringing a session to a close and helping the client make the transition to postsession activities or the next session.

Finally, social workers need to address a number of ethical and legal issues that may emerge during practice-related conflicts around agency gag rules preventing the sharing of important information with clients, conflicts between personal and professional values, and the duty to warn others if the social worker believes a client may be dangerous. The importance of using consultation and staying up-to-date on evolving issues, legislation, and court decisions was stressed.

## *Related Online Content and Activities*

Visit *The Skills of Helping Individuals, Families, Groups, and Communities,* Seventh Edition, CourseMate website at **www.cengagebrain.com** for learning tools such as glossary terms, links to related websites, and chapter practice quizzes. The website for this chapter also features additional notes from the author.

# Competency Notes

The following is a list of Council on Social Work Education (CSWE) recommended competencies and practice behaviors for social work students defined in Educational Policy and Accreditation Standard (EPAS) and addressed in this chapter.

**EP 2.1.1a** Identify as a Professional Social Worker and Conduct Oneself Accordingly (p. 189)

**EP 2.1.1b** Practice personal reflection and self-correction to assure continual professional development (pp. 153, 157, 178)

**EP 2.1.1c** Attend to professional roles and boundaries (p. 181)

**EP 2.1.1e** Engage in career-long learning (pp. 153, 157)

**EP 2.1.1f** Use supervision and consultation (pp. 153, 157, 162, 169)

**EP 2.1.2a** Recognize and manage personal values in a way that allows professional values to guide practice (p. 157)

**EP 2.1.2c** Tolerate ambiguity in resolving ethical conflicts (p. 215)

**EP 2.1.3b** Analyze models of assessment, prevention, intervention, and evaluation (p. 148)

**EP 2.1.3c** Demonstrate effective oral and written communication in working with individuals, families, groups, organizations, communities, and colleagues (pp. 148, 178)

**EP 2.1.10a** Substantively and affectively prepare for action with individuals, families, groups, organizations, and communities (p. 148)

**EP 2.1.10b** Use empathy and other interpersonal skills (pp. 148, 162, 169, 178)

**EP 2.1.10c** Develop a mutually agreed-on focus of work and desired outcomes (p. 148)

**EP 2.1.10d** Collect, organize, and interpret client data (pp. 148, 162)

**EP 2.1.10e** Assess client strengths and limitations (p. 148)

**EP 2.1.10f** Develop mutually agreed-on intervention goals and objectives (pp. 148, 162)

# Endings and Transitions

By examining the ending and transition phase of practice, this chapter completes our look at the phases of work for individuals. The chapter explores the unique dynamics and skills associated with bringing the helping process to a close and helping the client to make appropriate transitions. Practice examples will illustrate how this can be the most powerful and meaningful phase of work, as the client makes the third decision—to deal with core issues that may have only been hinted at in the earlier phases. In this chapter, we also examine the danger of this phase becoming a moratorium on work, in which both the client and the worker participate in an illusion. Specific skills to increase the possibility of positive endings and transitions will be described and illustrated.

# Making the Third Decision

Recall that, in the beginning phase, clients face a first decision. They must decide whether they are prepared to engage with the worker—to lower defenses if needed and to begin to work. In the second decision, clients agree to deal with difficult issues, to take some responsibility for their part in problems and to face the emotional pain involved in work. In the third decision, clients must decide whether to deal with the most difficult issues as they approach the end of the working relationship.

The ending phase offers the greatest potential for powerful and important work. Clients feel a sense of urgency as they realize there is little time left, and this can lead to the introduction of some of the most difficult and important themes of concern. The emotional dynamics between worker and client are also heightened in this phase as each prepares to move away from the other. Termination of the relationship can evoke powerful feelings in both client and worker, and the worker can often connect discussion of these to the client's general concerns and tasks. The ending phase holds tremendous potential for work, yet ironically this phase is often the least effective and can be characterized by missed appointments, lateness, apathy, acting out, and regressions to earlier, less mature patterns of behavior. Moreover, the worker—as well as the client—shows these behaviors at times.

## General Difficulty in Ending Important Relationships

In many ways, the ending sessions are the most difficult ones for both worker and client. The source of the strain stems from the general difficulty we have in dealing with the end of important relationships. Our society has done little to train us how to handle a separation; in fact, the general norm is to deny feelings associated with it. For example, when a valued colleague leaves an agency, the farewell party is often an attempt, usually unsuccessful, to cover the sadness with fun. The laughter at such parties is often a bit forced. Similarly, children and counselors who have developed a close relationship in summer camps usually end by resolving to meet again at a winter reunion, which often does not take place. When someone moves to another city and leaves a close and valued friend behind, the two may occupy themselves with elaborate plans for keeping in touch by mail, phone calls, and visits rather than mutually acknowledging the fact that the relationship will never be quite the same.

## Ending the Worker–Client Relationship

The worker–client association is a specific example of this larger problem. It can be painful to terminate a close relationship; when you have invested yourself meaningfully in a relationship, have shared some of your most important feelings, and have given and taken help from another human being, the bond that develops is strong. Strean (1978) has described the difficulties involved in terminating a close working relationship:

> Whether a social worker–client relationship consists of five interviews or a hundred, if the worker has truly related to the client's expectations, perceptions of himself and transactions with his social orbit, the client will experience the encounter as meaningful and the worker as someone significant; therefore, separation from this "significant other" will inevitably arouse complex and

ambivalent feelings. Still, a long-term relationship with a social worker will probably include more intense emotions at termination than a short-term one.

A prolonged relationship has usually stimulated dependency needs and wishes, transference reactions, revelation of secrets, embarrassing moments, exhilaration, sadness, and gladness. The encounter has become part of the client's weekly life, so that ending it can seem like saying good-bye to a valued family member or friend. (pp. 227–228)

The ending process in a helping relationship can trigger the deepest feelings in both worker and client. As such, both can do powerful work during this phase, as well as ineffective work if the feelings are not dealt with. In this chapter, we explore the dynamics of the ending phase, identify some of the central skills required to make effective endings, and discuss how workers can help clients make transitions to new experiences.

## The Dynamics and Skills of Endings

**EP 2.1.10b**
**EP 2.1.10f**
**EP 2.1.10k**

Schwartz (1971) described the ending phase in the group context:

In the final phase of work—that which I have called "transitions and endings"—the worker's skills are needed to help the members use him and each other to deal with the problem of moving from one experience to another. For the worker it means moving off the track of the members' experience and life process, as he has, in the beginning, moved onto it. The point is that beginnings and endings are hard for people to manage; they often call out deep feeling in both worker and members; and much skill is needed to help people to help each other through these times. (pp. 17–18)

### Flow of Affect in the Ending Phase

One of the dynamics that makes endings hard has already been mentioned: the pain associated with ending a relationship in which one has invested a great deal. In addition to the pain, a form of guilt might surface. Clients may feel that if they had worked harder in the relationship, played their part more effectively, and risked more, perhaps they could have done a better job. This guilt sometimes emerges indirectly, with the client saying, "Can't I have more time?"

As with many of the feelings in the ending phase, this sense of guilt is often shared by the worker, who may feel that he or she should have been more helpful to the client. Perhaps, if the worker had been more experienced, or more capable, he or she could have been more helpful with regard to some of the unresolved issues. Instead of understanding that the client will need to work continually on life's problems, the worker feels guilty for not having "solved" them all. Social work students often articulate this feeling as follows: "If only the client had a real worker!" Usually, they underestimate the help that they have given.

The flow of affect between worker and client often increases during the ending phase. Because of the general difficulty of talking about negative and positive feedback, both worker and client may have many unstated feelings that need to be dealt with in the final phase. Things may have been left unsaid because of taboos against honest talk about the role of authority. This theme needs to be discussed before the relationship can properly end. For example, the worker may have said and done things that made the client angry. The reverse might also be true, with the worker somewhat frustrated about the client's inability to take risks and to open up to the worker.

Providing this feedback, if it is related to the worker's real caring for the client, can serve to clear the air. Even if a client and worker have not been able to get along together, and both face the impending separation with a sense of relief, the discussion that takes place at the end should be real. What was it about the worker that the client could not relate to? In turn, the client should know what made it difficult for the worker. There may have been misconceptions on the part of either or both parties, and discussing these can help clear them up. This could be quite helpful to the client, who may choose to enter another helping relationship in the future. The importance of feedback to the worker is obvious. In addition, if the negative feelings are not dealt with, a client might transfer them to his or her next worker in the way that some of the examples on beginning showed in Chapter 4.

Even more difficult for worker and client to handle than the negative feelings may be the positive ones. It is not easy for any of us to tell those close to us, particularly people in authority, that they have meant a great deal to us. Moreover, many workers find accepting positive feelings with grace extremely hard to do. I have repeatedly observed workers respond to a client's genuine expression of thanks for all that the worker has done by protesting, "It wasn't really me, I didn't do that much, it was really all your work." One student in a social work training program asked during a class if it was all right for her to accept a fruitcake offered to her by an elderly client at the end of their work together. This was not a case in which a client was trying to pay a worker for her services, which were normally free. It was simply this woman's way of saying thank-you to a worker who cared. I asked the student if the fruitcake looked good and suggested that, if it did, the student ought to take it.

When I press workers about the cause of their embarrassment in such cases, they usually point to the general cultural barriers against appearing immodest, as well as their belief that they could not have really given that much help. The latter response reflects an underestimation of the effect of the help given. Clients respond with great feeling to a caring, honest worker; they are not usually as critical as the worker about what the worker might have done. Cultural barriers notwithstanding, mutual sharing of positive feelings at the end of a relationship matters a great deal because it enables both client and worker to value what has taken place between them and to bring it properly to an end. Both client and worker can carry feelings of regret for unspoken words long after they have stopped seeing each other, thus making the actual ending process protracted and more difficult. The problem with delayed endings is that they tie up energy that both parties need to invest in new relationships.

### Timing and the Ending Phase

The timing of this phase depends on the length of the relationship. For example, in weekly counseling that lasts a year, the final 8 weeks or so constitute the ending process. In short-term work—for example, six sessions—evidence of feelings about endings may emerge in the fourth or fifth session as the worker receives subtle cues to the client's reactions. Although these cues mark the beginning of the ending phase, thoughts about the end are present even in the beginning. Often, a client will inquire early in the process, even after a first session that was helpful, how long the sessions will continue. Time is an important factor, and clients will orient themselves accordingly. A long break in the work phase, whether caused by the worker's illness, a vacation, or perhaps a holiday season, can provoke ending feelings as the client associates the break with the ending to come. It is not uncommon to observe apathy, withdrawal, and other premature ending symptoms immediately after such a break.

It is important for the worker to draw the client's attention to these signals and initiate a discussion of whether or not the client has begun to think about the ending. Then the worker and the client can strategize about how to make sure they don't end prematurely and that they make good use of what might be the most important period of work rather than experience a moratorium on work.

## Stages of the Ending Phase

**EP 2.1.1f**
**EP 2.1.7a**

Schwartz has outlined the stages of the ending process as follows: denial, indirect and direct expressions of anger, mourning, trying it on for size, and, finally, the farewell-party syndrome. The reader who is familiar with the classic work by Kubler-Ross (1969) on the stages of death and dying will note similarities. Every ending represents a loss, not as powerful as death, but still evoking strong emotions. Each of the stages suggested by Schwartz is discussed in more detail, and the required worker skills are identified and illustrated.

### Denial

Because of the general difficulty of facing feelings associated with the ending of important relationships, the first stage often reflects denial. The client neither admits to the impending ending nor acknowledges his or her feelings about it. During this first phase, the client may refuse to discuss the ending, insist on a nonexistent agreement with the worker to continue the sessions long past the ending date, "forget" that an ending date has been set, or request that sessions be prolonged because the client feels "unready." Unless the worker raises the ending issue, the client may simply ignore it until the last session.

Workers, as well, may handle their feelings about endings through denial and avoidance. Many clients have greeted a new worker with stories of how their former worker simply told them during their last session that he or she was leaving the agency. These clients are often left feeling that their workers did not care about them. In reality, these workers' denials are often rooted in the fact that they cared very much but could not face their own feelings. If there is residual anger at the former worker who left abruptly, it is not unusual for the new worker to experience it during the first sessions.

If workers are to help their clients manage their feelings in the ending phase, the workers must be able to manage their own feelings. They must address feelings about ending with the client as well as with their setting, supervisors, and colleagues, if the worker is leaving. In my workshops, often a field instructor will present his or her problem with a student worker who is having trouble ending with clients at the end of the school year. When I inquire whether the supervisor has begun to discuss endings with the student, the supervisor is surprised to recognize that she or he has also avoided dealing with endings. Once again, more is caught by the student than is taught by the field instructor.

The ending process must provide enough time for the worker and client to sort out their feelings and use this phase productively. A sudden ending will be difficult for both worker and client and will cut necessary work short. Because the worker wants the client to experience the ending as a process rather than as a sharp closure, enough time must be permitted for this to happen. At the appropriate time, which depends in part on the length of the relationship, the worker should remind the client of the impending ending.

### Ending with a Foster Child Transitioning to Independence

An example from a child welfare setting will help illustrate this skill. The client was a young man who had been a ward of the agency for 8 years. The worker had been in contact with him for the previous 2 years. In 2 months, the client would be 18 years old, at which time he would leave the care of the agency. The client's reference to the "Aid" is short for the Children's Aid Society.

**Practice Points:**  The worker set the ending process in motion by reminding the client of the ending date.

WORKER: Before we start to talk about that job interview next week, I wanted to remind you that we only have 8 more weeks before you leave the agency. You have been with the "Aid" [the term used by clients to describe the Children's Aid Society] for a long time, and I thought you might want to talk about the change.

CLIENT: Only 8 weeks? I hadn't realized it was coming so soon. That's great! After 8 years I'm finally on my own; no more checking in, no more "Aid" on my back. You know, I'm going to really need that job now, and I'm worried about the interview.

WORKER: What's worrying you?

**Practice Summary:**  By commenting on the limited time left, the worker set the process in motion. The client's reaction reflected both denial of the impact and recognition of its importance. Schwartz describes the "graduation quality" of endings, when clients feel excited and ready to test their ability to make it on their own. The quick switch from the ending topic to the job interview represented resistance—the client did not want to talk about it right then. The worker was also reluctant to discuss it and thus allowed it to be dropped easily. In addition, the worker had identified the issue of ending only in terms of the agency, not in relation to his work with the client. This evasion signaled the worker's own ambivalence. Nevertheless, the statement of the impending ending was enough to set the process in motion.

### Active Resistance to Discussing the Ending Feelings

**Practice Points:**  In the following example, the worker presses for the ending feelings, but the client resists. Note how the worker reaches into the silence and inquires as to what the client is thinking. Jane is the worker, and Thelma the client.

JANE: I will be leaving the office at the beginning of May, which gives us four more times together. I thought we might want to talk about this.

THELMA: I don't understand—why are you leaving?

JANE: I'm not sure if you remember, Thelma, but I mentioned to you last October that I was a student, which means I will be leaving my placement in early May. (Silence)

JANE: Thelma, you have turned quiet. What are you thinking about?

THELMA: (After a pause) I don't know what I am going to do now. I don't understand why you have to go.

JANE: Are you worried about what is going to happen with you after I leave? (Silence)

THELMA: Yes, but you are not leaving for a month, right?

JANE: Yes. I know that we have been seeing each other for many months now, and talking about my leaving is hard—it is hard for me too—but we both need to share our feelings and thoughts about this. (Silence) I know that I am feeling a little sad. We have been through some tough times together. It's tough letting go.

THELMA: (Looking down, she picks up a piece of her child's schoolwork) Hey, did you know that Gladys will be going into grade two next year? Ivan and I went up to the parent-teacher meeting last Friday and the teacher told us then. She even showed us some of her schoolwork. She is doing so well. (Worker's note: I tried to have Thelma elaborate on her feelings about the ending of our sessions, but she denied and avoided the opportunities, and the remainder of the session covered some superficial topics and how her children were doing.)

**Practice Summary:**   Although the client moved away from the painful work, the worker's strong message through the demand for work sent a signal that this topic must be addressed. The worker understands and accepts the client's reluctance to continue, demonstrating a respect for the client's defenses. The stage has been set, and the worker will return to the ending theme in the weeks to come.

### Indirect and Direct Expressions of Anger

The denial stage is often followed by the client's indirect or direct expression of anger toward the worker. The circumstances of endings may vary; for example, the worker may be leaving the agency, as opposed to the client ending contact. Although these circumstances may affect the intensity of the angry feelings, they are usually present even in those situations in which the ending seems perfectly reasonable. The anger may be expressed directly, by the client challenging the worker who has changed jobs: "How could you leave if you really cared for me?" The ending is perceived as a form of rejection, and the worker must be careful to face these feelings directly and not try to avoid them.

Alternatively, the cues to the underlying feelings may be communicated indirectly— for example, by lateness or missed sessions. Conversations with clients may take on an element of antagonism, and the worker may sense the hostility. Sarcasm, battles over minor issues, or indications that the client is glad to see the relationship finally end may also be evidence of this reaction. However, under the angry feelings are often sad ones. It is therefore important to allow the expression of anger and to acknowledge it even though the worker's instincts make it hard to do so.

As with all stages of the ending process, the skill involved here calls for the worker to respond directly to the indirect cues. On perceiving these signals, the worker should point out the dynamics of the stage to the client. In the case of anger, the worker should reach past the indirect cue and encourage the client to express any angry feelings directly. The worker should also acknowledge the validity of the feelings and not attempt to talk the client into feeling differently. This direct acknowledgment is important even if the client does not take up the worker's invitation to discuss the anger but instead denies its existence. By identifying the stage of the ending process, the worker allows the client to increase her or his understanding and—therefore—control of the experience. This can free energies for productive participation in the ending-phase work. The worker must be honest in sharing any personal reactions to the client's anger.

***Residential Counselor Leaving to Attend Graduate School*** The following illustration involves a worker in a residential setting who was leaving the home to attend graduate school. The day after she announced she was leaving, a young female client had a blowup at home with her mother and her mother's girlfriend and had to be brought back to the center to be "in-house" (staying at the center instead of at home).

**Practice Points:** The example illustrates clearly the struggle for the worker, who must deal with her own guilt and pain about leaving a client with whom she has become very close and a setting in which she has enjoyed working. The teenage client regresses to her maladaptive way of handling her anger and acts it out.

> I was sitting with Jane, ready to check in, and I knew by the look on her face that last night was a hard one. I felt two things: first, "This is such bull—it is so easy for her to do well at home, especially since her brother is gone" and second, "I just don't want to have to deal with her being in-house." I had just announced the day before that I was leaving the program, and I was exhausted. She gave me her book, and as I was reading it she started to cry and yell, "I hate your stupid system, I hate this program, I hate you!" As I sat there reading about her night, listening to her yell at me, I thought, "This child will never change." I was ready to give up from my own exhaustion, but I couldn't let her know that.
>
> Jane's mom wrote that Jane had a really hard night. She refused to clean her room, started throwing things, and called her mom and her lover bitches and homos. When her mom told her to get in the time-out area, Jane hit her. When her mom's lover tried to intervene, Jane kicked her. Jane's mom and her lover eventually left her alone (she's too big for them to restrain) and she calmed down after a while and went to sleep.

**Practice Points:** Note that by acting out at home Jane returned to the residential center. Her anger at her mother, her lover, and the worker is openly expressed but the hurt at the loss is not. The worker reaches for the underlying cause of the acting out—her leaving. The worker's next intervention with Jane combines setting limits ("reminders") and reaching for her underlying feelings. The key to breaking through the cycle of anger is for the worker to share her own feelings about leaving the client.

> I knew she was going to have an in-house suspension, and she knew too. I just didn't want to deal with it. She was still crying and saying, "I hate you! I'm glad you're leaving!" All of this process took about 2 minutes and then I knew I had to speak. I tried really hard to get my tone of voice to be supportive, yet confronting, and I said, "What do you think made you have such a hard time last night?" She kept crying and yelling, "I don't know!" I thought back to my announcement yesterday and remembered her reaction. "Are you mad at me for leaving?" I asked. She said, "No! I don't care! I hate you! You're a bitch!"
>
> At this point, I was thinking, "Oh yeah! Well you're a brat!" but instead I said, "I understand that you are having feelings about me leaving and that's OK. What's not OK is that you swore at me. You have a reminder for that." (We use reminders for behavior management. When a kid gets a third reminder, he or she gets a time out.) "I know that my leaving is hard for you. Good-byes are always hard. You and I have worked together for a long time and we've had a lot of fun together. It's going to be hard for me to say good-bye to you, too. The important thing is that you tell me you're mad or whatever feelings you have. It's OK to feel that. It's not OK to swear and it's not OK to hit your mother."

She just continued saying over and over again, "I hate you." I felt irritated again. I said, "We have a choice: We can make the best of the next four weeks and really talk about what's going to be hard about saying good-bye to each other, or we can struggle and try to hate each other so it won't hurt. You know you're in in-house today because of last night, and we're going to use that time to do a little work around my leaving." With that, she cried louder and yelled, "No!" I could see how upset she was about this. She once told me I was the only person that she felt she could depend on, and here I was leaving her. I felt like saying, "OK, I won't go back to school, I'll stay here with you." She really pulls at me. So, knowing I had to say something else, I said, "This isn't easy for me either," and then I talked with her about how I felt about leaving her and saying good-bye to her.

We talked about fun things we had done together and looked at pictures, and all through it I kept assuring her that no matter what, I would never forget her. I was trying to keep good boundaries, but I started to really feel the sadness over my leaving. I was leaving a job I love, kids I love, and a team that had become my second family. I felt myself getting too emotional, so I cut the conversation short by saying, "We are going to be able to talk about this a lot before I leave." I was torn about what to do. I thought about continuing the conversation so she could understand that someone really did care about her and that her feelings about my leaving are all very normal. But on the other hand, I felt that if I had kept talking about it, I would've cried. When I said we'd be able to talk more about it, she said OK, got up, hugged me, cried, and said, "I'm going to miss everything about you." Well, that did it. I felt myself wanting to cry and my eyes were getting watery. I walked her over to the in-house area, got her settled, and then composed myself.

I wish that I could've let go of my own sadness. I am usually really good at sticking with hard feelings even though I can relate it to my own life. I sat through a check-in with a kid who was my absolute favorite kid I've ever worked with, and I had to tell him his mother was in the hospital. She went in while he was in school. I was his age when I found out my mother had cancer. He looked at me with tears in his eyes and said, "Is she gonna die?" I could sit with that. I was kind of annoyed that I couldn't stick with the conversation [with Jane]. I think this was different because it was so emotionally charged for me, the team, and most of the kids. I also wish I could've addressed her behaviors more directly, too.

**Practice Summary:**   This excerpt illustrates the importance of supportive supervision. The worker's instincts were on target; however, she was afraid of showing her emotions too directly and was concerned about crying. At the same time, the worker demonstrated good professional work as she analyzed her own struggle with this difficult ending. It is important that she did this, so that the process of her ending could be directly synthesized with the content of the work. Most children in residential settings are dealing with profound losses, and yet, the staff and the system often have great difficulty in dealing with losses themselves.

## Mourning

Underneath the anger expressed by the client often lie feelings of sadness. When these emerge, the client begins the mourning stage of the ending process. During this stage, the client experiences fully the feelings he or she may have been struggling hard to suppress. When this happens, some clients express their feelings directly to the worker, whereas others do this indirectly. A normally active and involved client suddenly seems apathetic and lethargic. Interviews are marked by long periods of silence, slow starts followed by minimal activity, and conversations that trail off rather than end. One worker described arriving at a woman's home to find the blinds drawn at midday and a general feeling of gloom pervading the usually bright room.

In part, the difficulty in working reflects the client's unwillingness to open up new areas just when the work seems about to end. In addition, the work left to the end is often the most difficult for the client, which adds to the ambivalence. Essentially, the feeling is one of sadness about the ending of a meaningful relationship. The denial and anger are past, and the ending must now be faced.

Two important skills in this phase involve acknowledging the client's ending feelings and sharing the worker's ending feelings. As we have seen, the skill of acknowledging and sharing the worker's feelings is both crucial to the helping process and difficult for workers to employ. In the ending phase, this difficulty is compounded by the intensity of feelings and our society's taboos against their direct expression. Workers have suggested that, even when they did pick up cues to the client's sadness, they did not acknowledge the feelings because they felt somewhat embarrassed. "How can I tell clients I think they are sad because we won't be seeing each other anymore? It sounds like I'm taking my impact on the client and blowing it out of proportion. And anyway, how will it feel if the client says I'm all wet—and that I didn't mean that much to the client at all?" The worker feels vulnerable to the risks of commenting on the importance of the relationship. This also holds the worker back from expressing personal feelings toward the client. As one worker said, "It doesn't sound professional for me to tell a client I will miss him. He will think I'm just putting him on. Won't that be encouraging dependency?"

In most cases, the reluctance to share feelings stems from the difficulty the worker has in coming to grips with his or her own sadness when separating from a valued client. The flow of affect between the two has first created and then strengthened a bond that the worker values. The significance of this relationship needs to be recognized as it comes to an end. Often, workers must take the risk of expressing their own feelings before clients will feel free to do the same. Both may feel vulnerable, but it is part of the worker's function, and a measure of professional skill, to be able to take this first, hard step.

***18-Year-Old Foster Child in Transition: The Last Sessions*** Let us look at an illustration of an 18-year-old foster child about to leave the care of the agency to make the often difficult and frightening transition to independence.

WORKER: You seem quiet and reserved today. You don't seem to have much to say.
CLIENT: I guess I'm just tired.
WORKER: And then again, this is almost our last session together. I've been thinking a lot about that, and I have mixed feelings. I'm glad to see you getting ready to go out on your own, but I'm really going to miss you. We've been through an awful lot together in the past two years. (Silence) How about you? Are you a little down about our ending too?
CLIENT: (Long silence) I guess we have gotten close. You've been my best worker although sometimes you were a real pain.
WORKER: Why do you feel I was your best worker? It can be important to talk about this.

**Practice Summary:**   After the mutual acknowledgment of feelings, the worker took another step by asking the client to reflect on the relationship. The client had experienced the breakup of many important close relationships and sharply felt the resulting rejection and pain. Many people develop armor against such vulnerability, which is reflected in unwillingness to risk getting close again only to experience another loss. Once again, an important synthesis between process and content is possible. Understanding this worker–client relationship can be an important aid to the client in his future efforts to make close contacts—that is, his transitions (discussed later in the chapter).

***A Social Work Student Ending her Field Placement***   In the following discussion and process recording, a social work student describes the difficulty of sharing her own feelings as she and her client approached the end of the field placement:

**EP 2.1.4d**

> Beginning termination was a difficult and emotional process for both me and my client, Joan. As I attempted to discuss the ending of our relationship, Joan stated that she wanted her next income assistance check mailed to her home address. I asked her why. Joan replied that by doing so, she would no longer have to go into the office for her check.

WORKER: Joan, I don't really understand that. You've always picked your checks up. In fact, you preferred it that way, didn't you?

JOAN: Well, yeah, but I'm getting tired of seeing the same people, and I think they're tired of seeing me every month. (Silence; Joan looking away.)

WORKER: Joan, is it that you don't want to see me at the end of this month? (Silence) Check days have been our "hi/keep-in-touch" days. I feel like you want to avoid seeing me on my last check day here.

**Practice Points:**   The worker recognizes the decision to not pick up her check is the indirect offering of the client's difficulty in saying good-bye. She reaches for it and begins the discussion of the mutual sadness over the separation. The student is completely honest about her feelings in a manner that must feel genuine and supportive to the client. She also begins the process of identifying the client's important growth and her strengths and asks the client to give her feedback on the kind of worker she has been. In turn, she will let the client know how she experienced her—both the strengths and the problems. This is important for the client who will soon start with another worker and can use this worker to help her understand how she uses or puts off helping professionals.

JOAN: Maria, what am I going to do without you?

WORKER: Joan, do you feel you really need me?

JOAN: I need somebody to talk to. Well, sometimes I feel like I don't. Other times I feel like I'm going to fall apart. I don't know what I'm going to do without you.

WORKER: Joan, I know we've been through a lot and shared a lot together, but, to be honest, I feel you're much stronger now than you were in the beginning, and I feel you can make it without me. That's not to say I think things will be easy for you, but I've seen a growth in your own self-confidence. You're beginning to take more risks, make your own decisions.

JOAN: Yeah, my self-confidence has increased slightly, hasn't it?

WORKER: It really has, Joan. I know it's going to feel weird and empty without me, but you know you've made a lot of new friends in the past few months at the center, at your new place. Sherri has been a real support and a good friend for you, hasn't she?

JOAN: Yeah, she has, she really has. But it won't be the same. I just know it.

WORKER: It won't be the same for me either, Joan. You know I've never had an ongoing involvement with any client before. It feels weird to think that I won't be your worker after May. Right now I can't describe exactly how I feel, but I know it's going to feel weird without you. I know I'm going to keep thinking about you, about how you're doing. I know I'm going to miss you and Don (Joan's son). (Joan is silent, looking down.) I feel you'll make your goal (to be self-dependent and off income assistance). It'll be slow and you'll have to take a lot of steps, but I really feel you'll do it. I wish I could be there to see that.

JOAN: Yeah, I'm going to make it!

WORKER: You sound determined. That's another change I've noticed.

JOAN: Yeah, I am more determined. I have to get off I.A. (income assistance). The changes in me have been because of you.

WORKER: Well, I may have helped you, but the changes came from you. (Joan shrugged her shoulders.) Joan, what kind of a worker have I been for you?

Joan stated: (1) that I was the first worker that ever shared personal feelings with her. She felt that this made it easier for her to discuss problems and to relate to me; (2) that I expressed a great deal of concern for her, but at times Joan felt I was overly concerned; (3) that in the first term I seemed to think I was always right, whereas in the second term I was easier to talk to, more relaxed, more open; (4) that whenever I was late, Joan felt I was treating her like "scum," even though I did apologize to her each time.

As Joan began to know me better, she realized that my apologies were genuine, that I really did care for her. I also relayed my feelings to her regarding our relationship. For example: (1) I struggled with her resistance; (2) as I noticed more strength and confidence in herself, I felt threatened—I wanted to keep "protecting" her; (3) I've learned a great deal about single parenthood, the hardships and difficulties associated with sole child-rearing, with no outside support. Near the end of the session, we began to discuss Joan's feelings regarding new beginnings with a new worker in a new office. Joan stated that, prior to me, she had two good workers. Both these workers were older and had children of their own. Joan hoped that her new worker would also be older; she felt this would help in the new beginnings. This issue was tabled for our next session. As I was leaving, Joan stated that she would see me on check issue day.

**Practice Summary:** The discussion about what the work has meant is interactional in nature: Both the client and the worker have been affected by the relationship and the evaluation of how things have gone, and what has been learned is important for both parties. The client needs to see the worker as being involved in a process of continual growth and learning—not, as many clients fantasize, as a "finished product." The worker exemplifies the values of reflection, analysis, learning, and growth. When the worker shares that, at times, she felt "threatened" by the client's growth, she forces the client to begin to see this worker (and possibly future workers) as human and vulnerable.

## Trying it on for Size

Earlier I referred to the "graduation" quality of the ending. As the client moves to the final sessions, the worker often senses an effort to test out new skills and the ability to do things independently. It is not unusual for a client to report having tackled a tough problem or dealt with an issue that, earlier, she or he would have first discussed with the worker. The worker senses the client's positive feelings of accomplishment and employs the skill of crediting the client. This consists of a direct acknowledgment of the client's ability to "go it alone."

When the client remains with the service and the worker leaves, discussion of the new worker often begins to dominate the conversation: "Who will the new worker be, and what will he or she be like?" This can represent "trying the change on for size" as well as an expression of anger toward the worker who is leaving.

I have experienced this process myself, when I have worked with students on a year-long course. The way we interact is, in some ways, a model of the process we study, although both the content and my role differ from those found in social work practice. Nevertheless, I can remember times during the final classes when I found it impossible to get into the conversation. When I would comment on the work being discussed, the students would look at me briefly and then continue to talk as if I were not there. After a few such attempts to enter the conversation, I would comment that it felt like I was not in the classroom; again, the students would merely look at me and then return to their conversation. As I sat back and listened, I could hear the students carrying on important discussion and analysis of practice within the peer group and without my help. This was a part of our ending process. They were trying it on for size.

## The Farewell-Party Syndrome

Schwartz uses the term *farewell-party syndrome* to refer to the tendency to "pad" ending discussions by concentrating only on the positive aspects of the relationship or even by planning a celebration. All working relationships have both positive and negative aspects to them. The worker must not allow the ending discussion to get so caught up in the positive feelings that an honest analysis of the content and process is bypassed. The worker should reach for negative evaluation to encourage the client not to hold a "farewell party." For example, "I'm glad you thought I was helpful to you but there must have been some times I was not so helpful. Let's talk about those as well."

The client and the worker may also use the farewell-party syndrome to avoid discussion of the powerful feelings associated with endings. There is nothing wrong, under certain circumstances, with having a "party" of some sort to mark the end of the relationship. One residential worker went skiing on the last day with a child for whom he was the key worker. Another foster care worker arranged to go to McDonald's for lunch to celebrate a last day. The problem arises when the celebration is used to mask or avoid the ending. This can leave too much unsaid and does not allow both worker and client to achieve closure. In the skiing example, the worker described how the teen started to drop hints about his feelings just as they reached the top of the chairlift, where they were to get off and start skiing down the hill. Finally, the worker had to say, "We have things to talk about. Let's take our skis off and go in for a cup of cocoa."

Thus far, I have detailed some dynamics and skills involved in handling the ending process with individuals. Parts III, IV, and V of this book examine further illustrations in the family, group, and community context and address some of the differences in the dynamics. In addition to the process of ending, the worker must pay attention to the substantive content that can make the ending important for the client's learning. In the next section, I review those skills of the ending phase that help the client to use the experience with the worker to make an effective transition to new situations that she or he may face alone.

# The Skills of Transitions

A new beginning is always inherent in the ending of a working relationship. For example, as the former foster child—who is now a young adult—leaves the care of the agency, she begins a new phase of her life and faces a new set of demands. Some of these demands are similar to those faced by any young person of the same age, but others are unique to someone who has been the ward of an agency. The ex-convict who completes the term of parole begins to function in society without the supervision and support offered by the parole officer. The patient who leaves the rehabilitation center must negotiate the outside world, even though she is still limited by the effects of her accident or illness. The former narcotics addict who leaves the treatment center must deal with many of the same pressures and demands on the street that helped lead to the addiction in the first place. This time, the ex-addict needs to make it without the support of either the worker or the drugs. The adolescent delinquent who leaves the protection of the wilderness camp may be facing a family that has changed little during his time away. For each of these clients, the time of ending is also the time of a powerful beginning.

The worker needs to pay attention to this process of transition during the ending phase by focusing on the substance of the work as well as on the process of ending. In work that has gone well, clients may have discovered new things about themselves, their strengths and weaknesses, their patterns of behavior under pressure, and their abilities to handle problems. They may also have learned new ways to view some of the important people and systems they must deal with. Ending should be a time to add up what has been learned.

Because the client's work is never really finished, clients end with some new ideas about how to deal with issues in their lives, as well as with an agenda for future work. By asking the client to identify the specific areas on which he or she needs to work, the worker communicates that the learning process does not end with the end of their relationship. The worker also sends a message that he or she feels the client will be capable of continuing the work.

Next, workers can help clients synthesize the process and content of the ending phase. As with all phases of the relationship, the interaction between workers and clients offers fertile areas of learning related to the contract. Workers can use the dynamics of the ending process to help clients generalize from their learning to new experiences.

Finally, workers can help clients make direct transitions to new experiences and to other workers and alternative sources of support that may be available for their use. These tasks of the ending phase are examined in the next three sections.

## Identification of Major Learning

Endings are a time to systematically evaluate the helping experience. The worker asks the client to reflect on their work together and to identify some of the things that have been learned. One week before the final session, for example, the worker could ask the client to prepare to share these important ideas during the final week. In the very first session, the worker asked the client for feedback on the issues that seemed to be of concern. Now that the sessions are ending, worker and client need to review jointly where things stand on these issues and others that may have emerged during their work together.

The worker must demand specifics; a general summing up is not enough. When the client says that the sessions with the worker were valuable because the client learned so much about himself or herself, the worker might respond, "Exactly what was it you learned that was important to you?" This process helps the client consolidate the learning. A second benefit accrues from the client's recognition of newly developed abilities. This can strengthen the client in preparing to end the relationship. The worker can participate in this process as well, because in any real interactive experience, the worker will learn from the client. What does the worker now understand differently about the client's problems and about the worker's personal and professional self? The summing up should include discussion of what both worker and client are taking away from the experience. The following example illustrates this adding-up process.

***Ending with a Voluntary Client who Hit her Daughter*** This young mother was referred to the counseling agency after she told her family doctor that she felt badly for hitting her daughter. The work had gone on for a number of sessions and after completing the last session the plan called for a two-month break and then a follow-up to see if the change was lasting.

> Social Worker's Notes: Christine originally came in because she felt so bad that she hit her oldest daughter whenever she became angry. It was established that she wanted techniques of parenting that would prevent her from hitting her child. We openly discussed her lack of bonding with this oldest daughter and the poor marital situation Christine found herself in. Christine tried but could not get her family to participate. This was to be the second-to-last session with a follow-up in February (2 months).

WORKER: Let's review a little where we started and where we are now.

CHRISTINE: The reason I came was because I had been hitting Raphaelle, much more than I felt good about. But things have been going very well. In the beginning I thought that if I could stop hitting her altogether, I would feel really happy about it. Well, I haven't struck her once, and I don't even feel like it. It is going very well.

WORKER: And it's been about three months.

CHRISTINE: It almost seems so far away now.

WORKER: You mean from the time we started?

CHRISTINE: Yes, it seems almost a little unreal—do you know what I mean? It's a little embarrassing.

WORKER: Well, it has been some time since October, but it was all very real then.

CHRISTINE: No kidding. But it feels good to end, because I don't feel I need it anymore—things are going well. But it does feel good that I can come back in February.

WORKER: Why did you say it is embarrassing?

CHRISTINE: It was embarrassing to even come in and state that I was hitting my children. I had to talk to my family doctor and explain it all to him. I wish I could have solved it within the family without outside help.

**Practice Points:** The worker helps the client to explore the process of change over time and to credit her growth starting with her decision to seek help. It's important to identify the still unfinished business with the husband who refused to attend but at least the client has been able to separate that issue from her response to her daughter.

WORKER: I guess it seems easier to solve this hitting now, eh?

CHRISTINE: Well, this is it, but I am glad I came because I might still be hitting Raphaelle. You know, just the commitment of getting help was the biggest factor.

WORKER: Asking for help makes you vulnerable, but ironically it also makes you stronger. Is there anything else that's different for you and Raphaelle?

CHRISTINE: For some reason, I look at her a little different. I see her having some problems, but I see her also as older. Remember how you said that she is becoming a teenager and won't take hitting anymore? I also think like she could be gone in 5 years. Where have all the years gone? (Showed sadness)

WORKER: What is happening for you right now? (Some discussion followed about Raphaelle.)

CHRISTINE: I guess I also feel that things aren't going so well between my husband and me. I suppose that will always be there.

WORKER: Well, you know I always did feel it was a shame that you couldn't get him to participate in these sessions. But maybe that's for another time and under different circumstances. Have things deteriorated between you two? I guess I am asking if you need to spend some time on this issue even though he won't come in.

CHRISTINE: No, not really. I guess I don't really want to dwell on the negative. I am glad for me and, as you said, that's what counts.

WORKER: Sure, but the door is open. I don't know how aware you were but a couple of times I really pushed hard for you to bring your husband into these sessions.

CHRISTINE: (Laughing) Oh, I felt it! (This was followed with some discussion about this issue.)

WORKER: You seem to have consolidated some strengths and determination. You seem to put your foot down. I guess it will take some adjustment for your relationship (with husband). Somehow you have to find a way to support each other. You do tend, it seems to me, to walk a bit of a tightrope sometimes, and, as a result, you end up having to give quite a bit, even when you need to get your own needs met.

CHRISTINE: You know how you said, last time, that I am a giving person? My husband just thinks I am a selfish manipulator. I think he is more right. But it sure is nice to hear.

WORKER: You mean that you are a giving person?

CHRISTINE: Yes. (A little teary)

WORKER: It's hard to hear, isn't it?

CHRISTINE: It's just not something I heard before. My husband says I do some nice things but doesn't say I am a nice person. I don't think of myself as a nice person.

WORKER: It can be your secret that you are a nice person.

CHRISTINE: (Laughing) What do you mean?

WORKER: Well, we'll say good-bye and we'll see each other only one more time in the end of February, but you'll remain a nice person, even though I won't say it anymore.

CHRISTINE: It's nice of you to say so and it's funny but you have to hear it to believe it, but I have also thought about it as well and that makes a difference. (We reviewed some of the main themes of the sessions and discussed what was helpful and what wasn't. We contracted to see each other at the end of February. We planned to have a short session in February to see if things were still OK with her and Raphaelle.)

The following is the end of our follow-up session in February, a short half-hour session in which Christine brought in a little book as a gift.

WORKER: Well, maybe we can just say good-bye?

CHRISTINE: Good-bye, John, and thank you.

WORKER: You're welcome; good-bye, Christine, good luck to you and your family. It's funny, but I feel a little sad about saying good-bye.

CHRISTINE: I feel a little bit sad as well. Just a little sad but I am also happy that I came and now I don't feel I need to come anymore. I felt good about having 6 weeks to see if I could keep it up.

WORKER: In retrospect, that does seem like it was good. Anyway, you have our telephone number, and don't hesitate to call even if it is to say hello.

CHRISTINE: Yes, thanks a lot for that. Bye, John, and good luck with your studies. You're not a bad social worker (laughing).

WORKER: Thanks, good-bye, Christine, and of course, thanks for that beautiful little book.

 **Interactive Skills of Helping**

Use the accompanying DVD or visit *The Skills of Helping Individuals, Families, Groups, and Communities,* Seventh Edition, CourseMate website at www.cengagebrain.com and enter your personal access code to watch this video

**ENDING AND TRANSITION SKILLS** This example presents a White worker and a middle-aged African American client who is dealing with a divorce, discussing the ending of their working relationship. The early difficulty in establishing an intercultural working relationship is explored.

## Identification of Areas for Future Work

The worker should convey to the client that the work will continue after the ending. It is all right for the client to have unanswered questions, to be faced with unsolved problems, and not to have life all figured out. In the previous example the client made significant progress in her relationship to her daughter but not with her husband. The worker had recognized that might be for future work. The client began the experience with certain problems or life tasks and has learned how to handle some of these more effectively than at the beginning. The experience ends with other problems or life tasks ahead. The difference now is that the client has learned how to deal better with these concerns.

If some of the uncertainties and accompanying ambiguity are detailed, the worker must resist the temptation to try to "solve" these last-minute concerns. Part of the learning experience involves being able to live with some uncertainties. The worker's task is to help the client inventory these unresolved issues, create an agenda for future work, and use their experience together to determine how the client can continue to work on these concerns. The worker must also resist the temptation to reassure the client who expresses doubts about competency. Acknowledging and understanding these fears of not being able to continue alone is more helpful. The worker needs to convey a belief in the client's potential to tackle future tasks without in any way attempting to minimize the feeling that the going may be rough.

***18-Year-Old Foster Child Transitioning to Independence: Final Session***  To illustrate this point, we return to the ending sessions of the 18-year-old who was about to leave the care of the child welfare agency. The worker had asked the client to identify those things he had learned as well as those areas he still felt he needed to consider. This excerpt from the final session begins as they review what the client has learned. Note the worker's request for specificity in what the client felt he had learned.

WORKER: What ideas hit you hard during our discussions together? What will stay with you?

CLIENT: I learned that I have to be more responsible for myself. That was important to me.

WORKER: Exactly what do you mean by that?

CLIENT: Well, I used to walk around with a chip on my shoulder. All my problems were someone else's fault. I was angry at my mother for giving up on me, it was always my foster parents who were the cause of my fights, and the "Aid"—well, I hated the place.

WORKER: And how do you see it now?

CLIENT: Well, I did have it tough. It wasn't easy moving from home to home, never having the kinds of things normal kids had. But I think I understand better that what happens to me from now on is pretty much up to me. I can't blame everyone else anymore. And the "Aid," well, for all my complaining, with all the changes in foster homes, the "Aid" has been the only place I can call home.

WORKER: I guess you have a lot of mixed feelings about this place, but now that you're leaving, a part of you is going to miss it.

CLIENT: (Silence) Even with all the complaining and all the crap I had to take, I'm still going to miss it. You know, I'm scared about being on my own.

WORKER: Sure, it's scary. What exactly are you afraid of?

CLIENT: I'm going to have to make it on my own now. I'm starting this new job, and I'm worried about how I'm going to do. And what if I don't make any friends in the rooming house? There are other people my age there, but it's hard to get to know them. It's not like a group home where you spend a lot of time together and you always have the house parents to talk with.

**Practice Points:**   As the discussion gets into the underlying fears associated with independence the worker demonstrates the skill of partializing so that the client can address them one at a time.

WORKER: So you have two questions to work on: how to make it on the job and how to make some new friends.

The two critical tasks identified in this discussion are major ones for any young adult and quite appropriate to this client's phase of life. As he moves into adulthood, he must tackle issues that relate to how he will fit into the working world, and he must also begin to shift his relationships from parental figures to his peer group. Having moved through the child welfare system makes these tasks more difficult for him than for others. His life has been marked by so many broken relationships that he has become reluctant to risk being hurt again.

In a project I directed at the University at Buffalo School of Social Work, we worked with a group of foster children who were ready to make this transition to independence. Interestingly, during the previous few years their workers had seen no reason to work with them, and thus they were termed "drawer" kids—their files were kept in the drawer but were considered inactive. What we found was that entering this ending stage and preparing for transition evoked many issues with which they needed help. The key was to recognize that they were ready to accept help once it was offered to them.

In the next segment, we continue this illustration to demonstrate how the worker–client ending process can directly relate to the content of the work.

## Synthesizing the Ending Process and Content

If we keep in mind that the worker–client relationship is one of many the client deals with in life, and is in fact just a special case among all relationships, then the experience can be used to illustrate important themes. The relationship can be viewed as a training ground for the client; skills that have been developed in dealing with the worker are transferable to other situations. The astute worker can tune in to identify connections between the worker's own interactions with the client and the work that will follow the ending.

For example, to return to our illustration with the 18-year-old, this client had to overcome his guardedness and establish a close relationship with the worker. It took a long time for the client to allow himself to be vulnerable, to risk being hurt. In effect, the client needed to learn what we must all learn: For our life to have meaning, we must risk getting close to people, even though this may mean getting hurt sometimes. If we go through life remembering only the hurt, then we may build a wall between ourselves and people who could provide comfort and support. The typical "graduate" of the child welfare system has been hurt so often that he or she often begins a new relationship with the expectation that it will not work out. Such children may seek out close ties (for example, by marrying early) but will hold back on really investing themselves. This worker recognized that intimacy is a central issue for clients who must now risk themselves with their peers (in the rooming house and elsewhere). Eventually they will face the same problem as they grow older and consider marriage.

**Practice Points:**   Let us return to the interview, as the worker tries to help the client learn from their experience together. The worker uses her own feelings and experience and by sharing them with the client frees the client to share his.

WORKER: You know, I think what we have gone through together might offer you some ideas about how to handle this friendship question. Do you remember how it was with us when we first met?

CLIENT: Yeah, I thought you would be just another social worker. I wondered how long you would stick around.

WORKER: As I remember it, you made it pretty tough on me at the beginning. I had the feeling you wouldn't let me get close to you, because you figured it wouldn't last too long anyway.

CLIENT: That's right! I didn't build it too high 'cause I knew it was only temporary.

WORKER: It was frustrating for me at first because I couldn't seem to get anywhere with you. You seemed determined not to let anything get going between us. Somehow, it worked out. Because I feel real close to you, it's going to hurt now not to be seeing you all the time. I knew from the first day that someday we would have to say good-bye and it would be painful. No matter how much it hurts now, I wouldn't want to have missed knowing you this way. It was something special for me, and I will remember you.

CLIENT: (Silence—obviously struggling with emotion) I'm glad you stuck with me. You're the only worker who really did.

WORKER: What can you take out of our experience that relates to you and the people at the rooming house, or wherever you meet friends—at work, the Y?

CLIENT: You mean the same thing could happen there? If I build the walls too high, they might not get through?

WORKER: You said before that you had discovered how responsible you are for a lot of what happens. I think that's true in this case as well. If you're afraid of risking yourself, of being rejected, of getting close to these people and then losing them, then you will be alone. Maybe the most important thing you have learned is that you can get close if you want to, that it does hurt when you say good-bye, but that's life. You pick yourself up and find new people to get close to again.

CLIENT: You mean like the kids at the rooming house?

WORKER: Right! And on the job and maybe at the Y, or other places where you can meet people your own age.

CLIENT: So it's up to me.

WORKER: It usually is.

**Practice Summary:** In many ways, the worker is sharing his own learning with the client. Every time the worker starts with a new client and finds himself investing feeling, he must do so with the knowledge that it will hurt to say good-bye. This is the gift a worker can give to a client. The best way for workers to handle their own feelings of loss is to share them in the ending with one client and then begin again with a new client.

## Transitions to New Experiences and Support Systems

As the worker brings the relationship to a close, it helps to identify what it is about their work together that the client valued and to discuss how the client can continue to receive this support. In the previous illustration, the worker helped the client think about how he might shift his need for support to a peer group. This suggestion made sense for his stage of development. In another case, a worker might help a client identify family or friends who could offer help if the client will use them; in this way, the client can employ the skills that he or she developed while using the worker. For cases in which a transfer is made to a new worker, some discussion of the strengths and weaknesses of the present working relationship can help a client develop a strategy to use the new worker more effectively. Community resources for social, vocational, and counseling needs can also be identified.

In addition, workers can convey to the client that the counseling process is not necessarily a one-time experience that leaves the client capable of facing all of life's crises. It is helpful for getting through a particular period and may be needed again at different points in life. For example, a young female child who is a survivor of sexual abuse may need immediate help to cope with the trauma and the resulting disruption of her family. New issues will emerge as she enters her teen years, and a mutual-aid support group may be helpful to her—and to her nonoffending parent as well—during this normally difficult transition stage. As a young adult, when she is getting ready to enter into partnerships of her own, and again later, if she becomes a parent, she may need support to cope with the normative issues of the transitions in age and status that are compounded by the unique issues facing survivors. An ending at any one stage should help the client realize she has not "solved" her problems but instead has learned how to use social support to cope with them. She should not see it as a sign of failure if she needs help again.

Finally, a physical transition to the new situation can also be made. For example, a joint session with the new worker can ease the change, or a worker from a residential center might accompany a resident on visits to a new foster home. In many circumstances, concrete steps can be taken in addition to conversation about endings and transitions.

# Variations on Endings

When I discuss these sorts of emotional endings with students and workers, usually at least one group member will courageously say, "These endings sound great, but what if you and the client really don't feel so bad about endings?" When I credit the commentator for being honest, another participant sometimes follows up by commenting, "What if you don't like the client and are actually glad to see the relationship come to an end?" In this section, we explore several variations on the ending model: endings of relationships that the worker feels never really got started, endings in which the worker is angry rather than sad about ending, endings associated with the worker's job loss, and endings associated with the death of a client—in one case, a suicide, and in another, a client in the last stages of AIDS.

### Ending a Relationship that never Really Began

**EP 2.1.1b**

When students review examples of powerful and emotion-laden endings with clients, they often feel guilty if their own experiences have not been similar. They share examples in which the working relationship never got off the ground. Intellectually, the student understands that the client may have played some part in the creation and maintenance of the illusion of work. Emotionally, however, the student often takes full responsibility for the "failure" because of feelings of guilt and incompetence. These feelings, in turn, may block the student from moving fully into the ending/transition phase of work, causing her or him to avoid the process of evaluating the experience with the client.

First, students need to gain a clear perspective on the interactional nature of their practice. No matter how effective and skillful they become, they will never be able to reach all clients. Second, social workers can only do the best they can at any particular moment in their professional careers. They cannot hold themselves responsible for not being able to give a client more than they did. Instead, they should guard against allowing their feelings to cause them to underplay the help they did give—just as big a mistake as overplaying their contribution. Once workers have developed perspective and received support from their supervisor and/or colleagues, the ability to manage these feelings can help them mobilize themselves to use the ending period as a time to provide additional help to the client. Support is crucial to the success of this process because students and inexperienced workers are vulnerable at this stage in their careers, and they will experience negative feedback as particularly painful.

In many cases, discussing the endings is even more important when the work has gone poorly than when it has gone well. The ending process centers on an honest evaluation of the working relationship. The worker needs to own up to his or her part in the process and also to help the client examine the part she or he played in keeping the work superficial. If handled in a nonaccusatory and constructive manner, this discussion can constitute the worker's most important contribution to the client's growth. Significant professional growth for the worker can also emerge from this conversation.

***Inner-City African American Teen with a White Worker in a Country Residential Setting*** In the following example, a worker levels with the client as the ending phase of work begins, making the demand for work that the worker failed to make during the beginning or middle phases of practice. In this example, the client is an African American, inner-city teenager who has been in a residential setting in a rural area of the state. The original referral was from the court system and the state's child welfare agency. Problems with the law, drug use, and family members are part of the teenager's history. Although the client has superficially conformed to the program, the worker, who is White, has always felt "conned" by the client but has failed to confront the issue.

**Practice Points:** The dialogue has been modified a bit, because the original transcript contained street jargon that the worker said was like a "foreign language" he had to learn. Both the jargon and the worker's feeling like an outsider were key signals of the core of the problem.

WORKER: We only have 2 more weeks left, and I think it is important that we discuss our time together. I realize that you are probably looking forward to finishing, because I don't believe you have found the program very helpful. I have to admit to feeling the same way. I think it is important that we discuss why it didn't work out. I'd like to know what you think I could have done to be more helpful, and I'd like to let you know what I think you could have done.

CLIENT: Man, I don't think you understood what it is like for me. This place is OK, no hassles, no problems. But when I get back home, it starts all over. The pressure is on to use when I'm on the street, and who's going to help me then? You don't have any idea at all. I mean, my ass is on the line back home, every day.

WORKER: I think you're right about that; I don't have any idea. I was hoping I could help you anyway, fix you up so when you went back home, you could handle it differently. Why didn't you level with me from the beginning—why did you just play along with me?

CLIENT: Are you kidding? You're the "Man"—I'm not going to level with you.

WORKER: I think I knew it was bull all along; I should have been more honest with you. I'm White, and you're Black. I have a job and a safe place to live, while you're just scratching to survive. I pretended that didn't matter.

CLIENT: Look, don't get me wrong. You're not so bad for a White dude. You just don't have a clue.

WORKER: You know, it would have helped if you had taken a risk, been a bit more honest and let me know what it was really like. I understand why you didn't, why you just conned me, said the right words, and I realize I could have pushed you harder, right from the beginning. But you had a part to play as well. You can keep on playing the game when you get back home, but it seems to me, that's when you are going to need some real help the most. You are going to have to trust someone sometime.

CLIENT: What good is that going to do me? Talk isn't going to help no one. I'm stuck in that hole and I'm not getting out. So I just gotta work on survival.

WORKER: It's like you're up against a stone wall, isn't it? No future, no hope—like you're trapped.

**Practice Summary:** As the conversation continued, the worker listened and acknowledged feelings that were present for the client but had been only hinted at earlier. Even though it was the ending of their work together, this conversation was real and might have begun to lay the groundwork for the client's future use of a helping professional. The focus turned to what resources the client might be able to tap back home when the pressure started again. The conversation also helped this worker to tune in better to the realities of oppression related to race, class, and gender that most of his inner-city clients faced. This would increase the chance that the worker could make a quicker start with the next client, pushing for honesty earlier while integrating support with a demand for work. The worker could also focus more on the realities of life in the city instead of thinking that the client's personality could be changed in the country. By acknowledging that their time together had mostly been an illusion of work, the worker turned the ending phase into a positive experience—perhaps some of his best work with this client.

In another example, an angry and openly resistant client responded to the worker's request for an honest evaluation of their work together by saying, with feeling, "The problem was that you were one hell of a real asshole." The worker responded, also with feeling:

Well, you know, you weren't much of a bargain to work with either! The fact is, you never gave me a chance, right from square one. I made my mistakes, I'll own up to that. But you should realize that as long as you keep your wall up, and won't let anyone inside, you are going to be all alone with this stuff. And that's a shame, because I think you're really hurting and could use some help.

**Practice Summary:**   It is quite possible that the client did not take in a word the worker said. Even so, the worker needed to level with the client. The hard part for this worker was to tune in to the source of his anger and frustration. If it is rooted in a sense of failure and incompetence, the disclosure may not help. If the worker can see past the client's defenses, and if the emotions come from concern for the client, then it may be the most helpful gift the worker can give. This is where supervision and peer support can help a worker who is ending with a difficult client.

***Research on Predictors of Early Termination in Counseling***  Lampropoulos, Schneider, and Spengler (2009), noting that premature or early termination of psychotherapy and counseling is a common problem, explored predictors of this problem. The method involved an archival study of 380 client files in a university counseling training clinic.

Approximately 50 trainee counselors provide counseling service in the clinic each semester. Half of them are enrolled in a terminal master's program in counseling…and see clients as part of their first or second practicum. The other half hold master's degrees in counseling or related fields and are enrolled in a doctoral program in counseling psychology….(p. 37)

The authors note a female-to-male ratio of 3:1 and that approximately 20 percent of counselors were minority students. The archival files of 380 clients (65 percent female and 35 percent male) who had sought counseling services in the clinic over a five-year period were examined. Of this client group, 17 percent were either students or relatives of university employees and the remaining 83 percent outpatients from the community.

Demographic and other data on these clients were collected during and immediately after the intake interview and again after termination of services. Only clients of three types of termination were included in the analysis: (a) clients who failed to return to treatment after the initial intake appointment (intake dropouts); (b) clients who ended treatment beyond the initial intake session but did not complete counseling (therapy dropouts); and (c) clients for whom their counselor ended treatment (completers) (p. 38). Of this group, 61 (16.1 percent) were intake dropouts, 218 (57.4 percent) were therapy dropouts, and 101 (26.6 percent) were completers.

The goal of the study was to determine what factors in the archival records might have predicted to which group a client would belong. A number of variables were examined including demographics (e.g., age, marital status, income, etc.), whether they had been in counseling before, and perception of the presenting problems (e.g., depression, marital stress, interpersonal, family, grief). Intake counselors also recorded their anticipated perceived difficulty in working with the clients. The sample ranged from low difficulty (54.5 percent) to medium (38.2 percent) and high (7.4 percent). They also recorded their perception of the urgency of the problem (e.g., must see the counselor right away, 21.6 percent, and noncrisis, 78.4 percent).

Intake workers (advanced doctoral students) also reported tentative Primary Axis I diagnoses using the American Psychiatric Association's (1994) *Diagnostic and Statistical Manual of Mental Disorders,* 4th edition (DSM-IV). For example, intake clients were assessed as having partner relational problem (39.8 percent), major depressive disorder (11.9 percent), anxiety disorders (6.9 percent), and so on. Finally, intake clients were assessed on the Global Assessment Functioning (GAF) Scale (Spitzer, Gibbon, Williams, & Endicott, 1996) with an average score of 64.04 on a range of 1 to 100, with a higher score indicating better functioning.

The researchers identified 12 potential predictor variables of the status of the clients in respect to early termination or completion of treatment. These included client age, education, annual family income, number of children in the client's living unit, number of the client's presenting problems, perceived client difficulty, GAF Scale score, prior treatment, gender, employment status, case urgency, and referral source (self or other). They reported that "The full, 12-predictor model was most useful for predicting the termination type therapy dropouts, yielding a 91.7 percent accuracy rate. However, the model was not useful for predicting the outcome categories intake dropouts (13.1 percent accuracy rate) and completers (19.8 percent accuracy rate). The overall classification accuracy of the full model was 60 percent (p. 39). Examination of the individual predictor items indicated that client age, annual income, perceived client difficulty, and the GAF Scale were most influential for dividing individuals into the group termination types.

The authors identify the limitations of the study and the tentative nature of the findings including the most obvious limitation: they were not able to assess the process—that is, the interaction between the therapist and the client—at either the intake or the treatment sessions. An argument could be made that the efforts by the intake workers to obtain significant amounts of data in the intake or "study" session, or the lack of skill of the counseling students may have contributed, in part, to the 16.1 percent intake dropout rate, the 57.4 percent therapy dropout rate, and the limited 26.6 percent completer rate. In the interactional framework presented in this book, the variable of interaction between the counselors at intake and during treatment might well account for a significant portion of the variance in the outcomes. A hint of this possibility emerged in the finding that for clients over 40, the age of the clinician did matter, with older counselors who had more life experience having more positive outcomes.

In addition, crucial data on the race and ethnicity of the clients were not available in the archival records although the majority of the clients were described as

"Caucasian." The fact that race and ethnicity data were not included in the records of the clinic could be a signal of lack of sensitivity to the importance of these variables and their impact on inter- and intracultural interactions.

## Endings caused by the Termination of the Worker's Job

**EP 2.1.1a**
**EP 2.1.1f**

As a result of severe cutbacks in federal and state funding of social services during the past decade, as well as the impact of managed care in health settings, endings caused by the professional's job loss are raised more frequently in my workshops with workers, supervisors, and managers. Supervisors describe workers who are depressed, cynical, and apathetic as they enter the final phase of work. Anger about the restriction of services and the job loss often leads the worker to want to ignore the ending phase issues, sometimes withholding disclosure of the termination of work until the last session with a client or even avoiding it completely. This lack of closure serves neither clients nor workers.

Clients are disempowered in such interactions and are denied the chance to deal with their ending feelings, to take some control over the endings, and to make an effective transition to life without their workers. The abruptness of the ending can negatively affect the transition to the new worker or service, or make the client reluctant to become emotionally invested with any other helping professionals. Clients are also denied the opportunity to challenge the loss of the services. In some situations, when clients have been made aware of what is happening, they have mobilized resources (other clients, family members, and so forth) to object to the loss and they have even been able to reverse or moderate the decisions that led up to it.

Workers pay a price for abrupt endings as well: They lose the opportunity to end professionally, which is one way to deal with some of their guilt about "abandoning" their clients. In addition, on later reflection, workers often report how helpful it was that their supervisor held them to a professional level of practice in the ending phase rather than allowing them to withdraw out of anger and depression. Of course, a crucial element in the process is the work done to create a supportive atmosphere in which workers know they can get assistance to manage their feelings.

In workshops I have led for frontline workers who face the potential or actual loss of their jobs, I have focused first on their anger and then on the pain and sadness that are usually also present (see Shulman, *Interactional Supervision*, 3rd ed., 2010). The guilt felt by remaining workers ("survivor guilt") needs to be dealt with so that their anxiety does not cause a flight-fight response. After some supportive work is done, staff can respond to my request to tune in to the impact of the cutbacks on their clients and to strategize how best to help clients to cope with loss while the workers struggle with their own feelings.

***Family Support Work with a Single Parent: The Worker Loses her Job*** In the following excerpt, a worker announces that she has lost her job and will be ending her work with the client, a single parent involved in family support work that focuses on problems with her teenager.

**Practice Points:**   Note that the worker shares her honest anger at losing her position but because of work done in supervision makes sure to stay focused on the meaning for the client. While it would be understandable if the worker wished to vent her anger and encourage the client's angry response, she also is determined to end a relationship with the client in a professional manner.

WORKER: I'm afraid I have some bad news for you. You may know that the state was considering cutting the funds available for support agencies like ours. Well, the cuts have come through, and, because of low seniority, I will be one of the first workers to lose my job. I'm afraid this means we only have 4 weeks left, and we are going to have to start to discuss how to end our work and connect you to other sources of help.

CLIENT: Oh my God, you must feel terrible. You mean they're letting you go, just like that?

WORKER: Actually, we have known there might be cuts for a few months. I didn't want to worry you because we just were not sure what would happen. But now we know, and you and I have to start to face it. I am feeling terrible about losing my job, and part of the reason for that is that I am going to have to say good-bye to clients I have gotten close to—and that includes you. (Silence) How about you, what are you feeling right now?

CLIENT: I'm furious at your agency. Just when I find a worker I can really like, they take you away. Does this mean I will get another worker? What will happen to me now?

WORKER: I want you to know I have really felt close to you, and it means a lot to me to hear that you will miss me too. I'm also angry, but underneath that I'm feeling a lot of sadness and loss. We need to talk about that over the next few weeks as well as where do you go from here. I must be honest. I don't think the agency really has had time to consider what we are going to do for clients like you. We never felt the cuts would be this bad, with so many positions lost.

I will try to find out what may be available to you, and, if you wish, I will put you in touch with my supervisor, who is staying on. That way you can ask some of the questions yourself. If it turns out that you cannot get the help you need here, we are going to have to see what else may be available in the community. Also, we better discuss where you can get help from other sources—your family and friends, for example. I can't make any guarantees about services because every other agency is also getting clobbered, but I will make sure we spend time on how you can cope no matter what we find out. You have grown a lot in the last few months, and I think you have more strengths than even you realize.

CLIENT: Those bastards! (Starting to cry) Don't they realize it's going to be hard on me to cope on my own? (Silence—the worker also starts to fill with emotion—the two sit quietly for a while, the client crying softly and the worker with tears in her eyes.)

WORKER: (After a short while) I'm not sure they do realize the impact of all of this on clients. If you want to discuss ways in which you can let them know, tell me. I'll be glad to help you communicate your views. Your needs are important, and they have to realize these decisions have serious impact on real people. In the meantime, let's start to talk about our work together, what you have learned, your strengths, areas where you still feel vulnerable, and what other sources of help you have available. I want to make sure we work hard right up to the end.

**Practice Summary:** There were many points in this dialogue at which the worker could have lost her sense of professional function. When the client asked the worker how she felt about the job loss, the rest of the conversation could have revolved around the worker's reactions. It did not, because the worker came right back to the impact on the client. When the client expressed anger at the agency, the worker might have joined in the anger, focusing on her own sense of the unfairness of the situation. Instead, she shared her own feelings of loss and reached for those of the client.

When the client asked, "What will happen to me now?" the worker could have expressed her resentment and bitterness by reflecting back the client's sense of hopelessness. Instead, the worker empowered the client, suggesting that she begin actively to make some demands on the system. The worker did not try to falsely reassure the client, but she did focus on the next steps available to the client if the formal systems failed her. In addition, when the client focused on her anger at the political neglect and lack of understanding, the worker offered to empower the client in finding ways to communicate her feelings, rather than reflecting her own sense of hopelessness by saying, "What's the use—you can't fight city hall."

Finally, instead of focusing just on the social action possibilities open to the client, the worker came back to the immediate issues and left the door open for further discussion. All in all, this worker should feel good about her efforts to help the client cope, her maintenance of a professional role, and her commitment to the client. It was all the more admirable given her understandable anger toward the political system and the community, which lacked the will to meet their commitments to vulnerable clients.

## Endings caused by the Death of the Client

Coping with the death of a client on a caseload or working with a dying client can be extremely traumatic for a worker. Although workers have always had to deal with the issue of death and dying as a normal part of their caseload (e.g., accidental deaths, suicide, terminal illness), the epidemic growth of health and social problems such as AIDS and crack cocaine addiction has increased the likelihood of such traumas. In the next sections, we explore the impact of a sudden death (a suicide) on the caseload as well as the implications of working with a client who is dying of AIDS. First, a word on the effect that traumatic events have on workers may help you understand these more specific circumstances.

***Traumatic Events and their Impact on a Worker's Practice*** The literature has addressed more recently the issue of secondary trauma. That is the impact over time on workers who deal with difficult cases such as sexual abuse of a child or working in a pediatric oncology ward dealing with very sick and at times dying children and their families. Secondary trauma is addressed in more detail in Chapter 17. In this section the focus is on the impact of a traumatic case on a specific worker, or on his or her colleagues.

A trauma, in the sense that it is used here, causes a deeply felt negative emotional reaction. This may be experienced immediately or—as is often the case—at a later date, when the impact of the experience reemerges. For example, one of my child welfare studies examined the impact of a traumatic event, such as the death of a child who is on caseload while in foster care or left at home with the biological parents (Shulman, 1991). Analysis of the data indicated that the trauma not only affected the practice of the caseworker, but it also may have affected the practice of other workers in the same office and region. The incidence of traumatic events in a region was positively associated with more children going into care, going into care more quickly, being less likely to return home, and staying in care longer.

A traumatic event on a specific worker's caseload also suggested such negative consequences for the worker as low morale and decreased practice skill with clients.

Other examples of traumatic events included a physical attack or threat of attack by a client on a worker, cutbacks in budgets that led to layoffs, and the death of a colleague. A social support system can buffer the impact of trauma; this system would need to assist not only the particular worker involved but all of the other workers in the office or agency as well. I have addressed the issue of supervision and management and the skills needed to assist staff in coping with these traumas and others elsewhere (Shulman, 2010).

My work with an affected office revealed a tendency by the staff to avoid the pain associated with the traumatic event through the flight-fight syndrome. The stress often increased when the administration responded (from their own anxiety) with the question, "Who is at fault?" Workers consistently report that, at such a time, what they desperately need is for supervisors and administrators to ask, "How are you doing?" Interestingly, under the direction of a social worker, a large Canadian bank developed a program to provide support to bank branch staff immediately following a traumatic armed robbery. The branch would be closed for a day, and the social worker would be flown in to meet individually and in groups with all staff for trauma counseling. The bank discovered that it experienced fewer sick leaves, less absenteeism, lower staff turnover, and even a reduction in the level of mistakes if it paid attention to the needs of its staff after a trauma. It is ironic that a corporate entity was able to recognize the benefits of support for its employees, while social and health services often seem not to understand this concept.

An ending of a working relationship that is brought on by the sudden and traumatic death of a client should immediately mobilize the resources of the agency to attend to the needs of the workers involved. In the next section, I outline some steps to help workers not only to deal with their own feelings but also to work effectively with the feelings of clients. (For a more complete discussion of the impact of trauma, see Shulman, 1991, 1984. For a discussion of the supervisor's role, see Shulman, 2010.)

## Suicide on a Caseload

The suicide of a client can powerfully affect a worker, as well as other workers and clients in the system. A sudden and permanent ending to a working relationship can evoke guilt in the worker. Even if he or she logically understands that such a decision was made by the client and was not the responsibility of the worker, self-doubt often remains. This doubt can affect a worker's current and future practice. In one example, a social worker in a veterans' hospital reported having difficulty ending his work with a veteran even after 5 years of counseling him. When the issue was examined closely, it became apparent that the suicide of another, similar client on his caseload, shortly after they had ended their work together, had made the worker overly cautious about ending before all of a client's problems had been "solved."

Further discussion revealed that the worker had received little help with his own emotions following the suicide, with most of the administrative responses geared to an investigation of the circumstances (e.g., whether the recording was up-to-date and all of the proper procedures had been followed). Even colleagues seemed to shun him, turning away in a form of flight from his pain. Some simply may not have known what to say. For others, the suicide may have raised anxiety about their own clients. Lacking a defined protocol to deal with staff in traumatic situations, and lacking leadership from supervisors and managers, the system's reaction to the suicide left the worker feeling abandoned. Unable to manage his feelings, he became less able to manage his practice-related problems—particularly, ending with clients.

The impact of such an event on an entire staff system was made dramatically clear to me during a 2-day workshop I led for the staff of a psychiatric ward for inpatient teenagers. During the first day, staff presented problems with one Native Canadian teenage patient who was emotionally isolated from other Caucasian patients, resistant to work, hard to reach, and in general considered to be the ward's deviant member. In this role, the client acts significantly differently from other clients in the system but may actually be sending an indirect message on behalf of the other clients. (The concept of the role of the deviant member will be discussed more fully in the chapters on family and group work.)

In discussing this patient, I tried to help the staff see him in a new way—as a patient who could be sending a signal to staff of issues and feelings related to the ward as a dynamic system, in which the behavior of each participant in the system (staff and clients) affects and is affected by the behaviors of all other members of the system. Staff moved quickly to integrate this new view of his behavior and to strategize about how to intervene differently with him and the other teens on the ward.

When I arrived to start the second day of the workshop, I noticed the staff speaking in hushed tones at the coffee urn. When I asked what had happened, they told me that the client they had presented had been home on a pass the previous evening, and that he had shot himself and died. I felt stunned at the news. I knew the staff was also in shock. When the session started, I acknowledged the impact of this traumatic event. I then suggested that, in order to deal with this event, we abandon the other examples we had scheduled for discussion. I told them I thought we could connect the discussion to the purpose of our workshop. I was conscious of the fact that I would be modeling for the staff a way to deal with the group of patients they would meet with that evening. I believed that the patients would be experiencing many of the emotions the staff felt in reaction to the suicide. How I handled the staff discussion should somewhat parallel the work they would need to do with the teens on the ward.

The work that followed that morning could be divided into three related phases. The first phase of the work involved expressions of grief, loss, and guilt. The second phase involved discussion of how to provide support to staff in these circumstances. In the third and final phase, we examined the impact on other clients and the implications for practice.

*Expression of Grief, Loss, and Guilt.* I began by telling them that, even though I did not know this child except for their brief description of him the day before, I felt stunned and tremendously sad about his loss of life. I asked if we could take some time so that each person had a chance to share what she or he was experiencing. Staff began to speak slowly and in quiet tones as they shared how upset they were by the event. One staff member, the patient's key worker who had particular responsibility for providing continuity of service, began to cry. She felt guilty about not having reached him sooner—she wondered how alone he must have felt on the ward, cut off from the other patients and staff. A colleague next to her offered support by putting her arm around her. Other colleagues cried as well. She went on to wonder if she had made a mistake in agreeing to allow him to go home on a pass. She said that if she had not let him go home, he might be alive today. I acknowledged her feelings and asked if the other staff could be helpful to her. I suggested that helping her might also be helpful to them, because I thought they all felt some of her emotions and doubts.

One staff member pointed out that they had all participated in the decision to allow weekend passes—it was a joint responsibility. Another pointed out that the patient had done well on his previous passes and that they had had no way of predicting this suicide. A third pointed out that, although they might want to review their procedures for assessing a client's readiness for passes, he thought it would be a mistake to stop the leave program suddenly or to become overly cautious and restrictive. Weekend passes worked well for most kids most of the time. Another staff member pointed out that this teen had brought his pain with him to the hospital—staff had not caused it. He might have committed suicide no matter what staff had done. One staff member noted that he was a Native patient and wondered if he had felt even more isolated on the ward with "White workers, White patients, and even White walls." (I had raised issues of race and culture during the workshop the previous day.)

A supervisor suggested that they put on their future agenda some discussion of the issue of race—a topic they usually ducked. He said he often felt cut off from the Native patients and parents and had to think about how to reach them more effectively. Some suggested the need to recruit Native staff, who might be able to relate more effectively. The conversation continued along these lines. There were long periods of silence and many moments when each staff member seemed to be lost in his or her own feelings and thoughts, as well as other moments when they seemed to be able to come together.

As the conversation continued, I felt a deepening of the staff's feelings of depression and sadness. Allowing time for these emotions to emerge and taking time to accept them were important. The initial instinct to reassure or move too quickly into next steps can preempt the space needed for the emotions to be felt and acknowledged. As is discussed in more detail in Part IV of this book, powerful healing can occur with group support that allows people to feel that they are "all in the same boat." Given the brief time we had left, I decided to help the staff focus on where they could go next as a way of coping with the loss.

*How to Provide Support to Staff.* I shared my own feelings about the depth of sadness we were experiencing and then wondered if it might be helpful to discuss how to help the key worker and all of the staff during the next few weeks. I thought this might be a way to develop a protocol for how to handle such traumatic events in the future. A number of suggestions emerged, including the acknowledgment that it was useful just to have some time together to share in the grieving. One worker asked the key worker if she felt up to meeting with the teen's family; if not, she would do it for her. The key worker thanked her but said that she felt she should do it herself.

Another worker revealed a similar incident he had experienced a number of years before in another setting. He said he still felt the pain, and this incident had brought it all back. He told of having been given time off to attend the funeral and said that this had been important to him and to the family. The supervisor indicated that this could be arranged if the key worker wished. She indicated that she would like the opportunity. Further discussion focused on their concerns about how the hospital administration might react. The whole group shared with their supervisor some suggestions about how he might handle the issue so that administration was tuned in to the needs of the staff during the next few weeks.

*Discussion of the Impact on their Practice with the other Clients.* From my perspective, focusing on the needs of the staff must receive the highest priority. If those needs are ignored, staff may not be able to focus on the needs of current and future clients. It is also important, however, to reach for the professionalism of staff and not let them get lost in dealing with their own pain. Focusing on the clients they can still help offers an important way in which workers can heal themselves and lessen their guilt over the client they feel they did not help. I asked staff to shift their focus from self to other—the remaining clients on the ward.

As this discussion proceeded, one could almost sense a lifting of the pall over the room. Staff seemed energized by a focus on what they could do as next steps. I summarized the suggestions that had emerged thus far and then asked if they could give some consideration to the teens who were still on the ward. If the staff reacted so strongly, how would the patients—many of whom may have had similar feelings as the patient who had committed suicide—react? One participant pointed out how, in the past, when there had been a suicide attempt, staff had tried to hide it from the patients. They were afraid that it might trigger other attempts. He indicated that he thought this was probably a mistake, because patients knew something was wrong and soon found out what had happened through the grapevine. By trying to hide it, they closed off the possibility of helping the teens deal with their reactions. He recognized that it was his own fears he was running from, and he proposed that they raise the issue at the evening's community meeting.

The remainder of the session was devoted to tuning in to the potential reactions of the patients and developing strategies to help them cope. I pointed out the parallels between the staff's experience during the workshop and the group experience they were about to lead. They recognized the importance of sharing their own feelings, allowing time to grieve, shifting to the impact of this death on each of the remaining patients, and discussing the mutual responsibility each patient and staff member had for the others. They decided to involve the patients in a discussion of what they could do if they ever felt so cut off and alone, and how they could try to be more supportive of one another.

At the end of the session, I congratulated the staff on their work and their professionalism. I told them they had experienced a rough shock to their systems but that I saw a lot of strength in their ability to help one another and to stay focused on their professional tasks with their clients. I wished them luck, and the session ended.

The three-step model discussed in this section—grieving, the need for support for the worker, and then moving to focus on clients—can help to conceptualize the stages of coping with trauma of any kind.

***Working with a Dying Client on a Week-to-Week Basis*** With the exception of those settings associated with terminal illness, such as a hospice—a residential setting for people who are in the final stage of a terminal illness—or a medical setting, such as an oncology (cancer) ward, most social workers traditionally do not deal with dying clients. Unfortunately, as a result of the continuing AIDS epidemic, this has changed. Participants in my workshops have increasingly raised examples of clients who are in some stage of this illness. Although the success of the triple-drug treatment has significantly affected survival rates, many clients with AIDS cannot take advantage of this new treatment because they have other medical problems that prevent the use of these drugs.

Others have detailed the stages of death and dying (Kubler-Ross, 1969) and the worker skills required to help a client take some control over the process. Our discussion here focuses on how having a dying client affects the working relationship, and how the worker can integrate process and content in this sort of case. The illustrative example comes from a worker who discussed in a workshop the stress involved in working with a male client with AIDS who was in the final stages of the illness. The client lived at home with the support of his lover, some friends, and family members. The worker introduced the example by asking, "How do you work with a client when you don't know from week to week if you will ever see him again?"

When the example was explored in detail, one of the client's major issues became clear: None of the people who mattered to him were willing to talk to him about his impending death. He felt he had come to grips with this ending of his life, but his efforts to raise the issue with his lover, friends, and family members had all hit a wall of denial. He was angry at them for not being willing to talk with him and for trying to "cheer him up." He was afraid he might die before he could complete some work with each of these important people.

I asked the worker if she had discussed with the client her feelings about not knowing if the client would be there for the next interview; she had not. It became clear that the worker, too, was distressed about this client's impending death. She was also having difficulty with her own ending work with him, thereby mirroring the client's problem with the other significant people in his life.

**Practice Points:**   With support from other workshop members, she developed a strategy to confront the issue with her client and to use the conversation about their relationship (the process) to help him with his concerns about family and others (the content). Following is her report of her next conversation with the client.

> I began our conversation by telling him there was something I needed to talk to him about that was very difficult for me to raise. I told him I had been trying to help him deal with a number of people who were denying that he was facing death, when I now realized I was doing exactly the same thing. I told him it was very difficult for me coming to see him each week, not knowing if he would be around for our next session. I had come to care a great deal about him, and it was hard for me to face his impending death. I was going to miss him.
>
> He was quiet for a few moments and then smiled. He told me he had been aware that I was avoiding the issue and had wondered if I was ever going to raise it. He said I had been very important to him, this past year, and that he wanted to make sure I knew how much he had appreciated my help. At this point I began to cry, unable to maintain my "professional" composure. After a while, I told him that I wondered if the other people in his life he wanted to talk with had similar feelings. Perhaps they too cared so much for him that it was hard for them to face losing him. I wondered if they were afraid they might upset him and were holding back their real feelings. I wondered if they were like me and were simply afraid of the pain of losing him.
>
> He was thoughtful for a while and said that was probably it. But what could he do about it, because at this point it was more painful for him not to talk about his death? I suggested that perhaps he needed to tell them that he understood why they kept avoiding the issue. Perhaps, if they knew how important this was to him and that he was really ready to face his death and wanted them to face it with him, they might find the strength to stop avoiding it. At this point, he started to cry, and I sat quietly. I asked him if he thought he might have some mixed feelings himself about having this conversation with these people. I noted that he was aware we were ducking the issue between us, but he had not raised it with me. I had to raise it with him. Was he sending mixed signals to these people who were so important to him? Could they be sensing his ambivalence? He indicated that he probably was not being as direct as he could be and was simply blaming them for changing the subject. I suggested we might discuss ways he could initiate this conversation more directly and how he could refuse to be put off by their initial denials. We worked on this for some time.
>
> At the end of the conversation, I told him that I wanted to be sure that we discussed our own work together and made sure we said all that we needed to, just in case. We agreed that we would focus on our work together next week as

well as how well he did with his family members. As I left, I told him I was glad we had spoken so honestly and I would see him next week. He smiled and said, "God willing."

**Practice Summary:** For the ending work to continue, the worker in this example needed to deal with her own ambivalence and start the process of expressing her real feelings. This signaled to the client that the worker was ready to face the client's real feelings about ending with others in his life.

## Ethical Issues Associated with End-of-Life Decisions

Although greater attention has been paid to social workers' involvement in end-of-life decisions during recent decades, particularly because of the growth in social work practice in palliative care, it still remains a complicated area for ethical decision making. A highly publicized case generated a storm of emotionally charged activity, when the parents of a young woman (Terri Schiavo) who had been medically comatose for years requested withdrawal of life support. It was quickly (and publicly) connected to the "right to life" issue of the antiabortion movement and was seized upon by politicians as a cause. The low point in the debate may have been when a senior U.S. senator, who was also a medical practitioner, viewed a video of the patient and declared that he thought she was conscious of her surroundings—without ever physically examining her.

Passage of state legislation, such as an assisted suicide bill in 1997 in Oregon (the Death with Dignity Act), can initiate conflict as well. In response to the Death with Dignity Act, federal officials challenged the legitimacy of the act and threatened possible license revocation of doctors who participated. One can see that, with regard to such emotionally and politically charged issues, social workers may face serious ethical decisions in their work with patients at the end of their lives.

***Client Self-Determination in End-of-Life Decisions*** Dolgoff et al. (2005) point to an effort to address this issue by the NASW Delegate Assembly in 1993 that approved a policy statement on "Client Self-Determination in End-of-Life Decisions." They list the central ideas contained in the statement as follows:

- The social work profession strives to enhance the quality of life; to encourage the exploration of life options; and to advocate for access to options, including providing all information to make appropriate choices.

- Social workers have an important role in helping individuals identify the end-of-life options available to them.

- Competent individuals should have the opportunity to make their own choices but only after being informed of all options and consequences. Choices should be made without coercion.

- Social workers should not promote any particular means to end one's life but should be open to a full discussion of the issues and care options.

- Social workers should be free to participate or not participate in assisted-suicide matters or other discussions concerning end-of-life decisions depending on their own beliefs, attitudes, and value systems. If a social worker is unable to help with the decisions about assisted suicide or other end-of-life choice, he or she has a professional obligation to refer patients and their families to competent professionals who are available to address end-of-life issues.

- It is inappropriate for social workers to deliver, supply, or personally participate in the commission of an act of assisted suicide when acting in their professional role.
- If legally permissible, it is not inappropriate for a social worker to be present during an assisted suicide if the client requests the social worker's presence.
- The involvement of social workers in assisted-suicide cases should not depend on race or ethnicity, religion, age, gender, economic factors, sexual orientation, or disability. (p. 209)

The authors assert that even the issuing of such a detailed policy statement did not remove ambiguity and ethical issues from the discussion. Some social workers claim that the statement suggests it is ethical to be involved, but others disagree. Dolgoff et al. (2005) claim that:

> The policy statement raises many questions, among which are the following: whose quality of life is supported by assisted suicide? Whose life harmed? What is competence in such a situation? How does one judge competency? Is coercion entirely absent when people are considering suicide? What should one do if the option chosen creates issues for other family members, significant others, friends, or other professionals? What should one do if there are conflicts among those involved—some wanting to maintain life at all costs, other supporting the person's decision? What does it mean to be present but not participate? Is this just another form of approval of the act? (p. 210)

It is clear that the passage of a policy statement with regard to such an emotional issue has not solved the potential dilemmas faced by practitioners in this area. It may, in fact, require the actions of the legislators and courts to help resolve the issue.

## Chapter Summary

The ending and transition phase of practice can be the most important part of the work, during which clients deal with some of their most significant issues. Because of the feelings involved in the loss of a relationship, this phase may become a moratorium on work unless the worker helps the client identify the stages of the process (denial, anger, mourning, trying it on for size, and the farewell-party syndrome) so that the client can maintain some control. Specific worker skills involved in the ending phase include pointing out endings early, identifying the stages of the process, asking for a mutual exchange of the feelings related to ending, pointing out process and content connections, and asking for an honest evaluation and summary of the work together. Skills of transition include identification of major learning and areas for future work, synthesizing process and content, and helping the client move on to new experiences and support systems.

Variations on the ending themes include situations in which the work has gone badly, the worker is fired, the work ends because of a traumatic event such as suicide, or the client is dying. A number of ethical issues and dilemmas were reviewed in connection with end-of-life issues and assisted suicide.

# Related Online Content and Activities

 Visit *The Skills of Helping Individuals, Families, Groups, and Communities*, Seventh Edition, CourseMate website at **www.cengagebrain.com** for learning tools such as glossary terms, links to related websites, and chapter practice quizzes. The website for this chapter also features additional notes from the author.

# Competency Notes

The following is a list of Council on Social Work Education (CSWE) recommended competencies and practice behaviors for social work students defined in Educational Policy and Accreditation Standard (EPAS) and addressed in this chapter.

**EP 2.1.1a** Advocate for client access to the services of social work (p. 245)

**EP 2.1.1b** Practice personal reflection and self-correction to assure continual professional development (p. 241)

**EP 2.1.4d** View themselves as learners and engage those with whom they work as informants (p. 231)

**EP 2.1.7a** Utilize conceptual frameworks to guide the process of assessment, intervention, and evaluation (p. 225)

**EP 2.1.10b** Use empathy and other interpersonal skills (p. 223)

**EP 2.1.10f** Select appropriate intervention strategies (p. 223)

**EP 2.1.10k** Facilitate transitions and endings (p. 223)

# Social Work with Families

Part III consists of three chapters that elaborate and illustrate the interactional approach to social work in the context of practice with families.

Selected concepts from family treatment theories are presented, and their application to social work with families is discussed. The *two-client concept* introduced in earlier chapters is applied to define the social worker's dual role with regard to each individual family member and to the family as a whole. The chapter then revisits the four-phase model of practice by exploring the preliminary (tuning in) phase and the beginning (contracting) model and applies them to family practice. Family assessment models that may be useful in the beginning phase are described. A detailed example of beginning work with a family that includes an angry and resistant father is provided. The variations on practice introduced by working with a single-parent family, as well as the impact of culture and community, are addressed and illustrated with an example of the first sessions between a White worker and a Native American family.

# The Preliminary and Beginning Phases in Family Practice

In this chapter, we build on the concepts explored in Parts I and II by applying the helping model to work with families and family problems. Although the core elements of the model are the same—the phases of work, the importance of contracting, the skills required to build a positive working relationship, and so on—significant variations arise when one attempts to provide help to families and family members. This chapter addresses such variations to help the reader make the transition from work with one client to work with more than one client at a time.

The chapter begins by examining how we define the word *family.* Social work with families includes family support, family counseling, and crisis intervention. Note that we make a distinction between social work with families and long-term, intensive family therapy. Although many social workers practice as family therapists, a discussion of that modality of practice is beyond the scope of this book. However, we will draw on ideas from a number of family therapy models and then apply these constructs to family treatment in the social work context.

The *two-client concept* that was introduced earlier is reexamined, this time with the second client being the family as a whole. Tuning in to the family, family assessment models, and a discussion of dealing with "family secrets"—along with the beginning phase contracting skills—are all explored. An exploration of a first session with a family that includes an angry and resistant father illustrates the engagement phase issues. The chapter ends with an examination of variations on the core practice introduced during work with a single-parent family, and the impact on the process of culture and community.

## What Constitutes a Family?

**EP 2.1.4c**

Social workers have a long history of working with families that predates the emergence of family therapy as a practice modality. In this chapter, the term *family* includes a wide range of associations, many of which do not fit the traditional two-parent family image. The increasing number of single-parent families, as well as families headed by gay or lesbian partners, has broadened our understanding of the concept of family. The discussion in Chapter 4 of culturally competent practice also introduced the idea that even the word for family in some populations refers to what the dominant culture would call the "extended" family.

Collins, Jordan, and Coleman (2007) addressed the difficulty of defining the word *family*:

> One of the most perplexing issues in learning about families derives from the deceptively simple question: "What is a family?" In part, the confusion stems from the changing nature of modern relationships. While the family is a group, it is a special type of group that cannot be easily captured in a single definition. However, attempts to define family meet with difficulties similar to defining femininity, fatherhood, or love. Everyone seems to have a personal definition of each, but a generally agreed-upon definition is difficult, if not impossible, to arrive at. (p. 9)

These authors point out that the definition of family has significant implications, for example, in deciding who receives agency family services and who can obtain benefits meant for "family members." They also point to the political nature of the discussion and how it can serve as a hot-button "values" issue that can be used for divisive purposes. They suggest that a "one-size-fits-all" mentality creates difficulties for families, and that the definition of family needs to be expanded (p. 11).

In this book, I argue that the lack of a supportive environment contributes to family disintegration. I celebrate family diversity. I believe that diversity—rather than being a threat to families—actually honors families. For example, the demand by gays and lesbians for legal recognition of their relationships *supports* the importance of families. Rather than acting as a deficit, diversity provides families with depth, character, and richness.

This approach is consistent with the definition of *family* found in the *Social Work Dictionary* (2003) and advocated by the National Association of Social Workers (1990):

> A primary group whose members assume certain obligations for each other and generally share common residences. The NASW Commission on Families

(Promoting Family Support Statements, 1990) defined a family as two or more people who consider themselves to be family and who assume obligations, functions and responsibilities generally essential to healthy family life. Child care and child socialization, income support, long-term care (LTC), and other caregiving are among the functions of family life. (pp. 154–155)

This is the definition of the word *family* that will be used in this book, with recognition that all readers may not agree.

## Social Work with Families: Family Support and Family Counseling

**EP 2.1.10f**
**EP 2.1.10g**

Social work with families usually falls into two general categories. In the first category, the practice is often called "family support work" or "family counseling." This activity is usually short-term and is designed to help families face normative crises, such as the first child reaching the teen years or a crisis provoked by the birth of a new baby. An environmental crisis, such as a parent's loss of a job, may also require professional intervention. More recently, the redeployment to a war zone of a husband or wife in the military would be an example. The work centers on helping a relatively healthy family get through a difficult time and using the experience to strengthen rather than erode the family system. Services may also be provided to couples without children. This general type of social work with families is often provided by voluntary family service agencies or private practitioners.

Child welfare agencies also provide family support services. Most child welfare agencies deal with families facing problems that range from the normative and environmental problems just described to more serious issues of abuse and neglect that require court involvement and protection of the children (e.g., foster care placement). In addition to the ongoing child protection social worker, a family support worker might be assigned to a family for a preventive intervention if the family is judged to be at risk or to help a family when a child is returned home.

For example, a social worker might work with a family by helping the parents strengthen their childrearing skills and find more effective ways to cope with aspects of their life that make parenting more difficult. Just as the worker would make referrals to other agencies for alcohol counseling, job counseling, and so on, he or she would also make a referral for ongoing marital counseling or intensive family therapy if needed. The work would be directed by the agency's mandate to work with families with children at some level of risk.

A family crisis may lead to the revelation of deeper, longer-term problems. In these cases, short-term family support work will often involve (1) helping the family identify the real problems, (2) creating a working relationship so that the family can begin to see helping professionals in a positive way, and (3) referring the family for more traditional forms of long-term family therapy.

The professional who provides this more intensive help may well be a social worker—many social workers work in family therapy practice within agencies or in group or private practices as managed care providers. The family support worker, as defined here, does not undertake the long-term, intensive family therapy task. The social worker, as family therapist, may assume this role; however, a focus on family therapy is beyond the scope of this book.

## Setting—Specific Work with Families

The second major set of circumstances in which most family support workers find themselves involves providing families with forms of assistance that are directly connected to the specific services offered by the worker's agency or host setting. For example, a hospital social worker in a medical setting might work with family members on their adjustment to a patient's illness or medical condition. A school social worker might undertake family work to help parents and a teenager deal with serious school failure problems or suspensions resulting from violent activity. A social worker in an elder-care agency may work with the adult children of an elderly client who is preparing to make the transition to a nursing home. This type of work centers on a particular problem or life crisis that both guides and limits the nature of the work. This differs from the first type of family work, in which the emphasis is on the family itself and the life crisis may be only one of several issues that affect family dynamics.

## The Unique Issues Associated with Family Dynamics

**EP 2.1.7a**
**EP 2.1.7b**

When working with families, several factors should be taken into account. First, families have a history that goes back many generations. Family members beyond the nuclear family, both dead and alive, often affect the present. That is, the nuclear family's relationship—or lack of relationship—to the extended family or the community may play a large part in its functioning. At times, one can sense in a family session that the missing or dead family member is virtually in the room exerting a powerful impact on the interaction. Workers occasionally have designated an empty chair for this missing family member as a way to visualize her or his presence.

Next, different family members exert different amounts of power in relation to one another. For example, between counseling sessions the children (or spouse) may face serious threats of retribution, including physical violence, as family members return to their lives. The social worker needs to take into account that the family has a life between sessions, and what is said during the session may have serious implications at home. If there are concerns, then protection of the family member or members must be a high priority.

Finally, the fact that stereotypes, roles, and communication patterns—in other words, the whole family structure—have developed and been reinforced on a daily basis, 24 hours a day, over many years, can create strong resistance to the "unfreezing" process needed for change. The family has had years to develop a family façade—a false front it presents to outsiders—and each family member has also had time to create the external role that he or she presents to the other family members. One of the major advantages of seeing whole families, as opposed to working with one member of a family at a time, is that it allows the worker to observe many of these factors in the family interaction (e.g., who sits where, who speaks for the family, etc.).

## Integrating other Models and Approaches into Family Practice

Many of the concepts and theories introduced in earlier chapters can be applied to understanding the family. For example, using the life-span framework, described in Chapter 2, the social worker can attempt to help family members identify the available baseline reserve capacity—both internal (within the family) and external—that could increase the family's ability to cope with the sources of stress. If, for example, the family crisis involves an elderly parent who can no longer cope independently because of physical deterioration, the work might involve identifying the developmental reserve capacity that is potentially available through interventions such as the services of a home-care aide or housekeeper.

Other practice models discussed in more detail in Chapter 17 provide constructs that are useful in this work. For example, cognitive practice interventions can help family members identify automatic thinking processes that cause them to misinterpret the reality of their family interactions, thereby allowing the family members to break maladaptive cycles of blame and conflict and to identify individual and family strengths and sources of support.

Feminist practice frameworks can help members of the family identify gender-stereotypical behavior that has led to the internalization of anger and frustration as well as to the generation of interactional-related depression on the part of parents or children. Solution-focused approaches that help family members identify their strengths and how they have coped in the past can also be used.

Resilience theory and research can offer suggestions to the worker and the family for potential interventions, such as the involvement of extended family members, elders, or other resources in the community (e.g., Big Brothers Big Sisters of America or similar volunteer organizations) that are designed to buffer the impact of a trauma (e.g., physical abuse) on children or parents. In this sense, the work is essentially restorative; it is designed to strengthen the family and to lead to more normal or positive growth and development.

## Selected Concepts from Family Therapy Theory

**EP 2.1.7a**

Family therapy theory can help us better understand family dynamics and choose effective interventions. There are many different views about how families function and what workers should do to help. One text on the subject describes 17 different models (Horne & Passmore, 1991). I will identify and briefly describe key concepts from a few of these models. It is not necessary to adopt a particular model in its entirety—concepts and techniques can be borrowed as needed and integrated into effective family work at any level.

### Psychodynamic Approach

One early contributor to family therapy theory, whose work has influenced many current theories, was Nathan Ackerman (1958). Our discussion will draw on his framework for viewing a family and will explore many of his practice strategies—including concepts he integrated from other theorists—to describe the role of the worker in family work. Ackerman viewed family work as a special method of treatment of emotional disorders that is based on dynamically oriented interviews with the whole family. He saw the family as a natural living unit that includes all those persons who share identity with the family and are influenced by it in a circular exchange of emotions. The family has a potential for mutual support that can be blocked by the communication problems and anxieties of individual members. This leads to family disorders and the family's inability to carry out its tasks.

Although Ackerman did not specifically define the role of the helping professional as mediation, many of his treatment skills can be perceived this way. For example, he recognized that treatment usually begins at a time of crisis, when the emotional equilibrium of the family has been upset. In the beginning stages of work, after contracting to help family members work together to improve their communications and deal with the family problems, the worker employs the skill of observation to identify the idiosyncratic language of the family.

Using personal emotions stirred by the feelings of the family members toward one another and the worker, he or she tests hunches about the family and its feelings by sharing them with family members. In this way, the worker helps the family move past the façade presented in the first stage toward a more honest disclosure of their interpersonal conflicts. For example, the worker might help the family move beyond viewing the family problem as a single child who serves as the family scapegoat. The child in this case is called the *identified patient* (IP)—the individual in the family system who is identified as having the problem. The process of moving past the façade has been described by other family theorists as reframing the problem to help the family see it in a new way.

The worker would identify unhelpful patterns and roles, and point them out to the family members. Roles might include scapegoat, victim, persecutor, and so on. Facilitative confrontation (similar to the demand for work) is used to break the vicious cycle of blame and punishment that usually characterizes disordered family relationships. The worker challenges the illusion of work using the "here and now" of the family session to bring out the central issues. Because the family acts out its dysfunctional patterns in front of the therapist, the process of the family session is directly synthesized with the content of the work. In Ackerman's model, the therapist controls interpersonal danger, selectively supports family members, and attempts at all times to present a model of positive interpersonal functioning.

## Bowen Family Systems Theory

Another early theorist whose ideas are helpful to understand in work with families is Murray Bowen (1961, 1978). Bowen also viewed the family as being guided in its activities by an emotional system that may have developed over many years. He stressed the importance of understanding and exploring the intergenerational contribution made to the development of this family emotional system. A key concept of Bowen's model is the importance of each individual being able to differentiate between emotional and thinking systems so that control can be maintained over behavior. (This is somewhat similar to one of the key concepts of the interactional model, in which clients are helped to manage their feelings so they can manage their problems.) Bowen also stressed the impact of anxiety on the family system. Increased anxiety—as a result of a perceived threat—can lead to efforts toward "togetherness" in the family as a maladaptive means of coping.

One example is the process of *triangulation,* in which one individual attempts to gain the allegiance of a second, aligning against a third individual as a means of coping with anxiety. Each parent might try to pull in the child for support against the other parent, for instance. This is a maladaptive way to cope with a problem and can result in significant negative consequences, as in the case of the child forced to choose between parents.

## Freeman's Implementation of the Bowen Model and the Stages of Practice

Freeman's work has been useful in explicating Bowen's theoretical model and describing and illustrating the method for its implementation (Freeman, 1981). In particular, his use of time to organize his discussion of family work (beginning family therapy, the family therapy process, and the terminating stage) makes it easy to fit useful concepts within the interactional model presented in this book.

Freeman points out that the family therapy process begins before the first interview, when the helping professional responds to the call to set an appointment. Rather than rigidly requiring all members of the family to attend a first session, the therapist can conduct a skillful and sensitive telephone discussion with the caller, usually the person who most often takes responsibility for dealing with the family's problems, and thereby discover important information about who is involved in the problem and gain clues as to who should be asked to attend the first sessions.

Instead of challenging the caller's ideas about who should attend, the therapist respects the feelings of the caller and agrees, for example, to see the parents alone at first. In this case, the worker does this to develop a working relationship that will encourage the parents to allow the therapist entry into the family. Freeman points out that the discussion of whom the caller perceives to be involved can be the start of helping the family members redefine who is involved in the problem and who should attend the sessions.

Freeman describes four phases of the first interview as follows:

- Warming up
- Defining the problem
- Reframing the family's thinking about the problem
- Obtaining the commitment to work as a family

The warming-up phase helps to reduce the family's anxiety. Defining the problem involves a form of contracting in which the worker tries to understand how all of the family members perceive the problem. The reframing phase involves helping the family see the problem in new ways (e.g., as a family problem and not merely the behaviors of the identified patient). Finally, the commitment-to-work phase lays the groundwork for future sessions.

The middle phase of practice is where Bowen's theory places special emphasis on intergenerational work. As individuals take more responsibility for their own actions, and the sessions are marked by less blaming and reactive behavior, the relative calm allows for the identification of subsystems within the interfamilial and extrafamilial networks toward which the family can direct its attention. It is at these points in particular that the multigenerational concepts are used to help families expand their boundaries. The worker tries to help the family understand the impact of the family history and use the extended family as a source of support.

## Person-Centered Approach

Another family therapy theory, termed the *person-centered* approach, builds on the ideas from the early work of Rogers (1961). In this approach, as described by Thayer (1982), the therapist works to establish a healthy psychological climate that family members can use to establish realness in family relationships, express true feelings, remain separate and yet identify with the family, develop effective two-way communication, start a healthy process for family development and problem solving, clarify societal effects on the family, clarify conflicts, seek solutions, explore values, make decisions, experiment with new behaviors, and develop a family model/direction unique to its needs and wants (p. 192).

The followers of this approach focus on the core helping skills that have been demonstrated repeatedly to facilitate change. These components of a healthy psychological climate include the therapist's genuineness (being real as a person), the therapist's caring and prizing of family members (unconditional positive regard for family members), and the therapist's willingness to listen carefully to what family members have to say (hearing and understanding family members' needs, wants, conflicts, fears, joys, loves, goals, values, hates, disappointments, dreams, sorrows, and worlds or realities). These core conditions will be familiar to the reader from Parts I and II of this book where they are described as the Rogerian conditions.

## Cognitive-Behavioral Family Therapy (CBFT)

Cognitive-behavioral approaches are viewed as a second-generation therapy that builds on and expands earlier behavioral approaches. At their core is the idea that individual family members—through a process of "self-talk"—develop cognitions about their family, their own role, and other individuals that have a profound effect on their behavior. This focus is on the thinking and doing elements of the interactional approach described earlier, in which how we think affects how we feel, which in turn affects how we act, in a reciprocal and cyclical manner. Problems in a family may arise from miscommunications as well as unrealistic expectations on the family or individual members. Maladaptive responses may be a result of the gap between expectations and the behavior of others rather than the behavior itself. Helping family members to understand these often unspoken cognitions and their impact on the family dynamics can help them take control of their behavior, perhaps by developing greater acceptance and more realistic expectations.

CBFT focuses on present behavior rather than past history and assumes that problem behavior in the family is functional, in that it serves some purpose even if it is maladaptive. Hanna (2007) describes the sequence of treatment using this model in the context of couple's counseling:

1. Define the primary conflict. Look for themes such as closeness/distance, responsibility, and so on.

2. Describe the negative interaction pattern. Obtain a clear picture of behavioral sequences.

3. Decrease blaming and increase vulnerability. Teach communications of fears, inadequacies, and uncertainties (e.g., "I'm afraid she will leave me").

4. Address other beliefs about significant others. Explore beliefs about why certain situations occur in the family, how family life should be, and what is needed to improve relationships.

5. Teach support and empathy for each partner. Assign readings and provide practice time in sessions.

6. Use behavioral contracting. Ask each partner to make a list of what the other can do to please him or her. Ask each partner to choose items from the list to begin positive cycles. Assess the couple's ability to solve problems and spend time in pleasurable activities. (p. 45)

## Multi-Systemic Therapy (MST) Model

The multi-systemic therapy (MST) model was first developed to treat children and adolescents involved in juvenile crime and substance abuse. The model draws on a number of other approaches. Hanna (2007) describes the process as follows:

The therapeutic process begins by linking the goals of the larger system that is caring for the adolescent. For example, the court system has its goals (e.g., prevent reoccurrence of crime and increase school attendance) and the family generally has other goals (e.g., "get the system out of our life," "make him mind," "get money to turn on the phone," etc.). These divergent goals are brought under a general umbrella (e.g., "help Jake succeed") that will enable each stakeholder to be part of the same plan. (p. 46)

This home-based treatment model stresses the development of a trusting relationship between the family members and the therapist, as well as the identification of specific action goals for each member of the family that are described in manageable steps and reflect the strength of the family members. Interventions with the system (e.g., the agency, school, or court system) are as important as working with the family. The therapist helps monitor progress and coach positive behaviors to move toward accomplishing the shared plan.

## GLBT Clients and their Families of Origin

More recently, attention has turned to the unique individual and social issues facing gay, lesbian, bisexual, and transgendered (GLBT) clients and their families of origin. Connolly (2005) addresses a number of these in the first issue (Volume 1, Number 1) of the *Journal of GLBT Family Studies.* She points out that "strong and pervasive familial and societal stressors impact the living and loving of [the] GLBT individual, couple, or family. These issues not only affect GLBT clients but their families of origin and extended families, resonating across the larger cultural and social terrain" (p. 5). Connolly focuses on the life stage events associated with "coming out of the client." She points out that:

Many GLBT clients discover their sexual orientation and gender identity later in the life span; others remember awareness from the beginning. That which is know to self is not always known to others, and why is an important process across contexts and the life span. (p. 6)

Connolly points out that there are a number of societal and familial constraints that may be unique in understanding the development of families with GLBT members. Drawing upon the emerging literature in this field, she identifies the following among others:

- Oppressive beliefs, attitudes, and behaviors against the GLBT population.
- Complications introduced by homophobia and stigma of the heterocentric social and extended family surrounding the GLBT person and the family of origin.
- Discrimination in employment, health care, the legal system, and social services.
- Internalization by the GLBT person of the social stigma.
- Growing up in a heterosexual family that assumes all children will be heterosexual.
- Disclosure of sexual orientation may be met with family hostility, siding with the external oppressor, and withdrawal of the family as a place of "refuge."

She further suggests that:

Considering the life cycle stage in which the discovery and post-discovery experiences occur is pivotal in the therapeutic process. Additionally, there are some questions one might ponder. Were discovery experiences as a result of self-awareness of the GLBT individual informed by a member of the family of origin, or as a result of a relationship outside of the family? (p. 8)

In addition to the stage of the life cycle in which discovery and disclosure occur, or the impact of nondisclosure as the GLBT individual tries to live a double life as a member of the family but also simultaneously an outsider, general theories of family dynamics and development must take this unique disclosure or nondisclosure of the sexual orientation variable into account.

The potential impact on the GLBT individual and the family of origin was brought home to me in a group I led for persons with AIDS in substance abuse recovery. (This group is described in detail in the group work section of this book.) A transgendered member, Tina, described her early understanding that she was a girl in the body of a boy. When she came out as a teenager and adopted feminine dress and presented generally as a female, the reaction in her small, rural community, her school, and in her nuclear and extended family was swift and brutal. The crisis culminated with her older brother holding a gun to her head and insisting that she immediately leave the community. Thus, her family became part of the external oppressor rather than serving as a source of solace and support.

Connolly addresses some of the clinical implications of understanding the unique nature of the GLBT-connected family issues. She suggests to therapists that:

Naming the process, recognizing injuries and attending to grief, understanding the affiliative nature of GLBT relationships, and respecting client's choice to disclose or not disclose are important considerations. (p. 150)

Of course, the experiences of the GLBT person and the reactions of the nuclear and extended family may be different in each case. Once again, there is diversity within diversity.

Connolly concludes on a hopeful note, pointing out that:

The GLBT person and family members adapt and transition, whether they stay connected, disconnect then reconnect, or separate from each other's lives. However, some families are able to use their awareness and disclosure to heal personal wounds and familial or cultural injuries. (p. 15)

## Core Concepts across Theories

Many of the core concepts in family therapy cut across theories. For example, multi-generational issues are important in most models, with Satir (1967) interested in "family fact chronology" and Keith and Whitaker (1982) referring to a "longitudinally integrated, intra-psychic family of three generations." The core issue of integration and differentiation—how to be part of a family as well as a separate individual—appears in most formulations, although the terms that are used may differ (e.g., Keith and Whitaker refer to "unification" and "separation").

All models see the family as more than the sum of its parts. That is, it (the entity known as the family-as-a-whole) has properties that impact its functioning even though they are not visible. For example, if all members share a norm that it's not all right to discuss a taboo subject—for example, a father with an alcohol problem—one can't see this property but one can infer it from the behavior of the family. If it is the "family secret" and no one discusses it openly, then the family members share in this norm and observe it by not discussing it. The family is also viewed as a dynamic system that interacts with its environment, though some models place more emphasis on the external interactions and others on the internal.

In most of the models, the reader will recognize a number of core ideas introduced in Parts I and II, such as the importance of contracting and identifying the common ground between clients and between clients and the system. Both the CBFT and MST models share a focus on the present rather than history and stress structure and action. Although not specifically cited, both of these approaches contain elements of an existential understanding of change; they stress that a person becomes stronger by acting stronger. In other words, you are what you do. If you act as though you have strength, no matter what your previous cognitions or emotions, you become stronger. This has also appeared in the literature as a "strengths perspective."

A number of theorists refer to the problem of triangulation, discussed earlier. Where they tend to differ is in their views of how to avoid the trap, change the pattern, or make strategic use of being the third party in the situation. The importance of developing a safe atmosphere is also stressed, although theories differ sharply with regard to the timing and methods of confrontation for upsetting the dysfunctional patterns.

The sections that follow include several constructs borrowed from family therapy theorists. Examples of family work drawn from a variety of social work settings will illustrate these concepts as well.

# Family Assessment Models

**EP 2.1.7a**
**EP 2.1.3b**

Thomlison (2007), working from a multi-systemic family practice orientation, describes certain key assumptions and concepts that organize information for assessments and designing services. Family systems practice requires you to (1) build on the resources within the family and community, (2) focus attention on the family-environment interactions, and (3) recognize the effects of environmental factors on family and child functioning. Families are not homogeneous groups. Each perspective in a family will be unique. Begin with an examination of the family relationships and the dynamics of family circumstances. What happens between individuals in a family influences family functioning and outcomes. Three influential components are (1) family relationship patterns, (2) family characteristics, and (3) sources of stress.

As Thomlison points out: "Families establish relationships, develop patterns and create ways of organizing themselves that are unique to every family unit" (p. 35). She continues, "How a family goes about organizing itself and meeting the needs of its members is as important as who does this and what is accomplished in the process" (p. 35). Family characteristics include the "personal characteristics of the parents, their family of origin experiences (historical events and current connections), and resources such as competencies, social support, and material support..." (p. 36). She describes sources of stress as including risk factors that are difficult to overcome. However, she also points out that "When stressors are overcome, protective factors develop based on a positive experience, and families develop resilience in coping with environmental stressors and demands" (p. 36).

## Families and the Organismic or Systems Model

This discussion of resilience and risk and protective factors mirrors that introduced in Chapter 2. This time, however, it is applied to both individuals in the family as well as the family as a whole. Most theorists—whether explicitly stated or not—view a family through the lens of the organismic or systems model. That is, the family is seen as an organism that is more than the sum of its parts, that is constantly interacting with its environment—both affecting and being affected by it, that has boundaries between the family and the environment and within the family itself, and that is capable of growth and change. These concepts and assumptions can also be found in the "ecological" approach included in such frameworks as the "life model" of practice described by Germain and Gitterman (1997) and the "strengths perspective" on families and family life.

This represents a central and core concept in working with families. Most often, when a family seeks or is referred to family counseling, the problem is described as resulting from the behavior or one member. The common refrain on the part of parents of "fix my kid" reflects this belief. For effective family practice to take place, the worker must step back and view the family as a dynamic system with the behavior of any one of its parts (members) affecting and being affected by the interaction with the others and the environment.

Collins, Jordan, and Coleman (2007) argue this point and define a family system as follows:

> According to family systems theory, all families are social systems and it this belief that guides understanding and work with families. Because family members are interdependent, behaviors therefore do not exist in a vacuum. As such, family systems theory helps us see how problems originate from family relationships and transactions. Work is done with the overall network of relationships within the family. Thus, one of the key beliefs of family systems theory is that problems that arise in families cannot usually be attributed to individual dysfunction or pathology. Rather, understanding family dynamics will help uncover the family processes that seem to foster and maintain the presenting problem. Therefore, problems such as parent-child conflict, behavior problems, mental health issues, and so on develop within the family context. (p. 41)

Any family assessment model needs to consider where the family (and the environment) is in its developmental stage, how well is it working, and what internal and external steps may be taken to mobilize the internal and external resources (e.g., extended family, intergenerational family unit, community agencies) needed for positive growth. Thus, a major emphasis is placed not on what is wrong with the family but on what is right; in this way, the family is viewed as a source of strength for change.

## Family Assessment Tools

A number of tools are available for family assessments, including genograms (charts that organize intergenerational relationships) and social network maps (maps that assess and chart the availability of social support for the family), family history reports, self-report instruments, and so forth. Further discussion of these would, however, be beyond the scope of this introduction to family practice.

**EP 2.1.4d**
**EP 2.1.3a**
**EP 2.1.10d**

Although any of these instruments may help social workers understand and chart important variables, caution must be taken with respect to their use. There is a difference between using a tool to obtain information and using it to organize information. By this, I mean that a family social worker who focuses in first sessions on completing a genogram or social network map may find that the tool actually gets in the way of engaging the family on its own terms. Much of the information will come out in the interviews and can be organized using any of these tools. Specific information can be obtained through direct questions as the family work continues. It is more important to focus on what the family members have to say, and to make the emotional connection that creates and strengthens the working relationship.

The important point here is that any tool should also be a tool for the family's use, not just the worker's. A rigid implementation of data gathering that does not fit the context of the family's concerns will be experienced by the family as the worker "acting on" the family rather than "acting with" the family. It is important that before a worker uses a tool to obtain information, the instrument be fully explained to family members, and that they participate in the decision to use it because they feel it would be useful to them.

***Family Interview as an Assessment Tool*** Another important tool in family assessment is the family interview itself. When held in the home, the social worker can get a perspective on the family function in its own environment that might differ from an interview in an office. Observation tools that are used during the first interview, such as where people choose to sit or what their posture conveys (e.g., arms crossed and resistant looking, mother's and father's chairs turned away from each other, a family member who chooses to sit away from the immediate family group, etc.), can reveal important information about the structure of the family and its communication patterns. Listening skills are another way to understand, for example, who takes the lead in the conversation (e.g., the mother describes the problem with the child while the father remains relatively passive) and how each family member and the family as a whole agree or disagree on the nature of the problem.

***Impact of a Crisis on Family Functioning*** Collins et al. (2007) suggest that:

> During assessment, the FSW assists the family, ideally with all members participating, to explore issues of concern. This exploration should lead to a deeper, more accurate understanding of the situation faced by the family. Each family member will have his or her own unique perspective of the problem and every individual perspective is important. For example, a problem defined by the family as a child spending time "hanging out with friends" may be a "conforming" issue for the parents, an "independence" issue for the target child, and an "exclusion" issue for siblings. Problems usually span behavioral, affective, cognitive, and experiential domains. In addition, some problems are more likely to arise in particular families at crisis periods in the family life cycle. (p. 120)

This was supported in an earlier study of child welfare by this author (Shulman, 1978), wherein data revealed that in a significant number of families that came to the attention of the provincial child welfare agency, the father had lost his job within the previous six months. The stress of unemployment exacerbated existing family stresses and created new ones.

***Sample Questions for a First Interview*** A number of questions may be helpful in a first session as part of the contracting process. Thomlison (2007) identified a list of possible questions drawn and adapted from the work of Wright and Leahey (1994, p. 149), which included the following:

What concerns bring you here?

What meaning does the problem have for each of you?

Why is the family coming for assistance now?

When did the problem begin?

Where did the information about the problem come from?

How might the family look, behave, or feel without the problems or concerns? (p. 67)

It usually takes some time to identify, with the family members, the nature of the problem. As with individual work, the whole family or individual members may raise "near problems," or what I called "first offerings" in Chapter 4, which define the issues in real but relatively superficial ways. It may take some time for the family members to develop trust in the worker as well as a feeling of safety that allows the real and often taboo issue to emerge.

In Chapter 8, I describe and illustrate the "family secret"—a problem that everyone in the family knows exists, such as a parental substance abuse issue or physical or sexual abuse. It may remain unspoken in the interviews and not appear on any of the assessment tool charts; however, it might be the engine that drives many of the family's problems. First interviews may appear to be about the "acting out" behavior of the teenager but then evolve into an understanding of how the teen has become the "family scapegoat" who expresses, for example, marital stress between the parents. If we truly understand the family group as a dynamic system in which the behavior of one member affects and is affected by the behavior of all the rest in a reciprocal manner, then it is wise not to get locked into the initial surface assessment. It is not unusual for workers to describe a situation in which the oldest child in the family moves out and the child who is next in the birthing order begins to act out in a similar or different manner. When the real, underlying problem is addressed, the child's behavior changes; the family no longer needs the child as a "ticket of admission" to family counseling.

## The Preliminary Phase—Tuning In to the Family

**EP 2.1.10a**
**EP 2.1.10b**
**EP 2.1.4b**

The concepts introduced in Chapters 3 and 4 that deal with the importance of tuning in and contracting apply to family work as well. A major difference, however, is that the worker must now also tune in to the entity called the family-as-a-whole. This requires the worker to consider each member of the family, but also to step back and view and understand the family as a dynamic system in which the behavior of each member affects and is affected by the behavior of the others as well as by the family culture. A family culture consists of the norms of behavior, rules of interaction, taboo subjects, roles played by individual members (e.g., the family scapegoat), and so forth. Much of the work done with families involves an attempt to influence a change toward a more constructive family culture that meets the common needs of all members while respecting the individual needs of each member.

### Tuning In to a Recently Immigrated Greek Family

The preliminary phase described in Chapter 3 identified a number of themes that the worker should consider when preparing to engage the client. To these themes, reviewed as follows, we add those introduced when working with a family. As an illustration, we will use an example described in detail later in this chapter, of a family support worker meeting a recently immigrated Greek family that consists of a father, mother, a daughter, and a 14-year-old son who has been identified as the problem because of his oppositional behavior and refusal to follow his father's rules.

The family has worked with the agency before, and the father has a reputation for being authoritarian, angry, and hard to work with. Previous workers have had confrontational contacts with him and found him resistant to seeing the problem as a family problem, insisting it is only the boy who has to straighten out and follow his rules. There has been some indication that the father has used physical discipline, although he denies having been excessive.

What follows are some of the issues that would be considered by this young, male worker during the preparatory tuning-in process.

### Agency Themes

- This client already has a confrontational relationship with the agency staff and may view me through his past experiences.
- I have to be alert to the mandated reporter issues because there have been questions about the use of physical punishment.
- I want to engage the father and the whole family but I also have a responsibility to protect the children. I need to be up-front about this if I'm going to develop any trust. A part of me would like to avoid this issue, but I can't.

### Authority Themes

- I am young and unmarried, and this father may see me as not understanding his concerns and feelings.
- He may think I'm going to side with his wife and kids and against him as he feels other workers have done.

### Family Work Themes

- I need to think about the issues involved for the son, who has just turned 14. He has developmental needs to establish some independence and to start to separate himself while still maintaining a connection.
- The father may experience this effort at independence as a loss of control but also the beginning of loss of his son.
- I should be prepared for the family structural issues with the father trying to dominate not only the children but his wife as well, who may have difficulty playing a role in the disciplinary process.
- I need to be open to the fact that his son may also have to take responsibility for his behavior.
- There may be cultural issues related to the ethnicity and the recent immigrant status of the family. I need to know more about this so I can understand the norms, roles, rules, and so forth that may be at work in this family.
- I have to be alert to my own family issues and how I may react to his (the father's) behavior and my own ideological views about how families should operate.
- I have to tune in to the fact that I'm a bit concerned about the father's reputation, and that I will need a source of help (supervision?) to keep me on track.

These are some examples of tuning in that might help the worker prepare for the first interview(s). As the reader will see later in this chapter, even when tuning in, the worker needs to catch his mistakes during the session, which I believe constitutes excellent work.

# The Two-Client Concept and the Worker's Role

One of the major differences in working with families rather than individual clients is that the worker is dealing with more than one person, or what is sometimes referred to as a "multiple client." Even though the model I've described called for conceptualizing the client in interaction with important systems, the worker usually had only one person to deal with at a time in most of the examples from Part II. As soon as the helping unit expands to more than two people, it becomes more complex and introduces new problems, new possibilities, and new demands on the worker's skills. One of the most common problems observed in family work results from worker identification with a subunit of the family system.

Perhaps the best way to describe the problem is to provide an example of how it typically emerges in workshops I conduct for helping professionals. The workshop participant in this case presented an example of a general problem: "How do you work with a family if the father is unmotivated and very defensive?" In response to my request, the worker described a family that included middle-aged parents (the father was an immigrant from Europe); a 15-year-old daughter (the identified patient), whom the parents viewed as the problem; and an 11-year-old son, whom the parents described as no problem at all. The father had called, indicating that they could not control their daughter and that he wanted the child welfare agency to "straighten her out or get her out." Although the particulars may differ, this type of situation and the conversation that follows is typical of hundreds of workshops.

After the description of the family and the circumstances of the worker's involvement, I asked for the details of the first session (word for word) as best the worker could recall. He described the father angrily taking the lead and confronting the daughter with accusations of misbehavior. These accusations were addressed to the worker almost as a prosecuting attorney might speak to a judge as he spelled out his case against the daughter. When I inquired how the daughter reacted, the worker said, "She was just sitting there, her head hanging down, very close to tears." When I asked for the worker's feelings at the moment, he replied, "I felt badly for her and could easily understand why she had trouble dealing with that father. He didn't seem to have any sense of how upset she was." I replied, "You must have also felt angry at him for his insensitivity. You were feeling her hurt and pain, and he seemed closed off from her." The worker agreed.

At one point, the worker described the father berating his daughter for running around with girls who "came in late, dressed like sluts, smoked dope, and didn't listen to their parents."

I asked how the worker responded, and he said, "I asked Maria [the daughter] if it hurt her to hear her father say those things, and she just nodded. I asked if she could tell her father that, and she just sat there, unable to speak and about to start crying."

I said to the worker, "You wanted the father to understand her hurt. Did it seem to get through to him?" The worker replied that the father was so dense, he couldn't hear a thing. The father simply escalated the anger, saying, "In Europe, children listen to their parents and respect them." I continued, "Which made you even angrier. What did you say to him?" The worker replied, "I told him that I thought he had to understand that he was in the United States now, and that teenagers here are quite different in many ways from the old country. I don't think it helped much, because he just sat there and glared at me. How do you get through to a guy like that?"

It is at moments such as these that it is possible to help workers see the problem in a new way.

Using a diagram with three circles—one for the daughter, one for the family, and one for the worker—I asked if the worker could put himself back into that moment and tell us where he was with respect to his emotional identification. Pointing to the daughter's circle, I said, "It would be quite understandable if you were really with the daughter." The worker replied that I was right. I then asked the workshop group, "Who was with the father?" After a few moments of silence, someone said, "He was all alone."

## The Mediation Role for the Social Worker

**EP2.1.10k**

This is the moment when the two-client idea, proposed by Schwartz (1961) in the context of group work, becomes helpful to understand the worker's function in work with families. To mediate the individual-social engagement effectively, in the special case of the family, the worker must understand the importance of conceptualizing and identifying with two clients simultaneously: the individual and the family system. Thus, in the conflict just described, for the worker to be helpful he must find a way to emotionally identify with (be with) both the daughter and the parents in the family system. By identifying with the daughter, however understandable his reaction might have been, the worker cut himself off from the parents—particularly the father—just at the moment when the father needed him the most. His response to the daughter was helpful in that he recognized her pain and articulated her feelings. If, at the same moment, he could have understood the father's feelings and responded with genuine empathy, the conversation might have sounded as follows:

FATHER: In Europe, children listen to their parents and respect them.
WORKER: So it makes it hard for you to understand what's going on now—why it doesn't seem to work the same way here in the United States.

In this moment, the worker needs to feel genuine empathy as he says these words. The worker must feel some of the father's struggle to figure out how to be a good parent when the world seems upside-down from the way in which he was raised. As indicated in the previous section, the worker will try in this first session to reframe the family's way of thinking about the problem. He will work to help the parents, as well as the children, move from blaming and confronting the daughter to seeing the problem as one that faces the whole family system. At this moment, however, the worker needs to be able to develop his working relationship with the parents, particularly the father. The worker must resist the pull toward triangulation, in which the family members may attempt to align the worker with their side. Instead, the worker must align himself with both clients—each individual family member and the family as a whole.

In fact, as the first full example described next will show, the father's behavior is in part an effort to find out just what kind of worker this is going to be. Because he already may have been feeling guilty about his parenting (something he may not admit even to himself), he probably began the session assuming that the worker would be on his daughter's side. When the father saw the worker's informal dress and guessed at the worker's age, a part of him said, "He's not much older than she is. How is he going to understand?" When the worker responded with the lecture on American culture, the father knew he had been right in his judgment.

The worker suffered from functional diffusion, or a loss of functional clarity that causes workers to diffuse their activity and implement a role (or roles) that is inappropriate for the moment. That is, the worker ends up trying to take on several different roles (e.g., teacher, cop, and preacher). Fortunately, functional diffusion is not a terminal illness and can be overcome with a dose of functional clarity. The worker is there to mediate the individual-social engagement, and thus the worker must understand his responsibility to be with—at the same time—each individual family member (including the father) and the family as a whole.

The importance of this can be seen clearly if one realizes that, in the example presented by the worker, at precisely the moment he tried to get the father to understand the daughter's feelings, he demonstrated his complete inability to feel with the father. Because the worker demonstrated a model of personal functioning, he said more to the father through his actions than through his words. He wanted the father to understand the daughter's behaviors, even those the father experienced as deviant, but he himself was having difficulty reaching behind the father's deviant behavior to understand the message he was sending.

## Countertransference in Working with Families

**EP 2.1.1b**

In reality, even with functional clarity, workers continuously find themselves overidentifying with one part of the family system and cutting themselves off from another. The countertransference process (discussed in Chapter 5) is never stronger than in work with families. Younger workers—some not far removed from situations similar to those experienced by the teenager in the family—must work hard to deal with their own feelings toward authoritative fathers or mothers if they are ever to begin to relate to these parental types as individuals instead of as cardboard caricatures.

This is a lifelong task that requires workers to use their professional experiences to understand their personal lives, and to use their personal experiences to better understand their professional practice. In this sense, each family represents an opportunity to learn more about one's own family of origin. Some family therapy theorists, such as Bowen (1978), incorporate family-of-origin work as a central part of the training for family therapists. As the therapist comes to grips with personal issues in relation to the family of origin, his or her insights can have a profound impact on work with clients.

Although it seems a truism that work on a social worker's own family issues (or any form of therapy) may add to her or his ability to work with families, this idea raises a controversial issue in social work training. Students have reported supervision sessions in which work on the actual practice problems was abandoned and the focus moved to the student's own family history, life issues, and problems. Take, for example, a student who grew up in an alcoholic family. Instead of reflecting on the specific ways this life experience may affect the student in moment-by-moment interactions with an alcoholic client-parent, the supervisor might focus on the student's history itself, thereby trading the educational focus of supervision for therapy. This provides an example of functional diffusion on the part of the field supervisor.

In the balance of this chapter, and in Chapters 8 and 9, several examples will illustrate the key concepts outlined in Parts I and II of this book and the first half of this chapter.

# The Beginning Phase: Contracting with the Family

**EP 2.1.10b**
**EP 2.1.10c**
**EP 2.1.10e**

The same contracting skills described in work with individuals apply as well to work with families:

- *Clarifying Purpose:* The worker shares his or her understanding of why they are meeting. This includes the agency or setting's purpose for offering the family session.

- *Clarifying the Worker's Role:* The way in which the worker will try to help the family.

- *Reaching for Feedback:* What the individual family members hope to get out of the sessions and what consensus, if any, the family can reach on common goals.

- *Addressing Authority Issues:* For example, the worker's role as a mandated reporter may need to be defined.

The contracting process is also influenced by the fact that the worker deals with more than one client at a time. The worker must be clear about purpose, and direct, open contracting remains important, as does obtaining feedback from the clients. However, each client may start with a different idea of the work to be done. A teenager may want to have more freedom, whereas a parent may want the worker to "change" the child so that he or she conforms more to the rules of behavior. The worker must be able to identify common ground as well as important differences between family members. As much as possible, the worker will try to identify and articulate the goals of the family as a whole when a consensus, however tentative, can be found. For example, all family members may want conflict to stop and to be able to enjoy family life again.

Because family members often attempt to treat the worker as a judge and jury, and try to get the worker to identify with their views and issues, the worker must also clearly define his or her role. This is where the two-client concept comes in: The worker must make clear that he or she is identified with each individual but also with the family as a whole. In the illustrations that follow in this chapter, we shall see how important explaining and maintaining this two-client role really is.

## The Problem-Oriented First Family Interview for the Beginner

Students and new workers can experience their first family interviews as stressful. They may have had an opportunity to work with individual clients and develop some beginning confidence in their ability to conduct a first interview. The first family interview, however, may be the first point at which they are called upon to work with more than one client at a time. They may have read about family practice and tried to integrate into their strategies the suggestions of supervisors and authors, including concepts from a number of models. They may have done their tuning in and may be prepared to respond directly when one parent asks the dreaded question: "And how many kids do you have?" They may have practiced role-playing a first session. Even better, they may have been given the opportunity to sit in and observe a first family session conducted by an experienced worker.

All of this helps, but when the moment comes and a new worker faces a family alone for the first time, consider what he or she must keep track of:

- Each individual member of the family
- The family as a whole (e.g., communication patterns; where people sit; nonverbal signals such as arms folded, suggesting resistance; etc.)
- The content of the conversation and the process of the interview
- His or her own feelings as the session progresses
- The clock (the session is usually time limited)

No wonder first family sessions can be somewhat intimidating!

Weber, McKeever, and McDaniel (1985) recognized how difficult and stressful first family interviews can be for students and new workers. They point out that the volume and diversity of resources can produce unsettling confusion:

> This confusion is often most apparent at the point of the first meeting with a family when bewildered and anxious trainees are obliged to take leadership, condensing the mass of clinical options into a practical, sensible, well-organized interview with a group of strangers. (p. 358)

In what they termed a "beginner's guide" for such sessions, they stressed simplifying the guidelines into an integrated step-by-step process. They described the primary goals of the first interview as follows:

1. Join the family, accommodating to the style of the family members and creating an environment in which family members will feel well supported.
2. Organize the interview so that family members will begin to gain confidence in the therapist's leadership.
3. Gather information about the problem in such a way that the family's transactions around the problem become clearer.
4. Negotiate a therapy contract, emphasizing the family's initiative in defining goals and desired changes. (p. 358)

These authors cite and build on the work of Haley (1978) in outlining a series of tasks that include attention to pre- and postinterview issues as well as tasks designed to accomplish the goals during the interview. Although one may disagree with specific techniques and strategies described in this model, and this author does with some, the overall framework can be helpful in thinking about the first family session. The integrated approach described by the authors begins with the telephone contact and forming of hypotheses (similar to tuning in) in the preinterview phase. The interview itself is divided into tasks that include greeting the family, a social phase (helping the family to feel more comfortable), identifying the problem, and observing family patterns. Postinterview tasks include revising hypotheses, contacting the referral person, and gathering records.

Although structure can be helpful, I agree with the authors that it may be necessary to abandon preconceived notions and plans, and to respond to the immediacy of the process as is illustrated in the example that follows.

***First Session with a Greek Immigrant Family: The Angry Father*** We now return to the Greek family first introduced in the tuning-in section of this chapter. In this example, we have an angry, volatile father and his 14-year-old son. This exchange illustrates how a worker can catch a mistake and correct it during the session.

The worker was a social work student in a family-support worker role at a large child welfare agency. Because of a complaint of physical abuse involving the teenager, the social worker who had protection responsibility made the first contact. The family support worker was called in to provide family counseling, to see if the family could be helped to deal with the problem while keeping the child at home. The material that follows is from the worker's report of the first contact.

### Description of the Curakis Family

**Father:** A Greek store owner. He was described to me as an angry, volatile, and violent man. Those who had tried to work with him described him as "a write-off," unworkable. He held very definite ideas of family life, including roles, expectations, etc. He came from a family where his father hit him often when disciplining. Obedience was valued.

**Mother:** A German teacher. She was a quiet, soft-spoken woman from an upper-middle-class background.

**Son:** A 14-year-old who was defiant toward his father. He smoked in front of him, in direct contravention of the father's orders. He performed well in school and had no apparent peer problems.

**Precipitating Incident:** Mother sought help after her husband repeatedly hit her son with his fist and once with a board. (Mother was not present during this incident. The story was shared by the son.) Father denies he hit the boy with anything other than an open hand.

**History:** During the family's previous contacts with professionals and family friends, as reported in the agency records, these workers and others scolded—in one form or another—the father for his behavior and showed sympathy for the boy. The most recent contact with a social worker was similar, with the additional threat to remove the boy from the house. The mother was planning to remove the child at the time of this first meeting, and did so the following day against the father's wishes. The father believed that the family and its functioning were his responsibility.

Both the husband and wife said that their marriage prior to the birth of their son had been fine, though Mrs. Curakis's voice was tentative. Discord arose shortly after the child's birth. From Mr. Curakis's point of view, his wife was too soft; from her point of view, he was too hard. Throughout the child's life, they could not agree on parenting procedures.

Mr. Curakis was the boss in the house. What he said was done. His wife was able to modify these edicts to a moderate degree in regard to herself, but only to a minor degree in regard to her son. At times of discipline, the father took command—often in a physical way. While this was happening, Mrs. Curakis would not become involved unless she felt that her son would be seriously hurt. However, after Mr. Curakis finished, she would take her son aside (in Mr. Curakis's absence), calm him, cuddle him, and in most instances contradict or modify what Mr. Curakis had said.

These actions on Mrs. Curakis's part were a constant irritant to the couple's relationship. She felt it was necessary to her son's development. He felt it was undermining his authority and was the reason the boy was acting the way he was. I gave the above history to indicate how—from the father's point of view and in reality—he had been undermined, excluded, and put down, and at the same time how his son was "sided with" (coalition)—against him—by family friends, social workers, his family doctor, and his wife.

\*\*\*

**Practice Points:**   It would be easy to see how the social worker in this example, after reading the agency records and making the initial assessment, might begin the interview already identifying with the family members versus the father. It would also be natural for the father to assume that this worker would be like all the rest. As the interview began, the father, son, and mother acted out their issues in a conflict over smoking. The worker skillfully responded to the process by recognizing it as a communication to him and used it to focus on the content.

*The Interview:*   The family had just been introduced to me by the social worker. The boy walked into the interview room smoking a cigarette. I introduced myself and began to give a brief introduction of myself and my role in the agency. As I was about 2 minutes into the introduction, the father began admonishing the boy for smoking. The boy said nothing at first. The father kept shouting. His statements became more derogatory and turned into a general attack on the boy's attitude. Mrs. Curakis, under her breath, said her husband's name, thereby asking him to stop.

I asked her if this is how the fights between her husband and her son often began. Mr. Curakis glared at me, at his wife, and then continued attacking his son (verbally). Throughout the next 10 or 15 minutes, I made numerous attempts at connecting with individual family members by empathizing, understanding, etc. I connected easily with Mrs. Curakis and her son but was unable to do so with Mr. Curakis. In fact, he was becoming more and more angry each time I spoke, regardless of whom I spoke to. But he was most hostile while I was speaking with the boy. Each time I began speaking to the boy, the father would, in a voice louder than mine, accuse the boy of some transgression. They would then get into a loud argument.

**Practice Points:**   During this early part of the session, the worker failed to pick up on the escalating clues of the father's anger and concern about the worker siding against him. His question to Mrs. Curakis might have been perceived by Mr. Curakis as another example of a worker's siding with his wife or son. As is often the case, as the client described problems with previous workers, he was actually indirectly raising concerns about the present worker. The worker's almost mechanical reflection of the client's anger does not get through to him. Then, in a skillful example of catching one's mistake while one is making it, as well as trusting one's feelings, the worker finally reached for the issue of the authority theme.

After a while, this pattern changed. Now, each time I spoke to the boy, Mr. Curakis would start arguing with the boy but end up shouting at me. At first, I did not realize this change; I only realized that I was beginning to understand what my colleague had warned me about. I was becoming impatient and angry with this "jerk." Almost mechanically, I said, "You are angry with me?" There was little or no concern in my voice.

The nonverbal cues did not seem to matter. The quality of anger changed. He was now focused on me, but he was not angry with me. For the next 15 minutes, he angrily related the years of no one understanding him, the sincere attempts he had made and was making to help his son grow up properly, the repeated incidents of "people" siding with his son against him after he had disciplined his son and how that had created the present situation, and how his wife and he could not get close because of it. I said something like, "And that makes it even more difficult, doesn't it?" in a sincere manner.

But he just continued letting it out. There was a pregnant silence—a very pregnant silence. I began to get uncomfortable and wanted to find something appropriate to say. Something that would summarize what he was trying to say. But I couldn't think of anything. Then a sentence came to mind: "And you think I'm going to be like all the rest." "That's right!" he shouted, almost coming out of his seat. He went on for a few minutes about his concern that when I talked to his son I was acting just like the others.

**Practice Points:** The worker's sincere apology is followed by a clarification of his perception of his role in working with the family. This could have, and should have, been stated right at the start of the session. Even if the worker had articulated his mediation role, however, there was a good chance that the father and other family members might not have been able to hear it.

There was a long silence. I was nodding, admitting to both of us that he was right. I apologized and told him that what I had done was not what I was trying to do. I went on to say that it was my job to be helpful to both of them, and, if I wasn't, then I wasn't doing my job the way I wanted to. I asked him to do me a favor. If he noticed me doing that again—to anyone in the family—to please let me know. I would appreciate it.

The remaining 10 to 15 minutes of the meeting were spent, to a large degree, discussing "old" parenting issues (between Mr. and Mrs. Curakis)—nothing significant. What was significant was that they were talking on a topic that they had avoided—except in argument—for many years. I asked them if they wanted another appointment. After a few moments' discussion, they decided they did as a family.

As they were on their way out, I said good-bye to the boy. He was a little less "cocky" but not very different. Mrs. Curakis seemed quiet, not quite at ease, but it looked like the universe she had been carrying around on her shoulders was reduced to a solar system. The biggest change was in Mr. Curakis. He shook my hand with both his hands, looked me in the eyes, and said, "Thank you, thank you, thank you very much." There were tears in his eyes. I put my other hand on his and said, "You're welcome." Tears welled up in my eyes.

When I walked into the front office after they left, some of the office staff shook their heads, thereby referring to what I must have gone through and what a "jerk" he was. (It seems that he had been quite gruff to the receptionist on the way in.) I told them that he was really quite a nice guy. There was a pregnant silence.

## Discussion of this First Family Session

In a first session with a family, as with an individual counseling session, contracting is crucial for setting the stage for work. The key questions on the minds of all the family members are: "Who is this worker?" "What kind of worker will he or she be?" and "What will happen here?" Because of this family's prior experiences with other helpers, they began with a stereotype of the worker that had to be dealt with head-on. The worker in this example tuned in to the potential feelings and concerns of the family members and was sensitive to the past experiences described in the brief history. Even so, when the father exploded at the son, all of the worker's best plans, opening statements, strategies, and so forth went up in smoke.

His first reactions were quite normal for a new worker. His skill was revealed in the quickness with which he caught the mistake—in the same session in which it occurred—and began to address the real issues raised by the boy who entered with a cigarette, the mother who displayed her passivity, and the father who said through his actions, "If you want to see what it's like around this family, just watch."

The worker had been set up by previous workers (even the office staff) to see the father as the stereotype he presented. The father was ready to see the worker as a stereotype as well. By responding directly to the anger and the implied question about how he was going to help, the worker broke the pattern. Previous workers had found this father hard to work with because of his anger. As the worker reached past the cardboard caricature presented by the father and responded to the process of the session rather than just the content, he began to develop a working relationship with one of the most important family members and revealed a side of the father previously hidden from other workers and the family members. In fact, the father's open expression of anger made him an easier client to work with, in some ways, than if he had hidden his real reactions and participated in an illusion of work, while all the time really thinking, "He's just like all of the rest of those workers: against me, and with the kid."

***Additional Contracting Steps Required*** Because of the urgency of dealing with the father, as well as the "which side are you on?" issue, other steps were left undone. For example, the worker still needs to be clearer about the purpose of these meetings and the specific role he will play. He started the process by trying to say that he wants to help all of them and not take sides. At a next session, he might want to say something about helping the family members talk to one another about how they operate as a family and understand how the other family members really feel. In addition, he will need to make sure that, in his effort to be with the father, he does not lose sight of the mother and the son.

***Reframing the Problem*** The worker will need to help the family reframe the problem as well. At first, they met to discuss their "problem" teenager. Even in the first session, however, the problem with the son quickly led to the problem between the parents. A family that needs help will often use a teenage child as a "ticket of admission" to the helping agency. In this case, the struggle over authority and the role of the father in the family was just as much of an issue for the husband and wife, but the wife found it easier, and perhaps safer, to deal with that struggle through the child. The pattern of relationship in the family is oppressive, because the father attempts to use emotional and physical intimidation to retain control over the family members. Some of this may be closely related to family and cultural background. This pattern will need to be confronted by the worker; however, such a confrontation may be more fruitful after he develops a relationship with the family.

***Guarding the Contract: Focusing on the Child Welfare Issues*** The worker needs to stay focused on how the parental struggle relates to the couple's ability to parent effectively, helping them to see the connections to their general relationship but not embarking on a course of general marital counseling (which would be outside of the agency-family working contract). Reassurance on this point may make it safer for both the husband and wife to drop the family façade—the false front discussed earlier.

Another issue that was not dealt with directly in this interview was confidentiality. A child welfare agency was involved, and a threat to apprehend (take into care) the teenage son had already been expressed. The worker will need to deal honestly with this issue; he has to report any information related to child abuse to the child protection social worker. This issue lay just under the surface of the first interview and must be raised and clarified. Under what conditions might the family support worker have to report child abuse to the social worker in this case? Avoiding such a discussion will not make the authority issue go away—rather, it will invest it with more power to block the work.

In summary, the worker made a start toward developing a working relationship with the family, especially its most potentially resistant member. Much work remains, and the outcome depends somewhat on how the worker handles his part and how ready the family members are to tackle their responsibilities.

# The Impact of Culture and Community

**EP 2.1.4a,b**

Whereas there are core similarities in all families, there are also important differences that relate to culture and community setting. In working with a family, it is important to understand the particular structures and norms that may be associated with ethnicity, history, geography, immigration status, race, and so forth. In addition, the worker must remain open to major areas of diversity within diversity. Within each general category are many different subgroups that must be taken into account. For example, to which tribe do we refer when we say Native American? When we refer to Hispanics, do we think of California Chicanos or New York City Puerto Ricans? Within the Asian American population, we need to differentiate among Chinese, Korean, and Thai, for example. In addition, we need to recognize that culture may be quite different within specific groups, and that any one family may be different from the general norms. These cautions were raised in Chapter 4, in which examples of culturally diverse practices with Mexican Americans, African Americans, American Indians, Canadian Indians, and issues in cross-racial practice were examined.

Janzen and Harris (1997) stress the importance of cultural sensitivity:

Families who seek help from social workers and other professionals hold diverse group memberships. They bring unique cultural traits that contribute to individual and group identity. Knowledge of how each family communicates between its members and to the outside world, its belief system, and its values will provide clues about how family problems originate and also suggest pathways to possible resolution. (p. 153)

The authors assert that knowledge of the family member's internal communication pattern, how the family communicates to the outside world, its belief system, and its values is essential to understand each member's behavior and to try to alter existing patterns in a way that will improve family functioning. They illustrate this with the following examples:

Consider the family member who is reluctant to express himself or herself freely when interacting with the therapist. For the Asian client, it might be the result of a traditional reticence in sharing feelings with someone outside of the family. The African American family member who displays the same behavior will most likely not be adhering to cultural values at all, but will be reacting to a lack of trust in the therapist, who represents the majority controlled institutional structure of contemporary society. (p. 153)

Even as we consider these suggestions, however, the caution against overgeneralizing needs to be repeated. In addition, many clients—regardless of their ethnicity—may be reluctant to share feelings with someone outside of the family, and potential mistrust of institutions may relate to both race and class.

Another note of caution needs to be raised in terms of respect for cultural sensitivity. Understanding cultural attitudes does not automatically mean that a person accepts them. For example, a recent immigrant family (or even second- and third-generation immigrants) may have brought with them gender-related views that conflict with our society's and our profession's core values on the status of women and children. When understanding the perspective and its impact on a family in certain circumstances, there are times when these values and attitudes, and the resultant actions by family members, need to be challenged. For example, learning that a family plans genital mutilation of a young female member—because this is an accepted and required practice in their country (and even in their ethnic community in this country)—does not relieve the worker of a responsibility to intervene and protect the child.

## Working with the Culture

**EP 2.1.4b**
**EP 2.1.10j**

It may be possible, at times, to work with the cultural or religious views rather than just oppose them. In a workshop I conducted, a social worker in the rural south described working with a "preacher" father who was accused of using a stick to punish his misbehaving child. When the child protection social worker questioned this, the father pulled out his bible and directed the social worker to a section that said to "spare the rod and spoil the child." The social worker, sensitive to these views in the population with which she worked, carried her own bible and quickly quoted a section that provided an opposing view. Thus, the worker had developed a method of working with the religious views of her clients rather than simply confronting them. The father was impressed and engaged with the worker in a discussion of the practice; he became open to exploring other alternatives. Eventually, if she could not reason with the father, a protective order might be needed.

In another example of work with an East Indian family that had recently immigrated to an urban area, the father dominated the discussion during the first session—a home visit—and made sure that his wife did not participate. It was clear that the culture in the family, in part also true in the community, supported the dominant role of the male and the submissive role of the female. The worker did not openly challenge this process in the first session but made clear her interest and openness to hear from all family members. When she arrived for her next appointment, the wife was waiting outside and asked the worker to talk with her out of sight of the home. She revealed her concerns about physical abuse of herself and her child as well as her fear of raising it directly during their session. The worker used this information, without reporting on the clandestine meeting, to challenge the father in the next session.

The reader is referred to Chapter 4, and to a number of other publications in the reference list, for more detailed descriptions of specific cultural and community values and norms and how they affect family life. For now, the key points are as follows:

- Cultural and community understanding and sensitivity can be crucial in engaging and working with families.
- We need to recognize diversity within diversity and not fall into the trap of overgeneralizing.
- Addressing intercultural (e.g., a White worker with a family of color) and intracultural issues (e.g., a Hispanic worker with a Hispanic family) is crucial in the engagement and ongoing stages of work.
- Sensitivity to these variables does not necessarily mean acceptance of them.

In the sections that follow, I focus on one minority group—American Indian—to illustrate the importance of understanding how racism and oppression can affect a family, and how a worker can use cultural awareness in practice.

## Racism, Oppression, and the Native American Family

**EP 2.1.5a**

One of the greatest tragedies in North America has been the impact of the White society on its "first peoples," the American Indians or Native Americans. The same can be said for the Native Canadian population. A strong family and community tradition, a whole culture, and a way of life were systematically stripped from a people in what has been described as cultural genocide. This is a special case of the struggle that each minority group faces, whether aboriginals or immigrants. Each must find a way to preserve what is of value to its own culture and still come to grips with a surrounding and dominating culture. When the group is of another race—Indian, Black, Chicano, Asian—the struggle is usually intensified by a persistent racism, sometimes subtle but other times open and direct.

In the Native community, from which the family in the following example is drawn, years of neglect, discrimination, and exploitation often lead to a breakdown in individual, family, and community functioning. Once-proud cultural traditions have been lost for many of the community's members. In particular, teenagers must go through a crucial step in their normative development in which they struggle to understand who they are and how they shall act. The separation and integration issue is just as important in relation to one's culture and community as it is in relation to the immediate family. In fact, the two struggles become intertwined in important ways.

Ambivalent feelings increase when the subculture—the peer group for a teenager—encourages and supports deviant behavior (e.g., the extensive use of alcohol, criminal activity, and so on) and the future appears to be bleak. When a teenager looks around and sees members of the adult community who appear to have given up, her or his internal struggle can lead to complete alienation from the larger society or, in a shockingly large number of cases, teenage suicide. Facing the problems, finding the strength to cope, and accepting as role models many of the adult members of the community who have refused to surrender to years of oppression represent another choice. For teenagers in this situation to make this transition, they will need all the help they can get from family, community (the local band and tribe), and their cultural heritage.

## Research Findings on Race and Practice with the Native Population

In a study cited throughout this book (Shulman, 1991), the issue of race and practice in relation to Native clients was explored. Two variables included in the analysis measured the worker's understanding of the Native culture (as perceived by clients) and the understanding of the impact of race on the working relationship (as perceived by the worker). Did clients believe that their workers understood the unique nature of their culture, and were workers aware of the powerful impact of race?

Both of these variables showed strong positive associations with the client's perceptions of a positive working relationship with the worker and the worker's helpfulness. These variables, as well as those that measured the attitude of the regional child welfare staff as a whole toward Native clients, also affected other outcome measures.

A first step in dealing with racism in practice is for helping professionals to face and accept the existence of their own internalized racism and sexism, which is a product of centuries of White, male, Euro-centered history, philosophy, medicine, psychology, and so on (Bulhan, 1985; Fanon, 1968). Only then can workers begin the task of monitoring and purging its impact on their practice. Each new client who is different from the worker can be part of the worker's education. Workers also have a responsibility to work on their own education.

## Oppression, Resilience, and the Psychology and Sociology of People of Color

With a clearer sense of the impact of oppression on the psychology and sociology of people of color, coupled with an understanding of the resilience factors that help people cope with oppression, the worker may be able to perceive these problems in new ways. The focus shifts from personal pathology and a reinforcement of oppressive stereotyping to a practice that helps the client perceive the devastating impact on self that can occur to any member of an oppressed group. In addition, the identification of baseline and developmental reserve capacity in individuals, the family, and the community offers opportunities to break the cycles that block growth and development. Techniques drawn from solution-focused therapy, for example, can help clients identify how they have coped in the past.

This perspective is important for work not only with people of color but also with other oppressed and vulnerable populations (e.g., women, the mentally ill, survivors of the Nazi Holocaust and their descendants, gays and lesbians, and so forth). Such a shift in perspective by the helping professional opens up the possibility of finding important areas of strength in the client, the community, and the culture. It also more clearly defines a professional responsibility social workers have to influence their own agencies, the community, and society away from oppressive practices.

**EP 2.1.10d**
**EP 2.1.4d**
**EP 2.1.4b**
**EP 2.1.10j**

*A White Worker with a Native American Family* Examples of adoption of self-destructive behavior and self-denigrating attitudes painfully emerge in the following example, as the parents refer to their son's "crazy Indian" and "dirty Indian" behavior. The worker's recognition of culturally based strengths appears in her attention to the importance to the son of his dancing and carving skills.

**Practice Points:** Culture and community are key issues as Jim, a 14-year-old Native teenager, struggles with this crucial, transitional crisis of identity as he moves through his teenage years. The worker must also deal with the fact that she is White. No matter what her attitudes and feelings are with respect to people of color, she is an outsider—a member of the oppressor group. White workers must be alert to the fact that, as one African American social work supervisor described in a training workshop, "For a person of color, the antennae are always up and on the lookout for racism." The efforts of the worker to engage Jim and his family are described in the record of service that follows.

**Client Description and Time Frame:** Father is 40; stepmother is 29; and son, Jim, is 14. The family is being seen as part of a probation program ordered by a judge because of Jim's arrests for breaking and entering.

**Description of the Problem:** Jim, in the throes of puberty, is searching very hard to establish his identity. Most of all, he wants to feel and be proud of his Native heritage, but the conflicting messages he has internalized about "being Indian" do not allow him to do so positively. His anger and confusion manifest themselves by his acting out: He has committed seven B&Es (breaking and entering) on the reserve, two of them specifically focusing on the Indian Band office. He has developed an alcohol problem. His acting out has alienated him from the elders of the band, who refuse to be involved in helping him with the court process, as is usually the case for juvenile delinquents of this band. I perceive his B&Es as cries for help with his home situation.

**Practice Points:** The worker skillfully tunes in to the meaning of the behavior rather than focusing on the behavior itself. In the next excerpt she demonstrates the "two-client" idea advocated in this chapter by also tuning in to the parents.

Jim's parents are disheartened and upset. They feel they have tried their best and have failed. They are considering sending him away to a residential school. Their medium of communication and major stumbling block between Jim and themselves is discussion of Native identity: All emotions, conflict, and disagreement are discussed under the heading "Indian." In my efforts to help this family, I must also deal with their feelings about me—a White, female probation officer. I realize I will have to become more than just a symbol of White authority.

***How the Problem Came to the Attention of the Worker(s):*** My first meeting with Jim and his parents was to discuss the B&E charges in the hope of sparing Jim court appearances. I had great difficulty keeping the session on focus: It was too painful a topic for everyone to discuss directly. Actually, Jim and his parents reenacted their communication pattern in front of me: The war was on. Jim's mother said angrily that these B&Es were "crazy Indian stuff." I tried to reach for the feelings of pain and disappointment behind the anger and said, "Jim's B&Es are hard on the family right now; they would be for any family, Indian or not." Jim's father said, "I knew nothing about them Indians."

Jim didn't give me a chance to say anything and counterattacked by angrily saying that his parents are Honkies in disguise but he is an Indian, he is a super dancer and carver and can drink and fight with the bigger guys on the reserve any day. I said that his parents might be proud about his dancing and carving. Jim's mother said, "Honkies or not Honkies, we know that Jim is a no-good Indian." The energy they put out fighting made me believe that there was a lot of concern and care hidden behind the anger. Their faces indicated they were clearly in pain.

**Practice Points:** As we have seen before the first session process, the nature of the interaction reveals to the worker the core content of the work to follow. The distress of the parents and Jim cause them to only see the surface feelings and to miss that caring underlies the anger for the family as a whole. As the worker writes about the interview she tries to identify her intent in her intervention (in bold).

***Second Session (an individual session with Jim):*** **I tuned in to Jim's feelings and tried to put his feelings into words.** Jim had a tough look on his face. He slid himself into a chair, his knees up close to his chest as if to protect himself. I said, "You look angry as hell today." No response. I waited out his silence. He said with a tone devoid of affect that he had a big fight last night after Indian dancing and that it lasted until 4 in the morning. I asked him if he'd gotten hurt (empathizing). He said no, he never gets hurt. He was drunk anyway. I was lucky he was sober this afternoon. I said, "Alcohol dims the pain. A 14-year-old drunk is a sad story to me." He said he knew. Jim said he had also siphoned gas out of a car last night. I said, "It is a lot for one night. Are you trying to tell me how bad you can be?" Jim looked at me intently. I said that behind his tough façade I thought there was a lot of pain. His voice changed. With a defensive tone he said, "Pain about what?" I said, "Maybe it is painful to feel you have to act like a hellion to get attention." He giggled and said it wasn't funny. I said, "I agree, it's not funny, it hurts."

**Practice Points:** Note that the worker integrates support (empathy) with confrontation by reaching for the painful feelings. The worker's message to Jim is that she really understands and is not going to participate in an illusion of work. She is making a demand for real work on real issues.

He cocked his head down. I waited out his silence. He said suddenly, "Nothing ever hurts anymore. Nobody cares about me anymore." I said, "Are you talking about home?" He said simply, "Yeah." **I recognized his indirect communication and tried to help him go from general to specific concerns.** Jim had done a rerun of the above 2 weeks in a row; that is, enumerating all the "bad" behaviors he had gotten into. I said it was the third weekend that he had asked me to give him hell. He said that if I didn't, nobody would.

I asked him if that's what he wanted his parents to do. He said, "No, I want them to understand me." I said that I knew things were rough for everyone at home right now; could he tell me what had taken place at home that hurt? He looked away and said in a low voice, "They called me a rotten Indian." The affect of pain was so strong that he could not elaborate on his feelings or the specific circumstances.

I said, "It hurts a lot doesn't it? I wish I could take the pain away from you." **I tried to share my feelings openly.** Jim said that he was sick and tired of being called a dirty Indian at home. The affect was anger. **I tried to reach for the specific feeling but got nowhere.** He said that all his parents talked about was "dirty Indians this, silly Indians that. Who do they think they are, anyway?" I said, "It may hurt to hear the word *Indian* coming from your own parents as a curse word." He asked me if I thought he was a dirty Indian. I said no, he was Indian all right, "but the two words together are a terrible combination." He said, "What about a silly Indian?"

I reached for his indirect communication and said, "You're checking out if I'm prejudiced, aren't you?" He said, "Yup." I said it was for him to judge. He said I would be on probation for a while. I said I knew. He said in a low voice that he didn't think I could understand. I said gently, "Do you feel you can't win: You can't be right and you can't be Indian?" **(Putting the client's feelings into words.)** He said suddenly, "I don't know what 'Indian' means. How am I supposed to grow up okay?" I put my arms around him and said that he was right. I wasn't sure I could understand fully what it means to grow up as an Indian. I said that his hurt was choking me up right now.

**Practice Points:** It's ironic that the worker is seen by Jim as on "probation," since she is a probation social worker. She has quickly reached the underlying issues and reframed them in terms that have meaning for Jim.

**I tried to help Jim view his parents in new ways.** Jim said that his parents put him through a grinder whenever he is home. I said that it sounds horrible, what does it mean? **(Reaching for elaboration.)** He said that his parents hassle him about every little detail about what he does at night. I jokingly said, "It's not such a horrible grinder after all!" He laughed. He said that really they don't care about him; they just want him on a leash. I said, "And you want to be more independent, don't you?" **(Recognizing the metaphor.)** He said, "Yup."

**Practice Points:** In order to be helpful, the worker uses the skill defined in earlier chapters as moving from the general to the specific by asking for an example.

I asked him to give me an example of the grinder. He said that last night he came home at midnight. They just had to know who he was with, where he had been. I said, "That sounds to me like they care about you. They worry about you, and frankly at midnight I would worry too." Jim pouted. I waited out his silence. He said, "I don't think they care. They're just angry." I said that maybe they felt both fear and anger. Did he think that they had any reason to be angry last night? He said, "Maybe so. Midnight is kind of late." I agreed. I asked him if he knew what his parents felt waiting for him. He said, "They always assume the worst. That's dumb."

I said, "We all do that when we're worried." He said, "I guess I give them reasons to be angry and I don't like it." I said sadly, "And they don't, either. I bet they feel just as bad as you do about yesterday."

**Practice Points:** In the next excerpt Jim gets into an underlying issue of his feelings about his mother being a stepparent, having married his father after his biological mother died. He expresses his anger in a strong manner; however, the worker recognizes or believes that he does not really intend to "kill" his mother. What emerges is an underlying problem often faced in families where one parent remarries and the children have to learn to connect to a new "parent." This can be a painful process for the stepparent and the child, but often it remains a taboo subject. It can be particularly difficult if the feelings of loss and grief on the part of the child are not dealt with. The feelings are there, but they are most often acted out in behavior.

**I supported him in a taboo area and tried to stay close to his feelings of anger and rejection.** Jim said that he was going to kill his mother one of these days. She isn't his real mom anyway. I asked him if he was angry about something she had done or angry because she isn't his real mom. (**Trying to partialize his concern.**) He said, "Both." I asked him what his mom had done for him to be so upset. He said, "She is really unreal; she phoned the school to insist that she be warned if I skipped out. It's none of her business. It's my dad's business, sure, but not her business." I kept the issue in focus and said, "Not hers because she is your stepmom?" He said, "Yup, I'm not her son. She's got no rights on me." I said sadly, "No right to care? She can't win, can she?" Jim said, "No, she can't win. She's the one who made us move from the reserve." I said I knew about that, that she wanted to make a better home for him and his dad. Jim nervously twisted his hair around his fingers and said that he would rather have his mom around than "her" care. I said that he had expressed real and deep feelings. (**Crediting his work.**) "It's real hard to get over one's Mom's death."

**Practice Points:** The worker has begun to identify the core issues for Jim and to develop a working relationship (rapport, trust, and caring). She is now able to offer her help by mediating the conflict and Jim is ready to accept it. She also skillfully challenges his comment about not believing in perfection and points to, and credits, his developing cultural skills that help to define him as Indian. She also reads the issue of her being White when he raises it indirectly.

**I tried to help Jim identify the affect obstacle and offered to mediate with his parents.** Jim said that he doesn't know how to tell his parents to stop calling him names when he does something wrong—names like "silly Indian." When they do, his blood boils and he goes out and gets drunk. He can't say anything. He just walks out. And he does start acting silly. I asked him to tell me exactly what he would like to tell his parents. He said that he just wants them to stop calling him names. But he can't say it to them. I said, "That's their way of criticizing you, isn't it?" He said, "Yeah. It's bad enough being told off when you do something wrong, but then calling me names like that, it's below the belt." I said, "It's like you're nobody all of a sudden." He said, "Yup." He had tears in his eyes.

I said, "Do you want me to help you talk to your parents?" He said, "Yeah." He couldn't do it alone. I said that I'd phone his parents, and if they agreed we'd try to talk about the name-calling and try to understand what is behind it from their side. Jim said that he didn't want to talk about the things he does wrong. I said that he forgets he does a lot of things real well too. We have to take the bad with the good. He said, "Yeah, but I'm far from perfect." I said that perfection is like a rainbow—nobody can reach it, we can only try. He said his parent didn't know that. I said I was sure they did, they just had high expectations for him. He said he didn't believe in high expectations. I laughed and said, "Baloney—you want to be the best at everything." He said, "How do you know?" I said that I had seen some of his carvings. They're beautiful. It was obvious to me that he was trying to be the best. Jim said a long drawn-out "oh." I brought the conversation back on focus and said, "So if your parents are willing, we'll talk about both sides." He said he was willing to try but that I was going to get myself into a lot of trouble with his parents. I said, "Because I'm White?" He said, "Yeah." I said I could only try, that things should go easier if I didn't take sides.

***Third Session:*** I tried to tune in to the feelings of ambivalence of the one (Jim) and the many (the family), tried to include everyone in the commonality of the experience, and clarified the contract. At the first meeting, I said that they must feel a bit uncomfortable about having a White probation officer coming into their home. Mr. Jones smiled and said, "You bet, you're the first one we managed to get in here." Mrs. Jones said that she didn't mind; today she'd had to clean her home for the health nurse anyway. I recognized her ambivalence and said that I knew how it felt—it's a hassle to clean house because a stranger is coming in. She nodded hesitantly. I said I felt a bit like an intruder today (**putting my personal feelings into words**), but that I hoped we would feel more comfortable once we knew each other better.

**Practice Points:**  Jim's posture and his stepmother's response act out their usual way of communicating, or really, not communicating. The worker tries to break the cycle and to enter the taboo area of stereotypes of the Native community. Note the father's reaction because he is still not sure about her as a White worker. It's important that the worker make clear her role in the conversation and that she is not just there to make Jim change his behavior nor is she going to join with the parents and side with them against Jim.

Jim's eyes were covered by his cap and his arms were crossed at his chest. I asked him what he was angry about. He said, "Nothing, leave me alone." Mrs. Jones firmly said that he couldn't talk to me like that. I said it was okay to be angry. Did they (Jim's parents) know what was making Jim so angry? Mr. Jones said that Jim is like that around home, not to worry. I said that maybe Jim is afraid that we might all gang up on him. "It's certainly not my intention." I said that I was there to have them talk about a real painful issue: Jim can't stand being called a dirty Indian and it hurts so much that he can't talk about it usually.

I got a nasty look from Mr. Jones. Mrs. Jones said she thought it was simple: I should forbid Jim from doing any of that crazy Indian stuff and then she'd stop calling him a crazy Indian. Mr. Jones agreed with her. I said that I knew they often worried about Jim, but I couldn't do that. That's not my role, and it wouldn't work anyway. Jim nodded sullenly. I said that I felt uncomfortable about the words "crazy Indian stuff." I asked Jim if he knew what his parents mean by that. He lifted his cap from his eyes and said that he knew for sure that "all Indians are dirty, crazy, violent, and lazy drunks."

Mr. Jones said, "Here he goes again, acting crazy. Everyone knows that Indians aren't violent and drunk." Jim giggled, and Mr. Jones cracked his knuckles. I said that perhaps Jim was hitting something very painful. That was the prejudice they had to live with day in and day out. Mr. Jones said I was damn right. Mrs. Jones said that's what she worried about, that Jim would become like "the rest of them Indians." I said, "You are Indian and you aren't violent, lazy, and crazy. Neither is Jim." Mrs. Jones said no, but that's because they'd moved away from the reserve. I said that maybe it was time to look at the positive things of the present rather than the bad things of the past.

**Practice Points:** Note in the next excerpt that the worker has done her homework on the Native culture and uses their idioms and expressions to join with them as they explore the underlying conflict. In this sense, she is joining with the family. She also understands that the father's comment about racist White teachers is also directed at her. Her response using humor helps to break the ice in this difficult area. Note also the connecting on this issue between Jim and his father.

**I tried to reach the feelings in their way, to establish contact, and to help the family members help one another.** Jim said, "You can't help but act on impulse, that's what my B&Es are all about." I said, "You forget to pray to the spirit of the bear, don't you?" Mr. Jones nodded and said I was right. He told us an Indian story about a little boy becoming a man becoming a bear. It was the opposite of Jim's progress at this point, but it emphasized his potential. Jim said that the story was OK, but that the elders had better ones. I said to Jim that maybe the story hit home a bit hard. I got nowhere.

Jim said that he had been kicked out of English today and that he wasn't much more disruptive than some of the White kids. I said that a little more disruption is all it takes to make a difference. (Silence.) Mr. Jones said that White teachers are racist. Mr. Jones [also] said that females are more racist than men. He would fight with a White man any day, but you can't fight with a White woman. I acknowledged my feelings and said that I was afraid the arrows might start flying toward me. We all laughed at the relief of tension. Jim said that the Indians only scalp White people who have no honor. Mr. Jones grinned. I recognized their offering and said that it felt good to hear I have honor. Their feelings for me are important to me, because I respect them.

**I tried to put the client's feelings into words for the benefit of the other family members so that they would gain a new understanding of one another.** Mrs. Jones asked me what I intended to do about Jim's alcoholism. I said Jim was doing his best to stay away from alcohol and the reserve, but sometimes he got so depressed about feeling bad about himself that he couldn't help it. Jim said I was right. He can't control himself when his parents call him a crazy Indian. Mr. Jones said that he and his wife mean well. They just don't know what else to say. I said, "I know, when you're worried words don't come easily." Jim said gently, "When I'm rotten, why don't you just say I let you down, Dad?" Mr. Jones put his arms around his son.

**Practice Points:** As Jim and his father begin to connect Mrs. Jones gets back into the discussion with her concern about Jim's carving and his future. In this next excerpt, we see the worker identifying with Jim and his father but losing emotional contact with his stepmother. Instead of simply defending Jim's carving, a better response would be to explore Mrs. Jones's underlying concern about Jim's future. It's easy to understand how the worker could lose sight of the need to be with all of the family members at the same time.

Mrs. Jones said that Jim was wasting his time carving; you can't make a living out of it. I said that I was really impressed by Jim's carvings. They are really beautiful. Mrs. Jones said that Jim spends too much time doing that. I said that it takes a lot of time to create a piece of art. Mr. Jones said he knew, because he tried when he was younger and couldn't do half as well as Jim. Jim was beaming. He asked his dad how good an Indian dancer he was when he was younger.

**Practice Points:**   The conversation now shifts to the impact of the environment, in this case the band and the band leaders, on the family. Participation in the community is a very important element of Indian culture. The family has been cut off from the band partly due to Jim's delinquent behavior.

I offered to mediate between the family and a system that made it harder to communicate between Jim and his parents as a result of his delinquencies. Everyone was silent. Mrs. Jones, especially, looked grim. I asked if I had offended them in any way. (Silence.) I said, "Anything I have done or said in relation to Jim?" "No," said Mr. Jones, "I guess we are taking it out on you." Jim said that he knew what it was all about. It's about the band. "You wish you were on good terms with the band, don't you?" Mrs. Jones said it wasn't possible. There was so much politics going on. Mr. Jones said they were arrogant.

Jim continued rocking in his chair and looked hurt. I said, noting his eyes, "You feel guilty about it; you want to cry. Your B&Es stand in the way, don't they?" He nodded. I said that I would talk to the band office. Maybe they would agree to supervise Jim's probation once I'm gone. Mr. Jones said, "They refused in the past; why would they accept now?" I said that they had had time to get over the shock, just as Jim had had time to do a lot of growing. Jim nodded.

*Current Status of the Problem—Where it Stands now:* The problem has shifted in urgency. Jim and his parents are starting to be able to discuss the problem of Indian identity with less anger and pain and are starting to be able to discuss other issues without approaching them from a perspective of ethnic origin. Jim's parents are beginning to be able to give positive strokes to Jim for his "Native Indian–oriented" achievements (e.g., his beautiful carvings and his proficiency in Indian dancing). They are striving to live together under the same roof without feeling that it is a battlefield of "good Indians" versus "bad Indians." Jim's anger has lessened, largely because he has regained the support of the elders in the band. He has stayed away from committing further delinquencies.

*Specific Next Steps:*

- For the next White worker: Do not shy away from discussing the racial element of the interaction, because it is a central element for Jim and his family and permeates all their lives.
- Continue family work around communication patterns. There are a lot of feelings of anger and sadness connected to Jim's natural mom's death that interfere between Jim and his stepmom.
- Continue to emphasize Jim's ability and desire to do well and excel rather than Jim's past record of delinquency; emphasize his parents' desire to be the best parents.
- Make an effort to enlist the band elders to help provide a social support system for Jim and his family.

**Practice Summary:**   The worker in this example has made a start toward breaking down the barriers between the parents and the child, the family and herself (and her White social service system), and the family and a source of support in the

Native community. Recognizing that a long history of communal support is central to the Native culture can be a crucial step in strengthening the family.

One finding of the child welfare study cited earlier (Shulman, 1991) was that regions of the provincial child welfare agency that established effective working relationships with the Native community had fewer Native children going into alternative forms of care or, if they did go into care, fewer leaving the Native community. (These working relationships involved friendship centers, homemaker and court workers, band chiefs and elders, and social workers.) Continued work with the family would need to integrate some discussion of the socioeconomic issues of oppression that contributed to the struggles within the family so that the problem could be reframed, from a personal pathology perspective to a social perspective.

## Chapter Summary

Defining the word *family* is complicated for a number of reasons; however, a few core elements are widely accepted. Social work with families includes general family support, family counseling, and crisis intervention. Unique issues are involved in work with families that distinguish this practice from work with individuals. There are also a number of different family therapy models that contain concepts that are useful in social work with families. The social worker's role in working with a family is defined as mediating the engagement between each family member and the family as a whole. The two-client concept is revisited, with the second client represented by the family as a whole.

A number of family assessment tools are described with an important caveat that the use of the tool in a first or early interview not serve to hamper the development of the working relationship. It is also suggested that the tool be fully explained to the family members and that it be used as their tool rather than just the tool for the worker's assessment. This is the difference between acting with the family as opposed to acting on the family.

The phases-of-work framework and the idea of tuning in—as well as the importance of contracting in the beginning phase—reappear in work with families. Models for family assessment can assist the worker in the engagement phase of contact. Additionally, the importance of understanding culture and community is stressed and illustrated by a White worker's practice with a Native American family.

## Related Online Content and Activities

Visit *The Skills of Helping Individuals, Families, Groups, and Communities*, Seventh Edition, CourseMate website at **www.cengagebrain.com** for learning tools such as glossary terms, links to related websites, and chapter practice quizzes. The website for this chapter also features additional notes from the author.

## Competency Notes

The following is a list of Council on Social Work Education (CSWE) recommended competencies and practice behaviors for social work students defined in Educational Policy and Accreditation Standard (EPAS) and addressed in this chapter.

**EP 2.1.1b** Practice personal reflection and self-correction to assure continual professional development (p. 275)

**EP 2.1.3a** Distinguish, appraise, and integrate multiple sources of knowledge, including research-based knowledge and practice wisdom (p. 269)

**EP 2.1.3b** Analyze models of assessment, prevention, intervention, and evaluation (p. 268)

**EP 2.1.4a** Recognize the extent to which a culture's structures and values may oppress, marginalize, alienate, or create or enhance privilege and power (p. 282)

**EP 2.1.4b** Gain sufficient self-awareness to eliminate the influence of personal biases and values in working with diverse groups (p. 271)

**EP 2.1.4c** Recognize and communicate their understanding of the importance of difference in shaping life experiences (p. 259)

**EP 2.1.4d** View themselves as learners and engage those with whom they work as informants (pp. 269, 285)

**EP 2.1.5a** Understand forms and mechanisms of oppression and discrimination (p. 284)

**EP 2.1.7a** Utilize conceptual frameworks to guide the process of assessment, intervention, and evaluation (pp. 261, 262, 268)

**EP 2.1.7b** Critique and apply knowledge to understand person and environment (p. 261)

**EP 2.1.10a** Substantively and affectively prepare for action with individuals, families, groups, organizations, and communities (p. 271)

**EP 2.1.10b** Use empathy and other interpersonal skills (pp. 271, 276)

**EP 2.1.10c** Develop a mutually agreed-on focus of work and desired outcomes (p. 276)

**EP 2.1.10d** Collect, organize, and interpret client data (pp. 269, 285)

**EP 2.1.10e** Assess client strengths and limitations (p. 276)

**EP 2.1.10f** Develop mutually agreed-on intervention goals and objectives (p. 260)

**EP 2.1.10g** Select appropriate intervention strategies (p. 260)

**EP 2.1.10j** Help clients resolve problems (p. 283)

**EP 2.1.10k** Negotiate, mediate, and advocate for clients (p. 274)

# The Middle and Ending Phases in Family Practice

## The Middle Phase in Family Practice

A model for understanding the middle phase practice session was presented in Chapter 5, with a focus on individual interviews. The same general principles and framework are useful in thinking about the middle phase and ongoing work with families, but we now introduce a striking difference. Whenever we deal with more than one client at a time—such as a family or, in later chapters, a group or community—we need to consider the communication process, stages of development, shared norms and taboos, rules of family interaction, and so forth of the family as a whole. For example, in addition to tuning in to what each individual family member may bring to a session, as we did during Stage I (described earlier as *sessional tuning in*), we now need to think about what the family "organism" brings as well.

As we think about sessional contracting at the beginning of any session, we need to be attuned not only to the indirect communications of each individual but also the direct and indirect

**EP 2.1.7a**

communications of the family unit. I mentioned in an earlier chapter that the client makes a number of decisions. The first decision is whether to engage with the worker (and, in the case of a family, with one another), which is associated with the contracting stage. Initial work is real and can have meaningful content; however, family members may conspire to raise "near problems" that are close to the core issues but not quite on target.

The key to the middle phase is whether the family makes a conscious or unconscious agreement to make the "second decision" and to begin to address more central, powerful, and emotional concerns. It is not unusual for clients to take one step back just before plunging in because of ambivalence and associated fears. Remember: Family members, unlike group clients, will most likely go home with one another after the session. A wife, husband, or child who raises a taboo issue such as a parental alcohol problem (sometimes referred to as the family secret) may have to deal with the consequences following the session. Thus, communications at the start of a session, during the sessional contracting phase, may appear to be ambivalent and very indirect. The sense of resistance is actually a sign that the family or family member is ready to take a next step but needs some discussion and reassurance about how the family will deal with the consequences.

The family may convey issues during the middle phase simply by the way they sit in the room—with the father, mother, or child suddenly changing places and sitting almost outside of the family group. This may send a signal of how the family member or the family is feeling at the moment; if this is recognized by the worker, it can be addressed. Because addressing process in the family group will move the family quickly into the content of the work, a worker's "demand for work"—or "facilitative confrontation"—on the family as a whole can serve as a turning point. To explore this middle phase, let's first review the framework shared in Chapter 5, with some modification and attention to the differences in family practice.

## A Framework for Analyzing a Family Session

**EP 2.1.7a**
**EP 2.1.10a**
**EP 2.1.10b**
**EP 2.1.10c**
**EP 2.1.10d**

Note the key differences from the earlier model (in Chapter 5), which essentially focused on communication between the client and the worker. Now, we must also consider the process between members of the family.

### The Work Phase Model

1. **Sessional Tuning In to Each Individual and the Family as a Whole.** Preliminary empathy is conveyed by the worker, based upon the previous session or sessions and/or environmental issues that may emerge. For example, the worker may address the potential impact of finding out that a member of the family has been called to serve in a war zone such as Iraq. Or, conversely, the family has found out that a family member will return after a long absence.

2. **Sessional Contracting with the Family as a Whole.** This requires the family support worker (FSW) to address issues raised directly or indirectly by an individual, as well as issues raised by the family group. Sessional contracting also involves helping the family members reach some consensus with one another in response to the question: "What are we working on today?"

3. **Elaborating Skills.** The FSW will help family members tell their stories to one another, not just to the worker. This skill involves helping them talk and listen to one another. For example, "I wonder if John can share how upset he was over the fight at school so you can get a better idea of what's going on for him." Or, "Mr. Jones, I know it's upsetting for you to hear about John's trouble at school, but if you could just try to listen a bit and let him get it out, we may be able to help with this problem."

4. **Empathic Skills Must Be Demonstrated for Both Clients—the Individual and the Family.** The empathic skills are designed to express empathy for each member of the family and the family as a whole. Skills include reaching for, acknowledging, and sharing expressed and unexpressed feelings. For example, "That must have been hard for you to share with your family, John, and I suspect it was also hard for all of you to hear it."

5. **Sharing Worker's Feelings.** This skill involves the worker sharing appropriate personal feelings in a professional manner. For example, "I have to admit that, after meeting with you for so many weeks, I have grown to really care about each of you and your family. I feel you have so much to give to one another, and it makes me sad to see all of the old arguments get in the way."

6. **Exploring Taboo Subjects.** This is a complex skill in which the worker uses a range of skills to create permission to discuss otherwise taboo subjects such as dependency, drug or alcohol use, sexual issues, and so forth. For example, "I think there is something you all need to talk about, but everyone is afraid to start. I believe it has something to do with how much drinking goes on in the house and how it's impacting each of you and your family."

7. **Making a Demand for Work.** These are the facilitative confrontation skills that address avoidance of real work and challenge the illusion of work. For example, "Each time we start to talk about difficult subjects, you two manage to start a fight. It's almost as if it's easier to fight with each other than to face your real feelings. I think it's time to stop."

8. **Pointing Out Obstacles.** This is a skill designed to help family members understand their communication and relationship process and, in particular, the obstacles that block positive growth. For example, "It seems to me that, each time you get close to reaching out to one another, someone gets scared and pulls back. It's almost as if you feel too exposed and vulnerable and are afraid of being rejected. I think that's going on for all of you."

9. **Identifying Content and Process Connections.** This is a meta-skill that involves pointing out how the process (the way the work proceeds among family members, the intimacy theme, or between the family and the worker, the authority theme) can be connected to the content of the work. For example, "Wow, look what just happened. You started to talk about Mom being ill, and John, you changed the subject and started to fool around. John, is this hard for you to talk about? The rest of you, is this the way you avoid the painful stuff—by letting John goof off?"

10. **Sharing Data.** The worker shares information, values, beliefs, and so forth that are related to the work of the family members, are otherwise not available, and are shared in a manner that is open to challenge. For example, "I can't generalize about this, but I can say that lots of families I work with

have the same struggles, the same feelings, and the same stress you are describing. They all think they are the only ones."

11. **Helping the Client See Life in New Ways.** This is a skill that is sometimes described as "reframing" but essentially offers family members a new and often more positive view of one another and the family as a whole. For example, "Can we take a minute and have each of you tell the rest of the family what you would like your family to look like? I mean, if this counseling works out, what would your family look like? Now no one can jump in and disagree. You each get a chance."

12. **Sessional Ending/Transition Skills.** These are the skills involved in bringing a session to a close and identifying the transitions to the next session or specific actions that the family members have agreed to take. For example, "I think you have all worked really hard tonight, but the really tough stuff came out just as we were coming to a close. Can we agree, I mean really agree, that we will begin next time with what John just raised?"

## Dealing with Family Secrets

**EP 2.1.5a**

Family often have a family secret that they feel is so terrible, no one will talk about it. A family secret is kept secret by an explicit or unspoken agreement in which all family members agree not to deal directly with a sensitive and taboo concern. Family violence, alcoholism, and sexual abuse are examples of family secrets that are often hidden behind a family façade. At times, the oppressor in the relationship uses emotional or physical threats to maintain the secret through coercion. Other common secrets are associated with physical and mental illness. Examples include family members who try to hide the onset of a potentially life-threatening illness, such as AIDS, cancer, or Alzheimer's disease. In some cases, the family knows about the illness but treats it as a taboo subject. Each family member may fear that the others cannot emotionally handle an open discussion. Although the guardian of the secret genuinely wants to protect the other family members, she or he is also protecting herself or himself. The result is an illusion of work, in which conversation takes place but nothing real happens.

Family secrets that are kept out of sight and not discussed can impair a family's ability to function in a healthy manner. The inability to discuss the subject area—the norm of behavior that has declared such discussion forbidden—blocks the family members' ability to deal with the issue and discover their inherent strengths.

### A Mother's Degenerative Illness: The Family Secret

**EP 2.1.1b**

In one example, a young mother suffered from a degenerative illness that had already caused her to go blind. She had experienced strokes and memory loss, and the prognosis was an early death. The father was no longer in the picture, and the three-generation family living in the home consisted of the mother (Ruth), her 8-year-old son (Billy), and the maternal grandmother (Millie). A norm of behavior had evolved in which all of the family members covertly agreed not to speak of the illness or its symptoms and, in particular, not to speak of the mother's future. The child was considered too young to understand. The grandmother worried that discussing the illness would make the young mother more depressed and perhaps trigger a stroke. The young mother worried about the burden the illness placed on the grandmother and how that burden might affect her health. Both the mother and grandmother were deeply concerned about what would happen to Billy if the other died first.

***Billy: The Identified Patient (IP)*** Although the tensions and stress in the family were carefully covered up, there was no way for the feelings to remain under the surface. Billy signaled the underlying problems by acting out the anxieties he felt about what was happening to his mother and his family. As his behavior worsened, his mother and grandmother could not handle him, so they sought help from a child-care resource to arrange a temporary placement in a foster or group home. This was a good example in which the member of the family becomes the "identified patient," the IP, when actually the child is sending a call for help for a family problem.

The mission of this agency was to provide assistance to families in dealing with their children's behavior problems or to offer resources for substitute child care. It was not, for example, a hospital social service department, for which the issue of the illness itself might be central.

The first response of the agency, along with the family worker involved, was to respect the grandmother's injunction against getting into the health issues. The grandmother involved the worker in a conspiracy of silence on the core issues. Given the child-focused service of the agency, the worker's agreement was understandable. Her early efforts focused on helping the mother and grandmother try to deal with Billy's behavior and on helping Billy control his activities. However, because this missed the real meaning of the deviant behavior and played into the family's use of Billy as the identified patient, little progress took place, and both the mother and grandmother expressed feelings of dissatisfaction with the results.

***Identifying the Family Secret and the Worker's Ambivalence*** The family worker realized that the core issue was the family secret, and she made several efforts to open it up. She pointed out to the mother and the grandmother that Billy's behavior might well stem from his anxiety in sensing something wrong within the family. However, at the first sign of resistance from the grandmother with regard to this suggestion, the worker backed off. The worker then had to examine her own feelings about death and dying that contributed to her willingness to go along with the illusion of work. As long as the family members sensed the worker's discomfort and resulting ambivalence, they would resist as well. By backing off, the worker indirectly signaled to the family her lack of readiness to help them with the issue. Once the worker had dealt with her own feelings, she could begin to see the resistance as a sign that the work was on target. When the meaning of the phrase "resistance is part of the work" became clear to the worker, she made a demand for work on the family members by persisting in raising the underlying issue.

***Confronting the Family: The Grandmother's Continuing Resistance*** Recognizing that she would need to confront the family about their conspiracy to keep the family secret, the worker took her courage in hand and challenged the obstacle. She confronted the mother and grandmother and tried to support them in opening up a discussion—first between the two of them and then between them and Billy. She explored the resistance by asking, "What makes it hard for you to talk about this with each other?" The taboo subject was finally out in the open, yet the grandmother refused to continue this line of discussion and closed off further discussions by saying, "When the time comes, we shall deal with it." In contrast, the mother responded by dealing more openly with Billy on the issue of her death. This discussion seemed to help the situation and resulted in a decrease in the child's acting-out behavior. However, the mother remained reluctant to discuss her death with the grandmother.

Although the worker could not help the family face the future at this time, she helped lay the groundwork by creating conditions in which the unspeakable could be spoken. Given the service of the setting, the work succeeded in that the child was freed of the responsibility to signal the family distress. The mother's and grandmother's denial was strong but understandable. In the final analysis, picking the time and place to face a harsh reality remained up to them.

## A Middle Phase Family Session

**EP 2.1.1b**
**EP 2.1.4d**

The example that follows will illustrate how one social worker tries to analyze and understand work with a family over time in the middle phase of practice.

### The Record-of-Service (ROS) Device

To describe this practice, I use a *record-of-service (ROS) device* (Garfield & Irizary, 1971). This is a written record that describes the client system, identifies the central problem area, describes and illustrates the practice over time, assesses the status of the problem after a period of work, and identifies future worker interventions to continue the work. A number of the examples in this book are abstracted from ROS assignments.

I use the ROS as an assignment for social work students to help them assess a particular problem faced by a client (individual, family, group, or community) and then to describe their efforts to address the problem over time. A full description of the record-of-service instrument, as well as a discussion of how it may be used in a practice class or fieldwork, can be found in the Instructor's Guide to this book and on the instructor's web page for this course (www.cengagebrain.com).

The record of service begins with the worker's description of the client and the time frame under discussion. A brief statement of the problem, as seen by the worker, is followed by examples of how this particular issue came to the worker's attention. Next is a summary of the work, using excerpts from process recordings to illustrate the worker's efforts to address the problem. The record of service concludes with an assessment of the current status of the problem (identified at the start of the record) and the worker's strategies for further intervention.

The worker's analysis of what she or he could have done differently is included in the description. The reader will be able to note how a careful self-analysis of practice can lead to significant, positive change in both the worker's interventions and the clients' responses. The device provides a means for a worker to incorporate an ongoing analysis of his or her practice.

*A Family with a 12-Year-Old Son in Trouble in School: The Role of the Stepfather in the Family* In the example that follows, a child welfare social worker brings in a family support worker to help a family whose 12-year-old son is having trouble staying in school. The family has a 2 1/2-year history of difficult times with the agency staff and is considered "hard to work with." As the worker's tuning-in comments indicate, he is aware of the past history and of the need to address it at the beginning of the relationship. He is also aware of the family's concern that the session will turn into marital counseling between the mother and her common-law husband of 5 years. In this case, a 15-year-old daughter raises a question for the family.

The example demonstrates how the worker tried to develop a working contract that respected the family's concerns, and then redefined the contract as it became clear that the parents wanted help to sort out how they dealt with the children.

A central issue, not uncommon in families with stepparents, is how involved the nonbiological parent should be. Often, the stepparent is wary about "butting in," and the biological parent wants to avoid burdening the stepparent. In the early sessions, the mother indirectly chooses to exclude the stepfather. After their confidence in the new family support worker grows, the mother and father are more open to including their relationship in the working contract.

## The Smith Family

### Client Description and Time Frame

*Composition:* Biological mother, Linda, 35; common-law husband of 5 years, Brian, 29; children: Marie, 15; Mike, 12; and foster child, Sally, 15. The time period covered is from November through April. The setting is a child welfare agency.

*History:* Linda, 35, natural mother of Mike and Marie, comes from a very unhappy background, had an alcoholic father, was abused by him, and lived in fear. School was a bad experience, and she prides herself on being very financially successful with only a grade-six education. She believes that Mike can do just as well if he can learn the basic "three *R*s." Brian, 29, has lived with Linda for the past 5 years as her common-law husband. He was born and raised in Europe, immigrated to the United States when he was 15 years old, and works successfully with a small business. He only gets involved with the children if Linda is desperate. Brian cannot accept the fact that Mike has a severe learning disability, and [Brian] feels that he must be made to sit down and learn. Brian has not spoken to the previous worker in 2 1/2 years, except to exchange greetings.

Marie, 15, is in the process of dropping out of school and trying to get into an accelerated program to get school finished quickly. Sally, 15, joined the household in January, had been Marie's best friend previously, and couldn't manage living with her own family. Mike, 12, has been at numerous resources and was expelled from school because he'd threatened several teachers and beaten up children at the school. The special education teacher supplied to Mike threatened to resign if she was required to tutor him. When I contacted the last resource he'd been in, I was informed that the family and Mike were "unworkable." With this and the information at the office, I was more than a little wary about being involved.

**Practice Points:** This is a good example of what I referred to in an earlier chapter as the "agency family." Given the history with social workers and teachers, it is important that the worker address the authority theme early and that she stay focused on the family system as a whole and not just Mike's problems at school. She needs to tune in to the issue of the lack of involvement on the stepparent's part and the need to engage him in the family work. Her recognition of her own wariness in working with this family is an excellent start in tuning in to her own feelings and how they may affect her work.

### Description of the Problem

Linda (the mother) was in a bind; she turned to the agency for assistance but was very hesitant to work with an agency that she felt was not responsive to her needs. Linda and her previous worker saw each other as adversaries, each trying to do what they thought was best for Mike. My record will follow how I worked to develop a culture in which Linda and the agency could identify their common ground of getting Mike back into school.

### How the Problem Came to the Attention of the Worker(s)

The Smith family was my first chance to work with a family, and Jane, the previous worker, went over the file with me. It soon became clear that whenever the social worker found a program that would consider taking Mike, Linda would agree to attend the intake interviews but would always end up saying it wouldn't work out. The pattern was that Mike would attend the program, but, after about a month, he stopped showing up. In frustration, the worker would tell Linda that Mike had stopped attending and Linda would respond that she knew this would happen. Mike appeared to stop attending the program when there were to be "family sessions." Linda's perception of these sessions was that her relationship with Brian would be examined and the two of them would be blamed for Mike's problems.

### Summary of the Work

In preparation, I did some resource hunting and came up with some possible programs that fit Linda's descriptions. I also did some preliminary tuning in. In considering the work to follow, I came up with several taboo areas:

- Telling Linda about parenting techniques
- Trying to probe Linda and Brian's relationship
- Trying to do a sales pitch for a resource
- Trying to steer Linda where I thought she should go

I realized that things must be getting desperate for Linda to call for help. Linda had been through the routine many times and knew the ropes much better than I did. I knew I had to level with the family about my agenda. In addition, I had to do work on the negatives before we could move forward. I had to let the family know that there might be nothing available for Mike.

**Practice Points:** It's easy to understand how previous workers may have been discouraged and frustrated by both Mike's acting out and Linda's apparent pessimism. We do not know how much work was done by the previous worker with Linda about her feelings of frustration and desperation. It's also unclear if the previous worker had taken the tack of "instructing" Linda on her parenting approach rather than joining her in the difficulty she faced as a mom. Note that in this excerpt the worker reaches for the step-dad's views even though he presents as if he were not part of the discussion (reading a book).

### *January*

I was nervous going into our first meeting. I was let in the door by Linda, who seemed tired and flustered and looked as if she were in pain. They'd just finished supper, and another social worker who was seeing Sally had left about 20 minutes earlier. Linda offered me a seat in the living room, turned off the TV, and called Mike, who sat next to me on the couch. To my amazement, Mike was a pleasant-looking 12-year-old who spoke as I'd expect a fellow his age would. I relaxed a bit, figuring he must either have been well drilled beforehand or was a top-blower. Marie sat about 6 feet away, looking at a book, but she was all ears. Brian sat at the far end of the dining room, reading and looking up occasionally. I opened the meeting by establishing role and purpose.

**WORKER:** Linda, you and I have spoken on the telephone and I'm wondering if the others know why I'm here tonight. What have you told them?

**LINDA:** Well, I told these guys that we're having a new social worker to find a place for Mike to go to school. He's 12 now and needs to get something—anything—so that he'll know how to read, do some math, and get a job. We need someone to find out where he can go and still be able to stay at home.

Linda continued speaking, and Brian had stopped his reading and looked interested, so I asked him what he thought about plans for Mike. He agreed that Mike needed to be in school and hoped that I could find a place. Linda jumped in suddenly, "Brian works really hard, and I do all the kids' schoolwork planning, you know." It seemed like Linda was trying to shut me off from talking with Brian, but I fought the urge to try to override her. Linda said, "Brian, why don't you make us some coffee?" He slowly disappeared into the kitchen and only appeared to deliver coffee; then he returned to the kitchen.

**Practice Points:** Once again, process (interaction) in the family reveals an important observation. Linda intervenes to cut off discussion with Brian, even sending him out of the room. One interpretation at this point would be that Linda is concerned about Brian feeling pressure about dealing with this difficult child and she is concerned that this may impact her relationship with him. She also may be concerned that the worker might raise marital issues which are not the purpose of the work other than how they relate together in dealing with Brian.

I wondered why Linda wanted Brian out of the discussion but didn't feel comfortable asking, so I turned to Mike and asked him what he'd like to get from school.

**MIKE:** The same things you've been talking about.

**WORKER:** Some regular schoolwork and some things to do with your hands, like mechanics and carpentry?

**MIKE:** Yeah, I'd really like that. I fix my bike all the time and I've made things, you know. Would you like to see something?

**LINDA:** Show Frank [the worker] your blue vase.

Mike got a blue ceramic vase from the knickknack shelf and proudly showed it. It was a nice piece, and I told him that I liked it. Marie was getting fidgety and I thought she wanted to get involved, so I asked her what she thought about plans for Mike. She spoke angrily.

**MARIE:** I don't want to talk about that. I want to talk about social workers and how they don't care about people. All they care about is making money and themselves.

She gave a rundown on all the things that had been tried and failed, and a list of social workers' faults. I was glad for our class work on checking out previous experiences and felt Marie's strength in speaking out.

**Practice Points:** It's at moments such as these that a young and inexperienced social worker might perceive Marie as her "enemy" because of her anger and respond to her defensively. Actually, Marie is the worker's ally, since she raises the authority theme directly and is serving as the "spokesperson" for the family on this issue. The worker's nondefensive response that recognizes the issue is really about her is a crucial first step in establishing the working relationship with the family.

WORKER: (Elaboration: moving from the general to the specific) Boy (I sighed), from what you've said, I'm sure you must be wondering if I'll be just like all the rest. I do want to find out exactly what Mike wants, as I know that there's no point in trying to force something on Mike that he doesn't want and that everyone doesn't agree to try. I hope that Mike and Linda will tell me, like you have, when I've missed the point or am not listening.

MARIE: Well, you are different. You're the first person who's asked Mike what he wants and not just come here and told us what to do.

I thanked Marie and felt like she'd done a lot of work for me, as everyone agreed to let me know if I was missing their point. I told them that I'd let them know if I thought they were missing my point or assuming without checking. This led to a discussion about years of misunderstandings and the frustrations involved.

### February

As the weeks passed, no facility was available for Mike. Our first meeting in February started with Mike meeting me at the door; he had two friends with him and was eager to talk and leave. I'd been looking for a tutor for Mike and had been unsuccessful.

MIKE: Have you found a tutor for me yet? It's getting to be a long time, you know, everyone says they're going to do something and then nothing ever happens.

WORKER: No, I haven't found anyone yet. Right now it looks like it could be several weeks before there'll be someone. Bet you're angry waiting to see who'll come.

MIKE: Yeah, you know, the longer things go, the worse they'll get; sometimes I just get mad and say to Mom—just tell her to stuff it if she can't get someone to help.

WORKER: I get really frustrated too. Sometimes it seems like forever before there's a tutor available.

**Practice Points:** An interesting observation in the excerpt that follows is that the worker sits down with Linda and helps her sort her receipts. Workers often complain of the difficulty of getting a family's attention with so much going on. This worker does not ask Linda to stop what she was doing but instead sits with her and helps. In another case, this worker carried out an excellent interview with a single-parent mom while helping her fold laundry. These ongoing family activities are often a signal to the worker of the stress the family feels about the session, and sometimes it may be easier to work within the activity than to try to bring it to a formal stop.

The worker will make another effort at bringing Brian into the discussion, which reveals that his contributions thus far may have been to blame Linda and her parenting skills, which explains why she was reluctant to have him involved.

In the kitchen, Linda was tallying her day's receipts, so I sat down and helped sort them out.

LINDA: No news, it sounds like, from your call.

WORKER: That's right. You sound like you've been through this before, Linda—fed up with the whole waiting business.

With that, we got into a discussion about hassles she's had with the agency, the school system, and other agencies. She asked if I'd go with her to find out exactly what had happened when Mike got suspended, and I agreed. Brian, who so often barely said two words, came in and sat opposite me at the table and looked as if he wanted to join the conversation.

I tried to include Brian and needed to recontract if he were to be included.

**WORKER:** Do you know what we've been talking about so far, Brian?

**BRIAN:** Yes, I could hear from the living room and want you to know that it's no good if you get someone for 2 hours a day. If Mike can get into doing something he wants, then he'll leave the schoolwork and never learn.

Brian went on to explain how he'd learned English when he arrived from Europe by studying 8 hours a day, and he began to attack Linda's parenting skills and blame her for Mike's failure. I could see Linda freeze up, and I referred to our contract.

**Practice Points:** This is an important moment in the work. The conflict issues are emerging between Linda and Brian; however, the worker, wishing to respect her agreement with Linda not to get into conflicts between them, leaves the decision to Linda. While this is respectful of Linda's need to control the discussion, the worker could also have pointed out that how Linda and Brian deal with each other in terms of their relationship to Mike is very much part of their work together. Mike will sense the conflict between them, even if under the surface, and some of his acting out may be related to this dynamic. The worker clarifies her offer of help between them, which is a form of recontracting.

**WORKER:** Linda, Brian is talking now about your differences, and we've agreed that you will decide if I'm to be involved in those discussions.

I could see the smoke inside Linda. I didn't want to lose Brian's impetus, but I wasn't going to break my agreement with Linda.

**LINDA:** Brian, you know I don't want to talk about this in front of others. It always leads to trouble.

**BRIAN:** We've got to talk about it or it'll always be the same. Nothing's going to change if we don't try something different.

Brian was visibly shaken; he motioned to his chest, indicating that he could hardly breathe, and stuttered badly as he told me of an old injury that causes this condition when he's angry. I still wanted Linda to have the say as to my participation.

**WORKER:** I still want you to ask me to wait in the living room, Linda, if you want to talk with Brian privately. I am willing to stay if you want; I might be able to help sort out some of the things both you and Brian are saying. This conversation sounds like it's been talked through a number of times without any solutions, just going around in circles with both of you getting really mad at each other.

**LINDA:** You can stay.

They talked about the differences in their upbringings and their expectations for their own family. They seemed to exaggerate their differences, and I pointed out many similarities, such as the belief that you have to be tough to survive and at the same time that they both wanted warmth and affection. Brian's gasping for breath made it almost impossible to get his words out. At that point, it seemed like they both wanted each other's support so badly but couldn't say it.

**WORKER:** You both sound so frustrated and both really want things to be good here. Linda, you sound like you could use some support from Brian. (I missed "vice versa.") Linda looked startled and said, "Yes, I could." Brian was done in, but heard, and excused himself from the room. Linda talked more about how hard it had been for her, and how she felt the kids were biologically hers so she should take all the responsibility for them. I told her we could talk more about that and thanked Brian on the way out for telling his part.

**Practice Points:** Because conversations between the husband and wife had broken down and turned to blaming and recriminations, Linda had feared opening up the "taboo" area. And yet, if the family system was going to work effectively, she would need all the help she could get from the whole family to tackle their problems—Brian included. By creating a positive and safe working relationship, and by focusing on the part of their relationship that dealt with the children, this worker helped set the stage for Linda's agreement to open the door on this important area of work. When Linda and Brian explore their different cultural backgrounds and family histories, they may find that they can better understand both their commonalities and differences. It is only a beginning, but a rather important one in reframing the problem.

In the excerpt that follows, the worker brings a tutor into the situation and meets with her, Linda, and Mike to discuss their working contract. When the tutor mentions the possibility of a family meeting to discuss Mike's school progress, both Mike and his mother choose a form of "flight" to escape the uncomfortable subject. The worker responds to the process of the session and calls everyone's attention to what happened. This allows the concerns about family sessions to be aired and the contract clarified. In the second excerpt, we see the worker begin the phase of transitions and endings, getting ready to connect the family members to new sources of help after he leaves.

### March

By March, I was able to get a tutor for Mike—Betty, who had worked with him 2 years before and was the only tutor the Smiths had identified as having been helpful. We met together to draw up Betty's contract. Mike was eager to have Betty work with him.

WORKER: Now, what do you two want Betty to work on during her time with Mike?

There was silence and many shrugs, looks at the ceiling, and "I don't know"s; then Linda asked me, referring to the contract, "What do you think should go down there?"

BETTY: No, no, no—it's not up to her to say what you want, it's up to you and Mike. There's no way I can work with you unless we agree on the contract. We can change as we go along, but you have to say what you want.

After more silence, Linda listed what she wanted. Betty added a weekly family meeting to discuss how things were going at school and at home for Mike and Linda. Suddenly, Mike started talking about the paint on the ceiling, and he and Linda spoke at full speed about the ceiling paint.

WORKER: Wait a minute—what's going on here? All of a sudden you two took off, and I don't know what's happening. What just happened here?
LINDA: Oh, nothing, I'm sorry.
WORKER: Mike, do you know what happened to you? You started looking at the ceiling all of a sudden.
MIKE: It's the family meetings—she doesn't like them. That's what happened before—she didn't want to go to them. (Linda looked shell-shocked.)
WORKER: What happened when you didn't have the sessions, Mike?
MIKE: I got kicked out.
WORKER: Are you worried that the same thing might happen again?

Mike went on to say that he wanted to have the school work out for him. Linda explained to him what she'd disliked about previous family meetings. After some clarification of Betty's role and purpose in the meetings, Mike thought it would work and was first to sign the agreement, looking proud of playing his part. Betty and I told them that they'd both taken big steps in leveling with us and each other.

**Practice Points:** The social work student's school year and her work with this family were coming to an end. The worker initiates the conversation and we can see the ending stages described in Chapter 6 emerging as the worker must say good-bye to the family. By beginning the discussion of how the relationship had developed, she is also starting to help the client prepare for the transition to a new worker—a transition about which the client is concerned.

### April

At a regular evening meeting in early April, we'd been talking about endings, and Linda had been shocked at first that the time was so short and then angry at me for leaving and frustrated about having to start all over again with another worker.

> **WORKER:** I remember our first meetings, Linda. I wasn't sure if we'd be able to work together at all. I feel that we've come through a great deal together and it's been pretty shaky at times—you know the times we've both got pissed off. You've all made me feel welcome in your home, I've come to like you very much, and I'm going to miss you.
>
> **LINDA:** Then why are you leaving? I know you have to leave. Who will be my new worker?
>
> **WORKER:** That's something I've been checking out. You've said that you've had a hard time whenever a new worker is involved. (Linda agreed and said that she wouldn't fool around and be nice to a new worker she didn't like.) That's one of the things I really like about working with you—you give it to me straight. I was always confident when I felt like I'd blown it that you'd tell me. That's a feeling I enjoy. Also, I was honored last week when you told me that you trusted me—I knew that was hard for you to say—that's when you added "almost."
>
> **LINDA:** Well, I do trust you. (She laughed and added "almost.")

I explained that I'd talked to my supervisor to find out who'd be getting the Smiths after I left, and we talked about getting together in order to clarify what would be happening. The conversation continued around some of the snags we'd hit, how things were resolved, and what obstacles might come up. It hadn't occurred to me until that evening how much I'd become involved with the family, and the conversation about leaving really hit me.

### Current Status of the Problem: Where It Stands Now

Linda has begun to see the agency as an ally and took the opportunity to suggest a joint meeting with Debbie, who'll be the new worker, to establish a working contract. Brian has joined in the last four out of five meetings and has said that he's willing to help with Mike when Linda asks. She's agreed to include Brian in the weekly family sessions.

### Strategies for Intervention

- Betty will continue working with Mike until the end of June and will be available in September for schoolwork and family sessions.
- Debbie and I will follow up on our meeting to discuss future plans, and she'll be available to the Smiths and Betty.

- Linda, Mike, Betty, and I will visit another possible resource this week and discuss future plans.

**Practice Summary:** Note that the worker's analysis of the current status of the problem does not consider it "solved." Very rarely are problems solved; in fact, I encourage workers to remove that word from their vocabulary. What the worker does instead is identify important changes in the state of the relationship between the family and the agency and among the family members themselves. The worker has helped to build a platform for ongoing work. In the lives of these clients, he has been only an incident—but an important one. Keeping this perspective helps workers avoid two common types of mistakes in analyzing practice: overestimating or underestimating the impact on a client.

# The Ending and Transition Phase of Family Practice

The general principles and interventions associated with the ending and transition phase described in Chapter 6 can also be applied in the family situation. Recall that, in the beginning phase, family members face a first decision. They must decide whether they are prepared to engage with the worker—to lower defenses if needed with both the worker and the other family members and to begin to work. In the second decision, family members must agree to take some responsibility for their part in problems and to face the emotional pain involved in work. If there is a family secret, it must be revealed and addressed. In the third decision, clients must decide whether to deal with the most difficult issues as they approach the end of the working relationship. When these issues involve long-term family dynamics that have been reinforced on a daily basis over a number of years, the ambivalence is understandable.

The ending phase offers the greatest potential for powerful and important work. Family members feel a sense of urgency as they realize there is little time left, and this can lead to the introduction of some of the most difficult and important themes of concern. The emotional dynamics between the worker and the family members are also heightened in this phase as each prepares to move away from the other. Termination of the relationship can evoke powerful feelings in both the client and the family members, and the worker can often connect discussion of these feelings to the client's general concerns and tasks.

## Goals of the Ending/Transition Phase

Collins, Jordan, and Coleman (2007) describe the central focus of termination as

> evaluating whether work with the family has resolved the presenting problem. A related purpose is ensuring that progress will be sustained—a process that can occur only if the families develop the skills they need to resolve future problems independently after the FSW's involvement has ended.

These goals are appropriate as long as we recognize that the presenting problem may turn out to be the first offering of another problem. New issues may emerge during the work. On the other hand, if the presenting problem leads to significant work on the underlying issues, then in most cases the presenting problem will be resolved.

In addition, the goal of equipping family members to deal with future problems independently is important but may not be possible for all future problems. In fact, even families that do well in counseling should understand that, as difficult life transitions and crises occur in years to come, a return to family counseling may not be a sign of failure but rather of success. For example, consider the loss of a job by the wage earner or the deteriorating health of an elderly parent or the last child moving out of the home. For each of these events, short-term counseling may be helpful and more effective because of the previous experience.

I would expand on the description of the central foci of termination to include the following:

- The initial presenting problem has been resolved.
- Other problems that emerge during the sessions have been at least recognized, if not resolved.
- Family members have identified structural, communication, and other issues that led to the increased stress associated with the problems.
- Family members have developed skills that allow them to address future issues more directly and to identify those that will require that they seek more help.
- Family members have developed a positive attitude toward seeking help and helpers, and see it as a sign of strength, not weakness.
- Family members have learned how best to use help if it is needed again.

## Emotional Reactions to the Ending Process in Family Counseling

As detailed in the earlier example with Mike, Linda, and Brian, and in Chapter 6, both the clients and the worker may have some resistance to bringing the relationship to a close. In some ways, the worker has become part of the family for a period of time, sharing in its experiences and offering support. If the work has gone well, the members of the family have learned some of the skills needed to provide that support themselves. However, concern may still exist about being able to deal with the problems without the worker. For the worker, the emotional connection can be strong, and there may be reluctance to give up the relationship. Workers have said that, because so many of the mandated families they work with are resistant, they like to "hold onto" those with whom the work is going well.

The importance of pointing out the ending early—to allow all members of the family unit to experience the termination as a process rather than as something being done to them—is heightened by the fact that the family will continue after the counseling is done. They will need to deal with the stages of ending, using the death and dying framework described by Kubler-Ross (1969) and also explored in detail in Chapter 6. These stages are summarized as follows:

- Denial
- Indirect and direct expressions of anger
- Mourning
- Trying it on for size
- The farewell-party syndrome

## Ending the Sessions before they Are Finished

Collins et al. (2007) point out that families sometimes terminate prematurely and may do so indirectly:

Some may simply not be at home for a scheduled meeting, and others may call and cancel at the last minute. They may be difficult to get hold of after a failed appointment and the family social worker begins to suspect that the family is avoiding further contact.... Another hint that families are considering dropping out is when instead of expressing dissatisfaction with family social work, they talk about practical problems of participating in family sessions, such as missed work, having to reschedule other appointments, and so on. When the social worker begins to notice a pattern forming (two consecutive missed appointments), we suggest raising the topic for discussion, if the worker is able to make contact with them. (p. 354)

Of course, the complicating factor is that the client is a family, and some of the actions just described may well be dictated by one member—for example, the father—if discussion begins to approach areas of discomfort or a family secret. The whole family may indicate unwillingness to proceed, but this may not be the real desire of all of the family members. If possible, the family social worker should arrange at least one last session to discuss how the counseling sessions were experienced by all of the family members, what was learned, what were the problems (particularly if they did not find the worker helpful), and what they might do if they need help again in the future.

**EP 2.1.4c**
**EP 2.1.5a**

Another indirect way to prematurely end family work is to experience a "honeymoon" period in which all of the problems appear to be resolved and additional work is not needed. Collins et al. (2007) refer to "faking good" as a way to end the sessions when they become too painful or get too close to difficult underlying issues (p. 354). With mandated clients, endings may come when the counseling is no longer required; in most cases, this suggests that the family counseling never really started. By that I mean that an "illusion of work" has been undertaken, in which the counseling sessions represented the clients' effort to satisfy some outside agent (e.g., the court) rather than having made a real commitment to work.

## The Impact of Ignoring Issues of Race, Class, and Culture in the Ending Phase of Family Practice

The family social worker also has to be open to the idea that his or her practice, for whatever reason, was not helpful. It would be a mistake to always assume that clients are "resistant" when they prematurely end counseling, rather than being open to the idea that the worker was not helpful. This may be particularly true if workers have not addressed or overcome inter- or intracultural issues. An example is poignantly described in an article entitled "Taking Sides: A White Intern Encounters an African American Family" (Jacobs, 2001). The author describes his work with an African American family and his efforts to have the father sign a paper that agrees with the intern's report to the court. The report stated that Jack, the son in trouble with the court for assaulting another teen, had been scapegoated by the father and therefore should be released from juvenile detention. The father resisted signing a paper he believed to be untrue and disrespectful of his parenting; however, the mother insisted that he sign it so that they could get their son out of detention. The author writes:

My memory of this scene, after a decade of seasoning as a clinical and family psychologist, still makes me wince. The father's seething look, the mother's voice of resignation, evokes guilt for me that I forced them to choose between their son and their pride. What I thought of as a kind of gallantry at the time—young clinician going the extra mile for an embroiled teenager—mostly strikes me now as hubris. Yet in my own development the case has provided me with an education through hindsight in integrating individual and family considerations with the impact of culture and race. It was only by proving to be a danger to the disadvantaged black people I was attempting to help that I learned the wayward power of being a privileged White professional on a mission. (p. 171)

The case example ends sadly, with the son being released as the father and mother are ignored and embarrassed in the courtroom by the White judge. A conflict between the father and son eventually escalated, and the son was sent to foster care after being threatened by the father with a gun during a heated argument. The author is courageous in analyzing all of the mistakes he made, mostly by ignoring the cultural implications of a Black family from a working-class background who live in a middle-class, White community and have to deal with a White court, a White judge, a mostly White agency, and a young White worker. At the time, it would not have been unusual for the young intern to close the case file with a comment that the father was "resistant" and "hard to reach."

## Ending a Relationship with a Family Because of a Change in the Worker's Job Status

In the following example, a worker deals with an ending and transition as a change in job status causes her to transfer a case. The agency is Big Brothers Big Sisters, and the worker has been helping the mother to obtain services for her child and to cope with her own difficult issues. The worker has also worked with the child and the mother together. Because the clients who use service may have experienced losses in their lives (e.g., death or divorce), the worker must pay particularly close attention to the demands of the ending and transition phase of practice. This is another example of how workers can integrate process and content.

WORKER: I have some news that I need to tell you.
CLIENT (MOTHER): Don't tell me you're leaving the agency.
WORKER: No, I'm not, but I will become supervisor of our new office, which will cause me to have to transfer the families I've been working with in this area.
CLIENT: I'm so happy for you, but it will be difficult for us not to have you as our social worker anymore.
WORKER: I have mixed feelings also, because I'm excited about the new position, but it will be hard for me to give up certain people, like you.

After hugging, I said I'd be in touch to arrange a meeting with her and the kids to begin talking about the change. Later that week, we set up an appointment. The mother came in talking about what a difficult time her son was having due to rejection by his father and now her son's Big Brother was also rejecting him. I asked if he was also feeling rejected by me. The mother said that he was angry about finding out about the change by getting a letter, and he no longer felt special. I apologized for that and explained that I had meant to tell him myself but didn't get a chance before the letter was sent. I added that he is special, and that I was planning to tell him and apologize.

After discussing more issues related to her son's depression and making suggestions for follow-up treatment with the next worker, I asked how the mother was feeling about meeting another worker. She replied that she was ready. I commented on how nonchalant and accepting she seemed about the change, and I mentioned that I was feeling sad. The mother acknowledged that, like her other son, she tends to deny difficult situations and then "fall apart" later on.

I said that I hoped I wasn't pressuring her, but that I thought it was important for her to recognize how she was acting. She started to cry and said she was glad to have known me. She spoke positively about our relationship and how much she had grown through her involvement with the agency. I told her that I would miss her cooperativeness, kindness, and appreciation, and that the next worker would be lucky. Mention was made of how it had been difficult to keep the professional and personal issues separate, and how our relationship would change. We then embraced again and made introductions to the next worker. The mother did call once after the day of my meeting with her child, but she has not called since.

## Chapter Summary

The framework introduced earlier for analyzing the middle phase of work, as well as the ending and transition phase, can be adapted to these phases in work with families. Often crucial to making the transition to the middle phase of practice is the worker's ability to help a family deal with a "family secret." Emotional reactions on the part of the family and the worker in the ending and transition phase can have a powerful impact on the process. At times, family counseling may be ended by the family—directly or indirectly—before the worker believes the work is finished. In such cases, the worker needs to be careful not to always blame the family members for ending counseling and must, at times, examine his or her own practice for a possible source of the perceived failure.

## *Related Online Content and Activities*

 Visit *The Skills of Helping Individuals, Families, Groups, and Communities,* Seventh Edition, CourseMate website at **www.cengagebrain.com** for learning tools such as glossary terms, links to related websites, and chapter practice quizzes. The website for this chapter also features additional notes from the author.

## *Competency Notes*

The following is a list of Council on Social Work Education (CSWE) recommended competencies and practice behaviors for social work students defined in Educational Policy and Accreditation Standard (EPAS) and addressed in this chapter.

**EP 2.1.1b** Practice personal reflection and self-correction to assure continual professional development (p. 297)

**EP 2.1.4c** Recognize and communicate their understanding of the importance of difference in shaping life experiences (p. 309)

**EP 2.1.4d** View themselves as learners and engage those with whom they work as informants (p. 299)

**EP 2.1.5a** Understand forms and mechanisms of oppression and discrimination (p. 309)

**EP 2.1.7a** Utilize conceptual frameworks to guide the process of assessment, intervention, and evaluation (p. 295)

**EP 2.1.10a** Substantively and affectively prepare for action with individuals, families, groups, organizations, and communities (p. 295)

**EP 2.1.10b** Use empathy and other interpersonal skills (p. 295)

**EP 2.1.10c** Develop a mutually agreed-on focus of work and desired outcomes (p. 295)

**EP 2.1.10d** Collect, organize, and interpret client data (p. 295)

# Variations in Family Practice

M ost social workers who work with families do so in a setting such as a school, hospital, family counseling agency, and so forth. Because of increased acceptance as providers by health insurance agencies, a growing number of workers are involved in private practice. This text serves as an introduction to generalist practice; for this reason, I will focus on setting-based family practice. Although family social work takes place in most settings, it is widely used in child welfare agencies and schools. These two settings will illustrate how the core ideas presented in Chapters 7 and 8 are adapted to setting and service.

Family composition may also affect family practice, as we have already seen in Chapters 7 and 8. This will be further illustrated by a focus on special issues that may be raised in work with single-parent families.

# The Impact of Setting and Service

A child welfare agency is a good example of a setting in which functional clarity plays a crucial role in family practice. Examples of contracting with the biological parents in a family and, in particular, of dealing with the authority of the worker and the agency were discussed in Part II of this book. In this section, family practice variations associated with work in a child welfare setting are explored through examples that involve practice with two foster-parent families, with an 11-year-old child in residential care, and with a teenage mother. In each of these examples, the work involves helping the client deal with her or his family-of-origin issues at a point at which she or he is not living with the family. The examples illustrate that clients take their families with them wherever they go, and that families of origin can have ongoing and continued influence on a client's current experiences.

In the cases described here, both the mandate of the setting and the specific client problems related to that mandate give focus and direction to the family practice. In effect, this chapter will revisit the contracting idea introduced in Chapter 4. There, we learned that the worker's practice with a client must center on the common ground between the service of the agency or host setting (e.g., a school) and the felt needs of the client. This apparently simple, but actually complex and powerful, idea provides a boundary and structure that free the client and the worker to be more effective. The worker needs to be asking himself or herself, at all times, "How does this conversation with family members relate to our service and to the family's particular problem?"

**EP 2.1.10c**

## A Family's Fear of Invasive Practice: Subverting the Contract

The work must be guided by the specific agency function and not subverted by the worker or the clients and turned into family therapy. Fear of this outcome often causes clients to be defensive and resistant in early sessions. A family that is meeting with a school social worker about their child's educational problems will not necessarily appreciate the conversation turning to the parents' marital problems. Identifying marital stress as a factor that affects the child's schoolwork would be appropriate, as would a discussion of how to handle its impact on the child. It would also be appropriate for the social worker to offer to make a referral for the couple's marital problem.

The client's fears of invasive practice are not completely unfounded. Social workers who are unclear about the boundaries of their practice sometimes use the initial reason for the contact as an entry for family therapy. In one extreme example, a family support worker in a child welfare agency described working with a couple on their sexual dysfunction issues. Although the worker was originally referred to the family to help them with parenting problems that had led to suspected child abuse, the sessions with the couple revealed sexual problems that the worker had undertaken to treat through counseling. When I asked about the connection between this work and the agency mandate, the worker admitted that there was no connection. She went on to say that she had taken a course in counseling people with sexual problems, and that this seemed like a good chance for her to practice. This worker's subversion of the working contract was inappropriate for many reasons, not the least of which was that while she was busy doing sexual counseling, she was ignoring the parenting-focused work that was in her domain.

### Rural Areas and Limited Services

**EP 2.1.1a**

In rural areas, where few services are available, workers must often be all things to all people. I have described these communities in workshops as being so small that you can't go to a bar in town on a Friday night without meeting half of your caseload. I have often been told that this is not an exaggeration, and that working in these areas creates a number of problems. In some cases, workers may have to provide a range of services as the "only game in town."

Even in these situations, when workers must offer help that extends beyond the normal service of the agency, they bear the responsibility of trying to close the gap between client needs and available services through professional impact on the community. In other words, while the social worker provides additional services that are unavailable to clients in a community, he or she must also work with colleagues, the political system, the community leadership, and so forth to establish new agencies and/or new services. (The strategies and skills for this aspect of social work are discussed in more detail in Part V.) In trying to provide all services to all clients, workers often become less effective in providing the services that are clearly their responsibility. Each of the illustrations that follow will highlight this crucial idea.

## The Child Welfare Setting

### Work with Foster Parents

**EP 2.1.6b**
**EP 2.1.8b**

Child welfare family work often involves collaborative work with the foster (or group home) parents or child-care workers in residential settings. (This is sometimes referred to as "ongoing" or foster care work, as compared to the initial investigation, intake, court work, etc.) Both the worker and the alternative parent often misunderstand the role of the social worker (Shulman, 1980). On one end of a continuum, foster parents may be viewed as clients. On the other end, workers may ignore important signals from foster parents concerning their need for support. In reality, foster parents and other alternative caregivers are collaborators in the process of buffering the traumatic experience of children who find themselves in short- or long-term care.

The positive impact of alternative caregivers is described in resiliency research (see Chapter 2), and the potential contribution to the foster child's plasticity is described in the life-span theory and research. These findings suggest that attention to the foster parents as contributors to the child's developmental reserve capacity can contribute significantly to the child's growth. The social worker can play an important role in mediating between the foster parents and the child, the agency, the natural family, the foster parents' own family, and other systems in the community, such as health care providers and the school.

## Potential Problem Areas in Work with Foster Parents

In my own work with foster parents and from my research studies, I have identified several areas in which problems may emerge. First, the foster parents may feel unappreciated and undervalued when the agency and the social worker make decisions without consulting them—the very people who may know the child best and will have to deal with the results of the decisions. Some foster parents report feeling particularly bitter when the agency or the workers tell them they are the most important members of the team and then proceed to ignore them.

Second, difficult foster children can raise problems in the foster family between a foster mother and father, or in relation to other children in the foster family. Foster parents have described feeling torn between the needs of their own children and the demands placed on them by needy foster children.

Finally, of all the issues raised in my workshops, two of the most difficult pertain to two kinds of worker overidentification with the foster child. The first results in unrealistic expectations for a return home, and the second results in anger and rejection of the biological parents. The following examples illustrate these two problems.

*Supporting the Foster Parent as She Supports the Foster Child* In the first example, the social worker tries to help a foster parent of a 9-year-old child deal with the child having been removed from his family.

**EP 2.1.10b**

**Practice Points:** The social worker's role is to try to provide a source of support for the foster parent as she attempts to help the child. By recognizing the foster parent's caring for the child and her difficulty in dealing with the child's pain, the social worker strengthens the foster parent in her difficult role.

> Mrs. Edwards, foster mother of 7 weeks to 9-year-old Tony, phoned me at 9:00 A.M. She told me in an angry, excited voice, "I had to call you and tell you that you need to hear the things that Tony told me this morning before he went to school. You people have things all wrong. I am convinced that the agency and that private school have done this boy and his family a grave injustice." I immediately thought to myself, "What has this kid cooked up now?" I said that this sounded serious and asked her to tell me more. She said that Tony insisted that his father had never beaten him and that his mother had never locked him out—he had just refused to go in the house and had gone away. Furthermore, Tony told her that he had decided to leave his last foster home 2 weeks early because he didn't want them to adopt him.
>
> I asked Mrs. Edwards why she thought Tony was telling her these things. She replied, "Because he wants me to help him get home—he trusts me and he's

hurting so bad that I told him that I'd get you to listen to him." I promised Mrs. Edwards that I would listen to Tony, but not on the phone as she suggested, because he played games on the phone and got her and himself upset in the process. I arranged to be there at 2:00 P.M. to talk to her before Tony got home from school.

**Practice Points:**   It's important that the worker not allow the foster parent's apparent panic to set off a similar reaction in the worker. It is not unusual for a worker when hearing this level of emotion and reaction from a foster parent to begin reacting with concern for maintaining the placement. Instead, it's important to understand that even though the foster parent is not a client in a strict sense of the word, the foster social worker's role does include providing support and helping the parent to understand the child's (and parent's) behavior. This is another example where the worker has to be with the child and the parent at the same time. Note her ability to empathize with the foster mother's reaction to seeing the child's sadness and pain.

When I saw Mrs. Edwards, we went over Tony's stories again. It appeared to me that Tony was using the information shared with him by another worker a month previously (when he decided to go home and not wait to be adopted) in an attempt to force me, through Mrs. Edwards, to get him home now. I reminded Mrs. Edwards of the tiny boy she had told me about, whom she had once fostered. He had been hospitalized after a beating from his mother, but had welcomed his mother when she had visited him in the hospital. Mrs. Edwards responded that it was the same with Tony—blood is thicker than water—but she felt it would help Tony for me to listen to his story. He needed to be believed.

I told her that I felt that Tony needed most to know that she and I were on his side and would help him to get home, but that going along with his tall tales was not helping him wait or helping him learn to get along with people. Mrs. Edwards replied, "But he's only a little boy, he feels all alone and wants to get back to his mother." I said, "You really hurt when Tony is hurting, don't you?" She agreed that she was a "softie" and that Tony really got to her with his constant appeals for help to get home.

**Practice Points:**   The worker in this excerpt avoided the mistake of identifying solely with the needs of the child. The two-client idea (the term *client* is used loosely when referring to this foster parent) is illustrated when the worker understands Tony's needs and those of the foster parent at the same time. In addition to providing emotional support, the social worker offers resources, including herself, to help the foster parent get the child through the stress of the court process. An agency will often tell foster parents that they are the most important members of the foster care team while simultaneously excluding them from any significant planning or decision making. This foster parent can instead be brought into a collaborative process by discussing a plan with the social worker. The worker should also convey the importance of involving the child in the discussion.

We discussed how the agency might see Tony through the waiting period until court on November 30. A child-care worker to take responsibility for Tony after school was not acceptable to her—Tony needed to come home to her and discuss the school day and do his homework. Talking to a psychiatrist not connected with the agency or with the court appealed to Mrs. Edwards, although she felt Tony should not be told that he was seeing a psychiatrist. She agreed when I pointed out that this would not be fair to Tony or the psychiatrist and could not work because of Tony's alertness. We decided to ask Tony what he thought about this idea.

**Practice Points:**   In the next excerpt the worker picks up on the indirect communication about reliability. When the foster parent says that Tony feels she is the only one he can rely on, the worker assumes she is indirectly being critical of the worker for her absence during the first month of placement. The worker accepts responsibility for this and contracts to be more available to both the child and the foster parent.

I suggested to Mrs. Edwards that Tony took advantage of her fondness for him and her wish for him to be happy. She replied that she knew he did, but he made her feel like she was the only one he could rely on. I told her that he could rely on me as well and that I could understand why he had doubts, since I had been absent during the most upsetting month of his stay in care—in other words, I had deserted him when he needed me. I told her I would try, with her cooperation, to spend more time with Tony and to reassure him that he would go home. I did not mention that she had balked at many of my attempts to see Tony during the early weeks of his placement in her home. Mrs. Edwards said that this should help a lot.

I told her why I thought that Tony was attempting to discredit the evidence used in court, pointing out that this was a plucky attempt on his part to take the responsibility for having been left in Canada by his parents, but reminding her that this information was in writing from Tony's mother, and that, although I was committed to returning Tony home, it could only be done through the court. Mrs. Edwards said she understood this.

**Practice Points:**   In the excerpt that follows after Tony arrives home the worker gently confronts him about his version of events shared with the foster parent. It's important for the foster parent to understand that in a desperate attempt to be sent home, even if it is a home that may have been abusing, Tony will say whatever he feels will get the foster parent on his side.

Tony arrived home from school, gave me a fleeting greeting, collected his Halloween candies, and ignored Mrs. Edwards's request that he tell me what he had told her that morning. He finally went outside, and Mrs. Edwards turned to me in consternation and commented that she couldn't understand this behavior. I told her that it was OK if he wasn't ready to share this with me, as he probably hadn't decided whether he could trust me or not. After two more excursions in and out of the room and a brief period at his homework, Tony offered me a candy and sat down with us. Once more, Mrs. Edwards urged him to tell me what was on his mind. Tony looked me straight in the eye and said, somewhat defiantly, "I told her I left Susan's 2 weeks early because I didn't want to be adopted by them." I told Tony that this wasn't the way I remembered it happening, and reminded him of visits and discussions about his leaving Susan's home, including his statements to me at the time. Tony wiggled a bit, conceded that was the way it had happened, shot Mrs. Edwards an amused glance, and looked at the floor. Mrs. Edwards's mouth was open. Then Tony looked up and told me firmly, "But my father never beat me!"

I told him that I wasn't going to get into a discussion of what had gone on in his family, because he had made his choice to return home and my job was to help him do this. I said to him, straightforwardly, "The fact is, your mother left you in Canada, didn't she, Tony?" He nodded, looking at the floor once more. I went on to say, "The law in Canada is that, when children are left by their parents, the case has to go court and the judge has to decide if you will go home or go for adoption. I'm asking the judge to send you home because your mother wants you and you don't want to be adopted." I asked Tony if that was what he wanted. He said yes, with fervor. I told him, OK, we all agree that's what we're working for.

**Practice Points:** Clients and foster parents may have the wrong perception about the decision-making process when potential neglect and/or abuse is involved. In the last analysis, the difficult decision about sending a child back home versus deciding on a "permanent order" that makes the child a ward of the state is always made by the judge. Social workers and other professionals can make the recommendation, but as one family court judge said to me during an early research project: "In the last analysis I'm the one who has to take the child away from his parents permanently and it is a very difficult responsibility." After reassuring Tony that the worker will help him with his goal of returning home, the worker returns to Tony and the issue of his acting out behavior at the home.

Now what could we do about the time between now and November 30? Tony observed brightly, "It's my birthday on November 7 and I'm having a party at McDonald's." I said that would be great, but what I meant was that things had to be a lot more peaceful in the Edwards home if Tony was to go home in good health and well behaved. Tony glanced at Mrs. Edwards, who chimed in, "I've been telling Donna that you're a hard boy to live with sometimes." I told Tony that I felt that a lot of his behavior toward Mrs. Edwards and the girls (her children) was way out of line, so much so that I wondered if he really wanted to stay there until he left for home. Tony had been looking at me, but when I referred to the misbehavior toward the girls, his eyes glistened and he smiled a smug secret smile that caused Mrs. Edwards to widen her eyes in dismay.

I told Tony that it was up to him to improve his behavior, since I knew that he was capable of this, and that I wanted to be able to tell his mother that he was happy, healthy, and well behaved when he left for home. When I asked Tony if he thought he could make this effort, he looked at Mrs. Edwards with an appealing smile and told me, "Yes, I'll try." We discussed whether or not it would be helpful to him to talk about his situation with someone outside the department and the court and, despite Mrs. Edwards's encouragement to do so, Tony declared that he didn't want to talk to anybody else. He then asked for permission to go outside and play.

Mrs. Edwards and I had a brief discussion of our talk with Tony, and she acknowledged that she had been taken in by him and that she now realized it had been deliberate. I, in turn, tried to get across to her the need to provide a structured, calm atmosphere in order to keep Tony on an even keel until he returned home. Although Mrs. Edwards verbalized intellectual understanding of this need, I was not assured that she could put it into effect, because of her own emotional needs.

**Practice Points:** The worker has begun to address the meaning of Tony's behavior but needs to focus further on the connection between Tony's acting out and his hope that he can return home. Teenagers have sat on the front porch of a new foster home, suitcase in hand, refusing to enter and demanding that they be returned to their natural parents. Foster children of all ages often act out in their alternative-care setting, thinking that if they are rejected there they will most certainly be returned home. When their acting out behavior affects the foster parent's natural children, it can lead to a call to remove the child. However, the acting out often leads to the child being placed in a new foster home instead of returning home. Foster parents need help to understand the meaning of the behavior, and the children need assistance—from the social worker and the foster parent—to deal with the pain of rejection.

*Foster Parent Anger over Erratic Visits with the Biological Mother* In the next example, an erratic visiting schedule with the biological parent has upset a young teenage boy in care and angered the foster parents. The family support worker (not the social worker responsible for the case) needs to help the foster parents deal with their own feelings so that they can help the child with his. The anger toward the biological parent is, in part, a cover for their pain at sensing the child's hurt. One role of the social worker is to help the foster family tune in to the meaning of the "deviant" behavior of the biological family members. In this sense, the foster parent also has two clients: the child and his biological parents. Before any work can be done, the worker must demonstrate a capacity to tune in to the foster parents. In the excerpt, the worker arrives at the foster home prepared to drive the child to his home for a visit only to find out the visit has been canceled. The worker's report follows:

EP 2.1.7a
EP 2.1.7b
EP 2.1.8b

> I drove up to Ann and Tom's home. Kevin was standing outside with a friend. He ran up to my car and said, "I'm not going." I said I didn't understand. "Going where? What do you mean?" He replied, "I'm not going away this weekend. No one can take me." I said, "I'm taking you." He said, "No. No one can take me to their house. My grandmother is taking two of my sisters, and she's tired and can't handle any more. My aunt is going away and my other aunt just moved and doesn't have a telephone." I said, "I'm sorry." He shrugged, looked away, and said, "That's okay. I've got stuff to do around here this weekend."
>
> I said, "I was looking forward to taking you up. I also wanted to meet your grandmother." He asked, "When can I go home?" I asked him, "To Edison?" which is where his mother and stepfather live. He nodded his head yes. I asked him if he had talked about this with his mother and stepfather. He looked at the ground and shook his head no. I asked him how his conversations with his stepfather were going. He said, "Good." I asked him if they had discussed the fight or had just blown it off like it didn't happen. He said they had blown it off.

**Practice Points:** In the next excerpt the worker tries to help the foster parents deal with the behavior of the biological mother and the child's stepfather, which has an impact on their ability to schedule their life but also affects them as they see the impact on the foster child.

> I told him to talk about it with his mother and stepfather and see what they said. Then, if everyone felt comfortable, I would talk about it with his child welfare worker and maybe we could arrange a visit. He walked back over to where his friend was waiting for him, and I went inside to talk to Ann and Tom. Ann immediately started talking about how she couldn't believe that his family

had cancelled his visit. She said, "They just don't want him. How could you do that to a child?" I said, "He must be very disappointed." She made a noise and said, "Yeah, he is." Then she started talking about how a previous foster child was supposed to come visit her this weekend, as well as Tom's son. She also made a comment about how it would be difficult to keep Kevin occupied to keep his mind off his disappointment.

I said, "Kevin's family canceling the visit must be hard for you too. You have other plans, and you thought that Kevin was going away for the weekend." She reluctantly agreed. She said, "I just wish they had given us more notice. He has been planning on going all week, and they just call up the night before and say, 'You can't come.'" I said, "You are right. Their not giving more notice is not fair to you or Kevin. I will call them next week and discuss visitation. You shouldn't be expected to always conform to their schedules; they need to compromise and work with you. Kevin's feelings need to be considered, too."

She appeared relieved that I would address this. Tom entered the room and also began discussing how "Kevin's family doesn't want him." He said, "That kid isn't going home, I can feel it in my gut." Ann expressed her anger and repeated, "How can you do that to a kid?" several times. I listened to them, but added, "We can't assume that his family doesn't want him." I asked Ann if she voices these concerns to Kevin. She said she does not. I told her that, as a person, she was free to vent her frustration with his mother to me, but as a professional, she must try not to let her anger get in the way of working with his mother. She said she understood.

**Practice Points:** The worker needs to integrate support for the foster parents (empathy) with a gentle confrontation that reminds them of their professional responsibility. Their anger at the parents and their concern for the feelings of the foster child are understandable; however, their role as foster parents requires that they develop the skills needed to tolerate deviant behavior and reach for the meaning behind it—easier to do with the child than the biological parent.

Tom expressed his feeling that Kevin needed to face the reality of not being able to go home because his family did not want him. I told him that I did not know what was going to happen when it was time for Kevin to leave our program, but I would ask the child welfare worker what the alternative to his going home would be. I also stated that he and Ann could help Kevin by developing some of his independent living skills. I took out a skills assessment, and we went over it together. We targeted some of the areas where Kevin might need their supervision, such as nutrition, what to do if there is an emergency, and so on. While we were going over this, Kevin came inside to tell Tom something. Tom asked him, "Are your ears ringing?"

Kevin looked confused and said, "No." Tom said, "Well, we are in here saying a lot of good things about you."

**Practice Points:** The worker was supportive and offered to intervene with the biological parents to address limit-setting and visiting issues. She could, however, have taken this conversation even further. After tuning in to the foster parents, the worker could have explored with them the meaning of this erratic behavior by the biological parents. Were they canceling the visit because they did not care or because they cared too much? What current stresses influenced their capacity to take care of Kevin? In addition, because contact between foster parents and biological family members can become extremely negative in such circumstances, the worker should consider with the foster parents how they might deal with the interaction. Was there a way to recognize the biological family's difficulty while sharing their own issues with regard to the missed visits and short notice?

The foster parents want the biological family to be more understanding of the child's feelings, and one way to do this would be for the foster parents to express some understanding of what the biological parents are going through. The interview continued with the worker addressing the feelings of the foster child. However, the intensity of those feelings of rejection resulted in the worker changing the subject to one that was less painful to the child (and to herself). This is an example of how a worker's use of an assessment tool can block the immediate work instead of deepening it.

Kevin smiled and ran out. I followed him outside a few minutes later to talk to him. We sat down, and I started by telling him a few of the things Ann, Tom, and I had discussed, such as his family contacting him earlier in the week if he couldn't go there for the weekend. I then said to him, "You must be disappointed about not going home." He said, "Yes." I reminded him that I was not opposed to his visiting Springfield (an aunt's hometown) if it could be worked out between him and his mother and stepfather. He said, "My aunt didn't call like she said she would."

We were silent for a minute. Then I told him that I had brought him some exercises to work on since he wasn't in school. He asked me, "What does this have to do with school?" I said, "Well, it's not reading, writing, or arithmetic, but these exercises will give you something productive to do." He said, "Well, if I get real bored, I'll take a look at them."

At this point, Ann yelled out the window at his friend who was still in the yard, and the friend started walking away. Kevin asked him where he was going, and he responded that he'd be back in a minute. I said, "I know there are a lot of distractions and you probably want to get back to what you were doing, but I have one more thing I want you to look at." I pulled out a family assessment. I said, "This is something to help you figure out ways your family interacts with each other. I made two copies for you so you could do one on your foster family and one on your other family." He said, "I don't know about my other family. I haven't been there so long." I said, "Well, do the best you can. We might be able to figure out things that need to happen in both families to help you feel more safe and comfortable." He said, "Okay. Leave it here and I'll do that one this week." Kevin started telling me about some of the yard work he and Tom were doing.

**Practice Summary.**   Working on a regular basis with children in pain can have a secondary effect on workers. In Chapter 17 we look at the issue of secondary trauma and the impact on workers who deal with pain and loss. It is not that they don't care and emphasize it is often that they care too much. This brief incident should be discussed with a supportive supervisor. Kevin was starting to talk about the rejections in his life and the worker had difficulty staying with the feelings.

## Work with Children in Residential Care

Children end up in residential care for a number of different reasons. For some, appropriate foster placements are not available or the children have been through a number of placements without success. The children may have special physical or emotional needs and need services only available in a residential setting. For some children, with a history of some forms of violence against themselves or others, residential settings are needed for containment. Whatever the reason for the placement, these children are physically and at times emotionally cut off from their families of origin.

A key element of treatment and care is the day-to-day contacts with residential counselors, medical and teaching staff, and others, who are responsible for helping the residents deal with the setting and each other. These staff members serve as substitute parents and their interaction with residents can have a most profound impact on the children. Informal activities, for example, in game lounges or at meals, or work training opportunities provide chances for staff to model a different kind of adult than those the children may have been used to in their families. Formal sessions, such as group "house" meetings to discuss the rules and procedures of living together, also offer an important opportunity to help residents develop more mature approaches to dealing with the different crises and conflicts in their lives.

***Understanding Acting Out Behavior as a Form of Communication*** Supervision and peer case conferencing in these settings are important because staff members have to deal with children who can be difficult in that they communicate their feelings by acting out. For example, one staff member in a workshop I led described a 12-year-old resident refusing to get out of bed on Monday morning to go to school. This provoked a confrontation and a battle of wills leading to the staff member restricting privileges and ordering detention in the "time out" room for the day.

**EP 2.1.1a**
**EP 2.1.1f**
**EP 2.1.9b**
**EP 2.1.10b**

In this case, the log kept by the weekend staff indicated that this had been the third weekend in a row where parents had promised to visit and not shown up. With help from a supervisor or the social worker, the staff member could be assisted in understanding the "deviant" behavior as a call for help. The youngster had learned to use the "fight" part of the "fight-flight" mechanism described earlier in the book to avoid facing painful feelings. Rather than getting into a battle of wills, a skilled counselor could point out that he or she knew the child was upset, angry, and hurt because of the lack of visiting but that getting into a fight this way was not going to really help. The child might still have privileges limited, but would know he or she had been heard.

In another example, it is not unusual to see residents exhibiting increased acting out behavior as a holiday season approaches. For some, the idea of going home to visit their families raises anxieties that are expressed through behavior. When the staff threaten to withhold the home visit privilege, this may, in some cases, be exactly what the resident wants whether aware of this or not. Children who are not going home can also act out their feelings of being abandoned and alone. In one residence for teenagers, two residents described going to a movie house on Christmas day and finding they were the only ones in the theatre. Social workers can often play an important role as members of the staff team in helping the whole system consider the impact of family, present or long gone, on the day-to-day activities of the children.

Social workers in such settings also provide individual and group counseling and serve as the connection between the children and the referring agency (e.g., child welfare), the court, the school (at the residence or in the community), the nuclear and extended family, and other systems that may be important to the children. Social workers may also work with the direct child-care staff, helping them to understand the behavior of the residents and intervening in their direct care professional roles, which most often do not include ongoing personal counseling. In effect, the work involves helping the child deal with the substitute residential family consisting of adults and peers.

Finally, one more often-taboo subject needs to be raised in considering issues that may arise in residential settings. Many of the children may come from significantly dysfunctional families and have experienced physical, emotional, or sexual abuse. Some, unfortunately, may have experienced abuse in the foster homes that were supposed to provide them with a safe haven. It is not uncommon for those who were abused to become predators themselves in a residential setting, seeking out weaker and more vulnerable youngsters for exploitation. Because of the discomfort of staff in this sexual area, behavioral signals may be missed that the setting itself is now replicating the abusive situations the children thought they were leaving behind when they left their homes. The abused become abusers and a cycle continues. An important role of social workers may be to help colleagues address these issues and to provide leadership in developing a program that attempts to break the cycle.

Thus, in a residential setting the social worker may work with the immediate and extended family as well as the residential family. The goal would be to help the resident deal with the immediate, ongoing and historical issues that may negatively impact on her or his life.

***Social Work Behind the Steering Wheel*** In this illustration, a worker helps an 11-year-old boy in residential care explore the connection between his feelings of loss and rejection and his ability to cope in the setting. In this example, the worker deals with the client's family issues even though the biological parents are not directly involved—one can do family work without working with the whole family. In this case the social worker has planned to take the child to visit a caring grandmother to help maintain some family connections.

**Practice Points:**   The example also illustrates how work with children often takes place in nonstructured settings. This could be called "steering-wheel" or "fast-food" social work. In residential treatment settings, where so many other children are around and competing for attention, a child needs to use these opportunities to capture the worker for his or her own needs. The issues, as in the example that follows, are often raised indirectly.

> On October 15, Danny and I visited his grandmother. She is a terrifically "grand-motherly" lady who obviously cares for Danny a great deal. She, in fact, has no use for her daughter for rejecting Danny. Danny's birthday was the next day, and the occasion for our visit was to pick up his present and for me to meet her. We spent about 2 hours there—a very pleasant afternoon—and Danny was relaxed on the drive home.

**Practice Points:**   On the drive home Danny uses an indirect way of getting to a painful family experience. The worker's first response is to preach to Danny about his behavior. Note that at one point the worker realizes he is not sure where the apparently casual conversation is going and thus begins to listen more intently.

> Our conversation turned to Halloween, which Danny said he was looking forward to because he didn't get to go out last year. I asked why. He said that last year he'd stolen 50 cents from a friend of his, and his mother found out and put him to bed right after supper. I asked him if he'd repaid the money, and he said yes he did, when he got some money later that week. I asked why he'd

taken money from his friend, and he said, "Well, he had money and I didn't." When I glanced at him he hung his head. I said, "Oh." But before I could make a further comment, he said that one time he'd stolen $4.65 from his mother and bought a whole shoebox full of bubble-gum cards. He said his teacher at school had found out about how he'd gotten them and made him rip them up and throw them away. His mother hit him and sent him to bed. This was relayed rather bitterly by him.

I was unsure at this point just where our pleasant car-ride conversation was headed, but I decided to explore how he was feeling about how he was handled by his mother versus how the teacher handled him. When I asked him how he felt about having to throw the cards away, he said "awful," because he wanted to give the cards to friends. I asked him if he thought it was fair, and he said yes, that he shouldn't have been allowed to keep them. When I asked the same questions about what his mother had done, he said that he got hit a lot whenever he'd done anything wrong, and it hurt when he got hit, but it also made him mad.

**Practice Points:**  With interventions that are designed to explore further why Danny is raising these issues, the worker quickly gets to Danny's experience of abuse at the hands of both his mother and his stepfather.

I asked him if he'd ever expressed this anger directly to his mother, and he said no—if he did, she (or her boyfriend) would have probably hit him more. He went on to say that Dale (his mother's boyfriend) had noticed 25 cents missing one night on returning from work and had really gotten angry. Although it was past midnight, Dale went into Danny's room and pulled him into the kitchen by his hair, and, in the final pull, Danny crashed into the table and knocked over a glass, which broke. Danny said he then had to sweep up the mess and was hit by his mother with a yardstick and sent back to bed.

**Practice Points:**  At this point in the interview, the worker was probably feeling the pain involved in the child's description of the abuse. An understandable resistance to exploring this pain, coupled with a lack of clarity about his role, caused the worker to respond as a "teacher-preacher": He used the child's description as an opportunity to teach a lesson. This missed the signal of the child's real work and illustrated the problem described earlier as *functional diffusion.* Fortunately, the worker caught his mistake—when the child gave him another chance—and made a "second offering" of concern.

Danny's voice in this recital was getting more and more strained, and he sounded angry. I didn't answer for a couple of minutes (for one thing, I wasn't sure of how to respond), and Danny calmed a bit. Then I said, "Well, it sounds like Dale and your mom were really fed up and angry with your stealing from them and other people. I guess I wouldn't like it much if you stole a lot around me either." He said, "I wouldn't steal from you, and besides, you don't hit me." I said, "No, I wouldn't hit you, even if I was really mad at you for stealing."

I obviously still wasn't getting his point, however, because he was very tense and tight in the seat. He then said, "What would you do if your kid was fighting at school and got hurt and had a bloody nose and you had to leave work to take him to the hospital?" This came out in a rush and he started to go on with his "hypothetical" example when I interrupted him and asked if that had happened to him, and he said, "Yes."

WORKER: What did your mother do, Danny?

DANNY: She got mad at me for fighting.

WORKER: Well, I wouldn't be very happy if you got into a fight at school.

DANNY: I don't blame you. Kids shouldn't fight.

WORKER: I guess I'd also be concerned about how your nose felt. It must have hurt a lot if you were going to the hospital.

DANNY: That's what I mean!

WORKER: (To myself) I think I finally got it.

DANNY: All she did was nag me about how she had to leave work to take me to the hospital and how it upset her to do it, and she never once asked me how I felt about having a sore nose!

WORKER: That must have felt really awful.

DANNY: Yeah!

WORKER: Like she didn't care about you, only the problems you caused her.

DANNY: Yeah, all she did was nag, nag, nag about having to leave work and how it was stupid to fight.

WORKER: I guess you already knew about the fighting; you had the sore and bloody nose to prove it.

DANNY: (Laughing) Yeah, and it was the only time she ever had to do anything like that, but she acted like I did it all the time, and I didn't. I know you're not supposed to fight, but kids do anyway sometimes.

WORKER: It must have been hard for you to act like a kid around your mother.

DANNY: Yeah, especially with Dale sticking his nose in all the time.

**Practice Points.** The issue of Danny's painful relationships with his family finally emerged, although it surfaced just as the worker drove into the center parking lot. This is often how the client asks, "Do you really want to hear about this? Do I really want to talk about this?" It is a good example of "doorknob therapy," only the doorknob is on the car. If the worker uses the arrival as an excuse to back off, the message to the client will close down the discussion. By continuing the discussion, the worker is saying to the client, "I'm ready if you are."

> At this point, we were a block away from the center, but instead of turning right onto the side street, I turned left into the parking lot of a park. He asked why I'd done that, and I answered that it seemed to me that we were having a pretty good talk and that I wanted it to finish a bit more naturally than by pulling into the parking lot and getting mobbed by the rest of the kids. He said all right and settled back in his seat.

WORKER: What do you mean about Dale "sticking his nose" into things?

DANNY: My mom and Dale would have meetings to discuss things and then they would vote on it.

WORKER: What did you vote on?

DANNY: We voted on my bedtime. I wanted to stay up 'til 9:00 P.M., but my mom wanted me to go to bed at 8:30 P.M., so we voted on it, and he voted for her.

WORKER: Wow, that sounds like they were sort of ganging up on you and pretending to be fair. He agreed and said that they did that a lot. I asked if he was glad to be away from his mother, and he said yeah—that she didn't know how to treat kids and that all she did was nag or get mad and then stay mad, and he alluded to an incident that we had talked about before. I said that he must have gotten pretty angry sometimes when he was at home. He said yes and started sobbing. He said that he wished that she was right here now so he could tell her how much he hated her. I said he could hate her all he wanted, and I didn't blame him.

**Practice Points:** At this moment the flood of emotions from Bobby causes the worker to identify with him; however, he fails to reach for the pain and the deep desire of Bobby to have a mother who loves him.

He said that sometimes he felt like going by where she lived and throwing rocks through all the windows. I said it must have been hard to be angry a lot of the time he lived at home and not be able to tell anyone. He said that he'd like to tell her now and talked about how he'd like her to be a target in a shooting gallery so he could shoot at her. He laughed then and said that was a joke. I said he was saying that he was really angry, joke or not. He had relaxed somewhat by this time and said yes, he was angry.

**Practice Points:** Having listened to the child's pain, the worker next made a connection between his family experiences and life at the center. The child had another social worker who focused on the ongoing relationship to family members. This worker would later share this information with the other worker, but, at this point, our worker was concerned with the relationship of the child to the center (staff, other residents, and so forth) and to other parts of the child's life, such as school. In the following comments, the worker attempted to acknowledge the painful feelings and to connect the discussion of the family experience to life at the center.

I said that he got angry a lot at little things around the center and sometimes screamed and raged at the adults. He agreed and said he thought it was good at the center because he could get mad and nobody held it against him. I said yes, it was OK at the center to get angry and let people know about it, but maybe sometimes he wasn't yelling at the person he was really angry with. He said yeah, that sometimes he was really feeling angry with his mom and the least little thing would set him off. I said that he must have his mother and home on his mind a lot, and he said that he thought about it "sometimes," especially bedtime, but during the day, too.

I said that I thought I understood some of how he felt and that I was feeling right then really sad and hurt for him, and is that what he felt like, especially before he got angry, did he feel sad and hurt by his mother? He said yes, that most of the time before he got angry he felt hurt and that would help get him mad. I said that maybe he could come and tell me when he was feeling sad or hurt because he was thinking about his mother and home. He perked up a bit at this and said sure, he'd try to do that, but why? I said that maybe if he did that, then he wouldn't have to get angry with the wrong person. He said maybe, but what would I do? I said, "Well, if you come and tell me when you feel hurt and sad, maybe we can just sit and feel hurt and sad together." He looked at me for a couple of seconds and smiled and said "OK." I gave him a small hug, and we started back for the center.

**Practice Summary.** In this last excerpt, the worker focused on helping the child to develop more adaptive ways of obtaining social support when he hurts. The flight-fight mechanisms for dealing with pain are counterproductive. The child needs to learn how to make close connections with others who can help to fill the gap in his life left by parental abuse and abandonment. The worker has made a nice connection between the feelings of the client and the purpose of their work together.

## Work with Teen Parents and Their Families of Origin

Children having children is a problem in North America. The stress of having to meet one's own teenage developmental needs, while simultaneously trying to meet the needs of a child, often results in a call for help through behaviors that bring the child welfare agency into the picture. In the following example, a family support worker attempts to help a teenage mother cope with her own feelings of rejection by her family of origin so that she can receive the support she needs as a parent under stress. The following excerpt is taken from the 15th session of counseling with Mary, a 17-year-old who is the mother of a 2-year-old daughter.

### Children Raising Children: Work with a Teenage Parent

**Practice Points:** In the following example, the client has avoided dealing with the painful issues associated with her estrangement from her family of origin. She has been raising what I referred to earlier in the book as "near problems"—real problems but not the core issues. The worker believes that the relationship—rapport, trust, and caring—has developed enough to allow her to confront the client and ask for real talk on this issue. Note that the worker is not fooled by the casual way the client describes a chance meeting with her father.

> Mary says that she has had little contact with her original family since she became pregnant. She has not wanted to talk about her family with me and has focused on her relationships with her boyfriend and foster mother. I felt that she might be ready to talk about her family, and I was looking for signals from her. Mary said that her father was shopping in the same store as she was this week. I asked what had happened. She answered, "Nothing." I smiled and asked her what happened when nothing happened. She laughed and said he pretended that he didn't see her. I asked her how she felt when he did that. She said, "I didn't care. He makes me laugh because he is so messed up." I said that when she says nothing happened, she seems to mean that they didn't speak to each other. I said I wonder if it really feels like nothing happened when her father passes her as if she didn't exist. She said that she really doesn't care.
>
> I said that I have known Mary since September and have seen her go through some really difficult situations. She has had some big fights with people close to her; she has had her boyfriend sentenced to 12 to 15 years in jail. However, in all this time, only once have I seen her with tears in her eyes. She asked, "When was that?" I answered that it was after the sentencing, when she said that her child would not have a father just like she didn't and that it was so important to her that her daughter have it better than she did. Mary thought a moment and said that I was right. She really has a lot of feelings, but she can't talk about it. I asked her why she thought it was so difficult to talk about it. She said because it is so painful. I agreed with her. I asked her what she thought happened to painful feelings that a person can't talk about. I asked her where the feelings go. She said that she keeps them buried inside. I asked her if they stay buried.

**Practice Points:** By persisting and making what I have called the "demand for work," the worker sends the message she is ready and she thinks Mary is also ready to get to the most difficult issues. When the client says she does not want to talk about these feelings, the worker responds skillfully by asking why she thought it was difficult rather than just accepting the resistance and moving off the difficult subject. She also helps the client to understand how ignoring the feeling does not make it go away.

She smiled and said she had a dream about her father after she saw him in the supermarket. In the dream, her father and mother were both in the store and, when they saw her, her father gave her mother some money and said to buy Mary whatever she needs. Mary said she knows what the dream means, but she doesn't want to talk about it. I said that she may not be able to talk about it today, but that she has done some really important work today. She took a tremendous step in moving from her statement that she has no feelings to saying she has a lot of feelings, but it is a difficult and painful subject to talk about. I said that she is sharing some feelings with me, but she is also saying that she needs to go slowly because it is so hard for her. I said that I would try to help her progress at a pace that is OK for her. I said that we know that there is some important work for us to do even if it is just a little bit at a time. Those bottled-up feelings are fighting to get out.

Mary was silent for a little while, and then she changed the subject. This was the first time that Mary discussed her father beyond the statement that they don't get along. I felt comfortable with the way I had handled this situation. I challenged her to work, gave her support, recognized her difficulty, gave her praise for beginning, and gave her permission to proceed slowly with my support. Finally, I gave her the opportunity to choose to continue or to change the subject, knowing that we have agreed that it is an important area for us to work on. In the two sessions we have had since this meeting, Mary has been able to talk in detail about her family relationships.

**Practice Summary:**  Emotional support is one way Mary can get the help she needs to provide good parenting to her toddler. The worker persisted in reaching for the feelings of loss in relation to her father but still allowed the client to remain in control over when and if they would be explored. It is not uncommon that raising the issue and giving permission to explore it while still reassuring that the client remains in control of the discussion is followed the next session with a full discussion.

In one of my child welfare research projects described earlier, clients reported that, in addition to emotional support, concrete support was also crucial (Shulman, 1991). To meet her own developmental needs, this client will require adequate financial support, child care, alternative schooling possibilities, respite care (someone to give her a break from child-care duties), and so on. If this mother chooses to keep her child, the "goodness of fit" between her developmental needs and these formal and informal resources may mean the crucial difference between success and failure (Germain & Gitterman, 1996).

# Family Practice in the School Setting

In this section, we examine family practice in a school setting. A common mistake mentioned earlier is to view the school setting as a place to provide mental health services rather than seeing the social worker's role as directly related to the educational mission of the school. If we use the mediating concept, we can envision a student reaching out for his or her education—with whatever ability he or she has available—and a school, administration, teachers, and staff committed to providing that education. This symbiotic relationship can be frustrated by obstacles that are associated with the student, the family, the community, the school, or its staff. In

Part V of this book, I illustrate the important work done by social workers to impact the school system itself. For now, the focus is on the student and the family.

*A High School Freshman with ADD*   A 15-year-old high school freshman had been diagnosed with an attention deficit disorder (ADD) that affected his ability to negotiate his educational experiences. The social worker in this setting attempted to mediate between the client and his family, as well as with other professionals in the system. Although our general understanding of ADD is increasing, family members and teachers often fail to understand the impact of this disorder and attribute the problems to "lack of trying" or "laziness." The following illustration, in the form of a record of service, examines the social worker's efforts over time as she became clearer about her specific role in the educational setting.

**EP 2.1.1a**

**Practice Points:**   Before we proceed, a comment is needed on the worker's use of activity to try to engage the teen. Activities can be used with children and teens as a medium to create a comfortable setting for conversation. However, this informal activity should not take the place of early conversation about purpose and role. In this case, the worker had not effectively contracted with the client and used the activity to fill the time. It is not unusual for workers to feel that they need to "establish a relationship" through small talk or an activity before they can get to work. Nothing could be further from the truth. The working relationship is a result of the work, which requires clear contracting. Although activities can be useful, they do not substitute for effective contracting. In spite of the lack of contracting, the client raised several important themes of concern.

### Client Description and Time Frame

The client is a 15-year-old freshman, male, Jewish student. The time frame was from October 19 to March 22.

### Description of the Problem

Jack is a young man who experiences considerable difficulty in dealing with his family and school system because of the effects of attention deficit disorder.

### Summary of the Work

*October 19 (Second Session)*
I wanted to find out how Jack was adapting to his new school. We began by talking about the fact that Jack had been absent last week. Since he is a freshman, I wanted to find out if he knew what he had to do to get his absence excused, and if he had gotten his makeup work from his teachers. When I asked Jack how his classes were going, he said that he had received a supplemental (warning notice) in civics. We talked about how he could get help on his homework from the Remedial Services teacher. I should have asked Jack more about the situation—how he was getting on with his teacher, how his parents reacted to him getting a supplemental. I could tell he was becoming uncomfortable but, rather than acknowledging that, I allowed him to change the subject. We talked about the World Series and the earthquake out in San Francisco.

*October 26 (Third Session)*
I asked Jack to choose the activity and take some responsibility for the session. I asked Jack to choose the game. He decided on checkers, and we began to play. After a few minutes, Jack asked me if I had taken drafting in high school. I said that I hadn't—was there a special reason he was wondering about it? Jack replied, "Because I'm having trouble in drafting—I can't finish any of the assignments."

I asked him what about drafting was keeping him from finishing the assignments, and he said, "It's just too hard." I asked him what part of it was hardest for him, and he said, "The measuring. If you have one line out of place, you get a zero." I said that I had taken mechanical drawing in junior high and that it is difficult and frustrating because it is so precise. Jack agreed but said that it wasn't really a big deal, because drafting was only the first 6 weeks of his Exploratory Shop class and it was almost over anyway. I said if it was frustrating him, I thought it was important. I offered to act as the mediator, but I didn't make Jack part of the process. I suggested that I talk with his drafting teacher and Remedial Services teacher to see if we could work together to make it easier for him. Jack agreed that I could do that.

**Practice Points:**  The two-client concept has been emphasized in most examples. In this one, the second "client" is the school system itself. In Part V of this book we examine in more detail the concepts and skills involved in working with this second client. Note how in the beginning the worker's identification with the client causes him to miss the issues for the teacher and the school.

This interview led to a lot of running around. However, I did not take time to tune in to the other members of the system. I had my own agenda. After having seen the difficulty Jack had with hand-eye/fine-motor coordination last week when we played the game with the blocks, I was not surprised to hear that he had trouble in drafting. I spoke with the drafting teacher, who showed me one of Jack's papers. All of the lines were crooked, and I could tell that Jack had erased many times to try to get the lines straight. The drafting teacher said he couldn't understand why Jack couldn't make the lines straight. I said that Jack obviously has some trouble with this, and that we needed to find out how to help him.

I did not empathize with the teacher. In fact, I felt annoyed that he hadn't recognized the trouble Jack was having and told someone in the Special Needs Department. I then went to talk with the school psychologist about all of the testing in Jack's file. I wanted to know why Jack was having trouble and what we could do to help him be more successful in drafting. The psychologist took one look at the test results and said that a child with Jack's deficits shouldn't even be in such a class, that all of the testing showed that he wouldn't be able to do it. I was somewhat flabbergasted by this statement and confused by the fact that Jack was put in this class in the first place if the testing showed he couldn't do it. I was intimidated by the psychologist's authority. I asked her if there were any more tests to be done or any methods we could use to help Jack learn to measure. She said that all of the testing had been done, and that Jack should be removed from the class. I knew that she was giving up on Jack, and I felt uncomfortable about this, but I didn't verbalize it.

**Practice Points:**  I believe the worker had trouble continuing the conversation because of the anger, self-recognized, toward the teacher. Once again, the worker would like the psychologist to tune in to Jack but is not tuning into the psychologist. This is a common problem, since while most professionals are told of the importance of "teamwork," they are rarely trained in the how—the interventions and skills—to make the team work. This will be discussed in detail in Part V when we deal with working with the system.

I then spoke with Jack's mother (who would have to give permission for Jack to drop the class). She said she wanted him to stay in drafting, that he probably wasn't trying hard enough. She said that he usually didn't try hard enough and wasn't motivated. I did not explore this statement or reach for the mother's feelings. At this point, I was identifying so strongly with Jack's predicament and how nobody wanted to help him that I was very angry with all of these authority figures. I said that I would see if Jack's Remedial Services teacher could help him learn how to measure.

I was very surprised that Jack's mother would not acknowledge that there must be more of a problem than just not trying hard enough when a 15-year-old can't draw a straight line, but I did not try to find out what was going on. I then went to see the Remedial Services teacher, who said that she had her hands full helping Jack with his other classes and didn't know anything about drafting anyway. I didn't offer the teacher any support. She suggested that I ask Jack's special needs math teacher to help him. So I went to see the math teacher, who said that he would help Jack learn how to measure. Jack remained in drafting class and did a little better during the remainder of the 6-week period until they switched to a new area of study.

**Practice Points:** While the worker may have obtained some help for Jack in this particular class, he had not addressed the real issue of the way the school and his family related to Jack around his special needs. On a systemic level, the issue may really have to do with how the school views and deals with all special need students.

Over the next several weeks, we settled into an illusion of work. Jack and I continued to play games in our sessions. Jack was very uncomfortable and restless if we did not play a game, but when we did, he would open up and talk about himself. It became apparent that his mother hassles him a lot, always trying to get him to try harder. Jack became more able to talk about his feelings.

### Last Week in January

Jack's mother called me and said that she was concerned because Jack had not been bringing any homework with him from school, and she thought he should have some. She said that Jack told her that he did his homework in Remedial Services, but she didn't know how that could be so, since he was getting such awful grades. I offered to act as the mediator between the systems, but I didn't actively include all of the parties involved. I said that I would mention her concerns to Jack, and if Jack agreed to it, I could go around and find out if he had been doing his work. She said that would be helpful to her and that it was really hard for her to get time off from work to go to the school. I told her I would call her back in a couple of weeks.

### February 1

I worked to maintain Jack's trust by including him. I told Jack that his mother had called me about him not having any homework. I told him that I had been careful not to reveal to his mother anything that we talked about in our meetings. Jack said that it was fine with him if I checked around with his teachers about his homework, because he was doing it anyway. We talked a little about how hard it is when your parents don't believe you.

I spent the next couple of weeks going around to all of Jack's teachers. I started out with the Remedial Services teacher and the special needs math teacher, both of whom said that Jack wasn't the best student, but he came to class and handed in his assignments. At this point, I think I was still overidentifying with Jack. I was looking for evidence that would show that he was doing his best, so I didn't explore very much with these teachers. When I talked with the mainstream teachers, they all said that Jack was doing OK work (in the C range), handing in his assignments, and behaving well. I found out that Jack did have some difficulty with hearing and remembering instructions given verbally by the teachers and that he would sometimes blurt out answers before the teacher finished asking the question. I knew from the research I was doing into attention deficit disorder that these were common symptoms, and I found myself a little annoyed that none of the teachers seemed to be helping Jack with this (for example, by writing things down on the board).

**Practice Points:**   How one defines the problem is crucial in most cases. Is the problem, as Jack's mother believes, that he is not doing his homework or is the problem the communication pattern between Jack and his mother around his schoolwork and his special challenges? I would maintain it is the second, so finding out if he is doing his work is not an answer to the problem. We also get a hint of the difficulty faced by the mother, a single and working parent, in being able to monitor and be actively involved in her son's school progress. The mother's insistence that the problem is Jack's motivation is also a clue to the difficulty she may have in accepting that he has a learning disability. For Jack to get the support and help he needs, this denial must be addressed. The worker's suggestion in the next excerpt that they all meet—Jack, his mother, the teachers, and so on—is a start to addressing the communication and understanding issues.

Before I had the chance to call Jack's mother back, she called me, saying that she had found two supplemental reports in Jack's pocket when she was doing the laundry. The reports were from the Remedial Services teacher and the Special Needs math teacher. I told her I was surprised that he had received reports from those classes because I had just spoken with those two teachers within the last couple of weeks, and they had given me no indication that they were planning to send home a notice. I volunteered to take the role of the mediator, this time suggesting that all parties take an active role. I suggested that perhaps it would be a good idea if we set up a time for a meeting. The meeting would include the two teachers, Jack, his mother, and me. I explained that maybe, if we sat down together, we could figure out some strategies to help Jack do better. Jack's mother agreed that a meeting was a good idea, but she said that she thought the problem was that Jack wasn't motivated enough. We agreed on a time for the next week, and I told her I would call back to confirm after I had spoken with the teachers and Jack. The teachers were open to the idea of a meeting, and, in our next session, Jack and I talked about it.

### March 8
Jack started out by saying that things were going better in school lately except that he didn't like Remedial Services. I asked him what he did not like about it. I made a demand for work, asking Jack to define his own needs. He said, "Well, she makes up all of these rules like we have to come in and sit down and go right to work. We can't talk to each other at all. In classes like shop, we get to talk to each other while we work." I asked him if it was hard for him to sit there and work the whole time without talking. He said that it was hard, and usually he ended up forgetting and talking anyway. I said that it's hard when people expect you to do something that's really hard for you, and he agreed.

We went on talking about the meeting. Jack asked if everyone was going to yell at him and be mad that he was not doing better. I told him that I couldn't promise that there wouldn't be any yelling, but that the point of the meeting was to find out what we need to do to help him learn better, and that sometimes when people care, they yell. I tried to reframe the situation. We then went on to talk about how this can tie in to his mother nagging him about school, that maybe it wasn't just because she wanted to bug him but because she really cares about him. We talked a little bit more about what Jack could expect the meeting to be like, and I told him that his input would be very important, that he had just as much to say as anybody else, and that I would support him.

I later called Jack's mother back to confirm the meeting and talked with her a little more about the purpose of the meeting. I found that we really had the same objective in mind, even if we had a different way of looking at it. I spent a lot of time over the next week doing research on ADD and tuning in to Jack, his mother, and the teachers.

*March 16*

Jack's mother arrived early for the meeting, which gave us a chance to get a little bit acquainted. I wanted to establish a rapport with Jack's mom, to tune in to her position and try to get her to work with me. I said that I was really glad that she had come, and that I could tell she was really concerned about Jack and I thought it was very positive that she was so invested in making sure that Jack did well in school. I told her that a lot of parents aren't that interested in how their kids are doing, and that having a parent who really cares makes a big difference for the kid. I also said I thought it must be really frustrating for her. I had seen Jack's file, and it was filled with years and years of evaluations and testing, yet things were still difficult. Jack's mother agreed and seemed to relax a little.

**Practice Points:**   The worker has shifted his focus and now seems to understand that the best way to help Jack might be to help his mother. One gets a sense that the worker is now with Jack's mother, the second client, more than he had been before.

Jack and the teachers arrived, and we sat down in the conference room. I wanted to defuse any of the defensiveness people were feeling and set the stage for some work to be done right at the beginning. I introduced Jack's mom to the teachers and said I wanted to thank everyone for taking the time to be here, that our objective was to figure out how to help Jack to do better in school. I said that I knew everyone was working really hard already on this and that we weren't here to criticize anyone or get down on Jack, and I thought that if we worked together we might come up with some new ideas. I said that Jack's input would also be important, and I wanted him to share his ideas with us too.

I said I thought we could start out by hearing from the teachers. I asked them to tell about how Jack was doing, and to talk about not only the things that needed improvement but also the things that Jack was doing well. Each teacher took a turn, and when they brought up behaviors that were related to the ADD, I made a point of stating that those behaviors were tied to the ADD and not lack of control on Jack's part.

Jack's mom spoke next, saying that she still thinks that the problem is that Jack needs to be more motivated and try harder. I made a demand for work, asking Jack to say what he really felt. I asked Jack what he thought about that. He said it was probably true. I said that I thought he was trying pretty hard already and that some of the things he was being asked to do were difficult for him. Jack looked relieved and agreed that he does try, but, no matter how hard he tries, everyone always asked him to try harder.

We then went on to talk about ways to help Jack remember to bring his books and pencil with him to class, and how his mom could help him at home. The teachers came up with some really good ideas, and, as the meeting ended, everyone thought the strategy was worth a try. We agreed to reevaluate the situation in about a month, and the teachers left. Jack, his mother, and I continued to work a little longer, talking about how they relate to each other at home. Once again, I tried to reframe their views of each other, and I gave them some suggestions about working together. This seemed quite successful, with Jack and his mom laughing a little and expressing some affection to each other.

*March 22*

I asked Jack to evaluate the meeting, to continue participating actively. We began by talking about the meeting with Jack's mother and teachers last Friday. I asked Jack what he thought about the meeting. He said that it was OK. I said that I thought it had gone well, that we had made some progress, but I had wondered what it had been like for him to sit in the meeting. He said that it hadn't been as bad as he thought it would be. I said that it is hard to sit in a meeting when it is about you, and that I thought he had done really well. Jack smiled. I asked him how things were going now with his mom. He said they were still arguing a little over school, but that the new ideas were helping.

### Current Status of the Problem: Where It Stands Now

A couple of weeks later, Jack's mom called me again to talk about how things were going. This time, I found myself really empathizing with her on the phone. In talking with her, I found out that in all the time that Jack has been diagnosed with ADD, no one had ever given her any real information about it or suggestions on how to deal with a kid with Jack's special needs. All this time, I assumed somebody had given her that information and advice. I offered to photocopy an article I had about guidelines for living with a child with ADD and a list of some good books on the subject. She sounded really interested, and I mailed the materials off to her.

It then occurred to me that, if nobody had spoken about these things with Jack's mother in all this time, probably nobody had spoken with Jack, which turned out to be the case. Since then, Jack and I have done some work on what ADD is, what might cause it, and what the treatment is. Jack said that, all this time, he thought that the ADD symptoms he experienced meant that he was stupid. I've learned never to assume that the obvious work has already been done. Even though we have not yet had our meeting to reevaluate the situation, Jack already seems to be doing better and feeling better about himself.

### Strategies for Intervention

- Work with Jack on strategies to cope with the ADD symptoms (i.e., ideas for helping him to remember things and to expand his attention span).
- Find information about a support group for parents of children with ADD for Jack's mother. This would help her learn more about ADD and talk with other parents about strategies to cope with and help Jack.
- Work with Jack on expressing his feelings with his mother in a more constructive way, to help their communication. Additionally, help Jack speak up more to his teachers and ask them to repeat directions or write them down on the board.
- Continue to work on the idea that the ADD symptoms are not Jack's fault.
- Help Jack learn to work effectively with his parents and teachers.
- Work on termination/transfer issues, including any ideas for talking with Jack's classroom teachers for the upcoming year and preparing them for his special needs.

**Practice Summary.** By staying focused on education-related issues, and by bringing into the picture as many members of the family and school system as possible, the worker mobilized all parties involved to help Jack overcome the deficit and succeed in school. The repeated statements by the mother that all Jack needed to do was try harder may have been a signal to the worker of an important area for discussion with the mother—her feelings about his academic problems and her difficulty in accepting that he may have physical barriers to success. The worker might want to explore the meaning of education to the mother's family and the cultural significance of education as well.

## Work with a Single-Parent Family

**EP 2.1.4a**

At minimum, having a professional "friend" with whom to discuss a child's progress can take a significant load off of a single-parent client. Our old view of the average family as a working father, a mother at home, and two to three children has become more myth than reality. The rate of growth of single-parent families is increasing. At one of my speaking engagements on the subject of working with single parents, I asked the audience—all helping professionals—how many of them were single parents, had been children in homes of single parents, or had close relations who were involved in single parenting. Almost two-thirds of the 500 people in the audience raised their hands.

Although single-parent and two-parent families have much in common, they differ in several ways that helping professionals should note. Single parents have to face many of the same normative crises faced by other families, but they have to face them alone. Most single parents are women, and a large percentage of these must either work (often in low-paying, low-status, dead-end jobs) or depend on welfare. Furthermore, the welfare reform law has set a 5-year limit for receiving welfare, so that many families face the possibility of losing—or have already lost—welfare payments. For many, the lack of affordable day-care facilities makes working, and therefore improving their financial situation, impossible. Between low pay and welfare, most single-parent mothers must try to live on income levels below the accepted poverty level—a factor that significantly increases the stress of raising a family alone. This, combined with the limited availability of decent-paying jobs, does not bode well for single-parent families.

Housing is another major area of distress for single parents. Many housing options are not open to them, and, as a result, they need to pay more of their income for housing than the general population does. A female single parent quickly discovers that her credit rating left with her husband, even if she had a positive relationship with her local bank while she was married. She may suddenly find herself in a catch-22: She needs a positive credit record to get credit, but she needs credit to get a positive credit record. Thus, if she wishes to purchase a home, she may run into discrimination that keeps her from improving her housing situation.

Single parents also face special problems in dealing with friends. Many single parents report that, after their divorce, former close friends change their attitudes toward them and take sides. Another common factor is the "Noah's ark syndrome," in which friends seem to operate under the general belief that people should come "two by two"; thus, they are less welcoming to a single friend. Old friends slip away, and new friends are harder to find. This problem, often compounded by the single parent's depression and lack of effort to create new support groups, leads to further isolation and loneliness. With these added pressures, a single parent often has difficulty finding time to meet her personal needs while still taking care of the needs of the children. Dealing with school meetings, dental appointments, homework, sports activities, and so on is difficult enough for two parents.

In addition, dealing with the feelings of one's children when one is so vulnerable can be hard to do alone. As a result, barriers start to grow in a family, and certain areas become taboo. One crucial taboo area may be the feelings of the children about the absent parent and the rejection they feel. As one woman said in a group I led for single parents, "It's hard for me to help my kids face their rejection, because I still haven't been able to face mine." The guilt felt by the remaining parent often makes an honest discussion with the children difficult. The children may show signs of distress through behavior cues appropriate to their age. For example, young children regress and wet the bed; latency-age children cut themselves off from friends, have school trouble, and get into fights; and teenagers get into trouble with the law or may become sexually overactive or begin to sample the readily available drugs. In such cases, the parent often senses the cause; however, the parent's guilt can create a significant communication blockage that prevents work on the problem.

Ongoing relations with the ex-spouse can also take a toll on the parent and the children. Often, the battles of the marriage or feelings concerning the split emerge with regard to custody issues, financial support issues, and struggles over loyalty. Children already hurt by a split between their parents, for which they may feel responsible, are further distressed by feeling they must take sides and cannot be loyal to both parents at the same time.

## Practice with Returning Veterans and Their Families

During the past 10 years U.S. military forces have experienced numerous combat tours in Iraq and Afghanistan, creating significant stresses and resultant trauma for themselves and their families. With recognition that ongoing and posttraumatic stress is having such a powerful impact, significant services have been mobilized to address the problems. Social workers and other helping professionals in existing VA hospital inpatient and outpatient programs, as well as contracted employees assigned for periods of time to provide services on U.S. and overseas military bases, have focused on issues involved in three developmental stages of deployment. Fenell and Wehrman (2010) describe them as follows:

> The model is divided into three developmental stages with each having distinct and identifiable stressors experienced by the service member and family: preparation for separation, separation and reunion. (p. 53)

The authors suggest that when families receive the news of the deployment the *preparation for separation* stage begins by helping children and adults express their fears and encouraging adults to respond directly to indirect cues from the children. Concrete steps required to prepare for the uncertainties are also explored during this stage. During the actual *separation* stage of the deployment, with the soldier in a combat zone, parents are faced with often overwhelming demands to provide caregiving to the children. Efforts need to be made to establish some form of communication (e.g., e-mail, chat, telephone); however, a balance between too little communication leading to increased anxiety or too much communication leading to distraction for the deployed soldier needs to be established and maintained. As with all stressful situations that are anxiety-provoking, the signals may emerge in indirect forms such as children having problems at school, parents experiencing depression or overuse of alcohol, and so on.

The third stage of the cycle, *reunion,* occurs as the family anticipates and prepares to be reunited. This is a time of excitement and anticipation, but it is also a time of concern for some families. The service member often returns from combat expecting the family to be the same as it was before the deployment; however, this is rarely the case. (p. 54)

Both the family members and the service member have changed during a 12- to18-month deployment, and adjusting to these changes can be complex and difficult. Sexual difficulties and abuse of alcohol and drugs are often reported, as are increased rates of suicides or suicidal ideations. With the significant number of service members returning with physical or emotional challenges, including amputated limbs or PTSD, counseling may be crucial to help in the adjustments that need to be made.

Both returning service members and their families may face these stresses behind a wall of denial and be reluctant to seek professional help. Alright and Rosellini (2010) suggest a number of questions that the service member or family member can be asked designed to determine the degree of need for counseling. They suggest that even one or two "yes" answers means the client may be opening the door to seeking help at a higher level of care. The questions are:

- Do you feel pushed and shoved to the breaking point at times?
- Do you ever feel like you can't think straight?
- Do you ever feel as if you might start screaming or crying and not be able to stop?
- Do you fly off the handle over little things?
- Do you feel overwhelmed much of the time?
- Is your stomach tied in knots or do you feel pressure and choking sensation in your throat or chest?
- Do nameless fears and a sense of doom plague you?
- Are things so bad that you want to hide or jump in your car and keep driving?
- Have you lost hope? Do you feel your efforts to make things better are futile, so you've given up trying?
- Do your thoughts scare you? Do you sometimes feel like you might hurt someone?
- Do you ever think you would be better off dead?

Even reviewing this list of questions brings home the powerful impact of these deployments as well as our responsibilities as citizens and mental health professionals to provide the help needed by both the deployed and their families who have sacrificed so much following their sense of duty.

## Chapter Summary

Family social work includes work that centers on agency mandates to address particular problems. Contracting and boundaries for service play a crucial role in these cases. The common ground between the services that arise from the agency mandate and the client's perception of need gives direction to the work. Taboo areas in the family present special challenges to workers trying to achieve specific goals. Family work can occur in many settings, such as child welfare agencies or schools. Unique issues in family practice with a single-parent family also need to be taken into consideration. Increasingly, family work with deployed soldiers and their families is moving to the forefront of social service needs.

---

## Related Online Content and Activities

 Visit *The Skills of Helping Individuals, Families, Groups, and Communities,* Seventh Edition, CourseMate website at **www.cengagebrain.com** for learning tools such as glossary terms, links to related websites, and chapter practice quizzes. The website for this chapter also features additional notes from the author.

---

## Competency Notes

The following is a list of Council on Social Work Education (CSWE) recommended competencies and practice behaviors for social work students defined in Educational Policy and Accreditation Standard (EPAS) and addressed in this chapter.

**EP 2.1.1a** Advocate for client access to the services of social work (pp. 315, 323, 330)

**EP 2.1.1f** Use supervision and consultation (p. 323)

**EP 2.1.4a** Recognize the extent to which a culture's structures and values may oppress, marginalize, alienate, or create or enhance privilege and power (p. 336)

**EP 2.1.7a** Utilize conceptual frameworks to guide the process of assessment, intervention, and evaluation (p. 320)

**EP 2.1.7b** Critique and apply knowledge to understand person and environment (p. 320)

**EP 2.1.9b** Provide leadership in promoting sustainable changes in service delivery and practice to improve the quality of social services (p. 323)

**EP 2.1.10b** Use empathy and other interpersonal skills (pp. 316, 323)

**EP 2.1.10c** Develop a mutually agreed-on focus of work and desired outcomes (p. 314)

# Social Work with Groups

In Part IV, we explore the interactional model of practice in the context of social work with groups. We describe the dynamics of mutual aid that can occur when a group of clients with common concerns is brought together for the purpose of helping one another. You will find that many of the processes and skills discussed in Parts II and III of this book can be used in the group context. We also explore some of the unique features of group method, as well as specific obstacles to mutual aid.

In Chapter 10, we explore the preliminary phase in group work starting with a discussion of the group as a mutual-aid system. The specific mutual-aid processes are discussed and illustrated. We also review the principles of group formation including the crucial preparatory work that needs to be done with prospective members as well as staff in the system. In Chapter 11, the beginning phase of group work practice is examined in detail. Chapter 12 explores the middle phase of practice, with special emphasis on the importance of working with two clients: the individual and the group. Finally, Chapter 13 examines the ending and transition phase of practice in relation to groups.

# The Preliminary Phase in Group Practice: The Group as a Mutual-Aid System

Although there are many different group purposes, models, and structures serving different populations in different settings, the potential for facilitating some form of mutual aid exists in all groups. The mutual-aid process in which members are a source of help for each other is a central concept in this framework for group work. I believe mutual aid can be integrated as an element in group practice that uses other theoretical frameworks (e.g., psychodynamic, solution-focused, cognitive-behavioral, motivational interviewing). The resilience discussion in Chapter 2 underlined how important social support can be as a buffer and a protective factor. The mutual-aid process in a group is a form of social support that can provide that help. Whether the group is a support group for the elderly, a substance abuse prevention or recovery group, or a counseling group for children who have lost a parent or someone else close to them, providing and receiving caring and help from other members is one of the major reasons we work with people in groups.

Since I will be discussing and illustrating how the mutual process works, and how the group leader helps to make it happen, I will use this chapter to describe and illustrate the dynamics of mutual aid that can occur when a group of people with a somewhat common agenda and similar concerns is brought together. The reader will find that many of the processes and skills discussed in this chapter are equally applicable when working with individuals and families; however, my focus is practice in the group context. I will also highlight the unique features involved in the use of group method, as well as specific obstacles that need to be overcome to create a mutual-aid system. I will outline the mutual-aid processes and examine the role of the group leader in the group.

## What Is Mutual Aid?

**EP 2.1.1b**
**EP 2.1.7a**

In a seminal article introducing the *mutual-aid* concept, Schwartz (1961) defined the helping group as follows:

> The group is an enterprise in mutual aid, an alliance of individuals who need each other, in varying degrees, to work on certain common problems. The important fact is that this is a helping system in which the group members need each other as well as the leader. This need to use each other, to create not one but many helping relationships, is a vital ingredient of the group process and constitutes a common need over and above the specific tasks for which the group was formed. (p. 18)

The idea of the group as a "mutual-aid system" in which the leader helps people to help each other is an attractive one, yet it raises many questions and doubts in the minds of students and workers whose experiences in groups, as members and leaders, have led them to question the potential of mutual aid. Exactly how can a group of people sharing the same set of concerns help each other? Isn't it a bit like the blind leading the blind? How will members be able to talk about their most intimate concerns before a group of strangers? What about the coercive power of the group? How can individuals stand up against the odds? What is the job of the group leader if the members are helping each other? These questions and others are legitimate. They sometimes reflect leaders' past group experiences, which may have been hurtful, nonproductive, or boring—far from being enterprises in mutual aid.

My response is that the potential for mutual aid exists in any group, but simply bringing people together does not guarantee that it will emerge. Many obstacles can block the group members' ability to reach out to each other and to offer help. Many of these are similar to those observed in individual counseling, but their effects can be magnified in the group context. Because all members will bring to the group their own concepts, based upon past experiences with groups (e.g., school, camp, committees), and because many of these past experiences may have been poor ones, the group leader is needed to help the group members create the conditions in which mutual aid can take place. The tasks of the group leader in attempting to help group members develop the required skills are related to these obstacles.

Developing mutual aid in a group is a complex process, with members having to overcome many of their stereotypes about people in general, groups, and the helping process itself. They will need all the assistance they can get from the group leader. Since the leader has also been affected by past group experiences, one of the leader's early tasks is facing her or his feelings and examining stereotypes. Without this self-examination, the leader may be unable to convey to the members a belief in their potential for helping each other. Faith in the strength of the group will make an important contribution to the group members' success in their struggles.

In the balance of this chapter, I will begin to address the leader's hesitancy and questions by listing some of the ways in which group members can help each other; these are the processes of mutual aid. The obstacles that can emerge to block this potential are briefly reviewed. An overview of the role of the group leader is then presented.

## The Dynamics of Mutual Aid

In the chapters that follow, the mutual-aid process will be described in detail and illustrated with examples from a range of groups. To assist the reader in conceptualizing mutual aid in a general way, a number of illustrations are presented here.

### Sharing Data

**EP 2.1.10e**
**EP 2.1.4d**

One of the simplest and yet most important ways in which group members can help each other is through the sharing of relevant data. Members of the group have had different life experiences, through which whey have accumulated knowledge, views, values, and so forth that can help others in the group. For example, in a married couples' group I led described in detail in Chapter 11, one of the couples is in their late sixties. They have experienced many of the normal life crises as well as those imposed by societal pressures (e.g., the Great Depression of the 1930s). As other group members who are in their fifties, forties, thirties, and twenties describe their experiences and problems, this couple is often able to share an insight that comes from being able to view these crises from the perspective of time. As the group leader, I often found myself learning from the experiences of this couple. We created in the group a form of the extended family in which one generation passed on its life experiences to the next. In turn, the older couple was able to use the group not only for their immediate problems but also as a place for reviewing their 50 years together. (This may be an important part of their work at this stage in their life cycle.)

In another group, working mothers were able to share ideas that have proven helpful in organizing their daily routines. The power of the Internet allows many group members to have access to information about resources that would never have been available before. Members shared the names of community services that they had discovered, and each mother tapped the experiences and the ingenuity of the others. Whether the data consist of specific tips on concrete questions (jobs, available housing, money management, and so on), values, or ideas about relationships, each member can contribute to the common pool of knowledge. The leader will also contribute data which, when combined with that of the others, provide a rich resource for the members.

In a group of persons with AIDS who were in early recovery from substance abuse (referred to as an AIDS/recovery group and co-led by this author), specific information about the recovery process and coping with AIDS and its treatment was shared on a regular basis. For example, one group member told another, "This is the start of your second year in recovery—the feelings year—so don't be surprised about all of the pain you are feeling because you don't have the drinking and drugging to cover it up." At another meeting, group members shared their experiences with the, at that time, new triple-drug therapy and provided information for those who were not in the trial groups about how to get connected.

**Practice Points:** In the example that follows, group members provided tips on how to increase one member's chances for acceptance into a special housing program for people with AIDS. My job as group leader was to help connect the group to the member to facilitate this form of mutual aid.

> I pointed out that, earlier, Theresa had mentioned her interest in getting into this independent living facility. I wondered if we might help her just by addressing that issue, as well. She told us she was concerned about putting an application in because she didn't think she had established enough credibility in her single-room occupancy housing. At this point, Jake and Tania started suggesting strategies and ideas about how to approach the living facility and what would maximize her ability to get in. They strongly encouraged her to make an application right now, since there were openings and a few months down the road these openings might close, and there would be no place for her. They said they thought it would be wonderful if she could move into the building.
>
> Tania (a transgendered member) pointed out that the building—if you looked at it—the building was supposed to be for people with AIDS, but, if you took a look at it, your guess would be that it was essentially for gay men. She said she was the only woman in the whole building—the only single woman in the whole building. She said to Theresa that if worse came to worst, you could always tell them it's discrimination, and that'll get their attention. She said, "That's how I got in."
>
> They continued to talk with Theresa about ways she could demonstrate her responsibility, things that she had done, her commitment to recovery, the fact that she wanted to leave the place she currently lived in. Even though it was supposed to be a safe building everybody knew drug dealing was going on there all the time, and it was scary to be there. She took it all in, thanked them for their advice, and said she was going to apply.

### The Dialectical Process

An important debate of ideas can take place as each member shares views on the question under discussion. Group members can risk their tentative ideas and use the group as a sounding board—a place for their views to be challenged and possibly changed. It is not always easy to challenge ideas in the group, and I will discuss later how such a "culture for work" can be developed. When this kind of group "culture" is present, the argument between two or more members takes on a dialectical nature. Group members can listen as one member presents the "thesis," and the other the "antithesis." As each member listens, he or she can use the discussion to develop a personal "synthesis."

An illustration of this process occurred in a couples' group I co-led when one couple in their late sixties discussed a problem they were experiencing with their grown, married children. They described their negative perception of the way in which their children were handling their marital difficulty and how this was affecting their marriage. As they spoke, I could see anger in the eyes of a younger couple in their twenties. They were experiencing difficulty with the wife's parents, whom they viewed as "meddling" in their lives. When I reached for the verbal expression of the nonverbal cues, the battle was on. The older couple had to defend their perceptions against the arguments of the younger couple, who could see the problem through the eyes of their children. In return, the younger couple had to look at their strained relationships with the wife's parents through the eyes of the older couple, who could understand her parents' perspective. For each couple, the debate, moderated by myself, led to some modification of their views and new insights into how the respective children and parents might be feeling. It was obvious from the discussion that other group members were making associations to their own experiences, using the dialogue taking place before them.

It is important to note that confrontation is a part of mutual aid. Instead of being suppressed, differences must be expressed in an arena where they can be used for learning. I believe that group members often present strongly held views on a subject precisely because they have doubts and desperately need a challenging perspective. The skills involved in helping group members to use these conflicts constructively in a mutually respectful and caring manner are explored later. This example also illustrates the fact that the group can be a laboratory for developing skills such as asserting oneself, so that the individual members can become more effective in their outside-of-the-group relationships. The conversation between the older and younger couples constituted a rehearsal for the important discussion that needed to take place with their respective children and parents. The group members were able to use the experience for this purpose when the leader pointed this out.

## Discussing a Taboo Area

Each group member brings to the group the *norms* of behavior and the *societal taboos* that exist in our larger culture. Norms are the rules of behavior that are generally accepted by a dominant group in society. These norms can be recreated within a counseling group or other system. The existence of the norms is evident when the group members behave as if the norms exist. For example, one norm of group behavior may be to avoid discussion in a societal taboo area.

In the beginning phase of work, the group recreates in this micro-society the general community "culture," consisting of norms, taboos, and rules that the group members have experienced outside the group. Thus, direct talk about such subjects as authority, dependency (on people and/or drugs), death and dying, and sex is experienced as taboo. One of the tasks of the group leader will be to help the group members develop new norms and feel free to challenge some taboos so that the group can be more effective. This is referred to as helping the group to develop a *"culture for work."*

Each group member will feel the urgency of discussing the subject somewhat differently from the others, and each group member will experience the power of the taboo differently. As the work proceeds and the level of comfort in the group increases (the skills for helping this to happen are discussed in later chapters), one member may take the first risk, directly or indirectly, that leads the group into a difficult area of discussion. By being first, the member allows the more fearful and reluctant members to watch as the taboo is violated. As they experience positive work, they are given permission to enter the formerly taboo area. Thus, all the group members are able to benefit from the particular sense of urgency, the lower level of anxiety, or the greater willingness to risk of the member who leads the way.

In my AIDS/recovery group, one member spoke about her own abusive past history and how she had escaped her family and turned to the streets and "to every kind of drug and drink you could imagine." She went on to describe her experiences prostituting in order to raise money for drugs and how she was not proud of herself or what she did. She said, "While I was on the street I was with many men but I was really with no man." These revelations opened the door for other members to share their own sexual experiences, often degrading and exploitive, as they went on "coke dates" to raise money for their drugs. The ability to discuss their emotions in a supportive, nonjudgmental environment appeared to have a cathartic effect, creating a culture in which other taboo issues were discussed, such as their own illnesses, their rejection by friends and family, painful losses of people close to them, and their own fears of debilitation and death associated with AIDS.

In another example of a counseling group for 8- to 10-year-old children, all of whom had lost a close relative (e.g., parent, grandparent), the session involved the use of drawing materials. The group leaders recognized that the taboo related to talking about painful issues such as death and loss was preventing a discussion of the members' feelings. Instead, the children were acting out their pain through maladaptive behavior. At the start of one meeting, one youngster drew a picture of his grandfather and then drew lines through it. The group leader pointed out the meaning of the drawing that his grandfather was dead, and the boy started running around the room saying he "doesn't want anyone to talk about his grandfather." A young girl in the group said he is running around because he doesn't want to talk about his grandfather's death. Another child said no one wants to talk about death, since when you talk about it you have bad dreams. The work began as they started to verbalize their feelings, having been led into the topic by the first boy's drawing.

## The "All-in-the-Same-Boat" Phenomenon

After the group enters a formerly taboo area, the members listen to the feelings of the others and often discover emotions of their own that they were unaware of, feelings that may have been having a powerful effect on their lives. They also discover the reassuring fact that they are not alone in their feelings, that group members are "*all in the same boat.*" Knowing that others share your concerns and feelings somehow makes them less frightening and easier to deal with. When, as a group member, one discovers that one is not alone in feeling overwhelmed by a problem, or worried about one's sexual adequacy, or wondering who one is and where one comes from (e.g., a foster teenager), or experiencing rejection because of "the virus" (AIDS), one is often better able to mobilize oneself to deal with the problem productively.

Discovering that feelings are shared by other members of the group can often help release a group member from their power. Guilt over "evil" thoughts and feelings can be lessened and self-destructive cycles broken when one discovers they are normal and shared by others. For example, a parent of a child with a physical or mental disability who hears that other parents may also feel that their child's condition represents "God's punishment" may be better able to cope with his or her guilt. This can be one of the most powerful forces for change resulting from the mutual-aid process. There is not the same impact when a leader in individual work tries to reassure the group member that the same feelings are shared by others. Hearing them articulated by others in the group sessions makes a unique impression.

In another example from the AIDS/recovery group, one member talked of her fears of being rejected by her boyfriend because she had AIDS and he didn't. Even though the boyfriend knew about her AIDS and seemed to accept it, she was afraid to ask for a stronger commitment from him because she thought he would turn her down and she would lose him. Although she was an attractive young woman, she feared that no one else could ever love her because of the "virus." A male member of the group responded, saying, "That's the thing you fear most—the rejection. I just disconnect my telephone and stay in my room because I know if I get close to someone, I'm just going to be rejected again."

## Developing a Universal Perspective

EP 2.1.4a
EP 2.1.4c
EP 2.1.5a

Expanding one's perspective is a special case of the all-in-the-same-boat phenomenon just described. Many group members, particularly those belonging to oppressed and vulnerable populations, may internalize the negative definitions assigned to them by the larger society. Thus, battered women, survivors of sexual abuse, persons of color, the mentally ill, or people with AIDS may assume the blame for their troubles and see their difficulties as a product of their own personal shortcomings. This can be reinforced by mental health professionals who focus on personal pathology while ignoring the socioeconomic factors that created and constantly reinforce the negative self-image.

In a group where common experiences of oppression are shared, it becomes easier for group members to recognize that a source of their problems in living may be external to themselves. Early in the women's movement, this process was exemplified in the *consciousness-raising groups* designed to help women become more aware of gender stereotyping and oppression issues that affected their lives. With a more universal perspective on one's problems, the additional burden of taking all of the blame for one's troubles may be lifted. The anger against the oppression—anger that often lurks just beneath the outward signs of depression, submission, and apathy—can be released and converted into positive energy for dealing with personal as well as social issues.

In an example described in some detail in Chapter 14, a group of young female survivors of sexual abuse support each other in recognizing the social roots of the gender oppression and violence they have experienced. In a pivotal meeting, the leader announces that a "Take Back the Night" march against violence toward women will occur in their town the following week and wonders if group members might want to participate. An important discussion between the women, which highlights how these women have been taught to accept their "victim" status, leads to their decision to attend the march as a group. This group experience, resulting from their ability to universalize their perspective, may well have been one of the most therapeutic aspects of the group.

In an example from the AIDS/recovery group, one woman talked about the sexual exploitation she had experienced both from her "Johns" while prostituting and from her boyfriends over the years. A transgendered female member of the group angrily declared that in her experience, sex is all most men are interested in and they will use and exploit you and your feelings, if they can, in order to get it. To underscore her point, she declared, "and I know, because I have been both!" After the group members stopped their good-natured laughing at her comment, there followed a discussion among the men and women of the group about intimate relationships, how hard it is to find people who really care, and how painful it is when you lose someone who does.

In a vocational counseling group for unemployed men and women, the discussion led to the recognition that all of the members had lost their jobs just when they had reached senior status in the organization and had been replaced by younger, lower-salaried employees. It became clear to them that they were "let go" not because they were no longer productive but that they were experiencing a pattern of age discrimination. This led to a discussion about not only how to continue their job search but also what legal remedies might be open to them and how to access them.

## Mutual Support

**EP 2.1.10b**

When the *group culture* supports the open expression of feelings, group members' capacity to empathize with each other is evident. With the group leader setting the tone through expression of personal feelings and understanding of others, each member is able to observe the powerful effect of empathy. Since group members share some common concerns, they are often able to understand each other's feelings in a deeper way than the leader. This expression of empathy is an important healing agent for both the group member who receives it and the one who offers it. As group members understand the feelings of the others, without judging them harshly, they begin to accept their own feelings in new ways. For a member struggling with a specific concern, the acceptance and caring of the group can be a source of support during a difficult time.

I have just used the expression "the acceptance and caring of the group," which introduces a new concept to be explored in detail in Chapter 13. The important element here is the group, the entity that is created when people are brought together. This entity, which I will call the group-as-a-whole, involves more than just the simple sum of the parts (members). For example, support in the mutual-aid group often has a quality that is different from support received in interaction with a single empathic person. It is more than just a quantitative difference of more people equaling more empathy. At crucial moments in a group, one can sense a general tone or atmosphere, displayed through words, expressions, or physical posture, that conveys the caring of the "group" for the individual. One can almost sense it "in the air." This seems to have a special meaning and importance to the individual group member. The properties of the group-as-a-whole are described in detail in Chapter 13, in which I will explore the idea of working with the group as the "second client."

In the following example of support, also from the AIDS/recovery group, the group member who is reluctant to confront her boyfriend for fear of losing him asks the transgender member how she looks.

**Practice Points:** I sense the underlying question related to the impact of having AIDS and articulate Theresa's feelings:

> Once again, Theresa asked Tania how she looked. She said, "You're a woman. I know, as a woman, you will be honest with me and just tell me what you think. Do you think I look okay?" Tania seemed confused and said, "Well, sure, you look wonderful." I said, "I wonder if Theresa is really asking, 'Am I pretty enough? Am I attractive enough? If my boyfriend leaves me, can I find someone else who could love me even though I have AIDS?'" She said, "That's it," and came close to tears. She said, "I'm so afraid, if I lose him, I won't find anyone else." She said, "I know I could have guys, and I know I could have sex, and I like the sex. I sure missed it during the time I was in prison, but can another guy love me?"
>
> The group members tried to reassure her that she was a wonderful person, and Tania said, "It's not what you look like on the outside, it's what you're like on the inside." And she said, "And you, honey—you've really got it where it counts."

In another example, also described in detail in Chapter 13, one member in a DWI (driving while intoxicated) group finally reveals that his trigger for his drinking is the memory of having driven his car while drunk, crashing, and the resultant death of his wife. The group leader describes how all of the men leaned forward toward him, physically and verbally supporting him as he struggled with his loss while also experiencing the feelings associated with their own losses due to their drinking.

## Mutual Demand

Central to this practice framework is the concept of the helping relationship consisting of elements of both support and demand, synthesized in unique, personal ways. The same is true in the group practice context. Mutual aid is provided through expectation as well as through caring. One illustration is the way group members confront each other. For example, in my couples' group two male members were able to challenge a third who was maintaining that the source of the problem was his wife, that she was the identified "patient," and he was coming to group merely to "help her out." Both of the confronting group members had taken the same position at our first session and had slowly modified their views. They had lowered their defenses and accepted the idea that the problem was a "couple" problem. This demand on the third member had a different quality coming from group members, rather than the group leader.

As the group culture develops, it can include expectations that members risk their real thoughts and ideas, listen to each other and set their own concerns aside at times to help another, and so on. These expectations help to develop a productive "culture for work." Another group expectation can be that the members will work on their concerns. At moments when group members feel overwhelmed and hopeless, this expectation may help them take a next step. The group cares enough about them not to let them give up. I have witnessed group members take some difficult action, such as confronting a boss or dealing more effectively with a close relative. When the action was discussed the following week, they indicated that one of the factors that had pushed them to make the move and take a risk was the thought of returning to the group and admitting that they hadn't acted. Mutual demand, integrated with mutual support, can be a powerful force for change.

In my AIDS/recovery group, members often used their insights and understanding about the recovery process, gained through participation in twelve-step groups such as Alcoholics Anonymous (AA) and Narcotics Anonymous (NA), to confront each other when their behaviors threatened their recovery. In one example, a group member who had just spent two weeks in a detoxification program after relapsing into cocaine use described how hard it was for him not to "hang around" the pool hall where all of his friends were. He described how he wavered each day, wondering if he could connect up with them and not relapse again. One of the other members, using an analogy obviously known by the others through their AA experiences, said, "You know, John, if you hang around a barbershop long enough" (pause), and the rest of the group, in a chorus, replied, "you are going to get a haircut!" The group members all laughed, and John replied, "I know, I know, you're right, I would definitely be risking my recovery."

## Individual Problem Solving

A mutual-aid group can be a place where an individual can bring a problem and ask for assistance. For example, in one group a young mother discussed the strained relationship between herself and her mother. Her mother lived nearby and was constantly calling and asking to come over. The group member had been extremely depressed and was going through periods where she neglected her work at home (dishes piling up in the sink, and so on). Each time her mother came over, she felt, because of her mother's actions, that she was being reprimanded for being a poor housekeeper and a poor mother to her young children. The resulting tension produced many arguments, including some between the husband and wife. The group member felt her mother still treated her like a child even though she was 27.

The group member presented the issue, at first indirectly and later with much feeling and tears. The group members reached out to offer support and understanding. They were able to use their own experiences to share similar feelings. The older members of the group were able to provide a different perspective on the mother's actions. They could identify with her feelings, and they pointed out how uncertain she might feel about how to help her daughter. Conversations and incidents described by the group member were discussed, and new interpretations of the interactions were offered. It became clear that the group member's perceptions were often distorted by her own feelings of inadequacy and her harsh judgments of herself. The problem was described by the leader (this author) from a new perspective, that of a normative crisis in life as the young couple sought new ways to relate to her parents, and the parents, in turn, struggled to find ways of being close while still letting go. There were other issues involved as well, related to some of the reasons for the group member's depression, such as her feelings of being trapped at home and trapped as a woman. These emerged in later sessions.

**Practice Points:**   It is important to note that as the group members offered help to the individual with the problem, they were also helping themselves. Each group member could make associations to a similar concern. All of them could see how easily the communications between mother and daughter were going astray. As they tried to help the group member clarify her own feelings, understand her mother's reactions in new ways, and see how the mutual stereotypes were interfering with the ability to communicate real feelings, the other group members could relate these ideas to their own close relationships. This is one of the important ways in which giving help in a mutual-aid group is a form of self-help. It is always easier to see the problem in someone else's relationships than in your own. The general learning of the group members can be enhanced through the specific problem-solving work done with each member. The group leader can help by pointing out the underlying common themes.

This mutual-aid process offers another example that challenges the false dichotomy often posed between meeting the needs of the individual or the needs of the group—that is, the feeling by group leaders that they must choose between the individual with a specific problem or attending to the group. This false dichotomy can lead to doing individual counseling in the group while the other members wait their turn or ignoring individual issues for fear of losing the group. As I will illustrate later in this chapter and in other chapters, if the group leader sees his or her job as helping individuals reach out to the group and helping the group to respond, then there is no need to choose between the one or the many. The group leader can be with both at the same time. This is another example of the "two-client" idea advocated in earlier chapters.

## Rehearsal

Another way in which a mutual-aid group can help is by providing a forum in which members can try out ideas or skills. In a sense, the group becomes a safe place to risk new ways of communicating and to practice actions the group member feels may be hard to do. To continue with the previous example, as the session neared the end, the group leader pointed out that the group member seemed hesitant about taking up the issue with her mother. The following excerpt from the process recording starts with the group member's response.

ROSE: I'm not sure I can talk with my mother about this. What would I say?

LEADER: That's a good question. How about trying it out right here? I'll pretend to be your mother calling to ask to see you. You can practice how you would respond, and the group can give some ideas about how it sounds. Does that sound all right?

ROSE: (She has stopped crying now and is sitting straight up in her chair with a slight smile on her face.) OK. You call me and tell me you want to have lunch with me and that I should keep the kids home from school so you can see them.

LEADER: (Role-playing) Hello, Rose, this is Mom.

ROSE: Hi, Mom. How are you and Dad feeling?

LEADER: Not so good. You know, Dad gets upset easily, and he has been feeling lousy. (The group member had indicated that her mother often used her father's health to try to make her feel guilty.)

ROSE: That's it! That's what she would say to make me feel guilty. (The group members are laughing at this point.)

**Practice Points:**   The discussion picked up, with the group members agreeing about how easy it is for others to make them feel guilty. The leader inquired how Rose would feel at that point in the conversation. It became clear that the rest of the discussion would consist of her indirect responses to what she perceives as her mother's "laying on a guilt trip." After some discussion of what the mother might have been really feeling and having trouble in saying (e.g., how much she and her father really care about Rose and how much she needs to see her—an admission she might find hard to make), the group strategized with Rose about ways to break the usual cycle of indirect communications. The key moment in the informal role-play came when the mother asked Rose to keep her children home for the mother's lunch visit. Rose had complained that the mother never wanted to see her alone; it was always with the children. She was always asking to have them at home when she visited. She thought her mother didn't trust her with the kids and was always checking up on her.

**Practice Points:**   At one point the leader, sensing ambivalence on Rose's part, confronted her by asking if she really wanted to talk to her mother.

LEADER: (Speaking as the mother) I wonder, Rose, if part of the reason I always ask to have the kids there is that I'm uncomfortable when we get together. I'm not sure what I would say to you for a whole two hours. I want the kids around to help fill the conversation.

ROSE: You know, I'm not sure what I would say to my mother either. I really don't know what to talk to her about.

FRAN: (Another group member) Can you try to tell your mother that you get upset when she asks you to keep the kids home because you want to have some time alone with her? Maybe your mother could understand that. (Silence)

LEADER: Rose, do you really want to spend some time with your mother?

ROSE: I'm not so sure I do.

LEADER: Then that's the first step. When you're sure, I think the words will come more easily. If you tell your mother how you really feel, it could be the start of some honest talk between you. Perhaps she could share some of her real feelings in response, instead of always doing it indirectly and in ways which are open to misinterpretation. Maybe if you could do this, then your mother would see this as a sign of your maturity.

**Practice Summary.** Rose tried to articulate her feelings more clearly but was obviously still having difficulty. She reported the following week that she had talked with her mother about how it made her feel when the mother tried to do things for her (e.g., wash the dishes when she came over), and the mother had responded by describing how she never really knew what to do when she came over—should she help out or not? Rose felt it cleared the air, even though other issues and feelings were not discussed.

The interesting thing about the role-playing device as a form of rehearsal is that is often reveals the underlying ambivalence and resistance that the group member feels but has not expressed in the discussion. The rehearsal not only offers the group member a chance to practice, but it also reveals to the group, the leader, and the other group members some of the feelings that need to be dealt with if the group member is to succeed in his or her efforts.

> In my AIDS/recovery group, at one point the group member who had raised boyfriend problems used the group to consider how to approach him with her concerns. One member helped by role-playing how Theresa could handle the conversation:
>
> We returned to Theresa, and I said, "Is the question really, Theresa, that you're afraid that he might not stay with you—that, if you actually confront him on this issue of the other women, that he might leave you?" She agreed that it was her concern. At this point, I wondered if it might help Theresa to figure out what she might say to her boyfriend. Theresa said that would be helpful because she didn't know when and how to say it. Then she laughed and said, "Maybe I should say it in bed." Tania said, "Oh no. Don't say it before sex and don't say it after sex." And I added, "And don't say it during sex." Everyone laughed at this point, and Tania, a professional stand-up comedian, did an imitation of having a conversation with Theresa's boyfriend, while pumping up and down on the couch as if she were in bed having sex with him.
>
> Tania then said, "You have to find a quiet time, not a time when you're in the middle of a fight, and you have to just put out your feelings." I asked Tania if she could show Theresa how she could do that. She started to speak as if she were talking to Theresa's boyfriend. I role-played the boyfriend, and said, "Oh, but Theresa, you're just insecure, aren't you?" Tania did a very good job of not letting me put her off and, instead, putting the issue right where it was—whether I (role-playing Theresa) was prepared to make a commitment or if I was too insecure.

**Practice Points:**   Ambivalence and fear often underlie our clients' inability to take a difficult step. In the earlier example in the previous section, the young woman was not really sure if she wanted to speak with her mother, even though she expressed disappointment at her mother not wanting to spend time alone with her. In Theresa's situation, ambivalence about confronting her boyfriend is related to not being sure she wants to hear the answer. This, in turn, is connected to the purpose of the group—the impact of having AIDS on their lives.

> Theresa said, "I know I have to talk to him, but, you know, he's told me that he's not sure he wants to be tied down, that he likes to have his freedom." Jake nodded his head and said, "Yeah, that's the problem, they want their freedom and they don't want to make a commitment, and you're afraid, if you push him, he'll leave you because you got the virus." Theresa said she realized she had to sit down and talk to him because it couldn't keep up the same way. She would just get too angry and do something crazy and screw up her recovery. She said when she had a fight with him on Thanksgiving he did call his sponsor and came back much more gently. She felt she had gotten through to him, but she had to find another way to get through to him and talk to him. Otherwise, this thing was just going to continue and it was going to tear her up inside.

### The "Strength-in-Numbers" Phenomenon

**EP 2.1.5a**

Sometimes it is easier to do things as a group than it would be as an individual. In one example described earlier, a group of female survivors of sexual abuse attended a "Take Back the Night" march. The "strength-in-numbers" phenomenon worked to decrease their feelings of isolation and individual risk involved, which encouraged the group members to make demands for their right to feel safe. An individual's fears and ambivalence can be overcome by participation in a group effort as his or her own courage is strengthened by the courage of others.

In a recent Public Television rerelease of the documentary "Eyes on the Prize," which chronicled a period of the civil rights struggle in the "Jim Crow" (segregated) southern states, one could see the enormous impact of large groups of people marching and demonstrating for the rights guaranteed to them by the Civil Rights Act that had been recently passed by Congress. The film documented in dramatic fashion the attacks on the marchers by the Mississippi State Police trying to stop the demonstration. This particular march was undertaken to continue a march led by a civil rights leader who had been shot along the way. The strength-in-numbers phenomenon was evident as the marchers continued on their way in the face of racist verbal and physical threats and attacks by Whites along the way. It was clear that even in the face of danger, the support of the group, marching and singing for their inherent rights, provided the fuel that helped to power their incredible courage.

### Summary of the Dynamics of Mutual Aid

A number of examples have been shared to illustrate how the dynamics of the mutual-aid process can work. Sharing data, the dialectical process, discussing taboo areas, the "all-in-the-same-boat" phenomenon, developing a universal perspective, mutual support, mutual demand, individual problem solving, rehearsal, and the "strength-in-numbers" phenomenon are some of the processes through which mutual aid is offered and taken. It is important to note that I am not suggesting that working in groups is a preferred method. The choice of individual or group counseling is influenced by many factors, particularly the comfort of the group members in dealing with their concerns on a one-to-one basis as opposed to within a group setting.

As I will explain in detail later, it is often helpful for a group member to have both individual and group counseling available so that both experiences can be used productively. Each would have a slightly different focus, and each could be expected to provide important stimulation for the other. For many group members, the group can offer (under certain circumstances) unique forms of help in dealing with their life problems. I have attempted to identify some of these mutual-aid processes, but it is important to realize that groups will not provide this kind of help just because they have been brought together. In the next section, I will examine some of the obstacles that can make mutual aid a difficult process indeed. These obstacles, and others, will be explored in detail in later chapters.

## Obstacles to Mutual Aid

**EP 2.1.7b**

In the early phases of a group's development, one potential obstacle to mutual aid is the apparent divergent interest each group member brings to the engagement. Even in a group with a narrow, clearly defined purpose, some group members may perceive their sense of urgency differently from the others. Even though the mutual threads of concern may exist, group members may not identify their common ground. Various group members may feel their concerns and feelings are unique and unrelated to those of other members. The attractions between members may be partial, subtle, and difficult to perceive. In many ways, the group is a microcosm of the larger society, and this diffusion of interest between "self" and "other" reflects the individual social encounter in society. Thus, as each member becomes oriented to the group engagement, that member will be asking, "How am I the same as or different from the other members?"

### Identifying the Common Ground

One of the early tasks of the group leader will be to help group members begin to identify their common ground. As the group develops a mature way of relating, individual members can begin to understand that they can learn and grow by giving help as well as receiving it. As each individual member develops the skills required to offer help and to take help, these same skills will be found to be related to their individual concerns outside of the group. For example, group members who learn how to identify their feelings and to share them in the group may be able to apply these skills in other intimate relationships with family and friends. Nevertheless, at the beginning stage and periodically during the life of the group, the inability of members to perceive their connections to the others will present an important obstacle.

### The Complexity of the Group-as-a-Whole

A second set of obstacles will emerge from the fact that even a small group can be a complex system that must deal with a number of developmental tasks if it is to work productively. As soon as more than one group member is involved, a new organism is created: the group-as-a-whole. This group is more than the simple sum of its parts (i.e., the individual members). For example, this new organism needs to develop rules and procedures that will allow it to function effectively. Some will be openly discussed, while others may operate beneath the surface by mutual although unspoken consent of the members. Roles may be subtly distributed to group members, such as scapegoat, deviant member, internal leader, and so on. Some of these role assignments will represent ways by which the group-as-a-whole may avoid dealing directly with a problem. For example, the group *gatekeeper* may intervene to distract the group each time the discussion approaches a painful subject. Many of the unstated rules for relating will be counterproductive to the purpose of the group. These factors, and others to be discussed in Chapter 13, are properties of this complex organism called the group and must be dealt with by the leader if the group is to function effectively.

### Difficulty of Open Communications in Taboo Areas

A final major source of potential problems for the group is the difficulty of open communication. I have already discussed some of the barriers that make it difficult for group members to express their real feelings and concerns. These are related to a social culture that has implicitly and explicitly developed a number of norms of behavior and identified taboo areas in which honest communication is hard to achieve. Each group member brings a part of this culture into the group, and thus the group culture, in early phases of work, resembles the culture of the social surroundings. This often makes it difficult for group members to talk with and listen to each other in areas of central concern. With the group leader's help, group members will need to develop a new culture—a culture for work—in which norms are modified and taboos lose their power, so that members may freely communicate with each other.

I have just outlined three major areas of potential obstacles to mutual aid: the difficulty individual members have in identifying their self-interest with that of the other group members, the complex tasks involved in creating a mutual-aid system, and the difficulties in communicating honestly. The existence of these potential obstacles helps to define the job of the group leader. These problems are not arguments against the use of groups as mutual-aid systems; rather, they represent an agenda for the group leader. If groups were not faced with these problems, and if people could easily join together to offer aid and support, then there would be no need for a group leader.

## The Role of the Group Leader

**EP 2.1.1c**

While the role of the group leader may vary depending on the type of group, purpose, membership, and so on, Schwartz (1961) suggested the general function of mediating the individual-group interaction. This leads Schwartz to argue one of his most central and useful ideas about group practice: that the group leader always has "two clients"—the individual and the group. The role of the group leader in this framework is to mediate the engagement between these two entities.

As the group process unfolds, the leader is constantly concerned both with each individual member and with the group. For example, as an individual member raises a specific concern, the leader will help the member share that concern with the group. Since it can be difficult for group members to describe their concerns, a number of crucial skills will be needed to implement this role. Some of these have been mentioned already in earlier chapters, and others will be discussed in more detail in a later chapter. These skills include, for example, reading indirect communications and responding directly; articulating group members' concerns and feelings, when needed; reaching for feelings; and encouraging elaboration. The goal will be to help individual group members talk to the group and clarify their concerns.

As the leader helps the one (the individual) talk to the many (the group), the interaction will also be monitored to see if the group members appear to be listening and relating to the individual. If they seem to be turned off, the leader will explore their feelings and reactions. Perhaps the individual's problem is painful to the group members, raising related feelings of their own and making it hard for them to listen. Whatever the realities may be, the group leader, with a clear sense of role, will pay attention to both the individual and the group at exactly the same time.

Attention to the group will require that the leader help group members to deal with the obstacles described earlier. For example, if the group culture is making it difficult for members to discuss their real feelings about a specific issue, then the leader can call this to the attention of the group members. An effort to bring the obstacle out in the open is a first step in helping the group members become more conscious of their own processes. With the assistance of the group leader, group members can discuss how the blockage of open communication in a sensitive area frustrates their work. With understanding comes growth as the group becomes more sophisticated about its ways of working. A new agreement, including new norms that are more productive, can be openly reached. In many ways the group leader serves as a guide for the group members faced with the complex task of developing an effective mutual-aid system. The important point is that this is the members' group, the work to strengthen it is theirs, and the group leader is there to help them to do it.

In a general way, these two areas of work characterize the group leader's responsibilities: helping the individual and the group relate effectively to each other, and helping the group become more sophisticated about its way of working, so that it releases the potential for mutual aid. Of course, this process is more complicated than this simple explanation implies. In the remaining chapters I will explore the underlying assumptions about how mutual-aid groups work and the tasks and skills required of the group leader. But first, I need to address the important work that must be done in preparing for group practice.

## Preparing for Group Practice

The preparatory (group formation) phase can be one of the most complex in work with groups, as a number of crucial issues must be dealt with before the first meeting takes place. The literature on group practice pays surprisingly little attention to the problems of this phase, beyond discussion of questions of group type (e.g., psycho-educational, educational, therapeutic, support), structure (e.g., frequency and number of sessions), group composition, and so on. As one example of a problem that is often ignored, it is not unusual for a group leader to decide that a group would be helpful and to approach colleagues for appropriate referrals. General agreement may be reached at a staff meeting to support the group; however, the leader waits two months without getting a single referral. In analyzing examples of this kind, I have consistently found that the leader had left out the important step of involving the colleagues in a meaningful way. I could often determine the moment in the staff meeting when the groundwork was laid for the frustration that followed.

In like manner, a group leader may launch a group and prepare for a first meeting with ten group members who have promised to attend. The evening of the meeting arrives, and after waiting 30 long and painful minutes for latecomers, the leader must face the reality that only two members have come. Once again, the source of the disappointment can often be traced to steps that were left out in the preparatory work with clients as the group leader or other group leaders began the referral process. In analysis of interviews and telephone conversations, it is often possible to identify the moment the group leader sensed the ambivalence of the prospective group member but did not reach for it—a skill I call *"looking for trouble when everything seems to be going your way."*

In the sections that follow, these and other group formation issues will be discussed, with an emphasis on describing and illustrating strategies that may increase the possibility of launching effective mutual-aid groups.

## Engaging Other Professionals in Developing the Group

**EP 2.1.9b**
**EP 2.1.10a**
**EP 2.1.8b**

An important first principle is to recognize that a group in an agency, school, hospital, or another institution must be related to the service. If a group leader attempts to establish a group because of a desire to develop new skills or because he or she has decided (without involving the rest of the staff) that there is a need for such a group, the group may be doomed to failure. A common example is the student who is placed in an agency for practicum experience and is taking a course in group work. Although simulated class groups are often used to meet the requirement for the student to lead a group, most would agree that a group leadership experience in the field practicum would be helpful; so the student endeavors to set one up in the field. Quite often the group never has its first meeting because the student's need for it is not a sound reason for developing a group. The idea for a group must begin with the identification of an area of potential unmet needs that the group method may be able to meet. The group must reflect the consensus of the department or team involved so that it is not seen as being personally "owned" by the group leader.

The difficulty or ease involved in establishing a group may depend upon the group experience of the setting. In those settings where groups are a common form of service and where all staff members take their turn at leadership, many of the problems of formation may be minimized. In other settings, where groups are unusual as a form of service, these problems may be intensified. For example, a group leader who attempts to introduce group work into a setting that has never had groups must recognize that a threatening situation may be created for other staff. As discussed in the Introduction, the fear-of-groups syndrome may be common.

Some group leaders may be concerned by the idea of facing more than one client at a time or doubt their abilities to lead groups. If they do not have a fund of good group experiences to draw upon or if they unsuccessfully attempted to establish a group when they were students, they may be hesitant about working with groups. The group leader attempting to initiate a group service must recognize that, on some level, colleagues may wonder whether, if the service is successful, they will be asked to carry a group next. This fear is often expressed indirectly with comments such as, "Groups would be great in this agency, but do we really have the time?" The development of group service can have an important impact on the staff system, and the group leader should make use of the tuning-in skill in preparing to negotiate the establishment of the group.

Staff resistance can also be noted when the administration of an agency or organization, because of the pressures of managed care or other cutbacks in resources, has decided to move into group work as a cost-cutting measure. In reality, group practice may actually increase costs, since it rarely serves as a substitute in those situations where individual counseling is required. In many cases, issues that emerge in the group for one member may generate the need for more intensive individual counseling, rather than less counseling, for other group members. Group work should be the practice modality of choice only if it is the best modality for the particular population and problem. When cost-cutting is the only rationale offered, staff resistance due to fears about competency is often masked by staff anger at the "top-down" imposition of group practice. Whether the reasons for developing group work practice are sound or spurious, there is little question that there has been a significant expansion of the use of group work in practice.

## Achieving Consensus on the Service

The idea of a group may emerge in a setting in many ways: client feedback, a group leader discovering a common concern among a number of individual clients, or a staff team discovering an important gap in the service. Wherever the idea of a group is initiated, it is important that all staff involved have the opportunity to comment honestly on the potential service. A common mistake is for a group leader to decide on the need for a group and then to set about "selling" colleagues on the idea. Rather than presenting their own views on the need for it and inviting feedback and discussion, group leaders may try to unduly influence their colleagues, creating the illusion that they are involving others in the process. The group leader might find an artificial agreement expressed through apparently unqualified support. Once again, the skilled group leader would not leave the session without first reaching for the underlying reservations. For example, the group leader might say, "It's great to see such quick support for my idea, but you know, it may cause some problems and inconveniences for the rest of you. Don't you think we should also talk about these?"

*Reaching for Underlying Staff Resistance*  The group leader often senses the underlying resistance but fears to reach for it. The belief is that if one leaves the negatives unexpressed, they will perhaps go away. They never do. These reservations, negative reactions, fears, and the like all come back to haunt the group leader in the form of conscious or unconscious sabotage of the group leader's plans. If the group is to become a reality, the group leader must insist that it be a service of the team, the agency, the school, or whatever, not just the group leader's personal group that happens to be taking place in this setting. Without real support from the rest of the staff, the group leader will be alone when problems emerge.

I have seen excellent work done with school principals, for example, when after the principal has given perfunctory agreement to allow a group to meet in the school, a community-based group leader has asked, "Would you be very upset if we couldn't offer this group to your kids?" After a moment's pause, the principal responded, "The only reason I OK these groups is that the people at the school board like to see them in the schools. Actually, staff and I often find they are more trouble than they are worth." Only at this point does the real discussion begin, and the group leader can start serious contracting with the agency or setting. If this stage is skipped over in the group leader's eagerness to gain a toehold, then the lack of real investment will hurt when the going gets rough in the group.

Fortunately, group leaders usually have the opportunity to go back after making a mistake and to try again. This is important, since group leaders who propose groups in a setting without connecting the purpose of the group to the general service of the setting are often seen as simply requesting space. When administrators and staff members perceive the connection between their service and the purpose of the group, they will be more likely to invest themselves in the group's development. A group leader offering to lead a group for children who have been identified by teachers as having trouble at school will be more easily accepted by the staff than one asking to lead groups for general discussion (e.g., "I would like to work with children who need a socialization experience").

*Confidentiality: Sharing Information with Colleagues* It is also important to discuss the issue of confidentiality with other staff. From the point of view of the helping role that is being elaborated in this book, the mediating approach, acting as a communication bridge between group members and the system is very much a part of the work. If the group leader begins work with staff by stating they will not be included in discussion of group content, their fears and anxieties may lead to direct or indirect efforts at sabotage. In one such case, a group leader in a group home for teens had completely ignored the residential group leader's concerns, particularly her fear of complaints, and had indicated that all discussions would be confidential. When the group leader arrived, the residential staff member rang a bell and shouted, to the group leader's consternation, "Group therapy time." In other examples, the group leader's colleagues have described the group to their individual clients in a way that served to heighten the clients' fears of involvement: "We are going to offer this group but you don't have to attend if you don't want to."

If the group leader's sense of function involves a commitment to helping in the process between client and system, including the agency, then this must be part of the contract. Child-care group leaders, teachers, and other group leaders must be viewed as colleagues, with each having a part in the operation. Discussions should focus on how the group leader and the other staff members will handle feedback. The meaning of the feedback and the way in which clients might use either the individual counselor or the group leader as a channel must be recognized. The agreement can include ways to achieve the optimum outcome, in which each will attempt to assist the group members' efforts to provide direct feedback to the other. I have found that this discussion often takes much of the threat out of the possibility of negative feedback and, instead, turns it into an important technical issue for both workers. The details of how the fears of the group members can be handled and how a group leader can effectively share feedback with other staff will be dealt with in later chapters.

When I explore why group leaders are reluctant to follow this course of action—that is, to treat other system people as colleagues and to work out agreements for mutual sharing of relevant information, they usually express concern about their colleagues' acceptance of such a contract. While there is some basis to this concern, I often find, in addition, they have their own fears about confronting a colleague with "bad news." How do you tell a fellow staff member, with whom you have coffee each day, that his client or student or patient doesn't feel he understands her? Confidentiality can then serve as a protection for the group leader but will eventually lead to problems.

Often group leaders reveal that they have developed stereotypes of their colleagues as "ineffective" counselors (poor teachers, insensitive doctors, and so on), so what good would sharing be? I can understand their reticence to take on this role, yet if the group leader accepts that the teacher, a fellow group leader, or whomever, is actually closed to change, such acceptance means that an important part of the service to members will no longer be available. The group leader will inevitably be in a serious quandary when the strength-in-numbers phenomenon described in the previous chapter leads the group members to share their real feelings. A situation will have been set up that makes it impossible for the group leader to do anything about the problem except empathize, ignore it, or defend the system. This often leads to apathy and disengagement on the part of the group members.

The question of confidentiality has broadened during this discussion to encompass a much larger issue: the role of the helping person within his or her own helping system. This will be explored with a number of examples in chapters to follow. For now, I would summarize my view as being that this concern may be a central issue for other staff members when group formation is discussed. I would want it out in the open, and I would want to contract with both staff and group members for freedom of communication of group content in a responsible manner.

## Identifying Group Type and Structure

EP 2.1.10g

Colleagues can also be helpful in considering the question of type of group and its structure. For example, will it be a group of fixed membership meeting over a period of time, or will it be an *open-ended group* in which different members arrive and leave each week? Special problems, dynamics, and strategies associated with open-ended groups will be discussed in Chapter 11; however, for some purposes and settings they provide a better alternative than a fixed-membership group. In contrast, a group for teenaged survivors of sexual abuse will need some time to establish the levels of trust required to explore painful and formerly secret experiences. An open-ended group with a continually changing membership would not be appropriate for such a population. Some members might be added after the initial sessions, but at some point, such a group would need to be closed.

Groups are sometimes formed from ongoing natural groups, such as in a residential setting or a school. A group home is a good example, since it represents a living group, operating 7 days a week, 24 hours each day. For two hours twice each week, house meetings are held at special times within the ongoing group life to focus on issues of group living, such as problems among residents and between residents and staff. These meetings represent structured incidents in the life of the ongoing group designed to improve the ability of all concerned to live and work together.

Another issue is related to the content of the group meeting. People can provide mutual aid through means other than just talking. Mutual aid can be provided through other "mediums of exchange" between people (Shulman, 1971). For example, senior citizens in a residential center might use activities that they have developed to structure their time, provide enjoyment or education, give them the opportunity to develop new skills, or just to enjoy the company of others. In Chapter 12 I will discuss in more detail the place of program activities in the life of the group and the group leader's tasks. In the formation stage, it is important to consider whether interaction through activity represents an important part of the purpose of the group and fits within the general mission of the setting.

Community-center-type activities offered during the school day to a group of children who are not doing well in their classes may be viewed by the school staff as a "reward" for acting badly, even if the group leader argues that the students are helped indirectly. When these activities are used in work with children as a substitute for discussions about class problems or because the group leader is concerned that the youngsters would not come to a "talking group," they may frustrate the essential work rather than assist it. This issue will be discussed in some detail in later chapters, but for now the important point is that a decision on group type (talk, activity, or both) needs to relate directly both to the mission of the setting and to the felt needs of the group members.

## Group Versus Individual Counseling

Another issue that can create problems for the group leader is the compatibility of group and individual counseling. Some group leaders take the position that group members should not be seen individually because that will lessen the intensity of the group experience. Individual counselors, as well, are often worried that clients will use their group session to discuss central issues. This can lead to a struggle over *"who owns the client,"* a misunderstanding of the interdependence of individual and group work, and an unacceptable attitude to client participation in decisions about service.

***The Interaction Between Individual and Group Practice*** On the first issue, clients may use both individual and group help for different issues, as they see fit. For example, as the group works on the concern of a particular member, the discussion may raise a similar concern for members who want a chance to discuss a special case of the general problem and may not have enough time in the group to do this. Individual sessions can provide this opportunity. Group discussion, rather than robbing the individual work of its vitality, will often enrich the content of the individual counseling sessions. As members address issues, as they understand how others are experiencing problems, they may be put in touch with feelings of their own that were not previously evident. Finding out that others have fears related to taboo areas, such as sex, may greatly speed up clients' willingness to discuss their own concerns in individual counseling.

In like manner, the work in the individual sessions can strengthen a client to raise a personal concern in the group. For some clients it may be too difficult to start to talk in a group context about some of their most private feelings and concerns. As they find they can share these with an individual group leader and not be harshly judged, they may be more willing to share these feelings in the group. Thus, the group and individual counseling can be parallel and interdependent, with the client free to choose where and when to use these resources for counseling. The question of client choice raises the second issue. In my view, these choices, at any particular moment, rest with the client. Feeling comfortable about dealing with issues in one context or the other, the client will make these decisions. The group leader may share opinions, offer support, and even provide concrete help (e.g., role-playing in an individual session to show how the client might raise an issue in the group).

With two and possibly more helping people working with the same client, good communication between the helpers becomes essential. Structures should be established that guarantee regular communication so that each understands how the client is choosing to deal with issues and so that the group leaders can help each other in their related work. For example, in a couples' group that I have led, two coleaders sat in on each session. They were seeing most of the couples on an individual counseling basis. In the "tuning-in" session we held prior to each group meeting, they summarized the specific concerns dealt with in the individual sessions. We used this preparatory work to anticipate potential group issues. I maintain a policy of not directly raising concerns in the group that were discussed in the individual counseling unless the couples wish them raised. The group member has to have control of what is raised in the group, how it is raised, and when it is raised.

Through the tuning-in process, I became more effective at picking up their indirect cues. Since coleaders sat in on the sessions, they were able to incorporate content from the group experience into their individual counseling. If they were not able to sit in, I shared copies of my group process and couple summary reports so that they would be aware of the couples' progress. When sessions were videotaped, the tapes were also available for their use. Rather than competing for client ownership, we had three professionals, each providing a service through different modalities. As pointed out in the earlier discussion on confidentiality, without freedom to share information, this open communication would not have taken place.

***Informed Consent and Colleague Communication*** This raises the issue of *informed consent*. Informed consent in the context of group work will be discussed in more detail later in this chapter. Informed consent is defined as follows:

> The client's granting of permission to the group leader and agency or other professional person to use specific intervention procedures, including diagnosis, treatment, follow up, and research. This permission must be based on full disclosure of the facts needed to make the decision intelligently. Informed consent must be based upon knowledge of the risks and alternatives. (Barker, 2003, p. 114)

In this instance, part of the informed consent process would be an explanation of how communications will take place between the individual counselor and the group leader. The client needs to grant permission for this cross-discussion and needs to know that he or she will be in control over what is shared. Other elements of informed consent will be discussed later in this chapter.

## Agency or Setting Support for Groups

In addition to support from colleagues, help from the agency or setting administration may also be needed. For example, special expenses may be incurred in carrying out a group program. Mothers' groups held during the daytime may require babysitting services. Recruitment publicity, transportation expenses, coffee, and other items may be involved in some group programs. In addition, the group leader developing a group may need support in the form of a reduction in individual cases and consultation from an outside consultant if one is not available on staff. These issues should be discussed when the group is formed.

In some settings, where groups have not been an integral part of the service, the approach to group counseling programs may require that the group leader take personal responsibility for their implementation. For example, group leaders are encouraged to develop groups if they can do so "on their own time." Many group leaders, eager to see the service begin or to develop new skills in group practice, accept this responsibility and soon regret it. If a service is part of the agency function, it should not have to be carried as a personal "hobby" by the group leader. Groups take time, and if group leaders do not see that the group is viewed as a part of their responsibilities, the additional demands upon them and their feelings about these demands will often affect their work with the group.

Even when agencies support the development of group services, they sometimes do so for the wrong reasons. Administrators may believe that seeing clients in groups can save time and so encourage a swing to group programs as a way of providing more service to clients without increasing staff. With cost-containment programs on the rise, there are some situations in which seeing clients in groups will save time. For example, orientation meetings for parents in a high school can be an effective way of starting communications with more than one person at a time. As pointed out earlier, however, more often than not the development of group services tends to increase the staff's workload, since new issues and concerns may be discovered that require additional individual counseling. Groups should be viewed as an important service in their own right rather than as a service substitute. A group leader will need time to follow up with individual members, to meet with other staff, to develop a system for recording the group work for agency accountability, and for personal learning.

To start a group service on a sound footing is better, even though the formation process may be slower and more frustrating. Time taken by the group leader to interpret the group's purpose as well as to identify the special needs and potential problems related to instituting new group services will pay off in the long run. In those cases where doubts exist about the benefits of group practice, the group leader can propose the group as an experimental service to be closely monitored and evaluated. Records can be kept on the costs and benefits. The agency staff and administration can use the first groups as a way of developing experience with a new form of service. The important point is that the group service be owned by the setting, not the personal project of a concerned group leader. With the latter, it is not unusual to have a good first group only to discover that the service dies when the group leader is no longer able or willing to provide it personally.

## Group Composition, Timing, and Structure

A conversation I had with a group of students who observed my weekly group sessions with a married couples' group helps to illustrate some of the myths and questions involved in planning a group. The married couples' group consisted of five couples in marital difficulty. The client group was videotaped and, with the group members' permission, was simultaneously observed by the students on a monitor in another room. The video of this 1st session and the 19th session of this group are available on the Instructor's Power Lecture DVD associated with this text. After each meeting, I met with the observers and my coleaders to discuss the session. At the end of a first session that was marked by excellent group member involvement, I was peppered by questions on how the group had been formed. The first request was for my principles of group composition that had led to such a lively, interactive group. One couple was in their twenties, another in their thirties, a third in their forties, a fourth in their fifties, and the oldest couple was in their late sixties and early seventies. I explained, much to the disappointment of the students, that these were the only five couples referred for the group.

Another student asked how I had decided on five couples. I pointed out that we were using a studio, and with myself and my coleaders, there was only enough room for five couples. Another effort to tease out principles followed as they inquired how we decided on the number of sessions. I pointed out that there were many long-standing issues involved, and a short-term group did not seem to offer enough time. "How did you settle on exactly twenty-three sessions?" was the next question. Once again I disappointed the group by explaining that we decided we couldn't do the advance work needed to start the group before October 15. We simply counted the weeks until the end of the academic year. We then went on to discuss the differences between what I felt to be the myth of scientific group composition versus the reality of how decisions were made.

The students wanted prescriptions and rules, and I argued, perhaps more strongly than was needed, that the rules were not really that clear. In reality, we often "take what we can get." Our experiences, and some research findings, have provided us with some guidelines. For example, we know that extremes often lead to problems. Groups can clearly be too large to provide opportunity for everyone to participate or too small to provide a consistent core of members. While groups can tolerate some degree of age range, as in my married couples' groups, extremes for some populations, such as teenagers, can create serious problems. For example, a 12-year-old foster child faces life tasks that differ significantly from the concerns of a 17-year-old foster child. One person of color in an all-White group may experience a sense of isolation that the addition of another might well alleviate. A group of survivors of sexual abuse may have significant difficulty in achieving intimacy if it is structured as open-ended, with new members constantly joining the group and other members leaving it.

The literature provides a fund of observations on questions of group composition and structure, but unfortunately it also provides conflicting opinions and evidence in support of rules. For example, there are conflicting reports on the optimum size for effective discussion groups, with support for different numbers argued persuasively. A balance has to be struck between ignoring these issues completely and depending too much upon rigid rules and structures.

For example, Corey and Corey (2006) suggest the following:

> What is a desirable size for a group? The answer depends on several factors: age of clients, experience of the leader, type of group, and problems to be explored. For instance, a group composed of elementary school children might be kept to 3 or 4, whereas a group of adolescents might be made up of 6 to 8 people. There may be as many as 20 or 30 children in developmental group guidance classes. For a weekly ongoing group of adults, about 8 people with one leader may be ideal. A group of this size is big enough to give ample opportunity for interaction and small enough for everyone to be involved and to feel a sense of "group." (p. 117)

Jacobs, Masson, and Harvill (2006) suggest a smaller group size would be appropriate for most groups:

> Group size can definitely affect group dynamics, so the leader should pay much attention to the decision of how many members to have in the group. The size of the group will depend in part on its purpose, the length of time of each session, the setting available, and the experience of the leader. We suggest 5 to 8 as the ideal number of members for most groups. For multicultural groups, the leader and the members may be more comfortable with groups of no more than 5. (p. 42)

The position argued here is that each setting must develop its own rules, based upon its experiences as well as those of others. Given this reality, a group leader must address a number of questions, using the experiences of colleagues and of other settings to develop some tentative answers. Each group represents an experiment that can contribute to the fund of experience the group leader will draw upon in starting new groups. Some of the questions requiring discussion are highlighted in the remainder of this section. I will not provide definitive answers to these questions, but rather, a way of exploring the issues.

## Group Member Selection

The crucial factor in selection of members is that there is some *common ground* between their individual needs and the purpose of the group. Whether this purpose has been defined broadly or narrowly, each member must be able to find some connection between a personal sense of urgency and the work involved. Even if this common ground is not apparent to the prospective members at the start, the group leader should have some sense of its existence. In the example of the couples' group, each couple was having severe marital problems. Another point in common was that all five couples had some commitment at the start to trying to strengthen their marriages. Couples who had already decided to separate and who needed help in doing so without causing additional pain to each other or their families would not have belonged in this group.

In an AIDS/recovery group I co-led early in the emergence of the epidemic, the five members included one White, gay male; a transgender woman; a heterosexual woman; and two African American males. Although their life experiences differed significantly, all of the members shared in common the disease of AIDS and all were in relatively early recovery (one week to a little more than one year) from poly-substance abuse (alcohol, cocaine, heroin, etc.) and had experienced some form of early trauma. Group members differed in their status with respect to AIDS. Two members were on what was at that time an experimental treatment that had lowered their AIDS viral loads (counts) to almost zero and had raised their T-cell (protective) counts to near normal. One client was waiting for her viral load and T-cell count to reach the point at which she could enter the experimental clinical trials with the new drugs. Another client was eligible, but refusing treatment. The health of the transgendered fifth member had been damaged so badly by her use of hormones and illegal substances that she was too ill for the experimental treatment. For this client, her viral load was climbing each week, her T-cell count was nonexistent, and she was experiencing a range of opportunistic infections common to later-stage AIDS. In spite of these significant differences, each member was able to relate to the others on the basis of their shared struggle with AIDS, with early substance abuse recovery, and with the interaction between the two.

***Group Composition and Age of the Members***  As the group leader defines the purpose of the group and considers potential members, common sense can help to identify potential differences that might create difficulty in reaching group consensus on the focus of the work. Group purpose will be important in thinking about age and group composition. For example, in the couples' group described earlier, the differences in the ages of the five couples provided unexpected dividends. Each couple was experiencing the crises associated with their particular phase of life and phase of their marriage; however, there were common themes cutting across all phases. In many ways, the older couples were able to share their experiences and perspectives with the younger ones, and the group often took on the appearance of an extended family. After one session in which some of the problems associated with the older couples' life phases were clearly delineated, the husband in the youngest couple said good-humoredly, "I'm beginning to wonder if this is what we have to look forward to going through!" The wife of the oldest couple, who had been married 49 years, responded, "Yes, but you will have the advantage of having had this group to help you face these problems."

Whether to include males, females, or both will similarly have to be determined according to the group's purpose. In those groups where gender issues are central, then gender may be a legitimate inclusion or exclusion criterion. For example, while there can be male and female survivors of sexual abuse, the impact of the abuse and the issues that have emerged from it may have gender differences and require a homogeneous gender membership. Chapter 13 explores a number of theories that help us to understand the entity I call the group-as-a-whole. One model described specifically refers to the dynamics in women's groups and explores feminist models of practice. Membership in these groups would be restricted to women.

I find some of the other factors often discussed when deciding on group membership, such as judgments about a member's "personality," somewhat questionable. For example, I have seen a group meticulously assembled with a proper number of relatively passive school children balanced by a manageable number of active ones. The theory was to guarantee interaction, with the active members stimulating the passive ones. In addition, some limit on active members was thought to help the leader with potential problems of control. Unfortunately, nobody informed the group members about their expected roles. The leader was observed in the first session desperately trying to deal with the acting out behaviors of the "passive" members while the "active" members looked on in amusement.

The fact of the matter is that clients do not act the same in every situation. A passive client in an individual interview or classroom may act differently when exposed to a new context. Clients will not remain in the "diagnosed" box—for example, active or passive—long enough to be clearly identified. Their reactions will be somewhat dependent on the actions of those around them, particularly the group leader.

***Race, Ethnicity, and Language*** The impact of diversity on practice was discussed in detail in Chapter 4. For this chapter, race, ethnicity, and language issues need to be considered when composing or leading a group. The counseling literature addresses the importance of understanding the multicultural context in group practice. Corey (2006) suggests:

> In a pluralistic society, the reality of cultural diversity is recognized, respected, and encouraged. Within groups, the worldviews of both the group leader and the members also vary, and this is a natural place to acknowledge and promote pluralism. Multicultural group work involves strategies that cultivate understanding and appreciation of diversity in such areas as culture, ethnicity, race, gender, class, religion, and sexual identity. We each have a unique multicultural identity, but as members of a group, we share a common goal—the success of the group. To that end, we want to learn more about ourselves as individuals and as members of diverse cultural groups. (p. 11)

Some authors who have focused on multicultural group work issues, such as DeLucia-Waack (2006), DeLucia-Waack and Donigian (2004), and the *Best Practices Guidelines* adopted by the Association for Specialists in Group Work (Thomas & Pender, 2007), have stressed the importance of attention to this issue. However, there is a paucity of research on the impact of diversity on counseling group composition decisions.

While not specifically addressing group composition, Rodriquez (1998) studied the impact of within-group value diversity on personal satisfaction, group creativity, and group effectiveness. He reported this finding: "After accounting for diversity in race/nationality, gender, and age, value diversity predicted greater personal satisfaction, and higher perceived group creativity and effectiveness" (p. 744).

Davis (1979, 1981, 1984, 1999) has addressed the impact of race on group composition and practice, basing his observations on anecdotal as well as empirical evidence. In reviewing the literature on the impact of racial composition, Davis (1981) identified a number of observed processes that emerge when a racial ratio changes and minority membership is increased. These included such processes as *cleavage, tipping points,* and *White flight.* In cleavage, the group splits into distinct racial subgroups. The tipping point is the number of minority members that creates anxiety in majority members, resulting in aggression toward members of the "out" group. Regarding White flight, he suggested that White persons are so often in the majority that when they are placed in a group in which they are in a smaller-than-usual majority—for example, with more than 10 to 20 percent persons of color—they may experience a mental state of being in the "psychological minority," at times leading to a White flight reaction (Davis & Proctor, 1989, p. 103). Conversely, members of the minority group faced with this ratio may experience being in the "psychological majority" even though their absolute numbers are less than 50 percent.

As with many such observations, these concepts of psychological minority and majority may not significantly affect the decisions related to the composition of one's group. Rather, they serve to attune the group leader to potential group dynamics resulting from a composition that may affect the group's functioning. Awareness of the process by the group leader, as well as a willingness to address these issues when and if they emerge, may help the group cope more effectively.

In summarizing the literature on race and group in the late 1980s, Davis and Proctor (1989) suggested that

> There is some evidence that whites and minorities may prefer different racial compositions: neither whites nor minorities appear to like being greatly outnumbered. The language spoken in the group may also be important. For example, if some members speak Spanish, while others do not, the nonbilingual speakers may become isolated. (p. 115)

Davis and Proctor (1989) also summarized the findings on group leadership:

> Leaders who differ in race from their group members may receive less cooperation. Biracial co-leadership may enhance communication in racially heterogeneous groups. However, biracial co-leaders must remain alert to the possibility of one leader being perceived as the leader and the other as his helper. (p. 116)

Finally, in addressing the paucity of empirical research, these authors stated:

> There is no evidence which suggests that group treatment is more or less suitable for any particular ethnic group. Furthermore, there is little evidence that either racially homogenous or racially heterogeneous groups are superior in their outcomes. Very few studies have attempted to assess the effects of the group leader's race on group member outcomes. Furthermore, reports from studies involving the race of the leader are mixed. However, these studies are consistent in that they have found that prior group leader experience in counseling with minorities appears to have beneficial effects for the group. (p. 117)

***A Prevention Intervention Program for Latino Children*** Although much of the discussion in this section has been on considering the impact of diversity or homogeneity on group composition, there are examples of group purpose in which race and language can be the central variable in composing the group. One recent example, reported by Marsiglia, Pena, Nieri, and Nagoshi (2010), involved implementing a mutual-aid support group program called "Real Groups" for fifth-grade Latino children referred by their teachers from predominately Mexican American schools located in the central city neighborhoods of a southwestern U.S. metropolitan area.

In a pilot study of an in-school, classroom-based, "keepin' it real" program, these 115 students were referred for an additional 8-week more intensive small-group program and then compared on outcome measures with their 306 Mexican-heritage classmates who did not receive the small-group intervention. The authors acknowledge limitations of the research design, for example, the lower existing substance abuse problems with fifth-graders and the possibility that teachers did not refer high-risk students for substance abuse, as intended, but rather, students with behavior problems. However, the program does provide a model for culturally specific group interventions with acculturating children using a mutual-aid model that is central to this book's group practice approach. It also provided suggestions for future research. I will focus on the model, rather than the research, which generated mixed results.

> The group sessions help students discuss, rehearse, and apply the Real resistance strategies to real-life situations connected with aspects of their culture of origin that protect them from risk, such as culturally supported antidrug norms....The group sessions provide members with opportunities to discuss, address, clarify, and redefine misconceptions and stereotypes about them and their communities of origin. (p. 108)

The model described by the authors encouraged group leaders (MSW students) to actively involve the members to own the group, to encourage supportive activities, and to provide direction for the discussion. This program used a structured manualized model to engage members in discussion. Key topics were:

1. When you do not know—fostering mutuality in relationships
2. What is in a name?—recognizing and asserting personal needs linked to culture of origin
3. Let's make room for everyone—balancing uniqueness with inclusion
4. Where are you from? —valuing the self and the history of migration
5. My neighborhood—valuing the self as a resource to others
6. Dream and act—maintaining a vision of the future and acting to realize that vision
7. My family and friends—cultivating a sense of belonging
8. You can count on me—connecting with support networks (p. 108)

The differences expected between the two groups were generally in the right direction but not at the required level of significance. In suggesting future research designs, the authors acknowledge the need to obtain data on the actual interactions in the groups, what I have been referring to as the "process" data, perhaps from the perception of participants as well as observers. Adding the ability to control findings for these process variables as well as including the specific interventions of the student leaders might have yielded more significant findings.

A common problem in research of manualized interventions is the assumption that all group leaders actually implement the manual as described and are able to respond spontaneously and skillfully to group process issues not described in the manual. Adding these elements, as well as including data on the demographics of the group leaders, might yield important inter- and intracultural information that can impact on outcomes. Even with these study limitations, the model itself provides a good example of a group where homogeneous membership in terms of ethnicity is important.

## Group Timing

There are a number of time-related factors to consider when setting up a group. How often will the group meet? How long will the meetings last? For how long will the group meet (e.g., six sessions, four months)? Once again, each of the answers must draw on common sense, the experience of the agency, and the literature, and all must be related to group purpose.

In the married couples' group, we chose to meet once each week, for two hours each session, over a period of 23 weeks. Meetings had to be held in the evening so that both partners could attend. The group was designed to provide long-term support to the couples as they dealt with their marital problems. The alternate option of intensive weekends, for example, was not considered. For couples in crisis, it seemed that the intensive, short-term experience might open up more problems while leaving the couples unable to deal with them. On the other hand, weekend workshops for marital enrichment groups, in which the relationships are strong to begin with, may be beneficial as educational and skill-development experiences.

The decision to meet weekly was based on the recognition that longer breaks between meetings might diffuse the intensity of the experience, making each session seem like a new beginning. Two hours seemed to be enough time to allow for the development of central themes and issues in the beginning phase of each meeting, while leaving enough time to deal effectively with specific individual and group concerns. More than two hours might be wearying for both group members and group leaders.

Whatever decisions are reached for a particular group, discussing and clarifying the plan with group members is important. Group members have a sense of the group's time frame and will be affected by the particular phase of the meeting or the phase in the life of the group. As pointed out earlier, the "doorknob therapy" phenomenon can accelerate the presentation of important issues; however, the members need to know when the time to reach for the door is close at hand. In my married couples' group, it was striking how as we approached the end of the life of the group each couple appeared to take one of the last five sessions in turn to deal with some of the most powerful issues in their marriage. It is possible for group members to work more effectively if they have less time to carry out their tasks.

Reid and Shyne (1969), for example, have discussed the impact of time on both the group leader and the client in their work on short-term treatment. There is a limit, however, to how much can be dealt with, so judicious balance needs to be developed, allowing enough sessions to deal with the anticipated themes of concern. This limit will come from experience as an agency evaluates each group, using the group members as part of the evaluation process. Group members can be used quite effectively in setting up the initial parameters by exploring their reactions to time proposals before the group is established. Feedback on the day of the week or the specific time for starting may help a group leader to avoid unnecessary conflicts.

***Form Follows Function in Group Formation***  An expression borrowed from architecture, "form follows function," is useful in thinking about time in the group formation stage. In building, this means that the design (form) of a specific building should take into consideration the use to which it will be put (function). Likewise, the form of the group in relation to time needs to be connected to group purpose. Agency conceptions about time can change as experiences with new group services are evaluated.

In one example, I served as a consultant to an agency providing extensive group services to persons with AIDS (PWAs) as well as their friends, lovers, and family members. These groups were offered early in the AIDS epidemic and before the use of the triple drug therapy treatments. Under the original plan developed by the agency prior to my work with them, a group would start with clients diagnosed as HIV positive and continue as members progressed through the stages of the illness (AIDS-related complex, or ARC) and AIDS itself. The group would continue as a mini-community as members became progressively more ill and most finally died. This structure seemed to make sense if the purpose of the group was to provide an alternative source of support for its members, many of whom felt cut off from other systems in their lives (e.g., family, work, and friends). In reality, the groups did not work this way. Most of the groups began to dissolve as members observed other members dying or becoming seriously ill.

The experience caused a rethinking of group purpose. Rather than the agency providing the substitute community, the groups were conceptualized as time-limited, with a focus on helping the members deal with transitions to the various stages of the illness (e.g., one group for recently diagnosed HIV-positive clients; another group for clients facing the onset of serious medical problems). Another group focused on living with AIDS. This was not always easy to do, as the course of the illness was neither always smooth nor predictable. However, instead of the agency attempting to provide the substitute community—a task that would eventually overwhelm the agency, given the number of potential clients involved in the pandemic of AIDS—the focus changed to one of helping group members mobilize existing support in their own family, friendship, and community systems.

Analysis of process in the groups indicated that group leaders had been too quick to accept their group members' contention that such support was closed to them and that only the group could provide it. Work in the groups became more demanding, and members were asked to look closely at their own efforts to connect with their social support systems. The move to time-limited groups had an important and positive impact on the nature of the work. Once the "function" of the group had been clearly defined, the questions of "form" were easier to resolve.

In my more recent experience coleading a group for persons with AIDS in early recovery from substance abuse, new issues of timing presented themselves. For example, with a number of our group members on the then new triple-therapy drug regime, and with their resulting improvement in health, we were viewing the group as one of the ongoing support systems designed to help the members cope with (for most of them) living with AIDS rather than dying from AIDS. Also, the recovery issues required more long-term support than if the members were dealing with AIDS alone. This group began in October of one year, focusing on helping members get through the extremely stressful holiday season of Thanksgiving, Christmas, and New Year's Eve when attending parties with friends and families posed a serious threat to their recovery efforts. The group reconvened in the new year and continued until a summer break period with the understanding that the members would assess the need to reconvene in the fall. Individual group members received ongoing support from my coleader, who served as their substance abuse counselor.

In one consultation session with private practice mental health group leaders, a group leader revealed he had been working with the same group meeting regularly for 6 years. This seemed excessive to me and I asked why it had gone on so long. With some difficulty the group leader finally shared that when he had ended a similar group earlier in his career a member had committed suicide. It became clear that he had experienced a vicarious trauma himself and that his judgment on the continuation of the current group was affected by personal and professional unresolved issues. I suggested he consider ending this group, working on how to help the members make a safe transition to other sources of support, and then find a group for himself to deal with his grief and fears for his clients.

## Group Structure, Setting, and Rules

There are a number of questions related to group structure and setting in the formation stage. For example, the meeting place needs consideration. Ease of access by public and private transportation might be a factor. Holding a session on sensitive and potentially embarrassing issues (e.g., child abuse) in a public setting where members might fear being identified could be a mistake.

The room itself should offer group members face-to-face seating (e.g., in a circle or around a table) and privacy. Comfortable chairs and surroundings often add to the group members' comfort during the first sessions. Even with larger information-focused groups, rather than setting chairs in straight lines, some sense of group involvement can be conveyed by simply curving the rows into semicircles in an amphitheatre style so that members can more easily see each other when asking questions or responding to the discussion. Work with children, on the other hand, where activity is going to be part of the work may require facilities that are relatively "activity-proof," so that members and the group leader can relax without constant worries about order and decorum.

Finally, group "rules" need clarification prior to the first group meeting. For example, limits on physical activity may be set with children's groups. Even with some adult groups it may be necessary to clarify the boundary on the use of physical force. In a group session for prison parolees, for example, one member pulled out a knife and began to clean his fingernails in a manner meant to be threatening to another member. The group leader recontracted with the members on the issue of bringing weapons to the session and made clear that threatening behaviors would not be tolerated.

Expectations about attendance are also important. The expectations the members have of the setting and the group and those the group leader has of the members should be discussed. In addition, what can each member expect from the others (e.g., confidentiality of material shared)? In my couples' group, for example, the three rules discussed in the first session are that each member is expected to come each week as long as he or she is not ill, that a couple wanting to quit the group will come back for one additional week to discuss it, and that confidentiality will be respected by group members. In the example of my AIDS/recovery group, meetings were held in a "clean and sober" residence (three members lived in this house). Members were not to bring substances to the group or be under the influence of substances when they attended.

There are many differences of opinion on the question of group rules. For example, some would argue that group members should not have contact with each other outside the meetings. The field of group practice is far from the point where we can come to agreement on these questions. My general bias is that group members own their own lives and that my group is simply an incident in their week (I hope, an important incident). I would, therefore, have difficulty insisting on a rule preventing them from having contacts outside the group. In fact, in many groups the bonds of mutual aid that have developed through telephone calls and informal contacts outside the group have been powerful supports for individual members.

Group leaders in some groups, who fear that group members may get involved in "acting out" outside of the group (having sexual contact, for example), appear to me to take more responsibility for the lives of the members than they should. In some groups, such as the AIDS/recovery group, such outside activity could be a distinct threat to the members' recovery at a particularly vulnerable time in their lives. These issues need to be discussed as part of the structure of the group.

In addition, group members should be free to bring their outside interactions into the group if they wish, since they can represent an important entry into the content of the group work. In general, the rules stated in the beginning of the group should be firmly rooted to the reality of the situation rather than the arbitrary authority or personal preferences of the group leader. They should be seen by group members as emerging from the necessities of the work. A full discussion of these rules should be included as part of the informed consent procedure.

Returning to my married couples' group which met in a room in a health science center, after the fifth week I discovered that group members were having a second meeting over coffee in the hospital cafeteria. I believe that their interaction as a "social group" was actually beneficial, allowing them to deal more effectively in the counseling group. There were times when I was not sure which meeting was helping more.

## Section Summary

A number of issues related to group composition, timing, setting, rules, and structure have been raised in these sections for the purpose of alerting the reader to questions requiring consideration prior to the start of the group. My opinions on these questions have been shared not as the truth, but rather as an illustration of how one practitioner develops his own views from his experiences and those of others. As with all the ideas shared in this book, the reader will have to test them against her or his own sense of reality and ongoing group experiences.

## Interviewing Prospective Members

After administration and staff support have been mobilized, potential obstacles to cooperation identified and discussed, and decisions made on the formation questions, then one more step remains: recruitment of group members. In contrast to individual and family work, very rarely does a group of clients arrive at the agency door and request services. It may happen with some naturally formed groups, as when a group of teens in a school approach the group leader for help. These are the exceptions rather than the rule. Most group counseling practice requires outreach, where the counseling service must be brought to the potential clients. Recruitment of group members is therefore a crucial element in the formation stage.

This process can also be complex, since clients feel a general ambivalence about taking help as well as unique concerns related to the group context. Some degree of ambivalence is usually present when people consider joining any group. I will focus this discussion on examples of mutual-aid groups designed to deal with problems of living (e.g., marital difficulties, parenting skills, alcohol or drug addiction, school difficulties) in the belief that some of the principles can be applied to other types of groups as well.

Clients may become prospective group members by identifying themselves in response to posters, newspaper stories, and letters from the agency, or other means of publicizing the existence of a group service. If handled well, the steps involved in making potential group members aware of the group can help to turn the potential client toward the service. For example, posters or letters should be worded clearly, without jargon, so that the prospective member has a clear idea of the group's purpose. This would be a first step in the informed consent process. It may be helpful to identify some of the themes of concern that may be related to the client's sense of urgency. If the embarrassment of the group leaders results in the use of euphemisms, or if the group leaders have the idea of changing the client "up their sleeves," a form of hidden agenda, and try to hide this by general and vague offers of service, prospective group members may be turned away. It can be helpful to test the letters or posters with colleagues and clients to get their sense of the meaning and suggestions as to how to make the wording direct but still nonthreatening. The group leader may be very surprised at a potential client's interpretation of the wording of the offer and, particularly, at the use of professional jargon unintelligible to the normal reader.

Other clients are referred by colleagues or other helping professionals or are selected by group leaders from their caseloads. Whatever the case may be, even when the client has initiated the contact, the gap between thinking about joining a group and arriving at the first meeting can be a big one. Many of the skills already identified can be helpful in increasing the chances of a successful start. Two areas I will now examine are working with colleagues after they have agreed to recruit group members (a real agreement), and telephone or in-person contacts between the group leader and prospective members.

## Strategizing for Effective Referrals

A group leader may have done an effective job with fellow staff members on the establishment of a group and even have their genuine support but still be disappointed by a relatively low number of referrals or clients showing up to a first meeting. An important question often overlooked is how the colleague will conduct a referral interview. It is a mistake to assume that even a motivated colleague will be able to make an effective referral without some joint work and strategizing as to how it might be done. For example, the colleague may have a general sense of the group purpose but be unable to articulate it clearly. One who has not worked with groups may not be sensitive to some of the underlying feelings and ambivalence that the client may share indirectly, thereby missing a chance to help overcome some of the obstacles blocking access to the group.

It is often helpful to suggest a "tuning-in" session, either one-on-one or with a staff group, in which group leaders pool their efforts to sensitize themselves to the concerns clients may have about joining the group and the indirect ways these may emerge. Staff can then share strategies for reaching for the underlying concerns through questioning or articulating them for the client. In addition, a brief role-play of the referral interview may reveal to the group leader that the colleagues are not able to articulate purpose, and work can then be done on this skill. For example, it might be heard differently if a school group leader describes a group as a place for the student to deal with the stresses from teachers, school, parents, and friends in a way that does not get him or her into trouble rather than suggesting that he attend an "anger management" group. Such a process may also bring to the surface ambivalent feelings on the part of the group leader or unanswered questions that need to be dealt with prior to the actual referral interviews.

***Recruiting Men Who Have Been Physically Abusive to Their Partners*** An example of this process is a referral workshop that I conducted for social service professionals in connection with the establishment of a new and (at that time) experimental group service for men who had physically abused their wives or partners. Recognizing the importance of professional referrals to launch the program and knowing that the referral process might be extremely difficult in this situation, we provided an opportunity for "tuning-in" and joint strategizing. To keep the discussion focused on skills, I asked for examples of difficult referrals of a similar nature.

One group leader described from memory a referral he had recently attempted with the common-law husband of a client. The client was a prostitute who had been beaten by the husband who was also her pimp, but she had refused to report the incident or leave him (the existence of many situations such as this had led to the project to establish groups for the men involved). As the group leader's interaction with the husband was analyzed, it became clear that he had never mentioned the physical abuse, attempting instead to lead the husband indirectly to agree to seek help.

When this was mentioned during the analysis of the example, the group leader revealed that he had feared angering the husband and risking that the husband might then take the anger out on the wife. An important discussion followed in which others spoke of their fears of possible retribution not only on the partners but also themselves. Of course, this raised ethical issues in terms of informed consent. The workshop participants felt they faced an ethical dilemma, since they wanted to protect the partner from further physical abuse and yet knew they would be misleading the potential group members on the purpose of the group.

Their dilemma was discussed and strategies developed for broaching the subject directly in a manner that tried to avoid exacerbating the abusing partner's defensiveness. The first group leader tried to role-play how to recruit the member while being honest. Without this preparatory work, group leaders would have been blocked, thus offering this group indirectly because of their fears. Of course, once the men arrived at the group, it would have become clear they had been misled.

Let us consider another illustration of the problem of stating group purpose. In a role-play of how to describe the group purpose, it became clear that the group leaders were describing the group in a way that would lead the prospective member to believe his worst fears—that the group was designed solely to chastise him for his behavior and to educate him to appreciate his impact on his partner. When I pointed out that the group leader seemed angry at the prospective group member, my comment released a flood of feelings, echoed by many in the room, of anger at the men. All of the professionals had agreed earlier that these groups could not be effective unless the men could both be held accountable for their violent actions toward women and also see the group as designed to help them as clients in their own right. This intellectual agreement evaporated in the role-play. It was replaced with an essentially punitive and thereby ineffective offer of service.

The opportunity for group leaders to discuss and be in touch with these natural yet often-denied feelings might have helped to ensure a presentation of the group that would turn prospective members toward the service rather than reinforce their resistance. It was recognized that for many of these men, even the most effective offer of service might not elicit a response. For some, it would take their partner leaving them or a court order to get them to come to the first meeting. Although this group example may be an extreme one, I believe that in most cases the group leader forming a group would be well advised to take some time with colleagues to discuss the technical aspects of making the referral.

## Group Leader Skills in the Initial Interviews

Group leaders often have initial contacts with individual members, in person or by phone, to discuss their participation in the group. These interviews can be seen as part of the exploratory process in which the group leader describes what the group has to offer and checks with the client to determine what may be needed. The skills described briefly earlier of clarifying purpose, clarifying role, and reaching for feedback are useful in this interview. Describing the structure of the group (how it will work) as well as timing helps to provide the information needed for the prospective member to make a decision about using the service. It also helps to fulfill another aspect of the requirement for informed consent.

In addition to the normal "tuning in" to the client's feelings about beginning a new relationship, it is also important to "tune in" to the specific concerns related to beginning in a group. The general population has been exposed to a number of reports on groups ranging from "group psychotherapy" to "encounter groups." In addition, clients may bring stereotypes of groups based upon their past experiences (e.g., class groups at school, camp experiences) that will have some effect on their feelings about attending. Questions about how people with the same problems can help each other will also be on their minds.

***Recruiting for a School Parent Group: Confronting the Illusion of Agreement*** Much of this hesitancy and fear may be just beneath the surface. It can be expressed in indirect ways, and the group leader must listen for it and reach directly for the indirect cues.

**Practice Points:** In the following example, a school group leader has been describing a parents' group and has found the parent apparently receptive. The cues emerge when the group leader gets specific about the dates.

Group Leader: We are going to have our first meeting in two weeks, on a Wednesday night. Can I expect you there?

Parent: (Long pause) Well, it sounds good. I'll try to make it if things aren't too hectic that week at work.

**Practice Points:** If the group leader quits right there and accepts the illusion of agreement, she may be guaranteeing that the parent will not show up. Even though group leaders can sense the ambivalence in the client's voice, they often refrain from reaching for the negative attitude. When I have inquired why group leaders refrain from exploring such cues of uncertainty, they tell me that they are afraid that if they bring the doubts out in the open, they will reinforce them— what I call the fear that if they reach for the problem they will bring it about. They believe that the less said the better. In reality, these doubts and questions are valid, and the group leader is missing an opportunity to help the client explore them.

Without this exploration, the client may simply not show up at the first meeting despite having promised to attend. When the group leader later calls, there is much guilt on the client's part and profuse explanations of his or her absence (e.g., "I really meant to come, only it got so hectic that day it just slipped my mind"; "Was it this week? I thought it was next week").

**Practice Points:** Returning to the interview with the parent, you should note the turn in the work when the group leader reaches for the cue.

**GROUP LEADER:** You sound a bit hesitant. Are you concerned about attending the group? It wouldn't be unusual; most people have a lot of questions about groups.

**PARENT:** Well, you know I never do too well in groups. I find I have a lot of trouble talking in front of strangers.

**GROUP LEADER:** Are you worried that you would have to speak up and be put on the spot?

**PARENT:** I don't mind talking about parenting; it's just that I get tongue-tied in a group.

**GROUP LEADER:** I can appreciate your concern. A lot of people feel that way. I can tell you right now that except for sharing your name and the names and ages of your children, no one will put you on the spot to speak. Some people always talk a lot at the early meetings while others prefer to listen. You can listen until you feel comfortable about speaking. If you want, I can help you to begin to talk in the group, but only when you're ready. I do this all the time with people who feel this way.

**PARENT:** You mean it's not just me who feels this way?

**GROUP LEADER:** Not at all. It's quite common and natural. By the way, are there any other concerns you might have about the group?

**PARENT:** Not really. That was the biggest one. Actually, it doesn't sound like a bad idea at all.

**Practice Summary.** Once again we see the importance of exploring the indirect cue so that the group leader has a clearer idea about the source of the ambivalence. Many group leaders would hesitate to explore the cue because they would feel it was a sign of polite rejection of the group (and the group leader). When asked why they assume this unnecessarily, they often reply that they are unsure about their own competency and the quality of the group. They respond to the client's ambivalence with their own feelings. In the case just cited, the fear of speaking in the group needed to be discussed. Knowing that the group leader understands and that it is all right to feel this way can strengthen the client to overcome an obstacle to undertaking group experiences.

In other cases, it may be memories of past group experience, or horror stories recounted by friends or relatives about harsh and confronting group encounters, or embarrassment about sharing personal details with strangers. The group leaders need to clarify the reality when possible, empathize genuinely with the fears, and still attempt to help the client take the first difficult step. With this kind of help from the group leader, many prospective group members will be able to overcome their fears and doubts and give the group a try. A source of great support for the client is the knowledge that the group leader understands his or her feelings.

***Recruiting Caregiver Family Members for Alzheimer Patients*** One other not uncommon type of resistance occurs when a group in a community mental health agency is offered to the caretaker, support person, or relative of a client. In one example, a group leader was recruiting a group for relatives of elderly Alzheimer patients who were caring for their family members at home.

**Practice Points:** Note that in the face of the initial, hinted reluctance, the group leader reached for the concern and said,

> "You sound hesitant about coming to the group, Mrs. Smith. Can you tell me why?" The client responded, with some feeling, "Just one more thing on the list for me to do to take care of my mother. I don't have time for myself!" The group leader replied, "Mrs. Smith, I think I can appreciate how demanding caring for your mother must be. But I don't think I made the purpose of this

group clear when I described it. This group is not for your mother. This group is for you. Other group members will also be feeling overwhelmed by the demands made upon them by their relatives with Alzheimer's, and part of what we can discuss is how you can get the support you need."

**Practice Summary.**    By reaching for the lurking negatives and the ambivalence, the group leader creates an opportunity to clarify group purpose to a potential member. A common trap that group leaders fall into when they hear the indirect or direct cues of some reluctance is to try to "sell" the group even harder.

## Screening Criteria for Group Practice

Earlier in this chapter I suggested that the crucial element for determining if someone would be a candidate for group practice was having an underlying common ground with other members so that they would feel a connection to the purpose of the group and to other group members. I also identified a number of demographic factors such as age, gender, and so on that, when related to group purpose, should be taken into account when composing a group. A previous section also examined how to engage potential members in individual interviews in order to encourage participation in the group and to actively involve other staff in making effective referrals.

But what about those individuals who may qualify according to the general criteria but are not really good candidates for group practice? This takes us to the issue of screening criteria that may be used in the initial interview that may lead the group leader not to include the particular client. A member who is a serious problem may drop out early, with an impact on the group as a whole, or continue in the group but cause others to drop out.

The literature is mixed on the question of whether we can, in a screening interview, identify potential members who will do well in the group, not drop out, and in fact be well received by other group members. One exception is an article by Gans and Counselman (2010) that identified a number of criteria that can be used in evaluating the potential success of a group member during a clinical screening interview. I should point out that they were referring to recruitment for long-term, open-ended, psychodynamically oriented group therapy and, in many cases, private group therapy practice. Still, some of the principles can be applied to the groups in agencies and settings described in this book. They point out that

> Group dropouts and, more generally, mismatches between an individual and the group demoralize the group or even lead to its demise, waste valuable professional expertise, time and energy, and often discourage those who have dropped out from ever seeking therapy again. Premature unilateral terminations, especially early, are unhappy experiences for both members and leaders. Thus, it behooves the therapist to employ screening methods that ensure the selection of the most suitable candidates for group psychotherapy. (pp. 197–198)

The authors contrast their experience over years of practice in which they have retained over 90 percent of their patients through 16 weeks in their long-term, open-ended weekly outpatient therapy groups. They acknowledge that many factors may have contributed to the retention rate, but they believe that "our close attention to several aspects of the pre-group screening interviews has been central, if not crucial to our success" (p. 198). They point out that how the prescreening interview is conducted may have an important impact on the beginning of the therapeutic alliance, which they acknowledge may be the most important predictor.

These authors also point to a number of factors that may influence dropping out, including a group's readiness to accept a new member, limitations on the leader's technical skills or the leader's ability to manage countertransference in relation to a difficult member, and the ability of the leader to manage the emotional impact of painful affect that, if expressed, would allow other group members to connect with the new member. (In the discussion of open-ended groups in Chapter 11 an illustration of the technical skills involved in bringing a new member into an ongoing group for men with AIDS illustrates the importance of working with the new member and the group.)

The authors suggest that a pregroup interview should include as many of the following as possible:

> (1) identification of potential or definite disqualifying factors; (2) elicitation, evaluation, and discussion of resistance and/or ambivalence to being a group therapy patient; (3) exploration of other group experience; (4) assessment of role playing (if used);[1] (5) analysis of countertransference contributions to clinical mistakes in the selection process; and (6) identification of problems specific to evaluating one's individual patient for combined therapy. (pp. 203–204)

The authors look at each of these areas and identify such practical disqualifying factors as ability to attend at the time of the meeting, travel distances to get to the meeting or work requirements that require travel, and child care. Additional factors include resistance or ambivalence, expressed through early acting out such as being late or missing the intake meeting or calling for the appointment months after the referral. They suggest exploring ambivalence even when it is only beneath the surface in a manner similar to the skill I called "looking for trouble when everything is going your way." Overly compliant patients may be another clue, such as when they say: "My therapist thinks I should be in group therapy."

Previous group experiences may leave the candidate with erroneous assumptions about group therapy expressed by a lack of asking questions when it would be natural to have some. A particular "red flag" is when the prospective group member will not give permission for the group leader to talk with either the former or current therapist. The authors also call for self-reflection on the part of the group leader on factors that might affect the decision to accept or reject the potential member (numbers 5 and 6 above).

Finally, the authors acknowledge shame felt by the potential member as a factor influencing a decision to participate and continue in a group treatment program, for example, one potential member who felt shame about her pedophile son. While this may not be a determining factor in influencing commencing and continuing in a group, it should be explored. They suggest:

> It is tempting to minimize such concerns or reassure the patient that the group will be understanding, rather than explore the depth of the patient's anticipated shame. While such dread needs to be respected, it does not have to constitute an absolute contraindication to group membership. (p. 209)

This section ends the discussion of steps that need to be taken in the preliminary stage of group practice. The next section reflects on some of the ethical issues that are unique to this phase of group work.

---

1. The authors are referring to a technique in which the interviewer suggests a number of events that might happen in a group, for example, a confrontation by another member, and then asks the interviewee how she or he might react.

# Ethical Issues in Group Practice

**EP 2.1.1c**
**EP 2.1.2a**
**EP 2.1.2b**
**EP 2.1.2d**

In this section the particular ethical issues raised by meeting clients in groups are addressed. Some of these are variations on issues discussed earlier, such as the clarification on the guarantees and limits of confidentiality in the worker–client engagement. These change dramatically when other clients are involved in the group. Thus, these issues must be given special consideration in the group formation stage.

In an introductory article to a two-part series exploring ethical problems and dilemmas for the group psychotherapist, Brabender (2006) points out that

> In the training of the group psychotherapist, considerable attention is devoted to the mastery of theory and technique that will enable the therapist to be effective in helping members to meet their individual and group goals. Cultivating the ethical group psychotherapist—training the therapist to be knowledgeable about ethical principles and be able to use them in everyday decision-making in the course of conducting psychotherapy groups—is a task that historically has been embraced with far less assiduousness. ... Yet, intensive attention to this dimension of training of the group therapist is warranted. When exposed, ethical and legal errors made by group psychotherapists endanger the public's trust in psychotherapy in general and group psychotherapy specifically. Further, effective group work requires ethical practice. (pp. 395–396)

Brabender notes that when group members observe that the group leader's decision making is not informed by ethical considerations, a crisis in trust and diminished group commitment is likely.

Although preparing for every eventuality is impossible, familiarity with basic expectations of professional practice will alert a group leader to potentially serious situations and possible missteps, thus encouraging consultation with colleagues or a supervisor. The expectations may be spelled out ranging from formal statements by agencies and other organizations to informal agreements concerning acceptable behavior on the group leader's part. In the section that follows this one, we continue by examining how laws and the legal system more sharply define ethical issues such as informed consent, confidentiality, and the duty to protect. While many of the ethical and legal issues can apply to counseling in any client modality (e.g. individual, family, group), I shall play special attention to those that are unique to group work practice.

Gumpert and Black (2006), referring to this unique nature of practice with groups, point out that it is

> a complex, multi-leveled practice modality that requires assessment and intervention of interactions among group members, each group member and the worker, each member and the group as a whole, and the group and the worker. At minimum, the group practitioner must have a broad perspective and knowledge and skills to intervene in relation to many levels within the group process. Given the complexity of group practice, it is logical that ethical issues and dilemmas unique to group process might arise. (p. 62)

## Guidelines for Practice in Group Work

Although many of the ethical guidelines for practice with individuals or families also apply to group work, seeing more than one client at a time presents unique ethical issues. For example, consider this variation on the confidentiality issue, introduced by the presence of other clients in group work, as raised in the *Ethical Guidelines for Group Counselors:*

- Members are made aware of the difficulties in enforcing and ensuring confidentiality in a group setting.
- The group leader provides examples of how confidentiality can nonmaliciously be broken to increase members' awareness and helps to lessen the likelihood that this breach of confidence will occur.
- Group leaders inform group members about potential consequences of intentionally breaching confidentiality. (American Association for Counseling and Development, 1989)

Although a group leader can make clear his or her position on confidentiality, the leader must also acknowledge that a "rule" of confidentiality cannot be imposed on group members. The group itself must discuss the issue and develop appropriate ground rules.

In a recent mailed and confidential survey of group leaders who were U.S. and Canadian members of the Association for the Advancement of Social Work with Groups (AASWG), participants were asked to rank 17 ethical issues according to the frequency with which they were confronted with these in their practice (Gumpert & Black, 2006). The 17 issues were identified in two focus group discussions prior to the survey. Of the 350 mailed surveys, 90 (return rate of 27 percent useable surveys) ranked the following 10 ethical issues as most relevant (in order of importance):

1. Communication among group members
2. Conflict between the best interest of group and best interest of individual members
3. Conflict between group norms and values and those of society
4. Unanticipated termination of a group member
5. Conflict between agency policy and best interest of group member
6. Breaches of confidentiality by group members
7. Conflict between member independence and interdependence among group members
8. Undemocratic group decision making
9. Professional incompetence of worker
10. Problems between coworkers that interfere with group process

Researchers in the field of group psychotherapy have raised complex issues associated with disclosures in multiperson practice (Roback, Purdon, Ochoa, & Bloch, 1992). The authors conducted a multidisciplinary survey of 100 members of the American Group Psychotherapy Association. Thirty-six of the respondents were group leaders. The survey described six hypothetical group therapy incidents that posed threats to the confidentiality of the group:

(1) A group member has disclosed outside the group highly sensitive material about another group member, (2) a group member has disclosed current involvement in nonviolent criminal activity, (3) a moderately depressed outpatient group member has threatened physical harm to his ex-wife, (4) a moderately

depressed inpatient group member has threatened physical harm to his ex-wife, (5) an adolescent group member has disclosed physical abuse that occurred for several years but is currently not present, and (6) an 8-year-old group member has disclosed an intention to run away from home, with no evidence of physical or sexual abuse. (p. 172)

Each of these examples takes on special significance because the disclosures took place in the group context. For example, in those states and circumstances in which confidential patient-therapist communications are protected, is the protection voided because of the presence of third parties, the other group members?

Respondents in the study answered four questions regarding each incident. These concerned the most appropriate context for dealing with the disclosure (group, individual, or both), with whom it should be discussed (therapist, group, or disclosing individual), who has primary decision-making responsibility for managing the situation, and what action the group leader should take.

Several of the study's findings provide insights into how group leaders would handle the ethical and practice issues associated with the six scenarios. For example, 80 percent of the group leaders indicated that they would not contact authorities in response to a disclosure of involvement in nonviolent criminal activities; however, 53 percent would encourage the group member to do so. Open-ended responses indicated that the nature of the crime and the potential threat to others would modify their response. Arson, for example, is much more serious than shoplifting.

Almost all therapists (94 percent) reported that they would contact the authorities if confronted with an outpatient's threat to harm others, and 92 percent would do so in response to an inpatient's threat. An interesting related finding was that gender affected the context within which such threats would be handled, with male group leaders more likely to deal with them within the group.

The same gender difference was found in the scenario in which a teenager disclosed prior physical abuse. Overall, 89 percent of the group leaders indicated that they would contact the authorities if confronted with such a disclosure. Approximately 50 percent of respondents would engage in each of the following four alternatives in response to a report of abuse that was no longer occurring:

(a) Discuss and assess the legitimacy of the allegation with the group member; (b) discuss with the member in group his or her feelings about the abuse and abide by what, if anything, he or she wants to do; (c) explain to the group the therapist's responsibility to report this information to the proper agency and proceed to do so; and (d) discuss with the group members their feelings about the abuse and honor their chosen strategy for resolving the situation. (Roback et al., 1992, p. 178)

Clearly there are numerous unique issues and complicated dilemmas that face even experienced and well-trained group leaders. In order to bring home the reality of the impact of these dilemmas, an example follows of work with a sexual abuse survivors group and the issue of the group leader as a mandated reporter.

***Survivors of Sexual Abuse Group and the Mandated Reporter*** Although the ethical issues and the guidelines for practice in situations in which someone is at risk are clear, and the group leader's responsibility as a mandated reporter removes much of the ambiguity, the process can still be painful for all concerned. Consider the following example from a group of eight women who were survivors of childhood sexual abuse. It was a long-term, open group, and although the group had been meeting for 2 years, this was the group coleader's first year. The student, a representative from the state child welfare agency, and a therapist from a local social service agency co-led the group.

**Practice Points:** The coleaders had clearly indicated the limits on confidentiality during the contracting in the first session. Once that is clear, the coleaders can assume that if a member shares information that requires reporting, the member knows the leaders are mandated to do so. Group members under these circumstances will often share the information with a conscious or unconscious desire that the leaders take the next step that they themselves find hard to take.

Confidentiality is a particularly salient issue, because, while the group was voluntary for these women, the fact of my being an employee of the child welfare agency was concerning for them until they got to know me and became comfortable with me.

The week prior to this meeting was very emotional, as one of the women had talked about concerns about how her son behaved when he returned from a recent visit with his father. The description of his behavior and the things that he said pointed to the father having digitally penetrated the boy's anus after they had showered together. I reminded the group of my role as a mandated reporter, and stated that I would be filing a report alleging sexual abuse of the young boy by his father. I told the mother that I thought that it was clear to me that the fact that she brought it up in group was her way of trying to get help. I praised her courage and her concern for her son.

Eileen, the mother of the young boy, did express some concern that her ex-husband, whom she was still emotionally attached to, was going to be mad at her. Mary, a young woman who was in the process of filing charges against her stepfather for her past sexual abuse as a child, expressed feeling empowered by what she saw as my immediate response to protect the child, because her mother had never believed her when she told her of the sexual abuse. After a short discussion, the group ended.

**Practice Points:** Although the leader's response was direct, honest, and required, and I believe she was correct in interpreting Eileen's raising the concern as a call for help, Eileen's reaction the following week is not uncommon. After returning to the home situation, the client now raises doubts about the event, second thoughts about having disclosed it, and anger at the group leader. The lack of defensiveness on the part of the group leader and the responses of other group members are crucial at this point.

At the start of the next group meeting, there was a long silence of about 2 minutes. Several members were glancing at Eileen, and she was moving about in her seat in an agitated manner.

GROUP LEADER: Eileen, you appear to be upset. Is something going on for you?

EILEEN: This is very hard for me. I'm really pissed at you, and I'm having a hard time confronting you. I spoke with Alice (her individual therapist) about what you did last week, and she told me that I should tell you how I feel.

GROUP LEADER: You sound very angry. I would very much like to hear what you have to say. (There is about 30 seconds of silence.)

EILEEN: Well, I thought what we said in group was supposed to be confidential! You took what I said in group when I was upset last week and then used it against me. How the hell am I supposed to ever trust you again?

GROUP LEADER: You feel I betrayed your trust by filing a report against Bobby, and you feel that it is not safe in the group because it is not really confidential.

EILEEN: Damned straight! How can I trust you anymore? Bobby is blaming me. I know my own son. I know when he's exaggerating and when he's not.

MARY: (Angrily) Right! I'm sure that's the same excuse that our mothers used when we were abused.

GROUP LEADER: Eileen, I wonder what it means to you that I reported Bobby. Do you think that it means that I don't trust you to protect your son, or that I think that you are a bad mother? (Eileen starts to cry. As she sobs, others squirm about in their chairs.)

EILEEN: (Looking up) Yes, it means that I am no better than my mother!

**Practice Summary.** In the group leader's analysis of this incident, she describes how, even though she knew she was doing the right thing and that she had no choice, it was painful for her to hear the client's anger. The group leader's skill was evident in not falling into the trap of explaining and justifying her action but instead exploring the source of the member's distress. Because the group leader had clearly described her role as a mandated reporter and had stated under what circumstances she would have to disclose confidential information, she could be reasonably certain that the member knew she would take action. Many nonoffending parents, who were themselves sexually abused and not protected by the other parent, report later that they wanted their group leaders to intervene to protect their children because they were unable to do so themselves.

## Confidentiality and Group Counseling: Unique Dilemmas

Lasky and Riva (2006), citing the work of Welfel (1998), outlined some of the unique confidentiality issues in group practice:

> In addition to disclosing personal information to a therapist, the group client discloses information to other group members with no guarantee that those others will keep that information private. The very effectiveness of the treatment is based on the interdependence and interaction among group members that entails the mutual disclosing of personal material. The group therapist has comparatively less control over how sessions progress, in terms of the nature and depth of material disclosed, or what happens between sessions, especially around issues of confidentiality. (p. 459)

The implications of the presence of these other members, who in most states are "third parties" which invalidates the principle of privileged communications between group leader and patient, are profound. Group members may not be aware, unless clearly informed in giving consent to receive the service, that other group members could be required to testify in civil or criminal proceedings. The authors point out that even in those few states that do protect the privilege in group sessions for the group leader and the members, many therapists are not aware of this privilege and other group members may not be as well. Even if aware, there are no consequences if other group members decide to waive this privilege and provide the information. Certainly, this is one of the most important distinctions between group and individual work. It heightens the need for a clear understanding of the principle of informed consent.

## Chapter Summary

In this chapter, I explored a number of ways in which group members can help each other through mutual aid, which is a process that can be employed in all types of groups. These included sharing data, the dialectical process, discussing taboo areas, the "all-in-the-same-boat" phenomenon, developing a universal perspective, mutual support, mutual demand, individual problem solving, rehearsal, and the "strength-in-numbers" phenomenon.

Three major areas of obstacles to the mutual-aid process in groups were defined and illustrated. These included the difficulty members may have in identifying their common ground, the tasks that must be accomplished by a group in order to develop a positive culture for work, and the general difficulty of open communication. The role of the group leader was defined as an extension of the mediating function described earlier in the book into the group context. The group leader was seen as mediating between two group members: the individual and the group-as-a-whole.

In this chapter I also explored three major areas of work involved in the formation stage of group counseling practice. The first focused on the skills required to work with one's setting and colleagues in order to engage them as active partners in the development of the group service. Strategies were suggested for coping with underlying obstacles that can lead to sabotage of group counseling efforts. The second area involved issues of group composition, timing, and structure. A model was suggested for exploring issues in advance in order to maximize the possibility of success in forming the group. The final area of work examined and illustrated the skills required to recruit members who may be ambivalent about attending a group session. In particular, the skill of looking for trouble when everything is going the group leader's way was identified as important for avoiding the illusion of agreement, in which the client promises to attend but doesn't show up. Some possible criteria for selecting group members were also discussed.

Finally, unique ethical and legal issues involved in group work practice, particularly in the beginning phase, were summarized.

Now that the group leader has completed the group formation tasks and the clients are ready to attend, the group leader needs to pay attention to the beginnings and the dynamics of first sessions. These topics are explored in the next chapter.

## *Related Online Content and Activities*

Visit *The Skills of Helping Individuals, Families, Groups, and Communities*, Seventh Edition, CourseMate website at www.cengagebrain.com for learning tools such as glossary terms, links to related websites, and chapter practice quizzes. The website for this chapter also features additional notes from the author.

# Competency Notes

The following is a list of Council on Social Work Education (CSWE) recommended competencies and practice behaviors for social work students defined in Educational Policy and Accreditation Standard (EPAS) and addressed in this chapter.

**EP 2.1.1b** Practice personal reflection and self-correction to assure continual professional development (p. 343)

**EP 2.1.1c** Attend to professional roles and boundaries (pp. 356, 380)

**EP 2.1.2a** Recognize and manage personal values in a way that allows professional values to guide practice (p. 380)

**EP 2.1.2b** Make ethical decisions by applying standards of the National Association of Social Workers Code of Ethics and, as applicable, of the International Federation of Social Workers/International Association of Schools of Social Work Ethics in Social Work, Statement of Principles (p. 380)

**EP 2.1.2d** Apply strategies of ethical reasoning to arrive at principled decisions (p. 380)

**EP 2.1.4a** Recognize the extent to which a culture's structures and values may oppress, marginalize, alienate, or create or enhance privilege and power (p. 348)

**EP 2.1.4c** Recognize and communicate their understanding of the importance of difference in shaping life experiences (p. 348)

**EP 2.1.4d** View themselves as learners and engage those with whom they work as informants (p. 344)

**EP 2.1.5a** Understand forms and mechanisms of oppression and discrimination (p. 348)

**EP 2.1.7a** Utilize conceptual frameworks to guide the process of assessment, intervention, and evaluation (p. 343)

**EP 2.1.7b** Critique and apply knowledge to understand person and environment (p. 355)

**EP 2.1.8b** Collaborate with colleagues and clients for effective policy action (p. 358)

**EP 2.1.9b** Provide leadership in promoting sustainable changes in service delivery and practice to improve the quality of social services (p. 358)

**EP 2.1.10a** Substantively and affectively prepare for action with individuals, families, groups, organizations, and communities (p. 358)

**EP 2.1.10b** Use empathy and other interpersonal skills (p. 349)

**EP 2.1.10c** Develop a mutually agreed-on focus of work and desired outcomes (p. 376)

**EP 2.1.10e** Assess client strengths and limitations (p. 344)

**EP 2.1.10g** Select appropriate intervention strategies (p. 361)

# The Beginning Phase with Groups

**M**any of the issues related to beginning work with individuals are equally applicable to first sessions with groups, with an important addition; the individual client must also deal with a new system—the group. The first two central questions for the client in the individual context are "What are we doing here together?" and "What kind of person will this leader be?" In the group context, a third question is added: "What kind of people will these other group members be?"

Many of the uncertainties and fears associated with new beginnings will be present in a first group session, but they will be increased by the public nature of the engagement. For example, a member's fear of being manipulated by someone in authority may be heightened by the thought that any potential inadequacy displayed, and the resultant humiliation, may be witnessed by peers. For this reason, among others, special attention to first sessions is important, so that a proper stage can be set for the work that will follow. The task of the group leader in these first meetings will be described, as in work with individuals and families, as *contracting*.

In this chapter I provide an overview of the general structure of a first group meeting, reviewing some of the underlying assumptions outlined in Chapter 1 and considering some of the unique dynamics associated with group work. The tasks of both the group members and the group leader are outlined, and a number of specific skills are identified. With this overview as a backdrop, the dynamics of a first group session are illustrated using a detailed analysis of a first session of a married couples' group led by myself. The issue of *recontracting* is also explored. This is the process in which the leader reopens the issues of contracting by providing a clearer statement of purpose or exploring the group members' resistance or lack of connection to the service. I will discuss the not-uncommon situation in which a leader joins an ongoing group in which a clear working contract has not been developed. The skills in working with the coleaders and the group in initiating a recontracting process are illustrated using a detailed example. This section of the chapter then addresses the potential strengths and problems involved in coleadership and strategies for dealing with them.

Finally, the chapter includes a brief discussion of variations on the beginning stage involved when one leads an "open-ended" group, with members starting, continuing, and leaving at different times; single-session groups; and online groups on the Internet.

## The Dynamics of First Group Sessions

EP 2.1.7a
EP 2.1.10c

In exploring each of the phases of group work—beginning, middle, and ending/transition—I will use the model of practice theory building described in Chapter 1. First, I will discuss what we know about people in general in relation to the phase described. In this case, it would be our general understanding about people attending a first group session. Then, based on this knowledge, I will explore what we would like to achieve based upon these assumptions. Finally, I will identify and illustrate strategies and interventions designed to achieve the valued outcomes.

### What Do We Know About First Group Sessions?

Most clients begin first group meetings, as they do all new encounters with people in authority, with a degree of tentativeness. Their normal concerns about adequacy and being up to the demands that will be made upon them can be heightened by the fact that the encounter is taking place in public view. Most clients bring to first meetings an extensive fund of group experience (e.g., classrooms, summer camp), many of which are associated with painful memories. We have all either witnessed or experienced the excruciatingly difficult moments in a classroom when an individual student has been singled out to answer a question, solve a math problem on the board, or give some indication of having completed the assignment. One could feel the embarrassment of a classmate when exposed to sarcasm as a punitive weapon in the hands of an insensitive teacher. In fact, whereas new encounters in a one-to-one counseling situation generate fears of the unknown, new group encounters tend to reawaken old fears based on past experiences.

Corey (2008) stresses the importance of the first meeting as follows:

> The initial stage of a group is a time of orientation and exploration: determining the structure of the group, getting acquainted, and exploring the members'

expectations. During this phase, members learn how the group functions, define their own goals, clarify their expectations, and look for their place in the group. At the initial sessions members tend to keep a "public image"; that is, they present the dimensions of themselves they consider socially acceptable. This phase is generally characterized by a certain degree of anxiety and insecurity about the structure of the group. Members are tentative because they are discovering and testing limits and are wondering whether they will be accepted. (p. 77)

An early clarification of purpose, required in individual and family counseling, is also central in the group context. It is only through presenting a clear structure that the leader can help to lower the members' anxiety. This concept is embodied in the expression "structure binds anxiety." The clients' first question will be: "What are we here for?" Once the boundary of the group experience has been clearly described, it will be easier for members to select appropriate responses. When the expectations of the group leader and the setting or agency within which the group takes place are clear, the group members' feelings of safety can increase. If purpose remains ambiguous, then all the fears of inadequacy will be increased. In effect, I am arguing that a dichotomy often suggested between "structure" versus "freedom" is a false one and that, in fact, structure can create freedom. Of course, it has to be a structure that is designed to create freedom, not one that will take it away. This will become clearer in the discussion to follow.

As the group starts, the group members will watch the group leader with keen interest. Having experienced the impact of powerful people in authority, they know it is important to "size up" this new authority figure as soon as possible. This leads to the clients' second central question: "What kind of person will the leader be?" Until the group members can understand clearly how this leader operates and the way in which they will be affected, they will need to test the leader directly or indirectly. Defenses will remain in position until members are certain that their individual safety is ensured.

All these dynamics are similar to the ones experienced in the beginning of any new helping relationship. The major difference in the group setting involves the presence of other clients. As the group session proceeds, each group member will also be appraising the others. Many questions will arise: Who are these other people? Do they have the same problems as I do? Will I be embarrassed by finding myself less competent than they? Do they seem sympathetic and supportive, or are there people in this group who may attack and confront me? While clients' primary concern in the first session is the group leader, questions about fellow members follow closely behind. Not only do members wonder what they can get out of the experience to meet their own needs, but they also wonder why it is necessary to get help in a group: "How can other people help me if they have the same problems as I have?"

Delucia-Waack (2006) points out that

> Providing specific information about what will happen in the group sessions and the role of the leader will help to reduce group members' anxiety. Their anxiety will also be reduced by participating in the screening interviews and the first session. Disclosing about their situation and finding that others have similar situations and/or reasons for being in the group is particularly helpful in alleviating initial anxiety related to group participation. Instillation of hope occurs through connections, identification of how groups work, and the discussion of specific activities to develop new skills. (pp. 95–97)

While there is unanimous support in the literature for the importance of clarifying purpose in first sessions, Kurland and Salmon (2006) point out that there are six common mistakes that group leaders make in the beginning phase of practice.

1. Practitioners promote a group purpose without adequate consideration of client need.

2. Practitioners confuse group purpose with group content.

3. Practitioners state group purpose at such a high level of generality that it is vague and meaningless, and therefore provides little direction for the group.

4. Practitioners are reluctant to share with the members *their* perceptions and ideas about the group's purpose.

5. Practitioners function with a hidden purpose in mind that they do not share with the group.

6. Practitioners do not understand purpose as a dynamic, evolving concept that changes over the life of the group. Instead, they view purpose as static and fixed. (p. 108)

With these cautions in mind, I now address what we want to achieve in first group sessions.

## What Would We Like to Achieve—Our Valued Outcomes?

**EP 2.1.4d**
**EP 2.1.10f**

With some of these issues in mind, the leader should design the structure of first meetings to meet the following objectives:

- To introduce group members to each other.

- To make a brief, simple, nonjargonized opening statement that tries to clarify the school's, agency's or institution's stake in providing the group service as well as the potential issues and concerns about which group members may feel some urgency.

- To obtain feedback from the group members on their sense of the fit (the contract) between their ideas of their needs and the setting's view of the service it provides.

- To clarify the group leader's role and method of attempting to help the group do its work.

- To deal directly with any specific obstacles that may obstruct this particular group's efforts to function effectively: stereotypes group members may hold concerning groups or people in authority, or group members' feelings of anger if attendance is involuntary.

- To begin to encourage intermember interaction rather than discussion only between the group leader and the group members.

- To begin to develop a supportive group culture in which members can feel safe.

- To help group members develop a tentative agenda for future work.

- To clarify the mutual expectations of the agency and the group members. For example, what can group members expect from the leader? In addition, what expectations does the leader have for the members (e.g., regular attendance, meetings starting on time)? Such rules and regulations concerning structure are part of the group contract.

- To gain some consensus on the part of group members as to the specific next steps; for example, are there central themes or issues with which they wish to begin the following week's or future week's discussions? How do the interests of the members fit with the content outline if the group content is already structured?
- To encourage honest feedback and evaluation of the effectiveness of the group.

At first glance, this list of objectives for a first meeting may appear overwhelming. A person new to leading groups might review this list and decide to stick to individual counseling. Actually, many of them can be dealt with quickly, and most are interdependent, in that work on one objective simultaneously affects the others. Obviously, however, these objectives cannot be achieved in the first session unless a clear structure for work is provided. The approach to creating such a structure, which is illustrated in detail in the remainder of the chapter, is offered as a general statement, recognizing that the order of elements and the emphasis may vary depending on the leader, the group members, the nature of their work together, and the setting.

## The Contracting Skills: Establishing a Structure for Work

**EP 2.1.10b**
**EP 2.1.10c**
**EP 2.1.10d**
**EP 2.1.2b**

The following is a list of skills and interventions designed to accomplish our valued outcomes, as described above, in the first session or sessions of a group. They are similar to the contracting skills described in earlier chapters; however, they are adapted to the group context.

- *Clarifying the Group's Purpose.* A simple, "nonjargonized" statement made by the group leader (usually incorporated into the opening statement to the group) that describes the general purpose of the group in terms the members can connect with. For example, instead of telling fifth-graders referred to a group because of their behavior in class that it is an "anger management" group, the leader might open by saying that each member was sent by their teachers because of their behavior in class that was getting them in trouble and probably making school not much fun for them. The leader could continue by saying that the purpose of the group is for each of them to help each other find ways to deal with their feelings, for example, their anger and sadness, and to figure out how to make school and their classes better for all of them.

- *Clarifying the Role of the Group Leader(s).* A statement of the role the group leader and coleaders will play provides some idea of how the group leader can help. In the school group, for example, it may be simply: "My job is to help each of you to talk to and listen to each other; to figure out what your problems in school are; and to help you help each other. I can also talk to your teachers, if you wish, and see if I can help them to understand you better."

- *Reaching for the Group Members' Feedback.* An effort made by the leader to determine the group members' perceptions of their needs and what they hope to get from the group. In the group context, I call this work "problem swapping." For example, continuing in the school group, the counselor might say: "How about it? Is school not much fun for you? Are your teachers and maybe your parents on your back? Are other kids giving you hard time and bullying you? Are you worried about passing or even getting suspended from school?" I call this intervention providing "handles for work" for the members, essentially potential areas for discussion, which frees them to grab on to the one that hits home.

They need to be phrased from the perspective of the group members and how they are experiencing their problems. It is important that they are not experienced as blaming. Such an opening also states the contract from the perspective of the children and the feelings and issues they struggle with that can lead to the problematic behavior. This contrasts with an opening in which the behavior itself is the problem and the children feel blamed. This might result from describing the group's purpose as "anger management." In addition to clarifying the kinds of things that can be discussed, the group leader is starting to demonstrate some empathy with the members, which is the beginning of developing the working relationship.

- *Identifying the Common Ground.* The group's beginning working "contract" includes the common ground between the services of the setting and the felt needs of the group members as well as the common issues shared by group members. Continuing with this example, after some sharing by members, the group leader could say: "It seems like all of you are having the same problems in class and at home. Maybe if we talk about these things you can all help each other. That's why the school asked me to set up this group, to help you find ways of dealing with these concerns and feelings that won't get you into so much trouble and maybe can get the teachers, your parents, and your friends off your back so maybe you can even start to enjoy school."

- *Supporting Members in Taboo Areas.* Helping group members talk about issues and concerns that are normally treated as taboo (e.g., sex, death, authority, dependency). For example, in our current program in an inner-city school setting, it could be something like:

  When I talk with kids like you I sometimes find out that they have had very sad things happen in their lives and in their families. Some kids have seen drive-by shootings or have had friends or families hurt by others. Some worry about the family a lot and even friends who are doing too much dope. Some are being pushed to join gangs even though they don't want to but they are afraid to say no.

- *Dealing with Issues of Authority.* The group leader's efforts to clarify mutual expectations, confidentiality issues, and the authority theme. The group leader has to make clear right from the start that what gets discussed in the group is confidential except if he or she learns that they are thinking about hurting themselves, hurting others, or doing something else that is illegal. The leader also has to make clear that it's part of his or her job to make sure that everyone feels safe in the group so that fighting in the group or even outside of the group cannot be allowed. This part of the work also addresses any questions they have about the leader as a symbol of authority—for example, when they ask: "Are you a teacher?"

The confidentiality issue must be addressed in the first session. In part, it relates to the earlier ethical discussion related to informed consent. In addition, the group leader is a *mandated reporter,* someone who is required by law to report when working with children, and in most states the elderly, if someone is at risk to themselves or to others.

Even as I describe and illustrate these basic contracting skills, the reader may have many questions in mind. For example, what if this doesn't go smoothly and the members start to act out? What if teenagers just sit there and stare at you? What if it is a mandatory group of DWI (driving while intoxicated) or DUI (driving under the influence) offenders sent by a judge, or men who have battered their wives and partners but don't believe they have a problem with anger and violence? All of these issues represent variations on the central theme and will be explored in detail throughout the later chapters in this book. Let me just be clear here that these skills, designed to achieve that long list of valued outcomes, in one form or another, are central to making a start in the work no matter what the setting, group membership, issues to be dealt with, and so on, may be.

The next section illustrates in some detail a first meeting using excerpts from a videotaped recording of the first session of a married couples' group I led a number of years ago. (This video is available on the instructor's Power Lecture DVD associated with this text.)

## Illustration of a First Group Session: The Couples' Group

The group was conducted under the auspices of a university health science mental health setting's outpatient clinic.[1] Five couples were referred from a variety of sources. All had experienced problems in their marital relationships, and in each of the five couples, one partner was identified by the other as the "patient." The youngest couple was John and Louise, in their twenties, with two young children. Rick and Fran were in their thirties and had been married for seven years with no children. Len and Sally were in their late forties, had been married for 20 years, and had children in their late teens and early twenties. Frank and Jane, in their fifties, were recently married after prior marriages and divorces. Jane's teenaged sons were living with them at this point. Finally, Lou and Rose were in their late sixties with a number of married children, who in turn had children of their own. Louise and Rose had recently been inpatients at the hospital. Sally had been seen at the hospital and was considering entering as an inpatient. Frank, Jane, Rick, and Fran had been referred to the group for marital counseling. Each of the couples had been interviewed individually by one of my two coleaders in the group; however, they were meeting me, the senior group leader, for the first time that evening. My two coleaders, one male (social worker) and one female (nurse), were also present.

### The Initial Stage of the First Session

The group meeting room was carpeted and had comfortable chairs set in a circle. The session was recorded on video cameras placed in an adjoining studio. Cameras and

---

1. It has been my practice to lead different types of groups over the years, and this was one identified by the hospital as important for their mental health and family services. Two full-time employees at the hospital were coleaders, although I had primary responsibility for group leadership. One coleader, a male social worker, had been a former student of mine. The other, a female psychiatric nurse, had offered to colead to expand her experience. The names of the group members have been changed in this text. Members of the group provided informed consent for the use of the group content for teaching and publication purposes and had an opportunity to view both sessions before they gave their final consent. As one member put it when giving final consent: "This group has been so helpful to us I want it to be used to be helpful for others." The names in this text are not the real first names on the DVD. This change was implemented because of the wider distribution of the text version of the sessions.

the camera operator were on the other side of one-way glass partitions. In addition, a group of graduate students were observing the video in another room as part of their group counseling course. The couples knew of the observation and had provided informed consent with the understanding that they could request that the cameras be turned off if they felt uncomfortable discussing an issue.

As the couples arrived, I met them at the door, introducing myself to each partner and encouraging them to take a seat. Len, Sally's husband, had to miss the first session, as he was out of town on business. Frank and Jane, who had expressed the most ambivalence and uncertainty about attending the group during the week, were not present at the beginning of the session. I began by suggesting that we go around the room so that the members could share their names, how long they had been married, and whether they had any children. I said this would be a way for us to get to know each other.

**Practice Points:** Note that I start to encourage the members to talk to each other and not only to me.

LOUISE: I am Louise Lewis. We have been married six years, and we have two children.
LEADER: Go ahead, John (speaking to Louise's husband sitting next to her), please share it with the group members. (I pointed to the rest of the group.)
JOHN: My name is John. (Pause)
LEADER: (Smiling) with the same kids!
JOHN: (Laughing along with the rest of the group) Yes, I hope so.

The group members continued around the circle, giving their names and the data on their families. The advantage of introductions is that they help group members break the ice and begin to speak from the start. In addition, the leader conveys to them the sense that knowing each other will be important. Often during these introductions someone will make a humorous comment followed by nervous laughter; however, even these first contributions can help the members settle down. It is important that a minimum of relevant information be requested at this point, since discussion of the working contract—the group's purpose, the coleaders' roles, and so on—has not taken place. Group members will have the opportunity later to share the reasons why they have come. This will come after clarification of group purpose, which will provide the necessary structure. An alternative approach would be to make a brief statement of purpose before asking for introductions. This could be particularly important if group members had no idea of the purpose of the group.

**Practice Points:** Although the members had provided informed consent for the videotaping and observation, I believed they needed another opportunity to address their decision. Following the introductions, I brought up the videotaping issue since I knew it might be on their minds.

LEADER: I realize you discussed the taping with my coleaders, but I thought I would like to repeat the reasons for taping these sessions and also to give you another opportunity to share your reactions. As you know, this is a training institution and we are involved in teaching other health professionals a number of skills, including how to work with groups. We find it helpful to use videotapes of groups such as these so that new group leaders can have examples to assist them in their learning. In addition, the coleaders and I will use these tapes each week as a way of trying to figure out how to be more effective in helping this group work well.

I went on to explain that they could request that the cameras be turned off at any point in a session if they would feel more comfortable. Also, if segments of the tape were kept, they would have an opportunity to view them and could decide if they wanted them erased. I asked if there was any response, and after a few moments of silence and some verbal agreement that there was no problem, I proceeded. I believed the tapes were still on their minds and would come up again; however, they were not quite ready at this point to accept my invitation.

***Clarifying Purpose and Role*** With this acknowledgement of the taping issue, I began the contracting process. The first skills involved were similar to those described earlier in this chapter: clarifying purpose, clarifying role, and reaching for client feedback.

**Practice Points:** I had prepared an opening statement in which I attempted to explain the stake the clinic had in providing the group, to identify their potential interest in the counseling of the group, and to state our roles as leaders. This statement had been reworded a number of times with the assistance of my coleaders until we felt it was jargon-free, short, and direct.

LEADER: I thought I would begin by explaining how we view the purpose of this group and the role that we would be playing, and to get some feedback from you on what you see the sessions to be all about. All of the couples in the group, and there may be one more here later this evening, are experiencing some difficulties in their marriages. This is a time of crisis and not an easy time. The way we see it, however, is that it is also an opportunity for change, for growth, and a chance to make a new marriage right within the one you presently have.

Now we know that isn't easy; learning to live together can be tough. That is why we have organized this group. Essentially, the way we see it, it will be a chance for you to help each other—a sort of a mutual-aid group. As you listen to each other, as you share some of the problems, some of the feelings, and some of the concerns, and as you try to help each other, we think you will learn a great deal that may be helpful in your own marriages. So that's pretty much the purpose of the group.

Now, for our role as group leaders, we have a couple of jobs. The first is that we are going to try to help you talk to and listen to each other, since it's not always easy to do that, particularly with people you don't know. Secondly, we will be sharing our own ideas along the way about close relationships, some of which may be helpful to you. Does that make sense? Do any of you have any questions about that? Does that sound like what you thought you were coming to? (Most heads were nodding; there were murmurs of "yes.")

LEADER: I thought to get us started, it would be worthwhile to take some time to do some problem swapping. What I would like you to do is to share with each other, for a little while, some of the problems and difficulties you have found between you as couples. I would like you also to share some of the things you would like to see different. How would you like the relationship to be? We can take some time to find out the kinds of issues that you're concerned about and then move from there. Would someone like to start?

***Reaching for Feedback on the Purpose: The Problem-Swapping Exercise*** The purpose of the problem swapping is twofold. First, it provides the feedback necessary to begin to develop the clients' side of the working agreement (contract). These are the issues and concerns that will be the starting point for the work of the group. It is quite possible that in the initial stage, group members will share "near" problems that do not bear directly on some of the more difficult and hard-to-talk-about issues. This is their way of testing, of trying to determine how safe it is to use the group. The group leader has to respect and understand their defenses as an appropriate way to begin a new experience. In this particular group, each couple actually indirectly raised a core issue in their relationship in this first session that only emerged clearly during the last five sessions—the ending and transition phase. The work in the middle phase was solid and dealt with other important but not as potent issues. Watching the video of the first session after the last session of the group I could see how they were indirectly sharing the problem and making what I have called the "first offering."

The second function of the problem-swapping exercise is to encourage intermember interaction. For most of their lives clients have participated in groups where the discussion has essentially been between the group member and the leader, the person in authority. This is a long-standing habit. They will need to learn new ways of relating in a group, and the problem-swapping exercise is a good way to start.

As each individual member shares a problem or a concern, the group leader pays attention to the two clients. By this point in this book, the two-client idea should easier to see as well as the pervasiveness of the concept. The first client is the individual who is speaking at the moment. The second client is the group. Attention is paid to the second client, the group, by monitoring their reactions as revealed by their eyes, their posture, and so on. The mediation function of the group leader can be seen in action during this exercise as he encourages individual members to speak to the group and share the concerns they are bringing to the forefront and at the same time helps group members respond to the individual. As group members hear others describing problems, they become better able to identify those issues for themselves. In addition, when they hear their own concerns echoed by other group members, there is some relief at finding out that they are "all in the same boat." The onus that each member may feel over having somehow failed as a human being and as a partner in a marital relationship can begin to lift as they discover that their feelings and their concerns are shared by others.

*Silence in the First Session* Silence is not unusual at this point in the first group session following the opening statement. This silence can represent a number of communications, a different one for each group member. Some may be thinking of what they are willing to share with the group at that time. Others may be shy and afraid to be the first one to speak. Still others are expressing their wariness of being put on the spot if they raise a concern, since they do not know how other group members or the leader will react.

These are the moments that inexperienced group leaders dread. The silence, they feel, confirms a recurring nightmare they have had about their first group session. They are worried that after they have made their opening statement and invited feedback, nobody will speak. It is not unusual for group leaders to take over the group at this point and to offer subjects for discussion or, in some cases, to present prepared films or presentations.

This, of course, leads to a self-fulfilling prophecy, where the message conveyed to the members by the leader is that although their participation is being asked for, there is no willingness to wait for it. An alternative, after a brief delay, is to explore the silence by acknowledging, for example, that it is hard to begin and that it is difficult to discuss such subjects with people one doesn't know. Often, this supportive comment frees a member to risk. If not, the group leader can ask if members might discuss what makes it hard to talk in a first group session as well as what would make it easier. This strategy is very effective because as the members discuss why it's hard to talk, they inevitably start the problem swapping as well. As they share what would make it easier, they are starting to develop a supportive culture for work.

***A Member Begins: The Authority Theme Emerges***   In the case of this couples' group, Lou, the member in his late sixties, had a strong sense of urgency about beginning to work and was ready to jump right in. He was seated directly to my left. (As will be discussed in more detail in Chapter 12, this chair, to my left, took on special significance with members choosing to sit in that particular chair at the start of a meeting during which they revealed powerful emotions. It was termed by a member as the "crying chair").

As Lou spoke, he directed his conversation to the other members. He began by describing the problem as his wife's depression. The affect was flat in his voice, and his wife sat next to him stone-faced, without any change in expression. This is a position she held throughout the session, almost until the end, not saying a word, although she appeared to be hearing everything said by others. As Lou spoke, the rest of the group listened intently, obviously relieved that he had started. If he not started, I would have acknowledged it was difficult to begin, which often is enough to encourage a response.

**Practice Points:**   Note that as Lou keeps referring to his wife, I concentrate on expressing my empathy for him. When he says it has been tough on her, I acknowledge that and say that it was hard for him as well.

LOU: To begin with, as you heard, we have been married for 45 years. Our relationship has been on a rocky road due in a great degree to tragedies that have happened to our family. While that was a real contributing factor, social conditions, economic conditions, and family relationships were also contributing factors. I'm making this very brief because most of this will come out later on. I think the outline on this will be enough for us to get our teeth into. As a result of the things I have mentioned, Rose, particularly, went into some real depressions. All the threads of her family seemed to go. As a result, it became difficult for her to operate. The problems were so strong, she decided she had to go to a psychiatrist. She went and I went with her for two and one-half years. The psychiatrist opened up some doors for her but not enough to really make her free to operate. The unfortunate thing about her depression is that it developed into hostility towards me and the children. Now as soon as the depression lifted, as far as she was concerned, things straightened out. As soon as her depression lifted, we had no problems. (This is said emphatically, facing the group leader.) We had differences of opinion, but we had no problems.

LEADER: It sounds like it has been tough for her and also tough for you.

LOU: Oh, yes! The unfortunate thing as far as we were concerned is that we did not have a psychiatrist who understood what the relationship was. He took our problems as a family problem. His suggestion after a while was that if we weren't getting along together, we should separate. I felt I really didn't like that because I knew that wasn't the problem. The problem was getting Rose out of her depression.

**Practice Points:**   Lou had begun presenting the problem the way one partner often does in a couples' group. The problem was essentially the other partner who, in some way, needed to be "fixed." This is the way one partner often experiences things, and it is important that the group leader attempt to understand and express that understanding of the members' feelings as they are presented. When I show this session to students, one will often confront me for "allowing" Lou to talk about his wife as the "identified patient." Many students in the class identify with his wife and become angry with Lou for not taking responsibility for his part in the problem. Some suggest I should have asked Lou to use "I statements." (This was a popular artificial contrivance in group work that required members to talk only about themselves—the "I"—rather than about the other).

I point out to my students that in the first few minutes of this session, this couple is acting out the very problem they have come to get help with. Lou is saying, "Do you want to see how I deny the problem and blame it all on Rose? Just watch me!" Rose is saying, "Yes, and watch how I sit here passively, letting Lou talk about me." I point out to the students that it doesn't make sense for me to get angry at these clients for having the very problem the group was established to deal with. Also, before I confront Lou, I have to build up a fund of support. In this case I attempt to do that by my comment about this experience being tough on his wife, and on himself. He talks about his wife, while I come back to him. Later in the session, this same client drops some of his defenses.

Some observers wonder about my letting Lou continue to talk instead of immediately involving other members. It seemed obvious to me that the second client, the group, was listening to what Lou had to say and did not mind his going on at some length. Group members begin first sessions with various patterns of behavior. Those who are used to being quiet and withdrawn in new situations will begin that way. Those who are used to speaking and jumping in quickly, such as Lou, will begin that way. Each member is entitled to their own defenses in the beginning, and it is important that the group leader respect them. When a group member speaks for a period of time, keeping to the subject, usually only the leader feels nervous. The other group members are often relieved that someone else has begun the discussion.

**Practice Points:** In this case, the tuning-in work from the individual session had alerted us to Lou's strong feelings toward helping professionals who he felt had not been helpful. He raises this at the end of the excerpt. Understanding that the authority theme and the question "What kind of group leader will this be?" are always present in a first session, I had strategized to reach directly if I felt there were indirect cues related to us, the group leaders. I did so at this point in the following way:

LEADER: Are you worried that I and the other group leaders might take the same position with you and Rose?

Lou: Well, I don't know (voice slightly rising with annoyance). I'm not worried; I'm past that stage (accompanied with a harsh laugh). I'm just relating what happened, because I know where I'm at (said emphatically). To be very frank, my opinion of psychiatrists is very low, and I can cite two hours of experiences of what I have been through, my friends have been through, to show you exactly what I mean. This was a good case in point, his making a suggestion that we should separate because of the problem.

LEADER: After 45 years I can imagine that must have hit you as a terrible blow.

Lou: Well, sure it did.

LEADER: Lou, do you think we could move around the circle a bit and also hear from the others as to what they see some of the problems to be?

**Practice Points:**   In retrospect, I think Lou responded somewhat angrily partly because of the way I made my statement, "Are you worried that I and the other group leaders might take the same position with you and Rose?" I wanted to open up Lou's concerns about what kind of leaders we would be; however, my attempt was neither direct nor clear enough. Instead of asking for further elaboration from Lou or, perhaps, asking if others in the group had similar experiences or relations, I suggested we allow others to exchange problems by "moving around the circle." It is important to encourage such an exchange of problems; however, further exploration of the authority theme was also important. Fortunately I had an opportunity to "catch my mistake" later in the session when I returned to the initial concerns raised by Lou. Lou responded to my suggestion that we "hear from the others" by turning to his wife.

Lou: Sure, you're on. Go ahead, dear. (He turns to his wife.)

Rose: I think I'll pass right now (said in a slow, even way, with no evidence of affect).

Leader: That's fine. How about some others? You don't have to go in order, and you know, you can also respond to what Lou just said if you like, as well as adding some of your own issues. We won't solve all of the problems tonight; I hope you realize that. (Some laughter by the group members) But what we would like to try and do is get a feel for how they seem to you right now. That can help us get a sense of what we need to talk about, and I think Lou has helped us get started. (At this point, John takes off his coat and seems to settle back in his chair.)

**Practice Points:**   Having witnessed how the leader responded to Lou, accepting and acknowledging his feelings, others in the group felt more ready to share. Note that Louise reinforces Lou's issues with helping professionals as well as sharing her problem. Note also that I ask Louise to focus on how the feelings she raises affects her relationship to her husband, since the marital relationship is what the group is about.

Louise: (John's wife, who is now speaking directly to Lou) I can understand what Lou means because depression has been our problem as well. I have gotten into such a state of depression that I can't function as a mother or a wife. I feel I have lost my identity. (This is all said with a very flat affect.) And I don't think that separation is the answer either. And I have had some pretty bad psychiatrists as well, so I can really feel for you when you say that, Lou. I can understand that. But the problem is to be able to sort out and find out what feelings I really have and recognize them for what they are and try to get myself out of the hole that I fell into, and that's the tough part.

Leader: How does it affect your relationship with John?

Louise: It's very strenuous. There is a lot of strain and tension when I'm sick and down and I put the responsibility for taking care of the household on John's shoulders. There is a breaking point for him somewhere there; I want to catch it before we get there. (Pause, leader is nodding and other members are listening intently) That's about it. (Brief silence)

John: Our biggest problem, or Louise's biggest problem, is due to her migraine headaches. She's had them ever since she was five years old. This is where the whole problem stemmed from, those migraine headaches and this new depression which she seems to have gotten in the last few months.

Leader: Anything special happen within the last few months?

JOHN: No, it has been actually a very quiet time this summer.

LOUISE: I think it is things that have been festering for a long time.

LEADER: For example?

LOUISE: I don't know. I can't put my finger on what they are.

LEADER: (Speaking to John) This depression came as a surprise to you, did it?

JOHN: Yes, it did.

LEADER: How do you see the problem, John? What would you like to see different in the relationship?

**Practice Points:** My effort to encourage John and Louise to become more specific about what has been going on recently is politely rejected. John goes on to describe how they don't do much together as a couple anymore and that he would like to see Louise get back on her feet so they can have some fun the way they used to. Discussion continued around the circle, with Fran and Rick looking at each other as if to ask who would go first. I verbalized this, and Fran begged off, saying that she didn't feel comfortable starting right away and that she would get in a bit later. Her husband, Rick, responded to my question by saying he was wondering why he was there because he knows that he has, or rather, they have, a problem, but what the problem is, is hard to define. Fran coached him at this point by whispering in his ear the word "communication." They seemed to agree that that's the problem, but when I asked for elaboration, Rick said, "That's not my problem; that's Fran's problem."

**Practice Points:** Rick then took a further step for the group by entering a taboo area and raising sexual intimacy. This was a surprise for me coming at the start of the first session. I had to press Rick a few times to get more specific and as a result he shared another surprising and usually taboo issue—physical fighting.

RICK: I guess if you get right down to basics, it would have to be sexual intimacy. I have been going along for a little over seven years, and now I find that I'm all alone. Fran's gone on a trip, and we're really in the very rocky stages of breaking up. (There is some emotion in his voice as he is speaking.) For the last six months, we have sort of been trying to recover, but it's still pretty shaky.

LEADER: It must feel pretty dicey for you right now.

RICK: Right. (With resignation in his voice)

LEADER: What would you like to be different? What would you like to see changed in your marriage?

RICK: (After a deep sigh to get his breath) There are times when everything is just fine, it seems to be going along smoothly, but just to say what I would like would be tough to put my finger on.

LEADER: How would you like the relationship to be with Fran?

RICK: I think I would like it to be peaceful at all times. We have been getting into a lot of fights and just recently we have been getting into a lot of physical fights. A peaceful relationship, that's what I would really go for.

LEADER: How about you, Fran, do you have any ideas now?

FRAN: No, can we come back to me?

LEADER: Sure.

**Practice Points:** As stated earlier, each group member (and in this case each couple) has to have control over how much they share. My approach is to ask for elaboration but also to be respectful of the member's defenses by not pushing too hard too early. The discussion continued with Sally talking about her marriage. This was difficult because her husband, Len, was not present. She described it from her perspective. Her description was filled with interpretations that had obviously been gleaned from years of involvement in various forms of analysis. The group listened intently to her stories. She also responded to Louise's comments about migraine headaches, mentioning that she had had them as well, and then she and Louise exchanged some mutual support. After Sally finished her description, there was a long silence as the group seemed unsure about where to go. Note in the following excerpt that I had decided to get back to the authority theme and Lou, who I felt I had cut off before.

**LEADER:** (Turning to Lou) I didn't mean to stop you before, Lou, if you want to get in again.

**LOU:** No, that's OK (laughing). I could go on for hours.

**LEADER:** Oh, they won't mind, you know (pointing to the group), they would be glad. (Most of the group members laugh at this.)

**LOU:** I want to give others the opportunity to speak because, after all, I have been married over 45 years, so I have an accumulation of incidents.

***Returning to the Authority Theme*** At this point, I picked up the theme that had been common to many of the presentations: "helping people" who had not really helped. I had reached for this theme earlier in the session in relation to the role played by me and my coleaders, but Lou had not accepted my invitation. I believe the relationship between the group and the group leader is a central question at the beginning of each new group. Some discussion needs to take place on this issue so that the group can begin to work on what I have referred to as the "authority theme," the relationship between the person who offers help and the person who takes help. It is a powerful factor in the first group session, and for the group to develop properly, the group leader must begin to deal with it.

**Practice Points:**   During the problem-swapping exercise, I had attempted to express my empathic responses to the concerns as they were raised, taking care not to express judgments on their feelings and actions. Even this brief period had built up a sufficient fund of positive relationship that I was able to reach for some discussion on this difficult theme. If the group was to start to develop as a healthy organism, it would need to begin to sort out its relationship to me as the leader and my coleaders as the persons in authority. Since this is a taboo subject, it would require considerable effort on my part to make it clear that the topic was open to discussion. I decided to return to the theme of helpers who had not helped. It is important to note that I returned to this issue directly by pointing out to the group members that I thought such a discussion might be important, so that they could be involved with full knowledge of the process.

The group discussion that followed, led by Lou who was an internal leader on this issue, was a critical factor contributing to a striking change in the group atmosphere and to its successful beginning. In a later chapter dealing with the individual roles members play in a group, I will discuss what I call the "deviant member." This is the group member who the leader experiences as an "enemy" because of the nature of the comments or, as in this case, the attack on helping professionals. I will argue later that the deviant member may actually be your ally, not your enemy. I think Lou serves this functional role by raising, with feeling and energy, the authority theme.

LEADER: I have noticed a theme that has cut across a number of your presentations that I think is important for us to talk about. A number of you have commented on helping people who have not been very successful—psychiatrists you have had in the past, doctors, and so on. (Group members all nod, saying yes.) Can you stay on that for a minute in terms of the things in your experiences that you found difficult? The reason I think it is important is because it would be a way of your letting me and my coleaders know what you would not find helpful from us.

**Practice Points:** This is the second time I reached for some comments about the group members' concern about us. This time, since a relationship was beginning, and since I reached in a way that was less threatening, they were ready to take me up. Lou volunteered to begin the discussion. He took us back to the year 1940 when he had his own business. He described some of the pressures on him concerning economic conditions and a rash he developed on his leg. His doctor referred him to a psychiatrist who was brand-new at the hospital. It was his first job. Lou's enthusiasm and feelings while describing this experience captured the attention of the group. They smiled and nodded agreement with his comments as he continued his story.

***Integrating the Late Couple and Maintaining the Discussion*** As he was about to describe his encounter with the psychiatrist, the door to the group room opened and the fifth couple, Frank and Jane, arrived late. It is not unusual for group members to arrive late for a first session. It usually presents a dilemma for the group leader: What do I do? In this case, I had the new couple introduce themselves, and I asked the other couples to give their names as well. I then briefly summarized the contract, explaining that we had been hearing about some problems to help get a feel for the concerns that had brought the couples to this session, and pointed out that one theme that kept recurring had to do with helping people who had not been very helpful. I said that we were focusing on this right now and that just before they had entered, we had been with Lou in 1940. With that, I turned back to Lou to continue, and the group picked up where it had left off.

**Practice Points:** I think that it is important to recognize the entrance of the new group members and help them connect to the group but, at the same time, I think it would be a mistake to take a great deal of time to start again. As will become clear later in this group session, these group members were late for a reason; their lateness was their way of handling a new and frightening experience.

Lou continued his story of his first encounter with the young psychiatrist, indicating that the psychiatrist had tried to lead him indirectly to recognizing that he had a marital problem. As Lou put it, "I was talking about the economic conditions and the problems of the time, and he kept coming back to the wife and the kids, and the wife and the kids, and the wife and the kids until I said to him, 'Are you trying to tell me my problem is with my wife and my kids?'" Lou went on to say that when the psychiatrist indicated it was, he stood up, called him a charlatan and quickly got out of the office as he described the enraged psychiatrist coming out from behind the desk and shaking his fist at him.

LOU: OK. I knew that my wife and my family were part of the problem, but I also knew that they were not at the core of the problem. They were a contributing factor because of the social and economic conditions. I went to this guy to get rid of this rash on my leg and not to have him tell me that my wife and my kids were giving me the problem. It took a while for the rash to go away, but eventually it did. That was item number one. I am going to skip a lot of the intervening incidents that had to do with families, and I will go to the one which we just experienced recently. We went to a psychiatrist in the community for two and one-half years—(and then with emphasis) two and one-half years! I knew I had to go with her to give her some support plus I wanted to find out what made her tick. I couldn't understand her depression. I had been down in the dumps and felt blue, but I had never felt depressed as she seemed to feel. He asked her a lot of questions, asked me a lot of questions, tried to have us do some play acting and had us try and discuss the problems. "You're not communicating" was his term. I didn't know what he was talking about when he said we didn't communicate, so we tried to communicate. But nothing really came of it because we saw we weren't communicating.

**Practice Points:**   As Lou related his experiences, he was describing a number of techniques that apparently had been used to try to help him and his wife deal with their problems. The central theme appeared to be that of a helping person who had decided what the problem was and was now acting in order to educate them as to its nature.

Lou was resentful of this approach and resisted it in most of the sessions. And yet, part of him deep inside knew that there was a problem that he attempted to deal with in his own way. He described an incident when he had taken a tape recorder home and recorded a conversation with his wife, listening to it later. His description of the aftermath of this tape recording contained the first overt expression of the sadness and the pains the couple had felt but were not ready to share.

**Practice Points:**   In this case, I believe it was necessary for Lou to share first the anger and the frustration at the helping people who had not understood him before he was willing to share his hurt and pain. My telling him to "take your time" and giving him some water was my natural response to his emotions. Note, once again, that I return consistently to Lou's emotions and how it felt for him.

Lou: We talked for about 15 minutes, and I realized when we played the tape back, that I was screaming at Rose. Now I never realized that I was screaming at her. But I heard my voice. (Lou clears his throat at this point and begins to choke up, obviously feeling emotions and trying to fight back his tears.) This is a little rough for me, can I have some water?

Leader: (Getting a glass of water from the decanter) Sure you can, Lou, take your time.

Lou: It's kind of tough to get over the fact that I was screaming at her. Then I realized that when I was screaming at her, I was treating her like a kid. I took this tape to the psychiatrist, and he couldn't hear the screaming. He got nothing out of it.

Leader: He didn't seem to understand how it felt to you to hear yourself screaming?

**Practice Points:**   Lou then relates an exercise introduced by the psychiatrist to assist them in their communication process. The suggestion that they reverse roles is attempted by Lou and his wife but it is evident that he was not feeling it was helpful as he was following the instructions. I suspect the psychiatrist was trying his best to be helpful but at that point, with Lou so upset at his own behavior, some explorations of Lou's feelings might have been more helpful.

LOU: That's right. He didn't even hear me screaming. The other thing he tried to get us to do which I found really devastating is he tried to get us to reverse roles; she should be me and I should be her. OK, we tried it. But while we were doing it, I was thinking to myself: "Now, if that isn't stupid, I don't know what is." (Turning to me at this point) But you're a psychiatrist; you know what the score is. How can you reverse roles when I'm not feeling like she's feeling and she doesn't feel like I do? How can I communicate? Well, it was things like that that had been going on for two and one-half years, and when we had finished, I was nowhere nearer being helped to be able to live with Rose than I was when we started. Now that's two and one-half years (with emphasis)! It isn't that we didn't try; both of us used to discuss this. Rose went back to the doctor, but I said I wouldn't go because I found I was just getting more frustrated.

At this point, there was some discussion on the part of group members about the use of the tape recorder. Rick thought it was a good idea and wondered if Lou had tried it again. Lou said he hadn't. The conversation returned to his feelings of frustration and his sense of not having been helped.

**Practice Points:**   My understanding of Lou's story was that he wanted to be sure that I and my coleaders would listen and try to understand. This was my opportunity to clarify our roles as group leaders with an emphasis on our ability to identify and empathize with their feelings. Although I had indicated what our role would be in the opening statements, I'm not sure anyone really heard and understood the statement. Now was the time to address it again.

LOU: I felt stupid. The psychiatrist kept telling me something, and no matter how hard I tried, I simply couldn't understand.
LEADER: You also seem to be saying, not only couldn't you understand him, but he didn't seem to understand you.
LOU: Well, yes. Peculiarly enough, that thought had not occurred to me. I felt, well you are a professional (facing the leader at this point), so what you're doing, you're doing on purpose. You know what you're supposed to be doing. And whether you understand me or not is immaterial. That's not what the game is. It's my responsibility to understand what you, if you are the psychiatrist, are saying. (There was anger in his voice.)
LEADER: If you're asking us (referring to the other coleaders) in this group, that's not the way I see it. I think that if we can be of any help to you or the other group members, the help will be in our listening and in our trying to understand exactly how you see it. The gimmicks and the things that seem to get tried on you is not my idea of how we can help. You'll have to wait to see if I mean that.
LOU: Yeah, we'll see.
LEADER: I think you folks have a powerful lot of help to give each other. And essentially, what I will try and do is to help you do that. And I'll share my own ideas along the way. But I have no answers or simple solutions.
LOU: Then, well, OK. (General silence in the group as this time the members appear to be taking in the meaning of the words)
COLEADER: I'd like to know, Lou, as we go along, how you see things. So, if you're feeling stupid or whatever, you'll let us know.
LEADER: It might be because we've said something dumb (some subdued laughter in the group).

**Practice Summary.**   Although I had described the group as a mutual-aid group in the opening statement, it was only at this point that the members really began to have a sense of how the group might work. Also, the clarification of the group leader's role contained in this exchange was actually "heard." Lou, playing the role of an internal group leader, was able to articulate the fears and concerns that group members felt about the potential power invested in the group leader's role. He provided the opportunity for an initial clarification of who we were as group leaders and what we did. Skills of accepting and understanding his feelings and his frustrations, and of helping to connect his past experiences to the present moment, were crucial in this session. The feeling in the group was that we had moved past the first step in building our relationship. The authority theme was not finished as a topic of discussion; however, one could sense that an important start had been made. Following this exchange, the group members were able to move into work on their contract with more energy, involvement, and intermember interaction.

On another note, I had indicated that each of the couples had indirectly raised a central issue in the first session which I could not hear and understand until it was raised at a much later session. In Lou's case when he said he was going to skip some of the other experiences with psychiatrists he was referring to a traumatic experience for him and his wife when speaking on the phone with their married son, living in another city, who was undergoing psychotherapy. The son had told his Lou's wife, Rose, that his psychiatrist had said that all of his problems were her fault and that he never wanted to see her again. According to Rose, the son said: "Don't ever come to see me or I will kill you!" As we discovered near the end of the group sessions, this was the precipitating event that led to Rose's severe depression for more than two years before and her recent hospitalization.

## The Middle Stage of the First Session

With a two-hour session it was possible to move past problem swapping, clarification of purpose, and the group leader's role into beginning efforts to focus on an example of what happens in a group.

***Frank and Jane and Issues of a Blended Family*** Interestingly enough, Frank and Jane, the couple who had arrived late, provided an opportunity to do this. Frank began to share, with some elaborative assistance from myself, a problem that they were experiencing in relation to his wife's teenage sons who were living with them. It was an interesting example of a group member raising a problem tentatively, moving quickly back and forth between the implications of the difficulty for the couple and his relationship to the children. He spoke of the sexual difficulty they had, while attributing most of it to his medical problem and also to the lack of privacy in their home. The bedroom door was not locked at any time, and the children would wander in without notice. As Frank was sharing this dilemma, he phrased it in terms of his problem with his stepsons, but one could hear throughout the discussion hints of the implications for his relationship to his wife. Each time I would acknowledge, even gently, the implication for the relationship, Frank would back off slightly, and both he and Jane would be quick to reassure the group of the positive nature of their communications.

**Practice Points:**   It is not unusual for group members to use the early sessions to raise "near" problems in a way that presents them as issues and at the same time defends them from discussion. This is in part an expression of the ambivalence of the member to deal with real concerns. It is also necessary for the group members to test the reaction of a group leader and the other members. Group members often feel it would be unwise to rush right in until they know how their feelings and thoughts are going to be treated, whether they will be met with support or confrontation, and whether it is OK to share their real feelings and concerns.

Not only are the group members worried about the leader and the other members, they are also concerned about their partners. In a group such as this one, you really have three clients: the individual, the group, and the couple as an entity. Each of the couples has developed a "culture" in their marriage that has included certain norms, behaviors, taboo areas, rules for interaction, and so on. The group will in many ways be a place for them to learn how to change that culture, or at least those parts of it that are not conducive to strengthening their marriage. With so many factors to consider, however, it is not unusual for group members to come close to a concern while watching to see how the partner, the other group members, and the group leaders will react.

Timing is important in a first session, and it would therefore be a mistake for a group leader to confront and to attack defenses at a point when the group member needs them. In addition, this example provides an opportunity to communicate to the group how mutual aid works as well as to involve the group in the decision to proceed with Frank's example. I also introduce the idea of going from the general to the specific, a skill identified in earlier chapters, by asking Frank to share some of the dialogue with his stepsons.

**Practice Points:**   As Frank began to describe his efforts to deal with the children about this issue of privacy, I suggested that they might use this as an example of one of the ways in which the group members might help each other: (speaking to the group) "Perhaps we can use this as an example of how we can be helpful. Frank can describe the conversation he had with his son and the rest of the group members might respond by suggesting how they would have reacted if they had been the son. We could do some thinking with Frank about how he might handle this kind of an issue." The group members agreed, and Frank went into some details of a conversation in which he sarcastically implied to the son that they needed some privacy. After a number of group members supported his right to privacy, the coleader pointed out that it would be difficult to take his comments seriously because he always seemed to be joking as he described things and never seemed as if he could really get angry. This triggered a response on the part of his wife, Jane.

JANE: Aha! That's it exactly. Frank has trouble getting angry. Ever since he has been a kid, he has been afraid to be direct and angry with people. I keep telling him, why don't you let yourself get angry and blow off steam? He says that he feels that it is just not the thing to do. You just don't do it. I do it all the time. I didn't use to, but now I do, and I get angry at least a couple of times a day.
FRANK: You know the kids are scared of you because you get angry so much.
LEADER: (Noticing that Sally appears to want to say something) Go ahead, Sally, get in.
SALLY: (Laughing as she speaks to Frank) You've got to meet my Len (the absent husband)! (The whole group, including Frank, erupted in laughter.) You sound like two of the same kind, and you're hard to live with.

**Practice Points:**   The discussion in the group has moved off the authority theme and we are into the work. With Sally's comment, the ability of the group members to laugh and not feel defensive, I think, emerged as the members truly began to understand how the group would work. In the next excerpt, as I did with Lou, I try to reach for Frank's feelings.

LEADER: Frank, what made it hard for you to speak seriously to your son right then?

FRANK: I don't know. Well, you know the image of a stepfather like in the fairy-tale books, he is like a monster. I've got a nice thing starting to build with these boys, and I don't want to ruin it.

LEADER: You are afraid they would get angry if you were direct and honest.

JANE: (Laughing, but with a touch of anger) It's all up in your head.

LEADER: You know, Jane, I think Frank really is worried about that.

FRANK: I do worry about that. I really do.

**Practice Points:** In response to the leader's question, "What are you afraid might happen?" Frank goes on to describe the relationship the children had with Jane's former husband, of some of his fears of being unable to prevent the continuation of the same coldness and the problems that he envisioned in that relationship.

FRANK: It was because I didn't want to hurt that relationship that I more or less symbolized what I really meant.

LEADER: You kind of hinted at what you felt rather than saying it directly.

FRANK: Well, it's like you are in a washroom and you saw a fellow peeing on the floor. You would probably say, "Hey, you missed, fella." (Group members and leaders roar with laughter at his story.)

Frank went on to describe how he finally had to speak directly with the son. He described, much to his wife's surprise, a very direct conversation in which he explained the problem to the son. Frank's point was that since that time, the son had been much more understanding about not interrupting.

***Lou the Internal Leader: How Do We Handle Anger in Our Relationships?*** At this point in the group session, Lou, who had been listening intently, moved in and took responsibility for the group process. In a striking illustration of internal leadership at an early stage in the group development, Lou moved directly from the general discussion of anger and indirect communication to the implications for each couple. The leader had noticed during the discussion that on a number of occasions Lou had attempted to whisper to his wife, Rose, and to ask her a question but she had refused to respond, and instead had sat impassive and expressionless.

**Practice Points:** Lou now used the group and this theme to deal with his concern—a concern that was common to all members. I believe that he was able to make this direct intervention and assume some leadership responsibility in the group because the way had been cleared through our earlier discussion of the role of the leader. This was an example of Lou accepting my invitation for the group members to begin to own their own group. This is an important shift, since the members usually start with the belief that it is the leader's group and he or she will be in control of the process.

LEADER: (Noting Lou's indirect communication of his desire to get into the discussion) Were you going to say something, Lou?

LOU: Something has come up here which I would like each couple in turn to answer if they can. (Turning to John, he asks his name, which John gives him.) I would like each couple to add to this in turn if they can. John, do you get really mad at Louise? I mean really mad, peed off? Do you yell at her, do you tell her off?

JOHN: Not really.

LOU: Why not?

JOHN: That's my style, that's the way I have been all my life.

LOU: Louise, how about you?

LOUISE: I'll probably hold back as long as possible and then usually end up to where I'm in tears, or slam cupboards or dishes, or give John a cold shoulder rather than coming right out and saying that I'm angry. (As Louise is speaking, Lou is nodding and saying yes.)

LOU: Why? By the way, I am referring to Rose and myself right now when I'm asking this question and I want to hear from everyone.

JOHN: It happens sometimes, but it is really rare that we actually yell at each other. (Louise shakes her head, agreeing.)

LOU: Are you afraid to get angry, either one of you?

JOHN: I don't think I'm afraid. I don't have a problem yelling at other people. It's kinda strange. I don't know why.

LOU: How about you, Frank and Jane?

Jane and Frank both discussed her getting angry regularly, blowing her top all the time. She indicated that it worried her. Frank said he had trouble getting angry directly at Jane and gave an example of her not sharing her load of chores (they are both working) and that he had been getting angry at that because it was setting a bad example for the kids, but that he had not told her. He paused when he said that, and then said, "I guess I hadn't said that to you until tonight."

**Practice Points:** As the conversation went on, I was monitoring the members, making sure they were involved and paying attention. Occasionally I would comment on some of the feelings associated with the comments.

LOU: (Directly to Jane) You have no aversions about getting mad, I mean spontaneously mad?

JANE: What other way is there to get mad?

LOU: You don't build anything up and then have it boil over?

JANE: Not anymore, not now.

**Practice Points:** For a novice leader, the fact that Lou had actually taken an internal leadership role in the group and was providing direction for the discussion would have been disconcerting. From my perspective it was a process that indicated to me that the group was off to a great, and unusually quick, start.

After a pause, I turned to Lou and said, "Stay with it." Lou responded, "Fine, because something is happening here that happens to us (pointing to his silent wife, Rose) and I would like to hear from everyone in the group on this." At that point he asked Fran, who had declined to speak thus far, if she got mad.

FRAN: I hold it for a little while, and then I start and I pick, and I can't stop at the issue. Often I can't even determine what the issue is at the time. Since I can't figure out what it is, I go through the whole gamut to make sure I get to the right one. And—maybe I should let Rick speak for himself—my opinion is that he's quiet. He listens to all of this without a comment back. That really drives me out of my mind. I can't stand the silence. If only he would yell! Even if I'm wrong, then I know I'm wrong. But like I said, I go over the whole ballpark because I know I may hit the right one, since the right one is in there somewhere. There's not much of a reaction, because Rick is the quiet type. He doesn't like to argue or fight. And the quieter he seems to get, the angrier I get. I have to push even harder. It's just recently, the last couple of months, that we've started to fight physically. We've been married for seven years, and this is just coming out now. Well, I didn't think that Rick had a breaking point and that he could get that mad. And I wasn't even aware that I could get that mad, but I can. I'm the pusher, I'm the one—the things that I could say could definitely curl your hair.

RICK: She basically said it all for me.

FRAN: And that's usual, too.

LOU: (Smiling in a supportive way) Your hair looks pretty straight to me, Rick.

RICK: (Sighing) It's been a long day. Yes, I am the quiet type, and I have a very long fuse, but once it gets to the end, look out. I've done some stupid things in my time, and they usually end up costing me. I guess I just reach my breaking point and take the frustration out somewhere. If it happens that Fran is taking hers out on me, I try and cool it as long as I can, but then I can only take so much of that, and we end up going at each other. That's about it.

LOU: Let me ask you a question, Rick. When Fran is at you like she does, is it that you don't want to or are you afraid of hurting her feelings so that she'll come back at you again and this thing will snowball, or is it that you have a reluctance and you feel you'll let her get it off her chest and then things will calm down again? Which of these is it?

RICK: I guess I'm just hoping that she'll get it off her chest and things will calm down again. But it doesn't work that way.

LEADER: (Turning to Lou) If I can just ask Rick this before you go on, Lou—what's going on inside of your guts when Fran is pushing that way? What do you feel?

RICK: (Takes a big sigh before he speaks) Well, I guess I'm trying to just block everything out of my mind. That's the reason I become quiet, even go to the point of reading the newspaper and just completely try to wipe it out.

LEADER: Because it hurts?

RICK: Right.

**Practice Points:**   This is a striking part of the session as Lou asks each couple in succession how they handle anger in their relationship. When I view the videotape of this session with students, they often ask me "Why did you let Lou take over your group?" They particularly note that I turned to Lou to ask him if I can ask Rick a question before he goes on. I have to point out to them that it is not my group. The students perceive Lou as trying to usurp my role as leader. I believe this comes from the students' insecurity. From my perspective, Lou is an "internal" leader and when he starts the questioning, I watch the other members closely and would intervene if they were distressed, but in fact they were not distressed at all. They were responding to Lou and I was feeling that the group had taken up my invitation to move past the authority theme and to begin to own the group. When students begin to realize what a contribution Lou is making to what turns out to be a dynamic first session, I jokingly suggest I should set up a "rent-a-Lou" service for their own groups.

Lou continued, turning to Sally, who also described how she saw herself in Fran, since her husband, Len, is like Rick, the quiet type. She described a number of similar examples, finally ending by saying, "I don't think I have ever found his boiling point. Heaven help me if I ever do."

LEADER: That must be as hard as having found it.

SALLY: Yes, I guess it is. The problem is that you hoard the hurts and when you get a chance, zap, you give them right back. The sad part is that I really don't think Len has a mean bone in his body.

***Rose Decides to Speak*** There is a long silence after this as the group waits in anticipation. The next speaker should be Rose, Lou's wife, who has not said a word nor changed her expression during the entire session. She has been watching and listening intently. Because of her silence, her comments at this point have a stunning impact on the group members as well as the group leaders.

ROSE: Well, I think there is a common thread running through with everyone and part of it is anger, and there may be some recriminations amongst the couples here. Some people have learned to live with it, but obviously, those of us here have not. And no matter how long you're married, it's still something you don't know how to handle. I found that I got very angry here and I wanted to tell Lou to stop talking about me that way.

LEADER: You mean here tonight?

ROSE: Yes, but I wasn't going to interrupt my husband to tell him that I didn't want him to say that or I didn't like what he was saying. So, I'm back to zero, not just one. I can pack my bags and go back to the hospital. (At this comment, her husband, Lou, flinches almost as if in pain and looks toward the leader.) And I don't feel comfortable talking about it.

LEADER: It's hard even now, isn't it?

ROSE: Yes, but I made up my mind I was at the point where I would pack my bags or talk.

LEADER: I'm glad you talked.

LOU: (His face brightening) Well, I have been thinking that that was about the only way I could get Rose to talk and to burst open.

ROSE: Sure, well, I knew that's what was going on.

LOU: She wasn't going to say anything to me. I asked her during the group if she was mad, and she said she was. I asked if she would say something, and she said no.

ROSE: Right, I said no.

LOU: Plus the fact that what goes on is that all our lives both of us have always been afraid of hurting each other.

ROSE: So, we kept quiet. Or else one spoke and said too much. I always felt that Lou had spoken lots more than I did. Now, I had an opportunity to do a lot of speaking at the hospital for five weeks, and certainly I found it helped me quite a bit. I told myself and the people there that I was going to try and remember to use everything they taught me. And there's really no way. Because different things come up and, say, they're not in the book that I went by.

LEADER: I guess you have to write your own book, then.

ROSE: That's right. I'm not very quick on my feet, and I don't think my mind operates very quickly either. But how to deal with anger seems to be everyone's particular problem. (There is a pause in the group as Rose's words sink in.)

## The Ending and Transition Stage of the First Session

**Practice Points:**   The two hours have sped by quickly and it is clear we must wind down the group and bring this first session to an end. My goal at this point is to summarize and credit their work as well as to make the transition to the next session. I also want to start the process of asking them to reflect on the session and provide some feedback to me and to each other.

LEADER: It's close to the end of our session, and I wonder if what we haven't done is identify a common theme and issue that we might want to look at in more depth next week. Perhaps you could be prepared to share some of the incidents and difficulties, because I think if you can bring some of those arguments from the outside into here, where it is a little safer, and where there are people around to help, maybe it's possible to learn to do what Rose did just now without hurting. Perhaps it is possible to say what you are really thinking and what you're feeling without having to store up the hurts. My own feeling is that any real, intimate relationship has to have both some loving and some fighting. That comes with the territory. But it's a hard thing to do. We simply haven't learned how to do it. So maybe this could be a safe area to test it out. Does that make any sense to the rest of you? (Group members nod.) Maybe we could pick up on this next week as something that we're interested in. How do you find a way of saying what you're really thinking and feeling toward each other without wiping each other out?

JANE: Is there a way to do that?

LEADER: I think so, but why don't we test that out here in the group? If there isn't, though, then I think we're in trouble, because I don't think you could really care for each other if you can't also get angry at each other. Does that make some sense to the whole group? (Once again, there is some nodding in agreement.) What we could do is different couples could bring some examples. Maybe you'll have a hard time during the week that's tough to handle. Well, we could go over that with you here in the group and see if we can find a way of helping you identify what you were really feeling and also be able to say it directly and clearly in a way that keeps communication open. I think this is the way it would work. Even if one couple raises a specific example, the rest of us could learn in helping them with that example. So, you would get something out of each week's session even if you weren't talking about your own marriages.

**Practice Summary.**   With a clear contract and some work in the beginning of the session that helped create the safe conditions within the group, group members felt free to begin to risk themselves. With Lou's help in addressing the authority theme, the group members were able to get into the work with more comfort. This authority theme will continue throughout the life of the group but at least we have made a start in dealing with it.

In addition, the group has moved directly to one of the core issues in marital relationships. What is striking is the way the group members themselves directed the emergence of this theme. Each group is different, since it reflects the strengths and experiences as well as the weaknesses of its members. Lou brought a sense of urgency and a willingness to risk himself to the group that helped it not only tackle the issue of authority directly and constructively but also helped it to move past its early defenses into the common concerns they had about their relationships with each other. Although the particular way in which this group worked during its first session is unique, I do not believe the level of its work or the speed with which it began is at all unusual. I believe it reflected the sense of urgency of the group members, the clarity of group purpose, and leader's role. The members were willing to attack the issue of authority directly, and the leader consistently tried to articulate the feelings expressed by the group members, even being slightly ahead of them. Given these core conditions, the impetus of the group members carried them toward productive work.

### *Wrapup and Session Evaluation*

**Practice Points:** Now that the session was nearly over and a consensus had been reached on a theme for additional work, the ending and transition phase of this session continued with an opportunity for evaluative comments. I wished in the first session to encourage members to talk about the way the group was working.

LEADER: We have five minutes left. This was our first session. I would like you to take a few minutes to share with each other and with us what your reactions are. What are your feelings and your thoughts? How has this session hit you? What will you say to each other on your way home in the car about this evening's session? It's important that you say it now.

ROSE: Well, I have the feeling that the first thing out the door, Lou is going to ask me what it is he said that made me angry. I can't define it right now. I'd have to pull it out of my head.

LOUISE: That's tough. That's really tough trying to figure out what it is that makes you angry. I feel that way, too. When I was an inpatient and someone showed me that I was angry at a resident and why I was angry, well that was fine; I was able to do a little bit of yelling and get it off my chest. But it's not always easy to put my finger on what it is I'm feeling.

LEADER: Maybe that's what we can do here—help you figure out what those feelings are. (Turning to Lou) What's your reaction? I'm really interested in your reaction because I have a feeling that you came in here thinking about all of the people in the past who haven't been helpful. Where do we stand so far?

LOU: So far I feel that we're beginning to break a little new ground. Actually, the most important thing that happened to me tonight was Rose getting mad.

LEADER: Is it easier to handle it when you know where she stands?

LOU: No, not really, I don't know where she stands. I knew she was mad; I asked her to tell me what she's mad about, but she said no. The reason I am feeling good about this is that she has just gone through five weeks as an inpatient, and I can assure you (voice cracking) I've just gone through the same five weeks.

LEADER: I think these things change step by small step and perhaps tonight made a beginning. Perhaps if you aren't too harsh with yourself and demand too much, you have a chance of doing it. I am glad it hit you that way. How about the others, what will your reactions be tonight?

FRANK: Whew!

JANE: (Laughing) I think we were so apprehensive about what would happen here tonight it wasn't funny.

LEADER: What were you afraid of?

JANE: Well, I guess it was the fear of the unknown, and yet when we got here, we immediately started to sense that here are people who are concerned, who care, and this came right to the fore.

LOU: Larry, I'd like to make a comment here. Our youngest son is 36 and one of the things he complained about to us was that "You never taught me how to argue with my wife." I wondered where in the world he got the idea that it was necessary to argue with each other. As time went on, I realized that we used to argue and keep things on the inside. My son today is having problems, and he even called me last night on the very same subject. The important thing he said was, "You haven't taught us how to argue." Oh, yes, not only that, but "You haven't taught us how to argue and to win the argument." (The group and leaders roared with laughter.)

Other members of the group were given a chance to comment. Frank pointed out that he and Jane were late partly because they were ambivalent about coming. He had been telling my coleader all week that he wasn't sure whether he really belonged here. As he described his conversations, he laughed along with the other members of the group. They all acknowledged that coming to the first session had been frightening. Frank went on to say that what impressed him was the people in the group; they all seemed to be a really "super bunch," and that helped a lot. Lou commented that it was reassuring to find out that he wasn't alone and that others had the same feelings.

### Reaching for the Negatives

**Practice Points:**   After some additional positive comments, I pointed out that it would also be important to share their negative reactions or questions; these were tough to share but were also important. Sally indicated her concern about whether or not the group would really help, if anything would really change. She was also worried about her husband Len having missed the first meeting. We talked about this, and I asked the group to strategize how we might bring Len into the second meeting quickly, since he would be feeling a bit like an outsider, having missed this first session. Once again, I was communicating a sense of their ownership of the group and their needed involvement in helping to make it work. It was not just my responsibility to help Len join the group in the second session; they had some responsibility as well.

I then told Sally that there were no promises, no sure answers or easy solutions. Marriage is hard work, as she knew, but perhaps through the group we might be able to offer some support and help with their difficult tasks. She nodded in agreement. Fran and Rick responded that they had felt a bit shy and found it difficult to talk in the group. John and Louise jumped in and reassured them, saying that they thought they had participated quite a bit. I pointed out that they had risked some very difficult and hard-to-talk-about subjects in the discussion with the group and gave them credit for that. Rick said that after a week or two he would probably find it easier getting in; I told him to take his time—that he would get in as he felt comfortable.

**The Rules of the Group**   As the evaluation seemed to be coming to an end, I pointed out that there were three rules we would follow in the group. I explained that members were expected to come each week and that it was OK to come even if your partner could not make it because of illness or some other reason. I said that material they shared with each other should be treated as confidential so that they could all feel that the other couples in the group would not be talking about them to outsiders. I also asked that if they wanted to drop out of the group at any time before the 23 sessions we had planned were over, they would agree to come back and discuss it with the group before quitting. All agreed that these seemed to be reasonable rules. I then complimented them on what I thought was an excellent start. I told them I could understand how nervous they must have felt at the beginning, since I felt a little of that nervousness, too, but that I thought they were off on some important work, and that boded well for our future. The session ended at this point, but people did not leave immediately; instead they milled around talking to other members and the leaders. Then, slowly, the group members left the room.

*Reflections on the First Session*

**Practice Summary.** This has been a detailed description of the first session of one kind of group. Perhaps the reader will immediately be thinking about some of the differences in the groups he or she has led. For example, these were generally articulate group members. They had volunteered to come to the group session and were not there under duress, having been mandated to attend. Of course, there are differences between groups depending upon the setting, the members, the purpose, and so forth. Some of these are illustrated later in this chapter with brief excerpts from first sessions of groups from different contexts. Nonetheless, the basic dynamics and skills involved in effective beginnings with groups cut across these differences. You will find in our examples that when these principles are respected, they more often than not lead to an effective start. When these principles are ignored, they haunt both the group leader and the group members. First sessions are important because they lay a foundation for the difficult tasks to follow. If handled well, they can provide a fund of positive feeling as well as a clear framework, both of which will influence the remaining sessions.

Returning to the comment made by more than one student after watching Lou taking the initiative in asking the couples about anger in their relationships: The video images reveal my facial expression, which clearly indicates my delight at his moving into a leadership role to the extent that I asked permission to interrupt. I pointed out that the fact that they accepted my invitation to take over in the first session was a very positive sign and an indication of the strength of the group members. This exchange often triggers an important discussion of the fear of an inexperienced group leader of "losing control of the group." It takes some experience and growing confidence for the group leader to realize that the process of "letting go" of control is central for leading effective groups.

## Recontracting After the First Session

**EP 2.1.1b**
**EP 2.1.4d**
**EP 2.1.10c**
**EP 2.1.10f**

Another common student reaction to the videotape of the couples' group just described is to feel somewhat intimidated. As they often put it, "My first session didn't go that way!" I reassure them that neither did my early efforts. Even if the neophyte group leader has done excellent preparatory work, is clear about the contract, and has role-played an opening statement with a supervisor, unexpected events and problems may occur. Retrospective analysis often reveals that the leader has left something out or the words did not resemble the carefully constructed and rehearsed opening statement.

New group leaders are understandably nervous leading their first groups and should not be too hard on themselves. They also need to realize that they usually have an opportunity to recontract with a group if they don't get it right the first time. Even if they are able to begin exactly as planned, group members may not hear or understand the opening statement. Contracting in an ongoing group always takes place over a number of sessions. The next two examples illustrate recontracting efforts.

Another common problem may be encountered when leaders join an already functioning group and have to recontract around their role as leader and the purpose of the group. Joining an ongoing group as a coleader and discovering that the contracting was never done or has been done badly can also be disconcerting. One student put it this way: "This sounds great in class, but I don't think the psychologist running our group has ever read your book!" In some circumstances, the ongoing group leaders have adopted a group practice model that operates under assumptions that differ from the interactional, strengths-perspective, mutual-aid model put forward here. The student needs to be reassured that there are many frameworks for helping and that this group provides them with an opportunity to see another model in action. Also, elements of the interactional model can often be integrated easily into other frameworks. In some examples, there simply is no model at all. Groups can be disorganized, unfocused, with members and the group leaders unclear about the purpose. Group sessions can resemble individual counseling in a group, with each member being "helped" by the group leader in turn. In the second set of circumstances, it becomes the group leader's job to try to influence the process with coleaders and members to recontract for a more effective group.

## Recontracting with Your Own Group

**EP 2.1.1b**
**EP 2.1.4d**
**EP 2.1.10a**
**EP 2.1.10b**
**EP 2.1.10c**
**EP 2.1.10g**
**EP 2.1.10m**

It is usually possible to come back at a later session and initiate the contracting discussion. In this section we have an example of a group leader getting a second chance as she learns from her first effort and, given the changeover of women in a battered women's shelter, she can start again.

***A Group for Battered Women in a Shelter*** In the example that follows we see a social worker from a community mental health setting leading an open-ended group in a shelter for battered women. She begins a first session of a psychoeducational group with a mixed message about the group's purpose. In her opening statement she briefly mentions a number of powerful themes related to the abuse and oppression that have brought these women to the shelter. In her structuring of the first session, however, she moves immediately to her agenda of providing information on "independent living skills." Rather than structuring time for problem swapping, which would have allowed the women some control over the agenda, the leader makes the decision for them. If one applies the oppression psychology outlined in Chapter 1, encouraging these women to take control of their own group could be seen as an important step toward "independent living."

**Practice Points:** A number of group members signal that they are at a different place in their needs related to this group. While independent living skills, job opportunities, and so on, are all important for these women, at this moment their sense of urgency may be more connected to their abuse and their living situations. The leader continues to control the first session, providing a sermon about the importance of "community support." As we will see, her understanding and skill evolves over the next few sessions as she recontracts with the women.

> **Session 1:** I said, "The purpose of this group is to provide you with some helpful information that you can use once you leave the house. The group will also provide you with an opportunity to talk about your feelings, experiences, and concerns that you might have about the different topics we'll be discussing. Tonight's topic is independent living skills." I went on to say, "Some of you are here because of abuse either by a boyfriend or a husband. You may find tonight that you have some feelings in common with each other. Some of you may be here for reasons other than abuse, and you may have your own set of circumstances that you'll want to share. My role is to help you to talk and to listen to each other. So I hope that we can all learn tonight not only from the material I have brought but also from the comments that we share with one another."

**Practice Points:** While the leader has made a direct opening statement, she has not allowed for any feedback or identification of issues that the women have brought to the group. She has her agenda and moves directly into it with a presentation about job training programs. Some members respond but others have a different sense of urgency and do not connect. The leader notes this but does not reach for the reason.

I began by giving the women information about two job training programs. One woman, Linda, talked about a job training program that she had attended and how she had landed a job afterwards. Two other women talked about the skills they had, one in accounting, the other in word processing and stenography. Four out of the seven women were interested. The other three women showed no interest at all. I didn't ask them why they seemed uninterested.

From there we moved on to the subject of community support. I stated that many people think asking for help is a sign of weakness. People, in many cases, think it's important to handle problems on their own. I said I disagreed with this type of thinking. I said people who think this way are oftentimes worse off because individuals aren't always equipped to handle situations that come up on their own. I said that people who look to their community for support could be better off in many ways. I then asked the women if they had any ideas or suggestions on where to find community support when they leave the house. No one had any suggestions off the bat, so I mentioned places such as churches, local community action programs, etc.

**Practice Points:** Although the leader wrote "we moved on to the subject," she should have written "I moved on"; clearly, the members did not move with her. The lack of response to her question is an indication they are not connecting with her information. In the next excerpt, an internal leader emerges to move the women to a discussion of the "here and now" of their experiences in the house and the pain of the abuse they carry with them. While the information the group leader wants to share is helpful and important, it is not addressing where the group members are at the moment.

One woman said she was very glad to be at the house. She said she came into the shelter wondering what the other women would be like and found out that many of the women were just like her. She said, "It feels good to be with people who have the same problem." She said that when she lived with her husband, he would be on her mind all day long. She would worry about what he would be like when he came home. Before she came to the house, she would stay with her parents when her husband became abusive. Eventually, her parents would talk her into going back with her husband. She said, "Here at the house, you get support. You're told he has a problem, not you." She said she was very glad to hear that. I said, "So it sounds as if you're relieved to be here." She said, "Yes."

Another woman said she used to wonder what her husband would find wrong when he came home. She also said he wouldn't allow her to talk with friends. I said, "You probably feel good that you don't have that pressure over you now." She agreed. In addition, she said she planned to attend Al-Anon meetings for support once she left the house.

**Practice Points:** In the next excerpt, one of the members sends a signal to the leader that the session is not meeting her needs. The leader's written comment about "reaction formation" indicates that she noted the negative feedback and reacted with internal anger and an external smile. The leader's early anxiety about doing a good job makes it hard for her to hear negative feedback. The group members' anxiety about their dependency upon the shelter may make it hard for them to share it. The discussion finally turns to money and issues of economic oppression that are closely tied to a major source of anxiety experienced by these women—economic survival.

One woman who had left the group for 15 minutes came back and said, "What did I miss out on?" Angela, one of the uninterested women, said, "Oh, you only missed out on some boring information." I should have asked her why she found the information so boring. Instead, I just smiled at her (reaction formation?). Then Janice, a night staff person, joined the group. Everything was fine until she started talking with the woman next to her. They continued to talk between themselves for about five minutes. I didn't know how to handle this situation.

When we started to talk about the area of financial management and I mentioned budgeting, one woman said, "What do I want to know about budgeting? I don't have any money to budget." Then she said that actually she did want to know about budgeting. She felt that someone should have sat down with her at the welfare office and shown her how to get the most for her money. Angela said she was always worried about having enough money to make ends meet, and she didn't see what good a budget would do. Angela has four children, one of whom is handicapped. The group began to talk about how she could get help for the handicapped child with cerebral palsy. The women suggested that she or her social counselor call a cerebral palsy foundation. I turned to Angela and said, "You must get very discouraged at times." She agreed.

**Practice Points:** Chapter 13 focuses in some detail on what I refer to as the *group-as-a-whole,* the entity that is formed when individuals are brought together. Bion (1961) provides an emotionality theory which suggests that in its early state, a group may have difficulty dealing with anxiety-producing emotions, and when faced with an issue such as economic security, one maladaptive response is for the group to go off into flight. This behavior in the group is a signal to the leader. The leader does not understand the meaning of the *"flight"* behavior in the following excerpt and, instead, thinks that she will need to do a better job at setting out the rules—a step that would cut off the expression of feeling, rather than dealing with it.

As the discussion continued about financial management, the discussion became some what chaotic. People were talking at once, cutting each other off. The women were skipping from topic to topic. I finally asked them to please talk one at a time. For the most part three women were doing all the talking. I could see that the other women were not paying attention. Next week I'd like to lay down some ground rules for discussion and emphasize the fact that everyone has important comments to make and we should take the time to listen to one another.

**Practice Summary.** With hindsight, the leader might have been able to address the second client, the group, by acknowledging that the discussion was hitting home for all of them. She could have identified the flight behavior—members talking all at once—as an understandable expression of the anxiety associated with the economic oppression and humiliation of being on welfare. These women had to demonstrate remarkable courage to overcome the economic restraints that our society places on them when they consider fleeing an abusive home. Inadequate financial supports function as a societal "shackle," helping to keep women chained to oppressive family situations. The leader might have responded to the group with the same empathy she had demonstrated moments before when she said to Angela, "You must get discouraged at times." The leader is surprised when another staff person intervenes with the offer of going to church the next Sunday. There is the possibility that this staff member responded to the flight with what she felt might help.

> Suddenly, Janice, a shelter staff person, asked if anyone wanted to go to church the following Sunday. This question was somewhat disruptive because we were talking about managing money at this point. She may have been responding to our discussion earlier about finding community support. It's difficult to say. The discussion became focused again when Linda asked for information about apartment hunting. One woman said that transportation was a big problem. Everyone chimed in on this. One woman said they should write a letter to the governor asking him to supply a car for the shelter. The women got excited at this point. I agreed that it sounded like a good idea, and I asked who would be in charge of writing the letter. Pam volunteered. Janice, the staff person, said they could talk about the letter the next day at the house meeting.

> I told them that we had discussed a number of important issues. I said I hoped they would be thinking about questions and ideas for next week's session on single parenting, and said I would see them next Wednesday night.

**EP 2.1.4a**

*A Chance for a New Beginning and a Different First Session* The next session described here is the fourth week following a number of sessions in which the leader allowed for more direction of the group to come from the group. As each session proceeds the leader becomes more comfortable; she is still providing a structured agenda but letting the group members take more responsibility for the direction of the conversation. Even the members who seemed bored and disconnected become engaged and actually begin to exert internal leadership. There are six new women at this session, giving the leader an opportunity to start again.

**Practice Points:** I include this excerpt as a way of saying to the reader that one can learn from mistakes and grow rather quickly as a group leader if one is open to feedback and willing to be self-critical (although not too self-critical). The leader's continued growth is evident when this session is compared to her first session of only three weeks before.

> **Session 4:** This week's group session consisted of six new women. Because of the new group composition, I told the women some information about myself, and then asked them to tell me their names, how many children they have, and how long they've been at the shelter. Then, I stated the purpose of the group session. I said, "This group will give you an opportunity to talk and to listen to one another. This is what's called a mutual-aid group. All of you here are experiencing some difficulty in your lives because of abusive relationships. This is not an easy time for you. In fact, it's a time of crisis. Because you've experienced similar difficulties, this group session will give you a chance to help each other. As you listen to each other, share some of your problems and feelings, I think you'll learn a great deal from each other."

**Practice Points:** Note the critical difference as the group leader moves from an opening statement to problem swapping instead of immediately presenting prepared material.

"In order to get the group discussion started, I'd like you to do some problem swapping—share with each other some problems and difficulties you've experienced in your abusive relationships. If you want to, you can share some of the things you'd like to see differently in your lives now. By problem swapping, we'll find out what your major concerns are, and then the discussion can focus on these issues. There's no sense in having a discussion if it's not about issues that you're concerned with." I said, "Who would like to start?" Joyce said, "My problem right now is that I don't have any money and the last time I tried to apply for welfare, they told me I wasn't eligible." The women talked about this for a few minutes and tried to offer Joyce suggestions about receiving welfare. Next, Linda said that her life was very disorganized. At this point, she doesn't know where she's going.

**Practice Summary.** The discussion continued going into some detail on their feelings of fear and oppression in the relationships they had just left. I will return to this group in a later chapter with a more detailed discussion of the way in which the relationship to their male partners was experienced by the women as a form of slavery. The key point here is that the content of the group emerges from the felt needs of the members. This does not mean the group leader never provides information, brings a film, or invites an outside speaker. This example illustrates how the contract with a group can evolve over time, and how the group process can educate a leader to deepen his or her understanding of group dynamics, group skills, and the themes of importance to the clients.

## Coleadership in Groups

**EP 2.1.8b**

Contracting issues are complex when starting a new group. They grow more complex when a leader joins an ongoing group that may have been operating for some time without a clear working agreement or with one that does not lead to effective work. In this situation, the new group leader has to deal not only with the members of the group but also with the ongoing leaders, who have an investment in the current status. Students often raise this as a perplexing problem when they report sitting in on group discussions as coleaders and observing clearly the problems associated with poor contracting, coleader conflict over the contract, or simply a lack of understanding of group process. Tensions develop as the students read about alternative models and listen in their classrooms to presentations that directly apply to their own groups. And yet, as a "mere student," they feel intimidated about intervening and effecting change. In a situation such as the one in the following example, their stress is increased when the team leader is also of another discipline, which introduces issues of status and power.

The discussion of joining an ongoing group brings us to the question of coleadership. Whenever the general subject of coleadership is raised by leaders, I inquire if they have had experience working with another staff member in a group. Almost invariably they have, and the experience was often a bad one. The list of problems includes disagreement on the basic approach to the group, subtle battles over control of group sessions, and disagreement during the group session over specific interventions—particularly those introduced by a coleader that seem to cut off a line of discussion one leader feels is productive.

Underlying all of these problems is a lack of honest communication between coleaders both within and outside the group sessions. Leaders often feel embarrassed to confront their coleaders outside the session and believe it would be unprofessional to disagree during the session. This stance is similar to the "not arguing in front of the children" syndrome that many parents experience. There is an unreasonable expectation that they must appear to agree at all times. This lack of honesty usually reflects the insecurity of both leaders and often leads to defensiveness and the illusion of cooperative work. In addition, because of the importance of the authority theme in all groups, group members are very sensitive to signs of disagreement between coleaders, whether they are openly expressed or lurk beneath the surface. Consider the irony involved, for example, if in the married couples' group described earlier, the coleaders had modeled dysfunctional communications. My point is that you can't hide it, anyway, so why not deal with it (i.e., differences)? Reflective practice, as described in the following section, offers one way to address the issues.

## Reflective Practice in Group Coleadership

Atieno (2008) cites authors who have identified *reflective practice,* the ability of counselors to reflect on their personal and clinical experiences, as critical to effective functioning of helping professionals. She cites Miller (2005) as identifying reflective practice in group work as

> about helping people to reflect on their experiences of themselves and each other in the workplace in a way that builds insight and awareness so that people have increased choices about action. (Miller, p. 367)

Atieno argues that the lack of reflective practice in coleadership can lead to many of the problems often experienced such as "mistrust, competition, power struggles, personal or theoretical disagreements, intimacy overload, envy among coleaders, and incompetence" (p. 237).

This author suggests that reflective practice in coleading groups involves a number of processes and that it evolves over time, requiring an investment of effort and commitment to the process on the part of the coleaders. These processes include:

- *An Intrapersonal Process:* "An internal dialogue in which coleaders critically and qualitatively contemplate their experiences in coleader and group interactions" (pp. 239–240).

- *An Interpersonal Process:* This "reflective practice can be described as a verbal interaction characterized by systematic negotiations and self-disclosure influenced by insights gained from coleaders' intrapersonal process." (p. 241)

- *An Evaluative Process:* "This evaluative function occurs at both the intrapersonal and interpersonal level. As coleaders reflect on the interpersonal patterns in their relationships and on their interactions with group members, they engage in a process of evaluating the quality of relationships. This process also involves coleaders examining their individual performances a leaders, their coleader performances, and the outcomes of their groups" (p. 242).

The ability to share this information between coleaders both outside of and, at times, in the group itself offers the possibility of an enhanced positive relationship between coleaders and increased trust, cooperation, and effectiveness. Where it can get difficult, as described earlier in this chapter, is when the thoughts and feelings are not always positive. If there also is a difference between the coleaders in experience, training, theoretical framework, or a power differential (e.g., a supervisor and student coleading a group), then honest sharing of the reflections on practice can be impeded. Many of the same skills required for effective practice may also be useful in implementing a reflective practice model in coleadership, as will be illustrated in an example shared later in this chapter. First, however, I want to discuss the potential positives in coleadership.

## Positive Potential in Coleadership

Coleadership can be helpful in a group. A group is complex, and assistance by another leader in implementing the helping function can be a welcome aid. In my couples' group, one coleader was female and a nurse. She was able to add perspectives to the work that were strikingly different from mine. For example, she reacted with a different mind-set to issues raised in the group related to women. Our ability to work well together was based upon a number of factors. First, there was a basic agreement about an approach to the helping process. While our theoretical frameworks differed and we used different conceptual models for understanding group member behavior and dynamics, we shared similar attitudes toward clients and a commitment to mutual aid and the importance of reaching for client strength. Within this common framework, our different conceptual models served, in fact, to enrich our work with the group.

Second, we structured time to discuss the group. We met before the start of the first group sessions to prepare strategy and also met before the start of each session to "tune in," using the previous session as well as any additional knowledge gained from individual contacts my coleaders may have had with the couples. Time was set aside after each session to discuss the group. (In this case, the discussion took place with a group of students training at the school who viewed the group sessions on a video monitor.) Every effort was made to encourage honest communication about the sessions and our reactions to each other's input. This was not simple, since I was the senior group leader, and it was not easy for coleaders to challenge me. As our relationship grew and trust developed, more direct communication was apparent.

Finally, we had an understanding that we would feel free to disagree in the group. In many ways, the nurse coleader and I were to be a model of a male/female relationship in action. It would be a mockery of our effort if we supported honesty and willingness to confront while maintaining professional "courtesy" toward each other in the group. Observing that coleaders could disagree, even argue, in a group and still respect and care for each other can be a powerful object lesson for group members.

Group members are very observant, and they can pick up subtle cues of tension between leaders, no matter how hard leaders try to hide them. This was pointed out in the mid-year evaluation session of this couples' group. A third coleader in this group was a former social work student of mine, and although he participated in the sessions up until that point, the presence of the other coleader and his feelings about working with a former teacher inhibited him. We had discussed this in the sessions with the student observers, who had been quick to pick up his hesitancy. In the mid-year evaluation session of the couples' group, I inquired how the members felt we could improve our group leadership during the second half of the year. Illustrating the perceptiveness of group members, Rose, our member in her late sixties (Lou's wife who had been silent during the first session described earlier), turned to my coleader and said, "I hope you don't take what I'm going to say personally. I think you have a lot to give to this group, and I would like to hear more from you. I don't think you should let Larry (this author and the senior leader) frighten you just because he is more experienced." He responded, "You know, Rose, I've been worried about my participation, too. It is hard for me to get in as often as I want to, and I'm going to work on it." In fact, this brief conversation was a turning point, with his participation in the group increasing substantially following it.

## Skill in Dealing with Coleader Conflicts in the Group

In this last example in this chapter, I focus on the work done by a student in a mental health setting as she tries to influence the senior coleader, a full-time employee from another discipline, into thinking about the group of psychiatric patients in a new and more strength-based manner. It becomes clear to her early in her work that the staff have a perception of psychiatric patients that underestimates their ability to work effectively in a group.

**Practice Points:**   At first, the student responds to her frustration with efforts that are not well received. After some reflection, and the writing of an assignment analyzing her work, she develops a more professional sense of how to work effectively with her colleagues. She begins to internalize the idea that the environment itself and its staff are the "second client." Her report begins with her efforts to clarify group purpose with Dr. Brown, the senior staff member.

> When I continued to press at another time for group purpose, Dr. Brown finally asked what I would suggest.

LEADER: Well, we could say something like, "This is a place where people can learn how to support each other and how to get along better."

DR. BROWN: Hmm. I think that might be too frightening for them to hear. Schizophrenics have a hard time with relating to others, and they may just get scared if we try to tell them they have to talk to each other. I don't think we really need to tell them anything. We can just make it very general.

LEADER: Like what?

DR. BROWN: Well, we could say there's just so much to talk about and we don't get enough chance to talk that much, so this is a chance for us to be with them.

> I did as he recommended at that point, but continued to bring up the topic in future group supervision meetings.

By this point in the process the student was expressing, in class, increased feelings of frustration and anger. She decided to use a written assignment to focus on her work with the doctor, recognizing that influencing her coleaders' and supervisors' perceptions about the group would require at least as much thought and skill as did her work in the group. This represented an important shift in her thinking from complaining about the existence of the problem to recognizing her responsibility to try to address it. At first, she still had difficulty tuning in to the concerns and feelings of her coleaders.

**Practice Points:**   The important change in her work, however, was her focus on taking some responsibility for her part in the interaction, which she can control. This is an example of good reflective practice.

I (the group leader) did eventually get some general answers about my coleader's purpose, but I failed to tune in adequately to the team leader's place in the setting and its implications for what he could feel free to do. In the example above, Dr. Brown gave evidence of an important concern: the psychological feelings of safety of the clients. In the following excerpt, Dr. Brown notes other concerns.

DR. BROWN: I think you'll find that they don't react the way you're expecting them to. If we push them too far, I'm not sure what they'll do.

LEADER: Right. I wouldn't want to push them too far. But I think they may be able to handle some attention to relationships, and then we can see what happens and back off if someone is getting too upset.

THE LEADER'S REFLECTIONS: By trying to convince him to do it my way, I failed to really give attention to his concerns or to explore what he thought might happen so that we might come up with some way to avoid it that really worked and that felt right to both of us. Since I wasn't really respecting his concern or trusting that it was a valid one, I was dismissing its importance and missing an opportunity to really tune in, to reach for the negatives, and to show empathy for the needs of the organization as well as of the clients. If I had this part to do over again, I would have asked for more information about his concerns, acknowledged them, and then tried working with him to solve the anticipated problems. In fact, I did get to do it over again in a later session, and did better at tuning in at that time:

LEADER: I thought it was great how they were able to challenge each other and really interact with each other.

DR. BROWN: Yeah, but I was concerned. Fred seemed to be getting upset at what was going on.

LEADER: Does he have any history of having problems when he gets anxious like that?

DR. BROWN: Yeah, actually he was at a forensic psychiatric unit a number of years ago for attacking somebody with a knife.

LEADER: Well, no wonder you're so concerned! I didn't know about that.

DR. BROWN: Yeah, it was a few years ago, but you never know with some of these people.

LEADER: We have never really talked about what we would do if someone became violent in the group. I've had some training in nonviolent self-defense, but what is the procedure on this unit?

LEADER'S REFLECTIONS: We were then able to talk about procedures and about other concerns about what could happen in the group. Again, I think I could have paid a little more attention to Dr. Brown's concerns by asking, "Do you think something like that might happen during group?" rather than by talking about procedures right away, but it did seem at least to acknowledge the importance of his concerns in a way I hadn't done before.

**Practice Points:** It is important that the tuning-in and empathic responses to colleagues be genuine. When training has led professionals to respond with a pseudo-empathy (speaking the words without feeling the feelings), an acute sensitivity to being "therapized" or "social worked," in the worst sense of the word, can be observed. This will result in a negative response. In this example, as the student was better able to examine and manage her own feelings in the situation, her capacity for genuine empathy with her colleague increased.

In the next excerpts, the student describes a strategy she has developed for influencing the team leader. Instead of confronting him with his "deficiencies," she invites him to join her in her own analysis of her work. She does this through the sharing of her process recordings, written for her supervision sessions, which include her own self-analysis of her practice.

After the first session, I began to share my thoughts on what I would like to be doing in the group with my coleader via process recordings. I began writing weekly a description of what happened in group, the main themes I saw, my overall impression, and my plans for follow-up, and I gave a copy of this to my coleader each week. I hoped that if I shared my thoughts with him in a written format, he might be better able to take in my ideas without having to respond to them right away. I also felt that I could show in more depth in these recordings the scope of what I envisioned for the group, and that by giving me a chance to show him the things I would have liked to say, even when I wasn't yet able to say them, he might come to trust my judgment more.

**Practice Points:** Note in the group leader's comments that follow that she chose to share her concerns and issues about her practice and to invite her coleader to discuss them with her. She was sharing her reflective practice and asking him to join her in the analysis. An example of what she shared with him follows, from the ninth group session:

**Description:** Helen started talking about her family and how her children and grandchildren kept her young. She also spoke about her job at the library and specific things she did there. I said it sounded like she really loved her job, and she agreed. She spoke more about this, addressing most of this to me, and I felt uncomfortable that the rest of the group was not being included, so I responded to her several times but then didn't pursue it further, hoping that others would be able to jump in then.

**Reaction/Analysis:** Not a great strategy, I see now! Perhaps I could have said how I felt and brought it to the group more, or said I thought it was interesting what Helen was talking about and wondered how other members were feeling as they heard Helen talk about her job, or asked her if she wanted anything from the group.

This strategy seemed to work well. When I saw Dr. Brown after he had read this, he said he had enjoyed reading it and looked forward to getting more. We then spoke more about the group and our plans for the next session. Although we rarely talked about the specific content of the recordings, it seemed that giving Dr. Brown the recordings did help him get to know me better and trust me more, and gradually we did come to working better together. I believe these recordings had a major impact on our relationship developing as well as it did.

**Current Status of the Coleadership Relationship:** Tremendous progress has been made in getting the team leader to accept some different possibilities for goals and formats for use with these patients. Through much discussion, he has been able to accept the possibility of their interacting with each other in a safe and empowering way, and, even more significantly, has begun to look at the system practices that work against the patients' being able to function independently in many areas. He has begun seeing possibilities for them to have more independence in the group that he didn't see before, and is showing interest in continuing to encourage that kind of independence. The structure of the group has been pretty well set by now, although the goals and purpose still need to be more clearly stated to group members and to the entire treatment team. There is a lot of work yet to be done, but a lot has been accomplished toward creating more empowering and effective goals and structure.

**Practice Summary.**    This example has not only illustrated a recontracting process over time, but it also has demonstrated the importance of the "two-client" idea, with the agency or setting as the second client. The attitude toward group practice in the setting was a reflection of the general attitude toward work with psychiatric patients. The student counselor was helpful to individual members of the group; however, her most important impact was on the system. Rather than just remaining distressed and angry about the deficiencies of the system, she began to see addressing these problems as central to her role. The effects of her impact on the system would be felt long after she had left her placement. She had also learned that in order to empower the client, staff must first deal with her or his own sense of disempowerment.

When I share this example or another like it I often hear: "But I'm only a student! Wait until I am a professional; then I can deal with my colleagues, my supervisor, or the agency/setting." I understand the hesitancy, since the student will be graded, wants to pass the field practicum, and wants to eventually graduate. In some circumstances, perhaps unlike the one described above, the coleader or the system may simply be too hard to impact. I tell my students that I believe it is important to take a next step and at least try. I think, as in the example above, skill in having professional impact needs to be developed. The helping professions have become very good at recognizing the strengths in our clients; however, we are not quite as good at seeing them in colleagues and the systems we work in. I point out to students that after they graduate they will still have a supervisor, they will still be evaluated, and they could still lose their job, so the magic of having the degree will not really protect them. So, I argue, they might as well start implementing and learning about this aspect of their professional role while they are students.

## A Final Comment on Coleadership

In the example above I addressed the issue of coleadership with a more senior coleader. It is not uncommon for coleaders to both be new to group practice. I believe it is difficult, but not impossible, for two beginning group leaders to work together. Their own anxieties are often so great that they often become more of a problem for each other than a help. Coleading with a more experienced leader provides learners with an opportunity to test their wings without taking full responsibility for the outcome. When mutual trust and sharing develop between coleaders, the leaders can be an important source of support for each other. The feelings of warmth and caring that develop between members and between the group leader and members must also exist between coleaders as they tackle the complex task of working with groups. If a good working relationship exists between coleaders, even two new ones, they can make the partnership work. Of course, the problems of coleadership, only partially elaborated in this brief discussion, must be kept in mind.

# Open-Ended, Single-Session, and Internet Online Groups

EP 2.1.6b

Now that I have presented the basic issues in the beginning phase of group work, the remainder of this chapter will focus on some of the variations introduced by open-ended groups, single-session groups, and the rapid emergence of computer or Internet groups.

## The Open-Ended Group

An open-ended group is one in which the membership is continuously changing. New members arrive and old members leave throughout the life of the group. This is in contrast to a closed group (or fixed-membership group), where the same people meet for a defined period of time. Members may drop out and new members may be added in the early sessions, but in general, the membership of a closed group remains constant.

Corey (2008) points out that

> As a result of managed care, many groups tend to be short term, solution oriented, and characterized by changing membership. Whether the group will be open or closed may be determined, in part, by the population and the setting. But the issue needs to be discussed and decided before the group meets, or at the initial session. (p. 70)

The decision to run a group as open-ended or closed depends on several factors, including the nature of the contract, the characteristics of the clients served, and the structure of the setting. For example, in a couples' group dealing with marital problems, the difficulty of discussing personal issues such as sexual incompatibility would increase if membership in the group were constantly changing. The same would be true in a group for survivors of sexual abuse, where disclosure of traumatic experiences is difficult in a group context. A stable membership is essential for such groups to develop the necessary mutual trust and culture for work.

On the other hand, an open-ended group is more appropriate for teenagers in a group home, where residents are entering and leaving at different times. The problems associated with shifting membership in this type of group are outweighed by the advantages of having all the residents present. Thus, the decision to operate open-ended or closed groups must be made with the unique characteristics of members, the group's purpose, and the setting in mind.

An open-ended group provides certain advantages. For example, a group that has developed a sound culture for work can bring in a new member quickly. As the new members listen to the discussion, their own willingness to risk may be accelerated by the level of openness of the others. In addition, those who have been in the group for a while can assist new members with issues they themselves have already dealt with. A technical problem associated with open-ended groups is that each session may be a new beginning for some members, an ending for other members, or both.

Corey (2008) points out that

> A disadvantage of the open group is that new members may have a difficult time becoming part of the group because they are not aware of what has been discussed before they joined. Another disadvantage is that changing group membership can have adverse effects on the cohesion of the group. Therefore, if the flow of the group is to be maintained, the leader needs to devote time and attention to preparing new members and helping them become integrated. (p. 70)

Toseland and Rivas (2005) address the question of the timing of adding new members.

> If a counselor can control when members begin and leave a group, the counselor should consider during the planning process when it is optimal to add new members. For example, the counselor may decide it is best to add new members during the first few sessions and then close group membership. Alternatively, the counselor might plan to add no more than one or two new members in any given meeting. (p. 172)

In short-term groups, where members do not remain for a long time, the leader can take responsibility for bringing in new members and acknowledging the departure of the old ones. In groups with longer-lasting membership, the group members themselves can discuss this process and develop a system for dealing with the changing group composition. This will be illustrated in the example in this section of bringing a new member into a group for persons with AIDS. Either way, the skills involved require that the leader be able to state the purpose clearly and briefly to a new member so that the ongoing work of the group can proceed in spite of the changes in membership.

Open-ended groups, particularly short-term groups, are characterized by the need for more leader guidance. Because the group has little continuity, the leader needs to actively provide the structural supports. This does not mean, however, that the group members are excluded from taking some responsibility for dealing with structural issues. One common example is when a new member joins a relatively stable open-ended group. Often, the new member initially feels like an outsider. In turn, the ongoing group members may resent a new member and be concerned about the possible impact on the group dynamics.

Ongoing members may not be direct about their feelings, because they sense it is not OK to feel that way. Their heads may say, "Because I am receiving help, shouldn't it be available to others?" At the same time, their hearts may say, "I like the group just the way it is, and I'm afraid a new member will screw it up!" Unless this issue is openly explored, their real feelings may be acted out in the way they relate to the new member. The leader may have some ambivalence as well, accepting the agency policy of keeping the group open, yet feeling concerned that a "good group" might change with the addition of an unknown new member. The result may well be an illusion of work, in which the leader announces a new member is coming the next week and the group quickly moves on to a different topic. Or, if the group raises objections, the leader may side with the new member and completely miss the concerns of the second client, the group.

The alternative is for the leader to tune in to his or her own feelings, as well as the feelings of the group members, and to use the skill described in Chapter 10 as looking for trouble when everything is going the leader's way. This is illustrated in the next example.

***Bringing a New Member into a Group for Persons with AIDS*** The following example from a group for people with AIDS illustrates how the leader asks the group members to take real responsibility for bringing in a new member.

**Practice Points:** The leader must first challenge the illusion of work as group members appear to have no problem with a new member joining. Rather than accepting the first positive responses, the group leader uses the skill described earlier as "looking for trouble when everything is going your way." The leader reaches for the potential lurking negatives.

**LEADER:** I wanted you to know that we have a new member joining the group next week. As you know, agency policy is that we stay open to new members if we have room. I'm not asking for a vote here, but since we have been maintaining a regular membership recently, I wondered how you all felt about adding someone new.

**JOHN:** It's not a problem. After all, we were all new at one point or another.

**LEADER:** I appreciate that thought, John, but in my experience, even though it isn't completely rational, ongoing members sometimes resent and even fear adding someone new to a group that's working well. I wonder if anyone feels that way.

**TED:** Does it mean we are going to go back to square one—I mean, starting all over? I've gotten to trust these guys, and I'm not so sure a new member is a great idea.

**LEADER:** That's exactly what I meant, Ted. How about the rest of you? You have worked hard to build a good group here, and it wouldn't surprise me if the new member might make a problem for you.

**RICK:** I'm not sure I want to see someone going through what we all went through when we first had that diagnosis. I mean, I'm past all of that now, and I want to work on other issues.

**Practice Points:** The leader's skill and understanding of his role and the role Ted may be playing as an internal leader allows him to credit Ted and reach for similar feelings on the part of other group members. This opens up important concerns under the surface of the apparent acceptance of a new member. The leader then partializes by listing these concerns.

**LEADER:** I think it's also a little scary to have someone come in who may reawaken all of the fear and anxiety. I hear three issues: Is the new member going to set us back to going over old issues? Are we going to lose our sense of trust in the group? And, how are we going to feel facing all of our initial feelings again? Let's discuss these and see if we can come up with a way to bring this new member in and cope with it effectively. I am willing to work with him in advance to help in the entry to the group, but I think you are all going to need to help as well. The faster we integrate him, the better chance we will not lose what we have.

**Practice Points:** At the leader's suggestion, the group members used the rest of the time to tune in to some of their own feelings when they first joined the group and what it was that either helped them to connect or put them off. As the members put themselves in the shoes of the new member, they developed strategies that both the leader and they could adopt in greeting the new member. These included acknowledging that he was coming into an ongoing group and that it might take some time for him to feel connected; making some room for him in the first session to handle the initial shock issues, while still making sure that they picked up on their own ongoing issues; letting him know he could get involved as he felt comfortable; and offering to provide a "buddy" from the group whom he could contact by phone if he wished.

After some further discussion, the leader raised another potential underlying issue associated with the entry of the new member. This was the fact that the space had opened up because of the sudden and unexpected death of one of the ongoing members. Even though it had been discussed when it happened, he explored with the group how their ongoing feeling of loss might affect their ability to attach to each other and to the new member.

**Practice Summary.**   The leader did not need to have this conversation for every new member who joined. Rather, the leader monitored the changing composition of the group and periodically raised the issue when circumstances required it. This concept is clearer if we conceive of the group as an organism, which is more than the sum of its parts. If we think of the group as an entity independent of its members, existing with a continuously changing membership, then the need to address its (the group's) tasks in relation to new members is clear.

## The Single-Session Group

Some groups are short-term and/or single-session groups. Examples include informational meetings or educational sessions (e.g., a session at a school designed to help parents assist their children with homework problems). These groups will often be larger than the small, face-to-face groups I have been describing thus far.

Jacobs et al. (2006) point out that clarity of purpose is particularly essential in a single-session group.

> The leader needs to be very clear about why the group is meeting and then plan a group that will accomplish the desired objective in the time allotted. The group's purpose may be to discuss and determine a treatment plan for a patient, to resolve a conflict, or to plan an event. Being clear will help the leader use the time effectively and accomplish the desired outcomes. Often at single-session group meetings, little is accomplished because the members keep switching topics and the leader fails to keep the discussion within the boundaries of the purpose. (p. 62)

Leaders of such groups often feel that the time limitations and size of the group will eliminate the possibility of group interaction or involvement. As a result they substitute direct presentation of the information to be shared, followed by a question period. Sessions structured in this way can be quite effective, but one drawback of straight didactic presentation is that people do not always hear, understand, or remember the material presented. If they are concerned about a specific issue or have feelings about attending the group, these may block their ability to hear.

A second problem is when too much information is shared, causing group members to actually tune out of the presentation as they suffer from information overload. Questions raised at follow-up sessions too often suggest that, although the leader has shared the data, the group members have not taken it in. I am sure every reader can remember a speech, a workshop presentation, or a didactic lecture in a class that they experienced as overloaded (e.g., too many PowerPoint slides with small print) or just boring. You can remember the event but not the actual content. The challenge for the leader is to structure a session in a way that allows participants to interact with the information given and make it more meaningful.

Size of group and restricted time do not automatically rule out active participant involvement, and many of the principles discussed thus far can be adapted to such situations. The leader should begin by thinking about each group if it were a "small group" and by attempting to adapt the basic model to the group's limitations. For example, the idea of phases of work is still helpful, but the beginning, work, and ending/transition phases all must be encompassed in one session.

Often I have found it helpful in an information meeting to reverse the usual order of talking first and listening later—that is, making a presentation and then asking for questions. Even a very brief, structured start to the meeting, following a statement of purpose in which the leader asks the group members what they would like to get out of the session, can make a major difference in their ability to connect to the presentation. Sharing some brief examples, what I have called earlier "handles for work," will help the group members think of their concerns in the area and also reassure them that they are not alone. Contracting in the opening phase of a session is critical, as the following example from a foster parent recruitment meeting demonstrates.

*A Single-Session Information Group: Foster Parent Recruitment* A major problem in child welfare is finding appropriate foster homes for children. The subsidies are usually too low, requiring the foster parents to cover some expenses from their own funds. In addition, many of the children referred to foster care have been seriously neglected and/or abused and the result may be acting out behavior. If the biological parent(s) are still involved, they may have supervised or unsupervised visiting rights. Reports of parents missing visitations or showing up under the influence of drugs or alcohol, with a resulting acting out by the children, are not uncommon.

Given some of the negatives, there are still many families who feel a deeply held obligation to help these children. The first information meeting is designed to encourage group members to consider becoming foster parents and to address concerns, real or imagined, or concerns heard in the neighborhood.

Note the following elements of the structure in this example:

- A clear statement of purpose and role
- Reaching for feedback and concerns
- Articulating a number of concerns as "handles for work"
- Recognition of the time available

I explained that the agency was holding these meetings to encourage families to consider providing a foster home for our children in care. The purpose of this first session was for us to share some information about fostering with the group, to try to answer their questions and to discuss the concerns they may have on their minds that might help them to determine if further exploration were feasible. I pointed out the group was large (over 40), and I realized that might make it hard for them to talk, but I hoped we could treat this evening as a conversation rather than a lecture. I would be interested as much in hearing from them as in sharing my own information. I then asked if this is what they had understood to be the purpose of the meeting. There was a general nodding of heads, so I continued.

I said I thought it might be helpful if I could begin by asking them what some of their questions were about fostering—some of the things that were on their minds. I would keep a list of these and try to make sure we covered them in our discussion. There was silence for a moment, and then a hand was raised.

**Practice Points:** In this example, the leader chose to obtain feedback from the group before beginning her presentation. If the hand had not been immediately raised, this would be a good moment for the leader, after a short pause, to provide some "handles for work." For example,

> Some folks who are new to fostering wonder about how much responsibility they will be taking on. It's not uncommon to wonder about the support they will receive from the agency—both financial, emotional and assistance dealing with the children. They wonder about contact with the biological parents as well as how having a foster child might impact their own children.

**Practice Points:**  This is the "listen first, talk later" approach mentioned earlier. One advantage to this approach is that it helps the leader identify and address members' needs. If people have an urgent concern about the subject, listening to any other conversation can be hard for them until that concern has been dealt with or at least acknowledged. Once they know they are "on the agenda," their energy is freed to invest in absorbing other data. Just throwing out these examples will often stimulate a response from group members who are reassured they are not alone in their concerns, that it's OK to have these questions, and that the group leader appears to understand and want to address the real issues.

The amount of time taken to raise questions or swap problems is determined by the overall time available. For example, in a 2-hour meeting one would not want to spend more than 15 minutes contracting and problem swapping, while in a 3-hour session, more time might be used to explore issues and develop a group consensus on the agenda. Timing is always important in group sessions, but it naturally takes on a special urgency in a single-session group. The leader needs to keep track of time and point out continually to the group the relationship between time and their work. For example, the leader might say,

> You are raising so many good issues that I think we could probably meet for a week. However, we only have 2 hours. I wonder if it is possible for us to focus on one or two central concerns and dig into them.

> Or the leader could explain,

> I would like some time at the end to discuss this evening's program, to evaluate the session, and to see what you feel you have gotten out of it. Can we be sure to leave the last 15 minutes to do this?

Group leaders often suggest many reasons for not involving clients in single-session or large groups more actively in the work. First, they are concerned that they have so much to cover they do not have time for group process. However, as pointed out earlier, most of us have noticed in our own educational experience, a teacher who is busy covering the agenda does not necessarily teach anything. We are often better off narrowing the field of work and limiting our goals. Effective work with a manageable agenda is preferable to going through the motions of trying to cover a wide area. The first skill in handling such meetings, then, is to narrow down the potential area of work to suit the time available. I will tell my own short-term groups that "I would prefer to try to cover everything well than to try to cover everything."

A second area of concern is that the group may raise questions that the leaders are not prepared to answer. This is a particular concern for new leaders, who are nervous enough as it is. They may have little experience in the field and have prepared extensively to deal with the specific areas they have predetermined as important. Their notes are written out in detail or they have prepared a PowerPoint presentation, and the last thing they want is someone asking a question for which they are unprepared. This is understandable, because it takes confidence to allow the group to shape the direction of the work. When leaders realize they are being judged by group members not on whether they have all the answers but rather on how well they involve the group in the process, they are often more willing to risk opening up the session in novel and unexpected directions. When they do so, they find they learn as much from such sessions as do the group members. Each session helps the leader to tune in and prepare for the next one, so that the ability to deal with the real concerns of the group grows with experience. Also, it is always possible to admit not knowing a specific piece of information and offer to find out the answer and contact theparticipant later.

A third area of concern, particularly with large groups, is that a single member may take over the group for individual or personal issues unrelated to the contract. Our discussion of deviant members in Chapter 13 will illustrate how the leader may need to be assertive in such a situation and guard the contract vigorously. This ability also comes with experience. Once again, the leader has to be willing to risk the hazards of such an approach if the benefits of more member involvement are to be gained.

## Internet Online Groups

Technology is having a growing influence on the way counseling is done—and in particular the use of the Internet for individual, family, and group practice. Kennedy (2008), in a lead article in *Counseling Today*, points out that

> More and more counselors have come to accept, even if sometimes begrudgingly, that their profession is not immune to technology's impact. Instead, they are actively looking for ways that technology can be of "help" to the helping professions. As such, new technologies are influencing how counseling is being accessed, delivered and taught. (p. 34)

Computer-mediated counseling is defined by Kennedy as "any type of counseling that uses a computer for delivery of services whether via e-mail, chat rooms, online support-groups or video conferencing" (p. 34).

One concern raised by members of the American Counseling Association (ACA) in an association survey is the "possibility of inadvertent violations of licensing laws if the client being treated online resides in a state different from that of the counselor" (p. 34). Kennedy cites Goodrich, who advises some precautionary measures when considering computer-mediated counseling. These include, among others:

- Encrypting conversations to ensure confidentiality.
- Performing risk assessments—know the contact information and locations of clients so these clients can be referred to local resources in cases of suicidal ideation or instances of other severe mental health risks.
- Being aware of client's access and basic computer knowledge.
- Being cognizant of legal issues.
- Knowing ethical codes for being a distance counselor.
- Acquiring proper licensure and credentials for distance counseling.

While still a relatively new approach to group practice, the use of the Internet for online groups, including chat groups, has been growing. Haug, Sedway, and Kordy (2008) point out that

> Over the past few years, computer-mediated interpersonal communication via the Internet has expanded rapidly. Online therapeutic approaches like Internet chat groups create new opportunities for the prevention and treatment of mental health problems. . . . Such groups offer the possibility of serving people with limited mobility, time restrictions and limited access to mental health services, including individuals living in remote areas, those lacking access to appropriate therapists, or those lacking access to other patients with similar problems to form a therapy group. The only requirement for a patient or therapist to

participate in the group is access to an Internet-connected computer and the ability to use this technology. (p. 36)

In this section of the chapter, I will discuss two of a number of types of communications currently used in online groups: (1) text-only groups, and (2) video groups.

***Internet-Chat Text Group Providing Follow-Up Mental Health Care*** Essential elements to qualify as an Internet-chat treatment group are that communications are synchronistic (there is the ability to have a direct response) and a therapist is present to guide the interaction. Haug et al. (2008) point out that

> The model for therapeutic chat groups is the traditional face-to-face group therapy setting in which group members (normally between 3 and 15) meet at prearranged appointment times with a therapist or other mental health professional. The online chat group interaction takes place in a "chat-room" where participants can simultaneously log on to a particular Web site to interact and communicate with each other. Compared to asynchronous forms of communication like e-mail or message boards, Internet-chats are more interactive as every sentence typed is immediately displayed on the screen for all the participants. (p. 37)

These authors state that there are both advantages and disadvantages to the use of Internet-chat groups. For example, there is a lack of facial expression and even emotional tone, since communications are text-based. Some ways of dealing with this include the use of emoticons (e.g., [?]) or sound words (e.g., hmmm). A number of other authors also have documented the difficulty of replicating face-to-face group process due to the lack of visual cues (see, e.g., Schopler, Galinsky, & Abell, 1997).

On the advantageous side, Haug et al. (2008) point out that

> The anonymity of the Internet may make it easier for individuals to disclose information about themselves since barriers such as age, gender, social status, and appearance are less present. (p. 27)

Noting that process research comparing face-to-face group treatment with online treatment has been rare or conducted with very small samples, these authors report their own study focusing on group evaluation and group process for a "stepped-care" program where 121 patients received inpatient group treatment followed by weekly therapist-guided Internet-chat groups. The study was able to control for previous contact in the hospital with other group members and/or the group therapist; however, all of the participants did share the inpatient group treatment experience. The central finding was that group processes did not differ significantly when the inpatient groups were compared to the Internet-chat groups.

> The study indicates that on the basis of a broad sample in an aftercare setting, group processes do not differ substantially between group traditional inpatient face-to-face groups and chat groups. We found that our group evaluations and processes increased over time in therapy. . . . The group evaluations in particular seem to follow a consistent upward course from the beginning of therapy until the end of chat aftercare. (p. 48)

***An Online Web-Based Video Support Group for Caretakers*** In another example of the use of technology in providing group services, Damianakis, Climans, and Marziali (2008) report the results of an online survey of eight social workers and one nurse exploring their experience in making the transition from face-to-face to Web-based video support groups for caregivers of family members with Alzheimer's,

Parkinson's, stroke, frontotemporal dementia, and traumatic brain injury. Groups were offered using a ten-session, one-hour-per-week model over a four-year period.

> The aim of these closed groups was to provide psychosocial support and to enhance caregivers' problem-solving and coping capacities while caring for their family members in their homes. (p. 103)

The researchers provided computer and webcam equipment for group leaders and participants. The group leaders were trained in the use of the equipment and provided a manual for Internet delivery of group treatment focusing on the particular illnesses (e.g., Alzheimer's) of those the caretakers cared for. The leaders' theoretical orientations included cognitive-behavioral, narrative, psychodynamic, and solution-focused. All of the therapists were experienced in working with geriatric populations. The online survey was composed of six open-ended questions dealing with their experiences in five key areas:

> (1) the experience of working online as compared to face-to-face, (2) the experience of transitioning from facilitative face-to-face groups to video Internet groups, (3) assessing the quality of relationships amongst group members and client outcomes, (4) advantages and disadvantages of working via Internet video conferencing, and (5) recommendations for other clinicians beginning to work online. (p. 104)

The researchers reported a generally positive experience as perceived by the therapists in spite of some technological challenges that impacted group processes. Online group interaction and therapeutic effectiveness was perceived as comparable to face-to-face support groups. The therapists reported that making the transition involved:

> (1) additional engagement of group members' in the pre-group phase,
> (2) attending to the group members' frustrations with glitches in the technology but also recognizing the potential advantages toward group bonding, and
> (3) adapting to change in group communication patterns as a result of structured technological sequencing. (p. 105)

While it is clear that the use of computer-assisted group work is still at the early stage in development and research, it is also clear that with the rapid growth of technology, Internet access, and new and more sophisticated software, this development needs to be closely monitored.

## Chapter Summary

The core skills of contracting in first sessions were examined in the group work context. Clarifying purpose, the group leader's role, reaching for client feedback, dealing with the authority theme, and so on, were all illustrated with a detailed analysis of the transcript of a first session of a married couples' group. Recognition that contracting does not always go well the first time and that it may take a number of sessions for the group to deal with all the issues were central to the discussion of recontracting—the process in which the leader raises contracting issues with an ongoing group.

In particular, strategies and skills for developing effective coleadership relationships were discussed with the "reflective practice" model shared as one example. This was illustrated in an example where a student coleader's ability to engage in a form of reflective practice with a senior staff member from another discipline had an important impact on group practice.

Some differences in the core elements in group practice include, among others, the unique processes and skills required in working with (1) an open-ended group, in which members join and leave the group continuously; (2) a single-session group, often large, which meets for informational proposes or in response to a particular event or trauma; and (3) the emerging use of the Internet for groups as well as initial and follow-up counseling.

## Related Online Content and Activities

 Visit *The Skills of Helping Individuals, Families, Groups, and Communities*, Seventh Edition, CourseMate website at **www.cengagebrain.com** for learning tools such as glossary terms, links to related websites, and chapter practice quizzes. The website for this chapter also features additional notes from the author.

## Competency Notes

The following is a list of Council on Social Work Education (CSWE) recommended competencies and practice behaviors for social work students defined in Educational Policy and Accreditation Standard (EPAS) and addressed in this chapter.

**EP 2.1.1b** Practice personal reflection and self-correction to assure continual professional development (pp. 414, 415)

**EP 2.1.4a** Recognize the extent to which a culture's structures and values may oppress, marginalize, alienate, or create or enhance privilege and power (p. 418)

**EP 2.1.4d** View themselves as learners and engage those with whom they work as informants (pp. 390, 414, 415)

**EP 2.1.6b** Use research evidence to inform practice (p. 426)

**EP 2.1.7a** Utilize conceptual frameworks to guide the process of assessment, intervention, and evaluation (p. 388)

**EP 2.1.8b** Collaborate with colleagues and clients for effective policy action (p. 419)

**EP 2.1.10a** Substantively and affectively prepare for action with individuals, families, groups, organizations, and communities (p. 415)

**EP 2.1.10b** Use empathy and other interpersonal skills (pp. 391, 415)

**EP 2.1.10c** Develop a mutually agreed-on focus of work and desired outcomes (pp. 388, 391, 414, 415)

**EP 2.1.10f** Develop mutually agreed-on intervention goals and objectives (pp. 390, 414)

**EP 2.1.10g** Select appropriate intervention strategies (p. 415)

**EP 2.1.10m** Critically analyze, monitor, and evaluate interventions (p. 415)

# The Middle Phase of Group Work

**EP 2.1.7a**
**EP 2.1.10a**
**EP 2.1.10d**
**EP 2.1.10f**

## The Middle or Work Phase in Group Work

In this chapter, I will revisit the impact of time on our practice, applying the concepts of the preliminary, beginning, middle, ending and transitions, this time to a single group session. As I did in Chapter 5 when I described the middle phase of working with individuals, to distinguish these elements from the phases over time, I will refer to them as *stages*. Just as looking at group counseling against the backdrop of time helps us to understand process over the life of the group, using the same backdrop for a single session is also revealing.

I begin in this chapter with a focus on the group leader's role. As pointed out in the chapter on beginnings and contracting, while strategies, interventions, and specific skills are important, they all need to be guided by the group leader's sense of role or function in the group. "What is my job in the group?" is the core question. While there may be a range of views in response to this question, and some believe the "role" changes depending on the group's purpose and setting, I will argue that the core job does not change; it is only elaborated differently. I also believe that being clear about role and being able to implement it consistently help a group leader deal with the unexpected events that always emerge in the life of the group.

In addition to the other responsibilities required in leading groups, a focus will be on how the leader helps individuals present their concerns and issues to the group and simultaneously assists the group members to respond. Once again I will be suggesting and illustrating the way in which indirect communications require the group leader to listen and understand what members of the group or the group-as-a-whole may be saying. In addition to helping individuals reach out to the group, I will focus on how the group leader helps the group to respond and be helpful.

Although the focus of this chapter is on the dynamic individual–group interaction, it is important to recognize that both the individual and the group require further detailed examination. In Chapter 13, I will analyze the individual's role in a group (e.g., Scapegoat, Monopolizer, and Gatekeeper) as well as exploring the concept of the group-as-a-whole.

These introductory sections will be followed by a detailed review of the work stages presented in Chapter 5; however, this time I will be adapting them to the group context and using group examples as illustrations. What will become clear to the reader is that there is a core to the helping process and that these basic ideas (the constant elements) need to be elaborated as they are adapted to different modalities of practice (the variant elements). Put another way, you can use what you already understand in work with individual and families by adapting these concepts and skills to the group context.

While most of the examples in this chapter address one form of group or another, the model presented can just as easily be applied to any form of group work. Variations on the theme are introduced by setting and type of group (psychoeducational, substance abuse recovery, task-focused, etc.), but the same four-stage framework will help to guide the interventions of all group leaders. All group sessions have beginnings, middles, and endings; and preparation for a group meeting by the group leader, before the actual meeting, is always important.

As will be evident in examples in this chapter and the chapters that follow, even in an educational or psychoeducational group where the leader is expected to share a good deal of information through presentation in some form or another, many of the general principles will apply. I have argued that simply speaking the words does not mean that group members hear, understand, remember, or invest any affect in the content—all of which are required for real integration and learning. If we reflect on our own educational experiences, we have most likely forgotten significantly more than we remember. However, a teacher who conveyed a passion about the subject or who was skillful in helping us to see the connection between the content to be learned and our own immediate sense of need is more likely to be remembered, as is the content of the course. A skilled research methods teacher who recognizes early in the class the anxiety felt by students as they attempt to learn what appears to be a foreign language (I call it talking Chi-Square) has a better chance of helping us to overcome this emotional obstacle. A social policy teacher who closely connects the historical development of such programs such as Social Security and Medicare to the current lives of our clients will get our attention. In a sense, even in an educationally focused group, where the role of the instructor can be described as mediating between the content of the course and the learners in the class, the notion of the two clients holds up. Sessional tuning in, sessional contracting, and so on are important in these groups as well.

I will start by focusing on the role of the group leader in the counseling or support group.

# The Role of the Group Leader

What do we know about communications in a counseling group or, in fact, in any group? There are a number of barriers to open communication in the group setting. These include ambivalence toward taking help because of the resultant feelings of dependency, societal taboos against discussion of certain topics (e.g., sex, substance abuse dependency), the members' painful feelings associated with particular issues, and the context of the helping setting (e.g., the impact of the helping person's authority). These blocks often cause a group member to use an indirect form of communication when sharing a problem or concern. This is similar to the use of indirect communications in individual or family work.

For example, members might hint at a concern (state a specific problem in a very general way), ask a general question in response to a presentation in a psychoeducational group that has a specific concern behind it, act it out (begin a session by being angry at the leader or other group members, using the anger to cover up the pain), employ metaphor or allegory as a means of presenting an issue (e.g., by telling a seemingly unrelated story), use art or other mediums (e.g., a child might draw a picture of an abusive parent), send the message nonverbally (e.g., by sitting quietly with a pained expression or sitting apart from the group with an angry expression), or present the issue with the classic "I have a friend with a problem."

In some cases the group member may present the opposite of a concern or feeling—for example, the member who responds to *check-in,* a technique used in some groups in which each member reports on any problems or how the week went, with a positive attitude and expression and says: "The last few days have been great, not like the beginning of the week." When (and if) the leader inquires about what happened at the beginning of the week, the story, attitude, and affect change dramatically and the real issue is raised.

The indirectness of these communications may cause the group members and the leader to miss important cues in the early part of the session. Alternatively, a member might raise a concern but do it in such a way as to hide the depth of feeling associated with it, thereby turning off the other group members. The leader's function is to assist the group in interpreting individual members' indirect communications.

## Reaching for Individual Communication in the Group

Because of the problems involved in individual–group communication, the leader should, in the early stages of each meeting, concentrate on helping individual members present their concerns to the group. The beginning of each group session should be seen as a tentative process of feeling out the group, endeavoring to determine which member or members are attempting to capture the group's attention for their own issues, and exploring how these issues may represent a theme of concern for the group. Even in a psychoeducational group that begins with a presentation, members may raise concerns indirectly through the questions they ask. For example, in a presentation to an adoptive parents' group on how children handle their concerns about their birth parents, one member might ask: "Do all adopted children want to know who their birth parents were?" The group leader who asks: "Has your child been raising this with you?" will find that the question was probably asked by the child during the previous week and the parent was unclear how to handle it. In a like manner, the group itself may be approaching a major theme of concern for that week, and the individual offerings may thus present specific examples of the central concern of the group.

Whether the concern originates with the single member or expresses the feelings of many, the leader's efforts in the early stages should be focused on answering the question, "What are they (the group members) working on in this session?" As in work with individuals and families, it is important for group leaders not to answer a question before they really understand the question. As the information is shared, group leaders need to monitor the group members' reactions. It would be a mistake for them to rush in with their own agenda simply because the first productions (comments) of the group members are unclear.

Likewise, it would be an error for the group leader to believe that simply because the group had agreed to deal with a specific issue or an individual's concern at the end of the previous meeting, or even at the start of a meeting, this will be the issue for the current session. Even if the discussion picks up exactly where the members had agreed it would at the end of the previous meeting, the leader should monitor the conversation in the early part of the session with an ear for either confirmation of the theme or hints that members are just going through the motions. In structured groups, such as a psychoeducational format, where an agenda for each session may be preplanned and a topic assigned for discussion, the group leader must still remain alert to the possibility that another or a related issue is emerging and needs to at least be recognized or that the topic presented has generated specific issues or strong emotions.

The important point is that the leader should be aware that even though the conversation may not seem directed toward the group's purpose, it is always purposeful. For clarity of exposition, I will focus here on examples where the early discussion is directed toward presenting a specific theme of concern. Later I will explore examples where the purpose of the early conversation is to raise an issue concerning the working of the group or the leader. In both cases, leaders should be asking themselves during the early discussion, "How does this conversation connect to our work?" or "What is troubling this particular member?" By doing so, there is a better chance of first hearing and then helping the individual relate a concern or raise an issue to the group.

*A Group for Grieving Children*   The following example involves a group for 10- and 11-year-old children who had lost a close family member. They were referred to the group because of behavior problems in school and elsewhere that signaled their difficulty coping with the death. The group members called themselves the "Lost and Found Group," since they had lost someone close but had found each other (Vastola, Nierenberg, & Graham, 1994).

**Practice Points:**   The authors describe how Mark, at the start of a group session following one in which members had begun to open up and discuss their losses, sends a mixed message using paper and pen. He repeatedly writes "Bob," the name of his grandfather who had recently died.

CARL: Mark, your grandfather died?
MARK: I don't want any damn body talking about my grandfather or I'll kick their butt.
LEADER: You sound pretty angry.
MARK: I'm not angry. I just don't want anybody talking about my grandfather.
LEADER: It's very difficult.
MARK: It's not difficult. I just don't want anybody saying that he died. (His anger is escalating.)

GLORIA: Nobody wants to talk about nobody dying.

DICK: Yes, we don't want to talk about that.

LEADER: How come?

GLORIA: That's why he (Mark) is running around. You can't force him if he doesn't want to.

LEADER: (Directed toward Mark) Is that what makes you run around—so you won't have to talk about something upsetting?

MARK: Nope.

LEADER: Maybe you feel it's too hard to talk about.

MARK: No, it's not hard for me to talk about anything…but that reminds you, and you could be dreaming.

CARL: Yup, you dream for about a week when you talk about your mother, then it takes about five days to try to get over it, but it comes back again and it stops and it comes back again. . . . Nightmares, I hate. I hate talking about my mother. (p. 87)

**Practice Summary.**   Through his behavior, Mark has demonstrated his difficulty in dealing with the loss. The group members move to his defense, because this is their problem as well. In effect, Mark is speaking for the other members who share similar feelings. The group leader's persistence sends a message to Mark (and the group) that she will not back off from this difficult issue. As she explores Mark's resistance by acknowledging the difficulty and asking what makes it hard to talk about his loss, the members begin to open up. It is interesting how often asking reluctant group members to discuss what makes it hard to address an issue actually leads to their addressing the issue. One can often interpret resistance as the group member or members saying to the group leader: "We need some help because this is a painful area."

In the preceding example, the leader was prepared to deal with the taboo subject of death and grieving—a very painful topic when children are involved. By responding to the behavior only, and attempting to set limits and stop Mark from running around the room, the leader would actually have been signaling her resistance to the discussion. The fight over the behavior would have been a means of avoiding the pain for both Mark and the leader. This is why it is so important for leaders to have access to supervision and support for themselves as they attempt to deal with these powerful issues (Shulman, 2010).

EP 2.1.1b
EP 2.1.1e
EP 2.1.1f

*Grieving Adults: Loss of a Friend, Partner, and/or Relative to AIDS*  Another example of behavior as communication comes from the beginning of a session of an ongoing, open-ended group for friends, lovers, and relatives who were grieving the loss of someone from AIDS. A woman who had just lost her son was attending her first meeting. The meeting started with a check-in ritual in which each member briefly shared what had happened to him or her during the preceding week. The new member began with an extremely rapid, nonstop monologue about how busy she had been keeping herself since her son died. She described a daily, hectic round of activity, showing very little emotion other than the hint of an underlying anxiety. She had clearly been in "flight" from her loss during the week and was indirectly communicating this flight by her opening conversation. It was as if she was saying, "Do you want to see how I am coping? Watch me!"

The leader responded by cutting her off, after a while, pointing out that they needed to hear from all of the members as a part of the check-in. Later analysis by the leader revealed that he had sensed her anxiety and simply had not been able to deal with it. Had he been able to be honest about his feelings at the moment, he would have shared how he experienced her presentation—being uncertain about how to help, feeling her sense of overwhelming loss, and wondering about proceeding with the check-in. Any or all of these comments might have opened the door for further discussion and expression of the emotion that was under her expression of anxiety.

The group members joined in the collusion, in a flight process of their own. They were at a different stage in their grieving, and this new member's behavior may have reawakened feelings they would have preferred to have left behind. This example also reveals some of the problems associated with rituals such as check-in, which can take on a life of their own when adhered to dogmatically. Instead of providing an opportunity to deal with individual members' concerns, they can become a way to avoid deepening the work. In retrospect, the leader could have acknowledged the indirect communications of the member and raised, with the group, whether they wanted to respond right away or wanted to continue check-in. Either way, acknowledging the feelings underlying the individual's acting out of her pain would have laid the groundwork for dealing with her loss and the feelings evoked in the second client, the group.

A final example from the same group for friends, partners, and relatives of a person who died of AIDS demonstrates how messages can be sent by more than just words. As the group started, the wife of a new couple attending their first meeting sat in the circle of group members but the husband sat outside of the circle by the door. When the leader invited him to join them, he responded: "I'm only here to drive my wife to the meeting." A powerful message was being sent about how the couple was handling the death of their son. The wife was facing the pain and doing the hard work on her own while the husband was hiding behind his pain, and behind his defenses by sitting outside of the group. This was a first session and the leader did not directly confront the message nor push the husband to join the group. Members are entitled to their defenses when they begin discussion; later, when the husband hears the other members dealing with their issues, and if the leader, when appropriate, invites the husband to comment, these defenses against the deep pain of losing their son to this disease may be lowered.

The emphasis in this first section has been on helping the individual reach out to the group. In many cases, particularly when the feelings expressed reflect those held by the group members, the leader's second client—the group—paradoxically appears to turn away from the individual. In the next section, I will discuss the meaning of this dynamic.

## Reaching for the Group Response to the Individual

It is easy to see how a leader can become identified with a particular member's feelings as a theme of concern is raised. If strong emotions are expressed, the leader may feel supportive and protective. Not surprisingly, if the other group members do not appear to respond to the individual, a common reaction from leaders is to feel upset and angry. The leader is shocked and surprised to observe group members apparently not listening, to see their eyes glazing over as they appear to be lost in their own thoughts, to watch as two members start to carry on their own whispered conversation, or to witness a sudden change in subject or a direct rebuff to the group member who has bared some innermost feelings.

At moments such as these, the leader's clarity of role and the notion of "two clients," the individual and the group, can be most critical. Instead of getting angry, the leader should view the group members' apparently disinterested response as a signal, not that they are uninterested in what is being said, but that the theme may be having a powerful impact on them. In other words, the group-as-a-whole may also be communicating in an indirect manner with the message to the leader being: "This is difficult for us to hear."

The tasks of the role for the leader as described here (one could call it a mediating role) call for the leader to search for the common ground between the individual and the group at the point where they seem most cut off from each other. This clear sense of function directs the leader to empathize with the group members' feelings underlying their apparent resistance at precisely the same time as expressing empathy with the individual group member. The group leader must be with both "clients" at the same time.

This is an observational and empathic skill that will develop over time. At first, new group leaders will respond to each individual as a separate entity apart from the group. When self-reflection or supervision reveals this tendency, new group leaders then tend to focus on the group but lose sight of the individual members. For example, a member raises an issue and the leader immediately inquires as to the reaction of other members, forgetting to get back to the original individual problem offering. With enough hard work, self-reflection, and learning from mistakes, the leader will find that one day he or she can "see" the group as an entity and each individual member at exactly the same time. I'm not sure how this shift happens, but it will happen if the leader has clarity about the need to be with the two clients and about the group leader's role.

***A Psychiatric Day Patients' Group*** The following example is from an adult, community mental health day treatment outpatients' group for members with a chronic mental illness. The focus is on family issues. In this fifth session, a member raises her depression on the fifth anniversary of the brutal death of her child.

**Practice Points:** The group members respond with silence, and the leader intervenes to support the second client—the group—and the individual member.

> At the beginning of our meeting, after group introductions and as people settled into their seats, Joan began speaking. She looked straight ahead of herself, eyes downcast most of the time, and occasionally made eye contact with me (one of the co-leaders) or looked furtively around the group as she spoke. Joan said, "Well, I just want to tell everybody that the fifth anniversary of my daughter's death (the daughter was raped and murdered) is coming up this week and it's bothering me a lot. It always has bothered me. I try to deal with it OK, but I just don't always know how. I get to thinking about it, and the more I think, the more I'm afraid that I'm going to lose it or do something against myself. I've tried to come to terms with it, but it's always hard when it comes around to when I lost her. So anyway, I've made arrangements to use the 24-hour bed (an emergency bed in the center) 'cause I'm too afraid when I get to feeling like this."

**Practice Points:** Note in the leader's next intervention how clarity of role and the two-client concept direct the leader to respond to the signal from the group—the silence—rather than rushing in to respond to Joan.

> There was complete and utter silence in the group. I remained silent for a few moments as well. As I looked around the group, the members too were looking straight ahead, or down at their feet or acting uncomfortable and as if they didn't know what to say. I said, "Wow, that's some pretty heavy issue that

you're bringing up. It seems like it is hitting people pretty hard." The group was still silent, and I paused, although, just as Elizabeth was about to say something, my co-leader said, "I'm wondering what people in the group are thinking or feeling about what Joan has just said, and if it's difficult to respond to it." There was a little more silence, and Joan went on, "Maybe I shouldn't have brought it up. Everybody here already knows that this is a problem for me. It's just that I felt so close to her. She was the one whose birth I remember. She was the one, instead of whisking her away and doing what they have to do right after they're born, they put her on me and I felt so much closer to her than the others. I remember it so much better. But maybe I just shouldn't bring it up here."

**Practice Points:** The group leader picks up on Joan's concern about the appropriateness of raising the issue and responds to her feelings, supporting her effort to use the group. She also helps to identify the common ground between Joan and the group, which is the pain of the loss of people you care about.

I waited a little and looked around the group once more and then said, "You're talking about a pretty big loss, here, and especially with it being your daughter, it's very appropriate to bring it to this group. Everyone has had some losses with people close to them; maybe some of them don't seem as earth-shattering as others, but we all know the experience of loss in our families, one way or another."

Then Elizabeth, who had been about to speak earlier, said, "Whew. That's just it. Thinking about your daughter and the 24-hour bed; that's pretty serious." Wendy spoke up, saying, "Yeah, that's scary. I mean I've been thinking about my accident (she had been in a car accident a few days before, and has a long-standing fear that she may kill herself in a car) and thinking about losing my sons in the divorce like I did. It really troubles me."

I said, "So, we're not only looking at family losses, but also at what we do to deal with them and look for ways to cope with them and feel safe."

**Practice Summary.** With the leader's help, the group members revealed that their silence did not reflect lack of feeling or concern for Joan. In fact, it was the opposite, as Joan's feelings about her loss triggered many of their own. Joan was reassured that the group was the place to bring these issues, and she was helped by knowing she was not alone.

As I have described the role of the group leader, many of the dynamics and skills required in individual counseling can be recognized. These are the common core of practice skill, the generic element. The variant elements of the work derive from the presence of one of these important systems—the group—and the need for the leader to pay attention to its responses.

### A Group for the Visually Impaired Elderly: The Death of a Member

**Group Purpose:** The group described in the following example meets once a week at an elder center for one hour serving as the members' primary and at times sole source of support (Orr, 2005).

**Group Membership:** The group consists of twelve visually impaired or blind elderly people, four of whom are also hearing impaired. They range from 61–92 in age. Ten members, male and female, are widowed and live alone.

**Practice Points:** The session described is one that follows their being informed by the van driver of the death of a member, Maddie, who was 75 and died of a massive heart attack the day before. Losses are very central in the life of people of this age. They have lost their former lives, in this case their eyesight, family members and friends, and so on. With so many living alone, they need a source of support to cope with the losses and to build up their "reserve" during this often painful time of life. The group conversation began without a formal opening.

TESSIE: I just can't believe Maddie died; I've been calling her house every day to speak to her husband, and no answer. I knew something was wrong (said softly and with despair). (Brief silence)

ROSE: Are you crying, Tessie?

TESSIE: I don't know whether I'm crying or not (said with frustration).

GOLDIE: Don't cry, Tessie; you'll only get all upset.

TESSIE: How can I not cry? Now it's Maddie; every week it's someone else (begins to cry openly). Rose leans over, reaches out to find Tessie, and puts her arm around her.

ROSE: But we are upset, Goldie, why shouldn't she cry? Why shouldn't we? I cried this morning when I found out in the van. We're all upset.

HANNAH: (Who is severely hearing impaired) Who's crying?

GOLDIE: (Whispers to the worker) We shouldn't tell Hannah; she lives in the nursing home; she gets upset when people die there. She doesn't have to know.

**Practice Points:** One can see Goldie as, in part, trying to avoid the painful feelings associated with the death and trying to protect a member as well. Depending upon the nursing home, Hannah may be in a place where the death of residents is not addressed because staff believe it can be too upsetting for residents. Someone dies, the doors to all the rooms are closed, the body is removed, and the next thing the residents know is a new person occupies the room. In reality, that is the part that is most upsetting; a death of a resident going unnoticed rather than an appropriate intervention with the remaining residents. At this point the leader intervenes to support Hannah's right to know and to receive support.

LEADER: (To Goldie) How do you think Hannah will feel when she finds out?

GOLDIE: (After a long pause) She'll be upset.

LEADER: I think Rose is right, that we're all upset. Hannah is part of the group.

GOLDIE: (Loudly to Hannah) Maddie died yesterday.

HANNAH: I knew something was wrong. I could feel it. Oh, my . . . that's terrible about Maddie.

**Practice Points:** The ambivalence about discussing the death of a member, a reminder to all of their other losses and their own inevitable deaths, emerges as one member suggests standing for a moment of silence and donating money to the center in her memory, and then another states:

RUTH: And then we can stop talking about it. Tessie's upset and Josephine's upset and I'm getting upset too. Talking about it won't help. We can go on to something else. We had something on the agenda.

**Practice Points:** The leader understands the part of each member that wants to avoid facing the reality of this loss and, as they do so, facing all of the other losses in their lives. She understands, however, that each member is going home for the weekend and the impact of this death when no one is around to provide support would be even greater. She makes what I have called an empathic demand for work and makes it in her own artistic way:

LEADER: What are we going to do with all that we're feeling, though, if we don't talk about it here, in the group? I'm thinking that it's Friday, and we've done a lot of talking over the past few months about how difficult the weekends alone are for so many of you, especially when something upsetting has happened. Are we going to take all that sadness and pain and emptiness home with us for the weekend? (Orr, 2005, pp. 480–483)

**Practice Points:** The leader consciously uses the word "we," since the loss of a member impacts on her as well. The resulting discussion deals with the difficulty of having no one to speak with at home, their own recent losses, and a powerful discussion of the recognition of their own mortality. At the leader's suggestion, the group also talks about what Maddie meant to them, not only the impact of her death. The leader also shares her own feelings and initiates a discussion of the difficulty she feels in not being able to say good-bye and come to closure. During this discussion, the leader walks over to Tessie and puts her arms around her. After further discussion and association to their own losses, the leader ends the meeting by saying:

LEADER: We've lost someone very special. Maddie touched each of our lives in a very special way. I think we've all touched each other's lives today. We've shared an awful lot of what we we're feeling. (p. 489)

## Reaching for the Work When Obstacles Threaten

In this section, the connections between the process (the way of working) and the content (the purpose of the group) are explored. For example, the flow of affect between the leader and group members—the authority theme—was identified earlier as a potential obstacle to work as well as a source of energy for change. Attention needed to be paid to these feelings; they had to be acknowledged before the work could proceed. This same issue was highlighted in our analysis of first group sessions, when the importance of discussing the leader–group relationship was underlined. In the group context, one also has to deal with the interchange that takes place between the members—what Schwartz refers to as the "intimacy" theme (Schwartz, 1961).

While both of these issues, authority and intimacy, are discussed more fully in the next chapter, they need to be mentioned now in the context of the middle phase of practice. For example, it may be important to discuss the process between members as a way of freeing individuals to trust the group enough to offer concerns in painful and sensitive areas. The group leader, often perceived as powerful and possibly threatening, must also establish a sound working relationship (therapeutic alliance) with individual members and the group-as-a-whole.

***Mothers of Children with Hyperactive Diagnosis*** Another way in which process and content are synthesized was described earlier in my discussion of the meaning of resistance. For example, the group member may appear to hold back from entering a difficult area of work, and the leader senses the member's reluctance to proceed. Such resistance was viewed as central to the work and a possible sign that the group member was verging on talking about an important area. The need to explore the resistance was suggested. In much the same way, a group may resist by launching a tacit conspiracy to avoid painful areas. This is often the reason the members of a group hold back in the early stages of a group meeting. Once again, the leader's task involves bringing the obstacle out in the open in order to free the group members from its power.

**Practice Points:**  In the following example of an educational and counseling group with mothers of children who have been diagnosed as hyperactive, the early themes had centered on the parents' anger toward school officials, teachers, neighbors, and other children, all of whom did not understand. They also acknowledged their own anger at their children. The leader empathized but she also pointed out a pattern of flight or avoidance of difficult subjects, by saying:

> "It is terribly frustrating for you. You want to be able to let your anger out, but you feel that if you do so, it will make things worse." After a few comments, the conversation became general again. I told the group members that they seemed to be talking in generalities again. Martha said it seemed they didn't want to talk about painful things. I agreed that this appeared to be hard. Every time they got on a painful subject they took off onto something safer. I wondered if the last session had been very painful for them. Martha said that it was a hard session, they had come very close, and she had a lot to think about over the weekend. Lilly said that she felt wound up over the last session, so much so that she had had trouble sleeping at night. I asked her to tell us what made it so upsetting for her. She said that she had felt so helpless when they had been talking about the school boards and the lack of help for children like her own. Doreen said it really wasn't so hopeless. She had talked to a principal and had found out some new information.

**Practice Summary.**  It is interesting to note that when the leader asked, "What made it so upsetting?" the answer to the question designed to explore the resistance brought the group back to its work. This is a simple, effective, and usually underused intervention for exploring and moving past resistance. When a group member says, "I don't want to talk about that!" the leader's response, "What would make it hard to talk about that?" is often all that is needed. As group members talk about what makes it hard to talk about it, they usually find themselves actually talking about it. In the current example, later in the same session, the leader picked up on the acknowledgment of the members' anger toward their children and the difficulty of talking about that anger, with similar results.

It is easier for leaders to explore resistance if they do not view it as a commentary on their lack of skill. When sensing resistance, group leaders often ask themselves, "What have I done wrong?" This is ironic because in many cases we sense resistance in the group because we have done something right. An important phrase that has helped me to explore rather than run from signs of resistance is: *resistance is part of the work*. If the group is going well and has started to deal with tough issues, then we should expect resistance. If we never get it, the danger is that we are engaged in the illusion of work—superficial conversation without affect. There are many phrases that can help the group leader explore the resistance, for example, "You are all quiet right now; is this hard to talk about?"; "The message I'm getting from you, all of you, is that you are not sure you want me to stay on this issue; are you finding it too hard to talk about?"; or "Every time we get to this issue you all seem to move away from it; any thoughts about why that is happening?" As pointed out earlier in this chapter, in many ways resistance is the group or group member's way of saying, "Help me out, leader; this is difficult for me."

# Avoiding Individual Counseling in the Group

One consequence of failure to recognize the role of the group leader as described above—that is, mediating between the individual and the group—is a problem raised frequently by beginning group leaders, particularly those who have done individual counseling. In an attempt to deal with an individual's concern, they find themselves doing individual counseling in the group. This is a common pattern in which the group leader provides individual advice to a member within a group setting. Suppose, for example, a member raises an issue at the start of a session and the leader responds with appropriate elaborative and empathic skills. The group member expands on the concern, and the leader tries to help deal with the problem while the other group members listen. When this problem has been explored, the leader then begins with another group member as the others patiently wait their turn. This contrasts with an effort to mobilize mutual aid for the group member by involving the other members.

After the meeting, the leader worries about having done individual counseling in front of an audience. In reaction to this feeling of uneasiness, the leader may strategize not to be trapped this way during the next session, thus making a different kind of mistake. Vowing to pay attention to the "group" aspect of group work, the leader attempts to do so by refusing to respond with elaborating skills when an individual opens the session with a direct or indirect offering of a concern. For example, one member of a parent group might say, "It's really hard to raise teenagers these days, what with all of the stuff they hear on the radio, that rap stuff, and what they see on YouTube." The leader quickly responds by inquiring if other members of the group find this to be true. One by one they comment on the general difficulty of raising teenagers. The discussion soon becomes overly general and superficial, and meanwhile the first group member is anxiously waiting with a specific concern about a fight with her daughter the evening before.

When trying to deal with individual concerns, leaders may find themselves doing individual counseling in the group, and when trying to pay attention to the group, leaders may find themselves leading an overgeneralized discussion. Both maladaptive patterns reflect the group leader's difficulty in conceptualizing the group as a system for mutual aid and in understanding the often subtle connections between individual concerns and the general work of the group. Schwartz's notion of the "two clients," discussed earlier, can help to resolve the apparent dilemma. He suggests that the leader simultaneously must pay attention to two clients, the individual and the group, and the field of action is concerned with interaction between the two. Thus, instead of choosing between the "one" and the "many," often a false dichotomy, the leader's function involves mediating the engagement between the two. In the next section we add time and the stages of work to our discussion of the role of the group leader and the dynamics of group interaction.

# Group Work Skill Factors in the Middle Phase

The work phase model was first presented in Chapter 5. We now revisit, expand, and illustrate the framework in the group context. The specific skills will be familiar to the reader from the earlier chapters. To remind you, the skills of the work phase have been organized into general categories called *skill factors*. A skill factor consists of a

**T A B L E   1 2 . 1**

------------------------------------------------------------------------------------------

## *The Work Phase Model*

**1. Preliminary Stage**

  • Sessional Tuning-In Skills

**2. Beginning Stage**

  • Sessional Contracting Skills

**3. Middle Stage**

  • Elaborating Skills

  • Empathic Skills

  • Sharing Leader's Feelings

  • Exploring Taboo Subjects

  • Making a Demand for Work

  • Pointing Out Obstacles

  • Identifying Content and Process Connections

  • Sharing Data

  • Helping the Group Members See Life in New Ways

**4. Ending and Transition Stage**

  • Sessional Ending

  • Sessional Transition Skills

------------------------------------------------------------------------------------------

set of closely related skills. The general intent of the leader who is using the skill is the element that is common to a given set of skills. For example, in this model, all behaviors associated with the efforts of the leader to deal with the group and group members' feelings are grouped together under the title "empathic skills." Table 12.1 lists the skill factors included in this middle phase model.

# The Preliminary Stage

## Sessional Tuning In

In the preliminary or preparatory stage, the leader attempts to develop anticipatory sensitivity, before each meeting, to themes that could emerge during the session. A review of the previous session, information passed on by group members or others, or the identification of subtle patterns emerging in the work can alert the leader to the members' potential current concerns. If a serious and possibly traumatic event has taken place, for example, the death of a member in a cancer survivors' group, the leader would tune in to the sense of loss but also the members' fear that they could be next. As another example, a powerful social trauma such as the 9/11 tragedy with the Twin Towers would have an impact on any group that met that day or even that week.

Sometimes the leader's tuning in takes place just before the start of the meeting. For example, at the first session of a three-session counseling group for single parents I led in a rural area, a member who arrived early spoke to another member of his difficulty in getting a babysitter in order to attend the meeting. I call this "preliminary chatter." It appears to be prior to the start of the meeting; however, if the group leader is listening, it is actually the start of the meeting, and the comments are meant for the leader to hear. In a similar manner, an apparently random comment by an individual to the group leader while walking to the meeting room may be a way of raising an issue.

The leader can develop some preliminary strategies for responding directly to such indirect cues. This involves the use of the skill described earlier as putting the member's feelings into words. In the situation above, I acknowledged in my opening statement that one of the difficulties when you are a single parent is just finding sitters so you can attend events such as this one and be able to take care of yourself. I mentioned the comments of the early member, and as the session evolved, his very difficult and painful struggle became a major piece of work for him and the group.

# The Beginning Stage

### Sessional Contracting

In the beginning stage of each session, the central task of the leader is to find out what the group member(s) or the group-as-whole is concerned about at the moment. Sessional contracting skills are used to clarify the immediate work at hand. As discussed in the previous section, sessional tuning in may make a major difference in the group leader's ability to "hear" what the member or members are working on. In some cases, the group leader may bring up issues that need to be addressed, and these will then be included in the contracting discussion. In a psychoeducational group or informational session, there may be an agenda already set for the meeting. Because group members often use indirect communication to indicate their concerns, leaders must take care to determine the members' current and perhaps more urgent agenda before moving quickly into the work. An illustration follows.

*A Preadoption Parenting Group* For example, in a preadoption information group, the leader might say: "I have scheduled a presentation on how and when to tell your child he or she is adopted. But before I begin, I wanted to check to see if there are also things on your mind you would like to discuss." In an actual example, they do not respond to the leader's invitation, but as the presentation goes on, the group leader picks up indirect cues that a major concern for them is how they will be judged as appropriate or not appropriate adoptive parents. Until that discussion surfaces, one can see the group members saying what they think the group leader wants to hear, creating what I have called an illusion of work, rather than saying what they really think and feel. When the group leader picks up the cues to this concern, and the members are reassured that if they made it this far they are considered to be good candidates, they get to the hardest questions for the couples: "How do I know if the child will love me?" and "How do I know if I will be able to love this child?" Once sessional contracting is clear, the work is both moving and powerful as group members address their real issues related to their ambivalence about adoption. The group leaders need to reassure them that these feelings and concerns are normal and do not eliminate them as prospective adoptive parents.

# The Middle Stage

When the sessional contract has been tentatively identified, the process shifts into the middle stage of the session. A priority in this stage, as described in an earlier section of this chapter, is the leader's use of elaboration skills to help the group member or members tell their story. Empathy skills encourage the sharing of the affective part of the message. The leader must also be ready to share the leader's feelings, in a professional manner, as spontaneously as possible. Because many concerns touch on taboo areas, the leader must be ready to help members overcome social norms that often block free discussion and to explore taboo feelings.

As the work progresses, it is not unusual to encounter some resistance from the group member or members, who are often of two minds about proceeding. One part of the person is always reaching out for growth and change, but another part is pulling back and holding on to what is comfortable and known. This ambivalence often emerges just as the work in the session starts to go well. It can be seen in evasive reactions (e.g., jumping from one concern to another), defensiveness, expressions of hopelessness, and other forms of resistance.

The leader needs to realize that resistance is a normal part of the work. As stated earlier, leaders often assume that group member resistance is a sign that the leaders have done something wrong, but ironically just the opposite is often true. Lack of resistance may mean that the leader has not pushed hard enough and the meeting consists of the "illusion of work," while resistance is often a sign that the leader is doing something right. If the leader thinks of resistant behavior as the members' way of communicating that there is a difficult area to face, hard emotions to experience, a problem with taking responsibility for behavior, and so forth, the leader will welcome resistance rather than fearing it.

It's almost as if the group member or members are saying: "Look here, group leader. We are getting close to a tough area and I need your help to explore what makes it tough." In the framework presented in this book, a premium is placed on exploring member resistance, or the ability of the leader to identify and discuss this resistance with the group member, which includes making a demand for work that can help the group member prepare to take the important next steps. Some other practice models suggest "rolling with," "circumventing," or simply "avoiding" areas that create resistance. In most cases, I disagree. Although I agree that timing is important—for example, respecting resistance in the early stage of work before a solid relationship is established—I believe it is a mistake to avoid it in the work or middle phase of practice. Such avoidance can lead to the illusion of work, in which the group member says what he or she thinks the leader or other members want to hear. It also means that the issues, concerns, and feelings signaled by the resistance remain unexpressed, unexplored, and unresolved. A group leader's unwillingness to explore resistance may be a result of not understanding its importance in the process or the leader's own conscious or unconscious reluctance to deal with the difficult area.

## Flow of Affect Between the Group Members and the Leader(s)

As the middle or work stage proceeds, obstacles may emerge that frustrate the members' efforts on their own behalf. For example, the flow of feeling between a group member and the leader may itself become an obstacle. As the leader makes demands for work, the group member may react to the leader, and this reaction in turn will affect the working relationship. Leaders and members must pay attention to such obstacles as they emerge. Because the leader–group member relationship resembles the member's other relationships, discussion of such obstacles can contribute to the member's understanding of his or her larger concerns. These obstacles are usually brought to light when the leader notices patterns in the work.

Another skill grouping is called identifying process and content connections. The central idea underlying this category of skills is that the process, or way of interacting between the leader and the group member, or between group members, often offers clues about the content of the work. In effect, the group member may (consciously or not) use the working relationship as a medium to raise and work on issues that are central to the substantive issues under discussion. For example, a group member working on developing independence of thought and action may demonstrate extreme dependence on the leader. It is as if the group member is saying, "Do you want to see what my problem around dependence and independence is all about? Watch me!" The point here is that behavior has meaning and sometimes we have to work hard to understand the real meaning behind the behavior.

## Elaborating Skills

The following skills are useful in helping group members tell their story and move from the initial offering to deepen our understanding of the issues they face.

*Containment* As a group member or members begin to tell their stories, group leaders too often attempt to "help" or invite group members to help before the whole story is told. This is especially true for people who are new to helping; the desire to help is so strong that they will often rush in with unhelpful suggestions that are not directed at the group member's actual concerns. The elaborating skill of containment is an interesting one, because it suggests that not acting—that is, a group leader's ability to contain himself or herself—is an active intervention.

As one who grew up in New York City, this author was used to a pattern of social communication in which one might begin to speak even before the other person had finished. While something of an exaggeration, nevertheless containment was an important skill to learn in my own professional development. This skill should not be confused with remaining silent in the face of silence (discussed later in this section). The group leader can be very active; however, the injunction is against jumping in with solutions or answers before the leader really knows the problem or questions.

*Focused Listening* Listening is something we do all the time; however, focused listening involves attempting to concentrate on a specific part of the member's or the group's message. I discussed earlier how complex even the simplest interchange of communication can be. In complex communications at the beginning of sessions, the group leader must focus on whatever the member or group is working on at that particular moment. By listening to the early communications with this purpose in mind, the group leader has a better chance of hearing the message.

A simple analogy is the difficulty of hearing two simultaneous conversations at a crowded social event. If one listens in a general way, all one hears is a loud buzz. If one attempts to focus on one particular conversation, however, it begins to stand out clearly, and the buzzing noise recedes. Similarly, when one is driving at night in a rural area, sometimes two radio stations are heard at once. The driver must tune in one station and tune out the other in order to really hear anything. In the same way, the "noise" of the member's early communications may make it difficult for the group leader to understand the single strand that represents the basic concern. Focused listening—directed toward determining the concern—often makes the theme stand out clearly. More specifically, focused listening, with the purpose of the group or the special purpose of the session clearly in mind, will allow the leader to hear content that might otherwise be missed.

A common mistake a group leader makes it to take control of the session when he or she does not immediately understand the meaning of the communication. In effect, a group leader may answer a question before he or she actually knows what the question really is. Focused listening involves an attempt to hear the communication as the member's effort to work, and to search for the connections when they are not apparent. The group leader can ask for the member's help. For example, "Could you help me connect this discussion with the concern you raised about your daughter at the start of the meeting?" Group members will often be able to do so, either immediately or after some reflection. They do not get the opportunity if the group leader has already decided they are simply not working and more group leader activity is needed.

Group leaders often ask me how to handle a situation in which there is no real connection and the member evades work by changing the subject. Focused listening will clarify this as well. The member is actually working by avoiding the work; this may sound contradictory, but the member is signaling resistance to a particular topic—perhaps because it is too painful or embarrassing—and this resistance is what the group leader should hear and address. Once again, *resistance is part of the work* if the group leader hears it for what it is—a call for help in facing difficult issues.

*Questioning* Questioning in the elaboration process involves requests for more information about the nature of the problem. As a fledgling high school journalist, I was encouraged to answer the "five Ws" early in my articles: the who, what, when, where, and why of the story. These are useful areas for exploring the details of a member's concern. For example, in an earlier illustration with the mother and daughter, I left the process at the point where the member responded to the group leader's effort to move from the general to the specific by describing a fight with her daughter.

**Practice Point:**   In the next part of the group session, we can see that the group leader's questions are designed to elicit more detail about what happened during the encounter.

MEMBER: I had some row last night when Sue came home at 2:00 A.M.
GROUP LEADER: What happened?
MEMBER: She had told me she was going to a movie with a friend, but when she didn't get home by 11:00, I was really worried.
GROUP LEADER: You were afraid something might have happened to her?
MEMBER: Well, you know I have had some problems in the neighborhood with men.
GROUP LEADER: What did you say to Sue when she came home?
MEMBER: I let her have it good. I told her she was irresponsible and that I was going to keep her home for 2 weeks.
GROUP LEADER: What did she say back to you?

**Practice Summary.**   As the conversation proceeded, the group leader helped the member elaborate on the details of the interaction, sharing these with the other group members. A term to describe this process between group leader and member is memory work, in which the member reaches back into her memory to recall the incident. In other situations, the group leader may aim her questions at getting a fuller picture of the member's concern.

*Reaching Inside of Silences* Silence during a group session may be an important form of communication. The difficulty with silence is that it is often hard to understand exactly what the member or group is "saying." In one situation, the member or all of the group members may be thinking and reflecting on the implications of the conversation. In another, a discussion may have released powerful emotions that are struggling to surface in the member(s). The members may be at the critical point of experiencing suppressed and painful feelings. Silence can indicate a moment of ambivalence as the member pauses to decide whether or not to plunge headlong into a difficult area of work. This is not uncommon when the conversation deals with an area generally experienced as taboo. Silence may also signal that the group leader's preceding response was off base in relation to the member's expressed concern. The group leader has "missed" the member's or group's message, and the silence is the polite way of saying so. Finally, the member or group may be angry with the group leader. Frequent silence in a group session may reflect a systematic attempt to express this anger passively by withholding involvement.

Because silences carry a variety of meanings, the group leader's response must vary accordingly. An important aid is the group leader's own set of feelings during the silence. For example, if the silence represents the emergence of difficult feelings, the group leader may have anticipated this reaction based on the content of the conversation or from the nonverbal communications the member sent. Posture, facial expressions, and bodily tension all speak loudly to the observing group leader and can trigger empathic responses. As such, the group leader may experience the same emergence of feeling as the member. At moments like this, the group leader can respond to silence with silence or with nonverbal expressions of support. All of these responses offer some support to the member while still allowing time to experience the feelings.

If the group leader senses that the member is thinking about an important point of the discussion or considering a related problem, responding with a brief silence allows the member room to think. Silence demonstrates respect for the member's work. However, a problem can arise if the group leader maintains the silence for too long. Silence can also be particularly troublesome if the group leader does not understand it or if it is used to communicate either a negative reaction or passive resistance. In such cases, the members may experience the silence as a "battle of wills." What started as one form of communication may quickly change to a situation in which the members are saying, "I won't speak unless you speak first." In this battle, both group leader and members always lose. The skill of reaching inside the silence matters most during these kinds of silences.

This skill involves attempts to explore the meaning of the silence. For example, the group leader who responds to a silence by saying: "You've all grown quiet in the last few moments. What are you thinking about?" is encouraging the member or members to share their thoughts. In another case, the group leader could try to articulate what the silence may mean. For example, the member who hesitates as he describes a particularly difficult experience might be offered this response: "I can see this is hard for you to talk about." Once again, the group leader's own feelings guide her or his attempts to explore or acknowledge the silence. The group leader must be open to the fact that the guess may be wrong and must encourage the member to feel free to say so.

Group leaders often find silences in group sessions to be difficult moments. They have been affected by societal norms that create the feeling that a silence in conversation is embarrassing, and they may feel that the most helpful thing to do is fill the gap. When one works with group members from different cultures, one is struck by the differences in these social norms. For example, some American Indian group members describe how talking to non-Indian counselors is hard because they never keep quiet. As one Native group member said to me, "The problem with White counselors is that they never stop 'nattering.'" She pointed out that Indian culture respects silence as a time to reflect, but non-Indian counselors continue to talk because of their own anxiety, without giving the Native person a chance to think. In some cases, the Indian member might simply be trying to translate the non-Indian group leader's English into the Indian language and then back to English.

***Why Are We Reluctant to Explore Silences?*** I shared my tentative research findings in Chapter 5 when I pointed out how reluctant workers in my study were to explore silences. The most common response after 3 seconds or more of silence, as observed on individual and group videotapes, was to speak and most often to change the subject. These findings reflect statistically my own observations that individual counselors and group leaders often seem reluctant to explore silences. In addition to the reasons already advanced, counselors have suggested that they often perceive silences to represent a problem in the interview or group session. If there is silence, the group leader must have done something wrong. The irony in the situation is that silence results more often from a group leader doing something right. The group leader often sees silence as negative feedback, even in those cases when it may mean other things.

A group leader's willingness to reach inside the silence when there is a possible negative response is directly related to feelings of comfort in the work and willingness to deal with negative feedback. Understandably, a group leader may be unsure about what to do with the feelings and concerns that might reside within the silence, and she or he may choose to change the subject rather than to reach inside the silence. At this point, after the group leader has successfully helped the member elaborate concerns, the discussion needs to move to the question of feelings and how to deal with them.

When these findings are shared with group leaders in training sessions, their reactions provide further clues to the apparent low frequency of use of this important skill. Many indicate that their skill training specifically cautioned them not to put a member's thoughts or feelings into words. They report having been encouraged to only ask open-ended questions and to avoid "putting words into the member's mouth" or "doing the group members' work for them." One group leader reported being told by a supervisor that it was "like tying a member's shoelaces for him." Although these are legitimate concerns, these repeated findings and my own experience as a teacher and trainer suggests that group leaders make more errors of omission (failing to articulate the feelings) than errors of commission (articulating the wrong feelings). I realize that this may be a controversial issue; however, these are my views.

**EP 2.1.1b,f**

***Moving from the General to the Specific*** This intervention has been mentioned in the sessional contracting stage, but it is important throughout the group sessions. Group members often raise a general concern that relates to a specific event. The general statement can be viewed as a first offering from the group member to the group leader. It may be presented in universal terms because the group member experiences it that way at the moment. The general nature of its expression may also reflect the ambivalence the group member feels about dealing with the concern in depth.

In one example, at the beginning of a single parents' group session I led, a mother stated, "It's hard to raise your kids these days when your mother is always criticizing you." Responding to the general theme, the group might have engaged in a discussion of changing mores, peer group pressure, drug availability, interfering in-laws, and so on. An example of moving from the general to the specific would be to ask, "Did you have a tough time with your daughter or your mother-in-law this week?" The group member's response in this case was to describe a fight she had with her 15-year-old daughter, who had returned home after 2:00 A.M. and refused to say where she had been. When she chastised her daughter, the child had called her grandmother who called this client and accused her of being too hard on her daughter. This second offering of the concern was a more specific and manageable piece of work; in other words, the general problem of raising teenagers is pressing in our society, but this group member and this group leader could not do much about it. However, this mother's relationship with her daughter and mother-in-law was open to change.

Behind most early general statements is a specific problem or feeling. If the group leader does not encourage elaboration, the concern might emerge at the end of the session as a "doorknob" communication (offered as the group member is leaving the meeting). The teenager in a group who casually comments during a general discussion that "parents just don't understand" may be reacting to an incident that morning. The patient in a community health clinic who mentions to the nurse that "doctors must work hard because they always seem so busy" may still be reacting to terse comments from the doctor that the patient was too frightened or overwhelmed to inquire about. In each case, the leader's skill would involve reaching for more specific information.

Helping professionals have suggested to me three major reasons why they might refrain from reaching for the specifics behind general comments. First, they are not aware of how specific work must be; that is, they do not realize that they can only give help in terms of the details of a problem. One cannot help a parent to deal with teenagers through general discussion alone. The learning will take place through the discussion of the specific interactions between parent and child. The group leader can help the parent and other group members develop general principles about their relationships with their children, but these principles must emerge from discussions of the specific events. Without the specific discussions, the group leader's attempts to generalize may be perceived by the mother and other group members as theoretical advice. Even in a parent-education group with organized lectures that follow a prescribed outline, it is important to explore how the concepts actually apply in specific examples. Some may be given by the group leader and others by the group members.

For example, the parent in the earlier encounter might describe a conversation with her daughter in which she did not share her distress and hurt but instead gave way to the surface feelings of anger. After a while, the group leader and the other members may be able to help the group member see how, in incident after incident, she finds it hard to be open with her daughter about certain feelings such as her fears and concerns for her daughter's safety. The group member may be able to understand this point because of the discussion of specific incidents and the reactions as well as the support of other parents in the group. The discussion should develop an experiential base on which the group member can build new understanding, a reframing of her perceptions about the problem, and possible solutions. The group member may not be able to do much about changing mores in our society, but she can conduct her next conversation with her daughter in a different way. Lack of understanding of the power of specific discussion may lead the group leader to overlook the usefulness of this elaboration skill. A similar conversation could take place in relation to dealing with her mother-in-law.

The second reason why group leaders do not reach for the specifics—even when they sense the concrete problem connected to the group member's general offering—is that they are not sure they want to deal with it. Group leaders in a community health clinic, for example, suggest that they do not reach for a patient's comment about busy doctors because they are not sure what they can do about it. As one put it, "I find the doctors too busy to answer my questions, so how can I help the client?" The source of the group leader's ambivalence may vary, but feelings of ambivalence are common. I believe that when group leaders feel more confident about offering help, they reach more easily for specifics. In the fifth part of this book I will provide examples in which the group leader is attempting to have a positive professional impact on other staff members who have significant interactions with group members within the setting (e.g., teachers) and at other systems (e.g., a clinic).

I propose a third, and less obvious, reason for failure to reach for elaboration that has to do with the parallel process between group leaders and supervisors described earlier. Often, a group leader or student raises a question with a supervisor such as "Do you have any thoughts about techniques for handling angry group members?" Unless the supervisor inquires, "Did you have a tough group meeting?" the remainder of the conversation may stay at a general level. If the modeling is sound, the supervisor will always move from the general to the specific, thus teaching by modeling this skill. In turn, the supervisor is aided by having an administrator reach for her or his specific concerns behind the general offerings. My research on supervision of supervisors, however, has indicated that this is rarely done (Shulman, 2010). A supervisor may get general help in a case conference on how to deal with a difficult student or employee, but rarely is the interactional process part of the conversation. It's no wonder then that the conversation in an individual or group supervision session often focuses on the case, and not the process.

## Empathic Skills

EP 2.1.10b
EP 2.1.10e

As group members tell their stories, group leaders may use a number of skills designed to keep the discussion meaningful by having group members invest it with feelings. Group members often share difficult experiences while seeming to deny the affect associated with them. For some, the experience may be so painful that they have suppressed the emotion to the point that their own feelings are not clear to themselves. For others, the emotions may seem strange or unacceptable, and they are fearful of discussing them with the group and the group leader.

Whatever the reason, the affect is there, and it will exert a powerful force on the member until it can be acknowledged and dealt with. In Chapter 5, I pointed out that group members can deal with affect in three different ways:

1. Group members' sharing of feelings with the group leader can release an important source of energy;

2. Group members can learn how emotions directly affect their thoughts and actions; and

3. Group members can develop skills that allow them to understand the sensations, accept them without harsh self-judgment, and disclose them to those who matter.

This can be described as the feeling-thinking-doing connection. How I feel affects how I think and act, and how I act affects how I think and feel. This interaction among feeling, thinking, and doing leads to the model described in this book, in which a group leader's skills for helping group members to manage their feelings takes on such importance in helping group members to manage their problems.

Expressing empathy with the member or the group can prove difficult for the group leader in many ways. The capacity to be in touch with the member's feelings is related to the group leader's ability to acknowledge his or her own feelings. Before group leaders can understand the power of emotion in the lives of group members, they must discover its importance in their own experience. Group leaders often find it hard to express empathy in specific personal areas. Group leaders are human, and they face all of the stresses and difficulties associated with daily living, including crises. When group leaders hear their own difficult feelings expressed by group members, the capacity for empathy can be blunted. The group leader's authority over the member may serve as another major block to empathy. For example, a group leader who is a mandated reporter and has had to report a possible child abuse situation revealed in a parenting group may find her or his empathic responses to the parent-member blocked at the time when they may be most needed.

Because of the difficulty of this skill area, group leaders must develop over time their ability to empathize. The capacity for empathy grows with experience. Group leaders who are open to this development can learn more about life from each group, which will help them to better understand the next group. I believe every group leader should emerge from a group experience somewhat changed. Group leaders also learn more about their own feelings and true reactions to the plight of others. Awareness of the sensitive areas in one's own emotional armor will help one avoid the denial or intellectualization of difficult emotions when they are presented. The group leader will more readily allow a member to share more difficult emotions as the group leader becomes comfortable with their effects, particularly those of negative feelings—both the group leader's and the member's—which form a natural part of any helping relationship.

Once again, supervision can play an important part in a group leader's emotional development. The concept of the parallel process suggests that the helping relationship between a supervisor and a group leader, or a practicum instructor and a student, parallels the relationship between the group leader (student) and the member. Thus, a supervisor must model effective empathic skills in the supervisory relationship. This is the meaning of the phrase "more is caught than taught"—supervisees watch their supervisors closely and learn a great deal from the nature of the interaction.

The three empathic skills described in the rest of this section are reaching for feelings, displaying understanding of the member's feelings, and putting the member's feelings into words.

*Reaching for Feelings* Reaching for feelings is the skill of asking the member or the group to share the affective portion of the message. Before proceeding, however, I should clarify one point raised briefly in a previous chapter. This process is sometimes handled superficially, in a ritualistic manner, thus negating its usefulness. The group leader who routinely asks a member, "How do you feel?" while not really being open to experiencing the feeling, may be perceived by the member as not really caring. Experienced group members have often reacted negatively to that repeated question. Of course, what they are reacting to is the group leader's intellectualizing, which is not effective practice. Genuine empathy involves stepping into the member's shoes and summoning an affective response that comes as close as possible to the experience of the other.

The reaching for feelings must be genuine, which means the group leader must be feeling something at the moment as close to the member's feelings as is possible. In most cases the group members will know when the leader's expression of affect is real or if it is just a technique. While learning to use a technique without the associated emotions is faster and easier than learning to experience the affect, it is the latter that has real impact in practice and in life. I often point out to my students that if they feel more comfortable prefacing a statement with "What I hear you saying is . . .," they should go ahead and do that, but they must actually try to feel the emotion. It's the client's sense of the leader's authenticity that really counts, and not the words that are used. Eventually, students will develop confidence and find their own words and their own voice.

***Displaying Understanding of the Member's Feelings*** The skill of displaying understanding of the member's feelings involves indicating through words, gestures, expression, physical posture, or touch (when appropriate) the group leader's comprehension of the expressed affect. The group leader attempts to understand how the member experiences the feelings even if the group leader believes that the reality of the situation does not warrant the reaction. Furthermore, the group leader needs to resist the natural urge to rush in with reassurances and attempts to help the member feel better. Efforts at reassurance are often interpreted by the member as the group leader's failure to understand.

An element of the healing process includes the member's sharing of feelings with a caring group leader as well as caring group members. This is an important difference in group practice. Having other group members who have similar problems and emotions, what I referred to earlier as the "all-in-the-same-boat" phenomenon, is an important source of help and healing. When the group leader openly and accurately empathizes, she or he models the process for other group members. Remember, this empathy can also be directed at the group itself, not only at individual members.

Group leaders often express their fear of strong emotions. They are concerned that a member might become too depressed and that the group leader's effort to bring the emotions to the fore could result in more problems. Note that the emotions themselves do not create the problems; rather, group members' inability to face their feelings or to share them with someone important does. The power that feelings can have over group members may be dissipated when these feelings are expressed and dealt with. The greater danger is not in the facing of feelings but in their denial. The only thing worse than living with strong emotions is the feeling that one is alone and that no one can understand.

The group leader's fear of being overwhelmed by emotions can be alleviated somewhat if the group leader is clear about the function and purpose of the engagement. The group leader's sense of function requires placing a demand for work on the member (as discussed in the next section). No matter how strong the member's feelings of hopelessness, some next step can always be taken. The group leader needs to experience the member's feelings of being overwhelmed (the empathy) while still indicating a clear expectation (the demand) that the member will do something about the situation. Belief in the strength and resilience of the member enables a group leader to make this demand.

With clarity of purpose in mind, the group leader can help the member find the connections between the emotions and the purpose of the discussion. Significant work with group members in painful areas can be done only after the expression and acknowledgment of feelings. The flow of affect and understanding between group leader and member, and between members, is a necessary precondition for further work. Empathic responses build a fund of positive affect that the group leader can draw on later. The metaphor of a bank account describes this process; I put money in and then I am able to draw it out when needed. This fund is a buffer that helps the members experience a group leader's later confrontation as a caring gesture.

***Putting the Member's Feelings into Words*** Thus far, I have described how a group leader might reach for feelings and acknowledge those that have already been stated. There are times, however, when a member or the group comes close to expressing an emotion but stops just short. The member might not fully understand the feeling and thus be unable to articulate it. In other cases, the member might not be sure it is all right to have such a feeling or to share it with the group leader. Putting the member's feelings into words is the skill of articulating the member's affect a half step ahead of the member. This occurs when the group leader's tuning in and intense efforts to empathize during the session result in emotional associations as the member elaborates a concern.

The example shared in the chapter on the preliminary phase of work illustrated this skill. The participant in the mother's group asked the group leader if he had children. The group leader responded: "I don't have any children. Why do you ask? Are you concerned that I may not be able to understand what you go through as a parent?" The mother had not said that exactly; the group leader had tuned in to that concern and expressed it for her. Instead of being "behind" the client by just asking how she felt, the group leader was half a step ahead of the client. I suggest a "half step," since I want to stay close to the expressed feelings and not get too far ahead of the client.

This is a controversial issue in the helping professions. Some advise one to never put a client's feelings into words because one might be wrong. Others suggest doing so encourages dependency. My teaching, practice, and research have all suggested otherwise. I believe we make more mistakes of omission, failing to risk our hunches about the client's feelings, than mistakes of commission, suggesting feelings that are not there. In any case, as stated repeatedly, we can always go back and catch our mistakes.

The findings of a number of studies reviewed in Chapter 5 offered additional support for the construct that describes how skill—including empathy—develops a working relationship with the member. The expression of concern for the member corresponds to the term *caring* in my own research. All of the behaviors associated with concern could be perceived as contributing to the member's perception of the worker as "caring as much about me as my children" and "here to help me, not just investigate me" (Shulman, 1978, 1991).

***Dealing with Despair and Long-Term Unemployment*** Job training and employment programs have an underlying assumption that once the participants have completed the exercises, learned to write resumes, developed interview skills, and so on, the jobs will be there for them. In reality, training programs such as these are often offered at a time when the job market may be shrinking, jobs are being sent overseas, and the general economy is not expanding. At the time this is being written (mid-2010), the United States is in the midst of one of the worst economies in decades, one that is even considered as being close to the great depression of the 1930s. In a time of recession, the emotion of "despair" may be understandable, unavoidable, and a major barrier to continuing to try to find work. In such an economy, the number of unemployed who move off the unemployment list because they are no longer seeking work can shrink, and the number of unemployed who are seeking work but remain unemployed can grow. In the example that follows, an internal leader raises these powerful feelings.

**Practice Points:** When a job training group is highly structured with written and verbal exercises as well as information presentation, it is possible to miss the underlying feelings of participants which may have a powerful impact on their ability to make use of the information and skill training. In the next example, we see the group leader first reacting defensively to a negative comment by a member in the second group session, but then catching himself in mid-session and exploring the meaning behind the words. It's not surprising because the group leader will also have feelings about the discouraging job situation when he tries to lead a group that tries to develop hope. This "deviant member" turns out to be an internal leader, raising important issues that need to be integrated into the discussion.

> Tim said he had something to say before we started the meeting. He went on to say that he had found last week's exercises and role-plays a waste of time. He felt it had avoided the real issues they faced in trying to get jobs. I felt angry and floored by his comment. I said: "Well, I'm sorry you didn't find the group that helpful. I hope this week will be more useful. It might help if you got more involved in the discussion instead of just being critical." The group was subdued after my comments and I had the sinking feeling that I was blowing it, but I had absolutely no way of figuring out how to stop myself and change directions. I just put my head down and plowed ahead with this week's scheduled presentation, sinking deeper as I went along.

**Practice Points:** The next intervention, when the group leader catches his mistake, is crucial. By apologizing, he models effective adult behavior in the face of criticism and opens the door for a real discussion. Catching a mistake in the same session is, in my view, very skillful practice indeed.

> About halfway through the session, I recovered enough to try to get back to Tim. I stopped the group and said: "I want to apologize to Tim. I told you folks that I wanted honest feedback on how the group was going, and the first time someone gave me feedback I didn't like hearing, I got defensive. Tim, will you give me another chance? What did you mean when you said we were not getting at the real issues last week? What are the real issues for you?" After some silence, Tim said it's all right to talk about job interviews and using the telephone for finding positions and resume writing; but what if you have given up all hope? What good is it to keep trying if all you get is a lot of rejections? I was quiet for a moment as I began to feel his despair.
>
> I asked if others in the group shared some of Tim's feelings. I said: "I wonder how many of you were also going through the role-play while you were wondering if it was worth all the effort?" After a brief silence, Tammy said she was feeling low as well, that it wasn't just Tim. I said that perhaps I was rushing into trying to discuss ways to find jobs, and I hadn't really taken enough time to let them talk about what was going on inside of them. I thought that was important to talk about as well, and I thanked Tim for having the guts to slow me down. I said we should talk about what they are going through, and then we can see if some of these exercises can be helpful at all.

**Practice Summary.** By treating the deviant member as an ally, the leader gave permission for the group to begin a frank discussion not only of how they were experiencing the group but also of their disappointing job searches. Others in the group felt the freedom to express their dissatisfaction, and as a result, the group members began to take responsibility for making the group more effective. The issue led some group members to point out the need to be determined in the face of adversity and not to allow all the rejections, as painful as they were, to stop them from making the effort. This also led to efforts to improve their job search skills, which was the essential purpose of the group.

## Sharing the Group Leader's Feelings

An essential skill relates to the group leader's ability to present himself or herself to the member as a "real" human being. Theories of the helping process that follow the medical paradigm have presented the ideal group leader as an objective, clinical, detached, and knowledgeable professional. In these models, direct expression of the group leader's real feelings is considered unprofessional. This has resulted in a concept of professionalism that asks the group leader to choose between the personal and the professional self. I believe this is another of the many false dichotomies that plague our practice; the real skill lies in integrating the personal and the professional.

***Integrating the Personal and the Professional*** The irony of the group leader not sharing appropriate feelings with group members is apparent: The group leader asks group members to take risks and to be open, honest, and vulnerable in sharing feelings, while—in the name of professionalism—he or she is doing just the opposite. The result is often the "mechanical" group leader who always maintains self-control, who has everything worked out, and who is never at a loss for words or flustered—in short, a person who is difficult to relate to in any helpful way. When group members experience the group leader as a real person rather than mechanical, they can use the group leader and the helping function more effectively. If the group leader shows no signs of humanity, the members will either constantly test to find the flaws in the façade or idealize the group leader as the answer to all problems. The member who does not know at all times where the group leader stands will have trouble trusting that group leader. The reader should remember the argument put forth earlier in the book. It must be an integration of the personal and professional, and counselors need to guard against inappropriate expressions of emotions. Clarity of purpose of the group and the role of the group leader will be helpful in understanding these boundaries.

Direct expression of feelings is as important for the group leader as it is for the members. A group leader who suppresses feelings must use emotional energy to do so. This energy can be an important source of help to the members if it is freed for empathic responses. The group leader cannot withhold his or her feelings and experience those of the members at the same time. The group leader may also become cut off from important forms of indirect communication in which members use the group leader's feelings to express their own. The concept of *"projective identification"* (Bion, 1961) will be discussed in more detail in Chapter 13 when we consider a number of group theories. For now, Bion suggests that a group or its members may project their own emotions onto the group leader. For example, if they feel defensive, they may make the leader feel the same way as a form of indirect communication. The members may not be aware of this process. Leaders who are ignoring their own feelings may be missing an important message.

***Nineteenth Session of the Married Couples' Group:*** **The Leader Is Angry** Consider the following example which comes from the nineteenth session of my married couples' group, described in earlier chapters and shared in detail later in Chapter 13. One couple had come close to breaking up the previous week, but because the group had agreed to deal with another couple's problem this session, the wife raised her concerns indirectly. At one point in the session, she began to share in an intellectual manner that completely avoided the expression of any emotion and was a sign of resistance. After listening for a while, I finally confronted her, with mildly angry, perhaps better described as exasperation, affect in my voice that challenged this illusion of work as a way of continuing to avoid dealing with the painful feelings between them. It's important to note that this was in the nineteenth session and long after I and my coleaders had built that fund of caring in our relationship I referred to earlier in this chapter. (In addition to the frustration with the member, I had recently broken my thumb, which was in a cast, and the painkiller prescribed by my doctor was wearing off during the session.)

My expression of my feelings broke through her intellectualizing and freed my energy to respond to the member's feelings. She immediately moved to an affective level and, in what became an important turning point in the work of the couple, and the group, she responded to my pointing out that she had an angry expression on her face by agreeing she was angry. When I asked her exactly what she was feeling, she responded: "Screw the whole damn thing," referring to her marriage, and began to cry. When she stood up to leave the room her husband followed her, and when they returned a few minutes later they finally addressed the core issues in their relationship. I believe it was my expression of frustration and exasperation that led to her ability to break through her veneer of intellectualizing. (This was the nineteenth session of the married couples' group that is on one of the DVDs available on the instructor's Power Lecture DVD).

***Expressing a Group Leader's Investment in the Success of the Member*** In the illustrations presented thus far, I have seen how the group leader's feelings of anger or frustration, when expressed openly in the context of a caring relationship, can help group members. This honest and spontaneous expression of feelings extends to a broad range of group leader responses. Another example is the feeling of investment a group leader can have in a member's progress. For example, consider a school counselor in a group for teenagers when one member states: "What's the use? I might as well just drop out of school." If the counselor indicates that she believes in him, cares about his success, and would be disappointed if he just quit, she may be sharing a feeling he very much needs to hear. Research on resilience cited earlier supports the idea that having even one person who believes in you and cares enough to set high expectations can be the crucial factor in coping with life and its stresses.

## Making a Demand for Work

In constructing this model of a middle phase session, thus far, I have presented the importance of six components: preparing for a session through sessional tuning in, establishing a sessional contract, identifying the individual member's or the group's agenda, helping members to elaborate concerns, making certain the members invest the work with feeling, and sharing the group leader's feelings. At this point, I should examine the question of ambivalence and resistance. Group members will be of two minds about proceeding with their work. A part of them, which represents their strength, will move toward understanding and growth. Another part of them, which represents their resistance, will pull back from what is perceived as a difficult process.

Work often requires lowering long-established defenses, discussing painful subjects, experiencing difficult feelings, recognizing one's own contribution to the problem, taking responsibility for one's actions, giving up long-held cognitive frameworks about life, and confronting significant people and systems. Whatever the difficulty involved, group members will show some degree of ambivalence.

Perlman (1957) describes member ambivalence as follows:

> To know one's feelings is to know that they are often many-sided and mixed and that they may pull in two directions at once. Everyone has experienced this duality of wanting something strongly yet drawing back from it, making up one's mind but somehow not carrying out the planned action. This is part of what is meant by ambivalence. A person may be subject to two opposing forces within himself at the same moment—one that says, "Yes, I will," and the other that says, "No, I won't"; one that says, "I want," and the other, "Not really"; one affirming and the other negating. (p. 121)

A crucial concept is that resistance is a part of the work. Less-experienced group leaders who do not understand this may back off from an important area. Their own confidence in what they are doing is fragile, so when the member shows signs of defensiveness or unwillingness to deal with a tough problem, they allow themselves to be put off. This is especially true if group leaders experience their own ambivalence about the area.

Communication of ambivalence in tough areas, however, can be seen as the member's way of saying, "This is tough for me to talk about." It can also be a question to the group leader: "Are you really prepared to talk with me about this?" It is one of those life situations in which the other person says he or she is reluctant to enter the taboo area, hoping you will not really believe him. The surface message is "Leave me alone in this area," while the real message is "Don't let me put you off." These are the moments in interviews when the skills of making a demand for work are crucial.

The notion of a demand for work is one of Schwartz's (1961) important contributions to our understanding of the helping process. He describes it as follows:

> The group leader also represents what might be called the demand for work, in which role he tries to enforce not only the substantive aspects of the contract—what we are here for—but the conditions of work as well. This demand is, in fact, the only one the group leader makes—not for certain perceived results, or approved attitudes, or learned behaviors, but for the work itself. That is, he is continually challenging the member to address himself resolutely and with energy to what he came to do. (p. 11)

The demand for work is not limited to a single action or even a single group of skills; rather, it pervades all the work. For example, the process of open and direct contracting in the beginning phase of work represents a form of demand for work. The attempt of the group leader to bring the members' feelings into the process is another form of demand for work. In a group for parents separated from their children, an angry father, commenting about the length of time he had not been able to see his kids because of a court order, said, "It's a long time for the kids." The group leader responded, "And for you, too." The father was talking about the child's feelings while the leader consistently commented on his feelings. This is another illustration of the empathic demand for work.

Note that this demand can be gentle and coupled with support. It is not necessarily confrontational. I underline this point because of a tendency for people to see confrontation as negative and uncaring. Some models of practice, particularly in the substance abuse area, have been designed to use confrontation to break down defenses. Instead of allowing a group member to address the issues and to move past denial, it often hardens the resistance. It is quite possible for the group leader to make an empathic demand for work—and, as emphasized earlier, confrontation is experienced as caring if carried out in the context of a positive working relationship.

I have categorized several specific interventions as demand-for-work skills:

- Partializing member concerns
- Holding to focus
- Checking for underlying ambivalence
- Challenging the illusion of work
- Pointing out obstacles

Each is related to specific dynamics in group situations that could be interpreted as forms of resistance. Note that the consistent use of demand-for-work skills can only be effective when accompanied by the empathic skills described earlier. As the group leaders express their genuine caring for the group members through their ability to empathize, they build up a fund of positive affect that is part of the working relationship or therapeutic alliance. Only when group members perceive that their group leader understands, and is not judging them harshly, can they respond to the demands.

An integration of empathy and demand for work is needed. On one hand, group leaders who have the capacity to empathize with group members can develop a positive working relationship but not necessarily be helpful. On the other hand, group members will experience group leaders who only make demands on their group members, without the empathy and working relationship, as harsh, judgmental, and unhelpful. The most effective help will be offered by group leaders who can synthesize caring and demand in their own way.

This is not easy to do, either in the helping relationship or in life. There is a general tendency to dichotomize these two aspects of relationships, and group leaders might see themselves as going back and forth between the two. For example, caring about someone, expressing it through empathy, but getting nowhere leads to anger and demands, with an associated hardening of empathic response. However, it is precisely at this point, when crucial demands are made on the member, that the capacity for empathy is most important.

With this stipulation clearly in mind, in the next section I explore four demand-for-work skills. A reminder to the reader: Although I will be referring to the group member, all of these dynamics and skills also can apply to the group-as-a-whole.

***Partializing Group Member Concerns*** Group members often experience their concerns as overwhelming. A group leader may find that a member's comments, perhaps during a check-in, consist of the recitation of a flood of problems, each having some impact on the others. The feeling of helplessness experienced by the member and the other group members is as much related to the difficulty of tackling so many problems as it is to the nature of the problems themselves. The member feels immobilized and does not know how or where to begin. In addition, maintaining problems in this form can represent a form of resistance. If the problems are overwhelming, the member can justify the impossibility of doing anything about them.

Partializing is essentially a problem-managing skill. The only way to tackle complex problems is to break them down into their parts and address these parts one at a time. The way to move past perceptions of helplessness and feelings of being immobilized is to begin by taking one small step on one part of a problem. This is one way the group leader can make a demand for work.

**Practice Points:** When a group leader listens to the concerns of the member and attempts to understand and acknowledge the member's feelings of being overwhelmed, the group leader simultaneously begins the task of helping the member to reduce the problem to smaller, more manageable proportions. This skill is illustrated in the following excerpt from a parents' group.

GROUP LEADER: You seem really upset by your son's fight yesterday. Can you tell us more about what's upsetting you?

MEMBER: All hell broke loose after that fight (her son had with a neighbor's child). Mrs. Lewis is furious because he gave her son a black eye, and she is threatening to call the police on me. She complained to the landlord, and he's threatening to throw me out if the kids don't straighten up. I tried to talk to Frankie about it, but I got nowhere. He just screamed at me and ran out of the house. I'm really afraid he has done it this time, and I'm feeling sick about the whole thing. Where will I go if they kick me out? I can't afford another place. And you know the cops gave Frankie a warning last time. I'm scared about what will happen if Mrs. Lewis does complain. I just don't know what to do.

GROUP LEADER: It really does sound like quite a mess; no wonder you feel up against the wall. Look, maybe it would help if the group could look at one problem at a time. Mrs. Lewis is very angry, and you need to deal with her. Your landlord is important, too, and I should think about what you might be able to say to him to get him to back off while you try to deal with Frankie on this. And I guess that's the big question, what can you say to Frankie since this has made things rougher for the two of you? Mrs. Lewis, the landlord, and Frankie—where should I start?

The demand implied in the group leader's statement is gentle yet firm. The group leader can sense the member's feelings of being overwhelmed, but she will not allow the work to stop there. In this example, one can see clearly three sets of tasks: those of the group leader, those of the member with the problem, and those of the other group members who need to respond. The member raises the concerns, and the group leader helps her to partialize her problems; the member must begin to work on them according to her sense of urgency; and the other members need to focus on helping with one issue as a time. This is the sense in which work is interactional, with the group leader's tasks and those of the members interacting with each other.

When a group leader partializes an overwhelming problem and asks a member to begin to address the issues, she or he is also acting on a crucial principle of the helping process: *There is always a next step.* The next step is whatever the member can do to begin to cope with the problem. Even when a member of a hospice group is dealing with a terminal illness, the next steps may mean developing a way of coping with the illness, getting one's life in order, taking control of the quality of one's remaining time, addressing unfinished business with family members, and so on. When social supports, such as adequate housing, are not available for a member, the next steps may involve advocacy and confrontation of the system or, if all else fails, attempting to figure out how to minimize the impact of the poor housing. Although the group leader may not be able to offer hope of completely resolving the problem, the group leader needs to help the member and the other group members find the next step. When a member feels overwhelmed and hopeless, the last thing he or she needs is a group leader or a support group who feel exactly the same way.

In one of my practice studies, partializing was one of the four skills for helping clients manage their problems that contributed to the development of the trust element in the working relationship (Shulman, 1991). The other skills in the managing problems grouping included clarifying purpose and role, reaching for member feedback, and supporting group members in taboo areas. The trust element of the relationship, in turn, contributed to the member's perception of the worker as being helpful. This is a logical finding, because counselors who help their group members to deal with complex problems are going to be seen as more helpful.

Furthermore, when used in the beginning phase of practice, the partializing skill ranked fifth out of eight skills in the strength of its correlation with the caring element of the working relationship. It moved to second place in relation to the trust element of the relationship, and to first in importance in terms of its impact on helpfulness. This association between partializing and the working relationship replicated a finding in my earlier study, in which the skill appeared to contribute to the outcome of helpfulness though its impact on relationship (Shulman, 1978).

Why, then, does use of the partializing skill positively affect relationship building? One explanation may be that the group leader's use of the partializing skill conveys several important ideas to the member. First, the group leader believes the tasks facing the member are manageable. Second, the group leader conveys the belief that the member can take some next step—that is, that the member has the strength to deal with the problem when it is properly broken down into manageable pieces. Third, because partializing also serves to focus the work clearly, it may be another form of clarifying role and purpose. In any case, the findings on the partializing skill suggest that counselors might do well, especially early on, to help group members identify clearly the component parts of the concerns they bring to the group.

These ideas are consistent with the more recent evolution of the strengths perspective and solution-focused approaches (discussed in more detail in Chapter 17). Essentially, the group leader conveys to group members a belief in their ability to manage their problems if they can address them step by step. Asking group members to reflect on times in their lives when they were able to deal with issues more effectively—one of the basic solution-focused techniques—is an effort to help change group members' cognition about their life and their abilities.

***Holding to Focus*** As a member begins to deal with a specific concern, associations with other related issues often result in a form of rambling in which the member has great difficulty concentrating on one issue at a time. Holding to focus—asking the member to stay on one question—is a second problem-solving skill that incorporates a demand for work. Moving from concern to concern can be an evasion of work; if the member does not stay with one issue, he or she does not have to deal with the associated feelings.

**Practice Points:** Holding to focus sends the message to the member and to the group that the leader intends to discuss the tougher feelings and concerns. This skill is illustrated in the earlier excerpt with the single parent. After the member decided to deal with Mrs. Lewis first (because of her fear of police involvement), the discussion continued:

MEMBER: When Mrs. Lewis came to the door, all she did was scream at me about how my Frankie was a criminal and that she would not let him beat up her son again.

GROUP LEADER: You must have been frightened and upset. What did you say to her?

MEMBER: I just screamed back at her and told her that her son was no bargain and that he probably asked for it. I was really upset because I could see the landlord's door opening, and I knew he must be listening. You know he warned me that he wouldn't stand for all of this commotion anymore. What can I do if he really kicks me out on the street?

GROUP LEADER: Can we stay with Mrs. Lewis for a minute and then get back to the landlord? I can see how angry and frightened you must have felt. Do you have any ideas about how Mrs. Lewis was feeling?

**Practice Summary.** By acknowledging the distress (support) and then returning to the issue of dealing with Mrs. Lewis (demand), the group leader helped the member stay focused on this issue instead of allowing the member's anxiety to overwhelm her.

*Checking for Underlying Ambivalence* One of the dangers in a helping situation is that a member may choose to go along with the group leader, expressing an artificial consensus or agreement, while really feeling ambivalent about a point of view or a decision to take a next step. Checking for underlying ambivalence is thus another important task of the group leader.

Group members may go along with the group leader in this way for several reasons. A member who feels that the group leader has an investment in the "solution" may not want to upset the group leader by voicing doubts. The member may also be unaware at this moment of his or her current doubts or the ones that might appear later, when implementation of the difficult action is attempted. Finally, the member may withhold concerns as a way to avoid dealing with the core of the issue. In this sense, the member shows another form of resistance that is subtle because it is expressed passively. In these circumstances, when words are being spoken but nothing real is happening, we have the illusion of work, which is the single most dangerous threat to effective practice. Having lived for six years in French Canadian Montreal, Quebec, I learned to call this the "therapeutic pas des deux"—a form of a dance in which counselors and group members develop marvelous ways of maintaining the illusion that something real is happening, each for their own reasons.

Sometimes group leaders are aware of a group member's underlying doubts, fears, and concerns but simply pass over them. As one group leader put it, "I knew we were just spinning our wheels, but I was afraid to confront the member." Group leaders believe that raising these issues may cause the member to decide not to take the next step. They believe that positive thinking is required, and they do not wish to heighten the member's ambivalence by acknowledging and discussing it. However, the reverse is often true. It is exactly at moments such as these that the group leader should check for the underlying ambivalence. This is what I mean by the skill I called earlier as "Looking for trouble when everything is going your way!"

When a member has an opportunity to express ambivalence, the group leader and other members have access to the member's real feelings and can be of help. When discussed with the counselor and the group members, negative feelings usually lose much of their power. Perhaps the member is overestimating the difficulties involved, and the group can help clarify the reality of the situation. In other cases, the next step will indeed be difficult. The group's help consists of empathic understanding of the difficulty and expression of faith in the member's strength and resilience in the face of these feelings. Whatever the reasons for hesitation, they must be explored so that they do not block the member's work outside the session.

Group leaders need to struggle against a sense of elation when they hear group members agree to take an important next step. For example, in working with a group member with a substance abuse problem, an enthusiastic group leader might accept the member's agreement to enter a treatment program and then be disappointed when the member does not show up for the intake appointment. Careful examination of the session reveals that the member sent signals that he was still in the "contemplative" stage and not yet ready to move into the "action" stage of seeking help. Group leaders often admit to sensing a member's hesitancy but believing that it can be overcome through positive encouragement. This mistake comes back to haunt the group leader when the ambivalence and fears emerge after the session.

All is not lost if, in the next session, the group leader can admit to having moved too quickly and can encourage the member to explore the mixed feelings, which are normal at this stage of the process. This provides a good opportunity to elaborate on the earlier comment that resistance is part of the work. It would be a mistake simply to think of member resistance as an obstacle to progress; rather, there are important "handles for work" within the resistance itself. In the example of the member with a substance abuse problem, as the group leader explores the member's resistance, important work themes may emerge: concerns regarding acceptance of a problem with substances, how employers would view him, feelings of shame, memories of traumatic events that serve as triggers, and so on. Other members of the group can be helpful if they share these concerns or have had them in the past and have been able to overcome them. This discussion does not take place unless the group leader encourages it.

In another example, a young university student who had been admitted to a psychiatric unit after a suicide attempt announced early in the first meeting that she would not discuss her boyfriend or her family because that would mean she blamed them. She simultaneously expressed resistance, and one of her central concerns related to guilt over her anger and resentment. Exploring why she did not want to discuss her boyfriend or her family could lead directly to her central theme of concern—the fact that she blamed her boyfriend and her family.

***Challenging the Illusion of Work*** As mentioned earlier, perhaps the greatest threat to effective helping is the illusion of work. Although helping can be achieved through nonverbal means such as touch or activity, much of the helping process takes place through an exchange of words. We have all engaged in conversations that are empty of real meaning. It is easy to see how this ability to talk a great deal without saying much can be integrated into the helping interaction. This represents a subtle form of resistance: By creating the illusion of work, the member can avoid the pain of struggle and growth while still appearing to work. For the illusion to take place, however, everyone must engage in the ritual. The group leader and the group members must be willing to allow the illusion to be created, thus participating actively in its maintenance. Group leaders have reported helping relationships with group members that have spanned months, even years, in which the group leader always knew, deep inside, that it was all illusion.

Schwartz (1971) describes the illusion of work in this passage about group practice:

> Not only must the group leader be able to help people talk but he must help them talk to each other; the talk must be purposeful, related to the contract that holds them together; it must have feeling in it, for without affect there is no investment; and it must be about real things, not a charade, or a false consensus, or a game designed to produce the illusion of work without raising anything in the process. (p. 11)

The skill involves detecting the pattern of illusion, perhaps over a period of time, and confronting the members with that pattern in a facilitative manner.

An example from a marriage counseling group illustrates this process. A couple had requested help for problems in their marriage. As the sessions proceeded, the group leader noted that most of the conversation involved problems they were having at work, with their parents, and with their children. Some connection was made to the impact on their marriage; however, they seemed to have created an unspoken alliance not to deal with the details of their relationship. No matter how hard the group leader tried to find the connections from the topic they presented to how the couple got along, the always seemed to evade him. Finally, the group leader said,

> You know, when I started out, you both felt you wanted help with the problems in your marriage, how you got along with each other. It seems to me, however, that all we ever talk about is how you get along with other people. You seem to be avoiding the tough stuff. How come? Are you worried it might be too tough to handle?

The group leader's challenge to the illusion brought a quick response as the couple explored some of their fears about what could happen if they really began to work. This challenge to the illusion was needed to help the couple begin the difficult, risky process of change. In addition, their resistance itself revealed a great deal about their underlying problems. They were demonstrating to the group and the leader how they avoided talking to each other about their real problems. The other group members participated in creating and maintaining the illusion because of their own underlying hesitancy to address their own relationships.

## Supporting Group Members in Taboo Areas

When moving into a helping relationship, the member brings along a sense of society's culture, which includes taboos against open discussion about certain sensitive areas. Taboos may be related to the general society or may be more specific to particular socioeconomic, ethnic, or community groups or families. Whenever we bring a group of people together, one thing we can be sure of is that a culture is immediately established from the first meeting with a set of norms of behavior, roles (leader, member, etc.), rules both stated and unstated, and taboo subjects. (The concept of group culture will be addressed in detail in Chapter 13).

For example, we are taught early in life that direct questions and discussions about sex are frowned on. Other areas in which we are subtly encouraged not to acknowledge our true feelings include, among others, dependency, authority, loss, and financial issues. The two examples in the next section illustrate the power of the taboo against discussing sex, incest, race, and authority.

*Identifying Taboo Subjects*  In one example of the impact of societal taboos, a social worker working with a teenager in a group for students exhibiting behavior problems in high school picks up hints that there may be a problem at home for one of the girls, including indirect suggestion of sexual abuse. The counselor, in an individual session, points out the obstacle by commenting to the girl after the session that a number of the girls she sees have experienced some form of abuse at home, and that this is always difficult for them to talk about for a number of reasons. The teenage girl does not respond in the moment; however, before the beginning of the next session, she discloses to the counselor that she has experienced incest with her father and has been too ashamed and afraid to tell anyone.

In another example of the impact of race and the authority theme, an African American high school student in a largely White school has difficulty discussing his experiences being bullied by White students with his White counselor. The counselor points out that it might be hard for the student to talk about what he is going through as a Black student in a mostly White school when his counselor is also White. By pointing out this obstacle, the counselor opens the door for the discussion that followed.

There are other taboo areas that can be identified by the apparent efforts of group members to avoid discussing them even when they are relevant to the purpose of the group. For example, feeling dependent is often experienced as being weak. The unrealistic image of a "real man" or a "real woman" presents one who is independent, who can stand on his or her own feet, and who deals with life's problems without help. In the real world, however, life is so complex that we are always dependent on others in some way. Most people experience the bind of feeling one way, consciously or not, but thinking they should feel another way. The norms of our culture include clear taboos that make real talk about dependency difficult. These include dependency on people as well as substances such as alcohol or drugs and gambling.

Money is considered a taboo subject as well. Many families deeply resent questions related to their financial affairs. Having enough money is equated with competency in our society, and poverty is embarrassing. Reluctance to discuss fees with professionals is one example of the effect of the taboo in practice. Group members sometimes contract for services without asking about the fee, feeling that it would be embarrassing to inquire. In a group example of mothers on welfare, one member raised her anger in the last meeting at another member who had promised to stop by her home and give her some money to help her get through the month. The second member apologized and said she meant to do it but found that she was also going to be short and was too ashamed to say so. The discussion in the group turned to the feelings related to self-worth and their interaction with poverty.

One of the most powerful taboos involves feelings toward authority. Parents, teachers, and other authority figures do not generally encourage feedback from children on the nature of the relationship. We learn early on that commenting on this relationship, especially negatively, is fraught with danger. People in authority have power to hurt us, so we can only, at best, hint at our feelings and reactions. In a group counseling situation, the fear is compounded by worrying about being embarrassed in front of peers. Revealing positive feelings to people in authority is almost as hard, because it is considered demeaning or, in the vernacular, "sucking up."

I already addressed the authority theme in the chapters on beginning as group members wonder what kind of person the group leader will be. Even if this is answered directly in the beginning, such as the illustrative responses to the question "Do you have children?" issues of authority remain. The taboo against openly addressing authority theme issues can create an important problem in the working relationship between the group leader and the members throughout the life of the group.

Loss represents another taboo subject—one that takes many forms and affects various types of group members and areas of work. For example, the loss of a relationship because of death or separation may be considered too difficult to discuss directly. A parent whose child has been born with a physical or mental problem may secretly mourn the loss of the perfect child he or she had wished to have. A survivor of childhood sexual, emotional, or physical abuse may mourn the loss of a normal childhood and his or her innocence. The adult child of an alcoholic may mourn the loss of the family once hoped for, but he or she may not feel free to discuss this because the family taught that the problem must be kept a family secret.

The elderly may grieve over the loss of family, friends, communities, and their good health and independence. In one example in a group meeting in a home for the elderly, members expressed dissatisfaction with the quality and variety of the food served in the dining room. The group leader helped them address this issue with staff but also opened up a discussion of the loss of their ability to cook their own favorite meals. Many of the messages of our society indicate that direct discussion of loss is not acceptable.

How does the group leader recognize a taboo exists? There is no sign on the wall or a written agreement not to discuss a specific taboo topic. The group leader recognizes the existence of the taboo in the culture of the group because the group acts as if it exists. The topic of understanding the culture of the group will be explored in more detail in Chapter 13, but for now, the concept is that we understand the culture of our group (norms of behavior, informal rules, roles taken on by members, taboos, etc.) because the group acts as if the culture exists. Thus, the properties of a group are invisible unless we infer them from the actions of the members. How do we know a group has a specific shared norm of behavior and an unstated agreement not to raise a taboo subject? We know it because the group members consistently avoid discussing the topic even though it is relevant to the work. On recognizing the taboo, the group leader brings it out in the open and begins the negotiation of a new norm of behavior for the group session.

***Changing the Culture of the Group*** To help a members discuss taboo feelings and concerns, the group leader has to work with the group members to create a unique "culture" in the group. In this culture, it is acceptable to discuss feelings and concerns that the members may experience as taboo elsewhere. The taboo will not be removed for all situations, however. There are some good reasons for us not to talk freely and intimately on all occasions about our feelings in taboo areas, as the discussion on sharing group leader feelings showed (e.g., a group leader's sexual attraction to a member).

Discussing taboo subjects during the group session is meant not to change the members' attitudes forever and in all life situations, but rather to allow work in the immediate situation. The group leader enables such discussion by monitoring the interaction of the work with the members and listening for clues that may reveal a taboo-related block in the process. Past experiences with group members and the tuning-in process may heighten the group leader's sensitivity to a taboo that lies just beneath the surface of the session.

The group leader needs to guard against a subtle subversion of the contract that can easily occur if the discussion of the obstacle becomes the focus of the work. The purpose of the helping encounter is neither to examine the reasons why the taboo exists nor to free the members from its power in all situations. Clarity of group purpose and the leader's role can assist the group leader to avoid the trap of becoming so engrossed in the analysis of the process that the original task becomes lost.

***Dealing with the Authority and Intimacy Themes*** Earlier I suggested that at any one time, the group would be dealing with its work (contract) or its way of working (the authority theme and the intimacy theme). I need to examine these issues of authority and intimacy, which also are usually taboo subjects, to understand their impact on the group.

Schwartz (1971) describes the authority theme as a reference to "the familiar struggle to resolve the relationship with a nurturing and demanding figure who is both a personal symbol and a representative of a powerful institution" (p. 11). As the member uses the group leader's help to deal with this task, positive and negative feelings will arise. At times, the member will think fondly of this caring and supportive figure. At other times, the member will feel anger toward a group leader who demands that the members address painful feelings and take responsibility for their own part in the events of their lives. Group leaders are not perfect individuals who never make mistakes. Even the most skilled group leader will sometimes miss a member's communications, lose track of the leader's role and begin to sermonize, or judge a member harshly without compassion for the real struggles involved in change. Reactions and feelings on the part of the member will result.

As one enters a helping relationship, problems with the authority theme should be anticipated as a normal part of the work. In fact, the energy flow between group leader and members, both positive and negative, can provide the drive that powers the work.

Two processes central to the authority theme are transference and countertransference. Drawing on Freud's psychoanalytic theory, Strean (1978) describes their effects on the group leader–member relationship as follows:

> This relationship has many facets: subtle and overt, conscious and unconscious, progressive and regressive, positive and negative. Both client and counselor experience themselves and each other not only in terms of objective reality, but in terms of how each wishes the other to be and fears he might be. The phenomena of "transference" and "countertransference" exist in every relationship between two or more people, professional or nonprofessional, and must be taken into account in every counselor-client encounter. By "transference" is meant the feelings, wishes, fears, and defenses of the member deriving from reactions to significant persons in the past (parents, siblings, extended family, teachers), that influence his current perceptions of the counselor. "Countertransference" similarly refers to aspects of the counselor's history of feelings, wishes, fears, and so on, all of which influence his perceptions of the member. (p. 193)

Unfortunately, the authority theme is one of the most powerfully taboo areas in our society. Group members have as much difficulty talking about their reactions and feelings toward their group leaders as they do discussing subjects such as sex. When these feelings and reactions remain undiscussed, the helping relationship suffers. These strong feelings operate just below the surface and emerge in many indirect forms. The group member or the whole group becomes apathetic, is late for meetings, or does not follow up on commitments. The group leader searches for answers to the questions raised by the member's or group's behavior. Group leaders may attempt to understand this behavior in terms of a member's "personality." However, the answers to the group leader's questions are often much closer to home and more accessible than the intangible notion of personality. The answers often may be found in the interactional process between the group leader and the members.

The skill of dealing with the authority theme involves continual monitoring of the relationship. A group leader who senses that the work is unreal or blocked can call attention to the obstacle and respond directly to it if she or he thinks it centers on the authority theme. Once again, as with other taboo subjects, the group leader is trying to create a culture in this situation in which the member perceives a new norm: "It is all right to treat the group leader like a real person and to say what you think about how the group leader deals with you." The group leader can begin this process in the contracting stages by responding directly to early cues that the member wants some discussion about what kind of group leader this will be. The new culture will develop slowly as the member tests this strange kind of authority who seems to invite direct feedback, even the negative kind. As the members learn that the group leader will not punish them, the feedback will arise more often and more quickly than before. Also of importance, the members get to see a nondefensive group leader demonstrate the capacity to examine his or her own behavior and to be open to change—exactly what the group leader will be asking the members to do. This is another example of integrating content and process.

Issues can also arise between members that remain under the surface and serve to create and support the illusion of work. As difficult as it may be to address issues with the leader, it can be equally difficult to deal with other members. Confrontation is hard when we have been generally taught to be polite and to avoid negative interactions. A member who is angry or hurt by another member's comment may hide these feelings while acting them out in withdrawal or indirect digs at the offending party.

Transference between members can be another issue. Corey and Corey (2006) address the issue of transference and multiple transferences in the group context:

> Members may project not only onto the leaders but also onto other members in the group. Depending on the kind of group being conducted, members may identify people who elicit feelings in them that are reminiscent of feelings they have for significant people in their lives, past or present. Again, depending on the purpose of the group, these feelings can be productively explored so members become aware of how they are keeping these old patterns functional in present relationships. The group itself provides an ideal place to become aware of certain patterns of psychological vulnerability. Members can gain insight into the ways their unresolved conflicts create certain patterns of dysfunctional behavior. By focusing on what is going on within a group session, the group provides a dynamic understanding of how people function in out-of-group situations. (p. 211)

**EP 2.1.6b**

***The Author's Research on Dealing with Taboo Subjects***  In my early study, the skill of supporting clients in taboo areas was one of four skills that distinguished the most effective counselors from the least effective, from their client's perspective (Shulman, 1978). In the more recent study, this skill was only the sixth most used out of the eight skills examined (Shulman, 1991). Clients reported that their workers used this skill between "seldom" and "fairly often." This is not unexpected, because workers face the same taboos that group members do. Group leaders need experience and supervision to find the courage to speak directly about many of these issues.

The introduction of time to the analysis of this skill yielded some interesting findings:

- Supporting clients in taboo areas, when used in the beginning phase of work (first sessions), was the third strongest skill (out of eight) that correlated with the client's perception of the worker's caring ($r = .52$).

- The correlation for the use of the skill in the middle phase of work was slightly higher ($r = .58$).

These findings were expected, because support of any kind, particularly in sensitive and painful areas of work, could contribute to the client's perception that the worker was concerned about him or her. This provides some justification for the argument that it is better for the group leader to take risks and be too far ahead of the members in addressing taboo subjects than to be overly cautious.

## Identifying Process and Content Connections

Two group leader skills are associated with identifying content and process connections: (1) identifying these connections and (2) pointing them out to the group member. Members who are aware of the way in which they use process to deal with content may be able to learn from that awareness and take control of their interactions with others. For example, recognition of the meaning of the dependency on the leader may free group members to become more independent in the helping relationship by taking more responsibility for the work. In turn, this serves as a training medium for the group member to practice new skills of independence—skills that can later be transferred to other significant relationships.

In an example of helping group members see a connection between the group process and the content of the work, an African American high school student suspended from school for violence was confronted by a White group leader during a group session at the Vision-Integrity-Structure-Accountability (VISA) Center I established at the University at Buffalo. When the leader skillfully addressed the just-below-the-surface taboo intercultural issue that had emerged between the Black teenager from the inner city and the White group leader from the suburbs, it was a major step in strengthening the working relationship. With an understanding of the connection between process and content, the discussion quickly moved to the conflicts between this student and his White teachers and administrators, who he experienced as racist. Thus, process (relationship to the group leader) and content (being Black and dealing with White teachers and administrators) were integrated.

This discussion may help the student make a better assessment of when he actually experiences racism or when he, for many good reasons drawn from his life experience, may see it when it is not always there. It may also help him find more adaptive ways of coping with these highly charged interactions that will create fewer problems for him. He may still have to confront racist professionals and students, but he may be able to develop more effective strategies and interventions in his response.

Another example cited in the Introduction of this book, in which an angry mother in a mutual-aid support group for mothers with chronically ill children in a hospital attacked a new leader during the first meeting. I suggested then that the mother was actually showing the leader how she used anger to avoid dealing with her painful feelings, and how she pushed helpful people away when she most needed them. This demonstrated how addressing the process (the authority theme) directly connected to the work of the group.

***Process and Content That Relate to the Authority Theme*** I suggested earlier that at any one time, the conversation in a group session is related to either process or content. However, because of the indirect nature of member communications, it is often hard to know which is really under discussion. For example, take a single parent in a group whose purpose is to work on issues related to dealing with children, employment, and relationships with friends and family. A member may begin a session apparently talking about content—how none of her friends or relatives understands her painful emotions. The issue is real to her, but she has also been angry with the group leader since the previous session, when the group leader missed or minimized her signals of distress.

This example emphasizes the importance of turning in and group leader tentativeness in the sessional contracting stage of a group meeting, discussed earlier in this chapter. The group leader who is tuned in to the member's pattern of indirect communications around issues of authority may be better prepared to hear that the discussion is really about process (the group leader's ability to understand) rather than content (friends and relatives). If the group leader prematurely assumes that the discussion is only content related, the session may turn into the illusion of work, with the process issues buried under the surface.

Thus far, the terms *content* and *process* have been described and illustrated; however, the concept of the integration of the two requires further elaboration. One common mistake made by group leaders is to fail to see the possible connections between process and content that allow for synthesizing of the two. Group leaders often describe being torn between process and content. They describe trying to balance the two, spending some time on process (how the group is working) and some time on content (what the group is all about). What they do not always realize is that they have fallen into the trap of accepting the false dichotomy of process versus content. When group leaders embrace this false dualism, they cannot avoid getting stuck. Instead, the group leader must search out the connections between process and content so that the discussion of process deepens the work on the content, and vice versa.

Returning to our single-parent example, the group leader who looks for this synthesis may recognize (usually between sessions, rarely during a session) that the way in which the member indirectly raised her anger and hurt feelings at the group leader's lack of compassion is a good example of the way this member deals with friends and other important people in her life. When her needs are not met, she gets angry because she expects other people to intuitively sense her feelings. She does not take responsibility for being direct about her pain and thereby helping others to understand. In this case, if the group leader opens up a discussion of the authority theme, the member can gain a deeper understanding of the skills she must develop to create and maintain a social support system. The member can be held accountable for her own responsibility in the relationship with the group leader as well as in relationships with other significant people in her life. Thus, I see in this example that the content of the work can be synthesized with process issues, and the process issues can be integrated into the content. After discussing the authority theme, the group leader can move from the specific issue of the member's way of dealing with the group leader or other members to the general issue of how the member seeks to have needs met by friends and family.

In another example, one group leader explored the difficulty a married member was having in allowing himself to feel dependent on the female group leader and the discomfort he felt at expressing his need for help. The difficulty seemed to relate too many of his notions of what a "real man" should feel. The work on the authority theme led directly to discussions of how hard it was for him to let his wife know in a direct manner how much he needed her.

In each of these examples, dealing with the authority theme served two distinct functions: It freed the working relationship from a potential obstacle and led directly to important substantive work on the contract. But this can only happen if the group leader rejects the process-content dichotomy and instead searches for the potential connections between the two.

The reader may have noted how often I challenge what I call false dichotomies and phony dualisms. This one is: "Do I deal with group process or content?" Once a group leader sees the connection between the two, the leader no longer needs to choose one versus the other.

## Sharing Data

The group member must also be allowed access to the leader's own relevant data. Contrary to some views, which require a form of neutrality on the part of the leader,

I argue that the leader's sharing of data such as facts, opinions, and value judgments is an important part of the helping process. In some groups, educational and psycho-educational groups, for example, sharing data is the purpose of the group. Even in these groups, the leader needs to consider when sharing data is appropriate and how the data are shared. In order to be sure that the group leader is not acting on a "hidden agenda," that is, attempting to manipulate group members, four conditions apply. The leader must take care to share only data that is:

- otherwise unavailable to the group members;
- relevant to the members' work;
- shared openly; and
- shared in such a way that the group members are left free to accept or reject the leader's views.

I define group leader data as facts, ideas, values, and beliefs that group leaders have accumulated from their own experiences and can make available to group members.

Sharing group leader data is important not only because of the potential usefulness to the member, but also because the process of sharing the data helps to build a working relationship. The member looks to the group leader as a source of help in difficult areas. If the member senses that the group leader is withholding data, for whatever reason, this can be experienced as a form of rejection. As a member might put it, "If you really cared about me, you would tell me what you know."

Although the skills of sharing data may sound simple, several misconceptions about how people learn—as well as a lack of clarity about the helping role—have served to make a simple act complex. The problems can be seen in the actions of group leaders who have important information for the member but withhold it, thinking that the member must "learn it for himself." These problems are also apparent in the actions of group leaders who claim to allow group members to learn for themselves while they indirectly "slip in" their ideas. This is most easily recognizable in group sessions wherein the group leader leads a member to the answer that the group leader already has in mind. This is a form of the "Socratic method" in which the knowing person asks questions designed to lead the unknowing person to the right answer. The belief is that learning takes place if the member speaks the words the group leader wants to hear. It is my observation, both as a group leader and a teacher, that students quickly sense this process and instead of working on an issue, they work hard on trying to figure out what the group leader/instructor wants them to say.

In the balance of this section, I shall identify some of the skills involved in sharing data and discuss some of the issues that often lead group leaders to be less than direct.

***Providing Relevant Data*** The skill of providing relevant data is the direct sharing of the group leader's facts, ideas, values, and beliefs that relate to the member's immediate task at hand. The two key requirements are that the data be related to the working contract and that they be necessary for the member's immediate work.

Regarding the first requirement, if the group leader is clear about the purpose of the encounter and that purpose has been openly negotiated with the member, then the group leader has a guideline as to what data to share. A problem is created when the group leader wants to teach something indirectly to the member and uses the interchange to subtly introduce personal ideas. This mistaken sense of function on the group leader's part is rooted in a model in which the group leader attempts to change the member by skillfully presenting "good" ideas. The problem is that the member soon senses that the group leader has a hidden agenda, and, instead of using the group leader as a resource for the member's own agenda, he or she must begin to weigh the group leader's words to see what is "up her sleeve."

This hidden purpose often creates a dilemma for the group leader in sharing data directly. On one hand, sharing may help the member. On the other hand, imposing an ideology on the member treats the member as an object to be molded. This group leader's ambivalence comes out in the indirectness with which the ideas are shared. If data are related to an openly agreed-on purpose, however, the group leader is free to share them directly.

The second requirement for directly sharing data is that the data be connected to the member's immediate sense of concern. Group members will not learn something simply because the group leader feels it may be of use to them at some future date, even if it relates to the working contract. The attraction people feel toward ideas, values, and so forth is related to their sense of their usefulness at the time. One reason for the importance of sessional contracting is that the group leader needs to determine the members' current sense of urgency and must share data that the members perceive as helpful.

*A Group for Preadoptive Couples*  From my observations of educational groups for preadoptive couples, I can offer an example of sharing data that are not immediately relevant. Individual or group work is often employed for the dual purpose of evaluating the couples' suitability as adoptive parents and helping them to discuss the adoption. Group leaders will often prepare a well-developed agenda for group meetings that touches on all the issues that they feel the couples will need to face as adoptive parents. Unfortunately, such an agenda can miss the immediate concerns that preadoptive parents have about adoption and about agency procedures for accepting and rejecting potential parents. In the following illustration, preadoptive couples in a second group session respond to the group leader's query, "Should one tell adopted children they were adopted, and when and how should we do this?"

**Practice Points:**  The important point to remember is that these couples are still waiting to hear whether they are going to get children, and all are expecting infants. The issue of whether to tell the child will not present itself until a few years after the child has been adopted.

MR. FRANKS: I think you have to tell the child or you won't be honest.
MR. BECK: But if you tell him, then he probably will always wonder about his real parents and that may make him feel less like you are his parents.

(This comment starts a vigorous discussion between the men about how a child feels toward his adoptive parents. The group leader uses this opportunity to contribute her own views indirectly; she already has in mind an "acceptable" answer to her question.)

GROUP LEADER: I wonder, Mr. Beck, how you think the child might feel if you didn't tell him and he found out later.

Recognizing that he may have given the wrong answer to the group leader, who will also judge his suitability to be an adoptive parent, Mr. Beck quickly changes his position.

MR. BECK: I hadn't really looked at it that way. I guess you're right—it would be easier to tell right away.

**Practice Summary.**   When the group apparently reached the consensus that the group leader had intended from the start, she shifted the discussion to the question of when and how to tell. This is an example of what I have called the illusion of work. Unfortunately, the urgency of the issue of "telling" was not an immediate one. Preadoptive couples are more concerned with how they, and their family and friends, will feel toward their adoptive child. This is a sensitive subject, particularly because preadoptive couples are not sure about the agency's criteria for acceptance. They often worry that they will be rejected if they don't express the "right" attitudes and feelings. This cuts them off from a supportive experience in which they might discover that most preadoptive parents face the same issues, that it is normal for them to have doubts, and that the agency will not hold this against them. In fact, parents who are in touch with their feelings, including such feelings as these, are often the ones who make excellent adoptive parents. Because the group leader was so occupied by "teaching" ideas for future use, she missed the most important issue.

Compare the previous example with the following excerpt. In this case, the parents raise the question of "Should one tell?" and the group leader listens for cues to the present concern.

MR. FRIEDMAN: (Responding to a group member's argument that the kids would not feel that the adoptive parents are their real parents) I can't agree with that. I think the real parent is the one that raises you, and the kids will know that's you even if they are adopted.

**Practice Points:**   Note how the group leader now opens the door for discussion of a taboo subject by raising their doubts about their feelings toward the child. In addition, she normalizes these feelings, thus giving permission for a real discussion of a tough issue.

GROUP LEADER: You have all been working quite hard on this question of how your adopted child will feel toward you, but I wonder if you aren't also concerned about how you will feel toward the child? (Silence)
MR. FRIEDMAN: I don't understand what you mean.
GROUP LEADER: Each of you is getting ready to adopt a child who was born to another set of parents. In my experience, it is quite normal and usual for a couple at this stage to wonder sometimes about how they will feel toward the child. "Will I be able to love this child as if it were my own?" is not an uncommon question and a perfectly reasonable one, in my view.
MRS. REID: My husband and I have talked about that at home—and I feel I can love our child as if he were our own.
GROUP LEADER: You know, I would like the group to be a place where you can talk about your real concerns. Frankly, if you're wondering and have doubts and concerns such as this, that doesn't eliminate you from consideration as an adoptive parent. Being able to face your real concerns and feelings is very much in your favor. You folks wouldn't be in this group if we hadn't already felt you would make good adoptive parents. It would be the rare situation in which I would have to reconsider.

**Practice Summary.** The group leader shared some important data with these group members that was relevant both to the general contract of the group and to their immediate sense of urgency. They learned that their feelings, doubts, and concerns were not unusual; that the agency did not reject prospective adoptive parents for being human and having normal worries; that the group was a place to discuss these feelings; and finally, that their presence in the group indicated that they were all considered good applicants.

This comment was followed by a deeper discussion of their feelings toward their prospective child and the adoption. These included their concerns over possibly getting a child from a "bad seed," their fears regarding the reactions of friends and family, and their anger about the delays and procedures involved in dealing with the agency. As one member put it: "Having your own child only takes 9 months. This adoption process never ends!" The data shared by the group leader in these areas were more meaningful to these parents than was information about future problems.

***Providing Data in a Way That Is Open to Examination and Challenge*** Group leaders are sometimes fearful of sharing their own fears, values, and so forth because of a genuine concern with influencing group members who need to make a difficult decision. The unwed mother, for example, who is trying to decide whether to abort her child, to have it and keep it, or to have it and give it up for adoption faces some agonizing decisions—none of which will be easy. Each option holds important implications for her future. The skillful group leader will help such a member explore in detail these implications and her underlying feelings of ambivalence.

During this work, the member may turn to the group leader at some point and say, "If you were me, what would you do?" Group leaders often have opinions about questions such as these but hold them back, usually responding to the question with a question of their own. I believe it is better for group leaders to share their feelings and reveal their opinions, and then to allow the member access to their views as representing one source of reality. For example,

> When you ask me that question, you really put me on the spot. I'm not you, and no matter how hard I try, I can't be you, since I won't have to live with the consequences. For what it's worth, I think the way you have spelled it out, it's going to be an awfully tough go for you if you keep the baby. I probably would place the child for adoption. Now, having said that, you know it's still possible that you can pull it off, and only you know what you're ready for right now. So I guess my answer doesn't solve a thing for you, does it?

Group leaders who withhold their opinion do so because they fear that the member will adopt it as the only source of reality. Rather than holding back, however, a group leader can simultaneously allow the member access to his or her opinions while guarding against the member's tendency to use them to avoid difficult work.

***Providing Data as a Personal View*** Thus far, I have described how a group leader can provide data to group members in a way that is open to examination by making sure that the member uses the data as just one source of reality. An additional consideration is to make sure that what is shared is presented as the group leader's own opinion, belief, values, and so forth, rather than as fact. This is one of the most difficult ideas for many group leaders to comprehend, because it contradicts the normal societal pattern for exchanging ideas. Group leaders have an investment in their own views and will often attempt to convince the member of their validity. We are accustomed to arguing our viewpoint by using every means possible to substantiate it as fact. New group leaders in particular feel that they must present their credentials to group members to convince them that they know what they are talking about.

In reality, however, our ideas about life, our values, and even our "facts" are constantly changing and evolving. A cursory reading of childrearing manuals would convince anyone that the hard-and-fast rules of yesterday are often reversed by the theories of today. I have found that inexperienced group leaders are often most dogmatic in areas where they feel most uncertain.

The skill of sharing data in a way that is open for examination means that the group leader must qualify statements to help group members sort out the difference between their reality and the group leader's sense of reality. Rather than being a salesperson for an idea, the group leader should present it with all of its limitations. A confident and honest use of expressions such as "This is the way I see it" or "This is what I believe, which doesn't mean it's true" or "Many people believe this, but others do not" will convey the tentativeness of the group leader's beliefs. The group leader must encourage the member to challenge these ideas when they do not ring true to the member.

## Helping the Group Members See Life in New Ways

A specific form of data is important enough to be included as a separate skill category. These are the skills with which the group leader helps group members reexamine perceptions (cognitions) about themselves, their life situations, or important people or systems in group members' lives (e.g., husband, parent, school). This group of skills can be central to a form of practice called cognitive-behavioral therapy (for a fuller discussion of this approach and others, see Chapter 17).

To summarize briefly, group members have developed their views of life subjectively. Given the difficulties involved in communications, they quite possibly have distorted other people's actions or have internalized perceptions of themselves and their life experiences that lead to negative cognitions and feelings and self-defeating behaviors. By exploring alternative views in collaboration with the group members, the group leader attempts to help a member rethink his or her life situation and correct negative and inaccurate "automatic thoughts" and perceptions. This approach is also consistent with some of the solution-focused techniques and strategies. The term "reframing" is also often used when thinking of this skill.

After a period of bad experiences, the blocks in the reality of the relationship become the member's (and sometimes the system's) only view of reality itself. The group leader needs to help the member explore this maladaptive pattern and to break the cycle that prevents the member from connecting to people and systems that are important for success. At these moments, a group leader offers the possibility of hope and a next step by sharing a view of others in the system that allows the member to glimpse some possibility of mutual attraction. This is only possible when group leaders themselves see these possibilities, described earlier as the areas of common ground. For example, when a group leader helps a teenager see that his parents' setting of curfew limits may show that they care for him and recognize that he is growing up, the group leader has not solved the problem, but at least he has shed a new light on the interaction.

# The Ending and Transition Stage

**EP 2.1.10l**

I now come to the skills factors involved in dealing with the ending and transition stage of any group session. Endings and transitions of group sessions present important dynamics and require the leader's attention. In addition, issues that have been raised indirectly throughout the session may emerge with some force when the group member is preparing to leave (the classic "doorknob therapy" phenomenon, discussed earlier). Finally, transitions need to be made to next sessions and future actions. Sessional ending and transition skills are used by the leader to bring a session to a close and to make the connections between a single session and future work or issues in the life of the group member.

As with beginnings and middles of any group meeting, endings contain unique dynamics and special requirements for leader skills. I call this stage the *resolution stage*. It is not unusual to find leaders carrying out their sessional contracting and demonstrating sensitive work with members in the group with regard to their concerns, but then ending a session without a resolution of the work. By "resolution of the work," I am not suggesting that each session end neatly, with all issues fully discussed, ambivalence gone, problems solved, and next steps carefully planned. A sign of advanced skill is a leader's tolerance for ambiguity and uncertainty, which may accompany the end of a session that has dealt with difficult work. If uncertainty is present for a member or members at the end of a session, the resolution stage might consist of identifying the status of the discussion. The five skills discussed in the balance of this section include summarizing, generalizing, identifying next steps, rehearsing, and identifying "doorknob" communications.

Before I examine these skills, a word on member activity between sessions is in order. Leaders sometimes act as if members have no life between sessions. They review a group meeting and then prepare to pick up the next session "where I left off." The leader needs to realize that the member has had life experiences, contacts with other helping systems, new problems that may have emerged during the week, and time to think about problems discussed in the previous session. After giving much consideration to how to help a member with a particular problem, a leader may be surprised to discover that the member has resolved the issue between sessions. It would be a mistake not to recognize and legitimate these between-session activities. Solution-focused practice incorporates inquiring about between session activities as a major strategy. That is one reason why the sessional contracting skill, described at the beginning of this chapter, is so important.

## Summarizing

Often, the group members are learning about life and trying to develop new skills to manage life in more satisfying ways. It can be important to use the last moments of a session to help the member or members identify what has been learned. How does the member add up the experiences? What new insights does the member have about understanding relationships to others? What has the member identified as the next, most urgent set of tasks? What areas does the member feel hopeless about and need more discussion on? I believe that the process of summarizing can help a member secure what he or she has learned. Sometimes the member summarizes the work, other times the leader does it, at other times the group members take on the task, and sometimes they do it together. Note that summarizing is not required in all sessions. This is not an automatic ritual but a skill to be employed at key moments.

## Generalizing

Earlier discussion stressed the importance of the skill of "moving from the general to the specific." It can also be important to move in the opposite direction. For example, a parent raises a specific problem with her teenage son, and after some work on the immediate problem, the leader may help the individual and the group to identify the general principle involved. As the mother gives details, problem by problem and system by system, the leader helps her to generalize the experiences and to recognize how her learning applies to a whole category of experiences. In this way all group members can relate the insight or skills to their own often-close versions of the same issue, and the specific group member has learned how to use his or her learning in similar situations. This is a key skill of living, because it equips the member to continue without the leader or the group and to use the newfound skills to deal with novel and unexpected experiences.

## Identifying the Next Steps

We have all experienced, at one time or another, frustration when we participate in some form of work that goes nowhere because of lack of follow-up. A good example is a committee or staff meeting in which decisions are made but the division of labor for implementing the decisions is overlooked, and no action follows. The leader must make a conscious effort to help the member identify the next steps involved in the work. No matter what the situation is, and no matter how impossible it may seem, some next step is possible, and the leader will ask the member to discuss it. I call this the principle of "there is always a next step." The next step may be a small one or a hard one, but it will be available when all else fails.

Next steps must be specific; that is, the general goal the member wishes to achieve must be broken down into manageable parts. The next steps for an unemployed mother on welfare who presents the need to find a job in a work retraining group might include exploring day-care centers for her child and meeting with an employment counselor. The next step for a couple in marital counseling who feel their relationship is worsening might be to identify specific areas of difficulty for discussion in the group the following week. In essence, the identification of next steps represents another demand on the member for work.

Lack of planning by the member does not always represent poor life-management skills; it may be another form of resistance. Talking about a tough subject may be difficult, but doing something about it may be even harder. By demanding attention to future, specific actions, the leader may bring to the surface another level of fear, ambivalence and resistance that need to be dealt with.

Sometimes the expression of understanding, support, and expectation by the leader is all the member needs to mobilize resources. There may be no easy way for the member to undertake the task, no simple solution, and no easy resolution when two genuinely conflicting needs arise. For the member, verbalizing the dilemma to an understanding and yet demanding leader and to the group may be the key to movement. At other times, the member needs help figuring out the specifics of how to carry out the act. For example, the member might need some information about community resources.

## Rehearsing

Talking about confronting another person with regard to difficult, interpersonal material is one thing, but actually doing it is quite another. Agreeing to undertake a job interview may be quite a difficult next step. A member who protests "I don't know what to say" may be identifying an important source of blockage. A leader can help by offering the safe confines of the group as a place for the member to rehearse. The leader or a group member takes on the role of the other person (boss, teacher, husband, mother, doctor, and so forth) and feeds back to the member possible reactions to the member's efforts. All too often, the leader skips this simple and yet powerful device for aiding a member by saying, "When the time comes, you will know what to say." Words do not come easily for most people, especially in relation to their most difficult feelings. With the help of the leader and group members, the individual may be able to say what must be said and, with some successful rehearsal under her or his belt, may feel a bit more confident about doing it. A leader who thinks she has done a marvelous job in helping a member learn to deal effectively with an important person may find that additional work needs to be done when the member formulates the words to be used.

## Identifying "Doorknob" Communications

A "doorknob" communication is shared as the member leaves the group session, often with his or her hand on the doorknob, or during the last session or sessions. This commonly observed phenomenon, described in the literature of psychotherapy, refers to any comments of significance raised by the member toward the end of a session when there is too little time to deal with them. We have all experienced a session with a member, or a conversation with a friend, when—after a relatively innocuous discussion—he says, "There is just one thing that happened this week." Then we hear that he lost his job or found out that his girlfriend was pregnant or received an eviction notice or noticed a strange lump in his groin. Reflecting on the session, the leader may see that the first clues to the concern were presented indirectly during the beginning stage. On the other hand, there may have been no clues at all.

A doorknob comment signals to the leader the member's ambivalence about discussing an area of work. The concern is raised at a time when it cannot be fully discussed. It may be a taboo area or one experienced as too painful to talk about. Whatever the reason, the desire to deal with the concern finally overwhelms the forces of resistance. The urgency of the concern, coupled with the pressures created by the lack of time left in the interview, finally results in the expression of the issue. This kind of comment is actually a special case of obstacles that block the member's ability to work. As with all forms of resistance, it is a natural part of the process and provides the leader with an opportunity to educate the member about the member's way of working.

This discussion of sessional ending skills brings to a close our analysis of the work phase. The purpose of this analysis has been to identify some of the key dynamics in giving and taking help that follow the negotiation of a joint working contract. An example of work with mothers of children diagnosed as hyperactive illustrates the importance of making the demand for work and transitioning to the ending stage.

### Mothers with Children Diagnosed as Hyperactive

**Practice Points:**   In the illustration that follows, a leader with a group of mothers with children diagnosed as hyperactive helped the members move toward more realistic next steps in their work as a mutual-aid group. In making this demand for work, the leader was endorsing the power of resilience, suggesting that no matter how hopeless the situation may seem, the group members could begin by taking steps on their own behalf.

There was a lot of exchanging of problem situations, with everyone coming out with her problems for the week. There seemed to be some urgency to share their problems, to get some understanding, and moral support from the other members. Through their stories, themes emerged: an inconsistency in handling their children's behavior (lack of working together with husband); the tendency to be overprotective; and their hesitancy at trusting their children. The issue of "nobody understanding" was again brought up, and I recognized their need to have someone understand just what it was that they were going through. Betty said that her son was never invited to play at the neighbors' houses, because he was a known disturber. Others had the same experiences with neighbors who didn't want their hyperactive son or daughter around. I expressed the hurt they are feeling over this, to which they agreed.

**Practice Points:**   After acknowledging the importance of others understanding, the group leader notes the members moving to the more difficult area of their own feelings toward their children.

After further discussion about the impact of their children on others (teachers, neighbors, children) they moved to a discussion of how their children's behavior affected them. Rose said that she ends up constantly nagging; she hates herself for it, but she can't stop. Her son infuriates her so much. Others agreed that they are the biggest naggers in the world. I asked what brought the nagging on. The consensus was that the kids kept at them until they are constantly worn down and they gave in to them. Also if they wanted the children to do something, they had to nag, because the children wouldn't listen. I said that the children really knew them, how they reacted, and also exactly what to do in order to get their own way. They agreed, but said that they couldn't change that they couldn't keep up with the badgering that these children could give out.

**Practice Points:**   The group members have expressed two divergent ideas: on the one hand, they "couldn't change," and on the other, they could not "keep up with the badgering" from their children. They quickly moved to a discussion of medications as a source of hope for change. The leader pointed out that their hope in this solution was mixed with their recognition that the drugs were addictive and that they could not provide an answer in the long run. This is an example of another process in groups that Bion (1961) calls "pairing," in which the discussion of the group members appears to raise the hope that some event or person in the future will solve the problem.

For these group members, drugs provided this hope but also gave the group members an opportunity to avoid discussing what they could do to deal with the problem. In a way, it represented a "primitive" group response: attempting to deal with the pain of a problem by not facing it. As the session moved to a close, the leader sensed the heaviness and depression of the group members caused by their feelings of hopelessness. She had empathized with these feelings but now needed to make a demand for work on the members, asking them to explore what they could do about the problem.

**Practice Points:** When the members raised another hope for a solution in the form of an outside expert who would help, the leader pointed out their real feelings that no "outsider" could help and that they needed to find the help within themselves. In this way, the leader helped them resolve a difficult and painful discussion by conveying her belief in their strength and her sense of the concrete next steps open to them.

There was further discussion around the children's poor social behavior and the mothers' own worry about how these children will make out as adults. What will become of them? Will they fit in and find a place for themselves in society? I was feeling the heaviness of the group and pointed out what a tremendous burden it was for them. Our time was up, and I made an attempt to end the meeting, but they continued the discussion. I recognized their urgency to solve the problem and the need to talk with each other and get support from each other. Marilyn said that it was good; she came away feeling so much more relieved at being able to talk about how she felt, and she certainly was gaining some new insight into herself.

Discussion diverted to the problem with the children and how they were to deal with it. I asked what they wanted to do. Edna suggested they ask a behavior modification therapist to help them work out solutions. Others thought it was a good idea. I said that was a possibility, but I wondered if in wanting to get an "expert" involved, they were searching for someone to solve their problems for them. They agreed. I asked if they thought all these experts could do this. They said that it hadn't happened yet. I wondered if I could use the group for the purpose it was set up, to help each other problem-solve. I suggested that next week we concentrate on particular problems and work together to see what solutions we could come up with. They seemed delighted with this and decided that they should write down a problem that happened during the week and bring it in. Then we could look at a number of problems. Consensus was reached as to our next week's agenda, and the meeting ended.

Most of the examples thus far have involved groups where talking has been the central process. For some groups, particularly children's groups, activities such as games and drawing, may provide the medium through which mutual aid can be facilitated. Since we ended this session with the parents' group with discussion of work with their children, it seems appropriate to transition now to a children's group as an illustration of practice over time and the place activity has in group work.

## Activity in Groups

*Activity group* is a term usually applied to groups involved in a range of activities other than just conversation. *Program* is another term used to describe the activities implemented in such groups, such as the expressive arts (poetry writing, painting, dancing), games, folk singing, social parties, cooking—in fact, almost any recreational or social activity used by people in groups. In one of my earlier articles, I examined the ways in which people relate to each other, suggesting that to dichotomize talking and doing is a mistake (Shulman, 1971). Relationships between people were best described by a *mixed transactional model*. Let me explain.

In the complex process of human interaction, people express feelings, ideas, support, interest, and concern—an entire range of human reactions—through a variety of mediums. A mixed transactional model presents the idea that all of these mediums—words, facial and bodily expressions, touch, shared experiences of various kinds, and other forms of communication (often used simultaneously)—should be included when one considers the means by which transactions are negotiated and consummated. Leaders should not fragment human interactions by forcing them into categories such as "talking" and "doing" but should focus instead on the common denominators among transactions, defined here as exchanges in which people give to and take from each other. Group leaders are concerned with helping people who are pursuing common purposes to carry out mutually productive transactions.

In my analysis of the ways in which group members might use shared activity for mutual aid, I rejected grandiose claims that suggested specific activities might lead to creating "spontaneous or creative individuals" or "strengthened egos." Instead I suggested the need to describe the specific and immediate functions that the activity in question may play in the mutual-aid process.

## Functions of Activity in a Group

Here are five identified functions of activity in a group:

1. *Human Contact:* activities that focus on meeting a basic human need for social interaction (e.g., golden-age clubs for isolated senior citizens).

2. *Data Gathering:* activities designed to help members obtain more information central to their tasks (e.g., teenagers, preparing for employment, arranging a series of trips to business or industrial complexes).

3. *Rehearsal:* a means of developing skills for specific life tasks (e.g., a teenage party creating an opportunity for members to practice the social skills necessary for the courtship phase of life).

4. *Deviational Allowance:* activities creating a flow of affect among members that builds up a positive relationship, allowing members to deviate from the accepted norms and raise concerns and issues that might otherwise be taboo (e.g., young teenage boys who have gotten to know each other and the leader through many shared activities being more willing to accept a leader's invitation to discuss their real fears about sex and identity).

5. *Entry:* specific activities planned by a group as a way to enter an area of difficult discussion (e.g., the playacting of young children as they create roles and situations that reveal their concerns of the moment, or artwork expressing issues for people in recovery from addiction).

## Two Categories of Activity Groups

Besides these functions, we can see activity groups in terms of two general categories of groups in which activities are used as a medium of exchange. In the first, the activities themselves constitute the purpose of the group. Examples include a teenage club in a school or community center or an activity group in a day-treatment center for the mentally ill. The group exists for the purpose of implementing the activity. A second category includes groups established for curative or educational purposes, in which an activity is employed as a medium of exchange with specific healing or educational goals in mind. A group for children who are dealing with grief through the use of drawing or art therapy is an example. Another would be a group for persons in substance abuse recovery who are asked to draw illustrations, for example, of how they see their addiction and/or draw how they envision their recovery would look. These two categories will be covered separately, because each raises special issues.

## Activity Groups Where the Activity Is the Purpose

In the example of the first type of group, the most typical problem is that the leader or the setting ascribes therapeutic purposes to the group that constitute a hidden agenda. The group members may think they are attending a school club, but the leaders view the group as a medium through which they can change the members. This view reflects an early and still dominant view of program activity as a "tool of the leader," which grew out of early efforts to distinguish the professional social work group leader from the recreational leader. The professional, so the thinking goes, would bring to bear special skills in selecting programs that would result in the desired behavioral changes. Take, for instance, the problem of the child who was scapegoated in a group. In this early model, the leader might ascertain what area of skill this child had and then select or influence the group to choose an activity at which the scapegoated child would shine. All of this was done without the knowledge of the group members, and the meaning of the scapegoat phenomenon was ignored.

My own training was rooted in this view of practice. In one setting, my agenda involved attempting to influence group members (teenagers) toward their religious association. The agency was sponsored by the Jewish community, which was concerned that second-generation teenagers might be "drifting away" from their religious heritage. Program was the tool through which I was to influence the members by involving them in agency-wide activities—for example, in connection with religious holidays and celebrations. When such activities were conducted with the direct involvement and planning of the members, they offered powerful opportunities for deepening a sense of cultural connection and community.

Unfortunately, at times I was so busy attempting to covertly "influence" the membership that I ended up missing the indirect cues group members offered about their real concerns related to their identity as a minority group in a Christianity-dominated culture. There were important moments when the concerns of the community and the felt needs of the group members were identical; the common ground was missed by me because of the misguided view that I could influence the process covertly.

If the agency or setting has other agendas it feels are important for groups, then these must be openly presented in the contracting phase, and the group leader must attempt to find whatever common ground may exist. However, just as the leader will guard the group's contract from subversion by members, he or she must also guard it from subversion by the setting or agency. Members will learn a great deal about relationships, problem solving, and other areas as they work to create and run their groups; however, the leader must see the group as an end in itself, not a tool to be used for hidden professional purposes.

## Activity Groups with Direct Therapeutic or Educational Purposes

The second category of activity in groups, where the activity has a direct therapeutic or educational purpose, often includes expressive arts. Corey (2008) addresses one form of this use of activity called "expressive arts therapy." This specific approach is based on the work of Natalie Rogers (1993) who expanded on the person-centered approach of her father, Carl Rogers (1961), by addressing the use of expressive arts to enhance personal growth for individuals and groups.[1]

> Group facilitators, counselors, and psychotherapists trained in person-centered expressive arts offer their clients or groups the opportunity to create movement, visual art, journal writing, and sound and music to express their feelings and gain insight from these activities. (N. Rogers, 1993, cited by Corey, p. 260)

Corey cites Rogers's principles underlying the expressive arts therapy, which include, among others, the following:

- All people have an innate ability to be creative.
- The creative process is healing. The expressive product supplies important messages to the individual. However, it is the process of creation that is profoundly transformative.
- Self-awareness, understanding, and insight are achieved by delving into our emotions. The feelings of grief, anger, pain, fear, joy, and ecstasy are the tunnel through which we must pass to get to self-awareness, understanding, and wholeness.
- Our feelings and emotions are an energy source. That energy can be channeled into the expressive arts to be released and transformed. (N. Rogers, 1993, p.7)

While expressive art therapy as developed by N. Rogers is a broad personal growth model, for my purposes here I want to emphasize how the creative arts can be linked to emotional expression and discovery as part of what I termed earlier a mixed transactional model.

***Classroom-Based Poetry Club for Young Children*** An example of the use of expressive arts, described by Malekoff (2007), was the development of a classroom-based poetry club in an alternative school for young children (5-, 6-, and 7-year-olds) identified as having serious emotional disturbances. Malekoff emphasizes working closely with teachers and attempting to integrate group purpose and academic goals. For example, in kindergarten the goals were:

- Uses grammatically correct language in complete sentences
- Participates in discussion, listens, takes turns
- Expresses originality and inventiveness
- Comprehends a story (poetry)
- Recalls a story (poetry)
- Identifies feelings and how to express them. (p. 126)

**Practice Points:** One age-appropriate example described by Malekoff was beginning each session with a ritual, a "guess-what poem," which was a poem that described something for the members to discover together:

> Key words were left out of the poems to create mystery. The group's assignment was to guess what the poem described. After the poem was read, the group was instructed to huddle up, like a football team might, and discuss what they

---

1. Corey acknowledges writing this section on creativity and creative expression in collaboration with N. Rogers.

thought the poem was about. Finally, when they thought they had arrived at the correct answer they would say so. The first poem was about a giraffe. (p. 127)

The children had to guess it was a giraffe after listening to poetic lines such as:

- Because they hold their heads up high
- Because their necks stretch to the sky
- Because they're quiet, calm, and shy

**Practice Summary.**   Malekoff describes the children enjoying the huddling with their arms around each other's shoulders, the discussion, the decision, and then the "high-fives" when they succeeded in guessing a giraffe. After that, the assignment was for each to create their own "guess-what" poem and share it with the others. Longer-term projects involved the members completing open-ended sentences about themselves, described as "poems-under-construction." Members refined their work each week and then included them in a *Poetry Club Journal* as part of an ending project. The group members shared gift-wrapped copies of their journal with teachers, the principal, and other staff in the school.

***Children Dealing with Their Parents' Separation and Divorce***   This second category of activity group in which specific purposes other than the activity are the major focus and the activity is used to help achieve these ends is illustrated in another example. In this group, the leaders helped 8- and 9-year-old children deal with the trauma of separation and divorce through activities using drawing, puppets, and discussion of scenarios as mediums of expression.

I am sharing this example in some detail for a number of reasons. First, it is a good illustration of how relatively new group leaders analyze their work over time and develop increasing skill in exploring painful feelings with children. The first step for them, and most new group leaders, is recognizing their own resistance to this difficult work. Also, it reveals the use of a wide variety of activities including drawing, puppets, completing real and imagined scenarios provided by the group leaders, and simple completion exercises in response to drawings (e.g., a sad or a happy face) or questions: "What are the good things about separations and what are the bad things?" Finally, it is an example of the strength and courage of young children dealing with a shattering experience in their families once they understand that the caring adults and the other children are willing to listen and help.

**Practice Points:**   As you read the following excerpts, note these elements:

- The leaders become more courageous in reaching for painful feelings as they recognize their own resistance.
- The leaders use a wide range of activities including drawing, puppets, and responses to prepared scenarios and scenarios created by the children.
- The leaders listen carefully to the cues, both direct through conversation and indirect through activities, and reach for their underlying meaning.
- The members become more comfortable with the leaders and each other and progressively deal with a range of emotions including sadness and anger.
- The members are in control of the pace of disclosure, with the leaders gently prodding them as they come close to the most serious and painful areas of discussion.

**Type of Group:** This is an ongoing group to give children the opportunity to discuss their fears, to face change, and to find solutions to the painful crisis of their family disruption.

**Members:** 8- and 9-year-olds; White; lower and middle income; two girls and one boy.

**Dates:** 10/31 to 11/28

**Summary of the Work**

*First Session*

I was anxious about starting a group whose members were so young. My coleader, Joanne, had a lot of experience working with children and did not share my anxiety, and this offered me some relief. She had some written activities for children from a former group she had run, and she and I together modified the activities to meet the needs of this group, knowing that it was important to allow for input from the members as well. Two of the members showed up early. For the first session we had expected three members and had been told one member would arrive late. We had a snack prepared and tried to make the two members comfortable, explaining that we would wait for the third member to arrive before actually starting group.

I felt a need to reach out to these two members. I introduced myself, asked their names and ages and where they went to school, and encouraged them to help themselves to the snack. Henry (age 9) and Stacy (age 8) were initially shy but with this invitation helped themselves to juice and crackers. Stacy began talking about her family. Time passed; the third member never arrived. Joanne and I decided to formally start the "group," recognizing that, with only two members, we might need to alter some of our planned activities to decrease the intensity for these two children. I asked if they knew why they were here. I wanted to get a feel for what they had been told about the group and note any reactions. Both were able to share that it was because their parents were "going through a separation."

**Practice Points:** Once again we observe the problem of the group leaders not making some form of opening statement that will let the members understand what the group is all about—rather than just indicating why they were sent to the group. For example: "When parents go through a separation or a divorce, it can be very difficult for the children involved. They can feel sad and sometimes angry as well. Sometimes they feel they have to take sides with their mother or their father, which is hard when they love both. We have this group as a place where you can help each other and we can help you get through this difficult time by talking about what it's like for you or having activities, like drawing, that will help you let us and the other group members know how you are feeling. We are going to start by doing some things that will help us to get to know each other."

Although the children might not take all of the information in such an opening statement in, and recontracting would most likely be necessary, at least the purpose of the group and the purpose of the activity would be explained.

We began our first activity, which involved having the members draw or write their responses to benign questions: something they like, something they don't like, an animal each would like to be and one they wish they had, and then share their work as an effort to increase their comfort level with sharing. Henry drew a picture of not liking when kids fight, which he said was happening at school. I wondered, given this was a group dealing with separation and divorce issues, if he also had not liked when his parents fought—how that felt, the position it put him in. Stacy said she does not have to worry about this because "everyone in my class likes me."

**Practice Points:** The group leader begins to make an effort to connect the child's comment about fighting to the fighting experienced in the family. Another connection, also possible, is that when children are sad and upset about fighting and separations, sometimes they get angry and that can lead to fighting in the school. Putting out both interpretations will help the child elaborate on this "offering" about fighting.

I wanted to set a precedent in this first group that there would be an expectation that members would speak with one another and that by doing so members might find new ways of problem solving. I asked Stacy if she could give Henry some advice about how to avoid ge   tting into situations where fighting might occur. Her response to Henry was to fight back if you had to. She said that is what her father had taught her to do.

A wish that both Henry and Stacy drew was illustrated by a great amount of money (green rectangles). I missed the significance of this wish until a review of the literature helped me to understand how money, in the children's minds, could fill the void that each of them feels.

**Practice Points:** Another interpretation of drawing money could be that since the separation, and even before, having enough money might have been a powerful issue between husband and wife. By asking why they were drawing money, the leaders might have been able to help them express the feelings behind the drawings. Both leaders are new to this work so it will take some time to develop the appropriate interventions.

The next activity involved each member drawing a picture of his or her family. Henry had great difficulty here. He drew a door, then a window, then asked to go to the bathroom. Stacy drew her entire family: all five members were smiling, Mom and Dad were next to each other, and a big heart encircled all of them. Henry's inability to draw his family members and Stacy's wishful illustration seemed to reflect some avoidance and some denial, respectively. (Henry did complete his drawing on his return and drew a smiling child with his mother's arm around him.)

Because of their ages and the fact that this was the first group session, as with issues mentioned earlier, I chose not to explore the significance of how this activity was played out. I knew these would be ongoing and necessary themes to explore, as the artwork demonstrated, and that my coleader and I would need to help these children name their feelings if the group was to be effective. I knew, too, I would need to pay attention to my own resistance or hesitation to explore these emotional, painful issues.

**Practice Points:** Since the children know in a general way what the group is all about, we can assume the drawings relate to the family distress. The group leader may be on target when she identifies her own resistance to acknowledging the reason she refrained from commenting on the connection. One option would have been to just identify the expressed feelings—for example, "It can be hard to draw your family when they don't feel like a happy family anymore" or "I guess you may be drawing a happy family because that is what you would like your family to be." Both comments simply acknowledge the message and do not require "probing" in a first session. It is often the case that the group members are ready to begin but when the content is painful, it is the leaders who are hesitant.

The group leader's recognition of her own resistance to explore painful issues is an important step in helping her to reach for the members' underlying feelings of hurt, anger, and tremendous loss. At times such as these, leaders need supervision or consultation to help them explore their own resistance. These children are astute observers of adults around them and have already received the message that the feelings are taboo and not to be discussed. When they perceive that these adults are ready to hear them, the chances of their responding will greatly increase.

### Second Session

**Practice Points:**   Although the intent of involving group members in explaining the purpose of the group is understandable, given the early stage of the group and the lack of clarity in contracting with the continuing members, it would be better to make a clear statement to the new member first and then involve the others. Note that Sara knows why they are there but is unable to really describe the purpose of the group or how their being in it will help.

Henry, Stacy, and Tara (age 9) participated in group today. Because Tara had missed our first group, I asked Henry and Stacy if they could share with her what took place in the first session. Both Henry and Stacy were able to tell Tara the activities we had done, and Henry even recalled the details of each of the drawing activities. Joanne and I asked the members if they could recall why each of them was here. Tara was able to say, as Henry and Stacy had the week before, that she knew it was because her parents had separated.

**Practice Points:**   The leaders now move into an activity that is more focused on the purpose of the group. Again, in hindsight, it would not have been hard to explain to even these young children why they were being asked to focus on the word *divorce.* It also could have been explained that by hearing each other, they could help each other.

For this session, the plan was to focus on the word *divorce.* The children were asked to brainstorm words that come to mind when they hear this word and determine whether the words have positive ("good") or negative ("bad") meanings to them. The members eagerly responded to this activity. Each took turns writing a word or phrase on the blackboard, and after they finished, we discussed what they had written. Their list was quite comprehensive: the "good" list included "no more fighting" and "parents still love us," and the "bad" list included "separation," "lots of crying," "children feel sad," and "some people think it's their fault." Because *children* was a big word and Stacy had trouble writing it, Henry suggested that she simply write, "We feel sad." I heard this as his ability to identify with her statement and bring its context closer to home.

When Henry wrote, "Some people think it's their fault," I asked him, "Which people?" I wanted to reach into his words and bring what he was saying closer to the group. He responded by mentioning "the children," which led us into a discussion as to whether each of the members had ever felt it was their fault that their parents had separated/divorced. None of them believed that it was; each sounded as if she or he was repeating messages heard from their parents about not feeling responsible.

**Practice Points:**   The work is starting to deepen; however, the group leader holds back on a gut feeling that could be very helpful. For example, she could have said: "I wonder if you hear from your parents that it wasn't your fault, but even so, it still feels like it was your fault. It would be hard not to feel that way."

Following this discussion, the members drew pictures illustrating aspects of what had just been discussed. Henry's picture was incredible; the top of the page said "Separation" and under this heading, he drew a crying child, alone, in the middle of the page with Mom walking off the right-hand side of the page and Dad walking off the left side. All you could see was one leg and one hand of each parent. It was a powerfully vivid and moving depiction of Henry's understanding of "separation."

The last part of the session involved reading a series of statements and the members deciding if these statements were true or false. Somehow, animal puppets had gotten passed around, to the leaders as well, and we all agreed to respond through the puppets. I did not know if it was due to difficult subject matter or the lateness of the hour, or perhaps a combination of both, but the group all seemed to be responding at once. I asked that one puppet speak at a time. I recognized that this exercise was the most sensitive one in which the group had participated so far.

**Practice Points:** The strong need of the children to deal with these feelings, at least with understanding adults such as the leader, leads them to use the activity as a powerful form of communications. The group leader's intervention to set the rules may actually be emerging more from her discomfort than theirs. As an alternative to repeating the rule, she could point out what is going on in the group: "You know when we talk about these sad things it can be hard to talk one at a time. You get so full of feelings you can't really hold them in. Maybe I can help by calling on you one at a time. Would that help?"

Again I noticed, however, that discussion seemed to travel between each member and my coleader or the members and me. I once more tried to encourage discussion among the members. Each time someone responded to a statement, I would say, "Stacy and Henry, Tara thinks this statement is true because . . . what do each of you think?" My effort at this time only resulted in their responding to me.

**Practice Points:** Sometimes the right intervention can seem so simple in retrospect. For example, if the leader trusted her gut she could observe to the children that each time they speak or respond to a question they speak to the leaders and not each other. She could ask them why they thought that was so. A discussion of the process would most likely reveal that they don't understand how other kids with the same problem could be helpful. This could lead to the contracting piece left out at the start—what is mutual aid all about? How can kids who have the same problems and feelings help each other?

I wished that this last exercise could have been given more time. The statements had evoked a lot of feeling and a lot of sharing, but the session was over. In comparison with the previous week's session, I did feel discussion of feelings associated with separation and divorce had taken place and that through their words, pictures, and puppets, much had been shared. It was only the second group and the first group for the three members together. I am actually struck, as I write this, at the courage and vulnerability the members displayed. I hoped that next week's session would provide another opportunity for the members to share their feelings and recognize their capacity for mutual aid.

### Third Session

Joanne asked the group what changes when parents separate or divorce. I overheard Stacy and Henry both say the word *disappears.* I commented that they had both used this word and asked each of them to share what they meant by this word. I was trying to create a bridge by showing the members there was similarity in their response.

**Practice Points:** By astutely listening and asking the children to elaborate on the use of the word *disappear,* the leader opens up a new, powerful, and poignant theme in the group. It's not only physical items that disappear, but important people do as well. The leader is also respectful of the differences between the children and rather than putting Henry on the spot she acknowledges how different separation can be for different families.

Stacy said that things disappear, like the couch or the television—one parent gets the couch, one the television. I looked to Henry for his response, and he immediately offered that a parent can disappear. Because I had learned through Joanne that Henry's father had left 4 years earlier, I knew there was a lot of feeling behind what Henry had shared. The two other members in the group had both parents very much in their lives, as well as brothers and sisters and new partners for their parents; Henry had only his mother. I do not believe the other members were aware of the significance of Henry's remark and therefore were not sensitive to what he had shared. I struggled with how to proceed. I chose to mention how divorce can be different in different people's homes. I discussed that for some people divorce may mean new people in their lives if mom or dad gets a new boyfriend or girlfriend and that this can be positive or negative; I also said that it can mean being single for a parent, which can be lonely for the parent and maybe for the child; and I added that it can mean leaving a place one has lived; leaving school, friends, grandparents, other family members; or perhaps moving to a place where one is closer to relatives or family friends. This created discussion among the children as they began to relate stories about their parents' partners, their grandparents, and their friends who were also experiencing parental separation/divorce.

**Practice Points:** Once again we see the group leaders using a creative idea to help the group members connect their feelings with issues related to the divorce. By writing them down and then sharing them, a structure is provided to discuss and share these feelings. It is sad that their view of the "best" thing about divorce is that family fighting has stopped.

Our activity for this session involved giving each member a sheet of paper with three faces on it, one face reflecting happiness, one reflecting sadness, and one reflecting fear. Each child was to write underneath each face the best, worst, and scariest thing about divorce, respectively. The children immediately responded to this task; all were clearly concentrating on what they were writing. When they were finished writing, they shared what they had written. All of them agreed that "no more fighting" was the best thing about divorce, a theme they had perhaps recalled from the previous week.

A variety of answers were written, and both Joanne and I encouraged each of the members to think about whether what the others had written applied to them. Not surprisingly, the children could identify with several of the examples. They all agreed with Tara's comment that another "best" thing about divorce is that "your parents still love you" and with Henry's comment that a "worst" thing about divorce is that "some kids think it's their fault." While many of these themes had been discussed the previous week, I saw that the members were incorporating some of what was being shared in our group. In addition, this week it seemed there was more feeling behind the words. I wondered if Joanne and I were functioning well as leaders and creating a safe environment in which the children's feelings could emerge, as the group seemed to be feeling more comfortable with one another, and in turn, more comfortable sharing.

**Practice Points:** In addition to tuning in to the general themes raised each week, and to the developing group process themes, the leaders are tuned in to the impact of the calendar. Family separation and family functioning is affected by the holidays.

The holidays may have been the times when the fighting was more pronounced, and the losses of family members and family structure will be more potent as Thanksgiving approaches. In the time before the conflict, holidays may have been important and positive family experiences that have been lost and may be missed.

### Fourth Session

With the Thanksgiving holiday occurring this week, I thought it would be appropriate to focus our fourth session on how the members were feeling about the upcoming holiday and what it represented to them in terms of how and with whom they had spent it in the past, what has changed for each of them, and what they anticipated for this holiday. I spoke with my coleader about this idea, and she agreed that it would be useful and that we could modify any activity to include this event. As has been described, each week so far had revisited discussion about expressing feelings of sadness, anger, and happiness in response to divorce. While in some ways it seemed redundant, my coleader and I recognized that the purpose of this group was to get the members to feel increasingly comfortable acknowledging and voicing their feelings. The Thanksgiving holiday seemed a perfect vehicle to elicit current struggles each member might be experiencing.

When this session started, I noticed that all three members immediately began chatting, eating their snack, and asking about today's plans in a more animated display than I had seen in previous weeks. I used this opportunity to get right down to work, and I asked what was happening this week that made this week special. Each child mentioned that it was Thanksgiving. I asked if they could tell the group how each one would be spending the time. All three members began speaking at once. I asked the group if we could review the group contract. Tara and Henry raised their hands. I explained that raising hands was not necessary; but that it seemed that they had the right idea. Tara said that only one person should speak at a time. I commented that it seemed all three of them had something interesting to say and that I did not want to miss anyone's contribution. Stacy asked if she could go first, because she was the youngest. The children described how they would be spending the holiday and then drew pictures of how they envisioned feeling on that day.

All three members reported that the previous Thanksgiving had been their favorite Thanksgiving; Joanne and I looked at each other skeptically, because we knew that for Stacy in particular, her parents' marriage had already been in serious trouble. Each child commented that they were with family and had good food. Stacy talked in great detail about her grandmother's soup. I recalled Stacy's difficulty in focusing on her personal situation in our first group session.

I mentioned that holidays can be very special because for many people they are spent with loved ones, but that they can also be difficult when families change or when someone wants to be in two places at once. The members continued to draw. Tara commented that she has an aunt who draws well, but not as well as Henry.

Despite the members' inability to tolerate what I was attempting to raise, this was the first time I had heard an unsolicited comment from one group member to another. While this may have demonstrated a member's aligning with another member rather than dealing with the issue at hand (flight), other examples of this interaction occurred in the session that supported my initial sense that the members seemed more connected and willing to speak to one another. Nevertheless, Joanne and I looked at each other and agreed we needed to move on to another activity; the members had become absorbed in their artwork and needed a push.

**Practice Points:** As the group develops the leaders introduce other creative activity forms that can facilitate the work. The sharing of vignettes can provide some structure for exploring difficult feelings. Once again, it would not be difficult to explain to the children, in simple terms, how the vignettes work and why they might be helpful.

Joanne and I took turns creating vignettes, and the members had to decide whether someone described in the vignette would feel happy, sad, angry, or disappointed. We spontaneously created scenarios that seemed relevant to what the children might be facing this week. I went first and offered: "Mary's father is supposed to pick her up at 10 A.M. on Thanksgiving. He calls her at 11 A.M. to say he can't make it because he's decided to go to his girlfriend's house. Mary feels . . ."

The scenarios became more complicated as Joanne and I introduced stepparent and stepsibling issues and other conflicting themes that might involve the members. Each child responded quite positively to this activity. They were spirited and engaged, and each contributed sound reasons for feeling as the character might have felt. Often the members personalized the scenarios by saying how he or she would feel. After Joanne and I had each done two scenarios, Tara asked if she could make one up. Stacy followed. She described a situation where a mother's boyfriend was angry at a child and threw the child down the stairs. She wanted to know how the mother should feel.

Henry and Tara responded together that the mother would be sad the child was hurt. I felt an urgent need to make a stronger statement, as well as model for the members the acceptability of their own strong feelings. I added, in a very firm voice, that if I was the mother, I would be furious that my boyfriend had hurt my child and that no matter how my child behaved, no child deserved to be hurt and that my boyfriend's behavior was absolutely unacceptable. Recalling the activity we had played in a previous session, Stacy acted like the judge and said I had given the best response for that scenario. It was a scenario Joanne and I would need to be alerted to.

**Practice Points:** The scenario shared by Stacy raised a warning flag for the leaders that they need to address in an individual session. The group leaders are mandated reporters, and even an indirect communication of possible abuse must be explored, and if confirmed, shared with the appropriate child welfare agency. Even if the individual conversation does not provide confirmation, the leaders should alert the child protection office so that a more thorough investigation can take place. In retrospect, the discussion about confidentiality, so crucial in any beginning session, was not reported in this record of group meetings. If not explicitly expressed before, it should be addressed after this comment. A more complete discussion of confidentiality and mandated reporting issues can be found in Chapter 4.

The children's vignettes were complicated and revealing. Each member seemed to be an internal leader—creating a vignette and listening to each person's discussion as to why someone might feel as he or she did. This activity seemed to reduce the amount of denial and avoidance I had sensed earlier; by removing the focus from the three members, which in a group of three may have simply been too intense, the members could be more spontaneous in exposing their feelings. Time had run out, and the members did not want to leave. I told the group that everyone had made wonderful, creative, and sensitive contributions and that we would talk more next week. I wanted to praise and reinforce their willingness to take risks and to take ownership of their group by conceiving their own stories.

*Fifth Session*

My coleader and I decided to focus this week's session on anger. Prior to group, she and I had agreed that we would use vignettes again because they seemed to be an effective way of getting each of the members to reveal their own feelings, sometimes in the guise of sharing through what the characters might feel and sometimes through making identifications with the characters as to how they, the members, would feel.

The group opened as it did last week; the members were snacking and chatting with each other and seeming comfortable as they discussed how they had spent their Thanksgiving holiday. The members asked what we were going to do today, and Joanne responded that we would be talking about anger. I felt a need to review why we were all together and to remind the group that there was a shared purpose to our meeting. I asked the group what we had been discussing in our previous weeks together and what it was that brought us all together. Tara immediately responded, "Divorce." I nodded and then asked if anyone could be more specific. Stacy said we talked about "happy, sad, and mad." I asked the group if this is different from what they do in school and, if it is, in what way. Everyone said it was different and that in school people do not discuss their feelings. I asked the group why they thought this was so. A silence followed.

I thought that the members might be feeling uncomfortable and that their silence reflected their own discomfort and sense of isolation regarding their ability to discuss their family situations freely at school, and perhaps even in the group. I missed an opportunity to acknowledge their discomfort and instead tried to educate them and normalize their experience about the common occurrence of divorce. I asked the members if they knew other children at school whose parents were separated and divorced. My coleader pointed out that almost half of all marriages end in divorce. Not surprisingly, the intellectualized response by my coleader, and perhaps by me, generated little response, and my coleader and I moved on to our planned activity.

**Practice Points:** The leaders here took the children to the edge of an important discussion. The question about what makes it hard to talk about these subjects was on target; however, the children's silence in response moved the leaders away from this conversation. This was the moment when reaching into the silence, perhaps by offering some specific possible reasons why it is hard, could help the children deepen the conversation. The group leader showed important insight in her learning process as she recognized her own intellectualizing response. Perhaps the silence and intellectualizing arose because talking about anger—the focus of the session— was particularly difficult for both the leaders and the children.

We asked the children what makes them angry about divorce. They came up with several responses. I tried to draw them out to have them reveal the depth that they had in previous sessions, and I pointed out connections to other responses when similarities were evident to me. Joanne and I then took turns creating vignettes that we knew would resonate for the members in our group. What followed was a lengthy discussion about absent parents, new partners in their parents' lives, and contending with the children of these partners.

Tara and Henry both described wanting to kill a new baby who was born to "Walter's mother and her boyfriend," characters in a scenario. I thought it was important to acknowledge the expression of their feelings and again tried to elicit from them why they might want to kill this baby, whom else might they be angry at, what would happen if they really did kill the baby, and what their loved ones might feel about them. Following this opportunity for them to play out this scenario, I asked if it was really OK to kill a baby. The members all said no. I then asked if anyone could think of other solutions to this dilemma, because killing a baby is really not OK. I hoped that this would instill confidence in the members' own capacity to problem-solve. Henry and Stacy smiled. Tara, who had a newborn in her home, did not. Henry, an only child, said maybe "Walter" could play with the baby; I asked Henry what that would do. He replied, "Walter might like it." I acknowledged that Walter might enjoy having a younger sibling after all, even though his feelings might remain mixed. This seemed to give Tara permission to discuss that it is hard having only younger siblings and that she wished she were not the oldest in her family.

One of the vignettes created a scenario of a friend wanting to talk to someone about his parents' divorce. I asked the group whom this friend could speak with. Henry said that he would tell this person to speak to a counselor or teacher. I said that this was a very good suggestion. I then highlighted for the group that each of them could be very supportive to a friend because they have gone through a similar situation and that it might help the friend to feel less alone. We again began discussing why talking about these feelings is difficult. I noticed that all three children had moved into the corner and were focused on a doll house, standing with their backs turned toward Joanne and me. This time I was not going to miss the opportunity to acknowledge their discomfort. I said to the group, "I have asked all of you a question. Is it hard for you to talk about this stuff right now?" I was stunned by the honesty of their reactions. Henry immediately nodded, and Stacy and Tara said, "Yes." I chose to reach further to have them identify their discomfort. "How come?" I asked. There was no answer, and this session was over. I again wanted to praise their willingness and bravery to take risks and share their feelings. I commented, "That's OK. You've all been doing a great job today talking about issues that are hard for everyone. It's not easy, and you've all been very brave."

**Practice Summary.** As the group sessions approach an ending, preparing for termination sessions with a group of children for whom the loss of adults has been central will be important. A good start will be for the leaders to tune in to their own feelings, given that the record reveals they have become close to these children and the children to them.

*A Knitting Group for Homeless Teen Mothers: Empowering Members and the Group Leader* This final example of an activity group is unusual, interesting, creative, and impressive. Rebmann (2006) writes about her first-year placement as an MSW student in a residence for homeless teen mothers. The author puts the activity in the context of empowerment both for her group members and herself describing an initial negative reaction to the group from her field placement supervisor. Citing Freund (1993) she describes herself and the group "moving from dependence, to self-assertion and risk-taking, to communal cooperation by individuals and the group-as-a-whole" (p. 5). Rebmann identifies many of the issues facing these clients:

Homeless teen mothers of color confront issues of poverty, homelessness, racism, motherhood, and education. They negotiate relationship with boyfriends, the baby-daddies, friends, family, teachers and social workers. Often when a client is acting particularly difficult, the staff at the TLP [Teen Living Program] remind themselves that if these girls had anywhere else to go, they wouldn't be here. The average stay for these girls, before finding permanent housing, was ten months to two years, depending on their age when they entered the program, the younger girls staying the longest. (p. 7)

The project emerged at a life skills group during a time when each person, including the leader, was asked to say something positive about themselves. When the leader, wearing (in her words) "a rather unflattering hand-knit green sweater that was about ten sizes too large for me" (p. 8), proposed the group, the girls were excited and asked to be taught to knit as soon as possible. They then listed the many items they wanted to create for themselves and their children. The leader assured them she would see what she could do.

This interest in knitting occurred at the halfway point in the placement. The student/author identifies some general difficulty in communication with her supervisor, who did not approve of the activity and refused to fund it even after requesting a budget from the student. The disempowered student group leader returned the purchased supplies and gave up on the idea of a knitting group, adopting a passive acceptance of the organizational obstacles. The group's and the leader's disempowerment was increased when the group leader was informed that her group time would be taken over for three weeks by an outside conflict-management team that wanted to try their techniques on this population. The author describes what happened:

> The subsequent three sessions were torturous. The girls were used to guest speakers but were confused by the presence of staff members. They responded minimally to the prompts of the facilitators when they probed for examples of conflicts to role play. They arrived to group for the candy but then participated through shrugs and "I dunnos." (p. 11)

The author describes what amounts to active and passive aggressiveness as the girls fiddle with cell phones, talk to each other, or verbally attack staff about rules they disagreed with (e.g., curfew) but could not change. The outside facilitators seemed at a loss on how to intervene, and the student group leader retreated into passiveness "buried in the couch."

It's at this point that the group leader begins to assert herself, first, by using her case management meeting with one girl, Patricia, who expressed the most desire to learn knitting, and bringing in her own leftover materials. The group leader described this as her "covert and unsanctioned mission." The first step was to teach her how to "tie a slipknot and put it on the needle" and then how to "cast on." (I have to admit that at this point in reading the article I, a nonknitter, was impressed but lost.) A chant was created together: "in the hole, to the back, wrap around, pull it through" (p. 13). When Patricia started, so did the shouting: "Stupid mofo get on there . . . c'mon you monkey!" The group leader had warned her to be prepared for the yelling, and Patricia asked: "Is this the yelling that happens in knitting?" The leader said yes and sat next to her for 45 minutes until they had "cast on an entire row."

The next time they met Patricia had brought Ann with her, a 20-year-old Jamaican woman. With some difficulty, and some shouting, Ann tried with less success than Patricia who was getting the hang of it. At one point when Ann was discouraged about how "ugly" her knitting looked, the leader reminded her of the sweater she had worn the first night they had talked about knitting. She pointed out that the sweater was really ugly, to which Ann agreed, but that the leader was proud because she had done it herself. Over the next few weeks other girls joined in, and it was clear many used the knitting activity as a social activity to talk with the other girls and the leader. Some of the early knitters, like Patricia, were able to take a teaching role with new girls and begin to help them develop their skills. With the knitting materials spread out on the floor, the activity became less covert but still unsanctioned. The student worried when the supervisor walked in on the noisy activity, and she went into the supervisor's office to receive the expected reprimand. That's not what happened:

"Wow?" she [the supervisor] exclaimed . . . are they really into it? She questioned excitedly. . . . To my great surprise she was very enthusiastic about the whole intervention. I took a list and explained what had been going on and how eager the girls had been to learn. My supervisor responded by sanctioning the lessons and offering for the program to pay for supplies. (p. 19)

This example has a number of important lessons. As pointed out earlier, an activity can be the medium through which important forms of mutual aid can take place. Young homeless mothers can be empowered to make something for themselves and their children. The parallel process I have identified in supervision (Shulman, 2010) is illustrated as the author experiences disempowerment in her supervision, and that is then extended to her client group. I have long wondered how social workers who feel oppressed, hopeless, and helpless in their own agencies can help clients who feel the same way in their lives. This student used stealth to empower herself and her clients, which has some drawbacks in any system. In Chapter 15, I will focus on the skills of helping clients to negotiate the agency that may offer some better (and safer) alternatives.

These two illustrations of work with activity-focused groups bring to a close our description of the work phase model in a mutual-aid group. Having presented the general model of the individual–group interaction, I can now examine the elements in depth and explore some variations on the theme. In the next chapter, I will examine the individual's role in the group, concentrating on how members are informally assigned to play functional roles such as scapegoat, deviant, and internal leader. I will also explore the needs of the group-as-a-whole and the way in which the group leader can help the group work on its central tasks.

## Chapter Summary

Our discussion in this chapter illustrated a number of points. First, we saw how the group leader needs to work with the individual and the group as they reach out to each other in the beginning stages of a session. Second, we found that mutual aid deals with general themes of concern as well as specific problems of individuals. The examples in this chapter illustrated how groups can move from the general to the specific and from the specific to the general. The last excerpt illustrated the importance of striving for resolution and transition as meetings draw to an end.

In an effort to describe this complex process in simple terms, I have had to oversimplify the central ideas. The work phase session does not proceed in four stages as neatly as I have outlined it here. Furthermore, the skill categories are not mutually exclusive. For example, as the sessional contracting proceeds, the leader will use elaborating, empathic, and demand-for-work skills. The advantage of describing this complex process in an oversimplified form is that it gives us a model with which to orient ourselves as I explore each stage and each skill factor in further detail.

I would like to reinforce an idea that will have already come to the reader's attention. This model of the middle phase of a group meeting could just as easily be written in the context of individual or family work, or other forms of counseling and task groups.

Finally, the chapter explored the unique issues involved in using activities in groups and provided an example of working with a children's group over time and a knitting group for homeless teen mothers that led to empowerment for group members and the student/leader.

# Related Online Content and Activities

 Visit *The Skills of Helping Individuals, Families, Groups, and Communities,* Seventh Edition, CourseMate website at **www.cengagebrain.com** for learning tools such as glossary terms, links to related websites, and chapter practice quizzes. The website for this chapter also features additional notes from the author.

# Competency Notes

The following is a list of Council on Social Work Education (CSWE) recommended competencies and practice behaviors for social work students defined in Educational Policy and Accreditation Standard (EPAS) and addressed in this chapter.

**EP 2.1.1b** Practice personal reflection and self-correction to assure continual professional development (p. 440)

**EP 2.1.1e** Engage in career-long learning (p. 440)

**EP 2.1.1f** Use supervision and consultation (p. 440)

**EP 2.1.6b** Use research evidence to inform practice (p. 473)

**EP 2.1.7a** Utilize conceptual frameworks to guide the process of assessment, intervention, and evaluation (p. 436)

**EP 2.1.10a** Substantively and affectively prepare for action with individuals, families, groups, organizations, and communities (p. 436)

**EP 2.1.10b** Use empathy and other interpersonal skills (p. 456)

**EP 2.1.10d** Collect, organize, and interpret client data (p. 436)

**EP 2.1.10f** Develop mutually agreed-on intervention goals and objectives (p. 436)

**EP 2.1.10l** Facilitate transitions and endings (p. 481)

# Working with the Individual and the Group

The model presented thus far suggests that the group leader always has two clients: the individual and the group. In this chapter an artificial separation of these two clients is employed to deepen your understanding of each in interaction with the other. First I will focus on the individual within the group, discussing how clients bring their personalities to bear in their group interactions. The concept of role is used to help describe how individual personality is translated into group interaction. Many common patterns of individual-group relationships are described and illustrated; for example, I look at scapegoats, deviant members, gatekeepers, and monopolizers. As these individuals are isolated for closer analysis, you will see that understanding individual clients without considering them in the context of their group interaction is often impossible.

In the second part of this chapter, I will examine the concept of the group-as-a-whole. This is the entity that is created when more than one client is involved at a time. I will introduce an *organismic model* and illustrate some of the group leader's tasks when he or she must intervene to help in the growth of the second client, the group.

# The Concept of Role in a Dynamic System

**EP 2.1.3a**
**EP 2.1.3b**

Two ideas central to the discussion of the individual in a group are role and dynamic system. Ackerman (1958) describes the ways in which the term *role* has been used and proposes his own definition:

> Sociology, social psychology, and anthropology approach the problems of role through the use of special concepts and techniques. They apply the term in two distinct ways, meaning either the "role" of the person in a specific, transient, social position or the characteristic "role" of the individual in society as determined by his social class status. Working in the psychodynamic frame of reference, I shall use the term to represent an adaptational unit of personality in action. "Social role" is here conceived as synonymous with the operations of the "social self" or social identity of the person in the context of a defined life situation. (p. 53)

Ackerman suggests that the individual has both a private "inner self" and a social "outer self" that emphasizes externally oriented aspects of his or her personality. I use this idea of social role in the following way: When clients begin a group, they present their outer selves as their way of adapting to the pressures and demands of the group context. Their pattern of action represents their social role. Ackerman argues that incongruity between the reality of the inner self and the outer self presented in a group can cause tension. In many ways, the task of the group leader involves helping individuals find the freedom to express their inner selves in the group. The central idea is that each member brings to the group an established pattern of translating a unique personality into social action.

## The Impact of Oppression on Social Role

**EP 2.1.4a**
**EP 2.1.4c**
**EP 2.1.5a**

When we consider oppressed and vulnerable groups, we can integrate Ackerman's notions about role into the oppression psychology concepts described in Chapter 2. The outer self of survivors of oppression represents their adaptive behavior to the defined situation of oppression. We can understand the incongruity between the outer self, which they present in social situations, and the inner self as one of the defense mechanisms employed in an effort to cope. This resulting incongruity is a form of alienation from self-identity, as described by Fanon (Bulhan, 1985). The effort in the mutual-aid group is to help members use the group to integrate their inner and outer selves and to find more adaptive mechanisms to cope with oppression, including personal and social action. The small group is a microcosm of the larger society. If we consider the impact of oppression, our understanding of the role played by a survivor of oppression within a group context deepens.

Keeping in mind the concept of individual roles, we can view the group as a dynamic system, in which the movements of each part (member) are partially affected by the movements of the other parts (the other members). This view is rooted in the classic work of Kurt Lewin (1935, 1951), who is often considered the founder of group dynamics. Thus, members bring their outer selves to this dynamic system of the group and then adapt to the system through their social roles. All group members engage in this process of adaptation.

More recently the concept of *impression management (IM)* has emerged as a model for the way in which people present themselves to others to effect how they wish others to perceive them. This model is rooted in the early classic work of Erving Goffman (1959) whose book *The Presentation of Self in Everyday Life* explored the way we consciously or unconsciously shape the image projected to others. More recently, social psychologists have been exploring the topic of self-presentation, impression management, and interpersonal behavior in a number of contexts; see, for example, Learly (1996) and Schlenker (2003). These theorists describe efforts on the part of individuals to control how they and their ideas are perceived as essential elements of human interaction.

## Formal and Informal Roles in the Group

Patterned social roles are most easily illustrated using an example from a formal, organized task group, such as a students' association. To function effectively, the association usually identifies specific tasks that group members must assume and then assigns these jobs by some form of division of labor. For example, the association may need a chairperson or president, a secretary, a treasurer, and a program coordinator. The essential idea is that group roles are functionally necessary and are required for productive work. In taking on any of these roles, specific members will bring their own sense of social role to bear. For example, depending on their experience, background, skills, and sense of social role, various members would implement the role of chairperson differently. Because the group is a dynamic system, the group and its individual members will also affect the chairperson's implementation of this role to a certain extent. The actions of the chairperson are best described as the product of the interaction among the individual's sense of social role, the role of chairperson as defined by the group, and the particular dynamics of the group and its members.

The roles just described are formal. Every group also creates less formal roles to help in its work, even though these might never be openly acknowledged. It's important to remember at this point that when I use the word *group,* I am referring to this entity I call the group-as-a-whole which is created by members but is more than the sum of its parts. For example, in a group led by a professional group leader who guides the discussion as an external leader, one or more internal leaders may emerge as if they had been formally elected. The individuals who assume internal leadership in a group play a social role within the group that includes this function. By responding positively to them, group members encourage the internal leaders' assumption of this important role. The key and in fact crucial concept here is that the group itself has something to do with assigning and encouraging the playing of the individual role. Think back to groups you have participated in. Remember the class clown who you and your classmates encouraged by your laughter? Think back to your formal and informal social groups and how one or another member played a leadership role and, by following him or her, you recognized that person's leadership.

Other, less constructive functional roles can emerge in a group; these reflect maladaptative rather than healthy development. For example, *scapegoats* are often selected by the group because they possess the personal characteristic that members most dislike or fear in themselves. Thus, a group of young teenage boys who are worried about sexual identity may select as the group scapegoat the teen that seems least "macho" or at least less sure of himself in his presentation. The members, of course, do not hold an election for such roles. It is not as if the group members held an informal meeting, prior to the group session, and asked for volunteers to be the group scapegoats, internal leaders, deviant members, and so on. If the group has a need for these roles, however, they will go through a subtle, informal process to select members to fill them. The dysfunctional aspect of employing a scapegoat is that it often leads the group members to avoid facing their own concerns and feelings by projecting them onto the scapegoat.

Similarly, individuals do not raise their hands and volunteer to act as scapegoats, pointing out that they have successfully played the scapegoat role in their families and social groups for most of their lives. The scapegoat in the group usually subtly volunteers for this role, because it is consistent with that individual's concept of his or her social role. Adapting to groups by playing this social role is as dysfunctional for the individual scapegoat as it is for the group as a whole. Once again, the idea of the group as a dynamic system helps us to understand the process of scapegoating in a dynamic way. (The next section explores the role of scapegoat in greater detail.)

In the sections that follow, I will look at informal roles that are developed in groups, such as scapegoats, deviant members, monopolizers, and gatekeepers. In each case, the discussion focuses on analyzing the dynamics as they reflect the individual's social role within the group. In addition, I will examine the skills of the group leader as he or she implements the individualizing part of the work while simultaneously addressing the second client, the group.

## The Scapegoat

**EP 2.1.4a**
**EP 2.1.5a**

The discussion of individual roles in the group begins with the *scapegoat* because it is one of the most common—and one of the most distressing—problems in work with groups. The scapegoat is a group member who is attacked, verbally or physically, by other members. These members usually project onto the scapegoat their own negative feelings about themselves. The scapegoat role is often interactive in nature, with the scapegoat fulfilling a functional role in the group. Whether it is the overt scapegoating that takes place in groups of children and adolescents or the more subtle type that occurs in adult groups, the impact on the group and the group leader can be profound. As I explore this particular role in detail, I shall introduce several important concepts regarding social role in the group and the function of the group leader. These central ideas will reemerge as I examine other roles. This discussion can then serve as a general model to analyze individual roles in the group.

First, we must consider the history of the term *scapegoat*. Douglas (1995) attributes the origin of the term to the 15th-century biblical scholar and translator Tyndale. Tyndale's translation of sections of Leviticus referred to an ancient ritual among the Hebrews that was practiced on the Day of Atonement. Two live goats were brought to the altar of the tabernacle. One was killed as a sacrifice and skinned with the skin of the goat called a "scape"; after the high priest transferred his own sins and the sins of the people onto the scape of the first goat, it was placed on the second goat which was taken to the wilderness and allowed to escape. Douglas suggests, "If Tyndale had read into the Hebrew idea that the goat was 'suffered to escape,' then his coining of the word 'scapegoat' becomes much clearer" (1995, p. 8). Douglas describes the scapegoat ritual as essentially a process of purification, which means—in essence—that its practitioners felt that they were contaminated by the transgressions of their daily lives, and that the ritual of scapegoating would disperse that contamination and reinstate them as clean in their own eyes and, more importantly, in the eyes of their god (1995, p. 14).

Whole populations, such as African Americans, Hispanics, Jews, the mentally ill, physically disabled, immigrants, and gays and lesbians, have experienced extreme forms of scapegoating as part of the systematic oppression described in Chapter 2. These have included the projection of negative stereotypes as an underlying justification for slavery, as well as more current forms of economic and social oppression; anti-Semitism and the Holocaust, in which millions of Jews (as well as many homosexuals, gypsies, and others) were systematically killed; and gay-bashing activities in which gays and lesbians are physically attacked on the street or serve as the butt of homophobic jokes. More recently, the immigrant Hispanic population, both legal and illegal, has served as political scapegoats for politicians trying to use this group to tap into underlying stereotypes and biases held by a portion of the larger population, and shocking and random physical attacks on immigrants have occurred in some communities.

Bell and Vogel (1960) have described the dynamics of this phenomenon in the family group, emphasizing the functional role played by the scapegoat in maintaining equilibrium in the family by drawing all of the problems onto him- or herself. Many scapegoats in groups have been socialized into this social role by their family experiences and are ready to assume it in each new group they enter.

Scapegoating is also discussed by Garland and Kolodny (1965), who provide an interesting analysis of the forms of scapegoating that are prevalent in practice:

> No single phenomenon occasions more distress to the outside observer than the act of scapegoating. Frequently violent in its undertones, if not in actual form, it violates every ethical tenet to which our society officially subscribes. As part of that society, the group worker confronted with scapegoating in the midst of interaction often finds himself caught up in a welter of primitive feelings, punitive and pitying, and assailed by morbid reflections on the unfairness of fate which leaves one weak and others strong. (p. 124)

In an early article of mine I address the common mistake in practice I called the *preemptive intervention*, in which the group leader moves into the interaction between the scapegoat and group in a way that preempts the opportunity for either the group or the individual to deal with the problem (Shulman, 1967). Most often, when the group leader protects the scapegoat, the hostility of the other group members merely takes more covert forms. Appeals to fairness or requests to give the member a chance do not seem to help, and the group leader is usually left feeling frustrated, the scapegoat hurt, and the group members guilty.

As we think about scapegoating in the group, the concepts of social role and the group as a dynamic system provide us with clues to the meaning of this interaction. We cannot understand the behavior of the scapegoat simply as a manifestation of his or her "personality." Rather, it is a result of the interaction between the scapegoat's sense of social role and the group's functional needs. The relationship between the individual role and the group need becomes clear if the group loses its scapegoat—if, for example, the member drops out of the group. As though operating on an unconscious command, the group immediately searches for a new candidate to take the scapegoat's place. One member is usually waiting to do so. It is not uncommon in the family dynamics that when a scapegoat child grows up and leaves home, another child moves into the role.

An example from work with a group of teenage girls in a school follows. The key concept for the reader to keep in mind is to avoid taking sides and to *be with the individual and the group at the same time*. Another important concept is to see the scapegoating process itself as a form of communication to the group leader. This entity I call the group-as-a-whole is indirectly, and most likely unconsciously, sending a message about the members' internal struggle. Thus, once again, there is no dichotomy between process and content.

***African American and Hispanic Teenage Girls in a School*** This example illustrates the scapegoating process, some of the pitfalls the group leader faces, and effective strategies for intervention. In the example, we see a new group leader's interventions with a group of teenage girls over a 2-month period in a school setting. The group leader was White, and the girls were African American and Hispanic. The group leader started this work by developing insights into the scapegoating process and tuning in to her feelings.

**Practice Points:** Her protective responses toward the scapegoat were subtle; she tried to deal with the problem indirectly because of her concern with the possibility of hurting the member who was being scapegoated. Although she never directly confronted the scapegoating process, she did deal with the concerns of the second client, the group, which led the group to have less need for a scapegoat.

> **Client Description and Time Frame:** This is a seventh-grade girls' peer support group of 12- and 13-year-old adolescents (three African American and two Hispanic girls) from a racially mixed, low-income part of the city. The time frame is from December 5 through February 6.
>
> **Description of the Problem (from the group leader's perception):** This group is projecting its dependency needs onto one individual, causing the group to remain in the beginning stage of development. This individual, Rachel, acts out these dependency needs for the group. Rachel does her own thing, not involving herself in any group activities and keeping to herself. The group's investment in the role of the scapegoat both hinders and helps the development of the group as it pushes toward its next stage, intimacy.
>
> **How the Problem Came to the Attention of the Group Leaders:** On January 23, I observed that Rachel sat away from the other members of the group and refused to join in the group activity (which was painting) and was unwilling to speak. This behavior brought a negative reaction from the group, and the other girls hypothesized about why she was acting like a loner. The group soon ignored this behavior when Lisa brought up a "hypothetical" situation in which she was involved. Lisa stated that she was tired of a girl she used to be friends with and now does not like anymore. Lisa asked the group for advice about what to do and how to tell this girl.
>
> At this point, I realized that the girl she was discussing was Rachel. When questioned by the other girls as to who this girl was, Lisa would not say. At this moment, I was very unsure of my position as a group leader and what I should do about the situation. My first instinct was to see this as an issue that needed to be dealt with by Rachel and Lisa only, but, in thinking about it further, I decided it was indeed a group problem, especially considering our group goal of improving peer relations. It became clear to me that this need for the role of a scapegoat was an issue for the entire group.

**Practice Points:** The group leader's first tendancy to see this as a problem between Rachel and Lisa is not unusual since she does not see the group-as-a-whole in a dynamic manner. She also is just beginning to understand the integration of process and content. That is, this apparent conflict between the two girls, handled in an indirect manner, is not at all uncommon for girls at this age and thus represents an opportunity to address the larger issue of peer relations.

### Summary of the Work

*December 5 (First Session)*

We were discussing the purpose of the group, and I asked them what they thought some of the rules should be. Most of the members jumped in and offered suggestions, many of them expressing concern about confidentiality and "secrets." Rachel and Kim sat on either side of me, neither of them saying anything, but they nodded when Lisa and Amy asked them what they thought of a rule or an idea they suggested.

I attempted to engage Rachel and Kim in conversation, and I gave the group permission to make their own rules. I asked them both what they thought we should do as a group if someone broke our rule of confidentiality. They both replied by looking confused and shrugging their shoulders. Rachel said, "I don't know—what do you mean?" Lisa immediately jumped in, asked Rachel if she was "deaf or what?" and gave her idea of a "punishment," causing Rachel to sink in her chair and look down at the floor.

I could sense what was going on, but I did not know how to respond to it. Looking back, I can see that these were all issues related to the theme of authority. I did not want to discourage anyone from saying what she wanted, and I did not want to push anyone into talking if she did not want to. I was simply thrilled that anyone was saying anything, and that they were enthused about the group.

**Practice Points:** The group leader's honesty in this early session is refreshing. She is both pleased that any conversation is taking place but also unclear about how to implement the group's purpose and especially about her role. She is clearer in the next session as she tries to help Kim reach out for help from the group. However, as the group gets into the details and as the conversation flows, the leader is still unclear about how to respond.

*December 12 (Second Session)*

Kim had a problem, and I supported her bringing it to the group. Kim told the group that she had a problem and that she wanted to ask everyone what she should do about it. She had been involved in a fight earlier that week and now she had to go to court. She said she was afraid that she would be sent to a school where "they are real strict and don't let you do nothing you want to do." She asked me what she could do about this and asked if I could help her by talking to the principal for her. I told her I was glad that she brought this to the group. I asked the group what they thought about the situation. Lisa stated that, if the situation happened to her, she wouldn't worry about it because she knew her mother would not get mad at her and would not care. I completely missed the boat on this statement! Kim was discussing the entire incident with Mary, and the group became interested in the details of the fight. I became interested in who did what to whom and who was responsible for what, trying to determine if Kim was indeed going to be punished severely by the court system.

**Practice Points:** In hindsight, Lisa's comment about her mother not caring is also very potent. While it may not be appropriate for this moment, at some time the group leader may want to get back to this issue. How about the other girls? Would their mothers care if they got into trouble?

Kim told the group that the reason she got into the fight was because someone in the school had spread the rumor that she was pregnant. She said that she had to let everyone know that she was not, and so she had no choice but to get into this fight with the person who started the rumor. The group agreed that she did have to fight this girl because, after all, she had no business saying such things, and she ruined Kim's reputation. (I missed an important issue the group was raising and asked the group to work on the more obvious issue.) I asked the group about other things they could do to avoid fighting in such a situation and did not focus in on the pregnancy issue, which, in retrospect, I think was the real problem.

**Practice Points:**   With so many issues emerging at once, it would help if the group leader could partialize the problems raised by the girls and then help them to address them one at a time: the fight, the court, parental reaction to the pregnancy, rumor spreaders, and, of course, the pregnancy itself. The group leader does note that Rachel, the group scapegoat, sits quietly during the discussion and picks a seat next to the leader. Taking this seat can be a communication of needing protection.

Almost everyone in the group was actively involved in a discussion of who can and cannot be trusted in their class, and who the people are in the school that spread rumors. I missed the significance of Rachel not participating in the discussion. I realized toward the end of the group that Rachel did not participate actively in the conversation and, in fact, had sat next to me again. I also was able to recognize the fact that I was quite uncomfortable addressing the issue.

**Practice Points:**   During a later session, the group leader realized that she had missed the central theme of concern for Kim. Although Kim raised her problem in terms of the fight and the resultant discipline, this was actually a first offering of her deeper concern—the fact that she was pregnant. The issue did not resurface until the fifth session. The next session followed the Christmas break for the group leader as well as a session before the break where the members expressed disappointment in not continuing to meet. Their competition for the attention of the leader emerges in some distress that one member, Rachel, is able to get out of class early to meet the leader. As the scapegoating of Rachel emerges indirectly, the leader senses it and feels a need to protect the scapegoat.

### January 23 (Fourth Session)

Before group started, Rachel came in and told me that Lisa had been acting unfriendly toward her and that this upset her a great deal, because they were supposed to be best friends. We discussed some ways that she could confront Lisa on this and the friendship in general. Rachel told me that she wanted to meet two periods a week instead of one. I encouraged her to bring this up in group.

When everyone arrived for the group, the girls all asked why Rachel got to get out of class early to come and talk to me. They appeared annoyed that Rachel may have received "special attention" but soon forgot this discussion when Lisa brought up a problem. I supported Lisa for coming to the group for advice, but I missed an underlying issue. Lisa told me that she had a problem and asked if we could please talk about her this week. She went on to say that this was a hypothetical situation and that it did not involve anyone they knew. Lisa said that she has a friend who is always doing everything she does, is always wearing the same clothes she wears, says the same things she says, and even likes the same boys she likes.

**Practice Points:**   The specific conflict with Rachel emerges once again—what might be considered an escalation of the message to the group leader. The response to scapegoating described in the previous section, the preemptive intervention to protect the scapegoat, is evident in the following example. The leader thinks she is the only one who knows what's going on, but actually most if not all of the group members know. They are waiting for a signal from the group leader that they can address the issue.

I sensed that Lisa was talking about Rachel, and I felt a strong urge to protect the individual being scapegoated. The group members jumped in on this subject and stated how they all hate this behavior. Rachel sat in the corner of the room, watching the group and looking out of the window. I suggested that maybe this friend really likes Lisa a great deal and wants to be like her. Kim jumped in and agreed with me and told Lisa that she should feel complimented. I made a demand for work. I asked the group what they would do in this situation. I made the assumption that I was the only one who knew the entire picture and acted accordingly. Everyone was very involved in the pictures they were drawing and did not seem to feel like discussing the subject.

**Practice Points:** It is moments such as these, when the group leader identifies with Rachel, the scapegoat, that lead to the crucial question. If the leader is with Rachel, who is with the group? The obvious answer is no one. Once again, a false dichotomy traps the leader, since her most helpful role is to be with the individual and the group at the same time. She is attuned to Rachel's discomfort but not connecting to the feelings of the group as expressed by Lisa.

In retrospect, I see that the group knew exactly what was going on and that it was my own feelings of discomfort that allowed me to avoid the issue. I avoided the main issue being raised in an attempt to protect the scapegoat. Lisa insisted on getting my opinion on the subject, even though I threw it out to the group for answers. I picked up on a conversation that Kim and Mary were having, and began talking with Cindy about a teacher they disliked. Lisa put her problem back on the table for discussion. I was feeling very annoyed at her insistence, and I told her that we had answered her question and that she could come and discuss it with me later if she wanted to. As the members left that day, Lisa pulled me aside and told me that this person was Rachel and that she did not want Rachel to know. I was able to support her as an individual group member; I told her that I would be free to speak with her later that morning and gave her a pass to get out of class.

**Practice Points:** The pattern of scapegoating is not directly addressed. Rachel, the group members, and the group leader all know it is going on. The group leader's reluctance is rooted in not wanting to hurt Rachel, yet the persistent pattern of scapegoating is more painful than any direct discussion might be. Group leaders are often afraid to open up an issue such as this because they are not sure what will happen and where it will go. The group leader's indirect efforts to deal with the problem match the group members' own use of indirect communications, thus frustrating the growth of the group. As the group culture becomes more positive, the group members are able to deal with some of their issues and lessen their need for a scapegoat. Kim will introduce a major personal issue with the not uncommon "I have a friend . . ." first offering.

### *January 30 (Fifth Session)*

I supported Kim for bringing a problem to the group. Kim brought up a problem she was currently dealing with and asked the group for advice. She said that she has a friend who thought she was pregnant. Her friend's cousin told her to drink "this awful stuff" to get rid of the baby. She said her friend did not want the baby, but that her friend's boyfriend wanted it very badly. Now her friend does not know what to tell her boyfriend. I reached for the group's feelings. The group immediately confronted Kim and wanted to know if she was speaking about herself. Kim said it was a friend. I said that this must be very difficult and was a scary situation to be in. I verbalized the group's nonverbal behaviors. I acknowledged that there seemed to be a great deal of tension around the subject of pregnancy and that it was a difficult topic of discussion. Cindy said that her mother would kill her if she ever came home pregnant and that she felt sorry for this girl. I pointed out to the group that the problem was not only an individual issue but also an issue for the group. The members appeared uneasy discussing the topic of pregnancy and were willing to change the subject and talk about something else.

**Practice Points:** The group leader's growing sense of her role is evident as she immediately addresses the second client—the group. Their avoidance of a difficult and taboo subject is a signal that they need some indication from the leader that this topic is OK and that the leader is not afraid to discuss it. In the leader's comment about Kim's courage and the group's emotion, we see the group leader's integration of the job of being with the two clients at exactly the same time: Kim who is pregnant, and the group members who are impacted by her comment.

The group tried to avoid the issue by concentrating on who among their classmates they thought could be pregnant. I made a demand for work. I stated to the group that a member had raised an important question and that it was an issue that demanded their attention. I asked the group what they would tell their boyfriends in a similar situation. Lisa stated that she would simply dump him and not tell him, since he must be crazy to think a 12-year-old should have a baby. Rachel stated that she did not have a boyfriend, and Mary said that she would tell him and hope he did not leave her. At this point, Kim broke in and told the group that it was herself that she was talking about. I said that everyone might be feeling a great deal of emotion, and that it must have taken a great deal of courage and trust to come to the group with this issue. The members focused in on the situation, giving Kim advice and reflecting the situation onto them, and they talked about what they would do in such a situation.

In this session, the group did not appear to need the scapegoat; the conversation was intense, and everyone worked together on the issue at hand. I began to feel that the group was progressing, and I felt much more in tune with my own feelings about things that happened in the group. I was able to catch myself more quickly and did not feel such a strong urge to protect everyone.

**Current Status of the Problem: Where It Stands Now (group leader's perception):** The group has entered the intimacy stage and we are able to do "real work" and discuss issues that they want to talk about. Scapegoating still occurs at times, but I am able to recognize it and address it at some level. I have found that, when I call attention to the scapegoating, it is no longer an issue (at least at that time). Rachel has been integrated into the group more often and has not been in the role of the scapegoat in our last few sessions.

The group is able to discuss issues that are of concern to them, such as boys, friendship, and the violence that they frequently see in their neighborhoods. Other issues are still very difficult for them to talk about, such as racism, what it's like to be Black or Hispanic in the city, and the fact that I am a middle-class, White group leader in a group for minority girls. The theme of authority remains an issue for the group—they have a difficult time understanding that they have control of this group. I need to work on letting them know this more often.

**Practice Summary.** Note that this student group leader identifies race as an issue for the girls in their daily lives and also as an issue between the girls and herself. She even includes it in her assessment of where the problem stands, although she identifies it as an issue that the members have difficulty discussing. Her struggle to deal with this crucial issue is not uncommon, and she will need support and supervision to recognize that her group members' difficulty in exploring the potentially explosive area of race reflects her own reluctance. When they are clear that she is ready, they will respond.

By understanding the dynamics of scapegoating, the group leader can more easily avoid the trap of siding with either the individual or the group. This natural response misses the essential message: that the group and the scapegoat are using the process as an attempt, albeit maladaptive, to offer a theme of concern. Because scapegoating may be the only way the group members know to deal with their thoughts and feelings, the group leader should not get too upset with either the group or the scapegoat. The group leader's task involves helping the group and the scapegoat to recognize their patterns and to find a new way to deal with concerns that are common to both. By viewing both the individual and the group as clients in need, the group leader can become better at understanding and empathizing with the feelings the two share.

### Strategies for Addressing the Scapegoating Pattern

**EP 2.1.4c**
**EP 2.1.7b**
**EP 2.1.10b**
**EP 2.1.10g**
**EP 2.1.10m**

Work with the scapegoating pattern involves several steps.

- First, the group leader observes the pattern over time.
- Second, group leaders must understand their own feelings in the situation to avoid siding with or against the scapegoat.
- Third, by using the tuning-in skill, group leaders can attempt to search out the potential connections between the scapegoat and the group. What is about themselves that they don't like and are projecting onto the scapegoat?
- If the group leaders are not clear about these connections, they can ask the group to reflect on the question.
- Finally, the next step involves pointing out the pattern to the group and the scapegoat. Thus, the group leader asks the group to look at its way of working and to begin the struggle to find a more positive adaptive process.

When group leaders challenge this scapegoating process, they should not criticize either the group or the scapegoat for having developed this way of dealing with their underlying feelings. In fact, the capacity for empathy and understanding of how hard it is to face these feelings is the very thing that allows the group leader to make this demand for work. This demand includes two tasks: asking the group to consider why it is scapegoating and asking the scapegoat to reflect on her or his reasons for volunteering for the role. Discussion of this process is designed to free the members to explore further their underlying feelings. It is important that the focus of the discussion continue to be directly related to the purpose of the group. This is not group therapy. It would be a mistake to encourage ongoing discussions of the individual's (Rachel's) life pattern of being a scapegoat. It also would be problematic if the group now became engaged in analysis of its process—how it is working—while losing sight of the original purpose of the group. When the discussion is honest, invested with feeling, and touches all of the members, the group will no longer need a scapegoat. The discussion may help the members moderate their harsh judgments of themselves that lead to the need for a scapegoat. In turn, the scapegoat may discover that his or her feelings are not unique.

I need to make one final comment on some models that advocate a more indirect mode of intervention. In childrens' groups, for example, that use program activity such as arts, crafts, or sports as part of the group activity, some models suggest that the group leader plan an activity that he or she knows the scapegoat can perform well. In my view there are a number of problems with this strategy. First, it assumes the leader plans the activities instead of working with the group members to plan. Second, it does not address the underlying issues that result in scapegoating. The leader is not recognizing that the scapegoating process is a communication from the group. Finally, it is a form of indirect influence since the members do not know that the group leader has a hidden agenda. This may be a minority viewpoint, but I believed it was important to share it.

# The "Deviant" Member

One of the most difficult clients for group leaders to deal with is the one they experience as the "deviant" member. In this discussion, the term *deviant* is used broadly to describe a member whose behavior deviates from the general norm of the group. This deviation can range from extremely inappropriate and disconnected behavior (e.g., a participant who refuses to stop talking at the first meeting or a member who manifests psychotic behavior) to one whose actions deviate only mildly or sporadically (e.g., a member who stares out the window while the rest of the group is deeply involved in a discussion).

In my practice, I have made two major assumptions about such behavior. First, deviant behavior is always a form of communication. The group leader's problem lies in figuring out what the member is saying. This difficulty is compounded by the fact that group leaders often experience the behavior as directed toward themselves, thus activating powerful emotions in the group leaders. For example, group leaders may see acting out behavior in a children's group as a test of the leader's authority, which at times, it is.

Second, deviant behavior in a group may express a communication that has meaning for the group as a whole. That is, just as the group may use a scapegoat as a means to deal with difficult feelings, a deviant member may serve an important social role for other group members. This assumption is related to the view of the group as a dynamic system. In this section, I explore these two assumptions.

## Extreme Versus Mild Deviance

Again, we can consider deviant behavior on a continuum that ranges from extreme to slight. On the extreme end would be a client or group member who evinces bizarre behavior that is totally inappropriate for the group. This can happen when meetings are open to the community or the screening of prospective members has not taken place. When this happens in a first session, the impact on the group leader and the group is profound. As the member speaks, one can sense the group shrinking in embarrassment and at times in fear. The leader needs to take responsibility for gently but firmly asking the member to withhold comment or, in extreme cases, to leave the session. Group members are not prepared, in an early session, to deal with extreme deviance and therefore depend on the group leader to clarify the boundaries and to enforce the limits if needed.

*Foster Parent Recruitment Group Example* In one such example, a woman attending a single-session, foster parent informational recruitment session responded to the group leader's opening contract statement and requests for group feedback by beginning a long, and essentially unrelated, tale of personal tragedy. When the group leader tried repeatedly to clarify the contract or to discover how the woman's concerns might relate to the discussion, she met with no success. The woman refused to allow others to speak and went on in detail about her personal problems and her fears that people were after her—even that the room was bugged.

**Practice Points:** The discomfort in the eyes of the group members was clear. The group leader, herself uncomfortable, finally moved to control the situation.

GROUP LEADER: Mrs. Pane, it is obvious that you're having a tough time right now, but I simply can't let you continue to use this group meeting to discuss it. I'll have to ask you to leave, but I would be glad to talk with you further about your concerns at another time.

MRS. PANE: You f—ing social workers are all alike. You don't give a s—t about us, you're no different from the rest. You took my kids away, and I want them back.

GROUP LEADER: I'm sorry, Mrs. Pane, I can't talk with you now about that. You will have to leave, and I can discuss this with you tomorrow.

Mrs. Pane finally left, and the group leader turned to the group to acknowledge how upset she was feeling about what had just happened. The group members expressed their own feelings. After emotions had settled, the group leader picked up the group members' reactions to Mrs. Pane as a parent of children in the care of the agency. This led to a discussion of parents, their feelings about placements, and contacts between natural parents and foster parents. Once again, we see a skillful example of how to integrate process (the acting out behavior of a disturbed biological parent) and content (possible contacts with biological parents).

The group leader followed up the next day with Mrs. Pane and did get to see her. There was a long, sometimes rambling and disjointed conversation during which the group leader consistently tried to reach Mrs. Pane and acknowledge her feelings. Mrs. Pane turned to the leader as she left and said, "I'm sorry for what I said last night. You know, it's just that I'm so angry—I miss my kids so much." Mrs. Pane's behavior at the meeting was an extreme example of the use of deviant behavior to express deeply held feelings. The group leader could not allow the session to be captured by Mrs. Pane, and using all of her courage, she protected—or using another term, guarded—the group's contract.

## Reaching for the Underlying Message of Deviant Behavior

It is striking how often group leaders are surprised to find relatively normal reactions and feelings underlying initial deviant behavior that they have taken as personal attacks. For example, a group member whose first comment is to challenge the need for the group itself or who responds defensively about his or her own need for help may seem deviant at first but not after the source of the behavior comes to light. All that is needed, at times, is to confront the group member directly and to ask about the meaning of the behavior. Three key concepts for the reader to keep in mind in the example that follows are:

- *The need to tolerate deviant behavior*
- *The importance of reaching for the underlying message*
- *Understanding the "deviant" as, at times, speaking for the group*

*A Group for Children Having Trouble in School* Consider the following example from a group for children who were having trouble in school. The meetings were held at the school in the afternoon, and John started acting up as he entered the meeting room. He picked a fight with Jim, knocked over the desk, and appeared ready to tackle the group leader next.

GROUP LEADER: John, what the hell is up? You have been roaring mad since you walked in here. (John remains silent, glaring, with his fists clenched.) Did you just come from a fight with someone? Or was it Mr. Smith (the teacher)? Did you have an argument with him?

JOHN: (Still angry, but slightly more relaxed) He's always picking on me, the bastard.

GROUP LEADER: Okay, now slow down and tell me what happened. Maybe we can help you on this one. That's what the group is all about.

**Practice Summary.** The group leader was able to reach for the meaning behind this behavior instead of getting caught up in a battle of wills with John, because he understood his own role, was clear about the purpose of the group, and understood that children often raise their problems indirectly by acting out. If the helping professional does not listen carefully and attempt to understand the feelings behind the behavior, it will only escalate. In the example above, the group leader attempts to understand what happened just before this outburst which leads to the feelings underneath and raises an agenda for work for the whole group.

The group member does not always immediately respond to the group leader's efforts to reach past the behavior; however, he or she often understands the group leader's meaning and will sometimes respond to the invitation later. Clarity of role is important, because if the group leader is concentrating solely on his or her limit-setting function (e.g., stopping the fight), he or she may miss the other part of the work. The skill often involves setting the limit and reaching for the meaning of the behavior at exactly the same time.

## Deviant Behavior as a Functional Role

As mentioned earlier, deviant behavior may in some way reflect the feelings of the group as a whole. This notion stems from the idea of the group as a dynamic system, in that the movement of one member is somewhat affected by the movements of the others. The deviant member can be viewed simply as a member who, for various reasons, feels a particular concern or emotion more strongly than the others in the group do. This greater sense of urgency causes the deviant member to express the more widely held feeling, often in an indirect manner.

Schwartz (1961) refers to the function of the deviant member in the client group as follows:

> Such clients often play an important role in the group—expressing ideas that others may feel but be afraid to express, catalyzing issues more quickly, bringing out the negatives that need to be examined, etc. This helped us to see that such members should not immediately be thought of as "enemies" of the group, diverting it from its purposes, but as clients with needs of their own, and that these needs are often dramatic and exaggerated versions of those of the other group members. (p. 11)

It is critical, therefore, that the group leaders not dismiss a deviant group member too quickly as simply acting out a personal problem. This would constitute the mistake of attempting to understand the behavior of one member of a dynamic system (the group) apart from the behavior of other members of the system. Although this member may bring this particular social role to all groups, one cannot understand him or her simply as a separate entity. The first hypothesis should always be that the member might speak for the group as a whole. In fact, this member who is often experienced by the leader as an "enemy" may in fact be an important "ally." In the first session of the couples' group described in earlier chapters, the older member (Lou) who attacked "professionals" was carrying out the important task of dealing with the authority theme, which was an issue for the whole group. His concerns and fears about how I and my coleaders would run the group were clearly shared by other members.

**Practice Points:** The following examples demonstrate two specific ways in which deviant behavior operates functionally: in opening up a discussion of group purpose and in deepening the work already in progress.

***Counseling Group at a Mental Health Center: What's the Purpose of This Group?*** In the following excerpt, a member attacks the purpose of the group in a session at a psychiatric center:

MR. WRIGHT: (Who has been quiet for most of the first two sessions, although he seemed to have a critical look on his face) I think this is really all a bunch of crap! How in the hell is it going to do us any good sitting around and talking like this?

MRS. SAMUELS: Well, you know, you really haven't had much to say. Maybe if you spoke up, it would be more worthwhile.

**Practice Points:** For most inexperienced group leaders, the force of this attack would be taken personally because the group leader would feel fully responsible for the success of the group. It would not be unusual for the group leader to view Mr. Wright as negative, hostile, and resistant and to set out to challenge him or encourage the group members to "take him on." For example, the group leader might wrongly say, "Mr. Wright doesn't seem to think the group is too helpful. Do the others feel that way, or do they feel the way Mrs. Samuels does?" Depending on how this question is asked, it could be heard by the group as an invitation to take on Mr. Wright. However, if Mr. Wright's behavior is viewed in the context of the dynamic interaction, and if the group leader sees him as a potential ally, he might instead help him to elaborate.

GROUP LEADER: I think it's important that we hear Mr. Wright out on this. If there are problems with the group as he sees it, maybe we can work them out if we talk about them. What's bothering you about the group?

MR. WRIGHT: Well, for one thing, I don't think we are leveling with one another. We're not really saying what's on our minds. Everybody is too busy trying to impress one another to be honest.

GROUP LEADER: You know, that often happens in the first few sessions of a new group. People are unsure of what to expect. How about it, have any of the others of you felt that way?

MR. PETERS: I didn't last week, but this week I thought the discussion was a bit superficial.

**Practice Summary.** By treating the deviant member as an ally rather than as an enemy, the group leader gave permission for the group members to begin a frank discussion of how they were working. Others in the group felt the freedom to express their dissatisfaction, and, as a result, the members began to take responsibility for making their group more effective. This kind of discussion is essential for all groups, but it is often considered impolite to be direct in such settings. Members do not want to "hurt the group leader's feelings" or the feelings of other members. As the group proceeded, the leader found that Mr. Wright—rather than not wanting to work—had several pressing issues he wished to deal with. His sense of urgency had forced him to speak out. Often, in a group, the member who seems most negative and angry is the one who wants to work the hardest. It is easy to understand, however, how the group leader's feelings might make it hard to see Mr. Wright in a more positive way.

***Deepening Discussion in a Parenting Group*** Expressions of deviant opinions in a group often serve as a lever for the group leader to deepen a discussion. For example, in one psychoeducational group on parenting skills, a major argument occurred when Mr. Thomas expressed the view that "all of this talk about worrying about the kids' feelings is nice for social workers but doesn't make sense for parents. Sometimes, the back of the hand is what they need." The other members pounced on Mr. Thomas, and a verbal battle ensued. Once again, for new group leaders who are not clear about their function, the expression of an idea that runs counter to their view of good parenting would arouse a strong reaction.

**Practice Points:** A new and inexperienced group leader might be particularly angered by the jibe about social workers and might set out to "educate" Mr. Thomas. Instead, this leader saw Mr. Thomas as expressing a feeling that was, in part, true for all of the parents but was not considered "proper" in this group. The principle articulated in the scapegoating section, being with the individual and the group at the same time, reemerges in this excerpt. The leader reached to support Mr. Thomas:

GROUP LEADER: You are all attacking Mr. Thomas's position quite strongly; however, I have a hunch there must be many times when all of you feel the same way. Am I right? (Silence)
MR. FISK: There are times when the only feelings I'm interested in are the ones he has on his behind when I let him have it.

**Practice Points:** With the group leader's help, Mr. Thomas gave permission for the parents to begin to discuss the reality of parenting, which includes anger, loss of temper, and frustration. The group leader continued by asking Mr. Thomas why he felt he had to express this position so strongly.

GROUP LEADER: You know, Mr. Thomas, you come on so strong with this position, and yet you don't strike me as someone who doesn't care about how his kids feel. How come?
MR. THOMAS: (Quietly, looking down as he spoke) Feelings can hurt too much.
GROUP LEADER: What do you mean?
MR. THOMAS: It wasn't easy to talk with my kids when their mother died.
GROUP LEADER: (After a silence) You really know what that is like, don't you? (Mr. Thomas just nodded.)
MR. SIMCOE: I've never had to handle something that tough, but I know what you mean about it being hard to listen when your kids are pouring out the hurt.

**Practice Summary.** In summary, the deviant member who challenges the authority of the leader, provides negative feedback on the work of the group, raises a point of view contrary to the group's norm, or fights strongly and with emotion for a position may play an important functional role in the dynamic system of the group. The deviant member can be an ally for the group leader if the leader can deal with personal feelings and listen to the deviant member as a messenger for the group. This concept will be reinforced in many of the examples in this and later chapters. In the previous example, we can see how a deviant member may turn into an active participant over time.

## The Internal Leader

Group leaders who are unsure of their role often experience internal leaders as a threat to their own authority, even viewing them as deviant members. However, if the mutual-aid process is central to the work, leaders should understand that the work is going well when an internal leader emerges. The mistake of viewing the internal leader as a deviant member is most evident in work with teenagers and children, when the internal leader challenges the authority of the group leader.

**EP 2.1.1b**

*Dealing with Acting Out Adolescents: A Community Center Group* The following excerpt is from the first meeting of a group I led during my first year of professional training. As part of my field practicum I wrote process recordings of the group meetings for discussion with my supervisor. I share this example for several reasons. First, students need to realize that all group leaders start out with similar feelings and make most of the same mistakes. Many students who read examples or see videotapes of my work with married couples, single parents, or people with AIDS do not know about the many mistakes I made, and still make, during my professional development. Second, this particular group—acting out adolescents—can be one of the most painful and stressful groups to lead. I still vividly remember dreading the early sessions, which seemed like a perpetual battle of wills—a battle both the group and I were destined to lose. Third, it provides a good illustration of how the group leader may at first see an internal leader as an enemy rather than an ally. Finally, it is an example of a community center group in which activities are a central part of the work. These kinds of groups often make up the bulk of group practice in some settings.

The group consisted of acting out adolescent boys (13 and 14 years old) who were members of a Jewish community center club. I had been warned that they were a difficult group and that they had given other group leaders a tough time in the past. Although the group was set up so that the club members planned their own activities, the agency had structured the first night by planning a mass sports program in the gym.

**Practice Points:** The first issue on the group members' minds was "What sort of leader will this be?" but my supervision had mistakenly led me to think that I must "demonstrate my authority in the first session and assert myself as leader," which in effect began the battle of wills.

> Only five boys had shown up by 7:45 P.M., so we spent the first 10 minutes talking about the club last year. At this point, Al showed up and completely changed the tone of our meeting. It seemed as if the first five boys had been waiting for the catalyst that had finally arrived. Al was bubbling over about the school football game he had played in that afternoon. It was their first win in 3 years.

When I asked how it had gone, he described it abruptly. He then wanted to know what we were doing that night. When I explained the prearranged evening program, he became very negative about it. "Rope jumping (one of the competitive events) is for girls," he replied. I told him boxers use rope jumping for training, and he replied, "I'm not a boxer, and I'm not a girl." Although the other boys had not been overly enthusiastic about the evening program when I had described it earlier, their tone changed sharply as they agreed with Al.

Lack of clarity of role and initial nervousness led me to defend the program and to see Al as competition for leadership of the group. The group leadership model I had been trained under suggested that my skill in working with groups was in my knowledge of activities and programs and that I had to directly or indirectly influence members to go along. The framework was actually manipulative in nature although I did not recognize it at that time. For example, as pointed out earlier, if there were a scapegoated boy in the group, rather than dealing with it directly, as in the earlier example with the girls' school group, I should select an activity the scapegoat could do well. No one would know that I had this goal "hidden up my sleeve." By the term *manipulation* I mean the group worker's secret use of power. I would be using my role as adult and leader to influence members without their knowing it. I later understood that this was problematic and would lead to distrust rather than trust.

**Practice Points:**   Getting back to my practice as a student, contracting was unclear, and an important discussion about the role of the group leader in relation to the group members was missed because of my own fears and misconceptions. As the meeting proceeded, I got myself deeper into trouble:

> I tried to discuss next week's program with the guys. Girls from another club started pressing their faces against the window of the door, and, before I could stop him, Al was racing to the attack. The contagion was immediate, and what had been a quiet group of boys was now following its leader. I jumped up and asked them to ignore the girls. Instead, they chose to ignore me. I went over to the door, closed it, and politely guided them back to the desk. This time, when they sat down, Al's feet were on the table (one of the wooden-finish types). Five more pairs immediately joined Al's (the testing was in full swing). All I could think of was my supervisor's advice which amounted to "show them who's boss." I asked them to remove their feet, because they could damage the table. Joe and Ken responded, but the others didn't. I tried to maintain a light and firm stand. They slowly responded, stating that last year's leader let them keep their feet up that way. Another said there were a lot of things their leader let them do last year that I probably would not. I said that I would only allow them to do those things that were acceptable to the agency. One of the boys asked me what an agency was. I explained I meant the center (first week of fieldwork and I was already overprofessional and using jargon). It was time to hit the gym for the games (much to my relief).

It is clear that my sense of role—that of "taming the group" and setting and enforcing limits—led me to miss important issues. Discussing the last leader's role would have been helpful. In addition, their relationships with girls were an emerging and uncomfortable theme for this group, given their age. Their behavior was very age- and stage-of-the-life-cycle appropriate, only I was missing the meaning of it. Al was the only club member to dance with girls later in the evening during the social part of the program. He asked about having a party with a girls' group, and I put off his request by saying, "We would need to plan this ahead of time." Al provided leadership in several areas, expressing the feelings and concerns of the group, but because I missed the importance of his role, a battle over "who owned the group" resulted, with me thinking that I did.

**Practice Points:**  Because I missed the signals, the indirect testing continued. Al led the members in throwing paper around the club room and leaning out of the windows, spitting on other center members as they left. I kept trying to set limits while not allowing myself to get angry (which was considered unprofessional). Finally, my instincts got the better of me.

I said that I would like to say a few words before we finished. I was attempting to reestablish the limits I had set earlier, but my own feelings got the best of me. I explained that this evening was really difficult for me and that probably it was for them too. I said that, if we couldn't relax enough to discuss further programs, there probably wouldn't be any. At this point, I said something that surprised me as I said it. I said their behavior better improve, or they could find themselves a new leader. They replied by saying that, compared with the group members who hadn't shown up this evening, they were well behaved. My reaction to this group was mild panic.

**Practice Points:**  It is easy to understand my panic in this situation. My idea of being professional was to be able to "handle" the group without losing my temper. Actually, in these moments at the end of the meeting when I revealed my real feelings, I was starting to develop a working relationship with the group members. After a few more sessions of off-and-on-again testing, I moved to discuss the issue of the authority theme and to help the group members develop their own internal leadership and structure.

I told the boys that, because I had been with them for 5 weeks, they might be interested in hearing what I thought about the group. They perked up at this. Bert said, "You love us," and everyone laughed. I said that, during this time, I had been able to talk to each one of them individually and seemed to get along well. However, when we got together as a group, we couldn't seem to talk at all, right from the beginning. In spite of what they said, I thought that each one of them was concerned about stealing, acting wise all the time, and being disrespectful. Al said (very seriously this time) that it was different when they were in the group. I asked why that was so. Bert asked all the guys if they had stolen anything, and they all agreed that they had.

**Practice Points:**  In the next excerpt I confront the taboo I believed existed in speaking up and challenging the negative behaviors. This would be considered "sucking up" and peer group acceptance was crucial for this age and stage of the life cycle. My honesty opened the door for them to address the authority theme, which really amounted to the question: "Whose group is this?" My training had led me to believe it was mine but my experience was rapidly telling me it had to be their group.

After some discussion, I told them I thought they were really afraid to say what they thought in the group. Bert said he wasn't afraid. I asked about the others. Al mockingly put up his fists and said, "I'm not afraid of anyone in the group." I laughed with the rest and said I thought it was easy to be brave with your fists but that it took a lot more courage to say something you thought the other guys would not like. I said it was their club, and, although it was important to me, it was really more important to them. Joel made a wisecrack, but he was silenced by Ken, who said, "That's just the kind of thing he (pointing to me) was talking about."

As the discussion continued, the boys explained that they often didn't like my suggestions for activities, and I encouraged them to say so in the future, because it was their club. A surprising amount of feeling emerged about the kidding around in the group, much of it directed at one boy who acted out a great deal but was not present that night. They talked about how they could plan their own programs. The group members suggested that I could bring in ideas from other clubs and that they would then decide what they wanted. At this point, Al suggested they have a president. After some discussion about the respective positions, a president (Al), vice president (Bert), and treasurer (Ken) were elected. A social committee was also formed to speak with the girls' club to discuss a party.

At this point in the meeting, I realized we were actively talking about something with no kidding around and no testing of me. I felt at ease for the first time. I commented to them about this. Al said, "We won't be able to do this all the time." I said I realized this and that there still would be a lot of kidding around. It would be all right as long as they could pull themselves together at times to get their work done. Al said that would be his job, and that I could help by telling them when they got out of hand. I agreed.

At the end of the process recording, I commented that "all of the boys gave me a warm good-bye" as I left the building. From this point on, much of the work shifted to helping the group members develop their own structure. For example, I met with Al before sessions, at his request, to help him plan the agenda and to discuss his problems with chairing the sessions.

**Practice Summary.** These group sessions were a painful initial lesson on the need to clarify my role and recognize the group's internal leadership. I had experienced Al as the group's deviant member when, in reality, he was its internal leader. I had told them it was their group, but my early behavior had contradicted this; following a different paradigm of practice, I believed it was really my group for implementing my purposes. I encouraged them to plan activities when I already had the "appropriate" activities in mind. I experienced Al as my enemy, when he was actually my main ally. Later in this chapter I will provide further illustrations of my work with this group, in which I describe what the group taught me about helping group members to negotiate the system—in this case, the school, their families, and the community center itself. I have always been grateful that they had not given up on me and had begun my group leadership education in an admittedly painful at times but very important way.

# The Gatekeeper

The previous section pointed out that the deviant member is often the one who feels the strongest sense of urgency about a particular issue. In a sense, the deviant behavior is an effort to move the group toward real work. The internal leader often serves this function in a healthier, more direct way. A group can be ambivalent about work in the same way an individual can be, and members can take on the function of expressing that ambivalence for the group. This is sometimes seen in the form of a gatekeeper role, in which a member guards the "gates" through which the group must pass for the work to deepen. When the group discussion gets close to a difficult subject, the gatekeeper intervenes to divert the discussion.

In one adult support group, every time the discussion appeared to approach the issue of the group leader's (instructor's) authority and behavior, one female member would light up a foul-smelling cigarillo or in some other way attract the group's ire. (This was prior to the emergence of the generally accepted no-smoking policies.) The group would rise to the bait, and the more difficult authority theme would be dropped. After observing this pattern, at one meeting the group leader pointed it out, describing what he saw: "You know, it seems to me that every time you folks get close to taking me on, Pat lights up a cigar or says something that gets you onto her back. Am I right about this?" The group rejected the interpretation and turned on the leader with anger, thus beginning to deal with the authority theme. Later in the session, Pat commented that the group leader's observation might be accurate, because she had always been fearful of seeing her parents fight and probably had done the same thing in childhood. It was not appropriate in this group to discuss the reasons for the pattern—neither Pat's nor the group's—nor did the group members need to agree with the observation. The mere statement of the pattern offered the group an opportunity to face the leader directly, and Pat no longer needed to carry out this role.

People often use humor to protect the gates to difficult and painful areas. A group member, usually one who has learned to play this role in most areas of her or his life, will act out, crack a joke, make a face, and so forth in an effort to get the group members and the leader laughing and distracted. This will be described later in this chapter as a form of "flight." Note that humor can also be used to help advance the work of the group and does not always represent a means of gatekeeping. It helps, at times, to be able to laugh when facing painful work.

Professional staff groups, for example, at times use what I call *macabre humor* to deal with their tensions related to their work. For example, they may tell stories about clients, or others, that they would never share publicly. However, when this is the only means of releasing tension, and the underlying feelings that result from the stresses and traumas are not dealt with, such humor can lead to social worker burnout rather than preventing it. I have addressed this maladaptive reaction to secondary trauma, for example, in a book on supervision (Shulman, 2010). With the client group, the group leader needs to observe the pattern over time and to note the results of the use of humor. If the humor consistently results in an illusion of work, the gatekeeper function is a likely explanation. In the example that follows of a group for teenage female survivors of sexual abuse, the reader should note the following:

- *The gatekeeper's acting out behavior always is associated with painful discussion*
- *The role of blocking discussion of these painful areas is reinforced by the group*
- *When the culture is changed and the taboo partially lifted, the gatekeeper is no longer needed*
- *The gatekeeper turns out to be the member with the most reason for guarding the gate*

***Teenage Survivors of Sexual Abuse*** In a group for adolescent girls who were survivors of sexual abuse, the group leader was careful to make sure that each girl had control over if and when she disclosed the circumstances of her own abuse. Whereas they had no control over their abuse as young children, it was important that they had control over disclosing it. One girl would act out when the discussion became serious and painful in response to a disclosure. She sang ribald songs, jumped on a table and danced provocatively, and otherwise exhibited sexualized behavior. The group eventually developed a more trusting culture through the disclosures of the details of abuse by a number of members. With the more positive and safer culture, the leader addressed the gatekeeper's behavior and reached for its meaning. The girl then revealed the extent of her abuse, in which her father had taken her to bars, had her literally dance on tables, and passed her around to patrons, trading sex for drinks. The gatekeeper is often the group member who has experienced the issue even more powerfully than the others and has the most to protect. In this case, the gatekeeper also had the greatest need for support and her "deviant" behavior was a loud call for help.

## The Defensive Member

Defensiveness represents its own social role, although other social roles may involve defensiveness as well. The defensive member refuses to admit there is a problem, to accept responsibility for his or her part in a problem, or to take suggestions or help from the group after a problem has been raised. The "yes, but . . ." syndrome is not uncommon as the defensive member has all of the reasons why he or she cannot deal with a problem and responds to every suggestion with a sentence that begins: "Yes, but. . . ." Group members often respond to a defensive member by attacking the defense and eventually giving up and ignoring her or him.

Lewin (1951) described a model for change that can be applied to defensiveness on several levels—individual, group, family, and organizational. Stated simply, the individual personality in relation to its environment has developed a *quasi-stationary social equilibrium* in which some form of balance has been achieved. For the defensive member, denial has worked as a way to deal with painful problems. This would be roughly equivalent to the "precontemplation" stage of change (DiClemente et al., 1991). The three steps for change involve "unfreezing" this equilibrium, moving into a phase of disequilibrium, and freezing at a new quasi-stationary equilibrium. Moving through a period of disequilibrium is essential for real change but also can be frightening. The important point is that defenses have value to the individual, and to expect the unfreezing process to be easy misses the essence of the dynamics. The more serious the issue—the more deeply the individual feels a challenge to the sense of the core self—the more rigid the defense. Like resistance, a group member's defensiveness is a signal that the work is real. To begin the unfreezing process, the group leader or group must challenge the individual. However, the individual will need all the support, understanding, and help possible to translate unfreezing into movement and then into a new and healthier level of quasi-equilibrium.

Group leaders often underestimate the difficulty of what they and group members are asking people to do when calling them to move past defensiveness and denial. The difficulty of this process needs to be respected. Only a delicate integration of support and demand can create the conditions in which the group member may feel free enough to let down his or her barriers. The reader should note the following in this next example:

- *The group leader is with both the individual and the group*
- *The group leader attempts to help the individual reach out to the group and to help the group respond*
- *The group leader recognizes that defensiveness and resistance are part of the work*

*A Defensive Father in a Parents' Group* In the example that follows, a father describes a conflict with his 18-year-old son that has resulted in the son's leaving home and the family's being in turmoil. As the situation plays out in some detail, other parents point out that the father has been stubborn and failed to listen to what his son was saying. They try to pin him down to alternative ways of relating, but to each he responds in a typical "Yes, but . . ." pattern, not able to take in what they are saying.

**Practice Points:** Finally, after a few minutes of this, the group grows silent. The group leader intervenes by pointing out the obstacle.

GROUP LEADER: It seems to me that what has been going on here is that Ted has raised a problem, you have all been trying to offer some answers, but Ted has been saying "Yes, but . . ." to each of your suggestions. You look like you are about to give up on him. Are you?

ALICE: We don't seem to be getting anywhere. No matter what anyone says, he has an answer.

GROUP LEADER: Ted, I think you must feel a bit backed into a corner by the group. You do seem to have a hard time taking in their ideas. How come?

TED: I don't think they can appreciate my problem. It's not the same as theirs. They all seem to be blaming me for the fight, and that's because they don't understand what it really is like.

GROUP LEADER: Maybe it would help if you could tell them how this struggle with your son makes you feel.

TED: I gave this kid so much, raised him since he was a baby, and now he treats his mother and me like we don't matter at all. I did the best I could—doesn't he understand that?

GROUP LEADER: I think it's tough when you feel you love your child the way you do and you still see him as your kid, but he seems to want to pull away. You still feel responsible for him but you also feel a bit impotent, can't seem to control him anymore. Can any of you appreciate what Ted is feeling right now?

The group members moved to support Ted in his feelings, with others recounting similar experiences and feelings. The focus had shifted for a moment to the common feelings among group members rather than the obstacle that seemed to frustrate them.

**Practice Points:** The group leader sensed that Ted needed to feel understood and not be judged harshly by the other parents, precisely because he tended to judge himself more harshly than any of them. Having established this support, the group leader reached for the feelings underlying the resistance.

GROUP LEADER: Ted, if I were you, I think I would spend a lot of time wondering what went wrong in the relationship. I would be wondering how this could have happened when I had tried so hard—and if I could have done things differently. Is that true for you?

FRAN (TED'S WIFE): He stays up nights; he can't get to sleep because he is so upset.

TED: Sure, it's tough. You try your best, but you always wonder if you should have been around more, worked a little less, had some more time . . . you know?

GROUP LEADER: I guess that's what makes it hard for you to believe that anyone else can understand, and you feel so lousy about it yourself. Can the rest of you appreciate that it would be tough to listen if you were in Ted's shoes?

RAY: I think we are in Ted's shoes. When I see him getting stubborn in this group, I see myself and my own defensiveness.

**Practice Summary.**   The group discussion focused on how hard it was to take advice in the group, especially when the members themselves felt uncertain. As the conversation shifted, the group leader could sense Ted physically relaxing and listening. After a while, Ted asked the group to take another crack at his problem. He said, "This is really tough, but I don't want to lose the kid completely."

Often, defensive members need more time than a single session to feel safe enough to "move." Group leaders will often find that the member has thought deeply, after the meeting, about the way he reacted, so that readiness to change and unfreezing appear in a later session. This is the client's part in the procedure; once again, the leader can only take responsibility for establishing the best possible conditions for change—the rest is up to the client and depends on many factors. One of my studies found that clients' acceptance of a problem contributed to their motivation to change as well as their ability to take and use help (Shulman, 1991).

In another example in the middle phase of work with a group of teenagers, a defensive member in the group was also responding with "Yes but . . ." to every effort to help her. The group leader had a good relationship with her, having built up a fund of positive feeling in the relationship. At one point, she gently confronted her by asking if there was any way they could reach her on this issue or was she so closed that they (the group) should just leave her alone and try another time. The member thought for a moment and then replied: "No, you can keep trying." At that point, in control of the process, she began to hear what they were saying.

For some clients, the stress of the issue is so great, or the issue so loaded, that they cannot accept any help at that particular point. Although such situations are frustrating and often sad, they exist. Accepting this is one of the most important things a new counselor can do. He or she must avoid taking responsibility for the client's part in the proceedings. Nonetheless, group leaders often feel guilty because of lack of clarity on this point and feelings of failure, and this guilt leads group leaders to feel angry with a defensive client for not cooperating. Note, in our example of the parent group, that the anger from the other group members appeared to be a result of their seeing some of their own feelings and attitudes exaggerated in the defensiveness of the member. In fact, the more they pushed him, the more they heightened his defensiveness.

## The Quiet Member

The quiet member is one who remains noticeably silent over an extended period of time. In small groups, the group leader and the other group members notice after only a few sessions that someone has said very little or nothing at all. A quiet member can create problems for the group, because the other members do not know what thinking and feeling goes on behind the façade. Group members will tend to believe that the quiet member is sitting in judgment of them, does not share their problems, or feels that others in the group talk too much. Group leaders, too, often grow uncomfortable, feeling that a member who is not speaking may not be involved.

The silence of a member in a group is similar to the silence in a one-on-one interview. It is a form of communication that, as we have seen, can be difficult to understand. For some group members, it simply means that they are uncomfortable speaking in the group. This is one of the most common explanations. Others may feel left out or uninvolved in the group because they feel that their problems are different. Some sit in judgment of the group's activity (as was the case in one of the deviant member illustrations dealing with the defensive parent). In my experience, sitting in judgment is the least-stated reason for silence but, interestingly, is often the most frequent interpretation of silence by the active group members and the group leader; this probably reflects their own feelings. The two examples presented shortly will examine the quiet member who is afraid to speak and the quiet member who is left out. First, let us see how the group leader can help the group when they react to a quiet member.

## Group Leader Strategies

Believing that all members need to speak an equal amount is a mistake. Social roles developed by individuals include patterns that involve active participation through speech as well as active participation through listening. A member may get a great deal out of a discussion without directly participating. On the other hand, small groups carry a sense of mutual obligation: Members who risk themselves feel that others should do the same. In fact, the silent member often feels uncomfortable about "taking" and not "giving." In addition, many silent members have been so used to being quiet in groups for so long that they have not developed skills required for intervention. Some quiet members say that they are always too slow with their thoughts. The group moves too fast for them, and, by the time they can get in, the idea has been stated and the group has moved on. Others say that, after they have been quiet in a group for several sessions, they are afraid the group members will "fall out of their chairs if I open my mouth." Whereas all members should be able to move into a group at their own pace, and although equal participation is not a goal, the quiet member often needs some assistance to participate in the group.

Group leaders sometimes try to deal with this problem either directly—through confrontation—or indirectly. Each tactic can backfire. For example, if a member has been quiet because of discomfort in speaking, a group leader who suddenly turns and says, "I notice you haven't spoken yet in the group and wondered what was on your mind?" may find the member even further immobilized by embarrassment. This direct confrontation may be exactly what the quiet member feared would happen.

Indirect means can be just as devastating. The group leader has noticed a member not verbally participating in a discussion and turns and says, "What are your ideas about this question, Fran?" A member who is afraid of speaking often finds that any ideas she did have completely disappear in this moment of panic. The other indirect technique, of going around the room to get all group members' opinions when it really is only the quiet person's opinion the group leader seeks, may be experienced as manipulative and artificial by members. This is an example of what I described earlier as "acting on" the client rather than "acting with" the client.

The task, then, is to be direct and nonthreatening at the same time. My own strategy is based on the belief that people have a right to their defenses and their characteristic patterns of social interaction. As the group leader, my job is to mediate the engagement between each member and the group, so I feel a responsibility to check with a quiet member and see how that engagement is going. If there is an obstacle between the member and the group, I can offer to help.

***The Member Who Is Afraid to Speak*** As we have seen, members sometimes are merely afraid to speak. They have likely always held back in groups. The following conversation took place after the second meeting of a group. Richard had been particularly silent in both meetings, although his eyes seemed to indicate that he was involved.

GROUP LEADER: Do you have a second to chat before you go?

RICHARD: Sure, what's up?

GROUP LEADER: I noticed you haven't spoken in the group these two sessions, and I thought I would check to see how it was going with you. I know some people take longer than others to get involved, and that's all right. I just wanted to be sure there were no problems.

RICHARD: Well, you caught me.

GROUP LEADER: What do you mean?

RICHARD: I managed to get through all of my years in school without ever saying anything in class, and now it looks as if I've been caught.

GROUP LEADER: Is it hard for you to speak in a group?

RICHARD: I always feel unsure of what I'm going to say, and, by the time I've figured it out, the group has gone past me. Sometimes, it's just hard to get in with everyone speaking at once.

GROUP LEADER: Look, I can tell from your eyes that you are actively involved in the discussion. However, after a while, you will probably feel uncomfortable not speaking, and then it will get harder and harder to talk.

RICHARD: That's the way it usually is for me.

GROUP LEADER: Not just you, you know. Lots of people feel that way. If you would like, I can help by watching for you; if I sense you want to get into the conversation by the look on your face, or your body, or if you give me a signal, I can reach for you and help you in. Would you like me to do that?

RICHARD: That sounds all right. If I give you a signal, you'll call on me?

GROUP LEADER: Exactly! I find that has helped people in the past.

**Practice Summary.** The key here was turning control of the group leader's intervention over to the member. At the next session, Richard avoided the group leader's eyes for the first 15 minutes; he was probably afraid of giving a false signal. He sat rigidly with his arms at his sides, also because he was afraid a sudden motion might be misinterpreted. The discussion was heated, and the group leader kept glancing at Richard. After a while, the group leader noticed Richard leaning forward a bit, with his eyebrows arched, looking at the group leader. The group leader simply said, "Come on in, Richard." The group paused, and Richard began to speak. Once again, it is important that the group leader always act *with* the client and avoid acting *on* the client.

***The Member Who Feels Left Out*** Another type of quiet member is one who feels that his or her particular concerns and issues may not be of interest to the group, or that his or her problems differ from those of the others. Such members do not share problems with the group members, and, after a while, they feel left out and the group members wonder what is happening. In the following example, Mrs. Trenke, who had shared some difficult experiences with the group, stated that she felt let down when the group did not respond to her feelings. Mrs. Davidson, who had been quiet in the group, supported Mrs. Trenke's comment.

**Practice Points:** The group leader encouraged Mrs. Trenke to elaborate:

The group leader said, "Maybe we could hear how Mrs. Trenke felt let down by the group?" Mrs. Trenke continued, "I felt that I was not a part of the group and that I was not going to get anything out of it." Mrs. Davidson cut in, "Yeah! We didn't listen to other people's troubles because we had enough of our own!"

The group leader turned to Mrs. Davidson and said, "Have you felt let down and left out of the group?" "No," said Mrs. Davidson, "I don't feel I have the same situation—they have husbands." (Mrs. Bennet reached out and touched Mrs. Davidson on the arm.) The group leader asked Mrs. Davidson how she felt about not having a partner. Mrs. Davidson replied, "Sad, depressed—I wonder if he could be as proud of the kids as I am?" She went on to say that maybe things would be different if her husband were still alive—maybe they could have made a go of it.

Once the issue was on the table, the group leader suggested that it had been a problem for a while and that the members would like to know what it felt like to be alone. Mrs. Bennet, in the "gatekeeper" role, interrupts the work by challenging the importance of dealing with feelings.

**Practice Points:** The group leader points out the process, recognizing that all of the group members would have some difficulty with the pain raised by Mrs. Davidson. Most likely, that was the feeling and thoughts inside of the silence.

The group leader said he felt that Mrs. Davidson had felt cut out of the group for some weeks. Mrs. Davidson agreed. Mrs. Bennet said that was probably due to the fact that she had not been able to share with the group the concerns she had. All agreed. The group leader responded after a silence and said, "I feel the group would like to know what it is like, what it feels like to be alone. What do you need help with?" Mrs. Bennet cut in, "There you go on that feeling theory again." The group leader asked if it worried Mrs. Bennet when we talked about feelings. "No," she said, "but is it important?" The leader said that it seemed important because everyone in this group was having trouble talking about and sharing feelings while at the same time they were interested in what others were feeling. "Do you see what we have done here? When we began to find out about Mrs. Davidson's feelings, someone suggested that we avoid it and we all agreed. Let's go back to Mrs. Davidson's feelings!"

Mrs. Davidson said, "I feel like an s-h-i-t (spelled out) at home with the kids." The group leader cut in and said it was all right with him if she said shit—but why did she feel that way? "It rips me right across here (indicating midsection) when they are fighting. I've had nothing but fighting all my life—first in my own home, then with my husband, and now with my kids." "How do you see the fighting? What does it mean to you?" asked the group leader. "I feel on my own, all alone." Mrs. Trenke cut in, "I know that feeling. I had it with my husband—we used to argue. . . . What can I do? Why is it always me?" The group leader asked if Mrs. Davidson could share a specific problem with the group, and she did. It involved setting limits, then wavering on them and letting the kids have their own way.

***Men's Group: A Member Reaches Out to the "Quiet Member"*** As is often the case, simply acknowledging the lack of involvement by the member is enough to encourage the sharing of her concerns. Sometimes the initiative for reaching out to a quiet member starts with the group. It is not unusual, after a period of time, to have a group member turn to one who has been silent and ask, "What have you been thinking?"

**Practice Points:** Once again, the leader's concern for the two clients—the individual and the group—and clarity of role can assist the group and the member in an important discussion.

RAY: I have been thinking about you, Fred. You have not said anything in the group so far. How come? (All eyes turned to Fred.)

FRED: (Looking very uncomfortable) Oh, I've been listening.

LEADER: (Addressing Ray) Does it concern you when Fred doesn't speak?

RAY: Yeah, I begin to wonder if I'm talking too much or he thinks I'm making a real ass out of myself.

LEADER: Have others in the group wondered about that as well? (Nodding of heads) I think it makes other people uncomfortable when you don't speak much, Fred, because they can't figure out what you're thinking. Could you react to that?

FRED: Actually, I've been sitting here thinking how much all of your problems are just like mine. I've wanted to share some, but I don't feel comfortable talking in a group.

LEADER: This wasn't easy for you right now, was it?

FRED: No, it wasn't easy at all, but I'm glad it came out.

RAY: Maybe if I shut up a bit, you would have more of a chance to talk.

LEADER: I don't think so, Ray. Some people speak more in a group and others do a lot of work by listening. You also seem concerned about what others have to say, so I hope you wouldn't feel you needed to hold back. How about the rest of the group?

LOU: You raise interesting points, Ray, and it helps the group keep going. I would miss you if you just clammed up. (Ray smiles at this.)

LEADER: I can watch the talk in the group, and if I see someone trying to get in, I'll help make room for him. Is that all right? (Members of the group nodded in agreement.)

FRED: I'll get into the conversation. I just need some more time.

RAY: That's OK. Don't feel pressed. You can get in when you feel comfortable.

**Practice Summary.**   Once the communications had been clarified, the problem of the silent member receded. Fred did get into the discussion the following week, raising a concern to the group and meeting with a positive response.

## The Monopolizer

The previous section on the quiet member brings up the opposite type of group member: the person who talks a great deal and is sometimes referred to as a monopolizer. My observation is that people who talk a lot are often more of a problem for the group leader than they are for the other members. In first sessions in particular, group members are pleased to see someone pick up the discussion. A problem arises, however, when the person who is talking does not also listen to others, cuts them off, and creates a negative reaction in the group. The group leader, who sees this happening as a pattern, rather than just the talkative response of a nervous group member at an early meeting, can raise the issue directly. One way would be to simply ask the member if she or he can hold off for a bit and give others a chance to get in. In most cases just pointing this out directly and gently is enough to help the member become more conscious of the need for some restraint. It is also helpful to recognize that the member, like the rest of the group, must feel the issues and problems strongly and is anxious to get some help.

It the pattern persists and the group leader can sense through verbal or nonverbal signals that group members are unhappy with the repeated monopolizing of the conversation, a stronger intervention is needed. If the group leader directly points out what is happening and opens up a discussion of the process, usually this helps to ease the problem. If the group leader inquires why the member acts this way in the group, the individual will often reveal that talking is a way of covering up feelings, avoiding a problem, or expressing concern about actions in the group. The overly verbal member's words are often a way of handling the same feelings that the quiet member handles, but in a quite different manner.

One pattern in groups is for the member to start to talk about an issue that seems unrelated to the theme of the discussion. Once again, understanding the meaning of this apparent changing of the subject is important. In some situations the discussion has hit a painful point and the apparent monopolizer takes on a gatekeeper role as described earlier. A direct response would be for the group leader to point that out once the pattern is established and ask the member if it is hard to hear others talk about the issue and/or the feelings. In others, the member is so overwhelmed with his or her feelings and issues that he or she appears not to have room for anyone else's issues. A direct response might be for the leader to say: "John, I think sometimes you, and maybe all of us, get so overwhelmed by our own pain it is hard to listen to someone else's."

While some models of group practice prescribe indirect interventions such as "cutting off" the member, I believe a more direct approach that addresses the pattern is more respectful and helpful to the monopolizing member as well as the rest of the group. For example, as a member goes off on what appears to be a tangent, the leader could say: "John, I'm not clear about the connection between what you are raising right now and the theme of the discussion. Can you help us see the connection or can anyone else in the group see the connection or John, is this an issue you want us to get back to?" I don't believe it is enough to simply discipline or teach group behavior without understanding the underlying meaning.

***A Psychoeducational Parents' Group for Children with Traumatic Brain Injury*** The following brief excerpt illustrates how immobilized both the group leader and the other group members can feel when faced with a monopolizer. This member, Dawn, acted out her anxiety by responding to a doctor's presentation with an unstoppable stream of talk.

AGENCY TYPE: A rehabilitation center for children and adolescents
GROUP PURPOSE: A psychoeducational group to educate the group members about their children's medical and therapeutic conditions, as well as to inform them of safety precautions for children who have had a traumatic brain injury
GENDER OF MEMBERS: Three men and eleven women (including group leader)
AGE RANGE: Mid-20s to early 40s

> As soon as Dr. Thomas began to explain that children who have experienced traumatic brain injuries tend to be impulsive, Dawn started to describe what had happened with her child to demonstrate that she agreed with the doctor. She went on and on for almost 10 minutes, and nobody intervened. Then, she started to talk about her other child, Lisa, and what had happened at home during the past weekend. I turned to Dawn and said, "Dawn, I know you have many things to say, but why don't we go back to Eileen's behavior?" Dawn replied, "I know. I know. But let me finish. This is related to Eileen, too." People in the room rolled their eyes, but I did not object. She spoke for another 3 minutes or so and finished her story by saying, "So I told my children that school is always

number one." I jumped in and said, "Good. Why don't we ask Melissa (the hospital tutor) about school?" People, including Dawn, laughed. When Melissa finished reporting on Eileen's school issue, I encouraged Dawn to ask Melissa questions. Then, I announced to the treatment team that we were running out of time so I would like to ask everyone to be short and precise. They nodded.

**Practice Summary.** In retrospect, this first meeting focused almost entirely on the concerns of one member. Although the other group members signaled their displeasure by rolling their eyes, the group leader, perhaps feeling unclear about how to intervene, let Dawn continue unchecked. Ironically, the doctor's presentation dealt with "impulsivity" of the children and we have evidence of an impulsive parent group member. The leader would have been helpful to Dawn and the other members if she had intervened more directly and firmly. In a session such as this one, the monopolizer often feels embarrassed afterward for having dominated the conversation, and the other members wonder about the value of the group. In a first session, the group leader must take responsibility for providing structure. The leader is guided by the following strategies:

- *Being direct but in a supportive manner*
- *Taking responsibility for maintaining structure*
- *Exploring the meaing of the monopolizing if it continues (becomes a pattern)*
- *Attending to the thoughts and feelings of the second client—the group*
- *Being aware of the integration of process and content*

In doing so, perhaps the leader could say:

> Hold on a second, Dawn. I know your child's injury and this discussion provoke a lot of feelings in you, and you probably feel you want as much help as you can get for your own child. But we need to allow room for everyone to ask their questions and make their comments, so I'll play traffic cop if it's OK with the rest of you.

If Dawn continued to test, such as by saying, as she did in the session, "Let me just finish," the group leader would need to say something like "Nice try, but we need to give someone else a chance." Continued persistence would require some discussion of the significance of being so full of one's own feelings that very little room remains for anyone else's. For example, "I know it's hard to hold back when you feel so upset about your daughter." There is also a good chance that Dawn has just acted out the problem she has with friends and other family members—overwhelming them with her issues and not being able to respond to theirs. "I wonder if this is the way you ask for help from your friends and family members. I suspect at times it is hard for all of you to hold back when you feel so desperate about the situation. Am I right about that?" Once again, we see the integration of process and content.

If the group leader handles such interventions directly, openly, without anger, and—where possible—with nonhumiliating humor, he or she will reassure the group that the group leader will not let the monopolizing member subvert the purpose of the group or act out his or her anxiety. The problem is that such interventions go against societal norms, which encourage passively allowing the monopolizer to go on at length, intervening indirectly with little success, or intervening from anger as the group leader feels frustration at one member's domination of the group. In most cases, the monopolizer wants the group leader to set limits, because structure helps to bind anxiety and helps the member feel more in control over what must be a devastating situation. Interestingly enough, there is a good chance that setting limits on the children's impulsive behavior is exactly what the parents need to do. The group leader needs to model it in the group, since once again, "more is caught than taught."

# The Group-as-a-Whole

In the first half of this chapter I have explored the various roles individuals play in a group setting—the interplay of one member within a dynamic system. In the remainder of this chapter, I take a more detailed look at the group as an entity much like an organism, with its own properties and dynamics, and then I explore a strategy for the leader's intervention in relation to it. Next, I trace the tasks of the group as it attempts to deal with the relationships of members to the leader (the authority theme), relationships among members (the intimacy theme), the group's culture for work, and the group's internal structure (communication patterns, roles, and so forth). A fifth task requires the group to relate to the environment—the setting that houses the group (the school, agency, institution). I address this task later in this chapter, when I examine the role of the group leader in helping the client (the group, in this case) negotiate the environment. The reader should note that I refer to "the group," since I view it as an entity that is more than the sum of its parts (members).

A large body of group theory and research is available to the practitioner who wishes to better understand group dynamics. Our focus in this chapter is not on describing this body of literature, but rather on the practitioner's use of theoretical models and research results to develop his or her own integrated model of group practice. To illustrate this process, I have selected three classic theoretical models and one relatively new framework for discussion in relation to the group tasks: developmental (Bennis & Shepard, 1956); emotionality (Bion, 1961); environmental (Homans, 1950); and feminist self in relation (Schiller, 1993, 1993; Fedele, 1994). While there are more recently published group theories, most in my view build their constructs on these earlier models. I decided it would be helpful for the reader to have an understanding of the foundation the three classic theoretical frameworks have provided. As will be seen in the discussion, each of these theories has ideas relevant to all of the group tasks.

## Describing the Group-as-a-Whole

It is not easy to describe this second client called the group-as-a-whole. In part, the difficulty comes from the fact that we cannot actually see the properties that describe a group. When we watch a group in action, we see a collection of individuals. Compare this to a solid object, such as a chair. When we are asked to describe its properties, visual references such as materials (plastic, wood, chrome), parts (back, seat, legs), shape, size, and so on immediately come to mind.

Describing the properties of a group is more difficult. For example, *cohesion* in a group can be defined as a bond among members: a sense of identification with one another and with the group as a whole. An observer cannot see a property of the group called "cohesion," but if we observe a group for a time, we can see all of the members acting as if the group were cohesive. Other properties of groups include shared norms of proper behavior and taboo subjects. We cannot see a group norm or a taboo, but we can see a pattern of behavior from which we can infer that a norm or taboo exists. For example, in our couples' group examples earlier, I noted the members avoiding discussion of issues related to sex even though the members had indicated that there were problems in this area. From this pattern of behavior we are able to infer that sex is a taboo area in our society, and as a result, a norm has developed that it not be openly discussed. This norm was replicated in the couples' group and, in fact, it also existed between the partners, which was one of the reasons it was difficult to deal with.

For beginning group leaders, when they look at the group what they see is a collection of individuals. As a leader begins to understand the properties of the group concept and to recognize collective behavior as an expression of the group's properties, the leader begins to "see" this organism I call the group-as-a-whole. With practice, it is possible to see the collection of individuals and to see the group as well. With experience, and I am not suggesting a significant amount of time here, it becomes possible for the leader, at one and the same time, to see each individual and the group-as-a-whole. This is a conceptual breakthrough that significantly enhances a group leader's ability to pay attention to the two clients—the individual and the group.

## The Group as an Organism

EP 2.1.3a
EP 2.1.13b
EP 2.1.6b
EP 2.1.7a
EP 2.1.10g

We need to start by exploring the very idea of a group. When attempting to describe something as complex as a group, using a model is helpful. A model, as discussed in Chapter 1, is a concrete, symbolic representation of an abstract or real phenomenon. Most of us have been to a planetarium and sat in a room watching spheres in the ceiling circling a sun. Unless we were very young, we understood that this was not our solar system but a model that represented it. Having this model helped us to understand the real thing.

To develop a model to describe a group, we must find an appropriate metaphor. Two common metaphors used in the literature are the machine and the organism. In the mechanistic model, the observer uses processes such as "input," "throughput," and "output" to describe the group. This was a popular model to describe organizations, work groups, and so on in the mid-20th century. Alternately, many theorists interested in human social systems have adopted the organismic model as the most appropriate. The choice of an organism rather than a machine as a model reflects the organism's capacity for growth and emergent behavior. These terms describe a process in which a system transcends itself and creates something new that is more than just the simple sum of its parts.

To apply this idea to the group, we need to identify what is created when a group of people and a group leader are brought together that goes beyond the sum of each member's contribution. What properties exist that are unique descriptions of the group, rather than descriptions of the individual members? An example of such a property is the creation of a sense of common purpose shared by all the members of the group. This common purpose is a catalyst for the development of a tie that binds the members together.

Group culture is a second example. As the group process begins, activities in the group are governed by a group culture made up of several factors including accepted norms of behavior. In a first session, the group culture generally reflects the culture of the larger society from which the members have been drawn. As sessions continue, this culture can change, allowing new norms to emerge and govern the activities of the members. Consider how important this can be, for example, in a group for adult children of alcoholics. The parent's problem with alcohol may have been the "family secret" that everyone knew but never discussed, certainly not outside of the family. This taboo is recreated in the group in the first sessions, and changing this norm will be essential for effective work. Thus, common interests and group culture are two examples of properties of the group that transcend the simple sum of its parts, the individual members.

A third example would be the creation of roles as discussed in the first part of this chapter. When behavior is considered dynamically, then the properties of the group include assignment of roles such as deviant member, scapegoat, gatekeeper, and so on.

A final example is the group's relationship with its environment. As the group is influenced by its environment—for example, the agency, school, hospital, or community—or the group leader as a representative of the agency, it must develop adaptive behaviors to maintain itself. This pattern of adaptive behavior is yet another example of a property of the group. I will be suggesting later in this chapter that one cannot think of the group without understanding that it is interacting with its environment all of the time. In fact, the immediate or larger environment may be having a more powerful impact on the group and member behavior than anything the group leader says or does. For example, in a psychoeducational group for children in a school, it may well be that the group members' behavior is in part in reaction to the way teachers and other staff relate to the students. If group leaders ignore the impact of the environment, then they may be dealing with the symptoms and not the actual problem. In another striking example, students in a violence prevention project I directed witnessed a traumatic event from their classroom windows—an attempt at an armed highjacking of a car parked in the street. Shots were fired and students hid under their desks. How could the environment not affect the group meeting held later that day?

To summarize, we cannot actually see a group as an entity. That is why a model, such as the organism, is helpful. What we can see, however, are the activities of a group of people who appear to be influenced by this entity called the group. For example, when group purpose is clear, we can explain the members' actions as contributions in pursuit of that purpose. Again, group pressures, group expectations, and the members' sense of belonging all influence the members' behavior. The fact that a member's behavior changes as a result of believing in the existence of the group makes the group real.

In the balance of this chapter, the key ideas to note are the following:

- *I shall refer to the group as an entity*
- *Employ the organism as a metaphor*
- *And focus on the group's developmental, internal, and external tasks*

## Developmental Tasks for the Group

Two major group tasks have already been mentioned without each having been specifically described as such. These illustrate how a group can have tasks that differ from the specific tasks of each member. In Chapter 11 on group beginnings, I addressed what could be called the group's formation tasks. The group needed to develop a working contract that reflected the individual members' needs as well as the service stake of the sponsoring setting. In addition, a group consensus needed to be developed. This consensus reflected the common concerns shared by members as well as an agreement as to where the work might start. Reaching consensus on the work is a task that is unique to work with multiple clients (groups, families, couples, and so on), because individual clients simply begin where they wish—there is no need to reach a consensus with other clients. The group's formation tasks also include initial clarification of mutual obligations and expectations. The effectiveness of the group depends on how well it accomplishes these formation tasks. The skills of the leader in helping the group to work on these formation tasks were described in Chapter 11 as contracting skills and illustrated with a range of first meetings.

A second critical group task involves meeting individual members' needs. For the group to survive and flourish, it must have individual members. Members feel a sense of belonging and develop a stake in the work of the group when they can perceive that their own related needs are being met. If these needs cease to be met, members will simply drop out of the group, either by not attending or by not participating. In Chapter 12 on the work phase in the group, we saw how easily the group can miss the offered concerns of a member or turn away from these concerns when they hit the group members too hard. In still other examples, individual members did not immediately see the relation between the work of the group and their own sense of urgency. Earlier in this chapter, we saw how members can play functional roles in the group, some of which cut them off from being able to use the group to meet their own needs. In each of these cases, leaders attempted to help members use the group more effectively, reach out and offer mutual aid more effectively, or both simultaneously. All of these efforts were directed toward helping the group with its task of meeting individual members' needs. Thus, in order to grow and survive, a group must address the tasks of formation and meeting individual members' needs.

Other sets of tasks linked to the developmental work of the group are those in which the group works on its relationship to the leader (the authority theme) and the relationships among members (the intimacy theme). Schwartz (1971) describes these two critical tasks as follows:

> In the culture of the group two main themes come to characterize the members' ways of working together: one, quite familiar to the caseworker, is the theme of authority in which the members are occupied with their relationship to the helping person and the ways in which this relationship is instrumental to their purpose; the other, more strange and threatening to the caseworker, is the theme of intimacy, in which the members are concerned with their internal relationships and the problems of mutual aid. It is the interplay of these factors—external authority and mutual interdependence—that provides much of the driving force of the group experience. (p. 9)

The group's ability to deal with concerns related to authority and intimacy is closely connected to the development of a working culture, established through common interests and group norms of behavior.

Finally, the group needs to develop a structure for work that will enable it to carry out its tasks effectively. For example, responsibilities may have to be shared through a division of labor, and roles may need to be assigned formally or informally.

The following five major task areas will be introduced in the balance of this chapter:

- *The relationship to the leader (the authority theme)*
- *The relationship among members (the intimacy theme)*
- *The development of a working culture*

- *The development of a structure for work*
- *The relationship to the environment*

Obviously, these tasks overlap a great deal: Work on one area often includes work on the others. Although somewhat artificial, the division is still helpful. Recall that discussion of these tasks will draw on elements of group theory from three foundation models and one relatively new model, and will focus on constructs that seem relevant, applying them to practice examples.

# The Relationship to the Leader: The Authority Theme

In Chapter 11 I discussed the authority theme, the relationship between the leader and the group members, as an important issue to address early in the life of the group. I suggested that the question: "Who is this leader and what kind of person will he or she be?" is on the minds of all group members as they begin in the group. Even if the issue is addressed directly in the first sessions, the authority theme does not simply go away. It remains as an important theme to be explored at different points in the life of the group. This next section explores this theme using a classic theoretical framework that still guides group practice today. The reader familiar with more recent group developmental models will recognize their debt to Bennis and Shepard (1956).

## The Bennis and Shepard Model—The Issue of Authority

Bennis and Shepard (1956) address the themes of authority and intimacy in their model of group development, and several of their key concepts are useful in explaining group process. Their observations, however, are based on their work with laboratory training groups (T-groups), in which graduate students studied group dynamics using their own experiences as a group. As a result, some ideas in their theory may be group-specific and therefore might not apply to groups of the type discussed in this book. Our analysis will illustrate how a practitioner can use what he or she likes from a good theory without adopting it whole.

The examples that follow illustrate the two sides to group members' feelings: On one hand, they are afraid of the leader and the leader's authority; and on the other hand, they want the leader to take responsibility for the group. Bennis and Shepard (1956) attribute these two sets of feelings to two types of personalities in the group: the *dependent member* and the *counterdependent member*. They believe that the dependency invokes great uncertainty for members, and that the first major phase of group development, the *dependence phase*, involves work on this question. They describe three subphases within this first phase.

- In the first subphase, *dependence-flight*, the group is led by the dependent leaders, who seek to involve the leader more actively in control of the group.

- In the second subphase, *counterdependence-flight*, the counterdependent leaders move in and attempt to take over the group. The group often shows anger toward the leader in this phase. Two subgroups develop—one that argues for structure and another that argues against it.

- In the third subphase, *resolution-catharsis*, members who are unconflicted—independent and relatively untroubled by authority issues—assume group leadership.

According to Bennis and Shepard, this "overthrow" of the leader leads to each member taking responsibility for the group: The leader is no longer seen as "magical," and the power struggles are replaced by work on shared goals.

In considering this model it is important to understand that the groups studied by the authors were marked by group leaders who were extremely and purposively passive in the beginning, which, in my view, increased the members' anxiety about the authority theme. The theory was that if the leader were passive, and I mean remaining silent and unresponsive to group member appeals for some form of intervention, the group would eventually have to take responsibility and develop its own internal leadership. The authors described this as a *barometric event* that impacts the group and marks the shift from one phase to the next, for example, when the leader is "overthrown."

My observation of groups such as these during and since my own graduate training has been that the first and most powerful barometric event was actually the passivity of the leader. The second was the lack of a clear external purpose other than that of examining the group's process. Even today some groups are structured this way and referred to as "process" groups. Thus, much of the interactions that followed were directly a result of the leader's early passivity and a lack of clear external purpose. At the same time, the idea that groups have to first address the authority theme and "overthrow" the leader, and then take responsibility for the group and deal with the intimacy theme, are useful constructs. This is a good example of how one can take part of a theory without adopting it whole. Although many of the specifics of the Bennis and Shepard model are restricted to the particular groups observed, we can apply to all groups the general outline of this struggle over dependency.

The five issues of the authority theme explored in the discussion that follows include:

- *Who owns the group?*
- *The group leader as the outsider*
- *The group leader's demand for work*
- *The group leader's limitations*
- *The group leader as a caring and giving person*

In the first example that follows, we can see the early emergence of the authority theme over the question of "Who owns the group?"

***Who Owns the Group?—The Couples' Group and the Authority Theme*** In the second session of the couples' group, the members were watching to see if I would carry out the role I had described in the first session. However, my intervention was actually an example of acting on instead of acting with a member. Once again, Lou, the 69-year-old member, signaled the members' concern about this issue.

**Practice Points:** Note that I catch my mistake and use this as an opportunity to further clarify the authority theme, with my encouraging members to catch me when I made a mistake.

> One couple was presenting a problem that they were having that involved the husband's grown children from another marriage. I noticed each spouse was telling the group things about the other, rather than speaking directly to each other. I interrupted Frank, the member in his 50s who had remarried to Ann, and suggested he speak directly to his wife. After a noticeable hesitation, he began to speak to her, but he soon returned to speaking to me. I interrupted him again. Once again, he seemed slightly thrown by my action.

As this was going on, I noticed that Lou was looking distressed, staring at the floor, and covering his mouth with his hand. After watching this for a time, I reached for the message. "Lou, you look like you have something to say." He responded, "No, that's all right. I can wait 'til later." I said, "I have the feeling it's important, and I think it has something to do with me." I had been feeling uncomfortable but was unaware why. Lou said, "Well, if you want to hear it now, OK. Every time you interrupt Frank that way, I think he loses his train of thought. And this business of telling him to speak to Jane is just like the stuff I described last week." I was surprised by what he said, and I remained quiet while I took it in.

Frank said, "You know, he's right. You do throw my line of thought every time you interrupt that way." I said, "I guess I ended up doing exactly the kind of thing I said last week I would try not to do. I have not explained to you, Frank, why I think it might help to talk directly with your wife rather than to me. I guess you must feel my comments, because you don't really understand why I'm suggesting this, as sort of pushing you around." Frank said: "Well, a bit." Lou said, "That's exactly what I mean." I responded, "I won't be perfect, Lou. I will also make mistakes. That's why it's so important that you call me on it, the way you just did. Only why wait until I ask?" Lou said, "It's not easy to call you; you're the leader." I said, "I think I can appreciate that, only you can see how it would speed things up if you did."

**Practice Summary.**   This second week's discussion was even more important than the first, because the members had a chance to see me being confronted with a mistake and not only acknowledging it but also encouraging Lou to be even more direct. The point made was that they did have rights and that they should not let my authority get in the way. At this point, you may be thinking that to reach for or encourage such negative feedback would be difficult for a beginning group leader. Ironically, the leader needs this kind of honesty from group members most when she or he is least confident and least prepared to hear it. Beginning group leaders should expect to miss these signals in sessions, but as their confidence grows, they should start to reach for the negatives later in the same session or in the session that follows. This is what I meant earlier in the book by the suggestion that we shorten the distance from when we make mistakes to when we catch them. Catching mistakes in the same session or the next session, in my view, is very skillful practice.

The authority theme appeared many other times in similar discussions, for example, about the agenda for our work. When I appeared to return to an area of work without checking on the group's interest, members would participate in an obvious illusion of work. When I challenged the illusion, we could discuss why it was hard for them simply to let me know when they thought I was leading them away from their concerns.

**Practice Points:**   Issues of control also emerged in connection with responsibility for the effectiveness of the work. In the next example, one couple had spent an unusually long time discussing an issue without getting to the point. I could see the reactions in the group and inquired about what was going on.

Fran, the member in her 30s, responded by saying it was getting boring, and she was waiting for me to do something. Because this was a middle phase session, I found myself annoyed that everyone was waiting for me. I said, with some feeling, "How come you are waiting for me to do something? This is your group, you know, and I think you could take this responsibility, too."

**Practice Summary:** The resulting discussion revealed that members felt it was risky to take one another on (the intimacy theme), so they left it to me. We were able to sort out that members, too, needed to take responsibility for the group's effectiveness. We discussed what the members were worried about if they were more direct with each other. In another striking example of how process and content can be integrated, I asked them if that was the same reason they had trouble confronting each other as couples. A major theme throughout the group sessions was how hard and risky it felt to be direct with each other, particularly in uncomfortable areas of their relationships.

## The Group Leader as the Outsider

Issues of control are just one aspect of the general theme of relationship to the leader. A second area concerns the leader's place as an outsider to the group. This arises particularly in groups in which the leader has not had life experiences that are central to the group members' themes of concern.

For instance, in a group for parents of children who have been diagnosed as hyperactive, the question arises of whether the leader who has no children can understand them and their problems. This is a variation on the similar question raised in the discussion of the beginning phase in work with individuals. The following excerpt illustrates this aspect of the authority theme struggle in the group context.

### Parents of Hyperactive Children: The Leader as the Outsider

**Practice Points:** Note the importance of the group leader not becoming defensive and acknowledging that she was an outsider and had much to learn from the parents. This is most often seen by the group members as a sign of strength and not, as inexperienced group leaders believe, a sign of weakness.

> Discussion got back again to causes of hyperactivity. Ann, who had thought it was hereditary, explained that her husband thought that he had been hyperactive as a child, except that nobody gave him the title. Marilyn said that her husband had also said that he had been like her son and had felt that her son would grow out of it. The group picked up on this idea and seemed to like the possibility. I was asked by Betty what I thought. I said I didn't know the answer, but that, from what I did know, not enough research had been done. The group began throwing questions at me, related to general conditions and medications, and I couldn't answer them. I admitted that I knew very little about hyperactivity. I was certainly nowhere near being the experts that they were.
>
> Someone asked if I had children. I said that I didn't. Beatrice wondered what work I had done with hyperactive children and extended this to children with other problems. I answered as honestly as I could. She wondered whether I was overwhelmed by their feelings. I replied that she and others present were really concerned about how I felt toward them, and whether I really understood what it felt like to be the mother of a hyperactive child. She agreed. I added that last week, when I had said I was feeling overwhelmed, I was really getting into what it felt like to have such a child. It was pointed out to me that I was the only one in the group who didn't have a hyperactive child—that I was really the outsider. Beatrice offered to lend me her son for a weekend, so that I could really see what it was like. Everyone laughed. (I think they were delighted at this.) I said that

they were telling me that it was important that I understand what it's like, and I wondered whether I was coming across as not understanding. They didn't think so. I said that the more they talked, the better feeling I got about what they were going through. Toward the end of this, there was a lot of subgroup talking going on, and I waited (thankful for the break).

## The Group Leader's Demand for Work

The third area of the authority theme relates to the group's reaction to the leader as a person who makes demands. For the group to be effective, the leader must do more than contract clearly and be empathic. The group will often come up against obstacles, many of which relate to the group members' ambivalence about discussion of difficult areas. As the leader makes demands, group members will inevitably generate negative feelings. If the leader is doing a good job, group members will sometimes become angry with the leader for refusing to let them off the hook. If group members are *never* angry at their group leaders, the leaders are probably not doing their job. Conversely, if group members are *always* angry at their leaders, that's a problem as well. Recall the earlier-described false dichotomy between support and confrontation, and the idea of building up a "fund" of caring to draw upon when making a demand for work is required.

Of course, clients also have positive feelings associated with the fact that the leader is empathetic and cares enough about the group to make these demands. The negative feelings, however, need to be expressed; otherwise, they can move beneath the surface and emerge in unconscious expressions, such as general apathy. As we have seen, the leader must feel comfortable in her or his role to be willing to deal with this negative feedback.

### Posttraumatic Stress Disorder Vietnam Veterans Group

**EP 2.1.1b**
**EP 2.1.4a**
**EP 2.1.4d**
**EP 2.1.10g**

In the example that follows, we see the delicate process of developing a good working relationship between a group of still-traumatized, male Vietnam veterans in an outpatient clinic of a VA hospital and a young female graduate student who takes on the role of new coleader, along with her supervisor. In a bold and creative manner, she challenges the men to address their internalized negative feelings that result from the way they were treated when they returned home from the war. Although the responses to today's returning Iraq war soldiers is strikingly different—because most of the antagonism of antiwar protesters is directed toward the administration, not the soldiers—there are still lessons to be learned from this example.

**Practice Points:**   Note the following in these excerpts:

- *The group leader's courage in addressing the issue of her gender*
- *Her capacity for empathy with their struggles on the issue of pride*
- *Her tenacious reaching for the group members' strength and finding it*
- *How the earlier-described connections between how we feel, think, and act interact with each other*
- *Her recognition that the group's relationship to its environment (the hospital and community) is central to the work*

The first sessions described below deal with the issue of a new coleader who is young and female. I believe these sessions lay the groundwork for her to make a later demand for work on the members, so they are described in some detail.

**Type of Group:** Posttraumatic Stress Disorder Vietnam Veterans Group

**Age Range of Members:** Early 50s through early 60s

**Gender, Ethnic Background, Sexual Orientation, and Racial Information:** On average, this biweekly group comprises 10 male individuals. Each member has been diagnosed with posttraumatic stress disorder (PTSD), and some receive a service-connected disability for this diagnosis. At the present time, the group is closed, and all members have been involved for a minimum of 2 years.

**Dates Covered in Record Form:** 9/14/06 to 11/9/06

**Group Task:** Relationship to the environment

**Problem Statement:** Beginning in mid-September 2006, this group was presented with a cofacilitator for the first time after a number of years. As a new authority figure in the group, my role as a young, female intern and group cofacilitator needed to be clarified. After the completion of this process, my goal was to confront the shame, hurt, and guilt when these veterans returned home to the United States after serving in Vietnam and receiving a very negative public response.

**How the Problem Came to My Attention:** After attending my first brief group session for approximately 20 minutes, in a nervous state of mind, there were mixed statements and body language presented that signified a welcoming to their group but also a level of uneasiness by some of the group members. I realized that I would need to promptly address these issues.

### Summary of the Work

I entered the group room mid-session because I was in between mandatory hospital trainings. My supervisor greeted me and introduced me as the visitor they were expecting. I addressed this comment by saying, "Hello, my name is Nicole. It is very nice to finally meet all of you." The male veterans all responded with a friendly hello and welcome, and one man, George, directed me to have a seat wherever I liked. After allowing the man who was speaking to finish the rest of his story, I further introduced myself. I spoke to the group by telling them that I am a second-year graduate student and explained that my role at the VA Hospital was as an intern. I explained I would be attending their group through next May, when I graduate. I explained that Barbara, their group leader, is my supervisor, and mentioned that I had hoped to be employed at the VA in the future, after I graduate.

There was silence after I stated my role. This was followed by my supervisor requesting that each member tell me a little about himself and his background. To my surprise, the veterans were not shy about offering information until it came to George, the third group member to speak. He began to introduce himself by saying, "You know, I feel like there is tension going on in the room because you are very pretty. I don't know if the others are feeling this way, but I just wanted to get this off of my chest." Completely caught off guard—feeling my face become flushed out of embarrassment and noticing that no one was responding to George's statement—I responded by saying, "Well, thank you." I immediately felt that my appearance was a hindrance to the group members. As a young, inexperienced leader, I also feared that I would not be able to be looked upon as a leadership figure, but only as a sexual object.

**Practice Points:** The student's reaction was understandable, and it would have been hard to respond any differently. However, in reflection, one of the issues these men faced was their response to women and their somewhat inappropriate way of handling such encounters, and this may have been signaled by George. It was almost as if George was saying: "Do you want to see how inappropriate we can be dealing with women?" This issue would have to wait for another session, but one can see how process, once again, can connect to content. It's also apparent that one can be insightful after the fact but that it is not so easy when the group leader is experiencing the moment. One man raises the issue of the intern as an outsider and she responds directly without defensiveness.

The second-to-last man introduced himself and then asked me two questions in a forceful tone of voice regarding my comprehension of the subject he was discussing. He said, "Do you understand?" I responded with, "I think so," even though I felt somewhat confused. I stated, "I realize that I am new here and still have a lot to learn. I recognize that I am young and I may have some questions, so I hope that everyone will teach me even if some of my questions appear to be silly." The group members were very understanding as they responded with "sure" and "no problem." I still wondered if they questioned how someone could help them if she or he didn't understand their experiences.

The last man to speak, named Dennis, was very friendly and reassured me that none of the group members would ever hurt me. I responded to Dennis by letting him know that was greatly appreciated, but I was not under the assumption that they would hurt me. The group members spoke over one another with muffled responses of "Don't worry" and "Yeah." This comment made me feel as though the group members thought I viewed them in a frightening and negative manner.

**Practice Points:**   Once again, with hindsight, we can see that the comment about not hurting the leader was also an indirect communication about the group members' concern as to how people reacted to them as Vietnam veterans. After presenting this excerpt in class, the student addressed this issue, at least in part. Note that she has tuned in to possible concerns on the part of the group members and shares her hunches directly.

During the third session, I initiated the group conversation by speaking to Dennis, who had previously stated that none of the group members would ever harm me. I presented to him that I was not clear as to what he meant by this and expressed that I felt that it was necessary that we speak about this because I did not want the group members to feel that I had any negative impressions of them. I explained that I had three different interpretations of the statement. Due to my age and my not fully understanding all war terms and experiences, I wondered if they either felt their discussions would be too traumatizing for me or that I feared them because I knew that they had killed people. I wondered if they thought I had negative images of them based on the nonsupportive media their war received and movies produced later that did not present the total reality of the war and their experiences.

Dennis disagreed with my perceptions and revealed to me that he did not want me to believe that the group members were nasty and miserable men who disapproved of my presence in their group. He stated, "In reality, we are all big teddy bears." I expressed to the group that I was not intimidated by them, that I trusted that no one would hurt me, and that I greatly appreciated everyone treating me nicely.

I brought up the statement I had made in the first session that I hoped the group members would teach me if I had questions because I was still learning. I specified to them that I recognized that this was their time to share their feelings with one another, explained that I was aware that their group session was time limited, and stated that I wanted them all to get the most beneficial experience out of their session without me interrupting to ask irrelevant questions. The men responded with comments including, "It is okay to ask questions," "Feel free to ask questions because you young people can help educate others about our experiences and real feelings," and "It is not a burden to our time limit."

**Practice Points:** Once again, with courage, she returns to the comments about her attractiveness in the first session by directly raising them with George.

I directed my attention to George, who had mentioned that he felt tension in the room because of my appearance. I instantly noticed that George appeared a little nervous when I brought this subject up, because he sat up and looked pink in the face. I described to him that I was not trying to make him feel uncomfortable or put him on the spot, but I wanted to know if my presence in the group initiated the same feeling of tension in anyone else. The group remained silent. I stated that I personally felt a little uncomfortable when that statement was made and wanted to know if my presence as a young female was going to impact the group in a way that would not allow them to disclose information as easily as they were able to before my entrance into the group. The group members replied that they did not feel this way and that they were used to working with an attractive female leader before my entry into the group.

**Practice Points:** This student's directness and willingness to reach for the meaning behind the previous comments demonstrated her strength and willingness to risk. Her honesty about her discomfort, a form of sharing her feelings, also contributed to the beginning of the working relationship and their respect for her in response to her respect for them. She still misses the implications of the comment in respect to their relationships to women and others outside of the group; however, she is making sound progress in developing the working relationship. In the excerpt that follows, she begins the process of exploring their internalized negative feelings.

Based on group conversation concerning the humiliation and dishonor Vietnam veterans received when they returned home, it was evident that the members lacked feelings of pride for their military service and were embarrassed to admit that they served in Vietnam. I opened the fourth session with the topic of Veterans Day approaching in the next couple of weeks. I asked the men if they could describe whether they observed the holiday in a positive or negative manner. I specifically asked whether they could reflect on feelings of pride and/or shame on this special day. I received a number of negative responses. These included remarks such as, "It is a holiday that observes veterans from all wars except the Vietnam War," "If it was a real holiday, then only veterans would receive special sale prices on this day," "How could I observe this holiday and feel pride if I was afraid to even admit that I served in Vietnam?" "It is just another day to me," and "The only place I would feel safe celebrating this holiday is with other Vietnam vets who understand one another's experiences." The men came to a general consensus that they did not feel pride or increased levels of self-esteem on Veterans Day.

I asked the veterans if they could discuss specific events that influenced them to feel shameful on this holiday and in general. The veterans discussed their disappointment at how they were treated by their families and their employers when they returned home, the names they were called, the lack of interest people had in trying to understand their war experience, no one seeming to recognize that they had to do what they were commanded to do while in the military, and how difficult it was to adjust to civilian life because the average citizen did not seem to understand the reality of the Vietnam War. I stated to the group that I had great respect for them serving in Vietnam, and that it angered me to know how badly they were treated when they returned home. I indicated that I was beginning to understand the severity of the traumas witnessed and experienced while in the war and commented that I gave them all a lot of credit for staying strong inside and seeking help through this group and individual counseling.

**Practice Points:** Because the Vietnam War was more than 40 years in the past, it is hard for young leaders to understand the turmoil in the country and the size and intensity of the antiwar movement and its impact on already traumatized veterans. This student would have experienced the wars in Iraq and Afghanistan, and although there were many in this country who objected to the original wars and the continuation of the wars, these feelings did not generally carry over to the returning troops. This was in sharp contrast to the response to the Vietnam veterans.

This conversation provides an important education for the student and allows her to demonstrate her empathy and respect for the group members. This expression is important because it lays the foundation for her to make a demand for work—the group members will know it comes from caring and with an understanding of how hard the steps she asks them to take will be. In her most impressive moments, she refuses to accept the word "no" and insists that they take the steps needed to face their demons. Using humor and persistence, she even confronts them when they try to avoid public exposure by hiding and smoking. I commented to her on her assignment paper when she handed it in: "You are very strict." The key here is that—by making a demand that they be strong—she sends the message that she believes they are strong.

It was at this point that I asked the veterans to please bring in their medals from the war and wear an item of clothing such as a hat that identified that they served in the war to the next session, because it was two days before Veterans Day. I described to them that I wanted them to be proud of their duty in the military, and that I hoped that they would be able to acknowledge that they could be recognized as Vietnam veterans without being retaliated against by the public. The veterans agreed to this after complaining that they really didn't want to do it and that they did not know where they had put their medals. I explained to them that we needed to work together to overcome these feelings and thoughts that have burdened their lives for many years.

The fifth session began with the veterans passing around their medals and certificates. To my surprise, six out of eight people who attended brought in their medals, seven men were wearing Vietnam hats, and one man brought in a catalog from which those who had misplaced their medals could order replacements. One veteran brought in red poppy pins, which represent veteran appreciation, and a roll of brand-new Canadian quarters, because every year a new word is printed on the back of the coin to represent veterans.

**Practice Points:** The exercise suggested by the group leader helped the men begin to address their lost pride in their efforts that had been overcome by the response on their return home. Her next step is to ask them to take their veteran selves outside of the group room and face the public.

After the sharing process, I told the group that I wanted them to go down to the cafeteria or to the main waiting room near the outpatient entrance as a group for 20 minutes with their Vietnam apparel on. I disclosed to the group that I had chosen these specific places because they were areas in which there would be veterans from different wars, employees, and friends and family members who were not veterans. Their immediate response was a rejection of this suggestion. The group made comments such as, "People in the halls are going to hide or put on protective gear if they see a group of Vietnam vets, because we are a bunch of crazies." I told them I knew that they could do it because they have one another for support. I persuaded them to hold their heads up high and be confident regardless of whether they were questioned about traveling through the hospital as a group. I made the group aware that I would be coming down to check on them in about 5 minutes to make sure that they really did go to one of the locations.

When I went down, I found the group outside smoking, and they had not gone to either location. They responded, "How did you know we were out here?" I joked with them and said, "If I can't have a cigarette, you can't either!" They commented, "Wow, I'm surprised you were able to walk out here and confront a whole group of males alone!" I laughed and said, "Just because you may feel that others are scared around you as a group, I'm not!" I then told them that we should go down to the cafeteria and get some coffee as a group.

We did this together and the veterans ended up staying longer than planned and talked to me and others eating in the cafeteria. The veterans showed an interest in speaking to me on a personal level without the presence of my supervisor. They questioned what I thought of working with their war population and what other things I was doing in the mental health clinic. I felt that this helped to increase our comfort level and establish a stronger rapport.

**Practice Points:** The growth in the therapeutic alliance is evident as the men begin to see this counselor as someone they can use for individual concerns as well. After pushing hard for the men to take the difficult public step, the group returns to the group room and the leader begins to explore their reactions to the experience.

When we returned to the group room, I raised the question, "In recognizing that you all were avoiding this experience by going out to smoke in an area where no others were present, was it as difficult of an experience as you originally perceived it to be?" The veterans stated that they were shocked to not receive any negative comments and to be as comfortable as they were together in an identified group of Vietnam veterans. The men responded positively to my asking whether or not this was a beneficial experience for them. One individual responded by recognizing that being in their group allowed them to normalize their feelings, but up until now, they had never left the safe space of their group room to perform an outside activity as a group. I asked if they would feel comfortable in the future doing a new activity outside of their group room again. They responded in agreement to this.

**Where the Problem Stands Now:** I feel that I have successfully addressed and clarified my role as a new helping figure. I have shown that I am confident in attending to taboo subjects and interested in reaching for further clarification with the group members regarding my role and subjects discussed. I became self-assured that the rapport between me and the group had strengthened to a deeper level when the men felt comfortable enough to ask me self-disclosing questions and speak to me in the cafeteria from an educational perspective. It communicated to me that they were interested in getting to know me as a person and were willing to devote part of their limited group time to assist me in further understanding their feelings and experiences while in Vietnam and after returning home. I feel that positive change has occurred in the group and will continue to be reinforced when new interventions are presented and activities outside of the safety of the group room are conducted.

**Practice Summary.** The student group leader has both developed a positive working relationship with the men—working across gender, age, and experience—and demonstrated her faith and belief in their ability to change. The excerpt of her practice over time has demonstrated her courage in addressing the issue of her gender, her capacity for empathy with their struggles on the issue of pride, her tenacious reaching for the group members' strength and finding it, and how the connections between how we feel, think, and act interact with each other. This example could also have been used later in this chapter as an example of helping the group negotiate its environment.

## The Group Leader's Limitations

A fourth issue is the need for the group to come to grips with the reality of the leader's limitations. Members hope that the leader, or some other expert, will be able to solve their problems. This is, in part, a result of the emerging dependency of the group. Once the group members realize that the leader has no solutions, their own work really begins. However, this realization is painful for the members and often for the leaders as well.

**Practice Points:** At the end of one particularly painful and depressing discussion in the parents' group dealing with their children's hyperactivity, when the members recognized that the drugs and the professionals were not going to "make the problem go away," a member appealed to the leader to cheer them up.

*Parents of Hyperactive Children: Can Someone Cheer Me Up?* We were way over our time. I started to sum up some of the feelings that came out today. I said that they had really been saying all along how helpless they felt that they couldn't do anything to help the children, and how hopeless they were feeling that there wasn't a solution for them. Marilyn said to me that that's how they felt, depressed and helpless. She said that I always came up with something at the end to make them feel better. I had better come up with something really good today, because they needed it. I said that I was feeling the same way, thinking to myself, "What can I say that's going to take the depression and hurt away?" I told her that I didn't have a magic formula, that I wished that I could suggest something. I knew how much she and all of them wished that I could help them with a solution. Rose said that they were feeling depressed, but they shouldn't blame themselves. I said that perhaps part of the depression was related to the fact that they themselves hadn't been able to help their children more, and they felt terrible about it. She seemed to be so terribly depressed, more than ever before. I know because that's exactly how I felt.

There was not too much discussion on the way out, as I didn't to know what to say to them (usually we joke around a bit). Marilyn said to me that I let her down—I didn't come up with my little blurb to pep them up. I said that she was feeling very depressed and she looked to me to say something to make things easier. I said that she wanted a solution, and I didn't have one. She said to me that perhaps I did, and I was holding back. I said to her that she was very disappointed in me that I hadn't been able to make things easier. I wished that I did have the magic solution that they all wanted so desperately, but I didn't have one. After this, the members left.

## The Group Leader as a Caring and Giving Person

A final aspect of the authority theme requires the group to deal with their reactions to the leader as a caring and giving person. The group members watch as the leader relates to them and to the others in the group. They can see the pain in the leader's face if he or she feels the hurt deeply; after a while, they can sense the genuineness of the empathy. This side of the leader provokes powerful responses in the group, and a mutual flow of positive affect results. An interesting discussion in my couples' group illustrates the importance of this aspect of the authority theme, as well as the group's awareness of this issue.

***The Couples' Group and the "Crying Chair"*** In the session before the Christmas break (the eighth session overall), one member arrived late and distraught. She sat down in the empty chair to my left, and, for the first time in the group, she shared a frightening medical problem her husband was facing. Until then, this member had appeared to be "without problems," because her husband was, in her mind, the identified patient. I comforted her while she told her story, and I tried to help her verbally and nonverbally—touching the back of her hand, communicating my empathic responses to her feelings. The group also reached out with support. In the second part of the session, after the immediate issue had been somewhat resolved and the member was in better shape, we carried out a planned midpoint evaluation of the group.

**Practice Points:** In discussing the way we worked as a group, one of the members raised the authority theme. Note how they had recognized an ongoing process in the group that I had missed.

> Fran said, "I knew that this was Jane's night to get help the minute she walked in the door." (Jane was the member who had been crying.) When I inquired how she knew, she said, "Because she sat in the crying chair." She went on to point out that all of the people who had cried in sessions—4 of the 10 group members—had sat down in that chair at the beginning of the session. In fact, some had sat apart from their spouses for the first time in the group. Other members nodded in recognition of the accuracy of Fran's observation. I inquired whether they had any thoughts about why that was so. Rose said, "Because that's the chair next to you, and we sit there to get some support when the going gets rough." I responded, "Could you talk a bit about what it is about me that causes you to sit there or feel I can support you? This is important as part of our evaluation, but it can also tell us something about what it is you might want from one another."

**Practice Points:** The request for specifics was designed to encourage discussion of the members' feelings about the leader reaching out to them with caring. In addition, as is often the case, the process in the group can serve to assist group members in understanding their own relationships more clearly. My record continues:

> Louise said, "It's because we can feel free to say anything to you, and you won't judge us. We can tell you our feelings." Rose continued, "And we know you really feel our hurt. It's not phony—you really care." Lou, the 69-year-old member who had been most critical of helping professionals in the first session, and had cried himself sitting in that chair, said, "It's safe next to you. We can share our innermost feelings and know that you won't let us get hurt." As I listened to the members, I felt myself deeply moved by the affect in their voices, and I shared that with them. "You know, it means a great deal to me to have

you feel that way—that you can sense my feelings for you. I have grown to care about you quite a bit. It's surprising to me, sometimes, just how hard things in this group hit me—just how important you really have become."

**Practice Points:**   The authority theme is a two-way street, and the leader will have as much feeling toward the members as the members have toward the leader. The countertransference dynamics need to be made a part of the discussion. The honest feelings of the leader, freely expressed, are often the key to aiding the group as it comes to grips with its relationship to the leader.

### Authority Theme Summary

In summary, some aspects of the authority theme to be dealt with during the life of the group include the leader's control, responsibility, and status as an outsider, and the group's reactions to the leader's demands, limitations, and caring. Although the phases in which a group deals with issues are never neat and orderly, a pattern emerges: As the issues of authority are dealt with, the group becomes more ready to turn to its second major developmental task, the relationships among members (the intimacy theme).

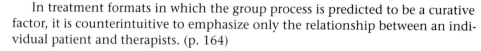

## Group Member Relationships: The Intimacy Theme

A second major theme and driving force for a group is the intimacy theme. This refers to the way in which the members relate to each other. Recent research has highlighted that in addition to the therapeutic alliance to the leader (the authority theme), a therapeutic alliance has to develop to this entity called the group-as-a-whole (the intimacy theme).

### Cohesion and Therapeutic Alliance to the Group-as-a-Whole

**EP 2.1.6b**

Recent research, for example, in the group psychotherapy field, has been paying increased attention to the concept of the group-as-a-whole and exploring both group development issues and their impact on outcomes. For example, while the concept of the "therapeutic alliance" between a therapist and patient has been examined, and its positive impact on outcomes has been evident in the literature, it has not been as widely examined in terms of alliance to the group-as-a-whole. Lindgren, Barber, and Sandahl (2008) have argued that

> In treatment formats in which the group process is predicted to be a curative factor, it is counterintuitive to emphasize only the relationship between an individual patient and therapists. (p. 164)

In their own pilot study of patients diagnosed with burnout-related depression who received short-term psychodynamic group psychotherapy, they found an association between patient report of group alliance (using the group version of the California Psychotherapy Alliance Scales) and two of their three outcome measures.

> After controlling for initial level of outcome measures and group membership, mean alliance was significantly predictive of decreases in anxiety and global symptoms, but not in depression. Alliance to the group-as-a-whole explained 50% to 55% of variance in change of global symptoms and anxiety after control of initial symptom level and group membership, and 22% of the variance in change of depression. (p. 173)

There was an interesting finding that relates to the model presented in this chapter, that groups first develop the working relationship with the leader (the authority theme) and then with other members (the intimacy theme). The researchers found that alliance to the group-as-a-whole was lower in the early sessions of the research groups but became stronger in the middle or work phase of the group. In addition, the association of middle phase group alliance with the outcome measures was significantly stronger than the alliance at the beginning phase. While this pilot study had a number of limitations, including the number of patients in the final analysis (19), the authors suggest that an increase in process research of the group-as-a-whole would be helpful.

In another study of group therapeutic alliance and cohesion by Joyce, Piper, and Ogrodniczuk (2007), the authors examined the impact of each on outcomes in short-term group therapy.

> In the group context, then, treatment benefit may be facilitated by the patient's relationship with the therapist (alliance), the patient's sense of cohesion with the other patients, the patients' experience of cohesion to the group as a whole, or some combination of these relationships. In this study, our aims were to explore, first, how global measures of the alliance and cohesion may overlap and, second, how they may jointly influence group therapy outcome. (p. 270)

In order to pursue these aims, the researchers used measures of cohesion that assessed the quality of the patient's relationship to the group as a whole [commitment] and the quality of the relationships with the therapist and other members [compatibility], from the perspective of each group member and the group leader (p. 273). Patients were matched on two personality variables and then randomly assigned to either an interpretative or a supportive group therapy, and each group was assigned a therapist. Of the 107 patients who completed the 12 sessions (32 attended less than 8 and were considered dropouts), a relatively equal number were in each group. The two groups were equally successful in achieving a number of positive outcomes including, for example, relief of grief symptoms.

The authors reported, among others, the following significant outcomes:

- The patient-related and therapist-related alliance variables had a modest degree of overlap. Patients and therapists had similar views of the level of alliance.
- The therapist's view of the alliance was moderately associated with the patient's rating of commitment to the group and to the other members' rating of the patient's compatibility.
- The patient-rated alliance was directly associated with improvement on all three outcome factors: general symptoms, grief symptoms, and target objectives/life satisfaction.
- The group alliance variables were more consistently associated with outcomes than cohesion variables.

While both studies report important limitations, nevertheless they mark an interesting venture into operationalizing key concepts such as group alliance, compatibility, commitment, cohesion, and so forth—and their impact on each other and on outcomes. As this research continues, it will add to our understanding of this entity called the group-as-a-whole. It should also offer insights into the mechanisms of change in group practice. In the next section, I return to the classic Bennis and Shepard model, but this time in relation to the intimacy theme.

## The Bennis and Shepard Model

Once again, Bennis and Shepard's (1956) theory can provide helpful insights. In addition to concerns about dependency, a second major area of internal uncertainty for group members relates to *interdependence*. This has to do with questions of intimacy—that is, the group members' concerns about how close they wish to get to one another.

In Bennis and Shepard's model, the group moves from the first phase, concerned with dependence and marked by a preoccupation with authority relations, to the interdependence phase, characterized by issues of peer group relationships. The two sets of member personalities that emerge in relation to this issue are the overpersonal and counterpersonal group members; these parallel the dependent and the counterdependent personalities of the first phase. Once again, three subphases are identified:

- the *enchantment-flight subphase*, in which good feelings abound and efforts are directed toward healing wounds;

- the *disenchantment-flight* subphase, in which the counterpersonals take over from the overpersonals in reaction to the growing intimacy; and

- the *consensual validation* subphase, in which the unconflicted members once again provide the leadership the group needs to move to a new level of work characterized by honest communication among members.

As pointed out earlier, the specifics of the Bennis and Shepard model relate most directly to the dynamics of training groups (T-groups). However, ambivalence toward honest communications among members can be observed in most groups. After dealing with the authority theme, the group often moves through a phase marked by positive feelings among members, as the enchantment-flight subphase suggests. As the work deepens and members move beyond simply supporting one another and begin to confront one another, more negative feelings and reactions arise. As members begin to rub up against one another in their work, these feelings are quite natural and should be an expected part of the process. However, group members have learned from their experiences in other situations (e.g., family, groups, classes they attended as students) that talking directly about negative reactions to the behavior of others is not polite and is risky. This conditioning is part of the leader's experience as well. Often, then, the leader and the group become angry with members but nonetheless withhold their reactions.

Without direct feedback from the group, individual members find it difficult to understand their impact on the group, to learn from that understanding, and to develop new ways of coping. If we remember that the small group is a microcosm of the larger society, then how a member relates in the group may offer important clues to how the member deals with significant others in his or her family, school, place of work, and so on. The leader's task is to draw these interpersonal obstacles to the attention of the members and to help the group develop the ability to discuss them. Leaders often fear opening up discussion of the angry feelings they sense in the group, because they are concerned that things will "get out of hand," they will be overwhelmed, individuals will be hurt, and the life of the group will be threatened. Actually, the greatest threat to the life of the group is overpoliteness and the resulting illusion of work. Expression of anger can free the caring and other positive feelings that are also part of the group's intimacy.

Of course, the leader needs to take care that the contract of the group does not get subverted. Sometimes, the discussion centers on intermember relationships, thereby losing sight of the original reason the group was formed. This is one of my major criticisms of the type of groups (T-groups) studied by Bennis and Shepard: They have no external group purpose other than to analyze the interactions among members. They are usually described as educational groups, wherein members can learn about group dynamics and their own interpersonal behaviors. A second possibility to which the leader must be alert is that the member involved may attempt to use the group to deal with a personal pattern of behavior in groups, another attempt at subversion of group purpose.

This contrasts with group simulations, for example, in a class on group work practice, where a clear group purpose exists (e.g., parent support group simulation) and students take on the roles of members and one student acts as the group leader. These can be very helpful when students are in situations learning about group work but not having a group experience in practicum.

***College Student Counseling Group and the Intimacy Theme*** In the following illustration from a counseling group for college students experiencing difficulty in adjusting to their first year on campus, one member developed a pattern of relating in which she consistently cut off other members, did not really listen to them, and attempted to raise her own questions and concerns directly with the leader.

**Practice Points:** The leader sensed that she was relating only to him. The other group members showed elevating nonverbal signals of anger at her behavior, which she did not perceive. The record starts after a particularly striking example of this behavior.

> I noticed the group members had physically turned away as Louise was talking. Their faces spoke loudly of their negative reaction. I decided to raise the issue: "There is something happening right now that seems to happen a lot in this group. Louise is asking a lot of questions, cutting some people off as she does, and I sense that the rest of you aren't too happy about that. Am I right?" There was silence for a moment, and Louise, for the first time, was looking directly at the other group members. I said, "I know this isn't easy to talk about, but I feel if we can't be honest with one another about how we are working together, we don't stand a chance of being an effective group. And I think Louise would want to know if this was true. Am I right about that, Louise?" She answered, "I didn't realize I was doing this. Is it true?" Francine responded, "Frankly, Louise, I have been sitting here getting angrier and angrier at you by the minute. You really don't seem to listen to anyone else in the group."

**Practice Points:** The leader opened the door by pointing out the pattern in the group and breaking the taboo against direct acknowledgment of an interpersonal problem. This freed members to explore this sensitive area. The reader should remember that this was not a first session. This kind of confrontation before the leader had started to develop a working relationship and before the group members had experienced some positive work might have shut everyone down rather than opening the discussion up. A point to remember is that timing is crucial.

> After Francine's words, there was a moment of silence, and then Louise began to cry, saying, "You know, I seem to be doing this in all areas of my life. All of my friends are angry at me, my boyfriend won't speak to me, and now I've done it again. What's wrong with me?" The group seemed stunned by her expression of feeling.

**Practice Points:** Because this was the first real discussion of an interpersonal issue in the group, the leader needed to clarify the boundary of the discussion, using the contract as his guide. I call this intervention *"guarding the contract"*; it is designed to prevent a member from subverting the working agreement by raising other issues. The group felt guilty, and Louise felt overwhelmed. The leader acknowledged both of these feelings.

"I guess you all must feel quite concerned over how strongly this is hitting Louise?" Members nodded their heads, but no one spoke. I continued, "Louise, I'm afraid this has hit you really hard. I should make it clear that we won't be able to talk about the other areas in your life that you are finding tough right now—that wouldn't be appropriate in this group. I'd be glad to talk to you after the group, however, and maybe, if you want, we could explore other avenues of help. For right now, could you stick to what is happening in this group? How come you seem to be so eager to ask all the questions, and why do you seem so cut off from the group?" Louise was thoughtful for a moment and then said to the group, "I guess it's just that I'm feeling really concerned about what's going on here at school and I'm trying to get some help as quickly as possible. I want to make sure I get as much from Sid (the leader) as I can." I paused and looked to the group. Francine responded, "You know, that's probably why I got so mad at you, because I'm the same way, and I'm sitting here feeling the same feelings—I want to get as much help as I can as well." Louise: "Well, at least you were straight with me, and I appreciate that. It's much worse when you can sense something is wrong, but people won't level with you."

**Practice Points:** After the exchange between Louise and Francine, the group seemed to relax. Louise's readiness to accept negative feedback without defensiveness had an impact on the group. In other circumstances, members may feel more vulnerable and would need all the help the leader could give in terms of support. When Louise was able to express the underlying feelings she experienced, other group members were able to identify with her, and this freed their affect and concern. Louise could sense their concern for her, making it easier for her to feel more a part of the group rather than relating only to the leader. The leader proceeded to underscore the importance of honest communication among members and then guarded against preoccupation with process by reaching for the implicit work hinted at in the exchange.

"I think it was really tough just now, for Louise and the rest of you. However, if the group is going to be helpful, I think we are going to have to learn how to be honest with one another. As Louise pointed out, it can be tougher not to hear sometimes. I think it is also important that we not lose the threads of our work as we go along. I noticed that both Louise and Francine mentioned their urgency about getting help with their problems right now. Could we pick up by being a bit more specific about what those problems are?"

**Practice Summary.** Francine accepted the invitation by expressing a concern she was having about a specific course. From that point on, Louise was more attentive to the group and appeared a good deal more relaxed. The few times she interrupted, she good-naturedly caught herself and apologized. The leader spoke to her after the session and arranged an appointment for personal counseling. Members from that point on also appeared more involved and energetic in the discussion.

A group needs to develop a climate of trust that will allow the members to lower their defenses. A powerful barrier to trust can be raised and maintained by what members leave unsaid. Group members can sense both positive and negative reactions by other members. The effect of these reactions increases when they remain beneath the surface. On the other hand, open expression of these feelings can free members, who feel more confident when they know where they stand with the group.

Leaders usually experience intermember issues as particularly difficult. As they develop group experience, they become proficient at reaching for issues related to the authority theme; however, they take longer to risk dealing with the intimacy theme. So powerful are the taboos and so strong is their fear of hurting, and of being hurt in return, that they will try many indirect routes before finally they finally risk honesty. The reluctance may be partly rooted in leaders' feelings that they are responsible for "handling" anything that comes from reaching for intermember negatives. As this excerpt has illustrated, a group that has developed even a small fund of positive feelings is better equipped to handle its own problems. The group needs the leader's intervention to act as a catalyst, giving the members permission and supporting them as they enter the formerly taboo area.

## The Stone Center: Intimacy and the Relational Model

Another theoretical model that helps us to understand the intimacy theme is the relational model. This model has emerged from the work done at the Stone Center in Wellesley, Massachusetts, which is dedicated to studying the unique issues in the development of women and methods for working effectively with them. The center has built on the early work of Jean Baker Miller whose publication entitled *Toward a New Psychology of Women* (Miller 1987; Miller & Stiver, 1991) laid the groundwork for the relational model.

Much of the evolving work in this area can be found in publications and a series of working papers from the Stone Center. This framework is often classified under the general rubric of self-in-relation theory. In one example of a group work elaboration of this model, Fedele (1994) draws on three central constructs repeatedly found in relational theory:

- *Paradox* (an apparent contradiction that contains a truth)
- *Connection* ("a joining in relationship between people who experience each other's presence in a full way and who accommodate both the correspondence and contrasts between them")
- *Resonance* ("a resounding; an echoing; the capacity to respond that, in its most sophisticated form, is empathy") (p. 7)

*Paradox* Referring to therapy, Fedele (1994) identifies several paradoxes: "Vulnerability leads to growth; pain can be experienced in safety; talking about disconnection leads to connection; and conflict between people can be best tolerated in their connection" (p. 8). She also identifies additional primary paradoxes in therapy as the paradox between "transferential" and "real" relationships in therapy and the "importance of establishing a mutual, empathic relationship within the context of the unequal therapist-client relationship" (p. 8). She says,

> These dilemmas are dramatically apparent in group psychotherapy. The therapists and group members collaborate to create an emotional relational space

which allows the members to recapture more and more of their experience in their own awareness and in the group. The feelings of the past can be tolerated in this new relational space. It allows us to reframe the experience of pain within the context of safety. The difficulty of creating an environment that allows vulnerability in a group format involves the complexity of creating safety for all participants. (p. 8)

In applying this theory to group therapy, she identifies the "basic paradox" of a simultaneous yearning for connection accompanied by efforts to maintain disconnection as a form of protection from being hurt—a need generated from earlier painful experiences. The paradox of "similarity and diversity" describes a tension between connection to universal feelings and fears of isolation because of difference. Fedele points out that

The mutuality of empathy allows all participants to feel understood and accepted. The leader, creating a safe relational context, fosters connectedness within that safety by working to enlarge the empathy for difference. (1994, p. 9)

Another related paradox is the fact that the very process of sharing disconnection can lead to new connection. For example, "When members phone the leader to report anger or dissatisfaction with the group, the leader can encourage them to share this experience in the group. Often, if one feels the disconnection, it is very likely that one or more of the other members experience similar feelings and resonate with the feelings of dissatisfaction" (p. 10). Thus, when members share the sense of disconnection, these feelings can lead to connection.

Finally, the paradox of "conflict in connection" describes the importance of managing conflict and keeping anger within the context of safety and acceptance of divergent realities. As Fedele points out: "One way to view anger is to see it as a reaction to the experience of disconnection in the face of intense yearning for connection" (1994, p. 11).

*Connection* In describing the second major construct of relational theory, the idea of "connection," Fedele (1994) says,

The primary task of the leader and the group members is to facilitate a feeling of connection. In a relational model of group work, the leader is careful to understand each interaction, each dynamic in the group as a means for maintaining connection or as a strategy to remain out of connection. As in interpersonal therapy groups, the leader encourages the members to be aware of their availability in the here-and-now relationship of the group by understanding and empathizing with their experiences of the past. But it is the yearning for connection, rather than an innate need for separation or individuation, that fuels their development both in the here-and-now and in the past. (p. 11)

*Resonance* Finally, the third major concept, "resonance," asserts that the "power of experiencing pain within a healing connection stems from the ability of an individual to resonate with another" (Fedele, 1994, p. 14). She suggests that resonance manifests itself in group work in two ways:

The first is the ability of one member to simply resonate with another's experience in the group and experience some vicarious relief because of that resonance. The member need not discuss the issue in the group, but the experience moves her that much closer to knowing and sharing her own truth without necessarily responding or articulating it. Another way resonance manifests itself in a group involves the ability of members to resonate with each other's issues and thereby recall or reconnect with their own issues. This is an important element of group process in all groups but is dramatically obvious in groups with women who have trauma histories. Often, when one woman talks about painful material, other women dissociate. It is a very powerful aspect of group work that, if acknowledged, can help women move into connection. It can also cause problems if women become overwhelmed or flooded. The leader needs to modulate this resonance by helping each member develop skills to manage and contain intense feelings. (p. 14)

Many of the constructs of this theory, particularly its group work implications, fit well with the mutual-aid framework presented in this book. The description of the process of resonance closely resembles the dynamic described as the "all-in-the-same-boat" phenomenon. As another example, Linda Schiller (1993), was able to use the self-in-relation framework to rethink a classic theory of group development known as the Boston model (Garland et al., 1965), adapting it to a feminist perspective. We will return to a discussion of gender-related models when we discuss feminist group practice in Chapter 17. More recent insights from the Stone Center publications will be shared which raise questions about the appropriateness of this model for all groups for women, since the initial observations were made with a largely White and middle-class population.

### A Support Group for Women with Cancer

**Practice Points:** In the example that follows, from a community-based support group for women with cancer, we can use the relational model to explain the patterns of interaction over time. We see examples of paradoxes, connections, and resonance in each session of the work.

> **Members:** Four 45- to 58-year-old White women from different ethnic and socio-economic backgrounds. All have been diagnosed with breast cancer and are either in the midst of treatment or have just finished.
>
> **Dates Covered in Record:** 11/14 to 12/5
>
> **Group Task:** Individual need satisfaction
>
> **Description of the Problem:** The task of this group is for members to reach out to one another to find support for painful issues related to their cancer diagnoses. One member in particular seems to be expressing the pain and anger for the group. The problem that I began to recognize was that this member was carrying a great deal of emotion about her cancer diagnosis. She demonstrated her emotion through anger and distrust projected onto group members and the medical staff in general. I suspect that all members shared similar feelings to some extent but were unable to recognize them as related to their illness. My coleader and I found ourselves faced with two problems:
>
> (1) We needed to find appropriate ways to address the emotions expressed by the angry member, or what appeared to be the deviant member, to get at the underlying message, and (2) we needed to help the group as a whole find the freedom to express and address their painful feelings rather than allow this individual member to bear the responsibility.

**How the Problem Came to the Attention of the Leader(s):** Through conversation and the telling of individual stories, it seemed apparent from the beginning of the group that this woman was distrustful of people in general. I had originally suspected that she was someone who generally had not found people trustworthy throughout her life. After the second session, I began to wonder if this quality was not somehow related to her recent cancer diagnosis as well. She called my coleader and expressed a desire to quit the group because her "ways of dealing with [her] illness [were] diametrically opposed to the other members' ways."

At this time, she also mentioned the name of one member specifically. Although she continued to attend, it was apparent that she was carrying anger with her, especially toward the member she had named. She would roll her eyes or mutter something under her breath whenever this woman spoke. The other members did not acknowledge this, nor did the woman to whom the behavior was addressed.

### Summary of the Work

*Session 1*

After introductions I went over confidentiality issues as well as the rules and the purpose of the group: "This was a support group for women with breast cancer. It was created because of their requests in the oncology clinic, and I hoped that it would become a safe place for all of them to share their experiences and feelings about their illness as well as a place in which they could learn from one another." My coleader then stated that she, too, hoped to make this a safe place for the women to share their stories, and then she invited each one to talk about her experiences.

Each member told her story, offering an account of what she had been through. I noticed that none of the women expressed their stories with much emotion, only offering descriptive accounts of their experiences. However, one woman, Joan, did stand out in her account. She expressed distrust of the medical system and said that, so far, she had not found any of the doctors or nurses helpful. "I do my own research and reading. I can't count on them to give me the answers. They're in and out in a flash." Another woman, Judy, added that she had a similar experience in the past and ended up switching doctors. Joan snapped at Judy, making an excuse for not being able to switch doctors, and said, "I just deal with it."

**Practice Points:** If we consider our discussion of the group as a dynamic system and each member playing a role, then the behavior of Joan can be understood as her potentially raising the feelings associated with the diagnosis they all experience and the underlying concern about whether they can trust their doctors. This is a difficult issue for the coleaders, since they must relate to the medical staff and must feel somewhat uncomfortable about the negative comments about doctors. This is evident as they do not pick up on this issue.

Once each woman had shared with the group, my coleader asked if any of them had been in groups in the past. Only one woman had been in a prior group, and she talked about how each member in that group had died. The room was silent. Instead of letting the silence stay and then addressing its meaning, I asked the woman what it felt like to be starting another group. She commented that it was a little scary and added, "But we have to keep going on. We have no other choice." I then asked the other members what it felt like to hear her talk about the other group.

They all commented about how it must have been an awful experience for her. My coleader pushed, "Does it make you start to think about your own mortality?" A couple of members said that they had not really given it much thought, and Joan said that it did make her think about it, but that was all. Instead of pursuing this, both my coleader and I let the conversation drift back to the members' telling Barbara how it must have been hard to be part of that group. Again, Joan had given us an opportunity to recognize her as really wanting to do the work in the group. First, she brought up the anger, and then she acknowledged thinking about death. Both are very real issues for all the members in this group. We failed to pick up on her desire to work.

We ended the meeting with my coleader offering a summary of what she felt she had heard as being common among the women's experiences. Death and anger were not mentioned. We both thanked them for coming to the group.

**Practice Points:** In Joan's reaching out and at the same time seeming to use her anger—for example, by snapping an angry response to Judy—to push people away, she demonstrates the basic paradox in the relational model of the simultaneous yearning for connection accompanied by efforts to maintain disconnection as a form of protection from being hurt. The coleader reinforces the taboo in the group in relation to death and anger by not mentioning it in her summary. In the next session, we see the leaders attempt to encourage connection and resonance as Joan brings up how overwhelming dealing with her own cancer and taking care of others can be. This time it is Judy who demonstrates disconnection as she responds to Joan's emotional presentation by moving to an intellectual discussion.

### Session 2

We asked each member to give a brief check-in so that everyone could get an idea of how the others were doing. Joan was the last one to check in, and she brought up the fact that her daughter was going through chemotherapy at the time and that she herself was presently taking care of a depressed friend. This opened up a discussion for all the women to find something in common. It turned out that each of them was caring for elderly parents; thus, all these women were acting as caretakers while dealing with their illnesses. I asked, "What's it like to not only have to worry about your own health and ability to live from day to day, but to have to worry about taking care of someone else as well?" Barbara said, "You gotta do what you gotta do." Everyone agreed.

Judy then began to change the subject to talk about how, when she was not caring for her mother, she was working on a proposal that addressed research on tobacco and cancer-related issues. She wanted to know if any of the other women would be interested in helping her out. Barbara and Gayle inquired about it, while Joan sat quietly, appearing to be somewhat annoyed. Neither my coleader nor I said anything. I did not realize at the time that this was Judy's way of avoiding the work of addressing painful feelings, the group's way of going along with it, and Joan's silent plea to do the work.

**Practice Points:** As is usually the case, the group members will offer the leaders another chance at addressing the real issues. In thinking about the group as a dynamic system with members playing various roles, then Joan is actually trying to move the group deeper into the work through the expression of emotions, although the anger covers her pain. Judy is the member who reminds everyone, including the leaders, that this is hard to talk about by moving away from painful subjects. This time the leaders address the process but fail to name the members and to identify the roles that they play.

The women continued to talk about their own efforts in keeping busy, and then Joan chimed in, "I haven't been able to go back to work because of the amount of chemotherapy I receive. I have enough trouble trying to take care of everyone else and myself." Judy responded by stating that she knew how she felt because she wished she had more time to work on her proposal. She then went into how long a proposal takes to draft. Joan rolled her eyes. The other members seemed to fall into Judy's trap again.

My coleader said, "I've noticed that the group sort of shifts a focus off of issues that seem to bring up some painful emotions for each of you. Have you noticed that, Sandra? Has anyone else noticed that?" Gayle asked what she meant. She explained, without using names, that whenever the group got close to having to share how experiences or "realities" were affecting them, they seemed to shift to talking about less emotional topics. She then said, "I wonder why this happens."

Here we began to point out the pattern that the group was establishing in addressing painful issues. What we failed to do was to recognize and use Joan's experience in the group as a way to name the painful feelings that the members avoided discussing. Gayle stated that she hadn't noticed this. Judy and Barbara stated that they had not noticed either. Each of them was sort of smiling an embarassed smile. Joan would not look at the group members; she just let out a very heavy sigh that caused everyone to look at her. No one said anything.

**Practice Points:** In the relational theory framework, the authors describe the importance of monitoring connection and resonance, keeping in mind that members can get "flooded" by emotions. Judy and Joan may be expressing the flooding in different ways, and the model would urge the leaders to help each member develop the skills to "manage and contain" intense feelings. While the leaders press Joan to respond, they still avoid the expression of anger which still remains a taboo in the group. Avoiding difficult issues is a group problem, and Judy and Joan are simply representing the ambivalence of wanting to connect on these issues and at the same time wanting to avoid them.

Barbara commented on how quiet it had gotten. This broke the silence, and the other members began to admit that they "might" have been avoiding painful issues. Joan still sat quietly. I remarked that she had been very quiet for a while and that our time was running out. I wondered if she wanted to share anything with the group. She said no. My coleader said that she imagined her silence meant something. She said, very angrily, that it was sometimes easier to "just not talk." The group then began to inquire and stated that the reason they were together was to help one another and that, if they could help Joan, they wanted to. Joan just shook her head and said that she was fine. We, again, avoided bringing up the anger that was present. Maybe we (my coleader and I) did not want to deal with it?

The group then began to talk about some side effects of chemotherapy. Judy was the only one in the group without hair. She expressed feeling fine about not having it: "It will grow back." Others talked about hair thinning and other side effects that they had read about. Joan joined in the conversation minimally. We still ignored the possible significance of her deviation from the group norm.

**Practice Points:** The call from Joan about wanting to quit the group easily fits another paradox in the relational model, in which the very process of sharing disconnection can lead to new connection. The leaders encourage Joan to bring her concerns to the group as a means to create the connection she both yearns for and resists.

In retrospect, what I think we were missing was that Joan represented the ambivalence of the group to face painful issues. In addition, we failed to really note what Judy represented to her, and possibly to other members. Judy is the only one who has completed chemotherapy and/or radiation, she is the intellectualizer (or initiator of flight), her baldness is a reminder of what might happen to others in the group, and she is getting back into her work and other parts of her life that she has put on hold, unlike the other members who are still faced with much uncertainty. The leaders make an empathic demand for work by asking directly who provides emotional support after members describe other forms of help.

### Session 3

The group opened again by checking in with each of the members. Joan appeared somewhat more cheerful than I had expected. Barbara brought up feeling worn out about caring for her mother and herself. This opened up a discussion about how they each were giving support to other people. Directing the question to any member, I asked, "Who gives you support?" Judy began to talk about how her friends used to provide her with transportation and/or come over with meals when she was sick from treatment. Each of the other women shared her "support" stories as well. I finally stated that the kind of support that they had all just talked about was support around concrete needs: food, rides, and so on. I then asked who gave them emotional support. The room got silent. Judy began to intellectualize. Joan rolled her eyes and shook her head. I pointed out that they were "doing it again," referring to their established pattern of avoiding painful issues.

Everyone but Joan smiled embarrassedly. I said to them that everyone was smiling but Joan, and I wondered what they were really feeling. They were silent. I said that I imagined it was hard for all of them to be here and to talk about their illness, especially when they are still in treatment. My coleader took this opportunity to ask the group what it was like for them to still be in treatment and to have a member present who was through with it. Joan remained quiet. Gayle got tearful and began to pour out that she was "scared shitless" of what might happen to her hair, of how sick she might become, and of how there's no real guarantee the chemo would work. I stated that I had just seen more emotion pour out of her than I had seen before. I named what I saw: "You seem like you're feeling sad and scared and angry all at once." She had tears rolling down her cheeks.

**Practice Points:** In the next excerpt the group leaders finally confront Joan and do not let her off the hook when she expresses her anger directly.

I looked at Joan, who was tearful. My coleader asked the group, "What do you do with all of these feelings every day?" Joan made a sound of irritation. My coleader asked her what that sound meant. Joan just shook her head. My coleader stated that Gayle's outpouring of emotion was understandable and that she thought it must be hard for her to carry those feelings around. I then took the opportunity to narrow the focus to the anger, because it seemed to be an emotion shared at that moment by more than one member (both Gayle and Joan).

At this time, I ended up taking advantage of an opportune moment to address Joan's anger without making her feel alone with it. When I mentioned that it must be hard to deal with the anger and asked how they managed it, Joan started right in about how angry she was at the hospital and about her depressed friend. The discussion continued until Gayle said that she just wished that she could get back to where she was before she got sick. Through this discussion, the group was able to talk about its anger, an emotion that all of them admitted to feeling. They acknowledged that it "might" be about their "unlucky" confrontation with cancer, but no one would give a definitive "yes" on that.

As the group ended that day, there was a sense of peace in the room. On reviewing my notes from this session, it appeared that much work was done to break through the obstacles that the literature speaks to. By reaching for the underlying feelings and the meanings of the nonverbal messages, we were able to open up some painful areas that the group obviously felt ambivalent about sharing. We were also able to take the individual's issue (the anger) and bring it out as a common feeling among all the group members, rather than leaving it in one person's possession. One thing that was not addressed, though, was Joan's anger directed at Judy. I think we were too afraid to touch this.

**Practice Points:**   The work thus far has been building up to the next powerful shared emotion that Joan has been indirectly raising week after week. Her stunning comment about "power" takes the group to the heart of their issues, their pain and their feelings of helplessness.

*Session 4*

The group started as usual with check-ins. The members shared some events that had taken place that week regarding new drugs that two of them were put on. A discussion opened up around side effects again, and this led Joan to discuss her anger about her visit with her doctor that week, as he had been "in and out in a matter of minutes." At this point, Barbara said to Joan, "You seem so angry at the doctors. I wish that your experience with them wasn't so dreadful. It makes it much easier if you feel like you are in good hands." The group began to discuss this thought, and Joan sat back and listened. She did not appear angry, just deep in thought. My coleader asked her what was going through her mind. Joan said, "I just feel like my life is in their hands. They have all the power; the cancer has the power, the drugs have the power, I have none."

For the first time, the group members started to really talk about feeling helpless to their cancer diagnoses. After we had recognized and called attention to Joan's nonverbal messages, the group was able to benefit once again from Joan's ability to bring a common issue to the forefront. In addition, the members were beginning to feel comfortable bringing up the issues themselves.

**Practice Summary.**   While the leaders have recognized that Joan plays an important role in the group, they fail to see that Judy does as well. If they acknowledge this interaction, the direct and indirect expressions of anger from Joan toward Judy, they will probably discover that the part of Judy that Joan is angry at is the part of her own feelings that would also like to live in some form of denial. We are most angry at others when their behavior touches a part of us that feels the same way. In an example of connection and resonance emerging from disconnection, as the relational model would describe it, the leaders do open the door to the powerful feelings of helplessness in dealing with a possibly life-threatening disease that underlie Joan's surface anger and are shared by the other members.

***Why Leaders Avoid Dealing with Anger Between Members*** The previous example illustrates how difficult it is for group members, and at times, group leaders, to deal with anger between members directly. In the misconception about relationships in general and groups in particular, the myth exists that anger is negative and is to be avoided. Anger is an emotion just like any other, and it needs to be faced and addressed if we are to get to the underlying feelings. When avoided, anger stays beneath the surface and blocks the opportunity for connection and resonance.

Kendler (2002) pointed out how difficult it is for group leaders, particularly new ones, to openly address anger and conflict in a group and calls for a process of personal introspection that allows group leaders to understand their fears.

No amount of professional experience will ever fully banish the group leader's fear of addressing conflict in groups. Nevertheless, the distinctive potential and power of a group to foster personal growth and to allow mutual aid to thrive among its members absolutely relies on the leader's comfort and skill in doing precisely that.

Leaders with groups need to make conscious efforts to come to grips with their own fears and struggle to do so even after years of group work experience. Time and experience in leading groups surely and gradually help leaders to overcome their aversion to conflict so as to be able to hone their skills and interventions. But time and experience alone are not enough to bring leaders to a level of personal awareness and professional appreciation of conflict as a positive force in the life of a group. (pp. 25–26)

In developing their readiness and skills to address conflict in the group, I have observed that leaders often first achieve some measure of comfort in dealing with conflict related to the authority theme and anger toward themselves as leaders. It is then that they are more able to address conflict and anger between members, what I have referred to as the intimacy theme. Kendler makes five recommendations for addressing conflict in groups:

(1) do not cut off confrontation too early, before members have arrived at the heart of the conflict; (2) do not allow confrontation to continue for too long, to a point at which members denigrate each other or to a point at which the nonparticipating members who silently observe the conflict are no longer able to tolerate its presence; (3) empathize with and validate the feelings of each member; (4) point out the communalities in the group; (5) refer to the overarching purpose of the group. (p. 26)

Of course, this still leaves questions for group leaders of when, whether, and how to confront or manage such conflict. I will return to this author in Chapter 17 on dealing with posttraumatic stress groups and her illustration of how she answered these questions in a group she led for New Yorkers coping with the September 11, 2001, terrorist attacks on the World Trade Center.

The descriptions of the difficulties that group members face in dealing with two major developmental tasks—the relationship with the leader and the relationship among members—refer to an even more general task, the development of a culture for work. In the following section, I explore the question of group culture in more detail.

# Developing a Culture for Work

The term *group culture* has been used thus far in its anthropological/sociological sense, with a particular emphasis on group norms, taboos, and roles. Earlier in this chapter I addressed the concept of role in some detail, so I will focus here on norms and taboos.

## Norms and Taboos

Hare (1962) has defined group norms as rules of behavior, or proper ways of acting, that have been accepted as legitimate by members of a group. Norms specify the kinds of behavior that are expected of group members. These rules or standards of behavior to which members are expected to conform are for the most part derived from the goals a group has set for itself. Given a set of goals, norms define the kind of behavior that is necessary for or consistent with the realization of those goals (p. 24).

Taboos are commonly associated with primitive tribes who developed sacred prohibitions that made certain people or acts untouchable or unmentionable. As I have discussed, the term *taboo* in modern cultures refers to social prohibitions related to conventions or traditions. Norms and taboos are closely related; for example, one group norm may be the tradition of making a particular subject taboo.

As groups are formed, each member brings to the microsociety of the group a strongly developed set of norms of behavior and shared identification of taboo areas. The early culture of the group therefore reflects the members' outside culture. As Hare (1962) points out, the norms of a group should be consistent with those necessary for realization of its goals. The problem, however, is that the norms of our society and the taboos commonly observed often create obstacles to productive work in the group. As seen earlier, the taboo related to discussion of death and dying may block productive work in a cancer support group. A major group task then involves developing a new set of norms, thereby freeing group members to deal with formerly taboo subjects.

We have already addressed the problem of helping group members develop their culture for work. For example, authority and dependency are generally taboo subjects in our culture; we do not talk freely about our feelings regarding either. Group experiences in classrooms over many years have taught us not to challenge authority and have alerted us to the dangers involved if we admit feelings of dependency on a person in authority in front of a peer group. The discussions of the authority and intimacy themes earlier in this chapter described the group leader's efforts to help the group discuss these taboo areas and to develop a new set of more productive norms. The effort is directed neither at changing societal norms nor at exorcising taboos. There are sound reasons for norms of behavior, and many taboos have appropriate places in our lives. The work focuses instead on building a new culture within the group, but only insofar as it is needed for effective group functioning. Transfers of this experience beyond the group may or may not be relevant or appropriate.

For example, members in a couples' group had to deal with taboos against open discussion of sex, an area critical to the work of the group. The frankness of the group discussion freed the couples to develop more open communications with each other outside of the sessions. This change in the culture of their marriages was important for them and was therefore an appropriate transfer of learning. On the other hand, if the couples used their newfound freedom to discuss issues of sexual functioning at neighborhood cocktail parties, they might quickly discover the power of peer group pressure (or perhaps be invited to more parties).

To illustrate the leader's function of helping the group work on its important tasks, I shall examine a number of efforts of leaders to develop a group culture. Then I examine the impact of ethnicity on group culture. This section uses the group theory outlined by Bion (1961) to illustrate again the way in which practitioners can draw on the literature to build their own models of group functioning. The reader familiar with more recent formulations about emotions and groups will recognize, once again, that they had roots in the early and innovative work of Bion.

## Bion's Emotionality Theory

Bion (1961) can help explain difficulties with addressing emotions, a characteristic common to groups. His work was based on observations of psychotherapy groups, led by himself, in which he played the relatively passive role of interpreting the members' behaviors. Once again, as with the earlier theory, some elements of his model are specific to this type of group, whereas other aspects lend themselves nicely to generalizing.

A central idea in Bion's theory is the *work group,* which consists of the mental activity related to a group's task. When the work group is operating, one can see group members translating their thoughts and feelings into actions that are adaptive to reality. For example, in the illustration from a parents' group for parents of hyperactive children described earlier in this chapter, the work group was operating when the members spoke honestly about the deep and painful emotions they often experienced. As Bion describes it, the work group represents a "sophisticated" level of group operation. In the living with cancer group just described, the honest discussions of the members' fears about the treatments, their anger, their feelings of helplessness all would represent what Bion would call the work group in action.

It is important to note that when Bion describes the work group, he is not speaking of a subgroup within the group or even of a separate group. This is a common misunderstanding of his theory. What he means by the work group, and other "basic assumption groups" described in the following paragraphs, is that the group members are acting as if they had come together under the basic assumption to do their work—or to avoid work—whatever it may be. So later, when I describe Bion's "basic assumption dependent group," it is still the same group of people; however, their behavior now looks as if they came together not to work but to act on the basic assumption to be dependent upon the leader. It is possible for a group session to start off as a work group, as we have seen in previous examples, but then, when a difficult emotion is raised, turn in an instant into the dependent group looking for the leader to help them resolve their pain. In the earlier example when the mothers of hyperactive children pleaded with the leader to cheer them up, that would be an example of what Bion described as the dependent group in action.

Bion believes most groups begin with a more "primitive" culture, in which they resist dealing with painful emotions. Group development is therefore the struggle between the group's primitive instincts to avoid the pain of growth and its need to become more sophisticated and deal with feelings. The primitive culture of the group's early stages mirrors the primitive culture in our larger society, in which the direct and open expression of feelings is avoided.

In the following example of a parents' group, the leader described how the problem came to her attention, pointing out how the more painful subjects were dropped as the group took flight into a discussion of more superficial issues. This conforms to one of Bion's key ideas. He believes that the work group can be obstructed, diverted, and sometimes assisted by group members who experience powerful emotional drives. His term *basic assumption group* refers to the idea that group members appear to act as if their behavior were motivated by a shared basic assumption about the purpose of the group—an assumption other than the expressed group goal.

***The Fight-Flight Basic Assumption Group: Avoiding Difficult Discussions*** One of the three basic assumption groups Bion identifies is the fight-flight group. In a primitive group, when the work group gets close to painful feelings, the members will unite in an instantaneous, unconscious process to form the fight-flight group, acting from the basic assumption that the group goal is to avoid the pain associated with the work group processes through flight (i.e., an immediate change of subject away from the painful area; using humor to blunt an issue) or fight (i.e., an argument developing in the group that moves from the emotional level to an intellectual one). Bion is taking a concept from individual psychology and biology, the inherent fight-flight reaction to danger, and applying it to this organism called the group. It may well be an unconscious reaction with group members not aware of how they are avoiding difficult work. For example, we saw in the previous chapter how the "clown" in a group used humor as a distraction just when difficult material was about to emerge.

This process in the group context parallels the ambivalence noted in work with individuals when resistance is expressed through an abrupt change of subjects. Bion's strategy for dealing with this problem is to call the group's attention to the behavior in an effort to educate the group so that it can function on a more sophisticated level. This process is illustrated in the next example. In reading this example, you should focus on the following:

- *The way in which the group goes into Bion's fight-flight mode whenever the discussion gets to painful issues*
- *The importance of the leader pointing this out*
- *The leader's expressions of empathy that build the foundation for making the demand for work*
- *The leader's efforts to make a demand for work that gets to the underlying issues*

***Parents of Hyperactive Children: Accepting Difficult Feelings*** The first illustration is of a leader's efforts to help a group of parents of hyperactive children share their painful and angry feelings about their children's problems. This is the same group cited earlier to illustrate the need for group members to deal with feelings that result from demands for work.

**Description of the Problem:** The members found it very difficult to talk about their own feelings about their hyperactive children. Instead, they continually focused on what other people—such as teachers, neighbors, husbands, and relatives—felt about the children. Despite their reluctance to focus on their feelings, they occasionally gave me clues that this was their underlying concern, and, as this was also part of the contract, I felt we had to explore their feelings and work on them.

**How the Problem Came to the Attention of the Leader(s):** During the first few meetings, the members continued talk about how important this group was for them, as it gave them a chance to get together to discuss their problems related to their hyperactive children and get support from one another. The feeling was that no one, not even their husbands or wives, understood what they were going through and how they felt. Any time they would begin to talk about their own feelings, they resorted back to discussing medications, school, and so on—in other words, safe topics. Yet the need to talk about how they felt was always raised by members in different ways. This pattern began in session two, when one member raised the question of hyperactivity due to emotional deprivation at an early age. The group superficially touched on it but dropped the subject, resorting back to something safe. As the members' pattern of flight became more obvious to me, I could help them understand what they were doing, and thus help them deal with their feelings.

**Practice Points:** As I return to the leader's record of service on this problem, we will see that her early efforts were directed at systematically encouraging the expression of feelings and acknowledging these with her own feelings in an attempt to build a working relationship. As the pattern of using flight, or in Bion's terms, the emergence of the fight-flight group, developed, the leader drew on this working relationship to point out the pattern of avoidance and to make a demand for work.

### Session 3

I listened to what the members were saying, and I encouraged them to talk about their feelings toward their hyperactive children. Marilyn told us that, since she had begun coming to the sessions, she noticed that she had changed her attitude in relation to her hyperactive son, and now he was responding more positively toward her. She had always thought of him in terms of being a normal child, and it had frustrated her that he was unable to react as normal children do. In fact, she had set up expectations for him that he couldn't meet. I encouraged her to continue talking about her feelings toward him. She said that she supposed she really couldn't accept the fact that he was hyperactive, and then, after coming to the meeting, she began to accept this. I asked how she felt now. She felt better, but the hurt was there.

**Practice Points:** By the fifth session, the group had come close to discussing some of the more difficult underlying feelings; however, each time they had come up, they had used the flight mechanism to avoid the pain. Some of the feelings experienced by these parents ran so counter to what they expected themselves to feel that they had great difficulty in admitting the feelings to others and at times even to themselves. The leader had developed a fund of trust during the first sessions through her efforts to understand the meaning of the experience for the members.

In the following excerpt, she draws on that fund and makes a demand for work by pointing out the members' pattern of flight. Even as she does this, she tries to express her empathy with the difficulty the group experiences in meeting this demand.

### Session 5

The group sometimes picked up on their feelings, and I tried to put a demand for work on them—that is, to stick with the subject and to really talk about their feelings. I pointed out their underlying anger and did not allow them to take flight. Betty started talking about George and the school again, and the others became very supportive, offering concrete help. She expressed anger at the school but also talked about George and how he didn't fit in—he couldn't read and cope with the courses, and he didn't care. I detected that some of her anger was directed toward him, and I asked how she felt toward him at this point. She said that she pitied him. I wondered if she wasn't also feeling somewhat angry at him for causing her so many problems and irritating her so much. I said that there were times when George made her very angry. Mildred agreed that she has reacted negatively, too.

**Practice Points:** The leader's synthesis of empathy and demand helped the group modify its culture and create a new norm in which the members would not be judged harshly for their feelings—even those they felt were unreasonable. As they expressed feelings of anger toward their children, the group members moved to a new level of trust and openness. With the leader's help, they described moments when they felt like "killing" their child, and, under her gentle prodding, they explored how they experienced having an "imperfect child" as a reflection of themselves as bad parents. This attitude, in turn, affected the children's sense of acceptance by their parents, which sometimes led to further acting out. Understanding and accepting these feelings was a first step toward breaking this vicious cycle. The leader's comments at the end of the session acknowledged the important change in the discussion:

> I recognized how hard it was to talk about their feelings, and how much pain they felt. I credited them for their work and tried to create feeling among them that I understood. Denise had been talking about her own feelings about her son, and she seemingly had her feelings well under control. She had said that she was very sensitive and had trouble talking about it. I said that perhaps she was saying that she, too, had feelings that the others had mentioned, but she found them very hard to discuss. The others said that it was hard to talk about their concerns, to admit that these children weren't the same as the others, that you wanted to be proud of them but couldn't.
>
> I agreed that it was hard—they were living the situation 24 hours a day, and they had feelings about these children. The members discussed how much they were criticized by their relatives and were very upset. I said that people just did not know what it was like to be a mother of a child like this, and also they did not feel the pain and frustration that the parents felt. I waited, and there was silence. I noticed that our time was up long ago, and I said that they had done some very hard work. It was not easy to talk as they had today, to share the feelings of depression and hostility toward their children, and to admit that they had wanted to kill them at times. I wondered how they felt now. Marilyn said that she couldn't understand everything I tried to get them to do, but I made her think and try new things, and also I made her look at things differently. I said that it wasn't easy for them to do this, I knew that, and I often felt their pain.

**Practice Summary.**   We have already seen, in an earlier excerpt, how the leader needed to help this group articulate its anger in response to her demands for work. Bion might describe those exchanges as examples of the flight pattern of reaction in the fight-flight group. Another basic assumption group, as described by Bion, is the dependent group, in which the group appears to be meeting to be sustained by the leader. This is another form of avoidance of the work group and was illustrated in the earlier excerpt in which the group wanted the leader to "cheer them up." The third and final basic assumption group in Bion's theory is the pairing group. Here, the group, often through a conversation between two members, the "pair," avoids the pain of the work by discussing some future great event. The event can be the discovery of a new drug or procedure that will cure the person who is ill. Another example would be the arrival of some person or organization that will solve the problem. The discussion in this group of "new drugs" or "outside experts" who might provide a solution to their problems is an example of the pairing group in action.

Bion's emotionality theory, his concept of the work group and the three basic assumption groups (dependent; fight-flight; pairing), is rooted in the idea of a group unconscious capable of acting even without the group members' awareness. One doesn't have to accept the strongly psychoanalytical core concepts of the model to be able to observe the processes he describes. We have seen examples in this book where arguments between members (fight) or inability to stay focused (flight) emerged when painful issues were being discussed. We have seen numerous examples where group members hoped that the leader (dependent) could help them solve or resolve the problem so they would not have to deal with the associated feelings. We have also seen in the previous example how much easier it was for the group when two members (pairing) talked about a new miracle drug that might change their children so they could be "normal." Bion's writings are often dense, complex, and at times mystical; however, these basic concepts I have described ring true and have helped me to "see" and understand this organism called the group and the many ways it deals with or avoids dealing with emotions.

## Helping Members to Develop a Structure for Work

As a group develops, it needs to work on the task of building a structure for work: the formal and informal rules, roles, communication patterns, rituals, and procedures developed by the group members to facilitate the work of the group. Some rules are established by the agency or host setting and are not within the control of the group members. At times, the group leader may try to help a group change a rule when conflict persists. In other cases, the rules emerge from the members themselves. The following example illustrates this process.

***An Outpatient Group for Young Recovering Addicts*** In the following example, one member of an outpatient group for recovering addicts raises the issue of bringing her baby to the group sessions. Underlying the issue of structure are several other concerns for this client, as well as questions for the leaders about the need for additional agency support for the group.

The setting is an outpatient alcohol and drug clinic in a hospital. This is a group for young recovering addicts. The purpose of the group is for the members to learn from and support one another as they cope with a sober lifestyle. Two men and two women are at the first meeting, and up to four more members could be added. The members range in age from 19 to 27 years old. The two women are Black; one of the men is Black, and the other is White. The coleaders are White, and one is a counselor at the clinic.

**Practice Points:** Although the agency rules were explained to the client, she decided to raise the issue in a meeting, hoping to achieve support for her position. Note how the leader explains the agency position and then turns to the group members for their views on the matter.

> We had just finished going over the group rules, and the group members were quiet. Beth (my coleader) asked the group members if they wanted to add any more rules. There was a brief silence, and then Amanda said (to Beth), "You know what I would like to have for a rule?" Beth nodded and said that maybe Amanda could explain what she meant to the group. Amanda turned back to the group and said that she had a 3-month-old baby. The social service department had the baby now, but she hoped to get the baby back soon. She was not sure that she could find someone she trusted to watch the baby while she came to group. This was her first child, and she had been separated from her for so long that she didn't want to leave her. She said that when she was in group, she would worry about the baby, and that she had asked Beth in the pregroup interview if it might be all right for her to bring the baby along, but that we (Beth and I) had told her that she couldn't bring the baby. Amanda looked at Beth.
>
> Beth said that, traditionally, the clinic hasn't had very many female clients, and that this issue hadn't come up before at the clinic, so she hadn't given Amanda an answer right away but had talked to me and to the other staff members; she said that she and I had thought that it could be disruptive and distracting to have a baby in the group. Amanda, still speaking to Beth, said that probably

the baby would just sleep most of the time. Beth said that the problem was that the baby wouldn't be 3 months for very long. Beth said that maybe Jen (another member) had some thoughts about the issue. Amanda turned to Jen. Jen smiled and said that she could remember when her daughter and her son were babies, and that she had never wanted to leave them. She said that it's hard to leave your baby, but if there's a baby in the room, it's hard to ignore it even if it is asleep, because babies are so cute you always want to pick them up or play with them or touch them, so having a baby in the group could be disruptive.

**Practice Points:**   Note how the supportive comments of the other members and their focus on Amanda's need are easier for her to hear. She is also raising through this request for a rule change a number of other potential issues. These include:

- I'm really a good mother and am concerned about the baby.
- I want the social service department to let me keep my baby once it's returned.
- It's going to be hard for me to address my own needs and those of the baby at the same time.

Amanda appeared to take this comment in thoughtfully, and then she turned to Leo and Herb and said, "What do you think?" There was a brief silence, and then Leo said that he didn't personally have children, but that he had a real soft spot for children and old people. He said that, from what he could tell, it was going to be hard for Amanda to leave her baby, and he could see why. He said it seemed like Amanda was between a rock and a hard place, because if she brought the baby, it might distract her and the rest of the group, and if she didn't bring the baby, it might also distract her because she would be thinking about her baby and worrying about her. He said that it was important for Amanda to take time to focus on her own recovery, and bringing the baby to the group could get in the way of that as well as be distracting.

Amanda seemed satisfied with this and turned to Herb, who said that he basically agreed with Leo. Herb said that he liked kids a lot, but that he thought that a baby probably would be distracting and that it would be good for Amanda to take the group time to focus on herself. Amanda said that she could understand where everyone was coming from, and she still felt like she didn't want to leave her baby, but she'd do the best she could to get a babysitter. Leo suggested that maybe Amanda shouldn't get too worked up just yet, because it would be a few more weeks before she got the baby back and maybe a solution would turn up between now and then. He finished off by saying, "Easy does it," prompting Herb and Jen to follow quickly with two more Alcoholics Anonymous slogans. Everyone, including Amanda, wound up laughing. Then there was a brief silence.

**Practice Points:**   The next intervention by the leader recognizes that she has two clients: the group members and the agency. Amanda's conflict raises a question about agency support for clients with similar issues. The leader's clear sense of her role leads her to suggest she will follow up with the agency on the need to consider additional supports.

**EP 2.1.1a**

I agreed with Leo and said that it was good that this issue had come up because it might be the first time it had come up in the clinic, but it almost certainly wouldn't be the last time. I said that I thought it showed a gap in the clinic's services, and it was something Beth and I could explore a little more and see if we could find a solution for. The members nodded, and Beth mentioned that there was a babysitting service in the hospital during the day, but that there clearly was a gap in the availability of services at night. Amanda said that she had not known about the daytime service, and it made her mad to know it wasn't offered at night. She said she thought that probably a lot more women would come to the clinic if there were someone here to watch their kids. The other group members agreed. Beth said that maybe something could be worked out, such as cooperative babysitting, and she asked me if I would bring that up at the staff meeting on Monday morning, because she isn't there on Mondays. I said I would be sure to, and I'd let them know what happened.

**Practice Summary.** The discussion of the rules often raises many issues for the client—in this case, Amanda's concern about caring for her baby and not losing it to the child welfare agency again. The leader remains responsible for enforcing the agency policy on the issue of Amanda bringing her baby to the group. In this example, the leader involves other group members in addressing the rule and its impact on Amanda and the group. Most important, the leader's sense of the mediating role between client and system leads her to begin immediately to identify potential systems work on the issue of providing child-care resources so that members can attend the group without being concerned about neglecting their children. This would be consistant with the concept of the two clients—in this case, the group member as one client, and the agency and its policies as the second. In exploring the other issue that may be being raised indirectly by the member—that is, her concerns about the demands on her life that emerge from her parenting responsibility—the leader provides an example of how process and content can be integrated. By bringing the baby to the group, the client may be indirectly saying, "Look how hard it is for me to take care of my own life and the baby at the same time." The leader might also want to explore this as a theme of concern for Amanda and for other members as well.

# Helping Group Members to Negotiate the Environment

The discussion thus far has focused on the internal tasks of the group. However, a group does not exist in a vacuum, but is located in an institution, a school, an agency, or in a community. As I explore the group task of negotiating the environment, I will use the term *open social system*. This term is used to suggest that the boundary between the group and its environment was not closed. In fact, the activities of the group will have some effect on the relationship between the group and the environment. In turn, the interaction with the environment will have an impact on the internal operations of the group. In this section I will explore this additional group task: negotiating the environment.

With the exception of the chapter on contracting, I have been discussing the group almost as if it is cut off from the external world. In the contracting chapter I focused on finding the common ground between the service of the setting and the needs of the group members. Contact between the group and its external system continues after the beginning phase and is one of the ongoing realities to which the group must pay some attention. Two aspects of this group and environment interaction are considered in this section. First, the group-environment relationship in terms of mutual obligations and expectations is discussed. The example is from a community center setting in which an acting out group of young teens, an activity group described earlier that I led in my first field practicum, finds itself in trouble with the agency because of its aggressive behavior.

***Adolescents: Acting Out Behavior in the Community Center*** The example involves the young teenage club described earlier in my discussion of internal leadership in the group. The setting was a middle-class community YM&YWHA (Young Men's and Young Women's Hebrew Association), and the group had a long history of acting out behavior at the center. This group was one of my first as a student. I was in the building working on recording one evening when I was told by a staff supervisor to "get the kids in your group in line," since they were acting out in the game room. He was obviously angry at them.

My first reaction was panic; I had been working hard to overcome our rocky start together, trying to undo my earlier mistakes of attempting to impose limits and establish my authority. I had just been getting somewhere in this effort and saw this confrontation as a potential step backward. When I explained this to the supervisor, his reaction was, "What's wrong? Do you have trouble setting limits and using your authority?" As any student in training knows, a supervisor questioning your "problem" evokes a powerful response. I decided to face my responsibility, as defined by the supervisor, and went off to do combat in what I knew would be a battle of wills. Feeling upset about what I was doing only made me come on stronger.

I found the guys running and screaming in the halls, and I yelled at them to "cut it out." They slowed down for a minute and I said to them, "Look, if you guys don't cut it out, I'm going to throw you out of the building." I continued, "What kind of way is that to behave, anyway? You guys know better than that. I thought I was getting somewhere with you, but I guess I was all wrong." My words seemed to be an additional catalyst and I found myself chasing them through the building, catching them one at a time, and escorting them outside.

My mistake was a natural one. I was not clear about the concept of deviant behavior as communication at that time, so I did not attempt to find out what was wrong—why they were so agitated. Even if I had been clear about that, my functional confusion would have prevented me from dealing with them effectively. In the same situation today, I would be able to explain my functional role more clearly to my supervisor, suggesting that I speak to the boys to see what was going on and to try to cool them down long enough to talk to the supervisor about what was happening in the building and why. If I were unsuccessful, then the supervisor could throw the group outside and I would go with them. I would have explained to the supervisor that at the point the boys were thrown outside, I would be available to them to figure out what had happened and to find a way to deal more effectively with the Y, since they would want to be accepted back. The Y was concerned about this group's behavior, and this would be an opportunity to do some work on the relationship between the group and the Y.

I am not suggesting there would never be a time when I felt bound to set limits on the boys and act on behalf of the agency or society. In the course of our time together, there would be many such occasions. For example, if physical violence were threatened, it would be my job to set limits and try to stop it so that we could develop safety for all members in the group. However, at this moment, when they were thrown out, they needed their leader the most. As I found out later, that day had been report card day at school, and most of the boys in the group were afraid to go home that evening and face their parents because of bad grades and reports of similar behavior problems in school. The acting out behavior was an indirect call for help. A marvelous opportunity for work had been missed.

### The Homans Social Systems Model—Relating to the Environment

A group theorist who could have helped me conceptualize the problem differently is Homans (Homans, 1950). In his classic book *The Human Group,* Homans presents a general theory of human interaction using five well-known field studies of social interaction to illustrate his ideas. He describes three major elements of behavior, which he terms interaction, sentiment, and activity. Interaction refers to any contact between people, sentiment to feelings or drives, and activity to any action. Thus, Homans could take a descriptive social study and break it down into these three components: interactions, sentiments, and activities. His interest centers on the interdependence of these elements of social behavior; for example, how sentiment in a group can affect interaction and, in turn, how interactions can affect sentiment. In the group example just described, the boys' feelings (sentiments) about their poor grades and anticipated criticism from parents affected the way they related (interactions) to each other, which in turn generated behavior (activity) of the acting out type.

Homan's second major theoretical contribution is also important here. He viewed activities, interactions, and sentiments within two interdependent systems—the "internal" system and the "external" system. The internal system consists of the interactions, sentiments, and activities within the group and their mutual interdependence. The external system consists of the same three basic elements (interaction, sentiment, and activity) between the group and its environment—in this case, the Y. It is important to note that Homans does not use the term *external system* to refer to the system itself (in this case, the Y). This is a common use of the concept system and a common misunderstanding in respect to Homans. The external system, to Homans, would be the three elements of interaction, sentiment, and activity between the group and the Y, not the Y itself.

The boys had developed a pattern of acting out within the Y that generated negative sentiment on the part of staff, which in turn affected the interactions between Y staff and the group, which in turn generated more negative sentiment, and so on. Any effort to deal with the group members' behavior within the group must take into account the impact of the "external systems" of the school, family, and the agency. While I have oversimplified Homan's theory, I think the central elements demonstrate once again how a theoretical construct can help a leader conceptualize a problem in a new way.

The issue of helping the group to negotiate the environment will come back to the forefront in later chapters. I will argue that the social worker who believes he or she can take the group into a room and work with it with no regard to environmental issues will be missing an important aspect of the helping role and an opportunity to have a powerful impact. More on this idea will appear later in this book.

## Chapter Summary

This chapter examined common examples of individual roles in the group. The concept of social role helps to explain patterned reactions by scapegoats, deviants, and gatekeepers, as well as by defensive, quiet, and monopolizing members. In each case, the group leader can best serve the group by understanding the individual member in terms of the dynamics of the group. For example, illustrations of how a perceived "deviant member" might actually be speaking for a larger number of group members suggested the importance of not trying to understand this behavior as just a product of "personality."

The scapegoating process in a group was defined in a similar manner with the group projecting onto the scapegoat their own internalized negative feelings and the scapegoat, in some cases, volunteering for the role. The key element in the chapter was the concept of the group leader being with the "two clients"—the individual and the group—at the same time.

The leader's second client, the organism called the group, must go through a developmental process. Early tasks include problems of formation and the satisfaction of individual members' needs. The concept of the group-as-a-whole is receiving increasing research attention with some focus on the impact of the development of group cohesion and what is called the therapeutic alliance to the group as a whole. Problems of dealing with the leader as a symbol of authority (authority theme) must be faced, as well as the difficulties involved in peer group relationships (the intimacy theme). Attention needs to be paid to the culture of the group so that norms can be developed that are consistent with the achievement of the group's goals. Taboos that block the group's progress must be challenged and mastered if the discussion is to be meaningful. A formal or informal structure must be developed. This structure will include assigned roles, assigned status, communication patterns, and a decision-making process.

Three classic group theories and one more recent theory were presented as models to help the group leader understand the group, its developmental needs, as well as its relationship to the environment. Effective work in the group will develop a sense of cohesion, which in turn will strengthen future work. Finally, the group exists within a dynamic system—the environment—and one of the leader's tasks is to assist with the interaction between the group and its social surroundings.

---

# Related Online Content and Activities

 Visit *The Skills of Helping Individuals, Families, Groups, and Communities,* Seventh Edition, CourseMate website at **www.cengagebrain.com** for learning tools such as glossary terms, links to related websites, and chapter practice quizzes. The website for this chapter also features additional notes from the author.

---

# Competency Notes

The following is a list of Council on Social Work Education (CSWE) recommended competencies and practice behaviors for social work students defined in Educational Policy and Accreditation Standard (EPAS) and addressed in this chapter.

**EP 2.1.1a** Advocate for client access to the services of social work (p. 568)

**EP 2.1.1b** Practice personal reflection and self-correction to assure continual professional development (pp. 518, 540)

**EP 2.1.3a** Distinguish, appraise, and integrate multiple sources of knowledge, including research-based knowledge and practice wisdom (pp. 503, 533)

**EP 2.1.3b** Analyze models of assessment, prevention, intervention, and evaluation (p. 503)

**EP 2.1.4a** Recognize the extent to which a culture's structures and values may oppress, marginalize, alienate, or create or enhance privilege and power (pp. 503, 505, 540)

**EP 2.1.4c** Recognize and communicate their understanding of the importance of difference in shaping life experiences (pp. 503, 512)

**EP 2.1.4d** View themselves as learners and engage those with whom they work as informants (p. 540)

**EP 2.1.5a** Understand forms and mechanisms of oppression and discrimination (pp. 503, 505)

**EP 2.1.6b** Use research evidence to inform practice (pp. 533, 548)

**EP 2.1.7a** Utilize conceptual frameworks to guide the process of assessment, intervention, and evaluation (p. 533)

**EP 2.1.7b** Critique and apply knowledge to understand person and environment (p. 523)

**EP 2.1.10b** Use empathy and other interpersonal skills (p. 512)

**EP 2.1.10g** Select appropriate intervention strategies (pp. 512, 533, 540)

**EP 2.1.10m** Critically analyze, monitor, and evaluate interventions (p. 512)

# Endings and Transitions with Groups

B y examining the ending and transition phase of practice, this chapter completes the discussion of the phases of group work. The chapter explores the unique dynamics and skills associated with bringing the helping process to a close and helping the group members to make appropriate transitions. Practice examples will illustrate how this can be the most powerful and meaningful phase of work, as group members make the third decision—to deal with core issues that may have only been hinted at in the earlier phases. This chapter also examines the danger of this phase becoming a moratorium on work, in which both the group members and the group leader participate in an illusion of work. Specific skills to increase the possibility of positive endings and transitions will be described and illustrated.

# The Ending Phase of Group Practice

**EP 2.1.10l**

Recall that, in the beginning phase, group members face a first decision. They must decide whether they are prepared to engage with the group leader and each other, to lower defenses if needed, and to begin to work. In the second decision, the transition to the work phase, group members agree to take some responsibility for their part in problems and to face the emotional pain involved in work. In the third decision, group members must decide whether to deal with the most difficult issues as they approach the end of the working relationship.

The ending phase offers the greatest potential for powerful and important work. Group members feel a sense of urgency as they realize there is little time left, and this can lead to the introduction of some of the most difficult and important themes of concern. The emotional dynamics between group leader and member are also heightened in this phase as they prepare to move away from the other. Termination of the relationship can evoke powerful feelings in both members and the group leader, and the group leader can often connect discussion of these to the member's general concerns and tasks. The ending phase holds tremendous potential for work, yet ironically this phase is often the least effective and can be characterized by missed meetings, lateness, apathy, acting out, and regressions to earlier, less mature patterns of behavior. Moreover, the group leader—as well as the members—shows these behaviors at times.

In many ways, the ending sessions are the most difficult ones for both the group leader and the members. The source of the strain stems from the general difficulty we have in dealing with the end of important relationships. Our society has done little to train us how to handle a separation; in fact, the general norm is to deny feelings associated with it. For example, when a valued colleague leaves an agency, the farewell party is often an attempt, usually unsuccessful, to cover the sadness with fun. The laughter at such parties is often a bit forced.

Delucia-Waack (2006) suggests the importance of addressing endings even in psychoeducational groups and addresses factors that may cause leaders to ignore the importance of this phase.

> Group leaders often underestimate the importance of the termination session and the consolidation of learning for a variety of different reasons. One is that psychoeducational groups tend to be so brief that it is difficult to consider giving a whole session to a topic that is not teaching a new skill or strategy. . . . [Also,] termination brings up grief and loss issues, and sometimes group leaders may not want to experience emotions that go along with this stage, so they avoid it if at all possible. (p. 129)

Chen and Rybak (2004) also address the issues of loss in what they refer to as the "termination stage."

> The characteristics of the termination stage in a group are similar to those of the golden age in a person's life. Ridden throughout is a theme of loss and grief. A lot of feelings are triggered by the ending of the therapeutic relationship. Ending can be filled with sadness. Although the entire group experience may feel like a small life lived with others who have become significant in one's life, its ending may feel like a big loss. When sensing the ending approaching, some members start to feel a sense of separation anxiety. (p. 318)

The group leader–group members association is a specific example of this larger phenomenon. It can be painful to terminate a close relationship; and when you have invested yourself meaningfully in a relationship, shared some of your most important feelings, and given and taken help from another human being, the bond that develops is strong. Strean (1978) has described the difficulties involved in terminating a close working relationship.

> Whether a leader-member relationship consists of five interviews or a hundred, if the leader has truly related to the member's expectations, perceptions of himself and transactions with his social orbit, the member will experience the encounter as meaningful and the leader as someone significant; therefore, separation from this "significant other" will inevitably arouse complex and ambivalent feelings. Still, a long-term relationship with a leader will probably include more intense emotions at termination than a short-term one.
>
> A prolonged relationship has usually stimulated dependency needs and wishes, transference reactions, revelation of secrets, embarrassing moments, exhilaration, sadness, and gladness. The encounter has become part of the member's weekly life, so that ending it can seem like saying good-bye to a valued family member or friend. (pp. 227–228)

Corey and Corey (2006) also emphasize the importance of the work to be done in this stage of the group.

> The final phase in the life of the group is the time for members to consolidate their learning and develop strategies for transferring what they learned in the group to daily life. At this time members need to be able to express what the group experience has meant to them and to state where they intend to go from here. For many group members endings are difficult because they realize that time is limited in their group. Members need to face the reality of termination and learn how to say good-bye. If the group has been truly therapeutic, members will be able to extend their learning outside, even though they may well experience a sense of sadness and loss. (p. 265)

## The Dynamics and Skills of Endings

EP 2.1.3a
EP 2.1.10b

Schwartz (1971) described the ending phase in the group context:

> In the final phase of work—that which I have called "endings and transitions"—the group leader's skills are needed to help the members use him and each other to deal with the problem of moving from one experience to another. For the group leader it means moving off the track of the members' experience and life process, as he has, in the beginning, moved onto it. The point is that beginnings and endings are hard for people to manage; they often call out deep feeling in both group leader and members; and much skill is needed to help people to help each other through these times. (pp. 17–18)

### Flow of Affect in the Ending Phase

One of the dynamics that makes endings hard has already been mentioned: the pain associated with ending a relationship in which one has invested a great deal. In addition to the pain, a form of guilt might surface. Group members may feel that if they had worked harder in the relationship, played their part more effectively, and risked more, perhaps they could have done a better job. This guilt sometimes emerges indirectly, with members saying, "Can't we have more time?"

As with many of the feelings in the ending phase, this sense of guilt is often shared by the group leader, who may feel that he or she should have been more helpful to the group. Perhaps, if the group leader had been more experienced, or more capable, he or she could have been more helpful with regard to some of the unresolved issues. Instead of understanding that members will need to work continually on life's problems, the group leader feels guilty for not having "solved" them all. Students often articulate this feeling as follows: "If only the group had a real group leader!" Usually, they underestimate the help that they have given.

Because of the general difficulty of talking about negative and positive feedback, both group leader and members may have many unstated feelings that need to be dealt with in the final phase. Things may have been left unsaid because of taboos against honest talk about the role of authority. This theme needs to be discussed before the relationship can properly end. For example, the group leader may have said and done things that made the member angry. The reverse might also be true, with the group leader somewhat frustrated about the members' inability to take risks and to open up to the group leader.

The group leader providing this feedback, if it is related to the group leader's real caring for the member, can serve to clear the air. Even if the leader and the group members have not been able to get along together, and they face the impending separation with a sense of relief, the discussion that takes place at the end should be real. What was it about the group leader that the group members could not relate to? In turn, the members should know what made it difficult for the group leader to connect with them. There may have been misconceptions on the part of either or both parties, and discussing these can help clear them up. This could be quite helpful to the members who may choose to enter another helping relationship in the future. The importance of feedback to the group leader is obvious. In addition, if the negative feelings are not dealt with, group members might transfer them to their next group leader.

Even more difficult for group leaders and members to handle than the negative feelings may be the positive ones. It is not easy for any of us to tell those close to us, particularly people in authority, that they have meant a great deal to us. Moreover, many group leaders find accepting positive feelings with grace extremely hard to do. I have repeatedly observed group leaders respond to a member's genuine expression of thanks for all that the group leader has done by protesting, "It wasn't really me, I didn't do that much, it was really all your work." One student asked during a class if it was all right for her to accept a fruitcake offered to her by an elderly group member at the end of their work together. This was not a case in which a member was trying to pay a group leader for her services, which were normally free. It was simply this woman's way of saying thank you to a group leader who cared. I asked the student if the fruitcake looked good and suggested that, if it did, the student ought to take it.

When I press group leaders about the cause of their embarrassment in such cases, they usually point to the general cultural barriers against appearing immodest, as well as their belief that they could not have really given that much help. The latter response reflects an underestimation of the effect of the help given. Group members respond with great feeling to a caring, honest group leader; they are not usually as critical as the group leader is about what the group leader might have done.

Cultural barriers notwithstanding, mutual sharing of positive feelings at the end of a relationship matters a great deal because it enables both members and the group leader to value what has taken place between them and to bring it properly to an end. Both the members and the group leader can carry feelings of regret for unspoken words long after they have stopped seeing each other, thus making the actual ending process protracted and more difficult. The problem with delayed endings is that they tie up energy that both parties need to invest in new relationships.

### Timing and the Ending Phase

The timing of this phase depends on the length of the relationship. For example, for weekly group sessions that last a year, the final 8 weeks or so usually constitute the ending process. In short-term work—for example, six sessions—evidence of feelings about endings may emerge in the fourth or fifth session as the group leader receives subtle cues to the members' reactions. Although these cues mark the beginning of the ending phase, thoughts about the end are present even in the beginning. Often, a member will inquire early in the process, even after a first session that was helpful, how long the sessions will continue. Time is an important factor, and group members will orient themselves accordingly. A long break in the work phase, whether caused by the group leader's illness, a vacation, or perhaps a holiday season, can provoke ending feelings as the member associates the break with the ending to come. It is not uncommon to observe apathy, withdrawal, and other premature ending symptoms immediately after such a break.

It is important for the group leader to draw the member's attention to these signals and initiate a discussion of whether or not the members have begun to think about the ending. Then the group leader and the members can strategize about how to make sure they don't end prematurely and that they make good use of what might be the most important period of work rather than experience a moratorium on work.

## Stages of the Ending Process

Schwartz (1961) has outlined the stages of the ending process in group work as follows:

- Denial
- Indirect and direct expressions of anger
- Mourning
- Trying it on for size
- The farewell-party syndrome

The reader who is familiar with the classic work by Kubler-Ross (1969) on the stages of death and dying will note similarities. Even though there is some question about the Kubler-Ross model itself, the discrete stages as described above, and the fact that they rarely proceed in a linear manner, nevertheless practice experience tells us the model is useful for understanding group dynamics in this phase of work. Every ending represents a loss, not as powerful as death, but still evoking strong emotions. Each of the stages suggested by Schwartz is discussed in more detail, and the required leader skills are identified and illustrated.

## Denial

First is the denial of the ending, in which group members appear to ignore the imminent end of the group. This is related to the general difficulty of facing feelings in all areas of our lives associated with the ending of important relationships. If the reader considers endings of personal relationships, it is possible to recall how hard it was to face them.

In the group context, the members are ending with the leaders—whom hopefully they have experienced as caring and supportive professionals—as well as ending with the other members. If the reader will recall the married couples' group led by this author that was illustrated in previous chapters, a number of excerpts revealed how close members were able to become to one another as they shared their life experiences. About halfway through this group, held in a room in the Health Science Center at the university, I discovered that the group members were getting together for coffee in the cafeteria after the regular session ended. The mutual-aid process had created a bond between these five couples—so different in their ages, life experiences, and social situations—that was also coming to an end. The group had become a safe place where they could get help with their difficult family struggles. They would be losing the group leaders, but they also would be losing one another.

Following my own advice, given later in this chapter, I pointed out at the 20th session that we only had four sessions left before the group would come to an end. I indicated that if they had something to say in the group, the next four sessions would be the time to do it. One member of the group disagreed with me and indicated that I had said in the first session that the group would continue until the end of May, not the end of April. He said: "We actually have 8 sessions left." The other group members agreed with him. Since all of the sessions had been videotaped I decided to play the next week the section of the first meeting where I indicated we would end the last week in April. After the tape stopped, the same member said: "See, you said the end of May." Denial was in full force and even the video evidence would not budge the members. My statement did, however, set the process in motion as we moved to the next stage the following week.

## Anger

Denial is often followed by anger about the ending, which emerges in direct and indirect forms and is often focused on the group leader, who group members feel is abandoning them. At times, conflict between members of a group during this phase of work is actually an indirect way of expressing anger toward the group leader.

***Ending a Children's Group in a School Setting: The Anger Stage Emerges*** In an example from a children's group in a school setting, one group leader describes the session that follows the one in which he told the group he must leave in a few weeks not by his choice. There is no response in that session; the members continue with their activities as if they had not heard. The group had been established for boys who were in trouble for fighting and other forms of acting out behavior.

Over the course of the school year, they had moved into being able to talk about their issues, such as their anger at teachers and parents, rather than acting them out through negative behaviors. At the start of the session the week after the announcement of the group leader's departure, the boys appeared to regress and began acting out, fighting, and not responding to the group leader's efforts to set limits. At one point, in a symbolic action, the internal leader of the group put masking tape over his mouth, an action that was quickly followed by the other members. The boys turned and shook their fists at the group leader. Finally, the group leader, who had also been in a stage of denial, said:

> "I know you are all angry at me for leaving, and that, underneath that anger, you are sad. I have to let you know I am sad as well. We have gotten very close to one another over the year. But we have been a talking group most of the year, and I hope you can take the tape off and we can talk about my leaving."

Adults can express their anger by missing group sessions or through dismissive comments about the value of the group. Regression may begin as group members report being unable to deal with problems in their lives that they had been able to address earlier in the life of the group. This regression may be an indirect call for help: "Don't leave us yet—we are not ready."

## Mourning

The mourning period is usually characterized by apathy and a general tone of sadness in the group. This can be seen as a grieving period, as the reality of the ending begins to hit home. In the couples' group, in the second session that followed my reminder to group members that we only had four sessions left, and now only two, I entered the usually brightly lit group room to find that no one had turned on the overhead lights. In addition, each of the members sat silently, looking mostly at the floor, and did not participate in catch-up conversation with one another as usual. I articulated my first reaction by saying, "What's going on? This feels like a wake." One of the members—Lou, our 69-year-old member who had been angry at professionals during the first session reported in Chapter 11—said, "This is a wake. In a few weeks, the group will be over." This was followed by a discussion of the implications of the group ending for the members and the beginning of the transition phase work in terms of how they would get help in the future and on whom they could depend for support.

What I found most interesting with regard to this ending was the fact that my coleaders and I would meet before and after the session with a group of students who observed the group on a monitor as part of their group course (with the informed consent of the group members). When I entered the observation room to meet with the students after this particular group session, I suddenly realized that I was going to have to deal with two group endings on the same evening. When I mentioned the wake-like feeling in the observation room—which mirrored the feeling in the group meeting room I had just left—one of the students said, "I have felt so close to these people and their lives that it's tough to think about this ending." A second student commented that she had seen one group member in a supermarket checkout line and almost went over to say hello before she remembered that the group member had never actually seen her. Another student asked, "What am I going to do on Thursday evenings"?

## Trying It On for Size

In the "trying the ending on for size" stage, the group members operate independently of the group leader or spend a great deal of time talking about new groups or new group leaders. I noticed this in my teaching (an educational group) when a second-year, last-semester seminar class was coming to a close. A student was making a presentation on the concept of continuing their learning when I made a comment. The class members turned toward me, looked for a moment, and then went right back to their discussion as if they had not heard me. When this happened a third time, I realized they were getting ready to graduate and would no longer have a professor to help them out. They would need to depend more heavily on their colleagues, and I could see that they were trying this on for size. I commented on this by pointing out what I thought was happening. They turned, looked at me, and then went right back to their conversation. I realized I needed to just sit back and watch and to be pleased with how they had learned to depend on and use one another.

### Farewell-Party Syndrome

Finally, in the farewell-party syndrome, group members appear to protect the group by avoiding discussing its negative aspects. The group leader may ask for feedback on how the group has functioned: What were the positives, and what were the negatives? How had the group leader done, and how well had the members accomplished their goals? When the feedback is almost all positive, this is a sign of the farewell party—no group is *always* great. The group leader needs to reach for the negatives so that the group members do not "pad" the experience by only reflecting on the positives.

It is also not unusual for group members to suggest throwing an actual farewell party in an attempt to avoid the pain of the ending. What is often left out is a discussion of the loss that accompanies the ending of the group. I am not arguing against a good, old-fashioned farewell party; however, it should not be a substitute for saying good-bye.

In another illustration of avoidance, consider a staff member leaving a residential institution. Staff members may have real farewell party while avoiding dealing with the affect associated with the staff member leaving. Also consider that loss is central to the issues faced by the children in the residence. They may have already lost their parents, siblings, home, and so on. Losing a residential counselor is another loss for some of these children and needs to be openly discussed. If staff members have not addressed their own feelings about the loss of their colleague, they may not be able to address those of the children.

## Group Leader Strategies with Regard to Ending

Group leader strategies for dealing with endings in group work are similar to those in work with individuals and families. They are as follows:

- The group leader should bring the ending to the group members' attention early, thereby allowing the ending process to be established.
- The stages should be pointed out as the group experiences them, with the group leader reaching for the indirect cues and articulating the processes taking place: denial, anger, mourning, and so on.
- Because the group ending has meaning for the group leader as well, he or she can bring personal feelings and recollections to the group.

- Discussion of the ending feelings should be encouraged, with the group leader participating fully in the exchange of both positive and negative reactions.

- The group leader should also help the group members be specific as they evaluate their work together. For example, when a member says, "It was a great group!" the group leader should ask, "What was it about the group that made it great?"

- Finally, the group leader should reach past the farewell-party syndrome to encourage members to share negative feedback. For example, "I'm glad you all feel the group sessions were great, but they can't always have been great. Weren't there some that were not-so-great?"

Because members have different reactions to endings, the group leader should encourage the expression and acceptance of differing views. Not everyone in the group will experience it in the same way, and as pointed out earlier in this chapter, the ending may have more impact on some than others.

## Group Leader Strategies with Regard to Transition

The group leader must also pay attention to the transitional aspect of the ending phase. For example:

- If members are continuing with other group leaders, how can they begin the relationship in a positive manner?

- If members have finished their work, what have they learned, and how can they use their learning in their new experiences?

- If members have found the group helpful, how can they find similar sources of support in their life situations?

In this way, the group leader can ensure that the ending discussion deals with substantive matters as well as the process of ending.

In some situations, help can also take the form of a physical transition. In another school example in a group for sixth graders who were about to transition to middle school, the group leader arranged for the group to visit the school and meet with the principal and seventh-grade teacher. This also serves as an example of helping the group to deal with its environment.

Finally, the group leader should search for the subtle connections between the process of the ending and the substantive work of the group. For example, endings for a group of young mothers about to give birth may coincide with separation from their children if they have opted to give them up for adoption. In another example, teenage girls in a group for survivors of incest expressed strong feelings of anger toward their two female group leaders as the group was coming to an end after a year of hard and powerful work. The group members expressed feeling abandoned by the leaders. With the help of the leaders, the group members connected this anger to their anger toward their mothers who had failed to protect them from the abuse. This had been a taboo subject and only emerged in the last sessions—an example of "doorknob therapy." These and other connections can help to enrich the ending discussion. They represent the group members making the third decision referred to earlier. The next section illustrates these dynamics and skills.

## The Group Leader Takes a Leave of Absence: Transitioning to an Interim Leader

One more model of endings can take place when the primary leader needs to take a leave of absence and intends to return, with the group led by an interim leader. While there is an expansive literature on endings with leaders or members leaving, the temporary leave of absence is not as well addressed. With roles in settings and in personal lives becoming increasingly complex and demanding, this need for a leave can occur more often.

Pudil (2007) uses her own experience on a leave from an adolescent HIV-positive group to develop and illustrate the model. She suggests five steps that need to be planned and implemented when a leave is known about in advance:

1. Providing ample time for the announcement of the primary leader's (hereinafter referred to as the "PW") leaving.

2. Developing a system of transfer through meetings between the interim leader (hereinafter referred to as "IW") and primary leaders.

3. Introducing the group members to the IW.

4. Processing group member's feelings and reactions about the transfer.

5. Reintroducing the group members to the PW when the leave of absence ends and the IW departs. (pp. 218–219)

The author provides illustrations of the five steps drawn from the adolescent group with step 3, introducing the group members to the IW being one of the most complicated. The PW and IW agreed to keep the first meeting brief to allow time for the group members to voice their concerns and feelings after the IW left the room. The IW introduced herself, and each member did so in turn. Some of the introductions came closer to expressing the feelings of the members. For example, Akira said, "I'm Akira. I have one daughter and I'm currently pregnant. I live in Manhattan. I've been in the program for a long time and I don't like new people" (p. 224). It's not too hard to understand which "new people" she is referring to. Another member expresses the feelings of loss: "Hi, I'm Kim. I've been with Dr. C for a long time" (p. 225).

The PW invites the members to ask the IW any questions and is greeted by silence. After the IW left, the responses flowed as described by the leader:

> They stated their dislike for her and her laid back, quiet personality. The members decided that she was too different and would not be able to meet their needs, alarming the PW, but it is important to remember they were still reacting to the idea that the PW was taking a leave of absence. Also, because a large number of members kept their HIV status a secret, they had historically tried to keep new people at a distance, automatically assuming that new people would be judgmental and reject them; in fact they had been in situations that regularly exposed them to rejection. (p. 225)

The strategy adopted for the transition involved having the IW attend a number of sessions with the PW and colead. Eventually, the IW began to take an increasingly active role in leading the group. In addition, the group members were provided with a chance to indicate the direction they wished the group to go during the interim period. The most important process in effecting a positive transfer was their ability to openly express their emotions, their concern about investing themselves in yet another leader when they knew the PW was returning, and then the deeper connection to losses experienced in the past. A gradual reintroduction of the PW coleading a number of sessions after months of absence allowed the group to successfully make the transition back.

### Individualizing the Ending and Transition to Meet Individual Needs

Each individual member may experience the ending of the group differently depending upon his or her particular circumstances and life experiences. Gladding (2003) points out that regardless of how careful and thorough the leader is during the termination stage, occasionally a few group members may need more help. For these people, he suggests three options:

1. individual counseling, in which unique concerns can be given greater attention;
2. referral to another group or organization, in which more specific or specialized assistance can be rendered; or
3. recycling, in which the individual can go through a similar group experience again and learn lessons missed the first time. (p. 182)

Most authors, including those cited above, agree that the ending process in a helping relationship can trigger the deepest feelings in both group leaders and members. As such, both can do powerful work during this phase, as well as ineffective work if the feelings are not dealt with. This chapter explores the dynamics of the ending phase, identifies some of the central skills required to make effective endings, and discusses how group leaders can help group members make transitions to new experiences.

●-------------------------------------------------

## Three Additional Group Illustrations

The ending phase of work offers a powerful opportunity to deepen the work by integrating process and content. The losses involved in ending a group often provoke issues of intimacy and loss in other areas of the members' lives. By constantly searching for the connections, however faint, between the dynamics of the ending process and the substantive work of the particular group, the group leader can help the members use the ending as an important learning experience.

*Ending with Hearing-Impaired Teenagers' Group* In this illustration, a leader helps a group come to grips with her leaving and prepare for the arrival of a new leader. The group consists of teenagers who are hearing-impaired. The beginning phase of work had been difficult, since the counselor had needed to develop a way to communicate with the members and to help them communicate with each other.

**Practice Points:** Their concern about the new leader was heightened by their fears that an "outsider" might not accept them because of their "handicap." The group had operated using a combination of discussion and activities. The planned activity for that evening was tobogganing:

> When I arrived, the members were already there. The usual greetings were exchanged, and we sat down to wait to see if more members would come. Billy said, "I think we should wait ten minutes and then go." Kathy said she had spoken to several members, and they had indicated they wouldn't be coming, as

it was such an awful night. I remarked that it was pretty cold for tobogganing. It was too bad we didn't know what the weather would be like. Billy said he had brought his toque, which would keep him warm. He proceeded to model it, which caused all of the members to laugh.

At this point, Billy asked when the new leader was coming. I said that Barbara would be coming next meeting. Stephen said, "Is she like you?" I replied that she was a student like I me, she was young and very happy to be coming to the group. I turned to Kathy and said, "We are talking about the new leader who will be coming to our meeting next week." Kathy turned to Amelia and Anna and indicated by sign language that the new leader would be coming next week. Amelia mocked a crying gesture, which bought a chorus of smiles from the other members.

Stephen said, "Has she ever worked in a group like ours, like with deaf people?" Billy turned to Stephen, and said, "Well, Lucille never worked with deaf people before us." Kathy replied, "That's right."

Just as group leaders need to develop the ability to monitor the group-as-a-whole, the content and process of the discussion, and the clock, they must monitor each individual as well. In this group, because of the hearing disability of the members and their difficulty in seeing and reading the lips of the others, the leader must actively monitor signs of lack of involvement.

**Practice Points:**   In the next excerpt the leader reminds the group to include everyone, and also reaches directly for their concerns about losing her and about the possible attitude of the new leader.

Amelia, Jo-Ann, and Anna were craning their necks to find out what was going on. I pointed out that some members were being left out of our conversation, and we had to try to remember to include everyone. Billy made a mock gesture to the effect of "here we go again," and he motioned the three members to move in closer. I said, "It's tough work letting everybody know what's going on," to which Billy replied, "Yeah!"

I remarked that Billy and Stephen seemed sort of worried about the new leader coming in. Kathy smiled the sort of smile that says, "You hit the nail on the head." Stephen said, "We just want to know what she's like." I said that I think Kathy was thinking that, too. I said, "Was I right, Kathy?" to which she nodded her head.

Amelia mumbled something that I didn't understand. Billy turned to her and then translated to me. Amelia had said it was like starting our group all over again. Jo-Ann asked what was starting over. Kathy explained to Jo-Ann what was going on. Jo-Ann shook her head. Anna, who is totally mute, was looking as if she were in another world; I was aware that she did not understand our conversation. I smiled at her, and she grinned back. Billy looked at me and said "I'll explain to Anna."

The group counselor recognizes that for any group there would be interest in what the new leader will be like during the ending and transition period. In the case of these hearing-impaired young people, a new hearing person raises concerns about how they will be viewed—as individuals or as their disability.

**Practice Points:**   While reaching for the feelings of concern, the leader does not directly raise the issue of having a hearing person lead the group.

I then turned to Amelia and said, "You're nervous, like maybe it was like when you came to the meeting with me for the first time." Amelia mumbled, "Nervous? Nervous?" and turned to Stephen with a puzzled expression. Stephen very slowly said, "Remember what it was like the first time we came here?" Amelia gave him a look that said "I sure do." I said I guessed it was like that again, knowing a new leader is coming. Stephen nodded and said, "How come you're going?" then in a joking way added, "I guess you don't like us anymore." I said, "Of course I still like you." Stephen then patted Billy on the back. Billy said, "A good group, aren't we?" I smiled and said we'd been through an awful lot together. Kathy nodded her head, and this was a message that quickly got translated to all the members.

Kathy said, "Gee, I wish we could have a leader that would stay in our group." Stephen said, "Yeah." I said I guessed that maybe people were also angry because I was going. Stephen said, "No, no, that's not right." Billy said, "We've had a good time in this group." I said, "Just the same, I understand it's a hard thing to have to face going through getting to know a new leader again." Kathy said, "Yeah, we just got to know you." Amelia made another mock gesture of crying. In the meantime, Jo-Ann and Anna were talking in sign language and I think were quite out of the conversation.

**Practice Points:**   The leader's direct reaching for the anger at her leaving was too difficult a demand for the members at this moment. In flight from the painful feelings, they played a trick on her instead of responding directly:

Jo-Ann then said to Billy (in sign language), "When are we going to go tobogganing?" He translated for me. I said we had somehow passed the ten minutes Billy had suggested we wait, and I asked her, "Are you ready to go?" Jo-Ann shook her head. I said, "You had a tough time knowing what was going on," and repeated this several times until she understood. She smiled and nodded and then smiled at Anna. Billy and Stephen then said they were ready to go. Billy poked Kathy and said, "Ready?" Kathy nodded. I said I thought Anna was being left out. Billy translated it to her, and she nodded.

I said I would go and get the two office toboggans and I'd be back in a minute. When I came back, to my dismay the group had all disappeared. I looked in several rooms and then decided to sit down and wait. In several seconds, Billy came whistling in. I jumped to my feet and said, "Gee, what happened to our group?" Billy, in a mischievous way, said, "Gee, I don't know. I just went for a walk." He said, "Why don't we look in the hall?" I said I guessed the members would come back, at which point he, in an insistent way, said, "No, let's look in the hall," which we did. Five beaming faces appeared with Kathy saying, "Surprise!" Everyone laughed, as did I; however, I said, "How come the group wanted to leave?"

Stephen said, "We wanted you to look for us." Amelia grinned and said, "Were you worried?" I said, "Did you want me to be worried?" to which there were several nervous titters. I then said, "I think this group wants to leave me before I leave them," to which there were vehement no's. Billy said, "We were just joking." I said, "Still, I wasn't sure that everyone knew why I was leaving." Stephen said, "You're going back to Saskatchewan, isn't that where you were from?" I said I would be working on my research till June. Kathy said, "We'll still have a good group." Stephen poked Kathy and said, "You'll still be here." Kathy said, "All of us members will be here." I said that I thought they could continue to have a good group, but that would depend a lot on them. Billy nodded his head as if he understood. Kathy said, "Like you always say, we got to work at it." The group members laughed and shared this last piece of information, and then we got ready to leave.

**Practice Summary.**  This example brought back to me my own early reluctance to directly address the disabilities of my group members in my early camp experience. Even after one becomes so use to the physical aspects, for example, entering a camper cabin with braces, crutches, artificial legs, and so on hanging from the rafters and folded wheelchairs, a person who is not disabled may feel reluctant to discuss the disability. On reflection, I think my own hesitancy was (and perhaps still is) related to my understanding of the anger often below the surface of those who have experienced yet another form of stigmatization and oppression and my own biases and prejudices that are deeply and socially ingrained.

***A Support Group for Patients with Multiple Sclerosis*** In the first example that follows, a group leader opens up the discussion of her leaving with a group of people who have multiple sclerosis, or MS (the group will be continuing). The announcement of the impending ending initiates a powerful conversation about intimacy and loss related to the illness.

**Practice Points:**  Note that the group leader brings the group members back to their own endings in the here-and-now of the group experience. This example illustrates the following points:

- *Endings provoke a range of feelings that can be connected to the work of the group*
- *The members in this group talk about loss of a sense of self as well as loss of loved ones*
- *The group leader needs to bring the members back to the imminent loss of the group*

GROUP LEADER: As you know, I only meet with you one more time after today. You all will continue to meet until June. What are your thoughts about the group ending in a couple of months?
BOB: I am not looking forward to the summer because of the hot weather . . . it makes my MS flare up.
ALBERT: I know . . . I always feel tired and run down when it gets too hot. And then the group breaks up and I don't have anyone to really talk to about my MS. I used to look forward to the summer, but now I almost dread it.
BOB: I'm going to miss everyone too. I don't have anyone to talk to either. My wife is great, but she doesn't really understand what I am feeling.
GROUP LEADER: Do you guys keep in touch even when the group is not meeting during the summer months?
ALBERT: Not really . . .
FRED: I talk to Rob from the other group pretty regularly.
BOB: Albert, you live not too far from me. We should get together once in a while this summer. Or at least talk on the phone.
ALBERT: I like that idea . . . I do want to stay in touch.

**Practice Points:**  As the group approaches the end with only one more meeting with this leader, we see the "doorknob therapy" phenomenon described earlier emerge as one member raises the powerful issue of physical appearance and how others appear to regard him. Another member points out that the lack of visible symptoms also causes problems as others do not understand the pain of the disease. The leader encourages elaboration of both themes.

JAMES: (Who has been quiet up to this point) I used to dance and run track . . . and now I can't anymore. People look at me like I'm weird.

BOB: I always liked to dance too.

GROUP LEADER: James, you said people look at you weird. What do you mean by that? How does that make you feel?

JAMES: I get mad because I am not weird. I am just in a wheelchair. They don't know what I used to be able to do. All they see is what I look like on the outside.

GROUP LEADER: You're right. Strangers do not know who you are or what you are like, as we do. They don't know you as a person, and it isn't fair that they should judge you by your appearance or being in a wheelchair.

FRED: That's the trouble—no one can see the MS. They can't see the pain we feel in our legs or the burning we have in our joints.

ALBERT: (Who is one of the members whose MS is not as extreme; he still walks) People don't even know anything is wrong with me because I am not in a wheelchair. But I still experience the MS symptoms. When they flare up, I get tired and sometimes walk off-balance, like I am drunk or something.

**Practice Points:** As the ending approaches, this conversation indicates that the members have made what I called earlier the "third decision." They are going to discuss some of the most painful and difficult issues, and the leader will try, as best as possible, to empathize with them.

GROUP LEADER: It must be hard for you, Albert, because people cannot see your illness, and they may not understand when you try to explain your physical symptoms.

ALBERT: Yeah, that happens a lot. When people find out I have MS, they don't believe me, because I am not in a wheelchair and they automatically associate MS with being in a wheelchair.

FRED: I went through that a lot when I was first diagnosed. I fought going into this wheelchair for as long as I could. I was lucky to be able to work until I was 60. But a short time after I retired, I had to get the chair.

JAMES: Yeah . . . when I first got those symptoms, the Military Police on base used to stop me to ask if I was drunk because I staggered so much. That's when I first realized something was wrong. And then it just kept getting worse until I wound up in this wheelchair.

**Practice Points:** The group leader takes the discussion to another level by opening up an area that has been most painful for the members—the loss of loved ones. As this discussion evolves, note how the leader, also being affected by the strength of the feelings, picks up on their concern about symptoms, moving them off this painful theme.

GROUP LEADER: You guys have lost important things associated with your identity because of this disease. Many of you had to quit working before you wanted . . . some of you lost important relationships.

JAMES: That's what I miss . . . having a girlfriend. (He pauses.)

GROUP LEADER: (After it looks like he won't continue on his own) Tell us more, James.

**JAMES:** I just miss the company. I don't care about the sex. I just wish I had the companionship. I need someone to talk to, who will do things with me. I love my son and my parents, but I wish I had someone more my age to be with.

(Group leader's note: James is a young guy—in his early 30s—and, in addition to being confined to a wheelchair, he has speech difficulties and shaking in his arms and neck. In retrospect, I wish I had explored more about how the change in his appearance and increasing disability affect his romantic possibilities. He has an 8-year-old son, but I don't know what his relationship with the mother was or if she left him when he became disabled. I'm sure this is something all the men have had to face—changes in their manhood, and how society views a disabled man.)

**FRED:** I know, James. Companionship is important.

**BOB:** There are a lot of symptoms of MS that people don't see and we don't talk about. Like our bladder and bowel problems. It's very degrading and embarrassing not to be able to control them all the time. (The others all voice their agreement.)

**GROUP LEADER:** I know you were interested a few weeks ago in having Dr. C. (urologist) come to speak to you about these problems. Did she ever come?

**ALBERT:** Not yet.

**GROUP LEADER:** I will talk to the Nurse again and try to schedule her as a speaker in the future. (I bowed out of a sensitive and embarrassing subject here as well. I probably should have explored their feelings more with regard to this subject.)

**Practice Points:** Although the discussion is important and raises powerful issues, it skirts around the group's ending and the losses involved in the group. It is as if the members of the group are waiting to see if the group leader will come back to the issue she raised at the beginning of the meeting. She does.

**GROUP LEADER:** I want to talk some more about our ending. I know I've been mentioning it the last couple of times we've met. It's really hard when people come and go from your life.

**ALBERT:** Yeah, it is. It seems like we just started with you and now you are leaving already.

**GROUP LEADER:** I want you to know that it is hard for me too. I am in a field where I will have to say good-bye many times to people whom I have grown to care about. But I believe that, when I leave here, I will take a part of you all and internalize it, especially your courage. I have learned a lot from all of you about what it is like to live with MS, and how hard it is to deal with all the symptoms. But mostly I have seen how courageous and positive you are in light of all you have been through, and that encourages me. I believe I will be able to help other people in your position because of what you have taught me about dealing with a chronic disease like multiple sclerosis, and I thank you for this group and this experience.

**BOB:** I know you are going to do well. You are a kind person, and genuine and caring. I think I speak for everyone when I say we've enjoyed having you here. (The others nod and voice their agreement.)

**GROUP LEADER:** Thank you. That's nice to hear. I've really enjoyed being a part of this group and getting to know all of you. (The time was up, and we finished by saying good-bye and their talking about meeting again in 2 weeks.)

**Practice Summary.** As the ending approaches, there is always unfinished business between the group and the group leader that needs to be explored. Given the theme of internalized stigma, it was important for the leader to share her perspective of them as people of real courage. In the next example, we see a leader ending with a group over time.

EP 2.1.4b
EP 2.1.4c
EP 2.1.5a
EP 2.1.5b
EP 2.1.5c
EP 2.1.10a
EP 2.1.10b
EP 2.1.10e
EP 2.1.10l

***Adult Female Survivors of Childhood Sexual Abuse: Ending over Time*** As the previous examples illustrated, the ending and transition phase of a group takes place over time. The stages are noticeable during the last three or four sessions for an ongoing group, beginning with the group leader's reminder that the group is coming to an end. The next example provides excerpts from the last six sessions of a group for adult survivors of childhood sexual abuse.

The members of this group all experienced oppression on many levels. They were all sexually exploited as children, most often by people whom they knew and should have been able to trust. As women, they continued to experience oppression in relation to their gender. Some of the members were Hispanic and faced racism, which—when combined with sexism—strongly affected their lives. Finally, some were lesbians or bisexual, which also placed them in a group that commonly experiences prejudice and oppression. Thus, all of the group members carried a great deal of pain and internalization of their oppression.

As the group members moved into their ending and transition phase, and as they reviewed and evaluated their work together, note their courage, their love for one another, and their group leader's conviction about their inherent strength not only to survive oppression but also to overcome it and fight it. In many ways, the work of the group followed the three developmental stages described in Chapters 1 and 2, in which oppressed people attempt to free themselves from the oppressor within and the oppressor without.

In addition, the discussion of a new psychology of women (Miller, 1987; Miller & Stiver, 1991), which laid the foundation for the self-in-relation model of group process drawn from the work of the Stone Center (see Chapter 13), helps to explain some of the paradoxes evident in the work.

**Practice Points:** In particular, this example illustrates the notion that vulnerability can lead to growth, talking about disconnection leads to connection, pain can be experienced in safety, and the importance of resonance or empathy between members (Fedele, 1994). The group leaders are both experienced in group work in general and specifically in work with survivors, which is evident in their practice.

> **Member Description and Time Frame:** This 24-week group for adult female survivors of childhood sexual victimization is offered by a community rape crisis center and is led by two coleaders. The time frame of the meetings is August 28 to October 16. The seven members range in age from 22 to 28. All members are women from working-class or middle-class backgrounds. Two members are Hispanic, and the rest are White or are from various other ethnic groups. Two women are lesbians, one is bisexual, and four are heterosexual.
>
> **Description of the Problem:** As the group begins its ending stage, members are reluctant to face the pain and loss of the impending termination and the potential effect of this transition on their lives. As survivors of sexual abuse, many of the women feel acute fear and discomfort when confronted with strong feelings. They have described families of origin in which the development and ending of relationships have been poorly modeled, and they have learned to keep silent about their feelings and fears. The tasks of the group leaders will be to help build a group culture in which the taboo subjects of endings and losses can be

explored, freeing the members to grapple with the tasks of termination. We must help the group establish a norm that supports intimacy and risk but also profoundly respects each member's need for safety and self-protection.

**How the Problem Came to the Attention of the Group Leader(s):** As my coleader Jane and I prepared for termination, we tuned in to the potential problems of this stage, using both general knowledge of survivors' issues and our knowledge of the work and struggles of this particular group as a guide. Since the first sessions, safety had been vital to meaningful and productive work in the group. Members had worked hard to recognize when they felt unsafe or at risk and had learned to take steps to protect themselves. Because bonding and connection had been central to the group's creation of a safe and trusting culture, we hypothesized that the group might feel unsafe as members began to separate.

Practice Points: Note that even a group that had created a safe culture may need to work on that group issue again as the ending approached. The leaders are aware that this is still a vulnerable group of young women and that safety needs to be addressed regularly throughout the development of the group.

We believed that the group might need to create a different "safe culture" that could tolerate the coming ending. On August 28, we learned about the group's norms for saying good-bye and about subjects and feelings related to endings that were forbidden. Members responded with silence when asked direct questions about what the group's end meant to them, and informed us that they usually run away from and ignore endings.

### Summary of the Work

#### August 28

Linda was describing how she felt compelled to binge on salty and high-cholesterol foods lately and how it was very dangerous for her high blood pressure. I observed that, in the past, she had done this when she was having really strong feelings, and I asked how she was feeling these days when she seemed compelled to binge. She began to cry and said, "There's just so much pain, so much loss." She described her fear of losing her whole family if she confronted her mother (the perpetrator of her sexual abuse), the death of a cousin who had been missing and whose body had been found, the anniversary of a rape in which she had nearly been killed at age 18, her loss of me as her individual therapist, and the impending loss of the group, the first people who had ever believed in and supported her. In the face of this, she said that she was really isolating herself and wanted to eat.

Practice Points: This powerful list of events, some earlier and some more recent, has emotional impact on the group members and the leaders. Given the ending stage, the group leaders focus on the support within the group and how to continue to get it even after the group has ended.

I tried to enlist the support of the group to combat her isolation. I said, "Linda, it sounds like you're feeling overwhelmed by all this pain, and at the very time you could use some support, you're all alone. Is there any way the group can help you right now?" She responded that she isolates most when she's most in pain but that the group could help by reaching out to her, that she needs to be with people when she feels this way. Some group members responded with expressions of support and offers to talk on the phone or be with her. People shared how hard it was to see her pain but how important it was that she share it.

**Practice Points:** The group leader uses the opportunity of Linda's sharing about the simultaneous need for connection coupled with an effort to disconnect to address the rapidly approaching ending of the group.

I said that Linda had shared feeling really sad about the group, and I wondered how others in the group were feeling about the end approaching. There was silence. I waited, thinking they might need time to respond. Jane, the coleader, asked group members how they usually say good-bye. Group members responded: "I just take off, usually." "Hey, I don't say 'good-bye,' I say 'see you later.'" "I never say good-bye, I just disappear." "I try to pretend nothing's changed." Jane said that she felt it was important for members to understand how they usually cope with good-byes so that they could make choices this time about how they want to handle this ending. Issues of trust, intimacy, and loss had been important in the group's work, and we could do vital work in these areas during our final weeks. Time was up, and I said that we would be spending more time next week talking about the approaching end of the group and how people wanted to work on it.

**Practice Points:** The group leaders recognize that this stage in a group such as this one can be a time of the most important and powerful work or a moratorium on work as members and leaders avoid facing the painful feelings associated with separation. While wanting the group members to make the best use of the last sessions, at the same time the group leaders display their understanding of the importance of allowing these young women to have control over the issue of disclosing the details of their abuse. It is common that, as the end approaches—in what I have already called "doorknob therapy," group members will disclose their most difficult issues and "secrets." Not having had control over what was done to them in the past, often by family members, it is crucial that the group members have control over their disclosure.

### September 11

A major goal for Martha had been to spend time in the group telling the story of her abuse, but each time she had planned to do it, she had felt unable to go through with it. She had felt flooded with fear and pain. The group had processed why it was so difficult and suggested different ways she could prepare and cope with this "disclosure," but to no avail.

This time, what came up was that she felt unable to risk and be vulnerable in the group when it was so close to ending and she could be rejected and abandoned by the group members. She said that it no longer felt safe in the group. I said that perhaps what she was telling us was that this goal was not right for her right now, that keeping herself safe was most important, and that she was making choices about how she needed to protect herself.

**Practice Points:** Because child-victims often learn to feel that they are not worth protecting and can never feel truly safe, safety and self-protection had been important in the group's work. The group leaders recognize that this is not only Martha's issue but one for the whole group. They use this as an opportunity to address group norms as they approach the last sessions.

I said that we needed to strike a careful balance as we approached the ending, trying to work as hard as we could and risk as much as we could but also respecting each person's needs for safety. I told Martha that if she wanted to do her disclosure we would help her, but that no one would force her to do it. Martha and the group discussed this for a while, and then Jane talked about Martha's goal and goals in general and how it was important for us to review them and take stock of the work we needed to address in the next 4 weeks.

**Practice Points:**   In the next excerpt the group members move past denial and begin to express the anger associated with the ending phase. The group leaders' efforts to evaluate the group and the progress achieved by members may have been an unconscious way of avoiding this painful part of the process. Once the anger is expressed, the leader's response connects it directly to the ending.

> I asked if we could spend some time right now hearing from everyone about what they had accomplished so far, what they still needed to work on, and how they were feeling about the group ending. (I immediately sensed my error but didn't know how to correct it.) The group was silent. Jane then said that she understood how hard it was for the group but that it was important for us to take stock of where we were. We could still accomplish a lot but we needed to know. . . . Jodi burst in and said, "I just feel like telling you to shut up. You both keep talking and talking about this, and I'm feeling really angry. I wish you would let us move on to what we want to talk about and stop wasting time."
>
> I said that she was clearly feeling really angry, and that it felt to her like we were pressuring the group. I waited and then said that people often feel very angry when they face losing something that has been really important to them. I wondered if some of her anger was related to the ending itself. Rita said, "But we're not losing the group. We'll still see each other." Others agreed. I confronted the group's denial. "That's true," I said, "you can choose to continue your friendships as individuals and as a group, but this Monday night group is special, the way we work together here. It's like it has its own identity. That's what's going to end." Michelle said that she wouldn't know what to do with herself on Mondays anymore. Others joined in, saying how they would miss the group. Both group leaders reflected these feelings and shared their own feelings about the group ending.

**Practice Points:**   The group leader recognizes that she has pressed too much in asking about goals and is somewhat ahead of where the members are at the moment. She catches her mistake.

> I said that I had asked for a lot at once during my earlier question about goals. This was really hard to talk about and might require some reflection. Perhaps group members could review their progress and future needs during the week, and we could set aside time to discuss them next week. We would also need to talk in more depth about the final session. For now, I wondered if we could just spend some time talking about how it felt this moment to be dealing with this. We discussed this for the last few minutes of the session.

**Practice Points:**   By addressing the process of ending and the associated affect, the leaders create the conditions where members can make the third decision—the addressing of the hardest and most painful part of the work. In this case, Martha, who has been the one member unable to disclose up to now, finally shares her painful childhood experiences.

> *September 18*
> I reminded the group that we had planned to spend some time this week taking stock of what the group has meant to people and where we needed to put our energy during these final four sessions. People had put quite a bit of thought into this, and the group spent some time evaluating and prioritizing. Martha had clarified the issue of disclosure for herself. She had discovered that, in trying to force herself to

discuss the abuse before the group "audience" while feeling unsafe, she had been recreating the dynamics of her abuse as a child in which her father had taken her to bars where she had been sexually abused by various strangers while others observed. With the support and understanding of the group, she was able to carry out a disclosure related to this specific abuse, checking with the group whenever she began to feel unsafe. We credited her growing ability to protect herself while achieving her goals. Both Jane and I offered positive feedback about Martha's growth and her ability to both keep herself safe and move forward with her goals.

**Practice Points:**   The leaders next address the structure of the final session. While they share an example of how it has been handled in previous groups, they continue to make clear that the group is owned by the members and that they will have the last say in how the final session will be structured.

> Later, Jane raised the issue of the final session, explaining to the group members that it is generally structured around feedback, both negative and positive. She asked the group to consider a structure that has worked well for other groups, in which each group member in turn gives feedback to each of the other members and the group leaders. Past groups have chosen to write a special message to each individual so that the feedback would be kept and remembered. Some members were eager to do this, whereas others expressed considerable anxiety about evaluating themselves and others. I said that some people seemed eager to do this, but others seemed really uncomfortable with it. Ultimately, the decision of how to handle the last session lay with the group, but I wondered if we could explore how people felt about it right now. What made it seem scary, and what seemed positive about it? This was explored for a while.
>
> Then group members asked me to review information about the local "Take Back the Night" march with them. We had told them about the march against sexual violence against women a few weeks before and, after some exploration of their fears about participating in a public demonstration, they decided to march as a group. I supported the group's readiness to act independently and support one another in new experiences. I shared with them how good I felt that they wanted to march together, and I gave them the information they needed.

**Practice Points:**   An additional discussion of a feminist orientation to practice will be included in Chapter 17. One of the major themes will be the importance of empowerment of, in this case, young women who have experienced sexual and physical abuse. The march is an activity that allows the women, as a group, to assert their rights by overcoming their fears. This is an example of the "strength-in-numbers" phenomenon described in the earlier discussion of mutual aid.

> ### September 25
> As the group processed how the march had felt for them, Jane and I shared how powerful it had felt for us to see them there, marching, chanting, and singing. We also shared that it was hard for us to see them and know that the group was ending. The group was special for us, and it would be hard to let it go.
>
> (I fell for the illusion of work and let the group get off track.) Rita had been talking for some time about her problems and conflicts with her parents. At first, both group leaders and the group were active in discussing her problem, but I gradually began to feel that we weren't going anywhere and my attempts to involve the group proved fruitless. They seemed to have checked out. I now think that some of the anger Rita was expressing was indirectly aimed at the leaders and/or the group, but I missed this at the time because she had ample reason to be angry with her parents.

**Practice Points:**   In the next intervention, this experienced group leader demonstrates her ability to be with each individual in the group and the group-as-a-whole simultaneously—what I have described as the "two clients." Her observation that the group appears to have "checked out" is recognition of their nonverbal cues. As she reaches for the underlying feelings associated with the nonverbal cues of one member, Linda, she opens up the powerful feelings of loss as well as the emerging feelings of hope and strength for all group members.

I had noticed for some time that Linda seemed very agitated and seemed to be struggling to contain herself. Rita had come to a long pause, and I asked, "What's going on with you, Linda?" Linda seemed startled: "Who, me? Why? What's the problem?" I answered, "Well, Rita's been talking for a while now about her family, and I know your family has been a source of a lot of your pain. You seem really upset right now, and I wonder what's happening." Linda began to talk of having a great deal of pain all the time. She said that her losses had totally overwhelmed her lately, and she just didn't know how she was going to make it. I immediately felt the group come back to life.

Linda and various group members talked for some time about how hopeless she felt. I reached for her ability to cope with her pain. "I'm just hearing that you have so much pain and sadness right now, Linda, and I wonder what you are doing with all this hurt." She said that she was crying a lot, just letting herself feel the sadness, and that she was also writing in her journal and writing poems. She mentioned that she had just written a poem today about her pain and where it was taking her.

Several people asked her if she would read it, and she did. It was called "Children of the Rainbow," and it described how beams of light are shattered and broken as they pass through a drop of water and how they emerge to form the vibrant colors of the rainbow. The poem said that she and all survivors in recovery are like beams of light; if they can make it through their pain, they will become vibrant, beautiful, and whole. Several of us had tears in our eyes (me included), and there was a powerful silence when she finished.

I remained silent to let the group control this moment. People thanked her for sharing such a personal, painful, and hopeful part of herself. I had been Linda's individual counselor for some time, and I was finding it very hard to leave her and the agency. I acknowledged her feelings, shared my own, and credited her ability to cope. I shared that I found the poem very moving, that I could feel that she had incredible pain, but that her art and ability to create were powerful vehicles for carrying her forward and transforming her pain. The group ended soon after.

**Practice Points:**   In the next session we can see the impact of Martha's finally being able to disclose her abuse in the group as well as her empowerment by participating in the Take Back the Night March. This process helps her to now to assert herself by confronting her father who was her abuser.

### October 2
Martha told the group that she had confronted her father with the abuse since the last group. We were all amazed, because this had been a goal that Martha had not hoped to attain for several months, if not years, in the future. Her abuse had been very sadistic, and her father had continued to hold incredible power over her when he was able to have contact with her. She had been with Linda before he called and described "just feeling very powerful and safe. I was able to see Linda and my roommate right there, and I could hold the whole group right in my mind and feel you supporting me and helping me to be safe. I've never felt anything like that before. And he was weak! He was the one who seemed powerless."

Martha had burned a picture of her father after the call as a way of exorcizing his control over her, and she had brought the ashes to group. Later, the group gathered and flushed the ashes down the toilet. Both leaders credited Martha's incredible and rapid growth and related it to the ending and how she had taken control of how she wanted to accomplish her goals and approach the end of group. The group gave Martha feedback and discussed how it felt to be part of her sense of safety.

**Practice Points:** In the next brief excerpt the group leader, after the fact, makes an important connection between a member's anger at her psychiatrist and the anger toward the group leaders. This is an important point of growth for the group leader.

Next, Donna raised the issue of her psychiatrist and how he had told her to get on with her life and stop indulging herself with her depression and dwelling on her abuse. The group responded with explosive anger. I allowed my own anger and the real differences between my approach and the approach of the psychiatrist to blind me to the part of the group's anger that might have been directed at me, had I invited it. We did good work in helping Donna evaluate her therapy, but we missed another chance to explore the group's anger about the ending and our role as group leaders. I think that this group felt so special to me, and I was finding termination from individuals, the group, and the agency so hard, that I kept myself unaware of their anger.

*October 16: Final Session*
Each member and group leader had prepared written feedback for the other members and group leaders, and members took turns reading their messages to one another. (Group leaders passed out written individual feedback and gave verbal feedback to the group as a whole.) The material was very personal and moving and related the work of the group to strong feelings about ending. Group leaders assisted members in preparing to read and helped the group to respond. Some members cried and expressed deep feelings of pain and loss. Group leaders also responded directly to their own feedback.

A few of the women chose to hand out the personal feedback and speak to the group generally while members read the personal material. Although I believe that the material was genuine, it focused on positives only, and both group leaders missed the opportunity to reach for negative feedback, falling for the farewell-party syndrome.

**Practice Points:** Although this important task was not accomplished, the group leaders did accomplish their goal of creating a safe culture in which members could risk being intimate and trusting as the group ended. Once again resonance and connection through disconnection is apparent.

Martha had read each note and closed with 'Love, Martha.' At one point, Rita said, "This is really hard, but I have to ask. You said 'Love' to everybody, but you didn't say it to me. I'm sure you just forgot, but I have to say, it hurts. Don't you love me too?" She began to cry with these last words. Martha had clearly just forgotten and turned to Rita, saying, "I'm so glad you told me. I was just finding this all so hard that I didn't even realize . . . I do love you. I'm sorry it hurt that I forgot you. Here, let me write it on yours."

I asked Rita how it had felt to risk this question, and I said that I remembered that she had entered the group 6 months ago saying she never let herself be vulnerable with others. Rita responded that this was a safer place than she had ever been in before. She had shared her story, her shame, and had been vulnerable with people here. She knew she could trust us. "It's true," added Martha, "I've never been any-where that was safe the way this is, even more than individual therapy." Michelle added, "This place is like the safe home we never had. You guys were almost like parents for us. You were honest with us, and we learned to be honest with each other. And it never mattered, we could feel good, feel bad, disagree with each other and be mad, but it was OK. We could learn to be ourselves. You were there for us the way our parents should have been." Soon after, we ended the group. There was a long "group hug" at the suggestion of the members, and we ate some cake a member had ordered. The message on the cake said, *"Survivors—Striving and Thriving!"*

**Practice Summary.** The metaphor of Linda's poem, in which survivors in recovery are viewed as "beams of light; if they can make it through their pain, they will become vibrant, beautiful, and whole," is extremely powerful and moving. It captures beautifully the struggle of these young, oppressed, and vulnerable women to free themselves from the self-image of being "damaged goods" that had been imposed upon them by those who should have been nurturing them. Their courage in joining a "Take Back the Night" march, when they felt so personally uncomfortable doing so, was an affirmation of their willingness to fight and overthrow their oppressors. It was a social parallel of their individual revolutions against oppression described in one member's efforts to confront her offending parent. The unique power of mutual-aid groups is amply demonstrated in the content of their work together and in the "Survivors—Striving and Thriving" lettering on the cake at their final session.

This last example completes the illustrations of the ending and transition stage. This chapter also brings to a close the focus on the four phases of work.

# Ethical Issues Related to Endings

**EP 2.1.6b**

Mangione, Forti, and Iacuzzi (2007) echo the importance of addressing endings and suggest there are ethical issues to be considered.

Loss and endings are potent factors in our client's lives, and potentially in their healing and growth. Therefore, we have the intersect of a cultural ethos that is not mindful of endings, clients with histories of complicated and conflictual endings, and at least some schools of psychotherapy postulating that well-worked endings are critical to client welfare. . . . Given the inherent difficulty and emotional upheaval that endings evoke, group psychotherapists need to be in possession of ethical tools for addressing the emotional tensions and conflicts that can arise in their clients and themselves and that can affect clinical decision making. (p. 27)

These authors also point to the importance of respecting racially, ethnically, and culturally diverse differential understandings and reactions to endings.

In a culture that emphasizes continuity of relationships, an ending may be viewed as an interruption, not a permanent alteration. In another cultural group an ending may be seen as a permanent severing. Ethical difficulties can arise when these divergent views arise in the context of ending a therapy group. (p. 28)

In a survey of members of the American Group Psychotherapy Association on ethical issues related to endings, conducted by these authors, 275 therapists (11 percent of the membership) responded. Half of these were in private practice and half in settings such as hospitals, schools, clinics, or university settings. These were their findings on key issues:

- Virtually all of the seasoned therapists felt that endings were important and spent a good deal of time both preparing for and processing them.
- Fifty-nine percent endorsed discussing ending expectations in pregroup screening, and 13 percent said they did not talk about termination at all.
- Just over one-third, 36.2 percent, said that ending should be jointly decided by therapist, client, and the group.
- Over one quarter of the respondents had experienced verbal or acting out appeals from members to extend the group and felt the need to extend the group in response to members getting more symptomatic even though they understood the ethical issues involved in changing the agreed-upon framework.
- Twenty percent of the sample had extended a short-term group at the request of the clients despite ethical concerns. Fourteen percent expressed ethical concerns about not extending a group when some clients were in distress and follow-up was not available.
- In response to an offered scenario of a member leaving unexpectedly, three-quarters would want to discuss their perspective on the departure with the group members; however, the same number were aware of the obligation to protect client privacy if they did so.
- A small percentage of respondents had experienced a group member committing suicide and they expressed the need for support for themselves as well as an opportunity to discuss the event with group members and to share in the grieving.
- Over half of the respondents had asked a member to leave the group primarily on the basis of disruptive behavior or a poor fit between the individual and the group.
- Over half of the respondents had experiencing having to leave a group often because of life situations (e.g., pregnancy) and at times because of more complicated issues such as experiencing a physical threat from a group member. (pp. 28–34)

This survey, as well as my own practice experience, suggests that endings can indeed be complicated, and they can raise ethical challenges for the group leader. An opportunity to explore these issues and having the advantage of a collegial ethical review committee as well as a risk management model in place can be extremely helpful.

## Chapter Summary

The ending phase of group work can be a powerful one as members bring to the forefront some of the most important and difficult issues in a process sometimes described as "doorknob therapy." However, because of the powerful issues involved in bringing a group to a close, both intimacy and authority themes need to be addressed to avoid the endings becoming a moratorium on work.

Group leaders need to help group members identify and move through several common but not universal ending stages: denial of the ending, anger over the ending, mourning, trying the ending on for size, and the farewell-party syndrome. Group leader interventions in this stage include: pointing out the ending early, reaching for feelings, identifying the stages of the ending, sharing the leader's feelings, making a demand for work to prevent avoidance of facing the ending, and, when appropriate, connecting the ending process with the purpose of the group.

The group members also need to consider transitions to new experiences and individual member "next steps" as the group is brought to a close. Special dynamics arise when the group leader leaves and the group continues.

------------------------------------------------------------

## Related Online Content and Activities

 Visit *The Skills of Helping Individuals, Families, Groups, and Communities,* Seventh Edition, CourseMate website at **www.cengagebrain.com** for learning tools such as glossary terms, links to related websites, and chapter practice quizzes. The website for this chapter also features additional notes from the author.

------------------------------

## Competency Notes

The following is a list of Council on Social Work Education (CSWE) recommended competencies and practice behaviors for social work students defined in Educational Policy and Accreditation Standard (EPAS) and addressed in this chapter.

**EP 2.1.3a** Distinguish, appraise, and integrate multiple sources of knowledge, including research-based knowledge and practice wisdom (p. 576)

**EP 2.1.4c** Recognize and communicate their understanding of the importance of difference in shaping life experiences (p. 590)

**EP 2.1.5a** Understand forms and mechanisms of oppression and discrimination (p. 590)

**EP 2.1.5b** Advocate for human rights and social and economic justice (p. 590)

**EP 2.1.5c** Engage in practices that advance social and economic justice (p. 590)

**EP 2.1.10a** Substantively and affectively prepare for action with individuals, families, groups, organizations, and communities (p. 590)

**EP 2.1.10b** Use empathy and other interpersonal skills (pp. 576,590)

**EP 2.1.10e** Assess client strengths and limitations (p. 590)

**EP 2.1.10l** Facilitate transitions and endings (pp. 575,590)

# Macro Social Work Practice: Impacting the Agency/Setting, the Community, and Effecting Social Change

P art V consists of two chapters that focus on the social worker's macro practice in relation to other professionals in the agency or setting (e.g., teachers or doctors), community organization practice (geographic or milieu), social action (individually or through professional associations), and social policy efforts for social change. Continuing with the theme of the social worker having "two clients," we explore ways in which a social worker in clinical direct practice, or one who concentrates on macro direct or indirect practice, can have positive impact acting with or on behalf of clients.

In Chapter 15 we discuss and illustrate the worker's efforts to help the client negotiate the system. The underlying framework that has thus far described the individual in interaction with the social surround reappears and the mediation and advocacy functions are stressed. The skills and dynamics described in the first four parts of the book reappear in the analysis of working with other professionals. This chapter also focuses on the social worker's responsibility to professionally impact his or her own setting or agency and the larger community.

Chapter 16 describes the development of social work practice in the community with a focus on empowerment-oriented and progressive practice frameworks. Basic principles for effective community practice are described as is the underlying philosophy of community organization in the social work context. A number of models of community work are discussed from "grassroots" organizing to the use of the computer to strengthen digital democracy.

The final section of Chapter 16 returns to the framework of time—the phases of work—to illustrate the community organization principles and models in the beginning, middle, and ending/transition phases. Once again, it is striking how the communication, relationship, and problem-solving skills described throughout this book lend themselves to macro practice in the community. Put another way, a good macro practitioner needs a solid grounding in the same practice skills employed by clinical practitioners as well as other skills appropriate for this level of practice. The converse argument can be made for clinical practitioners and their need for macro skills.

Finally, Chapter 16 extends this examination of macro practice by reaching back into our profession's historical roots and arguing for a generalist practice that includes efforts to effect social change through social and political action.

# Professional Impact and Helping Clients Negotiate the System

In Parts I to IV of this book, we explored the helping model in the context of work with individuals, families, and groups. Much of the emphasis was on preparing and helping clients to deal with important systems. In Part V, we consider another level of interaction—the relationship between clients and the social institutions with which they come into contact, such as schools, hospitals, housing agencies, political systems, and residential care centers.

# Macro Practice

EP 2.1.1a

The two chapters in this part of the book begin to examine what is commonly called "macro" social work practice. For some social workers this is an area of specialization, as contrasted with those who work in what is commonly termed "micro" or clinical practice. I take a generalist view that suggests that all social workers have some responsibility for macro activities even if they are essentially involved in direct clinical practice working in an agency, a setting such as a hospital or a school, or in private practice.

To begin, we need to define the term *macro*. Long, Tice, and Morrison (2006) defined it as follows:

> Macro means large-scale or big. In social work, it involves the ability to see and intervene in the big picture, specifically with larger systems in the socio-economic environment. Macro social work practice can include collaboration with consumers to strengthen and maximize opportunities for people at the organizational, community, societal, and global levels. (p. 3)

The authors document the historical roots of this element of social work practice and suggest that the strengths perspective fits well with the principles of macro practice.

Brueggemann (2006) provides a brief history of macro social work and suggests:

> From the beginning of the social work profession, the welfare of the social environment has been our primary concern, and macro social work has been one way social workers have engaged in that effort. Many early social workers concerned themselves with strengthening communities, making government organizations more democratic, working at city, state, and national levels to create better social policies, being active in social movements, and extending themselves to international concerns as well. (p. 4)

Brueggemann defines a wide spectrum of macro social work that includes:

- Community Social Planning
- Community Development
- Community Organizing
- Program Development in Organizations
- Social Work Administration
- Organizational Development
- Social Policy and Politics
- Social Action and Social Movements
- International Social Work (pp. 10–12)

In the two chapters in this part of the book, we will introduce basic concepts related to four of these areas of practice: organizational change, community organizing, social policy and politics, and social action.

# A Social Systems Approach

As we examine this level of individual-social interaction and the worker's function and skills required to facilitate it, we shall see that we can apply many of the concepts already presented. The use of an approach based on systems theory makes this possible because different levels of systems have universal properties, and insights into one level can serve as hypotheses for understanding another.

Chapter 2 introduced the systems or ecological approach as a general framework for understanding the client in his or her broader social context. Parts II, III, and IV focused on the worker's efforts to help the client negotiate the various important systems in her or his life (e.g., family, school, the mutual-aid group). We saw that the worker always has two clients—the individual client and the system—and that many of the principles developed in work with one can apply to work with the other. Practice examples included illustrations of social workers attempting to have professional impact on doctors, residential care workers, other social workers, and so on. In this chapter and the next, work with other professionals, organizations, and community systems comes to the foreground of the discussion.

This level of systems work, an essential element of all practice, has distinguished social work as a profession, although other related professions, for example, the group work specialist in the counseling field, can also claim a social justice and social action history (see Singh & Salazar, 2010). There also has been a surge in the counseling literature of interest in social justice practice.

## Toward a Unified Social Work Practice Theory

If we reach back into our social work history, Hearn (1962) was one of the first social work theorists to describe the potential value of general systems theory to the development of a unified social work practice theory. He said,

> If there are principles which apply to organismic systems in general, and if individuals, groups, organizations, and communities may be regarded as such systems, then these principles collectively might find their place in a unified theory of practice. This would provide a common framework for conceiving the individuals, groups, organizations, and communities as "clients," or as the means by which service is rendered to "clients." (p. 67)

Hearn suggests here that we use our understanding of one level of system to better understand another level. As an example of this idea, recall our discussion of the dynamics between a family and its deviant member; often, the behavior evidenced in this role is sending a message for the family as a whole. Recall also that the functional role of the deviant member in the small group works in the same way. In this chapter and the next, we take the same concept of the role of the deviant member and apply it at the organizational and community levels.

For example, in my consultations with large organizations, such as hospitals, I often find a service that is considered the deviant member of the system. This is the department that is constantly in turmoil, faces frequent staff changeovers, is in conflict with other departments, and so on. In a child welfare agency, the protection unit often plays this role. In county or state-wide agencies, one local office is identified, at times, as the problem office.

Following our analogy, we can interpret the behavior of an organizational department the way we would do so for the deviant member of a group. Thus, as hospitals come under increasing stress because of cost-containment efforts resulting from managed care, specific departments might act out the stress of the whole system. As with the small group and the family, the deviant member is usually the unit that is having the most difficulty coping with the general stress. In hospitals, it is often the emergency room, the intensive care ward, or the surgical service department that plays this role. These parts of the system normally have high-stress operations.

In a larger entity, such as a state in the United States or a province in Canada, a state-wide agency, such as the child welfare service, may send the signal of stress for all of the other human services systems. As another example, scapegoating is also common; some social service systems regard others as "less professional" and project their own problems onto the workers in those systems.

Once this systems approach is integrated into a social worker's theoretical framework, he or she can view all levels of systems dynamically and as potential targets for intervention. In addition, this point of view gives direction to conceptualizing the social worker's function and identifying the required skills. This chapter examines the individual-system interaction in much the same terms used thus far and describes the social worker's role in terms of mediation, which may include advocacy and confrontation. Examples from several settings will show work with clients who sometimes individually and at other times in groups are endeavoring to negotiate systems and their representatives (e.g., teachers, principals, doctors, housing authority administrators). You will see that many of the skills already identified are as helpful in dealing with system representatives as they are in dealing with clients. Because change also often involves confrontation with the system and social pressure, we discuss these processes as well.

This chapter also demonstrates how a worker can use experiences with clients to guide efforts to affect agency policies, structures, procedures, and programs to better meet the needs of clients. This specific responsibility to influence the larger systems—the second-client concept—is historical and gives the social work profession its unique and crucial role in our society. In short, social workers need to stop complaining about the system they work in or deal with (e.g., school, hospital, agency, community) and start doing something about influencing change in it.

## The Individual-System Interaction

**EP 2.1.9a**
**EP 2.1.10k**

In a modern, industrial, and largely urban society, the relationship between individuals and society has grown quite complex. A large number of institutions and agencies have been established to deal with the individual on behalf of society. For example, welfare agencies care for those who cannot support themselves (although some efforts at "welfare reform" have brought that function into question), schools provide the education needed for individuals to become integrated into the community and to play a productive role, hospitals provide medical care for physical illness, and psychiatric centers treat people with emotional disorders. However, the very institutions set up to solve problems have become so complex themselves that they have generated new problems. Social, medical, and educational systems can be difficult to negotiate even for individuals who are well equipped to deal with them, let alone for those with limited education and resources. The services established for people are often so complex that clients find making use of them difficult.

In addition to complexity, other factors compound the individual-system interaction. For one, many services inherently approach clients ambivalently. Thus, although welfare has been established to meet the needs of the poor, it is often administered in a way that reflects a judgmental and punitive attitude. For example, welfare recipients are often made to feel that their checks are public "doles," gifts from a generous community rather than a right, and that acceptance of welfare is a sign that the individual is neither a productive nor an important member of society.

Changes in the welfare legislation over the past years have reinforced such views. Anecdotal reports indicate that welfare-to-work efforts may help some recipients—in a good economy, and when appropriate day care, training, and other supports are in place. These reports also suggest that the undifferentiated application of the new rules to families and individuals who cannot make the transition may result in unacceptable hardships for the most vulnerable members of our population.

More recently, with a severe economic downturn and the loss of jobs by millions, similar accusations that receiving unemployment insurance encourages recipients not to seek jobs fly in the face of the reality. Attacks on individuals receiving long-term support, even when they have made major efforts to find employment in a disastrous economy, are actually an organized attack on social support programs.

A third factor contributing to breakdowns in the individual-system relationship is the size of bureaucracy. For example, finding the right department in a large government agency can be a frustrating, even overwhelming, task. Entering a large high school as just one student in a class of 2,000 can easily lead to getting lost in the system. This may prevent the student from getting the special help needed for successful completion of a program. (Many school systems have begun to recognize this and are attempting to create smaller middle and high schools or to break down large schools into smaller units.).

A fourth complication is the difficulty of human communication. For instance, a student may, even in a small setting such as a specific class, feel that the teacher does not care, and the teacher, in turn, may feel the same way about the student. Both may well be mistaken. In another example, a student of color may experience a White teacher as racist and punitive. In some cases this perception may be accurate. In others, it may reflect the tremendous complications involved in communication and relationships between members of different races and cultures.

You can surely provide your own examples in which the size and complexity of a system, difficulties in communications, or the ambivalence of the system toward its clients cuts them off from services they require. Because the individual who needs to use the system is also complex, feels some ambivalence toward the service, and has difficulty in communications, breakdowns become almost inevitable.

Of course, we know that simply establishing a service to meet a need does not guarantee that the need will be met. Recognizing this reality led Schwartz (1961) to propose that the function of the social work profession is to mediate the individual-social engagement. He suggests that this is the historical reason for the development of the social work profession: to stand as a buffer between clients and the systems they need to negotiate. Other professionals (psychologists, nurses, and so forth) may appropriately play this role; however, only the social work profession, according to Schwartz, embraces this role as a functional responsibility, that is, an essential part of the work.

# Mediating the Individual-System Engagement

**EP 2.1.9b**
**EP 2.1.10k**

One of the major problems facing workers in implementing this role is their own feelings. They tend to overidentify with the individual client against the system and its representatives. In our earlier discussion of work with the family and work with scapegoats in the group, we saw how workers, because of their own life experiences, often identify with one side in an engagement.

Because we have all known complex bureaucracies, authoritarian and insensitive administrators, teachers who seemed not to care, and the like, such an initial reaction to a client's problem with a system is understandable. I have seen workers develop a fine sense of tolerance for deviant behavior on the part of clients, an ability to see past a façade and reach for clients' underlying strength, and an understanding of clients' ambivalence. Yet these same workers lack tolerance for deviant behavior, are fooled by façades, and cannot accept ambivalence when they see these same characteristics in a system or representatives of the system.

Sometimes anger is the only appropriate response, and confrontation the only answer. However, workers often react in this way before they have attempted to understand the dynamics involved, and so they may respond to teachers, doctors, or welfare workers as if they were stereotypes. At the very point when a client needs the worker's help in negotiating a system, the worker may respond in a way that further cuts off the system from the client. The worker may then point to the system as impossible to reach, rather than examining personal feelings and critically analyzing his or her own part in the proceedings.

**EP 2.1.4a**
**EP 2.1.4b**
**EP 2.1.4c**
**EP 2.1.5a**

***Native Worker and a White Teacher in a Public School System*** A striking example of how workers can move beyond their initial reactions arose in a workshop I conducted for Native Canadian Indian women who work as social aides for their local bands. Their job was to help the members of the bands in their dealings with many White-staffed agencies and institutions (schools, welfare, and the like). I should point out that at the beginning of the workshop, I directly acknowledged our differences in race, gender, cultural background, and even geography, since I was a White male who came from a university in a large city in the province. I suggested I would need their help in understanding the specific issues they faced as Native workers in a rural area. Although nothing was said at this point, I noticed some affirmative nodding of heads. I believe this initial statement helped later in the discussion to bridge potential gaps.

One Native worker presented an example of her efforts to help a Native teenager who was close to failing a course taught by a White teacher. This worker had often attacked the inadequacy of the school. The following record presents the conversation between the worker and the White teacher.

WORKER: I hear you're having problems with Albert's English.
TEACHER: It's not my problem, it's his.
WORKER: I do think you're leaning on him too hard.
TEACHER: Look, if he wants to get anywhere, he'll have to shape up. I really don't have the time to argue. If he wants to pass English, he'll have to try harder.
WORKER: Speaking about time, we do pay some of your wages, you know. I do think you could be a little more lenient.
TEACHER: I'll try to keep that in mind.
WORKER: You do that.

**Practice Points:** In discussing this brief interchange, the workshop participants, all Native Indian workers, felt that the worker had come on too hard with the teacher. Both appeared to be defensive: The teacher may have felt the worker wanted her to let Albert pass in spite of his poor performance, and the worker felt that the teacher did not really care about Albert.

The group agreed that the relationship between the worker and the teacher was in poor shape and that, as a result of the interview, not much hope remained for an improved relationship between the teacher and Albert. The teacher had gained neither a better idea about Albert's feelings nor a sense of what was interfering with Albert's learning. In addition, the worker interpreted the teacher's expectations for Albert's performance as a rejection of Albert. However, many workshop members pointed out that some teachers made no demands on Native Indian students at all; they just passed them along—a real form of rejection and racism. The workshop group members strategized how the worker might go back to meet with the teacher, negotiate a contract for their relationship, and try to begin again.

**Practice Points:** Although the worker seemed to agree, I sensed her hesitation, particularly in respect to admitting to the teacher that she had come on too strong. I reached for her underlying feelings:

WORKSHOP LEADER: You seem hesitant. I get the feeling you're not anxious to go back and try again. Am I right?

WORKER: (After a very long silence) It would hurt my pride to go back and talk to that teacher. (Another long silence)

WORKSHOP LEADER: Could you explain why it would hurt?

WORKER: I don't think you understand. Thirty years ago, I was one of the first of five Indian children to go to that school when it was all White. . . .

**Practice Points:** I believe my earlier acknowledgment of my differences from the workshop participants allowed the conversation to continue and to get into painful areas. The presenter went on to describe her experiences in a White-dominated school in which she and other Indian students were made to feel ashamed of their race and their heritage. They had been forbidden to speak their Native language, were ridiculed by teachers and White students for their poor dress and manners, and were generally made to feel like outsiders. One example of the cultural shock was related to the use of silence. When asked questions in class, some Indian students would take a long time to respond because they were thinking about the answer (as was the custom in conversations they heard in their families) or trying to translate into their Native language and then back to English. Teachers who did not understand the importance of silence would often interpret the delay as indicating the student did not know the answer, and they would move on to another student. After a while, the Native students did not even try to speak, and the teachers failed to ask them anything.

**Practice Points:** In the workshop group, others shared their own experiences. Some participants gently pointed out that it is not the same today and that some of the White teachers try hard to understand their students. I tried to acknowledge the feelings of the worker.

WORKSHOP LEADER: I guess every time you walk into that school it must bring back a great deal of pain and feelings of humiliation. I can understand now why you would feel it would be a blow to your pride. I'm not sure if I can help right now.

What is hitting me hard is that for you to work differently with this teacher, you have to deal with your feelings about the White world—all the hurt you have experienced—and that's a tall order.

Other workshop members moved in at this point and the discussion focused on how they needed to avoid the tendency to see the world of today's Indian teenagers as being exactly the same as the one they had dealt with. There were still many similarities, and evidence of ongoing prejudice and oppression clearly existed. The anger they felt toward present injustices was clearly stated. Nevertheless, if they were to help things be different for their children, they had to do something to try to change things themselves.

**Practice Summary.** In this specific case, the workshop members felt it would not help Albert if the worker simply gave up on the school. For Albert to make it, someone had to open up communications between his teacher and him. The worker agreed that she could see this and said she would have to think about what she would do.

Keeping in mind my social justice role as a social worker, I pointed out that this example opened up a larger question about the relationship between the children of the band and their parents and the staff of the school. Had they thought about the possibility of trying to do something on a band- and school-wide basis? Were other Native Indian parents also feeling somewhat intimidated by the school? Perhaps the school staff felt cut off and intimidated by the band. Would this be an area to explore? Discussion continued on the implications of this specific case for the general problems of Indian children in the school.

Moving from the specific example to more general problems, or moving from "case" to "cause," is an important line of work that the next section will explore. For now, understand that the worker's feelings can have a powerful effect on perception of the system and its representatives. If the worker only sees that part of the system that shows resistance, then the worker may fall into the trap of missing the part of the system that is still reaching out.

**EP 2.1.8b**

Of course, workers do not need to have gone through this specific sort of experience in order to feel intimidated by a school setting. For example, one graduate student of mine described his first day of fieldwork. He was placed as a student social worker in the same elementary school he had attended as a child. On his first morning he met his former fourth-grade teacher in the hall, and she said, "Terry, what are you doing here?" He replied, "I'm the new student social worker." He described her face as broadening into a big smile as she said, "Isn't that nice?" He blushed and felt that the possibility of doing any effective work with this teacher was finished. A first step, therefore, in functioning more effectively in systems work is for the worker to become aware of her or his personal feelings about a system's representatives, particularly those in positions of authority. This is essential.

***Work with the School System When a Student Is Suspended*** The following more detailed example, about a youngster who was suspended from school, illustrates the mediation role in action and the importance of the two-client concept. The worker demonstrated her ability to be with the youngster, his mother, and the system representatives in the engagement. This was the key to her success.

The client was a 61-year-old woman who had contacted the worker at a community psychiatry department of the local hospital. The worker had been seeing her son in a group at the hospital, and the client, Mrs. Jones, had called to inform the worker that she was not able to get her son Bobby accepted into school, despite a court order requiring her to do so. The worker described the client as being somewhat inept at handling school matters and vague about why the school was failing to comply with the court order. The worker felt that Mrs. Jones was worried and depressed about the school problem. She visited the client at her home to help her talk about her problem.

**WORKER:** I know that with all of the criticism you have had regarding your children, it is very hard for you.

**MRS. JONES:** (Looking depressed) I am trying my best. I don't want the courts to send Bobby away, but the school won't let him return and he is getting into more trouble.

**WORKER:** It's like going around in circles—everyone's telling you what to do, and no one is showing you how.

**MRS. JONES:** Now they will say I'm neglecting Bobby. (In an exasperated manner) The court says put him in school; the school says he can't go. I don't know what to do!

She continued to talk about her inability to understand why the school has refused to allow Bobby to return. While we were talking, the other children were yelling and screaming. Mrs. Jones was very edgy. Several times she grabbed the little ones to make them be quiet. I said she seemed overwhelmed and I asked how I could help. She said I could do better if I talked to the school. She didn't understand "those people." Maybe I could. She explained how difficult it is for her to travel to school when taking care of all the other children. I said I would speak to the school staff and keep in close contact with her as to what was happening. She seemed relieved and thanked me.

**Practice Points:**  It is important for the worker to express empathy and support for this overwhelmed mother. Note, also, how the worker offers to directly intervene on behalf of the mother and child with the school system. At some point the mother will need help in dealing with the school herself, but at this point the worker appropriately offers to take on this role. Her first step is to talk directly to Bobby.

I later talked to Bobby to see how he was feeling. He was out on the block when I spoke with him, and he seemed unhappy but perked up a little when he saw me. His immediate comment was, "You going to get me in school?" I gave him some information about the steps I had in mind and added that I knew he and his mother had been trying very hard. My comment led to further discussion.

**BOBBY:** I know why the school doesn't want me.

**WORKER:** I'd like to know why.

**BOBBY:** The teachers don't like me, and they don't want me in that school.

He was sulking and seemed quite torn inside. He looked at me, and his eyes were watery. I reached out and probed for what he was feeling.

**WORKER:** I know it's hard, but get it out of you; tell me what you are feeling.

**BOBBY:** (Who was crying) I want to go back into school. There's nothing to do on the block! The court is going to send me away, and my mother keeps hollering at me!

We talked at great length about his feelings, and he continued to express his fears about getting into school. If he gets into school, he is not sure he will do well. He is afraid the same experiences will repeat themselves. Mostly, I just listened, giving support where I could.

**Practice Points:** The worker reached for Bobby's feelings and provided supportive empathy. But as we have seen in examples earlier in this book, empathy alone is often not enough. The worker makes a facilitative confrontation, or a demand for work, letting Bobby know he will also need to work on his part in the problem.

**WORKER:** I know it's hard, Bobby. I want to help you by trying to help your parents as well as the school to see that you want to do the right thing. But it's not easy. You'll have to help me do this.

**BOBBY:** I'll try.

**WORKER:** You're trying already. It must have been very hard for you to tell me what you were thinking.

Bobby was silent, but I felt he understood what I was saying. When I was leaving, he reminded me of the group's trip that evening, and I said I would be there.

**Practice Points:** The worker had begun the process by contracting with Mrs. Jones and Bobby about how she could help. She tried to get a sense of how they saw the difficulty and attempted to encourage their expression of feeling about the problem. After these conversations, you might expect that the worker might have gone to the school to do battle for Bobby. With a court order in the background, the worker might have tried to use the power of the court to force Bobby back into school. This effort might have worked, but the worker recognized it would have been a short-lived victory. If the problems between Bobby and the school system were not dealt with, they would just return to haunt him later, and he would soon be suspended again. In addition, while the worker might have been able to force the school to take Bobby back, she wanted more from them—she wanted them to work to help Bobby stay in. To enlist their aid, she needed to treat the staff at the school as allies, not enemies, in the struggle to aid Bobby. The school would be her second client.

Instead of creating a self-fulfilling prophecy by attacking the school representatives and provoking a defensive and negative response, the worker began the first contact with the school guidance counselor by contracting, employing the skill of clarifying purpose. Often, because of their hidden agendas, workers begin their systems work without a clear and direct statement of what they are about. Lack of clarity as to purpose can be just as threatening and unproductive with systems representatives as it is with clients. This worker also encouraged the guidance counselor to elaborate her perceptions of the problem. A worker who saw the counselor as the enemy and overidentified with Bobby might have begun a counterattack after the counselor's first responses. As the worker reported,

I visited the school for the purpose of getting clarification on the reasons why Bobby was not allowed in school and to trace the source of his difficulty there. I met Ms. Gordon, the guidance counselor, and after briefly describing my involvement with the family, I told her what I was after.

**WORKER:** The court has requested that Bobby be returned to school. Mrs. Jones has informed me that the school has refused to readmit him.

**MS. GORDON:** I know that the court has ordered Bobby back to school. However, when he was suspended, it was done by the district superintendent. Therefore, only that office can admit him to school.

I then asked for some clarification as to the meaning of Bobby's suspension. I wanted to know if it was common for suspended pupils to have to wait so long for readmission. She said Bobby's situation was different because he had been so disruptive (emphasis on *disruptive*) in school. She was emphatic about his fight with the lunchroom teacher last year. Further discussion revealed that there was a possibility that Bobby had been provoked. This came out when I shared with her Bobby's feelings about the situation. I revealed some of Bobby's characteristics that I felt the school should know about. My purpose was twofold: (1) I knew Bobby's record at that school would follow him, and I wanted to clear it up; (2) because of the demands placed on teachers, a child's struggles with the school and himself can often go unnoticed.

**Practice Points:** In response to the worker's direct statement of purpose and her willingness to listen, the guidance counselor began to open up with the worker. The worker listened and attempted to empathize with the counselor and her difficulties. It is in this sense that the worker tries to "be with" the client and the system at the same time. It would be easier not to hear the problems facing the system, but just as with any relationship, there must be genuine understanding before making demands is possible. Also, the best way for the worker to get the counselor to understand Bobby is by beginning to understand the counselor.

**Ms. Gordon:** I have noticed that Bobby is a sensitive boy, and under all his toughness there's a scared child.

Ms. Gordon seemed frustrated by her inability to reach for the positive aspects that Bobby has, and I suspected that she was feeling defeated and threatened by my probing into the particulars surrounding Bobby's suspension. I said to her, "There's probably a desire on your part to be more responsive. You probably feel uncomfortable about not reaching Bobby." Ms. Gordon, in a sincere but hesitant manner, had this to say:

**Ms. Gordon:** Many of the teachers are insensitive, and there is a lack of cooperation on the part of the principal. Also, there is a large population of disruptive children who are frequently sent to the office. The lack of sufficient personnel for these children inhibits us from doing our job.

She continued for some time, talking about her frustrations. I made several unsuccessful attempts to refocus the discussion on Bobby. I then decided it was best to allow her to ventilate her feelings. I listened while she told me how she tries to help the children and how in the past she has had some real struggles in terms of getting the teachers to relate to the disruptive students. In an exasperated manner, she said, "The pupils do need help, but it is hard for the teachers to give it to them—especially with so many!" I chose this opportunity to get back to Bobby's problem.

**Practice Points:** While it is important to listen and genuinely empathize with the counselor, the demand for work is needed to make sure the conversation does not lose sight of Bobby and his problem.

**Worker:** Ms. Gordon, I can understand how frustrating it is for you and the teachers, but it is also frustrating for Bobby. He wants to belong to the school, and I know that the school wants to help him.

**Ms. Gordon:** (Very concerned) I will not send any record of this to Bobby's new school. I wouldn't want to prejudice the teachers against him. I will write in the records that Bobby is a sensitive boy who is bright and capable but who needs some special help. I feel this will give him a better chance of adjusting.

Ms. Gordon then gave me some names of people to contact at the district office. She said she had enjoyed talking to me because it is rare that she gets a chance to talk about her frustration. I suggested that we could talk some more, and this comment led to a long discussion about obtaining a social worker for the school.

**Practice Points:** Because of the worker's stance and skill, and her clarity of role, the guidance counselor became an important ally in the effort to get Bobby back into school. Workers often wonder about the use of empathic skills with other staff. They ask, "Isn't it like 'social working' a staff member, and won't they resent it?" I believe that when they say this, they are using the term "social working" in its worst sense and that what they are referring to is an insincere, ritualistic empathic response, which the other staff members quickly experience as an attempt to manipulate them. In this case, there are real difficulties in dealing with children like Bobby in a school system, and if the worker expects the counselor and the staff to listen to Bobby, to understand his difficulties, and to empathize with his feelings, she must do the same with them.

Of course, the guidance counselor and other staff people at the school are not clients; the worker needs to keep in mind that they are professional colleagues, each with different functions in relation to the same client. However, mutual respect and understanding between colleagues and a willingness to understand the complexities of a situation matter greatly if the worker is to help Bobby and his mother, as well as have a positive effect on the interaction between Bobby and the school. In process recordings of work with systems representatives, workers often run into trouble in the sessions just after the point where the problems in the system start to be shared. Workers demand empathy for clients despite refusing to empathize with colleagues.

**Practice Points:** The worker in this example next approached the supervisory level for further information. When she found out there might have been some reactions to her involvement, she reached for possible negative reactions at the start of the conversation. She understands the grapevine in a school system would have sent a message about her that preceded her visit. In this case, her previous skillful work with the guidance counselor pays off in laying the groundwork for a positive reception.

At the district office, my strategy was to find out just what or who was preventing Bobby's return to school. I spoke with Ms. Reardon, guidance coordinator. Upon introducing myself, I was told that she had heard of me. I was surprised and asked what she had heard. She said she had seen my name on several court reports as the family social worker for St. Luke's Hospital. Ms. Gordon had also called and told her I was coming. Ms. Reardon seemed nervous, and I decided to explore her feelings about my involvement:

**WORKER:** Here I am trying to get back in school a child who has been out for a long period of time. You must feel somewhat annoyed by my efforts.

**MS. REARDON:** At first I felt that way, but my conversation with Ms. Gordon changed my mind. I am impressed with anyone who is interested in listening to problems of the school as well as the child.

**WORKER:** You must have had some bad experiences with social workers?

**MS. REARDON:** (With some irritation) Too many social agencies attack the schools. They make a big stink, and when the child is returned to school, they drop out of the picture. I don't like the fact that Bobby has been out of school so long, but I am waiting for a report from Child Guidance before returning him to school.

**Worker:** I know you want the best for Bobby as well as for any child. With so many demands on counselors, it is easy for a child to get lost.

**Ms. Reardon:** This is true. There are so many students like Bobby who have been out of school long periods of time. The parents think we don't care; but the children need so much and the teachers are unable to give it. We need help!

I then attempted to focus on Bobby's situation and at the same time recognize the global problems of the school system. I said I knew how difficult the school situation is.

**Worker:** We need social workers and psychiatrists right in the school, and most of all we need sympathetic teachers. But I am concerned with what we can do together for Bobby.

**Ms. Reardon:** (Seeming rather embarrassed) Oh! Forgive me! It's just that I had said to Ms. Gordon that I would explore the possibility of getting social services in at least one of the schools in the district.

**Practice Points:** This is a good example of moving from case to cause. Bobby is front and center for this worker, but there are many students like Bobby. The worker demonstrates her responsibility for working for social change by her offer to work with school staff on obtaining additional support services.

I invited her to a meeting that Ms. Gordon and I were going to have to work to secure services for the school. I then made some suggestions about what we could do for Bobby. I asked her to call Child Guidance to determine when the report would be ready. When she phoned, she discovered that Child Guidance was under the impression that the court was going to do a psychiatric evaluation. Ms. Reardon then phoned the court and spoke to the probation officer, who informed her that their psychiatric evaluation was to be done on the parents only, and Child Guidance was to do the one on Bobby. Ms. Reardon told me, frustrated, "No one really communicates with each other." She angrily phoned Dr. Bennet, head of Child Guidance, and obtained a commitment to do a psychiatric on Bobby.

**Practice Points:** After acknowledging the problems, the worker made a demand for work by concentrating on the immediate problem facing Bobby. The supervisor's conversation with the probation officer was one illustration of how the complexity of the system can often lead to clients "falling through the cracks." In the following excerpt, the worker sensed the coordinator's underlying ambivalence and reached directly for the feelings. She wanted to be sure that her conversation with the coordinator was "real," because any unexpressed doubts would return to haunt Bobby later. An important additional step was the worker's recognition that she would have to begin a working relationship with the staff in Bobby's new school; she thus suggested modifications in the coordinator's description of the worker's role, in order to prevent misunderstanding. This is an example of the skill of recontracting, which is just as important with system representatives as it is with clients.

I told Ms. Reardon of my earlier conversations with Bobby and Mrs. Jones and expressed their desire to have him back in school right away. Ms. Reardon said she also wanted him in school immediately, but I sensed some reservations. I reached for her ambivalent feelings.

WORKER: Part of you seems to want him back, and part of you doesn't.
MS. REARDON: You're right. I'm concerned about what school to send him to. Most of the other schools in the district are loaded with problem kids. There is one school that is better than others, but they are somewhat rigid. I want Bobby to have the best possible chance, but that's the only school that has room for him.

I offered a plan of action and reached for some feedback:

WORKER: If you could introduce me to the principal of the new school, perhaps we could work together with the teachers in a supportive role to broaden the chances of Bobby making a satisfactory adjustment.

**Practice Points**:   By engaging Ms. Reardon as an ally, the worker now has her support in dealing with the new school. The administrator shares some problems at the school to help the worker avoid possible mistakes that would create difficulties. Note, in particular, how skillful the worker is when the administrator suggests in a letter she is drafting that no decisions be made without consulting the worker. A less sophisticated worker would be pleased with this suggestion, but this worker anticipates that it could create problems with the principal. She suggests a change in wording.

Ms. Reardon felt that this was a good plan. She thought the school would appreciate my help. However, she suggested that I work with the school social worker and the teachers because they might resent my working directly with the principal. I said that I didn't fully understand what she was trying to tell me. She explained that the principal and the teachers have a "pretty rocky relationship," and she didn't want to get in the way of my attempts to help. She wrote a letter to the principal explaining who I was and what role I would have in working closely with the school to help Bobby. She ended the letter by stating that I should be consulted before decisions were made regarding anything Bobby has become involved in. I suggested that the letter be reworded so as not to give the impression of taking away decision powers. I told her to simply ask that I be involved as a resource person to enable them to make more informed decisions.

I gave recognition to Ms. Reardon for her assistance in getting movement on the reinstatement of Bobby:

WORKER: I know it isn't an easy decision to return Bobby to school, but I will be around to help when you need me.

As I was leaving, Ms. Reardon said I should contact her about the meeting to get social services in Ms. Gordon's school.

**Practice Summary.**   This worker recognized that getting Bobby back into school was just the beginning of the work, certainly not the final solution to the problem. She managed to keep in contact with the school and to monitor Bobby's progress so that when trouble arose, she would be there to help. In this important part of her work, her earlier efforts to develop a positive working relationship with the school staff paid dividends, giving her a basis of trust from which to work.

These first steps by the worker, predicated on the assumption that it was best to reach for the system's strength and to "talk softly" rather than begin with a confrontation, led to the client's reconnection to the school system in a new and more helpful way. In addition, the worker made a major contribution toward strengthening not only her own professional relationship with the school system, but also the relationship between her hospital and the schools. She would likely reap important benefits from this careful systems work if she needed to deal with this school system again. In addition, the worker's recognition of her responsibility for working with other professionals around the larger issue of availability of resources for children like Bobby reflects the broader social work function in action. Examples in the next chapter illustrate the steps involved in moving from Bobby's "private troubles" to the "public issues" affecting all of the children like Bobby.

Finally, although the worker was acting appropriately in working for Bobby's mother to overcome the immediate roadblocks to Bobby's readmission to school, the worker should also try to strengthen the relationship between Mrs. Jones and the school system. Other problems will come up and the worker may not always be available.

Specifically, she should explore Mrs. Jones's description of the school's staff as "those people." Mrs. Jones was an African American, and the worker was not. An underlying issue of racism may exist, or may be experienced as existing. Certainly, Mrs. Jones may think that an African American parent would not be respected by a largely White school system. She may have found it difficult to be direct about this issue with the worker, and the worker may have been uncomfortable about raising it with her.

***Family Court Group for Parents of Truant Children: Race, Class, and Conflict with Teachers in a School*** In order to better address the crisis in inner-city schools, family courts have developed specialized delinquency courts that include staff and graduate students to work with the truant students and their families. The court program integrates the use of authority with support for children at risk. It is often the case that the parents feel blamed for their children's behavior by the court and the school staff. Instead of a collaborative relationship between parents, teachers, and administrators, it can become confrontational. In the example that follows, members of a support group for parents and students raise a serious conflict they are having with the school administration and, in particular, one hostile teacher. What follows is the student/social worker's record of her work with this group over time. The reader can draw on the earlier discussion in the chapter on the group-as-a-whole in that this represents the group task of negotiating the environment—the school.

**Member Demographics:** There are nine parents in the group. Seven of them are female and two are male, one is Euro-American and eight are African-American, seven are single parents, the Euro-American woman was married to one of the African-American men, eight of the members are in the 30–40 age range, and one is age 50 or older. All reside in urban, low-income, high-crime neighborhoods. The parents were seated on couches and chairs in a circle. Because of space limits, the children would sit at a table at the other end of the same room, talking, eating breakfast, and playing games.

**Dates Covered:**     From 2/29 to 4/29

**Problem:** The problem the group faces concerns negotiating with the school system to develop a more cooperative relationship in addressing problematic student attendance. The parents experience being blamed and not listened to by the school. It is a problem because of the connections between the youths' behavior, their parents, and their school. This group of low-income, primarily African-American parents faces the task of improving their sense of self-efficacy and power. A group format is effective in helping vulnerable and oppressed groups be able to do that. By improving their communication skills, and access to information and linkages to other community resources, it is hoped that the parents will feel more individually and collectively powerful.

**How the Problem Came to my Attention:** The group initially presented as in need of information on and assistance with parenting. However, the group revealed that its immediate problem was in its relationship with the school system. Several observations of the group were made. The themes that arose were blame, scapegoating, helplessness, socioeconomic classicism, and racism toward the parents resulting from the frustrations with school teachers and administrators. Prior interactions left group members feeling disempowered, isolated from one another and their community, and unsure of their own strengths and abilities in many aspects of their lives, including parenting.

**Practice Points:** The work begins with the contracting skills required in every level of practice. The worker, taking the lead from the family court approach, begins with brochures and what might be viewed by members as a criticism of their parenting. The resistance is quickly evident; however, the worker recognizes what their behavior is saying to her.

### Session 1

I introduced myself as a student intern working in Family Court. I told the group that my role here would be to help them determine what they needed to help them and their sons by talking with them and gathering information for them on things like parenting, disciplining children with ADHD, housing, on how to lower their gas bills, and/or whatever else they could think of. I then passed around brochures on parenting tips and on disciplining children with ADHD. Several of the members had a polite but amused look on their faces. Each of the members introduced him- or herself as I asked, but none of them looked happy about it—they all had resistant and mistrusting facial expressions.

Some of them just stuffed the brochures in their purses without even glancing at them. I realized that this was probably not what they needed or wanted. I then asked each person to introduce themselves by name and child, reason for being here, and what s/he hoped to achieve.

The parents indicated they were at the group because of their sons' problematic attendance and behaviors and attributed full blame to the children. Parent D said that she was there because her son was bad. She looked toward him and said, "Look at all the troubles you've caused. . . . I have to be here, be punished, embarrassed, because of you. . . . Just wait until you get home." Parent A told her grandson, "You are just like [biological parent] . . . no good!" Parent C said her son "is lazy, bad, doesn't care, won't listen [etc.]" The group was then silent for a few moments. Then, the mother of D said that she spoils her son a little and could use some help learning new disciplining and other parenting skills.

**Practice Points:** Once again, the initial process is revealing of what goes on in the family and how the parents are trying to deal with the children through blame and criticism. Remember, this is how the family court has been dealing with them. Note also that the children, sitting across the room, are hearing this but are not involved by the worker.

The mother of F said that she and her husband are strict with their son, but that the school singles him out. Parent D said that her son is just plain bad, both at school and at home. Parent A nodded and said, "Mine, too." I told them, "You must all really love and care about your sons and their educations and futures because you all took the time off from work and volunteered to be a part of this program." Several parents nodded. I believed that doing this would help them feel empowered and motivated to change something they were or were not doing as parents. In other words, I assumed that their children had attendance problems because of them—the children and their parents. I would later find out that this was not accurate.

The session ended at this point because the first case was called into session. As the families left for the day, I thanked and commended them for coming, and said that I was looking forward to seeing them again next week. After everyone left, I realized that I never addressed the authority theme or developed a clear contract with them.

**Practice Points:**   Given that the sessions are held in the context of family court and that the children are facing some form of charge against them, the worker is correct in her observation about the need to address the issue of authority. She also initiates the problem-swapping stage of a beginning group session that was skipped at the first meeting. She needs to understand what it is like for them if she expects to help them understand what their children may be going through.

### Session 2

After greetings, I passed around brochures on parenting and disciplining. Then, I said that as a student who does not have any children, I wanted to learn and understand what it was like for them as parents of the boys. I asked the group if they would tell me what it was like for them. Parent D said that it was really hard. She said that she is a single mother of three children and works very hard to support them. So, it really makes her angry when her son gets into trouble or does not do his homework. She said that she wanted her kids to have a better life and not have to work as hard as she does. Several other parents nodded or verbalized in agreement.

Parent C added that she feared losing her job that she recently started because of having to miss a morning each week. Parent A said that she knew what they meant and that she was fed up because first she went through it with the child's mother and now has to go through it with him. She said that she never graduated from high school and at least wants her grandson to do that. She said that the child was smart but "just plain no good." I asked her what she meant by him being "no good," what he did or does that is "no good." She said that he does not do his chores or listen to her. He just comes home from school, goes straight to his room, and refuses to come out. She said that even in the morning, she cannot get him to come out and go to school.

I wanted to ask her about how that makes her feel but waited because I was hoping some of the members would chime in. Some verbalized validation by saying "um hum" or "uh uh." I said, "Wow, that must be frustrating." Parent A said that it's made her mad and hurt because it is disrespectful. I asked the group if anyone else also experienced something like that with his/her son. Mother of E said that she did sometimes, but that she resolved this by getting E's father involved. The other members seemed to tune out. Even though I noticed it—that something was going on either because of marital status, race, or interracial marriage, I did not reach for it.

**Practice Points:**   In hindsight, having the children at the meeting could have been used to some advantage if the structure included some involvement in the conversation. For example, perhaps the children feel the same way about school that the parents feel. Would it be helpful to facilitate some child-parent conversation so that parents can understand that the "deviant behavior" on the children's part was also sending a message? Note that in the next session, the discussion moves from a focus on the children and the parents' problems to their relationship to the school and their critical feelings.

### Session 3

I wanted to encourage addressing the intimacy theme. I tuned in and felt that the group did not seem to be developing the cohesion that it should and that something needed to be done so mutual aid could begin to develop.

I began the session by asking the group how the week had gone for them. Parents of E said that their son began an after-school program volunteering at the local animal shelter, and that he seemed to like it very much. He had been going to class every day and finishing his homework right away so that he can continue volunteering. Parent C said that her son was sent home early one day because his teacher said that he got into a verbal altercation with another student and she kicked him out of class. She said that another student had started it by throwing paper at her son, and the teacher knew that but still punished only C. When C told the assistant principal what happened, he sided with the teacher.

I told Parent C that she sounded a little angry about it. She said that she was because she did not think it was fair for only her son to be punished when another child started the paper throwing. She said that she knows her son has been at fault and that he should not have yelled at the other student, but she felt it was unfair to single out her son for punishment. Parent D asked, "Was it Mrs. X?" Parent C said that it was. Parent D just shook her head and said "um um." I asked who Mrs. X was.

**Practice Points:** The conversation begins to get personal as the parents recognize a particular teacher with whom they have had problems. They only hint at this, and the worker reaches for the message.

Parent D said that Mrs. X is also her son's teacher and that she singles him out too. She said that because D got into a fight with another boy earlier in the school year and has been absent a lot, Mrs. X is particularly harsh with him and told him once that she did not care who started an event but that he would still be responsible if he was in any way involved. Another time Mrs. X told D that he was just plain bad and would never be any good. I said, "Wow." Mother of E said that her son used to be in Mrs. X's class and that she treated him similarly. She said that because they are "truancy court boys," Mrs. X and the assistant principal single them out and blame them for everything. Parent B validated that this was true. She said that even though she worked for the school, Mrs. X and the assistant principal treat X and her like nothing they say is true and like they are beneath them. She said that she has tried to talk with Mrs. X but that Mrs. X told her that she was tired of these kinds of boys and parents who did not know how to parent. Mrs. X told her that she would not believe a word any of these boys or their parents said, but that if one of them is involved in any trouble or disruption in her class, out they go.

**Practice Points:** With the door open, the feelings of frustration and anger pour out. How can children expect to function well in school when their parents feel so angry at this teacher and the assistant principal?

Parent B said that Mrs. X talks down to parents, and made her feel bad about herself that day. Other group members were nodding their heads, saying things like "me too," and making verbal affirmations. I asked if anyone else tried talking with the teacher, assistant principal, or other person in the school. Parent A said "oh yeah," and others were nodding and saying "um um." I asked Parent A if she would share with the group what happened. Her story was similar, except that it was with the assistant principal, who she felt would not give any credence to her side of the story and made her feel bad. I said that it sounded like everyone felt like the school—at least one teacher and the assistant principal—had not been fair or respectful toward them. I said that maybe we could all think about how this might be changed and talk about our ideas next week. Everyone nodded.

### Session 4

A few parents said that they did not know what to do because no one listens to them. Parent D said that she felt the principal cared and would listen, but that it was hard to get in contact with him. Parent B said she was the staff member who acted as the liaison with the PTA and she thought that if they got involved with the PTA, they could have their issues addressed within that context and gain the PTA's support to then approach the school administration. Parent C said that she was a member of the PTA and told the group a story about how another issue some parents had was resolved. She said that she could show them how to do it, particularly since she had now lost her job from having to take time off every week. The other members said they would be interested in doing that and seemed to have an increased level of energy. Parent B said that she would talk with other leaders of the PTA and find out when their next meeting was and whether they could have their issue placed on the agenda.

**Practice Points:** The difficulty facing this group of parents is real. One parent had worried in the first meeting about losing her job while missing work to attend these meetings and that is exactly what happened. The increased level of energy most likely comes from starting to feel empowered; however, the worker realizes she will have to help them plan their approach to the PTA. These parents often feel overwhelmed and are vulnerable when attacked by school staff who challenge them and their parenting.

### Session 5

After a school social worker told the court personnel at truancy court that Parent B was "crazy" and made other derogatory remarks about her, I suspected that she (Parent B) may have been feeling down and discouraged and had not followed up with the PTA. I wanted to encourage the group to clarify the specific issue they wanted to ask be placed on the PTA's agenda and to plan their presentation(s).

Parent B said that Mrs. X was also on the PTA. Parent B said that she is a teacher's aide. Last week, she felt Mrs. X was out of line in the way she spoke to one of the students and the student's parents. Parent B told her that she and Mrs. X had a verbal altercation over it. Parent B said that Mrs. X told her she was a "lowlife bitch" and that she better learn to keep her mouth shut if she knew what was good for her. Parent B said that she felt scared about her job security after that and had not asked anyone about the PTA meeting yet. She sounded and looked sad and lacking in confidence. The group also looked as if they just got the wind knocked out of them.

I said that it was understandable to feel scared, but that Mrs. X had no right to say those things to her, that it was not okay. I asked the group what they thought about it. Parent D said, "No. It isn't right, but it's the way things are." Dad of E said that it was "not right" and Parent B should not take that from Mrs. X and should tell the principal about it. Other members agreed. Parent B said that she wants to but is afraid that Mrs. X will make her life miserable and cause her to lose her job, which would then negatively impact her son. Some other members nodded in agreement and understanding. A few moments of silence followed.

Parent C said that they should go talk to the parent association first because having their support would make it more likely to have their issue addressed by the

PTA, and Parent B would have their support, too. Parent C felt that otherwise, if they continued to allow things like this to happen, nothing would ever change. She said that she was sick and tired of it and was not going to sit around and do nothing anymore. Parent B said that she thought that was a good idea and would arrange for them to meet with the parent association.

**Practice Points:**   One can see the strength-in-numbers phenomenon emerge as group members are encouraged to unite to address the threats to themselves, their children, and, individually, to Parent B. The worker is tuned in to the fact that standing up for their right to be treated with respect has a special threat for Parent B—the loss of her job.

### Session 6

I felt that I and the group may not have given Parent B sufficient support and time to explore how her altercation with Mrs. X impacted her. I wanted to return to that for a moment and to find out what happened since then. I also wanted to encourage the group to identify next steps and divide tasks, as well as maintain the trust and relationship they had developed because I would only be with them for two more weeks since the semester was ending.

I said to Parent B that when she was telling us about what she experienced with Mrs. X, I sensed that she was feeling a lot of pain. I told her that I thought maybe we breezed over it too quickly, so I was wondering how she was doing. She said that she had felt humiliated by Mrs. X and was feeling down about it, but that she felt better after talking with the other parents. She said that was able to make an appointment for the group to meet with the parent association and gave everyone the date. I was thinking that I should ask the group to think about what they would say to the association. However, Parent C said that they (the group) should begin thinking about what they are going to say at the meeting. Parent B agreed and said that there might be information they would need to research, so they should decide on what to talk about as soon as possible.

**Current State of the Problem:** The group was just beginning to develop trust and have confidence in their abilities. At the end of my work with the group, members seemed to feel stronger and more confident in expressing themselves. They were better able to contribute their ideas and share their feelings. They seemed to feel energized. However, I think members had to experience some concrete results to strengthen their self-confidence, and that having the association support them would provide this kind of feedback. A challenge for the group will be in not losing their motivation and hope if their ideas are not accepted. I wanted to keep the group focusing on moving forward with self-advocacy rather than allowing individual members to just explore their experiences and feelings about specific incidences.

**Next Steps:** I will encourage the group to:

1. Organize, plan, and practice their presentation.
2. Consider how they might respond to a negative reception from the parent association to some or all of their ideas.
3. Be an active voice in the PTA by encouraging members to participate in its leadership.
4. Continue developing and maintain their relationships with each other.
5. Learn more about their community, and to learn how they can participate in strengthening it.

6. I will continue helping to empower the group and its members by contributing ideas, information, and support.
7. Encourage the group to empathize with school personnel and the stresses they must feel in the system.

**Practice Summary.** While the worker is clearly helping these parents begin to feel empowered, she does not address her relationship with the school and the school staff. It would be important to know if she has approached the principal, for example, to brief him on the progress of the group. While she needs to respect individual confidentiality, leaving it to the members to address the tough and scary issues, she can help him understand the general feelings of parents in a situation like this and how she is trying to help. She needs the principal and other administrative and teaching staff as allies in the process. Perhaps a chance to talk with teachers or even informal conversations in the lunchroom would help. If she adds working to develop her relationship with the school staff, she will be in a better position to help her group members and their children.

## Confrontation, Social Pressure, and Advocacy

If we think of agencies and institutions as social systems, by employing the organismic model used earlier to describe the group, some of the processes observed in small groups may also apply to larger systems. One such idea is Lewin's (1951) description of systems as maintaining a quasi-stationary social equilibrium in which customs and social habits create an inner resistance to change (see Chapter 13). This resistance to change is found in the individual, the family, the group, the community, agencies, and institutions. In the model presented thus far, the worker has endeavored to open up communications between clients and relevant systems (between the individual and the group, for example) in order to help overcome the obstacles to the inherent common ground. The worker has at all times been reaching for the desire for change within both the client and the system.

Because of their inherent resistance to change, systems and their representatives do not always respond with a willingness to deal with the obstacles. Even a worker who understands the system's problems and who makes every effort to influence the system in a positive manner may make no progress. In such situations, confrontation and social pressure are required. That is, some additional force is needed to overcome the system's resistance to change and to show the system it needs to respond in new ways to the client. This additional force upsets the quasi-stationary equilibrium and makes the system more open to change.

This argument resonates with crisis theory, which suggests that individuals and families are most open to change when a crisis makes maintaining a situation untenable. Under conditions where negotiation has failed or has been declined, the resistance of the system's ambivalence is so strong that it dominates the interaction. Something is needed to upset the dysfunctional equilibrium.

***Finding Housing for an Overwhelmed Client: A Canadian Example*** The following example illustrates how a worker did just this by acting as an advocate for an overwhelmed client who was facing a housing crisis after being ignored by an unyielding bureaucracy. As with the previous example, the worker was not hired as a client advocate per se, but considered advocacy part of his role as a worker. In this case, the worker was employed by a child welfare agency in a large Canadian city. His client was a French-speaking woman named Mrs. Belanger, age 35, who was a single parent with four children. She had requested placement of her children with the agency because of her severe depression after her husband left her.

After several interviews, the worker saw one of Mrs. Belanger's precipitating crises: She had been forced to move twice within the past 6 months because of changes in ownership of the buildings she lived in. Adequate and affordable accommodations were not available. As an alternative to accepting the children for placement, the worker proposed the following plan: Mrs. Belanger would continue seeing a psychiatrist to help her with her depression; the worker would arrange for homemaker services to help her with the children; he would also work with her to try to solve the housing problem. The client agreed. The worker felt this was a good example of a situation in which, with personal support and help in dealing with the housing system, the client had the strength to maintain herself and her children. By not providing adequate housing for this family, society bore part of the responsibility for the problem. Thus, the worker began a 4-month odyssey that provided a lesson in the complexity of the housing system and evidence of the power of persistence.

**Practice Points:** As a first step, after consulting with Mrs. Belanger, the worker addressed a letter to the city housing authority. An excerpt from that letter follows:

*September 26*
This letter is on behalf of Mrs. Belanger and her application for a 3-bedroom unit. Certainly this is a matter of urgency, as Mrs. Belanger and her children have been obliged to move twice in a very short time as her landlords have sold out. There is cause for serious concern, as Mrs. Belanger's health demands a stable environment. Due to the limits of her financial situation and her health, her choice of adequate shelter depends on your assistance.

Mrs. Belanger, as I know her, is a quiet, reserved woman with very good housekeeping standards and well-behaved children. It is my opinion that she would be a very good tenant. To keep her family together and maintain the home, it is imperative that she relocate to a suitable unit in a French-speaking area of her choice as soon as possible.

Thank you for whatever assistance you can offer to the Belanger family.

**Practice Points:** As the worker developed his case for Mrs. Belanger, he enlisted the aid of allies. The first was the psychiatrist who was treating the client. The psychiatrist's letter to the placement manager read as follows:

*September 26*
The above-named client, who is on your waiting list for housing, has been under my direct care for 2 years. She has exhausted her own possibilities in seeking housing for herself and her four children. It is imperative and urgent that suitable accommodation be found this month, as otherwise her mental health may decline once again with repercussions for herself and the children.

**Practice Points:** A return letter indicated that the client did not meet the residency requirements for housing within the city limits. The area Mrs. Belanger lived in was technically in another municipality surrounded by the larger city. The placement manager suggested that the worker should contact the provincial (Canadian equivalent of a state) government housing authority for help. The worker repeated the letters to the housing authority of the smaller municipality. The response indicated that because of a shortage of housing in the French-speaking area—a shortage that the municipality had done little to rectify—the only help available to Mrs. Belanger was an apartment in an English-speaking area. Mrs. Belanger could not speak English, and as a result, she would have been socially isolated in this area, which would have compounded her problems.

The worker made sure to consult with Mrs. Belanger at each step of the process to be sure she understood and agreed with the next steps. She felt identified with her present housing area and feared moving into an English-speaking housing project. They agreed to try to have the residency requirements waived in order to obtain housing in the city. A second letter was sent to the placement manager of the city housing authority with additional letters of support from the homemaker service. In addition, the worker arranged a meeting with the mayor of the smaller municipality, at which time he raised the problem of Mrs. Belanger and received assurances that the mayor would do his best to help.

Despite such promises, the months dragged on with no action. The worker arranged a meeting with the placement officer of the city housing authority and his client. His impression was that the officer was not as interested in the client's dilemma as he was in applying the regulations. As the worker encountered one frustration after another, he noted his own increasing depression. After only 2 months in the shoes of the client attempting to negotiate government bureaucracies, he felt it would not be long before he began to show clinical symptoms of depression. This increased his anger at the way his client and her children were lost in the complexity of agencies supposedly established to serve their needs. With the agreement of Mrs. Belanger and his supervisor, the worker wrote the following letter to the federal government representative (Member of Parliament):

*November 21*
I am writing on behalf of one of your constituents, Mrs. Belanger, who is having serious difficulty in finding adequate accommodations within her budgetary limitations. The enclosed letters indicate a series of steps that we have taken on behalf of the Belanger family in support of her application for low-rent housing. I urgently requested that her doctor and visiting homemaker outline their involvement to support the request. Letters were delivered and immediate personal interviews were held with the mayor, Mrs. Johnson of the Provincial Ministry, and Mr. Rolf of the Housing Authority. Unfortunately, we have come to a dead end.

As you will note in the accompanying letter from Mrs. Helflin, Mrs. Belanger has exerted many frustrating efforts on her own behalf. She, too, has been unsuccessful. She has been forced to move twice within the past year, due, in both cases, simply to a change of landlords through sales. Another move will occur at the end of the month, as she has received a notice to vacate. These necessary moves, due to no fault of Mrs. Belanger and her children, are very seriously affecting her health, as is documented in the attached letters written by various agencies on her behalf. Needless to say, the housing problem and a resulting depression of the mother can only have negative consequences for the children. Our concern is to prevent what will inevitably occur as Mrs. Belanger's health deteriorates further: placement of her children in foster homes.

I am asking that you intervene immediately on behalf of your constituent. I have no doubt that you will be far more effective than my efforts have been.

Over the telephone, the secretary of the Member of Parliament promised to look into the situation. The urgency of the problem increased as Mrs. Belanger received an eviction notice. She was to be out of her apartment by the end of the week. It was at this point in the process that the worker presented this case at a workshop I was leading for his agency's staff on systems work—the skills involved in helping clients negotiate agencies and institutions. He reviewed his efforts to date, reading excerpts from the letters and describing his interviews from memory. At the end of the presentation, he shared his utter frustration and anger at what was happening to his client and his feeling of powerlessness to do anything about it. I could tell from the reactions of his colleagues, and the looks on their faces, that they were feeling the same sense of impotency as they reflected on similar cases from their own caseloads. An excerpt from my workshop notes follows:

WORKSHOP LEADER: I can tell this case has come to mean a great deal for you. It probably symbolizes all of the cases where you feel deeply about the injustices your clients face and how little you seem to be able to do about it. It must hurt and make you feel bitter.

WORKER: What good is all the talk about systems work if Mrs. Belanger ends up with lousy housing and depressed, and then turns her kids over to us?

WORKSHOP LEADER: I don't think it is over yet. There is always some next step you can take. Does anyone have any ideas?

WORKSHOP PARTICIPANT: The only thing I would feel like doing is screaming about how mad I am about this.

WORKSHOP LEADER: Well, why don't you? If Mrs. Belanger is willing, isn't it time somebody brought her problem to the public's attention? How are they going to know about this kind of thing happening to people if you don't tell them?

WORKER: I'm a representative of the agency. How can I go to the papers?

WORKSHOP LEADER: Sounds like you need to do some work within the agency to gain support for taking a more public step. Have you spoken to the agency director about that possibility?

WORKER: No, I haven't. I assumed the agency wouldn't want this kind of publicity.

WORKSHOP LEADER: Why don't you ask your director? He's right here.

**Practice Points:** In the conversation that followed, the director indicated that he felt social pressure was needed at times, and that this seemed to be one of those times. He defined the parameters within which he felt his staff could operate. He wanted to be informed about cases as they progressed and to be assured that all steps had been taken before going to the press. After that, he would cooperate with staff if they felt that public awareness was the only step left. The director and the worker agreed to meet after the workshop to plan how to use the media in this case. What I found interesting was that the worker had assumed, without asking, that the agency administration would reject going public.

Workers often take this position, and in some cases they indeed run into stiff opposition. This means that they have some work to do within their own agency systems to obtain allies and to try to change a policy that categorically rejects the use of agency social pressure on behalf of the client. If unsuccessful, they may have to consider changing jobs or taking other steps to bring about changes in agency policy.

It would be a mistake, however, to assume the rejection in advance without even trying. In such a case, the worker avoids getting involved in a confrontation but can still blame the agency for the problem. Workers have said that it takes a lot of courage to challenge their own agency system, and I agree. Social change is never easy. However, a sense of professional identification that extends beyond being an agency staff member requires that workers take some risks along the way.

After a discussion with the client in which she agreed with the strategy, the worker contacted the local reporter who covered the social services in that city. The following edited excerpt is from the newspaper story on the case of Mrs. Belanger, entitled "'Take My Children,' Mom Pleads."

### November 29

If Mrs. B. doesn't get help within the month, she will be forced to turn her children over to the Children's Aid Society. Ron Strong, a Children's Aid Worker, said the separated woman's plight is critical as she and her four children continue to survive on a $464-a-month mother's allowance she receives. This has been her only source of income since her husband left in April.

The problem is housing. The family finds itself forced to move this weekend for the third time this year because the house in which they are living has been sold. She has two boys and two girls between the ages of 8 and 12 and needs a three-bedroom accommodation that will not eat up half the monthly income, Mr. Strong said.

An added problem is that Mrs. B. only speaks French and must live in a French-speaking area. She has been living in ———, which, Mr. Strong said, is causing her another problem.

In living outside the community boundary, technically she is not eligible for a housing unit under the Housing Authority until she has been living in the city for a year. "And the Provincial Housing Corp. has no units in other sections of the city—only further out—and even then they haven't offered her anything," Mr. Strong said. "She has given up all hope," he said. She has already asked the Society eight times if they will take the children.

"The Society is trying to prevent taking them," Mr. Strong said. "I have been working almost full time to find some solution to the problem." Is there a solution?

"City Housing can waive the eligibility in December, and they must do it— there is no other route to go," he said. "If it doesn't happen, the Society will have to take the children." "She is a good mother and tenant," Mr. Strong said. "But another month and the situation will move to emergency proportions."

**Practice Points:**   A few days after the appearance of this article, the worker and Mrs. Belanger met with the federal representative, the Member of Parliament, who was somewhat upset at the publicity. Nevertheless, he offered his support. A call was received soon after from the placement officer of the city housing authority informing the worker that the one-year residency requirement was being waived. Soon after, Mrs. Belanger was offered a suitable apartment. Interestingly, the psychiatrist treating Mrs. Belanger reported that during the time she and the worker were involved in the fight for housing—a period of almost 4 months—her psychotic symptoms disappeared. Acting in her self-interest and starting to affect others, rather than being passively acted on by the system, proved quite therapeutic. The experience appeared to be good for the worker as well, as some of his symptoms of depression, sometimes known as the "child welfare worker blues," were also relieved.

**Practice Summary.** This example shows that mediating between a client and the social system sometimes requires the worker to act as an advocate for the client. In this example, the worker made sure that the client was involved in each step of the decision-making process. In dealing with the system (the agencies), he was acting as if he believed they could provide the services if social pressure were employed. In a sense, he used pressure to make a demand for work and reached for the strength of the system. Another key factor was that he acted openly and honestly along the way. My view is that, although tactics involving deceit may seem helpful in the short run, they always return to haunt the worker in significant ways. The worker involved allies wherever he could (the psychiatrist, homemakers, and so forth). He was persistent and did not give in after encountering the first obstacles. Nor was he fooled by the system's efforts to "cool him off" by passing the buck or making vague promises of action. He made sure to involve and inform his own agency system, so that his agency (the director, supervisors) would feel part of the process. Most important, he maintained a belief in the idea that there is always some next step that can be taken. The basic principle that there is always a next step is central to our practice and to our lives.

## Establishing a Working Relationship with the System

Because we do not have detailed process recordings of the conversation between the worker and the representatives of the systems he dealt with, we cannot analyze the use of skills that characterized the work. However, Heyman (1971) addressed the questions related to worker skills used in establishing a relationship with the systems representative at points of conflict. Using the example of a social worker identified with tenants about to implement a rent strike, he describes in detail the way a worker attempted to play a mediating role and provide assistance to the landlord, which in turn could prove helpful to his clients. The key to the worker's effectiveness was that he was always open to the side of the landlord's ambivalence that ran counter to the strong forces of resistance to accepting the worker's help. As long as workers do not view the system as completely closed, one-dimensional, and without ambivalence, they can employ all of the helpful skills identified thus far.

The earlier example concerning the housing system raised another area of concern for the agency. Mrs. Belanger was one example of a client experiencing problems with public housing. However, many poor people in town who were not clients of the agency also had these problems. This worker had invested a great deal of time in this case, something that clearly would not be possible for every case on a worker's caseload, let alone the larger population. What would happen to a Mrs. Belanger who did not have a worker-advocate? In this way, the individual example of the problem facing Mrs. Belanger raised for the agency and its professional staff the general problem of housing for the poor. Almost every individual case raises some issue of public policy. Although workers cannot tackle all such issues at one time, they have a responsibility to deal with some of them. In this agency, a social policy committee was established to provide leadership in identifying and developing staff programs for dealing with the social policy implications of the problems facing individual clients. Next in this chapter, we explore this aspect of the professional's dual responsibility for both clients' private troubles and society's public issues.

# Professional Impact on the System

**EP 2.1.8a**

In the rest of the chapter we discuss ways in which social workers can have professional impact on policies and services within their own and other agencies and institutions as well as on broader social policies that affect clients. We also examine how social workers can bring about positive change in the interprofessional relationships within a setting and between settings. Illustrations of social workers attempting to influence larger systems, professional teams, and so on will demonstrate the functional role of mediation that lies at the core of the interactional model.

The term *professional impact* is defined in this chapter as the activities of social workers designed to effect changes in the following two areas:

1. Policies and services in their own agency and other agencies and institutions, as well as broader social policies that affect clients

2. The work culture that influences interstaff relationships within their own agency and with other agencies and institutions

This breakdown is somewhat analogous to the division cited earlier between the content of the work and the process (way of working).

Interest in the first area emerges directly from the worker's practice experience. As workers address the concerns of individual clients, they become aware of general problems affecting categories of clients. For example, in our recent illustration, the worker saw that Mrs. Belanger's particular difficulty was a specific example of the general problem of inadequate public housing. The worker's attempt to heighten his agency's interest in the problem of housing and his efforts to influence housing policies as part of his role as agency worker and as a member of a professional association are examples of professional impact on the agency, community institutions, and social policies. Similarly, a worker may point out, to the agency administration, an agency policy that negatively affects service to his clients; this is also an attempt to have professional impact within the system.

The second arena for professional impact is the work culture that exists within the agency staff system and between staff members of different agencies. When dealing with clients, workers constantly meet and interact with other professionals. Services to clients are directly affected by how well interdependent staff members work with one another.

The staff system in an agency develops a culture similar to that of a group. The barriers to the effective development of staff culture are also similar. In fact, my observations of staff systems have indicated that difficulties between staff members often occupy the greatest portion of staff time and energy. When one asks staff members what their prime source of frustration is (particularly in large and complex systems and especially if the staff is interdisciplinary), they usually answer, "Other staff." Similar problems often exist between staff members of different agencies within the community that are supposed to be working in partnership to meet clients' needs. Some clients suffer because workers in two settings are no longer talking to each other. Efforts by staff members to improve interstaff relationships and to create a more productive culture for work constitute the second area for professional impact.

In addition to providing direct service to clients, then, helping professionals have a functional responsibility for attempting constructive impact on these two major areas—policies and services, and the work culture of the system. Of course, a worker cannot deal with every social policy, program, or staff interactional issue that emerges from the work; indeed, merely identifying all of the concerns would be a major task. Nevertheless, a worker can tackle a limited number of issues, one at a time. For instance, a group of colleagues can begin working on an issue even though it may take months or even years to resolve. Recall from Part II that the process of taking a problem and breaking it down into smaller parts (partializing) and then attacking the problem by taking a first step, followed by a second, and so on, is helpful for clients. This same process is also useful for tackling questions of professional impact.

## Factors That Make Professional Impact Difficult

Nonetheless, attempting professional impact is not easy. Let us review some of the factors that can make it hard. In addition to the magnitude of the problems, workers have to deal with many of their own feelings about change. Workers too often feel helpless, viewing themselves as incapable of exerting meaningful influence. Our socialization experiences have generally encouraged us to conform to social structures. Families, schools, peer groups, and work settings do not always encourage individual initiative. Although all systems have a profound stake in encouraging members to differentiate themselves and to make contributions by challenging the system and asserting their individuality, neither the system nor the members always recognize this need, let alone act on it. Encouraging members to be an integrated part of the system is an important imperative; however, the system often achieves this at the expense of individual initiative. Efforts to integrate individuals can develop system norms that encourage conformity.

*System Resistance and the Precontemplation Stage* Given such life experiences, many workers tend to view taking responsibility for professional impact as a major change in their relationship to systems in general and to people in authority in particular. Even if workers are willing to strive for social change, experiences in agencies often discourage any further efforts. When workers face resistance to their first attempts, they often fail to recognize the agency's potential for change and give up.

The same worker who skillfully deals with resistance from a client, understanding that resistance is a central part of the change process, forgets this insight when dealing with the agency system. A worker who understands the importance of recognizing the precontemplation stage of change for clients may ignore this and immediately move into the action stage when the agency or setting is not ready. If workers remember that agencies are dynamic systems, open to change but also simultaneously resistant, then an initial rebuff does not necessarily mean closure to the worker's effort. Change may require persistence on the worker's part. Timing is also important. Like individuals and groups, agencies grow and change over time. An attempt to deal with a problem at one point may be blocked, but the agency might welcome the same effort at a later stage in the agency's development.

Persistence is important, and a willingness to keep working on a problem even if initial work is to no avail can make the difference in bringing about change. In a workshop I conducted for administrators on supervision and management, one administrator asked me if I had ever heard of the "rule of three." Intrigued, I asked for elaboration. He replied that:

> The first time someone raises an issue there are so many on your plate you don't really listen. If they raise the issue a second time, then you listen but you

may not do anything about it. If they come back a third time you need to pay attention and see if something can be done about it.

He went on to say that most staff do not come back a second time, and very few a third.

In short, although good administration would involve listening the first time, given the reality of large, complex, often-challenged system, coming back a third time may be the only way to have an impact and achieve change.

***Fear of Retribution*** In many situations, workers are simply afraid to assert themselves. If the agency culture has discouraged previous efforts, or if workers feel they will be viewed as "troublemakers" and that their jobs may be on the line, then they will be reluctant to raise questions about services or policies. In some cases, such as extreme defensiveness of administrators or political pressures on the agency, these fears are well founded. Workers in such situations have to decide for themselves, in light of their personal situations and their feelings about the professional ethical issues involved in the problem, whether they are willing to take the risk. If an effort to bring about change is risky in a particular setting, then workers would be wise to gather allies before they try.

***Risking Tenure When Challenging the University Administration*** While I have advocated these views over the years in my teaching and writing, I have done so from a relatively safe position as a tenured faculty member in a university. Tenure is designed to create the freedom to take risks in teaching, research, and participation in university governance. Many years ago, while acting as chair of the Faculty Council in a university whose employment I left a number of years ago, all of my theories, practice principles, and skills related to professional impact were put to the test over an issue of academic freedom. After exhausting all avenues of negotiation, the Faculty Council faced the need to release a controversial report. When I received a letter from the university administration containing a thinly veiled threat to revoke my tenure and fire me if I proceeded, I felt the full impact of the risks involved in attempting to confront an unyielding system. The Faculty Council report was issued without execution of the threat. Although my position on the responsibility of the social worker to improve her or his system has not changed, this experience has reminded me why acting is not possible in some situations.

***Stereotyped Views of Administration*** In other situations, workers remain uninvolved because they hold preconceived notions about the agency or setting administration, not because any actual experience in the agency has led them to fear reprisal. Nonetheless, trying to make a professional impact often requires courage. Lack of time also greatly affects a worker's ability to challenge the system. Some agencies demand impossible caseloads; in such circumstances, becoming involved in agency or social change seems completely unrealistic. However, simply dealing with the working situation would be a first effort at systemic change. Often, outside organizations such as professional associations or unions are the best mediums for effecting such changes.

In summary, the complexity and magnitude of issues tend to discourage professional impact efforts. Workers' general feelings about asserting themselves, as well as specific experiences in agencies, may act as deterrents. Fear of losing their jobs or experiencing other retribution may also be an obstacle to involvement. Finally, unrealistically high caseloads may obstruct workers' attempts at professional impact.

# From Individual Problems to Social Action

**EP 2.1.10h**

**EP 2.1.5c**

In developing his position on the function of the social work profession, Schwartz (1969) argues that the worker must be concerned with both the specific problems faced by the client and the social issues raised by those problems. Objecting to a professional trend of splitting these two concerns, so that some professionals deal only with the problems of the individual (clinicians) while others focus solely on problems of social change (activists), he argues that every professional has a responsibility for addressing both concerns. He cites C. Wright Mills (1959) as one who refused to accept this dichotomy between individual concerns and issues of policy:

> In our own time, C. Wright Mills has seen most clearly into the individual-social connections identified with social struggle. He pointed up the distinction between what he called the "personal troubles of milieu" and the "public issues of social structure," and noted that trouble is a private matter, while issue is a public one. Most important, he stressed that each must be stated in the terms of the other, and of the interaction between the two. (Schwartz, 1969, p. 37)

Schwartz points out that splitting these two worker responsibilities is impossible if "we understand that a private trouble is simply a specific example of a public issue and that a public issue is made up of many private troubles" (Schwartz, 1969, p. 37). Recognizing that agencies and social institutions can be complex and ambivalent, he suggests the worker's function should be to act as a "third force" or a "hedge against the system's own complexity" (p. 37).

> Where . . . such a function originates within the agency itself, the image is that of a built-in monitor of the agency's effectiveness and a protection against its own rigidities. From such a position, the social worker moves to strengthen and reinforce both parties in the client-agency relationship. With the client—and with mutual aid systems of clients—the worker offers the agency service in ways designed to help them reach out to the system in stronger and more assertive ways, generalizing from their private experiences to agency policy wherever possible and avoiding the traps of conformity and inertia. In many instances, the activity thus produced is similar to that desired by the advocates—except that the movement is towards the service, and the workers are interested in the process rather than having lost faith in it. With the system—colleagues, superiors and other disciplines—the worker feeds in his direct experience with the struggles of his clients, searches out the staff stake in reaching and innovating, and brings administration wherever possible into direct contact with clients reaching for new ways of being served. (p. 38)

Earlier in this chapter, we saw several examples of workers helping clients reach out to the system "in stronger and more assertive ways." The following examples show the worker raising general issues with the system that result from his or her experience with clients.

## Illustrations of Agency Change

The worker who is alive to the dynamic tension between clients' needs and the agency service will look for opportunities to generalize from direct practice experience to policy issues. Noticing a particular problem emerging regularly in the caseload may signal a need for modification in agency service. For example, one worker who dealt with clients who were parents of young unmarried mothers noted the strain that the parents seemed to feel. When she shared her observations with other workers in her department, a highly successful group was developed for these clients. Several illustrations of this process follow.

***Hospital Emergency Room Service*** For a hospital worker, repeated comments from patients in her ward group about the strain of their first contact in the emergency room (as in lack of attention for hours, which heightened their anxiety and that of their relatives, and difficulty in getting information) led her to explore the problems with the emergency room staff. The record of the start of this work follows.

> I asked for a meeting with the head nurse of Emergency. I met Ms. Thomas at the end of her shift, and I commented on how tired she looked. She told me it had been a particularly rough day complicated by two car accidents with four victims. I acknowledged that I could see it was really hectic and thanked her for taking some time to talk with me. I explained that I had been meeting with ward groups on 2 East and that a common theme had been patients complaining about their entry into the hospital through the emergency room.
>
> I told her I was raising this because I thought she would want to know about the problems and also I wanted to better understand the difficulty from the staff's point of view so I could handle this issue when it arose at meetings. Ms. Thomas seemed irritated at my statements, stiffened physically, and said she and her staff didn't have time to sit and talk to patients the way social workers did.

**Practice Points:**   Although the worker expressed some early empathy for the head nurse and phrased the opening statements in as nonjudgmental way as she could, the immediate response was defensiveness. Having prepared for this, the worker immediately addressed this response and clarified an offer of help.

> I quickly reassured her that I was not coming down to criticize her or her staff. I told her that I had worried that she would misinterpret my intentions, and I thought that she had done just that. Would she give me a chance to explain? I said, "I realize it's no picnic down here, and part of the reason I stopped in was to see if there was any way social service could be of more help. Working under pressure the way you do is rough." Ms. Thomas seemed to relax a bit, and I asked how I might be able to help. She said she thought it would be helpful to have a social worker around more often. I told her that might be one way. I wondered if we could arrange a meeting with the other staff members where I could share the feedback and get their reactions. I had no set ideas yet but perhaps if we put our heads together, we could come up with some. She agreed, and we set a time to meet.

**Practice Points:**   The worker's directness and statement of purpose helped to clarify the boundaries for the discussion. She responded directly to the indirect cues of defensiveness by sharing her own concerns. By acknowledging the real difficulties and offering to examine how she, in her function as social worker, might help, the worker quickly changed the situation from one staff member criticizing another to one in which two staff members, each with their own function, carry on the work of using patient feedback to examine their services. The meeting that followed was successful, with staff members telling the social worker about the difficulties they were facing. In addition, they identified changes they could make in response to the patient feedback. The worker, for her part, developed an open-ended group in a quiet corner of the waiting room for waiting patients and relatives. The group met for half an hour at midmorning to allow patients and relatives to ask questions and to deal with some of their anxieties about the emergency situation. Both staff and patients found the group to be helpful.

At a later date, the worker suggested that occasional meetings be held with patients, before they left the hospital, to discuss their experiences in the emergency room and to provide feedback for hospital staff. The bimonthly meetings proved to be effective. Both the social worker and the other staff members in Emergency approached other parts of the hospital to enlist their aid when required. For example, a trial program was established with young volunteers to run a children's group in the adjacent outpatient clinic waiting area to address the problem of bored children roaming the halls.

**Practice Summary.**   In both the case of the group for parents of unwed mothers (described earlier in the chapter when a worker noted the clients' common needs and worked with colleagues to develop the group) and the example of the emergency room problems, a sense of dual responsibility for dealing with both the specific problems and the policy issues led the workers to take their first steps. In these examples, the workers made use of direct client feedback in their efforts to influence service. Sometimes the feedback is more indirect, so that the worker must examine the relationship between client problems and agency service closely to observe the connections. In such situations, again, the worker can apply some of the dynamics used to understand processes in the group and family. For example, earlier chapters pointed out how deviant group members may be signaling a problem in the group-as-a-whole. Problems in a system, such as irregular or "deviant" behavior by groups of clients, may also be providing an indirect form of feedback.

*Rehabilitation Institution for Paraplegics*  One example from a number of years ago of using principles from group work to understand more complex systems is drawn from a rehabilitation institution for paraplegic patients. I was providing consultation to the staff at the center when this problem was raised by one group leader. The institution had a rule against patients going home on weekends, because of a government policy that paid for a patient only on days they slept at the hospital. Systematic work by the staff and administration, including organizing feedback by patients to government officials, led to a change in the policy, and weekend passes were authorized. Three months after implementation of the new policy, the administrator called in the worker to raise a problem. He pointed out that patients were returning to the hospital with serious bedsores and that if this continued, he would have to suspend the pass program. Before instituting such a change, however, he asked the worker to meet with the patients' council to discuss the issue. The administrator had been criticized before when he had instituted changes without patient consultation and was thus hoping to avoid another confrontation.

The following excerpt is from the worker's meeting with the patient council.

WORKER: Dr. Mansfield met with me and told me that many patients are returning with bedsores. He is deeply concerned about this and feels he may have to revoke the weekend-pass policy.

LOUIS: (With great anger) He can't do that. If he takes away that privilege, we will wheel down to his office, and he'll have a sit-in on his hands.

JOHN: Who does he think he is anyway? We fought hard for that right, and he can't take it away. (Others murmur in angry agreement.)

WORKER: I can understand why you are so angry. The pass is really important to you. It's important to see your families. But, tell me, I don't understand: Why is it so many people come back with bedsores? (Long silence)

TERRY: (Speaking slowly and staring at the floor as he does) Here at the center the nurses turn us in our beds all the time. When we get home, our families do not.

WORKER: (Suddenly understanding) And you are too ashamed to ask them, isn't that it?

**Practice Points:** In the discussion that followed, the group members talked poignantly about their feelings concerning their newfound dependency. Many felt they had lost their "manhood" and were ashamed to need help suddenly for going to the bathroom and for turning in their beds. So, they simply did not ask for help. As they discussed their families' reactions, it emerged that their wives were often too embarrassed to ask what kind of help they needed. It soon became clear to the worker that the problem of bedsores was an indirect communication of the need for an important new area of service: addressing the issue of dependency, patients' and family members' feelings about it, and how to handle it. The worker's next step was to ask for a meeting of the various department heads so she could report back on her session with the council.

WORKER: A most interesting issue was raised when I talked to the patients about the bedsores, and I wanted to share it with you to get your reactions and ideas.

After the worker recounted the discussion, the staff fell silent as the department heads thought about the implications of this feedback for their areas. The worker suggested it might be helpful to explore this question of dependency as it was handled throughout the institution and to see if some special attention could be paid to the problem.

**Practice Summary.** Once again, the worker took the stance of involving her professional colleagues in mutual discussion of an issue relevant to their work. From this discussion emerged a plan for raising the issue in the various departments and developing new services to deal with the problem, such as groups for relatives of recently paralyzed patients that would specifically focus on their reactions to the accident and their questions about their ongoing relationships, particularly how to handle the feelings of dependency they were sure to encounter. Programs for patients were also developed, and staff training implications were discussed. Because the worker was open to the idea that her setting was a dynamic system and that change was possible, she could enlist the aid of her colleagues to set important changes in motion.

***Sexuality in a Home for the Aged*** Another example in which a social work student's mind-set dramatically affected how she described a problem is taken from a home for the aged. At a staff conference, a ward aide raised a problem concerning one patient who was regularly masturbating in public places. This was affecting both staff and other residents, and the social work student was asked to speak to her about the problem. The discussion at the staff meeting was brief, and the discomfort of staff that had noticed this behavior and had been at a loss as to what to do was evident. Not happy about having to see the woman, the student was not sure what she could do, but after some discussion with her supervisor, the student began to see that her discomfort, and the discomfort of the staff, was related to the fact that sexual issues were never raised at the home. In fact, the staff system operated as if all of its residents were past the point of sexual interest. This had a great deal to do with the staff's view of the aged and their embarrassment about considering the question at all. The result was lack of attention to the real sexual needs of residents. This was, in many ways, a form of institutional oppression. In entering the institution, the adult resident was cut off from opportunities to engage in any form of sexual activity.

The student began to check out her hunch that this was a signal of a larger issue. When she approached various staff members and raised her feelings, she was amazed to find that she had unlocked several major issues that the staff had not addressed. Staff members were uncomfortable about this area and had not known how to raise the question. For example, there were elderly senile men who continually tried to get female residents and staff into bed with them. Staff joked about these occurrences, although their real feelings reflected discomfort and the joking was actually a form of flight. After a preliminary survey, the student returned to the meeting with her findings. The result was a decision by staff to develop a survey to identify the problem as seen by staff and residents, to discuss ways to deal with the feelings of the staff, and to develop new approaches for handling the issue with residents. The staff attended a workshop, run by outside consultants, on geriatric sexuality. The student social worker's sense of the connection between "private trouble" and a "public issue" opened up important work in a formerly taboo area.

## Professional Impact and Interstaff Relationships

**EP 2.1.3b**
**EP 2.1.3c**

The second area of professional impact concerns the work culture that influences staff relationships both within and between agencies. This is partially analogous to the "process" aspect of the helping relationship, but I am referring here to the way in which staff members relate to one another. Let me clarify several points. First, I am concerned with working relationships. Staff members need to deal with one another effectively while pursuing their own jobs. Personal friendships may develop within a staff system, and they may enhance the working relationship, but it is not necessary to be friendly with a colleague in order to work well together. Poor interstaff working relationships usually have a strong negative effect on the provision of services to clients. For example, an interesting early research project by Stanton and Schwartz (1954) indicated an association between staff tensions and evidence of psychiatric symptoms in patients in a psychiatric hospital.

Consider as another example, the interstaff relationships in a residential center for teenagers, which are usually out in the open in such a setting. Most of the residents have come from dysfunctional families and the last thing they need to deal with is dysfunctional staff. Conflicts between the psychologists and residential aids or the ongoing conflicts between the night shift and the day shift are endemic in my experience. In addition to the impact on residents, the emotional drain on staff members and the amount of time and energy expended on such issues can be extraordinary.

Second, the responsibility for strengthening staff working relationships and for dealing with obstacles that block effective collaboration rests with supervisory and administrative staff. If we think of the staff system as a group, then we can use the discussion in Part II to develop a model of the supervising and administrative functions. In workshops I have conducted for supervisors and administrative staff, I have helped participants analyze problems in the staff system by using many of the constructs and models described earlier. For example, staff systems often have a member who plays the same role as the deviant in the client group. In larger systems, as we have seen, a whole department or section may take on the scapegoat role, with the system avoiding its problems by projecting them onto its weakest part.

Through analysis of process recordings, one can identify all the skills described thus far—contracting, elaborating, empathy, demand for work, and the rest—as useful for staff management functions. Helping staff members develop a positive working culture is thus analogous to dealing with the intimacy theme described earlier in this book. A discussion of the use of this model in supervision and staff management can be found in my supervision text, *Interactional Supervision,* 3rd edition (2010). Although further discussion of supervision issues lie beyond the scope of this book, understand that the functional responsibility for dealing with problems in the staff system rests with the supervisors and administrative staff. Nonetheless, in spite of this general position, each member of a staff system can contribute to effective staff interaction. This is part of his or her responsibility for positive professional impact.

## The Agency as a Social System

In one of my earlier publications, I described the agency as a social system and argued for the importance of paying attention to interstaff relationships:

> The complex organism called "agency" consists of two major subsystems: staff members and clients. The client subsystem is further divided into smaller units, such as families, groups, wards, cottages. The staff subsystem is subdivided along functional lines. We have administrators, social workers, supervisors, clerical staff, and so on. In order to analyze a part of a complex system we must set it off with a boundary—an artificial divider which focuses our attention. In social work, it has been the client subsystem. We study family dynamics, ward behavior, group process, and so forth. While this is necessary, there is the danger that we can take this boundary too seriously. We examine our client interactions as if they were in a "closed" system in which interactions with other subsystems did not have significant impact. For example, we will try to understand the deviant behavior of some hospital patients as their problem rather than seeing this behavior as a signal of a problem in hospital care. Or we will describe our clients as "unmotivated" when they stop coming to our agencies rather than interpreting their dropping out as "voting with their feet" against poor service.
>
> If we view our agencies as open, dynamic systems in which each subgroup is somewhat affected by the movement of the other subgroups with which they come in contact, we cannot isolate our clients as discrete entities. Instead, we must see the total interaction between clients and staff as an essential part of the helping process. In turn, to the degree that staff interactions have a direct impact on the agency service, they must also be placed on our agenda. The way in which staff members' relations affect the "productivity" of the agency is thus directly connected to issues of client service. (Shulman, 1970, p. 22)

Staff relations can profoundly affect service. The cultural barriers that prevent open discussion of problems in the staff system are similar to those described in the chapters on group work. In any complex social system, conflicts of interest, hidden agendas, residues of bad feelings, misunderstood communications, and so forth are bound to arise; nonetheless, the system treats discussion of these concerns as taboo. The organizational theorist Argyris (1964) describes how the formal organization stresses "cognitive reality" (as opposed to expressions of real feelings), unilateral control in human relations, and the artificial separation of "process and task." He points out how this interferes with genuine interpersonal feedback; openness to new ideas, feelings, and values; owning one's own views and tolerating others; experimentation and risk taking—all factors that vitally affect the productivity of an organization. Organizations continue to function in spite of these problems, operating under what Argyris calls a pseudo-effectiveness that corresponds somewhat with the previously described illusion of work. The most important conversations about the real problems in the system then take place in the halls, over lunch, or within subgroups gathering over drinks on Friday afternoons to complain about staff members they find impossible to work with. Obviously, client service must suffer under such conditions.

Recognition of the importance of the way in which staff members work with one another has grown. For example, Braeger and Holloway (1978) wrote an excellent book dealing with this area of practice. They focused on the problems involved in effecting "changes from below" and explored forces affecting stability and change, the initial assessment stage, and the change process itself. They stressed, as do I, the importance of developing "allies" in the process so that the voice of the social worker is strengthened by others.

## Problems Associated with "Process-Focused" Staff Meetings

In contrast, agency efforts to deal with such problems sometimes use approaches borrowed from the "sensitivity training" movement, such as weekend retreats, encounter groups, and ongoing T-groups (training groups). Outside organizational development experts are often enlisted to assist staff in developing more authentic communications. Under some circumstances, these efforts can pay important dividends, but often they create more problems than they solve. Staff members may be stimulated in the artificial atmosphere, created by the trainer, to share thoughts and feelings with which other staff members or administrators cannot cope. When the session has ended and the trainer has left, the ongoing repercussions of this honesty can deepen rifts and intensify bad feelings. In addition, staff members who may have felt "burned" by the experience are confirmed in their views that any attention to process is destructive, and their resistance to any form of open discussions of interstaff relationships is heightened. Periodic opportunities for a general review of the working relationships in a setting can be helpful only if the setting is already operating at a sophisticated level of open communication on an ongoing basis.

## Dealing with Process in Relation to a Problem or Issue

Because most staff systems do not yet operate on that level, an alternative process is needed. Rather than attempting a full-scale analysis of the working relationships in a system—a threatening process at any time—focusing on specific problems directly related to service issues is often more helpful. By this I mean that the discussion should not deal with the question "How do we work together?" but rather "How do we work together on this particular case or in this area of agency or client concern?" This discussion needs to be built into the ongoing operation of an agency, as opposed to being reserved for special retreats or meetings. By keeping the discussion related to specific issues, one can avoid the trap of becoming personal, as in staff members dealing with each other's "personalities." Agency staff meetings are not "therapy" sessions, and staff members have a right to relate to each other in their own unique and hopefully respectful ways. The only issues appropriate for discussion are those directly concerned with the business of the agency. It is precisely the fear that sessions will turn into personal encounter groups that generates resistance by staff members to a discussion of process.

Focusing on specific issues on an ongoing basis allows a staff to develop the skills needed to be honest with one another at their own pace. As staff find that risking their honest thoughts and feelings produces effective results, they gradually lower their defenses, building on their first experiences to increase their capacity for authentic communication. As stated earlier, this process is greatly facilitated when administrative and supervisory staffs are skilled at helping staff members deal with one another. Of course, this is not always the case. (I have addressed this issue from the perspective of the supervisor and manager in another publication, *Interactional Supervision*, 3rd edition [Shulman, 2010].) In either situation, staff members can develop their own skills in relating to others individually and as a group in order to improve the agency culture for work. Although strong leadership speeds the process, change can begin anywhere in the system, as the examples that follow will show.

These examples present several common situations faced by social workers. In the first, a staff member tries to sort out her relationship with another staff member who shares work with her regarding a particular client. In the second, a unit in a large organization takes a first step at opening up communications in a system and is surprised to find that this leads to major changes. In the third example, staff members in one system face their responsibility for developing a better working relationship with staff in a related agency. This final example deals with the problem of discovering that a particular client is being served by a multitude of agencies and workers, none of which ever talk to each other. Some of you will find these problems familiar.

***Interdisciplinary Collaboration in Work with a Client*** A common area of tension between staff members occurs when different workers deal with the same client. The strains are often intensified if the workers come from different disciplines, such as a conflict between a social worker and a psychiatrist. One variation of this struggle appears in the form of a contest over "who owns the client." In larger systems, one group of professionals often becomes quite concerned if they believe another group is impinging on their role. Status is often at stake. More recently, with cost-containment efforts in full force, loss of a professional responsibility can threaten the continued employment of a whole professional group.

In one example, when nurses began to lead ward groups in a hospital, other professionals (social workers and psychologists) felt their traditional territory threatened. This type of conflict has emerged with new force more recently, as the impact of managed care has led various professional groups to attempt to carve out their "territories." In this specific case, efforts to discuss the questions of role in order to resolve the conflict failed because of the vagueness and generality used by the two professional groups when asked to describe what they did.

Often, one cannot attend an interdisciplinary meeting and hear a single sentence that does not contain jargon. When a professional group is clear about its function and the way in which that function is implemented in a particular setting and with particular clients, members feel much less defensive and do not need to resort to jargon. Interprofessional conflicts over territory often signal lack of functional clarity within each group and a lack of supervisory or administrative leadership. A first step toward resolving such conflicts is for each professional group to develop its own sense of role and then present it—not with reams of jargon, but by sharing specific examples of their work in action. In this way, different groups can become more aware of their similarities and differences concerning what they do with clients. Division of labor within a system can emerge from a joint discussion of what the clients' needs are and how each group can play the most effective role in meeting those needs in the context of the agency or setting service.

***Conflict Between a Social Worker and a Doctor: Who Owns the Client?*** Give-and-take can begin within the same staff, as members of different professional groups clarify how they will work together with specific clients. In the example that follows, a social worker dealing with Cindy, a 17-year-old girl attending a hospital clinic, is concerned about the lack of cooperation between the doctor on the case and herself. She feels he does not respect her contribution to the work, a complaint often voiced in interdisciplinary settings. Rather than simply complaining to colleagues, the worker confronts the doctor with the issue:

> I was alarmed that Cindy would cut off all contact with the clinic and thus a potential source of help. I was also concerned with how the doctor viewed the case, what his intentions were, and if he felt that my role and opinions in the case were relevant.
>
> I confronted him with these concerns and initially he reacted defensively, stating that he felt she needed an experienced psychiatrist and not a social worker. I replied that perhaps he was correct but that I felt at present she was having enough difficulty in accepting and receiving the aid of doctors, social workers, and school counselors, let alone a psychiatrist. (She had expressed some very strong and negative feelings about psychiatrists.) He calmed down, and I empathized with his difficulty in dealing with her during the interview.

**Practice Points:**   The social worker's direct confrontation (her words) on the issue (and we don't know what her tone was) created a defensive response. Instead of responding to the doctor's comment about a social worker's ability to help with her own defensiveness, by clarifying her concern and recognizing his feelings, the initial defensiveness is modified.

> I then attempted to get some clarification of our roles in relation to the client's treatment program. We discussed at length where we might cross each other up and confuse her and decided that we would consult one another before tackling certain problem areas involved in the case.

**Practice Summary.**   The important result of this discussion was not that the two professionals no longer experienced conflicts in their work but that they began to develop a working relationship in which they could anticipate conflicts or raise them with each other more quickly. The worker's taking the first step of raising the question lifted the strong taboo against direct discussion in this sensitive area. If staff members begin joint work with the understanding that there is bound to be some conflict and confusion, then they will be more likely to establish a maintenance system for early self-correction. Recall the importance, in coleading groups (discussed in earlier chapters), of honest communications between the coleaders.

***Interdepartmental Communications in a Large System*** A common problem in large systems is for subgroups of professionals, such as departments, to blame all the problems in the system on other departments. One group of staff members might even be identified as scapegoats or serve the "deviant member" function. Because of rules or politeness, as well as the fact that each department has some stake in maintaining the status quo, no formal discussion of the problems and the "problem" department follows. The talk in the informal system often consists of speculations on how things would be much better "if only the other department straightened out."

When the problem department is expressing a widely held concern, then its members will continue to bring the problem to the system's attention through indirect means. However, when this department finally starts to affect other departments directly, the response is often to deal just with the content of the issue. This is a mistake: Even if the specific issue is resolved, it will be replaced with another issue if the underlying problems are not addressed.

***Impacting the Staff System in a Residential Setting*** To illustrate this process and the way in which staff can use a specific confrontation to deal with the larger question of staff relations, I shall draw on an experience I had, early in my academic career, as a full-time field instructor for a school of social work (Shulman, 1968). In this case I was working with a unit of first-year social work MSW students placed in a residential institution for adolescents diagnosed in those days as "mildly retarded."

After 3 months in the setting, the students and I had observed many practices with which we disagreed, particularly the control procedures used by the cottage staff. The cottage life department was responsible for supervising residents and for maintaining the rules of the institution. The staff in this department was not professionally trained as residential counselors, and in fact most came with minimal education or from the army or law enforcement. They had a serious communication gap with the professionals (social workers, psychologists, educators, counselors). Informally, the professionals often expressed distaste for some of the more restrictive policies, but they never raised objections in formal meetings. Our unit went along with this state of affairs, content to carve out our area of service while ignoring the general problems.

This quasi-equilibrium was upset when a cottage supervisor refused to allow group members to attend a session led by one of my social work students. Some of the residents were on restriction (a punishment for behavioral offenses), and the cottage staff viewed the club group as a reward. The supervisor informed my student that he could only see his members one at a time and that he was to use the session to "give them a good lecture on how to behave." Our first reaction at our unit meeting the next day was shock at being instructed how to do our job. After reflection, however, and by analyzing the staff system of which we were a part, we began to see that this incident was a symptom of a larger problem of lack of communication between departments.

We could have easily "won the battle" by gaining permission to see our group members on our terms, because the administration wanted to maintain federally funded student-training programs at the institution. However, we would have further alienated cottage staff and would probably have found our program subverted in indirect ways. We chose, instead, to attack the larger communication problem, using this incident as a specific example. We clearly saw that a split in the institution between the training and therapy services formed a major obstacle to work.

The combination of overlapping boundaries and underdeveloped communications resulted in areas of conflict with limited opportunities for resolution. In such a situation, staff frustration grew, and a process of withdrawal had begun. Instead of increasing lines of communications, staff members made those that were open less meaningful by avoiding discussion of conflict issues. Cottage life staff, which bore the brunt of implementing the control function in the institution, became the convenient target for criticism. It became more difficult to mobilize the potential within the staff to make those adjustments that would keep the system in a "steady state." The most serious consequence of these problems was that the feedback essential for system adjustment was blocked.

Our strategy for action involved three lines of approach. First, I requested permission to attend a weekly meeting of department heads on the training side of the institution. This was the first formal bridging of the therapy-training gap and provided a forum for the discussion of conflict issues. By disregarding the taboo against real talk, I could raise concerns directly, and the resultant discussions served to clear up mutual misconceptions. It became clear that staff in all departments were reacting to people in other areas as if they were stereotypes, which led to consistently missed communications. Face-to-face contact made dismissing each other out of hand more difficult for staff. As communications opened up, the interdependence of department heads began to emerge, and the group became an arena for mutual aid. Members found they could help each other with their problems, particularly those in relation to the administration.

I should point out that developing relationships with other departments in the informal system of the institution also proved to be important. A recreation room contained two ping-pong tables, and a daily lunchtime ping-pong game had existed for a time. Participants lined up to play and the winner continued to play each participant in turn. It happened that some of the best ping-pong players were also department heads—the very same department heads I was meeting with in the formal system. I was also a good player, having worked part-time in my undergraduate college ping-pong room. I'm not sure if ping pong or the joint meetings contributed to the development of the good working relationships—perhaps it was both.

In a second line of work, each of the five students in the unit requested weekly meetings with respective cottage attendants to help bridge the communication gap. One result of these meetings was that students obtained a more balanced perspective on the problems faced by cottage attendants in dealing with residents. They found that their stereotypes of the attendants, developed by hearing only the residents' point of view and hardened by the general attitude toward cottage staff held in the institution, quickly faded as cottage attendants shared their "binds" in trying to do their jobs.

Students also took turns coming in on a weekend to get a sense of the issues facing staff and residents at these less structured times when other professionals were not around. As the students began to listen and to understand, cottage staff dramatically changed their views about student social workers. As the students better understood the realities of the attendants' jobs, they were perceived as "having their feet on the ground." This outreach effort continued in other areas of the system. For example, to gain a greater appreciation of the problems in the vocational training areas, students took turns alongside residents helping prepare meals or working in the center's laundry. These steps were greatly appreciated by staff in these areas.

The third line of work had the most dramatic impact. In an effort to break down the isolation between departments, we tried to improve communications with the social service department itself. I outlined the problem in a meeting with the head of social service, as indicated in my notes:

> I explained to Mrs. Paul that I was concerned because the students felt they were an enclave in the institution and that they were even cut off from social service. I told her that we felt that we had contributed to this isolation by not attending meetings and by not raising these feelings earlier. I asked if a meeting could be held with the department staff to discuss this and to see what might be done to rectify the problem. Mrs. Paul told me she was glad I raised this, because she had always felt uncomfortable about the lack of connection but wasn't sure about what to do to correct it. She said she was always afraid to raise it. I asked her why, and she indicated that she didn't feel she could make demands on the unit as she

would her staff, so she didn't want to seem to be pushing us for more involvement. I laughed and pointed out how we were both worried about the same thing but afraid to raise it. She agreed that other staff members might feel the same way, and we decided to make it an agenda item at the next social work meeting.

At the meeting, everyone could clear the air, as the staff members and the social work students raised their mutual concerns and discovered several misconceptions about each other's attitudes toward student involvement. They then discussed specific strategies for more meaningful student involvement in the work of the department. I generalized the question by pointing out that we felt an estrangement between social services and the rest of the institution, particularly cottage life. As an example, I related our recent experience of a cottage supervisor withholding permission from residents to attend a meeting and shared our beginning efforts to open up better communications. I asked if others felt the same way, and a flood of examples and feelings emerged.

It became clear that we were articulating common feelings held by the social work department members but never expressed. The balance of the meeting consisted of strategizing how we might reach out to the cottage life department to discuss the working relationship between social workers and cottage attendants. We extended an invitation to the head of cottage life and his frontline supervisors to discuss this problem, and we all agreed on a date. As the time approached, word of the meeting spread quickly, and comments in the informal system revealed some clues as to why such a meeting had not taken place before. It was variously described as a "showdown," a "shooting match," and a "confrontation," and all staff members were tense when the meeting time arrived. To our surprise, the heads of all of the other departments also attended the meeting on their own initiative.

Three meetings were held, and those expecting fireworks were not disappointed. Many work issues were aired for the first time, often with great feeling. Interestingly, my attending the training department heads' weekly meetings paid dividends at this point. A beginning working relationship had been developed that led various department heads to offer support when a particular area was under attack, including the activities of my student unit. As we owned up to the ways in which we helped to make the work of others more difficult and as we attempted to be nondefensive, the defensiveness of the other staff members lessened.

The focus of the discussion soon shifted from recrimination to identifying common problems, some needing to be dealt with by the departments and others requiring policy changes by the administration. As the list of concerns was drawn up, it became obvious that so much work was needed we could not even to begin to attack it at this meeting. The group decided to form four task forces to deal with each general category of problems. Line and supervisory staff from each department as well as at least one social work student sat on each task force so that all opinions could be represented in the discussions. In addition, the social work student members offered to serve as "staff" for the committee, keeping minutes of the discussion and performing other such tasks. The group formed a steering committee with a department head or supervisor from each area to monitor the process, and a deadline was set for reports.

At this point the group approached the administration for official support of this ad hoc effort. Some staff members had been concerned that the administrator might not value their efforts to institute change. They had developed a stereotyped view of the administrator as being someone who would object to anything that would disrupt the status quo, but when he was approached, his response was, "I'm always besieged by people telling me about all of the problems. It's a relief to have the staff coming to me with some solutions, for once." A memo to all staff clearly outlined his support for the project. What had begun as our student unit raising questions about our relationship to the social service department had become an institution-wide, formally sanctioned effort to attack long-standing problems. In addition, a new structure was developed that greatly enhanced interdepartmental communication at department head, supervisor, and line staff levels.

Thirty-eight recommendations for changes in policy and structure eventually emerged from the task forces. After line staff in each department approved the reports, the changes were instituted. A sample of the recommendations provides a sense of the range of the topics:

- Establishment of a representative resident council to meet monthly with the superintendent of the institution and department heads.
- Elimination of a "gold-card" system that rated residents on their behavior and controlled their access to the recreation program. This system had been generally described by staff as ineffective.
- A change in the dining room procedures to allow for coed dining.
- Allowing residents to have a degree of choice in selection of on-campus work assignments.
- The expansion of social services into evening and weekend time, when the greatest need was felt by staff and residents.
- The combining of the training and therapy services committee into one committee.

Of course, these changes did not solve all of the problems in the institution. The crucial result was that staff members discovered that they could talk to one another and that doing so might yield positive results. Structural changes (such as a resident council and combining training and therapy committees) would also increase the chances for better ongoing feedback from both staff and residents. Interestingly, and not surprisingly, as staff felt more empowered in the system, they were more open to empowering residents.

Most important, the experience released a flood of staff energy that apathy and a related feeling of hopelessness had suppressed. Staff learned that change could begin anywhere in the system and that they had to risk and invest themselves for those things they really wanted. The lesson was not lost on the social work students or their instructor.

## Impact on Relations with Staff at Other Agencies

While providing services to clients, workers make contact with staff from other private or public agencies working with the same clients. After repeated contact, patterns of staff relationships develop. When positive, these relationships strengthen the cooperation among professionals. When negative, because of either direct or indirect cues of hostility or lack of mutual trust, they act as barriers that can cut a client off from the required service.

***Emergency Services Workers in Conflict with Hospital Staff*** In one example presented at a workshop, emergency service workers described how they had been cut off from using the services of a hospital psychiatric department that was refusing to accept their clients with drug-related psychotic episodes when they brought them to the hospital. Because several workers had undergone similar experiences or had faced hostility from the hospital staff, the agency had written off the hospital as being noncooperative and no longer attempted to use it as a resource. A negative judgment about staff members of another agency thus can quickly become part of the agency culture. New staff members, who have had no experience with the other setting, are warned not even to try. In another illustration of this process, parole officers would not tell their parolees to use a particular government employment service because of past experiences that they felt had indicated a bias against their clients.

When the example of the uncooperative psychiatric service was examined in some detail and the actual conversations between workers and the hospital staff analyzed, it became clear that the workers had approached the hospital staff as if they expected to be rejected. I referred to this in earlier chapters as "looking for trouble and bringing it about." Their aggressiveness in dealing with the nursing staff, for example, was answered with hostility and defensiveness. The nursing staff viewed workers in an equally stereotyped way, and both sides began each encounter ready for a fight.

When I inquired if any efforts had been made, either individually or as an agency, to explore this poor working relationship, I was not surprised to find that the answer was no. The workers sensed the tension and hostility during the encounters, but they never directly reached for it to explore the reason for the difficulty. As a staff group, they had never thought to ask for a meeting with the hospital staff to discuss the obvious difficulties in communication. As often happens, the staff of each setting had decided, in advance, that the situation was hopeless.

Numerous examples of conflict between different staff groups suggest that the root of the problem is in the stress each group experiences in its work. The stress may come from the nature of the clients' problems. For example, dealing with teenagers who have had drug-related psychotic episodes is difficult at best, and the possibility of suicide makes this line of work particularly daunting. Lack of support for frontline workers in these high-stress jobs often leaves them unable to tune in to the feelings and concerns of workers in other settings. The conflict between staff groups often represents what Bion termed the fight-flight syndrome, described earlier in the text, when running from a problem or angry confrontation becomes a maladaptive means of coping with pain. During times of cutbacks in funds and services—so-called "restraint" programs—tensions among overworked, threatened, and unappreciated frontline staff members and their groups escalate. The unfortunate result is that the social services staff groups are cut off from one another just at the time when they need the most support. The cycle can be broken, however, if staff members begin to examine the process systematically rather than viewing the conflicts as personality based.

After the workshop analysis of the example dealing with teenagers and drug abuse, the agency workers held a meeting with the hospital staff. The skills of tuning in, contracting, and the other skills helped the social workers develop a strategy for opening up honest discussion without backing the hospital staff into a corner. Reports from workers after this session indicated that the hospital staff had been equally upset about the relationship with this agency. They had sensed the workers' hostility and particularly the workers' lack of understanding that the hospital was understaffed and somewhat overwhelmed by the cases brought in by the workers. The workers, in turn, shared their problems in dealing with such cases. Many of their problems were similar to those faced by the hospital staff—for example, providing help to a spaced-out youngster, receiving a report of active child abuse, and being expected to be involved in both cases at the same time.

The session resulted in a better delineation of the mutual responsibilities of the two settings and the development of a procedure for handling the immediate problems when either system was under strain. In addition, the groups agreed to cooperate in bringing the staffing problem to the attention of the respective agency administrations and supervisory government bodies. Although the problems were not solved immediately, the hospital and the agency workers were once again open to each other. In the earlier example of the parole officers and the employment agency, a joint meeting resulted in better understanding on both parts about the special problems involved in finding jobs for parolees and the establishment of a special group of workers to handle referrals and to provide a liaison with the parole service.

Clearly, workers can become so overwhelmed by the demands placed on them that they have little patience with problems in other systems. Often at key moments in a workshop dealing with the skills of professional impact, with a common example in front of us, I will ask: "Are you all so overwhelmed by your own stress that you have very little empathy left over for someone else?"

Communication breakdowns lead to the formation of stereotypes, which then become self-fulfilling prophecies. Client service suffers in the end. Workers argue that they do not have time for these efforts to improve working relationships between agencies, yet close analysis reveals that poor communication often results in greater expenditures of time than would be needed in order to face and resolve the problems.

***The "Too Many Cooks . . ." Problem*** Another example of professional impact concerns the common problem of "too many cooks." The following excerpt provides a good illustration. One worker reported an interview with a young mother of six children who was seen by the worker because of her potential for child abuse. After a good contracting interview, the worker tried to arrange a second session, but, much to her amazement, she discovered another problem faced by the mother:

WORKER: I'm glad you found this interview helpful. Can we get together on Friday?
CLIENT: I would love to, but I'm afraid I'm seeing Ted's probation officer Friday morning.
WORKER: OK, how about in the afternoon?
CLIENT: No, I have an appointment with the visiting nurse who is helping me out with my youngest.
WORKER: Would Monday be OK?
CLIENT: I don't know, the homemaker comes then, and the family support worker is here as well.
WORKER: (Beginning to feel a bit frustrated) Can you tell me your schedule for next week, and maybe I can find a time?
CLIENT: Well, Tuesday I'm supposed to see Leslie's psychiatrist at the mental health center, and Wednesday the family court worker wants to speak to me, and . . .
WORKER: My God, when do you have time for yourself?
CLIENT: You know, it's a real problem—but some of these people I have to see, and others are so nice, I don't want to hurt their feelings.
WORKER: Mrs. T, I wonder if all of these people know that you are seeing the others?
CLIENT: Probably not.

**Practice Points:** The problem setting a time to meet quickly reveals a central problem facing the client—that of too many professionals working with the client in an uncoordinated manner. Rather than becoming another one of these, the worker quickly recontracts to offer help in dealing with all of the systems.

**Worker:** Would it help if I tried to call a meeting of all the workers you are seeing, just so we can all find out what is going on with you, and perhaps work out some way to cut down on all of this?

**Client:** Please! Anything would help.

This interview is not unusual. Families with many problems often find themselves involved with such a complicated and intricate system of services that they need a worker just to help them sort it out. This worker called a meeting with the mother in attendance. Everyone was shocked to discover 14 different services and workers involved with the family, some of whom were providing overlapping services. They decided the social worker would serve as key worker for the mother and help coordinate the other services as needed. The group also discussed how the services could use registries better to stay informed of each other's work with the same families. A more recent term emerging for such coordinating activities is "wrap-around services"—referring to a process of wrapping services around a client or family—in which clarification of roles and communication plays an important part.

***Externalizing the Problem: It's Always the Other Person's Fault*** A final example summarizes in a way the process we have been discussing. In my training workshops, when I discuss issues of professional impact, workers usually follow a pattern of response. First, they tend to externalize and place complete blame for the problem on the "others" in the system. When I challenge this, they usually become defensive and angry. Often they claim that I simply "don't understand the particular situation." Detailed examination of the specifics of the interactions often leads to a lowering of defenses, particularly if I can be genuinely empathic with the difficulties involved and the feelings generated in the workers. Recognition that they may have had some part to play in the proceedings often leads to expressions of guilt about past or present experiences that workers feel they could have handled differently. This is followed by a renewed enthusiasm about the possibilities for action.

Situations that seemed hopeless may remain hard to deal with, but some possible next steps are evident. Workers are reassured when they realize that they need only take responsibility for their next steps and that the systems have responsibility for their own. Workers generally want to believe that there is a next step and that they can have some impact. Even though they may fight this idea initially, they would be very disappointed if I agreed with their apparent fatalism. I do not think workers need to be motivated to attempt professional impact on their systems. Rather, they need support for their existing impetus toward action.

# Chapter Summary

The social worker plays an important role in mediating the engagement between her or his client (individual, family, or group) and the systems that are important to them. Examples of mediation between clients and the school, hospital, and housing systems illustrate the two-client concept, in which the worker attempts to work effectively with both the client and representatives of the systems. At times, advocacy and confrontation are necessary strategies for "unfreezing" systems that prove to be unresponsive.

The worker needs to pay attention to opportunities for professional impact both to improve agency and community social policy and to promote better interstaff relationships. In so doing, workers must overcome initial feelings of apathy and hopelessness, avoid being overwhelmed by the enormity of problems, have faith in the potential of systems to change, and use interpersonal skills in improving relationships.

## Related Online Content and Activities

 Visit *The Skills of Helping Individuals, Families, Groups, and Communities*, Seventh Edition, CourseMate website at **www.cengagebrain.com** for learning tools such as glossary terms, links to related websites, and chapter practice quizzes. The website for this chapter also features additional notes from the author.

## Competency Notes

The following is a list of Council on Social Work Education (CSWE) recommended competencies and practice behaviors for social work students defined in Educational Policy and Accreditation Standard (EPAS) and addressed in this chapter.

**EP 2.1.1a** Advocate for client access to the services of social work (p. 604)

**EP 2.1.3b** Analyze models of assessment, prevention, intervention, and evaluation (pp. 605,636)

**EP 2.1.3c** Demonstrate effective oral and written communication in working with individuals, families, groups, organizations, communities, and colleagues (p. 636)

**EP 2.1.4a** Recognize the extent to which a culture's structures and values may oppress, marginalize, alienate, or create or enhance privilege and power (p. 608)

**EP 2.1.4b** Gain sufficient self-awareness to eliminate the influence of personal biases and values in working with diverse groups (p. 608)

**EP 2.1.4c** Recognize and communicate their understanding of the importance of difference in shaping life experiences (p. 608)

**EP 2.1.5a** Understand forms and mechanisms of oppression and discrimination (p. 608)

**EP 2.1.5c** Engage in practices that advance social and economic justice (p. 632)

**EP 2.1.7b** Critique and apply knowledge to understand person and environment (p. 605)

**EP 2.1.8a** Analyze, formulate, and advocate for policies that advance social well-being (P. 629)

**EP 2.1.8b** Collaborate with colleagues and clients for effective policy action (p. 610)

**EP 2.1.9a** Continuously discover, appraise, and attend to changing locales, populations, scientific and technological developments, and emerging societal trends to provide relevant services (p. 606)

**EP 2.1.9b** Provide leadership in promoting sustainable changes in service delivery and practice to improve the quality of social services (p. 608)

**EP 2.1.10h** Initiate actions to achieve organizational goals (P. 632)

**EP 2.1.10k** Negotiate, mediate, and advocate for clients (p. 608)

## CHAPTER SIXTEEN

# Social Work Practice in the Community— Philosophy, Models, Principles, and Practice

In this chapter, we examine the underlying philosophy, models of practice, principles of practice, and the role of the social worker as she or he works with clients in the community. The concept of community will be applied broadly, including neighborhood communities as well as milieu communities (e.g., residential institutions and psychiatric wards). Work with clients in the community is often considered one part of macro practice, in contrast with work with individuals, families, or support groups in a clinical setting, which is usually referred to as micro practice.

Many social work activities fall under the term *macro practice.* For example, a social worker may undertake social policy research designed to influence legislation. The social worker may never actually work directly with clients. This would be an example of what is called indirect macro practice: activities of a social worker on behalf of a community that do not involve direct work with clients. In contrast, working to organize tenants of a housing project to help them influence their housing conditions is an example of direct macro practice: social work that involves direct work with clients in pursuit of community goals and objectives.

This chapter focuses mostly on direct macro practice, with some attention given to indirect activities. The first part of this chapter explores the development of community social work practice and identifies the philosophy underlying this practice as well as the central practice principles. A number of models of community practice are also described. In the second part of this chapter, we return to the phases-of-work framework and provide illustrations of the community social worker in action.

## The Development of Community Social Work Practice

**EP 2.1.5a**
**EP 2.1.5b**

Mizrahi (2001) argues that there is a growing need for social workers with community practice skills. She points to the growth in community organizations that need well-educated practitioners who can focus on such issues as the impact on those who are "left out" during times of economic boom and are harshly affected during times of economic bust.

Cox (2001) traces the development of community practice in social work as it has changed and reemerged during the past 10 decades:

> The focus and emphasis of community work has changed to and from primary emphasis on (a) community organizing (community/locality based), (b) issue based social action efforts (local-state and/or national in scope), and (c) planning and coordination emphasis (service delivery systems-related efforts). Shifts in emphasis have been strongly related to political/social/economic circumstances of the period. (p. 39)

She points out that these different forms of community practice have existed at different times and have also overlapped, particularly during times of transition. Cox continues:

> Frequently, targets of concern evolved from the social aspects of community issues to the economic aspects of these issues, as in the civil rights movement. . . . Community practice . . . has also been characterized by degree of relationship to social movements, including the union movements of the 1920s and 1930s, socialist activity of the 1940s and 1950s, the civil rights movements of the 1960s and 1970s, the self-help movement of the 1980s, and now the new social movements of the 1990s. (p. 39)

# Empowerment-Oriented and Progressive Practice Models

EP 2.1.10k

Although many models of community organizing practice exist, our discussion in this chapter and the next will emphasize empowerment-oriented and progressive practice models, in keeping with the direct practice approach of this book. Cox (2001) draws on Lee's stated goal of empowerment practice as "socio-economic justice, reduction of institutional power blocks and social pollutions, changed socioeconomic structures and institutions to make them empowering structures" (Lee, 1994, p. 24). Cox sees the intervention strategies of empowerment practice as including a wide range of knowledge and skills used in other social approaches, including group work and community practice. Consciousness-raising processes with respect to personal, interpersonal, organizational, and political aspects of issues and egalitarian worker-client relationships are also critical components of most empowerment-oriented practice approaches.

Thus, although the focus of the work tends to be on community, larger systems, or political processes, many of the principles of practice and intervention strategies are similar to the work with clients described in earlier chapters. However, the goals, values, and strategies need to be attached to the function and role that are unique to the community social work professional. Although other professions may work to organize communities, I propose that the mediating function described earlier—the worker's standing between the client or clients and the systems that matter to them—offers a role for community social work that is consistent with the professional roots and historical development of social work. It is important to remind the reader at this point that "mediation" does not exclude confrontation when needed to at least get the system's attention.

Thus, we shall return to the two-client idea, with the second client being the social institutions and political systems that impact the lives of clients. The social work community organizer works with clients to empower them to engage effectively with larger systems that are often more powerful and at times threatening. As one strategy, workers may employ advocacy; however, at all times they should help clients develop the skills, strength, and confidence to advocate on their own behalf. Consistent with their functional role, social work community organizers should work skillfully to identify barriers that could impede the ability of clients to impact these important systems. When faced with clients' internal barriers, such as the need to develop leadership skills or the need to address real fears and concerns that involvement may be risky and result in retribution, social workers must address these issues directly in order to help clients overcome them. Examples in this chapter will include, among others, illustrations of organizing a tenants' group to confront a resistant public housing manager, a project to involve teenage leaders in a community, and empowering veterans in a psychiatric hospital milieu.

The worker in this model may also work with the system as the second client in need of effective intervention. As seen in the previous chapter, skillful implementation of this role often results in helping the service system, organization, or political system become more responsive to the needs of the client or client community. By first attempting to engage the system representatives effectively and to develop a positive working relationship, the social worker increases the possibility of assisting both the community and the system in identifying and acting on areas of common ground. The skills associated with making a "facilitative confrontation" when dealing with clients can prove just as important when dealing with difficult systems.

Not to be seen as naïve, I recognize that, no matter how effectively the worker tries, reaching some systems may be impossible. Powerful socioeconomic and ideological forces too often work to maintain an unsatisfactory status quo. This is why people often need advocacy and confrontation to move past system denial and resistance to change. The public housing tenants' group example later in this chapter illustrates advocacy and confrontation that challenges a resistant management with courage and skill.

## Principles of Effective Community Organizing

**EP 2.1.10e**
**EP 2.1.10i**

Effective social work community organizing respects the following principles:

- It is important to develop internal leaders from among the clients and not to take over the leadership when problems occur.
- In the final analysis, the client must control goals, objectives, and strategies, even though the social worker may have other views.
- A key role of the social worker is to help the group members develop and own structures and a culture for effective work. Many of the concepts related to group development described in earlier chapters (e.g., the authority theme, the intimacy theme, and formal and informal roles) will be just as relevant in a community-focused group.
- The social worker must respect the existence of barriers, both current and emerging from prior experiences, that may make taking the next step difficult for the client group until the members are ready. This respect involves recognizing and accepting the process of change, as well as an understanding of the stages cited earlier in the book. These include precontemplation, contemplation, preparation for action, action, and so forth (Prochaska & DiClemente, 1982).
- The social worker needs to know when to help clients to speak "softly" to systems in an effort to reach for the system's strength (i.e., to negotiate) and when to speak "loudly" to move a system to respond (i.e., to confront).
- Social workers must understand the importance of shifting from confrontation to collaboration once the system's attention and response have been obtained.
- The social worker needs to fully understand that all of the dynamics and skills described earlier as crucial for so-called "clinical practice" are equally important when the client is a community. The purpose and goals of the group may differ, but the process does not.

## Community Organizing Philosophy and Models

**EP 2.1.3a**
**EP 2.1.3b**

Social work, drawing on practice wisdom, has from its inception as a profession attempted to define a role that includes work with communities. In an early effort to conceptualize community organization, Rothman (1979) pointed out that this practice tended to play a peripheral role in social work and similar fields. He also described a "considerable degree of variation, transition, and confusion" in the theory development at that time (p. 25). To conceptualize this practice more clearly, he described three orientations regarding purposive community change:

Model A, locality development, presupposes that community change may be pursued optimally through broad participation of a wide spectrum of people at the local community level in goal determination and action. . . .

Model B, the social planning approach, emphasizes a technical process of problem solving with regard to substantive social problems, such as delinquency, housing and mental health. . . . Community participation may vary from much to little, depending on how the problem presents itself and what organizational variables are present. The approach presupposes that change in a complex industrial environment requires expert planners who, through the exercise of technical abilities, including the ability to manipulate large bureaucratic organizations, can skillfully guide complex change processes. . . .

Model C, the social action approach, presupposes a disadvantaged segment of the population that needs to be organized, perhaps in alliance with others, in order to make adequate demands on the larger community for increased resources or treatment more in accordance with social justice or democracy. It aims at making basic changes in major institutions or community practices. Social action as employed here seeks redistribution of power, resources, or decision-making in the community and/or changing basic policies of formal organizations. (pp. 26–27)

## Grassroots Community Organizing

**EP 2.1.4a**
**EP 2.1.6b**

The area of community practice on which this chapter focuses could be described as a hybrid of Models A and C that most closely fits the empowerment model described earlier. Another term commonly used to describe such a model is *grassroots organizing*. Staples (1984) provides a manual for organizers that starts with a basic philosophy and then describes strategies to implement an organizing effort. Following examples of government and corporate actions that directly and adversely affect people in disadvantaged communities, he suggests that these are typical problems faced by low- and moderate-income earners across the United States. The problems stem from people not having control of the institutions that affect their lives; this lack of control, in turn, stems from the unequal distribution of power, money, and prestige in U.S. society. This is true at the local level as much as in the state and national arenas. Inequality is a fact of life.

> To solve problems, people need to get some control over the concrete circumstances of everyday life. Organizing seeks to do this. The person who acts alone has very little power. When people join together and organize, they increase their ability to get things done. The goal is to strengthen their collective capacities to bring about social change. (Staples, 1984, p. 1)

Grassroots organizing implies active and involved leadership by members of the community. Given that most members of communities—even those who have already demonstrated leadership traits—have not been trained in organizing and leadership skills, a program of leadership training often precedes effective community organizing. Zachary (2000) conducted an exploratory case study of a major training project called the Parent Leadership Project (PLP), which was conducted by the City University of New York. More than 400 parent leaders participated during the course of the study period; most were female (more than 90 percent), African

American or Latino (more than 80 percent), and not college graduates (80 percent). The purpose was to assist parents to develop their knowledge of contemporary educational issues and their leadership skills so that they could be more effectively involved in influencing public schools.

Qualitative interviews with 40 participants during the summer of 1995 explored the aspects of the training that participants experienced as most helpful. Zachary's study participants identified the following elements as critical in developing their leadership skills and encouraging them to take significant risks: rituals of engagement; the sharing of power; a culture of participation characterized by safety, respect, and high expectations; and skillful, yet humble, facilitation to create solidarity and equality within the group (2000, p. 71).

This community organization model of social work practice is emphasized in Specht and Courtney's (1993) critique of a trend in the social work profession to abandon its traditional mission of work with the poor and the disenfranchised. They call for a return of the social work profession to its historic and "unfulfilled" mission: to build a meaning, a purpose, and a sense of obligation for the community.

> It is only by creating a community that we establish a basis for commitment, obligation, and social support. We must build communities that are excited about child care systems, that find it exhilarating to care for the mentally ill and the frail aged, that make demands upon people to behave, to contribute, and to care for one another. (p. 27)

Examples of community-based social work interventions that address several problem areas have emerged. For example, Mulroy (1997) describes an effort to build neighborhood networks to prevent child abuse and neglect. Mulroy and Shay (1997) illustrate how neighborhood-based collaboration of nonprofit organizations can lead to innovative prevention programs for child maltreatment. Amodeo, Wilson, and Cox (1996) describe lessons learned in an effort to develop a community-based alcohol and drug abuse prevention effort in a multicultural urban setting.

Although the grassroots organizing model is firmly rooted in social work history, the reality for many communities is that the staff members of community-action–focused agencies often are not professionally trained. There are at least three possible reasons for this. First, funding for direct community organizing by professionals has been sharply limited, which has resulted in a lack of positions for bachelor of social work (BSW) or master of social work (MSW) graduates. Second, the lack of professionally degreed social workers limits the abilities of students to obtain field placements that involve direct community intervention; accreditation requirements dictate that a student be supervised by an MSW with at least 2 years of practice experience. Some schools of social work attempt to deal with this reality by providing social work supervision as a complement to the task supervision at the agency. Finally—and, in my opinion, most importantly—community organizations often want their organizers to be from the community. If the organizers do not live in the community, it is helpful, but not required, for them to be racially or ethnically connected to the community in some way. Interest in grassroots community organization may grow given that the United States now has a president who worked as a community organizer in his home city of Chicago.

# The Phases of Work in Grassroots Community Practice

Once again, we return to the basic framework of time to examine the practice of a social worker. The four phases of work—preliminary, beginning, work, and endings/ transitions—are as useful for considering community practice as they were in individual, family, and group work. The examples that follow illustrate the general philosophy and principles of practice described in the previous chapter by applying them to work with community groups.

## The Preliminary and Beginning Phase of Community Practice

All of the dynamics and skills described to this point in the book are applicable to community practice, but the purpose of the group may be different (e.g., external issues that affect people personally versus personal issues that are the concern of the individual or family). Although community and social issues are usually closely connected to individual and family ones (e.g., the public housing problems described in the next example have a powerful impact on the families involved), if the group's purpose is to address the macro issues, the social worker needs to be concerned with helping group members keep this difference clear. The contracting skills highlighted throughout this book are as important in community (macro) practice as in clinical practice. The social worker may work individually with members of the group, but it is a mistake to allow the contract to be subverted—for instance, when a meeting called to address the social issues that face all tenants turns into an effort on the part of one member to deal with his or her particular family problems.

So, once again, we turn to the tuning-in skill, and this time we address the potential concerns with regard to involvement in a community organization group. In the example that follows, a very vulnerable population lives in public housing and fears the threat of retaliation by the housing management or staff if they rock the boat. However, they must face that fear openly, with the help of the worker, and overcome it if they are to take advantage of the "strength-in-numbers" phenomenon that is so crucial to social change efforts. The turning point comes when the worker seeks volunteers for a coordinating committee and is greeted by silence. As in the earlier chapters of this book, the use of tuning in to guide the worker in "reaching inside of the silence" and "exploring a taboo issue" is central to the group's development. The contracting skills of clarifying purpose and clarifying the worker's role, as well as the skill of reaching for feedback from members, are also illustrated.

*Contracting: A Tenants' Group in Public Housing* In the following example, a social worker contracts at a first meeting of public housing tenants he is attempting to organize. Public housing tenants are usually economically oppressed. They also often belong to minority groups or face gender discrimination as single mothers. When they accept public housing, they sometimes find themselves treated as second-class citizens, lacking even basic tenants' rights. Poor housing, inadequate maintenance, and nonresponsive bureaucracies add a new level of oppression and increase their sense of hopelessness.

As described in our discussion of oppression theory in Chapter 2, oppressed people may internalize this oppression as a negative self-image, and this can lead to their acting out the physical or emotional violence imposed on them. They often act out the violence on one another. Thus, they may become "autooppressors as they engage in self-destructive behaviors injurious to themselves, their loved ones and their neighbors" (Bulhan, 1985, p. 126). In turn, the oppressors use this self-destructive behavior as a justification for additional oppression.

Workers can break the cycle only by helping such clients to find their common ground and to assert themselves by confronting the oppression. In our example, the worker saw the tenants' group as a way to help the tenants deal with both the results of the oppression (e.g., their neighborhood conflicts) and the oppression itself. Oppression theory offers a helpful prism for understanding the problems raised in the first meeting.

The social worker in this example had done his preliminary phase work through door-to-door contacts and interviews, thereby gaining a sense of the issues of concern to the tenants. The meeting had been publicized using circulars and posters. Natural leaders in the housing complex had been identified through the interviews, and the worker had requested their help to get a turnout for this first session. Because the first session began without a structure in place, the worker made the opening statement to a room of 45 tenants.

> After introducing myself, I explained that I was a community social worker employed by the local settlement house and that my job was to work with citizens' groups to help them organize themselves to improve their community— that included their housing, schools, recreational services for kids, etc. After spending some time in this housing project, it became clear to me that the tenants had a number of gripes that they felt the management was not doing anything about. The purpose of tonight's meeting was to discuss these gripes and to see if they felt it would help to organize a tenants' group to deal with the management more effectively. I would try to help them get started and would stick with the group to try to help it operate effectively. However, it would have to be their group, because I couldn't do anything for them by myself. I asked what they thought about that.

The discussion began with group members complaining about poor maintenance, a haughty administrator who ignored simple requests, and so on. There was a great deal of anger in the room, which the worker acknowledged while he kept track of the issues that were raised. He did little to intervene other than to help the group members speak in order and respond to one another when appropriate. After a while, the members were speaking more to one another than to the worker. The discussion also moved to complaints the tenants had about one another (e.g., noise at night, loud radios, littering) and about gaps in service for kids (e.g., no safe place to play). The discussion was animated. When the list seemed complete, the worker returned to the question of his role.

**Practice Points:** The social worker set the stage for the discussion with his opening statement and his sharing of the areas they might address. He then encouraged the "problem swapping" and contained himself by not intervening too quickly. It is important that he keep emphasizing his role—that is, to help them deal with their issues and not to do it for them. His suggestion for a steering group is designed to begin to develop a sense of internal leadership for this early stage of group development.

> "You have many issues here that I think can be dealt with if you organize yourselves as a group. There are issues with management, issues with one another, and new services you feel are needed. Now, I told you at the beginning that I was getting you started, but that you would have to form your own group

to deal with these concerns. I would like to recommend that you select a steering committee tonight that could meet to discuss next steps. For example, they could discuss whether you need an association: If yes, what kind should you have, etc. What about it?" There were murmurs of agreement. I then asked for volunteers and was greeted by silence.

**Practice Points:**   In the remainder of the excerpt, we shall see how the worker reached into this silence for the underlying concern to which he had tuned in prior to the meeting. If it were easy to get together as a group to take on these problems, why had the tenants not done so on their own? The worker had tuned in to the residents' fear of reprisals if they became identified as "troublemakers" in the housing project, and he decided to reach for it at this point.

As the silence continued, I asked why they seemed hesitant to volunteer. With no response, I risked my hunch and said, "You know, I was thinking about this before the meeting, and I wondered if you might be concerned about reprisals if you get organized. You know, you are dependent on this place for housing, and if you were afraid that management might be upset, I could understand that." Mrs. Cain, who had been identified as one of the community leaders, spoke up at this point, "You know Mr. Brown used to raise a ruckus and complain all the time. He got drunk a while back and they used that to get him." I asked if they were afraid that this might happen to them. Discussion began to explore what might happen, their mutual fears, etc. Mrs. Cain finally said, "I guess we do take a chance, but if I knew you other folks would stand behind me and not run for cover if it got hot around here, I would think about doing it."

At this point, others indicated they would help out on the committee. I said, "It seems like some of your neighbors are willing to take some responsibility for leading this off and getting the group organized, but they want to know that you will back them up." Another member, a tall, older man with gray hair, who hadn't spoken all evening, said, "It's about damn time we stood up to the bastards!" Laughter broke the tension of the moment, and one could sense that an agreement had been reached.

I wanted to complete the contracting about my role before I finished the evening. "I want to be clear that I will help you folks get yourselves organized and help you work together, but it will have to be your group. You will need your own chairperson; you will have to make your own decisions." Group members murmured agreement to this. "We can discuss this later, but perhaps I might be able to speak to management at a later point and help them see how the group could be in their interest as well." The meeting ended as I complimented them for making a great start and set up a brief meeting with the steering committee to get ourselves organized.

**Practice Summary.**   This example demonstrates, again, the importance of process in dealing with groups and the importance of using the skills described thus far. The principles of contracting, clarifying purpose, clarifying role, and reaching for feedback were central to the effective start of this group. In addition to the contracting skills, the worker's tuning in and effective elaborating and empathy skills helped the group examine and overcome a major obstacle to their formation. If the worker had ignored their fears, tried to overcome them with a lecture on "strength in numbers," or simply jumped in and agreed to take the responsibility for the next steps *for* them instead of *with* them, the group development that is central to the worker's purpose would likely have been seriously delayed. Instead, his empathy and demand for work helped them to begin to find their own strength.

## Community Organizing Around a Specific Issue

Communities can be brought together to deal with what may be experienced by some as a specific threat or something that raises a significant and controversial issue. One example would be the expansion of casino gambling within an economic development area. Simmons (2000) uses an example of a 1992 proposal for the development of a casino in Hartford, Connecticut. The author points out that casino development is the type of proposal that ignites a "not-in-my-backyard" (NIMBY) reaction. In addition to the usual issues of scale, public funding, property values, "fit," safety, and infrastructure, Simmons suggests that casino development raises unique concerns:

> Casinos as venues for gambling raise an entirely new set of issues and elicit deep value conflicts. Gambling, itself, becomes a central controversy. Some forces want to debate gambling on purely economic grounds; others debate the issue from a moral perspective; and there are still others who are concerned about its social impacts without asserting a moral judgment. The discourse becomes extremely strident as powerful financial interests who develop casinos clash with opponents who hold strong views about the harm of gambling. (p. 48)

Simmons describes the complex interplay of powerful political and financial forces and the strong desire by some to see casino gambling as a force for economic development for a generally depressed downtown Hartford area. This issue came to a head after the 1992 opening of the giant and extremely successful Foxwoods Casino by the Mashantucket Pequot Indians on tribal land. The state of Connecticut took in $120 million from the arrangement that provided the Pequots with exclusive rights to operate slot machines. With this kind of money at stake, we can easily understand how the forces for expansion of casinos would be powerful and organized. Simmons describes in detail the battle fought in town meetings and informational sessions. The experience was both dramatic and exhausting. In the end, Hartford rejected the casino; this settled the problems that resulted from organizations and community groups taking opposing positions instead of uniting to battle for social justice issues, as they usually did. Simmons concludes:

> If proponents want to bring a casino to town, an uproar surely follows. Yet community organizations have considerable leverage in the fate of these projects because they can reveal the inflated claims of casino proponents and articulate an alternative vision of local economic development. More than most other "big projects," casinos provoke genuine arguments of costs and benefits, who will gain and who will lose. Community organizing can be critical in protecting a community from a highly questionable form of development. (2000, p. 67)

This example is but one of many that reflects a growing interest in how problem-specific community organizing efforts can enhance traditional treatment approaches.

## Rural-Based Community Organization Practice

The literature on community organization contains many examples from urban settings but fewer from rural areas. This distinction is important. As Soifer (1998) points out,

Socio-cultural, economic, and political differences between urban and rural areas are present. To be effective a rural social work practitioner must recognize and spend time learning about these differences. (p. 2)

Soifer provides an example of a rural-based community organizing effort in Vermont that combined several different community organizing models. The project arose in response to the many problems faced by low- to moderate-income and mobile home park residents. Foremost of these problems was that residents felt extremely intimidated by their landlords. Despite significant protections built into state law, residents feared retaliation and loss of their homes in a state with a tight housing market for people like themselves.

The approach taken to address the problem was the development of local tenants' associations that were linked statewide in an organization called Tenants United for Fairness (TUFF)–Vermont:

> The primary goal of the organization was to empower tenants to bring about qualitative improvement in their living conditions on a local, regional, and state level. . . . The methods used to achieve this objective include grassroots organizing, developing indigenous tenant group leaders, educating tenants about their rights under Vermont law, and mobilizing tenants to advocate for fundamental changes in state law concerning tenant-landlord issues. (Soifer, 1998, p. 3)

By August 1993, a network of 23 tenant associations representing 750 Vermont renters was organized. A statewide meeting of representatives that fall included training and educational programs. Soifer describes significant successful impacts on a state and local level. The step-by-step process involved in this organizing project included the selection of appropriate locations, door-to-door organizing drives, committee meetings, tenants' formation meetings, and organizational officers' meetings. Soifer (1998) believes that building an organizational basis for an action plan, as well as developing and implementing such a plan, depends on this process.

According to Soifer (1998), issues that separate rural community organization from its urban counterpart include the small size of many of the local organizing housing complexes (in this case, 15 units); driving distances, combined with poor roads and winter conditions, which make attendance at state meetings difficult; and the essential difficulty in using militant actions in small towns, where people must deal with neighbors, friends, and politicians they know on a first-name basis. Furthermore, high rates of poverty may be less visible in a rural area than in an urban one.

One additional difference, not mentioned by Soifer (1998), that I have observed in workshop presentations is the "only game in town" problem. Smaller and more rural areas tend to have fewer services and resources to address economic, health, education, and other issues. Work on major community organization projects is difficult without associated agencies that are willing to help. In addition, individual workers may have to provide a wide range of services, and this can lead to overwhelming caseloads and limited time for agency-sanctioned community organizing activities. Despite such significant obstacles, many social workers find ways—in their jobs or personal lives—to address the social issues that impact their clients.

## The Use of the Internet in Community Practice

Because of the growth in the ownership of computers and access to high-speed connections, community organizers have found new tools to implement their goals.

Whereas the term *community* might originally have been limited by geographic location, it now can refer to a cyber-community in which common interest and concerns bring members together.

Although this can be a powerful tool for organization and social change, many people with low incomes or limited education do not have the equipment, technology, and knowledge required to use it. This can result in what is called the "digital divide": a sharp distinction between those who can take advantage of "digital democracy" and those who cannot (Shelley, Thrane, Shulman, et al., 2004).[1] Thus, any effort to use this powerful tool for organization and social change among the poor and less educated, many of whom may have been left out of the computer revolution, needs to incorporate access to computers and computer training to empower community members to become actively involved.

Shelley, Thrane, and Shulman (2005) explored this issue in a study of 478 respondents drawn from Iowa, Pennsylvania, and Colorado. They were interested in the "digital divide in e-politics" and the impact of six blocks of variables:

1. Sociodemographic
2. Place effects
3. Voting
4. Attitudes toward technology use (VCR, cellphone, etc.) and computer apathy
5. Attitudes toward technology
6. Specific uses of the Internet

Their study found that the physical gap (e.g., home computers, high-speed Internet connections, etc.) reported in earlier studies continued, with certain populations lacking access to Internet connections. In addition, the blocks of variables previously described also impacted citizen participation. Shelley et al. conclude:

Before marginalized citizens can become e-citizens, public access to IT must be made available. Employment in low-wage service sector economy leaves many struggling to meet basic life needs and living their lives with little margin for error. Due to the intersections of race and class, poor minorities are at a significant disadvantage. Only 8% of Blacks and 9% of Hispanics are Internet users. Furthermore, just 5% of individuals without a high school diploma use the Internet, and only 18% of households with incomes below $30,000 are Internet consumers (Lenhart et al., 2003). Public access would ameliorate some of these class-based impediments. (2005, p. 24)

Nartz and Schoesch (2000) identify four models of Internet community practice: information dissemination, community building, mobilization, and community planning. They suggest that these models use six primary Internet tools:

1. *E-mail:* Allows users to compose messages and transmit them in seconds to one or more recipients anywhere in the world
2. *Text:* Allows users to read printed matter on pages of a website, and to navigate the sites and the Web via clickable links
3. *Search engines:* Help a user find information or resources by searching for keywords that the user specifies
4. *Listservs:* Allow users to receive and post messages about topics, with each message being sent to all subscribers to the list

5. *Newsgroups:* Allow users to go to one place on the Internet and view previous messages on topics and add new messages

6. *Chat:* Allows a group of users connected at the same time to send messages to each other in real time (p. 45)

These tools are powerful aids in the development of community action. More recently, social networking sites such as Facebook and the use of Twitter have become more widespread in use and can be used as mediums for connecting neighbors. Once again, the potential digital divide problem needs to be kept in mind. If that can be resolved, the ability for a few to mobilize, educate, and lead the many in community building and social policy change is evident. The Internet can give grassroots organizations the ability to confront and impact large organizations, government bodies, financial institutions, businesses, and so forth without being frustrated by the lack of matching financial resources and power. I believe that we have just begun to understand and use this powerful method in the fight for community and social justice.

## The Neighborhood as Community

The social science literature reflects growing professional interest in community concepts. One such area of interest centers on the concept of "neighboring" and its social, cognitive, and emotional components. Unger and Wandersman (1985) have reviewed the literature from several disciplines, including social psychology, environmental psychology, community psychology, and sociology. The authors define neighboring as involving "the social interaction, the symbolic interaction, and the attachment of individuals with the people living around them and the place in which they live" (p. 141). Their review identifies many important areas of social support:

- *Personal/Emotional Support.* The extent to which neighbors are willing to greet and visit with each other can serve as a source of social belonging and reduce feelings of social isolation often fostered within cities.

- *Instrumental Support.* Neighbors may serve as informal helpers for one another.

- *Informational Support.* Neighbors provide information to each other as they interact. This information may be helpful in locating needed resources.

- *Personal Social Networks.* Neighbors establish linkages with key individuals in their neighborhoods for individual benefit. They use these connections to find and further link themselves to resources in their neighborhood and wider community to solve problems.

- *Neighborhood Social Networks.* Neighborhood social networks are the linkages developed by a group of neighbors. (pp. 142–149)

Unger and Wandersman (1985) also describe cognitive mapping as "an activity neighbors routinely engage in. It has significant implications especially in transient and unstable neighborhoods for determining where neighbors feel safe to travel and where they choose to socially interact with others" (p. 150).

Finally, Unger and Wandersman (1985) address the affective bonds within a neighborhood:

Being a neighbor involves an affective dimension. As neighbors live in interaction or isolation within their neighborhood, various feelings often develop which characterize their relationship to neighbors and the neighborhood. These feelings may affect residents' satisfaction with their neighborhood and may influence their motivation to become involved in ways to solve neighborhood problems. . . . Three affective bonds are suggested: (a) a sense of mutual aid, (b) a sense of community, and (c) an attachment to place. (p. 154)

## The Role of the Worker in the Community

**EP 2.1.1c**

Clearly, work with the neighborhood as community will involve specific sorts of knowledge as well as skills. As in the earlier discussions of social work with individuals, families, and groups, the first question to be addressed is the role of the worker.

When working with communities, the worker often faces a more complex role because she or he must work within a task-focused group that has a formal structure. For example, if the group has a member who serves as a chairperson or president, and that person leads the discussion, what does the social worker do? Whereas we saw earlier that all groups informally develop internal leaders, in these task-focused community groups the internal leader may be elected and have well-defined responsibilities that are spelled out in the group's charter.

So, then, what is the role of the community social worker? Serving as one answer, Staples (1984) addresses the distinction between leading and organizing:

It is the organizer's job to get other people to take the lead. They have to be motivated and recruited, encouraged and convinced that they can really do it. Their knowledge and skills must be developed, their self-confidence bolstered, and their commitment to collective action deepened. Whoever acts as organizer shouldn't be a formal officer or the organization's public voice. S/he shouldn't make policy decisions or tell people what to do. (p. 8)

Ellis, Mallory, Gould, and Shatila (2006) offer a guide to effective community work in the form of a workbook that provides step-by-step strategies for effectiveness with organizations and communities. They stress the importance of systematic assessment, planning, and preparation for effective change. This work needs to include:

- Assessment
- Strategic planning
- Contingency planning
- Recruiting collaborative partners
- Gaining support and minimizing opposition
- Developing a public relations plan

The case examples provided later in this chapter will include illustrations of each of these elements of effective macro practice. They will also illustrate how the community organizer provides a resource for the leadership and community group members as they pursue their goals as opposed to taking the leadership role for her- or himself. Once again, we return to the core model of practice that uses time as a way to analyze our work.

Although I propose that the core dynamics and skills of all social work practice relate to community work, there are variant elements as well. For example, the unique role of the social worker is considered in work with a formal, internal leader of a group who may chair meetings. Additionally, a community group is focused on community and/or social issues rather than on personal problems. The personal problems of the members may lead to the need to address the larger issues; however, addressing them member by member is not the purpose of the group. This distinction is important, and one of the important tasks of the worker is to guard the contract so that a task group does not turn into a therapy group.

***SNCC: Starting Where the Client (Community) Is*** A classic example of the crucial nature of "starting where the client is" can be found in the work of the Student Non-violent Coordinating Committee (SNCC) volunteers who were early community organizers in the fight to overcome racism and segregation in the South in the 1960s. Their first year's effort involved attempting to overcome legitimate fears and to mobilize a voter registration effort in communities where African Americans were systematically denied the vote by the White power structure. The first year's effort was not fully successful. In the second year, the volunteers asked community members what they were most concerned about, and the quality of education for the children quickly emerged in response. Because of successful organizing during the second year with regard to the school issue, a working relationship developed along with a sense of empowerment. By the following year, these same communities were ready to work with the SNCC to address voting rights, which eventually contributed to the powerful civil rights revolution.

A problem that can be observed in social work community organization practice and literature is that, at times, the professionals believe they know what the objectives should be and the means to reach them. In some community groups, it is possible to observe members being directly or indirectly manipulated to achieve the worker's goals. These groups are destined for failure because the principles of members' ownership of the group and determination of its objectives are critical.

I have found it ironic that some of the early leaders in the community organizing field who advocated an empowerment model in relation to the larger political and power structure did not always recognize that substituting their own judgment for that of their members was actually disempowering.

## The Middle or Work Phase of Practice

In this section, we revisit many of the problems and issues described in the earlier chapters on group work. Now, however, we focus on task groups that have an external objective rather than on personal issues that were central to the groups discussed earlier. In the first example, we see the crucial difference created by an "internal" leader—in this case, an elected chairperson—who has the actual responsibility for managing the group and the process assigned to him by the group members. Internal leaders in community groups may lack the training, experience, and skills to provide leadership in a manner that engages all of the group's members and shares authority and responsibility. The example illustrates the important, active role played the social worker, who attempts to strengthen the leadership rather than take it over.

***Structure and Maintenance: A Citizens' Antipoverty Action Group*** In the excerpt that follows, we examine worker interventions with an antipoverty action group that was formed to encourage poor people to use strength in numbers to try to change some of the local welfare and school policies that affected their lives. More than 50 members signed up at an initial organizational meeting. Because 50 people cannot operate together without some form of organization, they clearly needed structure. One early task was to identify the roles required for effective operation. The term *roles* is used here more narrowly than before, relying on Hare's (1962) definition: "The expectations shared by group members about the behavior associated with some position in a group, no matter what individual fills the position, are called roles" (p. 24).

A small steering committee met to draft an outline of the group's structure and to identify functional tasks that group members needed to carry out: leadership (a chairperson), responsibility for relations with other community groups (a cochairperson), responsibility for the group's funds (a treasurer), and responsibility for maintaining the group's records and correspondence (a secretary). As the group developed, other roles became necessary and were created (e.g., committee chairpersons for special projects).

By creating these roles, the group engaged in the division of labor—the development of group structure in which the tasks to be performed are distributed among members in a formal or informal manner. Dividing the labor among group members allowed each member to carry some part of the burden, but not all of it. When division of labor and responsibility are not handled well—for example, when a chairperson attempts to do all the work—the overworked member can become overwhelmed while the other group members feel angry, left out, and apathetic. The greater the apathy, the more the chairperson feels the need to take responsibility.

In these circumstances, clarity about the worker's function is crucial. In addition to helping the members develop a structure for effective operations, the worker must monitor how well the structure is working and bring any problems to the members' attention. This group task, called *structure and maintenance*, refers to the work done by group members to develop, examine, and maintain in good working order their structure for work. In the example of the chairperson who does not share responsibility, the worker's function would be to mediate the engagement between the chairperson and the other group members.

**Practice Points:** The following excerpt illustrates this work in a steering committee session of an antipoverty action group. Group members had concerns about the chairperson's dominating the group as well as not following through on work that needed to be done in preparation for a protest confrontation. Challenging the internal leader can be as taboo a subject as challenging the external leader, the social worker, so the issue remains under the surface. Note how the social worker reaches into the silence to get the issue out in the open.

> I had gotten signals from a number of members that they were upset with the way things were going and especially unhappy with Sid's leadership. He had taken responsibility for a number of follow-up items and had not handled them well. As a result, the group faced some serious problems on a planned sit-in action that weekend. The meeting began as usual, with Sid reading the agenda and asking for any additions. There were none. Discussion began on a number of minor items. It finally reached the question of the plans for action, and I could feel the tension growing. Sara began, "Is it true, Sid, that we may not have the buses for Saturday?" Sid replied abruptly, "I'm working on that, so don't worry." There was silence. I said, "I think there is something going on here. What's up?"

**Practice Points:**   This is the point when clarity of role is crucial. Refer back to the discussion in the earlier chapter on the role of the social worker when there is conflict between the individual and the group. In this example we see the social worker recognizing that he has two clients—Sid the chair and the group—and that he has to be with both at the same time. The mediation role becomes clear in the emerging process. The worker is skillful in identifying the communication problem and in reaching under Sid's defensiveness for his real feelings.

Sara continued, "Look, Sid, I don't want you to take this personally, but there are a number of things screwed up about this Saturday and I'm really worried." Sid responded defensively, "Well, what do you expect? You know, I have a lot of responsibility to carry with not very much help." Terry broke in, "Every time we try to give you some help, you turn us down." Sid looked hurt. I intervened: "I think there has been a problem going on for some time, and you folks have not been able to level with one another about it. Sid, you feel you have to carry a lot of the burden around here and the group members don't really appreciate how hard it is for you. Am I right?" Sid nodded in agreement. I turned to the others. "I think the rest of you feel that you would like to pick up a piece, but you sense Sid seems to hang on—so you don't offer. Then you feel angry later when things don't work out." They nodded as well. I said, "Look, I know it's hard, but if we get this out, maybe we can work out a way of sharing the responsibilities that would be more helpful for the group."

**Practice Points:**   The community social worker needs to be clear that his or her function involves helping group members to work on their tasks. Workers with such groups are often just as uncomfortable about confrontation as the members. As a result, they may try to use indirect influence, or to take over some of the chairperson's functions, or even try to get the group to replace the chairperson. I have seen all of these mistakes in the work of less skillful social workers who are not clear about their role. This reflects a lack of understanding about group developmental tasks. Groups often run into such problems maintaining their structures for work. Indeed, if the group could work easily, without such obstacles, it would not need a social worker.

The real problem for a group such as this one arises when the members cannot openly discuss these difficulties as they emerge. As with the counseling groups described earlier in this text, a culture for work needs to be developed in which members can say what they really think and feel and avoid the trap of the illusion of work. There is a taboo in our society about direct expression of negatives; one way it has been described is as "an elephant in the room" that everyone sees but no one acknowledges.

This problem helps define the work of the helping professional: not managing the details of the structure itself, but facilitating the way in which group members develop and maintain their structure. In our example, the worker helped the group in this way, in this case by knowing that feelings have a great deal to do with most communication problems and that skill in this area can prove helpful. The work continued:

Although they were uncomfortable, they agreed to take some time to discuss the problem. I asked the group members why they had not leveled with Sid before. Rudy said, "Sid, we all like you a lot. That's why we asked you to be chairman. I didn't want to hurt your feelings. Since you became chairman, you seemed to forget the rest of us—and frankly, I started to get pissed off." I said, "Did you get the feeling, Rudy, that you weren't needed?" Rudy said, "That's it! All of a sudden, Sid was going to do the whole ball game himself." I asked Sid how come he felt he had to take all the responsibility. He said, "Look, this is my first time chairing anything. None of us has much experience at this stuff—I'm worried that we will fall on our faces. I've asked some people to do things, and they have screwed up, so I don't ask anymore. I just do it." I said, "Are you worried, Sid, that you're going to fall on your face?" He was silent and then said, "You bet." I waited.

Rita said, "I'm probably one of the people you feel let you down, aren't I?" Sid nodded. She continued, "Well, I meant to follow up and hold that subcommittee meeting. I just kept putting it off." I asked, "Have you ever chaired a meeting before?" Rita said, "No." I continued, "I guess you were probably nervous about it." She agreed that she had been nervous. Rudy said to Sid, "Look, Sid, I can understand your feeling worried about the group. We all feel the same way. But you really don't have to carry it all on your back. That's not what we expect of you. We can help out, and if we flop, we all flop." Sid relaxed a bit and said, "It would make it easier if I didn't have to feel completely responsible." I pointed out that the whole group was probably feeling shaky about their jobs and how well they could do them—just like Sid and Rita pointed out. "I don't think that's so unusual—in fact, I think that the fact that you are talking about this is a great sign. At least you can do something about the problem and not let it tear your group apart." They agreed that it was a start and spent the next 20 minutes analyzing the jobs to be done and redistributing the responsibilities.

**Practice Summary.** In addition to overcoming division-of-labor problems, groups must develop formal and informal communication patterns. In our current example, the group needed to decide who reported to whom, how often various subgroups would meet, who would get copies of the minutes, and how communications at meetings would be governed. Another task required the development of a decision-making process that would be efficient but still allow individual members to feel involved.

The worker paid attention to the formal structure, but he also observed the informal system at work. For example, shortcuts in communication were found that facilitated the coordination of subgroups within the structure. This had to be monitored because the informal communication system could also serve to subvert the formal system, thus becoming an obstacle in itself. The worker also observed the informal assignment of status to various members of the group. Members who performed their functions well and demonstrated the most-admired skills in the group gained higher status, and their contributions to discussions tended to carry more weight because of this. Because differential status could cause friction in the group, the worker needed to monitor the members' reactions to it.

In a sense, the worker is assigned the special responsibility of paying attention to the way in which the group works on these important structural tasks, monitoring the process to pick up cues that signal difficulties and helping the group members pay attention to these problems. Community social workers at times ignore these critical group tasks, however, concentrating instead on a strategy of action in relation to the outside systems (the welfare department, the school board, government officials, and so forth). After a while, these workers may find that the internal struggles of the group have grown so much that they have begun to sap the group's strength.

This decline results in a loss of group cohesion, the mutual attraction members feel for one another.

Attempts to develop greater cohesion through social activities (e.g., parties) or, even more commonly, by attacking another system and trying to unite members against a common enemy are only useful in the short run. Striking similarities exist between work with community (task-focused) groups and the work carried out with groups concerned with growth and development, support and stabilization, or therapy. The developmental group tasks are similar, and the skills required by the worker to assist this second client, the group, are similar as well.

***The Deviant Member: Community-Based Citizens' Advisory Board*** In previous chapters, we saw how the "deviant member" in a group can be viewed as a possible spokesperson, an ally for the worker rather than an enemy of the group. We saw that the worker should not identify with the group versus the individual but instead focus on helping the two clients. This clarity of role becomes particularly difficult when the deviant member expresses a point of view that differs from that of the worker.

One example of the functional role of the deviant member in a community group can be drawn from a community-based citizens' group charged with the responsibility of distributing a portion of community social welfare funds. Mr. Fisk developed a reputation in the group for being outspoken, angry, and intimidating, and usually taking a minority conservative point of view on an essentially liberal board. Given that the worker usually agreed with the more liberal view of the majority, she needed to overcome the strong temptation to work with the group against Mr. Fisk. In the first encounters, the worker lost sight of this role and attempted to rebut Mr. Fisk, thus siding with the majority.

The purpose of the board was to represent community opinion in the distribution of funds. On the agenda the evening of the meeting was the funding of a local women's center that was politically active and provided community social service. As the group worker expected, Mr. Fisk began by attacking the funding on the grounds that the center was essentially political. Feeling a strong attachment to the work of the women's center, the worker attacked Mr. Fisk's position by offering additional information in favor of the center. The debate between group members and Mr. Fisk continued, and he ended up losing the vote.

In a retrospective analysis of the process, the worker granted that, when Mr. Fisk spoke, some members silently nodded in agreement. Other members obviously disagreed. The group was also clearly uncomfortable about taking on Mr. Fisk because of the way he argued his point of view. As can easily happen, the worker was so intent on her agenda of getting the center funded that she ignored the communication problem in the group and jumped in to take sides. An alternative line of work might have been to help other members in the group express the feelings and thoughts behind the nonverbal signals, including those members who agreed with Mr. Fisk. The worker could bring into the open the difficulty in discussion caused by Mr. Fisk's strong presentation, but she would do this only to help the group members and Mr. Fisk in their communications.

With hindsight, it is easy to see that Mr. Fisk represented a larger body of opinion in the community, and, if the board were to do its job effectively, its decisions had to take into account a broad range of opinions. There was a good chance that some of the most ardent supporters of the women's center had some mixed feelings about funding the political action component, which was outside of the center's current mandate. In turn, Mr. Fisk and his supporters probably had a sense of the importance of the social service aspect of the center's work. If not, then the discussion would be enriched by a full debate on these ideas, in which the worker could help the members from both sides to say what they felt as well as listen to those who disagreed with them. The worker would be free to add her own views on the matter, but she should not abandon the crucial function of group worker. Often, in withholding personal views so as "not to influence the group," the worker ends up indirectly attempting to manipulate opinion to the desired outcome. Ironically, the same worker may feel and express a deep conviction in the importance of the community decision-making process. Once again, the deviant member, Mr. Fisk, could have been helpful in strengthening the debate on a contentious issue.

***Mothers on Welfare in Public Housing: The Role of Confrontation*** In the next example, we broaden our definition of the worker's community organization role even further by focusing on how she or he helps the members negotiate their environment. In this case, the group consisted of welfare mothers in a public housing setting somewhat similar to the one described in the earlier example. This time we explore the "third-force" role as the social worker attempts to work between the group and the systems that they must negotiate. We see how the worker's mediating role can include confrontation and advocacy when the system representative is not responsive.

In this example, the state welfare agency established the group to explore the problems faced by welfare families and to provide help with these problems when necessary. (This example of practice preceded the Welfare Reform Act and the welfare-to-work movement.) Seven women, aged 23 to 45, made up the group's membership. Discussion during the group's second session indicated that their problems with the Housing Authority and the housing project in which they all lived were central concerns:

MRS. BROWN: I don't have any complaint about the building or rent, but if we get more money from welfare for any reason, they (Housing Authority) raise our rent. But if our checks are reduced, they say they can't break our lease to reduce the rent.

MRS. MELTON: They also make us pay for things that people not on welfare do not have to pay for.

WORKER: Like what?

MRS. SMITH: During the summer, a man from the gas company came and put a tube on my stove so that I could move the stove, and the Housing Authority sent me a bill for $26.00.

WORKER: Did you call the gas company for repairs on your stove?

MRS. SMITH: No, he just came.

WORKER: Did you discuss this with the office?

MRS. MELTON: That doesn't do any good.

MRS. SMITH: I told them I couldn't pay the bill because I didn't have the money. They said I broke the pipe, so I had to pay the bill or move. So I paid it. But I didn't break any pipe.

MRS. LESSER: Last summer, the children were playing in the court and broke four windows in my apartment, and I had to pay for them. I called the office when they were broken and told them how they were broken, but I had to pay for them anyway.

MRS. SMITH: There is no such thing as wear-and-tear items that most landlords have to replace for tenants when you live in the project.

MRS. BROWN: That's what they tell us.

MRS. MELTON: If they come into your apartment and see the shades are worn, we have to pay for them.

WORKER: Do you know of any repairs or replacements that the Welfare Board will pay for?

MRS. SMITH: Yes, Miss D. told us to send in these bills and the welfare would pay for plumbing, shades, oven doors, and things like that.

WORKER: What does your lease say that the Housing Authority is responsible for replacing or repairing?

MRS. SMITH: It has all "don't" on the back and nothing else.

MRS. MELTON: They make us pay for everything, and I don't think this is fair.

**Practice Points:** As the worker listens to the litany of complaints, it becomes clearer that the real problem is the domination of tenants by the management of the housing complex. With these tenants dependent on their housing, their ability to confront what they experience as intimidation and lack of respect is understandable. As with the earlier example, the strength-in-numbers principle will be crucial. Note that worker first suggests reaching out to the manager, and when they indicate they do not think the manager will respond, the worker makes the "demand for work."

WORKER: Do you have a tenants' group that takes complaints to the office?

MRS. SMITH: Yes, but they (Housing Authority) choose the officers, and they don't do anything about the complaints. They call us troublemakers and try to keep us out of meetings. (Group members all agreed.)

WORKER: Would you like for me to invite Mr. Murray (housing project manager) to one of our meetings so that you can find out just what the Housing Authority is responsible for and what your responsibilities are?

MRS. MELTON: It won't do any good. He's great for listening and taking no action on complaints.

MRS. SMITH: Yes, let's ask him. But I don't think he'll come.

WORKER: Do you want him to come, or not? (Group members all indicated yes.)

**Practice Points:** As they discussed their relationship to the housing project, they found that they shared many of the same complaints. Strength in numbers made them believe some change might be possible despite their past experiences. In her enthusiasm for moving the work forward, however, the worker missed the underlying fears and doubts hinted at in the conversation. If taking on the housing project was so easy, why had they not done so before? At the next session, the worker corrected her mistake and began by trying to determine whether the housing issue was still the central concern.

Note that the worker did not determine which issues the group members should tackle. A common error in community organizing is for workers to choose, in advance, what issues citizens should focus on. They see their work as applying direct or indirect influence to convince the members to act on the hidden agenda. As seen in the earlier SNCC example, the driving force for the work must emerge from the clients' sense of urgency. The encounter may be rough, but the clients need to feel a commitment to the issue to carry them through. At the next meeting in our example, the conversation reflected some of the fears and doubts that had occurred to the group during the week. The silences hinted at these feelings.

To give the group members perspective on where they stood, the worker redefined the purpose of the group and gave a brief summary of the concerns expressed in the last three meetings before the holidays. The worker then asked group members what topic they would like to focus on. They agreed that their problems with the Housing Authority needed immediate attention (14 welfare checks had recently been stolen from the mailboxes).

WORKER: I called Mr. Murray's office, and his secretary said that she thought Mr. Murray would be willing to meet with the group. Maybe we should use this time to plan for the meeting with him. Make a list of questions you want to ask and what approach to use.

MRS. MCIVER: I would like to know if we can have more secure mailboxes or a different type of lock on them.

MRS. MELTON: Anybody could open these boxes—even a child with a stick or nail file.

MRS. KING: I'm there when the mailman comes, so no one gets my check.

MRS. MELTON: I can't sit by the box and wait for the man. I've got other things to do.

MRS. SMITH: Why should we have to wait? If the boxes were better, this would not be a problem.

MRS. MCIVER: I've complained about those boxes, but they (Housing Authority) say we talk too much about our business. He said the thieves know who gets the most money and when the checks come.

MRS. SMITH: That's common knowledge that the checks come on the first.

MRS. KING: I'd never tell anyone I was on welfare.

MRS. SMITH: People assume that you are on welfare if you live in the project.

MRS. STONE: Why can't the police be there on check day? Someone broke into my box, and I had to pay $2.50 for it.

MRS. MCIVER: That's right. They (Housing Authority) say we are responsible for the boxes whether we break them or not.

MRS. SMITH: That's not fair. Why should we have to pay for something we did not do?

MRS. MCIVER: Most people are afraid to call the police.

MRS. MELTON: You're right. You never know what those people (drug addicts) will do to you or your children.

MRS. MCIVER: You remember when that brick was thrown through my window? It was because I called the office (Housing Authority) about those big boys hanging out in the halls.

MRS. MELTON: They can sure make it bad for you.

MRS. MCIVER: The other tenants call you a troublemaker if you complain about noise or dirty halls or anything like that.

MRS. SMITH: I complain to the office all the time, not that it does any good. I don't care what the other tenants think. I've got my family to look out for.

MRS. BROWN: That's right! And look what happened to you last summer. (Laughter from the group)

**Practice Points:** The laughter of the group members is actually, in retrospect, a version of the fight-flight reaction discussed in the group work section. Humor is used to defray the real fears raised by the incident. With the worker's help, they began to address the risks involved in confronting not only the housing authorities but also neighborhood youths.

WORKER: What happened, Mrs. Smith?

MRS. SMITH: There were a lot of older boys outside my door making noise. I asked them to leave because my mother was sick, but they wouldn't do it, so I called the office. The police made them move, but they came back and turned on the fire hose and flooded my apartment. (Silence)

MRS. WRIGHT: They'll get you, all right. (The group agreed.)

**Practice Points:** The worker sensed the fear in the silences but did not reach for it. Workers in these situations are sometimes afraid to acknowledge underlying feelings of fear and ambivalence. One worker told me, "If I reach for it, I might get it, and then they would be so scared they would back out." This view underestimates the strength of people to face difficult and frightening tasks when they have a stake in the proceedings. Rather than frighten the group members off, the acknowledgment of the fears may provide the added strength needed to make the second decision about the confrontation. The first decision to act for their rights was made in the heat of the exchange of complaints.

The second decision, the real one, must be made after the members have had a chance to react to their own bold steps. They must reflect on the risks involved and feel the fear that is associated with taking an action such as this. Workers who do not pay attention to helping clients with these feelings often find that, when the crunch comes, clients are not ready to take the next step. Then the worker often takes over for the clients—for example, becoming the spokesperson in a confrontation—when, with more preparation, the clients might have handled the problem themselves. In this group, however, the housing manager's refusal to come to the meeting and a threat against one of the members by a local welfare rights group brought the issue to a head.

Plans had been made for Mr. Murray, manager of the Housing Authority, to attend this meeting. The worker told the group of her own meeting with Mr. Murray and his refusal to come to the group's meeting. A general attitude of pessimism, disappointment, and "I told you so" was expressed by all members. The worker has encouraged the group members to begin by "speaking softly" and reaching for possible engagement with the management. When this does not work the next step is to "speak loudly" through some form of confrontation.

MRS. MELTON: I think we should go over his head, since he refused to come. (All agreed.)

MRS. SMITH: Let's talk to Commissioner Long. He is Black and just recently appointed to the Housing Authority board. (All agreed.)

**Practice Points:** At this point in the meeting, Mrs. King arrived late, appearing upset. In response to the concerns of the worker and the other group members, she revealed that, because of her participation in this group, she had been threatened by members of a welfare rights group to which she and others belonged. What follows is an example of the problem that occurs when advocates take the position that the system—in this case, the welfare department and the welfare worker leading the group—is always the enemy. Rather than explore the genuine common ground between their own group's goals and those of the agency, they attempted to coerce members into quitting the group:

MRS. MELTON: I told you, Mrs. Payne, that he would not come. He does not care about us. None of them do. (At this point, Mrs. King came in, looking upset. She apologized for being late and stated that she almost had not come at all.)

WORKER: I'd rather that you be late than not come at all.

MRS. SMITH: What's the matter? Is Ronny (her son) all right?

MRS. KING: He's all right; that's not it.

MRS. MELTON: Don't you feel all right?

MRS. KING: (Silent for a few minutes.)

WORKER: If you'd rather not discuss it, we'll go on to our discussion about the Housing Authority.

MRS. KING: No, I'll tell you.

She then explained in detail how some members of the welfare rights group had come to her apartment, accused her of starting trouble with the people in the project by being in this group, and told her that she should leave the group. She denied the charges but stated that she was upset when they left and was worried that they might cause trouble for her because of her participation in the group. She stated that she got mad at herself this morning for letting them boss her around, so she got dressed and came to the meeting.

MRS. MELTON: How can they cause trouble for you? They don't have any power.

MRS. SMITH: How did they know you belonged to this group?

MRS. KING: I don't know. I didn't know any of the people. I've seen two of them who live in my building. I don't bother anyone. I stay to myself and mind my own business.

WORKER: Were any of you approached by this group? (All said no. Two of the five present belong to the welfare rights group.)

MRS. MELTON: Have they bothered you anymore?

MRS. KING: I don't really know. I had two slips in my box to come to the office (Housing Authority). The lady under me complained that I let water run down her walls from my apartment.

MRS. SMITH: I remember your telling me about that.

MRS. KING: I knocked over the pile of scrub water and it went through the holes between the radiator pipes. I said I was sorry, that it was an accident.

MRS. MELTON: They (Housing Authority) should close up the holes anyway.

MRS. KING: The other was that my son made too much noise.

WORKER: Have you received complaints before these?

MRS. KING: No.

GROUP: (Long silence)

**Practice Points:** This time, the worker had strategized to reach into the silence and explore the group members' feelings and to ask them to face the second decision, which can be frightening to people who are in an oppressed and vulnerable position.

WORKER: I believe that this has troubled all of you, and I can understand your concern. Let's take a few minutes and think about the group and your participation in it. How do you feel about it? Are you getting anything from the group? (Silence)

MRS. KING: I've been thinking about it a lot. I'm not going to let people tell me what to do. I don't really know what I'm getting from being here. I like to come, and I've been able to meet some new people. I think I understand your agency better.

MRS. MELTON: You see, Mrs. Payne, people are afraid of reprisals. I'm older, so they don't bother me. I get a lot out of these meetings. Things are clearer to me. And you helped me with those bills from the Housing Authority. Besides, this gives me a chance to get out.

MRS. DAVIDSON: I've learned a lot. I think my attitude about the caseworkers has changed. I know now that they are not all bad, and it's my responsibility to see that they know what my family needs. Certain things that I did not know about came up, and other policies were explained to me. I don't feel sorry for myself anymore, because I see other people's problems are worse than mine.

MRS. MELTON: I like coming here; a lot of things that were on my mind about welfare are clear to me now. You have helped me a lot. Besides, if we can get somewhere with the Housing Authority about our complaints, that alone will be a great deal.

MRS. KING: I've learned a lot about welfare, too, that I did not know before. I enjoy the group, and I'm going to keep coming. It's too bad more people don't come. It makes me mad to know that they will benefit from all our hard work.

GROUP: That's the truth.

WORKER: Then I take it that you want to go on? (All agreed.) I'll follow through and let you know before the meeting if we will have a guest.

**Practice Points:** After contact was made with the city commissioners, the project manager, Mr. Murray, changed his mind about meeting with the group. The group members found that, if they understood the political system, they could use it by applying pressure in the right places. Decisions concerning public housing are political in nature; as long as there are no public complaints, problems can be ignored. Using the political system as a tool for citizens is an important step for change. All too often, members of poor and oppressed groups give up hope of trying to deal with the "system." An attitude of "you can't fight city hall" predominates, leading citizens to give up on the institutions, structures, and agencies that are established to meet their needs. The worker must convey the idea that there is always a next step.

After the worker clarified the purpose of the meeting with Mr. Murray, the group members began their confrontation.

MRS. SMITH: I'd like to know what the Housing Authority considers wear-and-tear items. I don't think I should have to pay for shades that were worn when I came into my apartment or if they have been hanging for 5 years.

MR. MURRAY: If the shades are worn when an apartment is vacant, we replace the shades. All apartments are in good order when you people move in.

GROUP: (All disagreed.)

MR. MURRAY: When you move in, you sign a statement that everything is in good order. If you don't agree, don't sign it.

MRS. SMITH: I wrote on the list that the shades were worn. You replaced them, but you charged me for them. Ask Mrs. Payne—she gave me the money for them.

MR. MURRAY: You should not have been charged for those shades.

MRS. MCIVER: You see, that's what we are complaining about. We don't know what we should and should not pay for. Your men make us pay for everything. Even if we disagree, you take their word for it.

GROUP: That's right.

MR. MURRAY: You should come to me when you feel you are being charged unjustly.

GROUP: (Laughter)

MRS. SMITH: You're never there, and no action is taken if we leave a message.

GROUP: (Agreement)

**Practice Points:** As the meeting proceeded, the manager expressed his feelings about the tenants. It became clear that he had a stereotyped view of the tenants based on those who had damaged property and not maintained their apartments. Additionally, as a White manager speaking to a group of African American tenants, the phrase "you people" takes on a racist tone. In this case, the worker was also African American.

**MR. MURRAY:** The problem is that you people don't take care of your apartments. You let your kids wreck the place because you don't own it. You've got a responsibility, too, you know.

**MRS. MCIVER:** I resent that. Most of us keep our places clean. I know there are some people who don't care, but why should the rest of us have to suffer?

**MR. MURRAY:** We clean the grounds, make repairs, and paint the halls every 4 years. It's the tenants' responsibility to care for the upkeep of their apartments.

**MRS. BROWN:** Gin bottles, beer cans, and urine stay in the halls for days, and your men don't clean it away.

**MR. MURRAY:** Call me. I'll see that it gets done.

**MRS. MCIVER:** What about the mailboxes? Can't we have better boxes with pick-proof locks? Our checks are always stolen and boxes broken into and we have to pay for them.

**MR. MURRAY:** There's no such thing as a pickproof lock. I know the trouble you are having with your checks, and I'm sorry, but if we assume cost, then you people will break in every time you lose your key.

**MRS. MCIVER:** I disagree. I don't think the tenants would deliberately break into boxes.

**MR. MURRAY:** They do, and they will do it more often if I change that rule.

**Practice Points:** The White manager of this housing project with a majority population of people of color was treating tenants in a racist and stereotyped manner. His offers to take care of things were largely efforts to disarm this group, probably because of his fear of their strength in numbers. When the members felt they could not get past the defensiveness of the manager, they again resorted to political pressure, which had worked the first time. The manager responded by inquiring why they had not brought their complaints to him, and the issue of retribution was out in the open. The worker intervened to try to help the manager see that the residents were motivated to improve their living situation.

**MRS. SMITH:** Who makes appointments to the Housing Authority?

**MR. MURRAY:** The city commissioners make the appointments.

**MRS. SMITH:** Can one of us go to the commissioners to let them know our problems?

**MR. MURRAY:** My board meets once a month. It's open to the public. The board is autonomous. It sets its own rules within the federal guidelines. We will listen to your complaints.

**MRS. SMITH:** We want them to take some action, too.

**GROUP:** (All agreed.)

**MRS. MELTON:** We don't feel that the building representatives represent us. I did not know about the elections of officers.

**MR. MURRAY:** You were all told about the meetings, and I know it.

**GROUP:** (Disagreement)

**MRS. MCIVER:** (Member of one of the committees) Maybe the representatives do not take the time to tell all the people in their buildings.

MRS. SMITH: That man in my building does not represent me. He's not qualified; besides, he does not care about us.

MR. MURRAY: You people have lots of complaints, but you never bring them to the office.

MRS. MCIVER: Most people don't complain because they are afraid of trouble from the office.

MR. MURRAY: We have not put anyone out because of making complaints. I don't see why you should be afraid. There's no reason for it.

WORKER: What the group is saying is that the office has ways to put pressure on these people. The fear is here and cannot be changed overnight. These people are not here to attack you personally but the people who make these unjust rules. These people are motivated—that's why they are here. They want to improve their living circumstances. It's up to you and your board to help them.

MR. MURRAY: If the tenants think the representatives do not meet their approval, then I'll see to it that new elections are held.

MRS. MCIVER: The people don't feel that you are willing to meet with them. They don't feel that you are interested.

MR. MURRAY: I'll do what I can and take your complaints to the board. If you like, you may form your own committee.

MRS. SMITH: We will be at your next meeting.

**Practice Points:**   The meeting had to be called to an end because it had run 45 minutes past the scheduled time. The housing manager's reaction to the confrontation was predictable—inspections were suddenly ordered for all apartments. At the next meeting, the worker again attempted to explore the members' feelings about the reactions to their assertive behavior. Note the worker comes back a second time when they do not immediately respond to her question about how they feel.

MRS. SMITH: Everybody's talking about it (group's meeting with Mr. Murray) in the office. The janitor who came to inspect my apartment got mad because I refused to sign the inspection form. I told him why and he asked who had I been talking to: Mrs. Payne (the worker)?

GROUP: (Laughter)

MRS. BROWN: They think we are wrong. He (the maintenance man) said that there were over $6,000 in repairs this year in the projects, and that we were responsible for them.

MRS. KING: Andy (the maintenance man) said it's about time someone spoke up. Some of my neighbors are blaming us for the inspection because they have not been inspecting apartments.

GROUP: (All agreed.)

MRS. SMITH: I knew Mr. Murray would do something to get back at us.

GROUP: (All agreed.)

WORKER: Well, how do you feel about the things that are happening to you?

MRS. SMITH: I don't mind. I knew he would do something to get back at us. But with the agency (welfare) behind us, he knows he cannot get away with these things anymore.

MRS. BROWN: I heard they were inspecting the apartments, so I was ready for them. My apartment was really clean and in order.

MRS. MELTON: They (Housing Authority) have not inspected our apartments in 2 years or more. Why now?

GROUP: (Agreement. They seemed to make light of the situation and to take it as a joke.)

WORKER: But you still have not told me how you feel about all this, the criticism and pressure from the Housing Authority and your friends and neighbors.

MRS. BROWN: I don't mind. Something had to be done, so we are doing it.

MRS. SMITH: I don't mind being the scapegoat. I think we can still do a lot more. We will benefit if they (Housing Authority) approve some of our requests, as will those people who call us troublemakers. It's for them, too, not just us.

MRS. KING: The only thing I did not like was their going into my apartment when I was not home.

GROUP: (All agreed.)

WORKER: Were you notified of the inspection?

GROUP: No.

MRS. SMITH: They (Housing Authority) can come into your apartment anytime they want to—it's in the lease. They can do it as long as it's a reasonable hour.

MRS. KING: I still don't want them walking into my place.

WORKER: Were nonwelfare tenants' apartments inspected also?

GROUP: Yes.

MRS. KING: They wouldn't like it if it was their place.

MRS. MELTON: They did not miss a thing. We even had to pay for tassels on the shades and missing screws.

WORKER: In other words, they went over your apartment with a fine-toothed comb.

GROUP: (Laughter, agreement)

MRS. BROWN: They even took the screens out of the windows to be cleaned and fixed. I asked the man not to take mine because those windows are high and the children might fall out, and he said I should put parachutes on all of my kids. I could tell he was mad. (There was a great deal of conversation among members about what they did and did not sign for in regard to the inspection. Their general attitude was surprisingly light and gay.)

WORKER: Am I correct in assuming that you want to go on with the plans for the meeting tomorrow?

GROUP: (All agreed, saying, "Of course," "Why not?" and so on.)

MRS. SMITH: We all have asked the tenants in our buildings, but most people won't come because they are afraid of reprisals. They are always asking what we are doing and are interested.

WORKER: Are you afraid of the reprisals?

GROUP: (All chime in) No, of course not.

MRS. SMITH: No. I've always complained about things, not that it does any good. We think we are right. We are not asking for anything that is unreasonable.

MRS. BROWN: My friend said she would not come but would babysit so I could go. (Group all agreed that they were not afraid and would all be there Thursday night.)

**Practice Points:** The worker then suggested that they consider their strategy for the meeting. The members were concerned about speaking in public and asked the worker to read their requests. She refused, emphasizing the importance of tenants' speaking for themselves. The worker's belief in them was important. She offered to be there to help but said that it was their fight and she believed they could do it.

WORKER: What approach are you going to use?

MRS. MELTON: Can't we do like we did at our meeting?

**GROUP:** (All agreed.)

**MRS. BROWN:** Maybe one person should read the list of requests. Can't you do it, Mrs. P.?

**WORKER:** No, one of you should read it. The board will want to hear from you as tenants. What I will do is make a list of your requests and have one for each of you and the board members. Then they can ask you questions. I'll be with you and give you all the support I can, but it's up to you to present your side of the picture.

**MRS. KING:** That's a good idea, and it will help a lot if they ask us questions.

**MRS. MELTON:** Sometimes, I get all confused and can't say what I want to say.

**WORKER:** Let's all try to be calm and, above all, be polite.

**GROUP:** (Laughter. Personal joke on Mrs. Payne was told.)

**Practice Points:** Discussion continued about the painting of apartments, specifically with regard to the cheap quality of paint used, the lack of color selection, penalties for not painting, and the differential treatment of some tenants. The meeting adjourned with plans to meet Thursday night at 8:00 P.M. for the board meeting.

**Practice Summary.** At the meeting with the board, the members acquitted themselves well, and the board immediately approved 9 of their 11 requests. Two of the requests were complicated and required further study, but the board indicated that a positive response would be forthcoming. The members of the group and the worker were elated. By using the political system, the members found they could exercise their rights. The balance of power shifted and the pattern of inaction and conformity (because of fear) was broken; the positive reaction to the first steps taken by this group encouraged other tenants as well. Of course, many issues remained. The relationship with the project manager was still poor, but the worker strategized how to help him see that recognizing tenants' rights would serve his interests. The problem of intertenant friction also needed to be attended to, because peer pressure might well be the most important factor in getting tenants to take responsibility for better maintenance of the project. These next steps seemed more manageable to the group after their initial success.

In addition to the roles described thus far, the community social worker with a task group has many of the same functions described in the earlier chapters on working with clinical groups. Several of the dynamics described earlier, such as the emergence of the deviant member, arise in task groups such as the one described in the next example. This example also raises a fundamental issue that is common to community-based groups: What if the worker has a strong opinion about an issue or the direction the group should take?

*Mobilizing Adolescent Peer Leaders in the Community* In this next community group example, we examine a common type of program in which adolescents and teens in a housing project are organized to provide service to their community. The social worker focused on helping the teens to overcome their internalized sense of inadequacy, which had been reinforced by negative community stereotypes regarding their competency. The example demonstrates that each individual member of such a group brings her or his own strengths and problems to the process and that not all members will be able to achieve the hoped-for positive results. Standing in stark contrast to the success of the group on its community task are the poignant descriptions of the problems and setbacks experienced by members. It is a powerful reminder of how community and family pressures can exert a force, and how a "relapse" can occur even in the midst of community success.

*Type of Group*: Task group for adolescent peer leaders

*Age Range*: 13–19 years old

*Gender and Ethnicity*: Four male African Americans, one female African American, two female Hispanics, and one female Caucasian

*Dates Covered*: 10/15 to 1/13

### Description of the Problem

The peer leaders' lack of credibility in the community in which they worked and lived led to criticism from parents, the funding agency, the Housing Authority, and the Tenant Council. Few believed this group could organize positive events in this housing project, an attitude that undermined the peer leaders' potential and purpose.

### How the Problem Came to the Attention of the Worker(s)

During my twice-weekly training sessions with the peer leaders, the group would talk about the rumors and comments that their mothers, neighbors, Tenant Council, or Housing Authority Task Force were alleging against them. I watched the group go from joking about the newest rumor to growing discouraged, doubting their own abilities to create positive events. In late November, I announced to the group that the funding agency was going to drop this project because of the negative press that this housing project was beginning to receive in relation to teenagers.

### Summary of the Work

Thirty teenagers from this small housing project interviewed for the peer leader position. Eight were hired: four male and four female. At the first formal meeting, during their first day on the job, the contract became the tool that disclosed the group's task: negotiating its relationship to the environment.

Keith (17 years old, African American) mentioned that Mary, the Tenant Council chair, probably would not let them use this community center every day. Amy (15 years old, African American) elaborated on how the "green monster" yells and screams at them just for looking at her. I asked why they named her the "green monster." Bruce (15 years old, African American) answered by pointing to a green partitioned office in the corner of the center. Everyone laughed. I asked if there were any rules connected with our use of the building. They all grunted and chuckled, and Lucy (19 years old, Caucasian) enlightened me by asking if I had all day to sit and listen to her list them. I was reaching for their perceptions of their own environment as well as conveying my willingness to learn from them.

As the group began defining the problems they wanted to tackle and the events to work on, they became more aware of what a peer leader group is. The group struggled, however, with the idea of serving as positive youth role models. Jake (15 years old, African American), Amy's twin brother, mentioned that there is nothing for a teenager to do in this city. "All we do is go to school, come home, and get into trouble." Gwen (14 years old, Hispanic) added that the weekends are boring and "someone needs to make some changes around here." I asked who they thought should make these changes. I wanted to assist them with connecting their purpose as peer leaders to the task of creating change. Bruce answered by insisting that the Housing Authority were the only ones who could create change, because they had all the money. Danny (14 years old, African American), Keith's younger brother, jumped in and said, "Yes, if they were the cops we'd all be in the state pen." They then went on to exchange stories about their bad encounters with the Housing Authority.

I asked if they thought they could make some changes. Once again, I was hoping to help them make the connection between themselves and their purpose. Karen (13 years old, Hispanic) nodded her head yes, vigorously. The Housing Authority was perceived to have all the power, and they continued to have a difficult time envisioning their own abilities to create positive changes. I, too, was feeling oppressed by this powerful organization, but I also realized my need to know the Housing Authority Task Force, so I decided to attend meetings on an irregular basis.

**Practice Points:** In the excerpts that follow, the reality of living in a neighborhood in which crime, drug dealing, and murder are all too common is brought home dramatically to the social worker. These teens face many environmental stressors, and the worker must have faith in their resilience to survive and thrive in the face of adversity.

In early November, the group ran their first meeting with teenagers from the project. Forty-five youths showed up for the meeting. The basic goals were to build an organization of youths, brainstorm ideas for future events, and establish themselves as leaders among their peers. On the following Monday, I went prepared to process the success of their first organizing meeting; however, they came to work discouraged and quiet. I inquired about their gloomy faces. A few shrugged their shoulders, and then Danny looked over at Keith and said, "Just tell her."

Keith went on to tell me that he was arrested for assault on the weekend. I immediately responded by asking if Keith had been convicted. He informed me that he was given a court date in 2 months. I avoided details of the arrest intentionally, because I did not want to set myself up as the moral teacher or the judge. Lucy, however, was upset with Keith and asked him how he ever thought the group was going to look good if they all went around beating up people. This conversation lasted for 45 minutes and ended with major changes on their work contract. They decided that they needed to be accountable as positive role models "24/7" instead of just the 2 hours they worked each day. They also put in writing that, if any of them were arrested, caught in possession of illegal drugs, or caught carrying a gun, they were immediately terminated. They all agreed that Keith should not be fired, because he had not known about the rule.

**Practice Points:** It would be easy for the social worker to get as discouraged as the youth; however, it would be naïve to think that change can come so quickly. The issue is not whether or not they "regress" but, rather, how they handle an incident such as this one. Their recognition of their responsibility "24/7" is a positive step.

The group members must deal with yet another shock. After allowing them to discuss their feelings, the social worker asks them to reflect on the impact of the incident on their work as a group.

During the last week of November, one of their friends, Jed, was shot seven times and killed in front of the community center. Jed was a local hero because he had just signed with a record label and already had a rap album produced. He was also selling cocaine, which resulted in his death—a fact that the group refused to accept verbally. They romanticized Jed's death. It appeared to me that

Keith, Danny, and Jake were struggling internally with the decision to choose positive behavior over negative. The world that surrounds them daily is so full of pain and negative options. Their ambivalence about their role as peer leaders showed itself often in the group, putting them at higher risk for negative actions.

After an hour of talking about Jed's death, I asked them to think about how his murder affected them as a group. I saw this tragedy as an opportunity to clarify the need for peer leaders in this community. Keith said, angrily, that the world would do anything to keep the Black man down. Jake agreed, adding that Jed was going somewhere, and someone had to go and "take him out." Once again, I asked them to focus on the group as it related to Jed. I was aware of their avoidance to address the facts of the murder, such as the drug charges and the sad reality that the killers were also Black youths. It did not seem appropriate to address this at this time, because their grief was so new. Therefore, I felt a deep need to look at the relationship between themselves as peer leaders and an environment in which other youths are being killed.

After a brief silence, Gwen said that no one really "gives a fuck" about them. Danny jumped in and shared that his mother thought they were all a bunch of hoodlums, and that she is surprised that any of them could even get out of bed in the morning. No one laughed. Bruce added that he thought the whole community was against them, and that they all thought the members of this group were just like Jed. "We are just like Jed," blurted Jake. "I won't live past 18 years old." Silence fell over the group.

**Practice Points:** This is a powerful moment in the development of the group. The initial enthusiasm was easy but now, facing the reality of their situation, they will need to make the second decision—deciding to go on in spite of their fear, anger, and self-doubts. The worker does not jump in to reassure them but instead lets them experience the moment.

The silence was powerful. I was deeply affected by their comments. I was angry along with them. I was also sad as I felt their pain. "I'm tired of the killing!" shouted Amy. "First, my older brother is murdered, and then you (looking at Jake) were stabbed this summer, and now Jed, dead!" Amy turned to me and looked straight into my eyes and said, "Tina, no one gives a shit about us. What can we do to change anything?"

"Amy, you can prove to yourself by proving to others that you care very deeply about life and you want to see it improve," I responded.

I could see a lot of hope in the anger that we were all feeling. I felt like we were closer to sharing a common vision than ever before. I could see some lights clicking on in the midst of the pain and a new energy for the work being rekindled. I also felt a sense of urgency about our work. The time was now, and we needed to take the opportunity. Instead of a teen dance, or a party at Christmas, they decided to plan an event that would serve the whole community with an emphasis on celebration and healing. They needed money, credibility, and success.

The Holiday Bazaar would offer international foods, raffles, free presents for all the children, Santa Claus, a craft corner, face painting, a graffiti wall, and speeches delivered by Amy and Keith. They sent out press releases to several newspapers and TV channels. They especially wanted Channel 7 news to come, because they were the station that had covered the story on Jed. They liked the idea of the news team coming back to cover a positive story on youth. I overheard Amy telling the news reporter, "I believe the youth need to be heard in America. We have a lot to say and a lot to give you adults, so listen closely."

During the event, the director of the Housing Authority stood behind the microphone, asked for attention, and proceeded to deliver a speech to the community about how crucial he felt these peer leaders were for this housing project, and how proud he was of them. He then announced to the group, in front of their parents, friends, siblings, and neighbors, that the Housing Authority was giving the peer leaders $9,000 to continue their work.

The group was stunned by this announcement. Lucy, Amy, Keith, and Bruce flew over to me, confused and disoriented by the good news. They were firing questions at me, such as "Did he say he was giving us money?" "Did you know about this?" "What does he mean?" "Did you hear all the cool things he said about us?" I asked them how it felt to be such a success. I saw their shock at being delivered encouraging news from the Housing Authority, the very agency that they had felt so oppressed by during the past 3 months. I felt I needed to help them connect the director's announcement with their success. They were slow at internalizing good news and I was hoping they could absorb the glory as they were experiencing it and not just in retrospect. Finally, as the good news began to sink in, the peer leaders started hugging me and one another, exclaiming, "We did it!"

We broke for the holidays for 2 weeks and then held our first meeting after our big event on January 6. Jake had taped the 7-minute excerpt from the local news on the night of our event, so I arranged for all of us to view it. We watched it two times and then discussed what our favorite part of the event was. "Being told we could continue working," said Lucy. Bruce commented, "Yeah, I was shocked when the director got up there and said those cool things about us. I was scared that he was going to kick us out of the community center." We all laughed. I then told them I had some more good news. Not only did the Housing Authority commit to donating money, but the drug prevention funding agency also donated some. In unison, they shouted, "How much?" I was so excited to tell them that the amount was $10,000. I really wanted them to absorb their success as a group, so I lingered on the details. "That's $19, 000," Bruce declared. "We were hoping to raise $200 from selling the food and sodas. Shit, we really showed them." "Who is 'them'?" I asked.

I hoped we could reconcile some of the pain that months of criticism had brought them. I was also hoping that they would really start seeing themselves as creative and positive people. Naming the "enemies" and realizing that they, too, were capable of change could reveal to them some very important truths about their own personal power. We discussed every detail that was observed concerning their success as a youth organizing group.

**Practice Points:** The positive reactions of the community and the commitment of funding are a powerful force in helping the members begin to believe in themselves as agents of change. For the social worker, the success of the project and the news she is about to announce that the city is going to create five groups just like this one hits home to the part of her that also wants to feel she can have an impact on community. However, in her enthusiasm, she misses the impact of this announcement on the group.

During the next training session on January 13, we focused on our next big event. I started the group with a bit of new information that was being discussed in the Task Force meetings. "Because of your success as a group, the Housing Authority, in conjunction with the funding agency, wants to create five more peer leader groups in this city. They see the success of teenagers working to improve their own environments. Isn't that great? The youth voice in this city will be strong." I was personally so excited about this new development. From my perspective, this was the best news yet, because it would provide more jobs for youths and reach a large constituency.

The group was silent. I was surprised that they did not seem excited. Lucy then blurted, "What about us?" I was lost and said, "What do you mean? It's because of you that this is happening." I really missed the point here. Lucy continued, "What about us? They could be taking care of us and trying to improve our voice." "Yeah," Danny added, "they have completely forgotten about us." "We need a youth center," Bruce joined in. "We can't keep meeting in this ugly building, on these metal chairs." "We can't even hang up a poster in here," Keith added. "They won't even let us have snacks in this center."

These comments went on for 15 minutes before I asked what was wrong. I felt there was something else going on that I wasn't aware of. They were back to being upset with the agencies and their surroundings. They continued talking about not wanting to be forgotten. I then asked if they would like to help train other peer leader groups. I was beginning to see how much they needed to be recognized on an ongoing basis and how fearful they felt of having their victory taken away from them. Perhaps if they were given some status among these other groups, they might feel more in control.

They changed their tune completely after this comment. They started making plans about how to teach these other young rookies the ropes as youth organizers. They fantasized about their position as the top youth workers in the city and how the mayor would give them all outstanding citizen awards. I felt both sad and happy about their need to be accepted. I realized that the ongoing, daily reality of living as poor minorities in a housing project where they feared eviction was a very heavy burden that I so quickly forgot. Listening to them dream, however, was also beautiful. They had a very difficult time dreaming of a positive future.

### Current Status of the Problem: Where It Stands Now

The problem still exists. However, the opportunity for the group to see the very agencies that felt so powerful and oppressive be affected by the peer leaders' dedication has made them realize that they do have some control over their environment. The ongoing struggle of daily life, however, feels like an endless battle for some of the youths. Danny was fired in late January because he was caught by his mother in possession of cocaine. The only reason she reported her son was to beat the eviction letter. If tenants confess their mistakes before the council writes them a letter, they avoid eviction.

Jake is also struggling with his street-self. He was present when two of his friends were killed; he experienced the death of a brother, and another has recently been arrested; and he experienced violence personally when he was stabbed during the summer. Rumors are floating around that Jake bought a gun. We have no proof, and Jake denies the allegation. On February 8, Keith was convicted of an assault that he committed in October. He will be on probation for a year. Two weeks before the bazaar, Lucy married a 38-year-old man at the state penitentiary. He's been a "friend of the family" since Lucy was a child, and he is now serving time for rape charges. These hard realities have certainly impacted the group's newly attained credibility. Two steps forward and one step back.

### Specific Next Steps

I am now working 3 days a week with the peer leaders. We are currently planning a month of prevention in this city, during which the peer leaders will perform plays in the high schools, have a poster and essay contest, and host a banquet/entertainment night to which city officials and those who provided funds will be invited. The internal issues in the group, which are directly related to the environment in which they live, continue to undermine the group's work. However, much of my time is spent negotiating with parents and agencies to believe in these youths and encourage their efforts. Dealing with the dysfunction and the group dynamics is an area that demands much more attention and requires sensitivity and skill, but this is a whole new story.

**Practice Summary.**   What is so impressive about this example is the worker's never-failing faith in the capacity of the teens to overcome adversity. She understands the meaning of the deviant behavior that they have evidenced and still reaches for their strengths. As she points out, it will always be two steps forward and one step backward, but the general momentum for many of them will be forward.

## The Ending/Transition Phase of Practice: The Milieu as Community

In this section of this chapter on community work, we focus on the milieu as community and the ending and transition phase of community practice. For many clients, their community is a residential center or a hospital ward. Although treatment programs affect their lives, the day-to-day experiences of living and working with staff and other residents always have the most powerful effects. If a treatment group teaches about life empowerment but its members feel disempowered in the setting, the real message reinforces weakness rather than strength, pathology rather than resiliency. Clients already struggle with the internalized stigma associated with mental illness, and feeling disempowered in the hospital setting simply reinforces this view.

***Patient Empowerment Through a Newspaper in a VA Hospital***  In the example that follows, the social worker uses the medium of a ward newspaper to help psychiatric patients in a VA hospital to negotiate their community more effectively. The newspaper becomes a vehicle for communication with staff as well as a means for the members to discover their own strengths. It also becomes a medium through which the members can communicate their inner feelings about having to deal with the oppression associated with mental illness. The example takes us from the early, enthusiastic beginning phase, through the problems of the middle phase and the need to make the second decision, and finally to the way in which the worker (a student) helps the group and the system build in the structures needed to continue after she has left.

*Members:* White male veterans who are patients in a VA psychiatric setting

*Dates:* 9/30 to 12/2

### Description of the Problem

The task this group faces is one of negotiating the larger system in which it is situated, in order to produce a patient newsletter. Some of the challenges faced by the group are resistance from the larger system (the hospital), resistance within the group (fear of making waves), members' fear of retribution from staff, feelings of disempowerment, and suspicion from inside and outside of the group. The major problem centers on the feelings of disempowerment embodied by the group members. This is illustrated by their reluctance to express themselves honestly in the newsletter. A second, related problem is the hospital's low expectations of the patients and the ambivalence of the hospital toward change. The problem I face is to find a way to mediate between these two systems.

### How the Problem Came to the Attention of the Worker(s)

Several incidents led to this assessment. In the beginning phase of the newsletter, I observed a great deal of enthusiasm, both from group members and staff, but this enthusiasm began to falter after the first few meetings. Many of the members failed to complete the assignments for which they had volunteered, and support from the outside system was not forthcoming, as had been promised. Staff members discussed the need to censor the newsletter before it was distributed, which heightened and reinforced group members' fear and reservations. I realized that some of these issues would need to be addressed if the group were to proceed any further.

**Practice Points:** The principles of practice associated with the beginning phase require that the social worker begin with contracting and a clear statement of both purpose and role. In the first session we see the group members responding to this offer and making the first decision to get involved. Group work was a central method of working with these patients; however, most of the groups were experienced as illusions of work, with staff and members going through the motions in one type of group after another. It was the existence of so many groups that led the student social worker to conceive of the newspaper as something different. Initial reaction from staff, psychiatrists, nurses, and social workers on the ward was that there was little chance that these patients could be mobilized, but they wished the social work student the best of luck. This staff reaction to her proposal was a signal of the stereotyped view of the patients held by staff. The idea of a new group and one that would publish a newspaper attracted patient interest.

### Summary of the Work

The first session was exciting. It was filled with hope and expectations on the part of the worker as well as the members. It was a large group, with 17 members in all. There was a sense of expectation in the air. I had been preparing for the group for several weeks, and the newness of it was intriguing to the members. Most of the veterans had gotten to know me well enough to suspect that something different was happening—that this group would be different from other groups in the program.

In the beginning of the session, I explained to the group what I had in mind for the newsletter, in order to clarify its purpose. "As some of you already know, I had an idea to start a newsletter. The newsletter would be created by all of you. You would write the articles, decide what went into it, how often it would be published, and things like that. In other words, it would be your newsletter. I also thought of it as a way to help the members of this program get connected with one another and keep one another informed as to what kinds of things happen around here. We could send copies to your friends and families to let them know what kinds of things you do here. I would also contribute my own ideas from time to time and be available to help members with any problems they might have. There will also be some other students and volunteers who have offered to help in any way if you have trouble with writing. I'd like to hear from you now. Do you have any thoughts on this idea?"

**Practice Points:**   As discussed in the chapter on group formation and recruitment of members, the tendency on the part of the group leader is to ignore hints of ambivalence or doubts. The skill described as "looking for trouble when everything is going your way" would have been helpful in the first session if the worker had reached for the underlying issues she sensed but avoided. She will have another chance. One veteran playing the role of the "deviant member" raises the issue of the internalized stigma by sarcastically suggesting a title for the newspaper. The social worker, still anxious to get the group off the ground, chooses to avoid the signal.

Many members expressed interest and said it was a good idea, though I sensed some doubt on their part. I had the vague sense that they were just humoring me. Instead of confronting it directly, I went on, hoping that in time they would become more invested. Had I confronted it then, it might have opened up the discussion and raised some of the concerns and doubts they were feeling.

We decided on a name for the newsletter, and people volunteered for jobs. There was much debate about what to call the newsletter. One member, with a sarcastic tone, offered the Elite Newspaper of the East as a possible title. He seemed very angry. I added his title to the rest of the titles to be voted on, and I commented that I thought it was an interesting name. He did not respond, and I went on collecting other titles. I realized I had not picked up the message he was indirectly sending me. I had missed the opportunity to address some of the anger he was feeling, and I was not tuned in to what was urgent to him at that moment. I was unable to set aside my own agenda. Had I picked up on his anger, I would have been able to recognize that his feelings were representative of much of what the group was feeling. Fortunately for the group (and for me), this anger would surface again in later groups and help break through the illusion of work that had formed.

In the second session, the members volunteered one another for jobs. In a somewhat derisive manner, an older man named George volunteered Dana, one of the younger members, to be the editor. Dana was generally very quiet and reserved and seldom participated in other groups. I responded that I thought it was a great idea and asked Dana if he would consider accepting the position. He seemed pleased at this, and accepted. Everyone applauded. At this point, Harold, another older man, said that when he was in the army, he used to take a lot of pictures. I asked him if he wanted to be the photographer, and he agreed. The energy in the room seemed to increase, and everyone started volunteering for jobs. We decided to meet once a week as a group and to put the newsletter out once a month.

**Practice Points:**   The members have made the first decision to engage; this is the easy one. In addition to seeing the emergence of the deviant member role, there is now also evidence of scapegoating in the derisive nomination of Dana as editor. The sarcastic title for the paper in the first meeting, using the term *elite,* and the derisive suggestion for a passive member as editor can, in retrospect, be considered the first and second offerings of the underlying issues associated with the oppressor within and the stigma these men have internalized. These issues will emerge again as the group members face the more difficult second decision. The worker's tact in providing supportive encouragement still avoids addressing the more painful underlying issues.

In the fifth session she reaches for the real feelings, responding to the signals of apathy and boredom. Jim, the original deviant member, turns out to be the group's internal leader, expressing their anger and frustration. The social worker is very clear on the importance of maintaining her role by being with the group and the staff at the same time.

During the month, some of the members were very busy interviewing people and writing their stories. Others were not doing their jobs and were coming up with excuses for why they couldn't do them. I felt this was due to a lack of confidence in their abilities, so much of my work during this period focused on expressing my belief in their abilities to do the job. I began to recognize that a general theme was emerging with regard to how disempowered the members were feeling.

During the fifth session, I noticed that many of the members were having difficulty concentrating and seemed completely disinterested in the group. I reached for what was happening. "What is going on today? Everyone seems to be having trouble focusing on the topic. You all look bored and tired." Dan responded, "We all just went out for a long walk. We are tired." Richard added, "They keep us too busy around here, and all we do is go to groups. They never leave us alone." I asked if anyone else felt this way and, if so, whether they wanted to spend a few minutes talking about this. Many members responded by agreeing that there were too many groups and they were feeling overwhelmed.

I tried to validate their feelings by saying that sometimes there were a lot of groups to attend, and then I asked if they had ever spoken to the staff and voiced their concerns. Jim, the member who had been so angry in the first session, responded by saying that it did no good, that the staff didn't care what they wanted and treated them all like children. I knew I had to be careful here. My natural inclination was to side with the group members. I had often been angered by the patronizing manner in which these men were treated. It would have been easy for me to have jumped on the bandwagon and started criticizing the hospital, but I knew that would not have been useful. I responded instead by reaching for his feelings, saying, "It must feel pretty frustrating to be treated in this way. After all, you're not children, you're grown men."

**Practice Points**: In response to her skillful reaching for the "lurking negatives," she opens the door for the discussion of stigma and the way patients were treated by staff. This is the crucial step for helping them to make the second decision. She creatively points out that the newspaper might well be the vehicle for expression of some of their discontent.

This opened the door for a lengthy discussion about how it felt to be a psychiatric patient and to lose so much control over one's life. I tried to bring the conversation back into focus by suggesting that the newsletter might be a forum the men could use to voice some of their concerns. Roland, a member whom I have always thought of as very ingratiating to the staff, eager and cooperative, fearful of making trouble, and generally considered a "good" patient, said, "Oh no, we couldn't do that, they would never let us print it. Besides, it's not really so bad around here. The staff is all nice, and they treat us well." Another member was made anxious by the interchange and completely changed the subject. Time was almost up, so I said that, if the group wanted to, we could continue talking about this the next time we met.

**Practice Points**: As this potentially frightening issue emerges, Roland, playing the role of the "gatekeeper," expresses the part of all the group members that is fearful of confrontation with staff. The member who changes the subject illustrates the fight-flight reaction discussed in earlier chapters. These comments all emerge as the session ends in typical "doorknob" fashion. The worker is somewhat ambivalent as well, as evidenced by her not at least identifying the emergence of this theme of fear and the need to address it during the next meeting. With word getting out about the conversation, the group leader starts to address the turn of events with staff. She reaches for their underlying concerns beneath the joking.

> The next session involved a field trip we had planned, and the session after that, the recreational therapist joined the group. Apparently, the news had gotten out about our discussion. I told the staff I was encouraging the members to write about things that were meaningful to them and that, at times, this might involve an expression of criticism toward the hospital. They joked about how I was getting the patients all riled up. I sensed some suspicion beneath the humor, so I asked if they thought this was a bad thing. This brought the issue to the surface and opened up the opportunity for me to speak with the staff about some of the feelings the patients were having.

**Practice Points:**   With trust growing between the group leader and members, an element of what I have referred to as the working relationship (therapeutic alliance), members risk opening up other usually taboo areas related to treatments, lack of informed consent, and physical restraint and punishment. Roland again fills the role of gatekeeper. Jake's discussion about the drug side effect of impotence is another sign of developing trust, since sharing this with the female worker has to be difficult.

> During the next group session, we got back to the discussion and returned to the earlier topic. The members seemed distracted and uninterested. They were also having difficulties finishing the assignments for which they had volunteered. I asked them what was going on. Jimmy, a member who attended only occasionally, responded, "How do you expect us to do anything? I can't write; look at my hands." He held up his hands, which were shaking visibly. "They keep us so medicated around here, we can't even think straight." Jake agreed, "These doctors use us as guinea pigs. They try one medication after another on us. We are subjects in their experiments; they don't treat us like human beings." Roland began to get nervous. "Yes, but we need to take our medication because it helps us. I'm ready for my next shot. I get too agitated if I don't get my shot."
>
> Jake responded, saying the medication didn't help him and that it had ruined his life. He spoke of how he was not able to have a relationship with women or to live a normal life. He said, "Any member in this room will tell you that the medicines make you impotent. How are you ever supposed to meet a girl or think about getting married?" Several of the men nodded their heads in agreement. I said that must be very difficult for them and asked if they had ever let the doctors know about the problems they had with the medications. Jake again responded, "They don't care. If you refuse to take the medications, they will just lock you up." He went on to tell of how he had been forcibly locked up in the hospital. Several other group members agreed, telling stories of how they had been locked in the seclusion room, beaten up by orderlies, or admitted to the hospital against their will. They said that, when they told someone, the doctors responded by saying it was just a symptom of their paranoia. Jake said that he was learning not to fight, that he was not a young man anymore.
>
> I empathized with the things that the group members had gone through and said it must be really difficult to always have someone questioning their reality. I then suggested that Jake might want to write about his experiences for the newsletter. I hoped

to begin to help empower them and to show them a way to have their concerns heard. Jake expressed ambivalence about doing this. I said I could understand his reservations and that, if he wanted to, he could take some time and think about it or he could write it anonymously. This all proved to be more than Roland could stand.

**Practice Points:**   As the discussion deepens and the possibility of exposing some of the problems through the newsletter emerges, Roland responds with anger and we see the "fight" element of the fight-flight response designed to deflect conversation from the frightening idea of standing up for themselves in the system.

Under his breath, but loud enough for everyone to hear, he said, "Communist!" I was taken aback by this expression of anger from Roland. I was also not sure to whom he was talking. Jake responded angrily, "What did you call me?" Roland looked in his direction and said, louder this time, "A communist. You're nothing but a communist. The doctors are just trying to help us. You're always going around trying to stir things up." Jake was very angry at this; a veteran considers this to be the worst kind of insult. Jake responded to Roland, "I'm no communist, and don't you call me that. I have a right to say what I feel." I was afraid the situation might escalate into violence, because Jake was extremely angry. (I also felt my maternal instincts surface.)

I interjected, "Roland, it seems as if you see the situation in one way and Jake sees it from a different perspective. But I don't think it is useful for us to call one another names." I had intended to try to create a culture in which discussions of such matters were allowed and also one in which members respected and listened to one another. But, in rushing to Jake's defense, I was sending a message that I didn't believe he could take care of himself and that he needed my protection. This was not a useful message to send to someone who already feels oppressed. I might have done better if I had waited a little longer and allowed them to work things out themselves.

Roland apologized to Jake and said he was just a little "off" because he had not gotten his shot yet. Jake accepted this apology, and the conversation returned to a discussion of an article someone was writing for the newsletter. The session ended with me encouraging the members to consider writing about their hospital experiences for the newsletter.

### Current Status of the Problem: Where It Stands Now

I can safely say that the newsletter has become firmly established as a part of the program. I've noticed more staff members becoming invested in its continuation. There has been discussion of who will take over the project after I am gone. The director of the program requested a copy of the newsletter to be sent with his semi-annual report, and another staff member included it in a presentation she was giving about the program. I have witnessed some positive change, in that the system now relates to the veterans in a different manner. I notice some staff now saying "members" or "veterans" instead of "patients." Several staff members have expressed surprise with regard to the talent that the men are exhibiting. There is also less fear and suspicion about what kinds of things I am doing with the group. We are still working on the issue of censorship, as I continue to advocate for as little as possible to make sure the newsletter remains within the patients' control.

The group members are still working on how much they want to express themselves in the newsletter. Many of the members still feel very disempowered and alienated, but they have received a lot of positive reinforcement from the hospital community, which has led to a tremendous boost in self-confidence and self-esteem.

Some of the members of the newsletter group are working on submitting articles to a national journal that publishes works by disabled and hospitalized veterans. Others have expressed an interest in learning how to type so they can type the newsletter themselves. One member has decided to begin to study for his high school equivalency exam. This is truly an exciting process to watch.

### Specific Next Steps

- I will continue to encourage the members to use the newsletter as a forum to voice their concerns.
- I will attempt to create a safe atmosphere within the group, in which members can feel free to discuss things that are truly meaningful to them.
- I will continue to work with the larger VA system to sensitize it to some of the feelings, needs, and concerns of the veterans.
- I hope to continue to make the newsletter a project the members feel they can have ownership of.
- I will continue to search for connections between the system and the group to help create more open systems and a healthier environment for the veterans.
- At every opportunity, I will endeavor to empower the individual members as well as the group as a whole.
- Finally, I will continue to work on my skills as a group worker so I can "make more sophisticated mistakes" in the future.

It seems appropriate to conclude this example with some excerpts from the newspaper published by these veterans, the *War Memorial Gazette*. Their first issue did not deal directly with some of their concerns and feelings about the hospital and the staff; however, they did appear to employ indirect communications. For example, the comedy section of the first issue contained the following three jokes about psychiatrists:

### Jokes by Ed

1. What's the difference between a neurotic, a psychotic, and a psychiatrist? A neurotic builds castles in the clouds. A psychotic lives in them. A psychiatrist collects the rent for them.
2. How many psychiatrists does it take to change a light bulb? One, but the light bulb has to be willing to change.
3. This guy goes to the psychiatrist, and he talks to the psychiatrist, and the psychiatrist says, "You're crazy!" And the guy says, "I want a second opinion." And the psychiatrist says, "OK, I think you're ugly too."

As the members' confidence grew, they began to be more direct, including columns about their concerns over the ward policies and procedures balanced with interviews that highlighted members of the staff. In their third issue, they included editorial and poetry pages, excerpts of which follow.

This newsletter is a project of the Community Support Program of this Veterans Administration Hospital. The opinions and views expressed within do not necessarily reflect those of the staff or administration of the Hospital.

### Politicians

We as individuals should not form our opinions of a politician by their rhetoric and exposure by the media, but rather by their actual voting record, which should be publicly displayed. What is their background educationally, religiously, and what special interest groups support them physically and financially? This will determine their voting records and real selves. The news media should take more objective responsibility in this area.

### Personal Philosophy

I'm a Vietnam combat vet. I've been in and out of the Veterans Hospital for many years for physical and mental problems. This doesn't mean I haven't got a good IQ or common sense.

**On economics**, it's about time we as Americans bought American products to put Americans to work. Our products are better, as good, or maybe not up to foreign products. Every individual makes our economy and jobs with their purchases.

**On politics**, it's about time we look at our representatives and the policies they put forward. Are they voting for money, people, and special interest groups or for the American people? Stop the political slander and get to the economic issues. We have a beautiful system of checks and balances between the Congress, Presidency, and Supreme Court. We also have the right of petition if we disagree with what's going on. If we don't examine and vote, we stand a chance of losing this system.

### Poetry by Tom

*Feeling Blue*

When I'm out under the trees
I watch the flowers dance in the breeze
I feel the pain and sorrow that surround me
All I want is the sun to shine, the rain to fall
And no one to be left standing small.

*Saying Good-Bye*

For you there are always tears, the well is never dry
People live sadly, they must die
Think of a deep, deep sleep
Think of the trees swaying in the breeze
Think of a cool mountain stream you may see
Only in a dream
To find the answer you must be keen
Just be sure life was not just a dream.

*Teddy Bear*

I wish I was your teddy bear
I would squeeze away your tears
I would squeeze away your sorrows
I would squeeze away your fears
I would hug you ever so tight
Tell you I love you so
And Never, Never let you go.

The veterans published the *War Memorial Gazette* for more than 5 years (and may still be publishing it). It matured as a paper and earned the respect and support of the staff. When the veterans held a 5-year celebration of the inception of the paper, they invited the student who had helped them organize the paper, to thank her for her initiative and her faith in their abilities. The excerpts just cited serve as a tribute to the resilience and courage of clients and to the profound impact of one student who refused to give up on them or the system, her second client. This example sends an important and appropriate message to our profession, reminding us of the roots of social work and the importance of the two-client concept.

## Social Workers and Social Action

This chapter has focused mostly on how social workers work with communities and community groups to empower them to bring about change. I have suggested that it is important for the social worker to help community members develop the skills to bring about changes rather than take the leadership roles themselves. For example, in the earlier illustration of working with the public housing tenants' group preparing to meet with the Housing Authority board, the social worker resisted the temptation to speak for the tenants but instead worked with them to develop their own presentation. We could see in the report of the meeting how board members' hearing about the grievances directly from the tenants increased the impact.

### Social Action in the Community

Workers' contacts with clients often put them in a unique position with regard to community and social policies. These workers' firsthand experiences can provide insights into client needs, gaps in services, and the impact of existing policies that need to be brought to the attention of policy makers and the community. The complexities of our society often make it difficult for the wider community to know what is happening with the many "left-out" groups. In addition, society has some stake in not discovering the real nature of the problems. Once again, the functional role of mediating between the client and the system—this time, the community—can provide direction for the worker's efforts. These can consist of letters to a newspaper, briefs for government bodies prepared by the worker as an individual or as part of a professional organization, organized lobbying efforts in relation to specific legislation, and so forth.

One illustration of this process comes from my early practice in a small, suburban community on the outskirts of a large city. It was an example of a situation in which I was able to move from "case" to "cause." That is, a specific situation with two clients arose that led me to get involved in attempting to influence the policies of the town in which I worked. I was a youth worker in a Jewish community center that served a middle-class population. Over time, I noticed two teenagers who were attending our lounge program but who were not members of the center's client population. After I made contact with these youngsters and a working relationship developed, the boys began to discuss their gang activities in town. It became obvious that they were coming to the center in an effort to move away from their peer group because of fear of getting seriously hurt or in trouble with the law. As a new youth worker in town, I had not been aware of the existence of this problem and had not seen any reference to it in the local press. Conversations with other teenagers in the program confirmed the extent of the problem.

At about the same time, I was invited to participate in a mayor's committee on youth that had recently been established to plan the town's priorities in the area of youth programs. More than 100 workers and volunteers in local youth organizations attended the first meeting. As I listened to the presentations, it became clear that each organization was presenting a brief in support of its own activities. It was also clear that the youth gang population was not going to be part of the discussion. In fact, because of their difficult behavior, these youngsters were usually barred from participating in the organizations that were represented at the meeting. I attempted to raise the issue and was naïvely surprised by the reluctance of the group to admit the problem. My notes of the session describe the process:

> After being recognized by the chair, I said we were missing an important youth problem in town. I pointed out that no one had mentioned the gang problem, and yet it was one that must be troubling all of our organizations. There was a long silence. The chairman of the committee, a town councilman, said that he didn't think the town had a gang problem. He felt the gang trouble was usually caused by kids who came over from a neighboring town and that perhaps those were the youngsters I was referring to. He turned to the planning and research coordinator for the county government and asked if they were aware of any serious juvenile delinquency problem or gang problem in this town. He pulled a folder from his briefcase and outlined statistics that indicated very little difficulty in this area, with the exception of some limited informal gang activity in the neighboring town. The chairman of the committee then suggested that, because I was new in town, it might explain why I believed the spillover problem from the neighboring town was really our concern. I sat down, resolving to keep my mouth shut in the future.

I can still remember the embarrassment I felt in response to the patronizing tone of the chairman. A week later, after some reflection, I realized that a community was not much different from a family, and that admitting a problem was not easy. The community was in the precontemplation stage. Many of the members of the group were unaware of the extent of the problem, and reassurance from the officials was all they needed to return to such questions as the adequacy of the number of baseball diamonds in town. Some were aware of the problem but chose to deny the extent of the difficulty.

I decided to develop, before the next committee meeting, a way of bringing the problem to their attention more effectively. I also decided that I needed both allies and some initial ideas about how to deal with the problem. When the two teenagers met with me that week, I explained what had happened at the meeting and asked how they felt about taping a conversation with me about their gang activities, in which I would maintain confidentiality by leaving their names out; they agreed to help me. I also inquired whether there were any other people in the community with whom they had good relations who might be helpful in convincing the committee that the problem really existed. They mentioned a police sergeant who had been involved with the kids when there was trouble and who most of the youngsters felt was all right. I called the sergeant and met with him for lunch. My notes of that meeting follow.

> I detailed my involvement in this issue, including my abortive attempt to raise the problem. He told me that he had heard about it the next day and had a

good laugh at the response. When I asked him why, he told me he had been raising this issue with city hall for 2 years and getting nowhere. I asked him what he thought needed to be done. He felt the town very badly needed a youth bureau that could concentrate on working directly with the gang kids. He tried to make contact, but this was not officially part of his job, and his being a police officer created real conflicts. I told him I thought this mayor's committee might be a great place to bring pressure to bear on city hall, which would have a hard time ignoring a recommendation from its own committee. I asked if he would support me at the next meeting when I played the tape and raised the issue again. He said he could not raise the issue himself, for fear of sanctions, but he would attend. If the committee asked him questions directly, he could respond. We agreed that I would raise the problem and he would respond.

My next step was to record an hour-long conversation with the two teens. In the first part, I asked them to discuss the gang structure and activities in town. In the second, I asked them to talk about themselves, their hopes and aspirations, the problems they faced in trying to accomplish them, and what they thought might be helpful. I felt that it would be important for the committee members not only to be shocked out of their complacency but also to gain a sense of these teens as the community's children who needed their help. We reviewed the tape together, with the teens editing out parts they felt might reveal too much about themselves and strategizing with me about which parts I should play for the committee for the greatest effect. I then made an appointment to play the tape for the police sergeant to alert him to its content.

At the next session of the mayor's committee, I explained what I had done, and I requested time to play the tape excerpts. The committee members were intrigued, and they agreed. They listened with attention as the two boys, in response to my questioning, described in detail the gang structure in town, the names of each gang, whether they were White or Black, the number of members of each gang, their relation to larger gangs in the county, and the internal structure of the gangs. They then reviewed several gruesome incidents in town of recent gang fights at movie theaters, in pizza parlors, and at the local high school. They gave detailed descriptions of their involvement in "stomping" kids using hobnailed boots. I asked them how they felt about all of this, and one responded, "Lousy, but what can I do? If I don't go along with the gang, I would be on my own, with no one to back me up." The boys then talked about their future plans:

WORKER: What kind of work would you like to do?
TOM: I'd like to be something like a bank clerk, or work in an office somewhere. But you need high school for that, and I don't think I'm going to make it out.
WORKER: What do you think you will end up doing, then?
TOM: Probably, I'll end up like my brother—going to jail.

At the end of the tape there was another silence in the room, but this time the expressions on the committee members' faces indicated that they were stunned by the detailed description of the gang structure and moved by Tom's fatalism. One member asked if all the gang fights that had been described had actually taken place. The police sergeant was asked if he knew about these fights, and he confirmed that they had occurred. He was then asked if he knew about the gangs described, and, in response, he detailed his experiences with gangs during the past 2 years. The committee chair asked him what he thought they could do about the problem. The police sergeant described the possibility of a youth bureau such as had been created in other communities.

The story of the gang groups received front-page publicity in the town paper the next morning, along with an editorial that stressed the importance of dealing with this problem. Several recommendations emerged in the final report of the commission, including the establishment of a youth bureau and the development of special programs within the other youth organizations, as well as activity centers that would make the programs accessible to the gang population. The youth bureau was funded in the town's next budget, and the police sergeant accepted the job as the first director, with a field staff of two.

In this instance I had many advantages: dealing with a small town that was relatively open to influence, finding an effective ally in the sergeant, working with a ready-made forum provided by the mayor's committee, having the support and encouragement of my agency administration and board, and finding two youngsters who were willing to risk themselves. In other situations, moving from identifying a problem to changing policy might not be as easy.

## Advocacy Groups and Political Activity

There are times when social workers should take responsibility for direct or indirect advocacy in an effort to create social change. For example, social workers can support advocacy groups such as the political action groups that are sponsored by their state or provincial professional association. Joining and supporting single-issue groups financially or through the investment of time is another route. Although particular political and policy points of view may differ among social workers (e.g., pro-life and pro-choice positions), it is important for all social workers to get involved in one way or another to impact the "second client" at whatever level they can. As outlined in the Chapter 1 discussion on the historical roots of our profession, whether social workers are involved in micro or macro practice, family counseling or community organization, we have a professional responsibility to be socially and politically informed and to get involved.

Activity can take many forms and may include working on a campaign committee for a politician who advocates positions the social worker endorses on issues such as health care or the related issue of poverty and inequality in income distribution. A social worker in a practice area (e.g., public school social work) may have insights and experiences that can be helpful to a candidate in forming a platform or a position (e.g., on school reform and the need for increased services). Although no one can address all of the important social issues, it is important that social workers become actively involved in at least one issue that we deeply care about.

The argument that we are too busy with our direct clinical practice is no excuse. The position advocated here is that we are not actually doing clinical social work practice unless we are simultaneously concerned and involved with the public issues that impact the private lives of our clients. Inviting a group of inner-city students suspended for school violence to attend a support group, or what may be called an "anger management" group, without addressing the issues of racism in the schools, poverty, community gang activity, and community violence that these students face every day may be somewhat helpful for some students, but we are not addressing the issues that lead to the anger. The two-client idea that defines the unique role of social work requires that we try to find some way to begin to address the big-picture issues.

## Chapter Summary

The community social worker plays a specific role in working with task-focused community groups. Social work practice with community groups is called macro practice—in contrast to micro practice, which is clinical practice. Macro practice can include direct and indirect social work activity. *Community* is defined broadly to include a geographic area as well as an institutional milieu.

The concepts of group dynamics and the skills of working with groups introduced in earlier chapters that focused on micro practice also apply to work with community groups. Such work poses unique challenges as well, because the second client often has significant power and control over clients' lives. Models of community organizing include grassroots, social action, organizing around a specific issue, rural-based community organization practice, and using the Internet as a "virtual" community.

In work with task-focused community groups, the community social worker plays a particular role. The term *community,* as it is used here, is a geographic designation and includes an institutional milieu. The concepts of group dynamics and the skills involved in work with groups that were introduced in earlier chapters apply to work with community groups as well.

In addition to empowering community groups, social workers can also play a role in influencing community policy as they move from "case" to "cause." Political activity and participation in advocacy groups is another way to work for social justice.

## Related Online Content and Activities

Visit *The Skills of Helping Individuals, Families, Groups, and Communities,* Seventh Edition, CourseMate website at **www.cengagebrain.com** for learning tools such as glossary terms, links to related websites, and chapter practice quizzes. The website for this chapter also features additional notes from the author.

## Competency Notes

The following is a list of Council on Social Work Education (CSWE) recommended competencies and practice behaviors for social work students defined in Educational Policy and Accreditation Standard (EPAS) and addressed in this chapter.

**EP 2.1.1c** Attend to professional roles and boundaries (p. 662)

**EP 2.1.3a** Distinguish, appraise, and integrate multiple sources of knowledge, including research-based knowledge and practice wisdom (p. 652)

**EP 2.1.3b** Analyze models of assessment, prevention, intervention, and evaluation (p. 652)

EP 2.1.4a Recognize the extent to which a culture's structures and values may oppress, marginalize, alienate, or create or enhance privilege and power (p. 653)

EP 2.1.5a Understand forms and mechanisms of oppression and discrimination (p. 650)

EP 2.1.5b Advocate for human rights and social and economic justice (p. 650)

EP 2.1.6b Use research evidence to inform practice (p. 653)

EP 2.1.10e Assess client strengths and limitations (p. 652)

EP 2.1.10i Implement prevention interventions that enhance client capacities (p. 652)

EP 2.1.10k Negotiate, mediate, and advocate for clients (p. 651)

------------------

## *Endnotes*

1. The Stuart Shulman coauthor of this paper is this proud author's son. Although his academic route was through political science, his work then and continuing work now focuses on how to increase the impact of citizen input to government regulation. He has developed a software startup company (Texifter) that includes a program for analysis of citizen input required in the development of federal agency regulations.

# Practice Models and Evidence-Based Practice

I n the first five parts of this book, the text described the underlying philosophy and core assumptions about people, society, and social work practice that contributed to the development of this Interactional Model (IM). This was followed by the elaboration and illustration of the core (constant elements) of the model as it was implemented in work with different modalities: practice with individuals, families, groups, and communities. These represented variant elements that influenced the manner in which the core model was utilized. The particular setting, population, problem, and so forth added their own elements to the elaboration of practice.

In this Part VI and Chapter 17, a number of additional practice models are shared in the belief that we may draw ideas from a range of frameworks and incorporate them into our own models. While many of the concepts from these models and the evidence-based practices have already been integrated into the first five parts of the book, in this chapter we focus on them in more detail. A review of current views on evidence-based practice also may shape our interventions.

## CHAPTER SEVENTEEN

# Evidence-Based Practice and Additional Social Work Practice Models

The social work profession has a number of models and theoretical frameworks to draw upon for individual, family, and group practice. Although this book presents an interactional approach to practice, the underlying assumptions about human behavior in general and practice in particular are congruent with other models. For example, all of the practice models and theories shared in this chapter start from a strengths perspective in thinking about individual clients and groups. All of the models are based on the belief that individuals have the capacity to change how they think, change their emotions, and change how they act—and on the belief that changes in any of these elements (thoughts, feelings or actions) impact the others.

An example of this was seen in the illustration of the group of young women survivors of sexual abuse described in Chapter 14. Some of these women had perceived of themselves as "damaged goods" as a result of their childhood abuse experiences. This internalized view of themselves, along with the attached emotions, led to self-destructive behaviors such as the use of drugs and relationships with men who were abusive. As their understanding of their experiences changed and they no longer accepted the guilt for their abuse (e.g., "I must have been provocative toward my father"), and instead understood that what happened to them was not their fault, their feelings about themselves also changed. As they were able to take more adaptive steps in their lives, end abusive relationships, stop self-medicating with drugs, and even assert themselves by confronting specific abusers and by acting together to participate in a "take back the night" march, their strength increased as did their capacity for change. Constructs and strategies from cognitive-behavioral therapy, solution-focused practice, and feminist practice can all be identified in this example.

As an alternative to practicing a specific practice model, perhaps even following the directions of the model's protocol as outlined in a manual, specific concepts and techniques can be included in an integrated practice framework. For example, with clients in recovery from substance abuse, the worker could use a solution-focused intervention by asking the clients when in their lives they had been able to maintain their recovery for a longer period of time and what was going on at that time that helped them to do so. The all-in-the-same-boat phenomenon associated with a mutual-aid model in a recovery group could enhance this sort of reflection, since each member would be able to note similarities as well as differences.

In addition, core concepts from the mutual-aid model presented in Part III can be employed to understand group practice using other frameworks. For example, a crisis intervention group can be analyzed using the phases of work—preliminary, beginning, middle, and ending/transition (as in an example later in this chapter)—to identify the dynamics and skills associated with each phase. Social workers can draw upon a range of models as they create their own practice framework. In my view, the emphasis should be on finding what works for clients rather than on maintaining ideological purity or simply practicing in the comfort range of the worker.

A growing body of federally funded research has been helpful in identifying which models appear to offer advantages in dealing with specific populations and particular problems. The general rubric of evidence-based practice (EBP) has been used to describe frameworks that have been exposed to some level of rigorous testing and whose findings offer some support for their use in practice. Concepts from these models have been introduced in previous chapters, where relevant; however, in this chapter they are described and illustrated in greater detail. While they may have been in the background in previous chapters, they move to the foreground in this one.

The following section defines the criteria generally used to apply the designation EBP to a model. The sections that follow it provide an overview of EBP and briefly summarize three of the identified EBP models that already have made major contributions to our understanding of practice. This is followed by other models that, although not yet as well noted as EBP, nevertheless also actively contribute to our understanding of practice.

The specific models selected for this chapter were chosen because of my view that the concepts of the interactional approach and mutual aid could fit easily in their

**EP 2.1.3a**
**EP 2.1.6b**

versions and that their fundamental values were consistent with those espoused in this book. Other models exist that could have been included and also would meet these criteria; however, space considerations have limited the number shared.

# Evidence-Based Practice (EBP)

**EP 2.1.2b**
**EP 2.1.9a**

With so many models of practice available, every professional is faced with the need to evaluate various frameworks and strategies in order to modify practice in the best interest of the client. The term *evidence-based practice (EBP)* has been used to describe practices that have been determined to have some success, with some clients, at certain times, and with some outcomes.

Barker (2003) defined evidence-based practice (EBP) as follows:

> The use of the best available scientific knowledge derived from randomized controlled outcome studies, and meta-analyses of existing outcome studies, as one basis for guiding professional interventions and effective therapies, combined with professional ethical standards, clinical judgment, and practice wisdom. (p. 149)

The elements of this definition that help to define a model as an evidence-based practice model include the following:

- The best available scientific knowledge derived from randomized controlled outcome studies
- Meta-analyses of existing outcome studies
- Combined with professional ethical standards, clinical judgment, and practice wisdom
- Randomized controlled outcome studies that involve random assignment to treatment or no-treatment (or modified-treatment) groups with efforts to control for other variables that may impact the outcomes

McNeece and Thyer (2004) suggest a hierarchy of scientific methodologies that should be considered, with some offering more credible support for EBP validation than others. In rough order from high to low they are:

- Systematic reviews/meta-analyses
- Randomized controlled trials
- Quasi-experimental studies
- Case-control and cohort studies
- Preexperimental group studies
- Surveys
- Qualitative studies (p. 10)

## Ethical Considerations, Clinical Judgments, and Practice Wisdom

In addition, professional ethics, clinical judgments, and practice wisdom are integrated into the most effective EBP models. It would be hard, for example, to imagine an accepted EBP model that violated some of the basic ethical premises of the helping professions—for example, informed consent, as outlined in earlier chapters. In another example, some early models of treatment for addictive behavior involved extreme forms of confrontation designed to break down barriers and force acceptance of a problem. Miller and Rollnick (1991) addressed this issue. The authors point out that some therapy groups, particularly those organized around a Synanon therapeutic community model, have employed what is called "attack therapy," "the hot seat," or the "emotional haircut." After illustrating this with a particularly harsh and attacking example that has the therapist saying: "Now, Buster, I'm going to tell you what to do. And I'll show you. You either do it or you'll get the hell off Synanon property," the therapist in the example continues with a personally attacking and insulting verbal assault. Miller and Rollnick, referring to this illustration, comment:

> Approaches such as these would be regarded as ludicrous and unprofessional treatment for the vast majority of psychological or medical problems from which people suffer. Imagine these same words being used as therapy for someone suffering from depression, anxiety, marital problems, sexual dysfunction, schizophrenia, cancer, hypertension, heart disease, or diabetes. (p. 6)

This extreme-confrontation model would be an example of an approach that violates ethical standards, clinical judgment, and practice wisdom. Most professionals in this field would agree that denial of the existence of a problem is a reality, and that the client needs to face and accept a problem before it can be dealt with. Miller and Rollnick (1991) point out that confrontation is a goal, a purpose, and an aim. They continue, "The question, then, is this: What are the most effective ways of helping people to examine and accept reality, particularly uncomfortable reality?" (p. 13).

Whereas facilitative confrontation is an important element in any helping relationship, the emphasis is on the word *facilitative*. As described earlier in this book, confrontation that is integrated with genuine empathy and comes from caring is a crucial skill in a helping relationship. This concept emerges from both empirical research and practice wisdom.

As professionals consider claims that a particular approach is an evidence-based practice, it is important that they consider these crucial criteria: randomization, replication, professional ethics, effective assessment, and concepts that fit our established practice wisdom. Although our assessments and practice wisdom need to be challenged at times, our ethical standards are crucial to professional practice. The first three models described below have achieved the designation of being evidence-based.

A resource for identifying evidence-based practices in the substance abuse and mental health fields has been developed by SAMHSA, the federal government's Department of Health and Human Services Substance Abuse and Mental Health Services Administration (NREPP, 2006). This registry is available online at: http://www.nrepp.samhsa.gov/index.asp. The registry is described as follows:

> NREPP is a searchable database of interventions for the prevention and treatment of mental and substance abuse disorders. SAMHSA has developed this resource to help people, agencies, and organizations implement programs and practices in their communities. (p. 1)

## Manualized Interventions and a Note of Caution

One note of caution has to be raised on the issue of the implementation of manualized practices associated with EBP. For both research and practice purposes, it is common to develop a manual that provides a structure for the practitioner that guides the implementation of the particular EDP model. In multi-site research projects, manuals are used to ensure "dosage integrity," which means that the delivery of the model will be the same across sites. (The term *dosage* is borrowed from pharmaceutical research and refers to the way in which a particular drug is administered.) However, if the model and the manual are strictly observed in practice, it may, in some situations, prevent the use of innovative interventions or responses to unexpected events in the group.

In one example I observed, parenting groups were part of a national 16-site federally funded project designed to prevent the intergenerational transmission of substance abuse. Group leaders were instructed to deliver parenting information at fixed times in a group session and for a required amount of presentation time. The leaders' presentations were videotaped and the tapes analyzed to see if dosage integrity was maintained when compared to the other 15 sites. The rigidity of this manualized approach led the group leaders in this case to ignore parenting issues emerging from the group members as well as clear signals of reluctance (e.g., arms folded and angry expressions on participants' faces) to participate on the part of some mandated parents. Although the group leaders were experienced and normally would have addressed this initial resistance and tried to include the parenting issues raised by members, they felt restrained by the manual and the requirement of dosage integrity.

It was interesting to note that the video camera was trained only on the group leaders and their presentation, and no effort was made to view and rate the members' interactions with the leaders or each other. An assumption existed that I referred to earlier in this book: that words are magic. This is the belief that if the words are spoken by the group leaders, group members will hear, understand, invest affect in the concepts, and remember what has been said. This flies in the face of most of our lifelong learning experiences. This group would have benefited if the manual could have been adapted to the particular needs of the population and a level of spontaneity and artistry encouraged on the part of the group leaders.

The first three models and theoretical frameworks presented in this section of the chapter were selected because of they have been identified as EBP, having met the requirements above, and are consistent with the basic values of the mutual-aid model presented in this text.

## Motivational Interviewing (MI)

Examples of EBP-designated practices are found in major replications of a similar model funded by national organizations such as the National Institutes of Health. One example would be the use of motivational interviewing (MI) techniques to address addictive behavior (Miller & Rollnick, 1991).

Mason (2009) argues that MI can be understood as a more directive evolution of Carl Rogers's (1961) person-centered approach, since "it elicits the client's own intrinsic motivations for change; it is a supportive, empathetic, reflective and collaborative counseling style that honors client autonomy" (p. 357).

> Typically MI is differentiated from Rogers's style in that MI is directive, attending to and reinforcing selective change talk regarding the presenting behavioral problem. However, this distinction of nondirective versus directive counseling approaches may not be as clear as is commonly understood. (p. 357)

Mason cites the empirical research of Truax (1966), which asserted that Rogerian psychotherapy was actually just as directive as it was nondirective, stating:

> In Truax's detailed analyses of Rogers's therapy tapes, he indicated significant reinforcement effects (directive counseling) in the client-centered therapy, thereby bringing into question the complete nondirective nature of Rogerian therapy. This type of clinical behavior, such as reinforcing and encouraging positive statements, represents a style of clinical communication that is very similar to MI's more directive, albeit client-centered counseling. Notwithstanding, MI uses many, if not all, of the core ingredients that Rogers set forth in his work. (p. 357)

While echoes of Rogers's central conditions for effective treatment, such as empathy and genuineness and the use of reflective interventions, can be found in the discussions of MI, Miller and Rollnick (1991), in their use of MI techniques to address addictive behavior, focused on the issue of motivation:

> We suggest, then, that motivation should not be thought of as a personality problem, or as a trait that a person carries through the counselor's doorway. Rather, motivation is a *state* of readiness or eagerness to change, which may fluctuate from one time or situation to another. This state is one that can be influenced. (p. 14)

## Stages of Change

Miller and Rollnick (1991) build their framework on the stages-of-change model (Prochaska & DiClemente, 1982) cited and described in more detail earlier in the text. In brief review, the six stages of this model are:

- Precontemplation
- Contemplation
- Determination
- Action
- Maintenance
- Relapse

Key to the model is that the counselor uses interventions that are appropriate to the stage of change that is presented by the client. A counselor would not expect clients, for example, to begin to discuss actions to deal with the particular problem they are facing if they were still in a precontemplation or even contemplation stage. If the treatment approach involves the kind of confrontation described earlier in the Synanon example—when the client is in the precontemplation or even the contemplation stage—greater resistance is likely to be generated. Thus, while mandated clients could be forced to attend such a group, they could not be forced to change. At best, in a mandatory situation, the group member will go through the motions and participate in what I have called the illusion of work.

Miller and Rollnick (1991) assert:

> From time to time the balance tips, and for a span of time the person's statements reflect a good deal of what might be judged to be "motivation." At this "determination" stage, a client may say things like these:

I've *got* to do something about this problem!
This is serious! Something has to change.
What can I do? How can I change? (p. 17)

The motivational interviewing model suggests the therapist's tasks at each stage of the change process:

- *Precontemplation*: Raise doubt—increase the client's perception of risks and problems with current behavior.
- *Contemplation*: Tip the balance—evoke reasons to change, risks of not changing; strengthen the client's self-efficacy for change of current behavior.
- *Determination*: Help the client to determine the best course of action to take in seeking change.
- *Action*: Help the client to take steps toward change.
- *Maintenance*: Help the client to identify and use strategies to prevent relapse.
- *Relapse*: Help the client to review the process of contemplation, determination, and action, without becoming stuck or demoralized because of relapse. (p. 18)

## MI Interventions

The elements of the MI model that closely parallel the major assumptions and strategies of the interactional mutual-aid model central to this book include starting where the client is; working *with* the client and not *on* the client; recognizing the client's control over the outcome; developing a positive relationship through the use of empathy and other skills; and the importance of facilitative confrontation. Although emphases may differ, the similarities are evident. A brief summary of the model's motivational strategies, which Miller and Rollnick (1991) conveniently set forth, can be described (for mnemonic purposes) using the letters A through H, as follows:

- Giving ADVICE
- Removing BARRIERS
- Providing CHOICE
- Decreasing DESIRABILITY
- Practicing EMPATHY
- Providing FEEDBACK
- Clarifying GOALS
- Active HELPING (p. 20)

## MI Research

In the 2006 review of motivational interviewing research (NREPP, 2006), the national registry describes the core elements of the model as follows:

Motivational Interviewing (MI) is a goal-directed, client-centered counseling style for eliciting behavioral change by helping clients to explore and resolve ambivalence. The operational assumption in MI is that ambivalent attitudes or lack of resolve is the primary obstacle to behavioral change, so that the examination and resolution of ambivalence becomes its key goal. MI has been applied to a wide range of problem behaviors related to alcohol and substance abuse as well as health promotion, medical treatment adherence, and mental health issues. Although many variations in technique exist, the MI counseling style generally includes the following elements:

- Establishing rapport with the client and listening reflectively
- Asking open-ended questions to explore the client's own motivations for change
- Affirming the client's change-related statements and efforts
- Eliciting recognition of the gap between current behavior and desired life goals
- Asking permission before providing information or advice
- Responding to resistance without direct confrontation (Resistance is used as a feedback signal to the therapist to adjust the approach.)
- Encouraging the client's self-efficacy for change
- Developing an action plan to which the client is willing to commit

While most of the development and research of MI has been applied to individual treatment and has focused on treating addictive behavior, efforts have been made to translate the model into a group treatment modality. Van Horn (2002), describing a pilot-tested motivational interviewing group for dually diagnosed inpatients, points out that

Motivational interviewing is a brief treatment approach designed to produce rapid, internally motivated changes in addictive behaviors. Motivational interviewing shows promise for engaging clients with dual psychiatric and psychoactive substance use diagnoses in treatment. While initially developed as an individual treatment approach, key motivation enhancement principles may be applied to structured group interventions to facilitate its introduction to inpatient dual-diagnosis treatment. (p. 1)

Researchers have proposed adaptations of the core MI model to group practice in the substance abuse field, suggesting the development of a "core motivational group" as part of a treatment program (Ingersoll, Wagner, & Gharib, 2007). This framework uses topics such as the stages of change, decisional balance, exploring the pros and cons of changing and staying the same, supporting self-efficacy by exploring strengths, planning for change, and so forth in the group modality with a combination of presentations, group discussion, and group support.

In a study of the impact of the use of MI in a group-based motivational enhancement program prior to standard treatment, the authors reported that the 73 clients who attended the motivational group, compared to the 94 who did not, had significantly more positive outcomes (Lincourt, Kuettel, & Bombardier, 2002). When controlling for diagnosis, employment, and age, those in the motivational group had a higher rate of attendance to the overall program as well as treatment completion.

Finally, a randomized-controlled study was conducted with 161 alcohol-dependent inpatients who received three individual counseling sessions on their ward in addition to detoxification treatment and 161 inpatients who received 2 weeks of inpatient treatment and four outpatient group sessions in addition to detoxification. Both interventions followed the principles and strategies of motivational interviewing (John, Veltrup,

Driessen, Wetterling, & Dilling, 2003). The researchers found that group treatment resulted in a higher rate of participation in self-help groups at the 6-month-after-treatment point, but this difference disappeared after 12 months. There was no difference in the abstinence rate between the two groups.

Even though the adaptation of MI approaches in the group context is still early in its development and reports contain mixed results, it nevertheless offers a promising model for strengthening the initial engagement of clients and their willingness to participate in and complete treatment. Mason (2009) points out that

> Much of the research that has been conducted shows MI's effectiveness. However this method is not a panacea for all problems and is not without its limitations and concerns. Even though MI has been [shown] to be effective, explaining the "why" and "how" it works is yet to be fully understood. (p. 360)

Mason points out that MI is an approach that can be effectively used with other counseling styles and methods and that it was originally designed as a way to prepare clients for treatment and not as a self-contained method. He suggests, "MI can be used as a prelude to treatment, as added to or integrated with other counseling approaches, or as backup if motivational issues arise within a treatment context" (p. 360).

***Court-Mandated Group for Male Drunk Drivers: The Precontemplation Stage*** In the following example of a court-mandated group for clients convicted of driving while intoxicated (DWI), we see elements of MI integrated into the mutual-aid group practice model and observe how it is used as a "prelude" to treatment with a very resistant population. Note that the group leader does not attack the members' angry assertions in the first session that they are not alcoholics and don't think they should be forced to attend the group. Instead, she works with the resistance by having the men detail those things they did not want in the group, such as being called alcoholics or made to feel guilty. It was a number of sessions into the group, when they began to examine their "triggers" that led to drinking, that they were able to move into open contemplation of their problems and, for some, determination to do something that preceded the action stage.

In the first meeting, we see a fairly typical start to a court-mandated group for persons convicted of driving while intoxicated (DWI). Resistance and denial is in the air as the young female leader begins the session. Instead of confronting the resistance head-on and initiating the inevitable battle of wills, a not-uncommon approach in some models of substance abuse treatment, she recognizes the resistance as a symptom of the precontemplation stage of acceptance most of the men are in. In groups such as this one, group leaders often feel a threat to their authority (and agenda) when complaints emerge. In this case, you also have a female group leader dealing with a group of angry men, so gender issues can play out in the process.

*Purpose:* To introduce clients to support services; to encourage clients to explore their own use of substances and the role that alcohol and/or drugs play in their lives; to avoid rearrest

*Gender of Members:* Male

*Age Range:* 27 to 55 years

*Cultural, Racial, or Ethnic Identification of Members:* Two Irish males, one Indian male, seven European-American males

**Excerpt from Process Recording**

After going over the contract, I passed out a sheet that stated the purpose of the group and the topics to be covered. While some group members appeared to be reading the topics, others folded the sheet in half without a glance. I asked the group how they felt about the topics and if they had any questions. After a moment of silence one group member angrily stated, "You know, I shouldn't even be here. I was set up." (Nervous laughter from other group members.) He proceeded to tell his arrest story, while other group members appeared attentive. When he finished, I said, "It must be hard for you to be here when you don't even feel that the arrest was justified. I wonder if other people are feeling the same way."

**Practice Points:** Instead of ignoring the resistance or confronting the men, the group leader chooses to explore the resistance using empathy to begin to connect to their underlying feelings. The leader recognizes that the first member who challenges the need to attend the group is her "ally," not her "enemy." He raises feelings that are most likely experienced by all of the men. He, as well as most of the other group members, are in the precontemplation stage. Instead of getting into a "battle of wills" designed to prove they need the group, she uses an exercise to help the group begin to explore what powers their negative reaction and thus is able to capture their energy in pursuit of the group's purpose.

Another member spoke up, saying, "Well, what I don't understand is why we're going to talk about things like alcoholism and AIDS in a class for drunk drivers" (referring to the handout). "Yeah, we made one mistake, and now we're all alcoholics." Other group members joined in, expressing similar dissatisfaction with the topics. I replied, "You're raising some important points. It sounds like one of the things you're especially concerned about is being labeled. I wonder if we can come up with a list of some other things that you don't want to have happen in this group."

As I wrote on the board "Don't Want" and under it put "to be labeled," I asked members for further suggestions. Another member said "to feel guilty. I don't want to feel guilty for what I did." As I wrote "to feel guilty" on the board, I asked him if he could say more about this. He responded, "I mean, I know it was wrong, and I don't want to have people keep telling me it's wrong." Another member added, "Yeah, I feel like a criminal!" "Well, we are criminals, what do you expect?" another member commented. I asked, "Is it hard to see yourself in that way?" "Yeah, well, I guess we are criminals, but there are worse things we could have done."

**Practice Summary.** It is striking that the group leader's use of the listing of "don't wants" actually allows the men to express the important issues to be dealt with in the group. These include feeling guilty, feeling like "criminals," and concern about being branded as "alcoholics." Each of these represents powerful themes to be explored in the group. The group members are creating their own version of the agenda that actually, in many ways, mirrors the agenda of the leader and the agency. This example demonstrates the expression introduced in Part I of this book: "Resistance is part of the work."

*A DWI Group in the Contemplation Stage* In the excerpts that follow, we see the beginning phase and the transition to the middle phase in a group that is similar to the one just described. In this group, a number of the men have begun to face the fact that they have a problem, confronting the profound negative impact on their lives of their abuse of alcohol. They have moved into the "contemplation" stage in preparation for a transition to the "action" stage. One man, the "deviant member" Phil, holds out and refuses to engage. While the leader misses his early signals and sees him as the "enemy" to the group, internal leaders emerge to help both the man and the leader understand the behavior as a signal of the intense pain and guilt associated with a traumatic event.

**Practice Points:** The leader understands Phil's role as a "gatekeeper" but does not understand why Phil chooses to play this role. This is an example of the mistake of being with the group but not being with the individual. Once again we see that the "deviant member" is someone in the group who faces the same issues as the other members but who feels them more strongly. This recognition allows the whole group to move into a deeper level of work.

### Second Session

The group was struggling with their denial, Tom was starting to open up, but Phil was attempting to sabotage the movement of the group. It does appear that Phil is the gatekeeper, for every time the issue of drinking and driving is brought up he tries to prevent the process from occurring. I encouraged Tom to speak about his drinking and driving. Tom started talking about how he had three arrests in one year for drunk driving. I asked Tom if he could share with the group how he feels about this happening. He started to speak, but Phil jumped in and said that no one wanted to hear about this story. I tell Phil that Tom has the floor and ask him not to interrupt. I am starting to get upset that Phil is constantly interrupting, but I am hoping someone else will take a risk and say something.

**Practice Points:** Note that this is the moment that Phil needs the leader's help the most. Unclear about the "two-client" idea, the leader sides with group members who are angry with Phil and question his behavior.

Tom continues, saying he knows he needs help because he must have a problem, otherwise why all the arrests. Phil jumps in, but this time Pete speaks up and says that he has had enough of Phil and wants him to stop being rude. Inside I am excited that Pete, after having made overtures before as the internal leader, has stepped up to question Phil's behavior. I had asked myself how I might handle this challenge to my leadership (as a first-time leader) and my authority, but I realized the group had moved forward in the mutual-aid process and that the group's work was going well. This was a good opportunity to point out to Phil, and to the group, that he was diverting the group's attention away from the emotional issue of drunk driving. I asked the group if they think this is a sign that they are beginning to be a more cohesive group, and they replied yes, except for Phil.

**Practice Points:** As the group culture develops, the leader begins to understand how easy it is for the members to create the illusion of work. When he confronts them about triggers, thoughts, feelings, or events that lead to their drinking, the first reaction is a classic "flight" from pain through the use of humor and a "fight" reaction through a personal attack (as in the fight-flight element described earlier in connection with Bion's emotionality theory). The group leader understands this and comments on the difficulty the men are having with a painful subject. He still, however, has not tuned in to Phil.

### Third Session

While I think the group is starting to make progress, the illusion of work is holding the group members back. I make a demand for work by saying we are to discuss triggers that can cause them to drink. Jim speaks up and asks what I mean by triggers. Pete answers that was the Lone Ranger's horse. Tom jumps in and says that is what you use to shoot a gun with. I am not sure if the humor is a defensive tool to change the subject. I reply that this subject may have hit a sensitive spot, so I ask the group for feedback. Phil says that Jim asks the dumbest questions and wonders how Jim ever got his license. This is not the first time that Jim has been attacked when sensitive emotional issues are being brought to the surface. I am feeling some counter-transference issues rising in me, about Jim being a scapegoat, and I tell the group that they must be feeling pretty powerful when they attack Jim. I ask why they feel it is necessary to do this. (In retrospect, I see that I have taken Jim's side and have forgotten the group as a whole. I am surprised I did not lose the group at this point.)

Pete, the internal leader, makes a leap of consciousness and apologizes to Jim for acting the way he did. Tom, Sam, and Phil all say the same. Pete continues and says that he had never considered anyone's feelings before and asks me why. I open it up to the group. The one member who has been noticeably quiet, Bob, speaks for the first time since the beginning of the first session. He says it has to do with the topic of the day—triggers. Bob says that everyone has triggers that can set them off, but he sees triggers as coming from his past. He lived in an alcoholic and abusive home. I was taken aback by Bob's speaking up and what he had to say. I asked him if there was more he would like to say. He said he grew up never being allowed to say much, nor have an opinion, without suffering a negative consequence. It has taken him this long to overcome his fear enough to talk in the group, but after hearing the apologies to Jim, he feels safe in the group. I said he was very brave to speak up and describe his feelings.

**Practice Points:** In the fourth session we see the emergence of a strong internal leader who understands that Phil, the group's "deviant member," may be reluctant to talk because he is thinking about his own triggers. As is often the case, it is a group member who understands and empathizes with another member and helps the group take the next step in its development. In this excerpt we also see why Phil has been resistant from the first meeting and has played the role of trying to block addressing more intense issues and feelings. Returning to our discussion in earlier chapters of informal roles adopted by members and the concept of the group as a dynamic system, we can see Phil's behavior in the first three sessions as functional for the group not quite ready to risk in areas of intense emotion. As the group culture changes and it becomes safer to share, Phil no longer has to play this role. In addition, once again we see that the member who takes on this functional role is the one who has tried and so far failed to live with the strongest guilt over his past behavior.

### Fourth Session

I told the group that the last session showed the group is moving, and they should feel good about the work they have accomplished. I had a feeling that there was more work to be done with the issue of triggers, so I brought this out to the group. Pete said he had done some thinking over the week and wanted to know if the group could help him. All responded with a yes, except Phil. Tom asked Phil why he wouldn't, and Phil said he just didn't want to talk today. Bob said he thought Phil was struggling with his own triggers, and asked Phil if the group could get back to Phil's not wanting to talk after helping Pete. Phil, in a very quiet, subdued voice, said okay.

Pete said he wanted to revisit triggers because he feels that is where his major stumbling block is. Discussion was fruitful, and the group was beginning to take on a life of its own, dealing with intimacy and interpersonal relationships. Bob, Pete, and Sam were willing to look at these issues, while Phil and Tom were resisting any further intimate movements.

The group went back to Phil not wanting to talk, with Sam showing empathy and caring by saying that maybe Phil has some painful memories that have been triggered. The group as a whole struggled around how to help Phil. It seemed that the group had finally found a common ground to focus on—triggers. Other members took turns expressing how they have been affected by their triggers, how alcohol had taken over their lives, and the consequences. Bob talked about how he had lost his job, Sam said he had lost his job and his wife had divorced him, Pete said he had to go through bankruptcy, Jim finished by saying he had to spend eight months in jail for his drunk driving and this has affected how his children see him now. This was done with a lot of expressed emotions, with all members sitting in their chairs, but all leaning towards one another, as a way to begin to connect to the pains they had experienced due to alcohol.

**Practice Points:** As the group moves into a deeper and more emotional mode of work, we see the group leader practicing the skill of "containment" identified in the middle phase of practice. The members have moved past the authority theme, as described by Bennis and Sheppard, and are now into the intimacy theme.

They now turned to Phil, who looked like he had seen a ghost, and they asked if he was ready to share his triggers. Phil said that at first he had thought this group was foolish and felt that he had everything under control. We all sat with Phil's emotions. He started to cry, saying that he had for the first time since coming to group realized he was not alone in this fight over alcoholism. He said he felt this was a place for him to finally talk about his haunting nightmare. We all waited patiently, and I was overcome with the power of this group. Phil said that his trigger for all his years of drinking was he had never been able to forgive himself for driving the car and getting into an accident that had killed his wife. The group all sat in silence and cried for Phil and for their own losses.

### Where the Problem Stands Now

I believe we have created a new phase of work whereby the group is able to open up and express their painful feelings. I am surprised at how much progress they have made in moving to the middle phase of group work. The difficulty of denial, defensiveness, challenging me to be in control, members wanting to take control, and the different roles each member has played has been fascinating. There has been a slow change in the manner in which the members have interacted with one another, each playing a dramatic role in moving the group to its current place.

The culture of the group has grown to the point where they can begin to use empathic listening skills. This was not present in the beginning phase. I knew the group had the opportunity to experience the finding of a common ground, but I was not sure how we were going to get there. In retrospect, the problem statement does not have the same meaning as in the beginning. I now see their denial and resistance as a tool they use to cope, with alcohol being the method they use to hide their fears and feelings. The group had begun to deal with some of their most sensitive issues and losses in a more honest and trustful way than they had initially presented. The members carry within them a history of pain and denial, and their allowing this to surface has been a thrill to observe. I know there is much more work to be done, but to have experienced Phil's growth to the point of allowing others access to his feelings will stay with me forever. Just as the members are taking risks, I hope that I too can do the same in my role, challenging each of them to work more on their issues.

**Practice Summary.** While the leader admires the growth of Phil and the group, he should also acknowledge his own substantial growth. From a leader who at first identified with either the individual or the group he has developed the ability to be with both "clients" at exactly the same time. This will be a crucial step in his professional growth as he moves from the "contemplation" stage to the "action" stage in his practice.

# Solution-Focused Practice (SFP)

**EP 2.1.4b**
**EP 2.1.7a**
**EP 2.1.10c**
**EP 2.1.10e**

Another model of practice with elements that fit nicely in the interactional framework is called *solution-focused practice (SFP)* or *solution-focused brief therapy in group*. Corey (2008) points to the underlying positive orientation as a key concept:

> Solution-focused brief therapy is grounded on the optimistic assumption that people are resilient, resourceful, and competent and have the ability to construct solutions that can change their lives. . . . Clients are believed to be competent regardless of the shape they are in when entering therapy, and the role of the counselor is to help clients recognize the resources they already possess. Solution-focused therapists engage in conversations with their clients about what is going well, future possibilities, and what will likely lead to a sense of accomplishment. (p. 424)

Several of SFP's underlying assumptions and intervention techniques can be useful, particularly in the beginning phase of work. The practitioner needs to discern when they might be suitable or not for particular clients. This section provides a brief introduction to the model and identifies core techniques.

## Major Assumptions on the Nature of the Helping Relationship

The solution-focused model is built on the strengths perspective. As a form of "existential" practice, it focuses on the client's current issues and assumes that, with the help of the counselor, the client can identify and use inherent strengths that might be overlooked in a pathology-oriented practice. Put simply, the counselor thinks about what is *right* with the client rather than what is *wrong*. The counselor also believes that the source and methods of change will come from the client. This model emerged from an integration of the strengths perspective with interest in short-term treatment (deShazer, 1988; deShazer & Berg, 1992).

Some of the specific assumptions in the solution-focused practice model include the following:

- Intervention should focus on the present and what clients bring with them to the process.
- Achieving behavioral changes takes place in and affects the present, rather than resolving problems of the past.
- Although it focuses on the present, the model recognizes that longer-term treatment may require examination and resolving of past issues (e.g., survivors of sexual abuse).
- When engaging the client, counselors might acknowledge the person's discomfort but they do not engage in a prolonged discussion of etiology and pathology.

- Individuals have within themselves the resources and abilities to solve their own problems.
- Clients are often caught in feelings of powerlessness regarding their problems.
- Clients need to be helped to imagine what their future would look like without the problem—that is, if they were "unstuck."
- When working with mandated clients, the involuntary nature of the relationship must be acknowledged and used as the starting point for the work.

Prior to the engagement with the client and the first meeting, the counselor will make minimal use of history and agency records, preferring to let the client tell the story. This can help the counselor avoid stereotyping the client based on the judgments of previous counselors. Assume, for example, that a new counselor tells her colleagues that she is going to have Fred Jones in her group and her colleagues respond negatively: "Oh no, not Fred Jones!" Mr. Jones may be the person I referred to early in the book as the "agency client." Many of the counselors have worked with him and found him hard to reach. This is the client often assigned to new workers and students. The counselor's perception that this will be a difficult client helps to create conditions that can lead to a self-fulfilling prophecy.

As has been illustrated in a number of examples in previous chapters and in those in this chapter of work with mandated clients, the worker typically asks the members to share their views about the mandating agency's expectations and requirements. The worker recognizes and acknowledges that, although the agency or court can demand certain changes, clients serve as the final "authority" with regard to what they want or need to change in their lives. When the worker asks what the members want and the response is "Get the damn agency (or anyone) off my back!" the worker can respond, "OK, let's start with what all of you have to do to get the agency off your backs." Essentially, the client is invited to be the "expert" who informs the counselor about her or his situation.

## Role of the Solution-Focused Group Leader

Corey (2008) describes the solution-focused group counselor's role as follows:

> Solution-focused group counselors adopt a "not knowing" position as a route to putting group members into the position of being the experts about their own lives. In this approach, the therapist-as-expert is replaced by the client-as-expert, especially when it comes to what he or she wants in life. Although clients are viewed as experts on their own lives, they are often stuck in patterns that are not working for them. These practitioners disavow the role of expert, preferring a more collaborative or consultative stance, and they see their job as creating opportunity for clients to see themselves as experts in their lives. (p. 427)

One concern I have with the "not knowing" position is that if rigidly or incorrectly implemented, it can stop the group leader from sharing data—information, values, beliefs, and so on—that could be helpful to the group members. The core concept of the solution-focused approach, that the client is an expert in his or her own life, is central to the model I have presented in this book, and the idea that the key to change rests with the client is also consistent. I would rather, however, conceive of the group leader and clients both as experts, but about different things.

Clients are the experts about their lives, their troubles, possible solutions, and so forth, while the group leader is an expert in leading groups. The group leader's role includes teaching all members about how to help each other, and at times that may include the need to confront as well as support.

## Defining Techniques

Several specific techniques have been associated with the solution-focused model. All of them share a common focus on the client's strength and capacity for coping with adversity. The techniques that are applicable to individual, family, and group practice are as follows:

- *Asking about presession changes during the intake interview or recruitment interview for first group session*: The worker recognizes that change may have occurred even before the first session. The fact that a client has made an appointment to see a social worker or to find out about a group, voluntarily or not, may begin a change process. The social worker will be curious and inquire about how the client made these changes, and who was responsible for them.

- *Asking about between-session changes*: The social worker recognizes that the members have a life between sessions. Many factors will have influenced the client's life, and the worker will want to explore these at the beginning of the session. For example, the worker may ask the client, family, or group member, "What, if anything is better this week, compared with last week?" or "What issues are on your mind this week?" This is an element of the skill in the middle phase I called sessional contracting.

- *Asking about exceptions*: This technique asks the client to begin to examine when the problem did not occur in the past and what the conditions were that created these exceptions. For example, after a client receiving counseling for substance abuse discloses a relapse, the worker could ask: "You've relapsed and started drinking again at least three times over the past 5 years, but you've also been able to maintain your recovery for longer and longer periods. What was going on during the time you maintained your recovery, and how were you able to do that?" A variation on this question would be to ask about times when the problem was not that serious or severe, was less frequent, or lasted a shorter time. The goal is to search for and reinforce those factors that made a difference. This is a subtle but important shift from focusing on the problem to identifying potential solutions. In the group context, other members can identify their own exceptions and, if possible, the leader can point to similarities as well as differences. Also, member support for each other can help in maintaining hope and a strengths perspective in dealing with the problem.

- *Asking the "miracle question"*: Although there are different forms of the "miracle question," the most common is this: "Imagine you were to wake up tomorrow and a miracle had happened." The miracle would be that the client's life had changed for the better and the "problem" had been resolved. Questions such as "How would you first know that things were different?" or "What would others notice that would indicate that the problem was gone?" are designed to help the client conceptualize the desired change. A variation includes "Imagine this isn't so much of a problem" or "This session has helped you in just the way you thought it would" or "It is 3 months in the future, we have been working together, and problems have been resolved. How would you know this? What would be different?" The one caveat that the worker has to include when asking the question is that the client cannot answer that the problem itself did not exist. For example, a grieving widow cannot wake up the next day and find that her husband had not died.

- *Asking scaling questions*: This technique asks clients at a first meeting to identify the degree of the problem using a scale on which zero represents the worst end of a continuum and some other number represents the ideal. The group leader can then ask clients what number represents where they are in respect to this problem at a certain point in the work. In this way, group members may be able to identify incremental changes rather than see a problem as "solved" or "not solved."

- *Asking coping questions*: Another technique that emphasizes the clients' strengths and helps clients see themselves in new ways is to ask "coping" questions. For example, after a client has shared a serious problem and the social worker has acknowledged the problem, the worker might ask, "How have you managed to cope?" Another question might be: "Given how bad things are, how come they are not worse? How have you kept things from getting worse?" Once again, in a group context, others in similar situations can share their experiences in coping if the group leader invites members to contribute them to the discussion.

# Cognitive-Behavioral Therapy (CBT)

A third model considered to be an evidence-based practice borrows from cognitive-behavioral psychology and therapy. In cognitive-behavioral therapy, the therapist uses strategies and techniques designed to help clients correct their negative, distorted views about themselves, the world, and the future, as well as the underlying maladaptive beliefs that gave rise to these cognitions (Beck, Rush, Shaw, & Emery, 1979; Elkin, Parloff, Hadley, & Autry, 1985).

Earlier in this book, I pointed out the powerful interaction between how we feel and how we act. Essentially, cognitive-behavioral approaches, which build on social learning theories, suggest that how one thinks interacts with one's behavior. When feelings and cognitive distortions combine, they can result in maladaptive behaviors, which in turn strengthen the distortions, which then continue to affect the behavior. In cognitive-behavioral treatment models, the therapist helps the client identify and modify cognitive distortions and reinforces behaviors that are more adaptive for the client.

## Major Assumptions on the Nature of the Helping Relationship

Concepts drawn from a widely recognized and researched cognitive therapy model based on the work of Beck, who explored the causes and treatment of depression (Beck et al., 1979), can be usefully incorporated into the mutual-aid model of practice. Oei and Shuttlewood (1996) summarize the three dimensions of Beck's theory:

> First, life experiences lead people to form assumptions about themselves and the world ("schemata" or "underlying predispositions") that are then used

to interpret new experiences and to govern and evaluate behavior. "Some assumptions reached on the basis of past negative experience may become rigid, extreme, and resistant to change and, hence, are termed dysfunctional or counterproductive." (p. 93)

Second, Beck posed the existence of "automatic thoughts," short pieces of "internal dialogue" that are associated with negative emotions and can lead to self-statements such as "I am a failure." According to Beck, a pattern of frequent and "highly negative automatic thoughts" can develop into a vicious cycle that leads to depression, which then leads to more depressive cognitions. Third, automatic thoughts are seen as containing "errors of logic," which Beck termed "cognitive distortions." These can include overgeneralizing, disqualifying the positive, catastrophizing, minimization, and personalization.

> Beck's treatment approach "disrupts the vicious cycle of depression by teaching the patients to question negative automatic thoughts and then to challenge the assumptions (schemata) on which they are based." (Oei & Shuttlewood, 1996, p. 94)

***Cognitive-Behavioral and Supportive-Expressive Groups for Women Diagnosed with Breast Cancer*** In a recent review of the literature on the effectiveness of cognitive-behavioral and supportive-expressive group therapy for women diagnosed with breast cancer, Boutin (2007) reviewed 20 studies that examined the extent to which cognitive-behavioral therapy (CBT), supportive-expressive group therapy (SEGT), or a combination of these two treatments impact women with breast cancer. The 20 studies differed in methodology, with most (80 percent) using randomized assignment to the treatment or control groups. Studies also differed on the stage of the cancer and the ages of the women as well as the treatment options: SEGT, CBT, or a combination of the two.

Outcomes varied for different studies and different designs and included less mood disturbance, no survival rate difference, less depression, higher self-esteem, increased vigor and "fighting spirit," less affect suppression, decreased anxiety, less pain and suffering, and so on. Addressing the findings across studies, Boutin (2007) states:

> Despite evidence for success across all of the treatments, the patterns of results from the CBT, SEGT, and combination of CBT and SEGT studies are imbalanced. More repeated positive outcomes from studies implementing an experimental design were found for the SEGT treatments than for CBT as well as than the combination of CBT and SEGT treatments. Furthermore, studies with less experimental control were identified that support the outcomes of the more rigorous SEGT studies, but no supportive evidence was identified that supports the outcomes of the more rigorous CBT or combination of CBT and SEGT studies. A contributing factor for the imbalance in results is the corresponding imbalance in the number of studies published for each treatment. (p. 279)

Boutin identifies limitations in both the review and in individual studies. The differences in populations, length of time in treatment, and other factors, and the fact that treatment modalities were not directly compared with each other with the exception of one study, limit the ability to make inferences. Boutin does suggest that group treatment of using different modalities, particularly supportive-expressive group therapy, appears to have a positive impact on a number of important variables. An example of a CBT group that incorporates supportive-expressive group therapy within a mutual-aid framework follows.

***CBT Group for Chronic Mental Patients*** In an example of how a group leader can incorporate constructs from the cognitive-behavioral model into the interactional framework, Albert (1994) writes about a mutual-aid support group for chronic mental patients using a CBT approach. He describes a patient in a day treatment center—which had so many groups that patients often felt "grouped out"—who surprised staff by suggesting another group:

> She said, "We need to talk just about being mental patients, what it means, what it feels like." One patient after another seconded the motion. They wanted to address the mental patient identity. How were they thought of in their families and neighborhoods? How should they think of themselves? Was the mental patient stigma justified? Where did it come from? What were its effects? Although their "patienthood" was at the heart of what the patients had in common, it seemed to have remained an oppressive presence, at once too obvious and too painful to mention. (p. 109)

**Practice Points:** In one example from the group, patients were dealing with the ideation of permanent thinking—that when they are depressed, for example, treatment can seem "interminable and futile." This sense of failure and permanency, in turn, affects their ability to continue to cope.

> Sharon said, "I had the leaves raked into piles. Then the wind blew them all around the yard again. I thought, 'What's the use? They'll never get done. There will always be leaves.' Then I went back to bed. My body started feeling heavy. I couldn't get out of bed." I (the group leader) pointed out that Sharon had used the word "always" when speaking about her hospitalization, too. ["I'll always go back to the hospital."] I asked, "Is it true that there will always be leaves? Is the job never done?" Sharon said, "That's one way of looking at it."
>
> I asked the group for other ways. Members suggested that Sharon think about other tasks she has completed. [Disputation] Nick said, "Maybe you would have to redo the raking once or twice; maybe even three times—but not forever. [Disputation] I mean, you do what you can, then it snows and you're done." [Laughter] I repeated, "You do what you can." (Albert, 1994, p. 110)

The cognitive-behavioral approach is a good example of how most therapeutic frameworks, as long as they are based upon core assumptions and beliefs about client strengths, provide powerful ideas that can be integrated into other practice models. In addition, the emphasis by the cognitive-behavioral theoreticians on a practitioner-researcher model, in which the social worker continuously evaluates his or her own practice, is also healthy for the field because it accelerates the movement toward development of a more empirically based practice.

## Other Models and Theories

**EP 2.1.5a**
**EP 2.1.6a**

Models and theories discussed in this section are those that may not yet qualify as evidence-based practice but have elements that have proven to be consistently helpful, have achieved some research support, or are driven by shared practice wisdom and experience. They may be in the early research stage; however, they contain organized assumptions about behavior, valued outcomes, and intervention strategies that can be operationalized in a manner that can lead to consistent research findings. Although there are many models that would qualify for inclusion in this section, three have been selected as illustrations. These were selected because their core constructs and values are consistent with the framework presented in this book.

# Feminist Practice

Feminist group work practice consists of a number of models and frameworks that attempt to address the unique issues facing women in our society. These include issues of social and political oppression and the impact of having been generally placed in a subordinate position in respect to their gender. Efforts have also been made to develop a unique psychology of women in terms of how they relate and connect to others. Both of these approaches have direct impact on the structure and content of practice with women and will be explored and illustrated in this section. First, I begin with a brief introduction to a typology of feminist practice.

## Feminist Practice Typology

Feminist approaches to practice have diverged into several identifiable streams. Saulnier (1996, 2000) has attempted to identify these various viewpoints. Her typology includes the following models: liberal feminism, radical feminism, socialist feminism, lesbian feminism, cultural and ecofeminism, womanism, African American women's feminism, postmodern feminism, and global feminism. Although some may disagree with the specific categorization of the models and the associated descriptions, analyses, and critiques, Saulnier's contribution highlights this important area of theory development and identifies implications for social policy and practice.

Sands and Nuccio (1992) specifically address the emergence of postmodern feminist theory and its impact on practice. The authors describe how the feminist literature has identified three general categories of philosophical and political feminist orientations: liberal, socialist, and radical feminism. Liberal feminism emphasizes the attainment of political rights, opportunities, and equality within the existing political system. Socialist feminism attributes women's oppression to the interaction among sexism, racism, and class divisions, which are produced by patriarchal capitalism. Radical feminism finds patriarchy an omnipresent influence that needs to be dismantled (p. 490).

Sands and Nuccio then trace the emergence of postmodern feminism from its postmodern philosophical and French feminist theoretical roots. Although they acknowledge differences between the roots and the emergent thinking of this model, they point to a shared political agenda with American feminism:

> Regardless of whether a feminist has a liberal, socialist, radical or other perspective, she has a desire to change the social and political order so that women will no longer be oppressed. Thus, organizing and taking political action to redress injustices are significant dimensions of postmodern feminism. (1992, p. 492)

While the focus of this brief background is on the social justice and socio-political implications of the feminist approach, many of these concepts are translated into direct practice interventions as will be illustrated in later sections of this chapter. First, I want to explore some of the work in developing a women-centered psychology that has implications for practice.

## The New Psychology of Women and the Relational Model

A theoretical model that helps us to understand some of the unique dimensions of practice with women is the relational model. This model has emerged from the work done at the Stone Center in Wellesley, Massachusetts, which is dedicated to studying the unique issues in the development of women and methods for working effectively with them. The center has built on the early work of Jean Baker Miller whose publication entitled *Toward a New Psychology of Women* (Miller 1987; Miller & Stiver, 1991) laid the groundwork for the relational model. Much of the evolving work in this area can be found in publications and a series of working papers and books from the Stone Center. This framework is often classified under the general rubric of self-in-relation theory.

More recently, Freedberg (2009) addressed the issue of the compatibility between relational theory and feminist practice and social work. She suggests that

> Relational theory from a feminist perspective is fully compatible with the core principles and values of direct social work practice. It provides a contextual relationship view of self that is consistent with the person-in-situation ecological systems perspective of social work. This school of thought advances understanding of the emotional, social, moral, and cognitive development of women in particular. While most developmental theories devised by men emphasize the importance of disconnection from early relationships to achieve a separate self, women's experience, in large measure, contradicts such theory and suggests that a new model of development is needed. (p. 21)

The framework was described in detail in Chapter 13 when I suggested it could serve as one of the four models presented to help us understand the dynamics of the group-as-a-whole. I will briefly review some of the core elements that directly relate to group work practice. The reader is urged to return to the discussion in Chapter 13 for a more detailed presentation.

In one example of a group work elaboration of this model, Fedele (1994) draws on three central constructs repeatedly found in relational theory:

- Paradox (an apparent contradiction that contains a truth)
- Connection ("a joining in relationship between people who experience each other's presence in a full way and who accommodate both the correspondence and contrasts between them")
- Resonance ("a resounding; an echoing; the capacity to respond that, in its most sophisticated form, is empathy") (p. 7)

Referring to therapy, Fedele (1994) identifies several paradoxes: "Vulnerability leads to growth; pain can be experienced in safety; talking about disconnection leads to connection; and conflict between people can be best tolerated in their connection" (p. 8). In describing the second major construct of relational theory, the idea of "connection," Fedele (1994) says,

> The primary task of the leader and the group members is to facilitate a feeling of connection. In a relational model of group work, the leader is careful to understand each interaction, each dynamic in the group as a means for maintaining connection or as a strategy to remain out of connection. As in interpersonal therapy groups, the leader encourages the members to be aware of their availability in the here-and-now relationship of the group by understanding and

empathizing with their experiences of the past. But it is the yearning for connection, rather than an innate need for separation or individuation, that fuels their development both in the here-and-now and in the past. (p. 11)

Finally, the third major concept, "resonance," asserts that the "power of experiencing pain within a healing connection stems from the ability of an individual to resonate with another" (Fedele, 1994, p. 14). She suggests that resonance manifests itself in group work in two ways:

> The first is the ability of one member to simply resonate with another's experience in the group and experience some vicarious relief because of that resonance. The member need not discuss the issue in the group, but the experience moves her that much closer to knowing and sharing her own truth without necessarily responding or articulating it. Another way resonance manifests itself in a group involves the ability of members to resonate with each other's issues and thereby recall or reconnect with their own issues. This is an important element of group process in all groups but is dramatically obvious in groups with women who have trauma histories. Often, when one woman talks about painful material, other women dissociate. It is a very powerful aspect of group work that, if acknowledged, can help women move into connection. (p 14)

These three elements all have their parallels in the mutual-aid model in which ambivalence about closeness (paradox), the power of connecting with other members (connection), and mutual support through empathy (resonance) are described as elements in the mutual-aid process.

Following the early publications addressing the relational model, Stone Center researchers focused on an inherent and acknowledged bias in their original work. Jordan (1997), referring to the early work, said:

> [I]t represented largely white, middle-class, well-educated heterosexual experience. While we struggled not to reproduce the errors that occur when one subgroup speaks as if *its* reality is *the* reality, we inevitably were bound by our own blindspots and biases. We became more and more aware of the dangers of speaking about or for "all women." We were indeed speaking about "some women" or about partial aspects of many women's experience. Our appreciation of diversity needed to be broadened and deepened. (p. 1)

Jordan points out that the work in the later publications continued to elaborate on and explore the relational theory with an emphasis on topics such as sexuality, shame, anger, and depression as well as the complexity related to the diverse life experiences of women.

> While all women suffer in a patriarchal society where our experience is not presented in the dominant discourse, women in various cultural/ethnic groups suffer additional marginalization based on race, sexual orientation, socioeconomic standing, able-bodiedness, and age. Women who are marginalized also develop strengths that may differ from those of white, privileged heterosexual women. (p. 1)

### Feminist Group Work Practice

Butler and Wintram (1991), writing about the development of feminist group work at that time, caution against crossing the line in writing about women as problembearers as opposed to problem-solvers:

Effective therapy in groups should encourage women to value and develop inner strengths, regardless of societal norms. The institutional and social barriers that have impeded women are so wide-ranging that their erosion must occur on numerous fronts. Any feminist approach must harness the growing unrest among women with the aim of recognizing the dynamics of oppression whilst avoiding pathologizing them as vulnerable, weak and dependent. (p. 44)

The authors use their practice experiences working with inner-city women's groups in England to develop their model of practice designed to address the problems but also to develop solutions.

Our personal and professional experiences have shown us that women brought together can offer each other support, validation and strength, and a growing sense of personal awareness, in a way that is difficult to achieve otherwise. (p. 1)

Their experiences revealed common themes:

Fear, isolation and loneliness lay at the root of the experiences of many of the women with whom we were involved over the years. These three factors intertwine, forming their own perfect prism. The *fear* results from the threat of, or the actual occurrence of, physical, sexual and psychological violence. *Isolation* is caused by material constraints, such as lack of transport, money and child-care facilities, which all restrict mobility. There is no real contact with other people. Each woman convinces herself that she is the only one to know what she is feeling and experiencing. The *loneliness* that arises from such circumstances needs little elaboration, especially when a woman is told often enough that she is a failure, receiving little if any positive reinforcement for the endless domestic labour and low-paid work she may perform. Feelings of unreality, of going or being mad, are all common amongst people divorced from any point of reference. Solitude, in such circumstances, breeds powerlessness. (p. 2)

## Indicators of Oppression in a Feminist Practice Model

The description of the factors impacting these women echoes the key indicators of oppression in the psychology of Fanon (Bulhan, 1985). Fanon's model, as described by Bulhan, was drawn from the experience of slavery. The oppression model was elaborated in Chapter 2 as an underlying framework for understanding maladaptive ways of coping with oppression as the "oppressor without" becomes the "oppressor within." The discussion of resilience and the strengths perspective, in the same chapter, focused on oppressed populations as potential problem-solvers, as described by Butler and Wintram.

Bulhan (1985) identifies several key indicators for objectively assessing oppression. He suggests that "all situations of oppression violate one's space, time, energy, mobility, bonding, and identity" (p. 124). He illustrates these indicators using the example of the slave:

The male slave was allowed no physical space which he could call his own. The female slave had even less claim to space than the male slave. Even her body was someone else's property. Commonly ignored is how this expropriation of one's body entailed even more dire consequences for female slaves. The waking hours of the slave were also expropriated for life without his or her consent. The slave labored in the field and in the kitchen for the gain and comfort of the master. The slave's mobility was curbed and he or she was never permitted to venture beyond a designated perimeter without a "pass."

The slave's bonding with others, even the natural relation between mother and child, was violated and eroded. The same violation of space, time, energy, mobility, bonding and identity prevailed under apartheid, which in effect, is modern-day slavery." (p. 124)

The slave model is an extreme example of the violation of space, time, energy, mobility, bonding, and identity as indicators of oppression. Although the slavery experience of African Americans in North America must be considered a unique example of oppression, the indicators may be used to assess degrees of oppression for other populations as well. In this way, a universal psychological model can help us to understand the common elements that exist in any oppressive relationship. Note the emergence of the indicators of oppression in the example that follows.

### Battered Women's Group

**Practice Points:**   Consider the six indicators cited by Bulhan as you read a discussion among a group of women who have and are experiencing abuse from their partners. Note how the description of fear, isolation, and loneliness described by Butler and Wintram (1991) is echoed in this work with battered women.

> Candy said one thing that she didn't like was that her husband had to be number one all the time. He felt he should come first, even before the children. She said, "The man's got to be number one. Just like the president. He's a man and he's number one. You don't see any female presidents, do you?" I said, "Are you saying that a man had the right to abuse his partner?" She said no and then turned to the women to say, "But, who's the one who always gives in, in the family? The woman does." All the women nodded to this remark. Linda said, "To keep peace in the family." Candy said, "In the long run, we're the ones who are wrong for not leaving the abusive situations." She said she finally came to the realization that her man was never going to be of any help to her. In the long run, she felt that her children would help her out if she gave them a good life now. She feels very strongly about her responsibilities to her children.

**Practice Points:**   The comment about not seeing a female president was made a number of years ago when that seemed out of the question. The recent strong run for the Democratic nomination by a woman, Hillary Clinton, may be changing that view in spite of her loss. Cindy's powerful decision to leave her husband represents the "problem-solver" element in her behavior.

> Another woman, Tina, said that when she called the police for help, they thought it was a big joke. She said when she had to fill out a report at the police station, the officer laughed about the incident. The women in the group talked about their own experiences with the police, which were not very good. One woman had to wait 35 minutes for the police to respond to her call after her husband had thrown a brick through her bedroom window. I said, "Dealing with the police must have been a humiliating situation for all of you. Here you are in need of help, and they laugh at you. It's just not right."
>
> Linda talked about a woman in California who had been stabbed several times and the police didn't do anything about the incident. I brought up the recent case in Connecticut where an abused woman sued the police force and won millions of dollars. I said, "Because of this case, Connecticut police are now responding more quickly to abuse cases." I said, "I know this doesn't help you out now with your situations, but things are changing a little at a time."

I thought this story would provide the women with some reassurance and let them know that some public officials do not think abuse is a laughing matter.

**Practice Points:** The group leader's intervention is designed to address the feeling of powerlessness experienced by these women. The strength of their anger, finally fully expressed because of their ability to join with other women who can validate their feelings, and for some, freedom from the immediate fear of harm, emerges in the next comments. The devaluing of the work in the home, also identified by Butler and Wintram, is expressed.

Joyce said that she wanted to kill her husband. This desire had been expressed by an abused woman in a previous group session. Other women in the group said it wouldn't be worth it for her. "All he does is yell at me all the time. He makes me go down to where he works every day at lunchtime. The kids and I have to sit and watch him eat. He never buys us anything to eat." I said, "What would you do? Eat before you would go to see him?" She said, "Yes. Plus, he wants to know where I am every minute of the day. He implies that I sit around the house all day long doing nothing." Marie said her ex-husband used to say that to her all the time. She said, "But now I'm collecting back pay from my divorce settlement for all the work I never did around the house."

**Practice Points:** The trust and mutual support in the group allows Joyce to share her "secret" of sexual abuse experienced as a child. Her disclosure of the abuse to her current husband only results in further emotional abuse from him.

Then Joyce said she was going to tell us something that she had only told two other people in her life. Joyce said that she had been molested from the ages of five to seven by her next door neighbor, Pat. She said that Pat was friendly with her parents. Her mother would say, "Bring a glass of lemonade over to Pat." The first time she did this, he molested her. After that incident, when her mother told her to bring something over to Pat, Joyce would try to get out of it. But her mother insisted that she go over. Pat had told Joyce not to tell anyone what went on. At this point in the session, Joyce began to cry. I said that I understood this was a difficult situation for her to talk about. Candy said, "Joyce, it wasn't your fault." Joyce said she had kept this incident to herself for approximately 25 years. Finally, when she told her husband, he said, "You probably deserved it." Joyce said she felt like killing him for saying that. Candy said, "See, you can't depend on nobody else but yourself. You're better off just not talking to anybody because when you get down to it you can't really rely on anyone but yourself."

I said that I thought there were people that Joyce could talk to, including professional people. I said it was unfortunate for Joyce that when she finally decided to talk about her experience, her husband didn't give her the support she needed. I said that we were listening to Joyce and realized what a terrible experience she had suffered as a child. After Joyce talked a little more about the situation and calmed down, I asked if anyone also had experienced or seen abuse in their families when they were growing up. Candy said she saw her father beat her mother. She said she used to ask her mother why she put up with it. She said now she sees that it's easier to say you want to get out of a relationship than it is to actually do it.

**Practice Points:** The support of the group leads the members to begin to examine the "decision balance," a concept from motivational interviewing presented earlier in this chapter, between the problems of leaving an abusive situation versus the advantages of leaving. The group leader resists the urge to take a position on the matter, since she respects the fact that this is an issue only the women can decide. In this situation, the group leader is truly an outsider.

> Candy said, "I want to know whether we're better off leaving or staying in our abusive situations." I said, "Why don't we list on the blackboard the benefits of leaving and staying and see what we come up with." Candy said that leaving was better in the long run. By staying, the children will see their father abusing their mother. "What kind of example is that going to set for the children?" She felt her children would be happier by their leaving. Joyce said her children were happy to leave their father. She said, "They're tired of listening to him yell all the time." She said her son was more upset about leaving the dog behind than he was about leaving his father. Linda said another good reason for leaving is self-love. She said, "It comes to a point where you know he's going to kill you if you stay around." Linda said her boyfriend told her that he'd be happy to go to jail over killing her. Other good reasons for leaving that the women mentioned included: leaving an uncomfortable lifestyle, getting away from the pressure involved in an abusive relationship, and not having to take physical or mental abuse.

**Practice Points:** In her next comment, the leader demonstrates how far she has come from her early efforts to preach to the women, reaching for the reasons a woman might find to stay in the relationship. By not allowing herself to act on the natural instinct of wanting to convince the women to leave abusive relationships, she creates the culture where they can honestly face their ambivalence and get the help they need from each other.

> At this point, no one had mentioned reasons for staying in an abusive relationship, so I prompted the women to comment. The women said that money, belongings (many women leave their possessions behind when they seek shelter), and the convenience of the relationship were reasons for staying. Linda said, "Sometimes it's easier to stay because at least you know what's going to happen to you. If you leave, you don't have any idea what's in store for you. It's very hard."
>
> Since group time had run out, I finished up the session by saying that it looked like the reasons for leaving an abusive situation outnumbered the reasons for staying. Candy said, "Yes, it's easy to see that leaving is the best thing to do." I said, "Even though we can see from the list that leaving is better than staying, that doesn't mean it's easy to follow through on a decision to leave. There are many women who decide to go back to their partners after they've left." I told the women that I thought they were very strong for having made the decision to leave, and I wished them luck with their new way of life. I thanked them for participating in the group session and said their discussion seemed to help everyone in the group.

## Feminist Perspectives on Work with Other Populations

In another example of an application of feminist theory to practice, Holmes and Lundy (1990) present what they term a "feminist perspective" on work with men who batter. They provide specific prescriptions for intervention that are based on feminist theoretical and ideological assumptions. Other examples that draw on feminist perspectives include Berman-Rossi and Cohen (1989), who focus on work with homeless, mentally ill women, and Breton (1988), who provides an example of a "sistering" approach in a drop-in shelter for homeless women. O'Brien (1995) identifies the self-empowerment of a group of African American women, who were long-term public housing residents and activists, as a contributor to their resilience and effective mothering.

In an effort to merge a feminist perspective with a cognitive-behavioral approach (discussed earlier in this chapter), Srebnik and Saltzberg (1994) describe how internalized cultural messages negatively affect a woman's body image. The authors then propose interventions to influence thought patterns and dysfunctional behaviors.

In yet another example, Collins (1994) uses feminist theory to challenge the concept of codependency in substance abuse practice. The author refutes the idea that women need to view their relational strengths as pathology. Instead, she argues that they can get well by naming and discussing the injustices in their relational context.

In more recent work in this area, Wood and Roche (2001) draw on feminist and social constructionist positions, anthropology, and narrative ideas to describe and illustrate a framework for practice with groups of women who are being battered and raped by husbands and boyfriends. They emphasize the role of resistance and protest in developing self-representation and proclaiming it in definitional ceremonies (Wood & Roche, 2001). The example that follows illustrates the power of resistance, protest, and definitional ceremonies.

*"Take Back the Night" March* Most of the literature associated with the feminist model emphasizes the impact of oppression and the importance of refusing to accept the internalized image of oneself as powerless in its face. In a group that integrated clinical practice with social action, the group first introduced in Chapter 14, the leaders approached the ending phase of work with a group of survivors of sexual abuse. After many months of difficult and powerful work on the impact of abuse on their lives, the counselor suggests that they consider attending a local march against sexual violence directed toward women.

> Then group members asked me to review information about the local "Take Back the Night" march with them. We had told them about the march against sexual violence against women a few weeks before and, after some exploration of their fears about participating in a public demonstration, they decided to march as a group. I supported the group's readiness to act independently and support one another in new experiences. I shared with them how good I felt that they wanted to march together and gave them the information they needed.
>
> At the next session we supported the group's growing independence and shared our feelings with them. As the group processed how the march had felt for them, Jane and I shared how powerful it had felt for us to see them there, marching, chanting, and singing. We also shared that it was hard for us to see them and know that the group was ending. The group was special for us, and it would be hard to let it go.

Following their experience with the march, the group members decided to contribute samples of their poetry and art to an exhibit that dealt with issues of violence toward women. They also decided to contribute proceeds from the sale of their art to a fund devoted to support groups for survivors like themselves. This represents an example of a group combining the personal and the political, and deciding which part of their work was more "therapeutic" would be difficult. The cake they shared in their last session had even been decorated with the phrase "Survivors—Striving and Thriving!"

Finally, in an example of research in this area, Westbury and Tutty (1999) conducted a small, quasi-experimental study that compared women who were sexually abused as children and who were receiving individual and group treatment that included feminist techniques with women on a waiting list who were receiving only individual counseling. They found that the treatment group had significantly improved depression and anxiety scores, when compared with the waiting list group, as well as a near significant improvement in self-image.

## Working with Lesbians, Gays, Bisexuals, and Transgender Clients

**EP 2.1.4a**
**EP 2.1.5a**

In recent years, social work practice with lesbians, gays, bisexuals, and transgender (LBGT) clients has received greater attention both by the profession and within social work education. Writing in 2000, van Wormer, Wells, and Boes made the following point:

> Until recently the training of social work, like that of other mental health professions, included virtually no consideration of the knowledge and skills needed to work with gays and lesbians. To the extent that the needs of this highly invisible population were recognized at all, the focus was on causation and pathology. The change effort was directed to "the sexual deviant"; various forms of cures were tried. In recent years, as we have seen, social work has moved with psychiatry away from a view of homosexuality as an illness to be cured to a view of homosexuality as a viable alterative orientation. (p. 23)

It wasn't until 1977 that the Council on Social Work Education (CSWE) recommended that content on sexual diversity be included in the curriculum, and not until 1994 that this recommendation became a requirement. Even today, the influence of politics and religion significantly impacts how this issue is handled by schools and professional associations. We saw this manifested in the debate over exempting conservative religious schools from the CSWE requirement because those schools adhere to the position that homosexuality is a sin.

Van Wormer et al. (2000) assert that, at the beginning of the 21st century, social work had not yet developed an integrated approach to practice.

> Indeed, there are a great many books on lesbian, gay, and bisexual existence, enough to fill whole libraries. At the level of the popular press, issues relating to sexual orientation—for example, same-sex marriage, gays and lesbians in the military—have become more and more prominent in public discourse. Social scientific research on homosexuality has been prolific as well. But, apart from anthologies, no contemporary volume offering an integrated, social work approach had appeared. (p. xiii)

The authors suggest that the understanding of and practice with this population is affected by popular attitudes, religious views, and politics. They suggest that attitudes toward homosexual conduct have evolved from viewing it as "sinful," "criminal," and "sick," to being "a normal variation," and back to "sinful" again (van Wormer et al., 2000, p. 7).

## Definitions

Van Wormer et al. (2000) offer the following definitions of general terminology:

- *Sexual orientation* refers to the inclination of an individual toward sexual or affectional partners of the same sex, opposite sex, or both sexes.
- *Heterocentrism* is the term, parallel to ethnocentrism (as applied to ethnicity), to express the phenomenon of viewing the world through the eyes of the dominant group.
- *Heterosexual privilege* refers to the rights and advantages that heterosexuals have and take for granted every day: the right to marry a single person of the opposite sex, for example, or the informal privilege of holding hands in public.
- *Homosexuality* refers to sexual attraction between members of the same gender, often but not always accompanied by sexual behavior.
- *Gay* and *lesbian* are used in this book as parallel and equal terms to refer to male and female homosexuality, respectively.
- *Queer* is an insider term that is being reclaimed—as in, for example, queer art and queer theory. The advantage of this term is that it can encompass all sexual minorities. The disadvantage is obvious.
- *LGBT* stands for lesbian, gay, bisexual, and transgender people.
- *Bisexuality* refers to those individuals who can be attracted to either men or women or, as they say, to a person, not a gender.
- *Transgender* is a term that has come to be used to encompass several different types of sexual identities and sets of behaviors that involve taking on the attributes of the opposite sex. (pp. 18–19)

## The Oppression Perspective

In a culture in which being openly lesbian, gay, or bisexual is risky, in terms of social status, employment, and physical safety, it is not surprising that passing for straight—otherwise described as being "closeted"—is not uncommon. Fear of being "outed," or having one's real sexual orientation revealed, is also common. Recent examples exist in which politicians and others, who outwardly led what were considered normal heterosexual lives (e.g., married with children), have either denied their true sexual orientation or accepted it a reason to resign from their positions when revealed.

Although activist gay groups have worked hard to confront this oppressive culture through such activities as "gay pride" days and parades, legal challenges, and legislative initiatives, with some success, for many closeted and openly gay clients, Fanon's oppressor within, discussed in Part I of this book, is very much alive. The onslaught of negativity and homophobia can be unrelenting. The impact of listening to friends and colleagues, who may be unaware of one's sexual orientation, openly tell "fag" jokes takes its toll. For other oppressed populations, a greater awareness of the nature of sexism, racism, anti-Semitism, and so on has tended to drive some of this behavior underground. This is not yet true for antigay behavior, which is too often tolerated, although recent indulgences by national public figures in the entertainment field have been roundly attacked. Although patently ludicrous, the claim made by a major national religious leader that America was attacked on September 11 in part because of tolerance of homosexual behavior serves as an example; statements such as this reflect the acceptance of such beliefs within certain populations.

When stereotypical attitudes are held by the family members of gay individuals, in particular, it can be extremely painful. Petros Levounis (2003) describes his work as a gay psychotherapist with a gay patient named Stephen. He reports Stephen's description of coming out to his family:

> He came out to his mother when he was eighteen years old and expected a sympathetic response. Instead, she experienced a "nervous breakdown," locked herself in her room for days, and eventually sought professional help from a "psychologist who worked with hypnosis." She asked Stephen to simultaneously see the same therapist for individual psychotherapy in an attempt for them to address together the fallout of his coming out. Stephen complied only to find out, two months later, that his mother had quit therapy shortly after the initial visit: now, the only patient was Stephen, and, in his mother's words, he was "the one with the problem." "The whole thing felt like a setup," he recalls: he felt "bamboozled" by his mother and left the weekly treatment after two and a half months. This was Stephen's only prior experience with psychotherapy. (p. 18)

Of course, many young men and women who come out to family and friends find acceptance, love, and support, which helps to buffer the negative societal attitudes. For others, the response of family and friends can be both traumatic and lasting.

***Support Group for Persons with AIDS in Substance Abuse Recovery: Nonsupportive Family Members*** In a support group I led for persons with AIDS in early substance abuse recovery, Tania, who was a transgender client, described her traumatic experiences growing up in a small, rural, Midwestern town:

> I realized I was different and finally came to the conclusion that I was not just an effeminate boy but was really a woman in a man's body. I started to act more like the girl I felt I was which exposed me to ridicule at school, especially when I started to dress like a girl. When I told my family, they were shocked and angry at me and embarrassed. They tried to "straighten me out" but it didn't work. Finally, when I turned 16, my older brother grabbed me outside of the house and held a pistol to my head. He told me I had to leave town or he was going to shoot me. I knew he meant it. My being a girl scared them all. I decided to leave town, and I have never had contact with any of my family since that day. It was more than I could take.

At this point, Tania began to cry. A gay member of the group offered support and described how his family had rejected him and his homosexuality when he came out. Only his grandmother accepted him for who he was. Both members described a development of self-hatred for being who they were. This sense of self-doubt had begun to moderate only as they saw they were not alone, and they began to regain pride in themselves and how they had survived.

Van Wormer and Boes (2000) discuss their interpretation of parental responses:

> A primary fear of parents regarding their gay or lesbian children concerns their happiness in a society that stigmatizes homosexuality. Is there anyone who has not heard derogatory "fag" remarks and jokes? Gays, lesbians, and their loved ones endure cruel, hurtful words on a frequent basis from thoughtless and ignorant people. Homophobia is fostered by our religious, educational, and legal institutions. Gays and lesbians have lost jobs, been refused housing, denied hospital visitation to their informed partners, been beaten, raped, and killed by

homophobic heterosexuals or "wanna-be heterosexuals." Families have disowned their lesbian and gay children or siblings. Gays and lesbians have been devalued, been told they will burn in hell, and have been victims of aversion therapy. The roots of unhappiness are not due to sexual orientation but to hatred directed toward those who identify as or are perceived to be gay or lesbian. In spite of overwhelming homophobia, most lesbians and gays eventually state that they are happy. Indeed, research shows gays and lesbians to be as happy as are heterosexuals in the partner relationships. (p. 115)

For all clients, a strengths perspective may be important in helping to change their cognition and feelings about themselves. For clients who have experienced brutal oppression, it is essential.

## The Strengths Perspective for GLBT Clients

Van Wormer and Boes (2000) provide guidelines for how to apply a strengths perspective to gay/lesbian sensitive practice:

- *Seek the positive* in terms of people's coping skills and you will find it; look beyond presenting symptoms and setbacks, and encourage clients to identify their talents, dreams, insights, and courage.

- *Listen to the personal narrative*, the telling of one's own story in one's own voice, a story that ultimately may be reframed in light of new awareness of unrealized personal strength.

- *Validate the pain* where pain exists; reinforce persistent efforts to alleviate the pain (of themselves and others) and help people recover from the specific injuries of oppression, neglect, and domination.

- *Don't dictate: collaborate* through an agreed-upon, mutual discovery of solutions among helpers, families, and support networks. Validation and collaboration are integral steps in the consciousness-raising process that can lead to healing and empowerment (Bricker-Jenkins, 1991).

- Move from self-actualization to transformation of oppressive structure, from individual strength to a higher connectedness. (pp. 20–21)

## Strategies for GLBT Sensitive Practice: The School Social Worker Example

Elze (2006) describes how a school social worker can be GLBT sensitive in practice. This is a crucial stage of development for intervention, during which students attempt to come to grips with their sexual orientation, and the larger heterosexual population begins to develop its attitudes toward difference. Elze suggests that the social worker needs to demonstrate that he or she is an "ask-able" person in response to all students:

The strategies that signal to GLBT youths that you are a supportive person may precipitate questions from heterosexual youths and colleagues, providing opportunities for consciousness-raising. Always correct myths, stereotypes and other misinformation that students and colleagues articulate about GLBT people. Normalize sexual orientation diversity and gender variant behavior, and educate others to affirm diversity in gender expressions. When explaining to students what you do in your job, include sexual orientation, gender identity, and sexuality concerns as examples of the issues that students come and talk with you about. (pp. 861–864)

Elze (2006) also suggests that social workers incorporate the following approaches to practice with this population:

Use gender-neutral language when exploring youths' dating interests, romantic relationships, sexual behaviors, and concerns about sexuality in assessments and intervention sessions. Use words like "partner," "special person," or "girlfriend or boyfriend." You may ask, for example, "Have you been dating anyone? A girl? A boy? Girls and boys?" "Have you been feeling attracted to girls or boys, or to both?" When discussing sexual behaviors, ask all youths, "Have you been or are you currently sexually active with males, females, or with both males and females?" This is particularly important when talking with young people about risk reduction strategies related to HIV, other sexually transmitted infections, and pregnancy.

If a student responds angrily or with surprise at such a question, respond with a GLBT-affirmative statement, using a gentle, matter-of-fact tone of voice. Be aware that students with same-sex attractions may be testing you to see if you will agree with a homophobic statement. You also want to avoid causing young people to worry that you "saw something in them" that signaled to you that they might be GLBT. (p. 864)

Elze (2006) describes a number of best practice principles when working with GLBT youth, which are summarized as follows:

- When providing services to GLBT youths, respect the students' confidentiality.
- Follow your professional code of ethics.
- Do not assume that GLBT youths' problems are related to their sexual orientation or gender identity, and do not assume that they are not.
- Remember that these young people are, first and foremost, adolescents, and may bring to you such issues as clinical depression and other mental disorders, parental substance abuse or mental illness, parental unemployment and financial stress, and domestic violence.
- Affirm, validate, and accept youths' expressions of same-gender attractions, desires, and behaviors, of any self-identification, and any confusion the youth may be experiencing.
- With transgender youths, respect their wishes by using their preferred names and pronouns, and do not demand or enforce gender stereotypical behavior.
- Avoid labeling young people, but instead help them safely explore and understand their feelings, thoughts, and behaviors related to sexuality or gender identity.
- Follow the youth's lead in using terminology. However, be able to say the words "gay," "lesbian," "bisexual," and "transgender" with comfort and without hesitation.
- For a highly distressed youth who cries, "I don't want to be gay," encourage further expression of feelings and explore his or her underlying beliefs and attitudes. The distress is often grounded in myths, stereotypes, and fears of rejection and stigmatization.

- Help young people build self-esteem by correcting their internalized myths and stereotypes.

- Believe students when they share their experiences with discrimination and prejudice.

- Be aware that the risks of "coming out" vary from person to person. Do not assume that "coming out" is the best choice for everyone. Immigrant youths, youths with disabilities, and youths of color, for example, may have more to lose by self-disclosure, especially if they are already marginalized within their schools. (p. 865)

Elze (2006) also discusses the school's climate as a target for intervention. This may be the crucial first step as the social worker begins to address what I have referred to as the "second client." Teachers, administrators, school boards, parents, and the community may or may not be supportive of activities directed toward helping GLBT students cope more effectively and changing the school climate. Recent incidents in which the showing of films where children describe having "two mommies" have aroused passionate protests, and the banning of any material that attempts to neutralize negative views and stereotypes, are indicators of just how important this work will be.

***Homosexual Veterans with AIDS—Dealing with the Effects of Oppression*** In the example that follows we see many of the oppression concepts as well as the strengths perspective in group work with homosexual veterans with AIDS. This example focuses on the impact of societal oppression on the development of a group culture. In this case, the group members are gay veterans who are HIV positive or have been diagnosed with AIDS. Once their sexual orientation is established, these clients find themselves treated as outsiders by the larger, heterosexual population. They experience prejudice, discrimination, and assaults on their minds, hearts, spirits, and bodies. They can be the butt of nasty private and public humor (e.g., television and movie stereotypes), which if expressed about other oppressed groups—for example, persons of color—would be considered racist and unacceptable.

Only more recently, as a result of growing militancy, organizational skills, and self-assertion by organized gay and lesbian groups, have laws been passed in some states to ban discrimination on the basis of sexual orientation. While the taboo against recognizing homosexuality has been modified, as evidenced by the number of successful television shows with openly gay characters and actors, the strong homophobia emotions are easily aroused. The strong and emotional reaction to proposals for gay unions and gay marriage in recent years serves to support the idea that homophobia is still a strong current in our culture. The tendency to internalize the negative self-image of the oppressor society and to adopt defensive strategies, some of which are maladaptive, can be seen among some members of these populations as well.

Passing for heterosexual by staying "in the closet" about one's sexual orientation has been one means of surviving in an oppressive and often threatening society. While major strides have been made in establishing a general culture that supports open declaration and presentation of a gay or lesbian sexual orientation, leading many individuals to "come out" and declare themselves, many still keep their orientation hidden from friends, family, cocounselors, and the community. Such denial leads to Fanon's sense of alienation, as described by Bulhan (Bulhan, 1985), from self, culture, and community, which can cause emotional pain and damage. When the disease AIDS strikes the negative connotation attached to the illness by our society increases the experience of oppression. The long period of time in which this disease was ignored by local and federal governments—a situation that changed only with the spread of AIDS to the majority, White, heterosexual community—is a powerful sign of the depth of oppressive attitudes. Against this backdrop of oppression there have been encouraging signs of organized resistance by the gay and lesbian community, conforming to the third and healthiest stage of reaction to oppression, as described in Chapter 2.

A stark reminder of this discrimination was faced by every member of the group discussed in the following record of service. They had all served in the armed forces of the United States, where public acknowledgment of their sexual orientation would have led to dismissal. This policy, while modified slightly by the "don't ask, don't tell" position, introduced by the Clinton administration as a compromise, was in force in principle at the time of this writing, although it is not always enforced in practice. (The policy itself has been recently challenged with a federal judge striking it down as a violation of antidiscrimination legislation. In the current congress legislation was just passed that ended the policy.) For most of the men in this group, their homosexual orientation was kept secret from the army, from friends, and from their families. Now that they are HIV positive or diagnosed with AIDS, they face many difficult struggles that have been put off in the face of an oppressive homophobia.

**Practice Points:** The reader should note the following key points in these excerpts:

- In an ongoing health-related group in which members have advancing symptoms, discussion can become difficult as they begin to worry about their own futures.

- Clear examples of flight (humor and distractions from important discussions about the advance of their illness) and fight (anger at the medical establishment) emerge at key moments.

- Intracultural issues emerge for the leader, who is also gay, that lead to his own fight-flight reactions.

*Client Description and Time Frame*: Support and stabilization group for men, 28–65 years old. All the members have HIV infection and consider themselves to be gay in some capacity. All the members are United States veterans.

*Dates Covered in Record*: 10/16–11/20

**Description of the Problem**

The group members resist openly addressing issues around HIV/AIDS infection. Although the members identify with being gay, discussions of homosexual lifestyle issues are purposely avoided. Most importantly, the painful feelings associated with watching a fellow group member's health decline are suppressed by the group and not discussed. The group described here preceded the success of the "triple-therapy" drug treatment and the associated diminishing of symptoms of AIDS and increased hope for at least a greater ability to live with AIDS if not for an eventual cure.

**October 16th**

I wanted the group to address their feelings on seeing one of the group members with an advanced stage of AIDS. I knew that Mr. Rooney was having a hard time coming to group due to the fact that some of the members had the physical signs of advanced AIDS. Roughly half the group members were fairly new to this ongoing group of two years. I hypothesized that they too were struggling with their own acceptance of their diagnosis and were very disturbed at the sight of Mr. Jergen, the member with advanced symptoms, who was hacking, wheezing, and struggling for air when he spoke.

Mr. Rooney, one of the new members, was so uncomfortable with this that he had skipped the meeting prior to this one. When I confronted him about this outside of the group, he confirmed my suspicions and only reluctantly agreed to attend the session today. Having just been released from the hospital with a bout of shingles, Mr. Rooney discussed this experience with the group. In being careful not to single out Mr. Rooney, I asked the group how it feels to see each other becoming sick and being forced to spend time in the hospital. There was silence. Mr. Bane asked how bad Mr. Rooney's outbreak of shingles was. Just then, Mr. Downey arrived 20 minutes late, weighted down with lots of packages.

I copped out and allowed the "flight" reaction and the distraction of the late arrival to gloss over my demand for work. Jerry (coleader) allowed this to take place also in asking what Mr. Downey had brought in all of his packages.

**Practice Points:** The group leader in this example is also gay and has experienced many personal losses to AIDS. This would be an example of intracultural practice described earlier in this book. Examination of the working circumstances in this hospital revealed a lack of social support for staff that contributed to their participation in the same "fight-flight" behavioral reactions as many of their clients. The counselor's retrospective analysis helps him to understand his own participation in the illusion of work.

In the next excerpt, the fight reaction, also designed to avoid pain, emerges as the members attack the poor quality of medical care they feel they are receiving. Since institutional oppression in relation to medical care is a reality for this population, some of what Fanon referred to as "adaptive paranoia" is understandable and necessary. Persistence of this angry reaction on the part of the group members, in the face of evidence to the contrary, can be understood as the "fight" reaction. While the group members are furious at what they consider poor treatment because they have AIDS, at this stage in the epidemic with the close association between AIDS and homosexuality, believing they are being discriminated against because of their sexual orientation may also be present but not surfacing directly.

**Practice Points.** The leader misses the underlying meaning of the struggle and, instead, confronts the group members, trying to help them see the facts in the case. It is only in retrospective analysis that the leader recognizes the pain and fear that lay just below the anger. In effect, his effort to convince the group members represented his own version of fight-flight.

### November 6th
I was forced to confront behavior that allowed a misunderstanding to continue. Mr. Williams needs an operation on his hernia and financially cannot afford to seek alternative medical services outside this agency. After several weeks of scheduled pre-op, appointments, and what was perceived by Mr. Williams as bureaucratic red tape, his operation was canceled. During this period, Mr. Williams took every opportunity in group to discuss the delays he was experiencing, his blame on the system and the inconvenience of having to live with the hernia. For a while the group began to become incensed with what this implied, i.e., discrimination around not treating someone with HIV infection.

At this juncture Jerry (coleader) and I became involved in attempting to come up with a rationale for the indefinite postponement of Mr. Williams's surgery. It was the opinion of the chief of infectious diseases that Mr. Williams's overall health, even without regard to the HIV, was so poor that his risk was greater to have the surgery than to live with the hernia. This was then explained to Mr. Williams's satisfaction by the chief of infectious diseases (Dr. Smith). During the very next group session, Mr. Williams, when asked by Jerry as to his health, began again with blaming the system for his inability to get his surgery. It was at this point that I reminded Mr. Williams of his discussion with Dr. Smith and assured the group that no discrimination had occurred around his HIV infection.

It was during this session that Mr. Tippet had returned to group from a three-week vacation. He asked Mr. Williams whether or not he had received his operation. Mr. Williams shook his head in disgust and said that the "bureaucrats still haven't gotten it together." Mr. Tippet was enraged at the seemingly bad treatment Mr. Williams had received from the hospital. I waited for a group member to confront Mr. Williams. Mr. Tippet went on about the injustice of it all and looked at me. I said, "It was my understanding that Dr. Smith spoke to Mr. Williams and explained that there were other serious medical considerations apart from HIV that put Mr. Williams more at risk by having the surgery." I asked Mr. Williams for validation. He nodded in agreement. Mr. Tippet thanked me for the clarification and said he felt better about the hospital.

**Practice Points.**   The group leader is surprised that the facts of the situation seem to be ignored in the expression of anger toward the "system." He feels it is necessary to represent the hospital and the medical staff rather than explore the apparent disparity between their anger in this specific case and the medical reality.

I felt that Mr. Tippet could not be allowed to continue to think it was the fault of the system for the indefinite delay in Mr. Williams's surgery, especially when the rest of the members were made known of the truth during Mr. Tippet's absence. I was shocked and upset to think that Mr. Williams would choose to continue in this behavior. I could not allow this misconception to continue. It would have created collusion between Mr. Williams and the rest of the group, with the exclusion of Mr. Tippet. If I had this to do over again, I would have put aside my own feelings, considered the second client, and said something like, "It must be very difficult to be forced to manage several different ailments at the same time." Nearly all of these gentlemen could relate to that scenario.

**Practice Points:**   The group leader was surprised when the other group members did not confront the member who was angry at the system. This is not surprising at all if, in the terms of Bion's theory, we consider Mr. Williams the group's fight-flight leader. Rather than confronting this member, the group will generally encourage his angry reactions. In the next excerpt, the group leader does address the stigma around homosexuality and we see the impact of the oppression on the group members' ability to openly deal with their disease and their sexual orientation.

### November 13th
I wanted to allow the group to explore the feelings attached to the stigma around the HIV infection and the homosexual orientation. Mr. Tippet revealed that only one member of his family knew of his disease. Several other members expressed the same personal situation. Mr. Tippet said that he could only see himself telling one of his sisters about his HIV infection. I said, "Should you decide to tell her, what will

you say if she asks how you think you got it?" Mr. Tippet replied, "Well, I'll tell you, Dan; once a man reaches the age of 62 and never marries, then I think it's pretty easy to figure it out." I smiled and asked how he thought his sister would react to the news. Mr. Tippet said he thinks she would be "OK" with it. I asked what the others thought. Mr. Bane began with his own situation regarding disclosure to his brother in a letter he had sent to the Midwest. I allowed him to go on and Jerry subsequently questioned him further regarding the particulars around the disclosure.

I should have encouraged the group at that moment to look at the feelings associated with the taboo of homosexuality and the attached stigma of an AIDS diagnosis. Something like, "How hard is it for us to talk about this now? Maybe if we can talk about where these bad feelings about being gay come from, then discussing HIV infection with loved ones may not seem like such an impossible task."

**Practice Points:**   As the leader becomes more comfortable with opening up discussion in the up-to-now taboo area around their homosexuality and family acceptance, he also decides to address openly the group members' feelings when faced with the deteriorating health of other members. The leader encourages a member who can no longer attend because of his health to come one last time to say good-bye.

### November 20
I wanted to attempt to re-explore the feelings behind seeing a few of the members develop full-blown AIDS. Two of the veteran group members had been unable to attend the last few sessions as it became just too much for them logistically to come in. My supervisor and I paid one of these gentlemen a home visit. Mr. Jergen agreed on the next Tuesday to attend the group in conjunction with his scheduled appointments with the HIV clinic. With the aid of a wheelchair he came in early to attend group with the intent to say good-bye to the other members.

During the session, Mr. Jergen explained that he was taking his leave of the group as it had become too much for him physically to attend. He went on to say that his absence recently illustrated this but that he agreed with my supervisor and me, and he wanted to come in one last time to terminate with the group.

I asked the older members of the group how it feels to see the other original members getting sick and dropping out. Mr. Meany, who rarely speaks up, said that he has been in group for over a year and a half now and that, "At first you tend to feel bad for those who become sick and scared for yourself. You don't want to face it." He went on to say that, after one becomes sick a couple of times and gets well again, you begin to see others getting sick in a different way. Mr. Meany said, "You still feel for those that are too sick to come to group, but you begin to count your blessings that you feel good today." There was silence. I thanked Mr. Meany for his input.

Mr. Victor (who is asymptomatic) said he was also taking his leave of the group because he wants to be around other HIV-infected people that aren't sick. He wants the more upbeat experience from "The Center" downtown. He went on to say that he still feels he needs the support but that he has been with this group for almost two years and believes it is time to move on. Jerry (coleader) said we are sorry to see you go and hope that you decide sometime in the future to come back. Mr. Victor said that he may do that. Much to my surprise, the remaining time in the session was spent vividly discussing the gay affairs each member had while they were in the service.

### Current Status of the Problem

The group has managed to get at some of those feelings associated with witnessing the decline of a fellow member's health. Mr. Meany's comments were a beginning for the group to attempt to break through that negative group norm. In their defense, there exists no similar example in modern history of how to act when faced with a disease that has the stigma AIDS carries and offers, in most cases, only a slow and, in many instances, painful progression towards death.

**Practice Points:** If this was written today, there would be more discussion of living with AIDS and less of the inevitability of an early death, although I doubt if the stigma issue would be very different. The group leader continues his analysis:

> Society tells us at best to pity those afflicted with this disease and, at worst, to blame the victim. These men take with them into group the views of our society and an internalized guilt (stigma) for being "deviant" in their homosexual behavior. I believe, based on the last process excerpt (November 20th), that ground has been broken in beginning to discuss openly issues around homosexuality and the inevitable progression of the disease which afflicts all the members in some capacity.

**Practice Summary.** While the group has been able to make some breakthroughs, there is evidence of the impact of the losses faced by the leaders affecting their own denial. Working in situations such as this one (with advanced illness, death and dying, etc.), it is important to develop a support group to assist the worker, coleaders, and other staff in the system in dealing with all the losses they are experiencing. The need for such help became obvious to this group leader after a subsequent meeting, when the very ill member, who was attending a session in conjunction with a clinic visit, deteriorated so quickly that he had to request admission to the hospital. This had a powerful impact on the group members and the leader. In fact, the leader reported that shortly afterward, he had an argument with the patient's admitting nurse, which he later recognized was caused by his struggle to deal with his own pain. This led to first steps to begin his work with the system.

# Religion and Spirituality

**EP 2.1.2b**

The helping professions have been taking an increased interest in the area of religion and spirituality in their practice. Formerly most evident in pastoral counseling of one kind or another, religion and spirituality have moved toward inclusion on many mainstream practice models.

Van Hook (2008) lists four reasons for incorporating spirituality into practice:

- First, those counseling models which stress the meaning of systems in the lives of individuals and families including spirituality and religion require counselors to understand the paradigms that shape how clients view their world (p. 37).

- Second, there is a growing recognition by health professionals that spirituality and religion play important roles in the lives of people from a wide variety of cultural backgrounds (p. 38).

- Third, a growing body of literature points out the positive role that spirituality and more specifically religion can play in promoting both mental and physical health (p. 38).

- A fourth reason for including spirituality in the counseling process is that spirituality has been identified as promoting resiliency (the process by which people manage not only to endure hardships but also to create and sustain lives that have meaning and contribute to those around them) (p. 40).

Moody (2005), in his introduction to an edited collection of papers on the application of religion and spirituality to the aging population, points out that the precursor of early practice had roots in religious movements. Only recently have the helping professions begun to seriously explore the impact of religion and spirituality on the lives of clients and has the topic gained greater acceptance in the academic world. Spirituality and religion had been marginalized as outside of our scientific model. Now, aided by the increased focus on work with the elderly in which religion and spirituality have been found to play an important role, this area has taken on new importance. It would be difficult to find professional training programs that do not include a course (or courses) on the topic.

## Definitions

Moberg (2005) points out the difficulty of defining *spirituality*. He cites Aldridge (2002, pp. 25–54), who summarized nine definitions of spirituality . . .

> that emphasize *meaning and unity* as the essence of spirituality, eight that interpret it as a dimension of persons, that *transcends* self or any experience at hand, three that focus upon it as *a motivating force or belief in a power* apart from a person's own existing, three that link it with *breath and its activities,* and four emerging from postmodern interpretations as something *nonobservable and meta empirical.* There is no universally accepted definition, but we clearly are moving toward a universal consensus that there is a "something" about people that we can call "the human spirit" and therefore a reality that we can label as *spirituality.* (p. 13)

Moberg suggests that all of the definitions of spirituality, and even the scales developed to empirically measure it, only touch on aspects of the concept. He also suggests that for most, although not all, spirituality and religion are so closely related that the terms may be easily linked. He argues that most of the empirical work has been on the topic of religion because the term *spirituality* is more elusive and difficult to "observe," and has only recently become a topic of research.

Van Hook (2008) points out:

> The incorporation of spirituality into the healing process does not represent a specific treatment technique, but instead is recognition that spirituality can play a vital role in the healing process and that it is important to find appropriate ways to support this particular aspect of healing. Spirituality as part of the therapeutic reprocess opens the door to an important reality of human existence and taps the strengths and issues that are present within the individual. (p. 31)

Drescher (2006), in a chapter that addresses spirituality in the face of terrorist disasters, offers the following distinguishing definitions of religion and spirituality:

> For the purpose of this chapter we will define religion as "a system of beliefs, values, rituals, and practices shared in common by a social community as a means of experiencing and connecting with the sacred or divine." And we will define spirituality quite broadly as "an individual's understanding of, experience with, and connection to that which transcends the self." The object of the

understanding, experience, and connection may be God, nature, a universal energy, or something else unique to a particular individual. A person's spirituality may be realized in a religious context, or it may be entirely separate and distinct from religion of any sort. In most cases, however, religion can be understood as a spiritual experience, with spirituality a more broad, generic way of describing the experience. (p. 337)

Although some may question the use of a concept that is "meta-empirical" or difficult to define, there is no question that spirituality and religion can have a profound impact on our clients and therefore must be considered as part of our practice. It may be less a "model" of practice and more a recognition of the importance of these concepts in the lives of those with whom we work. Whereas Moberg (2005) points to the growing body of research findings that relate religion and spirituality to mental and even physical health, he also suggests caution when moving from the research findings to interventions. In particular, ethical issues may emerge that need to be considered. He issues the following caveat:

But spirituality deals so much with personal choice and other transcendental issues of the existential being itself that we may never know all of its components. There very likely are significant differences between individuals who adopt spiritual or religious behaviors out of a desire to obtain the typical accompaniments of faith and those who do so out of an intrinsic personal faith without regard to "rewards," the latter receiving its fruits, but the former not.

Eventually, some prescribed therapies may prove harmful, while others that are proscribed may be recognized as aspects of positive spirituality. (p. 32)

Another concern about the potential negative impact of religion and spirituality is voiced by Van Hook (2008) who describes examples of the "shadow side" of this powerful resource and stresses the importance of assessment in determining who may or may not benefit.

An individual who contracts HIV through a homosexual relationship could find it difficult to seek help from a religion community that condemns such relationships. A person whose depression makes her or him feel alienated from God could feel burdened by additional guilt. People with perfectionist concepts of what is expected of them by the spiritual tradition can feel cut-off when he or she has failed to meet these standards. (p. 41)

### Intervention Examples: The Spiritual/Religious Autobiography

There may not be a spirituality/religious "model" of practice in the same sense as those models that were described earlier in this chapter; there are, however, interventions that foster respect for these ideas and for the structuring of new rituals and activities to address them. Encouraging members of a group, for whom religion or spirituality is important, to write a spiritual autobiography is one example. Schein et al. (2006) describe the exercise in a group context in a text on catastrophic disasters as follows:

The spiritual autobiography is an exercise that provides opportunity for personal reflection and sharing among group members. It is designed to enhance the third primary goal of group sessions by increasing the sense of social support among members. Because trauma frequently isolates survivors and leaves them thinking that no one else has experienced what they have or could possibly understand their experience, sharing spiritual history in the context of various life events reveals to members frequently how alike they are. (p. 357)

This concept was described earlier in this book as the "all-in-the-same-boat" phenomenon—one of the mutual-aid processes.

In the exercise described by Schein et al. (2006), a chart is used that has a timeline along the bottom, from left to right. Symbols are used to describe either positive or negative events, such as a heart that represents relationship events (marriage, divorce, birth, and death), an upward-pointing arrow that represents positive events, and a downward-pointing arrow that represents negative events. The symbols are placed in the decade in which the events occurred. The left axis represents the importance, intensity, or value of spirituality or religion in a person's life at the time of the event, with a range from low to high. The group members each end up with their own personal autobiography in chart form. Connecting the symbols with a line provides a graphic view of the rise and fall of these influences in relation to these events (p. 358). Members then use the charts to share their autobiographies with one another.

In an individual practice example of how religion and spirituality may emerge in a counseling session, a client, referring to her teenaged son's problems with the law, said, "It's in God's hands now." The worker replied, "But maybe God wants to work his will through you." In another, a father accused of using excessive force in punishing his son responded to a social worker by opening a bible and citing a passage suggesting that if you spared the rod, you spoiled the child. The worker, experienced in working with this population, opened her own bible and read a passage that called for restraint. In both examples, the workers integrated interventions into their practice that were specifically related to the clients' sense of spirituality and religious beliefs.

This mode of practice is still in an early stage, but as it develops the challenges will be to ensure that it is client-centered and not counselor-centered; that it is respectful of boundaries and ethical issues; that it does not proselytize and evangelize rather than work within the client's existing religiosity and spirituality; and that it remain faithful to the role of the social work profession. It will be interesting to note how practice in this area differs from or is similar to a related profession, pastoral counseling. We will return to this discussion in the following section, in which we briefly examine practice with clients in response to traumatic events.

## Practice in Response to Trauma and Extreme Events

During a training session I conducted with child welfare counselors in Hong Kong, one member of the group pointed out to me that the two Chinese characters for the term *crisis* mean "danger" and "opportunity." Most theories about crisis and response to disaster use a similar concept. The "danger," of course, is the potential for physical and emotional impact after experiencing any form of trauma. The "opportunity" refers to the unfreezing that occurs during or after a traumatic event, which leaves a client open and vulnerable to either a positive or negative change.

When disasters occur, such as the terrorist attacks on September 11, 2001, and a storm such as Hurricane Katrina (including the slow and disorganized outside response), the entire community may experience some level of trauma and, ultimately, posttraumatic stress. One does not have to be in the direct path of the disaster to experience the emotional impact, although those directly affected clearly are the most vulnerable.

In a coincidence, when I was originally writing this section, I received the following e-mail from a staff member at an antiviolence project I was directing in an urban, inner-city middle school:

> I was at the school today, and things are just so sad and bizarre! Last week a classroom witnessed an attempted carjacking in front of the school. Apparently two groups of men with shotguns came at the car from different directions, and the owner of the home/car released his pit bulls into the front yard, which caused the men to leave. The teacher of the classroom instructed all the kids to get down under their desks, which they did. She then instructed one youth to crawl out of the classroom to go get the principal while she stayed with the class. Jane, our site coordinator, and the other two full-time staff in the resource center, debriefed the classroom, but they were not instructed to do this until later, when the classroom was back to work (a bit of a delayed response).

This provides an example of a small-scale traumatic event, although not insignificant for the students and staff in this classroom. Witnessing drive-by shootings, gang fights, robberies, rapes, and other physical attacks can take a toll on any group of children or adults. Although the term *extreme event* is most often used to describe a disaster, including the unchecked spread of a disease, a terrorist attack, or a devastating storm, I suggest that there are less obvious, persistent, and slow-moving extreme events in many communities that come to our attention only when they make the headlines. These more frequent, lower-profile events may affect as many or more children and adults than the widely publicized disasters. Violence, or the threat of violence, exists in many urban and suburban schools, and in higher education, but only when there are deaths and serious injuries involved does our attention focus on the event. The incident in 2007 at Virginia Tech provides one recent example of this category of high-profile tragedy.

An example of a school-based program to address persistent trauma in Israel has been reported by Baum (2005). This program was designed to help Israeli children who were regularly exposed to ongoing trauma and stress from attacks on civilian populations. The author describes a national school intervention program designed to train teachers to deal with the persistent and long-term stress related to bombings and other forms of physical attack. The goal was to train teachers to work with class groups on an ongoing basis to help "build resistance" and "resilience." Initial and tentative analysis of the data supported a positive impact on teachers' attitudes and their confidence to implement the program. If the program is supported by ongoing research, and the teacher training results in positive outcomes for the Israeli children, this preventive approach could be useful for Palestinian, Iraqi, and Afghan children, and for any children who live in a persistent threatening environment— even in the inner cities of the United States. Of course, for all of these children the real issue is how to resolve the conflicts and restore a sense of peace and security.

In the section that follows, I will briefly introduce an evolving model of group practice that incorporates elements from crisis theory, disaster theory, and crisis intervention.

## Crisis Theory and Crisis Intervention

Mitchel and Everly (2006) describe three main characteristics that are evident in any crisis:

1. The relative balance between a person's thinking and emotions is disrupted.

2. One's usual coping methods fail to work in the face of the critical incident.

3. Evidence of mild to severe impairment occurs in the individual or group involved in the crisis. (p. 428)

Mirabito and Rosenthal (2006) explore the issue of practice at the micro, mezzo, and macro level in the wake of the September 11 attacks on the World Trade Center. As faculty members at a university located in lower Manhattan, they describe the experiences of counselors on a number of levels. Drawing upon the literature, they begin by setting out the underlying knowledge base for the intervention approach by exploring crisis theory. They refer to a model developed by Ell (1996) that includes the following:

- During a crisis, individuals frequently experience a state of acute emotional disequilibrium, which is marked by physical symptoms, cognitive impairment, and social disorganization.

- The state of acute situational distress that accompanies a crisis upsets an individual's usual steady state. It is important to emphasize that this state of disequilibrium is not a pathological condition. Moreover, crisis can happen to anyone at any time of life.

- During the state of disequilibrium that accompanies a crisis, individuals will naturally strive to return to a state of homeostasis or balance by mobilizing personal, familial, social, and environmental supports.

- While struggling to return to the previous state of homeostasis, individuals experience a time-limited state of psychological, emotional, and, possibly, physical vulnerability that can be extremely difficult and distressing.

- During the heightened state of vulnerability that accompanies a crisis, individuals are often more receptive to and better able to utilize professional intervention.

- After the resolution of a crisis, individuals return to a state of functioning that may be either the same as, better or worse than the original state of equilibrium prior to the crisis. (p. 44)

When considering the stress that results from a crisis, Mitchel and Everly (2006) identify four major categories: general stress, cumulative stress, critical incident stress, and posttraumatic stress disorder (PTSD). The authors suggest that general and critical incident stresses are normal reactions that people can usually overcome. The cumulative and posttraumatic stress, on the other hand, can produce significant life disruptions if not treated. They describe the goals of crisis intervention as follows:

1. To stabilize and control the situation

2. To mitigate the impact of the traumatic event

3. To mobilize the resources needed to manage the experience

4. To *normalize* (depathologize) the experience

5. To restore the person to an acceptable level of adaptive function (p. 430)

## Crisis Intervention Stress Management: Group Examples

Mitchel and Everly (2006) identify four major crisis intervention stress management (CISM) group interventions in response to a terrorist event:

The two large-group interventions are called demobilization and crisis management briefings and are used to provide information and guidance. The two small-group interventions, called defusing and CISD [critical incident stress debriefing], are useful in assisting a small group to discuss or process a shared traumatic experience. (p. 436)

The authors describe the demobilization intervention as a brief, large-group information session that focuses on personnel (e.g., the first responders) following their work-related exposure. The session provides information on possible symptoms, tries to normalize the experience, provides information on receiving additional help, and starts the process toward recovery.

A crisis management briefing is a large-group information session for people exposed to a distressing traumatic event. Accurate and practical information is supplied on the details of the event and on what is being done by the appropriate authorities to deal with the event (e.g., law enforcement, health, and fire services). This briefing may involve mental health personnel as well as community leaders.

Defusing is a small-group process to be used within hours after a homogenous group has endured the same traumatic event. It is a shortened version of the critical incident stress debriefing (CISD) that is sometimes described as "storytelling" time. The goal is to normalize reactions and provide information about possible symptoms and resources. (The authors point out that early intervention is an area of contention in the field, with some studies arguing that the possibility of "retraumatizing" exists during a defusing session, and that not discussing the incident may be helpful to some in delaying a longer-term negative impact. Other studies provide support for this process.)

Finally, Mitchel and Everly (2006) describe CSID as a specific, seven-phase group crisis intervention process provided by a specially trained team. CSID is designed for a homogenous group, to mitigate the impact of a traumatic event on group members. It is typically provided several days after the crisis and lasts between two and three hours. The extended time allows a more detailed discussion of the event than the defusing. (p. 437)

In addition to the goals of the immediate defusing group (normalizing, providing information on potential physical and psychological impact), this session can serve as a screening tool to determine if any members of the group need additional individual attention or a referral for therapy or counseling.

These authors provide a description of the seven phases and a detailed discussion of the goals and interventions for each. Although their depth of detail is beyond the scope of this discussion, the seven phases described are the following:

- Introduction
- Fact phase
- Thought phase
- Reaction phase
- Symptoms
- Teaching
- Reentry (2006, pp. 456–459)

## Trauma Groups

Attention to small-group process principles can strengthen groups that address trauma-focused issues. Davies, Burlingame, and Layne (2006) offer this view:

> Trauma treatment is complex and often requires interdisciplinary teamwork to address its multifaceted nature. Few circumstances are more complex than the aftermath of large-scale catastrophic events that result in hundreds, if not thousands, of individuals in need of care. In such cases, a variety of trauma treatment models may be employed, some of which target victims' initial reactions; others focus on the intermediate and long-term sequelae. (p. 385)

The authors cite research literature to support the notion that group treatment is as effective as individual or other forms of treatment to deal with trauma stress. They also point out that the result of a meta-analysis of relevant studies suggests that it is not the particular model of group treatment (e.g., cognitive-behavioral) that accounts for positive outcomes. Different models have been proven effective, ranging from those that emphasize didactic presentation to those that emphasize "process."

Many of the elements that have been shown to matter across practice models include those identified earlier in this book. These include, for example, a positive relationship with the group leader (the therapeutic alliance), experiencing the commonality of the reaction to the event (I referred to this earlier in Chapter 10 as the "all-in-the-same-boat" phenomenon), emotional support from others in the group, information (data) that helps place the trauma in perspective, and so forth.

Different models identify specific exercises that can be implemented in the group to assist trauma survivors to develop effective coping skills. One illustration of these skills, forgiveness exercises, is described in a later section of this chapter.

## Practice with Children Addressing the Trauma of 9/11

We have become increasingly aware of the unique impact of traumatic events on children, either an immediate event such as 9/11 or more persistent chronic trauma such as community violence. Pfefferbaum (2005) point out that

> A host of stressors, both natural and human-caused, have the potential to evoke symptoms. Naturally occurring stressors include, for example, tornadoes, earthquakes, and medical illnesses. Human-caused events include accidents, domestic and community violence, murder, terrorism, and war. Some of these are singular events; other involve chronic or repeated exposure. Trauma exposure appears to be common in children. (p. 19)

The author points out that most data are retrospective self-reports; a number of factors have not been well examined. Referring to the need for additional research, she suggests one example:

> Of great interest, particularly with the advent of major terrorist events in this country, are indirect forms of exposure and the PTSD spectrum. The impact of exposure has been measured primarily in relation to PTSD symptoms or reactions, potentially obscuring important differences between normal reactions and those that have clinical significance. . . . The child's subjective response is central to our understanding of the post-trauma process and the course of recovery, the relationship between the biology and psychology of the disease, the relative importance of specific symptoms, and treatment planning. Finally, the child's emotional response to a traumatic event or experience does not depend

on exposure alone. A host of individual, family, and social factors influence the relationship and must be considered in the context of exposure in both clinical practice and research. (p. 24)

Cohen (2005) echoes the call for additional research on the impact of trauma on different categories of children and the effects of specific treatment responses:

More research is needed to identify effective treatments for traumatized children, including those exposed to a variety of different traumatic events, those with comorbid psychiatric conditions, including substance abuse disorders, and those with serious functional impairments in a variety of domains. Research is also needed regarding the critical components and dosage of TF-CBT [trauma-focused, cognitive-behavioral treatment], the efficacy of alternative promising treatment models including those provided in the acute aftermath of mass disasters, and the efficacy of psychopharmacological agents used alone or in combination with psychosocial treatments. (pp. 117–118)

***A Group for Children Directly or Indirectly Influenced by 9/11*** Malakoff (2008) describes a group example of an effort to treat the long-term impact of trauma for those children who were directly or indirectly influenced by the events of 9/11. He points out that

The terrorist attacks of September 11, 2001 (9/11), demonstrates in the most horrific terms that violence, grief, and trauma know no bounds and have become a fact of life in communities across the United States. The aftermath of 9/11 involves a complex healing and recovery process for those who were directly affected, one that addresses the basic assumptions about self and community. September 11, 2001, has also had direct and rippling effects on the millions who saw it on television, know about it, and grieve with those who were there. Children and adolescents are particularly vulnerable to the consequents of this devastating life experience. (p. 32)

The impact of repeatedly watching the collapse of the towers on television, no less being involved through the loss of a family member, neighbor, or even living in the lower Manhattan neighborhood, can involve profound emotional and cognitive effects that linger long after the event itself. Malakoff describes some of these consequences as follows:

The troubling impact of the neurobiological and psychosocial consequences for trauma and violence include post-traumatic stress disorders and responses such as impaired cognitive, behavior, and psychosocial development, dysfunctional thinking and processing, altered attention and concentration, anxiety, depression, dissociation, aggression, violence, suspicion, mistrust, sense of foreshortened future, isolation, and changes in peer and family relationships. (p. 32)

Malekoff (2008) points out that a key question is how to regenerate a sense of interdependence and community. He suggests that mutual-aid support groups using verbal and nonverbal activities that can help children "calm down" and "soothe themselves in fun ways" can help to prepare them for addressing more anxiety-raising memories. He then describes a number of strategies used to help children who lost fathers in the 9/11 attack to deal with difficult emotions and memories while still finding ways to remember the positive feelings toward those they lost. Some of these included the following:

- *Creating a Board Game to Remember Dad.* Used with a group of preteens who created a board game in which squares described emotions and cards dictated activities such as acting out particular events related to the person who died. Even the game pieces were designed by the children to represent something memorable about their dads (e.g., a football to remember watching games on Sunday with Dad).

- *Cognitive-Behavioral Strategies in Group Work to Empower Young People to Cope with Intrusive Thoughts.* Activities that assist the child in taking control by regulating difficult feelings, soothing and calming oneself (e.g., drawing a stop sign on the back of a school book and dividing it into slices representing safe places or ideas or activities, calling a friend, or playing a video game), or that engage their imagination (e.g., a park, a family vacation home, etc.).

- *Helping Young People to Make Waves: Giving Voice Through Group Work.* These can include involving them in community affairs where they can have some positive impact. Another example was a counselor preparing to present a paper at a national conference of bereavement counselors and asking members of her group what she should say helped. Their list was as follows:

  - Grown-ups need to know that kids have a voice.
  - Grown-ups need to listen.
  - Groups are important to feel better and not to feel alone.
  - Grown-ups need to be patient and to know that grieving takes a long time.
  - It is okay to laugh. Laughing doesn't mean you forgot about your lost loved one, or aren't still hurting.
  - It is okay to have fun. After all, "that is what our dads would want." (pp. 38–41)

Malekoff parallels group work principles and empowerment principles when working with children and youth in the aftermath of disaster. These include:

- Provide protection, support, and safety.
- Create groups for survivors that reestablish connections and build a sense of community.
- Offer opportunities for action that represents triumph over the demoralization of helpfulness and despair.
- Understand that traumatic grief is a two-sided coin that includes both welcome remembrances and unwelcome reminders. (pp. 44–46)

## Forgiveness Exercises

Another approach developed for work with victims of terrorist attacks in group treatment is termed *forgiveness exercises*. Drescher (2006) writes:

> Exercises centered on forgiveness can be potentially important in working with victims of terrorist disasters. Because of the attributions of evil and malevolence attached to intentionally perpetrated traumatic events such as terrorist disasters, survivors and family members of victims frequently struggle with feelings of hatred, rage, and vengeance that are difficult to get rid of and may interfere with functioning. Forgiveness exercises strongly support the second primary goal of the group: cognitive processing of the meanings associated with the traumatic events. Group members may feel "stuck" with these feelings and unable to move forward. (p. 360)

The author suggests that "forgiveness interventions can focus on forgiving oneself, others (possibly even the perpetrators of terror), and even God" (2006, p. 361). Drescher suggests that clear definitions of forgiveness are crucial:

> Members must understand that forgiveness does not mean condoning an act of terror or forgetting the victims. Moreover, there is no requirement that *reconciliation* with the perpetrator be part of the process. The primary purpose of forgiveness intervention is to allow the survivors to loosen the hold that the event and the related emotions have on them and begin to move forward. The goal is to help people get "unstuck." (p. 361)

The author proposes that steps in the process include the following:

- Clarify responsibility to deal with distortions or factual errors and self-blame or survivor guilt.
- Create an environment in which beliefs that are theological in nature (e.g., "This is God's punishment of me") be gently challenged without challenging the theological foundation.
- Help group members to move toward the decision to forgive, emphasizing that this is always a personal choice.
- Finally, reinforce the decision to forgive through, for example, retelling the story in a new context or reassuring members that the reemergence of old feelings is a normal part of the healing process.

Drescher (2006) appropriately mentions the controversy associated with the forgiveness approach, particularly with respect to female survivors of malevolent male-perpetrated trauma, such as incest, in which a significant differential in powers exists.

Some alternative models suggest that maintenance of a healthy level of compassion and anger is a more positive goal. Lubin and Johnson (2008), in a clinician's manual for trauma-centered group psychotherapy for women, address the issue of forgiveness of the perpetrator and the potential challenges involved. In response to a group member's question, "Am I supposed to forgive my perpetrator?" they suggest the following:

> Some behaviors are not forgivable. You do not have to forgive the perpetrator. This is up to you. What we are talking about here is your capacity and readiness to forgive yourself. Many traumatized individuals blame the trauma on themselves and some of their self-destructive behavior may be an attempt to punish themselves. If you can remind yourself and accept that you were short-changed, maybe you can forgive yourself. (p. 59)

The concept of forgiveness can also be understood as an element of spirituality and religion. Van Hook (2008) points out that forgiveness of self and others can be a powerful therapeutic tool. An appreciation for diversity and culture leads her to caution as follows:

> While forgiveness is supported by many religious traditions, the meaning of forgiveness varies depending on the tradition. As a result, counselors need to seek understanding of the meaning of forgiveness within the client's tradition. . . . In Judaism only the injured can grant forgiveness. Within Eastern religious traditions, harmful actions are viewed within a concept of worldwide suffering. (pp. 56–57)

Forgiveness has also emerged on a societal or national level through the use of "truth and reconciliation" processes, in which the perpetrators of acts of violence against whole populations accept their guilt and national reconciliation is the goal. The effort in South Africa to move past the atrocities committed by the White power structure during apartheid is one example.

# Impact of Trauma on the Professional: Vicarious and Secondary Traumatic Stress (STS)

**EP 2.1.1f**

The first part of this section examines the impact of a traumatic extreme event (e.g., 9/11) on the professionals involved in providing help. In the second part of this section, I will explore the impact of a different kind of traumatic event (e.g., the death of a client on a child welfare caseload) and the ongoing secondary traumatic stress of working in an area of practice that places the professional in regular contact with clients who have experienced physical, emotional, or sexual abuse. The assumption is that both specific traumatic events and ongoing traumatic practice can lead to negative impacts on professionals who will need some form of help from supervisors or colleagues or both. The argument is that the professionals who provide support to others must have access to sources of support for themselves.

When considering the impact of a disaster, it is important to understand how it can affect the helping professional who may have been exposed to the disaster or worked with survivors. Mirabito and Rosenthal (2006) provide this view on those who assisted survivors of September 11:

> Many of the professionals who volunteered to assist in the aftermath of September 11 did so in the dual capacity of professional helpers and individuals who were themselves affected in many different ways. Struck with their own grief, mourning, and shock, they struggled to make sense out of the extremely disturbing events. Moreover, they attempted to recover from the effects of the disaster as quickly as possible in order to begin to help others. (p. 55)

This is an important issue because helping professionals can experience a delayed impact following direct exposure to an immediate traumatic event, vicarious traumatization, and secondary trauma symptoms that result from work with the survivors. Vicarious traumatization refers to the changes in the helping professional when repeatedly exposed to the impact of trauma on clients.

In addition to the secondary trauma symptoms experienced by professionals dealing with mass disasters such as the 9/11 attack, there is evidence of compassion fatigue, sometimes referred to as burnout, experienced when exposed to long-term work in trauma-related areas. Professionals who deal with child abuse or sexual abuse groups, for example, may evidence personal and professional changes as they experience the emotions of the trauma victims in individual or group treatment.

## A Single-Session Vicarious Traumatization Model for Trauma Workers

Clemans (2004) describes an example of a single-session psychoeducational group model for trauma workers to assist them in understanding and recognizing vicarious trauma in their own work experiences. The two-hour sessions were organized using a mutual-aid model with presentations, exercises, and discussions. These sessions were provided to agency-based trauma workers in settings dealing with rape crisis/sexual assault, domestic violence, and child welfare/child protection. The groups were called "VT Seed Groups," and the purposes were described as follows: "to provide workers with an overview of VT; to assess its occurrence among workers; and, through the process of mutual aid, to generate effective strategies to respond to VT" (p. 61).

Each group was divided into four separate sections, each one attempting to answer a specific question:

1. Getting started (Why are we here and what can I expect?)
2. Providing a context (What is VT?)
3. Recognizing and responding to VT (How can I help myself and, in turn, my clients?)
4. Ending and transition (How did we do?)

The group leaders made use of a "stem sheet exercise," a writing exercise in which each participant shared their personal feelings about their trauma-specific work. Participants were asked to write in response to prompts such as: "A specific way I am personally affected by my work with victims of domestic violence is . . ." or "One specific way I cope (either negatively or positively) with the stress of my work is . . ." (p. 64). Participants were then asked to introduce themselves and to share selected responses from their sheets. Responses were used to frame both the process and content elements of the group session.

- B (participant reading from her sheet): My name is B. I work in a domestic violence shelter. One specific way I cope with the stress of my work is by sleeping a lot.
- R (participant reading from her sheet): My name is R. A specific way I am affected by my work with rape victims is that I have become so overprotective of my 13-year-old daughter. (p. 64)

The authors describe elements of mutual aid that emerged from the discussion such as the "all-in-the-same-boat" phenomenon, the normalization of their responses, and the ability to discuss taboo subjects such as the use of sleep or alcohol to deal with stress (citing Shulman, 2006).

This opening was followed by presenting a brief definition and history of VT, three characteristics, and three specific effects, followed by case vignettes and discussion. Each vignette was read aloud by a member and introduced a theme: vulnerability and fear; difficulty in trusting; and a changed worldview. Strategies for coping were then discussed including awareness (paying attention to feelings), balance (maintaining a healthy connection between work and home and outside activities), and connection (creation of positive connections with others). The ending phase of the session asked the participants to write a letter to themselves about the "lessons learned" and to make a commitment to address and transform VT. An evaluation of the group followed.

## Secondary Traumatic Stress (STS) in Child Welfare Practice

Note: The discussion in this section draws upon Chapter 12 of the author's book entitled *Interactional Supervision*, 3rd edition (Shulman, 2010).

As social workers in a state child welfare office arrive for work on a Monday morning, they can immediately sense an atmosphere of crisis. They learn that a young child on the caseload, who had recently been returned to his parents after months in foster care, was killed over the weekend. The local manager is attempting to keep up with the urgent demands from the central office staff requesting the immediate faxing of all documentation on the case. There are telephone calls from the local press requesting interviews, and a local politician has also called. The worker who carried the case is sitting at his desk looking distressed as he attempts to review his case records in preparation for a visit from the central office investigation unit, which staff often refers to as the "death squad." He is sure they are going to be looking for fault and perhaps for a scapegoat. He reads his files but is not able to get past the initial paperwork as his mind keeps wandering to the death of the child and the guilt he feels.

His supervisor is busy on the phone dealing with the supervisor from an associated contracted agency reminding her that they had documented problems with the family and therefore were not at fault. Social workers talk to each other in hushed tones but carefully avoid the worker whose client has been killed. They get busy reviewing their own records to make sure they are up to date and that they have not missed taking the appropriate steps or completing the mandated visits. A hectic, hyperactive atmosphere pervades the office as everyone seems intent on determining who's at fault just at the time when all of the staff most needs someone to ask how they are doing.

This is a typical response to the crisis of an immediate traumatic event. Unless the system at all levels can respond in a more supportive manner and can recognize the impact of the trauma on all staff, the practice behavior of all of the workers in the office—perhaps even in the region or the state—may be affected for months and even years after the incident. (Shulman, 2010, p. 307)

In addition to recognizing the impact of immediate trauma, we are increasing our understanding of the more long-term, persistent secondary traumatic stress (STS), also referred to as emotional exhaustion, that can affect workers in particularly difficult arenas of practice such as "childhood abuse, criminal victimization, natural disaster, and war and terrorism" (Bride, Jones, & MacMaster, 2007, p. 70). The authors, citing Figley (1995), described STS as follows:

It has become increasingly apparent that the effects of traumatic events extend beyond those directly affected. The term *secondary traumatic stress* has been used to refer to the observation [that] those who come into continued close contact with trauma survivors, including human service professionals, may experience considerable emotional disruption and may become indirect victims of the trauma themselves. (p. 70)

Secondary traumatic stress, although less dramatic, can also have a negative impact on staff and services. Working with battered women, sexually or physically abused children, seriously ill adults or children, and others can take its toll on individual staff and an agency as a whole. The term *burnout,* a symptom of STS, has been used to describe a syndrome exhibited by workers dealing with intense stress over a period of time and lacking support. Although most used in the child welfare literature, it is also seen in reference to workers in any high-stress field of practice and, in particular, in large government agencies.

When the stress gets too high, I have observed a form of hyperactivity on the part of workers and supervisors, administrators, support staff, and others. The hyperactivity is both a reaction to the demands of the job (for example, 10 unanswered telephone message slips sitting on a worker's desk, all marked urgent) and a means for the worker to protect against experiencing his or her emotional reactions. If a worker keeps going fast enough, he or she does not have to feel the pain.

Some staff members have a delayed reaction to stress and experience these feelings later, while driving home. Another common reaction is to accuse other staff members or the agency as being responsible for the stress. (Shulman, 2010, p. 309)

## Impact of STS on Delivery of Services: The Child Welfare Example

The impact of these events, either individually or cumulatively, can not only affect the person of the professional but can also affect her or his direct practice. In my research on practice and supervision in child welfare (Shulman, 2010), I found that traumatic events (e.g., the death of a child in care or the physical attack on a professional) had a profound emotional impact on both the worker and workers in the same unit or even the same geographic area. This impact directly affected practice for a time following the event unless group support was offered and the issue was addressed, often through the intervention of a supervisor.

For example, in one of my studies in the province of British Columbia, Canada, when a high-profile death on a caseload was reported in a region of the province, the number of children served in that region sent into care increased and the willingness of workers to recommend that children be returned to their biological parents decreased (Shulman, 1993b, 2010). There were also significantly longer periods of time in alternative-care arrangements. In contrast, in those district offices in a region where some form of mutual-aid support groups were created by the supervisor or other administrator, and the participants were given an opportunity to deal with their own feelings and concerns and how they impacted practice, burnout, and turn-over of staff, less appropriate decisions around placement of children decreased.

When traumatic events, such as the death of a child in care, have received wide publicity, and implied blame has been, often unfairly, placed on the workers, if the response of provincial or state and local administrators is experienced by the professionals as "Who is at fault?" rather than "How are you (the staff) doing?" the negative impact on the professionals and their practice is heightened. The inference I have made from my work with students, professionals in the field, and my research is that more effort needs to be made to care for the caretakers if we expect them to care for their clients.

*A Mutual-Aid Support Group for Workers Dealing with Trauma* The following example is from my work in leading a support group at a child welfare agency immediately after the high-profile death of a child on the caseload at the hands of her biological mother. The client was seen once by the worker, who made many efforts to follow up on the case but could not find the mother or the child. A doctor who had been seeing the child indicated he thought the mother had taken the child on vacation to another state. The case received wide coverage in the local press, which compounded everyone's stress. I was asked to meet with the staff group to help them to cope with their reactions to the incident.

This incident and others have led me to propose a three-stage model for addressing traumatic stress issues of any kind. The three stages are:

1. Grieving and expressing related emotions

2. Developing action protocols

3. Examining the impact on practice

In the grieving stage, staff needs an opportunity to share with each other the profound feelings associated with the event. The staff members experience the all-in-the-same-boat phenomenon and provide support to each other in this first phase. In second phase, development of action protocols, the group discusses what steps can be taken immediately and in the future to address issues emerging from the event. For example, a physical attack on a worker in the field would lead to a discussion of steps the agency could take to respond to the trauma as well as to provide additional protection if possible. It is the third stage, exploring the impact on practice, that often appears to be missed in many well-meaning efforts to address traumatic events. As will be seen in the example that follows, this third stage is crucial in assisting staff members to recover from the event.

The meeting began with my contracting with the group. I stated my purpose to them as follows:

"You have all been going through a very rough time recently. The purpose of this session is to help you share your grief with each other, to consider ways you can be supportive during what will be a stressful time, to explore the impact this tragedy may have on your practice, and to discuss the implications for your other clients." I invited the staff to start by sharing some of their reactions.

**Grieving phase:** One worker responded, "I can't feel it yet. I have wanted to cry all week, but I just can't." Another said, "I haven't stopped crying at home—but I try to pull myself together when I come into work." A third commented, "I know it's crazy, but somehow I feel guilty—almost as if we were the perpetrators." Another staff member commented on how angry they felt when on the first day they were besieged with requests for documentation.

The worker at the center of the storm, who had dealt with the mother, said, "I know it's important to have my documentation—and I had it up to date in this case. I received a lot of support. But what if it wasn't up to date? There are times we all get overwhelmed and fall behind. You shouldn't be able to turn it on or turn it off—I need help no matter how I may have handled the case."

A local administrator described how easy it was to get caught up in the hectic activity around documentation and that now, in retrospect, it was clear that it was partly a way of avoiding the pain. I pointed out how it seems that each level was reacting from deep emotion in response to the case. Another worker said it would have been helpful if we had just all sat in a room together on that first day: "We didn't even have to talk—just to be there for each other." Still another worker said, "I haven't really faced it yet. . . ." After a few moments of silence, she began to cry and was joined by a number of staff members and myself.

**Developing action protocols:** In response to my request, they started to explore what steps each one of them could take to respond to this stress, how they could be helpful to the worker involved, and what they needed in the way of help from each other and the agency.

A number of specific suggestions emerged, ranging from a worker who offered to interview the child's other family members so that the involved worker would not have to do it, to secretaries (who were part of the group) talking about how they could provide a buffer for the worker over the next number of weeks. He replied, "That would help a lot. I find myself getting lost at times.

I'm sitting at my desk and writing out a note, but after 15 minutes I realize I haven't written more than one sentence." I pointed out that it would take some time to get back to normal on this one, and probably some of the feelings would not simply go away.

Discussion moved to attempting a realistic assessment of what workers could and could not do in cases such as this.

One worker said, "We have to get really clear about the limits of our abilities; we are simply not going to be able to stop children dying no matter how well we do our job." Another pointed out how helpful the supervisor had been through all of this to all of the workers, not just the one involved. They felt she was with them, taking responsibility for the case, not just trying to "cover her ass." The worker said to her, "When you told me not to worry, that you would stand with me on this one and wouldn't let me face it alone, it was extremely important to me."

**Exploring the impact on practice:** As we came to the last part of the morning, I asked them if they had the energy to discuss the implications for their current work with their clients. I pointed out that clients read the papers and watch television. They would know about this case, and it might have some impact on them. Some of the more experienced workers said they did not have the energy for discussing their clients; they were not ready. Others (mostly the younger workers) responded to my invitation and observed that some of their clients had commented to them about the case, but they had been too upset to notice. They said they wanted to discuss what they could do.

The group agreed, and at my request one worker described her conversation with a young mother of about the same age and in a similar situation to the mother in the case. When the worker arrived at her home, the client held up the newspaper and asked about the case. The worker responded by saying it was confidential and she could not talk about it, thus closing off the conversation.

I asked the workers to consider what the client might be worried about. They quickly saw the indirect cues in her comments raising concern about her own situation. Could she get angry enough to hurt her own child? The worker role played how she could explore these concerns during her next contact. Others provided similar examples of cues they were hearing but ignoring because of their own feelings. As the discussion turned the corner and began to focus on their professional responsibilities, a noticeable change was evident in the atmosphere in the room. The sadness was still there, but energy seemed to be returning and hopefulness along with it.

The group was positive about the discussion during the evaluation. They asked the worker if he knew how upset they had been, and he replied that he did now. It helped to have their support. He went on to say that he did not feel "out of the woods yet." He was afraid of what might happen if a scapegoat was needed. One worker said, "I kept thinking that you are such a good worker, and it still happened to you. My God, it could happen to me." Another worker broke the tension by pointing out how they were all rapidly catching up on their overdue case notes. I credited them with the support they provided to the worker and to each other and hoped that they could keep providing it over the next few months.

# Chapter Summary

A number of evidence-based practice (EBP) models were described and illustrated. The three presented were motivational interviewing (MI), solution-focused practice (SFP), and cognitive-behavioral therapy (CBT). These three meet the requirements for designation as EBP theories in that they use the best available scientific knowledge derived from randomized controlled outcome studies, and meta-analyses of existing outcome studies, as one basis for guiding professional interventions and effective therapies, combined with professional ethical standards, clinical judgment, and practice wisdom. It was suggested that some degree of flexibility is important so that implementing a manualized model does not prevent the group leader from responding in creative ways to the productions of the group and unexpected events.

A number of other models were also summarized, including feminist practice, spirituality and religion, and trauma and extreme event intervention, along with interventions designed to assist workers who experience secondary trauma. Models developed to deal with traumatic and extreme events (e.g., 9/11) as well as the ongoing persistent trauma evident in many communities were discussed and illustrated. Crisis theory, crisis intervention, trauma groups, forgiveness approaches, as well as the impact on professionals of dealing with ongoing and immediate trauma (e.g., compassion fatigue) were discussed. A single-session vicarious traumatization group model was shared as a source of support for workers who deal with trauma victims as well as a mutual-aid support group for workers experiencing a death on a caseload.

The reader has been and is encouraged to draw from any helpful practice model those elements or principles that can be integrated into an effective mutual-aid support group.

## Related Online Content and Activities

Visit *The Skills of Helping Individuals, Families, Groups, and Communities,* Seventh Edition, CourseMate website at **www.cengagebrain.com** for learning tools such as glossary terms, links to related websites, and chapter practice quizzes. The website for this chapter also features additional notes from the author.

## Competency Notes

The following is a list of Council on Social Work Education (CSWE) recommended competencies and practice behaviors for social work students defined in Educational Policy and Accreditation Standard (EPAS) and addressed in this chapter.

**EP 2.1.1f** Use supervision and consultation (p. 746)

**EP 2.1.2b** Make ethical decisions by applying standards of the National Association of Social Workers Code of Ethics and, as applicable, of the International Federation of Social Workers/International Association of Schools of Social Work Ethics in Social Work, Statement of Principles (pp. 700, 735)

**EP 2.1.3a** Distinguish, appraise, and integrate multiple sources of knowledge, including research-based knowledge and practice wisdom (p. 699)

**EP 2.1.4a** Recognize the extent to which a culture's structures and values may oppress, marginalize, alienate, or create or enhance privilege and power (p. 725)

**EP 2.1.4b** Gain sufficient self-awareness to eliminate the influence of personal biases and values in working with diverse groups (p. 711)

**EP 2.1.5a** Understand forms and mechanisms of oppression and discrimination (pp. 716, 725)

**EP 2.1.6a** Use practice experience to inform scientific inquiry (p. 716)

**EP 2.1.6b** Use research evidence to inform practice (p. 699)

**EP 2.1.7a** Utilize conceptual frameworks to guide the process of assessment, intervention, and evaluation (p. 711)

**EP 2.1.9a** Continuously discover, appraise, and attend to changing locales, populations, scientific and technological developments, and emerging societal trends to provide relevant services (p. 700)

**EP 2.1.10c** Develop a mutually agreed-on focus of work and desired outcomes (p. 711)

**EP 2.1.10e** Assess client strengths and limitations (p. 711)

# Glossary

**act out** To communicate thoughts and feelings through behavior, often in a disruptive manner.

**active mistake** A response by a worker than may be off target but, because it is an active rather than passive mistake (inaction), allows the worker to grow. Social workers are encouraged to make active rather than passive mistakes.

**activity group** A term usually applied to groups involved in a range of activities other than just conversation. *Program* is another term used to describe the activities implemented in such groups, such as the expressive arts (painting, dancing), games, folk singing, social parties, cooking, and so on.

**advocacy** In social work, championing the rights of individuals or communities through direct intervention or through empowerment (Barker, 2003, p. 11).

**"all-in-the-same-boat" phenomenon** A mutual-aid process in which group members gain support from discovering that other group members have similar problems, concerns, feelings, and experiences.

**ambivalence** Mixed feelings about a problem, person, or issue. For example, a client may wish to finally deal with an issue, but because of the painful feelings associated with it, the client may also wish to deny that the problem exists.

**anger over the ending** A stage in the ending/transition phase whereby individuals, family members, or group members appear to be angry at the worker because of the ending of the relationship. This appears in direct or indirect forms.

**authority theme** Issues related to the relationship between the client (individual, family, or group) and the social worker.

**baseline reserve capacity** The individual's current "maximum performance potential" with existing internal and external resources.

**basic assumption groups** Bion's (1961) idea that group members appear to be acting as if their behavior were motivated by a shared basic assumption—other than the expressed group goal—about the purpose of the group.

**beginning (or contracting) phase** The engagement phase of work, during which the worker contracts with the client by clarifying the purpose of the engagement, by clarifying the role he or she will play, and by reaching for client feedback on the content of the work. Authority issues are also dealt with in this phase.

**bisexuality** Individuals who can be attracted to either men or women or, as they say, to a person, not a gender.

**burnout** A common problem in stressful practice situations in which the worker's emotional reactions lead to leaving the job or maladaptive behaviors such as overworking or closing off all emotional reactions.

**caring** One element of the construct "working relationship"; the client's sense that the worker is concerned about him or her and that the worker wishes to help with those concerns the client feels are important.

**casework in the group** A common pattern in which the group leader provides individual counseling to a client within a group setting. This contrasts with an effort to mobilize mutual aid for the client by involving the other members.

**causal path analysis** A form of statistical analysis that allows the researcher to create a model of a process that involves predictor variables having some impact on outcome variables. The analysis allows the researcher to determine the direction (path) of the influence and the strength (coefficient) of the influence. Thus, it is a useful tool for empirically based theory building.

**check-in** An exercise used in some groups at the start of the session, in which each member briefly shares what has happened to him or her during the preceding week.

**checking for underlying ambivalence** Exploring client ambivalence that may be hidden by an artificial agreement.

**clarifying the worker's purpose and role** Establishing the purpose of the contact, the various services offered by the agency or setting, and the specific ways in which the worker can help.

**cleavage** A process in a group in which the members split into distinct racial subgroups in response to a changing racial ratio. It can occur with an increase of the minority or when "out" group members increase beyond the tipping point.

**closed group** A fixed-membership group in which the same people meet for a defined period of time. Members may drop out and new members may be added in the early sessions, but in general, the membership of the group remains constant.

**code of ethics (NASW)** The National Association of Social Workers code of ethics that is the explication of the values, rules, and principles of ethical conduct that apply to all social workers who are members of the NASW.

**cognitive-behavioral psychology and therapy** In cognitive-behavioral therapy, the therapist uses strategies and techniques designed to help clients correct their negative, distorted views about themselves, the world, and the future, as well as the underlying maladaptive beliefs that gave rise to these cognitions.

**cohesion** The property of the group that describes the mutual attraction members feel for one another.

**common ground** The overlap or commonality between the specific services of the setting and the felt needs of the client.

**confidentiality** The right of a client not to have private information shared with third parties.

**consensual validation** The third subphase of the interdependence phase of group development (Bennis & Shepard, 1956), in which the unconflicted members once again provide the leadership needed for the group to move to a new level of work characterized by honest communication among members.

**containment** The skill of refraining from responding immediately to a client's comment or question.

**content** The substance of the work, consisting of ideas, issues, problems, concerns, and so on that are part of the working contract.

**contracting process** A worker-initiated effort, usually in the beginning phase of the work, to establish the purpose of the contact, to explain the worker's role, to gain some sense of the client's issues (feedback), and to deal with issues of authority.

**correlation** A nondirectional measure of association between two variables, with the correlation (*r*) ranging from –1.0 to 1.0.

**cost containment** Efforts on the part of administrators to lower the cost of services. They are often introduced because of reduced funding by private and government agencies or third-party payers such as health insurance companies.

**counterdependence-flight** The second subphase of the dependency phase of group development, in which the leader attempts to take over the group and group members are in flight, exhibiting beaviors indicating fear of the leader's authority (Bennis & Shepard, 1956).

**counterdependent member** A member of the group who, during the counterdependence-flight subphase of group development, acts as if she or he is not dependent on the group leader and attempts to take over the group (Bennis & Shepard, 1956).

**countertransference** The complex feelings of a worker toward a client.

**crisis** A term used by social workers in two ways: (1) an internal experience of emotional change and distress, and (2) a social event in which a disastrous event disrupts some essential functions of existing social institutions (Barker, 2003, p. 103).

**crisis intervention** The therapeutic practice used in helping clients in crisis to promote effective coping that can lead to positive growth and change by acknowledging the problem, recognizing its impact, and learning new or more effective behaviors for coping with similar predictable experiences (Barker, 2003, p. 103).

**culture for work** An explicit or implied set of values, taboos, rules of interaction, and other concepts that are shared by the group members and that positively affects the group's ability to work at its tasks.

**cyber-community** An online community in which common interests and concerns bring members together.

**data gathering** One of the functions of group activities; designed to help members obtain more information central to their tasks.

**dealing with issues of authority** The worker's efforts to clarify mutual expectations, confidentiality issues, and the authority theme.

**demand for work** The worker's confrontation of the client to work effectively on her or his tasks and to invest that work with energy and affect.

**denial of the ending** A stage in the ending/transition phase whereby individuals, families, or group members appear to ignore the imminent end of the sessions.

**dependence-flight** The first subphase of the dependency phase of group development, in which group members are in flight, exhibiting behaviors indicating dependence on the leaders (Bennis & Shepard, 1956).

**dependence phase** The first phase of group development, which is marked by group members' preoccupation with authority issues (Bennis & Shepard, 1956).

**dependent group** One of Bion's (1961) basic assumption groups. The group appears to be meeting in order to be sustained by the leader rather than working on its purposes.

**dependent member** A member of a group who, during the dependence-flight subphase of group development, acts as if she or he is dependent on the group leader, wanting the leader to take control of the group (Bennis & Shepard, 1956).

**detecting and challenging the obstacles to work** Perceiving and then confronting directly the obstacles that impede the client's work.

**developing a universal perspective** A mutual-aid process in the group in which members begin to perceive universal issues, particularly in relation to oppression, thus allowing them to view their own problems in a more social context and with less personal blame.

**developmental reserve capacity** Refers to an individual's resources that can be activated or increased.

**deviant member** The client who acts significantly differently from other clients in the system (such as the family or group) but may actually be sending an indirect signal of feelings and concerns on behalf of the other clients.

**deviational allowance** One of the functions of group activities; designed to create a flow of affect among members that builds up a positive relationship, allowing members to deviate from the accepted norms and raise concerns that might otherwise be taboo.

**dialectical process** A mutual-aid process in which group members confront each other's ideas in an effort to develop a synthesis for all group members.

**digital divide** A divide usually based on income and class in between those who can take advantage of "digital democracy" and those who cannot.

**direct macro practice** Social work involving direct work with clients in pursuit of community goals and objectives.

**discussing a taboo area** A mutual-aid process in which one member enters a taboo area of discussion, thereby freeing other members to enter as well.

**disenchantment-flight** The second subphase of the interdependence phase of group development, in which the counterpersonals take over from the overpersonals in reaction to the growing intimacy (Bennis & Shepard, 1956).

**displaying understanding of the client's feelings** The skill of acknowledging to the client, through words or nonverbal means, that the worker has understood how the client feels after the affect has been expressed by the client (e.g., the worker's response to crying).

**division of labor** The development of group structure in which the tasks to be performed are distributed among members in a formal or informal manner.

**"doorknob" communication** A client communication usually shared at the very end of a session (hand on the doorknob) or in the last sessions. This is one of the sessional ending and transition skills.

**duty to warn** The legal obligation by social workers and other professionals to warn a third party when they, in exercising their professional skill and knowledge, determine that a warning is essential to avert danger arising from the medical or psychological condition of their client.

**dynamic interaction** Interaction in which the parties involved affect each other reciprocally—that is, with the movements of one party affect the other(s), moment by moment, in the interaction.

**dynamic system** A system in which the behavior of each participant in the system (e.g., staff and clients) affects and is affected by the behaviors of all other members of the system.

**elaborating** Helping the client tell his or her story.

**empathy** Helping the client share the affective part of the message.

**empirically based practice theory** A research-based description of a social worker's valued outcomes and interventions, which are based on a set of underlying assumptions about human behavior and social organization and on a set of professional ethics and values.

**empowerment practice** Practice that attempts to achieve socioeconomic justice, to reduce institutional power blocks and social pollution, and to change socioeconomic structures and institutions to make them empowering structures.

**empowerment process** A process through which the social worker engages the client (individual, family, group, or community) in order to improve their circumstances.

**enchantment-flight** The first subphase of the interdependence phase of group development, in which good feelings abound and efforts are directed toward healing wounds (Bennis & Shepard, 1956).

**ending and transition phase** The termination phase of work, in which the worker prepares to end the relationship and to help the client review their work together as well as to prepare for transitions to new experiences.

**entry** One of the functions of group activities; designed as a way to enter an area of difficult discussion.

**ethics** A system of moral principles and perceptions about right versus wrong and the resulting philosophy of conduct that is practiced by an individual, group, profession, or culture (Barker, 2003, p. 147).

**evidenced-based practice** The use of the best available scientific knowledge derived from randomized controlled outcome studies, and meta-analyses of existing outcome studies, as one basis for guiding professional interventions and effective therapies, combined with professional ethical standards, clinical judgment, and practice wisdom (Barker, 2003, p. 149).

**exploring client resistance** Identifying and discussing, with the client, the meaning of the signals of a client's resistance.

**external leader** The social work group leader who derives his or her authority from external sources such as the sponsoring agency. This is in contrast to the internal leader, who is a member of the group.

**facilitative confrontation** Drawing on the fund of positive work with the client to use confrontation to make the work of the client easier.

**family** A natural living unit including all those persons who share identity with each other and are influenced by it in a circular exchange of emotions (Ackerman, 1958).

**family-as-a-whole** The organism created that is more than the sum of the parts (members) of the family. It includes norms of behavior, rules of interaction, taboo subjects, status, and so on.

**family façade** A false front presented by the family in early contacts with the worker. The façade demonstrates how the family collaborates in hiding its problems from the social environment.

**family secret** An explicit or unspoken agreement in which all family members agree not to deal directly with a sensitive and taboo concern. Family violence, alcoholism, and sexual abuse are examples of family secrets often hidden behind a family façade.

**family support (family counseling)** A type of support that is usually short-term and designed to help families facing normative crises, such as the first child reaching the teen years, the birth of a new baby, or the loss of a job. The work centers on helping a relatively healthy family get through a difficult time, using the experience to strengthen rather than erode the family system.

**farewell-party syndrome** The tendency on the client's part, in the ending/transition phase, to avoid the pain of ending by planning some form of celebration. Also, the tendency to express only positive reactions about the experience, rather than being critical.

**fear-of-groups syndrome** The anxieties experienced by workers as they prepare to work with groups for the first time.

**feeling-thinking-doing connection** A process in which how we feel affects how we act and think, and how we act affects how we think and feel.

**feminist social work** The integration of the values, skills, and knowledge of social work with a feminist orientation to help individuals and society overcome the emotional and social problems that result from gender discrimination (Barker, 2003, p. 161).

**fight-flight** The natural tendency on the part of any organism to respond to a threat by either attacking it (fight) or running from it (flight). In human relationships, fight-flight usually (but not always) characterizes a maladaptive response to emotional pain that can lead to the avoidance of real work. Family violence is an example of fight, and drug and alcohol addictions are examples of flight.

**fight-flight group** One of Bion's (1961) basic assumption groups. When the work group gets close to painful feelings, the members sometimes unite in an instantaneous, unconscious process to form the fight-flight group, acting from the basic assumption that the group goal is to avoid the pain associated with the work group processes through flight (an immediate change of subject from the painful area) or fight (an argument developing in the group that moves from the emotional level to an intellectual one).

**first decision** The client's commitment to engage with the worker in a meaningful way and begin to develop a therapeutic alliance.

**first offering** An indirect communication from the client offering the worker a clue about the nature of the client's concerns. Often followed by a second (more direct) and even third or fourth offering designed to increase the signal's clarity.

**focused listening** Concentrating on a specific part of the client's message.

**function** In social work, the specific part the professional plays in the helping process.

**functional diffusion** A loss of functional clarity that causes a worker to diffuse her or his activity and implement a role or roles inappropriate for the moment.

**gatekeeper** A group member who may intervene to distract the group each time the discussion approaches a painful subject.

**gay and lesbian** Parallel and equal terms to refer to male and female homosexuality, respectively.

**generalist practice** A social work practitioner whose knowledge and skills encompass a broad spectrum and who assesses problems and their solutions comprehensively (Barker, 2003).

**generalizing** Using specific instances to help the client identify general principles (such as the importance of being honest about one's feelings in different situations). This is one of the sessional ending and transition skills.

**generic social work** The social work orientation that emphasizes a common core of knowledge and skills associated with social service provision (Barker, 2003, p. 174).

**grassroots community organizing** Grassroots organizing implies active and involved leadership by members of the community.

**grounded theory** An approach to theory building, first described by Glaser and Strauss (1967) in the field of sociology, in which formal and informal observations from the field are used to develop constructs of the theory. Formal research is conducted to test propositions and to generate new ones.

**group culture** The norms, taboos, rules, and member roles that guide the generally accepted ways of acting within the group. In a group's early stage, the group members usually recreate a group culture representative of the larger community. This culture can be modified over time to become more conducive to effective work.

**handles for work** Concerns and problems, suggested by the worker in an opening or contracting statement, that offer possible areas of connection between the client's needs and the agency's services.

**helping the client see life in new ways** Skills designed to help clients modify their cognitions about themselves and their world (e.g., reframing a situation in a more positive way).

**heterocentrism** The term, parallel to ethnocentrism (as applied to ethnicity), to express the phenomenon of viewing the world through the eyes of the dominant group.

**heterosexual privilege** The rights and advantages that heterosexuals have and take for granted every day.

**holding to focus** Asking the client to stay focused on one theme as opposed to jumping from issue to issue. It is one of the demand-for-work skills.

**holistic theory** A theoretical approach that includes a broad range of variables—personal, interactional, contextual, and time related—in describing social work practice.

**homosexuality** Sexual attraction between members of the same gender, often but not always accompanied by sexual behavior.

**hospice** A residential setting for people who are in the final stage of a terminal illness.

**human communications** A complex process in which messages are encoded by a sender, transmitted through some medium (such as words or facial expressions), and received by the receiver, who must then decode the message. The response of the receiver involves encoding a new message and transmitting it, which keeps the cycle going.

**human contact** One of the functions of group activities; designed to focus on meeting a basic human need for social interaction.

**identified patient (IP)** The client in a family system who is identified as having the problem.

**identifying process and content connections** A skill set allowing the worker to see how the client uses the working relationship (process) as a medium for raising and working on issues central to the substantive issues under discussion (content).

**identifying the next steps** Helping the client use the current discussion to develop ideas about future actions. This is one of the sessional ending and transition skills.

**identifying the stage of the ending process** The skill of naming for the client the stage of the ending process for the purpose of helping the client to feel more in control of the endings. These stages are denial, indirect and direct expressions of anger, mourning, trying it on for size, and the farewell-party syndrome.

**illusion of work** A process in which the worker and the client engage in a conversation that is empty of real meaning and affect. It may be a form of passive resistance in which the client tries to please the worker by pretending to work.

**indicators of oppression** Bulhan (1985) identifies several key indicators for objectively assessing oppression. He suggests that "all situations of oppression violate one's space, time, energy, mobility, bonding, and identity" (p. 124).

**indirect macro practice** Activities of a social worker on behalf of a community, such as research or legislative report writing, that do not involve direct work with clients.

**individual problem solving** A mutual-aid process through which group members help one member solve a particular problem, receiving help themselves while offering it to another.

**informational support** Neighbors provide information to each other as they interact. This information may be helpful in locating needed resources.

**informed consent** "The client's granting of permission to the social worker and agency or other professional person to use specific intervention procedures, including diagnosis, treatment, follow up, and research. This permission must be based on full disclosure of the facts needed to make the decision intelligently.

Informed consent must be based upon knowledge of the risks and alternatives" (Barker, 2003, p. 114).

**instrumental support** Neighbors may serve as informal helpers for one another.

**intake worker** The worker who usually makes the first contact with a client and conducts some form of assessment of suitability for services.

**interactional model** A model of practice that emphasizes the interactional nature of the helping process. The client in this model is viewed as a self-realizing, energy-producing person with certain tasks to perform, and the social worker as having a specific function to carry out. They engage each other as interdependent actors within an organic system that is best described as reciprocal, with each person affecting and being affected by the other moment to moment. The worker-client relationship is understood within the social context and is influenced by the impact of time.

**interdependence phase** The second phase of group development, which has to do with questions of intimacy—that is, the group members' concerns about how close they wish to get to one another (Bennis & Shepard, 1956).

**internal leader** A member or members of the group who assume a leadership role in a situational or ongoing basis. This role needs to be confirmed by the other group members.

**intimacy theme** Concerns related to the interactions among the members of a group.

**key worker** A worker, usually in a residential setting, who has particular responsibility for providing continuity of service to a particular client.

**LGBT** An acronym that refers to lesbian, gay, bisexual, and transgender people.

**life-span theory** A theory that suggests that development throughout life is characterized by the joint occurrence of increases (gains), decreases (losses), and maintenance (stability) in adaptive capacity.

**listen first, talk later** An approach used in work with information groups, in which the leader first listens to the group members' questions, issues, and concerns, and then presents the required information.

**looking for trouble when everything is going the worker's way** The skill of exploring hidden ambivalence or a negative response when a client immediately responds positively to a difficult suggestion.

**macabre humour** Used by staff to deal with their tensions related to their work.

**macro practice** *Macro* means large-scale or big. In social work, this practice involves the ability to see and intervene in the big picture, specifically with larger systems in the socioeconomic environment. Macro social work practice can include collaboration with consumers to strengthen and maximize opportunities for people at the organizational, community, societal, and global levels.

**mandated reporter** A professional who is required by law to report if certain categories of clients (e.g., children and the elderly) are at risk (posing a threat to themselves or others or experiencing serious abuse or neglect).

**mandatory client** A client who is required to engage in services involuntarily, usually because of an agency policy (as in preadoptive groups), a court (as in male batterers' groups), an employer (as in alcohol counseling), or a family member (as in support groups for spouses of addicts).

**mediation** The proposed functional role of the social worker helping clients and their systems identify their common ground. The term is used in a broad sense and can include other activities such as confrontation and advocacy.

**medical model** The four-step process of organizing one's thinking about practice, commonly described as study, diagnosis, treatment, and evaluation. Also, sometimes used to describe a "pathology" model for diagnosing client problems.

**micro practice** Social work with individual clients, families, or support groups in a clinical setting.

**microsociety** A description of the small group as a special case of the larger individual-social interaction in society.

**middle (or work) phase** The phase of work in which the client and the worker focus on dealing with issues raised in the beginning phase or with new issues that have emerged since then.

**mixed transactional model** A way of seeing social work in terms of transactions, or exchanges in which people give to and take from each other through different mediums of exchange, including words, facial and body expressions, touch, shared experiences of various kinds, and other forms of communication (often used simultaneously).

**model** A concrete, symbolic representation of an abstract phenomenon.

**model A** A social work approach that presupposes that community change may be pursued optimally through broad participation of a wide spectrum of people at the local community level in goal determination and action.

**model B** A social planning approach that emphasizes a technical process of problem solving with regard to substantive social problems.

**model C** The social action approach that presupposes a disadvantaged segment of the population that needs to be organized, perhaps in alliance with others, in order to make adequate demands on the larger community for increased resources or treatment more in accordance with social justice or democracy.

**monitoring the group** The skill of observing the second client—the group members—by watching for verbal and nonverbal clues as to their reactions while a member is speaking.

**monitoring the individual** The skill of observing individual group members, remaining alert to verbal and nonverbal clues signaled by each individual. This is an acquired skill. When this skill is integrated, a group leader can simultaneously monitor the group and each individual.

**monopolizer** A member of a group who talks a great deal and appears to monopolize the conversation. The monopolizer is usually described as someone who does not listen well to others.

**motivational interviewing** A technique to address addictive behavior focusing on the issue of increasing client motivation and drawing upon the stages-of-change model.

**mourning period** A stage in the ending process of a group, usually characterized by apathy and a general tone of sadness.

**moving from the general to the specific** Helping a client share specific details about an issue first brought up on a more general level.

**mutual demand** A mutual-aid process in which group members offer each other help by making demands and setting expectations on personal behavior.

**mutual support** A mutual-aid process in which group members provide emotional support to one another.

**near problems** Legitimate issues raised by clients, early in the relationship, to establish trust before raising more difficult and often threatening issues.

**neighborhood social networks** The linkages developed by a group of neighbors.

**neighboring** The social interaction, the symbolic interaction, and the attachment of individuals with the people living around them and the place in which they live.

**nonverbal forms of communication** The transmission of a communication without the use of words; for example, a posture or facial expression, a client getting up and leaving an interview, or an affectionate touch.

**norms of behavior** The rules of behavior generally accepted by a dominant group in society. These norms can be recreated within a social work group or other system. The existence of the norms is evident when the group members act as if the norms exist.

**open-ended group** A group in which new members can join at any point and ongoing members may leave at different times. For example, a ward group on a hospital may have new members join when admitted to the hospital and others leave when discharged.

**opening statement** The worker's statement, during the first contact, that attempts to identify the purpose of the encounter, the worker's role, and possible areas of connection with the felt needs of the client.

**oppression psychology** A theory of the impact of societal oppression on vulnerable populations.

**organismic model** A metaphor suggesting a capacity for growth and emergent behavior—that is, a process in which a system transcends itself and creates something new that is more than just the sum of its parts.

**outreach process** A process through which the social work service is brought to potential clients.

**outreach program** A program that attempts to bring services directly to clients, usually in their own homes or neighborhoods.

**pairing group** One of Bion's (1961) basic assumption groups, in which the group, often through a conversation between two members, avoids the pain of the work by discussing some future great event.

**parallel process** The way in which the process on one level (such as supervisor-worker) parallels the process on another level (such as worker-client).

**partializing the client's concerns** Helping the client deal with complex problems by breaking them down into their component parts and addressing the parts one at a time.

**personal/emotional support** The extent to which neighbors are willing to greet and visit with each other can serve as a source of social belonging and reduce feelings of social isolation often fostered within cities.

**personal social networks** Neighbors establish linkages with key individuals in their neighborhoods for individual benefit. They use these connections to find and further link themselves to resources in their neighborhood and wider community to solve problems.

**plasticity** Defined as the individual's ability to be flexible in response to stress.

**pointing out endings early** The skill of reminding clients, far enough ahead of the last sessions to be helpful, that the working relationship is coming to a close. How early this is depends on the length of the working relationship, among other factors.

**practitioner-researcher** A social worker who is continuously involved in evaluating his or her own practice and developing generalizations from the practice experience.

**preliminary (or preparatory) phase** The phase of work prior to the worker engaging with the client. Usually used by the worker to develop a preliminary empathy about the client's issues and concerns.

**privileged communications** Worker-client communications are held to be privileged, so that the social worker cannot disclose them without the client's permission, even in the course of legal proceedings. Specific exceptions to privilege are usually listed in the state legislation that establishes the privilege.

**process** The interaction that takes place between the worker and the client during an interview, or between the client and another client, which characterizes the way of working versus the content of the work.

**professional impact** The activities of social workers designed to effect changes in (1) policies and services in their own agency and other agencies and institutions, as well as broader social policies that affect clients, and (2) the work culture that influences inter-staff relationships within their own agency and with other agencies and institutions.

**program in group work** The use of activities other than just words as a medium of client exchanges in the group.

**pseudo-effectiveness** Defined by Argyris (1954) as the ability of the organization to create the illusion of effective operation.

**psychosocial history** The client's story, taking into account personal, psychological, and social factors that may have some bearing on the current life situation. This is usually obtained during an intake interview or early history.

**putting the client's feelings into words** The skill of articulating the client's feelings, in response to tuning in or perceiving the client's indirect communications, prior to the client's direct expression of affect.

**quasi-stationary social equilibrium** A term used by Lewin (1951) to describe a stage in the change process at which a person is in balance with his or her social environment. This balance can be upset by external or internal forces, resulting in a state of disequilibrium that can lead to change and a new quasi-stationary equilibrium.

**queer** is an insider term that is being reclaimed—as in, for example, queer art and queer theory. The advantage of this term is that it can encompass all sexual minorities. The disadvantage is obvious.

**questioning** In the elaboration process, the worker's requests for more information from the client regarding the client's problem, including who, what, where, when, and why.

**quiet member** A member of the group who remains noticeably silent over an extended period of time.

**rapport** One element of the construct "working relationship"; a general sense on the client's part that he or she gets along well with the worker.

**reaching for feelings** The empathic skill of asking the client to share the affective portion of the message.

**reaching for the client's feedback** Inviting a client to share his or her concerns related to the purpose of the contact and the agency service. This may be a simple question or a statement of specific illustrative examples of possible concerns (see *handles for work*).

**reaching inside of silences** The skill of exploring the meaning of a silence by putting the client's possible feelings into words (for instance, "Are you angry right now?").

**recontracting** The process in which the worker reopens the issues of contracting by providing a clearer statement of purpose or exploring the group members' resistance or lack of connection to the service.

**record of service** A written record that describes the client system, identifies the central problem area, describes and illustrates the practice over time, assesses the status of the problem after a period of work, and then identifies next worker interventions to continue the work.

**reframing the problem** The process, described by family theorists, as helping the family see a problem in a new way. One example of this would be helping the family move beyond viewing the family problem as concerning a single child (the identified patient) who may be serving as a family scapegoat.

**regression analysis** A statistical procedure for projecting the impact of predictor variables on outcome variables.

**rehearsal** (1) The process in which the client has an opportunity to practice a difficult next step in an informal role-play, with the worker usually playing the role of the other person. This is one of the sessional ending and transition skills. (2) A mutual-aid process in which group members help one another by providing a forum in which members can try out ideas or skills. (3) One of the functions of group activities; designed to develop skills for specific life tasks.

**resiliency** The human capacity (individual, group, and/or community) to deal with crisis, stressors, and normal experiences in an emotionally and physically healthy way; an effective coping style (Barker, 2003, p. 369).

**resistance** Behavior on the part of the client that appears to resist the worker's efforts to deal with the client's problems. Resistance may be open (active) or indirect (passive). It is usually a sign of the client's pain associated with the work.

**resolution-catharsis** The third subphase of the dependency phase in group development, in which group leadership is assumed by members who are unconflicted (independent) (Bennis & Shepard, 1956). This "overthrow" of the worker leads to each member taking responsibility for the group: The worker is no longer seen as "magical," and the power struggles are replaced by work on shared goals.

**resolution stage** The stage of work in which a session is brought to some form of closure or resolution, which may include recognizing the lack of closure and determining next steps.

**role** In the psychodynamic frame of reference, an "adaptational unit of personality in action" (Ackerman, 1958, p. 53).

**scapegoat** A member of the group attacked, verbally or physically, by other members who project onto the member their own negative feelings about themselves. The scapegoat role is often interactive in nature, with the scapegoat fulfilling a functional role in the group.

**second decision** The client's decision to continue engaging with the worker in the middle phase of work. This decision is made in the face of challenges such as dealing with painful issues and accepting personal responsibility for addressing issues.

**self-determination** The right of clients to make their own choices and decisions; an ethical principle in social work.

**sessional contracting skills** The skills usually employed at the start of a session to clarify the immediate work at hand. These include exploring client resistance, identifying process and content connections, and helping the client see life in new ways.

**sessional ending and transition skills** The skills designed to bring a session to a close and to make the connections between a single session and future work or issues in the life of the client. These include summarizing, generalizing, identifying the next steps, rehearsal, and identifying "doorknob" communications.

**sessional tuning-in skills** The skills designed to sensitize the worker, prior to each session, to the potential themes that may emerge during the work. These include tuning in to the client's sense of urgency, to the worker's own feelings, to the meaning of the client's struggle, to the worker's realities of time and stress, and to the worker's own life experiences.

**sexual orientation** Refers to the inclination of an individual toward sexual or affectional partners of the same sex, opposite sex, or both sexes.

**sharing data** A mutual-aid process in a group when members share accumulated knowledge, views, values, and so forth that can help others in the group.

**sharing worker data** Sharing facts, ideas, values, and beliefs that workers have accumulated from their own experiences and can make available to clients.

**sharing worker's feelings** The skill of appropriately sharing with the client the worker's own affect. These feelings should be shared in pursuit of professional purposes as the worker implements the professional function.

**skill factor** A set of closely related worker skills.

**skills** Specific behaviors on the part of the worker that are used in the implementation of the social work function.

**societal taboos** Commonly shared injunctions in our society that directly or indirectly inhibit our ability to talk about certain areas (e.g., sexual abuse, death and dying). More generally, taboos are social prohibitions that result from conventions or traditions. Norms and taboos are closely related, because a group norm may be one that upholds the tradition of making certain subjects taboo.

**solution-focused practice** This model is built on the strengths perspective. It focuses on the client's current issues and assumes that, with the help of the social worker, the client can identify and use inherent strengths that might be overlooked in a pathology-oriented practice.

**spirituality** Devotion to the immaterial part of humanity and nature rather than worldly things such as possessions; an orientation to people's religious, moral, or emotional nature (Barker, 2003, p. 414).

**"strength-in-numbers" phenomenon** The mutual-aid process in which group members are strengthened to take on difficult tasks (such as challenging agency policy) through the support of other group members.

**structure and maintenance** The work done by group members to develop, examine, and maintain in good working order their structure for work (roles, rules, culture, and so on).

**structure for work** The formal or informal rules, roles, communication patterns, rituals, and procedures developed by the group members to facilitate the work of the group.

**summarizing** Helping a client to identify the main themes of discussion during a session. This is one of the sessional ending and transition skills, to be employed at key moments, not necessarily in every session.

**supporting clients in taboo areas** Encouraging a client to discuss a sensitive or difficult area or concern (e.g., sex, loss).

**symbiotic assumption** The assumption of a relationship between the individual and his or her nurturing group in which each needs the other for the life and growth of each, and each reaches out to the other with all the strength possible at a given moment.

**symbiotic diffusion** Obscuring of the mutual need between people and their social surroundings by the complexity of the situation, by divergent needs, or by the difficulties involved in communication.

**systems or ecological approach** A view of the client that takes into account his or her dynamic interaction with the social context.

**systems work** The set of activities in which social workers attempt to influence the systems and systems representatives (e.g., doctors, administrators, teachers) that are important to their clients.

**taboo** See *societal taboos*.

**theoretical generalizations** Testable propositions that receive repeated support from research.

**therapeutic alliance.** A generally accepted concept contained in most practice theories suggests that the activities of the helping person can help him or her develop a positive working relationship with the client.

**third decision** The decision clients make to deal with their most difficult issues as they approach the end of the working relationship.

**tipping point** The "saturation point" in the changing racial ratio of a group that leads majority group members to respond with anxiety and aggression toward the "out" group. Reaching the tipping point can generate such processes as cleavage and White flight.

**transgender** Several different types of sexual identities and sets of behaviors that involve taking on the attributes of the opposite sex.

**triangulation** A process in which one party attempts to gain the allegiance of a second party in the struggle with a third party (e.g., the parents and the therapist versus the child; the mother and an older child versus the father) as a means of coping with anxiety.

**trust** An element of the construct "working relationship"; the client's perception that she or he can risk sharing thoughts, feelings, mistakes, and failures with the worker.

**trying the ending on for size** A stage in the ending/transition phase in which clients or group members operate independently of the worker or spend a great deal of time talking about new groups or new workers.

**tuning in** The skill of getting in touch with potential feelings and concerns that the client may bring to the helping encounter. For this to be done effectively, the worker has to actually experience the feelings, or an approximation, by using his or her own life experiences to recall similar emotions.

**two-client construct** View of the social worker as always having two clients at any moment in time (e.g., the individual and the family; the member and the group; the client and the system).

**unconflicted member** A member of the group who is independent and untroubled by authority.

**values** The customs, beliefs, standards of conduct, and principles considered desirable by a culture, a group of people, or an individual (Barker, 2003, p. 453).

**vulnerable client** A client who is particularly exposed to the impact of oppression and stressful life events because of personal and/or social factors (such as lack of a strong social support system of family or friends, or limited economic resources).

**White flight** The process of White members leaving a group when the racial composition ratio of the group changes, resulting in an increase in minority group members beyond the tipping point.

**who owns the client?** A maladaptive struggle in which helping professionals appear to fight over "ownership" of functional responsibility for a client.

**work group** The mental activity related to a group's task (Bion, 1961). When the work group is operating, one can see group members translating their thoughts and feelings into actions that are adaptive to reality.

**worker data** See *sharing worker data*.

**working relationship** A professional relationship between the client and worker that is the medium through which the social worker influences the client. A positive working relationship will be characterized by good rapport and a sense on the part of the client that he or she can trust the worker and that the worker cares for the client.

# References

Ackerman, N. (1958). *Psychodynamics of family life* (3rd ed.). New York: Basic Books.

Addams, J. (1961). *Twenty years at Hull House*. New York: Signet.

Albert, J. (1994). Rethinking difference: A cognitive therapy group for chronic mental patients. *Social Work with Groups, 17,* 105–122.

Albright, D. L., & Rosellini, G. (2010). Treating veterans and their families: What civilian counselors need to know. In *Terrorism, trauma, and tragedies: A counselor's guide to preparing and responding* (3rd ed., pp. 59–63). Alexandria, VA: American Counseling Association.

Aldridge, D. (2000). *Spirituality, healing and medicine: A return to silence*. London: Jessica Kingsley Publishers.

Alexander, R., Jr. (1997). Social workers and privileged communication in the federal legal system. *Social Work, 42,* 387–391.

American Association for Counseling and Development. (1989). *Ethical guidelines for group counselors*. Alexandria, VA: Author.

American Psychiatric Association. (1994). *Diagnostic and statistical manual of mental disorders* (4th ed.; DSM-IV). Washington, DC: Author.

Amodeo, M., Wilson, S., & Cox, D. (1996). Mounting a community-based alcohol and drug abuse prevention effort in a multicultural urban setting: Challenges and lessons learned. *Journal of Primary Prevention, 16,* 165–185.

Appleby, G. A., Colon, E., & Hamilton, J. (2001). *Diversity and oppression, and social functioning*. Boston: Allyn & Bacon.

Argyris, C. (1964). *Integrating the individual and the organization*. New York: Wiley.

Atieno, J. E. (2008). Reflective practice in group co-leadership. *Journal for Specialist in Group Work, 33*(3), 236–252.

Atkinson, D. R., Maruyama, M., & Matsui, D. (1978). The effects of counselor race and counseling approach on Asian Americans' perceptions of counselor credibility and utility. *Journal of Counseling Psychology, 45,* 414–423.

Barker, R. (2003). *The social work dictionary* (5th ed.). Silver Spring, MD: National Association of Social Workers.

Baum, N. L. (2005). Building resistance: A school-based intervention for children exposed to ongoing trauma and stress. In Y. Danieli, D. Brom, & J. Sills (Eds.), *The trauma of terrorism: Sharing knowledge and shared care—An international handbook* (pp. 487–498). New York: Haworth Press.

Beasley, M., Thompson, T., & Davidson, J. (2003). Resilience in response to life stress: The effects of coping style and cognitive hardiness. *Personality and Individual Differences, 34,* 77–95.

Beck, A., Rush, A., Shaw, B., & Emery, G. (1979). *Cognitive theory of depression*. New York: Guilford Press.

Bell, N. W., & Vogel, E. F. (1960). The emotionally disturbed child as the family scapegoat. In N. W. Bell & E. F. Vogel (Eds.), *A modern introduction to the family* (pp. 382–397). New York: Free Press.

Bennis, W. G., & Shepard, H. A. (1956). A theory of group development. *Human Relations, 9,* 415–437.

Berlin, S. B. (1983). Cognitive-behavioral approaches. In A. Rosenblatt & D. Wald Fogel (Eds.), *Handbook of clinical social work* (pp. 1095–1119). San Francisco: Jossey-Bass.

Berlin, S. B. (1984). Single-case evaluation: Another version. *Social Work Research and Abstracts, 19*(1), 3–11.

Berlin, S. B., & Kravetz, D. (1981). Women as victims: A feminist social work perspective. *Social Work, 26,* 449.

Berman-Rossi, T., & Cohen, M. B. (1989). Group development and shared decision making working with homeless mentally ill women. In J. A. Lee (Ed.), *Group work with the poor and oppressed* (pp. 63–74). New York: Haworth Press.

Bernstein, S. (1965). *Explorations in group work*. Boston: Boston University School of Social Work.

Bernstein, S. (1970). *Further exploration in group work*. Boston: Boston University School of Social Work.

Beutler, L. E., Moleiro, C., & Talebi, H. (2002). How practitioners can systematically use empirical evidence in treatment selection. *Journal of Clinical Psychology, 58*(10), 1199–1212.

Bion, W. R. (1961). *Experience in groups*. New York: Basic Books.

Boutin, D. L. (2007). Effectiveness of cognitive behavioral and supportive-expressive group therapy for women diagnosed with breast cancer: A review of the literature. *Journal for Specialist in Group Work, 32*(3), 267–284.

Bowen, M. (1961). The family as a unit of study and treatment. *American Journal of Orthopsychiatry, 31,* 40–60.

Bowen, M. (1978). *Family therapy in clinical practice*. New York: Jason Aronson.

Boyle, D. P., & Springer, S. A. (2001). Toward a cultural competence measure for social work with specific populations. *Journal of Ethnic and Cultural Diversity in Social Work, 9,* 53–71.

Brabender, V. (2006). The ethical group psychotherapist. *International Journal of Group Psychotherapy, 56*(4), 395–414.

Braeger, G., & Holloway, S. (1978). *Changing human service organizations: Politics and practice.* New York: Free Press.

Breton, M. (1988). The need for mutual-aid groups in a drop-in for homeless women: The sistering case. In J. A. Lee (Ed.), *Group work with the poor and oppressed* (pp. 47–60). New York: Haworth Press.

Bricker-Jenkins, M. (1991). The propositions and assumptions of feminist social work practice. In M. Breicker-Jenkins, N. Hooyman, & N. Gottlief (Eds.), *Feminist social work practice in clinical settings* (pp. 271–303). Newbury Park, CA: Sage.

Bride, B. E., Jones, J. L., & MacMaster, S. A. (2007). Correlates of secondary traumatic stress in child protective services workers. *Journal of Evidence-Based Social Work, 4*(3/4), 69–80.

Brueggemann, W. G. (2006). *The practice of macro social work* (3rd ed.). Belmont, CA: Thomson Brooks/Cole.

Bulhan, H. A. (1985). *Franz Fanon and the psychology of oppression.* New York: Plenum Press.

Burkard, A. W., & Knox, S. (2004). Effect of therapist color-blindness on empathy and attributions in cross-cultural counseling. *Journal of Counseling Psychology, 51,* 387–397.

Butler, K. (1997, March/April). The anatomy of resilience. *Networker,* pp. 22–31.

Butler, S., & Wintram, C. (1991). *Feminist group work.* London: Sage Publications Ltd.

Butterfield, E. (2003). Intersectonality: New directions for a theory of identity. *International Studies in Philosophy, 35*(1), 1–12.

Carter, J. A. (2002). Integrating science and practice: Reclaiming the science in practice. *Journal of Clinical Psychology, 58*(10), 1285–1290.

Castex, G. M. (1994). Providing services to Hispanic/Latino populations: Profiles in diversity. *Social Work, 39,* 288–296.

Chen, M., & Rybak, C. J. (2004). *Group leadership skills: Interpersonal process in group counseling and therapy.* Belmont, CA: Wadsworth/Thomson.

Christian, M. D., & Barbarin, O. A. (2001). Cultural resources and psychological adjustment of African American children: Effects of spirituality and racial attribution. *Journal of Black Psychology, 27,* 43–63.

Chung, R. C.-Y., & Bemak, F. (2002). The relationship of culture and empathy in cross-cultural counseling. *Journal of Counseling and Development, 80,* 154–159.

Clay, C., & Shulman, I. (1993). *Teaching about practice and diversity: Content and process in the classroom and the field* [Videotape]. Produced and distributed by the Council on Social Work Education.

Clemans, S. E. (2004). Recognizing vicarious traumatization: A single session group model for trauma workers. *Social Work with Groups, 27*(3), 55–74.

*Code of ethical practice.* (1991). Boston, MA: Board of Registration of Social Workers, 258 CMR-25.

Cohen, J. A. (2005). Treating traumatized children: Current status and future directions. In *Acute reactions to trauma and psychotherapy: A multidisciplinary and international perspective* (pp. 109–121). New York: Haworth Press.

Collins, B. G. (1994). Reconstructing codependency using self-in-relation theory: A feminist perspective. *Social Work, 38,* 470–476.

Collins, D., Jordan, C., & Coleman, H. (2007). *An introduction to family social work.* Belmont, CA: Thomson Brooks/Cole.

Congress, E. P. (1994). The use of culturagrams to assess and empower culturally diverse families. *Families in Society, 75,* 531–540.

Connell, J. P., Spencer, M. B., & Aber, J. L. (1994). Educational risk and resilience in African American youth: Context, self, action, and outcomes in school. *Child Development, 65,* 506–520.

Connolly, C. M. (2005). The process of change: The intersection of the GLBT individual and their family of origin. *Journal of GLBT Family Studies: Innovations in Theory, Research, and Practice, 1*(1), 5–20.

Constantine, M. (2007). Racial microaggressions against African American clients in cross-racial counseling relationships. *Journal of Counseling Psychology, 54*(1), 1–16.

Contrato, S., & Rossier, J. (2005). Early trends in feminist therapy theory and practice. In M. Hill & M. Ballou (Eds.), *The foundation and future of feminist therapy.* New York: Haworth Press.

Corey, G. (2008). *Theory and practice of group counseling* (7th ed.). Belmont, CA: Thomson Brooks/Cole.

Corey, M. S., & Corey, G. (2006). *Groups: Process and practice* (7th ed.). Belmont, CA: Thomson Brooks/Cole.

Council on Social Work Education. (2003). *Curriculum policy statement.* New York: Author.

Cox, E. O. (2001). Community practice issues in the 21st century: Questions and challenges for empowerment oriented practitioners. *Journal of Community Practice, 9,* 37–55.

Coyle, G. (1948). *Group work with American youth.* New York: Harper.

Daly, A., Jennings, J., Beckett, J. O., & Leashore, B. R. (1995). Effective coping strategies of African Americans. *Social Work, 40,* 240–248.

Damianakis, T., Climans, R., & Marziali, E. (2008). Social workers experiences of virtual psychotherapeutic support groups of family caregivers for Alzheimer's, Parkinson's, stroke, front temporal dementia and traumatic brain injury. *Social Work with Groups, 31,* 99–116.

Danieli, Y., Brom, D., & Sills, J. (Eds.). (2005). *The trauma of terrorism: Sharing knowledge and shared care—An international perspective.* New York: Haworth Press.

Davidson, K. W. (1985). Social work with cancer patients: Stresses and coping patterns. *Social Work in Health Care, 10*, 73–82.

Davies, D. R., Burlingame, G. M., & Layne, C. M. (2006). *Integrating small group process principles into trauma-focused group psychotherapy: What should a group trauma therapist know?* New York: Haworth Press.

Davis, L. E. (1979). Racial composition of groups. *Social Work, 24*, 208–213.

Davis, L. E. (1981). Racial issues in the training of group workers. *Journal of Specialists in Group Work,* volume 1, issue 2, 155–160.

Davis, L. E. (1984). *Ethnicity in social group work practice.* New York: Haworth Press.

Davis, L. E. (1999). *Working with African American males: A guide to practice.* Newbury Park, CA: Sage.

Davis, L. E., & Proctor, E. K. (1989). *Race, gender, and class: Guidelines for practice with individuals, families, and groups.* Englewood Cliffs, NJ: Prentice-Hall.

DeLucia-Waack, J. L. (2006). *Leading psychoeducational groups for children and adolescents.* Thousand Oaks, CA: Sage.

DeLucia-Waack, J., & Donigian, J. (2004). *The practice of multicultural group work: Visions and perspectives from the field.* Belmont, CA: Thomson Brooks/Cole.

deShazer, S. (1988). *Clues: Investigating solutions in brief therapy.* New York: Norton.

deShazer, S., & Berg, R. (1992). Doing therapy: A poststructural revision. *Journal of Marital and Family Therapy, 18*, 71–81.

Devore, W., & Schlesinger, E. G. (1991). *Ethnic-sensitive social work practice* (3rd ed.). New York: Macmillan.

Devore, W., & Schlesinger, E. G. (1996). *Ethnic-sensitive social work practice* (4th ed.). Needham Heights, MA: Allyn & Bacon.

DiClemente, C. C., Prochaska, J. O., Fairhurst, S. K., & Velicer, W. F. (1991). The process of smoking cessation: An analysis of precontemplation, contemplation, and preparation stages of change. *Journal of Consulting and Clinical Psychology, 59*, 191–204.

Dolgoff, R., Loewenberg, F. M., & Harrington, D. (2005). *Ethical decisions for social work practice* (7th ed.). Belmont, CA: Brooks/Cole.

Douglas, T. (1995). *Scapegoats: Transferring blame.* New York: Routledge.

Drescher, K. D. (2006). Spirituality in the face of terrorist disasters. In L. A. Schein, H. I. Spitz, G. M. Burlingame, P. R. Muskin, & S. Vargo (Eds.), *Psychological effects of catastrophic disasters: Group approaches to treatment.* Binghamton, NY: Haworth Press.

Dreschler, J., D'ercole, A., & Schoenberg, E. (Eds.). (2003). *Psychotherapy with gay men and lesbians.* New York: Harrington Park Press.

Duff, C. T. (2010). Counsellor behaviours that predict therapeutic alliance: From the client's perspective. *Counselling Psychology Quarterly, 23*(1), 91–110.

Egeland, B. R., Carlson, E., & Sroufe, L. A. (1993). Resilience as process. *Development and Psychopathology, 5*, 517–528.

Elkin, I., Parloff, M. B., Hadley, S. W., & Autry, J. H. (1985). NIMH treatment of depression collaborative research program: Background and research plan. *Archives of General Psychiatry, 42*, 305–316.

Ell, K. (1996). Crisis theory and social work practice. In F. Turner (Ed.), *Social work treatment: Interlocking theoretical approaches* (4th ed., pp. 168–190). New York: Free Press.

Elze, D. (2006). Working with gay, lesbian, bisexual and transgender students. In C. Franklin, M. B. Harris, & P. Allen-Meares (Eds.), *The school services sourcebook: A guide for school-based professionals* (pp. 861–870). New York: Oxford University Press.

Engstrom, C. (2009). Social workers' ability to assess how clients experience investigation sessions—with and without the ASI. *Journal of Social Work, 9*(3), 309–323.

Fanon, F. (1968). *The wretched of the earth.* New York: Grove Press.

Fedele, N. (1994). *Relationships in groups: Connection, resonance, and paradox* (Working Paper Series). Wellesley, MA: Stone Center.

Fenell, D. L., & Wehrman, J. D. (2010). Deployment counseling: Supporting military personnel and their families. In *Terrorism, trauma, and tragedies: A counselor's guide to preparing and responding* (3rd ed., pp. 49–51). Alexandria, VA: American Counseling Association.

Figley, C. R. (Ed.). (1995). *Compassion fatigue: Coping with secondary traumatic stress disorder in those who treat the traumatized.* New York: Brunner/Mazel.

Fischer, J. (1973). Is casework effective? A review. *Social Work, 18*, 5–20.

Flanders, N. A. (1970). *Analyzing teaching behaviors.* Reading, MA: Addison-Wesley.

Fonagy, P., Steele, M., Steele, H., & Higgitt, A. (1994). The Emanuel Miller Memorial Lecture 1992: The theory and practice of resilience. *Journal of Child Psychology and Psychiatry and Allied Disciplines, 35*, 231–257.

Freedberg, S. (2009). *Relational theory for social work practice: A feminist perspective.* New York: Routledge, Taylor and Francis Group.

Freeman, D. S. (1981). *Techniques of family therapy.* New York: Jason Aronson.

Freud, S., & Krug, S. (2002, September–December). Beyond the code of ethics, part 1: Complexities of ethical decision making in social work practice. *Families in Society: The Journal of Contemporary Human Services, 83*(5/6), 474–482.

Freund, P. D. (1993). Professional role(s) in the empowerment process: Working with mental health consumers. *Psychosocial Rehabilitation Journal, 3*, 65–73.

Galloway, V. A., & Brodsky, S. L. (2003). Caring less, doing more: The role of therapeutic detachment with volatile and unmotivated clients. *American Journal of Psychotherapy, 57*, 32–38.

Galper, J. (1967). Introduction to radical theory and practice in social work education: Social policy. *Journal of Education in Social Work, 12*, 3–9.

Gambrill, E., & Pruger, R. (1997). *Controversial issues in social work ethics, values, and obligations.* Boston: Allyn & Bacon.

Gans, J. S., & Counselman, E. F. (2010). Patient selection for psychodynamic group psychotherapy: Practical and dynamic considerations. *International Journal of Group Psychotherapy, 60*(2), 197–220.

Garfield, G. P., & Irizary, C. R. (1971). Recording the "record of service": Describing social work practice. In W. Schwartz & S. Zalba (Eds.), *The practice of group work* (pp. 241–265). New York: Columbia Press.

Garland, J. A., Jones, H. E., & Kolodny, R. L. (1965). A model for stages of development in social work groups. In S. Bernstein (Ed.), *Explorations in group work* (pp. 17–71). Boston: Boston University School of Social Work.

Garland, J. A., & Kolodny, R. L. (1965). Characteristics and resolution of scapegoating. In S. Bernstein (Ed.), *Explorations in group work.* Boston: Boston University School of Social Work. (Published later under the same title by Boston: Charles River Books, 1976; Hebron, CT: Practioner's Press, 1984.)

Garmezy, N. (1993). Children in poverty: Resilience despite risk. *Psychiatry, 56,* 127–136.

Garmezy, N., Masten, A. S., & Tellegen, A. (1984). The study of stress and competence in children: A building block for developmental psychopathology. *Child Development, 55,* 98–111.

Garvin, C. (1969). Complementarity of role expectations in groups: The member-novice contact. In *Social work practice* (pp. 127–145). New York: Columbia University Press.

Gary, L. E., & Leashore, B. R. (1982). High-risk status of black men. *Social Work, 27,* 54–58.

Garza, Y., & Watts, R. (2010). Filial therapy and Hispanic values: Common ground for culturally sensitive helping. *Journal of Counseling and Development, 88*(1), 108–113.

Germain, C. B., & Gitterman, A. (1996). *The life model of social work practice: Advances in theory and practice* (2nd ed.). New York: Columbia University Press.

Gilgun, J. F. (1996). Human development and adversity in ecological perspective, part 1: A conceptual framework. *Families in Society, 77,* 395–402.

Gilligan, C., Lyons, N. P., & Hammer, T. J. (1990). *Making connections: The relational worlds of adolescent girls at Emma Willard School.* Cambridge, MA: Harvard University Press.

Gim, R. H., Atkinson, D. R., & Kim, S. J. (1991). Asian-American acculturation, counselor ethnicity and cultural sensitivity, and ratings of counselors. *Journal of Counseling Psychology, 38,* 57–62.

Gladding, S. T. (2003). *Group work: A counseling specialty* (4th ed.). Upper Saddle River, NJ: Merrill/Pearson Education.

Gladis, M. M., Gosch, E. A., Dishuk, N. M., & Crits, C. P. (1999). Quality of life: Expanding the scope of clinical significance. *Journal of Consulting and Clinical Psychology, 67*(3), 320–331.

Glaser, B., & Strauss, A. (1967). *Grounded theory.* Chicago: Aldine.

Guiffrida, D. A., & Douthit, K. Z. (2010). The black student experience at predominantly white colleges: Implications for school and college counselors. *Journal of Counseling and Development, 88*(3), 311–318.

Gumpert, J., & Black, P. N. (2006). Ethical issues in group work: What are they and how are they managed? *Social Work with Groups: A Journal of Community and Clinical Practice, 29*(4), 93–99.

Gutheil, I. A. (1992). Considering the physical environment: An essential component of good practice. *Social Work, 37*(5), 391–396.

Guttmann, D. (2006). *Ethics in social work: A context of caring.* Binghamton, NY: Haworth Press.

Hacker, A. (1992). *Two nations: Black and white, separate, hostile, unequal.* New York: Scribner.

Håkan, J. (2010). Therapeutic alliance and outcome in routine psychiatric out-patient treatment: Patient factors and outcome. *Psychology and Psychotherapy: Theory, Research and Practice, 83*(2), 193–206.

Hakansson, J., & Montgomery, H. (2002). The role of action in empathy from the perspective of the empathizer and the target. *Current Research in Social Psychology, 8,* 50–62. Retrieved from http://www.uiowa.edu/.

Hakansson, J., & Montgomery, H. (2003). Empathy as an interpersonal phenomenon. *Journal of Social and Personal Relationships, 20,* 267–284.

Haley, J. (1978). *Problem-solving therapy.* San Francisco: Jossey-Bass.

Hancock, A. M. (2007). When multiplication doesn't equal quick addition: Examining intersectionality as a research paradigm. *Perspectives on Politics, 5*(1), 63–69.

Hanna, S. M. (2007). *The practice of family therapy: Key elements across models* (4th ed.). Belmont, CA: Thomson Brooks/Cole.

Hardy, K. V., & Laszloffy, T. A. (1992). Training racially sensitive family therapists: Context, content, and contact. *Families in Society, 73*(6), 364–370.

Hare, P. A. (1962). *Handbook of small group research.* New York: Free Press.

Haug, S., Sedway, J., & Kordy, H. (2008, January). Group processes and process evaluations in a new treatment setting: Inpatient group psychotherapy followed by Internet-chat aftercare groups. *International Journal of Group Psychotherapy, 58*(1), 35–53.

Hearn, G. (1962). *The general systems approach to understanding groups.* New York: Society of Public Health Educators.

Herrenkohl, E. C., Herrenkohl, R. C., & Egolf, B. (1994). Resilient early school-age children from maltreating homes: Outcomes in late adolescence. *American Journal of Orthopsychiatry, 64,* 301–309.

Heyman, D. (1971). A function for the social worker in anti-poverty programs. In W. Schwartz & S. Zalba (Eds.), *The practice of group work* (pp. 167–180). New York: Columbia University Press.

Holmes, D. M. (2006). Spirituality courses become part of medical school curriculum. In *University at Buffalo New Release*.

Holmes, M., & Lundy, C. (1990). Group work for abusive men: A profeminist response. *Canada's Mental Health, 38*, 12–17.

Horne, A. M., & Passmore, J. L. (1991). *Family counseling and therapy* (2nd ed.). Itasca, IL: Peacock.

Hulko, W. (2009). The time and context-contingent nature of intersectionality and interlocking oppressions. *Affilia: Journal of Women and Social Work, 24*(1), 44–55.

Ingersoll, K. S., Wagner, C. C., & Gharib, S. (2007). *Motivational groups for community substance abuse programs*. Richmond, VA: Mid-Atlantic Addiction Technology Transfer Center.

Jacobs, B. (2001). Taking sides: A white intern encounters an African American family. In S. McDaniel, D. Lusterman, & C. Philpot (Eds.), *Casebook for integrating family therapy* (pp. 171–178). Washington, DC: American Psychological Association.

Jacobs, E. E., Masson, R. L., & Harvill, R. L. (2006). *Group counseling: Strategies and skills* (5th ed.). Belmont, CA: Brooks/Cole.

*Jaffee v. Redmond*, 116 S. Ct. 1923 (1996). [Lexis, U. U. 3879]

Janzen, C., & Harris, O. (1997). *Family treatment in social work practice*. Itasca, IL: Peacock.

John, U., Veltrup, C., Driessen, M., Wetterling, T., & Dilling, H. (2003). *Motivational intervention: An individual counseling vs. a group treatment approach for alcohol-dependent in-patients. Alcohol, 38*, 263–269.

Jordan, J. (1991). Empathy, mutuality, and therapeutic change: Clinical implications of a relational model. In *Women's growth in connections: Writings from the Stone Center*. New York: Guilford Press.

Jordan, J. (1993). *Challenges to connection: Work in progress* (Working Paper Series, No. 60). Wellesley, MA: Stone Center.

Joyce, A. S., Piper, W. E., & Ogrodniczuk, J. S. (2007). Therapeutic alliance and cohesion variables as predictors of outcome in short-term group psychotherapy. *International Journal of Group Psychotherapy, 57*(3), 269–296.

Keith, D. V., & Whitaker, C. A. (1982). Experiential/symbolic family therapy. In A. M. Horne & M. M. Ohlsen (Eds.), *Family counseling and therapy*. Itasca, IL: Peacock.

Kendler, H. (2002). "Truth and reconciliation": Worker's fear of conflict in groups. *Social Work with Groups: A Journal of Community and Clinical Practice, 25*(3), 25–41.

Kennedy, A. (2008). Plugged in, turned on and wired up: How technology and the computer age are changing the counseling profession. *Counseling Today, 51*(2), 34–38.

Kim, B. S. K., Ng, G. F., & Ahn, A. J. (2009). Client adherence to Asian cultural values, common factors in counseling, and session outcome with Asian American clients at a university counseling center. *Journal of Counseling and Development, 87*(2), 131–142.

Kirk, S. A., Siporin, M., & Kutchins, L. (1989). The prognosis for social work diagnosis. *Social Casework, 70*, 295–304.

Kobasa, S. C., & Pucetti, M. C. (1983). Personality and social resources in stress resistance. *Journal of Personality and Social Psychology, 45*, 839–850.

Kubler-Ross, E. (1969). *On death and dying*. New York: Macmillan.

Kuhn, T. H. (1962). *The structure of scientific revolution*. Chicago: University of Chicago Press.

Kurland, R., & Salmon, R. (2006). Purpose: A misunderstood and misused keystone of group work practice. *Social Work with Groups: A Journal of Community and Clinical Practice, 29*(2/3), 105–120.

Lambert, M. J., Hansen, N. B., & Finch, A. E. (2001). Patient-focused research: Using patient outcome data to enhance treatment effects. *Journal of Consulting and Clinical Psychology, 69*(2), 159–172.

Lampropoulos, G. K., Goldfried, M. R., Castonguay, L.G., Lambert, M. J., Stiles, W. B., & Nestoros, J. N. (2002). What kind of research can we realistically expect from the practitioner? *Journal of Clinical Psychology, 58*(10), 1241–1264.

Lampropoulos, G. K., Schneider, M. K., & Spengler, P. M. (2009). Predictors of early termination in a university counseling training clinic. *Journal of Counseling and Development, 87*(1), 36–46.

Lasky, G. B., & Riva, M. T. (2006). Confidentiality and privileged communication in group psychotherapy. *International Journal of Group Psychotherapy, 56*(4), 455–476.

Learly, M. R. (1996). *Self presentation: Impression management and interpersonal behavior*. Boulder, CO: Westview Press.

Lee, J. A. (1994). *The empowerment approach to social work practice*. New York: Columbia University Press.

Levounis, P. (2003). Gay patient—gay therapist: A case report of Stephen. In J. Dreschler, A. D'ercole, & E. Schoenberg (Eds.), *Psychotherapy with gay men and lesbians*. New York: Harrington Park Press.

Lewin, K. (1935). *Field theory in social science: Selected theoretical papers*. New York: McGraw-Hill.

Lewin, K. (1951). *A dynamic theory of personality: Selected theoretical papers*. New York: McGraw-Hill.

Li, X., Stanton, B., Pack, R., Harris, C., Cottrell, L., & Burns, J. (2002). Risk and protective factors associated with gang involvement among urban African American adolescents. *Youth and Society, 34*, 172–194.

Lidz, C. (1984). *Informed consent*. New York: Guilford Press.

Lincourt, P., Kuettel, T. J., & Bombardier, C. H. (2002). Motivational interviewing in a group setting with mandated clients: A pilot study. *Addictive Behaviors, 27*(3), 381–391.

Lindgren, A., Barber, J. P., & Sandahl, C. (2008). Alliance to the group-as-a-whole as a predictor of outcome in psychodynamic group therapy. *International Journal of Group Psychotherapy, 58*(2), 142–163.

Loewenberg, F., & Dolgoff, R. (1996). *Ethical decisions for social work practice* (5th ed.). Itasca, IL: Peacock.

Long, D. D., Tice, C. J., & Morrison, J. D. (2006). *Macro social work practice: A strengths perspective.* Belmont, CA: Thomson Brooks/Cole.

Lu, Y. E., Organista, K. C., Manzo, S. J., Wong, L. & Phung, J. (2001). Exploring dimensions of culturally sensitive clinical styles with Latinos. *Journal of Ethnic and Cultural Diversity in Social Work, 10*, 45–66.

Lubin, H., & Johnson, D. R. (2008). *Trauma-centered group psychotherapy for women: A clinician's manual.* New York: Haworth Press.

Lueger, R. J. (2002). Practice-informed research and research-informed psychotherapy. *Journal of Clinical Psychology, 58*(10), 1265–1276.

Lum, D. (1996). *Social work practice and people of color: A process-stage approach* (3rd ed.). Pacific Grove, CA: Brooks/Cole.

Lum, D. (1999). *Culturally competent practice: A framework for growth and action.* Pacific Grove, CA: Brooks/Cole.

Mailick, M. D. (1991). Re-assessing assessment in clinical social work practice. *Smith College Studies in Social Work, 62*(1), 3–19.

Malekoff, A. (2007). What could happen and what couldn't happen: A poetry club for kids. *Social Work with Groups: A Journal of Community and Clinical Practice, 29*(2/3), 121–132.

Malekoff, A. (2008). Transforming trauma and empowering children and adolescents in the aftermath of disaster through group work. *Social Work with Groups: A Journal of Community and Clinical Practice, V.32, 1,2*, 29–52.

Mangione, L., Forti, R., & Iacuzzi, C. M. (2007). Ethics and endings in group psychotherapy: Saying good-bye and saying it well. *International Journal of Group Psychotherapy, 57*(1), 25–40.

Marsiglia, F. F., Pena, V., Nieri, T., & Nagoshi, J. L. (2010). Real groups: The design and immediate effects of a prevention intervention for Latino children. *Social Work with Groups, 33*, 103–121.

Mason, M. J. (2009). Rogers redux: Relevance and outcomes of motivational interviewing across behavioral problems. *Journal of Counseling and Development, 87*(3), 357–362.

Massachusetts NASW Chapter. (1996). [Monthly newspaper.]

Masten, A. S. (2001). Ordinary magic: Resilience processes in development. *American Psychologist, 56*, 227–238.

McGloin, J., & Widom, C. S. (2001). Resilience among abused and neglected children grown up. *Development and Psychopathology, 13*, 1021–1038.

McNeece, C. A., & Thyer, B. A. (2004). Evidenced-based practice and social work. *Journal of Evidence-Based Social Work, 1*(1), 7–26.

Mendez-Negrete, J. (2000). "Dime con quien andas": Notions of Chicano and Mexican-American families.

*Families in Society: The Journal of Contemporary Human Services, 81*, 42–48.

Miller, J. B. (1987). *Toward a new psychology of women* (2nd ed.). Boston: Beacon Press.

Miller, J. B. (1988). *Connections, disconnections, and violations* (Working Paper Series). Wellesley, MA: Stone Center.

Miller, J. B., & Stiver, I. P. (1991). *A relational framing of therapy* (Working Paper Series). Wellesley, MA: Stone Center.

Miller, J. B., & Stiver, I. P. (1993). A relational approach to understanding women's lives and problems. *Psychiatric Annals, 23*, 424–431.

Miller, S. (2005). What's like being the "holder of the space": A narrative on working with reflective practice in groups. *Reflective Practice, 6*, 367–377.

Miller, W. R., & Rollnick, S. (1991). *Motivational interviewing: Preparing people to change addictive behavior.* New York: Guilford Press.

Mills, C. W. (1959). *The sociological imagination.* New York: Oxford University Press.

Mirabito, D., & Rosenthal, C. (2006). *Generalist social work practice in the wake of disaster: September 11th and beyond.* Belmont, CA: Thomson.

Mitchel, J. T., & Everly, G. S., Jr. (2006). Critical incident stress management in terrorist events and disasters. In L. A. Schein, H. I. Spitz, G. M. Burlingame, P. R. Muskin, & S. Vargo (Eds.), *Psychological effects of catastrophic disasters: Group approaches to treatment.* Binghamton, NY: Haworth Press.

Mizrahi, T. (2001). The status of community organizing in 2001: Community practice context, complexities, contradictions, and contributions. *Research on Social Work Practice, 11*, 176–189.

Moberg, D. O. (1955). Research in spirituality, religion and aging. In H. R. Moody (Ed.), *Religion, spirituality, and aging: A social work perspective.* Binghamton, NY: Haworth Press.

Moody, H. R. (Ed.). (2005). *Religion, spirituality, and aging: A social work perspective.* Binghamton, NY: Haworth Press.

Mulroy, E. (1997). Building a neighborhood network: Interorganizational collaboration to prevent child abuse and neglect. *Social Work, 42*, 255–264.

Mulroy, E. A., & Shay, S. (1997). Nonprofit organizations and innovation: A model of neighborhood-based collaboration to prevent child maltreatment. *Social Work, 42*, 515–524.

Murray, C. (2003). Risk factors, protective factors, vulnerability, and resilience: A framework for understanding and supporting the adult transitions of youth with high-incidence disabilities. *Remedial and Special Education, 24*, 16–26.

Nartz, M., & Schoesch, D. (2000). Use of the Internet for community practice: A Delphi study. *Journal of Community Practice, 8*, 37–59.

National Association of Social Workers. (1990). *Promoting family support statements.* Washington, DC: Author.

National Association of Social Workers. (1999). *National Association of Social Workers code of ethics*. Washington, DC: Author.

National Institute of Mental Health. (2003). Treatment of depression collaborative research program: Background and research plan. *Archives of General Psychiatry, 42*, 305–316.

NREPP. (2003, 2006). SAMSSA's National Registry of Evidence-Based Programs and Practices, http://www.nrepp.samhsa.gov/.

Nugent, W. R. (1991). An experimental and qualitative analysis of cognitive-behavioral intervention for anger. *Social Work Research and Abstracts, 27*(3), 3–8.

O'Brien, P. (1995). From surviving to thriving: The complex experience of living in public housing. *Affilia, 10*, 155–178.

Oei, T. P. S., & Shuttlewood, G. J. (1996). Specific and nonspecific factors in psychotherapy: A case of cognitive therapy for depression. *Clinical Psychology Review, 16*, 83–103.

Orr, A. L. (2005). Dealing with the death of a group member: Visually impaired elderly in the community. In A. Gitterman & L. Shulman (Eds.), *Mutual aid groups, vulnerable and resilient populations, and the life cycle* (3rd ed., pp. 471–492). New York: Columbia University Press.

Perlman, H. H. (1957). *Social casework: A problem-solving process*. Chicago: University of Chicago Press.

Pfefferbaum, B. (2005). Aspects of exposure in childhood trauma: The stressor criterion. In E. Cardena & K. Croyle (Eds.), *Acute reactions to trauma and psychotherapy: A multidisciplinary and international perspective*. Binghamton, NY: Haworth Press.

Pilsecker, C. (1979). Terminal cancer. *Social Work in Health Care, 4*, 237–264.

Polowy, C. I. (1997). *NASW law notes for social workers* [pamphlet].

Prochaska, J. O., & DiClemente, C. C. (1982). Transtheoretical therapy: Toward a more integrative model of change. *Psychotherapy: Theory, Research and Practice, 19*, 276–288.

Proctor, E. K., & Davis, L. E. (1994). The challenge of racial difference: Skills for clinical practice. *Social Work, 39*, 314–323.

Pudil, J. (2007, January). I'm gone when you're gone: How a group can survive when its leader takes a leave of absence. *Social Work with Groups, 29*(2/3), 217–233.

Radloff, L. S. (1977). The CES-D scale: A self-report depression scale for research in the general population. *Applied Psychological Measurement, 1*(3), 385–401.

Rak, C. F., & Patterson, L. E. (1996). Promoting resilience in at-risk children. *Journal of Counseling and Development, 74*, 368–373.

Ramos-Sanchez, L., & Atkinson, D. R. (2009). The relationships between Mexican American acculturation, cultural values, gender, and help-seeking intensions. *Journal of Counseling and Development, 87*(1), 62–71.

Reamer, F. G. (1990). *Ethical dilemmas in social services* (2nd ed.). New York: Columbia University Press.

Reamer, F. G. (1998). The evolution of social work ethics. *Social Work, 43*, 488.

Reamer, F. G. (2000). The social work ethics audit: A risk management strategy. *Social Work, 45*, 355–366.

Rebmann, H. (2006). Warning—there's a lot of yelling in knitting: The impact of parallel process on empowerment in a group setting. *Social Work with Groups, 29*(4), 5–24.

Reed-Victor, E., & Stronge, J. (2002). Homeless students and resilience: Staff perspectives on individual and environmental factors. *Journal of Children and Poverty, 8*, 159–183.

Reid, W. J., & Shyne, A. W. (1969). *Brief and extended casework*. New York: Columbia University Press.

Reitzes, D., & Reitzes, D. (1986). Alinsky in the 1980s: Two contemporary Chicago community organizations. *Sociological Quarterly, 28*, 265–283.

Richards, M., Browne, C., & Broderick, A. (1994). Strategies for teaching clinical social work practice with Asians and Pacific Islanders. *Gerontology and Geriatric Education, 14*(3), 49–63.

Richmond, M. (1918). *Social diagnosis*. New York: Russell Sage Foundation.

Richters, J. E., & Martinez, P. E. (1993). Violent communities, family choices, and children's chances: An algorithm for improving the odds. *Development and Psychopathology, 5*, 609–627.

Roback, H. B., Purdon, S. E., Ochoa, E., & Bloch, F. (1992). Confidentiality dilemmas in group psychotherapy: Management strategies and utility of guidelines. *Small Group Research, 23*, 169–184.

Rodgers, K. B., & Rose, H. A. (2002). Risk and resilience factors among adolescents who experience marital transitions. *Journal of Marriage and Family, 64*, 1024–1037.

Rodriquez, R. L. (1998). Challenging demographic reductionism. *Small Group Research, 29*, 744–759.

Rogers, C. R. (1961). *On becoming a person*. Boston: Houghton Mifflin.

Rogers, C. R. (1969). *Freedom to learn*. Columbus, OH: Merrill.

Rogers, N. (1993). *The creative connection: Expressive arts as healing*. Palo Alto, CA: Science & Behavior Books.

Rosenberg, M. (1978). *Logic of survey analysis*. New York: Basic Books.

Rothman, J. (1979). Three models of community organization practice: Their mixing and phasing. In F. M. Cox, J. L. Erlich, J. Rothman, & J. E. Tropman (Eds.), *Strategies of community organization* (pp. 25–45). Itasca, IL: Peacock.

Salmon, R., & Graziano, R. (Eds.). *Group work and aging: Issues in practice, research and education*. Binghamton, NY: Haworth Press.

Sands, R., & Nuccio, K. (1992). Post-modern feminist theory and social work. *Social Work, 37*, 489–494.

Satir, V. (1967). *Conjoint family therapy.* Palo Alto, CA: Science and Behavior Books.

Saulnier, C. F. (1996). *Feminist theories and social work: Approaches and applications.* New York: Haworth Press.

Saulnier, C. F. (2000). Incorporating feminist theory into social work practice: Group work examples. *Social Work with Groups, 23*, 5–29.

Scannapieco, M., & Jackson, S. (1996). Kinship care: The African American response to family preservation. *Social Work, 41*, 190–196.

Schaefer, D. S., & Pozzaglia, D. (1986). Living with a nightmare: Hispanic parents of children with cancer. In A. Gitterman & L. Shulman (Eds.), *Mutual aid groups and the life cycle.* Itasca, IL: Peacock.

Schein, L. A., Spitz, H. I., Burlingame, G. M., Muskin, P. R., & Vargo, S. (Eds.). (2006). *Psychological effects of catastrophic disasters: Group approaches to treatment.* Binghamton, NY: Haworth Press.

Schiller, L. Y. (1993). Stages of group development. In *Women's groups: A relational model.* Paper presented at the 15th Annual Symposium of the Association for the Advancement of Social Work with Groups, New York.

Schlenker, B. (2003). Self-presentation. In R. Learly & J. P. Tangney (Eds.), *Handbook of self and identify* (pp. 492–518). New York: Guilford Press.

Schopler, M. D., Galinsky, M. J., & Abell, M. D. (1997). Connecting group members through telephone and computer groups. *Health and Social Work, 22*, 91–100.

Schwartz, W. (1961). The social worker in the group. In *New perspectives on services to groups: Theory, organization, and practice* (pp. 7–34). New York: National Association of Social Workers.

Schwartz, W. (1969). Private troubles and public issues: One social work job or two? In *The social welfare forum* (pp. 22–43). New York: Columbia University Press.

Schwartz, W. (1971). On the use of groups in social work practice. In W. Schwartz & S. Zalba (Eds.), *The practice of group work* (pp. 3–24). New York: Columbia University Press.

Shallcorss, L. (2010). Managing resistant clients. *Counseling Today, 52*(8), 40–43.

Shelley, M., Thrane, L., & Shulman, S. (2005). Lost in cyberspace: Barriers to bridging the digital divide in e-politics. *International Journal of Information Policy, Law and Security, 1*(2).

Shelley, M., Thrane, L., Shulman, S., Lang, E., Beisser, S., Larson, T., et al. (2004). *Social Service Computer Review, 22*, 2–14.

Shulman, L. (1967). Scapegoats, group workers, and the pre-emptive intervention. *Social Work, 12*, 43.

Shulman, L. (1968). *A casebook of social work with groups.* New York: Council on Social Work Education. (Published in Swedish by Student Litteratur, 1971; French edition published by Association Nationale des Assistantes Sociales, 1977.)

Shulman, L. (1970). Client, staff, and the social agency. In *Social work practice* (pp. 21–40). New York: Columbia University Press.

Shulman, L. (1971). Programs in group work: Another look. In W. Schwartz & S. Zalba (Eds.), *The practice of group work* (pp. 221–240). New York: Columbia University Press.

Shulman, L. (1978). A study of practice skills. *Social Work, 23*, 281.

Shulman, L. (1979a). *The skills of helping* [Videotapes]. Montreal: Instructional Communications Centre, McGill University.

Shulman, L. (1979b). *A study of the helping process.* Vancouver: University of British Columbia, School of Social Work.

Shulman, L. (1980a). Leading a first group session [DVD]. Insight Media, http://www.insight-media.com/IMGroupDispl.asp.

Shulman, L. (1980b). Social work practice with foster parents. *Canadian Journal of Social Work Education, 6*, 71.

Shulman, L. (1981). *Identifying, measuring, and teaching helping skills.* New York: Council on Social Work Education and the Canadian Association of Schools of Social Work.

Shulman, L. (1982). *The skills of helping individuals and groups.* Itasca, IL: Peacock.

Shulman, L. (1984). *The skills of supervision and staff management.* Itasca, IL: Peacock.

Shulman, L. (1991). *Interactional social work practice: Toward an empirical theory.* Itasca, IL: Peacock.

Shulman, L. (1993a). *Interactional supervision* (2nd ed.). Silver Spring, MD: National Association of Social Workers.

Shulman, L. (1993b). *Teaching the helping skills: A field instructor's guide.* Alexandria, VA: Council on Social Work Education.

Shulman, L. (2002). Learning to talk about taboo subjects: A lifelong professional task. In R. Kurland and A. Malekoff (Eds.), *Stories celebrating group work: It's not always easy to sit on your mouth.* New York: Haworth Press. (Copublished simultaneously in *Social Work with Groups, 25*(1)).

Shulman, L. (2010). *Interactional supervision* (3rd ed.). Silver Spring, MD: National Association of Social Workers.

Shulman, L. (2011). *Dynamics and skills of group counseling.* Belmont, CA: Brooks/Cole, Cengage Learning.

Shulman, L., & Buchan, W. (1982). *The impact of the family physician's communication, relationship, and technical skills on patient compliance, satisfaction, reassurance, comprehension, and improvement.* Vancouver: University of British Columbia.

Shulman, L., & Clay, C. (1994). *Teaching about practice and diversity: Content and process in the classroom and the field* [Videotapes]. Alexandria, VA: Council on Social Work Education.

Shulman, L., Maguin, E., Syms, C., Sheppard, S., & Manning, A. (2006). *The VISA Center: A report on a program for students suspended from the Buffalo Public Schools for violent and/or aggressive behavior, substance abuse, or weapons possession.* Buffalo: The University at Buffalo School of Social Work. www.socialwork.buffalo.edu/research/visa.asp.

Singh, A. A., & Salazar, C. F. (2010). The roots of social justice in group work. *Journal for Specialists in Group Work, 35*(2), 97–105.

Simmons, L. (2000). High stakes casinos and controversies. *Journal of Community Practice, 7,* 47–69.

Smalley, R. E. (1967). *Theory for social work practice.* New York: Columbia University Press.

Smith, A., & Siegal, R. (1985). Feminist therapy: Redefining power for the powerless. In *Handbook of feminist therapy: Women's issues in psychotherapy.* New York: Springer.

Soifer, S. (1998). A rural tenant organizing model: The case of TUFF Vermont. *Journal of Community Practice, 5,* 1–14.

Specht, H., & Courtney, M. E. (1993). *Unfaithful angels.* New York: Free Press.

Spitzer, R. L., Gibbon, M., Williams, J. B., & Endicott, J. A. (1996). Global Assessment of Functioning (GAF) scale. In L. I. Sederer & B. Dickey (Eds.), *Outcome assessment in clinical practice* (pp. 76–78). Baltimore: Williams and Wilkins.

Srebnik, D. S., & Saltzberg, E. A. (1994). Feminist cognitive-behavioral therapy for negative body image. *Women and Therapy, 15,* 117–133.

Stanton, A. H., & Schwartz, M. F. (1954). *Mental hospital: A study of institutional participation in psychiatric illness and treatment.* New York: Basic Books.

Staples, L. (1984). *Roots to power: A manual for grassroots organizing.* New York: Praeger.

Stern, S., & Smith, C. A. (1995). Family processes and delinquency. *Social Service Review,* 703–731.

Stevens, J. W. (1994). Adolescent development and adolescent pregnancy among late age African-American female adolescents. *Children and Adolescent Social Work Journal, 26*(6), 433–453.

Strean, H. (1978). *Clinical social work theory and practice.* New York: Free Press.

Swank, E., Asada, H., & Lott, J. (2002). Student acceptance of a multicultural education: Exploring the role of a social work curriculum, demographics, and symbolic racism. *Journal of Ethnic and Cultural Diversity in Social Work, 10,* 85–103.

Taft, J. (1933). Living and feeling. *Child Study, 10,* 100–112.

Taft, J. (1942). The relational function to process in social case work. In V. P. Robinson (Ed.), *Training for skill in social casework.* Philadelphia: University of Pennsylvania Press.

Taft, J. (1949). Time as the medium of the helping process. *Jewish Social Service Quarterly, 26,* 230–243.

Tanner, D. (2007). Starting with lives: Supporting older people's strategies and ways of coping. *Journal of Social Work, 7*(1), 7–30.

*Tarasoff v. Regents of the University of California,* 551 P.2d 334 (1976).

Thayer, L. (1982). A person-centered approach to family therapy. In A. M. Horne & M. M. Ohlsen (Eds.), *Family counseling and therapy* (pp. 175–213). Itasca, IL: Peacock.

Thomas, R. V., & Pender, D. A. (2007). *ASWG best practices guidelines.* Association for Specialists in Group Work. Retrieved from http://www.asgw.org/.

Thomlison, B. (2007). *Family assessment handbook: An introductory guide to family assessment and intervention* (2nd ed.). Belmont, CA: Thomson Brooks/Cole.

Thornton, S., & Garrett, K. (1995). Ethnography as a bridge to multicultural practice. *Journal of Social Work Education, 32*(1), 67–74.

Thyer, B. A. (1987). Contingency analysis: Toward a unified theory for social work practice. *Social Work, 32,* 150–157.

Thyer, B. A., & Thyer, K. B. (1992) Single-system research designs in social work practice. *Research on Social Work Practice, 2*(1), 99–116.

Toseland, R. W., & Rivas, R. F. (2005). *An introduction to group work practice.* Boston: Allyn & Bacon.

Tracy, E. M., & Whittaker, J. K. (1990). The social network map: Assessing social support in clinical practice. *Families in Society, 72*(8), 461–470.

Trimble, D. (2005). Uncovering kindness and respect: Men who have practiced violence in intimate relationships. In A. Gitterman & L. Shulman (Eds.), *Mutual aid groups, vulnerable populations, and the life cycle* (3rd ed., pp. 352–372). New York: Columbia University Press.

Truax, C. B. (1966). Therapist empathy, warmth, genuineness, and patient personality change in group psychotherapy: A comparison between interaction unit measures, time sample measures, and patient perception measures. *Journal of Clinical Psychology, 71,* 1–9.

Truax, C. B., Wargo, D. G., Frank, J. D., Imber, S. D., Battle, C. C., Hoehn-Saric, R., Nash, E. H., & Stone, A. R. (1966). Therapist empathy, genuineness, and warmth and patient therapeutic outcome. *Journal of Consulting Psychology, 30*(5), 395–401.

Van Hook, M. P. (2008). Spirituality. In A. L. Strozier & J. Carpenter (Eds.), *Introduction to alternative and complementary therapies* (pp. 39–63). New York: Haworth Press, Taylor and Francis Group.

Van Horn, D. (2002). A pilot test of motivational interviewing groups for dually diagnosed inpatients. *Journal of Substance Abuse Treatment, 20*(2), 191–195.

van Wormer, K., Wells, J., & Boes, M. (2000). *Social work with lesbians, gays, and bisexuals: A strengths perspective.* Needham Heights, MA: Allyn & Bacon.

Vastola, J., Nierenberg, A., & Graham, E. H. (1995). The lost and found group: Group work and bereaved children. In A. Gitterman & L. Shulman (Eds.), *Mutual aid groups, vulnerable populations, and the life cycle* (2nd ed., pp. 81–96). New York: Columbia University Press.

Watt, J. W., & Kallmann, G. L. (1998). Managing professional obligations under managed care: A social work perspective. *Family and Community Health, 21,* 40–48.

Weaver, H. N., & White, B. J. (1997). The Native American family circle: Roots of resiliency. *Journal of Social Work, 2*(1), 67–79.

Weaver, H. N., & Wodarsky, J. S. (1995). Cultural issues in crisis intervention: Guidelines for culturally competent practice. *Family Therapy, 22*(3), 213–223.

Weber, T., McKeever, J. E., & McDaniel, S. H. (1985). A beginner's guide to the problem-oriented first family interview. *Family Process, 24*(1), 357–363.

Weick, A., & Vandiver, S. (1982). *Women, power, and change.* Silver Spring, MD: National Association of Social Workers.

Welfel, E. R. (1998). *Ethics in counseling and psychotherapy: Standards, research, and emerging issues.* Boston: Brooks/Cole.

Werner, E. E. (1989). Children of the garden. *Scientific American, 260,* 106–111.

Westbury, E., & Tutty, L. M. (1999). The efficacy of group treatment for survivors of childhood abuse. *Child Abuse and Neglect, 23,* 31–44.

Williams, E. E., & Ellison, F. (1996). Culturally informed social work practice with American Indian clients: Guidelines for non-Indian social workers. *Social Work, 41*(2), 147–151.

Willis, R. A., Mallory, K. C., Gould, M. Y., & Shatila, S. L. *The macro practitioner's workbook: A step-by-step guide to effectiveness with organizations and communities.* Belmont, CA: Thomson Brooks/Cole.

Wilson, G., & Ryland, G. (1949). *Social group work practice: The creative use of the social process.* Boston: Houghton Mifflin.

Wood, G. G., & Roche, S. E. (2001). Representing selves, reconstructing lives: Feminist group work with women survivors of male violence. *Social Work with Groups, 23,* 5–23.

Wright, L., & Leahey, M. (1994). *Nurses and families: A guide to family assessment and intervention* (2nd ed.). Philadelphia: F. A. Davis.

Zachary, E. (2000). Grassroots leadership training: A case study of an effort to integrate theory and method. *Journal of Community Practice, 7,* 71–93.

Zuroff, D. C., Kelly, A. C., Leybman, M. J., Blatt, S. J., & Wampold, B. E. (2010). Between-therapist and within-therapist differences in the quality of the therapeutic relationship: Effects on maladjustment and self-critical perfectionism. *Journal of Clinical Psychology, 66 & 67,* 681–697.

# Case Index

# Author Index

# Subject Index

Note: 1. Subjects may also be located in the Index of Case Examples.
2. Letters 'f' and 't' following the locators refers to the figures and tables cited in the text.

Crying
  by clients, 9, 52, 71, 81, 92, 109, 153,
    174, 176, 178, 182, 203, 228–229,
    246, 249, 273, 291, 311, 338, 352,
    384, 397, 445, 462, 493, 547, 551,
    585–586, 592, 596–597, 611, 710,
    722, 727, 750
  in group session, 547, 587–597
  by workers, 37, 178, 229, 249, 252, 280
Culturagrams, 127
Culturally competent practice, 75
Culturally diverse practice, 129–140
  African Americans, 132–134
  in beginning phase, family practice,
    282–283
  defined, 129
  education/training for, 139–140
  issues in, 138–139
  Mexican Americans, 131–132
  Native people, 136–137
Culture
  dangers of ignoring, 309–310
  family support work and, 282–292
Culture for work, 345, 561–566
  See also Work culture, systemic
Cyber-community, 660

**D**

Data gathering, 486
Dealing with issues of authority, 98, 392
Death and dying
  denial of, 225–227
  dying clients, 251–253
  effect of, on worker's practice,
    247–248
  endings from, 247–253
  end-of-life decisions, 253–254
  psychiatric group and, 442–445
  suicide, 248–253
Death with Dignity Act, 253
Defensive member, 523–525
  See also Denial; Resistance
Defusing, 741
Delinquency courts, 617–623
Delinquents, 285
Demand for work
  defined, 25
  empathy and, 189
  in family counseling, 296
  group leader's, 540–46
  skills related to, 188
  strengths perspective and, 25–26
  in work phase, 186–194
Demobilization intervention, 741
Denial
  cancer and, 560
  of endings/transitions, 225–233, 308
  See also Defensive member
Dependence-flight, 536
Dependence phase, 536
Dependency, 195, 536, 566, 635
Dependent group, 563
Dependent member, 536
Depression, 397–399, 714
Detecting and challenging the obstacles to
  work, 194
Developing a universal perspective,
  348–349
Developmental group tasks, 534–536
  culture for work, 561–563

relationships among members, 549–553
relationship to worker, 534–535
structure for work, 563–565
  See also Group formation
Developmental psychology, 55–60
Developmental reserve capacity, 59, 60
Deviational allowance, 486
Deviant member
  communicative behavior of, 513–515
  community organizing and, 667–668
  extreme versus mild behavior of,
    513–514
  role of, 515–518
  in system, 605
  as worker's ally, 667
Diagnosis, 103
Diagnostic and Statistical Manual of Mental
    Disorders (DSM), 125
Dialectical process, 345–346
Dichotomies, false
  empathy versus demand for work, 189
  individual concerns versus social policy,
    632
  personal versus professional self, 35,
    37–38, 178
  process versus content, 201
  structure versus freedom, 104
  talking versus doing, 485
  See also Paradoxes
Digital divide, 660–661
Direct communication, obstacles to,
    69–70
Direct macro-practice, 650
Discussing a taboo area, 346–347
Disenchantment-flight, 550
Displaying understanding of the client's
    feelings, 36, 92, 173–175
Distortions, cognitive, 714
Diversity within diversity, 75, 127, 282
  See also Culturally competent practice;
    Culturally diverse practice
Division of labor, 212, 482, 504, 535,
    639–640, 664, 666
Divorce, 489–498
Doorknob therapy, 100, 151, 214–215, 370,
    592
  in group practice, 483–485
  in work phase model, 214–215
Drawing, 491–492
Driving while intoxicated (DWI), 350, 393,
    706
Dualisms, false. See Dichotomies, false
Duty to warn, 217–218
Dynamic interaction, 4, 101, 516
Dynamic systems theory, 10

**E**

Education. See Training, for culturally
    sensitive practice
Elaborating skills, 162–169, 296
  in group practice, 451–456
Elderly, 377, 636
"Elephant in the room," 665
Emergency service workers, 644–645
Emotions. See Crying; Feelings
Empathic skills, 169–177, 296, 614
  in group practice, 456–480
Empathy
  and demand for work, 188
  development of, 82–83, 172–173

research on, 176–177
in work phase, 149
  See also Tuning in
Empirically based practice, 719
Employment, patterns of, 21–22
Empowerment, 26, 683–691
Empowerment practice, 651
Empowerment-oriented model, of
    community organization, 650, 653
Enchantment-flight, 550
Endings/transitions
  abrupt, 245
  in community organization, 683–691
  in couples' group session, 396
  death and, 247–254
  difficulties of, 222
  dynamics of, 223–233
  emotional reactions to, 308
  in family counseling, 307–311
  flow of affect in, 223–224
  future work after, 237–239
  goals of, 307–308
  in groups, 578–597
  job termination and, 245–247, 310–311
  paradoxes of, 222
  poor relationships and, 241–245
  premature, 309
  process-content connections in, 239–240
  results identification and, 234–237
  sessional, 210–219
  skills of, 234–241
  stages of, 225–233, 308, 578–581
  timing and, 224–225
Ending phase in group practice
  dealing with ending, leadership
    strategies, 582
  importance of, 575–576
  negative feelings of, 577–578
  stages in, 578–582
  transitional aspect, leadership strategies,
    582–584
End-of-life decisions, 253–254
  client self-determination in, 253–254
  ethical issues, 253–254
Entry, 486
Ethics
  audit/risk management strategy for, 44–45
  defined, 41
  duty to warn and, 217–218
  and end-of-life decisions, 253–254
  factors in decision-making, 43–45
  informed consent and, 140–141
  problems and dilemmas in, 42–43
  professional, 40
  sharing data and, 217
  therapeutic methods and, 701
  values versus, 40–41
  See also Code of Ethics
Ethnic groups
  African Americans, 48, 56–58, 64–65,
    132–133, 506, 617, 663
  European immigrants, 154, 273,–275
  Hispanics, 131
  Mexican Americans, 131–132
  Native people, 93, 129–130, 167, 282–292,
    608–609
  Puerto Ricans, 127, 129, 282
  See also Race
Ethnic-sensitive practice, 127
European immigrants, 154, 273–275

Evidence-based practice, 699–702
   CISM (Crisis Intervention Stress Management) group examples, 740–742
   clinical judgements in, 700–701
   competency notes, 752–753
   concept of, 700
   crisis theory, 740–741
   ethical considerations, 700–701
   extreme events, practicing, 738–739
   forgiveness excercises, 744–746
   GLBT clients, handling of, 728–730
   manualized practices, 701–702
   online contents, 752
   practice wisdoms in, 700–701
   religion, 735–738
   summary, 752
   trauma groups, 741–742
   traumatized children, effective treatments, 742–744
   *See also* Cognitive-behavioral therapy; Feminist practice; Motivational interviewing; Solution-focused practice (SFP)
Exceptions, 713
Exploring client resistance, 149
Externalization of problems, 647
External leader, 504, 664
Extreme events, 738–746

**F**
Facilitative confrontation, 296, 701
Falling through the cracks, 615
Family
   African Americans and, 132
   complexity of, 21
   definition of, 21, 259–260
   dynamics of, 261
   economic effects on, 22
   Mexican Americans and, 131–132
   multigenerational issues in, 264, 267
   Native people and, 137, 284–292
   secrets of, 267, 297–299
   *See also* Family support work
Family-as-a-whole, 267, 271
Family counseling. *See* Family support work
Family façade, 261, 281, 297
Family secrets, 267, 297–299
Family support (family counseling), 3–4
Family support work
   assessment in, 268–271
   in child welfare setting, 315–329
   contracting phase in, 276–282
   culture and, 282–292
   description of, 260
   endings/transitions in, 307–308
   first interviews in, 276–277, 270
   in school setting, 329–336
   setting/service impact on, 314
   setting-specific, 261
   theory and, 262–268
   tuning in, 271–272
   two-client concept and, 273–275
   worker's personal experiences and, 275
   work phase in, 294–307
Family systems theory, 263
Family therapy, 260
Family therapy theory, 262–268
   Bowen's family systems theory, 263

Cognitive-Behavioral Family Therapy (CBFT), 265
   Freeman's implementation, 263–264
   Multi-Systemic Therapy (MST) Model, 265–266
   Person-Centered approach, 264–265
   psychodynamic approach, 262–263
Fanon's psychology, 15–17, 48–49
Farewell-party syndrome, 233, 581
Fast food social work, 324
   *See also* "Steering wheel" social work
Fear-of-groups syndrome, 358
Feedback
   endings/transitions and, 223–225
   negative, for social workers, 154
   reaching for, 107, 154, 160
Feelings
   articulation of client's, 72, 74, 91, 148, 175–176
   clients' ways of dealing with, 169
   as communication obstacle, 69
   endings/transitions and, 223–224
   flooding of, 558
   reaching for, 173–174
   significance of, 169
   skills for helping clients manage, 91, 167, 185
   of social workers, 35, 37, 73–74, 84, 153–155, 178–186, 202–203, 296, 547–548
   understanding of client's, 174–175
   workers' sharing of own. *See* Self-disclosure
   *See also* Crying
Feeling-thinking-doing connection, 170
Feminist practice
   on batterer, 723–724
   family and, 262
   and group work, 719–720
   and new psychology of women, 718
   oppression indicators, 720–721
   relational model and, 555, 718–719
   sexual abuse survivors group and, 712–714
   typology of, 717
   on women's group, 718–720
Feminist social work, 717
Fight-flight, 563–564
Fight-flight group, 563–564
First decision, 36, 99, 295
First interviews
   conduct of, 106
   in family counseling, 270–271, 278
   for group work, 567
   importance of, 99
   interaction in, 7–9
First offering, 152
Flight-fight reactions, 69, 153, 248, 325, 563–564
Flooding, of emotions, 558
Focused listening, 164–165
Forgiveness, 744–745
Foster children, group work with, 238
Foster parents
   and child welfare setting, 315–329
   problems regarding, 315–316
Foxwoods Casino, 658
Functional clarity, 275, 314
Functional diffusion, 275, 325
Future work, identification of, 237

**G**
Gag rules, on health care, 216
Gambling, 658
Gangs, 58, 691–694
Gatekeeper, 521–523
Gays, 725–735
   definition, 726
Generalist practice, 29
Generalizing, 211–212, 628
General-to-specific movement, 163–164
Generic social work, 29
Genograms, 269
GLBT sensitive practice, 728–735
   oppression perspectives in, 726–728
   *See also* Gays; LGBT
Glossary, 755–763
Grassroots community organizing, 653–654
Grassroots organizing, 653–658
Grounded theory, 6
Group culture, 533, 561–567
Group formation, 357–358, 534
   agency/setting support for, 363
   group versus individual work, 362–363
   and new members, 426–429
   preparation for group work, 357–358
   process of, 359–361
   staff system and, 358
   type/structure and, 361–362
Group leaders
   as caring/giving persons, 547–548
   and coleadership, 419–425
   external, 504
   role of, 356–357
   group control and, 537–539
   internal, 401, 518–521
   limitations of, 546
   as outsiders, 539–540
Groups
   activity, 485–500
   agency/setting support for, 363
   and all-in-the-same-boat phenomenon, 344, 347–348, 396, 738
   common purpose of, 533
   communication in, 356, 550
   composition of, 366–367
   defined, 343
   developmental tasks for, 534–536
   dialectical process in, 345–346
   dynamics of, 344–355, 388–391, 503, 539, 550
   environmental influences on, 534
   fear of, 358
   feedback in, 360
   formation of, 367–358
   as machines, 533
   mutual demand in, 350
   mutual support in, 349–350
   new members to, 426–434
   open-ended, 426–434
   as organisms, 268, 533–534
   problem solving in, 351
   prospective members of, 373–379
   purpose of, 370, 375, 378, 391, 445
   rationale for, 359
   recontracting with, 414–419
   rehearsal in, 352–354
   relational model and, 553–555
   roles in, 356

Posttraumatic stress disorder, 540–546
Practice theory, 4–5
Practitioner-researcher, 716
Pre-contemplation stage, 630
Preliminary and beginning phase, Family practice. *See* Assessment model; Family therapy theory; Middle phase in family practice; Tuning in
  agency themes, 272
  authority themes, 272
  competency notes on, 292–293
  countertransference in, 275
  family counseling, 260
  family support, 260
  family working themes, 272
  family, defined, 259–260
  GLBT-connected issues., 266–267
  issues in, 261
  mediation role, worker, 274–275
  online contents, 292
  other practice models, 261–262
  summary, 292
  tuning in, 271–272
  two-client concept, 273–274
  work setting, 261
Preliminary phase, individual practice
  competency notes on, 95–96
  direct and indirect communications, 69–72
  online contents, 95
  summary, 95
  therapeutic alliance, 78–83
Privileged communications, 141–143
Problems
  externalization of, 647
  skills for helping clients manage, 98, 109, 190
Process, 638
Process-content connections, 149, 201–205, 239–240, 296
  *See also* Acting out the problem
Process-focused staff meetings, 638
Professionalism, 37–38, 84, 178–179
  assumptions, impact on, 17–26
  client-system interaction, 7–10
  concept of, 27–33, 30–33
  Dynamic Systems Theory, 10–14
  ethical decision making, 43–45
    competency notes on, 45–46
    online contents, 45
    summary, 45
  ethical problems and dilemmas, 42–43
  feminist views on, 14–15
  personal versus, 37–38
  problems in early sessions, 2–4
  work skill and working relationship, 33–36
Programs. *See* Activity groups
Program in group work, 487
Progressive practice model, of community organization, 651–652
Projective identification, 461
Protecting the child, 70, 78, 122, 173, 260, 272, 283
  *See also* Mandated clients
Psychiatric setting
  interagency cooperation in, 644–647
  veterans in, 540–546
Psychosocial history, 102
Public housing, 655–658, 668–677

Puppets, 489
"Putting client's feelings into words," 72, 74, 91, 148, 175–176

## Q

Quasi-stationary social equilibrium, 523, 623
Queer
  definition, 726
Questioning, 165–166
Quiet member, 525–529

## R

Race
  cross-racial interactions, 138–139
  dangers of ignoring, 309–310
  group composition and, 367–368
  parent-school relations, 617–623
  teacher-student relations, 608–610
  worker-client relations, 93, 285, 617
  *See also* Ethnic groups
Racism
  African Americans and, 133
  institutionalized, 51
  in medicine, 20
  Native people and, 284
Radical feminism, 717
Rapport, 78
Reaching for feelings, 173–174
Reaching for the client's feedback, 98, 144
Reaching inside of silences, 91, 121, 166–169
Recontracting, 414–419
Record of service, 299, 731
Reflection, 74–75, 173
Reframing, 151, 297
Reframing the problem, 281
Regression analysis, 92
Rehearsal, 213, 352–354
Relational model, 553–561
  connection, 554
  paradox, 553–554
  resonance, 554–555
Religion, 735–738
  counseling models, 735–738
  *See also* Spirituality
Research findings
  on contracting, 109–110
  on partialization skill, 190–191
  on racism, 284
  on social work practice, 38–40
  on taboo areas, 196–197
  tuning-in, importance of, 91–92
  worker's response, silence, 167–169
Reserve capacity, 59–60
Resilience theory, 54–60
  cognitive hardiness, 59–60
  developmental psychology and, 55–59
  family and, 262
  life-span theory and, 59
  models in, 54–55
  social work implications of, 60–65
  variable-focused versus person-focused, 54–55
Resiliency, 15
Resistance, 112–125
  of African Americans, 127
  to change, 623
  exploring, 149, 192, 445
  family and, 261

in social systems, 630
  worker reaction to, 117
  in work phase, 148–149, 186–187
  *See also* Defensive member
Resolution-catharsis, 536
Resolution stage, 210
Resonance, 554
Respect, 134, 138
Restorative justice, 24
Retribution, worker-agency relations and, 631
Risk, resilience and, 54–64
Roles
  defined, 503, 663–664
  formal versus informal, 504
  in groups, 354, 503
  oppression and, 503
Rural communities
  community organization in, 659
  social work in, 314–315, 659

## S

Scaling questions, 714
Scapegoating
  dysfunctional aspect of, 505
  group work and, 506
  history of, 505
  role of, 504–505
  teenage girls example of, 505–513
  working methods, 512–513
Schemata, 714–715
School setting
  family support work in, 328–329
  social worker interaction with, 609–617
  student problems in, 610–617
Secondary traumatic stress (STS)
  examples, delivery of services, 749–752
  in child welfare practice, 747–749
  trauma, impact on professionals, 766
Second decision, 36, 99, 103, 147, 295
Second offerings, 325
Self-determination, 42–43, 253
Self-disclosure, 76, 181, 178–185
  about life experiences, 181
  and anger at client, 178–179
  boundary issues and, 182–183
  criticisms of, 178–179
  in family counseling, 296
  and investment in client success, 180–181
  research on, 184–186
  sexual feelings and, 183–184
Self-in-relation theory, 13, 553, 555
Self-interest, 21–23
Separation, marital. *See* Divorce
September 11, 2001 attacks, 738, 750, 746
Service plan, 107
Sessional contracting skills, 158–161, 295
Sessional ending/transition skills, 210–215
Sessional tuning-in skills, 152–158
Settings, family practice
  competency notes on, 339
  impact of, 314
  invasive practice, clients fear on, 314–315
  online contents, 339
  rural areas, 315
  single-parent family, 336–337